Handbook of
Divorce and Relationship
Dissolution

HANDBOOK OF DIVORCE AND RELATIONSHIP DISSOLUTION

Edited by

Mark A. Fine
University of Missouri—Columbia

John H. Harvey
University of Iowa

LEA

LAWRENCE ERLBAUM ASSOCIATES, PUBLISHERS

2006 Mahwah, New Jersey   London

Senior Editor:	Debra Riegert
Editorial Assistant:	Kerry Breen
Cover Design:	Kathryn Houghtaling Lacey
Textbook Production Manager:	Paul Smolenski
Full-Service Compositor:	TechBooks
Text and Cover Printer:	Hamilton Printing Company

This book was typeset in 10/12 pt. Times Roman, Italic, Bold, and Bold Italic.
The heads were typeset in Americana, Americana Italic, and Americana Bold.

Lawrence Erlbaum Associates, Inc., Publishers
10 Industrial Avenue
Mahwah, New Jersey 07430
www.erlbaum.com

Library of Congress Cataloging-in-Publication Data

Handbook of divorce and relationship dissolution / edited by Mark A.
   Fine, John H. Harvey.
     p. cm.
   Includes bibliographical references and index.
   ISBN 0-8058-5128-3 (casebound : alk. paper)
   1. Divorce.   2. Separation (Psychology)   3. Man-woman relationships.
I. Fine, Mark A.   II. Harvey, John H., 1943–

   HQ814.H27   2006
   523.46—dc22   2005017773

Contents

Preface

We decided to compile this handbook as we were finishing our last book, *Children of Divorce: Stories of Hope and Loss*, published in 2004 by Lawrence Erlbaum Associates. As we reviewed the voluminous literature on divorce, we noted several important gaps: there was inadequate information on processes associated with relationship dissolution; there was relatively little in the literature on non-White, middle class, and heterosexual married couples; and there was far less material on nonmarital relationships than on marriages. Most importantly, there was no single source that brought together scholarly information on relationship dissolution. Thus, we decided to edit this handbook to address these deficiencies and to provide an authoritative source that brings together into a single volume the available scholarship on divorce and dissolution. Our audience is intended to include researchers and graduate students from any of the disciplines addressing divorce and relationship dissolution (e.g., family studies, psychology, sociology, child development, communication, anthropology, and nursing) advanced undergraduates, practitioners involved with divorce and dissolution, and policy-makers.

We asked the very best known scholars in this field to contribute chapters to the book. Those who were able to contribute were asked to attend to issues of process, diversity, and nonmarital relationships in their chapters, and all did. Many shared their very latest work in this handbook, and we were fortunate that many shared some of their newest theoretical insights in their chapters. Because multiple disciplines have contributed to our knowledge base regarding divorce and dissolution, we deliberately and thoughtfully chose contributing authors who were from such varying disciples as psychology, family studies, sociology, and communication studies. Our book is distinctive in its expansive coverage; attention to issues of diversity and process; consideration of nonmarital relationship dissolution in addition to divorce; and its multidisciplinary and eminent group of contributors and commentators.

To provide the integrated and extensive coverage that we thought was lacking in the field, we developed an ambitious outline of topics to be covered. Our eight sections and 28 chapters address introductory issues (1 chapter); demographic and historical aspects of divorce and relationship dissolution (3 chapters); causes, underlying processes, and antecedents of divorce and relationship dissolution (10 chapters); consequences of divorce and relationship dissolution (5 chapters); coping with divorce and relationship dissolution (3 chapters); variations in divorce and relationship dissolution patterns and processes (3 chapters); and applied issues pertaining to divorce and relationship dissolution (3 chapters). At the end of the volume, we present commentaries by three well-known scholars in the area—Robert S. Weiss, Ellen Berscheid, and Alan Booth. Each had access to earlier drafts of all the chapters, and each provided a rich mixture of comments about the volume as a whole, reflections on individual chapters, and some observations on the field as a whole. We hope that there are fruits of wisdom and kernels of interest embedded throughout this book for any serious student of divorce and relationship dissolution.

We express our appreciation to Debra Riegert, Senior Editor at Erlbaum, whose encouragement helped us through the production process. Debra has been the editor on both of our books and has been a very supportive advocate. We also appreciate the professionalism and competence of other Erlbaum staff, including the production editor.

We express our sincere gratitude to all of the individuals whose efforts have culminated in what we hope will be the definitive source on divorce and relationship dissolution issues, including our chapter authors and commentators; our colleagues who have supported each of us in numerous ways over the years, including Larry Kurdek, Larry Ganong, Marilyn Coleman, Steve Duck, Dave Demo, Katherine Allen, Hal Kelley, Ellen Berscheid, Jud Mills, Amy Wenzel, Terri Orbuch, and Ann Weber; and, most importantly, our families, children (Aubrey and Julia for M.F.; Patrick for J.H.), and partners (Loreen Olson for M.F.; Barbara for J.H.), whose patience during the many hours when we were working on this handbook was integral to our being able to bring this project to completion.

—Mark A. Fine and John H. Harvey

List of Contributors

Kari Adamsons
Department of Human Development and
Family Studies
University of North Carolina at Greensboro

Tamara D. Afifi
Department of Communication Arts
and Sciences
Pennsylvania State University

Erida C. Alfaro
Department of Family and Human
Development
Arizona State University

Paul R. Amato
Department of Sociology
Pennsylvania State University

Bonnie L. Barber
School of Psychology
Murdoch University

Robin Barry
Department of Psychology
University of Iowa

Denise S. Bartell
Department of Human Development
University of Wisconsin—Green Bay

Margit Berman
Department of Psychology
University of Minnesota

Ellen Berscheid
Department of Psychology
University of Minnesota

Karen R. Blaisure
Department of Family and Consumer
Sciences
Western Michigan University

Alan Booth
Department of Sociology
Pennsylvania State University

Sanford L. Braver
Department of Psychology
Arizona State University

Edna Brown
Institute for Social Research
University of Michigan

Mali Bunde
Department of Psychology
University of Iowa

Eric Clausell
Department of Psychology—Clinical/
Community Division
University of Illinois

Marilyn Coleman
Department of Human Development
and Family Studies
University of Missouri—Columbia

David H. Demo
Department of Human Development and
Family Studies
University of North Carolina at Greensboro

Steve Duck
Department of Communication Studies
University of Iowa

Robert E. Emery
Department of Psychology
University of Virginia

Diane Felmlee
Department of Sociology
University of California—Davis

Frank D. Fincham
Department of Child and Family Sciences
Florida State University

Mark A. Fine
Department of Human Development
and Family Studies
University of Missouri—Columbia

Patricia Frazier
Department of Psychology
University of Minnesota

Lawrence Ganong
Department of Human Development
and Family Studies
University of Missouri—Columbia

Margie J. Geasler
Department of Family and Consumer
Sciences
Western Michigan University

Matthew R. Goodman
Department of Psychology
Arizona State University

Julie H. Hall
Department of Psychology
University at Buffalo, The State University
of New York

Matthew Hall
Department of Sociology
Western Washington University

Kellie Hamrick
Department of Communication Arts
and Sciences
Pennsylvania State University

Jason Hans
Family Studies
University of Kentucky

John H. Harvey
Department of Psychology
University of Iowa

Shelley Irving
Department of Sociology
Pennsylvania State University

Karen Kayser
Graduate School of Social Work
Boston College

Gay C. Kitson
Department of Sociology
University of Akron

Erika Lawrence
Department of Psychology
University of Iowa

Margaret M. Mahoney
School of Law
University of Pittsburgh

Masahiro Masuda
Department of Human Culture
Kochi University

Terri L. Orbuch
Department of Sociology
Oakland University

Institute for Social Research
University of Michigan

Ramona Faith Oswald
Department of Human and Community
Development
University of Illinois

Kay Pasley
Department of Child and Family
Sciences
Florida State University

Satya S. Rao
Graduate School of Social Work
Boston College

Eunyoe Ro
Department of Psychology
University of Iowa

Amy E. Rodrigues
Department of Psychology
University at Buffalo, The State University
  of New York

Stephanie S. Rollie
Department of Communication Studies
University of Iowa

Liana C. Sayer
Department of Sociology
Ohio State University

David A. Sbarra
Department of Psychology
University of Arizona

Maria Schmeeckle
Department of Sociology and Anthropology
Illinois State University

Jenessa R. Shapiro
Department of Psychology
Arizona State University

Xiaoling Shu
Department of Sociology
University of California—Davis

Susan Sprecher
Department of Sociology and Anthropology
Illinois State University

Ty Tashiro
Department of Psychology
University of Minnesota

Jay Teachman
Department of Sociology
Western Washington University

Lucky Tedrow
Department of Sociology
Western Washington University

Adriana J. Umaña-Taylor
Department of Family and Human
  Development
Arizona State University

Anita L. Vangelisti
Department of Communication Studies
University of Texas at Austin

Robert S. Weiss
Gerontology Institute
University of Massachusetts, Boston

Julia T. Wood
Department of Communication Studies
University of North Carolina at Chapel Hill

Handbook of
Divorce and Relationship
Dissolution

I

Introduction

1

Divorce and Relationship Dissolution in the 21st Century

Mark A. Fine
University of Missouri—Columbia

John H. Harvey
University of Iowa

OUR PURPOSE IN EDITING THE HANDBOOK

As we worked collaboratively on our earlier book, *Children of Divorce: Stories of Loss and Growth* (Harvey & Fine, 2004), we conducted a thorough review of the divorce literature. To our surprise, we discovered that there was no single source that brought together into a single volume the wealth of information that the scholarly community has now gathered about divorce. This led to our decision to develop this handbook for researchers, graduate students, practitioners involved with divorce and relationship dissolution, and other interested constituencies.

In addition to a lack of integration across sources, we found three major gaps in coverage. The first gap was that there was relatively little information on the *processes* involved before, during, and after divorce. By *processes*, we are referring to the so-called hows and whys: the day-to-day events that are involved in divorce, the ways that various family members (and even outside institutions) behave toward each other, the changes over time that occur, and even the meanings that the participants assign to the various divorce-related events. Most of the literature on divorce has dealt with such issues as the demographic aspects of divorce, the psychosocial outcomes for individuals experiencing divorce, and how divorce relates to a variety of other social and psychological phenomena. As a result, we have several chapters in the handbook that are specifically focused on processes; we asked all authors to attend to such issues as they prepared their chapters.

The second gap we identified was a lack of information on divorce and relationship dissolution across diverse groups of individuals. Much of the literature has focused on White, middle-class samples of individuals; groups varying on such dimensions as race, sexual orientation, and gender composition have received far less attention. Consequently, we commissioned chapters on African American, Latino, and gay and lesbian relationships, as well as a chapter on the role of gender in divorce and dissolution. However, we did not want to relegate all of our attention to issues of diversity to an isolated set of chapters; we asked all authors to attend to issues of diversity as they prepared their chapters. Unfortunately, because of a lack of information on diverse relationships in the literature, our authors were limited in how much attention they could devote to issues related to diversity.

The third gap that we observed is that there has been far less scholarly attention devoted to the dissolution of nonmarital relationships than to divorce. Further, the scant focus on nonmarital relationships has been on the dating relationships of college students far more than cohabiting relationships. However, with increases in nonmarital cohabitation rates (Teachman, Tedrow, & Crowder, 2000; Teachman, Tedrow, & Hall, chap. 4, this volume), the dissolution of nonmarital relationships has taken on even more importance. As a result, we asked all authors to address both divorce and nonmarital relationship termination, to whatever extent permitted by the literature.

THEORIES AND METHODS USED IN THE STUDY OF DIVORCE AND RELATIONSHIP DISSOLUTION

A wide variety of theories are referred to in the chapters in this handbook. For example, among others, the following theories or models are used either to ground the empirical research reviewed or to integrate the research literature presented in the chapter: stress and coping; risk and resilience; social exchange and resource; investment; behavioral theory; crisis; vulnerability, stress, and adaptation; cognitive theory; cognitive-behavioral theory; cognitive-developmental theory; account-making; coping with loss; family systems; ecological theory; symbolic interactionism and identity; disaffection; social penetration; disillusionment model of dissolution; perpetual problems model of dissolution; stage models; relational depenetration; cognitive-emotional adaptation; social network; stress-related growth; relational deterioration model; deinstitutionalization of marriage; feminist theory; and gender.

Is the use of so many different theoretical perspectives a strength of this field or a deficit? In different ways, it is probably both. It is a strength in that there is a wealth of different perspectives on divorce and relationship dissolution—in the midst of the diversity of perspectives is, one would hope, a complementarity and synergy that is beneficial for the development of our knowledge base. Creative and innovative solutions to new research questions are more likely when an array of varying theoretical perspectives is available to address them. However, the multiplicity of theories is a deficit in that the lack of a singular, unifying perspective makes it more difficult to integrate findings across studies. Our knowledge base expands most rapidly to the extent that different scholars use similar perspectives; for example, it is easier to build on earlier research when investigators develop the same operational definitions of important constructs (e.g., marital quality or relationship stability). Furthermore, within these varying theoretical perspectives, many constructs have been defined in quite different ways (e.g., relationship stability has been defined either in terms of whether or not the relationship continues over time or the extent to which individuals have thoughts of ending the relationship). To their credit, many of the authors in this handbook have developed integrative theoretical models to bring greater clarity and integration to their topic.

There is a similar level of variability in the methods used to gather the empirical information reviewed in the chapters. As is the case in the social sciences in general, the majority of the studies that have informed our knowledge base on divorce and relationship dissolution have been quantitative. Quantitative approaches have included such methods as the use of Census data, national secondary data sets (e.g., the National Survey of Families and Households), surveys, correlational studies, longitudinal studies, and experimental designs. Qualitative methods—including interviews, ethnographies, and narrative accounts—have also provided and are likely to increasingly provide unique and important insights. This methodological

diversity is a strength in that different methodological approaches yield data that can potentially compliment each other. Robert Weiss, in his commentary at the end of the handbook,
advocates for a sequential combination of quantitative and qualitative approaches to furthering
our understanding of divorce and relationship dissolution.

THEMES EMERGING IN THE HANDBOOK

As we begin to frame the vastness of this book, we have identified the following themes in the
various chapters.

Variability and Diversity

This theme permeates the volume. As we will see in the chapters, variability is found in the
manifold reported causes and consequences of dissolution, in the diverse populations being
studied and described, and in the varied reactions to dissolution issues. There are chapters
that address how the dissolution process for African American and Hispanic couples is similar to and different from that for White individuals (see chap. 23 by Orbuch & Brown and
chap. 25 by Umaña-Taylor & Alfaro, respectively). There also is a chapter that addresses how
relationship dissolution in gay and lesbian couples is both similar to and different from heterosexual couples. Change over time and variability are found in the chapter by Amato and
Irving on the history of dissolution and divorce, including the various cultural change factors
such as industrialization, urbanization, and women's entry into the workforce during and after
World War II. Change is also found in the future projections discussed by Teachman, Tedrow,
and Hall, including predictions about how cohabitation will continue to play a role in how
people enact their close relationships. As will be suggested in the chapter by Sprecher, Felmlee, Schmeeckle, and Shu on social networks, heterogeneity is also found in the increasing
number of multicultural relationships and the particular dynamics they bring to the table in
understanding close relationships.

Variability and diversity are found not only in demographic trends but also in the numerous
processes theorized to be part of the overall package of dissolution experiences. For example,
Braver, Shapiro, and Goodman, in their chapter in this volume on the effects of divorce on
parents, reached a conclusion that is rare in the literature—that divorced men, on average, may
actually fare worse financially in the long run than divorced women; Sayer, in her chapter
on the economic aspects of divorce and relationship dissolution, reached the more typical
inference that women fare worse than men. Clearly, these differing conclusions in these two
chapters suggest, among other possible explanations, that there is considerable variability in
the financial sequalae of divorced men and women. In addition, how people adapt to dissolution
varies greatly. Terms such as *enhancers*, *good enough*, and *the defeated* have been coined to
describe the varying ways that people adjust to dissolution.

Complexity

Complexity is another theme that leaps from the pages of this book. Certainly, this is the central
theme behind the different chapters on why dissolution and divorce occur. We will learn in
the chapter by Hall and Fincham, for example, that even though infidelity may play a role in a
couple's decision to separate, it may not be the critical factor in determining whether divorce
actually occurs. Reported causes for dissolution are myriad, and they even vary with the times
(e.g., the discussions of how much individuals stressed self-fulfillment as a great quest behind
their decision to dissolve relationships in the 1960s and 1970s).

Divorce and dissolution patterns also show complexity. Ganong, Coleman, and Hans, in their chapter on redivorce, note that the median length of one's first marriage is 8 years, followed by 3 years of being single, and then 7 years of remarriage, followed by the second divorce. This pattern likely would still leave the individuals involved in their midlives, thus setting the stage for possible further cycles of marriage and divorce toward the senior years of life! With the baby boom generation as principal architects of these trends for current midlife people, might we not expect a major increase in divorce for this generation of individuals during their senior years?

We also will learn about the complex role that the social environment plays in how close relationships are started, continued, and ended. These environments, filled with friends and family members, are shown to affect relationships in major ways. Then, when divorce or dissolution occur, a person's social network often changes in dramatic ways, with substantial loss of previous acquaintances and even confidants (referred to in the chapter by Sprecher and colleagues as "atrophy in the social network").

How to Achieve a Realistic, Practicable Adaptation to Dissolution and Divorce

This issue is addressed in virtually all of the chapters. The key question is, if dissolution is to occur, how do the partners and any children involved best adapt to the circumstances? As we will discover, the circumstances may be daunting. We will learn, however, that there are many approaches, some quite recent, that have snowballed in the arena of helping couples achieve better outcomes, particularly when children are involved. Chapters on mediation (by Sbarra & Emery), educational interventions (by Blaisure & Geasler), growth and resilience after loss (by Tashiro, Frazier, & Berman), and the law and divorce (by Mahoney) are instructive about new ideas and policies aimed at facilitating the exit process and the reestablishment of lives in the aftermath of dissolution. Barber and Demo reviewed the literature on the effectiveness of several intervention programs for children whose parents have divorced, and they found that several programs have yielded positive results.

There are numerous suggestions for adaptation in the various chapters. There are so-called collaborative divorces now in which couples are coached toward mutually acceptable outcomes by third parties; these individuals are mediators in some cases, and they are therapists, lawyers, and clergy in others. This development is leading to a major industry of professionals who help people divorce, presumably in better ways than they would otherwise. We will learn from Sbarra and Emery in their chapter on mediation that it appears to be having a generally positive impact on partners who engage in it, who do not have to battle one another with separate lawyers in court. We may wonder whether there will be a mushrooming of expenses associated with these newer, nonadversarial professional services, just as there are when attorneys are involved in the traditional adversarial process.

Relatively new ideas such as trauma growth after dissolution are presented in the handbook, and there is an extension of Duck's well-known stage model of relationship dissolution in the chapter by Rollie and Duck. Although we will gain some perspective on how people may grow and even prosper in these situations, it still will not be clear what the package of characteristics and processes is for those who do generally grow from the experience versus those who do not seem to grow much, or may even become the defeated. The chapter by Tashiro et al. on stress-related growth provides some clues.

There are a few chapters that have discussions of account-making and narrative development (see the chapter on account-making by Harvey & Fine) as a way of coping with feelings of abandonment, anger, and hopelessness that may accompany dissolution. There is discussion in the chapter by Wood and Duck of gender differences, and similarities, in these coping processes. The interesting term *grave dressing* is presented by Rollie and Duck in the context of people's attempts to develop a story about the loss and move to new points in their lives.

The idea of successful adaptation is in the air in 21st-century analyses of dissolution. We even have a chapter by Masuda on postdissolution relationships. Such relationships, and the binuclear family (i.e., the family that has been reconstituted after divorce or dissolution), are a thoroughly modern phenomenoa that likely will grow in number, just as the new category of people who are divorced and are going back to try to find and renew relationships with long-lost lovers has grown exponentially by use of the Internet (e.g., Kalish, 1997).

Children of Divorce

The editors of this volume have been quite involved of late in analyzing issues associated with children of divorce (e.g., Harvey & Fine, 2004). Although we did not intend for this handbook to widely reflect the questions being addressed regarding children of divorce, many of the chapters (see the chapter by Barber & Demo on the consequences of divorce for children) and Booth's commentary on children of divorce refer to these questions and to the debate about whether divorce does irreparable harm to children, or what the continuum of effects is for children. This specific theme overlaps with the earlier theme of adaptation. In this vein, there is the recognition that, when divorce occurs and children are involved, the family remains, albeit as a binuclear family. Commentators address how this newly constituted family has the responsibility of putting the children's interest high in the priorities of coping with the divorce.

As noted in the chapter by Ganong et al. on redivorce and stepfamilies, there often is a significant feeling of loss and grief for those experiencing dissolution or divorce. Children, in particular, may show such reactions. Parents need to be sensitive to children's feelings that they have lost a family, a newly absent parent, neighborhood and school friends, and possibly a home in the divorce. Such experience may make children feel stigmatized and abnormal relative to those in their social networks.

Several chapters focus on how parents may successfully engage in coparenting after divorce (Adamsons & Pasley), how stepfamilies may establish their own effective identities (Ganong et al.), and how people may use cognitive-emotional approaches (Harvey & Fine), including accounts and narratives, to help understand and manage the chaos that may surround the lives of children involved in a divorce or dissolution situation.

The Politics of Dissolution and Divorce

This theme is found most prominently in contemporary debates about the effects of divorce on children. The discussion goes well beyond research evidence to include strong beliefs about what is true or best for people. As the reader will see (e.g., in the chapter by Amato & Irving on divorce and relationship research in historical context), such currents are prominent in historical and contemporary analyses of dissolution and divorce. In this volume, these currents are implied in some of the chapters concerned with general issues and historical trends, as well as in the final commentaries. Political considerations obviously cloud public policy about gay and lesbian marriage and whether the government has a duty or right to try to create laws that make divorce more difficult to obtain. In the chapter by Amato and Irving, there is discussion of the sanctity of marriage and what that may mean regarding public policy about divorce. There also is commentary about the use of terms such as *broken homes* and *failed marriages* and how such ways of discussing dissolution may be deleterious to the families involved. Although this handbook was not designed to address the many issues that are more political than scholarly in this area, it would be folly to argue that some of those issues are not either explicitly or implicitly found within its pages. What we hope is that the type of analysis that is central to this volume will be informative to policymakers and the general public who are genuinely searching for the best answers to policy questions about the family and divorce in the 21st century.

Obviously, our depiction of the themes found herein includes considerable overlap. The first two themes of diversity or variability and complexity may be viewed as overarching themes that encompass the more specific themes of how to achieve a realistic, practicable adaptation to dissolution, children of divorce, and the politics of dissolution and divorce. Each of the latter themes certainly epitomizes considerable diversity and complexity.

TOPICS REQUIRING MORE COVERAGE IN THE FUTURE

No single source can provide exhaustive coverage of all relevant topics, and this handbook is no exception. Here, we indicate areas that we believe warrant more attention in future work. First, because of our focus on the processes involved in divorce and dissolution, which by definition involve relationships, the majority of our coverage is of interpersonal factors. Intrapsychic issues, such as partners' mental health and partner cognitions regarding termination-related events, receive relatively less coverage. Second, an exciting development is recent research on biosocial aspects of relationship processes (Booth, Carver, & Granger, 2000; also discussed by Booth in his commentary), and these warrant more attention in the future. Third, spirituality and religiosity are mentioned in several chapters. For example, in the chapter by Orbuch and Brown on African American relationship dissolution, they note the importance that religion and church activities have in African American families; Rodrigues, Hall, and Fincham (in their chapter on predictors of divorce and relationship dissolution) point out that divorce and dissolution are related to low levels of religious participation. However, because of this only modest coverage, religion and religious activity, as well as spirituality more broadly, warrant more attention in future research.

Fourth, this handbook considered psychological, socioemotional, cognitive, relational (see Bartell's chapter), and financial consequences (see Sayer's chapter on the economic aspects of divorce and dissolution) of relationship dissolution for children and parents, but other types of consequences (e.g., catastrophic) could have been considered more, as could the impacts of dissolution for other groups of relationship partners, such as those without children and those in later life. Fifth, despite our inclusion of several chapters devoted to relationship dissolution among minority couples, more ethnic and diverse family types deserve consideration. As prime examples, we encourage researchers to attend to relationship dissolution in Asian American couples, as well as among couples from various religious preference, sexual orientation, socioeconomic, and national origin groups. Finally, a topic that deserves much more attention is the role of violence and aggression in relationship dissolution. The chapter by Lawrence, Ro, Barry, and Bunde provides an excellent overview of the literature on dissolution in physically aggressive relationships, but we know that relationship violence is both underreported and understudied. The control and power issues involved in relationship violence also influence couple dynamics in nonviolent relationships, and these dynamics have to be studied in more depth (Olson, Fine, & Lloyd, 2005).

We also encourage additional work on applied issues related to divorce and relationship dissolution. Our book addresses legal and policy issues, mediation, and parent education, but more attention has to be focused on other types of intervention, such as psychotherapy, postdivorce family therapy, remarriage education, financial planning, and family life education. These different approaches to intervention, to varying degrees, are integral components of the new divorce industry and require more scholarly attention.

ORGANIZATION FOR THE HANDBOOK

The book is organized into eight sections, including three commentaries. Section 1 is composed of this introductory chapter; section 2 contains three chapters that focus on demographic and historical trends in divorce and relationship dissolution. Kitson shares her insights into the history of research on divorce and discusses how this history can inform current research. Amato and Irving provide a unique history of the demographic aspects of divorce dating back to the Colonial era in the United States. Teachman, Tedrow, and Hall take on the difficult task of projecting into the future (from historical data) with respect to demographic aspects of divorce and relationship dissolution. Collectively, these three chapters provide far more information, dating back further into the past and into the future, than typical analyses of trends in the last quarter century, as well as a human element in Kitson's chapter regarding the early origins of divorce research.

The third section targets the causes, underlying processes, and antecedents of divorce and relationship dissolution. Our goal in this section is ambitious, as we attemp to describe factors that either cause or predict later divorce *and* to characterize the processes that occur before, during, and after the divorce or termination of the relationship. Chapter 5, by Rodrigues, Hall, and Fincham, summarizes and integrates the knowledge base regarding the factors that predict divorce and relationship dissolution. Masuda, in chapter 6, addresses the issue of friendship following relationship dissolution among premarital couples. Chapters 7 and 8, by Vangelisti and Hall and Fincham, respectively, deal with two understudied phenomena—hurtful communication and infidelity, respectively—and how these affect relationship processes during relationship termination. Duck and Wood, in chapter 9, explore the dynamics of gender in relationship dissolution and argue for scholars to be more careful about honoring the distinction between *sex* and *gender*.

Change over time is an essential aspect of the dissolution process. Three chapters touch on this dynamic aspect of the process—chapter 10, by Harvey and Fine, on the social constructions of accounts of how the relationship terminated; chapter 11, by Kayser and Rao-Kelter, on the process of disaffection, or how a partner grows out of love; and chapter 12, by Duck and Rollie, on the benefits and limitations of stage models of divorce and relationship dissolution. In the latter chapter, Duck and Rollie extend Ducks's (1982) very widely cited stage model of relationship dissolution. We are very pleased to have an "exclusive" on this theoretical advance.

Adamsons and Pasley, in chapter 13, explore the phenomenon of coparenting after divorce and relationship dissolution. Coparenting has become a popular concept of late, and Adamsons and Pasley take a critical look at the literature. In the final chapter in the section, chapter 14, Lawrence, Ro, Barry, and Bunde focus on the critical issue of relational violence in their look at relationship distress and dissolution in physically aggressive relationships.

Section 4 addresses perhaps the most controversial of the issues involved in divorce and relationship dissolution—the consequences of divorce and relationship dissolution. Barber and Demo, in chapter 15, examine the very polarizing literature on the effects of divorce and relationship dissolution on children through their discussion of four "tiers" of research traditions, and Braver, Shapiro, and Goodman, in chapter 16, review the consequences of relationship termination on parents and reach some perhaps surprising conclusions regarding sex differences in financial well-being following divorce. In chapter 17, Bartell focuses on the effects of relationship dissolution on young adults' romantic relationships and uses a cognitive-developmental model to help explain the mechanisms underlying these effects. Tashiro, Frazier, and Berman, in chapter 18, refreshingly take a rare look at the positive consequences of the termination process—stress-related growth following divorce and relationship dissolution—and Sayer, in chapter 19, reviews the important area of finances and economics pertaining to divorce and relationship termination.

Section 5 focuses on the diverse ways that families cope with divorce and relationship dissolution. In chapter 20, Ganong, Coleman, and Hans target stepfamily living and the consequences of redivorce for couples in stepfamilies. Communication processes are critical components of any coping response, and Afifi and Hamrick, in chapter 21, integrate the literature on communication processes that promote risk and resiliency in postdivorce families. The final chapter in this section, chapter 22, by Sprecher, Felmlee, Schmeeckle, and Shu, explores social networks and how they affect and in turn are affected by relationship dissolution. One's social network is an essential influence on the process of coping with relationship termination, and this important area of research is reviewed in this chapter.

Consistent with our intention to address variation in divorce and relationship dissolution processes, section 6 contains three chapters that explore this issue. In chapter 23, Orbuch and Brown review the literature on divorce and dissolution in the context of race or ethnicity, whereas Oswald and Clausell, in chapter 24, review our knowledge base with respect to relationship dissolution among gay and lesbian couples. In chapter 25, Umaña-Taylor and Alfaro focus on relationship termination issues for Latino individuals.

Applied issues are addressed throughout the handbook, but they are the primary focus of the chapters in section 7 on applied issues pertaining to divorce and relationship dissolution. In chapter 26, Mahoney discusses recent trends in laws pertaining to divorce. Sbarra and Emery, in chapter 27, review the literature on the increasingly popular intervention of divorce mediation. Finally, educational programs for divorcing parents, which have become a thriving industry, are examined by Blaisure and Geasler in chapter 28. Blaisure and Geasler have conducted several large-scale surveys of such programs and provide the most recent information in this chapter.

Finally, in section 8, three noted scholars—Robert S. Weiss from the University of Massachusetts, Ellen Berscheid from the University of Minnesota, and Alan Booth from The Pennsylvania State University—have provided commentaries of the material in the book. The commentators were asked to address some aspect of the process of divorce and relationship dissolution, either based on material in the book, their own research and scholarship, or both.

CONCLUDING THOUGHTS

We hope that this book is successful not only in bringing together the very best scholarship related to divorce and relationship dissolution, but also in stimulating future research on this important topic and in bringing some scholarly attention to the public debates on issues related to divorce and relationship dissolution.

REFERENCES

Booth, A., Carter, K., & Granger, D. A. (2000). Biosocial perspectives on the family. *Journal of Marriage and the Family, 62,* 1018–1034.

Duck, S. W. (1982). A topography of relationship disengagement and dissolution. In S. Duck (Ed.), *Personal relationships: Vol. 4. Dissolving personal relationships* (pp. 1–30). San Diego, CA: Academic Press.

Harvey, J. H., & Fine, M. A. (2004). *Children of divorce: Stories of loss and growth*. Mahwah, NJ: Lawrence Erlbaum Associates.

Kalish, N. (1997). *Lost and found lovers: Facts and fantasies of rekindled romances*. New York: Morrow.

Olson, L. N., Fine, M. A., & Lloyd, S. (2005). A dialectical approach to theorizing about violence between intimates. In V. Bengsten, A. Acock, K. Allen, P. Dilworth-Anderson, & D. Klein (Eds.), *Sourcebook of family theories and methods: An interactive approach* (pp. 315–331). Newbury Park, CA: Sage.

Teachman, J. D., Tedrow, L. M., & Crowder, K. D. (2000). The changing demography of America's families. *Journal of Marriage and Family, 62,* 1234–1246.

II

Demographic and Historical Aspects of Divorce and Relationship Dissolution

2

Divorce and Relationship Dissolution Research: Then and Now

Gay C. Kitson
University of Akron

At the time, it did not seem to be such a big deal, but I was there near the beginning of the upswing in divorce research in the 1970s. It was an exciting period. As a beginning scholar not knowing any better, however, I took it for granted. I was happy working on longitudinal research on divorce adjustment with Marvin Sussman (Kitson & Sussman, 1982), but I certainly did not appreciate the magnitude of the upswing in U.S. divorce rates or that, as a result, this era would become a highly productive period in divorce research. Even more than I have experienced since, researchers were generous with one another in sharing tips, thoughts, and encouragement.

This chapter reflects on divorce research trends of earlier decades to illustrate how some of the research themes of today have built on or grown beyond these earlier works, and, in some cases, appear to be revisiting them. Issues that currently seem self-evident were not then, and others that seemed settled are less so now. Because most journals encourage a focus on more recent research to ensure that authors are up to date, this earlier foundation is often less apparent. An understanding of this background helps to put the foci and controversies of today in context. These earlier works can also help to identify recently ignored issues and approaches or types of analyses that can be replicated today with larger, often longitudinal, data sets and more sophisticated analytic techniques.

My primary focus is on divorce and to a lesser extent relationship dissolution in the United States. When I use the term *divorce*, I also mean dissolution of marriage. This chapter is not a literature review but an examination of some themes and reflections on them. As a result, I cite only some works that illustrate my points. More detailed reference lists may be found in many of the citations.

As an organizing device, I highlight some of the important contributions of four scholars whose work I think played an important role in the field of divorce research, particularly in the area of adjustment to divorce: William J. Goode, E. Mavis Hetherington, Judith S. Wallerstein, and Robert S. Weiss. After describing some of each author's work, I also explore certain themes or directions of the field that I see as related to their research.

ESTABLISHING THE BACKGROUND

After declining from, at that point, an all-time high after World War II, U.S. divorce rates began to increase in the mid-1960s. By the early 1970s, they had already gone up substantially before reaching their all time peak, to date, in 1979 and 1981 (see Figs. 4.1 and 4.2 in chap. 4). Although divorce rates have decreased since then, they are still high. Recent life-table estimates indicate that 30% of U.S. couples divorce within 10 years (Bramlett & Mosher, 2002) and that, for those aged 45 years or younger, 50% of first marriages will end for men and 45% to 50% will end for women (Fields & Kreider, 2000). Because such estimates ignore the breakup rate of long- and short-term heterosexual and same-sex cohabitation, the actual rates of relationship dissolution are undoubtedly higher.

With the increase in the divorce rate and changes in the legal requirements from fault-based divorce to no-fault divorce or dissolution of marriage, researchers in the 1970s began to study divorce in greater detail. In both 1975 and 1976, as young researchers working on the topic of divorce, Lenore J. Weitzman and I organized informal evening gatherings of divorce researchers at the American Sociological Association annual meetings in, respectively, San Francisco and New York City. Because of the locations of the meetings, other scholars who were not sociologists were also able to attend. Some of these people had already published on divorce, and all would subsequently do so. Neither of the organizers kept a list of the participants, but among the attendees were Bernard Bloom, Emily Brown, Kathleen Camara, David Chiriboga, Stanley Cohen, Julie Fulton, Paul Glick, Doris Jacobson, Gerald Jacobson, Joan Kelly, Arthur Norton, Helen Raschke, Graham Spanier, Marvin Sussman, Judith Wallerstein and Robert Weiss. Some of the individuals who were present at one or the other of the meetings, such as Jacobson, Wallerstein, and Kelly, also established clinical practice programs that have been widely copied. Weiss's work describing Seminars for the Separated, an approach using support groups for the separated and divorced, is still used today, and Cohen became executive director of the Association of Family and Conciliation Courts. Thus, these attendees, as did others who were active during that period, greatly influenced the direction of and discourse about clinical practice on divorce. In the following sections, I use the work of four researchers to illustrate some of these trends.

WILLIAM J. GOODE: SOCIAL CHANGE

Goode, a Pennsylvania State University doctoral graduate in sociology, one of whose high school teachers in Texas was Lyndon Johnson (Caro, 1982), made contributions in a number of research areas. Much of his work on marriage and family examined or reflected on the impact of social change on marital relationships. In the face of increased interest in divorce after World War II, Goode did research on divorce in Detroit, Michigan, where he was then a faculty member at Wayne State University. Goode modeled his book's format on Emile Durkheim's *Suicide* (Weitzman, 2003). It was published as *After Divorce* (Goode, 1956; also known as *Women in Divorce*, 1965, in the paperback version). Goode's book, in my opinion, set a foundation for much of the thinking about divorce in the late 1960s and early 1970s. His work was based on interviews with Detroit women in 1948 who were single mothers aged 20 to 38 years. According to information drawn from divorce court records, the women had been divorced from 2 to 26 months; Goode's aim was to simulate a longitudinal study with data collected in a cross-sectional design. The book detailed the demographic characteristics, process of marital dissolution, and divorce adjustment of his sample. Goode used role theory to examine adaptation to the multiple roles a divorced person faced. Although this perspective has not been widely used since, Raschke (1977) used a role approach as did Johnson and Wu (2002) in a pooled time series analysis of divorce adjustment in which they found the role approach accounted for more variance in their models than did their measures of selectivity and the crisis approach.

With his multidimensional, processual approach to the topic, Goode included a chapter detailing "steps to the divorce" and the self-described complaints that led to the divorce, as well as the timing of what he called the trauma of the divorce, that is, the behavioral indicators of distress such as trouble sleeping and low work efficiency. He further examined the reaction of friends; the economic divorce; what he called "the children of divorce" in a chapter on the mothers' reports of their offspring's reactions; the postdivorce relationship with the exspouse; dating; and remarriage.

Bohannon (1970) subsequently labeled the interrelated experiences of divorce as the emotional divorce (the period of predivorce estrangement); the legal divorce (the grounds for the divorce and legal process); the economic divorce (money and property); the coparental divorce (custody, visitation, and the single-parent household); the community divorce (the reactions of friends and others); and the psychic divorce, or the establishment of a sense of autonomy as a person outside of the marital relationship. Although much research has subsequently focused on psychological well-being (as Amato chose to do as an organizing device in his 2000 review of the consequences of divorce), these dimensions still serve as a useful model for looking at the totality of adjustment to relationship breakup.

Goode's thorough book contributed, in my opinion, to a period of research quiescence on the topic: What else was there to know? Besides, decreased divorce rates in the 1950s, which continued into the early 1960s, meant marital breakup was no longer as much of a social problem as it had been in the period after World War II when Goode's book was published.

In fact, it was not until the mid-1970s in the United States that divorce surpassed death as the major reason for the end of marriage (Uhlenberg & Chew, 1986). Because of the generally negative societal view of divorce as an event to be prevented, and the widespread use of secondary data, research in the early 1970s was still substantially focused on the societal and demographic causes of divorce (Kitson & Raschke, 1981). As a result, divorce in this period was often studied as a by-product of other research topics. If someone were looking at, say, fertility, the data might also be used to look at both fertility and divorce (e.g., Coombs & Zumeta, 1970).

SOME TRENDS IN MARITAL DISSATISFACTION AND DIVORCE

During this period, adjustment to divorce was less emphasized. In fact, as recently as the 1990 *Journal of Marriage and the Family* decade review, divorce was discussed in terms of causes (White, 1990) and consequences (Kitson & Morgan, 1990). The studies that began in the 1970s generally used divorce records-based samples; they focused more on adjustment than much of the previous research had, or on the processes that people went through as they considered and then (often) acted on a decision to divorce (Bloom, Hodges, & Caldwell, 1982; Bloom, Hodges, Caldwell, Systra, & Cedrone, 1977; Chiriboga, Catron, & Associates,1991; Kitson, 1985, 1992; Spanier & Thompson, 1984; Weitzman, 1985). As with Goode's (1956) work, these studies had the advantage of being able to look in depth at the process of divorce generally in a cohort of people who separated and divorced at a similar time, but they had the disadvantages of reporting only on a limited geographic area and using retrospective reports of events before the divorce was filed, even if the individuals were followed longitudinally postfiling. Much of this research also explored men's reactions to the breakup. Additional research on fathers and fathering and divorce did not become more common until the 1990s (Amato & Gilbreth, 2001; Arendell, 1995). Despite the increase in joint custody and the increase in the number of single-father families, from 393,000 in 1970 to 2 million in 2000 (Fields & Casper, 2001), data are still relatively limited on the father's role in childrearing, a gap that should be filled. In addition, Williams and Umberson's (2004) report that men may experience more long-term psychological difficulties in divorce than women suggests further reason for study.

Good Enough Marriages

Although pathways and adjustment to divorce have been increasingly explored, less is known about less-than-satisfactory but continuing marriages. Such information would be useful now, at a time when states and the federal government are promoting marital preparation and enrichment and covenant marriage designed to make marital dissolution more difficult.

In a chapter on family disorganization in a book on social problems—still quite a common way to look at divorce at the time—Goode (1966) detailed the various ways in which family units dissolved. He also described internal dissolution, or "empty shell marriages," in which couples continued to live together although they found their relationships to be emotionally unsatisfying. At about the same time, in research based on a not methodologically well described series of open-ended interviews, Cuber (1969) studied different conceptions of, if not happy, at least contented, upper-middle-class marriages of at least 10 years duration in which the couples had lived together without considering divorce. The descriptions of these relationships seemed useful. They included passive-congenial, devitalized, and conflict-habituated marriages. Hetherington and Kelly (2002) also presented a taxonomy of marriages. With a greater awareness of the heightened psychological distress associated with staying in an unsatisfactory marriage versus divorcing for adults (Williams, 2003) and for children (Emery, 1994; Rodgers & Pryor, 1998), more should be learned about such families and relationships.

Worldwide Divorce Increase

During the 1960s and 1970s, researchers became more aware that it was not only U.S. divorce rates that were increasing (Glendon, 1987; Phillips, 1988). In 1963, Goode's book *World Revolution and Family Patterns* highlighted that the process was a worldwide one as societies industrialized and urbanized and couples chose their own marital partners. In some societies, such changes led to decreases in divorce rates; in other societies, they led to increases. With more discussion of legal issues and cohabitation, Goode updated and continued his analysis of worldwide trends in divorce in 1993.

As Goode (1963, 1993) and others have demonstrated (Aghajanian, 1986; Moskoff, 1983), efforts to "prop up" marriage by restricting the availability of divorce have had a consistent rate of failure around the world. With such efforts, divorce may temporarily decrease, as it also has in war and during the Great Depression, but as soon as restrictions are lifted or social and economic conditions improve, a pent-up increase in divorce occurs.

Difficulties in collecting, translating, and assimilating cross-cultural data and the differences in its quality and timeliness in different societies still make cross-national comparisons difficult. Such comparisons continue to be needed and should move more to the examination of cultural differences and similarities in the divorce and postdivorce process. In this way, the influences of cultural acceptability and societal unrest could be incorporated to explore how or if social and psychological differences in divorce adjustment exist cross-culturally.

Research Methods

To illustrate the changes in analysis techniques and the increased ability to manipulate large quantities of data over the past decades, Goode's (1956) initial analyses for his Detroit study involved McBee cards, which were cards with punches around the edges to reflect survey responses. A metal rod was thrust through the cards to sort out those with a similar punch pattern, and then those cards were counted. Goode then graduated to the use of an electronic card sorter that could count and, with manipulation, cross-tabulate IBM cards (W. J. Goode, personal communication). This technique also highlights the quality of the contribution of his 1956 book at a time when the resources available to do so were more limited.

Today, with the use of personal computers with their own sets of statistical programs and the public availability of census and other large-scale data sets, analyses are more sophisticated. Research has moved ahead in various ways, but it is important to recognize what a shift in direction this represents. As Price-Bonham and Balswick (1970, p. 967) observed in the first of the *Journal of Marriage and the Family* decade reviews on divorce and remarriage, research in the 1960s in family demography, the divorce process, and remarriage had often produced "oversimplified generalizations" and was "often limited to a single-factor approach rather than a multiple-factor approach" that more appropriately attempted to "ascertain the interdependent nature of the relationships" studied. Such analyses began to be more possible to do in the 1970s.

Such improvements also helped in the development of longitudinal studies that allowed for prospective analyses to follow those who eventually divorced (see, e.g., Booth & Amato, 1991). However, such data are generally part of a larger battery of questions so that less detail is available about individual topics, such as divorce. In addition, the multiple secondary use of such data sets means that the sampling, attrition, and measurement biases of the research—and this is true of all studies—are compounded and magnified through the repeated use of the data sets.

Despite the detail and richness that qualitative research can provide, research on divorce has been, with some significant exceptions (Arendell, 1995; Kurz, 1995; Hackstaff, 1999), predominantly quantitative. Although there is greater recognition of the utility of qualitative research when used in combination with the quantitative approach, qualitative approaches are still often not well regarded; nor are those, such as divorce-records based studies, that are not nationally representative. At a time when the forms of couple relationships appear to be changing, a greater recognition of the contributions that each kind of research can contribute—perhaps even in combination—would lead to a fuller understanding of the relationship breakup process.

The Demography of Divorce

Characteristics of Those Who Divorce

Goode's detailed analyses of the demographic characteristics of his divorced sample presaged a period of increased demographic research. In the 1970s, trends in marriage and divorce were just beginning to be reported. For example, divorce was more likely for those individuals with lower age at marriage and less education and income. It had previously been assumed that higher status couples were more likely to divorce than those of lower status, a belief Goode (1956) found to be inaccurate in methodological studies before beginning his 1948 study. The study of divorce rates in marital cohorts who were successively followed from their dates of marriage was introduced (see Glick & Norton, 1973, for a discussion). This approach more clearly demonstrated differences in the likelihood of divorce in a "marital lifetime" (defined as 40 years) in cohorts married differing lengths of time (Bramlett & Mosher, 2002; Norton & Moorman,

1987). Compared with that period, more recently, the age at marriage has increased, and the proportion of married individuals has decreased; as of 1996, just 51.1% of the U.S. population was married (Kreider & Simmons, 2003).

In other trends from this earlier period, compared with previous rates of divorce, couples with children became increasingly likely to divorce. In addition, as more married women became employed, their independent sources of income made divorce more of a possibility for those in unhappy marriages (Cherlin, 1981; Glick & Norton, 1973, 1977; Norton & Glick, 1979; Teachman, Polonko, & Scanzoni, 1999).

Remarriage

As divorce increased, so did remarriage rates and research about it. The decade reviews of the *Journal of Marriage and Family* are often barometers of changing perspectives on and increases in research in various marriage and family topics. Not until 1990 did researchers feel that enough studies had accumulated to examine remarriage as a separate research area in the decade reviews (Coleman & Ganong, 1990; Coleman, Ganong, & Fine, 2000).

It became clear that individuals in remarriages often had difficulty quickly establishing a new, cohesive family group (Ahrons, 1981; Cherlin, 1978; Ihinger-Tallman & Pasley, 1987). In more recent years, more divorced individuals have chosen to cohabitate instead of remarrying (Casper & Bianchi, 2002), and more remarriages are ending in a second divorce (Bramlett & Mosher, 2002).

Cohabitation

What was "news" demographically in the 1970s has since been considered, until fairly recently, settled knowledge. The findings of that earlier demography of marriage and the family are now being called into question. The age at marriage has increased and the number of marriages and remarriages has decreased. The number of individuals cohabiting has increased. According to the 1995 National Survey of Family Growth, 41% of women aged 15 to 44 years have ever cohabited (Bramlett & Mosher, 2002). The 2002 U.S. Population Survey reported that 15%, or 2.5 million couples out of 16.5 million cohabiters (persons of opposite sex who share living quarters), have children under the age of 15 living with them (Fields, 2003).

Some countries, particularly in Latin America, have long had traditions of cohabitation (Goode, 1993), and others, such as Sweden, have a more recent history of increased cohabitation (Trost, 1979). However, in the late 1970s, only 2% to 3% of the U.S. population reported cohabiting (Glick & Norton, 1977). According to data from the National Survey of Family Growth, as of 1995, 7% of couples were cohabiting, with 41% reporting they had ever cohabited (Bramlett & Mosher, 2002). Such relationships are more unstable than marriages (Bumpass & Lu, 2000).

Furthermore, as these changes were occurring, less national data on marital status were available. As Coltrane and Adams (2003) reported, the National Center for Health Statistics stopped supporting state marriage and divorce registration statistics and the national reporting of these; the reasons for doing so included lack of complete coverage, poorer quality data, and cost-related issues. In addition, in 1995 the Current Population Survey stopped its cyclical 5-year marital history supplement that began in 1980 (Bramlett & Mosher, 2002). Thus, although relationship changes are a foot, less clear data are available.

The lack of data on the number of and the absence of records of cohabiting breakups creates an increasingly inaccurate picture of the magnitude of the relationship dissolution rate for heterosexual and same-sex couples beyond those who are married and divorced legally. In addition, the social, economic, and psychological consequences of breakups for couples and the children who are involved in cohabitation are difficult to determine beyond the use of volunteer samples. Efforts that have been instituted or proposed in other countries to provide legal protections for couples (Goode, 1993) would help in identifying those whose consensual relationships ended. For example, Canadian provinces have begun to establish provisions for property and spousal support for cohabiters, with some provinces addressing issues such as insurance and social security benefits (Wu & Hart, 2002–2003). In a limited number of U.S. locations, cohabiting couples can register with local authorities (Seltzer, 2000). In an exploratory study, Willetts (2003) used such registries to determine why a small sample of heterosexual individuals chose to have licensed partnerships. Without the availability of accurate public records about them, however, the increases in long-term cohabitation hinder researchers' ability to examine the breakup of heterosexual and same-sex unions and the consequences of such dissolutions.

Couples are continuing to choose cohabitation despite the legal and financial benefits to marriage, U.S. federal efforts such as The Defense of Marriage Act, and the encouragement of marriage and marriage education, particularly for those on welfare. Analyses of the reasons for increasing numbers of cohabiting relationships that do not or only slowly move toward marriage suggest that couples' reluctance to formalize these relationships may be attributed, in part, to lack of a firm economic base for the marriage and lack of conviction about the commitment level of the partner (Cherlin, 2003; Jamieson et al., 2002).

ROBERT S. WEISS: THE EMOTIONAL PROCESS OF DIVORCE

Robert S. Weiss, a University of Chicago doctorate in sociology, began his graduate education in mathematics at the University of Buffalo, then moved to mathematical statistics at the University of Michigan, and then switched to sociology for his master's degree (R. S. Weiss, June 13, 2004, personal communication). He subsequently taught research methods in his position at Brandeis University before moving to the Harvard Medical School and then to the University of Massachusetts–Boston. Although Weiss has done quantitative research, particularly on widowhood (Glick, Weiss, & Parkes, 1974; Parkes & Weiss, 1983), it is his qualitative research (1975, 1976, 1979, 2001) on separation from the spouse in divorce and widowhood that is my focus here. Weiss (1993) has also written about conducting qualitative research.

For his separation and divorce research, Weiss drew from interviews with members of Parents Without Partners, the widowhood research with which he was involved, and a program he developed that he called Seminars for the Separated. The seminars were used as a field placement for psychiatrists, psychologists, social workers, and nurses in the Community Psychiatry program at Harvard (R. S. Weiss, personal communication, August 4, 2004). The seminars provided an informal, educational, and self-help environment for the recently separated or divorced to learn about their emotional reactions to their relationship breakups and the issues with which they were faced.

Part of the genesis for including Weiss' divorce research in the larger category of loss events is based on his use of clinical writing on object relations, particularly those on attachment and loss (Bowlby, 1977a, 1977b, 1980; Jacobson, 1983; Parkes, 1972); he also participated in a seminar led by John Bowlby at the Tavistock Institute in London (see his commentary at the end of this volume).

In his work, Weiss described how adults, like children (Bowlby, 1969, 1973), experienced attachment, or secure emotional bonds to particular others. For a married couple, when the partner is present or reliably available, the other partner feels a sense of comfort and security. In marital separation or divorce, however, a person may find that the familiar and formerly comforting marital partner is no longer available, but still, confusingly, the person may want to seek out the former partner. As a result of the lack of the reliable availability of the former partner, attachment is disrupted, resulting in separation distress, or anxiety; this manifests itself in restlessness, sleeplessness, depression, and a desire to search for the lost partner. The sense of loss can be befuddling as a person experiences the seemingly contradictory emotions of wanting to share new experiences with a person he or she is simultaneously glad to be rid of. These feelings, Weiss (1975, 1976) suggested, were due to the loss of attachment. Weiss, as did Goode (1956) earlier, suggested these feelings were likely to be weaker for the person who chose to leave the relationship versus the person who did not want to leave. Thus, Weiss illustrated how those persons who were separating or divorcing could often simultaneously feel relieved and mournful at the end of their relationships.

Weiss's approach highlighted the emotions that the breaking up of important relationships can cause. This formulation suggests that it is the breaking of the bonds of attachment that produces psychological distress. Thus, although studies of psychological distress in divorce may not measure this emotional dimension directly, they are likely to be picking up some of the consequences of this sense of dislocation through their use of measures of psychological symptomatology.

In addition, for many individuals, divorce represents a sense of failure at an important adult social role, leading to reflections about how one could have chosen a partner so badly or been deceived so greatly (Kitson, 1992). This approach, which Kitson called loss and change, suggests that the breaking up of relationships, regardless of how common such breakups are in a society, can be emotionally distressing.

Weiss's approach illustrates the stress and coping perspective. In the paragraphs that follow, I discuss this perspective more fully, as well as several other explanatory models of adjustment to divorce.

Stress and Coping

Today, the stress and coping model of response to life events is widely accepted. This approach became more prominent in divorce research as researchers moved to explore the processes and consequences of marital breakups, not just the causes. As did Weiss, this perspective states that divorce is a stressful life event with negative physical and psychological effects for many of those who experience it. Even positive events, such as a desired divorce, can produce distress. According to this perspective, most people adjust over time to the changes in their lives brought about by the events of divorce (Booth & Amato, 1991; Chiriboga et al., 1991; Jacobson, 1983; Kitson, 1992).

Because the stress and coping model is now so widely accepted, it is hard to realize that this was still a fairly new perspective in the 1970s. For example, the ubiquitous Holmes and Rahe (1967) life events ratings scale and its successors were just being introduced (e.g., Dohrenwend, Krasnoff, Askenasy, & Dohrenwend, 1978; Myers, Lindenthal, Pepper, & Ostrander, 1972). Toward the end of the decade, Pearlin and Schooler (1978) described the structure of coping whereas Rutter (1981) discussed the need to specify the concept of stress as it reflected on coping and development. At the time, research on crises in family studies focused on the ABC-X crisis model by Hill (1958) and then the double ABC-X elaboration of this model by McCubbin and Patterson (1983). Although Boss (2002) drew on Hill's work to develop her model of family stress, this approach has, for the most part, been eclipsed by the stressor approach (Wheaton, 1990, 1999; Williams & Umberson, 2004).

Although it is well accepted now, the concept of stress is not always well understood. For example, in critiquing Amato's (1993) analysis of conclusions to be drawn from research on children and divorce, Demo (1993, pp. 44–55) observed that, like many in family studies "who take a problem-oriented perspective, he [Amato] views life changes as stressful, when in fact many changes are positive." Change, as reflected in a divorce, is a stressful event. The *degree* of stress and whether it is positive or negative varies, not its presence or absence.

Selectivity

The idea of divorce as "problem behavior" has had a long history that still continues, as indicated by the selectivity approach. The titles of earlier books by psychiatrist Edmund Bergler illustrate this view quite well: *Unhappy Marriage and Divorce* (1946) and *Divorce Won't Help* (1948). Bergler's thesis was that, without psychotherapy, preferably psychoanalytic in nature, those who divorced would continue to have neuroses, regardless of the individuals' marital status. As his earlier formulation illustrates, this approach perceives some individuals as having physical or psychological disabilities that make them less fit to marry, remain married, adjust adequately to the end of their relationships, or remarry successfully (Bachrach, 1975). Selectivity is still discussed (Waite, 1995; Waite & Gallagher, 2000) or is seen as part of the reason for family decline (Popenoe, 1993), as concerns about the practicability of marriage have increased again as they did in the late 1940s.

For centuries, in many places in the United States and elsewhere, divorce was viewed culturally, socially, and legally as deviant, stigmatized behavior—and it still is, to some extent. Halem (1980) traced this "pathological" view through three U.S. historical periods. First, in the 1600s and 1700s, those who divorced were viewed as having moral and religious failings that made them unfit to keep their marriage vows. Second, in the 1800s, the view was that social conditions made individuals unable to manage their relationships, homes, and children appropriately. Third, in the 1940s and 1950s, the view was that psychological failings, such as personal and mental health problems, made people incapable of living in a compatible way with a spouse. It was not that each view superseded the other, but that each, even now, plays a role in the thinking of at least some people, including policy-makers. Hackstaff (1999) has suggested that, today, despite lingering elements of a "marriage culture," the United States has moved to a "divorce culture" in which attitudes and behaviors reflect the idea that marriage is seen as optional and contingent and divorce is an acceptable outcome.

As Thornton and Young-DeMarco (2001) noted, national survey data illustrate that the stigma of divorce is less than it was 30 years ago. However, as they did earlier, that national morbidity and mortality rates are higher for separated and divorced persons compared with those who are married, widowed, or single suggest long-term consequences for individuals who experience such breaks in relatiohships (Kitson, Babri, Roach, & Placidi, 1989; Schwartz et al., 1995). The question, however, is why. Is it the pileup of stress that dissipates slowly for some, or is it the characteristics of those who divorce that make them less fit to have married at all and, therefore, understandably, more prone to problems after they divorce?

Selectivity theory is now being used to broaden researchers' understanding of those who decide to continue to cohabit than to marry. The results are mixed: Some find selection effects whereas others do not (Lamb, Lee, & DeMaris, 2003; Simon, 2002; Simon & Marcussen,1999). Nevertheless, such efforts illustrate the continuing hardiness and extension of this approach.

Normative Approach

The normative approach sees divorce and remarriage as normal and expected, or standard; that is, the events are so frequent today that people's choices should not be seen as problematic but as part of the life course like graduation, job entry, and widowhood (Ahrons & Rodgers, 1987; Allen, 1993: Coleman & Ganong, 1990; Demo, 1993). According to this approach, relationship dissolution is a change, but it cannot or should not be seen as potentially negative because at least some family member or members benefit from the break. Although it is admirable in that it highlights the problem focus that has permeated so much research on divorce, this perspective confuses normal or frequent with normative, or expected or accepted, behavior. This formulation also ignores the linkage of change and stress. While attempting to recognize the potential reduction in distress produced by more accepting attitudes toward marital breakup and highlighting the societal biases that crept into earlier and some recent research, this formulation assumes divorce and remarriage are more structural than emotionally upsetting events. This is an assumption that has not been supported. Virtually all research reports heightened psychological distress during marital separation and, at the least, the early stages of divorce and remarriage, and longer-term difficulties for some.

Stress and Selectivity

Along with the growth of knowledge about the stress perspective, it has been my feeling that the growing number of members of the middle and upper middle class who divorced, including researchers, led to greater focus on the stress approach. These researchers had the self-awareness and knowledge—as well as a personal stake—in saying that the experiences of divorced persons did not reflect selectivity. Research, however, suggests some role for selectivity and a major role for stress in adjustment to relationship breakup (Amato & Booth, 1997; Kitson, 1992; Lorenz et al., 1997).

The issue of which of these perspectives is more accurate is still not settled. Comparative, longitudinal studies that look at separated and divorced individuals in different countries or subcultures within the United States with known differences in attitudes about divorce could begin to disentangle the effects of these formulations.

E. MAVIS HETHERINGTON AND JUDITH S. WALLERSTEIN: CHILDREN AND DIVORCE

An underlying concern of much divorce research (and also the reason for the focus of much of the research on women, who are generally the custodial parents) is the impact of divorce on the children of those who end their relationships. Beyond the perceived moral value of marriage, marriage provides a societal purpose by keeping people tied to one another in small groups that are generally protective of their own, conservative in their view of the need for change, and, thus, less prone to engage in acts that are disruptive to society. A related issue about children and divorce is the consequence for society if what is felt to be the best structure for socializing children is threatened—the two-parent (and some would say heterosexual), legally, continuously married couple. To perpetuate themselves, societies need to continue to produce members who, as they mature, can take on the tasks needed (Kitson & Morgan, 1990). If, as the data suggest, relationship breakups for couples with children help produce even a minority of children who as adults do not meet their potential, this is not only a personal but also a societal loss. It is the fact that children are the unwitting participants in the divorce process of their parents that has fueled part of the continuing concern about them. To illustrate the background out of which the research by Hetherington and Wallerstein appeared, I describe the state of research before their work.

Herzog and Sudia: Review of Research on Children and Divorce

In the 1950s and 1960s, research on children whose parents had divorced was beset with various problems. In a widely circulated government report, Herzog and Sudia (1970) reviewed research on the topic of children in fatherless families, many of which were the result of parental divorce or separation. Herzog and Sudia had a list of criticisms of and suggestions for additional research that was extensive. It is instructive to summarize their points, some of which still have not been adequately addressed even today. They noted that one third of the studies they reviewed looked only at boys, perhaps because of a concern for boys' potential for engaging in juvenile delinquency (this was also prior to the growth of the feminist movement and the resulting increase in research on girls and women). Other foci of these older studies reviewed by Herzog and Sudia included problems of self-esteem and identity for the children; difficulties associated with the low socioeconomic status of the families; and children's school achievement, although they noted that little was available on college academic achievement. Despite knowledge that children's reactions to events differ depending on their developmental stages and that, even in the same child, reactions can vary as the child ages, few of the studies Herzog and Sudia reviewed were longitudinal. More of the research focused on family process and interaction than on family climate, and it used single outcome measures rather than multiple ones.

Herzog and Sudia also observed that much of the research involved poor measurement techniques, there was little research replication, and many of the often clinically based studies were without control groups. They further observed that deleterious distinctions were made between "broken" and intact families. There was also little research on single mothers themselves, despite the fact that women were generally the primary caregivers for the children. (See the meta-analysis by Amato & Keith, 1991, for citations to some of the studies reviewed by Herzog and Sudia; Amato's 2001 meta-analysis extends the 1991 one; also see Rodgers & Pryor, 1998, who also review such research.)

The Research of Hetherington and Wallerstein

It was in the research context of Herzog and Sudia described herein that new research on children and divorce began to emerge. It is hard to realize now what stunning developments the early articles and book by Wallerstein and Kelly (1974; 1975;1980) were. Joan Kelly, who initially worked on this study (Kelly & Wallerstein, 1976; Kelly, 1982; 1988), subsequently shifted more of her focus to mediation (Kelly, 1989; 1996). The Wallerstein and Kelly qualitative, longitudinal, clinically focused research was based on a convenience sample of 60 Marin County, California divorcing families who came initially for a 6-week preventive intervention counseling service that they understood was part of a research project. None of the children in the study had been in psychotherapy, although some of the parents had. Multiple methods of study were used. All of the family members were repeatedly interviewed; self-report questionnaires were administered; and the children were involved in play therapy sessions. Clinical ratings were developed from the data (Tschann, Johnson, & Wallerstein, 1989; Wallerstein & Blakeslee, 1989). Although not identified as such, their work took a systems and developmental approach. Its intrapsychic emphasis highlighted that the behaviors and actions of divorcing and divorced parents affected their children. A child's reaction to his or her parent's divorce also depended on the child's level of development when the divorce occurred and his or her later developmental stages. The research contributed to a greater understanding of adolescents and young adults. Furthermore, the authors noted, even very young children had reactions. It was a substantial achievement to highlight these issues. As clinicians, their research was predominantly published in journals read by clinicians and other practitioners, but the research was also widely cited by others.

Publication of Hetherington's divorce research also began about the same time (Hetherington, Cox, & Cox, 1976). Her initial work, the Virginia Longitudinal Study, involved a convenience sample of families of 4-year-old preschool children. Half of the participants came from mother-custody divorcing families, and half came from intact families. A matched sample of families in which remarriage had occurred was later added. Taking a systems and life course approach, her research also used multiple methods of data collection, including open-ended and fixed-choice questions for the parents, observations of the children, and interviews with the children's teachers. Hetherington subsequently did research on two other samples, one of stepfamilies in Philadelphia and the other a national sample that included married and step-families with twins and fully related, half-related, and unrelated stepsiblings. Hetherington's research has primarily appeared in publications read by academic researchers.

Hetherington and Wallerstein addressed some of the issues that Herzog and Sudia (1970) found problematic in prior research. Concerned about the depth, breadth, and length of the often negative changes that they observed in the children and adults they studied, each continued to do research on the families they had originally begun to follow in the 1970s. Now each study encompasses 25 years of data (Hetherington & Kelly, 2002; Wallerstein, Lewis, & Blakeslee, 2000). Hetherington, as the editor of *Child Development* in the 1980s and editor or coeditor of volumes of research on divorce, single parenting, and remarriage (Cowan & Hetherington, 1991; Hetherington, 1999a, 1999b; Hetherington & Aratesh, 1988), also played an important role in bringing greater visibility to the research of others in this area of study.

Criticisms

The works by Hetherington and Wallerstein were widely quoted but also drew much criticism. These criticisms included the relatively small size and regional nature of their samples, the social class and ethnic composition of their participants, subject attrition, and, if controls were used, the adequacy of the subject matches. A contributing factor to the controversy was also the fact that, although she stepped back from this stance in her latest child guidance book for divorcing and divorced parents (Wallerstein & Blakeslee, 2003), Wallerstein made increasingly sweeping generalizations about the negative impact of divorce on children and said that parents should consider staying in marriages if there was no parent psychopathology present. This stance fueled further academic controversy, with, for example, Cherlin (1999) emphasizing a variety of factors that could contribute to the difficulties of divorce. These included the role of predivorce difficulties of the parents or children in addition to the impact of the multiple events triggered by the divorce, and even a possible interaction of genetic and environmental factors that made some individuals more prone to divorce and postdivorce difficulties. A series of articles edited by Braver and Cookston (2003) weighed in on the controversy forcefully and, overall, disapprovingly about Wallerstein's work. For example, Coltrane and Adams (2003) maintained that Wallerstein's generally negative view of the consequences of divorce for children had been highjacked by others who wanted to push their own agenda of tougher divorce laws.

Widening Their Focus

Although Hetherington and Wallerstein each kept a foot in publishing for a professional au-dience, both authors in recent years have moved beyond the academic audience to trade pub-lications, in which their aim has been to provide information to lay audiences about divorce and adjustment to it. To help make their work more understandable to these audiences, each involved professional writers in their projects. Hetherington worked with journalist John Kelly (Hetherington & Kelly, 2002), and Wallerstein wrote with Sandra Blakeslee, a *New York Times* reporter (Wallerstein & Blakeslee, 1989, 1995, 2003; Wallerstein et al., 2000). This approach widened the audience for their work and shifted the tenor of the discussion of their findings to an even more public and contentious one than it had been previously in academe. The media tried to pitch the books as "a battle of superstars" (Corliss & McLaughlin, 2002, p. 40) and pitted the two authors against one another as producing contradictory results, as exemplified in Merkin's (2002) lengthy *New Yorker* review. The following quote from an article in *The New York Times* illustrates the tenor of these articles:

> "We're not against each other," Dr. Hetherington said. "When I read Judy's books, I always learn something. But you know Judy has a gloom and doom approach to divorce."

> "I don't have a gloom and doom approach," Dr. Wallerstein responded, "but I do think we've underestimated the cost on the child." (Duenwald, 2002, p. F6)

Despite all the controversy, as noted in *Time* magazine by Corliss and McLaughlin (2002, p. 40), "The real difference may not be in their methods (the statistician vs. the shrink) [Hetherington and Wallerstein, respectively], but in temperaments (hopeful vs. fretful)." Interestingly, in terms of their conclusions about the long-term difficulties children experienced, the two authors were not far apart in their estimates of those young adults who were adversely affected. Hetherington (Hetherington & Kelly, 2002, p. 7) concluded that 25% of the young adults originally studied as children had "serious social, emotional, or psychological problems," compared with 10% from nondivorce families; Wallerstein (Wallerstein et al., 2000, pp. 332–333) reported that 30% were "doing poorly, with functioning significantly impaired and below average."

Exemplars of Schools of Thought

As Corliss and McLaughlin observed, part of the difference in the approaches by Hetherington and Wallerstein relates to their disciplinary backgrounds and the wider controversies surrounding these. The works of Hetherington and Wallerstein come, respectively, from the academic and clinical foundations of psychology.

Hetherington trained in clinical psychology at the University of California at Berkeley and spent much of her academic career as a professor at the University of Virginia (Hetherington, 2001). Her work has taken a behavioral approach, with her more recent work using the risk and resiliency perspective. Wallerstein's initial education was as a social worker. She then trained at the Menninger Clinic, a center for psychoanalytic training, and later received a doctorate in clinical psychology from Lund University in Sweden (Wallerstein, 2001). She lectured for many years at the School of Social Welfare at the University of California, Berkeley. Her primary identity is a clinical one, with a strong focus on her psychoanalytic foundations and intrapsychic issues. Wallerstein's work and that of her colleagues is arguably the best known clinically based divorce research on parents and children in the United States today. It is the more cited study in the popular media, whereas Hetherington's work is more widely cited in the *Social Science Citation Index*, indicating, as Coltrane and Adams note (2003, p. 367), that "peers are more likely to view Hetherington as an academic expert on divorce." I would also argue that academics are more familiar and comfortable with Hetherington's research approach.

Academic Versus Clinical Psychology

Histories of psychology in the United States divide the field into academic and clincial psychology (Hothersall, 1995). Academic psychology has focused primarily on experimental and quasi-experimental techniques, behaviorism, cognition, and outgrowths from these. In more recent years, feminism has affected the entire field. Clinical work has aimed to help distressed patients and those in troubled relationships and has developed and assessed approaches to aid therapists in their work.

Psychoanalytic Approach

Not only is Wallerstein's background clinical, but it draws from the psychoanalytic tradition that was initially based on Sigmund Freud's work. Although Westen (1998) observed that much of Freud's work is outdated or wrong, certain aspects of it have infused much of modern psychodynamic clinical thinking. Although researchers or readers may not always be aware of the foundation for these ideas, they are apparent in many of the topics in research on divorce today. Westen included the following five ideas of Freud as making continuing contributions: (a) the role of unconscious mental processes that make much of mental life unaware, leading people to find some of their thoughts and behaviors mystifying to themselves; (b) the role of conflicting or ambivalent feelings in relationships; and (c) the initial formation of adult personality in childhood, with childhood experiences affecting interpersonal relationships and, if a person is troubled as an adult, the kinds of psychological symptoms he or she might develop. Westen went on to mention (d) the important role of object relationships theory in how individuals respond to events or other persons; and (e) how personality development begins to manage sexuality and aggression as individuals move from immaturity and dependency to maturity and independence.

U.S. academic psychology has not, however, paid much attention to these ideas. As Collins (1994, p. 31) observed, "The American behaviorists declared that the subject of scientific psychology should be laws of overt behavior, not introspective efforts to get at that illusive and prescientific concept, the mind."

According to Hall and Lindzey (1954, p. 143), academic psychologists viewed the psychoanalytic approach with "reserve or downright hostility," with this disdain having rational and irrational components. The issues that Hall and Lindzey raised are still relevant today. They observed that the rational components included psychoanalysts' lack of concern with control groups, fuzzy empirical definitions of concepts, and statements of data relationships that were hard to support or disprove. Hall and Lindzey (pp. 143–144) felt that the irrational component derived

> from a kind of professional jealousy that strongly resents contributions by individuals not trained in the discipline of psychology, a persistence in common-sense or normative views of behavior which are so strikingly violated by many psychoanalytic precepts, and stubborn adherence to a naive positivism that considers nothing worth note that does not meet relatively high standards of rigor and control.

Despite the discomfort many other social scientists have with the approach, a psychoanalytic section of the American Psychological Association has grown substantially in recent years and now has more than 4,000 members (Division 39–Psychoanalysis, 2004) out of 150,000 in the organization. Nevertheless, the distinction between academic psychology and clinical practice continues.

Thus, some of the controversy surrounding the work of Hetherington and Wallerstein is related to their disciplinary homes, who accepts which tradition, and how willing people are to see the contributions of each tradition despite disagreements about methods and emphases. The criticisms of their work also ignore what these researchers did in the context of the time they were trained and began to work: They changed the tenor of the work on children and helped to put children whose parents had divorced front and center as an important concern in terms of research and public policy. This concern continues today.

By the standard of replication—which is the hallmark of the social sciences—both Hetherington and Wallerstein have contributed substantially. Others, using different methods and often more representative samples, have found that divorce is initially disruptive for all family members and that some children may be adversely affected into their adult lives.

The realization of the potential long-term impact of parents' divorces on their children and what elements might have contributed to this have led to a steady stream of studies on the intergenerational transmission of divorce that has spanned the past few decades. (Representative examples include Amato & Booth, 1997; Amato & DeBoer, 2001; Cherlin et al., 1991; Kiernan & Cherlin, 1999; Kulka & Weingarten, 1979; Mueller & Pope, 1977; Rodgers & Pryor, 1998.) Such studies have generally found a small but significant intergenerational effect, with approximately 5% more adult children whose parents divorced experiencing a divorce than those whose parents did not divorce.

Using national, longitudinal data, researchers have estimated that the life chances of at least 15% of young adults whose parents divorced were adversely affected by dropping out of school, premarital pregnancy, poor jobs, and young marriages (Chase-Landsdale, Cherlin, & Kiernan, 1995; Cherlin et al., 1991; Cherlin, Chase-Landsdale, & McRae, 1998; McLanahan & Sandefur, 1994). Among the factors implicated in these findings are the lowered economic resources of such children, multiple postdivorce transitions (Amato, 2003), the lack of good role models for intimate relationships, and continuing postdivorce parental conflicts (Maccoby & Mnookin, 1992).

Societies can ill afford the continuing drain of potentially productive children as adult citizens that results from the relationship choices of their parents. It is, after all, not just divorce events that can adversely affect children's development and life chances. The divorce and postdivorce periods may be areas in which some of these potentially deleterious effects can be reduced relatively effectively by continuing recognition of the impact of these events— including the emotional toll—and the development of appropriate predivorce and postdivorce interventions to counter them.

CONCLUSION

So, Where Are We Now?

I once read a quote—the author and source of which I long ago lost—that observed, for sociologists, "History is what happened yesterday." The quote applies to the study of divorce as well. We are told that shifts in family life are more likely in periods of social change. On the basis of what Goode (1956, p. 4) called the "classical family of Western nostalgia" drawn from our mental picture of rural family values in an idyllic time and Coontz's (1992) dissection of U.S. family changes to illustrate that they did not occur as we thought they did, we may still be sorting through the results of earlier changes as we examine the state of marriage and divorce today. Nevertheless, if it ever was so, today social change is not a now-and-again occurence but a continuing process. It is still too early to understand what even the past 40- to 50-year period means in terms of family change. However, since I began doing research on divorce in the 1970s, among the large-scale changes and dislocations that have occurred in the United States are shifts in moral standards; a lessening and then increasing role of certain types of religion in personal and public life; the continuing expansion of metropolitan areas and the increasing segregation of racial and ethnic minorities into central cities; the growth and greater voice of ethnic and racial groups; substantial immigration; technological advances, including the widespread use of reliable contraceptive techniques; increases in women's rights and their paid employment; the shift to a service economy; numerous military incursions and regional wars; and, now, a hovering threat of domestic terrorism. The impact of such changes then ripples through relationships. With so much that has changed, it is perhaps not surprising that the rates of divorce and relationship dissolution still remain high despite various efforts to prevent or slow them down. At the same time, for those remaining married, many marriages have extended in length from 40 to 50 and 60 years. For most, such long marriages are a new phenomenon (Skolnick, 1991). In some ways, it is even more amazing that so many have been able to maintain their marriages in the face of such changes than that others have failed to do so.

One striking development illustrated in this chapter is the inclusion of relationship dissolution as part of the discussion of the breakup process. In the past 30 to 40 years in the United States and other Western societies, cohabitation has become more visible, frequent, and publicly accepted; it has spread across social classes and the age range, with increasing numbers of children born in or brought into these relationships.

Although cohabitation research is beginning to move beyond demographic profiles to provide more information about the relationships themselves (see, e.g., Ciabattari, 2004; Raley & Wildsmith, 2004), we still do not know much about this process. Several qualitative studies have begun to fill in some of the blanks (Jamieson et al., 2002; Willetts, 2003), but more are needed. Research on gays and lesbians—who seek the legal right to marry at a time when others who have the choice to marry increasingly choose not to—has also increased substantially, but as Patterson (2000) observed, here too there is little qualitative work to provide a fuller picture.

Where Do We Need to Go?

Structural and Psychological Issues in Relationship Dissolution Research

After a period in which a number of studies looked at processes of divorce and adjustment in their totality, more recent research seems to be bifurcated. Some studies have taken a more psychological bent whereas other studies have shifted back to a focus on structure and causes—why things are as they are—not on what the impact is of the events that have occurred. As a result, there is more examination of causes or correlates of the decision to end relationships, aspects of the adjustment process, or a focus on public policy issues such as child support. Although it is useful and interesting to determine the basis for relationship breakup and its mental health impact, a focus on such issues perpetuates a problem-oriented perspective on the issue of divorce. When public policy-makers become involved in the issue, the question becomes whether the government should prevent relationship events that some see as detrimental or ameliorate the results of conditions that do occur. Both the kinds of structural issues Goode examined in earlier years and psychological issues—more broadly defined than mental health—have to be examined.

The Normative Nature of Divorce?

At the same time, however, the meaning of being divorced appears to be changing. I am not so sure that divorce is actually viewed by many as part of the normal life course. It is not built into most people's expectations of life events such as graduation or employment or retirement. Difficult events, such as unemployment, chronic illness, or early death, hardly ever are. If, as appears to be the case, it is virtually universal to have at least some initial period of emotional reaction to a breakup, does the greater frequency of divorce mean it is less distressing to experience these reactions now because the event is so common, or normative? Does it take less time for adults and children to adjust? Are there fewer long-term consequences for those who experience breakups?

Times have changed and we cannot go back to earlier times. We can, however, address these issues in studies that compare individuals from communities in the United States with those in societies in which divorce is less widely practiced or accepted.

Where there are available public records about relationship breakups, these should be used in combination with methods such as those use by Kurdek (1998) to identify same-sex couple cohabiters. Divorced persons identified in large-scale representative surveys could then be interviewed to gather more detailed data. Although public records-based samples drawn from divorce records lose the prospective perspective of being able to identify those in a representative sample who will end their relationships, they can provide greater depth and breadth of knowledge about the short- and long-term process of adjustment. The combination of these methods might be beneficial to researchers.

Race and Ethnicity

Although demographic research has provided more data on racial and ethnic differences in divorce and breakup patterns, we know less about the role of these factors in adjustment to divorce. There is relatively little research on Blacks and Latinos and divorce adjustment, and even less on Asian Americans. With divorce more frequent among Blacks, Kitson (1992) found that black participants in the study reported less sense of stigma about divorce and fewer adjustment difficulties than did the White participants. This finding has to be retested with a broader array of ethnic and racial groups with differing likelihoods of divorce.

Much of the in-depth divorce adjustment research has been based on small court or convenience samples, which has meant, generally, that few minority participants were studied. In part this has been due to where and how the studies were done and by whom. Some of the researchers (who generally were not bilingual) also conducted their in-depth studies in settings with fewer minority members. Even representative national samples, often providing less in-depth data, have had difficulty obtaining a sufficiently large number of minorities to examine differences in response to divorce by race and ethnicity, unless oversampling was done. In addition, researchers may have, again unwittingly bought into the still-lingering cultural assumption that minorities' relationship breakups were "a problem" and focused on the causes of breakups in order to prevent them in the future.

If part of the difficulties in adjustment are due to subcultural patterns and resources, it is curious that in such a large, diverse society as the United States so little research has explored this issue, particularly when divorce is more frequent among Blacks and less frequent among Latino and Asian Americans (Bramlett & Mosher, 2002). Such a distribution provides an opportunity to understand the pressures that may differentially influence the decision to divorce and adjustment. In his decade review, Amato (2000, p. 496) concluded his examination of the limited data on adjustment to divorce by race and ethnicity by noting that research does "not suggest strong racial difference in divorce adjustment in the United States." More examination of this issue is needed, as research is more mixed than he suggested (see, e.g., Fine, McKenry, & Chung, 1992; Kitson 1992; Williams, Takeuchi, & Adair, 1992). The roles of race and ethnicity in divorce and its adjustment are still important research gaps that have to be filled.

Economic Issues

Compared with other Western countries, the United States generally has provided low levels of government support for women and their children (Goode, 1993). As a result, U.S. research and policy have focused on how to obtain more private support, primarily from the father, and whether the payments could or should be increased (Garfinkel, McLanahan, Meyer, & Seltzer, 1998; Garfinkel & Oellerich, 1989; Sorenson, 1997). Because of increasing concerns about these issues, in 1980, the U.S. Bureau of the Census began to collect data on child support and alimony. Although they are still high, rates of noncompliance in payments have since decreased to below 50% (Casper & Bianchi, 2002).

More research that looks at the continuing economic impact of making and receiving support payments for men and women who often have new families or partners would be useful. Similarly, data on how women and children cope economically with sometimes irregular or no payments would be helpful. The gap in research on single-parent fathers also requires attention.

Other Issues in Research Methods

In addition to the topics and methods discussed here, Rodgers and Pryor (1998, p. 45), in their analysis of research on children and divorce in the United Kingdom (which also discussed some U.S. studies), listed other methodological shortfalls and factors requiring study. These concerns included studies with inadequate sample size to be able to provide appropriate statistical power; the lack of statistical tests in some analyses and their inappropriate use in others; the needed examination of children's physical health and development and of their differing vulnerabilities and resilience; evaluation and intervention studies; and a righting of the "insufficient attention to their [children's] perspectives and rights," especially at the time of marital separation. Even if "only" 15% to 30% of children are adversely affected by such breakups, societies can ill afford that potential drain of productive future workers when some of this effect is a generally unintended consequence of their parents' decisions.

The aim of this chapter has been to discuss some of the ways in which divorce and relationship dissolution research has grown and changed in the past decades. It is helpful to see where we have been in the context of where we are now in identifying neglected topics or those that are ripe for reinvestigation. The irony is that what seemed to have been settled knowledge in the 1970s and 1980s is less settled today. The characteristics of those who marry and divorce appear to be changing. With fewer couples choosing to marry and more cohabiting, even our knowledge about how much relationship instability exists is limited.

Although marriage may still be the normative expectation for how couples should live together and bear and raise children, as we have seen, the numbers of couples actually choosing this household structure has decreased. At the same time, those deciding to end their marriages remains at high levels. Among those who marry, Heaton (2002) has demonstrated that increased age at marriage, and to a lesser extent increased education, has produced greater stability for these marriages. This is related to who chooses—or is able to choose—to marry.

As an organizational device in this chapter, I focused on the work of four researchers whose work I think broadened the field considerably: William J. Goode, E. Mavis Hetherington, Judith S. Wallerstein, and Robert S. Weiss. Obviously, I could have selected others whose works were also instrumental in developing the field. I selected these people because each made substantial contributions to our understanding of the events of divorce as a process and of adjustment to relationship breakdown. Goode, Wallerstein, and Weiss added to our knowledge of the often increasingly estranged nature of marital relationships prior to the decision to divorce. The decision to divorce is not generally an easy or quick one. Weiss and Wallerstein emphasized the role of emotions on adjustment. Goode broadened the discussion of marriage and relationship dissolution by observing that similar processes were occurring worldwide in cohabitation, marriage, and divorce. Goode and Weiss focused on adults, whereas Hetherington and Wallerstein centered their work on children and the developmental issues they experienced in their childhoods and early adult years. Hetherington's primarily quantitative work drew from the tradition of academic psychology; Wallerstein's qualitative approach developed out of the clinical realm, including a focus on more global evaluations of individuals. The contentious nature of the discussion about Hetherington and Wallerstein's works, depends in part on the deep divisions between academic and clinical psychology, particularly the use of an intrapsychic approach, and continuing controversy concerning the merits of quantitative and qualitative research techniques.

Recognition of Contributions, Not Just Research Deficits

Although all research should be evaluated by the best practices, it is also important to recognize where, when, and with what perspective earlier researchers worked. We need to recognize what such researchers contributed, not just what they got wrong or what became outdated. Perhaps the most important standard of research evaluation is replication (Kitson et al., 1982). Do researchers using similar, or even dissimilar, approaches find the same or comparable results? Although there are still many divorce issues that should be studied and disagreements about the magnitude and lengths of effects, findings *are* replicated: The majority of children and adults adjust adequately to divorce and remarriage with the passage of time, but a minority do not. This question remains: What can and should be done to ease the short- and long-term consequences of relationship breakups? This issue continues to be important to examine.

LESSONS LEARNED

As cultures change and new theoretical and research techniques develop, the issues studied in social science research shift. In the paragraphs that follow, I discuss some of the ways that keeping past research and nascent research ideas just beginning to arise in mind can aid in developing new research on relationship dissolution.

Mining the Past

Tracing through some of the approaches and issues previously studied in marriage and divorce research helps us to see from where some of today's research foci have come. In addition, such a search also illustrates which issues are no longer emphasized but might usefully be reexamined with newer theories, samples, or methods.

I once heard a graduate student presentation at a national meeting in which the student indignantly noted that George Simmel, a German sociologist from the late nineteenth to early twentieth century, did not focus on the issue of gender and how this variable affected his study of small groups. The student's discussion of Simmel's work seemed to assume that Simmel had walked out of his office yesterday and was oblivious to his surroundings and important cultural issues. The presenter's approach illustrates that the use of the past must recognize its context. In Simmel's time and place, his focus was understandable, if regrettable by our standards, and reconsideration of his ideas today does lead to new issues to study.

Using Other Sources for Leads

Many new research topics develop in stages. Sometimes a clinician will write about his or her observations of new issues observed in practice. Noticing changes around them, others may begin to use convenience samples on the topic. After this stage, larger scale studies with more representative samples may begin. Checking what may seem more out-of-the-way sources may help a researcher to begin to develop a broader background on a new issue.

Listening to Others

Another source of ideas is listening to what others say in casual conversation, interviews, or transcripts of interviews. For example, Robert Weiss felt that what fellow course members were saying at a Tavistock Institute workshop did not jibe with what he had seen in his work with Parents Without Partners; this reaction led him to the idea of Seminars for the Separated. The impetus for my research on couples who file for divorce and change their minds came from telephone calls from potential participants in a longitudinal divorce study. In declining to be interviewed, people would say things like, "We're reconciled, and I'm so happy I don't want to talk about it" or "We've reconciled, and I don't want to mess things up by discussing it." I began to wonder what such seemingly fragile relationships were like and discovered there was little research literature on the topic. This observation subsequently led to publications and a grant on the topic (Kitson, 1985; Kitson, Holmes, & Sussman, 1983; Kitson & Langlie, 1984).

Peering Into the Future

Identifying new topics or approaches early in their development is not always easy. With the lead time it takes for research to be conducted and articles and books to be published, using other less traditional data sources such as computer Web sites and chat rooms to identify new topics can help. Reading the Lifestyle, Arts, and Leisure sections of newspapers can help spot new trends. Major East and West Coast papers such as *The Los Angles Times, The New York Times*, and *The Washington Post*, which are published in cities where many trends begin, are particularly useful.

Listening to Yourself

Your own experiences are another source of research information and guidance. If your experiences of cohabitation, divorce, or the postdivorce period do not match what others are saying and writing, give some thought to the differences. Vaughan (1986) describes her experiences of "uncoupling" from her spouse as a basis for her subsequent research. Research that is based on your own experiences can be useful, but it can also be a hard source to use if you are not at a point to be able to step back enough to listen to others' disparate experiences without attempting to force them into your own perspective. Topics that touch us deeply, such as abuse, divorce, serious illness, or death, can be especially difficult to do research or work on over time because of the strong personal emotions they can arouse (Kitson et al., 1996). Vaughn (1986, p. 201), for example, in describing her uncoupling research, noted that it was "emotionally turbulent." This included the writing process, "which required not simply merging the files but dwelling on and integrating data from many sources, [and] was an immersion not only in the life experience and human vulnerability of others, but my own."

The devil may be in the details, as the saying goes, of just how much effect divorce and remarriage have, for whom, and with what consequences for individuals and society. In addressing these issues, however, it is important to keep in mind the history of our research, the strides that have been made, and the larger disciplinary issues that are involved in many of the continuing controversies about divorce and remarriage today.

ACKNOWLEDGMENTS

I am grateful to Paul Brinich, Cheryl Elman, and Diane Moran for their discussion of issues I have raised in this chapter; Mary Aaby, James Kitson, and Lynn White for their comments on an earlier version of the chapter; and Jean Garcia for her word processing of the manuscript. Although Mavis Hetherington, Robert Weiss, and Judith Wallerstein each reviewed the manuscript for factual errors, the interpretations and conclusions drawn about their work are mine. Scholar William Goode, who played such an important role in the field of divorce research, died in 2003.

REFERENCES

Aghajanian, A. (1986). Some notes on divorce in Iran. *Journal of Marriage and the Family, 51,* 749–755.

Ahrons, C. R. (1981). The continuing co-parental relationship between divorced spouses. *American Journal of Orthopsychiatry, 51,* 315–328.

Ahrons, C. R., & Rodgers, R. H. (1987). *Divorced families: A multidisciplinary developmental view.* New York: Norton.

Allen, K. R. (1993). The dispassionate discourse of children's adjustment to divorce. *Journal of Marriage and the Family, 55,* 46–50.

Amato, P. R. (1993). Children's adjustment to divorce: Theories, hypotheses, and empirical support. *Journal of Marriage and the Family, 55,* 23–38.

Amato, P. R. (2000). The consequences of divorce for adults and children. *Journal of Marriage and Family, 62,* 1269–1287.

Amato, P. R. (2001). Children of divorce in the 1990's: An update of the Amato and Keith (1991) meta analysis. *Journal of Family Psychology, 15,* 355–370.

Amato, P. R. (2003). Reconciling divergent perspectives: Judith Wallerstein, quantitative family research, and children of divorce. *Family Relations, 52,* 332–339.

Amato, P. R., & Booth, A. (1997). *A generation at risk: Growing up in an era of family upheaval.* Cambridge, MA: Harvard University Press.

Amato, P. R., & DeBoer, D. D. (2001). The transmission of marital instability across generations: Relationship skills or commitment to marriage. *Journal of Marriage and the Family, 63,* 1038–1051.

Amato, P. R., & Gilbreth, J. (1999). Nonresident fathers and children's well-being. *Journal of Marriage and the Family, 61,* 557–573.

Amato, P. R., & Keith, B. (1991). Consequences of parental divorce for children's well-being: A meta-analysis. *Psychological Bulletin, 110,* 26–46.

Arendell, T. (1995). *Fathers and divorce.* Thousand Oaks, CA: Sage.

Bachrach, L. I. (1975). Marital *status and mental disorder: An analytical review.* (DHEW Publication No. ADM 75-217). Washington, DC: U.S. Government Printing Office.

Bergler, E. (1946). *Unhappy marriage and divorce.* New York: International Universities Press.

Bergler, E. (1948). *Divorce won't help.* New York: Harper.

Boss, P. (2002). *Family stress management: A contextual approach* (2nd ed.). Thousand Oaks, CA: Sage.

Bloom, B. L., Asher, S. J., & White, S. W. (1978). Marital disruption as a stressor: A review and analysis. *Psychological Bulletin, 85,* 867–894.

Bloom, B. L., Hodges, W. F., & Caldwell, R. A. (1982). A preventive program for the newly separated: Initial evaluation. *American Journal of Community Psychology, 10,* 251–264.

Bloom, B. L., Hodges, W. F., Caldwell, R. A., Systra, L., & Cedrone, A. R. (1977). Marital separation: A community survey. *Journal of Divorce, 1,* 7–19.

Bohannan, P. (1970). The six stations of divorce. In P. Bohannan (Ed.), *Divorce and after* (pp. 29–55). Garden City, NY: Doubleday.

Booth, A., & Amato, P. R. (1991). Divorce and psychological stress. *Journal of Health and Social Behavior, 32,* 396–407.

Bowlby, J. (1969). *Attachment and loss: Vol. 1. Attachment.* New York: Basic Books.

Bowlby, J. (1973). *Attachment and loss: Vol. 2. Separation: Anxiety and anger.* New York: Basic Books.

Bowlby, J. (1977a). The making and breaking of affectional bonds: Part I. Aetiology and psychopathology in light of attachment theory. *British Journal of Psychiatry, 130,* 201–210.

Bowlby, J. (1977b). The making and breaking of affectional bonds: Part II. Some principles of psychotherapy. *British Journal of Psychiatry, 130,* 421–431.

Bowlby, J. (1980). *Attachment and loss: Vol. 3. Loss: Sadness and depression.* New York: Basic Books.

Bramlett, M. D., & Mosher, W. D. (2002). *Cohabitation, marriage, divorce, and remarriage in the United States.* (Vital and Health Statistics, series 23, No. 22). Washington, DC: U.S. Government Printing Office.

Braver, S. L., & Cookston, J. T. (Eds.) (2003). Special collection: Controversies, clarifications and consequences of divorce legacy. *Family Relations, 32,* 314–317.

Bumpass, L., & Lu, H. (2000). Trends in cohabitation and implications for children's family contexts in the United States. *Population Studies, 54,* 29–41.

Caro, R. A. (1982). *The years of Lyndon Johnson: Vol. 1. the path to power.* New York: Knopf.

Casper, L. M., & Bianchi, S. M. (2002). *Continuity and change in the American family.* Thousand Oaks, CA: Sage.

Chase-Lansdale, P. L., Cherlin, A. J., & Kiernan, K. E. (1995). The long-term effects of parental divorce and the mental health of young adults: A developmental perspective. *Child Development, 66,* 1614–1634.

Cherlin, A. J. (1978). Remarriage as an incomplete institution. *American Journal of Sociology, 84,* 634–650.

Cherlin, A. J. (1981). *Marriage, divorce, and remarriage.* Cambridge, MA: Harvard University Press.

Cherlin, A. J. (1999). Going to extremes: Family structure, children's well-being, and social science. *Demography, 36,* 421–428.

Cherlin, A. J. (2003). Marriage: Current status and alternative futures. Paper presented at the annual meeting of the National Council on Family Relations, Vancouver, British Columbia.

Cherlin, A. J., Furstenberg, F. F., Jr., Chase-Lansdale, P. L., Kiernan, K. E., Robins, P. K., Morrison, D. R., & Teitler, J. O. (1991). Longitudinal studies of effects of divorce on children in Great Britain and the United States. *Science, 252,* 1386–1389.

Cherlin, A. J., Chase-Landsdale, P. L., & McRae, C. (1998). Effects of parental divorce on mental health throughout the life course. *American Sociological Review, 63,* 239–249.

Chiriboga, D. A., Catron, L., & Associates. (1991). *Divorce: Crisis, challenge, or relief?* New York: New York University Press.

Ciabattari, T. (2004). Cohabitation and housework: The effects of marital intentions. *Journal of Marriage and Family, 66,* 118–125.

Coleman, M., & Ganong, L. (1990). Remarriage and stepfamily research in the 80s: New interest in an old family form. *Journal of Marriage and the Family, 52,* 925–940.

Coleman, M., Ganong, L., & Fine, M. (2000). Reinvestigating remarriage: Another decade of progress. *Journal of Marriage and Family, 62,* 1288–1307.

Collins, R. (1994). *Four sociological traditions.* New York: Oxford University Press.

Coltrane, S., & Adams, M. (2003). The social construction of the divorce "problem": Morality, child victims, and the politics of gender. *Family Relations, 52,* 363–372.

Coombs, L. C., & Zumeta, Z. (1970). Correlates of marital dissolution in a prospective fertility study. *Social Problems, 18,* 92–102.

Coontz, S. (1992). *The way we never were: American families and the nostalgia trap.* New York: Basic Books.

Corliss, R., & McLaughlin, L. (2002, January 28). Does divorce hurt kids? *Time,* p. 40.

Cowan, P. A., & Hetherington, E. M. (Eds.). (1991). *Family transitions.* Hillsdale, NJ: Lawrence Erlbaum Associates.

Cuber, J. F. (with Haroff, P. B.). (1969). *Sex and the significant Americans: A study of sexual behavior among the affluent.* Baltimore: Penguin Books.

Demo, D. H. (1993). The relentless search for effects of divorce: Forging new trails or tumbling down the beaten path. *Journal of Marriage and the Family, 55,* 42–45.

Division 39–Psychoanalysis. (2004). Retrieved May 28, 2004, from www.apa.org/about/division/div39.html.

Dohrenwend, B. S., Krasnoff, L., Askenasy, A. R., & Dohrenwend, B. P. (1978). Exemplification of a method for scaling life events: The PERI life events scale. *Journal of Health and Social Behavior, 19,* 205–229.

Duenwald, M. (2002, March 26). 2 portraits of children of divorce: Rosy and dark. *New York Times,* p. F6.

Emery, R. E. (1994). *Renegotiating relationships: Divorce, child custody, and mediation.* New York: Guilford.

Fields, J. (2003). *Children's living arrangements and characteristics: March 2002* (Current Population Reports, Series P20-547). Washington, DC: U.S. Government Printing Office.

Fields, J., & Casper, L. M. (2001). *American's families and living arrangement: March 2000* (Current Population Reports, Series P20–347). Washington, DC: U.S. Government Printing Office.

Fields, J. M., & Kreider, R. (2000). *Marriage and divorce rates in the U.S.: A multi-state life table analysis. Fall 1966, SIPP.* Paper presented at the annual meeting of the Southern Demographic Association, New Orleans. Cited in L. M. Casper & S. M. Bianchi (2002), *Continuity and change in the American family.* Thousand Oaks, CA: Sage.

Fine, M. A., McKenry, P. C., & Chung, H. (1992). Post-divorce adjustment of black and white single parents. *Journal of Divorce and Remarriage, 17,* 121–134.

Garfinkel, I., McLanahan, S., Meyers, D. R., & Seltzer, J. A. (Eds.). (1998). *Fathers under fire: The revolution in child support enforcement.* New York: Russell Sage Foundation.

Garfinkel, I., & Oellerich, D. (1989). Noncustodial fathers' ability to pay child support. *Demography, 26,* 219–233.

Glendon, M. A. (1987). *Abortion and divorce in western law.* Cambridge, MA: Harvard University Press.

Glenn, N. (1997). A reconsideration of the effect of no-fault divorce on divorce rates. *Journal of Marriage and the Family, 59,* 1023–1025.

Glick, P. C., & Norton, A. J. (1971). Frequency, duration, and probability of marriage and divorce. *Journal of Marriage and the Family, 33,* 307–317.

Glick, P. C., & Norton, A. J. (1977). Marrying, divorcing, and living together in the U.S. today. *Population Reference Bureau, 32,* 3–39.

Glick, P. C., & Norton, A. J. (1973). Perspectives on the recent upturn in divorce and remarriage. *Demography, 10,* 301–314.

Glick, I. O., Weiss, R. S., & Parkes, C. M. (1974). *The first year of bereavement.* New York: Wiley.

Goode, W. J. (1956). *After divorce.* Glencoe, IL: The Free Press.

Goode, W. J. (1963). *World revolution and family patterns.* New York: The Free Press.

Goode, W. J. (1965). *Women in divorce.* New York: The Free Press.

Goode, W. J. (1966). Family disorganization. In R. K. Merton & R. Nisbet (Eds.), *Contemporary social problems* (2nd ed., pp. 479–552). New York: Harcourt Brace & World.

Goode, W. J. (1993). *World changes in divorce patterns.* New Haven, CT: Yale University Press.

Grief, G. L. (1985). *Single fathers.* Lexington, MA: Heath.

Hackstaff, K. B. (1999). *Marriage in a culture of divorce.* Philadelphia: Temple University Press.

Halem, L. C. (1980). *Divorce reform: Changing legal and social perspectives.* New York: The Free Press.

Hall, C. S., & Lindzey, G. (1954). Psychoanalytic theory and its applications in the social sciences. In G. Lindzey (Ed.), *Handbook of social psychology. Vol. 1: Theory and Method* (pp. 148–180). Cambridge, MA: Addison-Wesley.

Hawkins, A. J., Nock, S. L., Wilson, J. C., Sanchez, L., & Wright, J. D. (2002). Attitudes about covenant marriage and divorce: Policy implications from a three-state comparison. *Family Relations, 51,* 166–175.

Heaton, T. (2002). Factors contributing to increasing marital stability in the United States. *Journal of Family Issues, 23,* 392–409.

Herzog, E., & Sudia, C. E. (1970). *Boys in fatherless families.* Washington, DC: Office of Child Development, U.S. Department of Health, Education and Welfare.

Hetherington, E. M. (1989). Coping with family transitions: Winners, losers, and survivors. *Child Development, 60,* 1–14.

Hetherington, E. M. (1991). The role of individual differences and family relationships in children's coping with divorce and remarriage. In P. A. Cowan and E. M. Hetherington (Eds.), *Family transitions* (pp. 165–194). Hillsdale, NJ: Lawrence Erlbaum Associates.

Hetherington, E. M. (1999a). Should we stay together for the sake of children? In E. M. Hetherington (Ed.), *Coping with divorce, single parenting, and remarriage: A risk and resiliency perspective* (pp. 93–116). Mahwah, NJ: Lawrence Erlbaum Associates.

Hetherington, E. M. (1999b). (Ed.). *Coping with divorce, single parenting, and remarriage: A risk and resiliency perspective.* Mahwah, NJ: Lawrence Erlbaum Associates.

Hetherington, E. M. (2001). *Who's who in America.* New Providence, NJ: Marquis Who's Who.

Hetherington, E. M., & Aratesh, J. D. (Eds.). (1988). *Impact of divorce, single parenting and stepparenting on children.* Hillsdale, NJ: Lawrence Erlbaum Associates.

Hetherington, E. M., Cox, M., & Cox, R. (1976). Divorced fathers. *The Family Coordinator, 25,* 417–428.

Hetherington, E. M. & Kelly, J. (2002). *For better or for worse: Divorce reconsidered.* New York: Norton.

Hill, R. (1958). Generic features of families under stress. *Social Casework, 39,* 139–150.

Holmes, T. H., & Rahe, R. H. (1967). The social readjustment rating scale. *Journal of Psychosomatic Research, 11,* 213–218.

Hothersall, D. (1995). *History of psychology* (3rd ed.). New York: McGraw-Hall.

Ihinger-Tallman, M., & Pasley, K. (1987). *Remarriage.* Newbury Park, CA: Sage.

Jacobson, G. F. (1983). *The multiple crises of marital separation and divorce.* New York: Grune & Stratton.

Jamieson, L., Anderson, M., McCrone, D., Bechhofer, F., Stewart, R., & Li, Y. (2002). Cohabitation and commitment: Partnership plans of young men and women. *Sociological Review, 50,* 356–377.

Johnson, D. R., & Wu, J. (2002). An empirical test of crisis, social selection, and role explanations of the relationship between marital disruption and psychological distress: A pooled time-series analysis of four-wave panel data. *Journal of Marriage and the Family, 64,* 211–224.

Kelly, J. B. (1982). Divorce: The adult perspective. In B. Wolman & G. Stricker (Eds.), *Handbook of developmental psychology* (pp. 734–750). Englewood Cliffs, NJ: Prentice-Hall.

Kelly, J. B. (1988). Longer-term adjustment in children of divorce: Conveying findings and implications for practice. *Journal of Family Psychology, 2,* 119–140.

Kelly, J. B. (1989). Mediated and adversarial divorce: Respondents' perceptions of the process and outcomes. *Mediation Quarterly, 24,* 71–88.

Kelly, J. B. (1996). A decade of divorce mediation research: Some answers and some questions. *Family and Conciliation Courts Review, 34,* 373–385.

Kelly, J. B., & Wallerstein, J. S. (1976). The effects of parental divorce: Experiences of the child in early latency. *American Journal of Orthopsychiatry, 46,* 20–32.

Kiernan, K. E., & Cherlin, A. J. (1999). Parental divorce and partnership dissolution in adulthood: Evidence from a British cohort study. *Population Studies, 53,* 39–49.

Kitson, G. C. (1985). Marital discord and marital separation: A county survey. *Journal of Marriage and the Family, 47,* 693–700.

Kitson, G. C. (with Holmes, W. M.). (1992). *Portrait of divorce: Adjustment to marital breakdown.* New York: Guilford.

Kitson, G. C., Babri, K. B., & Roach, M. J. (1985). Who divorces and why: A review. *Journal of Family Issues, 6,* 255–293.

Kitson, G. C., Babri, K. B., Roach, M. J., & Placidi, K. S. (1989). Adjustment to widowhood and divorce: A review. *Journal of Family Issues, 10,* 5–32.

Kitson, G. C., Clark, R. D., Rushforth, N. B., Brinich, P. M., Sudak, H. S., & Zyzanski, S. J. (1996). Research on difficult family topics: Helping new and experienced researchers cope with research on loss. *Family Relations, 45,* 183–188.

Kitson, G. C., Holmes, W. M., & Sussman, M. B. (1983). Withdrawing divorce petitions: A predictive test of the exchange model of divorce. *Journal of Divorce, 7,* 51–66.

Kitson, G. C., & Langlie, J. K. (1984). Couples who file for divorce but change their minds. *American Journal of Orthopsychiatry, 54,* 469–489.

Kitson, G. C., & Morgan, L. A. (1900). The multiple consequences of divorce: A decade review. *Journal of Marriage and the Family, 52,* 913–924.

Kitson, G. C., & Raschke, H. J. (1981). Divorce research: What we know, what we need to know. *Journal of Divorce, 4,* 1–37.

Kitson, G. C., & Sussman, M. B. (1982). Marital complaints, demographic characteristics, and symptoms of mental distress in divorce. *Journal of Marriage and the Family, 44,* 87–101.

Kitson, G. C., Sussman, M. B., Williams, G. B., Zeehandelaar, R. B., Schickmanter, B. K., & Steinberger, J. L. (1982). Sampling issues in family research. *Journal of Marriage and the Family, 44,* 965–981.

Kreider, R. M., & Simmons, T. (2003). *Marital status: 2000.* (Census 2000 Brief). Washington, DC: U.S. Census Bureau.

Kulka, R. A., & Weingarten, H. (1979). The long-term effects of parental divorce in childhood on adult development. *Journal of Social Issues, 35,* 50–78.

Kurdek, L. A. (1998). Relationship outcomes and their predictors: Longitudinal evidence from heterosexual married, gay cohabiting, and lesbian cohabiting couples. *Journal of Marriage and the Family, 60,* 553–568.

Kurz, D. (1995). *For richer for poorer: Mothers confront divorce.* New York: Routledge.

Lamb, K. A., Lee, G. R., & DeMaris, A. D. (2003). Union formation and depression: Selection and relationship effects. *Journal of Marriage and the Family, 65,* 953–962.

Lorenz, F. O., Simons, R. L., Conger, R. D., Elder, G. H., Johnson, C., & Chad, W. (1997). Married and recently divorced mothers' stress events and distress: Tracing change across time. *Journal of Marriage and the Family, 59,* 219–232.

Maccoby, E. E., & Mnookin, R. H. (1992). *Dividing the child: Social and legal dilemmas of custody.* Stanford, CA: Stanford University Press.

McCubbin, H. I., & Patterson, J. M. (1983). Family stress and adaptation to crises: A double ABCX model of family behavior. In D. H. Olson & B. C. Miller (Eds.), *Family studies review yearbook* (Vol. 1, pp. 87–106). Beverly Hills, CA: Sage.

McLanahan, S., & Sandefur, G. (1994). *Growing up with a single parent: What hurts, what helps.* Cambridge, MA: Harvard University Press.

Merkin, D. (2002, April 22–29). Can this divorce be saved? *New Yorker,* pp. 192–194, 196–200.

Moskoff, W. (1983). Divorce in the USSR. *Journal of Marriage and the Family, 45,* 419–425.

Mueller, C. W., & Pope, H. (1977). Marital instability: A study of its transmission between generations. *Journal of Marriage and the Family, 39,* 83–93.

Myers, J. K., Lindenthal, J. J., Pepper, M. P., & Ostrander, D. (1972). Life events and mental status: A longitudinal study. *Journal of Health and Social Behavior, 13,* 398–406.

Norton, A. J., & Glick, P. C. (1979). Marital instability in America: Past, present, and future. In G. Levinger & O. C. Moles (Eds.), *Divorce and separation: Context, causes, and consequences* (pp. 6–19). New York: Basic Books.

Norton, A. J., & Moorman, J. E. (1987). Current trends in marriage and divorce among American women. *Journal of Marriage and the Family, 49,* 3–14.

Parkes, C. M. (1972). *Bereavement: Studies of grief in adult life.* New York: International Universities Press.

Parkes, C. M., & Weiss, R. S. (1983). *Recovery from bereavement.* New York: Basic Books.

Patterson, C. J. (2000). Family relationships of lesbians and gay men. *Journal of Marriage and Family, 62,* 1052–1069.

Pearlin, L. I., & Schooler, C. (1978). The structure of coping. *Journal of Health and Social Behavior, 19,* 2–21.

Phillips, R. (1988). *Putting asunder: A history of divorce in Western society.* Cambridge, England: Cambridge University Press.

Popenoe, D. (1993). American family decline, 1960–1990: A review and appraisal. And rejoinders. *Journal of Marriage and the Family, 55,* 527–555.

Price-Bonham, S., & Balswick, J. O. (1980). The noninstitutions: Divorce, desertion, and remarriage. *Journal of Marriage and the Family, 42,* 959–972.

Raley, R. K., & Wildsmith, E. (2004). Cohabitation and children's family instability. *Journal of Marriage and Family, 66,* 210–219.

Raschke, H. J. (1977). The role of social participation in postseparation and postdivorce adjustment. *Journal of Divorce, 1,* 129–139.

Rodgers, B., & Pryor, J. (1998). *Divorce and separation: The outcomes of children.* York, England: Joseph Rowntree Foundation.

Rutter, M. (1981). Stress, coping, and development: Some issues and questions. *Journal of Child Psychology and Psychiatry and Allied Discipline, 22,* 323–356.

Schwartz, J. E., Friedman, H. S., Tucker, J. S., Tomlinson-Keasey, C., Wingard, D. L., & Criqui, M. H. (1995). Sociodemographic and psychosocial factors in childhood as predictors of adult mortality. *American Journal of Public Health, 85,* 1237–1245.

Seltzer, J. A. (2000). Families formed outside of marriage. *Journal of Marriage and the Family, 62,* 1247–1268.

Simon, R. W., & Marcussen, K. (1999). Marital transitions, marital beliefs, and mental health. *Journal of Health and Social Behavior, 40,* 111–125.

Skolnick, A. (1991). *Embattled paradise: The American family in an age of uncertainty.* New York: Basic Books.

Sorenson, E. (1997). A national profile of nonresident fathers and their ability to pay child support, *Journal of Marriage and the Family, 59,* 785–797.

Spanier, G. B., & Thompson, L. (1984). *Parting: The aftermath of separation and divorce.* Beverly Hills, CA: Sage.

Teachman, J. D., Polonko, K. A., & Scanzoni, J. (1999). Demography and families. In M. B. Sussman, S. K. Steinmetz, & G. W. Peterson (Eds.), *Handbook of Marriage and the Family* (pp. 39–76). New York: Plenum.

Thornton, A., & Young-DeMarco L. (2001). Four decades of trends in attitudes toward family issues in the United States: The 1960's through the 1990's. *Journal of Marriage and Family, 63,* 1009–1037.

Trost, J. (1979). *Unmarried cohabitation.* Vasteras, Sweden: International Library.

Tschann, J. M., Johnson, J. R., & Wallerstein, J. S. (1989). Resources, stressors, and attachment as predictors of adult adjustment after divorce: A longitudinal study. *Journal of Marriage and the Family, 51,* 1033–1046.

Uhlenberg, P., & Chew, K. S. Y. (1986). The changing place of remarriage in the life course. *Current Perspectives on Aging and the Life Cycle, 2,* 23–52.

Vaughn, D. (1986). *Uncoupling: Turning points in intimate relationships.* New York: Oxford University Press.

Waite, L. J. (1995). Does marriage matter? *Demography, 32,* 483–507.

Waite, L. J., & Gallagher, M. (2000). *The case for marriage: Why married people are happier, healthier, and better off financially.* New York: Doubleday.

Wallerstein, J. S. (2001). *Who's who in America, 2001.* New Providence, NJ: Marquis Who's Who.

Wallerstein, J. S., & Blakeslee, S. (1989). *Second chances: Men, women, and children a decade after divorce.* New York: Ticknor & Fields.

Wallerstein, J. S., & Blakeslee, S. (1995). *The good marriage: How and why love lasts.* New York: Houghton Mifflin.

Wallerstein, J. S., & Blakeslee, S. (2003). *What about the kids: Raising your children, before, during, and after divorce.* New York: Hyperion.

Wallerstein, J. S., & Kelly, J. B. (1974). The effects of parental divorce: The adolescent experience. In E. J. Anthony & C. Koupenik (Eds.), *Children at psychiatric risk* (Vol. 3, pp. 479–505). NY: Wiley & Sons.

Wallerstein, J. S., & Kelly, J. B. (1975). The effects of parental divorce: Experiences of the preschool child. *Journal of the American Academy of Child Psychiatry, 14,* 600–616.

Wallerstein, J. S., & Kelly, J. B. (1977). Divorce counseling: A community service for families in the midst of divorce. *American Journal of Orthopsychiatry, 47,* 4–22.

Wallerstein, J. S., & Kelly, J. B. (1980). *Surviving the breakup: How children and parents cope with divorce.* New York: Basic Books.

Wallerstein, J. S., Lewis, J. M., & Blakeslee, S. (2000). *The unexpected legacy of divorce: A 25-year landmark study.* New York: Hyperion.

Weiss, R. S. (1975). *Marital separation.* New York: Basic Books.

Weiss, R. S. (1976). The emotional impact of marital separation. *Journal of Social Issues, 32,* 135–145.

Weiss, R. S. (1979). *Going it alone: The family life and social situation of the single parent.* New York: Basic Books.

Weiss, R. S. (1993). *Learning from strangers: The art and method of qualitative interview studies.* New York: The Free Press.

Weiss, R. S. (2001). Grief, bonds, and relationships. In M. S. Stroebe, R. O. Hansson, W. Stroebe, & H. Schut (Eds.), *Handbook of bereavement research: Consequences, coping, and care.* (pp. 47–62). Washington, DC: American Psychological Association.

Weitzman, L. J. (1985). *The divorce revolution: The unexpected social and economic consequences for women and children in America.* New York: The Free Press.

Weitzman, L. J. (2003). Si Goode remembered. *Footnotes, 33,* 1, 7, 10.

Westen, D. (1998). The scientific legacy of Sigmund Freud: Toward a psychodynamically informed psychological science. *Psychological Bulletin, 124,* 333–371.

Wheaton, B. (1990). Life transitions, role histories, and mental health. *American Sociological Review, 55,* 209–223.

Wheaton, B. (1999). The nature of stressors. In A. V. Horowitz and T. L. Scheid (Eds.), *Handbook for the study of mental health: Social contexts, theories, and systems* (pp. 176–197). Cambridge, England: Cambridge University Press.

White, L. K. (1990). Determinants of divorce: A review of research in the eighties. *Journal of Marriage and the Family, 52,* 904–912.

Willetts, M. C. (2003). An exploratory investigation of heterosexual licensed domestic partners. *Journal of Marriage and the Family, 65,* 939–952.

Williams, D. R., Takeuchi, D. R., & Adair, R. K. (1992). Marital status and psychiatric disorders among blacks and whites. *Journal of Health and Social Behavior, 33,* 140–157.

Williams, K. (2003). Has the future of marriage arrived? A contemporary examination of gender, marriage, and psychological well-being. *Journal of Health and Social Behavior, 44,* 470–487.

Williams, K., & Umberson, D. (2004). Marital status, marital transitions, and health: A gendered life course perspective. *Journal of Health and Social Behavior, 45,* 81–98.

Wu, Z., & Hart, R. (2002–2003). Union disruption in Canada. *International Journal of Sociology, 32,* 51–75.

3

Historical Trends in Divorce in the United States

Paul R. Amato and Shelley Irving
Penn State University

Throughout American history, marriage has been defined as a lifelong relationship between spouses. Of course, this definition represents a cultural ideal rather than a description of reality. Almost everyone knows that marital dissolution is common these days, and that nearly half of all first marriages are projected to end in divorce. Many people do not realize, however, that divorce has always been a fact of life in American society. Our goal in this chapter is to present a historical perspective on marital dissolution in the United States. We focus on three aspects of divorce that have changed significantly over time: (a) the frequency of divorce, (b) the legal regulation of divorce, and (c) public attitudes toward divorce.

Unfortunately, almost no historical information is available about the dissolution of non-marital relationships, including cohabiting unions. Living together outside of formal marriage, however, was not uncommon in the past, especially among the poor (Phillips, 1991). Moreover, prior to the Civil War, most slave couples, including those with children, were not allowed to marry. Living together was also common among couples in remote parts of the country who did not have access to clergy or a justice of the peace. To the extent that these frontier couples lived as "husband and wife," most states recognized their unions as common-law marriages. That is, these couples had the same legal rights and responsibilities as other married couples, even though they did not have a license or participate in a formal ceremony. (Given the ease of marrying these days, as well as the legal complexities that these unions present, most states have since abolished common-law marriage.) Because cohabiting couples that split up did not obtain legal divorces, we know little about the frequency or causes of dissolution among these informal unions. Consequently, although the material in this chapter focuses on legal marriage and divorce, readers should keep in mind that a large number of unions in the United States were formed and dissolved without leaving tracks in the historical record.

To organize the material in this chapter, we have divided historical periods into three eras: the Colonial era, the period between the Revolutionary War and the end of the 19th century, and the 20th century. In the conclusion of our chapter, we summarize several general trends that a historical survey of divorce reveals. We also include some thoughts on how a consideration of historical trends can inform our current thinking about divorce.

THE COLONIAL ERA: FROM 1620 TO THE REVOLUTIONARY WAR

The Frequency of Divorce

Although divorce was rare in Colonial America, historical records indicate that it occurred at least occasionally. At least 9 divorces were granted during the 72-year history of Plymouth colony (established in 1620), the first European settlement in New England (Riley, 1991). Surviving records indicate that divorce was most common in the New England colonies, especially Connecticut and Massachusetts. Divorce was established in Massachusetts Bay colony in 1629, and at least 44 divorces occurred there prior to the end of that century. Similarly, Connecticut made provisions for divorce in 1640, and at least 40 divorces occurred there over the next six decades (Phillips, 1991). At the time, the Church of England, along with most Catholic European countries, did not allow divorce. The Pilgrims, however, had left Europe to be free from conservative religious restrictions, and, consequently, most of the New England colonies—although under English rule—instituted provisions for divorce.

Divorce policies and practices were more conservative in the middle colonies, such as New York and Pennsylvania, than in the New England colonies. Nevertheless, these colonies occasionally granted divorces in cases of adultery, desertion, or bigamy. Divorce was not possible in the southern colonies, largely because the founders of these colonies (in contrast to the founders of the New England colonies) closely followed the teachings of the Anglican church. The southern colonies, however, did allow for limited divorces, or "separation from bed and board" (Jones, 1987).

Because Colonial governments did not recognize marriage between slaves, it was unusual for African Americans to obtain divorces. Nevertheless, at least two divorces involving African American couples occurred in Massachusetts, with one case involving slaves and the other involving free Blacks (Riley, 1991). Formal divorce among Native Americans was essentially nonexistent in the colonies, largely because Native American cultures had their own procedures for ending marriages.

Records from New England indicate that wives were more likely to initiate divorce than were husbands (Philips, 1991). This trend continues to the present day. Gender differences also occurred in the grounds for divorce. The majority of women's petitions referred to their husbands' desertion, whereas the majority of husbands' petitions referred to their wives' adultery. The former trend reflects the fact that husbands were more likely than wives to abandon their families, which was an option made possible by men's greater economic independence. The latter trend, however, does not imply that wives were more likely than husbands to engage in adultery—only that people believed adultery to be a more serious marital offence when committed by wives than by husbands (Basch, 1999).

Although most of the colonies allowed for marital dissolution, attitudes toward divorce (as we note later) were negative. For this reason, and because formal divorces were difficult to obtain, many couples resolved their marital problems though informal separations. Because these disruptions were undocumented, the true extent of marital breakdown during this period is impossible to estimate (Riley, 1991).

The Legal Regulation of Divorce

Each colony had different procedures for divorce (a pattern that continues to the present day, with each state enacting its own divorce statutes). For example, depending on the colony, divorces were granted by courts, governors, or colonial legislatures (Riley, 1991). Wherever divorce was allowed, however, it was permitted only on fault grounds; that is, one spouse had to prove that the other spouse had violated his or her marriage vows. Divorces were granted most commonly for reasons of adultery, desertion, or bigamy. Other grounds (available in some colonies, but not in others) included physical cruelty, threats to life, failure to provide, impotence, and refusal of intercourse (Basch, 1999; Riley, 1991). Adultery was considered to be the most serious marital offence, and it was the charge most likely to result in a successful divorce petition (Basch, 1999). Early courts took the notion of fault seriously and often ordered harsh punishments for "guilty" spouses, including whippings, fines, and incarceration in the stocks. Moreover, spouses found to be at fault for causing the divorce generally did not have the right to remarry (Jones, 1987).

The English government disapproved of these liberal practices and made numerous attempts to limit divorce in the colonies. The colonies differed, however, in the extent to which they complied with these demands. Massachusetts and Connecticut acted contrary to the English system, largely because the founders of these colonies were influenced by Protestant thought (which allowed for divorce). The middle colonies granted divorces only under extreme circumstances, and the southern colonies (following the English system) did not allow divorce under any circumstances. Despite variations in the extent to which colonies conformed with English law, it was only after the Revolutionary War that the American colonies were completely free to develop their own procedures for marital dissolution (Basch, 1999; Phillips, 1991; Riley, 1991).

Public Attitudes Toward Divorce

Despite the fact that most colonists strongly disapproved of divorce, the New England colonies quickly established divorce laws with relatively little public resistance. Most Puritans believed that troubled couples should be encouraged to reconcile, but many also believed that requiring hostile couples to stay together had the potential to undermine the social harmony of the community (Riley, 1991). In the eyes of many colonists, divorce was a necessary evil, even if scandalous and shameful (Phillips, 1991). Because adultery was the most commonly recognized cause of marital dissolution, many people assumed that divorced individuals (especially women) were adulterers and people of low moral character. For this reason, divorced individuals had relatively low status in most communities.

Despite these negative views, the topic of divorce appeared frequently in the popular literature of the time. For example, prior to the Revolutionary War, Tom Paine, who produced influential works on liberty and human rights, also wrote about the unfairness of loveless marriages from which individuals were unable to escape. Advice columns also became popular during the 1700s in magazines such as the *Columbian, Pennsylvania Magazine, Boston Magazine,* and *Gentlemen and Ladies Town and Country Magazine* (Basch, 1999). Many readers sent letters or questions about marital problems and divorce to these magazines, which suggests that, despite the low rate of divorce, the general public was concerned about the phenomenon of failing unions (Basch, 1999).

THE REVOLUTIONARY WAR THROUGH
THE 19TH CENTURY

The Frequency of Divorce

Divorce statistics for the late 18th century and the first half of the 19th century are of poor quality. Nevertheless, available records suggest that divorce became more common after the Revolutionary War. This increase probably occurred for several reasons. First, some observers have suggested that the revolutionary notion of "liberation from oppression" spread to affect people's views of unhappy marriages. For example, Basch (1999) stated, "No sooner, it seems, did Americans create a rationale for dissolving the bonds of empire than they set about creating rules for dissolving the bonds of matrimony" (p. 21). Second, during the Colonial era, in many places (such as Pennsylvania), divorces could be granted only by Colonial legislatures—a slow and awkward method. In the decades following the war, however, most states shifted jurisdiction for divorce to the courts. Because courts were more accessible to the public and could reach decisions more quickly than legislatures, marital dissolution became easier to obtain (Riley, 1991). Third, divorces began to occur in the southern states, where they had been illegal previously. Fourth, westward migration increased during the early 1800s, and the new territories and states had especially high rates of marital disruption (Phillips, 1991; Riley, 1991). As we describe in the paragraphs that follow, divorce laws in the West were relatively permissive, which prompted some people to migrate in search of easy divorces.

Shortly after the Civil War, the federal government began to collect divorce statistics for the first time, and these data confirmed what many people had expected: The divorce rate was rising. Some of this increase may have been due to the war itself. Wars tend to increase marital instability for several reasons, including the long separation of spouses, adultery that occurs during the period of separation (due to loneliness and unmet sexual needs), and the difficulty experienced by many veterans in readjusting to civilian life. Irrespective of the reason, the rising rate of divorce in the second half of the 19th century created a great deal of public controversy (as we subsequently note). Moreover, the United States began to gain a reputation as a divorce-prone society, and many Europeans believed that Americans not only had a fragile family system but also possessed weak moral values (Philips, 1991).

A useful way to track the frequency of divorce is to calculate the refined divorce rate, which is the number of divorces in a given year per every 1,000 married women. The divorce rate doubled from about 2 in 1865 to about 4 by the end of the century. Of course, divorce rates do not capture the whole story of marital breakdown. Throughout the 19th century, divorced individuals were stigmatized. Moreover, although the number of divorce petitions increased steadily, many of these petitions were unsuccessful (Riley, 1991). Divorces also were expensive, and the majority were granted to relatively affluent couples (Basch, 1999; Phillips, 1991). Because of the stigma of divorce, the courts' frequent refusal to grant divorces, and the expense of divorce, many couples resorted instead to informal separations (Riley 1991). For these reasons, official divorce rates substantially underestimate the true level of marital disruption during this period.

Nevertheless, the availability of reliable data on official divorces led to a series of empirical studies on this topic late in the 19th century. In one of the most comprehensive of these studies, Willcox (1891) examined the divorce rate in each state, along with the number of grounds for divorce allowed by each state and whether states restricted remarriage following divorce. By cross-tabulating these variables, he found that divorce rates did not appear to vary with either the number of grounds for divorce or restrictions on remarriage. These findings led him to conclude that legal regulations had little influence on the occurrence of divorce. Willcox also noted that two thirds of divorces were granted to women. Moreover, wives were most likely to file for divorce in states where women had more possibilities for economic independence (the northern states) or where wives were in demand (the western states). Wives were least likely to file for divorce in the southern states, where social and economic conditions for women were most restrictive. As Willcox stated, "Divorces are most frequent where women are most emancipated, and the percentage granted to the wife in such communities is excessive" (p. 68). Willcox also demonstrated that divorce was more common in the United States than in Europe, that childless marriages were more likely to end in divorce than were marriages with children, that divorces tended to occur in the early years of marriage, and that African Americans were less likely to divorce than were Whites. With the exception of the latter finding, all of these trends persisted into the 20th century.

The Legal Regulation of Divorce

After the Revolutionary War, most states quickly formalized their divorce laws. As we noted earlier, a major change in the legal regulation of divorce during the 19th century was the shift in the jurisdiction of divorce cases from state legislatures to the courts (Basch, 1999; Riley, 1991). States defined divorce law carefully, largely because of the seriousness with which people viewed marital dissolution. The general consensus among lawmakers was that divorce laws should rest on "causative reasoning"—that is, courts had to firmly establish the cause of the divorce (the spouse who was at fault). Because of the focus on fault, many couples that mutually agreed to part found it difficult to obtain a divorce (Basch, 1999).

Although laws in all states were based on the concept of fault, many states expanded the legal grounds for divorce to include cruelty, insanity, imprisonment, and habitual drunkenness (Phillips, 1991). For example, California, in 1851, allowed divorce on the grounds of adultery, extreme cruelty, desertion, neglect, habitual intemperance, impotency, fraud, and conviction of a felony. Two decades later, California law became even more liberal when the legislature decreased the required period for intemperance, desertion, and neglect from 3 years to 1 (Griswald, 1982). Despite the expanding grounds for divorce, as in the Colonial era, the primary reasons for divorce continued to be desertion and adultery.

As the 19th century progressed, cruelty became an increasingly common ground for divorce (Basch, 1999). There was much debate about what constituted cruelty, but with the shift of jurisdiction from the legislature to the courts, the definition of cruelty gradually expanded (Riley, 1991). California courts, at the middle of the 19th century, broadened the definition even further to include psychological as well as physical harm. Moreover, California courts argued that wives were especially vulnerable to emotional abuse on the part of their husbands, even if no physical harm was involved (Griswald, 1982). In 1824, the territory of Indiana added an "omnibus clause," that allowed divorce for "any misconduct that permanently destroys the happiness of the petitioner and defeats the purpose of the marriage relation" (Jones, 1987, p. 23). Several other states, mainly in the West (but also in New England), added omnibus clauses to their laws in the following decades.

As in the Colonial era, divorce laws differed from state to state. Southern states moved cautiously after independence, but, by the middle of the 19th century, most southern states allowed divorce on several grounds, including imprisonment, adultery, impotence, and desertion (Phillips, 1991). South Carolina, the most conservative state, did not establish divorce until 1868. Despite South Carolina's efforts to allow marital dissolution, their divorce clause was repealed in 1878, even though relatively few divorces had been granted during the preceding 10 years (Jones, 1987).

In contrast to the South, divorce laws were especially liberal in the western part of the country. Shortly after an area gained status as a territory, most governments created laws that allowed divorce on a wide variety of grounds (Phillips, 1991; Riley, 1991). As we already noted, Indiana was the first place to introduce an omnibus clause for divorce. Moreover, most territories had minimal residency requirements. In Indiana, in particular, divorce was especially easy for residents and nonresidents alike. Petitioners could put notices of their divorce petitions in newspapers and did not have to personally inform their spouses. This procedure created numerous problems, because many people were unaware that they were being divorced, were absent from the divorce hearings, and were unable to defend themselves. By 1859, Indiana had changed the residency requirement and taken steps to make divorce more difficult to attain, but this did not lower the number of petitions for divorce (Riley, 1991).

The existence of liberal divorce laws, combined with lenient residency requirements, led many unhappy couples to move westward to end their marriages. When territories were granted statehood, however, the new governments often adopted more conservative divorce policies, forcing unhappy couples to look elsewhere for easy divorces (Riley, 1991). This trend led couples seeking to end their marriages to move increasingly westward during the 1800s: to Ohio in the 1840s, to Indiana in the 1850s, to Illinois in the 1870s, and to the Dakotas, Wyoming, Utah, and Idaho in the 1880s and 1890s (Jones, 1987).

Public Attitudes Toward Divorce

As divorce became more widespread, and as the laws regulating divorce became less restrictive, the public became increasingly fascinated with marital disruption. Newspapers in the 19th century often reported the details of divorce trials, and these stories were followed closely by readers across the country. Moreover, trial pamphlets emerged as a popular genre. These pamphlets compiled information on popular divorce cases and included extensive editorials on the background and implications of these events. Cases involving adultery or cruelty were especially popular with readers (Basch, 1999).

Not surprisingly, many individuals were uncomfortable with this new reality, and, during the second half of the 19th century, divorce become a major issue of public controversy and debate. Horace Greeley, founder and editor of the *New York Tribune*, wrote numerous editorials on the problem of excessive individualism in American life. Greeley believed that the high rate of divorce was one of the major outcomes of this destructive focus on the self, and he warned that widespread marital dissolution would lead to "corruption such as this country has never known" (cited in Riley, 1991, p. 62). He and other critics believed that "easy" divorce had the potential to undermine the institution of the family and literally bring forth the collapse of American society. From this perspective, the larger good of social stability was more important than the dissatisfaction of married spouses. Despite these objections, however, most opponents of liberal laws agreed that divorce should be available for reasons of adultery or other extreme marital offenses (Phillips, 1991; Riley, 1991).

In 1881, concerned individuals founded the New England Divorce Reform League—the first organization with the specific goal of restricting liberal divorce laws. In 1885, this group expanded into a national organization, the National Divorce Reform League, and the name of this group was later changed to the National League for the Protection of the Family (Phillips, 1991). This organization aimed to counter liberal social policies and permissive social trends with respect to sexuality, prostitution, and alcohol consumption. Its main goal, however, was to encourage state governments to make marital dissolution more difficult to obtain. The group had some success, and, in response to public pressure, a number of states removed omnibus clauses from their divorce laws or made residency requirements for divorce more stringent (Jones, 1987).

Despite these conservative trends, it would be a mistake to conclude that public opinion was consistently against divorce during the second half of the 19th century. Many groups and individuals argued that widespread marrital breakdown—rather than divorce—was the real problem. These individuals supported liberal divorce laws because they did not believe that it was humane to force two people to remain in a relationship when one or both partners were miserable (Basch, 1999; Phillips, 1991; Riley, 1991). Many women's rights activists, such as Susan B. Anthony and Elizabeth Cady Stanton, supported the *further* liberalization of divorce laws. As Stanton stated, "I think divorce at the will of the parties is not only a right, but that it is a sin against nature, the family, and the state for man or woman to live together in the marriage relation in continual antagonism, indifference, and disgust" (cited in Basch, 1999, p. 69). Moreover, given that marriage was a patriarchal arrangement, many feminists saw divorce as a way for wives to escape from oppressive, perhaps dangerous, marriages. Not all women's rights activists, however, were in agreement on this point. Some feminists were cautious about the further liberalization of divorce laws, because of their concern about women's ability to support themselves outside of marriage, as well as the difficulty that older women faced in remarrying (Basch, 1999). In the 19th century women's movement, as in the larger society, people held a variety of opinions on these issues.

THE 20TH CENTURY

The Frequency of Divorce

During the first half of the 20th century, the divorce rate rose and fell in response to specific events and changing social circumstances. The divorce rate increased gradually during the early years of the 20th century, and then it surged in the years following World War I. Presumably, this occurred for the reasons noted earlier; that is, couples were separated for long periods, some married individuals engaged in adultery during the time of separation, and many veterans had difficulty fitting into civilian life after the war. In addition, there was a rapid increase in the marriage rate during the war years. Given that some of these marriages were contracted hastily (before men left for military service), it is not surprising that many ill-considered matches were made. The divorce rate declined during the Great Depression of the 1930s—a time when many unhappy spouses literally could not afford to divorce. World War II pulled the United States out of the depression, and, consistent with earlier trends, divorce rates spiked sharply upward during the war. In the aftermath of the war, the divorce rate declined, and by the end of the 1950s, the rate of divorce was back to where it had been 20 years earlier.

The 1950s represented a relatively "profamily" period in U.S. history. In addition to the stable divorce rate, the marriage rate was high and fertility increased dramatically—a period known as the baby boom. Several forces came together to create the stable, two-parent, child-oriented family of the 1950s: a strong economy, increases in men's wages, veterans' taking advantage of the GI bill to obtain university educations, the growth of home construction in the suburbs, and a desire on the part of many people to move beyond the tumultuous war years and to concentrate on home and family life (Cherlin, 1992).

After being stable for more than a decade, the divorce rate increased sharply during the 1960s and 1970s. It reached an all-time peak in 1980 and then declined modestly. Currently, the rate of divorce is about 20, which means that about 2% of all marriages end in divorce every year [(20/1,000) × 100]. Although the 2% figure may seem low, it is based on a single year. By applying duration-specific probabilities of divorce across all the years of marriage, it is possible to project the percentage of marriages that will end in divorce. Using this method, demographers estimate that about one half of first marriages, and about 60% of second marriages, will end in divorce (Cherlin, 1992). These figures represent a historically high level of marital disruption in the United States. In comparison, about one eighth of all marriages ended in divorce in 1900, and about one fourth of all marriages ended in divorce in 1950 (Preston & McDonald, 1979).

The Legal Regulation of Divorce

As we noted earlier, throughout American history, divorces were granted only when one spouse demonstrated to the court's satisfaction that the other spouse was "guilty" of violating the marriage contract. This process required that courts gather evidence, including witness testimony, either from people familiar with the family or from the spouses themselves. Under this system, the "innocent" spouse often received a better deal than the guilty spouse with respect to the division of marital property, alimony, and child custody. In other words, the law punished the spouse who was responsible for undermining the marriage (Katz, 1994).

Fault-based divorce did not allow for the possibility that two spouses simply might be unhappy with their marriage and wish to go their separate ways. Instead, by making divorce difficult, and by requiring one spouse to accept responsibility for violating the marriage contract, the law affirmed its commitment to the norm of marital permanence. Despite the difficulty and cost of proving fault in court, however, demand for divorce increased throughout the first half of the 20th century. To accommodate this growing demand, courts broadened the grounds for marital dissolution, and an increasing proportion of divorces were granted on the relatively vague grounds of mental cruelty. More specifically, in the mid-19th century, only 12% of divorces occurred for reasons of cruelty. This figure rose to 28% in 1920, 40% in 1930, 48% in 1940, and 59% in 1950 (DiFonzo, 1997).

In 1933, New Mexico was the first state to add "incompatibility" as a ground for divorce (DiFonzo, 1997). Twenty years later, Oklahoma instituted a form of no-fault divorce based on mutual consent (Vlosky & Monroe, 2002). Although fault-based divorces still were possible in New Mexico and Oklahoma, spouses could dissolve their marriages even if neither spouse had committed a serious marital offense. Several other states added no-fault options during the next decade, including Alaska in 1963 and New York in 1967 (Vlosky & Monroe). It is important to note, however, that fault-based divorce existed side by side with no-fault divorce in each of these states.

The most dramatic change in divorce law occurred in California in 1969, when the state legislature eliminated fault-based divorce entirely and replaced it with no-fault divorce. Under the new legislation, only one ground for divorce existed: the marriage was "irretrievably broken" as a result of "irreconcilable differences" (Glendon, 1989). Moreover, courts in California granted divorces even if one spouse wanted the divorce and the other did not—a system known as unilateral no-fault divorce. The assumption underlying unilateral no-fault divorce was that it takes two committed spouses to form a marriage. If one spouse no longer wished to remain in the relationship, then the marriage was not practicable. California also removed the notion of fault from the award of spousal support and the division of marital property (Parkman, 2000; but note that the notion of fault was retained to a certain extent, however, in decisions about child custody).

Other states quickly followed California's lead, and, by the mid-1980s, all 50 states had adopted no-fault divorce. Most states adopted versions of unilateral no-fault divorce. A few states introduced no-fault divorce, but only by mutual consent. In Pennsylvania, for example, if one spouse wants a divorce and the other does not, then a no-fault divorce can be obtained only after the spouses are separated for 2 years. Otherwise, the spouse who wants the divorce must prove fault. Despite the fact that some states require mutual consent, and despite the fact that some states have retained fault provision, the great majority of divorces in the United States today take place under unilateral no-fault divorce regimes (Katz, 1994).

States introduced no-fault divorce for several reasons. First, it was widely known that many spouses who wished to dissolve their marriages colluded to fabricate grounds for divorce. For example, spouses might claim that infidelity had occurred, even if it had not. The recognition that many couples were making a mockery of the law was one factor that led to divorce reformation (Katz, 1994). In addition, legal scholars increasingly accepted the proposition that spouses had a legal right to end their marriages if they were incompatible, had fallen out of love, or were no longer happy living together (Glendon, 1989). Finally, fault-based divorce is an inherently adversarial procedure. Many legislators believed that no-fault divorce would lessen the level of animosity between former spouses, and, hence, make it easier for them to cooperate in raising their children following marital dissolution (Glendon, 1989; Katz, 1994).

Some scholars believe that the liberalization of divorce laws stimulated further demand for divorce (for a review of this evidence, see Parkman, 2000). Other scholars disagree with this claim (e.g., Glenn, 1999). Nevertheless, even if legal changes encouraged some couples to divorce, this effect was modest. Most scholars believe that changes in divorce laws were more a consequence than a cause of marital breakdown (e.g., Cherlin, 1992).

Not everyone was happy with the shift to no-fault divorce, especially after the sharp increase in divorce during the 1970s. Some conservative reformers hoped to lower the frequency of marital dissolution by placing restrictions on unilateral no-fault divorce. For example, during the 1990s, legislators in nearly a dozen states that had unilateral divorce laws introduced bills that required the consent of both spouses for a no-fault divorce, provided that they had dependent children. In some attempted reforms, fault-based divorce would be available without mutual consent in cases of abuse, desertion, or adultery. Other bills attempted to lengthen the waiting period prior to divorce or to require marital counseling (with the goal of attempting a reconciliation) before divorce. Despite attracting a good deal of media attention, none of these bills was passed in any state (DiFonzo, 1997).

Divorce law reformers were more successful with the introduction of covenant marriage in three states. Louisiana was the first state to introduce this legislation in 1997, followed by Arizona and Arkansas. Under this system, couples choose between two types of marriage: a standard marriage or a covenant marriage. To obtain a covenant marriage, couples must attend premarital education classes and promise to seek marital counseling to preserve the marriage if problems arise later. Unilateral no-fault divorce is not an option for ending a covenant marriage. Instead, to terminate a covenant marriage, one spouse must prove fault, although a couple can also obtain a divorce after a 2-year separation. (For a detailed description of covenant marriage in Louisiana, see Thompson & Wyatt, 1999.) Although proponents of covenant marriage see it as a way to strengthen marriage and lower the divorce rate, only a small percentage of couples in Louisiana have chosen covenant marriages (Sanchez, Nock, Wright, Pardee, & Ionescu, 2001). For this reason, the introduction of covenant marriage has, so far, been unsuccessful in lowering the rate of divorce.

Public Attitudes Toward Divorce

As the divorce rate surged following World War I, divorce emerged again as a major social issue. During the 1920s and 1930s, articles on divorce appeared frequently in the media, including in magazines such as the *Saturday Evening Post, Vanity Fair, Ladies Home Journal*, and *Good Housekeeping*. Echoing the concerns of a half-century earlier, conservative writers felt that divorce posed a threat to the family and to the larger society, and that divorcing couples were placing their own needs ahead of the needs of their children. Many of these critics placed the blame for marital instability on increases in wives' employment, rising expectations for personal satisfaction from marriage, and the declining stigma of divorce (DiFonzo, 1997).

Many early family scholars also took a dim view of divorce. Developmental theories of the time, such as Freudian theory, assumed that children need to grow up with two parents to develop normally. For this reason, most social scientists in the first half of the 20th century saw the rising level of marital disruption as a serious social problem. Sociologists were concerned that one of the fundamental institutions of society—the family—was being undermined. In the 1920s and 1930s, social scientists published books with titles such as *The Marriage Crisis* (Groves, 1928), *Family Disorganization* (Mowrer, 1927), and *Marriage at the Crossroads* (Stekel, 1931). Curiously, few studies focused on children, presumably because the idea that divorce was bad for children seemed self-evident. Instead, researchers focused primarily on factors that promote or erode marital happiness (e.g., Burgess & Cottrell, 1939; Terman, 1938).

The debate over divorce subsided during the 1950s and early 1960s. As we noted earlier, this was a profamily time in American history, with high marriage rates, a stable divorce rate, and rising levels of affluence. Nevertheless, many people continued to see divorce as being unrespectable. As an illustration, Adlai Stevenson (who was divorced in 1949) served as the Democratic Party's candidate for President in 1952. During the campaign, Dwight Eisenhower (the Republican Party candidate) raised Stevenson's divorce as a campaign issue—an issue that resonated strongly among women voters (Rothstein, 2002). Partly for this reason, Stevenson lost the election.

Public attitudes toward divorce became more liberal during the 1960s and 1970s. For example, surveys indicate that *disagreement* with the statement, "When there are children in the family, parents should stay together even if they don't get along" increased from 51% in 1962 to 80% in 1977 (Thornton & Young-DeMarco, 2001). As noted earlier, Adlai Stevenson's divorce was a major campaign issue in the 1952 presidential election. In contrast, Ronald Reagan ran successfully for President in 1980, and the fact that his first marriage had ended in divorce was never raised as a campaign issue (Rothstein, 2002). By the end of the 1970s, the great majority of Americans viewed divorce as an unfortunate but common event, and the stigma of divorce, although still present, was considerably weaker than in earlier eras.

The growing acceptance of divorce was consistent with a larger cultural shift that occurred during the 1960s and 1970s. During these decades, personal happiness and self-fulfillment came to be seen as the main goals of marriage (Bellah, Madsen, Sullivan, Swidler, & Tipton, 1985; Cherlin, 2004; Popenoe, 1996). During the same time, people's expectations for sexual satisfaction with marriage also increased (Seidman, 1991). With the satisfaction of personal needs becoming the main criterion by which people judged their marriages, spouses tended to seek divorces when they became dissatisfied with their relationships, even if their marriages did not include serious problems such as cruelty or adultery. Moreover, rather than condemning the decision to divorce, friends and family members tended to support spouses who left unsatisfying marriages.

The last two decades of the 20th century, however, saw a reaction to the liberal views of the 1960s and 1970s. Two national surveys, one carried out in 1980 (Booth, Johnson, White, & Edwards, 1991) and the other carried out in 2000 (Amato, Johnson, Booth, & Rogers, 2003), provide the latest information on this issue. These surveys revealed that agreement with the statement, "Couples are able to get divorced too easily today," increased from 33% in 1980 to 47% in 2000. Correspondingly, agreement with the statement, "The personal happiness of an individual is more important than putting up with a bad marriage," declined from 74% in 1980 to 64% in 2000. Overall, scores on a scale based on these and other items (coded to reflect support for the norm of lifelong marriage) increased by more than one fourth of a standard deviation (0.27) during this 20-year period. Moreover, growing support for the norm of lifelong marriage was apparent among wives as well as husbands. A similar trend can be observed in the General Social Survey. This annual survey of the American population revealed that the percentage of people who believe that divorce should be more difficult to obtain increased from 44% in 1974 to 51% in 2002 (see http://webapp.icpsr.umich.edu/GSS).

Although attempts to scale back no-fault divorce during the 1990s were unsuccessful (as we noted earlier), legislative efforts to strengthen marriage (rather than restrict access to divorce) met with some success. Although not widely recognized at the time, the 1996 federal welfare reform legislation referred to promoting marriage and encouraging the formation and maintenance of two-parent families as explicit policy goals (Ooms, 2002). Since that time, several state governments have enacted legislation and programs to strengthen marriage. For example, Oklahoma (as part of the Oklahoma Marriage Initiative) currently provides publicly funded premarital education classes to a wide range of couples, including poor, unmarried parents. Florida decreased the fee for a marriage license, along with the waiting period between obtaining a license and getting married, for couples that have taken a premarital education course. Florida also requires all high school students to take a course on marriage skills. In Arizona, Florida, Louisiana, and Utah, couples are given marriage materials (booklets or videos) that include information on how to build strong marriages, the effects of divorce on children, and available community resources (see Parke & Ooms, 2002, for details on these policies.)

Despite this recent shift in attitudes and policy, it would be a mistake to conclude that the American public is generally against divorce. Instead, people appear to be deeply ambivalent. For example, in the 2000 survey described earlier (Amato et al., 2003), only a minority of people (17%) agreed with the statement, "It's okay for people to get married thinking that, if it does not work out, they can always get a divorce." However, as also noted earlier, the majority of people continue to believe that personal happiness is more important than remaining in an unhappy marriage. Similarly, a poll by *Time Magazine* in 2000 found that 66% of people believed that children are better off in a divorced family than in "an unhappy marriage in which parents stay together mainly for the kids." At the same time, however, 64% of people believed that children always or frequently are harmed when parents get divorced (Kirn, 2000). It appears that many people today hold contradictory, unresolved views on divorce.

Public confusion about divorce is reflected in (and may have been shaped partly by) debate among family scholars during the last two decades of the 20th century. Some scholars view the retreat from marriage and the corresponding spread of single-parent families as a cause for alarm (Glenn, 1996; Popenoe, 1996; Waite & Gallagher, 2000; Whitehead, 1993; Wilson, 2002). These scholars believe that American culture has become increasingly individualistic, and people have become inordinately preoccupied with the pursuit of personal happiness. Because people no longer wish to be hampered with obligations to others, commitment to traditional institutions that require these obligations, such as marriage, has eroded. Indeed, in a society that encourages the maximization of self-interest, people are more concerned about their own well-being than the well-being of their spouses or children. For example, Popenoe (1996) made this argument:

> Traditionally, marriage has been understood as a social obligation—an institution designed mainly for economic security and procreation. Today, marriage is understood mainly as a path toward self-fulfillment. . . . No longer comprising a set of norms and social obligations that are widely enforced, marriage today is a voluntary relationship that individuals can make and break at will. (p. 533)

According to Popenoe, people are no longer willing to remain married through the difficult times, for better or for worse, until death do us part. Instead, marital commitment lasts only as long as people are happy and feel that their own needs are being met.

Other scholars reject the notion that our culture has shifted toward greater individualism and selfishness in recent decades (Coontz, 1988, Scanzoni, 2001; Skolnick, 1991; Stacey, 1996). These scholars also are skeptical of claims that the proportion of unsuccessful marriages has increased. According to this perspective, marriages were as likely to be troubled in the past as in the present, but because obtaining a divorce was time consuming and expensive, and because divorced individuals were stigmatized, these troubled marriages remained "intact." Rather than view the rise in marital instability with alarm, advocates of this perspective point out that divorce provides a second chance at happiness for adults and an escape from a dysfunctional and aversive home environment for many children. Moreover, because children are adaptable and can develop successfully in a variety of family structures, the spread of alternatives to mandatory lifelong marriage poses few problems for the next generation. Coontz (2000) stated the following:

> The amount of diversity in U.S. families today is probably no larger than in most periods of the past. . . . Most of the contemporary debate over family forms and values is not occasioned by the existence of diversity but by its increasing legitimation. Historical studies of family life . . . make it clear that families have always differed. Many different family forms and values have worked (or not worked) for various groups at different times. There is no reason to assume that family forms and practices that differ from those of the dominant ideal are necessarily destructive. (p. 28)

Feminist scholars, in particular, have argued that changes in family life during the past several decades have strengthened, rather than undermined, the quality of intimate relationships. For example, Stacey (1996, p. 9) stated that "changes in work, family, and sexual opportunities for women and men . . . open the prospect of introducing greater democracy, equality and choice than ever before into our most intimate relationships, especially for women and members of sexual minorities."

GENERAL TRENDS AND EXPLANATIONS

Four General Trends

Looking at the broad sweep of American history leads to four general conclusions about divorce trends. First, despite the fact that the divorce rate in the United States increased during some periods and decreased during others, the overarching trend—starting in the 17th century and continuing through the 20th century—has been a gradual rise in the rate of divorce. The roots of our current high divorce rate are over 300 years old. The fact that half of all current first marriages end in divorce, therefore, cannot be a function of relatively recent social conditions, such as the shift to no-fault divorce. Instead, the seeds of widespread marital instability were present in American society from its very beginning. Any theoretical explanation for the current high rate of divorce must take this fact into account.

Second, the conditions that courts, state legislatures, and the public view as justifying divorce have expanded continuously throughout American history. During the Colonial era, divorces were granted for a limited number of causes, such as desertion and adultery. These grounds expanded significantly during the 19th and 20th centuries. The ground of cruelty is particularly noteworthy, as it referred to relatively severe forms of physical abuse in the early 1800s and later incorporated acts of emotional cruelty and unkindness. A particularly dramatic shift occurred in the 1970s and early 1980s, when all states accepted versions of no-fault divorce. This change eliminated the necessity of proving that the marriage contract had been violated and made it possible for couples to divorce for virtually any reason. Moreover, unilateral no-fault divorce (available in most states) meant that one spouse could obtain a divorce, even if the other spouse wanted the marriage to continue. The gradual expansion of the grounds for divorce suggests that the law was responding to an ever-increasing demand from the American public, along with rising expectations for what constitutes a good marriage.

A third noteworthy trend is the tendency for wives to initiate divorce more often than husbands. This gender difference existed during the Colonial era (Phillips, 1991), the 19th century (Willcox, 1891), and the 20th century (Braver, 1998; Kitson, 1992; Maccoby & Mnookin, 1992). Why are wives more likely than husbands to seek a divorce? One explanation is that men are more likely to behave badly within marriage than are women. For example, men are more likely than are women to engage in serous forms of violence, both inside and outside of marriage (Felson, 2002). Men also are more likely than women to abuse alcohol and other substances, and husbands are more likely than wives to engage in infidelity (See Hall & Fincham, chap. 5, this volume). Recent research shows that wives are especially likely to end their marriages because of their spouses' cruelty, adultery, or drunkenness (Amato & Previti, 2003)—a difference that appears to have been as true in the past as it is today.

In addition, in the Colonial era through the 19th century, husbands were considerably more likely than wives to desert their families, largely because men had more opportunities for economic independence. Given that desertion was one of the few grounds for divorce in many states, it is not surprising that wives were especially likely to file for divorce. However, with the industrialization of the American economy, women gained greater access to employment, and, correspondingly, the means to live independently from men (albeit at a lower standard of living). Economic autonomy made it possible for wives to leave their marriages, just as husbands had left (deserted) their marriages in earlier eras. Rather than deserting their husbands, however, wives were able to obtain divorces on the expanding grounds of cruelty, and later, on the basis of no-fault provisions. In other words, although wives have always been more likely than husbands to initiate divorce, their reasons for doing so shifted as social conditions changed.

The feminist perspective, which argues that marriage provides substantially greater benefits to husbands than to wives, provides another explanation for the tendency for wives to initiate divorce. This point was articulated by 19th century feminist activists, such as Susan B. Anthony and Elizabeth Cady Stanton, and it has been echoed in the writings of more contemporary feminist scholars (e.g., Bernard, 1972; Stacey, 1996). For example, Bernard argued that "marriage introduces such profound discontinuities into the lives of women as to constitute genuine emotional health hazards" (p. 37). Some empirical work supports the notion that marriage improves the mental and physical health of husbands and lowers the mental and physical health of wives (e.g., Gove & Tudor, 1973). The great majority of recent longitudinal studies, however, indicate that marriage generally improves the mental and physical health of *both* sexes (e.g., Ross, 1995; Waite & Gallagher, 2000; Williams, 2003)—a finding that contradicts the feminist hypothesis.

Despite the lack of empirical support for the feminist hypothesis (that marriage benefits husbands more than wives), this notion is partly consistent with our claim that men are especially prone to exhibit behaviors that undermine the quality and practicability of marriage. As we noted earlier, men are more likely than women to abuse alcohol and other substances, to engage in severe violence, and (especially in the past) to desert their families. Nevertheless, only a minority of husbands engage in these behaviors. In most cases, therefore, marriage benefits wives as well as husbands. However, in a minority of marriages, wives suffer from their husbands' antisocial behavior. Consistent with this interpretation, if we eliminate badly behaved husbands from the married population, then wives and husbands are equally likely to initiate divorce (Amato & Previti, 2003).

Finally, our review indicates that divorce always has been controversial in American society. During the Colonial era, sharp differences existed between New England and the southern colonies about whether divorce should be allowed at all. In the latter part of the 18th century, divorce became a matter of widespread and contentious debate in the media and among policymakers. After World War I, many observers (including many social scientists) believed that the family was in danger, with harmful consequences for children and society in general. During the last two decades of the 20th century, this debate emerged yet again among policymakers, the media, the general public, and family scholars. Curiously, many of the arguments that are advanced today (both in favor of and against divorce) are similar, if not identical, to arguments made in previous centuries.

The Deinstitutionalization of Marriage

We believe that these various historical trends—along with differences of opinion among contemporary family scholars, policy-makers, and the general public about the meaning and implications of these trends—can be explained with reference to the *deinstitutionalization* of marriage. The view was originally put forward by Ernest Burgess, a sociologist who wrote on marriage and family life in the first part of the 20th century (Burgess & Cottrell, 1939; Burgess, Locke, & Thomes, 1963; Burgess & Wallin, 1953). Burgess argued that marriage was in a process of transition from a social institution to a private arrangement based on companionship. By *institution*, Burgess meant a fundamental unit of social organization—a formal status regulated by social norms, public opinion, law, and religion. In contrast, the emerging form of marriage was based primarily on emotional bonds between two autonomous individuals.

According to Burgess, the industrialization and urbanization of the United States weakened the institutional basis of marriage. Prior to the second half of the 19th century, the United States was predominantly a rural society, and most adults and children lived and worked on family farms. During this era, marriage was essential to the welfare not only of individual family members but also to the larger community. Before the development of specialized services and institutions, family members relied on each other to meet a wide range of needs, including child care, economic production, job training, and elder care. Because cohesive families were necessary for survival, the entire community had an interest in ensuring marital stability. Once married, spouses were expected not only to conform to traditional standards of behavior but also to sacrifice their personal goals, if necessary, for the sake of the marriage. Of course, because marriages were patriarchal, wives made more sacrifices than did husbands. Nevertheless, through marriage, men and women participated in an institution that was larger and more significant than themselves. For these reasons, divorce was frowned on and was allowed only if one partner had seriously violated the marriage contract, such as by engaging in physical abuse or desertion.

By 1900, the United States had become industrialized, and two-parent breadwinner–homemaker families replaced farm families as the dominant family form (Hernandez, 1993). Burgess believed that industrialization and urbanization provided individuals with more control over their marriages. Several factors were responsible for this change, including the greater geographical mobility of families (which freed spouses from the domination of parents and the larger kin group), the rise of democratic institutions (which increased the status and power of women), and a decline in religious control (which resulted in more freedom to adopt unconventional views and behaviors). As we noted earlier, the growth of employment opportunities for women also gave wives more economic independence from their husbands. As parents, religion, community expectations, and patriarchal traditions exerted less control over individuals, marriage was based increasingly on the mutual affection and individual preferences of spouses.

Burgess referred to the new model (and ideal) of marriage as *companionate marriage*. According to Burgess, companionate marriage is characterized by egalitarian rather than patriarchal relationships between spouses. Companionate marriage is held together not by bonds of social obligation but by ties of love, friendship, and common interest. Unlike institutional marriage, which emphasizes conformity to social norms, companionate marriage allows for an ample degree of self-expression and personal development. Of course, people in the United States have always expected marriage to be a source of love and emotional support. Furthermore, growing support for companionate marriage can be traced from the Revolutionary War through the end of the 19th century (Griswald, 1982). However, the notion that marriage should be based *primarily* on mutual satisfaction began to gain widespread public acceptance only during the early decades of the 20th century. Psychologists, educators, and social service providers applied these ideas in their professional practice, and it was in this context that marital counseling emerged as a discipline, with its goal being to help couples achieve emotional closeness and sexual satisfaction through improved communication and conflict management. By the 1950s, the great majority of Americans, irrespective of social class, accepted the companionate model of marriage as the cultural ideal (Mintz & Kellog, 1988).

The concept of deinstitutionalization helps to explain the historical trends described in this chapter. Because marriages held together by mutual satisfaction are intrinsically less stable than are marriages held together by community expectations, legal requirements, and religious restrictions, the gradual decline of institutional constraints made the long-term rise in divorce inevitable. Moreover, as people's standards for a good marriage increased, so did the percentage of marriages that failed to live up to these standards. As a result, marriages that were seen as being tolerable in the 19th century came to be seen as intolerable in the 20th century. It seems likely that rising standards for a "good" marriage fueled public demand for divorce, which in turn placed pressure on the states and courts to liberalize the grounds for marital dissolution (see DiFonzo, 1997, for a historical argument along these lines).

Finally, it is not surprising that the gradual deinstitutionalization of marriage has been generating debate for three centuries. Public controversies usually revolve around strongly held values, and values related to marriage and family life are anchored deeply in the American psyche. Americans, it seems, have always had a love–hate relationship with divorce. On the one hand, people value the freedom to leave unhappy unions, correct earlier mistakes, and find greater happiness with new partners. On the other hand, people are deeply concerned about social stability, tradition, and the overall impact of high levels of marital instability on the well-being of children. The clash between these two concerns reflects a fundamental contradiction within marriage itself; that is, marriage is designed to promote both institutional and personal goals. Happy and stable marriages meet both of these goals without friction. In contrast, when unhappy spouses wrestle with the decision to end their marriages, they are caught between their desire to further their own personal happiness and their sense of obligation to others, including their spouses, their children, their churches, and their communities. Because tension between the values of freedom and obligation is inherent in marriage, controversies over marital stability will always be common in American society.

REFERENCES

Amato, P. R., & Previti, D. (2003). People's reasons for divorcing: Gender, social class, the life course, and adjustment. *Journal of Family Issues, 24,* 602–626.

Amato, P. R., Johnson, D., Booth, A., & Rogers, S. J. (2003). Continuity and change in marriage between 1980 and 2000. *Journal of Marriage and Family, 65,* 1–22.

Basch, N. (1999). *Framing American divorce: From the revolutionary generation to the Victorians*. Berkeley: University of California Press.

Bellah, R. N., Madsen, R., Sullivan, W. M., Swidler, A., & Tipton, S. M. (1985). *Habits of the heart: Individualism and commitment in American life*. New York: Harper & Row.

Bernard. J. (1972). *The future of marriage*. New York: World Book.

Booth, A., Johnson, D. R., White, L. K., & Edwards, J. (1981). *Female labor force participation and marital instability: Methodology report*. Lincoln: University of Nebraska–Lincoln, Bureau of Sociological Research.

Braver, S. L. (1998). *Divorced dads*. New York: Putnam.

Burgess, E. W., & Cottrell, L. S. (1939). *Predicting success or failure in marriage*. New York: Prentice-Hall.

Burgess, E. W., Locke, H. J., & Thomes, M. (1963). *The family: From institution to companionship*. New York: American Book.

Burgess, E. W., & Wallin, P. (1953). *Engagement and marriage*. Chicago: Lippincott.

Cherlin, A. J. (1992). *Marriage, divorce, and remarriage*. Cambridge, MA: Harvard University Press.

Cherlin, A. J. (2004). The deinstitutionalization of marriage. *Journal of Marriage and Family, 66,* 848–862.

Coontz, S. (2000). Historical perspectives on family diversity. In D. H. Demo, K. R. Allen, & M. A. Fine (Eds.), *Handbook of family diversity* (pp. 15–31). New York: Oxford University Press.

DiFonzo, J. H. (1997). *Beneath the fault line: The popular and legal culture of divorce in twentieth-century America*. Charlottesville: University Press of Virginia.

Felson, R. B. (2002). *Violence and gender reexamined*. Washington, DC: American Psychological Association.

Glendon, M. A. (1989). *The transformation of family law: State, law, and family in the United States and Western Europe*. Chicago: University of Chicago Press.

Glenn, N. D. (1999). Further discussion of the effects of no-fault divorce on divorce rates. *Journal of Marriage and the Family, 61,* 800–802.

Gove, W. R., & Tudor, J. F. (1973). Adult sex roles and mental illness. *American Journal of Sociology, 78,* 812–835.

Groves, E. R. (1928). *The marriage crisis*. New York: Longman, Green.

Griswald, R. L. (1982). *Family and Divorce in California, 1850–1890*. Albany: State University of New York Press.

Hernandez, D. J. (1993). *America's children: Resources from family, government, and the economy*. New York: Russell Sage Foundation.

Jones, M. S. (1987). *An historical geography of the changing divorce law in the United States*. New York: Garland.

Katz, S. N. (1994). Historical perspective and current trends in the legal process of divorce. *Future of Children, 4,* 44–62.

Kirn, W. (2000, September). Should you stay together for the kids? *Time Magazine, 156,* 75–82.

Kitson, G. C. (1992). *Portrait of divorce: Adjustment to marital breakdown*. New York: Guilford.

Maccoby, E. E., & Mnookin, R. H. (1992). *Dividing the child*. Cambridge, MA: Harvard University Press.

Mintz, S., & Kellog, S. (1989). *Domestic revolutions: A social history of American family life*. New York: The Free Press.

Mowrer, E. R. (1927). *Family disorganization*. Chicago: University of Chicago Press.

Ooms, T. (2002, August). Marriage and government: Strange bedfellows? Policy Brief No. 1: Couples and Marriage Series. Washington, DC: Center for Law and Social Policy.

Parke, M., & Ooms, T. (2002, October). More than a dating service? State activities designed to strengthen and promote marriage (Policy Brief No. 2: Couples and Marriage Series). Washington, DC: Center for Law and Social Policy.

Parkman, A. M. (2000). *Good intentions gone awry: No-fault divorce and the American family*. Lanham, MD: Rowman and Littlefield.

Phillips, R. (1991). *Untying the knot: A short history of divorce*. New York: Cambridge University Press.

Popenoe, D. (1996). *Life without father: Compelling new evidence that fatherhood and marriage are indispensable for the good of children and society*. New York: Martin Kessler Books.

Preston, S. H., and McDonald, J. (1979). The incidence of divorce within cohorts of American marriages contracted since the civil war. *Demography, 16,* 1–25.

Riley, G. (1991). *Divorce: An American tradition*. New York: Oxford University Press.

Ross, C. E. (1995). Reconceptualizing marital status as a continuum of social attachment. *Journal of Marriage and the Family, 57,* 129–140.

Rothstein, B. (2002, April 10). Marital strife: Do the voters really care? *The Hill,* p. X. Retrieved April 30, 2003 from http://www.hillnews.com.

Sanchez, L., Nock, S. L., Wright, J .D., Pardee, J. W., & Ionescu, M. (2001). The implementation of covenant marriage in Louisiana. *The Virginia Journal of Social Policy and the Law, 23,* 192–223.

Scanzoni, J. (2001). From the normal family to alternate families to the quest for diversity with interdependence. *Journal of Family Issues, 22,* 688–710.

Seidman, S. (1991). *Romantic longings: Love in America, 1830–1980*. New York: Routledge.

Skolnick, A. S. (1991). *Embattled paradise: The American family in an age of uncertainty*. New York: Basic Books.

Stacey, J. (1996). *In the name of the family: Rethinking family values in the postmodern age*. Boston: Beacon Press.

Stekel, W. (1931). *Marriage at the crossroads*. New York: Godwin.

Terman, L. M. (1938). *Psychological factors in marital happiness*. New York: McGraw-Hill.

Thompson, R. A., & Wyatt, J. M. (1999). Values, policy, and research on divorce. In R. A. Thompson & P. R. Amato (Eds.), *The postdivorce family: Children, parenting, and society* (pp. 191–232). Thousand Oaks, CA: Sage.

Thornton, A., & Young-DeMarco, L. (2001). Four decades of trends in attitudes toward family issues in the United States: The 1960s through the 1990s. *Journal of Marriage and the Family, 63,* 1009–1037.

Vlosky, D. A., & Monroe, P. A. (2002). The effective dates of no-fault divorce laws in the 50 states. *Family Relations, 51,* 317–324.

Waite, L. J., & Gallagher, M. (2000). *The case for marriage: Why married people are happier, healthier, and better off financially*. New York: Doubleday.

Whitehead, B. (1993, April). "Dan Quayle Was Right." *The Atlantic Monthly,* pp. 47–84.

Wilson, J. (2002). *The marriage problem: How our culture has weakened families*. New York: Harper Collins.

Willcox, W. F. (1891). *The divorce problem: A study in statistics*. New York: Columbia University Press.

Williams, K. (2003). Has the future of marriage arrived? A contemporary examination of gender, marriage, and psychological well-being. *Journal of Health and Social Behavior, 44,* 470–487.

4

The Demographic Future of Divorce and Dissolution

Jay Teachman, Lucky Tedrow, and Matthew Hall
Western Washington University

Alas, we do not have any facts at all about the future, and we shall not have any until we get there.
—Goode (1993, p. 13)

When asked to write a chapter about demographic trends in divorce and relationship dissolution, we envisioned a chapter that would focus heavily on *historical* trends, as well as major socioeconomic differentials that might supply information about the predictors of divorce and dissolution. The task seemed straightforward, and we looked at it as an opportunity to consolidate our thinking about recent research on the topic. As the task evolved, however, we came to be responsible for writing a chapter in which we discuss the *future* of demographic trends in divorce and dissolution. This turn of events caused us a few moments of panic because social scientists are notorious in their inability to predict the future (for discussions about the difficulty of the task, see Goode, 1993; Lipset, 1979; and Stinchcombe, 1982). The malleability of human behavior when combined with the uncertainty of social, economic, and political context makes prognostication a poor career choice, at least if one needs to be correct.

Yet the task is not without some attraction. Marriage and divorce are topics of considerable interest to the general public and the subject of considerable policy import. For example, as we write this chapter, there are two ongoing, high-profile debates that highlight the salience of the issue in contemporary American society. One debate concerns the implementation of various promarriage policies (from premarital counseling to tax incentives), and the second debate revolves around a possible constitutional amendment that would prohibit gay marriages. These debates are energizing academic, lay, and political communities to sharpen their arguments concerning these issues. Indeed, concerned citizens of all political stripes are making assumptions about the future of the family as one means to develop fuel in support of their arguments. The past frames the arguments being made, but the future lends a sense of urgency in calls for action. Thus, a chapter discussing the future of divorce and relationship dissolution may not be as easily ignored as a chapter focusing on some other topic.

Having accepted the task, however, we begin with a Goffmanesque disclaimer about the inevitability of being wrong when discussing likely future trends in divorce and relationship dissolution. Indeed, rather than making forecasts, we opt for safety and, for the most part, limit our task to providing a framework for thinking about the future, a rough paradigm for thinking about the "what ifs." That is, what might happen to divorce rates if a certain set of conditions change, or do not change? The available literature gives us important clues as to what we might expect to happen.

We further limit our task by focusing primarily on divorce, rather than relationship dissolution in general. There is, of course, a wide range of relationships that are at risk of being terminated (Scanzoni, Polonko, Teachman, & Thompson, 1989). These relationships may be sexual or nonsexual, coresidential or not coresidential, legal or non-legal, and so on. As demographers, we are more comfortable in discussing divorce or separation (the termination of a marriage) because we can draw on a long history of data and research on the topic, data that simply do not exist for relationships (such as cohabiting unions) that are not part of the U.S. vital statistics system. Moreover, there is almost universal consensus about the importance of marriage as a social institution. To be sure, the institution is changing, and alternatives such as nonmarital cohabitation are becoming increasingly common (and we will provide some information about cohabiting unions), but marriage remains the gold standard against which other types of relationships are most often judged.

In the first section of our chapter, we begin by reviewing historical trends in divorce (a topic covered in more detail by Amato and Irving in chap. 3, this volume). An understanding of the past is the best foundation for making educated guesses about the future; in the short term, at least, the best prediction is simply a continuation of recent trends. In this section, we necessarily spend a little time discussing the nature of marriage, how it has changed over time, and various explanations that have been provided about why the risk of divorce has changed over time. In the second section of the chapter, we provide a framework for thinking about changes in the risk of divorce. Our approach draws heavily on traditional demographic approaches to the decomposition of rates (also akin to regression standardization). Our approach may seem to be a bit technical to some readers, but we believe that it provides a nice framework for thinking about the sorts of changes that can occur that would affect rates of divorce. In the third section of the chapter, we examine the major demographic predictors of divorce (e.g., age at marriage, premarital fertility, and premarital cohabitation) and consider how changes in these predictors may alter future trends in divorce.

HOW CAN THE PAST INFORM THE FUTURE?

We begin by making the only clear-cut prediction possible for marital dissolution in the future: all marriages (and, for that matter, all relationships) will end. At issue is how they will end. Divorce (we include separation as a means to end a marriage and thus equate it to divorce) and death compete to end all marriages. Historically, death has won this contest. Over the past century, however, declines in mortality and increases in divorce have altered the relative advantage death has enjoyed in this race. For women born between 1888 and 1892, about 17% could expect to see their marriages end in divorce, with the remainder (83%) having theirs end in death (Schoen, Urton, Woodrow, & Baj, 1985).[1] For women born between 1948 and 1950,

---

[1] We present data for women because most of the information that we possess about divorce comes from information reported by women. As reported by Bumpass, Martin, and Sweet (1991), marriage histories reported by men are much less reliable than those reported by women.

about 42% can expect to see their marriages end in divorce, with death holding a slim lead at 58%. Reflecting recent stability in divorce (see what follows), Schoen and Standish (2001) used period data to estimate that 1995 divorce rates imply that a recently contracted marriage would have about a 44% chance of eventually ending in divorce.

Interestingly, for birth cohorts from 1888 to 1892 through 1928 to 1932, declines in mortality more than compensated for increases in marital dissolution such that women could actually expect to spend a growing percentage of their lives married (Schoen et al., 1985; Schoen & Standish, 2001), from 47% to 53%. Since the 1933 to 1937 birth cohort, however, increases in divorce (in conjunction with substantial increases in age at marriage) have reduced the percentage of life a woman spends married. In 1995, the data indicate that women can expect to spend about 41% of their lives married.

The steady rise in rates of divorce in the United States is shown in Fig. 4.1. This figure is based on data provided by Jacobson (1959) and Preston and McDonald (1979). We have simply extended the trend line to 2000. The figure presents the ratio of divorces to married women aged 15 and older (multiplied by 1,000) for each year from 1870 to 2000. The continuous line indicates the observed ratio, and the dashed line indicates the predicted ratio (based on a polynomial least-squares regression). Two points are readily evident from reading Fig. 4.1. First, the overall (predicted) trend in the rate of divorce has been upward. Less than 2 marriages in 1,000 ended in divorce in 1870, compared with about 18 marriages in 1,000 in 2000. Second, at various points in history, there have been substantial deviations in rates of divorce from the overall trend. For example, divorce was higher than expected following World War I, lower than expected during the Great Depression, and higher than expected following World War II. The 1950s and early 1960s once again saw lower than expected rates of divorce, followed by a substantial increase in divorce that led to higher than expected rates during the 1970s and early 1980s. Since about 1980, however, rates of divorce have stabilized and have even declined somewhat.

Shown in Fig. 4.2 is a slightly different representation of the over-time data on divorce (again borrowing from Preston and McDonald, 1979, and updated using more recent data taken from Schoen and Standish, 2001). Here, the proportion of marriages begun in each year between 1870 and 1995 that end in divorce (or, for more recent marriage cohorts, the proportion of marriages that is expected to end in divorce) is plotted. The same upward trend in divorce is noted, as well as the same deviations from the trend. Note, however, that the deviations appear to be much less substantial because the divorce figures are cumulated across the lifetime of a marriage cohort. That is, for a given marriage cohort, the risk of divorce is averaged over a number of historical periods, which may include periods of both below-average and above-average risk. For example, women married in 1960 would have been exposed to the relatively low divorce rates of the early 1960s, as well as the substantially higher divorce rates of the 1970s and the subsequent stability and decline in divorce rates in the 1980s and 1990s.

The rather significant swings in period divorce rates indicated in Fig. 4.1 suggest some caution about interpreting the immediate past for hints about the future. Indeed, Fig. 4.1 looks like a good example of the principle of "regression toward the mean." The overall trend has been upward, but the rate of divorce for marriage cohorts has not increased as much as that implied by the highest period rates, and it has not decreased as much as that implied by the lowest period rates. Recent declines in the rate of divorce may to some extent be taken as just another correction in rates of divorce that have fluctuated above and below the overall trend line for more than 100 years.

Figures 4.1 and 4.2 correspond to two different (yet related) ways that demographers account for changes across time in the occurrence of some event (here divorce): period and cohort (Cherlin, 1992; Thornton & Rodgers, 1987). Period influences subsume those factors that

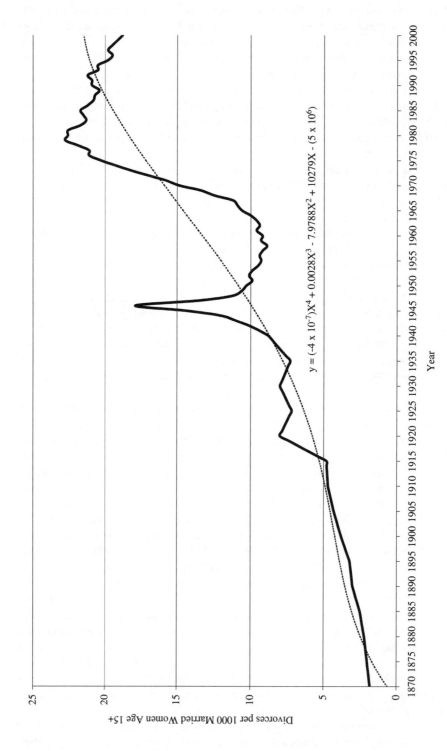

FIG. 4.1. Divorce per 1,000 Married Women Aged 15 and Older by Year, With a Fitted Fourth-Degree Polynomial: 1870–2000. (Adapted From Jacobson, 1959, and Preston & McDonald, 1979.)

$$y = (-4 \times 10^{-7})X^4 + 0.0028X^3 - 7.9788X^2 + 10279X - (5 \times 10^6)$$

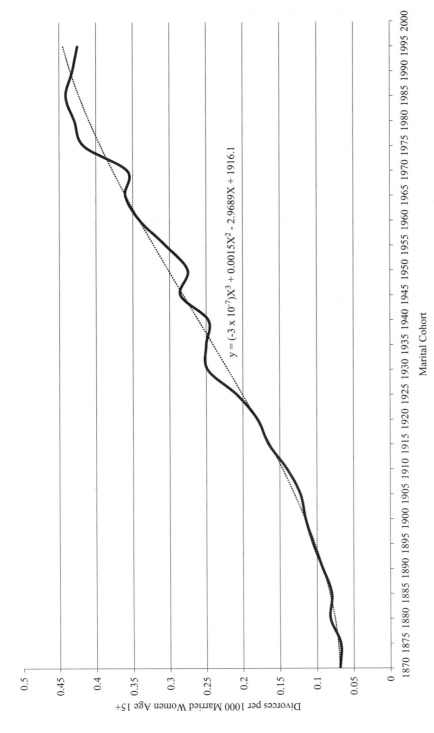

FIG. 4.2. Divorce per 1,000 Married Women Aged 15 and Older by Marital Cohort, With a Fitted Third-Degree Polynomial: 1870–2000. (Adapted From Jacobson, 1959; Preston & McDonald, 1979; and Schoen & Standish, 2001.)

affect the risk of divorce uniformly for all marriages at a given time irrespective of when those marriages were formed. For example, the dismal economic circumstances associated with the Great Depression are assumed to have depressed the risk of divorce for all married couples during the 1930s, irrespective of when their marriages were formed. Cohort influences, in contrast, focus on circumstances affecting divorce that are unique to a given marriage cohort (Carlson, 1979), circumstances that reflect the unique configuration of historical circumstances impinging on that marriage cohort. For example, marriages formed in the 1950s may have been uniquely affected by the convergence of relatively prosperous economic conditions and small cohort size that rendered their marriages unusually stable.

Adjudicating between period and cohort explanations is a difficult task at best, made even more complex by the necessary mathematical relationship that occurs between the two when combined with age (the age–period–cohort conundrum—see Glenn, 1976, and Feinberg and Mason, 1978). Nevertheless, not denying the possibility that cohort effects occur in conjunction with period effects (Ono, 1999), most analysts agree that period effects on divorce have dominated, at least over the span of time that reasonable data are available (the past 100–150 years in the United States). Period effects can and have been used to explain the long-run rise in divorce, as well as deviations from the long-term trend shown in Fig. 4.1 (Cherlin, 1992; Goldstein, 1999; Preston & McDonald, 1979; Ruggles, 1997; Teachman, 2002a; Thornton & Rodgers, 1987).

In their simplest form, at least as demographers tend to use them, period and cohort concepts are simple accounting mechanisms (also see Weiss' commentary at the end of this handbook). That is, they can be used to account for patterns of change across time, but without additional information they do not by themselves elucidate reasons explaining the observed pattern.[2] Deeper explanations require information about the nature of periods and cohorts—that is, the behavioral mechanisms that allow periods (or cohorts) to vary from each other. These behavioral mechanisms are necessarily tied to the nature of marriage, which when altered disrupt the balance of a marriage and lead to an increased risk of dissolution.

Most work focusing on changes in the nature of marriage that can be used to account for temporal changes in divorce can be characterized as emphasizing either structural or normative changes. Structural arguments most often focus on decline in the number of functions performed by families associated with the rise of extrafamilial institutions responsible for employment, education, health care, and so on (Coleman, 1990; Goode, 1993; Phillips, 1991). These changes in family functioning are thought to have led to devolution in the gendered division of labor that has historically generated the mutual and interdependent well-being of husbands and wives. Perhaps the most significant structural change noted by previous researchers is the movement of married women into the paid labor market, a trend that is argued to reduce the economic interdependence of spouses (Becker, 1991; Cherlin, 1992; Ruggles, 1997), thus increasing the risk of divorce.

Normative arguments, in contrast, emphasize the growth of individualism over time, an increase in value placed on personal gratification, and a decrease in a sense of family obligation (Amato & Irving, this volume; May, 1980; Phillips, 1991; Stone, 1977). As a consequence of these cultural changes, societal-wide norms regulating divorce have been replaced by norms allowing individual decisions based on rational choice—in which rationality includes efforts to maximize individual happiness. This cultural shift has led to a reduction in legal barriers to

---

[2]For example, period effects most often are accounted for by including a set of dummy variables in an equation that allow rates of divorce to vary from one period to the next. Although this procedure perfectly accounts for temporal variation in divorce, it does little to explain why such shifts occurred.

divorce, as well as a proliferation of adult alternatives to marriage (e.g., cohabitation, living alone). The net result of these shifts in normative orientation is a greater risk of divorce.

Of course, as other authors have noted (Goode, 1993; Phillips, 1991), both structural and normative shifts are likely to have occurred simultaneously as components of larger processes of industrialization and modernization. Indeed, it is likely that structural and normative changes have reinforced each other over time. For example, divorce in one generation becomes the engine of divorce in the next generation. As men and women adapt to the consequences of divorce, they set the stage for an even greater weakening of the historical interdependence of spouses. Divorce becomes an acceptable solution to domestic dissatisfaction, and the withdrawal from the labor force that generates economic dependence becomes a risky venture that few men and women are willing to take. Thus, we emphasize that changes in marriage and divorce are multidimensional, and failure to recognize this fact will only lead to a more limited understanding of changes that have occurred, as well as the plausibility of future paths that change may take.

For our purposes, therefore, we imagine a scenario wherein both the structural and normative bases of marriage have weakened over time. Husbands and wives have become increasingly less interdependent economically and public stigma associated with divorce has melted. Accordingly, spouses are increasingly making choices about staying together that are not limited by economic necessity and that are made in a context of permissive attitudes and a growing range of practicable living alternatives outside of marriage. This is a somewhat crude theoretical position, but it does remind us to consider a broad range of alternatives when thinking about the future of divorce.

A FRAMEWORK FOR THINKING ABOUT FUTURE DEMOGRAPHIC TRENDS IN DIVORCE

Just as our theoretical tool is crude, so is our framework for thinking about the future of divorce. The approach we take, by writing a simple regression model, may seem overly quantitative to some readers, but as demographers we are first concerned about being able to account for changes over time in the risk of divorce. If we can account for change, then we have a tool that may allow us some leverage for thinking about why change has occurred and what this may imply for the future. In particular, we can substitute expected changes into the model and arrive at some conclusions about what the future of divorce may look like.

To begin, imagine a set of data that corresponds to numerous marriages observed over a long period of time. Without worrying about any of the statistical concerns (assume that an appropriate estimation technique can be found), consider the following model estimated for these data:

$$Y_{it} = a + b_1 X_{it} + b_2 P_t + b_3 U_{it} + b_4 X_{it} \times P_t + b_5 U_{it} \times P_t + e_{it},$$

where Y_{it} is the risk of divorce for the ith person or couple at time t, X_{it} is a measured characteristic of the ith person or couple at time t (for the sake of making the argument concrete, say age at marriage), P_t is a period factor acting on all persons or couples at time t (in the simplest case, P_t would be represented by a set of dummy variables indicating historical period), U_{it} is an unmeasured characteristic of the ith person or couple at time t (e.g., an unmeasured personality characteristic that may be inherited and that renders the individual divorce prone), $X_{it} \times P_t$ is an interaction term involving the measured characteristic and period, $U_{it} \times P_t$ is an interaction term involving the unmeasured characteristic and period, and e_{it} is an error term reminding us that the model is stochastic (i.e., we can never hope to perfectly predict who will divorce). The coefficients b_1, b_2, b_3, b_4, and b_5 tell us the direction and strength of the relationships under consideration. Let us call this equation the *framework model*.

For readers who may be unfamiliar or uncomfortable with a regression approach, simply think of X_{it}, P_t, U_{it}, $X_{it} \times P_t$, and $U_{it} \times P_t$ as symbols that represent different types of variables and the coefficients b_1 to b_5 as weights indicating the importance of a given variable. The most important point to understand is that the rate of divorce (Y_{it}) is determined by some weighted combination of the different types of variables. Divorce is a multidimensional phenomenon that is determined by a multitude of factors, some of which may be different from one time period to the next.

Many readers will focus on the model as a way in which to ascertain the relative impact of a set of covariates on the risk of divorce (a completely legitimate interpretation of the model). Indeed, this is the most common use of the model. Another way to think of the model, however, is to take *expected values* (a statistical term that means taking the average). If we take the expected value (i.e., the average) of the framework model at time t, we arrive at the average level of divorce at that point in time under the assumption that everyone possesses the average value of each predictor variable (covariate).[3] When multiplied by 1,000, this calculation yields the period divorce rate as shown in Fig. 4.1 (assuming a representative sample of marriages).

We can then repeat the process for another point in time, either in the past or in the future, allowing ourselves to pose and answer certain theoretically interesting questions. For example, we can ask, What would the rate of divorce be at some point in the future if the average value of one or more of the covariates shifted upward (or downward) by some arbitrary amount? What would the divorce rate be if there were no change in the average value of the predictors, but there was some change in the regression coefficients (the relative weights assigned to each coefficient) linking the predictors to divorce? For example, what would the rate of divorce be if the average age at marriage increased by 2 years? What would the rate of divorce be if the average age at marriage did not change, but its effect (i.e., its regression coefficient or weight) on marital dissolution decreased by one half? Firebaugh (1997) describes this sort of statistical decomposition exercise in greater detail, and we refer the reader to his account for specific details in conducting a decomposition exercise. Amato, Johnson, Booth, and Rogers (2003) provide an excellent example of the application of this decomposition to changes in marital quality between 1980 and 2000.

As stated, the framework model is simple and many additions could be offered, such as additional interactions, additional variables, variables that change across time for an individual or couple (e.g., income), and so on. Nevertheless, the model serves our purposes of illustration. Moreover, even as simple as it is, the model is demanding with respect to data. Even in the United States, with a well-developed system of censuses and vital statistics registration, long-term data on divorce are scarce at best. The number of measured variables (the X_{it}) available is minimal and often inconsistent. Indeed, research that seeks to include information on divorce beyond the past three or four decades must use data requiring sometimes heroic assumptions. For example, Ruggles' (1997) examination of divorce in the United States over the period from 1880 to 1990 was actually based on aggregate census data that only provide information on current marital status.[4]

---

[3] For example, take the average value of the variables represented by X_{it}, P_t, U_{it}, $X_{it} \times P_t$, and $U_{it} \times P_t$, and multiply each by its respective coefficient (b_1–b_5). The summation of each of the resulting terms is the average level of divorce in the population.

[4] One concern with such data is that many currently married individuals could have been divorced at some time in the past, yielding an underestimation of divorce.

Most research on divorce estimates a simplified version of the framework model, that is,

$$Y_{it} = a + b_1 X_{it} + e_{it}.$$

In this model, the effect of a measured characteristic of the individual or couple on the risk of divorce is estimated (here, our example variable is age at marriage). Variables commonly considered in recent demographic literature include age at marriage, duration of marriage, education, income, premarital fertility, premarital cohabitation, parental divorce, race, and various measures of partner homogamy on these characteristics (Bumpass, Martin, & Sweet, 1991; Teachman, 2002a; White, 1990). Such a model is obviously much more limited than the full framework model because the effects of only one type of variable are considered. Per force, this simple model assumes no period effects on marital dissolution and no change in the effects of the measured covariates across time.

Occasionally, these are required assumptions given the available data (i.e., if the data only span a limited time period such as that covered by the two waves of data collected in the National Survey of Families and Households). Accordingly, the results of such models should be interpreted as being specific to the limited span of historical time covered by the data. The effects of unmeasured covariates (the U_{it}) are also ignored, potentially biasing the regression coefficient (b_1). This is a risk inherent in almost all nonexperimental research, but it is particularly important in the case in which we concern ourselves with examining change in the risk of divorce over time, because variables important in determining divorce in one era may not be important in a different era.

Recognizing the rapid change in the risk of divorce over time, researchers in a few studies possessing appropriate data have included an indicator of historical period (usually measured as a set of dummy variables for historical period or marriage cohort) in their models (Bramlett & Mosher, 2002; Ono, 1999; Teachman, 2002a; Thornton & Rodgers, 1987; Wolfinger, 1999). That is, using the regression analogy of the framework model, researchers obtain an equation of the following form:

$$Y_{it} = a + b_1 X_{it} + b_2 P_t + e_{it},$$

where P_t is added to the model and is most often a measure of time itself (perhaps a set of dummy variables indicating year or some other grouping of time) and not necessarily a more specific causal agent associated with time (such as specific attitudes or structural and economic conditions that lead to a change in the risk of divorce). In essence, this model allows the risk of divorce to vary according to individual characteristics (such as age at marriage) and period. Thus, this model is more flexible in allowing for individual variation, as well as change that occurs according to more general contextual conditions.

Unfortunately, although fully accounting for the effects of period on divorce, the model as described provides no information about the nature of the effect (for a notable exception, see Ruggles, 1997). That is, we are left with no information about what it is that has changed across time that led to a shift in the divorce rate. A more theoretically interesting and promising model would be one in which the content of a period effect was specified. That is, exactly which changes in structural and normative conditions are associated with differences in divorce across historical periods? In such a model, more specific indicators of the contextual conditions thought to be important (e.g., time-varying indicators of macroeconomic conditions) would replace the dummy variables (the P_t) indicating the different periods. This is a particularly important concern when one is seeking to make predictions about the future. Dummy variables can perfectly explain the past, but without some hint about what generates period changes in rates of divorce, one can have little hope for generating expectations about what to expect down the road.

Just as important, this model also fails to consider possible change in the effect of X_{it} over different time periods (i.e., it fails to include the $X_{it} \times P_t$ term in the model, whether an accounting measure of period is used or a more specific causal measure). In other words, the effect of X_{it} is assumed to be immutable across time (i.e., the regression coefficient for X_{it} is assumed to be the same at all points in time). Another way of stating this notion is that the effect of X_{it} is not allowed to vary according to the larger macrocontext. For example, the effects of age at marriage or premarital cohabitation and female labor force participation are assumed to be constant across all periods, even though these periods may tap very different contextual conditions surrounding marriage.

This is a very strong assumption, and it is somewhat surprising that more research has not investigated the possibility that the assumption is false. There are good theoretical reasons for expecting different historical periods (P_t) to set the context across which the effects of covariates (X_{it}) will vary. For example, taking a long view, Goode (1993) and Phillips (1991) suggest that the effect of income (mostly the income of husbands) on divorce has shifted from being largely positive to being largely negative. In the past, when divorce was frowned on and divorce laws were difficult to work around, only wealthy couples could afford the legal work required to end their marriage. More recently, with more liberal attitudes toward marital dissolution and substantially more lax divorce laws, divorce has become concentrated among less affluent couples whose marriages are stressed by economic uncertainty. This sort of shift implies a change in the effect of an individual-level covariate (an X_{it}) across different periods (P_t), which would be indicated by a significant coefficient for the interaction effect ($X_{it} \times P_t$).

Strong empirical evidence for a shift in the effects of major demographic predictors is lacking, however. Indeed, two recent studies have found little evidence for change in the effects of major demographic predictors of divorce such as age at marriage and premarital fertility over the past 40 to 50 years (Heaton, 2002; Teachman, 2002a). It may be the case that a longer term is necessary to witness change in the effects of predictor variables on divorce. More likely, though, it is necessary to consider a broader set of predictor variables than considered by Heaton and Teachman. For example, using Panel Study of Income Dynamics (PSID) data that contain detailed information on work histories (information not available in the data used by Heaton and Teachman), South (2001a) reported an increasingly positive effect across time of female labor force participation on divorce. Schoen (1992) provides another example in reporting a declining effect of premarital cohabitation on divorce among more recent marriage cohorts.

Of course, as already noted, the things that we do not measure (as noted here by the term U_{it}) are difficult to deal with in any context. When we are dealing with data across time, however, such variables are of particular concern because increased variation on a variable may suddenly occur. A prime example is premarital cohabitation. It is only in the past two to three decades that premarital cohabitation has become sufficiently common to be of concern to researchers focusing on divorce. Thus, excluding premarital cohabitation from models of the demographic predictors of marital dissolution prior to the mid-1960s (in essence, treating premarital cohabitation as an unmeasured covariate) was not likely of great consequence. For models estimated on more recent data, though, the exclusion of premarital cohabitation would likely lead to biased estimates of the effects of other predictors.

Even though it may seem odd for us to consider the interaction between an unmeasured covariate and period (the $U_{it} \times P_t$ term in the framework model), it can become an important consideration when we are examining change over time. A classic example is the literature providing evidence for the heritability of divorce (Jockin, McGue, & Lykken, 1996; McGue & Lykken, 1992). When rates of divorce are low, heritability is minimal. When rates of divorce are higher, heritability is greater. Apparently, heritability operates through the inheritance of personality traits that increase the risk of marital dissolution. When rates of divorce are low, these traits are not allowed to express themselves (miserable marriages remain miserable marriages). When constraints limiting divorce are relaxed and divorce rates climb, the effects of possessing an adverse personality trait on marital stability are not as likely to be suppressed (miserable marriages become divorces). Thus, an increasingly permissive attitude toward divorce (a period effect or P_t) sets the context within which a previously unimportant and unmeasured characteristic (personality or U_{it}) becomes linked to divorce (as indicated by a significant coefficient for the interaction term $U_{it} \times P_t$). This is an important consideration to which we return later when we consider the future of divorce.

Before moving on to consider how the framework model can help us think about the future of demographic predictors of divorce, we note the few authors who have used the model in attempts to decompose the recent leveling of the rate of divorce. The question posed by these authors is whether change in composition across time with respect to easily measured variables, or various X_{it}, can explain change, or lack of change, in the overall or average risk of divorce. The question is important given the fact that substantial change has occurred in the composition of American marriages that would lead us to expect a change in the overall divorce rate (e.g., more marriages are preceded by a spell of cohabitation, and more marriages are formed at older ages). Using aggregate data, Ruggles (1997) argues that the rise of nonfarm employment for women can explain virtually the entire rise in rates of divorce since 1880. Moreover, virtually all of the Black–White difference in rates of divorce over time can be explained by racial differences in male and female employment.

Focusing on more recent decades, and using a more detailed set of demographic predictors, Heaton (2002) found that upward shifts in age at marriage alone were sufficient to account for the leveling of divorce over the period from 1975 to 1995. Goldstein (1999), however, using different data and a still different set of variables, was unable to explain changes in the rate of divorce over a longer period of time, from 1955 to 1995. Although no clear picture emerges from the decomposition exercises that have been attempted, they alert us to the fact that overall rates of divorce may change simply because the composition of marriages shifts. For example, if age at marriage is negatively related to the risk of marital dissolution, then, all else being equal, the overall rate of divorce should decline if fewer young marriages are contracted. Of course, the effect of an increasing age at marriage could be nullified by an increase in marriages contracted by individuals possessing other characteristics positively linked to the risk of divorce (e.g., premarital cohabitation), or if the underlying relationship between age at marriage and divorce shifts.

WHAT THE FUTURE MAY HOLD

How can the framework model help us think about the future of demographic trends in divorce? The model alerts us to the fact that we should pay attention to the well-known and often measured predictors of divorce (the X_{it}), to potentially unmeasured predictors of marital disruption that might suddenly increase in importance (the U_{it}), large-scale period forces that drive changes in marital dissolution across time (the P_t), and interactions between measured and unmeasured covariates and period forces (the $X_{it} \times P_t$ and $U_{it} \times P_t$) that indicate change in the strength of the relationship between various predictor variables and the risk of divorce. More simply, we need to pay attention to potential changes in the composition of marriages and how the effects of the variables determining this composition may or may not change across time.

Period Forces

We begin by considering what may be the most difficult consideration. We ask, What might be the macrolevel period forces (the P_t) affecting marital dissolution? As we noted earlier in this chapter, there are two interrelated conceptualizations of macrolevel factors underlying change over time in rates of divorce—structural and normative. The predominant structural change thought to have generated period change in divorce over the past century or more is the partici- pation of wives in the paid labor market (Cherlin, 1992).[5] Indeed, there is remarkable similarity in the rise of rates of female labor force participation and divorce. For example, Ruggles (1997, Table 2) notes that rates of female labor force participation for married White women aged 20 to 59 years rose from 1.7% in 1880 to 70.9% in 1990. The corresponding increase for Black women was 12.5% to 72.0%. Over the same period, the divorce rate (divorces per 1,000 married women) rose from 1.8 to 20.9. The declining economic interdependence of spouses and the greater economic independence of women associated with labor force participation are thought to link the two series of data (Becker, 1991; Ruggles, 1997). Oppenheimer (1994, 1997a, 1997b) added changes in economic opportunities for men to the mix, but the argument remains one that is based on structural changes in the economy. The bottom line is that, over the long term, as nonfarm employment increased for women and wages and employment stagnated for men, rates of divorce rose.

The normative perspective focuses more on attitudinal changes that emphasize the value of personal fulfillment over commitment to the group (Bellah, Madsen, Sullivan, Swidler, & Tipton, 1985; Stone, 1977). Unfortunately, no long-term data exist on changes in norms and attitudes that can be linked to shifts in rates of divorce. Thus, research such as that conducted by Ruggles that provides an empirical link between rates of female labor force participation and rates of divorce cannot be tested against the competing hypothesis by using comparable attitudinal data. This is unfortunate, because it is plausible to expect that changes in norms and attitudes that may have permitted an increase in divorce are also at least partly responsible for gains in female labor force participation. Over more recent decades for which we have data about attitudes toward marriage, divorce, cohabitation, and premarital sex, there has been a general liberalizing trend (Axinn & Thornton, 2000; Cherlin, 1992; Thornton, 1989). Moreover, evidence exists that attitudes toward marriage and divorce can be used to predict the likelihood of marital dissolution independent of other personal characteristics (Amato, 1996; Amato & DeBoer, 2001; Sanchez & Gager, 2000; Sayer & Bianchi, 2000).

It may be the case that both structural and normative forces have operated in concert to affect marital disruption, but in a slightly different manner than that implied by the aforementioned arguments. Oppenheimer (1997a, 1997b) suggests that changes in the economic contributions of women may not destabilize marriages by reducing economic interdependence. Indeed, female labor force participation is not in itself a destabilizing factor in marriage. Rather, female labor force participation (or at least the possibility that women can find work outside the home), in an era increasingly accepting of divorce, simply provides the *opportunity* for women to end unhappy marriages (i.e., working outside the home does not necessarily create an unhappy marriage). Rogers (2004) and Schoen, Astone, Rothert, Standish, and Kim (2002)

---

[5]There is a degree of ambiguity in the framework model (or any model utilizing both individual-level and macrolevel data) when one is addressing variables such as female labor force participation. In some instances, if wives' participation in the labor market were measured for each couple, the variable would be considered to be one of the X_{it}, or a measured individual-level coviarate. As discussed here, however, it is assumed that female participation in the labor market is not measured for distinct couples. Rather, aggregate rates of female market activity are used to form one component of a period factor, that is, a period factor that is composed of the sum of many (here unobserved) individual characteristics (Blalock, 1984).

provide support for this notion. They found that wives' economic contributions to the family were linked to divorce only when marriages were unhappy. There appears to be little connection between wives' economic contributions and marital dissolution when marriages are reported as being happy. This perspective takes us in a slightly different direction by making us ask what makes marriages unhappy. Are there particular period forces, structural or normative, that generate increasing or decreasing chances that a marriage will be unhappy? What are the measured and unmeasured characteristics of individuals and couples that allow them to generate sufficient marital good will or marital commitment that will enable them to survive a long-term relationship in an era when economic and normative pressures to remain married are weak?

What does all this imply for the future of divorce? Why has the happiness of marriages become an important variable to consider? The long-term upward trend in divorce does not suggest the likelihood of a return to more conservative attitudes toward divorce. To the contrary, attitudes toward divorce are likely to remain quite accepting. Using a wide range of surveys (and admittedly different questions), Thornton and Young-DeMarco (2001) reported that attitudes toward divorce became dramatically more approving from 1962 to 1977 and have remained relatively stable over the 1980s and 1990s. In 1993, Thornton and Young-DeMarco reported that about 80% of young respondents in the Intergenerational Panel Study believed that divorce is an acceptable resolution to a poor marriage, even if young children are involved.

Somewhat paradoxically, young people still express views that indicate that they value marriage highly. Data from the Monitoring the Future Survey indicate that, among high school seniors in 1997 to 1998, over 80% of young women and over 70% of young men believed that forming a good marriage is important to them (Thornton & Young-DeMarco, 2001). Apparently, young Americans still see considerable value in married life, but they are steadfastly pragmatic about their chances for realizing a successful lifelong marriage. A culture of divorce in which a substantial fraction of all children experience the divorce of their parents and in which the majority of children spends some time in a single-parent family (Furstenberg, 1994) has tempered expectations about the permanency of marriage. At the same time, it is clear that Americans no longer see marriage as the only alternative for successful and rewarding adult living. The majority of American men and women accept nonmarital cohabitation, living alone, premarital sex, and childbearing outside of marriage as reasonable choices (Axinn & Thornton, 2000; Thornton & Young-DeMarco, 2001). Thus, although marriage remains highly valued for most Americans, it is increasingly a voluntary choice and faces growing competition in the form of alternatives for successful adult living. The most likely scenario for the future, particularly the near future, is a period in which continued high expectations among young Americans for a successful and rewarding marriage (a happy marriage) will continue to place pressure on marriages when divorce is commonly accepted as a solution to end relationships that are not meeting expectations.

We expect, therefore, that the importance of making a good marital match will grow. In an environment in which legal and normative barriers to divorce have waned considerably, individual choice has become much more important in determining the success (here, avoiding divorce) of a marriage. Marriages can no longer rely on external constraints to endure; they must rely on internal dynamics of negotiation and change as determined by the degree of marital match. In part, a good marital match depends on the degree of commitment brought to the union and certainty about those expectations, and these are at least partly a function of the characteristics that individuals bring to the union (either measured, the X_{it}, or unmeasured, the U_{it}). However, before we review recent trends on some of these important individual-level covariates, we ask whether widespread structural changes have occurred in the way that men and women form expectations about marriage—things that might be subsumed under the influence of P_t. These are the things that set the context within which a good marital match can be formed and assessed.

For example, Sayer and Bianchi (2000) suggest that the nature of the economic bargain struck by husbands and wives has changed. Historically, both men and women were expected to make an economic contribution to marriages (although not necessarily in the paid labor force). Around the middle of the past century, however, changes in men's employment patterns and increases in male wages allowed the development of the breadwinner–homemaker model wherein women were not expected to make a direct financial contribution to the family. Indeed, it may be the case that, under such expectations, wives' participation in the labor force would act to destabilize a marriage. Thus, the sharp rise in rates of divorce between 1965 and 1980 may have been at least partly a function of the disjuncture between the expectations of spouses and the reality of wives' labor market activities.

More recently, the declining economic position of men (Oppenheimer, 1997a, 1997b), accompanied by increasing economic opportunities for women, may have led couples to renegotiate the marital bargain, once again emphasizing the need for economic contributions by both spouses. Indeed, recent evidence suggests that women with more income or education are more likely to marry (Clarkberg, 1999; Goldstein & Kenney, 2001; but see Xie, Raymo, Goyette, & Thornton, 2003, for a contrary view). Sweeney (2002) found that the effect of female earnings on marriage was nonsignificant for women born early in the baby boom (1950–1954), but positive and significant for women born at the end of the baby boom (1961–1965). These trends in the pattern of union formation suggest another component of a period factor in the near future—a macrolevel context wherein marriages involve more collaboration around similar tasks and are less likely to revolve around separate male and female roles generating a sticky cement of structural interdependence.

Taken together, these period forces do not necessarily imply a change in the overall rate of divorce. Assuming that men and women continue to make adjustments in their expectations about marriage in favor of shared responsibility for economic provision, female labor force participation may no longer generate a disjuncture between expectations and reality in marriage (although it will still provide women with the opportunity to leave less-than-satisfactory marriages). Coupled with changes in the household division of labor that indicate greater participation on the part of husbands (Bianchi, Milkie, Sayer, & Robinson, 2000), more equal labor force commitment on the part of both spouses implies an increasingly gender-neutral organization of married life. However, marriages with less sharply defined gender roles are necessarily more egalitarian and thus likely to require more vigilance to maintain equilibrium (Brines & Joyner, 1999). As a consequence, the need for increased vigilance will heighten the need for individuals to be committed to the union and the need to make a good marital match, someone with whom it is possible to negotiate the details of everyday life without relying on the structural constraints generated by a highly gendered division of labor. We suspect that commitment and ability to form a good marital match, one that allows practicable marital negotiating, are unmeasured characteristics (the U_{it}) of future marriages that will affect divorce rates (we consider these characteristics as components of U_{it} because most large-scale demographic data-collection efforts do not attempt to measure these concepts directly). Marriages formed without sufficient commitment and that are not a good match will not be able to rely on economic interdependence and normative pressure to ensure their survival, making them more susceptible to dissolution.

We now turn our attention to potential future trends in important demographic covariates known to be associated with marital dissolution. Our selection of covariates is limited because we wish to focus on variables about which we have reasonably good data. Recognizing the growing importance of commitment to marriage (either in general or the specific union) and the need for generating a good marital match, we also constrain our discussion to variables for which we can make reasonable decisions about how they may be tied to these aspects of marriage. We organize our comments around the assumed direction of impact (positive or negative) associated with the covariates.

VARIABLES WITH ASSUMED NEGATIVE EFFECTS ON MARITAL DISSOLUTION

Age at Marriage

We begin with perhaps the most consistent predictor of marital instability, that is, age at marriage: Almost all previous research has found that young age at marriage leads to an increased risk of divorce. Men and women who marry at older ages have most likely engaged in a more extensive search for a spouse, resulting in a better marital match. Individuals who marry older are also less likely to experience rapid personal change that could destabilize a previously good match. Recent history suggests a rapid decrease in the number of Americans who marry at a young age. Between 1950 and 2000, the median age at first marriage for women increased from 20.3 to 25.1 years. For men, the comparable ages are 22.8 and 26.8. Recent attitudinal data showing that young people believe that it is important to wait at least 5 years after high school graduation before marrying suggests that this trend is not likely to reverse itself in the near future (Thornton & Young-DeMarco, 2001).

The trend toward later age at marriage is further supported by changes in the economy that make it more difficult for young men to establish sufficient economic security in order to be able to support a family (Oppenheimer, Kalmijn, & Lim, 1997), and the increasing proportion of young women who delay marriage until after finishing college and entering into their careers (Goldstein & Kenney, 2001). Continued late age at marriage, therefore, suggests a dampening effect on future rates of divorce (recall that Heaton, 2002, found that changes in age at marriage can completely explain changes in divorce rates over the 1975–1995 period). This dampening effect of compositional change may be offset to some degree, however, if an increasing need for equilibrium maintenance in marriages leads to an increase in the rate at which young marriages are dissolved (although Teachman, 2002a, found no change in the relationship between age at marriage and divorce over the 1950–1954 to 1980–1984 period).

Educational Attainment

Another factor potentially dampening future increments in divorce rates are levels of educational attainment. A number of studies have linked higher education to a reduced risk of marital disruption (Bumpass, Martin, & Sweet, 1991; Heaton, 2002; South, 2001a; South, Trent, & Shen, 2001; Teachman, 2002a). Between 1960 and 2000, the percentage of women having completed 4 or more years of college increased from 5.8 to 23.6 (U.S. Bureau of the Census, 2002). For men, the increase over the same period was from 9.7% to 27.8%. Increases in levels of education have also been accompanied by greater educational homogamy of spouses (Mare, 1991), and, assuming that education enhances negotiating skills, we suspect that both trends will act to reduce potential conflicts and misunderstandings between husbands and wives that might be tied to marital dissolution. As is the case for age at marriage, however, increases in rates of divorce among marriages formed by less educated men and women could act to offset the negative effect of compositional change associated with increased educational attainment on rates of divorce.

Premarital Cohabitation

Considerable research has linked premarital cohabitation to an increased risk of marital disruption (Bumpass, Sweet, & Cherlin, 1991; Schoen, 1992; Teachman, 2002a). There has also been an increase across time in the prevalence of premarital cohabitation. Only about 10% of marriages contracted between 1965 and 1974 were preceded by a spell of nonmarital cohabitation by at least one spouse (Bumpass & Sweet, 1989). This figure increased to 56% for marriages contracted between 1990 and 1994 (Bumpass & Lu, 2000). With continued late age at marriage, combined with attitudes that generally accept premarital sex and cohabitation, it is unlikely that premarital cohabitation will become any less common than has been the case in recent years. Indeed, the percentage of marriages preceded by a spell of cohabitation may continue to creep upward for some time.

At first glance, continued high levels of premarital cohabitation might suggest continued high levels of divorce, given previous research linking cohabitation to an increased risk of marital dissolution. However, we believe there are several reasons that this may not be the case in the future. First, there is evidence that the relationship between premarital cohabitation and divorce is waning (Schoen, 1992; see also Schoen et al., 2002, and Sayer & Bianchi, 2000, for analyses that failed to find a statistically significant effect of premarital cohabitation on divorce). Teachman (2003) found that women who limited premarital sex and premarital cohabitation to their future spouse did not experience a higher risk of divorce. Teachman argues that premarital sex and cohabitation are becoming a normal and accepted part of the courtship process in the United States and are no longer indicative of less commitment to the institution of marriage or the permanence of intimate unions.

Second, premarital cohabitation may serve as a sorting mechanism. That is, by cohabiting before marriage, spouses may be able to determine whether they are compatible. Unions that are not compatible are easily dissolved and never involve a marriage. Because a marriage is never formed, these unions do not inflate the divorce rate. This is an old idea and is admittedly a difficult pattern to detect, but it could be an important component in new marital search regimes.

Third, a spell of premarital cohabitation may provide a proving ground for couples to improve their relationship skills. As Brines and Joyner (1999) note, cohabiting unions are more likely to involve principles of equity that require more day-to-day negotiating to maintain a proper equilibrium. To the extent that this is the case, and the extent to which a larger number of marriages in the future will involve more negotiation between partners of nearly equal bargaining power, premarital cohabitation may prove to be a valuable proving ground for developing increasingly important relationship skills.

Female Labor Force Participation

The participation of wives in the labor market has undergone dramatic change over time. Between 1970 and 2000, the number of married women in the labor force with children increased from 39.7% to 70.8% (U.S. Bureau of the Census, 2002). The vast majority of research has assumed that the effect of female labor force participation is to raise divorce rates. Enough research has found a positive link between female labor force participation and divorce that it is not unreasonable to expect upward pressure on rates of divorce if women continue to march into the labor force in greater numbers. South (2001a) has even suggested that the effect on divorce of wives' participation in the labor market has increased over the past 25 years.

Nevertheless, there is sufficient recent research to suggest that the future may not be a simple continuation of past trends in the relationship between female labor force participation and marital dissolution. As indicated earlier, the effect of wives' labor market participation may not be causal. That is, labor force participation may not destabilize marriages; it may act only as a factor enabling women to leave unhappy unions. Again, there is growing research that this may be the case (Rogers, 2004; Sayer & Bianchi, 2000; Schoen et al., 2002). Accordingly, if marriage is increasingly dependent on the income of two spouses to maintain economic stability and changes in gender-role orientations are sufficient to support an egalitarian division of labor, particularly among men, the long-term effect of wives' labor force participation on union stability may be neutral or even negative.

In an environment in which both spouses are expected to work, we suspect that better marital matches will occur when spouses share relatively similar work experiences (e.g., income, prestige, and skill requirements). A similarity of work requirements and experiences should reduce the need to continually negotiate patterns of household labor and thus help ensure principles of equality. Sharing the world of work may also provide couples with a sense of mutual understanding and commonality that enhances and eases negotiations that do occur.

VARIABLES WITH ASSUMED POSITIVE EFFECTS ON MARITAL DISSOLUTION

Premarital Fertility

There are a number of demographic variables that have been positively linked to divorce and that have increased in prevalence over time. Moreover, there is little evidence that these demographic covariates are necessarily linked to improvements in mate selection or ability to negotiate in an increasingly egalitarian environment. For example, premarital fertility has increased considerably over time. Abma, Mosher, Peterson, and Piccinino (1997) reported that the percentage of first marriages preceded by a birth increased from 8.3 for marriages contracted in the early 1980s to 21.6 for marriages contracted between 1990 and 1995. Moreover, other research indicates a generally positive effect of premarital fertility on divorce (Bramlett & Mosher, 2002; Heaton, 2002; Teachman, 2002a). With increasing pressure for both spouses to participate in the labor market, and with an increased need to engage in day-to-day negotiation of household tasks, the presence of a premarital birth injects an additional element of potential instability into a marriage.

We acknowledge, however, that the positive effect of a premarital birth on divorce may not be substantial if the marriage involves both biological parents. Indeed, if the birth occurred while the couple was cohabiting, it might simply represent continued evolution of the process of mate selection in the United States, and the couple may have had sufficient time to negotiate their relationship prior to marriage. The destabilizing effect of a premarital birth is most likely to occur when there is only one biological parent involved in the marriage, particularly in situations in which the absent parent or other kin remain involved in the child's life.

The Transmission of Divorce Within and Across Generations

We conclude this section by noting that divorce today may provide the fuel supporting more divorce in the future. There are two paths by which this can occur—within a generation and across generations. Within a generation, higher rates of divorce mean that more individuals are likely to enter a second or higher order marriage, and the available literature is consistent in finding that marriages in which at least one spouse has been previously married are at an increased risk of marital dissolution (Bumpass, Martin, & Sweet, 1991; Rogers, 2004; Schoen et al., 2002). In 1970, nearly 70% of all marriages involved a first marriage for both bride and groom (U.S. Bureau of the Census, 2002). By 1988, this figure had dropped to 54%.

Continued high levels of divorce will thus continue to fuel subsequent divorce. Moreover, there is little evidence to suggest that the effect of having experienced a divorce on subsequent risk of divorce will subside any time in the future. Individuals who have divorced may be a select group with preexisting (and unmeasured) characteristics that may lead them to be more prone to divorce. In addition, the process of divorce itself may indicate to individuals that marital dissolution may act to solve marital difficulties. One potential countervailing factor could be a continued slowdown in the rate at which individuals remarry. There has been a reasonably consistent downward trend in the proportion of divorced individuals who remarry, particularly for women and Blacks (Bramlett & Mosher, 2002).

Across generations, it has become increasingly clear that children are affected by the divorce of their parents. The range of outcomes caused by parental marital dissolution is wide, but one of the most consistent is an intergenerational transmission of divorce. A number of recent studies have documented the link between parental divorce and offspring divorce (Amato, 1996; Bumpass, Martin, & Sweet, 1991; Mueller & Pope, 1977; Pope & Mueller, 1976; Teachman, 2002b; Wolfinger, 1999, 2000). Although it is possible that experiencing parental divorce leads to the development of poor relationship skills that detract from the stability of marital unions, Amato and DeBoer (2001) presented findings that suggested that the effect of parental divorce is more closely tied to the comparatively weak commitment to marriage among children who have seen their parents' marriage end in divorce.

The upward trend in divorce in the United States has meant that an increasing number of children have seen their parents' marriage dissolve. Teachman (2002a) reported that less than 10% of marriages formed in the 1950s involved wives with divorced parents. For the 1990 to 1994 marriage cohort, this figure had risen to 27.4%. This latter figure would be even higher if husbands from disrupted families were considered. For example, Bumpass, Martin, and Sweet (1991) reported that, for marriages begun between 1975 and 1984, about 35% involved at least one spouse who had experienced parental divorce (for the 1980–1984 marriage cohort, Teachman reported that 17.4% of wives come from a family disrupted by divorce).

Of course, the effect of changes in the composition of marriage with respect to parental divorce also depends on the stability of the effect of this covariate on marital dissolution. Wolfinger (1999) presented findings that suggested that the effect of parental divorce on offspring divorce may have declined for marriages formed after the mid-1970s. He argued that divorce has become much less stigmatized and that children of divorce have become less traumatized by the event. Teachman (2002a), examining marriages formed between 1950 and 1984, however, found no evidence for decline in the intergenerational transmission of divorce.

RACE DIFFERENCES

Up to this point, we have paid little attention to racial differences in marital dissolution. In part, this stems from the fact that racial differences in marital dissolution are not well understood. We know that, on average, marriages among Blacks are the least stable, followed by marriages among Whites and Hispanics, with marriages among Asians being the most stable (Bramlett & Mosher, 2002). Differences between various Hispanic and Asian groups are not documented with any precision, however. We also know little about the underlying processes that may generate differences in divorce rates among racial and ethnic groups.

Notwithstanding these limitations in our understanding, it is clear that, to the extent that there are differences among race and ethnic groups with respect to marital disruption, the overall rate of divorce in the United States in the future will be a function of the composition of marriages with respect to race and ethnicity. For example, the proportion of the U.S. population that is Black has not changed dramatically over time, yet some evidence suggests that fewer Blacks may eventually marry (Teachman & Paasch, 1999). This compositional change would tend to drive the overall rate of divorce downward. Downward pressure on divorce rates might also occur if the proportion of the U.S. Asian population that marries continues to increase (U.S. Bureau of the Census, 2002).

Of course, change in overall divorce rates can occur through changes in the relationship between race or ethnicity and the risk of marital dissolution. Unfortunately, there is relatively little research that has attempted to document differences between race and ethnic groups in the determinants of divorce (see Martin & Bumpass, 1989, for results that suggest a few racial differences in the predictors of divorce, and see Teachman, 2002a, for an analysis that failed to find substantial race differences). Two pieces of evidence, however, suggest that the effect of being Black may not remain constant across time. First, there is reasonably good evidence that the impact of being Black on divorce can be largely attributed to the unfavorable economic conditions facing Black men (Sayer & Bianchi, 2000; Schoen et al., 2002; South, 2001b). To the extent that future economic conditions positively affect the relative economic position of Black men, as did the rapid economic expansion that occurred over the 1990s, rates of divorce will likely fall. Negative change in economic conditions leading to a decline in the still-precarious economic position of Black men will lead to an increase in divorce.

Second, Teachman (2002a) found that the effect of being Black on rates of divorce declined over the period from 1950 to 1995. Although part of this decline may be attributed to the changing economic circumstances of Blacks, Teachman suggests that a contributing factor is the increasing selectivity of marriage among Blacks. That is, because fewer Blacks are marrying, those who do marry are more likely to possess characteristics that are favorable to the success of their unions. A continuation of this trend would act to further suppress divorce rates in the future.

COHABITATION

We have spent most of our time discussing marital dissolution. We do not mean to deny the importance of cohabitation. Rather, we are recognizing the somewhat fuzzy status occupied by cohabitation in demographic data. Whereas marriages and divorces have long been part of the vital statistics system in the United States (although the collection and dissemination of detailed data on marriages and divorces was suspended beginning January, 1996), and marital status is a key population characteristic obtained in the census, estimates of cohabitation have, until recently, been largely indirect (Casper & Cohen, 2000). It is only in a number of recent survey efforts that information about cohabitation has become widely available.

Of course, scholarly interest in cohabitation has been spurred by its increasing prevalence. Over the 20 years between 1977 and 1997, the number of cohabiting couples is estimated to have increased from 1,097,000 to 4,856,000 (Casper & Cohen, 2000). Bumpass and Lu (2000) estimated that, by 1995, nearly half of all women under the age of 40 had cohabited, and more than half of all marriages were preceded by a spell of cohabitation. Cohabitation has largely offset the rather steep decline in rates of first marriage among men and women younger than 25 years of age (Bumpass, Sweet, & Cherlin, 1991; Bumpass & Lu, 2000). Young men and women are not marrying, but they are still living together. Moreover, an increasing proportion of nonmarital births are occurring to cohabiting couples (Bumpass & Lu, 2000; Raley, 2001), and there exists a lively debate about the meaning of cohabitation as a family status and what it means for both adults and children (Booth & Crouter, 2002; Rindfuss & VandenHeuvel, 1990; Seltzer, 2000).

Most cohabiting unions end either because the partners marry or they end their relationship (few cohabiting unions last sufficiently long for death to become a serious competing risk). Bumpass and Lu (2000) estimated that between 50% and 60% of cohabiting unions will result in marriage, with the remainder being very short lived (only about 10% remain cohabiting unions after 10 years). Surprisingly, there appear to be few demographic characteristics of couples that consistently predict union dissolution among cohabitors. Whereas characteristics such as age at union formation and race predict the risk of divorce, the same is not true for the dissolution of cohabiting unions. The most consistent predictor of the risk of dissolution among cohabiting unions is the income of the male. Unions in which the male partner earns more are much less likely to end in separation and are more likely to make the transition to marriage (Oppenheimer, 2003; Smock & Manning, 1997). Brines and Joyner (1999) found that cohabiting partners whose earnings and employment are more equal were less likely to end their union. Heterogamy in earnings, particularly when the woman earns more, was detrimental to stability.

Part of the reason that few predictors of union dissolution have been found may be the diversity of these unions. Some cohabiting unions are clearly formed as a precursor to marriage. Cohabitors who expect to marry are likely to do so in short order (Brown, 2000). Other cohabiting unions appear to be more like unions of convenience in which couples may not expect to form a marriage. Indeed, cohabiting unions are much more likely to occur among individuals with less education and fewer economic resources, characteristics negatively associated with the risk of marriage (Bumpass & Lu, 2000; Oppenheimer, 2003).

What does this brief demographic overview suggest about the future? Combined with continued delays in marriage and slower career development among young men (Oppenheimer, 2003), cohabitation is likely to become even more prevalent. Because cohabitation is also common following divorce, high rates of marital disruption will also fuel cohabitation. Bumpass and Lu (2000) reported that, over the period from 1980–1984 to 1990–1994, cohabiting unions became less stable. That is, they were less likely to result in marriage and more likely to end in separation. Bumpass and Lu attributed this trend to the growing acceptability of cohabitation. As a growing proportion of couples without serious commitment to a long-term relationship form unions, higher rates of union dissolution are likely to occur. Continued high rates of economic uncertainty, particularly for young men, are likely to exacerbate this trend, with only the most economically stable unions making the transition to marriage. This pattern may auger well for the stability of marriages if only the better matches continue on to marriage.

CONCLUSION

We finish where we started, with an admonition that the future is exceedingly difficult to predict, including the future of divorce. The range of factors that affect marital dissolution is just too wide, and changing too rapidly, to make definitive conclusions more than a few years into the future. The interaction between personal characteristics and period forces is nearly impossible to anticipate, and predicting unmeasured characteristics that might be related to the risk of divorce in the future can be a guess at best. What we have done is to develop a rough, but useful, conceptual model for thinking demographically about the future of divorce. The model proposed is along the lines of a simple demographic accounting design wherein changes in the overall rate of divorce can be attributed to change in the composition of marriages or change in the relationship between the characteristics of spouses and the risk of divorce.

As long as men and women (or as current deliberations illustrate, men and men or women and women) come together to form marital unions, divorce is inevitable. As we note, it is our belief that the future of divorce depends on the future of marriage. The processes by which men and women are selected into the institution are changing, as are expectations that these individuals hold for their marriages. The future of marriage and divorce is also likely tied to related changes in adult living. For example, the increasing propensity for couples to form nonmarital cohabiting unions may act as a screening device for marriage, selecting couples more prone to stability. In addition, we suspect that structural changes to the social and economic landscape will influence the financial obligations ascribed to each spouse and the nature of interdependence experienced within unions. It is most likely that future changes will continue to undermine economic interdependence as the glue holding together marriages, placing greater emphasis on indicators of commitment to marriage and finding an appropriate match.

The factors contributing to divorce discussed in this chapter are far from exhaustive, and we acknowledge that we have constrained our focus to more easily measured demographic characteristics such as age at marriage, premarital cohabitation, and premarital fertility. We assume, however, that new predictors of divorce will become evident in the future, and it is likely that new data-collection efforts will be required to collect the information necessary to test the impact of different kinds of variables. We anticipate that many of these variables will be less tied to traditional demographic measures unless they can be shown to tap various dimensions of commitment or search practices tied to the quality of the marital match.

For example, we suspect that indicators of effort expended in finding a good marital match might include items such as length, intensity, and type of courtship. Individuals who spend more time and energy in searching for an appropriate marital match are more likely to be able withstand the ups and downs associated with married life. This is not a new idea, and it is implicit in the way that many demographers use age at marriage as a predictor of divorce (i.e., men and women who marry at older ages are likely to have spent more time searching for a better match). However, we can conceive of better indicators of search effort, including the number and length of prior relationships, nature of shared activities during courtship, and so on.

Other indicators of a successful marital match may rest in degree of homogamy on important social characteristics such as religion, education, occupation, and family background (see Rodrigues, Hall, and Fincham's chapter in this volume on predictors of divorce and dissolution). Again, this is not a new notion, and several previous researchers have commented on the role played by homogamy in rates of marital dissolution (eg., see, Bumpass, Martin, & Sweet, 1991). In the future, however, as couples come to increasingly rely on interpersonal commitment to cement their marriages rather than larger structural constraints and a rigid gender-based division of labor, the degree of similarity on important characteristics around which daily lives are organized is likely to be an important consideration.

Finally, as indicated by Stanley, Whitton, and Markman (2004), simple indicators of interpersonal commitment, rather than commitment to the institution of marriage itself, may be important to consider when one is assessing risk of divorce. The degree to which spouses are dedicated to each other, are willing to take a "we" perspective as opposed to an "I" perspective, and a willingness to negotiate and sacrifice for the other may become central to staying married.

To some degree, these characteristics of a marriage indicating extent of marital match may be tapped by demographic measures commonly collected in surveys (if not vital statistics data). The education, income, occupation, and religion of spouses can be easily tapped in a survey to create indicators of homogamy. We suspect, however, that indicators of interpersonal commitment and ability or willingness to negotiate are more direct indicators of a successful marital match and will require development of measures for use in survey efforts not commonly applied in the demographic literature. It is possible that data-collection efforts measuring components of interpersonal interaction would be useful (see Gottman, Coan, Carrere, & Swanson, 1998) if they could be made sufficiently reliable in a nonlaboratory setting. Moreover, because divorce is a process that unfolds over a period that often covers several years, if not decades, measures have to be developed that can be easily embedded in longitudinal survey efforts.

REFERENCES

Abma, C., Mosher, W., Peterson, L., & Piccinino, L. (1997). *Fertility, family planning, and women's health: New data from the 1995 National Survey of Family Growth* (Vital and Health Statistics, Series P23, No. 19). Washington, DC: U.S. Government Printing Office.

Amato, P. (1996). Explaining the intergenerational transmission of divorce. *Journal of Marriage and the Family, 58,* 628–640.

Amato, P., & DeBoer, D. (2001). The transmission of marital instability across generations: Relationship skills or commitment to marriage? *Journal of Marriage and Family, 63,* 1038–1051.

Amato, P., Johnson, D., Booth, A., & Rogers, S. (2003). Continuity and change in marital quality between 1980 and 2000. *Journal of Marriage and Family, 65,* 1–22.

Axinn, W., & Thornton, A. (2000). The transformation in the meaning of marriage. In L. Waite, C. Bachrach, M. Hindin, E. Thomson, & A. Thornton (Eds.), *The ties that bind: Perspectives on marriage and cohabitation* (pp. 147–165). New York: de Gruyter.

Becker, G. (1991). *A treatise on the family.* Chicago: University of Chicago Press.

Bellah, R., Madsen, R., Sullivan, W., Swidler, A., & Tipton, S. (1985). *Habits of the heart: Individualism and commitment in American life.* Berkeley: University of California Press.

Bianchi, S., Milkie, M., Sayer, L., & Robinson. J. (2000). Is anyone doing the housework? Trends in the gender division of household labor. *Social Forces, 79,* 191–228.

Blalock, H. (1984). Contextual effects models: Theoretical and methodological issues. *Annual Review of Sociology, 10,* 353–372.

Booth, A., & Crouter, A. (2002). *Just living together: Implications of cohabitation on families, children, and social policy.* Mahwah, NJ: Lawrence Erlbaum Associates.

Bramlett, M., & Mosher, W. (2002). *Cohabitation, marriage, divorce, and remarriage in the United States* (Vital and Health Statistics, Series 23, No. 22). Washington, DC: U.S. Government Printing Office.

Brown, S. (2000). Union transitions among cohabitors: The significance of relationship assessments and expectations. *Journal of Marriage and Family, 62,* 833–846.

Brines, J., & Joyner, K. (1999). The ties that bind: Principles of cohesion in cohabitation and marriage. *American Sociological Review, 64,* 333–355.

Bumpass, L., & Lu, H. (2000). Trends in cohabitation and implications for children's contexts in the United States. *Population Studies, 54,* 29–41.

Bumpass, L., & Sweet, J. (1989). National estimates of cohabitation. *Demography, 26,* 615–626.

Bumpass, L., Martin, T., & Sweet, J. (1991). The impact of family background and early marital factors on marital dissolution. *Journal of Family Issues, 12,* 22–42.

Bumpass, L., Sweet, J., & Cherlin, A. (1991). The role of cohabitation in declining rates of marriage. *Journal of Marriage and the Family, 53,* 913–927.

Carlson, E. (1979). Divorce rate fluctuation as a cohort phenomenon. *Population Studies, 33,* 523–536.

Casper, L., & Cohen, P. (2000). How does POSSLQ measure up? Historical estimates of cohabitation. *Demography, 37,* 237–245.

Cherlin, A. (1992). *Marriage, divorce, remarriage.* Cambridge, MA: Harvard University Press.

Clarkberg, M. (1999). The price of partnering: The role of economic well-being in young adults first union experience. *Social Forces, 77,* 945–968.

Coleman, J. (1990). *Foundations of social theory.* Cambridge, MA: Harvard University Press.

Feinberg, S., & Mason, W. (1978). Identification and estimation of age-period-cohort models in the analysis of discrete archival data. In K. Schuessler (Ed.), *Sociological methodology* (pp. 1–67). New York: Jossey-Bass.

Firebaugh, G. (1997). *Analyzing repeated surveys.* Thousand Oaks, CA: Sage.

Furstenberg, F. (1994). History and current status of divorce in the United States. *The Future of Children, 4,* 29–43.

Glenn, N. (1976). Cohort analysts' futile quest: Statistical attempts to separate age, period, and cohort effects. *American Sociological Review, 41,* 900–904.

Goldstein, J. (1999). The leveling of divorce in the United States. *Demography, 36,* 409–414.

Goldstein, J., & Kenney, C. (2001). Marriage delayed or marriage foregone? New cohort forecasts of first marriage for U.S. women. *American Sociological Review, 66,* 506–519.

Goode, W. (1993). *World changes in divorce patterns.* New Haven, CT: Yale University Press.

Gottman, J., Coan, J., Carrere, S., & Swanson, C. (1998). Predicting marital happiness and stability from newlywed interactions. *Journal of Marriage and the Family, 60,* 5–22.

Heaton, T. (2002). Factors contributing to increasing marital stability in the United States. *Journal of Family Issues, 23,* 392–409.

Jacobson, H. (1959). *American marriage and divorce.* New York: Rinehart.

Jockin, V., McGue, M., & Lykken, D. (1996). Personality and divorce: A genetic analysis. *Journal of Personality and Social Psychology, 71,* 288–299.

Lipset, S. (1979). *America as a post-industrial society.* Chicago: University of Chicago Press.

Mare, R. (1991). Five decades of educational assortative mating. *American Sociological Review, 56,* 15–32.

Martin, T., & Bumpass, L. (1989). Recent trends in marital disruption. *Demography, 26,* 37–51.

May, E. (1980). *Great expectations: Marriage and divorce in post-Victorian America.* Chicago: University of Chicago Press.

McGue, M., & Lykken, D. (1992). Genetic influence on risk of divorce. *Psychological Science, 6,* 368–373.

Mueller, C., & Pope, H. (1977). Marital instability: A study of its transmission between generations. *Journal of Marriage and the Family, 39,* 83–93.

Oppenheimer, V. (1994). Women's rising employment and the future of the family in industrial societies. *Population and Development Review, 20,* 293–342.

Oppenheimer, V. (1997a). Comment on the "Rise of divorce and separation in the United States, 1880–1990." *Demography, 34,* 467–472.

Oppenheimer, V. (1997b). Women's employment and the gains to marriage: The specialization and trading model. *Annual Review of Sociology, 23,* 431–453.

Oppenheimer, V. (2003). Cohabiting and marriage during young men's career-development process. *Demography, 40,* 127–149.

Oppenheimer, V., Kalmijn, M., & Lim, N. (1997). Men's career development and marriage timing during a period of rising inequality. *Demography, 34,* 311–330.

Ono, H. (1999). Historical time and U.S. marital dissolution. *Social Forces, 77,* 969–999.

Phillips, R. (1991). *Untying the knot: A short history of divorce.* Cambridge, MA: Cambridge University Press.

Pope, H., & Mueller, C. (1976). The intergenerational transmission of marital instability: Comparisons by race and sex. *Journal of Social Issues, 32,* 49–66.

Preston, S., & McDonald, J. (1979). The incidence of divorce within cohorts of American marriages contracted since the Civil War. *Demography, 16,* 1–25.

Raley, R. K. (2001). Increasing fertility in cohabiting unions: Evidence for the second demographic transition in the United States. *Demography, 38,* 59–66.

Rindfuss, R., & VandenHeuvel, A. (1990). Cohabitation: A precursor to marriage or an alternative to being single? *Population and Development Review, 16,* 703–726.

Rogers, S. (2004). Dollars, dependency, and divorce: Four perspectives on the role of wives' income. *Journal of Marriage and Family, 66,* 59–74.

Ruggles, S. (1997). The rise of divorce and separation in the United States, 1880–1990. *Demography, 34,* 455–466.

Sanchez, L., & Gager, C. (2000). Hard living, perceived entitlement to a great marriage, and marital dissolution. *Journal of Marriage and Family, 62,* 708–722.

Sayer, L., & Bianchi, S. (2000). Women's economic independence and the probability of divorce. *Journal of Family Issues, 21,* 906–943.

Scanzoni, J., Polonko, K., Teachman, J., & Thompson, L. (1989). *The sexual bond: Rethinking families and close relationships.* Newbury Park, CA: Sage.

Schoen, R. (1992). First union and the stability of first marriage. *Journal of Marriage and the Family, 54,* 281–284.

Schoen, R., & Standish, N. (2001). The retrenchment of marriage: Results from marital status life tables for the United States. *Population and Development Review, 27,* 553–563.

Schoen, R., Astone, N., Rothert, K., Standish, N., & Kim, Y. (2002). Women's employment, marital happiness and divorce. *Social Forces, 81,* 643–662.

Schoen, R., Urton, W., Woodrow, K., & Baj, J. (1985). Marriage and divorce in twentieth century American cohorts. *Demography, 22,* 101–114.

Seltzer, J. (2000). Families formed outside of marriage. *Journal of Marriage and Family, 62,* 1247–1268.

Smock, P., & Manning, W. (1997). Cohabiting partners' economic circumstances and marriage. *Demography, 34,* 331–341.

South, S. (2001a). Time-dependent effects of wives' employment on marital dissolution. *American Sociological Review, 66,* 226–245.

South, S. (2001b). The geographic context of divorce: Do neighborhoods matter? *Journal of Marriage and Family, 63,* 755–766.

South, S., Trent, K., & Shen, Y. (2001). Changing partners: Toward a macrostructural-opportunity theory of marital dissolution. *Journal of Marriage and Family, 63,* 743–754.

Stanley, S., Whitton, S., & Markman, H. (2004). Maybe I do: Interpersonal commitment and premarital or nonmarital commitment. *Journal of Family Issues, 25,* 496–519.

Stinchcombe, A. (1982). On soft-headedness on the future. *Ethics, 93,* 114–128.

Stone, L. (1977). *The family, sex, and marriage in England 1500–1800.* New York: Harper & Row.

Sweeney, M. (2002). Two decades of family change: The shifting economic foundations of marriage. *American Sociological Review, 67,* 132–147.

Teachman, J. (2002a). Stability across cohorts in divorce risk factors. *Demography, 39,* 331–351.

Teachman, J. (2002b). Childhood living arrangements and the intergenerational transmission of divorce. *Journal of Marriage and Family, 64,* 717–729.

Teachman, J. (2003). Premarital sex, premarital cohabitation, and the risk of subsequent marital dissolution among women. *Journal of Marriage and Family, 65,* 444–455.

Teachman, J., & Paasch, K. (2000). The social and economic context of increasing demographic diversity of families. In D. Demo, K. Allen, & and M. Fine (Eds.), *Handbook of family diversity* (pp. 32–58). New York: Oxford University Press.

Thornton, A. (1989). Changing attitudes toward family issues in the United States. *Journal of Marriage and the Family, 51,* 873–893.

Thornton, A., & Young-DeMarco, L. (2001). Four decades of trends in attitudes toward family issues in the United States: The 1960s through the 1990s. *Journal of Marriage and Family, 63,* 1009–1037.

Thornton, A., & Rodgers, W. (1987). The influence of individual and historical time on marital dissolution. *Demography, 24,* 1–22.

U.S. Bureau of the Census. (2002). *Statistical abstract of the United States.* Washington DC: U.S. Government Printing Office.

Wolfinger, N. (1999). Trends in the intergenerational transmission of divorce. *Demography, 36,* 415–420.

Wolfinger, N. (2000). Beyond the intergenerational transmission of divorce. *Journal of Family Issues, 21,* 1061–1086.

White, L. (1990). Determinants of divorce: A review of research in the eighties. *Journal of Marriage and the Family, 52,* 904–912.

Xie, Y., Raymo, J., Goyette, K., & Thornton, A. (2003). Economic potential and entry into marriage and cohabitation. *Demography, 40,* 351–367.

III

Causes, Underlying Processes, and Antecedents of Divorce and Relationship Dissolution

5

What Predicts Divorce and Relationship Dissolution?

Amy E. Rodrigues and Julie H. Hall
University at Buffalo, The State University of New York

Frank D. Fincham
Florida State University

The need for the current handbook attests to the instability of romantic unions in today's society. Approximately one half of all first marriages end in separation or divorce (Bramlett & Mosher, 2002; Castro Martin & Bumpass, 1989; Rogers, 2004), with even higher rates of divorce for second marriages (Cherlin, 1992; Glick, 1984). Divorce is often preceded by separation, with 75% of separations resulting in divorce (Bloom, Hodges, Caldwell, Systra, & Cedrone, 1977). Although divorce rates have been declining since the early 1980s and marriages have become more stable in recent years (Heaton, 2002), divorce continues to wreak emotional and physical havoc on the families in which it occurs. Thus, identifying predictors of divorce and dissolution is an important task.

In this chapter we review sociodemographic, individual difference, and relationship variables that predict divorce or relationship dissolution. We devote particular attention to potential mechanisms that might explain the associations identified. Following identification and analysis of the various predictors, we consider implications for prevention programs and future research. We begin with a brief review of the theoretical frameworks that underlie relationship functioning and stability and that inform our analysis.

THEORETICAL BACKGROUND

Three theoretical orientations have laid the foundation for much of the research on this topic (see Huston, Caughlin, Houts, Smith, & George, 2001 for three alternative models). In addition, we review the vulnerability–stress–adaptation model (Karney & Bradbury, 1995), as it is the first conceptual framework to integrate existing theory and research.

Social Exchange Theory

Social exchange theory, which evolved from the interdependence theory of Thibaut and Kelley (1959), was first applied to the marital relationship by Levinger (1965). Interdependence theory emphasizes the dependence of each spouse on the marital relationship, and the ability of that relationship to fulfill individual needs. Kurdek (1993) hypothesized that couples in which one or both partners exhibited low levels of relationship dependence would be at higher risk for divorce. Levinger (1979) initially expounded on this idea and posited that marital success or failure is dependent on the attractions of the relationship, the barriers to abandoning it, and the presence of potential alternatives. The attraction of a relationship is positively related to the rewards associated with that bond, examples of which are family income, companionship, and sex. In addition, there is an inverse relationship between attractiveness and the costs associated with the union, which include things such as time and energy. Levinger (1979) recognized that individual perception was important by emphasizing the notion of subjective probability; the higher one's *anticipation* that a reward or cost will present itself, the greater impact it is thought to have on the attractiveness of the relationship. The outcome of marriage is also assumed to be influenced by the presence of barriers to leaving the relationship (e.g., financial or religious constraints) that encourage individuals to remain in a relationship. Social exchange theory also posits that marital stability is influenced by the presence of alternative attractions to the current relationship, such as independence or alternate romantic partners, attractions that can result in withdrawal from the relationship. Ultimately, relationships characterized by low levels of attraction, a small number of barriers, and attractive alternatives are likely to end in dissolution, according to proponents of social exchange theory.

An elaboration of this view was presented by Lewis and Spanier (1982), who considered marital satisfaction in addition to stability. Accordingly, marriages may be satisfying and stable, satisfying yet unstable, unsatisfying and unstable, or unsatisfying yet stable. Marital satisfaction is thought to be influenced by the attractiveness of the relationship, whereas the barriers to leaving and attractive alternatives impact marital stability. For example, a satisfying unstable relationship consists of a suitable level of attractions, yet the barriers are low and there are attractive alternatives. This addition recognizes the importance of describing relationships as more than merely stable or unstable.

Behavioral Theory

Behavioral theories of marriage are also rooted in interdependence theory (Thibault & Kelley, 1959), yet, as Karney and Bradbury (1995) noted, behavioral theory differs from the intrapersonal focus of social exchange theory, which emphasizes individual perceptions of attractions and alternatives. In contrast, behavioral theory adopts an interpersonal stance, which asserts that marital satisfaction is related to the exchange of overt behaviors between partners. The underlying premise is that the exchange of positive, rewarding behaviors enhances marital satisfaction, whereas negative, punishing behavioral exchanges decrease marital satisfaction (Wills, Weiss, & Patterson, 1974; for reviews see Kelly, Fincham, & Beach, 2003; Weiss & Heyman, 1997). This perspective has focused on behaviors occurring in the context of problem solving, in which distressed couples are more likely to engage in and to reciprocate negative behaviors than nondistressed partners.

Although the link between behavior and satisfaction has received considerable support, there is recognition that variables other than behavior are likely to be associated with marital satisfaction. Bradbury and Fincham (1990) have elaborated on the link between behaviors and satisfaction by considering the attributions that partners make regarding overt behaviors. Although these cognitive processes are not thought of as directly associated with marital satisfaction, they are believed to influence interaction behaviors that in turn affect marital quality (Bradbury & Fincham, 1990). In the theoretical framework proposed by Bradbury and

Fincham (1990), if the behavior of one's spouse appears to be low in negativity, unexpectedness, and self-relevance, the individual will produce subsequent behavior in the absence of additional processing. However, perceptions of high negativity, unexpectedness, and self-relevance will lead to attributions regarding the specific behavior, examples of which include the intentionality of the behavior and the positive versus negative intent of the individual. These attributions in turn influence subsequent behavior. Both situations are believed to influence and to be influenced by the short- and long-term satisfaction of partners.

Crisis Theory

Crisis theory originated from Hill's (1949) explanations of how families react to stressful events, and it has since been used in relation to marital outcomes. Hill proposed the ABCX model, which states that families have differing levels of resources (B) when dealing with stressful events (A), which are likely to be defined differently as a function of the familial context (C). According to Hill, the nature and outcome of the crisis (X) is determined by whether the available resources of the family (B) are adequate for the stressful event (A) as defined by the family (C). When related to the marital relationship, satisfaction and stability are a result of a couple's ability to recover from crises. Theoretically, the probability of negative outcomes increases as the stress surrounding the event increases; the way the event is defined in addition to available resources is thought to moderate this relationship.

An extension of this model was provided by McCubbin and Patterson (1982), with the recognition that the focus of the original ABCX model was limited to variables present prior to the crisis. In their double-ABCX model, McCubbin and Patterson recognized that crisis responding is unlikely to be a static process and posited that variables subsequent to the crisis are important to consider in understanding marital satisfaction and stability. Therefore, they proposed that variable A extends beyond the initial stressor to include everyday occurrences unrelated to the stressor, in addition to stressors that develop as a result of dealing with the original stressor. Similarly, the level of available resources (B) consists of not only the resources present at the start of the conflict, but also those developed through the course of dealing with the stressful event. Finally, the perception of the stressor or event is extended to include the perception of what this crisis situation means to each individual family member postcrisis. This perspective recognizes that the variables associated with marital satisfaction and stability in relation to crises or stressors are ever changing, and it admits to their importance in the revision of the ABCX model.

Vulnerability–Stress–Adaptation Model

Our discussion of social exchange theory, behavioral theory, and crisis theory shows that each suggests different predictors of marital instability. Although beneficial, each perspective alone is insufficient, as it is likely that marital satisfaction and stability may be predicted from a variety of factors. Karney and Bradbury (1995) have answered the call for an integrated framework with the presentation of the vulnerability–stress–adaptation model (see Fig. 5.1). In this model, marital quality is posited to be a function of three variables: enduring vulnerabilities, stressful events, and adaptive processes. Enduring vulnerabilities include the stable characteristics that each spouse brings to the union (e.g., personality characteristics and level of education). Stressful events, in contrast, encompass all the events or circumstances that are experienced by the couple (e.g., death of a family member, or loss of a job). Adaptive processes refer to the experiences encountered in the marriage, such as the behaviors engaged in during conflict

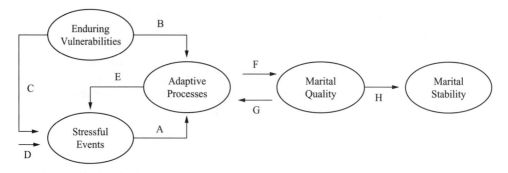

FIG. 5.1.   Stress–Vulnerability–Adaptation Model of Karney and Bradbury (1995).

or the appraisals surrounding these interactions. Karney and Bradbury posited that enduring vulnerabilities and stressful events influence marital quality indirectly through the adaptive processes, with the relationship between stressful events and adaptive processes presented as reciprocal. The adaptive processes, in turn, are expected to influence (or be influenced by) marital quality, which ultimately predicts marital instability. Therefore, this model attempts to incorporate variables that have previously been recognized such as stressful events (crisis theory) and overt behaviors (behavioral theory) with additional factors such as stable characteristics; it is important that it presents an integrated framework for their influence on marital quality and stability.

A number of the pathways in the model have already received considerable support (e.g., stressful events to adaptive processes), allowing the vulnerability–stress–adaptation model to act as a comprehensive integration of previously cited research findings. In addition, empirical investigations of the complex relationships between the variables are well under way. For example, Cohan and Bradbury (1997) examined the way in which stressful events contribute to marital quality and stability through adaptive processes. Their results suggest that the link between stressful life events and relationship quality and stability may be moderated, not mediated, by adaptive processes. Therefore, it appears that the vulnerability–stress–adaptation model has received considerable empirical support as a useful organizational framework. As investigations continue, researchers will move closer to integrating more fully the numerous predictors of divorce into a single framework.

Having laid the necessary theoretical groundwork, we now turn to the specific factors associated with divorce and relationship dissolution. We first consider sociodemographic and life course factors, which we follow with a discussion of individual difference factors; we conclude with an exploration of relationship–process variables that predict dissolution.

SOCIODEMOGRAPHIC AND LIFE COURSE FACTORS

Gender

Within the traditional heterosexual institution of marriage, divorce is obviously equally likely among men and women. However, striking gender differences emerge when we examine subjective and objective causes of relationship dissolution. Certain variables, such as affirmation by one's spouse, predict marital stability when they are measured in terms of husbands, but not in terms of wives; husbands who reported that they felt affectively affirmed by their wives were at lower risk for divorce than those who did not feel affirmed (Orbuch, Veroff, Hassan, & Horrocks, 2002). When asked what caused their divorce, men and women identify different variables, leading some researchers to suggest that there may be "his" and "her" divorces (Gager & Sanchez, 2003). Wives are more likely than husbands to cite emotional or relationship issues, spousal personality variables, spousal drinking, and abusive behavior as causes of divorce (see Amato & Previti, 2003, for a review). Husbands are more likely to identify external causes and to cite their own negative behaviors as being causally related to the divorce. Men are also more likely to report uncertainty as to what caused the divorce (Amato & Previti; Kitson, 1992). In this sense, gender can be viewed as a moderator of divorce and relationship dissolution. Thus, rather than exploring it as an independent predictor, we consider it throughout the chapter as a potential moderator of the association between other variables and relationship stability.

Race

African American couples are more likely than Caucasian couples to divorce during the first 14 years of marriage (Bramlett & Mosher, 2002; Bumpass, Martin, & Sweet, 1991; Heaton, 2002; Orbuch et al., 2002). This association holds even after interactional processes such as conflict and affirmation through which one's spouse is made to feel interesting, cared for, and important are controlled for (Orbuch et al.). Rates differ by sex, as some studies have shown that African American women, but not men, are at increased risk for divorce (DeMaris & Rao, 1992). However, among separated women, African Americans and Hispanic Americans were less likely than Caucasians to legally divorce (Bramlett & Mosher, 2002; Cherlin, 1998; Kposowa, 1998). There is also emerging evidence to suggest that marital dissolution is more likely among interracial couples (Bramlett & Mosher; Heaton). Unfortunately, there is little research exploring mechanisms involved in this association between race and divorce. A notable exception is a study by Amato and Rogers (1997), which found that being African American was associated with a higher likelihood of marital problems caused by being unfaithful or jealous, spending money, and drinking or using drugs.

According to sociologists, race can be seen as a structural factor, in that individuals from certain racial groups are systematically confronted with greater societal challenges or stressors (e.g., lower status, lower income, and lower education), which may spill over into the marital relationship (Orbuch et al., 2002). Indeed, when it comes to relationship dissolution, race tends to serve as a proxy for other sociodemographic variables, such as income, education, premarital birth, parental divorce, and cohabitation (Orbuch et al.). However, different racial groups may also attribute unique meaning to marriage and marital processes. For example, whereas wives' supportive or cooperative behavior is viewed favorably within Caucasian marriages, this same behavior has negative connotations within the African American community (Orbuch, Veroff, & Hunter, 1999). Thus, race must be considered not only as having a potential main effect on divorce or dissolution, but also as a potential moderating variable.

Society or Culture

In addition to examining individual characteristics, such as race and sex and their associations with divorce, researchers have broadened their focus to include the societies within which relationships are embedded. For example, there are regional differences in the prevalence of divorce in the United States, with a higher rate of divorce in the West than in the East, and a slightly lower divorce rates in the North than in the South (e.g., Glenn & Shelton, 1985).

Of interest is the assortment of proposed explanations for this discrepancy, which range from differences at the level of the individual to inconsistencies at the level of society. An example of an individual-level explanation is that individuals identified as Catholic or Jewish are less likely to divorce and tend to reside more heavily in the Northeast, whereas high divorce rates are characteristic of African Americans, who are more likely to live in the South, therefore accounting for the regional inconsistencies in the prevalence of divorce (Glenn & Shelton). In contrast, a popular explanation at the societal level concerns the level of social integration: Social integration theory emphasizes adherence to social norms. It has been suggested that this norm compliance results in a decreased tendency to separate when dissatisfaction emerges in the marital relationship, as divorce is often met with social disapproval. Glenn and Shelton, after controlling for variables such as religion and socioeconomic status, found that residential movement, which implies low levels of social integration, is positively correlated with marital dissolution. This finding offers support for social integration theory.

Finally, prevalence of divorce varies as a function of community size, with urban areas exceeding rural areas in the divorce rate (Wilkinson, Thompson, Reynolds, & Ostresh, 1982). Social integration theory has again received support as an explanation for this discrepancy (Shelton, 1987).

Investigating cultural variations in the divorce rate extends beyond the United States into the international realm. Although the elevated level of divorce in the United States has received considerable attention, in comparison with other nations the rate of marital dissolution within the United States may be viewed as moderate (Lee, 1982) and there are a number of nations that exceed our levels of separation (Hutter, 1988). However, worldwide comparisons suggest that Western nations such as the United States exceed Eastern cultures such as Japan and China in their rates of marital dissolution (McKenry & Price, 1995).

One potentially important characteristic that tends to distinguish Western from Eastern cultures is individualism versus collectivism. It is not surprising that collectivist nations such as Japan, which deemphasize individual freedom while emphasizing family life, have low levels of marital dissolution (McKenry & Price, 1995). In a similar vein, Hofstede (1980) showed that level of individualism, which views the interest of the individual as taking precedence over the interests of the larger group to which the person belongs, was positively related to the rate of divorce even after gross domestic product per capita was controlled for.

These investigations highlight the importance of considering a wide array of variables, such as geographic location and individualism or collectivism, when attempting to understand the broad cultural variables that may influence marital dissolution. As noted by McKenry and Price (1995), with changes such as economic development and female labor force participation, we are likely to see changes in the rate of marital dissolution throughout the world. Understanding the mechanism through which these variables exert their influence will be important for developing public policy designed to influence divorce rates.

Income or Employment

Income is inversely related to risk of divorce (e.g., Kurdek, 1993). However, Orbuch et al. (2002) did not find that income predicted divorce after they controlled for race and education. Although there is evidence to suggest that the ratio of the wife's income to the husband's income may have more implications for divorce risk than the couple's overall income, findings in this area have been mixed. Whereas some research has shown that the risk of divorce is highest when spouses have equivalent incomes (e.g., Heckert, Nowak, & Snyder, 1998), other findings have shown that similar incomes bring the lowest risk of divorce (e.g., Ono, 1998). A recent study by Rogers (2004) found that wives' income was positively and linearly related to the risk of divorce. In addition, the risk of divorce was greatest when wives contributed about half of the total family income. Rogers concluded that economic dependence and obligation predict marital stability, but when economic resources are equivalent, spouses are then freer to seek divorce.

In terms of employment, rates of divorce are elevated among couples in which the husband or both husband and wife are unemployed during the first year of marriage (Bumpass et al., 1991; Tzeng, 1992). Nonstandard work schedules are also related to marital stability. Presser (2000) found that, among families with children, working nights rather than days increased the risk of divorce. Interestingly, individuals from different socioeconomic groups tend to cite different causes for divorce (see Amato & Previti, 2003, for a review). Individuals of higher status are more likely to blame emotional or relationship issues, whereas those of lower status tend to cite more basic causes, such as financial problems or drinking.

Premarital Cohabitation

Premarital cohabitation is associated with lower levels of marital satisfaction and a higher risk of divorce (Amato, 1996; Booth & Johnson, 1988; Bumpass & Sweet, 1989; Bumpass et al., 1991; deVaus, Qu, & Weston, 2003; Heaton, 2002; Teachman & Polonko, 1990). Premarital cohabitation is more common among African American couples, couples with lower education levels, and couples reporting parental divorce or separation (Bumpass & Sweet; Orbuch et al., 2002). However, this differential risk between cohabitors and noncohabitors has been shrinking in more recent cohorts (deVaus et al.). After controlling for other divorce predictors, there was no significant difference between divorce rates for cohabitors and noncohabitors who had married in the early 1990s. In addition, the link between premarital cohabitation and divorce may apply only for those individuals who have been in more than one cohabiting relationship. Teachman (2003) found that premarital cohabitation was not associated with an increased risk of divorce when it was limited to the future spouse.

One potential mechanism that may account for this association between cohabitation and divorce is length of relationship. It has been posited that cohabitors have spent longer periods of time in the relationship, and thus report higher rates of dissolution (DeMaris & Rao, 1992). However, this argument has received only modest empirical support. Teachman and Polonko (1990) found that cohabitors displayed elevated rates of divorce relative to non-cohabitors when marital duration was considered from the wedding date. But when relationship length was measured from the date of cohabitation, only "serial cohabitors" (those who had cohabited more than once before marriage) had higher rates of divorce than non-cohabitors. However, other studies have found that premarital cohabitation predicts divorce even after controlling for relationship duration (Bennett, Blanc, & Bloom, 1988; DeMaris & Rao). An alternative account rests on selection bias. According to this account, premarital cohabitation is nontraditional, and thus attracts individuals with unconventional views of marriage and a greater openness to divorce (Bennett et al.; deVaus, Qu, & Weston, 2003). Other potential mechanisms include problem behaviors within marriage, as Amato and Rogers (1997) found that individuals who cohabitated experienced increased problems due to spousal moodiness.

Premarital or Marital Birth

Premarital childbearing is associated with an increased risk of divorce (Heaton, 2002; Martin & Bumpass, 1989; however, for an exception, see DeMaris & Rao, 1992). Although African American couples are more likely to have children before marriage than are Caucasian couples (Orbuch et al., 2002), the association between premarital birth and divorce appears to be weaker among African Americans (Martin & Bumpass). Interestingly, there is not a strong association between premarital conception and divorce (Teachman, 2002). However, the birth of a child during marriage is a protective buffer against divorce; DeMaris and Rao found that the odds of divorce were significantly reduced on the birth of the first child (DeMaris & Rao; White & Booth, 1985). What is also interesting is that this effect may be specific to the sex of the child, as Morgan, Lye, and Condran (1988) found that parents of girls were more likely to divorce than parents of boys (but see Devine & Forehand, 1996, for an exception). The presence of children appears to be related to accounts given for divorce. Amato and Previti (2003) found that couples with children were more likely to cite abuse or alcohol or drug use as causes of the divorce. This suggests that divorce is more likely in situations in which children are witnessing or being the victim of negative or violent behaviors by one of the parents.

Age at Marriage

Age at marriage is one of the strongest predictors of divorce within the early years of marriage, even after the presence of children is controlled for (Bumpass et al., 1991; DeMaris & Rao, 1992; Heaton, 2002; Martin & Bumpass, 1989; Moore & Waite, 1981; Tzeng, 1992). Although the risk of divorce decreases as age at marriage increases, this buffering effect lessens as age at marriage increases (DeMaris & Rao). This is not surprising, as 1 year during the teens represents a greater increase in maturity than does 1 year during a person's 20s or 30s. Age at marriage appears to be similar among African American and Caucasian couples (Orbuch et al., 2002), but it is lower among offspring of divorced parents (Amato, 1996; Keith & Finlay, 1988). Age heterogamy is also associated with divorce, as couples in which the husband is 3 or more years older than his wife are at an increased risk for divorce (Tzeng, 1992). This effect was not found for older wife–younger husband marriages or age–homogenous couples.

In regard to the mechanisms that link early marriage to divorce, it has been argued that individuals marrying at a young age may be less compatible with one another, less prepared for marriage, and lack economic resources (Booth & Edwards, 1985). Specific problem behaviors may also account for the link between age at marriage and divorce. Amato and Rogers (1997) found that marrying at a later age was associated with a decline in problems that were due to infidelity, jealousy, and use of alcohol or drugs—behaviors that have been shown to predict divorce. Interestingly, subjective accounts of divorce also tend to vary according to age at marriage. Individuals who married at older ages were more likely to cite incompatibility and a lack of a sense of family as causes of divorce (Amato & Previti, 2003; Kitson, 1992). Those who married young tended to blame marrying young, growing apart, and going out too much with friends. Drinking has been cited by those who married young (Amato & Previti, 2003), as well as by those who married at an older age (Kitson, 1992).

Education

Orbuch et al. (2002) found that level of education predicted divorce for African American and Caucasian wives, and Caucasian husbands; divorce risk decreased with greater education. No association between education and divorce was found among African American husbands. These findings held even after the researchers controlled for interaction variables such as affirmation (making one's spouse feel important) and conflict. Similarly, Bumpass et al. (1991) found that rates of divorce were lower among highly educated women, even after age at marriage was controlled for. Kurdek (1993) also found that low levels of education for either spouse predicted divorce within the first 4 years of marriage. In contrast, Kposowa (1998) found that greater levels of education among wives predicted a higher likelihood of divorce. Rather than considering education in absolute terms, we find that it is also important to examine educational heterogamy within couples. Rates of divorce are lower if the husband is in a higher educational category than his wife than they are among couples of the same educational status (Bumpass et al.; Heaton, 2002), and they are highest if the wife is in a higher educational category than her husband.

Few mechanisms have been proposed to account for the relationship between education and divorce. However, Amato and Rogers (1997) found that lower levels of education were associated with an increase in reported problems caused by jealousy and drinking or drug use, behaviors that are also predictive of divorce. In regard to subjective accounts, individuals with higher levels of education are more likely to cite incompatibility as the cause of divorce (Amato & Previti, 2003). It is also important to note that education tends to serve as a proxy for other sociodemographic variables, such as income, premarital birth, parental divorce, and cohabitation (Orbuch et al., 2002).

Length of Marriage

The risk of divorce appears to decrease as length of marriage increases (Fergusson, Horwood, & Shannon, 1984; Thornton & Rodgers, 1987). Many studies have focused on the newlywed years, as the risk of divorce appears to be greatest during the first 3 years of marriage and over one third of divorces occur within the first 5 years (National Center for Health Statistics, 1991). Becker (1991) has suggested that divorces early in marriage are predicted by changes in how one views one's partner, which are often the result of gaining negative information about the spouse after marriage. Divorces later in marriage, however, are the result of changes and life events that have affected the relationship. Indeed, individuals who divorce after long-term marriages tend to blame infidelity, growing apart, and problems with family cohesiveness (Amato & Previti, 2003; Kitson, 1992), whereas those in short-term marriages cite personality clashes and basic incompatibility.

Remarriage

The likelihood of divorce is significantly higher in second marriages than it is in first marriages (Amato, 1996). This trend is more extreme among African American women, women younger than 25 at the time of remarriage, and women from separated or divorced families (Bramlett & Mosher, 2002). Martin and Bumpass (1989) found that the risk of divorce was 25% higher in second marriages than first marriages, and they argued that individuals who remarry bring with them the same intrapersonal and interpersonal variables that led to divorce in their first marriage. However, White and Booth (1985) contended that second marriages are less successful because they generally present more complex family dynamics than first marriages.

Parental Divorce

The risk of divorce is elevated among individuals whose parents divorced or separated (Amato, 1996; Bumpass et al., 1991; Keith & Finlay, 1988; Pope & Mueller, 1976). Although African Americans are more likely than Caucasians to come from divorced or separated families of origin (Orbuch et al., 2002), Pope and Mueller found a weaker association between parental and offspring divorce among African Americans. There have been conflicting findings regarding sex differences in the effect of parental divorce, as Amato (1996) and Teachman (2002) found significant associations between parental and offspring divorce among wives but not husbands. However, other studies have found that rates of divorce were especially high among couples in which the husband came from a separated or divorced family but the wife did not (Bumpass et al., 1991). Similarly, DeMaris and Rao (1992) found that coming from an intact family was a protective factor for men, but not for women. Regardless, this effect of parental divorce on offspring appears to be additive, as Amato (1996) found that the risk of divorce was even greater when both spouses came from divorced families than when only one spouse did. In addition, the deleterious effects of parental divorce on marital stability may be most potent for children who are young at the time of divorce. Amato (1996) found that parental divorce occurring when children are under the age of 12 was associated with a 60% increase in the probability of divorce, as opposed to a 23% increase for children aged 13–19 years. Offspring over the age of 20 when their parents divorced actually showed a 20% decrease in the risk of divorce.

Several mechanisms for this association have been posited, with age at marriage and premarital cohabitation accounting for much of the variance (Amato, 1996; Bumpass et al., 1991). However, Amato found that problematic interpersonal behavior was the strongest mediator of the association between parental and offspring divorce. These behaviors ranged from being easily angered and jealous, to being critical, or not being home enough. Amato and Rogers (1997) replicated these findings, showing that parental divorce was associated with an increase in problems among offspring that were due to jealousy, moodiness, infidelity, irritating habits, the spending of money foolishly, and alcohol or drug use. Interestingly, after parental divorce, closeness to one's in-laws may serve as a protective buffer against offspring divorce. Timmer and Veroff (2000) found that, when wives came from a divorced family, increased closeness with the husband's family was associated with a lower likelihood of divorce.

Religiosity

Low religious participation and religious heterogamy are also associated with a greater risk of marital dissolution (Bramlett & Mosher, 2002; Bumpass et al., 1991; Heaton, 2002; Thomas & Cornwall, 1990). In regard to mechanisms for this association, problem behaviors within the context of marriage may account for the relationship between religiosity and divorce. Amato and Rogers (1997) found that lower church attendance was associated with an increased likelihood of reporting problems stemming from jealousy, moodiness, infidelity, irritating habits, the spending of money, and alcohol or drug use. In terms of subjective accounts of divorce, Amato and Previti (2003) found that more religious individuals were more likely to cite infidelity as a cause of divorce, and they were less likely to blame incompatibility. Amato and Previti stressed that this does not indicate that religious individuals are more likely to experience infidelity; rather, it may demonstrate that highly religious individuals divorce only under extreme conditions.

INDIVIDUAL DIFFERENCE FACTORS

Personality

Approximately 30% to 42% of the heritability of divorce risk stems from genetic factors affecting personality (Jockin, McGue, & Lykken, 1996). Personality issues are also commonly cited by divorced individuals as being causally linked to separation or divorce. Amato and Previti (2003) found that personality problems were the fifth most commonly blamed causes of divorce, and they were cited by approximately 10% of divorced individuals.

Among the personality variables that have been considered as predictors of divorce and relationship dissolution, *neuroticism* (a generalized tendency to experience negative affect, such as fear, sadness, embarrassment, anger, and guilt) has gained the strongest empirical support (Karney & Bradbury, 1995). Higher levels of neuroticism have been consistently linked to elevated rates of divorce. The impressive longitudinal study by Kelly and Conley (1987) that followed 300 couples over nearly 50 years demonstrated that neuroticism at the start of the study was associated with subsequent divorce. Kurdek (1993) replicated these findings in a 5-year longitudinal study, as did Jockin et al. (1996) in their genetic analysis of factors affecting divorce risk. These findings are strengthened by the fact that measurements of neuroticism taken during adolescence are predictive of women's divorce at age 32 (Kiernan, 1986). In addition, Kurdek (1992) found that these results generalized to cohabiting homosexual couples, as partners who separated reported higher levels of negative affect before the separation than did partners who stayed together.

However, some researchers, such as Bentler and Newcomb (1978), have failed to find an association between neuroticism and divorce in longitudinal studies of marital stability. Similarly, in a 4-year longitudinal study, Karney and Bradbury (1997) found that, although neuroticism was associated with initial levels of marital satisfaction, it was not related to marital dissolution or trajectories of marital satisfaction. Other researchers have also found that neuroticism is associated with marital dissatisfaction (Kelly & Conley, 1987; Terman & Oden, 1947), suggesting that neuroticism may not be uniquely linked to divorce after marital happiness is controlled for. Alternatively, neurotic individuals may be difficult to live with or may easily give up on marriage (Kurdek, 1993).

Low levels of *agreeableness* (the tendency to be altruistic, trusting, soft-hearted, sympathetic, warm, and generous) and high levels of *extraversion* (the tendency to be upbeat, energetic, assertive, active, talkative, and friendly) have also been considered as predictors of divorce and relationship dissolution. Kelly and Conley (1987) found weak associations between these personality variables and marital dissolution, whereas Bentler and Newcomb (1978) found that high extraversion predicted divorce for husbands only. Jockin et al. (1996) found that a positive emotionality factor (corresponding with extraversion) was predictive of marital dissolution for both men and women. However, other studies have failed to find a significant relationship between agreeableness, extraversion, openness, and divorce (Kurdek, 1993). *Conscientiousness* (the tendency to be efficient, thorough, resourceful, organized, ambitious, industrious, and enterprising) has also received some attention as a potential predictor of marital dissolution; Kurdek (1993) found that wives' lack of conscientiousness was associated with elevated levels of divorce.

Although these personality variables represent enduring characteristics, it has been argued that they exert different effects on a marriage at varying time points (Tucker, Kressin, Spiro, & Ruscio, 1998). Although not formally tested, the data from Kelly and Conley (1987) suggest that divorces within 20 years after engagement were predicted by husbands' impulsiveness and both husbands' and wives' neuroticism. Divorces after more than 20 years from engagement were predicted by husbands' neuroticism and extraversion. In a prospective investigation, Tucker et al. found that certain aspects of neuroticism and disagreeableness were related to the timing of divorce. Specifically, individuals high in anxiety and anger were at higher risk for earlier divorce (within the first 20 years of marriage) than later divorce. Similarly, spouses rated lower on conscientiousness were at risk for earlier divorce, though this was only marginally significant after age at marriage and education were controlled for. However, it is interesting to note that, although the other aspects of neuroticism (inadequacy and sensitivity) were associated with a higher risk of divorce, they were unrelated to the timing of divorce. Tucker et al. concluded that characteristics associated with disagreeableness and impulsivity or conscientiousness are risk factors for early divorce, whereas characteristics associated with neuroticism are risk factors for both early and late divorce.

Psychopathology

There is ample evidence of a cross-sectional association between psychiatric disorders and rates of divorce or relationship dissolution (Frank & Gertler, 1991; Thompson & Bland, 1995; Williams, Takeuchi, & Adair, 1992). However, two causal pathways are practicable, as psychopathology may be the cause or the result of divorce. Thus, longitudinal research is necessary to explore this association. There is emerging evidence supporting a causal link between individual psychopathology and elevated risk of divorce. Kessler, Walters, and Forthofer (1998) found that individuals reporting the onset of one or more psychiatric disorders before or during the course of marriage were more likely to divorce than individuals without any psychopathology. All psychiatric disorders, with the exception of social phobia and simple phobia, were associated with increased odds of divorce during the first marriage. Mania was associated with the greatest risk of marital dissolution for both men and women. Anxiety disorders showed the highest chance of divorce among men, followed by mood disorders and substance use disorders. Among women, substance use disorders were associated with the greatest risk of dissolution, followed by mood disorders and anxiety disorders. Generalized anxiety disorder, in particular, is associated with a higher risk of divorce in women's first and second marriages (Bramlett & Mosher, 2002). For both sexes, the chance of divorce increased according to the number of disorders endorsed. Alcohol and drug use have also been cited as a cause of divorce in subjective accounts of divorced individuals. Amato and Previti (2003) found that alcohol or drug use was the third most common cause reported by divorced individuals.

Thinking About Divorce

Although thinking about divorce is more common than actually getting a divorce (Kitson, 1992), it is arguably a necessary (though not sufficient) precursor to relationship dissolution. Thoughts of divorce may be triggered by marital dissatisfaction, incompatibility, or sexual problems, among others (Orbuch et al., 1999). Not surprisingly, many of the sociodemographic and process factors that predict divorce also predict thinking about divorce, suggesting that these thoughts may mediate divorce-related behaviors (e.g., contacting an attorney). Broman (2002) found that African Americans, younger individuals, parents, and those with lower marital satisfaction were significantly more likely to think of divorcing their spouse. Thoughts of divorce were indeed linked to actually getting a divorce; individuals who thought of divorcing their spouse at Time 1 were 2.46 times more likely be divorced 3 years later (Time 2); however, 90% of those who originally thought of divorce remained married at Time 2. Ethnicity moderated the association between thoughts of divorce and actual divorce, as thinking of divorce increased the odds of actual divorce for Caucasians but not for African Americans.

Self-Monitoring

There is emerging evidence to suggest that the degree to which one self-monitors is related to the likelihood of divorce. Self-monitoring, defined as the ability and motivation to modulate self-presentation (Snyder, 1974, 1987), is associated with divorce history; Leone and Hall (2003) found that the majority of married persons who reported at least one divorce were high self-monitors (70%; vs. 30% low self-monitors), whereas the majority of those who had never divorced were low self-monitors (63%; vs. 37% high self-monitors). Marital satisfaction and marital commitment are potential mediators of this association, as maritally satisfied spouses tend to be low self-monitors (Leone & Hall), and low self-monitors are more committed and less likely to seek out alternative relationship partners (Jones, 1993; Snyder & Simpson,

1984). However, additional research will be necessary to pinpoint the mechanism that links self-monitoring to relationship dissolution.

RELATIONSHIP–PROCESS VARIABLES

In addition to exploring the association between intrapersonal variables and divorce or dissolution, it is also important to discuss interpersonal or relationship-level factors, as these variables are considered to be more proximal to relationship outcomes (e.g., Amato & Rogers, 1997). Marital satisfaction, relational dependence, marital violence, and marital interaction are four areas most commonly related to divorce, and they are discussed in the following section. Although infidelity is one of the strongest predictors of divorce, we do not discuss it here; instead we refer readers to chapter 8, where the link between infidelity and relationship dissolution is explored in detail.

Marital Satisfaction

At first glance, the impact of marital satisfaction on dissolution appears straightforward; there is a well-documented positive relationship between marital satisfaction and marital stability (Gager & Sanchez, 2003; Karney & Bradbury, 1995; Kurdek, 1993; White & Booth, 1991). However, Broman (2002) found that marital satisfaction predicted divorce among Caucasians, but not African Americans. Interestingly, when spouses disagree about marital happiness, only marriages in which the husband is unhappier than his wife are at an increased risk of divorce (Gager & Sanchez, 2003). When wives are unhappier than their husbands, the risk of divorce is the same as when both spouses are happy. In Western cultures, happiness and satisfaction are integral to relationships and are thought to guide decisions regarding their future. Nevertheless, the association between satisfaction and stability is influenced by a variety of factors.

For example, the influence of satisfaction on the likelihood of dissolution has been found to be a function of the duration of the marriage, with more marital unhappiness being necessary for a marriage of a longer duration to end in divorce than a marriage of shorter duration (White & Booth, 1991). This is thought to reflect the higher barriers and lower levels of alternatives characteristic of long-lasting marriages, which make abandoning the relationship more difficult. In contrast, in newer relationships the barriers to leaving are lower and there is likely to be a greater number of attractive alternatives, which allows for a lower level of marital dissatisfaction to lead to dissolution.

Additional attempts to reach a greater understanding of the satisfaction–dissolution association have focused on unhappy but stable marriages. For example, Davila and Bradbury (2001) examined individual differences in attachment style and found that individuals concerned with abandonment and love worthiness were more likely to remain in unhappy marriages. As the authors note, this demonstrates a situation in which something other than satisfaction, namely insecurity, is contributing to marital stability. An additional investigation of stable, unhappy marriages found that the frequency with which individuals remain in unhappy relationships is low (Heaton & Albrecht, 1991), most likely because of the increasing adoption of a hedonistic view of marriage in Western culture. However, for these individuals, a number of variables were found to influence the relationship between happiness and stability, including duration of marriage, attitudes and beliefs surrounding marriage, and feelings of self-control. In sum, there is a strong link between satisfaction and dissolution, yet this relationship may be attenuated by an assortment of factors.

Relationship Interdependence and Dependence

Consistent with interdependence and social exchange theories, Rusbult (1983) found that partners in dating couples that separated reported lower levels of satisfaction, lower levels of investment, and a greater number of gratifying alternatives to the current relationship than did partners in couples that remained together. Kurdek (1992) replicated these findings with cohabiting gay and lesbian couples. In a study of married couples, Kurdek (1993) inferred interdependence from marital satisfaction, faith in the marriage, value placed on autonomy and attachment, and motives for being in the relationship. Husbands who were externally motivated to be in the marriage and wives who had few intrinsic motives were most at risk for divorce within the first 4 years of marriage. In addition, couples with discrepancies in terms of marital interdependence demonstrated elevated levels of divorce, and declines in marital interdependence were associated with divorce.

In an extension of interdependence theory, a dependence model of breakups posits that, even when relationship satisfaction is low, individuals may remain in these relationships if their needs cannot be satisfied elsewhere (Drigotas & Rusbult, 1992). Using a longitudinal examination of dating relationships, Drigotas and Rusbult showed that individuals who reported one or more alternative relationships in which to satisfy their needs were more likely to break up than those who were dependent on the current relationship for need fulfillment.

Marital Aggression

The startling prevalence of marital violence is well documented and appears to be more commonplace than previously believed. Straus, Gelles, and Steinmetz (1980) reported that the lifetime prevalence for marital aggression is 30%, with 15% of married couples reporting aggression in the previous year. Both age and income have a negative correlation with marital aggression; younger people and those with lower socioeconomic status are most likely to report marital violence (Straus et al.). However, as reported by Rosenbaum and O'Leary (1981), marital discord proves to be the variable with which marital aggression shows the strongest correlation.

Given the prevalence of marital aggression and its strong association with marital discord, a number of studies have examined the longitudinal impact of violence. Great attention is given to newlywed individuals, as these couples are characterized by higher levels of aggression (Suitor, Pillemer, & Straus, 1990) and they enable researchers to examine spousal aggression in its earliest phases. O'Leary et al. (1989) reported that individuals in relationships with stable levels of aggression showed significant decreases in marital satisfaction across a 30-month period. Quigley and Leonard (1996) examined the impact of aggression across 3 years and found that husband-to-wife aggression predicted decreases in wives' marital satisfaction. Given the strong association between marital quality and divorce risk (White & Booth, 1991), findings such as these lend support to the conclusion that marital aggression is a significant predictor of future divorce. Indeed, DeMaris (2000) found that male violence predicted separation or divorce; however, this effect was mediated by relationship quality.

Studies that directly examined the relationship between aggression and divorce have found that physically aggressive couples were more likely to end their marriage in separation or divorce than nonaggressive couples (Lawrence & Bradbury, 2001) and premarital aggression was predictive of wives' future steps toward dissolution (Heyman, O'Leary, & Jouriles, 1995). Rogge and Bradury (1999) also confirmed the relation between aggression and marital dissolution with their finding that, although dissatisfaction may be predicted by negative communication, the presence of marital violence foreshadows the occurrence of separation or divorce within the first 4 years of marriage. This finding suggests that the presence of aggression is associated with the rapid deterioration of the marital relationship. In short, the association between marital aggression and dissolution has received substantial support.

It is important that many individuals involved in abusive relationships fail to perceive themselves as maritally discordant and are likely to downplay the aggression (O'Leary et al., 1989). These findings have critical practical implications, as they suggest that partners at high risk of divorce as a result of aggression are likely to downplay the violence or make excuses, which may make them less likely to seek treatment for the problematic behavior. This highlights the importance of prevention programs that attempt to reach individuals and make them aware of the detrimental effects of violence, with the primary goal of preventing aggression.

Marital Interaction

Although marital research originated in the 1930s with the use of self-report and interview methods, it was not until the 1970s that researchers began to focus on marital interaction (for a historical account, see Fincham & Bradbury, 1990). Not surprisingly, spending time together is associated with lower levels of marital dissolution (Hill, 1988), but researchers have moved beyond merely studying the quantity of interaction to consider the quality of the interactions. This typically involves inviting participants into the laboratory, where they are asked to discuss a given topic, which may range from a source of conflict in their marriage to the events of the day to a pleasant topic. From these interactions, it has been repeatedly demonstrated that unhappy marriages exhibit greater levels of negativity and, to a lesser degree, lower levels of positivity (Matthews, Wickrama, & Conger, 1996).

A number of longitudinal investigations have demonstrated an association between marital interaction and dissolution. For example, in a 4-year longitudinal study of couples, Gottman and Levenson (1992) used the Rapid Couples Interaction Scoring System to classify couples as regulated or nonregulated on the basis of a conversation surrounding a marital problem. They used positive codes, such as positive problem description and humor, in addition to negative codes, such as complaining and criticizing, to classify speakers. Regulated couples were characterized by a larger ratio of positive to negative behaviors for both partners, whereas nonregulated couples had at least one spouse with a larger ratio of negative to positive behaviors. Nonregulated couples were more defensive, conflict engaging, stubborn, angry, whiny, and more likely to withdraw, in addition to being less affectionate, interested, and joyful. Importantly, nonregulated couples were more likely to consider dissolution, experience separation, or divorce than couples characterized as regulated. Therefore, couples in which the ratio of positive to negative behaviors is greater than unity are likely to experience stability, whereas dissolution appears to be predicted by equal or greater levels of negative as compared with positive behaviors. Similarly, among gay and lesbian couples, negative affect during conflict and lack of positive affect during an events-of-the-day discussion were associated with separation (Gottman et al., 2003). However, the association between affect and divorce may also vary depending on the length of the marriage. Gottman and Levenson (2000) found that negative affect during marital conflict predicted early divorce (within the first 7 years of marriage), but not later divorce (between the 7th and 14th year of marriage). However, a lack of positive affect during such conflict and during an events-of-the-day discussion was predictive of late but not early divorce.

Matthews et al. (1996) also investigated interaction as a predictor of divorce in well-established marriages (length, $M = 18$ years). They classified couples in relation to their levels of hostility and warmth. Hostility consisted of things such as rejecting behavior, insensitivity, and stubbornness, whereas examples of warmth included cooperation and enjoyment.

These researchers found that greater hostility and less warmth were associated with marital instability both directly and also indirectly by influencing partner perceptions of hostility.

Recently, in a longitudinal investigation of 130 newlywed couples, Gottman, Coan, Carrere, and Swanson (1998) elaborated on the finding that the balance of negative to positive behavior is associated with marital dissolution. They found that anger did not predict divorce, but that the combination of other high-intensity negative affects did, including belligerence, defensiveness, and contempt. Briefly, belligerence is an attempt to provoke a response by starting a fight or getting a rise out of one's partner, whereas defensiveness is characterized by portraying oneself as an innocent victim and claiming to be blameless. Finally, contempt involves things such as insult, mockery, judgment, and disapproval toward one's partner. Therefore, it appears that a combination of these negative behaviors proves to be detrimental to marital stability. However, the results of this study should be interpreted with caution, as various methodological and conceptual concerns have been raised about it, including the nonrandom selection of participants and the use of correlational data to draw causal conclusions (Stanley, Bradbury, & Markman, 2000).

In order to more fully understand the relationships among these variables, Gottman (1994) tested alternative models and found that divorce is predicted by a model in which contempt of the wife leads to defensiveness of both spouses, which leads to divorce. Marital dissolution may also be predicted by the low-intensity negative affect of wives. This low-intensity affect is a sum of whining, anger, sadness, domineering, disgust, fear, and stonewalling (which refers to a listener who is not providing the appropriate cues to the speaker that he or she is listening; Gottman & Krokoff, 1989). These results suggest that, even though negative affect (anger) may be associated with concurrent marital satisfaction (Gottman & Krokoff), this does not imply a longitudinal road to dissolution. Again, however, this finding has proved controversial, and it is widely accepted that the relation between current negative interaction in marriage and its future course is far more complex than the picture offered by Gottman (for a detailed discussion, see Fincham & Beach, 1999).

Additional investigations have focused on sequences of interaction, particularly the demand–withdraw pattern. This pattern occurs when one partner (the demander) nags or makes demands of the partner (the withdrawer), who avoids the situation and becomes defensive (Eldridge & Christensen, 2002). This pattern is related to concurrent marital dissatisfaction (Eldridge & Christensen) and to future levels of marital satisfaction. Specifically, the wife demand–husband withdraw pattern has been consistently linked with declines in marital satisfaction (Kurdek, 1995; Levenson & Gottman, 1985). Interestingly, it appears that the effects of this conflict resolution style may be moderated by the context of the withdrawal. For example, Smith, Vivian, and O'Leary (1991) found that premarital withdrawal in particular was associated with future decreases in marital satisfaction. Of interest is the finding that if the withdrawal occurred in the context of high levels of positivity, longitudinal marital satisfaction actually increased. Finally, Heavey, Christensen, and Malamuth (1995) showed that this pattern varies according to which partner's problem issue is discussed; when discussing an issue identified by the husband, there were no systematic differences in the roles taken by each spouse, but when discussing the wife's issue, women were much more likely to be demanding and men more likely to be withdrawing than the reverse. These studies highlight the longitudinal impact of patterns of interaction such as demand–withdraw in addition to the importance of the context in which these behaviors occur.

Research is also moving beyond the study of conflict and negative behavior (Fincham, 2003). For example, among married individuals the spouse is being shown to be a significant and valuable source of social support (Beach, Martin, Blum, & Roman, 1993) and that social support is influential in maintaining relationships (Barbee, 1990). Therefore, it is reasonable to expect that the way spouses lend social support to one another is also indicative of future marital stability. Pasch and Bradbury (1998) examined newlyweds while interacting in both a marital conflict and social support task. They found that, when wives displayed less positive behaviors and more negative behaviors while providing support to their partner, their relationship was more likely to be distressed in the future. In addition, wives' use of increased negativity in soliciting support was also predictive of relationship distress. Both findings remained even when conflict behavior was statistically controlled. This study highlights the importance of examining behavior other than marital conflict, such as social support, in order to more accurately predict marital outcome and understand the processes underlying marital success or failure.

IMPLICATIONS FOR PREVENTION

Identifying variables that impact marital stability presents psychologists with the opportunity to target for preventive interventions those populations of individuals who are at increased risk for marital dissolution. The importance of identifying such risk samples should not be underestimated, as recent investigations suggest that there is selection bias in prevention programs in that couples studied appear to be at no greater risk for dissolution than control couples within the community (Sullivan & Bradbury, 1996). Therefore, the variables identified earlier may prove useful in reaching the high-risk populations truly in need of prevention services.

In relation to prevention, a much-needed emphasis has been placed on designing prevention programs in collaboration with investigations of the longitudinal course of marital dissolution. One well-known example of this is evident in the Prevention and Relationship Enhancement Program (PREP). Markman (1981) identified premarital communication as one of the strongest predictors of future marital distress. This finding, in addition to others that highlight destructive interaction patterns, has laid the foundation for the goals and strategies of PREP. One of the most intensive focuses of the program lies in helping couples to first identify negative patterns of interaction, followed by communication skills training designed to reduce these detrimental behaviors. A number of strategies have been implemented as a way of improving conflict management, including the speaker–listener technique and time-outs. Briefly, in the speaker–listener technique, one person is designated as having the "floor," which clearly identifies the speaker and the listener. The speaker and listener are then expected to follow a set of rules that have been identified for their particular role. A time-out involves using a predetermined method of ending early communication or interaction styles that are harmful to the relationship (Stanley, Blumberg, & Markman, 1999).

Interestingly, not only do the underlying goals of PREP recognize the impact of detrimental communication to marital stability, the specific strategies endorsed also allow the prevention to be tailored to specific patterns of negative interaction. For example, Gottman et al. (1998) found that belligerence, contempt, and defensiveness lead to marital instability. Therefore, a couple that exhibits these behaviors could use the rules of the speaker–listener technique to address, and it is hoped, reduce this negativity. As noted earlier, the ratio of positive to negative behaviors predicts marital dissolution. In an effort to prevent negative behaviors from increasing in frequency, a time-out may be useful. Therefore, it appears that both the principles and practices of PREP have been successful at integrating empirical findings regarding marital dissolution with a practical prevention for couples.

PREP is just one example of a prevention program that has taken into consideration the variables that are likely to impact marital stability. This program and others like it represent a strong commitment to integrating research and practice. However, as noted by Kelly and Fincham (1999), areas such as personality characteristics and positive interaction have been identified as predictors of marital quality and stability (Karney & Bradbury, 1995; Pasch & Bradbury, 1998), yet they have been greatly overlooked in the area of prevention. Therefore, it appears that although prevention programs have been successful at incorporating specific predictors of marital dissolution into their underlying structure (e.g., the skills needed for conflict resolution), there are essential variables that have been neglected. In addition, although Stanley et al. (2000) support the use of basic science to inform couple interventions, they raise valid concerns about linking these two areas without ensuring the methodological and conceptual integrity of the basic research. The success of prevention programs is likely to increase as more factors are recognized as targets of prevention.

The previous discussion highlights the importance of allowing empirical findings to guide the future of marital prevention programs. However, it is also important to entertain the likely possibility that experiences with prevention may be useful in determining future research directions. For example, as previously alluded to, there is a strong likelihood that couples presenting for prevention programs are not at an increased risk for marital dissolution. It is possible to use various demographic variables such as age at marriage, race, and education to target populations at an elevated risk for dissolution. However, using demographic variables in this fashion is only successful to the extent that we understand the mechanisms underlying their relationship to increased marital dissolution. For example, recall that Amato (1996) examined the mechanisms underlying the association between parental divorce and future marital discord. He found that this relationship was mediated largely through the interpersonal behavior of offspring, such as communication difficulties, inability to trust, and coping with jealous emotions. Therefore, practitioners are in a position to first target a population at increased risk for marital dissolution— but this is only a first step. The second step is to build on mediational research like that presented herein. Such research allows the prevention program applied to this at-risk population to target specific interpersonal behaviors that have been identified as the underlying mechanism for the intergenerational transmission of divorce. This is just one example of the way in which a better understanding of the precise mechanisms leading to divorce can be beneficial in devising prevention programs. As research in this area develops, it will prove fruitful in both targeting specific populations and the appropriate mediating variables.

It appears that, although prevention programs have made significant advances in the integration of empirical findings, there are a number of challenging obstacles that must be overcome before we can be certain that the appropriate populations and behaviors are the target of prevention. For example, the potential emotional-state dependence of skills training is a limitation of skills-based prevention programs. This limitation was aptly captured by Wile (1993) when he stated "It is impossible to make I-statements when you are in the 'hating my partner, wanting revenge, feeling stung and wanting to sting back' state of mind" (p. 2). Fincham and Beach (1999) therefore focus on the "emergent" goals that characterize couples locked in destructive interactions. They note that, during destructive interactions, couples commonly switch from the cooperative goals they profess and believe most of the time to emergent goals that are adversarial in nature. For example, rather than focus on generating a solution to the problem at hand, partners locked in the destructive pattern of escalation may find themselves focused on defeating their partner—or at least not losing the argument to their partner. This sets the stage for couples to engage in negative behaviors even when they "know better." In other words, even well-learned relationship skills may fail when emergent goals change the focus of couple interaction from collaboration to competition.

The goal analytic approach of Fincham and Beach (1999) suggests that skills-based prevention alone is not a complete answer to marital breakdown and cannot provide couples with a sufficient basis for long-term marital satisfaction. Rather, the area of prevention is in need of an intervention that can modify problematic "emergent" goals and an important task is to develop and evaluate a goal-based prevention program.

FUTURE DIRECTIONS

In this section, we offer several recommendations to guide future research.

Depth Rather Than Breadth: Toward an Integrative Model of the Prediction of Divorce and Relationship Dissolution

Given that nearly 200 variables have been examined in longitudinal studies of marriage (Karney & Bradbury, 1995), it is not surprising that the literature on predictors of divorce and relationship dissolution is a vast and messy body of research. The result is that it has been nearly impossible to synthesize this research into a single model of divorce and relationship dissolution. In sacrificing depth for breadth, researchers have discovered many predictors of union disruption, but few mechanisms to account for these associations. A first step in integrating existing research and exploring mechanisms is to define the relationship between intrapersonal (sociodemographic and individual difference) variables and relationship–process variables.

Orbuch and colleagues (Orbuch et al., 2002) have argued that there are three possible ways in which these factors may be interrelated in the prediction of divorce and relationship dissolution. First, demographic–individual difference factors and relationship–process factors may independently predict relationship dissolution. Alternatively, relationship–process variables may mediate the association between demographic factors and divorce. This viewpoint has been supported by numerous researchers (e.g., Kelly & Conley, 1987), who suggest that intrapersonal variables affect marital stability through interpersonal processes. Broman (2002) agreed, concluding that demographic variables answer the question of "who gets divorced?" and process variables address "why do people get divorced?" However, a third possibility is that sociodemographic variables may serve as the context within which interactional processes occur and may moderate the relationship between process variables and divorce. This idea has also gained empirical support, as the associations between marital conflict and divorce appear to vary by gender and race (Orbuch et al.). It is improbable that any one of these three options accurately captures the relationship between intrapersonal and interpersonal variables in predicting divorce or dissolution. Rather, the nature of these associations likely varies depending on the specific variables being considered. Thus, it is imperative that researchers begin to consider both demographic and process variables within single studies. Gottman et al. (1998) are perhaps in the best position to explore this relation, yet they have failed to provide any data or analyses regarding the association between intrapersonal variables, interpersonal processes, and separation or divorce (see Stanley et al., 2000, for a discussion).

To expedite the integration of intrapersonal and interpersonal variables into a cohesive model of relationship dissolution, psychologists and sociologists must join forces and assimilate their knowledge. In reviewing the literature, we found it striking to see how few citations there were of sociological research in the psychological literature. Given the history of marital research in the field of sociology, and the fact that marriage is a social institution, it is simply irresponsible for psychologists to continue to ignore the field of family sociology. Whereas sociologists have long focused on demographic predictors of divorce, psychologists have tended to view demographic variables as nuisance factors that have to be controlled (Kurdek, 1993). In addition, the most informative studies that examined intrapersonal and interpersonal predictors of divorce have come from sociology.

In one example of such a study, Amato and Rogers (1997) posited that problem behaviors within marriage, such as anger, jealousy, and infidelity, partially mediated the association between sociodemographic–individual difference factors and divorce. They found that infidelity, the spending of money foolishly, alcohol or drug use, and jealousy at baseline were the leading spousal behaviors that predicted divorce during the following 12 years. More importantly, several demographic–individual difference factors were associated with these problem behaviors, thus supporting the idea of mediation. Age at marriage, premarital cohabitation, race, religiosity, education, and parental divorce were all significantly associated with one or more marital problems. Consistent with the criteria for mediation, adding marital problems to the model improved the prediction of divorce, above and beyond the effects of demographic–individual difference variables. However, Orbuch et al. (2002) found that marital interaction processes did not mediate the association between race and education and subsequent divorce. Nevertheless, it is important for the field to begin to build upon these studies that have focused on both intrapersonal and interpersonal variables, in order to improve the prediction of relationship dissolution.

Opposites May Attract, But Do They Stay Together?

According to the partner-discrepancy approach, differences between partners in terms of individual difference factors or levels of interdependence increase the risk of divorce (Kurdek, 1993). Indeed, Bentler and Newcomb (1978) found greater discrepancies in spousal personality traits at engagement among couples that later separated or divorced than among couples that stayed together. As discussed earlier, demographic heterogamy is also associated with elevated levels of divorce, as is heterogamy on relationship variables. Larsen and Olson (1989) assessed interspousal agreement on various relationship issues at the time of engagement, and they found greater discrepancies among couples that went on to separate or divorce than couples that remained married. Gager and Sanchez (2003) found that the association between spousal discrepancies on relationship issues such as happiness and divorce varied by sex. However, aside from this handful of studies, relatively little attention has been devoted to exploring the association between partner similarities or differences and divorce. There is a pressing need for longitudinal research, which can capture growth over time, to compare divorce rates of spouses who become more similar over time with those who become increasing different. This parallels our earlier suggestion of increasing depth rather than breadth, as there are already a number of variables that are robustly linked to divorce. However, it is now important to explore each of these predictors more carefully, including considering differences between spouses in such variables, as spouses from divergent backgrounds may interpret relationship events very differently. However, some have argued that it is not incompatibility that predicts distress or divorce, but rather how a couple handles incompatibility (Markman, Floyd, Stanley, & Storaasli, 1988). Thus, it is important to consider the full array of factors that may mediate the association between spousal heterogamy or homogamy and divorce, remembering that when we examine attitude and personality homogamy it is critical to control initial levels of the variables (Karney & Bradbury, 1995).

Pathways From Distress to Divorce: Why Do Some Unhappy Couples Divorce Whereas Others Do Not?

Perhaps it is not marital satisfaction in an absolute sense that predicts divorce, but, rather, the trajectory of marital satisfaction throughout the course of a relationship. Karney and Bradbury (1997) found that rates of change mediated the association between initial levels of marital satisfaction and divorce, such that dissatisfied individuals reported greater declines in satisfaction and higher rates of divorce than did maritally satisfied individuals. This finding is interesting when examined in light of unhappy stable marriages and may explain this latter phenomenon. It may be that even though these relationships are characterized by dissatisfaction, the course that relationship satisfaction has taken is not a sufficient condition for marital dissolution. This possibility highlights, yet again, the need for depth rather than breadth. Although marital satisfaction is associated with marital dissolution, it is time to expand upon this relationship with longitudinal studies that monitor changes in marital satisfaction. Multifaceted investigations such as these are likely to have important implications for prevention. Current prevention programs justifiably focus on marital satisfaction, but expanding knowledge of the specific trajectories of marital satisfaction that lead to dissolution is essential to improving their success. Therefore, as depth exceeds breadth and the potential mediators of the relation between satisfaction and stability are enhanced, practical as well as theoretical gains will accrue.

Subjective Versus Objective Causes of Divorce

Research on predictors of divorce can be approached from one of two perspectives. The majority of this work has explored intrapersonal and interpersonal variables that are empirically or theoretically associated with marital dissolution. However, predictors of divorce can also be identified from subjective accounts of separated or divorced individuals (Albrecht, Bahr, & Goodman, 1983; Amato & Previti, 2003; Bloom, Niles, & Tatcher, 1985; Cleek & Pearson, 1985; Kitson & Sussman, 1982). This approach has been criticized for many reasons, including an inability to predict divorce (White, 1990), unreliability and retrospective bias (Goode, 1956), and susceptibility to self-serving or self-presentation biases. In addition to these weaknesses, the fallibility of accounts given by dissatisfied marital partners must be taken into consideration. For example, there is a tendency for spouses experiencing dissatisfaction to attribute positive behaviors to variables outside of the person, whereas negative behaviors are attributed to internal characteristics of the spouse (Bradbury & Fincham, 1990). Given the hostility and bitterness that often accompany divorce, it seems unlikely that these attributions may increase in accuracy following separation. Therefore, it is imperative to understand the underlying attributions that may be driving these subjective accounts of the precursors to divorce. On a similar note, a fieldwork investigation by Hopper (2001) suggests that the spouse who initiated the divorce is likely to re-create the marriage as a negative and unhappy experience with an increased focus on problems and failures. Although it is likely that these relationships were characterized by high levels of negativity, it is also a way to justify ending a relationship that was at one time viewed as sacred and held in high esteem (Hopper). Therefore, it is important to take into consideration the justifications people might make for the less than optimal circumstances of their life.

Given these weaknesses, why might both subjective and objective accounts be desirable? Subjective accounts have revealed important information, including the fact that husbands' and wives' self-reported causes for divorce tend to be very different (Amato & Rogers, 1997), and that infidelity, incompatibility, and alcohol or drug use are the most commonly cited causes of divorce (Amato & Previti, 2003). In addition, the utility of this subjective approach is dependent on the purpose of the research. Subjective accounts are invaluable for informing marital interventions designed to prevent or avert divorce. In the therapeutic context, the couple's subjective reality looms large, and it is most proximally related to the risk of divorce. Individuals assign a cause to their marital difficulties, and to their divorce, and this cause becomes the cognitive framework within which they view their circumstances. These accounts for marital difficulties or divorce can also be informative in prevention, as they may help to target at-risk couples. Couples affected by infidelity, incompatibility, and alcohol or drug use are easily identified, and these issues can be the focus of preventive interventions. Similarly, demographic variables that correlate highly with commonly cited causes of divorce might be used to initially identify at-risk couples. This group can then be narrowed on the basis of those experiencing the common problematic behaviors. Such an approach might also make prevention and intervention efforts more relevant to participating couples, as objective predictors of divorce are rarely cited in subjective accounts (White, 1990). Thus, in order to fully understand the divorce process, we must begin to incorporate subjective accounts of marital dissolution (Amato & Previti, 2003).

Fairy Dust and Candy-Colored Clouds: The Role of Marital Expectations and Illusions in Divorce

The association between relationship beliefs and divorce has most commonly been explored in the context of children of divorce, although there is little evidence that these individuals hold dysfunctional beliefs about love and marriage (Sinclair & Nelson, 1998). Furthermore, even though marital interventions consistently focus on challenging dysfunctional relationship beliefs in order to alleviate marital distress (e.g., Epstein & Baucom, 2002), there is little research on relationship beliefs or expectations in the literature on predictors of divorce. Studies that have examined relationship beliefs have found that initial levels of dysfunctional beliefs and increases in the strength of such beliefs over time predict divorce (Kurdek, 1993; Kurdek & Kennedy, 2001).

According to the disillusionment model, marital stability is jeopardized when spouses' views of one another change, love and affection decline, and ambivalence increases (Huston et al.). Huston et al. found support for this model, as couples that divorced showed decreases in love and overt affection, decreases in perceived spousal responsiveness, and increases in ambivalence. Thus, as individuals' expectations of marriage or their spouses are unrealized, the risk of divorce may increase. Similarly, some individuals may enter marriage with unrealistic or idealistic expectations of marriage, and they may opt to divorce after becoming disenchanted. Indeed, positive illusions about marriage are adaptive, as evidenced by their association with marital satisfaction (e.g., Fowers, Lyons, Montel, & Shaked, 2001). Thus, when individuals are not able to maintain these illusions through their own cognitive efforts, the risk of relationship dissolution may increase. The association between dysfunctional relationship–partner beliefs and divorce is one that has only begun to be explored, and it is an important area for future research.

CONCLUSION

This chapter began by presenting the four theoretical orientations (social exchange theory, behavioral theory, crisis theory, and the vulnerability–stress–adaptation model) that have informed most empirical research on the causes of marital discord and dissolution. Following this brief background, sociodemographic and individual differences factors as well as relationship–process variables were presented as they relate to marital satisfaction and stability. The data suggest that African Americans as well as those in the South and West United States, Western countries, and individualistic nations are more likely to experience divorce. It was also concluded that lower income, unemployment, premarital cohabitation or childbirth, marrying young, fewer years of education, length of marriage, remarriage, parental divorce, and low levels of religiosity all predict marital dissolution. Personality variables that were explored as precursors to marital dissolution include high levels of neuroticism or extraversion, low levels of agreeableness, psychopathology, actively thinking about divorce, and self-monitoring. In recognizing that divorce may be attributed to more than the characteristics that individuals bring to the relationship, a variety of relationship variables associated with marital dissolution were identified, including dissatisfaction, aggression, and negative interaction. Finally, we discussed the practical implications of these findings for applied work and emphasized the importance of understanding moderating and mediating relationships, especially for maximizing the success of prevention programs.

We concluded our analysis by identifying numerous challenges that must be addressed to more fully understand precursors to marital success and failure. These include development of an integrative theoretical framework, investigation of the trajectory of marital satisfaction as it may increase our understanding of which dissatisfied couples ultimately divorce, and understanding the role that beliefs and expectations that partners bring to their relationship play in the subsequent evolution of the relationship. In addition, we emphasized the value of obtaining subjective accounts of the possible precursors to divorce from divorcing individuals and the need for research on the expectations one brings to marriage as they may be detrimental to future marital stability. We hope that we have provided an initial cartography of the terrain we need to cover in future marital research as we continue the journey toward uncovering the complex nuances that surround marital dissolution.

REFERENCES

Albrecht, S., Bahr, H., & Goodman, K. (1983). *Divorce and remarriage: Problems, adaptations, and adjustments.* Westport, CT: Greenwood.

Amato, P. R. (1996). Explaining the intergenerational transmission of divorce. *Journal of Marriage and the Family, 58,* 628–640.

Amato, P. R., & Booth, A. (1991). The consequences of divorce for attitudes toward divorce and gender roles. *Journal of Family Issues, 12,* 306–322.

Amato, P. R., & Previti, D. (2003). People's reasons for divorcing: Gender, social class, the life course, and adjustment. *Journal of Family Issues, 24,* 602–626.

Amato, P. R., & Rogers, S. J. (1997). A longitudinal study of marital problems and subsequent divorce. *Journal of Marriage and the Family, 59,* 612–624.

Barbee, A. P. (1990). Interactive coping: The cheering up process in close relationships. In S. Duck (Ed.), *Personal relationships and social support* (pp. 46–65). London: Sage.

Beach, S. R. H., Martin, J. K., Blum, T. C., & Roman, P. M. (1993). Effects of marital and co-worker relationships on negative affect: Testing the central role of marriage. *American Journal of Family Therapy, 21,* 312–322.

Becker, G. S. (1991). *A treatise on the family.* Cambridge, MA: Harvard University Press.

Bennett, N. G., Blanc, A. K., & Bloom, D. E. (1988). Commitment and the modern union: Assessing the link between premarital cohabitation and subsequent marital stability. *American Sociological Review, 53,* 127–138.

Bentler, P. M., & Newcomb, M. D. (1978). Longitudinal study of marital success and failure. *Journal of Consulting and Clinical Psychology, 46,* 1053–1070.

Bloom, B., Hodges, W. F., Caldwell, R. A., Systra, L., & Cedrone, A. R. (1977). Marital separation: A community survey. *Journal of Divorce, 1,* 7–19.

Bloom, B., Niles, R., & Tatcher, A. (1985). Sources of marital dissatisfaction among newly separated persons. *Journal of Family Issues, 6,* 359–373.

Booth, A., & Edwards, J. N. (1985). Age at marriage and marital instability. *Journal of Marriage and the Family, 47,* 67–75.

Booth, A., & Johnson, D. (1988). Premarital cohabitation and marital success. *Journal of Family Issues, 9,* 255–272.

Booth, A., Johnson, D. R., White, L. K., & Edwards, J. N. (1985). Predicting divorce and permanent separation. *Journal of Family Issues, 6,* 331–346.

Bradbury, T. N., & Fincham, F. D. (1990). Attributions in marriage: Review and critique. *Psychological Bulletin, 107,* 3–33.

Bramlett, M. D., & Mosher, W. D. (2002). *Cohabitation, marriage, divorce, and remarriage in the United States.* (Vital and Health Statistics, Series 23, No. 22). Washington, DC: U.S. Government Printing Office.

Broman, C. (2002). Thinking of divorce but staying married: The interplay of race and marital satisfaction. *Journal of Divorce and Remarriage, 37*(1/2), 151–161.

Bumpass, L. L., Martin, T. C., & Sweet, J. A. (1991). The impact of family background and early marital factors on marital disruption. *Journal of Family Issues, 12,* 22–42.

Bumpass, L. L., & Sweet, J. A. (1989). National estimates of cohabitation. *Demography, 26,* 615–625.

Bumpass, L. L., Sweet, J. A., & Cherlin, A. (1989). The role of cohabitation in declining rates of marriage. *Journal of Marriage and the Family, 53,* 913–927.

Castro Martin, T., & Bumpass, L. L. (1989). Recent trends in marital disruption. *Demography, 26,* 37–51.

Cherlin, A. (1922). *Marriage, divorce and re-marriage.* Cambridge, Mass: Harvard University Press.

Cherlin, A. (1998). Marriage and marital dissolution among Black Americans. *Journal of Comparative Family Studies, 29,* 147–158.

Cleek, M., & Pearson, T. (1985). Perceived causes of divorce: An analysis of interrelationships. *Journal of Marriage and the Family, 47,* 179–183.

Cohan, C. L., & Bradbury, T. N. (1997). Negative life events, marit interaction, and the longitudinal course of newlywed marriage. *Journal of Personality and Social Psychology, 73,* 144–128.

Conger, R., Elder, G. H., Jr., Lorenz, F. O., Conger, K. J., Simons, R. L., Whitbeck, L. B., Huck, S., & Melby, J. N. (1990). Linking economic hardship to marital quality and instability. *Journal of Marriage and the Family, 52,* 643–656.

Davila, J., & Bradbury, T. N. (2001). Attachment insecurity and the distinction between unhappy spouses who do and do not divorce. *Journal of Family Psychology, 15,* 371–393.

DeMaris, A. (2000). Till discord do us part: The role of physical and verbal conflict in union disruption. *Journal of Marriage and the Family, 62,* 683–692.

DeMaris, A., & Rao, K. V. (1992). Premarital cohabitation and subsequent marital stability in the United States: A reassessment. *Journal of Marriage and the Family, 54,* 178–190.

DeVaus, D., Qu, L., & Weston, R. (2003, April). *Does premarital cohabitation affect the chances of marriage lasting?* Paper presented at the eighth Australian Institute of Family Studies Conference, Melbourne, Australia.

Devine, D., & Forehand, R. (1996). Cascading toward divorce: The roles of marital and child factors. *Journal of Consulting and Clinical Psychology, 64,* 424–427.

Drigotas, S. M., & Rusbult, C. E. (1992). Should I stay or should I go? A dependence model of breakups. *Journal of Personality and Social Psychology, 62,* 62–87.

Eldridge, K. A., & Christensen, A. (2002). Demand–withdraw communication during couple conflict: A review and analysis. In P. Noller & J.A. Feeney (Eds.), *Understanding marriage* (pp. 289–322). Cambridge, England: Cambridge University Press.

Epstein, N., & Baucom, D. H. (2002). *Enhanced cognitive-behavioral therapy for couples.* Washington, DC: American Psychological Association.

Feng, D., Giarrusso, R., Bengtson, V. L., & Frye, N. (1999). Intergenerational transmission of marital quality and marital instability. *Journal of Marriage and the Family, 61,* 451–463.

Fergusson, D. M., Horwood, L. J., & Shannon, F. T. (1984). A proportional hazards model of family breakdown. *Journal of Marriage and the Family, 46,* 539–549.

Fincham, F. D. (2003). Marital conflict: Correlates, structure and context. *Current Directions in Psychological Science, 12,* 23–27.

Fincham, F. D., & Beach, S. R. (1999). Marital conflict: Implications for working with couples. *Annual Review of Psychology, 50,* 47–77.

Fincham, F. D., & Bradbury, T. N. (1990). Psychology and the study of marriage. In F. D. Fincham & T. N. Bradbury (Eds.), *The psychology of marriage: Basic issues and applications* (pp. 1–12). New York: Guilford.

Fowers, B. J., Lyons, E., Montel, K. H., & Shaked, N. (2001). Positive illusions about marriage among married and single individuals. *Journal of Family Psychology, 15,* 95–109.

Frank, R. G., & Gertler, P. (1991). Mental health and marital stability. *International Journal of Law Psychiatry, 14,* 377–386.

Frisco, M. L., & Williams, K. (2003). Perceived housework equity, marital happiness, and divorce in dual-earner households. *Journal of Family Issues, 24,* 51–73.

Gager, C. T., & Sanchez, L. (2003). Two as one? Couples' perceptions of time spent together, marital quality, and the risk of divorce. *Journal of Family Issues, 24,* 21–50.

Glenn, N. D., & Shelton, B. A. (1985). Regional differences in divorce in the United States. *Journal of Marriage and the Family, 47,* 641–652.

Glick, P. C. (1984). How American families are changing. *American Demographics, 6,* 20–27.

Goode, W. J. (1956). *After divorce*. Glencoe, IL: The Free Press.

Gottman, J. M. (1979). *Marital interaction: Experimental investigations*. New York: Academic Press.

Gottman, J. M. (1994). *What predicts divorce*. Hillsdale, NJ: Lawrence Erlbaum Associates.

Gottman, J. M., Coan, J., Carrere, S., & Swanson, C. (1998). Predicting marital happiness and stability from newlywed interactions. *Journal of Marriage and the Family, 60,* 5–22.

Gottman, J. M., & Krokoff, L. J. (1989). The relationship between marital interaction and satisfaction: A longitudinal view. *Journal of Consulting and Clinical Psychology, 57,* 47–52.

Gottman, J. M., & Levenson, R. W. (1992). Marital processes predictive of later dissolution: Behavior, physiology, and health. *Journal of Personality and Social Psychology, 63,* 221–233.

Gottman, J. M., & Levenson, R. W. (2000). The timing of divorce: Predicting when a couple will divorce over a 14-year period. *Journal of Marriage and the Family, 62,* 737–745.

Gottman, J. M., Levenson, R. W., Gross, J., Frederickson, B. L., McCoy, K., Rosenthal, L., Ruef, A. & Yoshimoto, D. (2003). Correlates of gay and lesbian couples' relationship satisfaction and relationship dissolution. *Journal of Homosexuality, 45,* 23–43.

Greenstein, T. N. (1995). Gender ideology, marital disruption, and the employment of married women. *Journal of Marriage and the Family, 57,* 31–42.

Greenstein, T. N. (1995). Gender ideology and perceptions of the fairness of the division of household labor: Effects on marital quality. *Social Forces, 74,* 1029–1042.

Greenstein, T. N. (1990). Marital disruption and the employment of married women. *Journal of Marriage and the Family, 52,* 657–676.

Heaton, T. B. (2002). Factors contributing to increasing stability in the United States. *Journal of Family Issues, 23,* 392–409.

Heaton, T. B., & Albrecht, S. L. (1991). Stable unhappy marriages. *Journal of Marriage and the Family, 53,* 747–758.

Heaton, T. B., Albrecht, S. L., & Martin, T. K. (1985). The timing of divorce. *Journal of Marriage and the Family, 47,* 631–639.

Heavey, C. L., Christensen, A., & Malamuth, N. M. (1995). The longitudinal impact of demand and withdrawal during marital conflict. *Journal of Consulting and Clinical Psychology, 63,* 797–801.

Heckert, D. A., Nowak, T. C., & Snyder, K. A. (1998). The impact of husbands' and wives' relative earnings on marital disruption. *Journal of Marriage and the Family, 60,* 690–703.

Heyman, R. E., O'Leary, K. D., & Jouriles, E. N. (1995). Alcohol and aggressive personality styles: Potentiators of serious physical aggression against wives. *Journal of Family Psychology, 9,* 44–57.

Hiedemann, B., Suhomlinova, O., & O'Rand, A. M. (1998). Economic independence, economic status, and empty nest in midlife marital disruption. *Journal of Marriage and the Family, 60,* 219–231.

Hill, M. (1988). Marital stability and spouses shared time. *Journal of Family Issues, 9,* 427–451.

Hill, R. (1949). *Families under stress*. New York: Harper.

Hofstede, G. (1980). *Culture's consequences: International differences in work related values*. Beverly Hills, CA: Sage.

Hopper, J. (2001). The symbolic origins of conflict in divorce. *Journal of Marriage and the Family, 63,* 430–455.

Huston, T. L., Caughlin, J. P., Houts, R. M., Smith, S. E., & George, L. J. (2001). The connubial crucible: Newlywed years as predictors of marital delight, distress, and divorce. *Journal of Personality and Social Psychology, 80,* 237–252.

Hutter, M. (1988). *The changing family: Comparative perspectives*. New York: Macmillan.

Jockin, V., McGue, M., & Lykken, D. T. (1996). Personality and divorce: A genetic analysis. *Journal of Personality and Social Psychology, 71,* 288–299.

Jones, M. (1993). Influence of self-monitoring on dating relationships. *Journal of Research in Personality, 27,* 197–206.

Karney, B. R., & Bradbury, T. (1995). The longitudinal course of marital quality and stability: A review of theory, method, and research. *Psychological Bulletin, 118,* 3–34.

Karney, B. R., & Bradbury, T. (1997). Neuroticism, marital interaction, and the trajectory of marital satisfaction. *Journal of Personality and Social Psychology, 72,* 1075–1092.

Keith, V. M., & Finlay, B. (1988). The impact of parental divorce on children's educational attainment, marital timing, and likelihood of divorce. *Journal of Marriage and the Family, 50,* 797–809.

Kelly, E. L., & Conley, J. J. (1987). Personality and compatibility: A prospective analysis of marital stability and marital satisfaction. *Journal of Personality and Social Psychology, 52,* 27–40.

Kelly, A. B., & Fincham, F. D. (1999). Preventing marital distress: What does research offer? In R. Berger & M. T. Hannah (Eds.), *Preventive approaches in couples therapy* (pp. 361–390). Philadelphia: Taylor & Francis.

Kelly, A. B., Fincham, F. D., & Beach, S. R. H. (2003). Emerging perspectives on couple communication. In J. O. Greene & B. R. Burlson (Eds.), *Handbook of communication and social interaction skills* (pp.723–752). NJ: Erlbaum.

Kessler, R. C., Walters, E. E., & Forthofer, M. S. (1998). The social consequences of psychiatric disorders, III: Probability of marital stability. *The American Journal of Psychiatry, 155,* 1092–1096.

Kiernan, K. E. (1986). Teenage marriage and marital breakdown: A longitudinal study. *Population Studies, 40,* 35–54.

Kitson, G. C. (1992). *Portrait of divorce: Adjustment to marital breakdown.* New York: Guilford.

Kitson, G. C., & Sussman, M. (1982). Marital complaints, demographic characteristics, and symptoms of mental distress in divorce. *Journal of Marriage and the Family, 44,* 87–101.

Kposowa, A. J. (1998). The impact of race on divorce in the United States. *Journal of Comparative Family Studies, 29,* 529–548.

Kurdek, L. A. (1992). Relationship stability and relationship satisfaction in cohabiting gay and lesbian couples: A prospective longitudinal test of the contextual and interdependence models. *Journal of Social and Personal Relationships, 9,* 125–142.

Kurdek, L. A. (1993). Predicting marital dissolution: A 5-year prospective longitudinal study of newlywed couples. *Journal of Personality and Social Psychology, 64,* 221–242.

Kurdek, L. A. (1995). Predicting change in marital satisfaction from husbands' and wives' conflict resolution styles. *Journal of Marriage and the Family, 57,* 153–164.

Kurdek, L. C., & Kennedy, C. (2001). Differences between couples who end their marriage by fault or no-fault legal procedures. *Journal of Family Psychology, 15,* 241–253.

Larsen, A. S., & Olson, D. H. (1989). Predicting marital satisfaction using PREPARE: A replication study. *Journal of Marital and Family Therapy, 15,* 311–322.

Lawrence, E., & Bradbury, T. N. (2001). Physical aggression and marital dysfunction: A longitudinal analysis. *Journal of Family Psychology, 15,* 135–154.

Lee, G. R. (1982). *Family structure and interaction: A comparative analysis.* Minneapolis: University of Minnesota Press.

Leone, C., & Hall, I. (2003). Self-monitoring, marital dissatisfaction, and relationship dissolution: Individual differences in orientations to marriage and divorce. *Self and Identity, 2,* 189–202.

Levenson, R. W., & Gottman, J. M. (1985). Physiological and affective predictors of change in marital satisfaction. *Journal of Personality and Social Psychology, 49,* 85–94.

Levinger, G. (1965). Marital cohesiveness and dissolution: An integrative review. *Journal of Marriage and the Family, 27,* 19–28.

Levinger, G. (1979). A social psychological perspective on marital dissolution. In G. Levinger & O. C. Moles (Eds.), *Divorce and separation: Context, causes, and consequences* (pp. 37–60). New York: Basic Books.

Lewis, R. A., & Spanier, G. B. (1982). Marital quality, marital stability, and social exchange. In F. I. Nye (Ed.), *Family relationships: Rewards and costs* (pp. 49–65). Beverly Hills, CA: Sage.

Markman, H. J. (1981). Prediction of marital distress: A five-year follow-up. *Journal of Consulting and Clinical Psychology, 49,* 760–762.

Markman, H. J., Floyd, F. J., Stanley, S. M., & Storaasli, R. D. (1988). Prevention of marital distress: A longitudinal investigation. *Journal of Consulting and Clinical Psychology, 56,* 210–217.

Martin, T. C., & Bumpass, L. L. (1989). Recent trends in marital disruption. *Demography, 26,* 37–51.

Matthews, L. S., Wickrama, K. A. S., & Conger, R. D. (1996). Predicting marital instability from spouse and observer reports of marital interaction. *Journal of Marriage and the Family, 58,* 641–655.

McCubbin, H. I., & Patterson, J. M. (1982). Family adaptation to crises. In H. I. McCubbin, A. E. Cauble, & J. M. Patterson (Eds.), *Family stress, coping and social support* (pp. 26–47). Springfield, IL: Thomas.

McKenry, P. C., & Price, S. J. (1995). Divorce: A comparative perspective. In B. Ingoldsby & S. Smith (Eds.), *Families in multicultural perspective. Perspectives on marriage and the family* (pp. 187–212). New York: Guilford.

Menaghan, E., & Parcel, T. (1990). Parental employment and family life: Research in the 1980s. *Journal of Marriage and the Family, 52,* 1079–1096.

Moore, K., & Waite, L. (1981). Marital dissolution, early motherhood, and early marriage. *Social Forces, 60,* 20–40.

Morgan, S. P., Lye, D., & Condran, G. (1988). Sons, daughters, and the risk of marital disruption. *American Journal of Sociology, 94,* 110–129.

National Center for Health Statistics. (1991). *Advance report of final marriage statistics, 1988* (Monthly Vital Statistics Report, Vol. 39, No. 12, Suppl. 2). Hyattsville, MD: Public Health Service.

O'Leary, K. D., Barling, J., Arios, I., & Rosenbaum, A. (1989). Prevalence and stability of aggression between spouses: A longitudinal analysis. *Journal of Consulting and Clinical Psychology, 57,* 263–268.

Ono, H. (1998). Husbands' and wives' resources and marital dissolution. *Journal of Marriage and the Family, 60,* 674–689.

Orbuch, T. L., Veroff, J., Hassan, H., & Horrocks, J. (2002). Who will divorce: A 14-year longitudinal study of Black and White couples. *Journal of Social and Personal Relationships, 19,* 179–202.

Orbuch, T. L., Veroff, J., & Hunter, A. G. (1999). Black couples, White couples: The early years of marriage. In E. M. Hetherington (Ed.), *Coping with divorce, single parenting, and remarriage* (pp. 23–43). Mahwah, NJ: Lawrence Erlbaum Associates.

Pasch, L. A., & Bradbury, T. N. (1998). Social support, conflict, and the development of marital dysfunction. *Journal of Consulting and Clinical Psychology, 66,* 219–230.

Pope, H., & Mueller, C. W. (1976). The intergenerational transmission of marital instability: Comparisons by race and sex. *Journal of Social Issues, 32,* 49–66.

Presser, H. B. (2000). Nonstandard work schedules and marital instability. *Journal of Marriage and the Family, 62,* 93–110.

Quigley, B. M., & Leonard, K. E. (1996). Resistance of husband aggression in the early years of marriage. *Violence and victims, 1,* 355–370.

Rogers, S. J. (2004). Dollars, dependency, and divorce: Four perspectives on the role of wives' income. *Journal of Marriage and Family, 66,* 59–74.

Rogge, R. D., & Bradbury, T. N. (1999). Till violence does us part: The differing role of communication and aggression in predicting marital outcomes. *Journal of Consulting and Clinical Psychology, 67,* 340–351.

Rosenbaum, A., & O'Leary, K. D. (1981). Marital violence: Characteristics of abusive couples. *Journal of Consulting and Clinical Psychology, 49,* 63–71.

Rusbult, C. E. (1983). A longitudinal test of the investment model: The development (and deterioration) of satisfaction and commitment in heterosexual involvements. *Journal of Personality and Social Psychology, 45,* 101–117.

Shelton, B. A. (1987). Variations in divorce rates by community size: A test of the social integration explanation. *Journal of Marriage and the Family, 49,* 827–832.

Sinclair, S. L., & Nelson, E. S. (1998). The impact of parental divorce on college students' intimate relationships and relationship beliefs. *Journal of Divorce and Remarriage, 29,* 103–129.

Smith, D. A., Vivian, D., & O'Leary, K. D. (1991). The misnomer proposition: A critical reappraisal of the longitudinal status of "negativity" in marital communication. *Behavioral Assessment, 13,* 7–24.

Snyder, M. (1974). Self-monitoring of expressive behavior. *Journal of Personality and Social Psychology, 30,* 526–537.

Snyder, M. (1987). *Public appearances/Private realities: The psychology of self-monitoring.* New York: Freeman.

Snyder, M., & Simpson, J. A. (1984). Self-monitoring and dating relationships. *Journal of Personality and Social Psychology, 47,* 1281–1291.

Spitze, G., & South, S. J. (1985). Women's employment, time expenditure, and divorce. *Journal of Family Issues, 6,* 307–329.

Stanley, S. M., Blumberg, S. L., & Markman, H. J. (1999). Helping couples fight for their marriages: The PREP approach. In R. Berger & M.T. Hannah (Eds.), *Preventive approaches in couples therapy* (pp. 279–303). Philadelphia: Taylor & Francis.

Stanley, S. M., Bradbury, T. N., & Markman, H. J. (2000). Structural flaws in the bridge from basic research on marriage to interventions for couples. *Journal of Marriage and the Family, 62,* 256–264.

Straus, M. A., Gelles, R. J., & Steinmetz, S. K. (1980). *Behind closed doors: Violence in the American family.* New York: Anchor.

Suitor, J. J., Pillemer, K., & Straus, M. A. (1990). Marital violence in a life course perspective. In M. A. Straus & R. J. Gelles (Eds.), *Physical violence in American families: Risk factors and adaptations to violence in 8,145 families* (pp. 305–320). New Brunswick, NJ: Transaction.

Sullivan, K. T., & Bradury, T. N. (1996). Are premarital prevention programs reaching couples at risk for marital dysfunction? *Journal of Consulting and Clinical Psychology, 65,* 24–30.

Teachman, J. D. (2002). Stability across cohorts in divorce risk factors. *Demography, 39,* 331–351.

Teachman, J. D. (2003). Premarital sex, premarital cohabitation, and the risk of subsequent marital dissolution among women. *Journal of Marriage and the Family, 65,* 444–456.

Teachman, J. D., & Polonko, K. A. (1990). Cohabitation and marital stability in the United States. *Social Forces, 69,* 207–220.

Terman, L. M., & Oden, M. H. (1947). *The gifted child grows up: Twenty-five year followup of a superior group.* Stanford, CA: Stanford University Press.

Thibaut, J. W., & Kelley, H. H. (1959). *The social psychology of groups.* New York: Wiley.

Thomas, D. L., & Cornwall, M. (1990). Religion and family in the 1980s: Discovery and development. *Journal of Marriage and the Family, 52,* 983–992.

Thompson, A. H., & Bland, R. C. (1995). Social dysfunction and mental illness in a community sample. *Canadian Journal of Psychiatry, 40,* 15–20.

Thornton, A., & Rodgers, W. (1987). The influence of individual and historical time on marital dissolution. *Demography, 24,* 1–22.

Timmer, S. G., & Veroff, J. (2000). Family ties and the discontinuity of divorce in Black and White newlywed couples. *Journal of Marriage and the Family, 62,* 349–361.

Tzeng, M. (1992). The effects of socioeconomic heterogamy and changes on marital dissolution for first marriages. *Journal of Marriage and the Family, 54,* 609–619.

Tucker, J. S., Kressin, N. R., Spiro, A., & Ruscio, J. (1998). Intrapersonal characteristics and the timing of divorce: A prospective investigation. *Journal of Social and Personal Relationships, 15,* 211–225.

Vannoy, D., & Philliber, W. W. (1992). Wife's employment and quality of marriage. *Journal of Marriage and the Family, 54,* 387–398.

Weiss, R. L., & Heyman, R. E. (1997). A clinical-research overview of couple interactions. In W. K. Halford & H. Markman (Eds.), *The clinical handbook of marriage and couples interventions* (pp. 13–41). Brisbane: Wiley.

White, L. K. (1990). Determinants of divorce: A review of research in the eighties. *Journal of Marriage and the Family, 52,* 904–912.

White, L., & Booth, A. (1985). The transition to parenthood and marital quality. *Journal of Family Issues, 6,* 435–449.

White, L. K., & Booth, A. (1991). Divorce over the life course: The role of marital happiness. *Journal of Family Issues, 12,* 5–21.

Wile, D. B. (1993). *After the fight: Using your disagreements to build a stronger relationship.* New York: Guilford.

Wilkie, J. R. (1991). The decline in men's labor force participation and income and the changing structure of family economic support. *Journal of Marriage and the Family, 53,* 111–122.

Wilkinson, K. P., Thompson, J. G., Reynolds, R. R., & Ostresh, L. M. (1982). Local social disruption and western energy development. *Pacific Sociological Review, 25,* 275–296.

Williams, D. R., Takeuchi, D. T., & Adair, R. K. (1992). Marital status and psychiatric disorders among Blacks and Whites. *Journal of Health and Social Behavior, 33,* 140–157.

Wills, T. A., Weiss, R. L., & Patterson, G. R. (1974). A behavioral analysis of the determinants of marital satisfaction. *Journal of Consulting and Clinical Psychology, 42,* 802–811.

6

Perspectives on Premarital Postdissolution Relationships: Account-Making of Friendships Between Former Romantic Partners

Masahiro Masuda
Kochi University

This chapter is designed to provide an overview of theoretical issues in relational processes after dissolution by focusing on account-making of premarital postdissolution relationships (PDRs). A PDR is a cross-sex nonromantic friendship or companionship established by former romantic partners, and this term refers to both a reestablished relationship between exspouses (a postdivorce relationship) and that after a breakup before marriage (a postdating relationship). This chapter consists of two major parts. The first part briefly reviews previous research on PDRs in general and points out a fundamental problem in the research tradition of this untraditional type of relationship: Relationship researchers still cannot sufficiently explain why some people voluntarily maintain relational interactions with their former romantic partners. Then, the second part introduces a part of my own exploratory research about communicative strategies legitimating premarital PDRs, which answers a research question derived from the review. Given the results of the research, the last section discusses the potential of the account-making approach to enhance future PDR research.

PROBLEMS IN POSTDISSOLUTION RELATIONSHIPS

A Relationship With No Name

In this chapter, I define a PDR as any cross-sex friendship established by former romantic partners. I do not insist that this is the best name for this relationship; however, as social scientists, we cannot start research before we give a name to the subject that we wish to investigate. Relationships with no proper names spoken in quotidian discourses are likely to be overlooked because personal relationships are experienced and studied through language usage (Wood & Duck, 1995), and because the existence of a name for a relationship connotes tacit understandings of the relationships shared by those who speak the same language. Ganong and

Coleman (1994) confessed that they have difficulties in finding appropriate relational terms for an extended family that exists because of divorce and remarriage, and they grumbled that the traditional notion of a stepfamily implies consequences of widowhood and therefore does not recognize divorce as its precursor. In their discussion on exspousal interactions in binuclear families, Ahrons and Wallisch (1987) argued that the relational term *exspouse*—a term with the prefix *ex*—exacerbates negative aspects of divorced families, which discourage researchers from paying more attention to the positive side of divorce.

Postdissolution relationship is also an awkward prefixed relational term that connotes something extraordinary in the relationship. Some people may even doubt its existence because its name contains contradictions; because the dissolution of a romantic relationship means the end of romantic bonding, if the expartners are still relating to each other, dissolution sounds meaningless. However, I would say that such an assumption overlooks the fact that relationship dissolution does not stop all relational interactions.

The nonromantic aspects of romantic relationships maintained after dissolution have been identified mainly by those researchers who study postdivorce relationships; that is, the relationships explored are those of exspouses after their divorce (e.g., Ahrons, 1994). Even though divorce terminates a marriage, it does not end the parent–child relationship; therefore, former spouses still continue to relate to each other as coparenting partners. In this case of postdivorce relationship, a relationship after dissolution is recognized as a by-product of the postdivorce parent–child relationship. In contrast, nonparental aspects of a postdivorce relationship have been no more fully examined than all nonromantic aspects of a postdating relationship, that is, a friendship between former premarital romantic partners. Thus, in the realm of relationship research, PDRs in general (not only postdivorce relationships but also postdating relationships) have yet to be recognized as dyadic relationships but only as parts of postdivorce family systems.

PDRs in general have been underacknowledged, not only because researchers tend to investigate relationships with well-known and well-defined names but also because the majority of people doubt whether PDRs really exist. Because social science is also a social enterprise and researchers' views usually represent cultural assumptions (Sampson, 1993; Wood & Duck, 1995), researchers are usually reluctant to take the risk of beginning research on something that most people, including themselves, have never or seldom thought of. The study of such relationships is assumed to suffer from some difficulties because such relationships challenge researchers' understandings of so-called ordinary personal relationships supported by the folk wisdom of *traditional* relationship norms. Unconventional relationships seem to violate or falsify the traditional understanding of "normal" relational processes. Thus, social scientists' observations of such relationships may cause tensions between what we believe as common sense and what we actually observe. If we researchers call attention to such tensions between underacknowledged relationships and their audience in the social network in which they are embedded, we can also simultaneously experience our common sense about personal relationships challenged by such relationships. PDRs in general challenge our implicit notion of relational development.

Unexpected Relational Development

Research on PDRs provides relationship researchers with an alternative view to traditional ones presuming the linearly sequential development of personal relationships (See Weigel & Murray, 2000), because PDRs are neither planned nor goal oriented. No romantic partners expect to establish their future PDRs when they initiate their romantic relationships. Processes of romantic relationships inherently produce unpredictability and sometimes even transform what once attracted partners into what makes them decide to leave (Felmlee, 1998). When we relationship researchers think of the development of a typical premarital romantic relationship, we usually assume sequential changes toward its anticipated successful goal—marriage (e.g., Huston, Surra, Fitzgerald, & Cate, 1981)—or its unsuccessful outcome—dissolution. Unlike other types of close relationships, a premarital romantic relationship is expected not to maintain its premarital status forever but to be oriented toward either of the two goals.

From such views, the dissolution of a romantic relationship might not be taken as a surprise based on linear models of sequential changes. However, its transformation into a platonic friendship might be a great shock and even a challenge for traditional views, which have not presumed that processes in premarital romantic relationships could be transformative as well as transitive. As I discuss in later sections, a platonic friendship has not been regarded as a typical status of a romantic relationship in its early phase rather than one of the potential outcomes of relationship dissolution. The end of a particular romantic relationship often connotes discontinuation of all processes, not just romantic ones; therefore, we seldom attempt to separate the adjective and the noun that compose the relational term *romantic relationship* and to replace *romantic* with another adjective such as *platonic*.

Research shows that the decline of a romantic relationship is not like a film of its development shown in reverse, as Altman and Taylor (1973) claimed in their social penetration theory, but that the disengagement can be rather a part of preliminary processes of new friendship as a PDR. Metts, Cupach, and Bejlovec (1989) investigated trajectories of the deescalation of romantic relationships, and they indicated that "factors prior to the onset of romantic involvement and factors associated with the disengaging period influence the possibility of alternative trajectory" (p. 273) to no further interactions. According to their findings, romantic partners' preliminary friendships help them deescalate their relationship to the level of friendship. For such a PDR, deescalating processes do not mean simply tracing backward from the romantic relationship to the preliminary friendship. PDR partners renegotiate their relationship in their deescalating processes and start their friendship anew.

The "Only" Justifiable Reason for PDRs in the Biased Research Tradition

The complexity in developmental processes of PDRs is not the only reason for the scarcity of PDR research. Unlike PDRs between former partners of premarital romantic relationships, exspousal relationships with children are relatively better examined because the latter type of PDRs are culturally legitimated and even encouraged by the magical term *coparenting*, which justifies interactions between exspouses for the sake of their children (Ahrons, 1994). This bias is not so unreasonable, because research provides some supportive evidence for an implicit association of postdivorce relationship with coparenting. For instance, Ambert (1988, 1989) presented longitudinal research on 85 excouples and found that the existence of children affected how exspouses contacted each other. Compared with excouples who were parents, nonparents were indifferent to each other. Thus exspousal relationships without children were less likely to be established than those with children. As a Japanese proverb says, "Children are a bond between husband and wife." This Japanese folk wisdom is true also in present-day North American culture and even after husband and wife are no longer legal spouses. Ironically, however, the researchers' excessive attention to this "children bond" left the nonparental aspects underacknowledged or forgotten.

Obviously, most research on postdivorce relationships is aimed at exploring how to save *family* after divorce, and therefore exspousal relationships are considered nothing more than a family-saving instrument. In this view, exspousal postdivorce relationships are subsystems of child-centered larger family systems (Goldsmith, 1981). Most researchers focusing on coparenting argue that marriage and family should be considered separately; a broken marriage does not mean a broken family. Ahrons (1994) proposes the notion of "good divorce" to protect children of divorced couples from negative effects, including society's prejudice. Although she laments the scarcity of research on nonparental exspousal interactions, she does not take the deficit seriously because her notion of family still resides in traditional concepts of the nuclear family, as her neologism "binuclear family" implies (Ahrons & Wallisch, 1987). Ahrons strongly argues that divorce is normal as long as the template of nuclear family is preserved from the view of children. In addition, her typology of exspousal relationships discusses how divorced parents interact with each other, and most of their interactions are based on parenting (Ahrons, 1994). Therefore, her interest in nonparental exspousal interactions derives from that in coparental interactions.

Ahrons' (1994) usage of the prefix *ex* is tricky; because she argues that divorce does not destroy family but extends it, the *ex* of exspouses does not mean "exfamily." Exspouses continue their relationships even after either or both of them get remarried, because the existence of children legitimates those exspousal relationships. Remarried exhusbands continue to relate to their exwives as long as they can support their children; when they cannot afford to do so, exspousal interactions become less frequent (Hobart, 1990). In binuclear families, parental roles of exspouses are considered much more central and their spousal ones more peripheral (Ahrons, 1980). Through her research on binuclear families, Ahrons (1994) attempts to prove her belief that we should pay more attention to so-called good sides of divorce because it is not necessarily disastrous to family. This good side refers to what is good for children; she seems to believe that so long as coparenting is successful, any sort of postdivorce relationship between exspouses may be acceptable.

Thus, it is reasonable that relationship researchers have mainly focused on developmental processes of coparenting PDRs because only the quality of coparenting can be assessed by apparent criteria representing so-called good family processes. For instance, Graham (1997) performed an analysis of turning points in postdivorce coparenting relationships. In her research, she asked her participants to assess their commitment to their relationships after their divorce on 5 point scales; the concept of postdivorce commitments may be self-evident in the coparenting relationships.

Preoccupation: Thinking of Exromantic Partners May Be Hazardous

Contrary to its supportive arguments for coparenting in postdivorce relationships, however, most research on exspousal interactions has regarded any nonparenting interactions as hazardous to exspouses because most researchers have assumed that postdivorce relationships in themselves are problematic and that coparenting relationships should be considered exceptional. Thinking of one's expartner is usually described by a stigmatized term such as *preoccupation*. In her literature review on the research up to the late 1980s, Masheter (1990) points out that most research on postdivorce relationships has regarded exspousal interactions as maladjustment to divorce, and that this view originates in stigmatized images of divorce, which damage an ideal image of the traditional nuclear family. Researchers on coparenting criticize this view by suggesting binuclear family as a good alternative style of healthy family (Ahrons, 1994); however, too much attention to coparenting ignores another image of exspouses as continuing partners in a dyadic relationship. Without the label of *parent*, postdivorce relationships are no longer treated as legitimate.

Most psychological research on exspousal postdivorce interactions has assumed that preoccupied feelings and thoughts about their former partner represent the exspouses' postdivorce mental distress. Most results show negative associations between attachment and psychological well-being (Berman, 1988a, 1988b; Tschann, Johnston, & Wallerstein, 1989), and most researchers have recognized attachment as preoccupation with exspouses, which are assumed to derive from affection (Berman, 1985) or disputation (Isaacs & Leon, 1988) that exspouses experienced before their divorces. However, Masheter (1991, 1997b) successfully differentiates preoccupations from attachment and points out that it is not attachment but preoccupation that hinders exspouses' postdivorce adjustment. Thus, attachment to former spouses is not necessarily problematic, unless it turns into preoccupation along with intrusive thoughts about them. Just thinking of the positive side of one's expartner is not hazardous at all.

In Search of the Reasons for the Continuation: Beyond the Dichotomy Between Coparenting and Preoccupation

As already discussed, the majority of previous researchers of postdivorce relationships seem to have believed that children are almost only permits for former romantic partners to redefine their relationship as friendship. Otherwise, the nonparenting aspect of exspousal relationships has been considered synonymous to psychological maladjustment. Although this naive dichotomous thinking is problematic in terms of its ignorance of other various aspects of romantic relationships, it gives us a clue to understanding PDRs: Any PDR requires some reasons for its continuation that are acceptable to its audiences. In the case of relationships between exspouses, it is the exspouses' children who connect them to each other. When researchers speculate that it is residuals of love that drive postdivorce partners with children to continue their relationship, they regard this reason as illegitimate. Such a perspective based on this simplified dichotomy sees children as if they were the only social joint or constraint.

I suggest that the notions of unconventionally divorcing processes of Hagestad and Smyer (1982) could help us get out of such a dichotomous view of postdivorce relationships. Hagestad and Smyer posit three aspects of a divorce: (a) emotional cathexis, (b) role attachment, and (c) shared routine. The research on coparenting emphasizes only the second aspect, and the research on preoccupation is preoccupied with the first aspect; this research tradition ignores the third aspect. Even though there have been few examples, it is highly probable that there may be exspouses who want to continue to share everyday work and activities as they did before the divorce. Partners have social networks other than children, such as mutual friends. Thus, more attention to expartners' shared routines should be indispensable for more elaborated perspectives on PDRs in general.

Dissolution of romantic relationships is not simply private but also *public*—just like other relational processes (Duck & Pond, 1989). Johnson (1982) emphasizes the necessity of accounting for dissolution because "a dissolution is a change which has been labeled, and the labeling enhances the difference, silences the sameness" (p. 69). In contrast, La Gaipa (1982) points out the importance of face-saving strategies used by the excouple in front of their social network, on the basis of the assumption that expartners will be antagonistic. Therefore, their social network expects them to establish a peaceful relationship that is saliently different from their previous status.

On the basis of their exploratory research on premarital postdating relationships, Foley and Fraser (1998) imply that difficulties in PDRs' public relations may be due to their lack of scripts, which are "hypothesized cognitive and performative structures which organize a person's comprehension of situated events and guide a person's performance of a situated set of actions" (Ginsburg, 1988, p. 29). Most people do not know any more how to deal with their friends' PDRs than how such PDRs develop. According to their findings, some individuals' PDRs were supported by their network members' expecting their whole networks to be kept intact; others, in contrast, had difficulties in how they negotiated with their network members. Foley and Fraser also raise another problem in the PDR supported by networks; their respondents revealed that their supportive network members expected them to get back together. Such an expectation could be another potential threat to a PDR as a redefined relationship. For some supportive network members, a PDR is seen not as a friendship but just as a romantic relationship in conflict, which will eventually restabilize. Thus, a PDR is a relationship to be accounted for to its network members until no member questions its redefined nature as a platonic friendship.

Dialectical Approaches to Redefining Processes in the Development of PDRs

PDR partners' redefining processes along with nonlinear qualitative changes of their relationships have interested those relationship researchers who apply structural dialectical approaches to the analyses of relational transitions. Structural dialectical approaches contrast former relational phases with new ones by emphasizing differences between these two, and they assume that redefining processes of PDR are structured by dialectical tensions between opposing forces such as the tension between past and present. Conville (1988, 1991) proposes the helical model of recursive evolutional phases in relational transitions. This model assumes that personal relationships develop through the following four phases: (a) security—temporary stability and consensus; (b) disintegration—noticing differences; (c) alienation—rejection of current status; and (d) resynthesis—connecting across differences. In his theory, dissolution is actually the third phase (alienation) rather than the end state it has traditionally been. The relational processes do not end here but are followed by resynthesis, security, disintegration, and another new alienation, because this patterned development is recursive.

Masheter (1994; also see Masheter & Harris, 1986) also pioneered dialectical approaches to her research on friendships with former spouses, that is, friendships rather than coparenting partners. In PDR partners' accounts of their relational developments, she has attempted to uncover the trajectories of how they redefine their relating styles. Unlike Conville (1988, 1991), who believes in the universal helical model that illustrates the whole development, Masheter pays much more attention to each PDR's episodes in its relational history. In her analysis, Masheter applied Baxter's (1990; also see Baxter & Montgomery, 1996) dialectical perspective, which assumes three basic dialectics (integration vs. separation, stability vs. change, and expression vs. privacy), and identified pairs of opposites that construct postdivorce relationships and partners' various strategies of coping with these contradictions. In her view, *cyclic alternation* is one of many coping strategies that enhance relational transitions.

Again, cyclic alternation does not necessarily mean tracking back to the friendship stage prior to the romantic involvement, or starting the relationship all over again. Both old and new relational constructs characterize the renegotiated relationships. Masheter (1997a) attempted to discover former couples' multiple pathways to their postdivorce friendships by her own inductive theory-building analysis. In addition to the deescalation suggested by Metts et al. (1989), she identified two more paths of relational redefinitions: One is *escalation*, which refers to the newly formulated friendship that had not appeared until the couple got divorced; the other is *modification*, which means the modified existing friendship consisting of both of the components derived from the excouple's predivorce friendship and the other added to their current postdivorce interactions. Predissolution interactions contain former couples' nonromantic routines during their romantic period as well as their preliminary friendships. MacLennan's (1998) inductive analysis of the interviews with both partners of dissolved premarital romantic couples describes how PDR partners' past interactions are seamlessly connected to their present ones. Relational processes that define PDRs do not deny all interactions in the excouples' romantic period. The change of the relational style is portrayed by the coexistence of the past and the present.

What Is Missing in the Previous Research on the Premarital–Nonparental PDRs?

Earlier, I discussed the advantage of dialectical approaches to the research on the development of PDRs; however, even dialectical approaches to PDRs' developmental processes have not yet shown any positive evidence for the practicability of premarital or nonparental PDRs in their social networks. In other words, previous PDR research has paid less attention to the social side of relationship dissolution: In general, dissolutive processes are not completed until the breakups are announced to and shared with the expartners' network members (Duck, 1982; Vaughn, 1986). This evokes one fundamental question: How do PDR partners successfully have their continued interactions understood as relational processes of newly redefined friendships, not as remaining romantic interactions?

Here I emphasize that establishing a successful PDR *is* one of the successful strategies of dissolving a romantic relationship. As Duck's phase model of relationship dissolution illustrates, (Duck, 1982; also see Rollie & Duck, chap. 12 this volume), the dissatisfied partners need to make their dissolution socially recognized and shared with their network members (the social phase), present that they are no longer romantic partners as previously known (the grave-dressing phase), and finally move on the next phase that lets them get ready for new relationships (the resurrection phase). Apparently, the social phase and later phases are crucial for PDR processes composed of two contradictory relational processes: disengagement and engagement of a relationship with the same partner. When a PDR is nonparental or premarital, its partners' nonparental status may require them to present other permits of their unconventional relationships, equivalent to so-called children bonds in parental postdivorce relationships. Nonparental or premarital PDR partners may need extra effort to have their new relationship recognized as friendship until they successfully show strong evidence for the stability of their friendship.

Previous research on PDRs has not attempted to identify publicly acceptable reasons for the establishment of nonparental or premarital PDRs, except for the exploratory study by sociologists Foley and Fraser (1998). They interviewed 30 individual members of former couples and asked the interviewees for the reasons for having postdating relationships. The majority of interviewees responded that they did not stop relating to their former partners because, for example, they continued to work together or because they and their PDR partners were part of the same social circle. This finding is comparable with major findings of the coparenting research that supports postdivorce relationships for the sake of excouples' children. However, the data from Foley and Fraser also suggested that there was another reason: "Several respondents simply did not want to give up the friendship that they had before and during the dating relationship" (pp. 212–213). This intriguing finding may provoke the society's suspicion that PDRs are still romantic. However, Foley and Fraser did not perform any further analyses than simply describing the "audience challenge," that is, difficulties that excouples have in presenting their unconventional relationships as authentic to their relevant audience (Monsour, Harris, Kurzweil, & Beard,1994; O'Meara, 1989).

EXPLORATORY RESEARCH ON
ACCOUNT-MAKING OF PREMARITAL PDRs

In this section, I introduce a portion of the results from my own exploratory research on premarital PDRs (Masuda, 2000–2001). This research examines PDR partners' accounts of their PDRs, and it particularly focuses on their rhetorical strategies of legitimating their unconventional relationships. A personal relationship is discursively constituted through everyday talk between its relational partners, (Duck, 1994) and the partners' relatedness is rhetorically addressed to the public (Shotter, 1992). Because no traditional theory of personal relationships applies well to the analysis of nontraditional relationships, researchers are expected to broaden the range of acceptable personal relationships and create a new theory that is applicable to nontraditional relationships in cooperation with relational partners as their research participants. Therefore, I directly asked 33 premarital PDR partners to talk about their friendships with their former romantic partners.

Research interviewing about unconventional personal relationships is a way of discursive positioning of such relationships in the shared cultural context (Gergen, 1994). For the partners, researchers are also a kind of audience to whom they need to present the legitimacy of their relationships. Because interview narratives are jointly constructed by both interviewees and interviewers (Bochner, 1994; Riessman, 1990), the examination of how partners of nontraditional relationships account for their relationships in research interview sessions is assumed to contain several arguments that legitimate their relationships.

Procedure

Participants

I invited research participants to a 30-min interview session by using the following two strategies: recruitment by flyers and recruitment through the classroom. I directed the recruitment carefully in order to invite only voluntary participants.

A total of 34 interview sessions were held; 2 of them were joint interview sessions attended by both partners of exromantic couples, and the other 32 were one-on-one interview sessions (including 3 extra interviews attended by 3 women who volunteered their second participation). The samples collected by the other one-on-one interviews break down into 5 men and 24 women (including the 3 women's first interviews); thus 7 men and 26 women were interviewed. All participants were students (undergraduate, graduate, or law) at a Midwestern research university at the time of the interviews.

The age of male and female interviewees ranged from 19 to 29 years old, and from 18 to 29 years old, respectively. The age of PDR partners of male interviewees and female interviewees ranged from 18 to 25 years old, and from 19 to 29 years old, respectively. Among the 33 interviewees including 2 excouples, 19 (58%) had dating (or marital) partners at the time of the interviews. In contrast, among the 36 PDR partners, only 7 (19%) seemed to be dating new partners as far as interviewees were concerned.

Among the 34 PDRs, 31 were reported as relationships between Caucasians. Of the PDRs, 22 were long-distance relationships, 17 originated in romantic relationships between high school students, and 9 had been romances at the university. The length of the period before the romance ranged from 0 to 120 months; its mean was 15.3 months ($N = 34$, $SD = 26.2$). The length of the romantic period ranged from 3 to 60 months; its mean was 15.9 months ($N = 34$, $SD = 13.2$). The length of the period between the dissolution and the reestablishment of the friendship ranged from 0 to 66 months; its mean was 6.1 months ($N = 34$, $SD = 11.5$). The length of PDR period ranged 1 to 85 months; its mean was 22.1 months ($N = 34$, $SD = 19.4$).

Throughout the recruitment processes, the criteria of qualification were emphasized in either oral communication or written notices. Participants in this research were expected to satisfy all of the following criteria: (a) The participants are those who currently have a friend of the opposite sex who was originally their premarital heterosexual romantic partner. Moreover, (b) the participants are those who are satisfied with their friendship with their exromantic partner; this criterion relies on each prospective participant's subjective attitude toward the relationship, and, therefore, the friendship qualifies if both individuals consider it a good friendship without hesitation. Although the second criterion sounds very arbitrary and ambiguous, it was necessarily included in the announcement because nominal friendships should be ruled out of my research. What I call a *nominal friendship* means a relationship that exromantic partners do not intend to maintain in the future, or a relationship in which broken couples are hoping to restart their romantic relationship with the same exromantic partner.

Interview Process

The interview protocols were semistructured and consisted of two main parts. The first part asked the interviewee about the history of his or her relationship with his or her PDR partner—from their first encounter through their establishment of their PDR. The second part consisted of nine questions on how the excouple negotiated, at the time of the interview, with their network members' reactions. The questions regarding the legitimation of their relationship to others were adapted from Werking's (1997) interview protocols for her research on cross-sex friendships. It took approximately 30 minutes for an interview session.

Data Analysis

All tape-recorded narratives, including conversations between the interviewer and the interviewee, were transcribed. All conversational interactions, overlaps, and interjections were included in the transcripts. The transcribed data were analyzed by analytic induction, which is a theory-building methodology for developing hypotheses and explanations of a phenomenon through inductive processes such as comparing tentative hypotheses from one data case with new ones from another (Lindlof, 1995). The interviewees' accounts of their PDRs were identified and classified by Spradley's (1979) domain analysis, which is an ethnographic analytical method designed to reveal the semantic relationships among folk terms and their referents (Coffey & Atkinson, 1996). It is useful especially in the exploratory research that investigates tacit knowledge in a particular speech community.

Results

As a result of my analysis, I identified five major domains of the justifications for the PDR: irreplaceability of the PDR, detachment of the past, denial of traumatic dissolution, nullification of the questions about the PDR, and inaccessibility of the PDR partner. As I discuss later in this section, however, the last domain does not connote the maturity of the PDRs.

Irreplaceability of the PDR: "He Is a Part of My Life"

The majority of the interviewees emphasized the importance of the maintenance of their friendships by a common expression: "She[He] is a part of my life." They told me that their shared knowledge about themselves, which they had cherished through their romances, made them feel secure in their current interactions with their PDR partners. For instance, Interviewee 25 (a 21-year-old woman) noted that she could never replace her PDR partner Sam with someone else because he was her first love, with whom she believed she was connected by a "special bond":

> He was such *a part of my life for so many years*, and then, I couldn't just have him not to be any more. And so, a really bad thing that I did was—I knew he still loved me after we broke up, and I think I—part of me—I still loved him, but I wasn't in love with him. And so, but he was so in love with me, and part of me found this like *great security in just knowing that...* . HE'S MY FIRST love; *he's the only person I've ever been in love with till this day*. I'm now 21 years old. And I've had one love of my life, so far. And it's him, I'm still,—like, he still holds such a special place in my heart. And he just came to see me this weekend. It was so cool we're totally friends now, you know. And it's good we still have this—like special bond, you know. Because, because I mean—*we've been growing up together*. (capitalized words are her emphasis; italic words are mine)

For Interviewee 25, therefore, the removal of her partner from her current life means the denial of the important part of her life history. As she describes, PDR partners are the trustworthy companions of their lives, who have observed their progress. Their mutually shared life histories make them reliable friends, especially in emergencies or crises of one partner. For instance, Interviewee 28 (a 20-year-old woman) told me that she had resumed her PDR with Nat because he had been the only person who completely understood her family's crisis:

> Uh-um, just because he's always been a good friend—he's one of my best guy friends. And uh-um, I had a lot of stuff like problems with my family and stuff like that, and he's, uh-um, *he's like one of the persons that was there through all of that, and he's known my family for a very long time*, so, I mean he just knew the whole situation.... I felt I could easily talk to him about it [her family's crisis] because he knew what had happened in the past.... A lot of hassles initiated our talking again, because *I knew that I could talk to him about it, and he was willing to listen again*. (emphasis added)

Interviewee 8 (a 21-year-old woman) was another interviewee who told me that her PDR partner Henry was the only reliable friend that she could access when she was in a serious personal crisis. In asking for his support, she began to rediscover his good nature as friend, that is, his humane personality, such that he was willing to support whoever needed care:

> So, you know, *he was the only one that I talked to, or could talk to. That is easy enough to talk to on a regular basis*, you know, being at school, friends at home, or always available to talk. And you know, it was always convenient, he is here in this city—just, *very, very concerned*, taking responsibility—*wanting to talk to anyone to help*. (emphasis added)

Not only the offered care but also the intention to care initiate PDR processes. Several interviewees said that they had developed their PDRs through one partner's support of the other partner who was struggling with challenges. Apparently, *care* can be identified as the key term that characterizes the nature of PDRs. Interviewee 21 (a 23-year-old woman), one of such interviewees, emphasized her special bond with her partner by an analogy with siblings, as this excerpt shows:

> Say, "No, we're just friends," you know, "Just buddies, hanging out," you know, "Having a good time," or just explaining to them that, you know, "*I do care about him a lot*, you know, he's a great guy," and, you know, "I love him, but *it's more like a brother than it is like a romantic kind of love*," you know, "When I see him, *my heart doesn't skip a beat*," or you know... but I do many things for him. (emphasis added)

In her accounts, Interviewee 21 neatly contrasts friendship love with romantic love by indicating two salient characteristics: caring and sexual arousal (Fehr, 1994; Sternberg, 1986, 1987). Interestingly, however, the interviewees did not disclose their conception of the differences between their current friendships and their past romantic relationships until I questioned it directly. The aforementioned excerpt was a rare case that shows an interviewee's voluntary reference to the sibling analogy, which avoids sexual connotations associated with cross-sex relationships (Werking, 1997). Most of the interviewees did not attempt to contrast friendship with romantic love when I did not ask them to do that. Rather, they simply emphasized the importance of their special bonds characterized by their exclusively shared experiences and caring.

Detachment of the Past: "We're Different Now."

Many interviewees in my research refer to the time that separates their present friendships from their past romantic involvements and their subsequent dissolutions, which were traumatic to some interviewees. Typically, the interviewees briefly noted that now they became "mature" (Interviewee 14's term) and that they did not feel like interacting with their PDR partner in their past styles. Therefore, in my interview with the excouple Zach (19-year-old man) and Zoe (18-year-old woman), I requested them to clarify the major difference between their current friendship and their past romantic relationships. What follows is the excerpt that shows their answer to my question:

Zoe (To Zach): Can you answer that? He treated me differently when we were together, uh-um, he was a type of person who is gonna wine and dine a girl and just make her feel important. And I think a friend doesn't try and make me feel important—I mean, I feel I'm important. But I don't think he tries—or wants me to feel important—like he does for the girlfriend. You know, *for the girlfriend he's willing to do anything to make her feel special, feel love, to make sure she feels happy, to make sure she feels comfortable—for whatever reason.* And I think it was just like the lifestyles. . . what do you think?

Zach: I think friends, uh, don't need, uh, *the best treatment in the world,* like. . . you know, you don't take your friends to go out to dinner. [What differentiates a romantic relationship from a friendship is] It's just nice gestures, and the little things that add more.

Zoe: *He was like so caught up in gentlemen things.* You know, like, opening doors or, something like that.

Zach: I agree.

Zoe: *But I didn't like them, then.* [Laugh]

Zach: *You liked that before.*

Zoe: [Laugh]. (emphasis added)

According to Zach and Zoe, the most significant difference between the two types of relationships that they have experienced is the difference between the scripts in their quotidian interactions, which have changed in accordance with the change of the status of relationships. Therefore, the changed scripts can be regarded as strong evidence for the qualitative change of their relational statuses from romantic partners to friends. The section of the excouple's conversation shown on the last three lines of the excerpt illustrates that their relational scripts have changed cognitively as well as performatively.

Those interviewees who had critical views of their PDR partners' weakness explained that their attitudes toward their partners' negativity changed in accordance with their relational transitions. For instance, Interviewee 8 (a 21-year-old woman) told me that she, as a good friend of her PDR partner Henry, was now able to tolerate his "bossy" personality that as his girlfriend she had detested:

> So, he's still bossy, he's still bossy now. But, I think also by that time, we had been able to move on—from the relationship we didn't have any—romantic ties any more. I didn't feel about him in the same way that I would do. *I didn't feel bad about the breakup any more....* I've always thought like that way—he's a much, better friend than any other boyfriend. (emphasis added)

As these two examples show, many interviewees present their current friendship by emphasizing how their views of their relationships with PDR partners have changed; PDR partners detach their past from their present on their own.

Denial of Traumatic Dissolution: "It Was a Clean Breakup"

Some interviewees in my data set reported that their dissolutions did not traumatize both PDR partners, because they had recognized the dissolution of romantic relationships as nothing more than the change of relational scripts. According to them, they discontinued their romantic relationships simply because their lifestyle changes did not allow them to maintain the scripts of romantic interactions that they had constructed. These PDR partners chose to switch the status of their relationships from romantic partners to friends rather than attempt to make their romantic scripts adapt to their new lifestyles. Their accounts of their PDR processes emphasized how clean (Interviewee 13's term) their breakups were. Such PDR partners do not have those audiences who attempt to blame one partner for hurting the other partner emotionally.

According to Interviewee 19 (a 21-year-old man), for instance, he and his PDR partner Nelle stopped dating simply because they did not believe a long-distance romantic relationship could work well after they were geographically separated. However, they thought there would be no problem in maintaining a long-distance friendship. Therefore, they did not experience any awkwardness in their dissolution and naturally replaced the old label of their relationship (*romantic relationship*) with the new one ('friendship'). In this account, the interviewee told me that this transition was easy because the dissolution was nobody's fault:

> [It was easy] just because we had such a good relationship, *only* [*because*] *it was apart by our distance*. So, uh-um, I think our friendship—*we operated it very well*. And about romantic level, because it was long time ago, we've been that changed. But I think starting a relationship was very easy, *just like, becoming best friends again*. (emphasis added)

Basically, the establishment of PDRs depends on flexibility, durability, and capacity of the relationships. Interviewee 21 (a 23-year-old woman) compares a relationship to a container: If partners' negative interactions in dissolving a romantic relationship break the "container," they cannot keep a good friendship in it any longer. Therefore, she emphasized that her PDR with Vince was a special case for her:

> *It's just a container*, then I'll be able to do so—it's kind of—"Let me try it out, it works," so. We've just become now—with attitudes that we're good friends.... But I think a lot of people, you know, once they get a feeling hurt, or, uh-um, something bad happens to break their relationship.... *I think [it's] just hard for people to forgive, and forget....* A certain boyfriend that I have—but I can't be friends with him, just because I'm still mad at him [Laugh]! ... *Maybe because we* [She

and Vince] *really didn't have a good reason for breaking up*, or maybe because we never had a—[because] we didn't date for a really long time, and [because] it was just a few months—so maybe [because of] that, [we can be] just a kind of true friends, you know. Maybe *just because I like him so much as a person*–his personality, [and because] we have so much in common. (emphasis added)

This excerpt indicates the importance of previous friendship-like interactions in PDR processes: Interviewee 21 said that she had realized she had not liked another exboyfriend at whom she was still mad. This implies that the failure in the establishment of PDRs may be strong evidence for the lack of the companionate aspects of previous romantic relationships. For instance, Interviewee 34 (22-year-old woman) criticizes her formerly close female friends who strongly discouraged her from her PDR with Donald because these friends had bitter experiences in their own PDRs:

> *Their [her formerly close friends'] personalities are—that they wouldn't do that [establish PDRs] themselves.* And therefore,...[they believe] what wouldn't work to them shouldn't work for me....Or they've been hurt a couple of times,...so, they just don't wanna see—anything harmful happen to me. (emphasis added)

Interviewee 34 attributes her friends' experiences to their problematic personalities. Given Interviewee 21's argument, however, what Interviewee 34 calls "personalities" actually seem to indicate these friends' companionate interactions with their fomer boyfriends. Even though the current data are not sufficient for conclusions, it may be possible that PDR partners defend their PDRs against their anti-PDR audiences by the argument that the maintenance of PDRs is the strong evidence for their true experience of romantic love in a narrow sense. Major psychological theories of love define romantic love as combination of both companionship and passion (e.g., Sternberg, 1986, 1987). Fehr (1988, 1993, 1999) argues that it is not passion but companionship that lay people in Western cultures recognize as the central prototype of love. From this viewpoint, one's denial of PDRs may represent no experience of the fundamental nature of love in one's past romantic relationships. Further research could usefully examine this presumption.

Nullification of Questions About the PDR: "I Have a Lot of Girl Friends"

Even though the number of cases is small, some interviewees justify their PDRs by their arguments that PDRs are as normal as other relationships are for these interviewees; their arguments nullify the significance of the audiences' questions about PDRs deriving from their curiosity. Like this, some interviewees present the counterevidence against their audiences' assumption that there should be something special in such an "unusual" type of relationship.

Interviewees 12 (a 20-year-old woman), 21 (a 23-year-old woman), and 31 (a 21-year-old man) argue that PDRs are not unusual for them because they have many cross-sex friends and feel more comfortable with such cross-sex friendships than other friends of the same sex. Indeed, they admit that they belong to the minority and that the majority of their network members have different opinions about cross-sex friendships in general; however, their regular interactions with their other cross-sex platonic friends reduce PDRs' saliency. In such cases, interviewees' accounts of their PDRs do not mean their justification of their PDRs; rather, these acts present their particular characteristics of their selves to their audiences by claiming that what is normal to them differs from what their audiences believe is normal. Because establishing cross-sex friendships has been part of their uniqueness, these interviewees are confident that their audiences will understand their PDRs if the audiences know them better, as Interviewee 31 explains:

> *The mentality in college is—not really [like] "[Men can] make friends with women," just, it's kind of like, "going out and dating them," and you know, [they might have been] experiencing different things [from mine] I guess.* But I just tell them everything all: "I've dated her already, and now it's just a friendship, that's what we're doing." Hmm, they finally have to believe it, there's no reason not to trust me, so, you know... and *they can think whatever wrong, that doesn't really matter to me.* (emphasis added)

There is another strategy to nullify the audiences' questions about PDRs, even though I have only one case in my data set. Interviewee 9 (a 19-year-old woman) always silences her audiences by pointing out that asking the reason for someone's friendship is not appropriate because this issue is located in the person's privacy. According to most interviewees, it is natural that people are interested in *how* the person got acquainted with his or her friend and therefore, it is preferable to be ready for this question. In Interviewee 9's view, in contrast, asking *why* the person maintains the friendship is an awkward question in everyday conversations, even if this person's friend is his or her exromantic partner. Interviewee 9 convinces her audiences that the *why* question is generally inappropriate in the following way:

> [Laugh] Because it's not really—*none of their business I guess.* I mean, just because [he is] a friend of mine, I mean, it's a friend of mine, *there's not a kind of [question like]—"Why is she a friend of yours?"* [Laugh] They (9's friends) are [just responding to this question in the way like] "Oh, OK." (emphasis added)

She makes her audiences notice the fact that they seldom ask "*why*" questions if the target person's friend is a person of the same sex, because the reason for the friendship is a private matter. She points out that this privacy must be respected even when the friendship is a PDR. Interviewee 9's strategy challenges the legitimacy of the audiences' questions about PDRs— and the appropriateness of my interview questions as well. I must confess that this interview was the shortest of the all the interviews I had.

Inaccessibility of the Partner: "I Want Him to Find a Girlfriend"

Even though it is controversial among my interviewees, the establishment of new romantic relationships with new partners is believed to stabilize PDRs and let people's curiosity about the PDRs fade away. Several interviewees noted that the establishment of their own or their PDR partners' new romantic relationships had functioned as turning points in their PDR processes that had facilitated their new commitments as platonic friends. Interviewee 14 (a 22-year-old man), who is the only married interviewee in my data set, described his engagement as "security" that prevents him and his PDR partner Nancy from resuming their romantic relationship. When he visited Nancy's college, she utilized this fact as strong evidence for the end of their romance in combination with using the label *exboyfriend*. She needed to emphasize his inaccessibility because she still had romantic feelings for him in those days. Here is the excerpt that shows this episode:

> She described me as her exboyfriend.... She made it very clear. And she let everyone know that I was involved with someone else. She would introduce me to one of her female friends, and she would make it a joke, saying, you know, "*But keep a distance, because he is involved.*" You know,

it's like—she was like pissed off at me for being involved with someone. You know what I am saying? She wanted to throw that in my face. *That she could no longer have [been involved with me]—she wanted to make that very, very clear.* (emphasis added)

As Nancy's attitude represents, the establishment of new romantic relationships creates a distance between former couples. On the other hand, Interviewee 17 (a 21-year-old woman), who established two PDRs, seems to believe that the psychological distance created by new romantic relationships stabilizes her 7 month PDR, the later established of her two PDRs. She told me that she was really concerned that her PDR partner Keith would not want to have any new girlfriends. She even attempted to serve as a matchmaker for him, as shown in this excerpt:

But I want him to find a girlfriend [at his college]. . . . I told him, you know, *"Look for Ann. She's really cool. She's a very fine girl"* and, [his response was] like, "No," he was like, "I don't really like anyone here. I don't like the girls here." You know, he's like—so, I think—I mean—I'm not saying that it's our friendship that's preventing him from maintaining other relationships, but he doesn't have a girlfriend. And he's very, very different. He doesn't like any of the girls there. (emphasis added)

It is very important for Interviewee 17 that Keith starts his new romantic relationship in a place far from the college town where she lives. In other words, she seems to believe that his new romantic relationship will—geographically—disconnect him from his past life, including his past romance with her. Because Interviewee 17 maintains two PDRs, I asked her about the biggest difference between that with Keith and that with the other PDR partner. She answered that she felt less secure in her PDR with Keith. She had no problem in her earlier established PDR, which was a 4-year friendship at the time of the interview.

As these two examples show, I would argue that the need for distance (not only psychological but also physical) implies that the PDRs have not been well developed. This assumption is compatible with the argument by Interviewee 5 (a 21-year-old woman) that a new romantic relationship as the tool for stabilizing a PDR "spoils" (her term) the PDR. In my interpretation, Interviewee 5 means to say that PDR partners should be able to keep an appropriate psychological distance between them without such an external obstacle as a new romance if these PDR partners have really negotiated their new scripts for the maintenance of their PDR.

Discussion

Although the number of cases is small, the findings from this exploratory research suggest that social scientists should pay more attention to how platonic friendships are "performed" (Goffman, 1959). In the PDR partners' accounts, they clearly explain the nature of PDRs as nonromantic friendships based on remaining companionate love.

Many interviewees' common phrase, "She[He] is a part of my life," emphasized how important and meaningful their companionships with PDR partners were for their lives. The interviewees noted how they and their PDR partners cared for and supported each other in their regular interactions as well as in crises. They also pointed out the advantage of having someone with whom they could share their experiences and life histories. In this sense, successful PDRs can be regarded as consummately beneficial relationships that satisfy all three types of relational partners' needs: material needs, that is, needs for practical aids and supports; cognitive needs, that is, needs to create a meaningful frame of reference for one's own social behaviors; and socioemotional needs, that is, needs for love, affiliation, and self-validation

(Solano, 1986). Furthermore, communicative processes such as self-disclosure that enable friends to share each other's self and life history serve to regulate their views of themselves and the meanings of their friendship and their daily interactions (Duck & Pittman, 1994; Fehr, 1996), and finally to invite each other "into an exclusive relational club where the most important issues of the day reside" (Duck & Pittman, 1994, p. 691). It is such exclusiveness that characterizes PDR partners' special bond, of which they are highly proud, and which they cannot replace with another friendship.

From the view of psychological theories of definitions of love (Hatfield & Rapson, 1993; Sternberg, 1986, 1987), the PDR partners in this study argued that they continued to love their former romantic partner in a qualitatively different way from how they had loved them before their dissolution: A part of their romantic love to their PDR partner in the past still remained as companionate love, although another part such as passionate love no longer existed. During the interviews, the majority of my interviewees did not seem to feel that they needed to contrast their current friendships with their previous romances until they were asked to do that. Moreover, they did not even seem to refer to their loss of sexual interest in their PDR partners until they perceived that their audiences still doubted the continuance of their past romantic relationships. Rather than the denial of sexual connotations, the majority of my interviewees simply emphasized how they *cared for* each other's social and emotional well-being. Caring in combination with commitments to the partner is considered to be companionate love (Sternberg, 1986, 1987).

Partners of a dissolved romantic relationship do not stop loving each other if they continue relating to each other with less romantic commitments. From the viewpoint of a relationship researcher, PDR partners' emphasis on companionate love seems to make their relationships more like a revised version of their previous romantic relationships, because companionate love is an important category or element of romantic love (Hatfield & Rapson, 1993; Hendrick & Hendrick, 1992). However, PDR partners do not seem to recognize this "theoretical" problem as their own. Ambiguity in companionate love is the *researchers'* problem, as Berscheid and Meyers (1996) point out. After all, companionate love cannot demarcate the border between romantic relationships and platonic friendships. It just characterizes unique qualities of each type of close relationship.

In this study, some PDR partners referred to their struggle with "audience challenge" (Foley & Fraser, 1998; O'Meara, 1989); however, only few of them described their efforts to avoid letting their audience doubt that their PDR could become romantic again. Most of my interviewees did not attempt to show me any positive evidence against the potential of another romantic involvement with their PDR partner. They might think that the "detachment of the past" argument could well represent their current attitudes toward their PDR partner. Some of them even showed their contempt for the "inaccessibility of the partner" argument as a proof for nonromantic relationships. Rather, all they presented to me as a stranger was simply how they maintained their friendships through their everyday communicative activities with their PDR partner (Duck, Rutt, Hurst, & Strejc, 1991). More research is needed to analyze how PDR partners deal with audience challenge, because this issue has generally been inconclusive in research on other nontraditional relationships such as cross-sex friendships (Monsour et al., 1994).

FUTURE DIRECTIONS OF PDR RESEARCH

I conclude this chapter by positing ideas for further theory development in PDR research. Indeed, this chapter focuses on friendships between former partners of premarital romantic relationships and emphasizes the uniqueness of the premarital PDR processes; however, I do not mean to contend that relationship researchers should discuss issues in premarital dissolution and those in divorce separately. This chapter is aimed at having postdating relationships promoted to the same position as postdivorce relationships in terms of significance in relationship research. In this last section, I propose future research directions for typologies of PDRs, which are expected to integrate research on premarital dissolution with that on divorce.

As Ahrons (1994) argues, typology is a way of illustrating diversity of relationships after relationship dissolution. Her typology classifies postdivorce relationships into five types, namely, perfect pals, cooperative colleagues, angry associates, fiery foes, and dissolved duos. She conceptually separates interactions and communication: *Interactions*, in her theory, are equivalent to the shared routine in the model of unconventional divorce by Hagestad and Smyer (1982) that I introduced earlier in this chapter; *communication*, in contrast, refers to the quality of communicative ways of maintaining shared routine interactions with exspouses. Ahrons identifies four types of interactors in postdivorce relationships, and three types of communicators: High interactors are those exspouses who maintain both parental and nonparental (i.e., companionate) aspects of their postdivorce relational interactions; moderate interactors continue coparenting with their former spouses while discontinuing other aspects of interactions; low interactors basically avoid mutual communication with their exspouses and minimize parental aspects of relational interactions; and no interactors discontinue contacts with their exspouses in spite of the existence of their children.

In terms of communication, high communicators are those former spouses who successfully make their relational interactions meaningful to both partners and other people in their social networks, including their children, and jointly organize their relational interactions as everyone in the network expects; low communicators, in contrast, cannot arrange their relational matters without unsolvable conflicts; and no communicators never have opportunities to interact with each other. Ahrons (1994) compares two types of postdivorce relationships based on higher level communication (perfect pals and cooperative colleagues) with two types of relationships based on lower level communication (angry associates and fiery foes). What distinguishes one from the other in each type is the amount of shared routine interactions: perfect pals (high interactors and high communicators) share their mutual networks and regular activities as friends, and they do not downgrade their companionate love with each other; both cooperative colleagues (moderate interactors and high communicators) and angry associates (moderate interactors and low communicators) continue their shared routine interactions to the extent that PDR partners believe such interactions should be necessary; and fiery foes (low interactors and low communicators) attempt to exclude their expartners from their social networks. Finally, dissolved duos is a type of relationship with neither interactions nor communication.

Indeed, it is apparent that more research is required to elaborate the conceptualization of shared routine interactions in premarital PDRs. However, I suggest that Ahrons' (1994) typology could be applied to analyses of premarital PDRs by renaming nonparental interactions and parental interactions "routines for keeping up continued companionships" and "routines for appropriately winding up parental commitments," respectively. Keeping-up routines are relational interactions to maintain former partners' remaining mutual closeness as constant companions; winding-up routines are performed only to take responsibility for what the expartners have been expected to do for some periods of time until such routines are appropriately accomplished. Moreover, I posit another type of postdissolution routine interaction named setting up routines; there are newly established routine interactions for setting up new friendships, which characterize qualitative differences of friendship interactions from their previous ones as romantic partners. It would not be so unusual that some premarital romantic couples that had frequent disputes with each other could turn into well-matched platonic friends after breakups.

The data from my exploratory research also show that some people could discover the good natures of their expartners after the breakups. Especially in such cases, therefore, postdissolution interactions function as communication for setting up new relationships as good friends rather than simply keeping up companionate aspects of broken relationships.

I contend that future research on PDRs should pay more attention to how PDR partners make sense of these three types of routines (keeping up, winding up, and setting up) in their accounts of their PDRs. As Duck and Pond (1989) argue, accounts of relationship processes help relational partners "to create life narratives through which they can 'market' their relationships to other people and explain what they think is going on in their lives" (p. 33). PDR partners perform a variety of mutually shared routine behaviors, and they present such routines to relevant audiences in their social networks in ways that enable their newly created meanings of PDR routines to be incorporated into their audiences' commonsense knowledge of normal relational processes. The three types of routines might be well described and explained in PDR partners' accounts of how they have developed their friendships. In this sense, the five rhetorical strategies of legitimating PDRs can be recognized as PDR partners' typical ways of making such routines meaningful and accountable. For instance, "irreplaceability of the PDR" justifies keeping-up routines by explaining why the partners need to share such routines with each other; "detachment of the past" clearly distinguishes the new characteristics of their current setting-up routines from their past routines; and "denial of traumatic dissolution" and "inaccessibility of the partner" demonstrate how they have been completing winding-up routines for their breakups. In contrast, "nullification of questions about the PDR" emphasizes that keeping-up routines in PDRs are nothing more than those in all other nonromantic close friendships.

This approach focusing on account-making (see chap. 10 by Harvey and Fine, this volume) is advantageous for relationship researchers to integrate PDR research with other research on divorce and dissolution. Here, I point out two potentials for future PDR research. First, this approach would be applicable to research on negative aspects of PDRs: Analyses of accounts of uncomfortable PDRs could also clarify fundamental problems in unsuccessful PDRs. In my exploratory research, I have identified only those legitimating strategies that construct PDRs established with friendliness because I recruited only those individuals who were satisfied with their PDRs; therefore, all accounts demonstrate positive and constructive keeping-up routines in PDRs. However, I am sure that future research on uncomfortable PDRs could reveal another type of accounts of continuing negative and destructive keeping-up routines that would depict a premarital version of angry associates, as well as unfriendly winding-up routines that could make PDRs so-called dissolved duos. Second, this approach could help relationship researchers synthesize research findings from various cultures in a way contrasting cultural values associated with people's acceptance or denial of PDRs. This approach directly examines people's talk about PDRs—what they think of PDRs, which is assumed to contain culturally distinctive codes of how to talk about PDRs in each culture (see Philipsen, 1992). In spite of the variety of such cultural codes in people's talk about PDRs, the functions of those codes would be common. Thus, I believe that the approach to account-making can be the strongest tool for international researchers on dissolution and divorce.

REFERENCES

Abelsohn, D. (1992). A "Good Enough" separation: Some characteristic operations and tasks. *Family Process, 31,* 61–83.

Ahrons, C. R. (1980). Divorce: A crisis of family transition and change. *Family Relations, 29,* 533–540.

Ahrons, C. R. (1994). *The good divorce: Keeping your family together when your marriage comes apart.* New York: HarperCollins.

Ahrons, C. R., & Wallisch, L. S. (1987). The relationship between former spouses. In D. Perlman & S. W. Duck (Eds.), *Intimate relationships: Development, dynamics, and deterioration* (pp. 269–296). Newbury Park, CA: Sage.

Altman, I., & Taylor. D. A. (1973). *Social penetration: The development of interpersonal relationships.* New York: Holt, Rinehart & Winston.

Ambert, A.-M. (1988). Relationship between ex-spouses: Individual and dyadic perspectives. *Journal of Social and Personal Relationships, 5,* 327–346.

Ambert, A-M. (1989). *Ex-spouses and new spouses: A study of relationships.* Greenwich, CT: JAI.

Baxter, L. A. (1990). Dialectical contradictions in relationship development. *Journal of Social and Personal Relationships, 7,* 69–88.

Baxter, L. A., & Montgomery, B. M. (1996). *Relating: Dialogues and dialectics.* New York: Guilford.

Berman, W. H. (1985). Continued attachment after legal divorce. Journal of *Family Issues, 6,* 375–392.

Berman, W. H. (1988a). The relationship of ex-spouse attachment to adjustment following divorce. *Journal of Family Psychology, 1,* 312–328.

Berman, W. H. (1988b). The role of attachment in the post-divorce experience. *Journal of Personality and Social Psychology, 54,* 496–503.

Berscheid, E., & Meyers, S. (1996). A social categorical approach to a question about love. *Personal Relationships, 3,* 19–47.

Bochner, A. P. (1994). Perspectives on inquiry II: Theories and stories. In M. L. Knapp & G. R. Miller (Eds.), *Handbook of interpersonal communication* (2nd ed., pp. 21–40). Thousand Oaks, CA: Sage.

Coffey, A., & Atkinson, P. (1996). *Making sense of qualitative data: Complementary research strategies.* Thousand Oaks, CA: Sage.

Conville, R. L. (1988). Relational transitions: An inquiry into their structure and function. *Journal of Social and Personal Relationships, 5,* 423–437.

Conville, R. L. (1991). *Relational transitions: The evolution of personal relationships.* New York: Praeger.

Duck, S. W. (1982). A topography of relationship disengagement and dissolution. In S.W. Duck (Ed.), *Personal relationships: Vol. 4. Dissolving personal relationships* (pp. 1–30). London: Academic Press.

Duck, S. W. (1994). *Meaningful relationships: Talking, sense, and relating.* Thousand Oaks: Sage.

Duck, S. W., & Pond, K. (1989). Friends, Romans, countrymen, lend me your retrospections: Rhetoric and reality in personal relationships. In C. Hendrick (Ed.), *Close relationships* (pp. 17–38). Newbury Park, CA: Sage.

Duck, S. W., & Pittman, G. (1994). Social and personal relationships. In M. L. Knapp & G. R. Miller (Eds.), *Handbook of interpersonal communication* (2nd ed., pp. 676–697). Thousand Oaks, CA: Sage.

Duck, S. W., Rutt, D. J., Hurst, M. H., & Strejc, H. (1991). Some evident truths about conversations in everyday relationships: All communications are not created equal. *Human Communication Research, 18,* 228–267.

Fehr, B. (1988). Prototype analysis of the concepts of love and commitment. *Journal of Personality and Social Psychology, 55, 557–579.*

Fehr, B. (1993). How do I love thee?: Let me consult my prototype. In S. W. Duck (Ed.), *Individuals in relationships* (pp. 87–120). Newbury Park, CA: Sage.

Fehr, B. (1994). Prototype-based assessment of laypeople's views of love. *Personal Relationships, 1,* 309–331.

Felmlee, D. H. (1998). Fatal attraction. In B. H. Spitzberg & W. R. Cupach (Eds.), *The dark side of close relationships* (pp. 3–31). Mahwah, NJ: Lawrences Erlbaum Associates.

Foley, L., & Fraser, J. (1998). A research note on post-dating relationships: The social embeddedness of redefining romantic coupling. *Sociological Perspectives, 41,* 209–219.

Ganong, L. H., & Coleman, M. (1994). *Remarried family relationships.* Thousand Oaks, CA: Sage.

Gergen, K. J. (1994). *Realities and relationships: Soundings in social construction.* Cambridge, MA: Harvard University Press.

Ginsburg, G. P. (1988). Rules, scripts and prototypes in personal relationships. In S. W. Duck (Ed.), *Handbook of personal relationships* (1st ed., pp. 23–39). Chichester, England: Wiley.

Goffman, E. (1959). *The presentation of self in everyday life.* New York: Anchor.

Goldsmith, J. (1981). Relationships between former spouses: Describe findings. *Journal of Divorce 4*(2), 1–2.

Graham, E. E. (1997). Turning points and commitment in post-divorce relationships. *Communication Monographs, 64,* 350–368.

Hagestad, G. O., & Smyer, M. (1982). Dissolving long-term relationships: Patterns of divorcing in middle age. In S. W. Duck (Ed.), *Personal relationships: Vol. 4. Dissolving personal relationships* (pp. 155–188). London: Academic Press.

Hatfield, E., & Rapson, R. L. (1993). *Love, sex, and intimacy.* New York: HarperCollins.

Hendrick, S. S., & Hendrick, C. (1992). *Romantic love*. Newbury Park, CA: Sage.

Hobart, C. (1990). Relationships between the formerly married. *Journal of Divorce and Remarriage, 14*(2), 1–23.

Huston, T. L., Surra, C. A., Fitzgerald, N. M., & Cate, R. M. (1981). From courtship to marriage: Mate selection as an interpersonal process. In S. W. Duck & R. Gilmour (Eds.), *Personal relationships: Vol. 2. Developing personal relationships* (pp. 53–88). London: Academic Press.

Isaacs, M. B., & Leon, G. (1988). Divorce, disputation, and discussion: Communicational styles among recently separated spouses. *Journal of Family Psychology, 1*, 298–311.

Johnson, M. P. (1982). Social and cognitive features of the dissolution of commitment to relationships. In S. W. Duck (Ed.), *Personal relationships: Vol. 4. Dissolving personal relationships* (pp. 51–73). London: Academic Press.

La Gaipa, J. J. (1982). Rules and rituals in disengaging from relationships. In S. W. Duck (Ed.), *Personal relationships: Vol. 4. Dissolving personal relationships* (pp. 189–210). London: Academic Press.

Lindlof, T. R. (1995). *Qualitative communication research methods*. Thousand Oaks, CA: Sage.

MacLennan, J. (1998, November). *Part of the question and part of the answer: Relationship redefinition after the breakup*. Paper presented at the 84th Annual Convention of the National Communication Association, New York.

Masheter, C. (1990). Postdivorce relationships between exspouses: A literature review. *Journal of Divorce and Remarriage, 14*(1), 97–122.

Masheter, C. (1991). Postdivorce relationships between ex-spouses: The roles of attachment and interpersonal conflict. *Journal of Marriage and the Family, 53*, 103–110.

Masheter, C. (1994). Dialogues between ex-spouses: Evidence of dialectic relationship development. In R. L. Conville (Ed.), *Uses of "structure" in communication studies* (pp. 83–101). Westport, CT: Praeger.

Masheter, C. (1997a). Former spouses who are friends: Three case studies. *Journal of Social and Personal Relationships, 14*, 207–222.

Masheter, C. (1997b). Healthy and unhealthy friendship and hostility between ex-spouses. *Journal of Marriage and the Family, 59*, 463–475.

Masheter, C., & Harris, L. M. (1986). From divorce to friendship: A study of dialectic relationship development. *Journal of Social and Personal Relationships, 3*, 177–189.

Masuda, M. (2000–2001). Accounting for post-dissolution relationships. *Dissertation Abstracts International, 61*(12-A), 4615A.

Metts, S., Cupach, W., & Bejlovec, R. A. (1989). "I love you too much to ever start liking you": Redefining romantic relationships. *Journal of Social and Personal Relationships, 6*, 259–274.

Monsour, M., Harris, B., Kurzweil, N., & Beard, C. (1994). Challenges confronting cross-sex friendships: "Much ado about nothing?" *Sex Roles, 31*, 55–77.

O'Meara, J. D. (1989). Cross-sex friendship: Four basic challenges of an ignored relationship. *Sex Roles, 21*, 525–543.

Philipsen, G. (1992). *Speaking culturally: Explorations in social communication*. New York: State University of New York Press.

Riessman, C. K. (1990). *Divorce talk: Women and men make sense of personal relationships*. New Brunswick, NJ: Rutgers University Press.

Sampson, E. E. (1993). *Celebrating the other: A dialogic account of human nature*. Boulder, CO: Westview Press.

Shotter, J. (1992). What is a "personal" relationship?: A rhetorical-responsive account of "unfinished business." In J. H. Harvey, T. L. Orbuch, & A. L. Weber (Eds.), *Attributions, accounts, and close relationships* (pp. 19–39). New York: Springer-Verlag.

Solano, C. H. (1986). People without friends: Loneliness and its alternatives. In V. J. Derlega & B. A. Winstead (Eds.), *Friendship and social interaction* (pp. 227–246). New York: Springer-Verlag.

Spradley, J. P. (1979). *The ethnographic interview*. New York: Holt, Rinehart & Winston.

Sternberg, R. J. (1986). A triangular theory of love. *Psychological Review, 93*, 119–135.

Sternberg, R. J. (1987). Liking versus loving: A comparative evaluation of theories. *Psychological Bulletin, 102*, 331–345.

Tschann, J. M., Johnston, J. R., & Wallerstein, J. S. (1989). Resources, stressors, and attachment as predictors of adult adjustment after divorce: A longitudinal study. *Journal of Marriage and the Family, 51*, 1033–1046.

Vaughan, D. (1986). *Uncoupling: Turning points in intimate relationships*. New York: Oxford University Press.

Weigel, D., & Murray, C. (2000). The paradox of stability and change in relationships: What does chaos theory offer for the study of romantic relationships? *Journal of Social and Personal Relationships, 17*, 425–449.

Werking, K. J. (1997). *We're just good friends: Women and men in non-romantic relationships*. New York: Guilford.

Wood, J. T., & Duck, S. W. (1995). Off the beaten track: New shores for relationship research. In J. T. Wood & S. W. Duck (Eds.), *Under-studied relationships: Off the beaten track* (pp. 1–21). Thousand Oaks, CA: Sage.

7

Hurtful Interactions and the Dissolution of Intimacy

Anita L. Vangelisti
University of Texas at Austin

Love and hurt are intrinsically interlinked.

—L'Abate (1999, p. 83)

Being hurt is an inevitable part of close relationships. What varies from relationship to relationship is not whether partners hurt each other, but how their relationship is affected by hurtful episodes. In some cases, hurtful events and hurtful interactions have very little influence on relationships. Partners who have hurt each other deeply find ways to forgive each other and remain relatively close. In other cases, however, interactions and events that hurt partners have devastating effects on their relationships. Those who are hurt may distance themselves from each other emotionally or physically and may go so far as to end their association with each other.

The purpose of the current chapter is to describe the role of hurtful interactions in the dissolution of intimacy. When friends, family members, and romantic partners hurt each other and the intimacy between them fades, they may or may not opt to end their relationship. The focus of the present chapter, thus, is not on the association between hurt and the structural dissolution of relationships, but rather on the association between hurt and relational distancing. In many cases, relational distancing is a step on the way to dissolution unless partners make efforts to stay close. I begin the chapter by describing various ways that hurt has been conceptualized in the literature. I highlight common components of these conceptions and put forth an argument for treating hurt as an interpersonal phenomenon. Then I define and discuss the action tendency associated with hurt—relational distancing. I follow this discussion with a review of research on factors that should influence the tendency of hurtful interactions to encourage or discourage relational distancing. Finally, in the last section of the chapter I explore issues that researchers might usefully address in the future as they examine the links between hurt and relational dissolution.

THE CONCEPTUALIZATION OF HURT

Hurt has long been regarded as a feeling that occurs when an individual is emotionally injured by another (Folkes, 1982; L'Abate, 1977). Although there is general agreement that hurt involves a sense of emotional injury, the defining characteristics of hurt and the underlying features that distinguish it from other emotions are not entirely clear.

Some of the first research mentioning hurt, as an emotion, examined it in terms of its relationship with other emotions. For instance, Shaver, Schwartz, Kirson, and O'Connor (1987) found that people saw hurt as being related to sadness. More specifically, the prototype analysis of emotion concepts conducted by these researchers indicated that *hurt* clustered together with terms such as *anguish* and *agony*. Shaver et al. suggested that the common element among these terms is that they all involve a degree of suffering.

In addition to identifying a sense of injury and suffering as common to hurt, researchers have begun to discuss other elements that may define hurt and distinguish it from other emotions. For instance, Leary, Springer, Negel, Ansell, and Evans (1998) argued that the feature common to all hurt feelings is relational devaluation—"the perception that another individual does not regard his or her relationship with the person to be as important, close, or valuable as the person desires" (p. 1225). In support of this argument, Leary et al. found that the intensity of hurt experienced by participants was associated with the degree to which participants felt accepted or rejected by the individual who hurt them. These researchers further suggested that the types of hurtful events described by their respondents, like the types of hurtful messages identified in earlier work (Vangelisti, 1994), "all appeared to involve real, implied, or imagined social disassociation" (p. 1233).

Although they noted that a single theme, relational devaluation, characterizes hurtful episodes, Leary et al. (1998) acknowledged that the experience of hurt is quite complex. Indeed, their data suggest that hurt typically involves a mixture of other emotions. Leary and Springer (2001) elaborated on the possible associations between other emotions and hurt: They measured a wide variety of negative emotions and found that those emotions, together, did not account for all the variance in hurt. On the basis of these data, they argued that although hurt often is accompanied by other negative emotions, it is a unique emotion in and of itself.

Vangelisti and her colleagues (2001; Vangelisti & Sprague, 1998; Vangelisti & Young, 2000) conceptualized hurt in slightly different terms. This group of researchers defined hurt as an emotion "blend" (Weiner, personal communication). They suggested that hurt involves both a degree of sadness at having been emotionally injured as well as a fear of being vulnerable to harm. Vangelisti and her coauthors argued that hurt is elicited as a consequence of a relational transgression—that people who are hurt perceive they have been emotionally wounded by something another person said or did. They also noted that relational transgressions do not uniquely evoke hurt, and they acknowledged that other emotions such as anger are elicited by perceived transgressions (Weiner, 1986). According to Vangelisti, the factor that distinguishes hurt from these other emotions is a sense of vulnerability (Kelvin, 1977). People who feel hurt, in other words, perceive that they are vulnerable to harm. They may react to their sense of injury and vulnerability with anger, fear, anxiety, or sadness, but their initial experience of hurt is elicited by being emotionally wounded and vulnerable.

In contrast to Leary and his associates, Vangelisti and her coauthors have not argued that all hurt is associated with relational devaluation. Indeed, Vangelisti and Young (2000) found that there are cases when people discuss being hurt by a relational partner (e.g., a friend, family member, or romantic partner) in relatively positive terms. For instance, some people who perceived that their partner hurt them unintentionally noted that their partner engaged in hurtful behavior in an effort to be supportive (e.g., "because he cares about me and my health" and "to help me do what would be right"). Others said that their partner's hurtful behavior was justified (e.g., "I hurt him and put him on the defensive" and "I deserved it for what I just said") or accidental (e.g., "She simply didn't know" and "He didn't think it would bother me"). Although these relatively charitable explanations for hurtful behavior were in the minority, they do suggest that relational devaluation may not typify all instances of hurt.

Feeney (2005) has combined aspects of Leary's and Vangelisti's approaches by suggesting that hurt is evoked by relational transgressions and that the transgressions eliciting hurt typically imply low relational evaluations. Like prior researchers, Feeney notes that a sense of injury is a defining element of hurt, but she argues that this injury is a consequence of threats to positive mental models of the self and others. Feeney's research suggests that, indeed, attachment dimensions are associated with hurt feelings. People in her study who were avoidant reported relatively low levels of hurt, fear, and general distress, whereas those high in anxiety reported more hurt, fear, shame, and general distress. Although Feeney's findings do not establish threats to positive mental models as a necessary or sufficient cause of hurt, they are suggestive and offer an important starting point for other researchers.

Clearly, questions concerning the relative usefulness of these different approaches to defining hurt feelings are complex. Although these questions are not likely to be resolved in the near future, researchers have identified several common components of the approaches. First, the experience of hurt is generally regarded as negative. Whether it is subsumed under the emotion of sadness (Shaver et al., 1987), defined as a combination of sadness and fear (Vangelisti, 2001), or distinguished as a unique emotion in its own right (Leary & Springer, 2001), hurt is regarded by those experiencing it as unpleasant and aversive. Second, hurt is an interpersonal phenomenon. People feel hurt because they perceive someone said or did something that emotionally injured them. As a consequence, appraisals of others' interpersonal behavior are necessary for the elicitation of hurt feelings (Vangelisti & Young, 2000). These appraisals may vary for individuals from different races, socioeconomic statuses, sexual orientations, and nationalities. In as much as this is the case, the elicitation of hurt also may vary for individuals in these different groups. Even if appraisals associated with the elicitation of hurt vary, though, the object of those appraisals remains the same: People evaluate interpersonal behavior when they are hurt. Third, hurt as an emotion can and should be distinguished from hurt as an outcome. When people say they are hurt, and when researchers report that their participants have been hurt, it is not always clear whether hurt is being referenced as an emotion or as an end-state involving some sort of psychological, physical, or relational injury. Disentangling the emotion from the end-state is not easy because the emotion of hurt involves a sense of being injured or wounded (Folkes, 1982; L'Abate, 1977). However, people can feel injured without sustaining any observable psychological, physical, or relational damage, and people can sustain psychological, physical, or relational damage, without feeling hurt. Separating the emotion from the outcome is important if researchers are to develop theories to predict and explain hurt feelings.

THE LINK BETWEEN HURT AND RELATIONAL DISTANCING

A number of theorists have argued that emotional responses can be characterized on the basis of people's tendency to approach or avoid the source of their feelings (Davidson et al., 1990; Gray, 1987; Horney, 1945). Although some researchers suggest that classifying emotions on the basis of the likelihood that they will elicit an approach or an avoidance response provides too broad an understanding of emotions (Cappella & Greene, 1982), most agree that the impulse to approach or avoid others is a defining feature of interpersonal relationships (Baxter & Montgomery, 1996) and that many, if not most, emotions encourage some form of approach or avoidance (Knobloch & Solomon, 1999). In fact, Frijda and his colleagues (Frijda, 1986; Frijda, Kuipers, & ter Shure, 1989) have argued that every emotion is associated with a tendency to engage in, or disengage from, interaction with the environment. According to Frijda et al., this "state of action readiness" does not dictate people's emotional responses, but it primes them so that, other things being equal, some responses are more likely than others. Because hurt involves feeling injured and vulnerable, the state of action readiness associated with hurt is characterized by avoidance or relational distancing.

On the basis of prior work (de Rivera, 1981; Kreilkamp, 1981), Helgeson, Shaver, and Dyer (1987) defined relational distancing as "a noticeable rift in an otherwise, or formerly, intimate relationship" (p. 224). Relational distancing, in other words, involves a movement away from intimacy. Although the prototypical case of distancing likely involves close relational partners who disassociate from each other over time, partners who are not very close also may distance themselves from each another. In either case, when relational distancing occurs, a relationship that was intimate will become less intimate—one that was not intimate will become even more remote.

Hurt feelings are characterized by a readiness to engage in relational distancing because hurt involves emotional pain. People who experience hurt feel they have been injured. Their impulse, in response to being emotionally injured, is to move away (figuratively or literally) from the source of their pain. By distancing themselves from the source of their pain, those who are hurt protect themselves and decrease their vulnerability to further harm.

It is important to acknowledge that experiencing a readiness to engage in relational distancing does not mean that all, or even most, people who feel hurt actually will distance themselves from the person who hurt them. Most spouses can recall instances when they hurt each other, but this does not necessarily mean that their relationship also has become more distant as a consequence. When Frijda and others (Frijda, 1986; Lazarus, 1991; Oatley, 1992) discussed the states of action readiness associated with various emotions, they did not describe those states as absolute precursors to particular behavioral, psychological, or relational responses. Instead, they suggested that the responses that emerge from a given state of action readiness are influenced by individuals' appraisals of the event that initially evoked their emotion. Thus, for example, research indicates that whether a hurtful behavior is appraised as intentional influences people's tendency to engage in relational distancing. Individuals who perceived that their hurt feelings were intentionally elicited were more likely to distance themselves from the person who hurt them than were those who viewed their hurt as unintentionally elicited (Vangelisti & Young, 2000).

Findings such as these suggest that the tendency of people who have been hurt to engage in relational distancing is influenced by the way they appraise or evaluate the behavior that initially hurt them. Although such appraisals provide information that can be used to predict people's responses to emotions such as hurt, they offer a somewhat limited view of the interpersonal processes associated with the elicitation of emotion (Parkinson, 1997). In other words, they are a useful tool for examining responses to hurt, but they are a relatively blunt tool. Indeed, the literature suggests that several other sets of variables should affect the tendency of hurtful interactions to encourage relational distancing or relational dissolution. These include (a) the characteristics of the hurtful event; (b) the affective, cognitive, and behavioral responses that people have to being hurt; (c) the enduring characteristics that individuals bring to hurtful interactions; and (d) the qualities of individuals' relationships with the person who hurt them. The studies examining these variables do not always directly assess people's tendency to engage in relational distancing, nor do they assess variables that might suggest important differences among individuals based on their race, socioeconomic status, sexual orientation, or nationality. However, the findings do point to a number of issues that researchers who are interested in examining the characteristics of hurtful interactions and relational dissolution should consider.

INFLUENCES ON HURT AND RELATIONAL DISTANCING

Characteristics of the Hurtful Event

When people are hurt, they perceive that something someone else said or did in the context of a social interaction caused them emotional pain. Research and theory suggest several characteristics of hurtful interactions that may influence the degree to which people distance themselves from the person who hurt them. These include the type of hurtful event, the frequency with which the event occurs, and the intensity of the event.

Type

Several researchers have explored the types of events or behaviors that elicit hurt (see Table 7.1). For instance, Vangelisti (1994) asked people to recall and describe interactions when someone said something to them that hurt their feelings. She found that informative statements, accusations, and evaluations were the most frequently reported types of hurtful messages received by individuals. Her data also indicated that informative statements tended to be more hurtful than other types of messages. Vangelisti suggested that the reason for this latter finding may have been that informative statements leave recipients with little or no recourse, whereas other types of hurtful comments can be challenged. If, for example, a wife informs her husband that she does not love him anymore, the husband is left with a relatively narrow repertoire of possible responses. He may experience a wide range of emotions, but there is not much he can say to dispute his wife's comment. By contrast, if a wife accuses her husband of being a liar, or evaluates his behavior as inconsiderate, the husband can dispute what she has said by arguing that it is untrue, providing explanations or justifications for his behavior, and so forth.

As noted by Leary et al. (1998), one limitation of Vangelisti's (1994) research is that it focused exclusively on situations in which someone said something that elicited hurt feelings and, as a consequence, it did not include nonverbal behavior or instances when the absence of a behavior or set of behaviors evoked hurt. To address these gaps, Leary et al. asked their respondents to recall and describe instances when someone else "said or did something" that hurt their feelings (p. 1226). They found that four types of events—criticism, betrayal, active disassociation, and passive disassociation—characterized the majority of hurtful episodes reported by participants and that two additional events—being unappreciated and being teased—were reported by a minority of participants. Although Leary et al. did not find differences among the events in terms of the degree of hurt they evoked, they did find that criticism elicited a lower sense of rejection than did the other events.

Feeney (2004) revised the typology developed by Leary et al. to apply it to romantic relationships.[1] She found that hurtful events occurring in the context of romantic partnerships

---

[1] Feeney required respondents to have been married or to have had a dating relationship for at least 3 months. Given that she used a student sample, most of her participants probably reported on hurtful events in nonmarital romantic partnerships.

TABLE 7.1
Typologies of Hurtful Interactions

Vangelisti (1994)		Leary et al. (1998)	Feeney (2004)
Message	*Example*	*Event*	*Event*
Inform: a disclosure of information	"You aren't a priority in my life."	Criticism	Active disassociation: behaviors that explicitly signal disinterest in the partner
Evaluation: a description of value, worth, or quality	"Going out with you was the biggest mistake of my life."	Betrayal	Passive disassociation: being ignored or excluded from the other's plans, activities, conversations, or important decisions
Accusation: a charge of fault or offense	"You're such a hypocrite."	Active disassociation	Criticism: negative verbal comments about one's behavior, appearance, or personal characteristics
Directive: an order, set of directions, or command	"Just leave me alone, why don't you?"	Passive disassociation	Infidelity: extrarelationship sexual involvement
Express desire: a statement of preference	"I don't ever want to have anything to do with you."	Being unappreciated	Deception: misleading acts
Advice: a suggestion for a course of action	"Break up with her so you can have some fun."	Being teased	
Joke: a witticism or prank	"The statement was really an ethnic joke against my ethnicity."		
Threat: an expression of intention to inflict some sort of punishment	"If I find out you are ever with that person, *never* come home again."		
Lie: an untrue, deceptive statement or question	"The worst part was when he lied about something."		

Note: Categories are listed in order of frequency.

could be classified into one of five categories: active disassociation, passive disassociation, criticism, infidelity, and deception. The partners in Feeney's study rated infidelity as more serious (e.g., as high in hurt, powerlessness, perceived intentionality, destructive victim behavior, and long-term effects on both the victim and the relationship) than other types of hurtful events and criticism as relatively low in seriousness. As Feeney noted, these findings fit with Vangelisti's argument concerning the degree to which those who are hurt are able to challenge or dispute the hurtful event: Because criticisms and accusations can be disputed by recipients, they may be seen as less serious than other hurtful events (i.e., infidelity) that leave the person who is hurt with little or no recourse.

Frequency

As suggested by Feeney (2004), the type of hurtful event that individuals experience offers some information about how they will respond to being hurt. On average, people who are hurt by a romantic partner's infidelity probably are more likely to distance themselves from their partner than those who are hurt by criticism. With this said, it is important to note that hurtful behaviors do not occur in a vacuum. They take place in the context of other behaviors. If a behavior that is typically viewed as extremely hurtful (e.g., infidelity) occurs in a relationship where there is a preponderance of positive behaviors, the person who is hurt should be less likely to engage in relational distancing than he or she would be if the same behavior was part of an ongoing pattern of hurtful interactions.

Most studies of hurt feelings have asked participants to recall and describe single hurtful events. As a consequence, relatively little is known about how patterns of hurtful interaction influence relational distancing. One study that did begin to address this issue examined people's perceptions of hurtful messages as part of an ongoing pattern of behavior (Vangelisti & Young, 2000). To assess the extent to which participants viewed a hurtful interaction as ongoing, the researchers measured two variables. One was participants' perceptions of the frequency with which they were hurt by the other individual (e.g., "He or she often hurts my feelings," and "It is typical of him or her to hurt my feelings"). The other focused on participants' perceptions of the other person's general tendency to hurt people (e.g., "A lot of people have been hurt by his or her behavior," "She or he often says or does things that hurt people"). The findings of this study indicated that both variables were positively associated with relational distancing: Individuals' perceptions of both the frequency with which the other person hurt them and the other's general tendency to hurt people were linked to participants' tendency to engage in relational distancing—even when perceived intent and relational quality were controlled.

Intensity

Another variable that very likely influences people's tendency to engage in relational distancing is the intensity of the comment or event that hurt their feelings. Message intensity typically has been defined as the emphasis or strength with which an attitudinal position is stated (McEwen & Greenberg, 1970). According to this definition, intense hurtful communication involves negative nonverbal cues (e.g., yelling or a harsh tone of voice) as well as extreme language (name-calling or swearing). Young (2004) examined the association between message intensity and individuals' appraisals of hurtful communication. She found that participants' ratings of message intensity predicted the way hurtful messages were evaluated: "How a message was stated was pivotal in determining recipients' appraisals of it" (p. 300). Comments that were stated harshly, abrasively, or that used extreme language were assessed by participants as more negative.

Although extant literature provides a clear guideline for defining the intensity of hurtful communication, the guidelines for assessing the intensity of hurtful events are less clear. One approach might be to use seriousness as a proxy for intensity. Many of the events rated by Feeney's (2004) participants as highly serious (e.g., as high in hurt, powerlessness, perceived intentionality, destructive victim behavior, and long-term effects on both the victim and the relationship) probably also would be rated by participants as intense. However, there are situations when an event may be serious (e.g., it may be viewed as intentional or as having long-term effects on the relationship) without being intense and vice versa. A more direct approach would be to use the definition of message intensity as a template for defining the intensity of events. The strength with which an event reflects an attitudinal position could be operationalized by the perceived harshness of the message or *meaning* associated with the event. Factors that might amplify the intensity of a hurtful event would include the abrasiveness of any verbal or nonverbal communication associated with the event, but they also would involve the meaning that people assign to the event itself. Thus, for example, a relational partner who views honesty as extremely important might see an act of deception as intense, whereas one who sees honesty as relatively unimportant might not. On the basis of Young's (2004) findings, it is reasonable to expect that highly intense hurtful events will be viewed by participants as more negative. The negativity associated with these events very likely will be linked to relational distancing.

Responses to Hurt

Clearly, the characteristics of hurtful events influence the tendency of people to distance them-selves from the source of their pain. Some events are more likely than others to prompt individuals to protect themselves. In addition to the characteristics of hurtful events, the im-mediate responses that people have to being hurt can either encourage or discourage relational distancing. These reactions can be discussed in terms of three levels. That is to say, individuals respond to being hurt on affective, cognitive, and behavioral levels.

Affective Responses

On an affective level, distinctions in the tendency of people to engage in relational distancing should be evident in the degree of hurt they experience. On average, individuals who feel extremely hurt should be motivated to distance themselves from the source of their pain—if for no other reason than to protect themselves from further harm. Indeed, Vangelisti and Young (2000) found a positive association between the degree of hurt that people felt and their self-reported tendency to engage in relational distancing. Similarly, Leary et al. (1998) found that the degree to which individuals felt hurt by an event was correlated with the extent to which the event temporarily weakened their relationship. It is important to note, however, that the correlations reported in both of these studies were weak. Furthermore, Leary et al. did not find a significant association between the degree of felt hurt and the extent to which the event permanently damaged individuals' relationships. These relatively weak correlations as well as the lack of association between hurt and permanent relational damage suggest that, as previously noted, hurt feelings do not invariably lead to relational distancing. As suggested by the work of Frijda (1986), states of action readiness such as relational distancing may predispose individuals to engage in certain responses to emotion, but they do not dictate those responses.

Vangelisti (2001) noted that variations in the link between people's tendency to engage in relational distancing and the degree to which they feel hurt can be illustrated by use of a 2×2 matrix. As we can see in Fig. 7.1, the intensity of people's hurt feelings makes up one axis

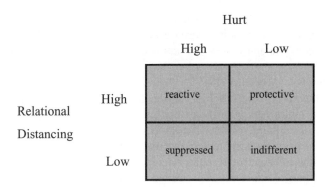

FIG. 7.1. Variations in affective responses to hurt and relational distancing.

of the matrix; the degree to which individuals engage in distancing comprises the other axis. The first cell is one characterized by a situation in which individuals feel a great deal of hurt and, as a response, engage in high levels of relational distancing. Because people in situations such as this one display a relatively measured response to the hurt they have experienced, this cell was labeled by Vangelisti as *reactive*. Although the response of these individuals appears to be reasonable (because they opt to distance themselves from someone who has hurt them deeply), the costs associated with relational distancing may make this response less than desirable. More specifically, when individuals in this situation distance themselves from the source of their pain, they are giving up a degree of intimacy. If they value the sense of intimacy that they have with the person who hurt them (regardless of whether it is a great deal of intimacy or not much at all), they may opt not to engage in relational distancing.

The second cell in the 2 × 2 matrix is one that Vangelisti (2001) labeled *suppressed*. Like those in the first cell, individuals in this cell experience a high degree of hurt. What distinguishes those in the first cell from those in the second is that those in the second cell engage in relatively little relational distancing. Prior research and theory suggest at least three cases when this situation may occur. The first is when the hurt experienced by individuals is so infrequent that it is deemed insignificant—particularly when compared with the rewards associated with the relationship. This is very likely to be the case when partners who are highly satisfied with their relationship (occasionally) hurt each other's feelings. When people who are highly satisfied are hurt, they may suppress their own feelings and control any urges they have to distance themselves from their partner because they place such a high value on maintaining the quality of their relationship. A second case when individuals may suppress their tendencies to engage in relational distancing is when they see the cause of the hurtful behavior as external and temporary. People who explain their partner's hurtful behavior as external and unstable should be relatively unlikely to distance themselves from their partner because they do not conceive of their partner as the primary source of their pain and because they do not see the cause of their pain as enduring. Furthermore, attribution theorists would argue that those who provide external, unstable causes for negative partner behaviors such as hurt are likely to be relatively satisfied with their relationships (e.g., Fincham, Beach & Baucom, 1987; Grigg, Fletcher, & Fitness, 1989; Holtzworth-Munroe & Jacobson, 1985). Their relatively high levels of satisfaction may provide these individuals with a reason to stay close to their partner. A third case when people may opt not to engage in distancing in spite of feeling a great deal of hurt is when they perceive they have few relational alternatives (Thibaut & Kelley, 1959). Some individuals who perceive they have few alternatives to their current relationship may be hesitant to engage in relational distancing because they believe that distancing themselves from their partner will leave them in a worse position than they currently are in. Others may perceive that they have few alternatives because they "deserve" to be hurt. Indeed, the literature on physical and emotional abuse in close relationships suggests that some individuals stay in relationships where they are continually hurt because being hurt is the only real alternative they see for themselves (Walker, 1979).

In contrast to the first two cells in Fig. 7.1, the third cell represents situations in which the intensity of people's hurt feelings is relatively low. Although individuals in these situations may have been involved in interactions that others see as hurtful, they do not experience much emotional pain. They do, however, tend to respond to their pain with relatively high levels of relational distancing. Because the responses characterized by this cell revolve around efforts to prevent further pain, Vangelisti (2001) called this cell *protective*. There are at least two cases when people may decide that the costs associated with the relatively small amount of emotional pain they have experienced exceed the rewards they would get from maintaining a close relationship with the person who hurt them. One of these might occur in the initial stages of a relationship. In these early stages, partners usually do not have a great deal invested in maintaining their association with each other. As a consequence, if they experience even a small amount of emotional pain, they may decide that the costs associated with their hurt feelings outweigh the benefits they might receive from future interactions. Another case when individuals might engage in protective responses to their hurt feelings is when they have been repeatedly exposed to hurtful interactions. Zahn-Waxler and Kochanska (1990) explained the processes by which repeated exposure to certain stimuli may result in exaggerated emotional responses. More specifically, they proposed a neurophysiological model of "kindling," which predicts that individuals' responses to emotions can become kindled or exaggerated over time. Originally posited by Meyersberg and Post (1979), this model suggests that, when individuals are repeatedly exposed to noxious stimuli (e.g., electric shocks), they become sensitized to those stimuli so that smaller and smaller doses of the stimuli are needed to evoke a response (e.g., seizures). Applied to situations when people feel hurt, the model implies that those who are repeatedly hurt may develop exaggerated responses to their emotional pain. Eventually, being hurt even a little may encourage them to engage in relational distancing.

The fourth and final cell depicted in Fig. 7.1 was labeled *indifferent*. This cell represents situations in which people feel relatively low levels of hurt and do not distance themselves very much from the person who hurt them. In some cases, the hurtful episodes experienced by these individuals may, in fact, be relatively harmless. When this is the case, the lack of relational distancing exhibited by people in these situations may represent a measured response to their hurt feelings. In other cases, however, individuals may be demonstrating subdued affective and relational reactions to hurtful episodes. For example, husbands and wives who are extremely dissatisfied with their marriage sometimes act indifferently toward each other (Knapp, 1984). Their extreme dissatisfaction may lead them to withdraw from their relationship so that, over time, the verbal barbs they throw at each other elicit relatively little emotional pain. In contrast to those who develop protective responses to their hurt feelings, these partners become habituated to being hurt—they develop relational calluses. Another possibility is that the subdued affective and relational responses characterized by this fourth cell are strategic. Over time, individuals may learn that minimizing their hurt feelings provides them with a way to stay close to relational partners who hurt them.

Cognitive Responses

In addition to examining the associations between affective responses to hurt and relational distancing, researchers have studied the links between relational distancing and cognitive responses to hurt. This line of work indicates that there are associations between the way people think about the hurtful interactions they experience and their tendency to engage in relational distancing. For instance, Leary et al. (1998) found that individuals' attributions for a relational partner's hurtful behavior were associated with the effects that the behavior had on their relationship. More specifically, people who reported that the other's hurtful behavior was not accidental were more likely to indicate that the hurtful interaction permanently weakened their relationship. Similarly, those who noted that the other person was intentionally trying to hurt them or that the other was trying to "get them back" reported permanent weakening of their relationship.

Vangelisti and Young (2001) also examined the links between individuals' perceptions of intent and their tendency to distance themselves from the person who hurt them. These researchers asked people to describe an interaction in which someone said something that hurt their feelings. They found that individuals who believed the other person intentionally said something to hurt them felt that the message had more of a distancing effect on their relationship than did those who felt the message was unintentional. In addition, when they examined the intensity of people's hurt feelings, Vangelisti and Young found an interaction between perceived intent and perceived frequency. Those who thought that the other person did not hurt them frequently felt relatively less hurt when they perceived the message was unintentional and more intense hurt when they thought the message was intentional. However, those who thought the other person hurt them frequently felt moderately hurt when they perceived the message was unintentional, but little to no hurt when they believed that the message was intentional. In short, people who were frequently hurt by a relational partner became callous to the partner's hurtful behavior: When they saw their partner saying something intentionally to hurt them, they felt almost no emotional pain.

Perceptions of intent provide a glimpse of the way people make sense of a relational partner's hurtful behavior, but they provide very limited information about the way people explain their own feelings. There is some evidence that the explanations that individuals provide for their own hurt feelings are associated with their tendency to engage in relational distancing. For instance, Vangelisti, Young, Carpenter-Theune, and Alexander (in press) found that people who explained their feelings by saying that a hurtful event denigrated their relationship (e.g., "it showed the other person didn't care about our relationship") or that it pointed to a personal fault (e.g., "it focused on a flaw I that I know I have") were relatively likely to engage in distancing; by contrast, those who explained their feelings by saying that the event involved mistaken intent or misunderstanding (e.g., "it showed the other person didn't understand me") were relatively unlikely to distance themselves from the person who hurt them.

Behavioral Responses

Several groups of researchers have examined the behavioral responses that individuals have to being hurt. For example, Vangelisti and Crumley (1998) asked people to provide detailed descriptions of the way they reacted to a hurtful situation they had experienced. Ten different responses emerged from these data (see Table 7.2.). The responses ranged from relatively aggressive behaviors such as verbally attacking the other person to more passive behaviors such as crying or being silent. After generating this list, Vangelisti and Crumley asked another group of individuals to rate their tendency to engage in each of the behaviors when they felt hurt. Three factors characterized participants' ratings. The first factor was labeled *active verbal* responses. It included behaviors that required individuals to engage in verbal interaction of some sort with the person who hurt them. Active verbal responses included using sarcasm, asking for or providing an explanation, verbally attacking the other person, and defending oneself. The second factor was labeled *acquiescent* responses. Behaviors characterizing this factor were relatively passive and included crying, conceding, and apologizing. Finally, the third

TABLE 7.2
Behavioral Responses to Hurt Feelings

Vangelisti & Crumley (1998)	Leary et al. (1998)	Feeney (2004)
Silence	Told the other person	Told the other person
Attack	Expressed anger	Expressed anger
Crying	Cried in front of the other person	Cried in front of the person
Defend	Cried later, when alone	Cried later, when alone
Sarcasm	Argued or defended	Argued or defended
Ask for or provide explanation	Said something critical or nasty	Said something critical or nasty
Ignore		Asked for an explanation
Apologize		Ignored the whole situation
Laugh		Apologized
Concede		Laughed
		Bottled up my feelings
		Got worked up and thought about the situation over and over

factor was called *invulnerable* responses. Invulnerable reactions were those that made it appear as if the person was not hurt. They included laughing, ignoring the event, and being silent. Among other results, Vangelisti and Crumley found that people who reported invulnerable responses to being hurt were less likely to engage in relational distancing. It is possible that invulnerable responses provide individuals with a way to maintain a degree of closeness to the person who hurt them. Alternatively, it may be that those who respond with invulnerable behaviors already see themselves as having a relatively distant relationship with the individual who hurt them and, as a consequence, do not feel the need to engage in relational distancing. The findings also indicated that there was a positive association between the degree of hurt people felt and their tendency to report acquiescent responses. The more intense hurt feelings of those who engage in acquiescent responses may render them unable to access a broad repertoire of behaviors. Rather than verbally interact with other person or act invulnerable, these individuals may simply "give in."

Leary et al. (1998) also looked at several behavioral responses to being hurt (see Table 7.2). They found that telling the other person about one's hurt feelings, crying (in front of the other person or alone), and saying something critical or nasty were positively associated with the degree to which people felt hurt. They also found some interesting results concerning gender. Men were less likely to tell the other person they were hurt and were less likely to cry when the person who hurt them was a man than when it was a woman. Women, however, did not differ in terms of they way they responded to men or women who hurt them. These findings have potentially important implications for same-sex couple relationships and friendships. Women who are hurt by their female partners may have a wider range of responses at their disposal than do men who are hurt by their male partners. Compared with men, women also may more frequently be able to verbally communicate their feelings to their same-sex partners.

Although she did not focus specifically on the questions regarding gender that were raised by the study by Leary et al. (1998), Feeney (2004) examined the behavioral reactions that partners involved in romantic relationships had to being hurt. She assessed the responses examined by Leary et al. as well as many of those examined by Vangelisti and Crumley (1998), as shown here in Table 7.2. By conducting a factor analysis and dropping several items, Feeney was able to collapse the responses that she measured into two factors. One, labeled *constructive* responses, consisted of items assessing the tendency of partners to tell the person, bottle up their feelings, ignore the whole situation, and ask for an explanation. The other, called *destructive* responses, measured the extent to which partners said something critical, nasty, or sarcastic, expressed anger, got worked up, or cried by themselves. Using these two factors, Feeney found that destructive responses to hurt feelings were associated with the tendency of the hurtful episode to have negative long-term effects on partners' relationship.

Characteristics of the Individual

The research reviewed up to this point suggests that characteristics of hurtful events as well as the way individuals respond to those events influence the likelihood that those who feel hurt will distance themselves from a relational partner who hurts them. Both the event itself and the way people react to it represent relatively specific variables that unfold in the context of hurtful episodes. However, people who are hurt also bring relatively global individual differences to hurtful interactions that affect the tendency of those interactions to either encourage or discourage relational distancing. Three individual differences that are particularly relevant to the association between hurtful events and relational distancing are attachment orientation, self-esteem, and rejection sensitivity.

Attachment

There is theoretical and empirical evidence to suggest that individuals' attachment orientation can influence the degree to which they feel hurt by others' behavior. For instance, Simpson (1990) found that those who are avoidant, particularly men, noted feeling much less distress after the dissolution of their relationships than did others. These same people may report feeling relatively little hurt after an interaction that others would deem emotionally painful (Vangelisti, 2001). Because they are wary of close relationships, individuals who are avoidant may protect themselves from being emotionally vulnerable to others.

Feeney (2005) recently conducted a study to address these issues. She discussed the attachment system as a "safely regulating system that maintains a balance between exploratory behavior and attachment (proximity-seeking) behavior" (p. 256). Given that hurtful events involve vulnerability to emotional injury or harm, Feeney suggested that they are particularly likely to activate behaviors associated with attachment. Then, on the basis of the work of Kobak and Sceery (1988) and Fraley and Shaver (1997), she argued that avoidant attachment is linked with rules and strategies that restrict the expression of distress, whereas anxious attachment reflects hyperactivation of the attachment system and, as a consequence, should be associated with greater fear of rejection. In line with her predictions, when Feeney asked people to recall hurtful situations, she found significant associations between attachment dimensions and the degree of hurt people reported. Individuals who were highly avoidant reported lower levels of hurt and distress and those who were highly anxious reported higher levels of hurt and distress.

What researchers may want to address next is the relative tendency of those who are avoidant and those who are anxious to engage in relational distancing following a hurtful interaction. Vangelisti (2001) suggested that people who are avoidant may be particularly likely to distance themselves from relational partners who hurt them. Given their tendency to distrust relational partners, those who are avoidant may engage in relational distancing at the slightest hint that they will be hurt. However, it also is possible that avoidant individuals will report engaging in little relational distancing because they believe their relationships with others who might hurt them already are relatively distant. This may be particularly the case for individuals that Bartholomew and Horowitz (1991) labeled as *dismissive avoidant*.

Although researchers typically expect different patterns of findings for those who are avoidant and those who are anxious, it is difficult to predict whether anxious and avoidant people will differ in terms of the patterns of relational distancing they exhibit in response to hurt. Individuals who are anxious may respond to their hurt feelings by clinging to their relationship with the person who hurt them and thus may not engage in relational distancing at all. Alternatively, the more intense hurt that anxious people feel (Feeney, 2005) may motivate them to protect themselves from further harm by distancing themselves from the source of their pain.

Self-Esteem

Theoretically, individuals who enter a hurtful interaction with low self-esteem should have more areas of vulnerability—or more acute vulnerabilities—than people who think well of themselves. Indeed, Murray, Rose, Bellavia, Holmes, and Kusche (2002) found that, when individuals with low self-esteem were exposed to threats to their personal relationships, they were more likely than those with high self-esteem to question their partner's affection and acceptance. Given the greater vulnerability of those with low self-esteem, they should report feeling more hurt, on average, than those with high self-esteem. At least one study has demonstrated that this is the case. The results of this study revealed a negative association between self-esteem and the degree of hurt felt by participants (Vangelisti et al., in press).

In addition to feeling more hurt than those with high self-esteem, people with low self-esteem appear to make sense of their hurt feelings in different ways than do those with high self-esteem. Researchers have long argued that individuals who are low in self-esteem are more likely to attribute negative events to internal, stable, causes (e.g., "because I'm a loser") than are those who are high in self-esteem (Weiner, 1979, 1987; Zautra, Guenther, & Chartier, 1985). Not surprisingly, then, when they asked people to describe a hurtful episode and explain why they felt hurt, Vangelisti et al. (in press) found that people with low self-esteem and those with high self-esteem explained their hurt feelings differently. More specifically, those low in self-esteem were more likely than those high in self-esteem to say that they felt hurt because an event denigrated their relationship with the person who hurt them (e.g., "it showed the other person didn't care about our relationship"), because it humiliated them (e.g., "it humiliated me"), or because it pointed to a personal fault (e.g., "it focused on a flaw that I know I have"). Compared with people who were low in self-esteem, individuals high in self-esteem were more likely to note that they were hurt as a result of being shocked by what the other person said or did (e.g., "it was something I was not prepared for").

Rejection Sensitivity

Downey and her colleagues (Downey & Feldman, 1996; Downey, Feldman, & Ayduk, 2000) described rejection sensitivity as a general tendency, on the part of some individuals, to anxiously expect rejection from relational partners. Although there have not been any studies looking at the association between hurt feelings and rejection sensitivity, a number of researchers, including Fitness (2001), Leary et al. (1998), and Feeney (2004), have argued that feelings of rejection are central to being hurt. Indeed, Leary et al. found that the degree of hurt people felt was positively associated with feelings of rejection. Given that individuals who are high in rejection sensitivity are particularly vigilant about rejection, they may feel hurt more often and may experience more intense hurt feelings than others who are lower in rejection sensitivity. In line with this prediction, Downey and Feldman found that those high in rejection sensitivity tended to perceive rejection from relational partners when none was intended.

Does rejection sensitivity increase the likelihood that people will distance themselves from relational partners who hurt them? Researchers have yet to address this question directly. Downey, Freitas, Michaelis, and Khouri (1998) have found that women who are highly sensitive to rejection tended to behave more negatively than others during conflict, and that this greater negativity on the part of the women was associated with their partners being more angry.

Whether or not this pattern of interaction is associated with, or results in, relational distancing has yet to be determined. What we do know at this point is that feeling rejected is linked not only to hurt but also to the tendency of hurtful events to permanently weaken individuals' relationship with the person who hurt them (Leary et al., 1998). The greater tendency of individuals who are high in rejection sensitivity to feel rejected may thus put them in a position that is ripe for relational distancing.

Characteristics of the Relationship

Like the individual differences that people bring to hurtful interactions, characteristics of people's relationships can be conceived as set of relatively global variables that may influence individuals' tendency to distance themselves from relational partners who hurt them. The characteristics of relationships create a context in which hurtful episodes occur. In this way, they are likely to influence not only the tendency of relational partners to feel hurt but also the way partners interpret hurtful events and respond to being hurt. The literature suggests that at least two relational characteristics are likely to play a role in hurtful interactions. They are relational satisfaction and structural commitment.

Satisfaction

A number of studies indicate that relational satisfaction is linked to hurtful interactions (e.g., Vangelisti & Crumley, 1998; Vangelisti & Young, 2000). For instance, there is a negative association between satisfaction and the intensity of hurt feelings that people report: Individuals who are satisfied with their relationship tend to report feeling less hurt by their partner than those who are dissatisfied. People who are relationally satisfied also have a greater tendency to judge their partner's hurtful behavior as unintentional than do those who are dissatisfied. In addition, those who are satisfied are more likely try to engage a partner who has hurt them in verbal interaction (e.g., by asking for an explanation, defending themselves, or even verbally attacking the partner) than they are to acquiesce to their partner or to act invulnerable. Given the efforts of those who are satisfied to verbally interact with their partner following a hurtful episode, it is not surprising that they also engage in relatively little relational distancing: Studies have revealed a negative association between relational satisfaction and people's tendency to distance themselves from a partner who has hurt them.

Although findings such as these demonstrate that relational satisfaction can affect the impact of hurtful interactions on relationships, they do not reveal much about the mechanisms by which satisfaction exerts this influence. A key issue for researchers to examine in the future is the extent to which (a) relational satisfaction creates a context for fewer hurtful events or (b) relational satisfaction serves as a lens for interpreting hurtful behavior. Theoretical and empirical evidence exists to support both positions. For instance, the literature on negative behavior in romantic relationships indicates that partners who are relationally satisfied tend to exhibit fewer negative behaviors toward each other than those who are dissatisfied (e.g., Barnett & Nietzel, 1979; Broderick & O'Leary, 1986; Gottman, 1979; Jacobson, Waldron, & Moore, 1980; Noller, 1982, 1985). By implication, these findings suggest that people who are satisfied may experience fewer hurtful events in the context of their relationships than those who are dissatisfied. Alternatively, research also shows that relational satisfaction tends to color individuals' judgments of their partner's behavior (e.g., Murray & Holmes, 1997; Murray, Holmes, & Griffin, 1996). Inasmuch as this is the case, those who are satisfied with their relationship may interpret behaviors that others would see as hurtful as relatively benign. When they are asked to report on hurtful events, satisfied partners may report fewer hurtful events and less intense feelings of hurt than those in dissatisfied relationships. By contrast, people who are dissatisfied may interpret neutral or even positive behaviors in relatively negative ways. They may perceive hurtful events where others do not and may ruminate, more than others, about the emotional injuries they receive.

Of course, the most likely scenario is that both of these processes occur: There probably are some instances when relational satisfaction creates a context for fewer hurtful events and others when it serves as a lens for interpreting hurtful behavior. If researchers find that both processes characterize hurtful interactions in romantic relationships, they may begin to investigate variables that predict the prevalence of one process over the other (e.g., patterns of communication in partners' family of origin may be associated with the tendency of partners to engage in hurtful behavior) as well as variables that predict shifts from one process to the other (e.g., the frequency of hurtful events may encourage highly satisfied partners to take off their so-called rose colored glasses and interpret their partner's behavior in less charitable ways).

Structural Commitment

Another relationship characteristic that is likely to affect the tendency of hurtful interactions to encourage or discourage relational distancing is structural commitment. Johnson (1999) described structural commitment as occurring when people feel that they *have* to continue their relationship—even if they would prefer not to. Individuals feel structurally committed to their partner when the costs of leaving (whether social or financial) constrain their ability to end the relationship.

Although there have been no studies directly examining the association between hurt and structural commitment, there are data suggesting that something akin to structural commitment may be important in influencing hurt and responses to hurt. When Vangelisti and Crumley (1998) examined people's behavioral reactions to hurt, they contrasted three types of relationships: These included romantic relationships, family relationships, and nonfamily or nonromantic relationships. The researchers' reasoning in distinguishing among these groups was that the passionate characteristic of romantic relationships and the involuntary nature of most family relationships would likely influence the ways individuals respond to hurtful interactions that take place in those relational contexts. Indeed, they found that this was the case. People who said they were hurt in the context of family relationships reported feeling more hurt than individuals in either romantic or nonfamily or nonromantic relationships. However, those who were hurt by family members did not engage in more relational distancing than the other two groups. The researchers suggested that family members may experience more hurt because they are particularly skillful at emotionally wounding each other—their lengthy relational histories may give them a rich store of ammunition for eliciting hurt. However, because family associations typically are involuntary, members may feel constrained to remain relatively close to each other. Family members may be hesitant to engage in relational distancing because they cannot easily dissolve or replace their family relationships.

A similar situation may occur in any type of relationship that is characterized by a great deal of structural commitment. Being structurally committed may give partners a license to hurt each other without having to incur the costs of relational distancing. That is to say, people who are high in structural commitment may have difficulty extricating themselves from partners who are hurtful. Certainly, the literature on physically abusive relationships provides evidence of this phenomenon (Johnson, in press). Women in abusive relationships often are structurally committed to their partners because their partners control most, if not all, of their social and financial resources. By staying relatively close to their abusive partners, these women have access to vital resources for themselves and their children.

CONCLUSIONS

The intent of the present chapter was to describe the associations between hurtful interactions and relational distancing. The various ways that researchers have conceptualized hurt were examined and common components of these conceptions were noted. Relational distancing was discussed as the action tendency associated with hurt. Finally, the bulk of the chapter provided a review of the literature on variables that should affect the tendency of hurtful events to encourage or discourage relational distancing.

Although the literature on hurtful interactions provides useful information about the possible associations between hurt and the dissolution of intimacy, it is important to acknowledge that there are a number of rather large gaps in the literature that researchers need to fill. For example, the physiological components of hurt feelings have yet to be explored. Eisenberger, Lieberman, and Williams (2003) recently found that the neuroimaging data associated with physical pain were very similar to those associated with social pain. Given that these researchers operationalized social pain as rejection, their findings have interesting implications for the study of hurt feelings. The findings suggest, as clinicians have argued for years, that emotional pain may have as much (or more) of an influence on individuals as does physical pain. Of course, physiological reactions to hurt are evidenced in a variety of ways. In addition to looking at neuroimaging data, researchers need to examine the degree to which people become physiologically aroused when they feel hurt. Individuals' tendency to become physiologically aroused and, perhaps more importantly, their ability to regulate their physiological arousal may be associated with their ability to engage partners who hurt them in constructive verbal interactions.

Another gap in extant literature involves socialization processes concerning hurtful interactions. How do children learn to hurt others? How do they learn to respond to being hurt? Certainly, the research on bullying in childhood can inform questions such as these. This research suggests, for example, that bullying and victimization are correlated with each other and are relatively stable over time (Rigby, 2002). Whether at home or on the playground, children appear to learn the roles of both bully and victim and, once they adopt those roles, they appear to maintain them. Do children learn strategies for how to hurt others and how to respond to hurt simultaneously? What encourages certain children to develop particularly sophisticated strategies for hurting others? What enables some to use prosocial responses to hurt and renders others unable to access those responses? Does the ability of children to regulate their physiological arousal when they are hurt influence their reactions? Obtaining responses to questions such as these would help researchers and clinicians not only to understand the ways children experience hurtful interactions, but also to explain the ways some adults enact hurtful episodes.

Yet another untapped area of research involves influences of different social contexts on hurt. Social contexts vary with regard to the degree to which they constrain individuals' responses to emotion. For instance, researchers suggest that many work settings restrict the range of emotions that employees may express (Hochschild, 1983). How, then, do people respond to the elicitation of hurt in work environments? How do employees maintain relationships with coworkers who repeatedly hurt them? Inasmuch as work environments restrict the expression of hurt, there are likely other social contexts that leave relational partners particularly vulnerable to emotional pain. Indeed, there may be a "sociology of hurt" such that people who are members of particular social groups or cultures are more susceptible to hurt than others.[2]

The possibility that there is a sociology of hurt suggests that researchers also should examine cultural influences on hurtful interactions. Given that hurt feelings are characterized by emotional injury and vulnerability, there are likely cultural differences in both what hurts

---

[2]The author is indebted to Mark A. Fine and John H. Harvey for this idea.

people and how people respond to hurt. Individuals from distinct cultural backgrounds are likely to vary in terms of what they see as injurious. For instance, cultural differences in certain standards for beauty (e.g., Nichter, 2000) may create situations in which a statement about a person's physical appearance is viewed as hurtful in one culture and as harmless, or even complimentary, in another. Further, because norms for the expression of emotions can vary somewhat from one culture to another (e.g., Scherer & Wallbott, 1994), people from different cultures likely display different behavioral responses to hurt. Whether these behavioral responses manifest themselves in different relational outcomes is an interesting question. Exploring cultural differences in the tendency of hurt feelings and responses to hurt to encourage relational distancing could provide researchers with valuable information about the processes that link hurt to the dissolution of intimacy.

REFERENCES

Barnett, L. R., & Nietzel, M. T. (1979). Relationships of instrumental and affectional behaviors and self-esteem to marital satisfaction in distressed and nondistressed couples. *Journal of Consulting and Clinical Psychology, 47,* 946–957.

Bartholomew, K., & Horowitz, L. (1991). Attachment styles among young adults: A test of a four-category model. *Journal of Personality and Social Psychology, 62,* 226–244.

Baxter, L. A., & Montgomery, B. (1996). *Relating: Dialogues and dialectics.* New York: Guilford Press.

Broderick, J. E., & O'Leary, K. D. (1986). Contributions of affect, attitudes, and behavior to marital satisfaction. *Journal of Consulting and Clinical Psychology, 54,* 514–517.

Cappella, J. N., & Greene, J. O. (1982). A discrepancy-arousal explanation of mutual influence in expressive behavior for adult–adult and infant–adult interaction. *Communication Monographs, 49,* 89–114.

Davidson, R. J., Ekman, P., Saron, C. D., Senulis, J. A., & Friesen, W. V. (1990). Approach-withdrawal and cerebral asymmetry: Emotional expression and brain physiology I. *Journal of Personality and Social Psychology, 58,* 330–341.

de Rivera, J. (1981). The structure of anger. In J. de Rivera (Ed.), *Conceptual encounter: A method for the exploration of human experience* (pp. 35–81). Washington, DC: University Press of America.

Downey, G., & Feldman, S. (1996). Implications of rejection sensitivity for intimate relationships. *Journal of Personality and Social Psychology, 70,* 1327–1343.

Downey, G., Feldman, S. I., & Ayduk, O. (2000). Rejection sensitivity and male violence in romantic relationships. *Personal Relationships, 7,* 45–61.

Downey, G., Freitas, A. L., Michaelis B., & Khouri, H. (1998). The self-fulfilling prophecy in close relationships: Rejection sensitivity and rejection by romantic partners. *Journal of Personality and Social Psychology, 75,* 545–560.

Eisenberger, N. I., Lieberman, M. D., & Williams, K. D. (2003). Does rejection hurt? An fMRI study of social exclusion. *Science, 302,* 290–292.

Feeney, J. A. (2004). Hurt feelings in couple relationships: Toward integrative models of the negative effects of hurtful events. *Journal of Social and Personal Relationships, 21,* 487–508.

Feeney, J. A. (2005). *Hurt feelings in couple relationships: Exploring the role of attachment and a sense of personal injury. Personal Relationships, 12,* 253–271.

Fincham, F. D., Beach, S. R., & Baucom, D. H. (1987). Attribution processes in distressed and nondistressed couples: 4. Self-partner attribution differences. *Journal of Personality and Social Psychology, 52,* 739–748.

Fitness, J. (2001). Betrayal, rejection, revenge, and forgiveness: An interpersonal script approach. In M. R. Leary (Ed.), *Interpersonal rejection* (pp. 73–103). New York: Oxford University Press.

Folkes, V. S. (1982). Communicating the causes of social rejection. *Journal of Experimental Social Psychology, 18,* 235–252.

Fraley, R. C., & Shaver, P. R. (1997). Adult attachment and the suppression of unwanted thoughts. *Journal of Personality and Social Psychology, 73,* 1080–1091.

Frijda, N. H. (1986). *The emotions.* Cambridge, England: Cambridge University Press.

Frijda, N. H., Kuipers, P., & ter Schure, E. (1989). Relations among emotion, appraisal, and emotional action readiness. *Journal of Personality and Social Psychology, 57,* 212–228.

Gottman, J. M. (1979). *Marital interaction: Experimental investigations.* San Diego, CA: Academic Press.

Gray, J. A. (1987). *The psychology of fear and stress* (2nd ed.). New York: Cambridge University Press.

Grigg, F., Fletcher, G. J. O., & Fitness, J. (1989). Spontaneous attributions in happy and unhappy dating relationships. *Journal of Social and Personal Relationships, 6,* 61–68.

Helgeson, V. S., Shaver, P., & Dyer, M. (1987). Prototypes of intimacy and distance in same-sex and opposite-sex relationships. *Journal of Social and Personal Relationships, 4,* 195–233.

Hochschild, A. R. (1983). *The managed heart: Commercialization of human feeling.* Berkeley: University of California Press.

Holtzworth-Munroe, A., & Jacobson, N. S. (1985). Causal attributions of married couples: When do they search for causes? What do they conclude when they do? *Journal of Personality and Social Psychology, 48,* 1398–1412.

Horney, K. (1945). *Our inner conflicts: A constructive theory of neurosis.* New York: Norton.

Jacobson, N. S., Waldron, H., & Moore, D. (1980). Toward a behavioral profile of marital distress. *Journal of Consulting and Clinical Psychology, 48,* 96–703.

Johnson, M. P. (1999). Personal, moral, and structural commitment to relationships: Experiences of choice and constraint. In J. M. Adams & W. H. Jones (Eds.), *Handbook on interpersonal commitment and relationships stability* (pp. 73–87). New York: Kluwer Academic/Plenum.

Johnson, M. P. (in press). Violence and abuse in personal relationships: Conflict, terror, and resistance in intimate partnerships. In A. L. Vangelisti & D. Perlman (Eds.), *Cambridge handbook of personal relationships.* New York: Cambridge University Press.

Kelvin, P. (1977). Predictability, power, and vulnerability in interpersonal attraction. In S. Duck (Ed.), *Theory and practice in interpersonal attraction* (pp. 355–378). New York: Academic Press.

Knapp, M. L. (1984). *Interpersonal communication and human relationships.* Boston: Allyn & Bacon.

Knobloch, L. K., & Solomon, D. H. (1998). *Responses to changes in relational certainty and uncertainty in dating relationships: Emotions and communication strategies.* Paper presented at the annual meeting of the International Communication Association, San Francisco, CA.

Kobak, R. R., & Sceery, A. (1988). Attachment in late adolescence: Working models, affect regulation, and representations of self and others. *Child Development, 59,* 135–146.

Kreilkamp, T. (1981). Psychological distance. In J. de Rivera (Ed.), *Conceptual encounter: A method for the exploration of human experience* (pp. 273–341). Washington, DC: University Press of America.

L'Abate, L. (1977). Intimacy is sharing hurt feelings: A reply to David Mace. *Journal of Marriage and Family Counseling, 3,* 13–16.

L'Abate, L. (1999). Being human: Loving and hurting. In A. C. Richards & T. Schumrum (Eds.), *Invitation to dialogue: The legacy of Sidney M. Jourard* (pp. 81–90). Dubuque, IA: Kendall/Hunt.

Lazarus, R. S. (1991). *Emotion and adaptation.* New York: Oxford University Press.

Leary, M. R., & Springer, C. A. (2001). Hurt feelings: The neglected emotion. In R. M. Kowalski (Ed.), *Behaving badly: Aversive behaviors in interpersonal relationships* (pp. 151–175). Washington, DC: American Psychological Association.

Leary, M. R., Springer, C., Negel, L., Ansell, E., & Evans, K. (1998). The causes, phenomenology, and consequences of hurt feelings. *Journal of Personality and Social Psychology, 74,* 1225–1237.

McEwen, W. J., & Greenberg, B. S. (1970). The effects of message intensity on receiver evaluations of source, message, and topic. *Journal of Communication, 20,* 340–350.

Meyersberg, H. A., & Post, R. M. (1979). An holistic developmental view of neural and psychological processes: A neurobiologic–psychoanalytic integration. *British Journal of Psychiatry, 135,* 139–155.

Murray, S. L., & Holmes, J. G. (1997). A leap of faith? Positive illusions in romantic relationships. *Personality and Social Psychology Bulletin, 23,* 586–604.

Murray, S. L., Holmes, J. G., & Griffin, D. W. (1996). The benefits of positive illusions: Idealization and the construction of satisfaction in close relationships. *Journal of Personality and Social Psychology, 70,* 79–98.

Murray, S. L., Rose, P., Bellavia, G. M., Homes, J. G., & Kusche, A. G. (2002). When rejection stings: How self-esteem constrains relationship-enhancement processes. *Journal of Personality and Social Psychology, 83,* 556–573.

Nichter, M. (2000). *Fat talk: What girls and their parents say about dieting.* Cambridge, MA: Harvard University Press.

Noller, P. (1982). Chanel consistency and inconsistency in the communications of married couples. *Journal of Personality and Social Psychology, 43,* 732–741.

Noller, P. (1985). Negative communications in marriage. *Journal of Social and Personal Relationships, 2,* 289–301.

Oatley, K. (1992). *Best laid schemes: The psychology of emotions.* Cambridge, England: Cambridge University Press.

Parkinson, B. (1997). Untangling the appraisal–emotion connection. *Personality and Social Psychology Review, 1,* 62–79.

Rigby, K. (2002). Bullying in childhood. In P. K. Smith & C. H. Hart (Eds.), *Blackwell handbook of social development* (pp. 549–568). Oxford, England: Blackwell.

Scherer, K. R., & Wallbott, H. G. (1994). Evidence for universality and cultural variation of differential emotion response patterning. *Journal of Personality and Social Psychology, 66,* 310–328.

Shaver, P., Schwartz, J., Kirson, D., & O'Connor, C. (1987). Emotion knowledge: Further exploration of a prototype approach. *Journal of Personality and Social Psychology, 52,* 1061–1086.

Simpson, J. A. (1990). Influence of attachment styles on romantic relationships. *Journal of Personality and Social Psychology, 59,* 971–980.

Thibaut, J. W., & Kelley, H. H. (1959). *The social psychology of groups.* New York: Wiley.

Vangelisti, A. L. (1994). Messages that hurt. In W. R. Cupach & B. H. Spitzberg (Eds.), *The dark side of interpersonal communication* (pp. 53–82). Hillsdale, NJ: Lawrence Erlbaum Associates.

Vangelisti, A. L. (2001). Making sense of hurtful interactions in close relationships: When hurt feelings create distance. In V. Manusov & J. H. Harvey (Eds.), *Attribution, communication behavior, and close relationships* (pp. 38–58). New York: Cambridge University Press.

Vangelisti, A. L., & Crumley, L. P. (1998). Reactions to messages that hurt: The influence of relational contexts. *Communication Monographs, 65,* 173–196.

Vangelisti, A. L., & Sprague, R. J. (1998). Guilt and hurt: Similarities, distinctions, and conversational strategies. In P. A. Andersen & L. K. Guerrero (Eds.), *Handbook of communication and emotion* (pp. 123–154). San Diego, CA: Academic Press.

Vangelisti, A. L., & Young, S. L. (2000). When words hurt: The effects of perceived intentionality on interpersonal relationships. *Journal of Social and Personal Relationships, 17,* 393–424.

Vangelisti, A. L., Young, S. L., Carpenter, K. E., & Alexander, A. L. (in press). Why does it hurt?: The perceived causes of hurt feelings. *Communication Research.*

Walker, L. E. (1979). *The battered woman.* New York: Harper & Row.

Weiner, B. (1979). A theory of motivation for some classroom experiences. *Journal of Educational Psychology, 71,* 3–25.

Weiner, B. (1986). *An attributional theory of motivation and emotion.* New York: Springer-Verlag.

Weiner, B. (1987). The social psychology of emotion: Applications of a naive psychology. *Journal of Social and Clinical Psychology, 5,* 405–419.

Weiner, B., & Handel, S. (1985). Anticipated emotional consequences of causal communications and reported communication strategy. *Developmental Psychology, 21,* 102–107.

Young, S. L. (2004). Factors that influence recipients' appraisals of hurtful communication. *Journal of Social and Personal Relationships, 21,* 291–303.

Zahn-Waxler, C., & Kochanska, G. (1990). The origins of guilt. In R. A. Thompson (Ed.), *Nebraska symposium on motivation* (pp. 183–258). Lincoln: University of Nebraska Press.

Zautra, A. J., Guenther, R. T., & Chartier, G. M. (1985). Attributions for real and hypothetical events: Their relation to self-esteem and depression. *Journal of Abnormal Psychology, 94,* 530–540.

8

Relationship Dissolution Following Infidelity

Julie H. Hall
University at Buffalo, The State University of New York

Frank D. Fincham
Florida State University

Tom and Diane have been dating exclusively for 3 years. Four months ago, Tom became sexually involved with a female coworker and has continued this relationship without Diane's knowledge. Diane recently overheard a phone conversation between Tom and his coworker and confronted him about it. Tom admitted to the affair but promised to end it and asked Diane for her forgiveness. He vowed never to stray from their relationship again, pledging his love and commitment to Diane. Diane initially agreed to give Tom another chance, but found that she was unable to put the incident out of her mind and decided to break off the relationship. Tom was upset, but agreed that they should go their separate ways.

Rick and Nancy have been married for 7 years and have a 2-year-old son. Early in their marriage, Rick had a brief affair with a neighbor that he revealed to Nancy and they were able to put behind them. However, several years later Nancy had a one-night stand with an exboyfriend, which she immediately regretted. She never told Rick about the affair, but has struggled with guilt and remorse over the incident. Nancy recently decided to disclose the infidelity to her husband, and he was extremely angered and hurt by this information and the fact that she had kept the affair a secret for so many years. Rick told Nancy that he needed some time to think about their future, but ultimately decided to rebuild their marriage. They went through counseling and over time Rick was able to forgive his wife. The couple regretted that the incident ever occurred, but felt that their relationship was even stronger after working through it.

How is it that two couples can experience infidelity in such different ways? Why is that infidelity led to relationship dissolution for Tom and Diane, whereas Rick and Nancy were able to reconcile and move forward? Admittedly, Nancy's fleeting indiscretion seems more minor than Tom's 4-month affair, but there may also be other factors at play. Dating couples are perceived as being more likely to separate after infidelity than are married couples (Roscoe, Cavanaugh, & Kennedy, 1988). In addition, couples are more likely to break up when infidelity is discovered "red-handed" as in the case of Tom and Diane than when it is voluntarily disclosed as it was by Nancy (Afifi, Falato, & Weiner, 2001). In light of these data, the differential effect of infidelity on these two couples seems obvious. However, the picture is not so simple, as there is also evidence to suggest that Rick and Nancy may have been more likely to separate than Tom and Diane. Men are less likely to forgive and more likely to break up with a sexually unfaithful partner than an emotionally unfaithful partner (Hall & Fincham, 2004; Shackelford, Buss, & Bennett, 2002). There is also a higher risk of relationship dissolution when both spouses have been unfaithful than there is when only one spouse has had an affair (Glass, 2003). Thus, it is evident that the impact of infidelity on a romantic relationship can be quite complex and multidimensional.

Given the multifaceted association between infidelity and relationship dissolution, it is crucial that researchers and clinicians not only explore the first-order effects of different variables on the likelihood of relationship termination, but also consider how such factors may interact to cause dissolution or reconciliation. In accordance with this important but admittedly lofty vision of contextualizing the decision to terminate a relationship following infidelity, in this chapter we explore the predictors of relationship dissolution following infidelity, as well as evidence of interdependence among these predictors. In this regard, we consider event-related factors, such as the type of infidelity and degree of involvement; cognitive factors, such as attributions and attitudes regarding extradyadic involvement and the other spouses' awareness of the infidelity; and individual or partner characteristics and relationship variables. After exploring the various determinants of relationship dissolution following infidelity, we consider the impact of extradyadic behavior on postmarital adjustment. In the penultimate section of the chapter, we examine the role of couple therapy and forgiveness in the aftermath of infidelity. Finally, we explore future directions for clinical work and research. However, we begin with a brief review of the infidelity literature to lay the foundation for later sections of the chapter.

THE CHEATING HEART: PREVALENCE, CAUSES, AND CONSEQUENCES OF INFIDELITY

According to conservative estimates, infidelity occurs in 20% to 25% of all marriages (Greeley, 1994; Laumann, Gagnon, Michael, & Michaels, 1994; Wiederman, 1997), and it can have a number of deleterious effects on a relationship and the individuals involved. Infidelity is the leading cause of divorce (Amato & Previti, 2003; Beitzig, 1989; Kitson, Babri, & Roach, 1985), and it often results in anger, disappointment, self-doubt (Buunk, 1995), and depression (Cano & O'Leary, 2000) among partners of unfaithful individuals. It has also been causally linked to domestic violence (Buss, 1994; Daly & Wilson, 1988). The scope of infidelity extends beyond the marital realm, with 65% to 75% of college students reporting engagement in some form of extradyadic involvement while in a serious dating relationship (Shackelford, LeBlanc, & Drass, 2000; Wiederman & Hurd, 1999). Further, therapists indicate that infidelity is the third most difficult problem to treat (Whisman, Dixon, & Johnson, 1997), and that forgiveness is a challenging but necessary part of the healing process (Coop Gordon & Baucom, 1999). Given the magnitude of this problem, researchers have devoted considerable energy to identifying the causes of infidelity in hopes of controlling or reversing these predisposing factors in at-risk couples.

However, such research has been plagued with methodological problems. Although prospective longitudinal studies are best able to address causality, the majority of infidelity research has focused on hypothetical scenarios or retrospective reports. In the former case, participants speculate about factors that would lead someone to be unfaithful. Unfortunately, it has yet to be established that these studies accurately predict the causes of actual infidelity. In the latter type of study, retrospective designs have been utilized to identify post hoc explanations of real-life infidelity, but these reports are often biased. Despite these methodological limitations, though, this body of research has yielded important information about variables that predict infidelity.

Predictors can be grouped into individual or relationship characteristics and contextual factors, and they are fairly consistent across dating and married samples. Roscoe et al. (1988) found that the perceived reasons for extradyadic behavior in dating relationships ran parallel to explanations for extramarital affairs. Individuals with permissive sexual values are more likely to engage in infidelity, and this permissiveness is more common among men, African Americans, and highly educated individuals (Smith, 1994). In addition, low religiosity is correlated with extramarital sex (Medora & Burton, 1981).

In terms of relationship characteristics, infidelity has been consistently linked to sexual or emotional dissatisfaction in one's primary relationship (e.g., Brown, 1991). However, this association may be moderated by partner sex or the nature of the infidelity. Evolutionary theory posits that men's desire for sexual variety stems from the basic need to spread their genes through procreation. Thus, men's affairs tend to be purely sexual in nature and may be unrelated to marital satisfaction (Atwater, 1982; Buunk, 1980; Glass & Wright, 1985; Pestrak, Martin, & Martin, 1985; Spanier & Margolis, 1983; Thompson, 1984). Women's affairs, however, are more emotionally charged, and women engaged in these affairs are more likely to be dissatisfied with their primary relationship (Atwater; Buunk; Glass & Wright, 1977, 1985). Length of marriage is also a significant predictor of infidelity, but this is confounded with marital satisfaction, which generally declines over time (Glass & Wright, 1977; Spanier & Margolis). Theoretical models of the relationship-oriented causes of infidelity have also gained empirical support. In accordance with equity theory, dating and married individuals are more likely to engage in infidelity when the relationship is inequitable or when they feel underbenefited than are partners in equitable or overbenefited relationships (Walster, Traupmann, & Walster, 1978). Among dating couples, low commitment was predictive of later physical and emotional infidelity, thus lending support to an investment model of infidelity (Drigotas, Safstrom, & Gentilia, 1999).

In regard to contextual predictors of infidelity, opportunities for extramarital involvement are associated with a higher likelihood of infidelity (e.g., Treas & Giesen, 2000). Opportunities can take the form of a high availability of potential partners (Johnson, 1970), frequent travel (Wellings, Field, Johnson, & Wadsworth, 1994), or living in a large city (Smith, 1994). In addition, substance-abusing spouses show greater infidelity (Hall, Fals-Stewart & Fincham, 2004) at both situational and global levels (Leigh & Stall, 1993). At the situational level, it is believed that alcohol intoxication may lead an individual to take sexual risks that would not be taken if the person were sober. At the global level, heavy episodic drinkers are more likely to have multiple sexual partners (Wechsler, Dowdall, Davenport, & Castillo, 1995); alcoholic patients, in addition to having multiple sex partners, show low rates of condom use and may trade sex for drugs or money (Scheidt & Windle, 1995).

The consequences of infidelity extend beyond the individuals involved in the infidelilty. With the rapid spread of sexually transmitted diseases (STDs), infidelity has become a significant public health issue. Not only are individuals who engage in unprotected sex outside of a committed relationship at direct risk of exposure to STDs, there is also emerging evidence that the primary partners of these individuals are at indirect risk of exposure to diseases such as HIV (Fals-Stewart et al., 2003). In the case of the "cheating heart," the stakes can literally become a matter of life and death.

The associations between the occurrence of infidelity and various so-called vulnerability factors raise an interesting issue. Given that infidelity is generally associated with relationship problems, which of these predicaments gives rise to relationship dissolution? Is dissolution truly a consequence of infidelity, or is relationship termination actually a consequence of relationship distress, of which infidelity is only a symptom? We must explore this distinction before proceeding further.

INFIDELITY AS A CAUSE OF RELATIONSHIP DISSOLUTION?

It is commonly assumed that relationship termination that follows infidelity is due to one or both partners' unfaithfulness. However, divorce has also been linked to a number of other factors beyond infidelity (e.g., incompatibility, alcohol or drug use), and many of the variables that are predictive of infidelity are also predictive of marital dissolution (Amato & Previti, 2003; Amato & Rogers, 1997; Booth & Edwards, 1985). These data make it difficult to discern whether infidelity is truly a cause of relationship dissolution, or whether it is just symptomatic of existing individual or relationship vulnerabilities that are also associated with divorce. One might argue that infidelity rarely occurs in the absence of individual or relationship characteristics that might also contribute to divorce. Thus, researchers must disentangle the numerous temporal and causal associations among vulnerability factors, infidelity, and divorce, in order to define the unique impact of infidelity on the decision to divorce.

Although 25% to 50% of divorcees report that a spouse's infidelity was the primary cause of their divorce (Kelly & Conley, 1987), individuals who separated or divorced following infidelity tend to attribute their breakups to a number of reasons aside from infidelity (Buunk, 1987). Thus, it is especially important to consider what infidelity may signify to a couple and what meaning the partners attach to it (Pestrak et al., 1985; Riessman, 1989). Did the infidelity occur on a whim, or did it stem from one partner's dissatisfaction with his or her marriage? Partners may be quick to attribute a subsequent decision to divorce to infidelity because it saves them from having to face other weaknesses in the relationship or in themselves (Buunk).

When a couple decides to separate after infidelity, how much of this decision can be attributed to the affair and how much must be attributed to other factors? This question is the precise reason why we must consider relationship dissolution in context, as the impact of infidelity differs according to the conditions under which it occurs. Amato and Rogers (1997) proposed a comprehensive model of the determinants of divorce, in which specific marital problems such as infidelity were proximally associated with divorce and demographic or life course variables were distally related to divorce. Infidelity, along with five other specific marital problems, partially mediated the association between demographic and life course variables and divorce. Although these individual and relationship factors were still uniquely related to divorce, infidelity was the strongest and most proximal predictor of relationship dissolution. This supports the notion that certain individual or relationship vulnerabilities predict the occurrence of infidelity, which in turn increases the likelihood of relationship dissolution.

It is evident that the role of infidelity in a couple's decision to terminate a romantic relationship is multidimensional, and it depends greatly on the context of the infidelity. It may moderate or mediate the association between a third variable and divorce, or it may be independently linked to relationship termination. These complexities require us to explore how the strength of the association between infidelity and relationship dissolution varies according to event-specific, cognitive, individual or partner, and relationship variables. However, it is important to bear in mind that the majority of research in this area has been cross-sectional in nature, which limits us to hypothesizing about the causal links among these variables, infidelity, and relationship dissolution.

PREDICTORS OF RELATIONSHIP DISSOLUTION FOLLOWING INFIDELITY

Event-Related Variables

The impact of infidelity on a couple's decision to separate depends in large part on the nature of the infidelity and how it was discovered. There are three distinct forms of infidelity, and each ranges on a continuum of mild involvement to major involvement. Emotional infidelity occurs when one's partner channels resources such as romantic love, time, and attention to someone else, whereas sexual infidelity refers to sexual activity with someone other than one's relationship partner (Shackelford, LeBlanc, & Drass, 2000). A third form of infidelity comprises the combination of sexual and emotional indiscretions. Although the majority of research on infidelity and relationship dissolution has focused on the most involved form of sexual infidelity, sexual intercourse with an extradyadic partner, there is evidence to suggest that these three forms of infidelity evoke different responses. Sexual infidelity is more likely to result in hostile or vengeful, shocked, nauseated or repulsed, humiliated, sexually aroused, or homicidal or suicidal feelings than is emotional infidelity (Shackelford et al.). In contrast, emotional infidelity is more likely to result in undesirable or insecure, depressed, helpless or abandoned, blameworthy, tired, or forgiving emotions than is sexual infidelity. Men report that they are more likely to break up with a dating partner who has been sexually unfaithful than one who has been emotionally unfaithful, whereas women report the opposite pattern (Hall & Fincham, 2004; Shackelford et al., 2002). Yet, within dating relationships, combined sexual and emotional infidelity is perceived as most likely to lead to a breakup (Hall & Fincham). Similarly, among married couples, the risk of relationship dissolution is greatest when a spouse is both sexually and emotionally involved with an extradyadic partner (Glass, 2003).

The degree of extradyadic involvement might also be predictive of relationship dissolution. Shackelford and Buss (1997) presented married couples with six hypothetical infidelity scenarios, and they asked each partner to rate the likelihood of ending the marriage in response to the other partner's infidelity. Infidelity behaviors ranged in severity and included flirting, passionately kissing, going on a romantic date, having a one-night stand, having a brief affair, and having a serious affair. There were no significant gender differences, and likelihoods varied in accordance with the severity of the infidelity behavior. Individuals anticipated being least likely to divorce in response to a partner's flirtation ($M = 2.5$–3.8%), and most likely to divorce because of a partner's serious affair ($M = 66.6$–69.0%). However, in a methodologically rigorous comparison of married or cohabiting individuals who ended their relationship or continued it after infidelity, Buunk (1987) found that the two groups did not differ in terms of the number of extradyadic relationships or degree of involvement (i.e., short term vs. long term). The risk of divorce is especially high when both spouses have engaged in infidelity and when infidelity continues after a course of marital therapy (Glass, 2003).

Although the nature and degree of infidelity are important in terms of predicting relationship dissolution, it is also crucial to consider how the infidelity is discovered. Afifi et al. (2001) found that the rates of relationship dissolution varied as a function of how a dating partner's infidelity was discovered. Of individuals who discovered their partner's infidelity by confronting the partner about his or her sexual fidelity, 86% terminated the relationship. Catching one's partner red-handed also led to high rates of relationship dissolution (83%), whereas 68% of those who heard of their partner's infidelity from a third party then ended the relationship. Unsolicited disclosure by the unfaithful party was least likely to lead to relationship dissolution. This may be because individuals who voluntarily confess their infidelity to a partner are more committed to repairing the relationship and are willing to make amends (Afifi et al., 2001). However, it may also be that these individuals provide more mitigating accounts of their infidelity (Mongeau & Schulz, 1997).

Cognitive Variables

However, even when the objective experience of infidelity is exactly the same for two couples (e.g., same degree of involvement, or the same method of discovery), the impact of the infidelity can vary greatly. This variability can stem from how the infidelity is interpreted by one or both partners, and what meaning is ascribed to the affair (Riessman, 1989). Among dating couples, maladaptive attributions regarding a partner's infidelity were associated with a higher risk of relationship dissolution (Hall & Fincham, 2004). Married individuals report that they would be most upset if a spouse's infidelity was the result of marital dissatisfaction, and least upset if the infidelity was done "on a whim," without an obvious reason (Wiederman & Allgeier, 1996). Among married or cohabiting couples who broke up following infidelity, individuals were more likely to report that their own and their partners' infidelity was motivated by aggression (e.g., revenge or anger) and deprivation (e.g., a void in the primary relationship) than were individuals who reconciled following infidelity (Buunk, 1987).

Interestingly, individuals whose relationships come apart following infidelity often ignore the role that their own infidelity may have played in the breakup (Buunk, 1987). When both partners have been unfaithful, individuals are more likely to attribute the breakup to their partners' infidelity than to their own (Buunk, 1987; Kinsey, Pomeroy, Marin, & Gebhard, 1953). This effect is most pronounced among men. However, this is likely due to self-serving biases rather than any empirical difference in the impact of one partner's infidelity compared with another's.

Attitudes regarding the acceptability of extradyadic involvement may also be predictive of relationship dissolution following infidelity. Although married or cohabiting individuals who broke up following infidelity did not differ in their disapproval of short-term extradyadic involvement from those who stayed together, the breakup group was more disapproving of long-term affairs (Buunk, 1987). These findings are difficult to interpret, as the breakup group's attitudes may have changed as a result of the relationship dissolution. Alternatively, those individuals with more permissive attitudes may not have broken up because they did not feel the need to choose between relationships when they could maintain both.

Implicit in our discussion thus far is the assumption that the uninvolved partner is aware of his or her spouse's infidelity, when actually this is rarely the case (Ellen, Vittinghoff, Bolan, Boyer, & Padian, 1998). Not surprisingly, the ramifications of infidelity are much more severe when the other spouse is aware of it; infidelity usually does not disturb the marriage until it is discovered by the other partner (Kinsey, Pomeroy, & Marin, 1948). Spousal awareness is higher among divorced or separated samples (e.g., Spanier & Margolis, 1983), suggesting that divorce is less likely when infidelity is not disclosed (Glass, 2003; Lawson, 1988).

Individual and Partner Variables

Infidelity may also have a differential impact on relationships depending on the characteristics of the individual partners. The sex of the partner, attractiveness, and personality have all been shown to moderate the association between infidelity and relationship dissolution. There is some evidence to suggest that divorce is more likely after a wife's infidelity than after a husband's infidelity (Beitzig, 1989; Kinsey et al., 1953). However, other researchers have found that the likelihood of divorce following infidelity does not vary according to the sex of the partner (Vaughn, 2002), and that men and women are equally disapproving of a spouse's infidelity (Spanier & Margolis, 1983). Nevertheless, overall, women are more likely to report that their divorce was caused by infidelity, specifically their partners' infidelity, than are men (Amato & Previti, 2003). Although the role of gender in the decision to divorce after a partner's infidelity is somewhat unclear, it is evident that men and women react differently to infidelity.

Men are more likely than women to feel content or relieved, homicidal or suicidal, happy, or sexually aroused in reaction to a partner's infidelity (Shackelford et al., 2000). However, women tend to show a more negative overall emotional reaction to infidelity than do men. Women are more likely than men to feel nauseated or repulsed, depressed, undesirable or insecure, helpless or abandoned, or anxious in reaction to a partner's infidelity. Furthermore, when asked to imagine a partner's infidelity, women report more self-doubt and disappointment than men (Buunk, 1995). Self-doubt was especially pronounced among women with lower self-esteem. However, women whose partners had been unfaithful in the past were less distressed by the prospect of additional infidelity (Buunk). This suggests that women may adapt to a partner's infidelity if it becomes a repeated pattern.

Mate value and attractiveness have also been considered as predictors of relationship dissolution following infidelity. When one partner is considered more desirable than the other, this discrepancy may contribute to the likelihood of divorce. Shackelford and Buss (1997) found that women who were higher in mate value or attractiveness than their husbands were more likely to predict that they would divorce if their spouse were unfaithful. From an evolutionary perspective, it is posited that these women would divorce after infidelity in order to find a mate with higher quality genes. However, men's predictions of divorce were unrelated to their wives' mate value or attractiveness.

Spousal personality characteristics are also predictive of relationship termination in the face of infidelity. Women who are married to emotionally unstable husbands or husbands lower in openness or intellect are more likely to predict that they would divorce if their spouse were unfaithful (Shackelford & Buss, 1997). This effect was found only for severe forms of infidelity such as brief or serious affairs, and not for more minor infidelity behaviors such as flirting or kissing. Interestingly, these men (i.e., low in emotional stability and openness or intellect) also reported that they would be more likely to divorce if their wife were unfaithful. Shackelford and Buss (1997) argued that the importance of men's personality characteristics is consistent with other literature on marital stability.

Shackelford and Buss (1997) also considered partner attributes and behaviors that were upsetting to the other spouse, and they found that these qualities were related to the likelihood of divorce. Husbands who complained of their wives' unfaithfulness and dishonesty were more likely to anticipate divorce if their wife had an affair. Meanwhile, wives' anticipations of divorcing an unfaithful husband were related to complaints of their husbands' inconsiderateness, abuse of alcohol, and emotional constriction.

Race and ethnicity are two additional variables that may moderate the likelihood of relationship dissolution following infidelity. Unfortunately, very little research has been conducted on this topic. Although rates of infidelity are higher among African Americans and Hispanics than among Caucasians (Amato & Rogers, 1997; Greeley, 1994; Treas & Giesen, 2000; Wiederman, 1997), rates of relationship dissolution following a partner's infidelity are not significantly different among minority and nonminority victims (Hall & Fincham, 2004). However, given the dearth of research in this area, diversity issues remain an important area for future research.

Relationship Variables

The association between infidelity and relationship dissolution may also vary depending on the nature or quality of the relationship. Although dating infidelity is considered more acceptable than marital infidelity (Sheppard, Nelson, & Andreoli-Mathie, 1995), relationship termination is considered a more likely consequence of infidelity in dating relationships than in marital relationships, potentially because the relative level of commitment is lower (Roscoe et al., 1988). In addition, the risk of divorce following infidelity appears to decrease with the length of marriage. Couples who experience infidelity in the early years of marriage are more likely to divorce than those who experience infidelity later in marriage (Glass & Wright, 1977; Pittman, 1989).

The likelihood of relationship termination following infidelity may also depend on the level of satisfaction within the primary relationship. Married or cohabiting partners who break up following infidelity recall lower relationship satisfaction than partners who stay together (Buunk, 1987). Similarly, couples who are less committed to each other and to working on their relationship after infidelity are more likely to divorce (Beach, Jouriles, & O'Leary, 1985; Glass, 2003). There is some evidence to suggest that emotional dissatisfaction is especially relevant for women in terms of the likelihood of dissolution, whereas sexual dissatisfaction is more salient for men (Betzig, 1989). In contrast, Shackelford and Buss (1997) found that women's marital satisfaction (general, sexual, and emotional) was unrelated to the anticipated likelihood of divorce after a husband's infidelity. However, men reporting lower emotional and composite marital satisfaction were more likely to indicate that they would seek divorce if their wife were unfaithful.

Additional negative relationship characteristics are also associated with a higher likelihood of divorce following infidelity. Women involved in high-conflict marriages are more likely to indicate that they would divorce a husband who engaged in a one-night stand or brief affair (Shackelford & Buss, 1997). Similarly, women whose marriages are less cooperative and agreeable, and more quarrelsome are more likely to report that they would divorce their husband after various infidelity behaviors. Shackelford and Buss argue that this is consistent with evidence that women are more sensitive to relationship problems than are men.

THE AFTERMATH OF INFIDELITY

Impact of Infidelity on Postrelationship Adjustment

The discovery of a husband's infidelity or divorce following such infidelity is associated with increased risk of a major depressive episode (Cano & O'Leary, 2000). However, this is unremarkable, given that divorced individuals generally report higher levels of depression, lower life satisfaction, and more health problems than married individuals (Amato, 2000). Thus, it is important to consider how infidelity may contribute to or exacerbate these problems.

Although divorce is predictive of depression, it may be that infidelity increases this risk; infidelity-related divorces may be even greater stressors than other divorces, because the heavy emotional and psychological toll associated with adultery is compounded with the distress of divorce. Indeed, individuals who divorce following infidelity are more distressed after the dissolution than those who divorce without infidelity (Kitson, 1992). They are also less well adjusted to the divorce and more attached to the former spouse than are those whose divorce was not related to infidelity (Amato & Previti, 2003). Adjustment scores are especially low when the infidelity was committed by one's spouse rather than oneself. Similarly, in an analysis of women's long-term adjustment to divorce, Thabes (1997) found that infidelity during the marriage contributed significantly to postdivorce depression. However, this study was restricted to women who had not remarried, and it is unclear whether the findings would generalize to remarried women or to men. There is preliminary evidence to suggest that women are more likely than men to be depressed, disappointed, and self-doubting after a partner's infidelity (Buunk, 1995; Shackelford et al., 2000; Sweeney & Horwitz, 2001).

However, the impact of infidelity on postdivorce depression may not be unidimensional; when examining initiator status (i.e., which spouse initiated the divorce) and spousal infidelity, Sweeney and Horwitz (2001) found little evidence that either of these factors directly affects postdivorce depression. Rather, it appears that initiator status moderates the effect of spousal infidelity on depression, such that individuals who initiate divorce from an unfaithful spouse are less likely to be depressed than those whose partner initiates the divorce. It may be that initiating divorce from an unfaithful spouse increases one's sense of control over the situation, thus mitigating the negative emotional impact of infidelity.

Infidelity may also be associated with poor adjustment among those individuals who commit it. Individuals, especially women, tend to feel extremely guilty after engaging in extradyadic behavior (Spanier & Margolis, 1983). When compared with same-sex spouses who had not engaged in infidelity, those individuals who had been unfaithful reported higher levels of depression or lower commitment levels (Beach et al., 1985). Thus, mental health issues may actually be a greater concern for the guilty party than for the spouse. It has been suggested that this depression stems from the unfaithful spouse's ambivalence about staying in the marriage, an ambivalence that may be maintained by the same lack of commitment that prompted the infidelity (Beach et al., 1985).

Despite the many negative outcomes associated with infidelity, some argue that it can have positive effects on the primary relationship. Infidelity helps some individuals, men in particular, to recognize that their primary relationships are more valuable and fulfilling than they had previously thought (Kinsey et al., 1948). Couples often feel closer after working through the infidelity (Olson, Russell, Higgins-Kessler, & Miller, 2002), and many report that their marriages improved following infidelity (Atwater, 1982). However, these findings may be due in part to individuals' efforts to minimize their own guilt if they were the ones who had the affair. In general, the overwhelming majority of evidence suggests that the deleterious effects of infidelity far outweigh evidence to the contrary. Given the distress that is associated with infidelity and with relationship dissolution, it is not surprising that many couples turn to therapy as they consider the future of their relationship.

Couple Therapy

Approximately 25% to 30% of couples in marital therapy report that infidelity is a concern (Green, Lee, & Lustig, 1974). Although many of these couples look to the therapist for guidance as to whether they should terminate the relationship or attempt to salvage it, this is an issue for the couple to decide as they go through therapy (Thompson, 1984). Glass (2002) has suggested that a general decision about the future of the relationship be made by the couple early in therapy, as it will guide the course of treatment. Couples are asked to decide whether the therapy should be labeled as marital, reconciliation, separation, or ambivalence therapy. The larger goals of treatment include establishing a safe therapeutic environment, understanding the meaning of the infidelity, creating good will or hope, and deciding whether to stay married or to separate (Glass, 2002). Therapy provides an opportunity for clients to express their thoughts and feelings about the affair in a constructive way, with an emphasis on active listening and empathic understanding (Thompson). It is important that this process not be rushed, so that clients do not make a decision about the future of the relationship without fully exploring the impact of the infidelity.

Although infidelity is both a common and a trying issue for therapists, marital interventions for addressing extramarital affairs have gained little empirical support. However, there is emerging evidence to suggest that the multitheoretical intervention of Gordon and Baucom (1999) may be effective in promoting recovery from such affairs (Gordon, Baucom, & Snyder,

1998, in press). This intervention is consistent with Glass's (2002) approach, in which the impact of infidelity is conceptualized through a trauma framework. Infidelity is traumatic in that it shakes individuals' fundamental assumptions about themselves, their relationships, and the world (Janoff-Bulman, 1992). This intervention integrates the trauma literature with a growing body of research on forgiveness, and it helps couples to move through stages of dealing with the impact of the infidelity, searching for meaning, and reaching recovery or moving forward. In the first stage (dealing with the impact of infidelity), the goal is to focus on the immediate problems caused by the infidelity, such as emotional dysregulation and the expression of anger and hurt. After the partners have explored the immediate emotional impact of the infidelity, the next stage involves contextualizing the infidelity by identifying the factors that may have contributed to the affair and increasing each partner's empathic understanding of the other's position. The decision of whether to end the relationship or stay together is not faced until the third stage, in which the partners are also encouraged to explore forgiveness, consider what they have learned from the experience, and reexamine their marriage. If they decide to reconcile, the remainder of therapy is devoted to troubleshooting, or exploring which issues are still problematic or may arise in the future. Alternatively, a decision to terminate the relationship is followed by efforts to help the couple separate as peacefully as possible, ideally with respect, empathy, and forgiveness.

The intervention by Gordon and Baucom (1999) has been reported to reduce depression, posttraumatic stress disorder symptomatology, and global marital distress, and to increase partner forgiveness (Gordon et al., in press). More general marital interventions have also shown modest effects in promoting recovery from extramarital affairs; couples undergoing traditional behavioral couple therapy or integrative behavioral couple therapy after infidelity were more distressed at the onset of treatment than other couples, but they improved at a greater rate (Atkins, 2003). Therapy generally facilitates communication between partners, and research has shown that couples who are able to discuss the infidelity in depth are less likely to separate or divorce (Vaughn, 2002). Therapy also provides a forum for the injured spouse to have his or her questions about the infidelity answered by the unfaithful spouse; when the unfaithful spouse is willing to answer such questions, there is a lower risk of divorce (Vaughn).

Despite the positive relationship outcomes associated with couple therapy, therapy will not necessarily promote or ensure reconciliation. Among couples in marital therapy, those who report infidelity are more likely to separate or divorce (Glass, 2002). Humphrey (1983) found that, among couples in therapy following infidelity, 46% of those in which the husband had been unfaithful were separated or divorced at the end of therapy, and 48% of those in which the wife had been unfaithful ended the relationship by the close of treatment. Nevertheless, regardless of a couple's decision to separate or stay together, therapy is an excellent vehicle for closure. Forgiveness is also becoming more prominent in the infidelity-intervention literature, as it has been shown to benefit both couples who reconcile and those who divorce.

Infidelity: A Forgivable Offense?

Many individuals have misconceptions about what it means to forgive a partner's infidelity. Forgiveness does not require an individual to excuse or condone a partner's extradyadic behavior, nor does it mean that a couple must reconcile. Infidelity is widely considered to be unacceptable in our society, and forgiveness does not ask anyone to believe otherwise. Rather, forgiveness is a process by which an individual replaces destructive responses towards one's partner, such as avoidance or revenge, with constructive behavior (McCullough, Worthington, & Rachal, 1997). Forgiveness is an instrumental component of the intervention by Gordon and Baucom (1999) for recovery from extramarital affairs. Within this intervention, the goal of forgiveness is for the injured spouse to gain a more balanced view of the offender and the infidelity, while decreasing negative affect toward the offender (including the right to punish him or her) and increasing empathy toward the partner. The cultivation of empathy may be especially important, given its key role in promoting forgiveness (McCullough et al.). Indeed, couples recognize that forgiveness is a necessary part of the healing process, and is equally important for couples that reconcile as it is for those who divorce (Brown, 1991; Olson et al., 2002). Brown has argued that both partners—the one who engaged in infidelity and the one who did not—must seek forgiveness for letting their marriage decline. However, it is important to recognize that forgiveness is a process, and thus may be a long and slow transformation (McCullough, Fincham, & Tsang, 2003); partners should not expect to forgive one another overnight.

Although forgiveness does not require a couple to stay together, it may make reconciliation more likely. In a study of infidelity in dating relationships, Hall and Fincham (2004) found that forgiveness predicted a lower likelihood of relationship dissolution and fully mediated the association between attributions and breakup. This suggests that, for many couples affected by infidelity, forgiveness is the vehicle through which they are able to reconcile. Thus, marital therapists treating infidelity can use forgiveness as a tool to salvage relationships, or at least enable them to end amicably. That is not to say that it is always in the best interest of a couple to remain together after a serious betrayal such as infidelity. Nevertheless, despite a couple's decision to break up or remain together, forgiveness can have significant emotional and physical health benefits (McCullough et al., 1997; Toussaint, Williams, Musick, & Everson, 2001; Witvliet, Ludwig, & Vander Laan, 2001). It may be that the poor adjustment shown by individuals whose partners have been unfaithful is due in some part to the anger and resentment that they still hold toward their expartner. Perhaps forgiveness would counteract these emotions and act as a buffer against such negative postrelationship adjustment; however, this remains an empirical question. In the next section of the chapter, we turn explicitly to other unanswered empirical questions, in an effort to identify directions for future research that might provide a more complete understanding of the complex association between infidelity and relationship dissolution.

FUTURE DIRECTIONS

As emphasized throughout this chapter, the decision to terminate a romantic relationship following infidelity must be considered in context. Although we identified many variables that may influence the likelihood of relationship dissolution, the absence of a larger theoretical or empirical framework makes it difficult to synthesize and interpret these associations.

The Need for a Contextual Framework

It is evident that there are many factors that make relationship dissolution more likely following infidelity, and it is fairly easy to interpret these moderators individually. For example, evolutionary theory posits that divorce is more likely following a wife's sexual affair because the husband's paternity is threatened (e.g., Shackelford et al., 2002). However, when one considers a given infidelity-related divorce in full context, with attention to the full range of event-specific, cognitive, individual or partner, and relationship variables, the roles of each of these individual factors in the decision to divorce are much more difficult to disentangle.

Shackelford and Buss (1997) argued that the various theories (e.g., equity theory, invest-ment theory, and evolutionary theory) and predictors of divorce following infidelity can be synthesized in a spousal cost-infliction model, in which individuals weigh the value of being in a given romantic relationship. Thus, infidelity forces the betrayed partner to evaluate the costs and benefits of remaining in the primary relationship and to compare them to those of divorce. According to this model, predictors such as degree of involvement, personality variables, and relationship satisfaction represent different levels of spousal cost infliction. For example, being married to an emotionally unstable partner is expected to inflict a variety of costs on an individual, thus making divorce a less costly and more beneficial alternative. This model is based on Lewin's (1951) work, later adapted by Buunk (1987), in which there are "push" (i.e., high cost and low benefits of primary relationship) and "pull" factors (i.e., low cost and high benefits of alternative relationship) that may lead to relationship termination. There is evidence that push factors may be more salient than pull factors in the decision to terminate a relationship follow-ing infidelity; individuals whose relationships ended following infidelity scored more highly on push factors than did individuals who remained in their primary relationships, whereas the two groups did not differ significantly on pull factors (Buunk). Although this attempt to synthesize the predictors of relationship dissolution within an overarching framework is commendable, the spousal cost-infliction model is limited in two major ways. First, this model is not specific to infidelity, and it could easily be applied in the absence of infidelity. Individuals may con-sider the costs and benefits of a given relationship under any conditions—not just following infidelity. In addition, this framework does not consider possible interactions among predictors.

The true test of a contextual framework will be in its ability to account for higher order effects among predictors, as there may not be simple linear associations between these variables and the decision to separate or divorce. For example, when one's partner has been mildly unfaithful (e.g., kissing someone else), attributes the infidelity to marital dissatisfaction, and is emotionally unstable, what is the likelihood of divorce? The possibilities for interaction effects are seemingly endless because predictors tend to co-occur. When the variables are considered that influence an individual's decision to terminate a relationship following infidelity, it will be critical to explore how certain factors may exacerbate, buffer, or have no effect on the impact of other variables. Undoubtedly, it will be difficult to formulate a contextual model that fully accommodates higher order predictors (interaction effects). The first step toward this goal is to expand current studies to explore interactions among predictors of relationship dissolution, as there are very few data in this area.

The development of an overall contextual model will also be critical in that it will allow researchers to detect overlap among predictors. When all variables that predict relationship dissolution after infidelity are considered simultaneously, redundancy among such variables will become apparent. For example, negative personality traits (e.g., low emotional stability) are predictive of lower relationship satisfaction and are also related to spousal complaints such as those considered earlier (Buss, 1991; Karney & Bradbury, 1995; Shackelford & Buss, 2000). If these variables were evaluated within a single model, it may become evident that they overlap considerably and have little unique predictive power when considered individually. Factor analysis will be useful in reducing the long list of factors that are predictive of dissolution following infidelity to a smaller, more informative group of independent components.

Further Exploration and Definition of Predictors

Given the need to consolidate the list of variables that predict relationship dissolution fol-lowing infidelity, it seems ironic that we would also suggest research to explore additional predictors and to further define existing ones. However, it would be premature to call for a moratorium on the exploration of variables that predict relationship dissolution following infidelity, because such predictors have received far less attention than the predictors of infidelity. One issue in particular that requires further consideration is documentation of the full range of behaviors that constitute infidelity, and movement away from focusing on only the stereotypic extramarital intercourse. Emotional infidelity has gained more attention in recent years, as more and more platonic workplace friendships are developing into emotional affairs (e.g., Peterson, 2003). Internet infidelity is also becoming recognized as a legitimate form of emotional betrayal (e.g., Shaw, 1997). It will be critical for future research to explore these forms of emotional infidelity and to determine how potent they might be in disrupting a relationship. *Sexual infidelity* is also somewhat of a hodgepodge term, as it constitutes minor indiscretions such as a kiss as well as major betrayals like intercourse. Thus, it will be essential in future work for researchers to make their conceptualization of infidelity explicit and to collect specific information from participants regarding discrete infidelity behaviors. To this end, it may become evident that different cohorts hold different views of what constitutes infidelity. Such efforts will lead not only to refinement of the construct of infidelity but also to greater precision in identifying infidelity behaviors that are associated with relationship dissolution.

Preventive Variables

The overwhelming majority of research in this area focuses on the so-called vulnerability factors, such as relationship dissatisfaction, which make separation or divorce more likely following infidelity. As a result, there is a large gap in the literature regarding variables that protect or act as a buffer against infidelity-related relationship dissolution. We know very little about couples whose affairs do not lead to divorce, and about the individual or relationship qualities or processes that protect against relationship dissolution. It would be a logical error to assume that "buffers" simply reflect the opposite of vulnerability factors. For example, one might conclude that marital satisfaction serves a protective function because marital dissatisfaction predicts divorce. However, it has become increasingly apparent that positive, satisfying marital processes reflect much more than the absence of negative processes (Fincham, 1998). Thus, future research must also explore the characteristics and mechanisms that prevent relationship dissolution following infidelity.

CONCLUSION

At the opening of the chapter, we considered two couples that shared the common experience of infidelity but made drastically different decisions about the future of their relationship. This example highlighted the importance of contextualizing such a decision, and considering the many variables that may determine how infidelity affects a romantic relationship. We went on to outline how the association between infidelity and relationship dissolution may vary according to event-related, cognitive, individual or partner, and relationship variables. This analysis was followed by an exploration of how individuals and couples deal with infidelity or relationship termination. We concluded the chapter by suggesting future directions for research in this area, with the overall goal of working toward a contextual model of the many factors that influence the decision to end a relationship after infidelity.

REFERENCES

Afifi, W., Falato, W., & Weiner, J. (2001). Identity concerns following a severe relational transgression: The role of discovery method for the relational outcomes of infidelity. *Journal of Social and Personal Relationships, 18,* 291–308.

Amato, P. R. (2000). The consequences of divorce for adults and children. *Journal of Marriage and the Family, 62,* 1269–1287.

Amato, P. R., & Previti, D. (2003). People's reasons for divorcing: Gender, social class, the life course, and adjustment. *Journal of Family Issues, 24,* 602–626.

Amato, P. R., & Rogers, S. J. (1997). A longitudinal study of marital problems and subsequent divorce. *Journal of Marriage and the Family, 59,* 612–624.

Atkins, D. C. (2003). *Infidelity and marital therapy: Initial findings from a randomized clinical trial.* Unpublished doctoral dissertation, University of Washington, Seattle.

Atwater, L. (1982). *The extramarital connection: Sex, intimacy and identity.* New York: Irvington.

Beach, S. R., Jouriles, E. N., & O'Leary, K. D. (1985). Extramarital sex: Impact on depression and commitment in couples seeking marital therapy. *Journal of Sex and Marital Therapy, 11,* 99–108.

Beitzig, L. (1989). Causes of conjugal dissolution: A cross-cultural study. *Current Anthropology, 30,* 654–676.

Booth, A., & Edwards, J. N. (1985). Age at marriage and marital instability. *Journal of Marriage and Family, 47,* 67–75.

Brown, E. (1991). *Patterns of infidelity and their treatment.* New York: Brunner/Mazel.

Buss, D. M. (1991). Conflict in married couples: Personality predictors of anger and upset. *Journal of Personality, 59,* 663–687.

Buss, D. (1994). *The evolution of desire: Strategies of human mating.* New York: Basic Books.

Buunk, B. (1980). Extramarital sex in the Netherlands. *Alternative Lifestyles, 3,* 11–39.

Buunk, B. (1987). Conditions that promote breakups as a consequence of extradyadic involvements. *Journal of Social and Clinical Psychology, 5,* 271–284.

Buunk, B. (1995). Sex, self-esteem, dependency and extradyadic sexual experience as related to jealousy responses. *Journal of Social and Personal Relationships, 12,* 147–153.

Cano, A., & O'Leary, K. D. (2000). Infidelity and separations precipitate major depressive episodes and symptoms of nonspecific depression and anxiety. *Journal of Consulting and Clinical Psychology, 68,* 774–781.

Coop Gordon, K., & Baucom, D. H. (1999). A multitheoretical intervention for promoting recovery from extramarital affairs. *Clinical Psychology: Science and Practice, 6,* 382–399.

Daly, M., & Wilson, M. (1988). *Homicide.* New York: de Gruyter.

Drigotas, S. M., Safstrom, C. A., & Gentilia, T. (1999). An investment model prediction of dating infidelity. *Journal of Personality and Social Psychology, 77,* 509–524.

Ellen, J. M., Vittinghoff, E., Bolan, G., Boyer, C. B., & Padian, N. S. (1998). Individuals' perceptions about their sex partners' risk behaviors. *Journal of Sex Research, 35,* 328–332.

Fals-Stewart, W., Birchler, G. R., Hoebbel, C., Kashdan, T. B., Golden, J., & Parks, K. (2003). An examination of indirect risk of exposure to HIV among wives of substance-abusing men. *Drug and Alcohol Dependence, 70,* 65–76.

Fincham, F. D. (1998). Child development and marital relations. *Child Development, 69,* 543–574.

Glass, S. P. (2002). Couple therapy after the trauma of infidelity. In A. S. Gurman & N. S. Jacobson (Eds.), *Clinical handbook of couple therapy* (3rd ed., pp. 488–507). New York: Guilford.

Glass, S. P. (2003). *Not "just friends:" Protect your relationships from infidelity and heal the trauma of betrayal.* New York: The Free Press.

Glass, S. P., & Wright, T. L. (1985). Sex differences in types of extramarital involvement and marital dissatisfaction. *Sex Roles, 12,* 1101–1119.

Glass, S. P., & Wright, T. L. (1977). The relationship of extramarital sex, length of marriage, and sex differences on marital satisfaction and romanticism: Athanasiou's data reanalyzed. *Journal of Marriage and the Family, 39,* 691–703.

Gordon, K. C., & Baucom, D. H. (1999). A multitheoretical intervention for promoting recovery from extramarital affairs. *Clinical Psychology: Science and Practice, 6,* 382–399.

Gordon, K. C., Baucom, D. H., & Snyder, D. (1998, November). Addressing infidelity: Preliminary results for a forgiveness-based marital intervention. In D. Atkins (Chair), *Infidelity: New developments in research and clinical intervention.* Symposium conducted at the meeting of the Association for Advancement of Behavior Therapy, Washington, DC.

Gordon, K. C., Baucom, D. H., & Snyder, D. K. (in press). An integrative intervention for promoting recovery from extramarital affairs. *Journal of Marital and Family Therapy.*

Greeley, A. (1994). Marital infidelity. *Society, 31,* 9–13.

Green, B. L., Lee, R. R., & Lustig, N. (1974). Conscious and unconscious factors in marital infidelity. *Medical Aspects of Human Sexuality, 8,* 97–105.

Hall, J. H., Fals-Stewart, W., & Fincham, F. (2004). *Risk of exposure to STDs among wives of alcoholic men.* Manuscript submitted for publication.

Hall, J. H., & Fincham, F. (2004). *Reactions to infidelity.* Manuscript submitted for publication.

Humphrey, F. G. (1983, November). *Extramarital relationships: Therapy issues for marriage and family therapists.* Paper presented at the annual meeting of the American Association for Marriage and Family Therapy, Washington, DC.

Janoff-Bulman, R. (1992). *Shattered assumptions: Towards a new psychology of trauma.* New York: The Free Press.

Johnson, R. E. (1970). Some correlates of extramarital coitus. *Journal of Marriage and the Family, 32,* 449–456.

Karney, B. R., & Bradbury, T. N. (1995). The longitudinal course of marital quality and stability: A review of theory, method, and research. *Psychological Bulletin, 118,* 3–34.

Kelly, E. L., & Conley, J. J. (1987). Personality and compatibility: A prospective analysis of marital stability and marital satisfaction. *Journal of Personality and Social Psychology, 52,* 27–40.

Kinsey, A. C., Pomeroy, W. B., & Marin, C. E. (1948). *Sexual behavior in the human male.* Philadelphia: Saunders.

Kinsey, A. C., Pomeroy, W. B., & Marin, C. E., & Gebhard, P. H. (1953). *Sexual behavior in the human female.* Philadelphia: W.B. Saunders.

Kitson, G. C., with Holmes, W. M. (1992). *Portrait of divorce: Adjustment to marital breakdown.* New York: Guilford.

Kitson, G. C., Babri, K. B., & Roach, M. J. (1985). Who divorces and why: A review. *Journal of Family Issues, 6,* 255–293.

Laumann E. O., Gagnon, J. H., Michael, R. T., & Michaels, S. (1994). *The social organization of sexuality: Sexual practices in the United States.* Chicago: University of Chicago Press.

Lawson, A. (1988). *Adultery: An analysis of love and betrayal.* New York: Basic Books.

Leigh, B. C., & Stall, R. (1993). Substance use and risky sexual behavior for exposure to HIV: Issues in methodology. *American Psychologist, 48,* 1035–1045.

Lewin, K. (1951). *Field theory in social science.* New York: Harper.

McCullough, M. E., Fincham, F. D., & Tsang, J. (2003). Forgiveness, forbearance, and time: The temporal unfolding of transgression-related interpersonal motivations. *Journal of Personality and Social Psychology, 84,* 540–557.

McCullough, M., Worthington, E., & Rachal, K. (1997). Interpersonal forgiving in close relationships. *Journal of Personality and Social Psychology, 73,* 321–336.

Medora, N. P., & Burton, M. M. (1981). Extramarital sexual attitudes and norms of an undergraduate student population. *Adolescence, 16,* 251–262.

Mongeau, P. A., & Schulz, B. E. (1997). What he doesn't know won't hurt him (or me): Verbal responses and attributions following sexual infidelity. *Communication Reports, 10,* 143–153.

Olson, M. M., Russell, C. S., Higgins-Kessler, M., & Miller, R. B. (2002). Emotional processes following disclosure of an extramarital affair. *Journal of Marital and Family Therapy, 28,* 423–434.

Pestrak, V. A., Martin, D., & Martin, M. (1985). Extramarital sex: An examination of the literature. *International Journal of Family Therapy, 7,* 107–113.

Peterson, K. S. (2003, January 9). Infidelity reaches beyond having sex. *USA Today,* pp. D8.

Pittman, F. (1989). *Private lies.* New York: Norton.

Riessman, C. K. (1989). Life events, meaning, and narrative: The case of infidelity and divorce. *Social Science and Medicine, 29,* 743–751.

Roscoe, B., Cavanaugh, L. E., & Kennedy, D. R. (1988). Dating infidelity: Behaviors, reasons, and consequences. *Adolescence, 23,* 34–43.

Scheidt, D. M., & Windle, M. (1995). The Alcoholics in Treatment HIV Risk (ATRISK) Study: Gender, ethnic, and geographic group comparisons. *Journal of Studies of Alcohol, 56,* 300–308.

Shackelford, T. K., & Buss, D. M. (1997). Anticipation of marital dissolution as a consequence of spousal infidelity. *Journal of Social and Personal Relationships, 14,* 793–808.

Shackelford, T. K., & Buss, D. M. (2000). Marital satisfaction and spousal cost-infliction. *Personality and Individual Differences, 28,* 917–928.

Shackelford, T., Buss, D., & Bennett, K. (2002). Forgiveness or breakup: Sex differences in responses to a partner's infidelity. *Cognition and Emotion, 12,* 299–307.

Shackelford, T. K., LeBlanc, G. J., & Drass, E. (2000). Emotional reactions to infidelity. *Cognition and Emotion, 14,* 643–659.

Shaw, J. (1997). Treatment rationale for internet infidelity. *Journal of Sex Education and Therapy, 22,* 29–34.

Sheppard, V. J., Nelson, E. S., Andreoli-Mathie, V. (1995). Dating relationships and infidelity: Attitudes and behavior. *Journal of Sex and Marital Therapy, 21,* 202–212.

Smith, T. W. (1994). Attitudes toward sexual permissiveness: Trends, correlates, and behavioral connections. In A. S. Rossi (Ed.), *Sexuality across the life course* (pp. 63–97). Chicago: University of Chicago Press.

Spanier, G. B., & Margolis, R. L. (1983). Marital separation and extramarital sexual behavior. *Journal of Sex Research, 19,* 23–48.

Sweeney, M. M., & Horwitz, A. V. (2001). Infidelity, initiation, and the emotional climate of divorce: Are there implications for mental health? *Journal of Health and Social Behavior, 42,* 295–309.

Thabes, V. (1997). A survey analysis of women's long-term, postdivorce adjustment. *Journal of Divorce and Remarriage, 27*(3/4), 163–175.

Thompson, A. P. (1984). Emotional and sexual components of extramarital relations. *Journal of Marriage and the Family, 10,* 35–42.

Toussaint, L. L., Williams, D. R., Musick, M. A., & Everson, S. A. (2001). Forgiveness and health: Age differences in a U.S. probability sample. *Journal of Adult Development, 8,* 249–257.

Treas, J., & Giesen, D. (2000). Sexual infidelity among married and cohabitating Americans. *Journal of Marriage and the Family, 62,* 48–60.

Vaughn, P. (2002). *Help for therapists (and their clients) in dealing with affairs.* La Jolla, CA: Dialogue Press.

Walster, E., Traupmann, J., & Walster, G. W. (1978). Equity and extramarital sexuality. *Archives of Sexual Behavior, 7,* 127–142.

Wellings, K., Field, J., Johnson, A., & Wadsworth, J. (1994). *Sexual behavior in Britain.* London: Penguin.

Wechsler, H., Dowdall, G. W., Davenport, A., & Castillo, S. (1995). Correlates of college student binge drinking. *American Journal of Public Health, 85,* 921–926.

Wiederman, M. W. (1997). Extramarital sex: Prevalence and correlates in a national survey. *The Journal of Sex Research, 34,* 167–174.

Wiederman, M. W., & Allgeier, E. R. (1996). Expectations and attributions regarding extramarital sex among young married individuals. *Journal of Psychology and Human Sexuality, 8,* 21–35.

Wiederman, M., & Hurd, C. (1999). Extradyadic involvement during dating. *Journal of Social and Personal Relationships, 16,* 265–274.

Whisman, M. A., Dixon, A. E., & Johnson, B. (1997). Therapists' perspectives of couple problems and treatment issues in couple therapy. *Journal of Family Psychology, 11,* 361–366.

Witvliet, C. V., Ludwig, T. E., Vander Laan, K. L. (2001). Granting forgiveness or harboring grudges: Implications for emotion, physiology, and health. *Psychological Science, 12,* 117–123.

9

What Goes Up May Come Down: Sex and Gendered Patterns in Relational Dissolution

Steve Duck
University of Iowa

Julia T. Wood
University of North Carolina at Chapel Hill

Both women and men form intimate relationships, and both sexes end some of those relationships. That much the sexes share. What they may not share is how they experience relationships, the reasons they are satisfied or dissatisfied with those relationships, and the ways they engage in ending relationships. In this chapter, we explore what is known about women's and men's and masculine and feminine understandings of close relationships, both when they are working well and when they are not. In the pages that follow, we discuss research that gives us insights into the somewhat different ways that the sexes and genders, in general, define and respond to relationship distress.

Our discussion is organized into three sections. First, we distinguish between two concepts that are often conflated: sex and gender. Second, we summarize findings from research on gendered patterns and preferences in intimate relationships to provide insight into how women and men understand and deal with relationship stresses and dissolution. In the final section of the chapter, we situate the sex- and gender-related patterns of relational decline and dissolution within broader cultural horizons.

DISTINGUISHING BETWEEN SEX AND GENDER

Although the terms *sex* and *gender* are often used as if they are synonyms, actually they are distinct in important ways. In any discussion of relationship dissolution, and more generally in considerations of social and personal interaction, the distinction has become more critical as later research has shown that early discussions attributing relational outcomes to sex are wrong at worst and overgeneralized at best. Sex, being different from gender as we indicate in the paragraphs that follow, is too broad and crude a distinction to correctly identify features differentially associated with relationship dissolution, or indeed with other relational features (Canary & Emmers-Sommer, 1997). Hence the discussion of the differences between sex and

169

gender will provide the foundation for a judicious understanding of sex- and gender-related dynamics in relationship dissolution.

Sex is a biological category—male or female—that is determined genetically. Gender refers to social definitions of masculinity and femininity at specific historical moments and in specific cultural contexts. Put another way, the term *gender* refers to the social meanings that others and we ourselves attach to sex. Gender is also the actions we take or do not take to embody or resist social meanings associated with male and female human beings. Gender influences expectations and perceptions of women and men, as well as the roles, opportunities, and material circumstances of women's and men's lives.

Although early research differentiated the relational endings of men and women (e.g., seeing men as first in, last out; Hill, Rubin, & Peplau, 1976), later research showed that the picture is more complex (Canary & Emmers-Sommer, 1997). Given that both men and women can adopt feminine or masculine perspectives on and performance styles in relationships (and many people combine elements of each gender style), the ending of relationships cannot be understood in terms of sex alone. It is therefore necessary to distinguish the two concepts—what is given (biological sex) and what is shaped by social experience (gender)—in order to see which relational characteristics and behaviors can be laid at the door of each construct.

Sex

A person is designated as of one or the other of the two sexes recognized in Western culture—male or female—based on genitalia (penis and testes in males; clitoris and vagina in females) and internal sex organs (ovaries and uterus in females; prostate in males). Genitalia and other sex markers are determined by chromosomes. The presence or absence of a Y chromosome determines whether a fetus will develop into what we recognize as male or female. Thus, XX results in a female, and XY results in a male. Occasionally, the chromosomes that determine sex diverge from the usual pattern. Some people have XO, XXX, XXY, or XYY sex chromosomes. Another variation from the usual sex pattern is intersexuality, which occurs when individuals are born with some biological characteristics of each sex.

Biology *influences* behavior in greater or lesser amounts, but it does not *determine* behavior, personality, social roles, and so on. In other words, biological sex does not force particular cognitions, feelings, or behaviors, although it may predispose a person toward them. Biology also does not determine the meaning that members of a culture assign to particular behaviors. More important than whether biological differences exist is how differences register socially. This moves us into the discussion of a second concept: gender.

Gender

Gender is a considerably more complex concept than sex. Gender is acquired through interaction in a social world, and it changes over time. One way to understand gender is to think of it as what we learn about sex. We are born male or female, but we learn ways to be masculine and feminine. Gender is a social, symbolic construction, which differs across cultures and varies over time within a given culture, and in relation to the other gender. We elaborate on these three aspects of gender.

Gender Is a Social, Symbolic Construction

The meaning of a gender depends on a society's values, beliefs, and preferred ways of organizing collective life. The frequent overlap between sex (male and female) and gender (masculine and feminine) reveals the tenacity of society's desire to ascribe social characteristics and abilities on the basis of biology and hence perhaps to see such social differentiation as "natural," immutable, and inherent.

Socially endorsed views of masculinity and femininity are taught to individuals through a variety of cultural means. From infancy on, most people are encouraged to conform to the gender that society prescribes for their sex and, just as important, to avoid acting, thinking, or feeling in ways prescribed for the other sex. Importantly for our argument here, both the sexes and genders are usually seen as opposites and as mutually exclusive, although research in the past 30 years has suggested that this dichotomous view is simplistic and misleading.

In relationships generally, and in the breakdown of relationships specifically, therefore, the sexes might be expected to engage in gendered styles of cognition and communication that reflect social prescriptions. In the processes of relational dissolution, gendered styles might be expected to influence the initiation of breakdown, resistance styles during breakdown, conflict management, and the effects of ultimate outcomes on self-esteem.

Views of Gender Differ Among Cultures

Because social definitions of gender permeate public and private life, they seem normal, natural, and right. However, we can grasp the arbitrariness of the meanings of gender by considering different ways in which different cultures define masculinity and femininity. Many years ago, anthropologist Margaret Mead (1935/1968) reported three distinctive gender patterns in the New Guinea societies she studied. Among Arapesh people, both women and men conformed closely to what the West considers feminine behavior. The Mundugumor tribe socialized both women and men to be aggressive, independent, and competitive. Within the Tchambuli society, genders were the reverse of current ones in America: Women were domineering and sexually aggressive, whereas men were considered delicate and were taught to wear decorative clothes and curl their hair so that they would be attractive to women. In other cultures, a person's gender is considered changeable (Kessler, 1998; Kessler & McKenna, 1978), so someone born male may choose to live and be regarded as female or feminine, and vice versa, and may alter his or her choices. In other societies, notably some Native American groups, more than two genders are recognized and celebrated (Brown, 1997; Nanda, 2004). Individuals who have qualities of multiple genders are highly esteemed.

In the United States, gender differs between racial or ethnic groups. In general, for African Americans, the gender roles attributed to women allow for more assertiveness than those attached to European American women, and African American men tend to be permitted and expected to be more communal than White men (Gaines, 1995; Rothenberg, Schafhausen, & Schneider, 2000; Smith, 1998). Again, then, to the extent that assertiveness plays any role in relationship dissolution, we might expect gender-based differences to arise in the experience.

Views of Gender Vary Over Time Within a Given Culture

Even within a single culture, the meaning of gender varies over time. Before the Industrial Revolution, family and work were intertwined for most people (Ryan, 1979). Thus, men and women often worked together to raise crops or run businesses, and they were jointly involved in homemaking and childrearing. Affection and expressiveness were considered normal in men as well as in women; dependability and vitality were attractive in women just as they were in men (Cancian, 1989).

With the Industrial Revolution, increasing numbers of men took jobs away from home and increasing numbers of women assumed primary responsibility for family life. Consequently, femininity was redefined as being nurturing, with women being dependent on men for income, focused on relationships, and able to make a good home. Masculinity was also redefined as being emotionally reserved, ambitious, successful at work, and, especially, earning a good income (Cancian, 1989; Risman & Godwin, 2001). If research shows that emotional reserve or nurturing plays a role in relationship dissolution, then we would expect gendered differences to be apparent and to overlap with sex only to the extent that the gendered behaviors were strongly attached to one sex alone.

Gender Is Relational

Finally, gender is a relational concept, because femininity and masculinity tend to be thought of in relation to each other; that is, it is difficult to conceive of femininity apart from masculinity and vice versa. Because masculinity and femininity continue to be perceived as substantially interdependent and complementary, as meanings of one gender change, meanings of the other tend to vary accordingly. With the Industrial Revolution, sheer physical strength was no longer as important to survival, so masculinity was redefined to emphasize intellectual ability and success in earning income. Simultaneously, femininity was redefined to contrast with and complement redefined masculinity.

To summarize our discussion of gender, consider Butler's (1990, 1993) assertion that there is nothing "normal" or "natural" about gender. She rejects the idea that gender exists prior to particular actions. Instead, claims Butler, gender comes into being as it is performed in everyday life. Individuals simultaneously enact and produce gender through a variety of mundane, performative practices such as dress, gestures, and verbal acts that embody—and, thus, confer an illusory realness on—normative codes of masculinity and femininity. Butler's view is supported by Deirdre (formerly Donald) McCloskey, a professor of economics who had hormonal and surgical treatments to change from being a man to being a woman. According to her, surgery and hormones changed her sex, but she had to learn gender; she had to learn to be feminine. She studied all of the small actions—gestures, facial expressions, postures, and so forth—that women typically use and practiced them until they were second nature to her. Reflecting on this, McCloskey (1999) wrote that gender is "an accretion of learned habits, learned so well that they feel like external conditions, merely the way things are. It is a shell made by the snail and then confining it" (pp. 83–84).

Although the distinction between sex and gender is "real" and important, it is difficult to offer substantial information about the effects of gender on relationship breakdown. It is difficult because the majority of research identifies only participants' sex. Gender is inferred, with questionable precision, based on sex, so there is much incautious writing in the academic reporting about sex and gender. The result is that one characteristic (sex) is usually measured and the other (gender) is assumed and focused on in discussing findings. This leads to confusing reports in the literature because it is not always clear whether the authors themselves are aware of the distinction between sex and gender. In other words, many studies that claim to be about gender are not about gender at all. Instead, they used sex as the criterion variable, and then they misstated results in terms of a variable (gender) that the authors never assessed. Following Canary and Emmers-Sommer (1997), we urge readers to attend seriously to this point and whatever common assumptions have been made about the role of *sex* or *gender* in relationships. Before conclusions can be drawn reliably, we need to take account of the distinction in the terms and then to revisit all previous studies that use one or the other term to ensure that they are correctly classified as investigations of sex or gender before conclusions drawn from them are reconsidered and confirmed. Having sounded that warning, we now proceed to explore sex and gender in intimate relationships before applying that analysis to dissolution specifically.

Although previous research on sex and gender in relationships must be treated cautiously for the reasons just outlined, we note that there are a number of relationship practices and styles that are believed to be associated with sex or gender, and these provide a backdrop for consideration of the processes that compose romantic relationships and also nonromantic relationships that are not covered in this volume. Although we do not see romantic relationships as restricted to cross-sex romances, there is very little research available on nonheterosexual romantic attachments. Therefore, most of what we say here is in fact derived from research on cross-sex romances, and most often the romances of college students.

GENDERED PATTERNS IN RELATIONAL DISSOLUTION

Our discussion of sex- and gender-related tendencies in relationships provides a foundation for a more detailed discussion of the processes entailed in relational dissolution. We rely on Duck's model of relational deterioration to organize our discussion of gendered patterns in the decline of relationships. This model, originally presented in 1982, has recently been updated (Rollie & Duck, chap. 12, this volume) to focus on process variables, to replace the language of "phases" with keener attention to processes, and to incorporate a more systematic depiction of the communication activity that defines and represents each labeled process. As we discuss each set of processes, we integrate research on gendered perceptions, inclinations, and strategies.

Relational Breakdown

Relational breakdown tends to be a subtle process, particularly during its early genesis. It refers to sufficiently troubling attributions, experiences, behaviors, cognitions, and discourse within the relationship to suggest the possibility of considering the relationship ending. Because dyadic breakdown typically is not dramatic or abrupt, partners in a relationship often do not notice or remark on it, especially during its embryonic phase, which is when partners might be most able to steer the relationship away from breakup if they recognize that an eventual break is a possible endpoint of present experiences and tensions.

Many early models of breakup treated the process as having one outcome. In other words, the breakdown process was treated as simply the initiation of an irrevocable slide toward the final breakup. In real life, it is not that simple. For instance, not all relationships that experience breakdown processes follow an inevitable and irreversible path toward breakup. Many a breakup is imagined without ever happening, and other potential breakups are prevented by changes in behavior or perspective. Researchers have not yet successfully examined relationships in which breakdown processes are halted or reversed.

Researchers have identified a number of gender- and sex-related differences in reasons for dissatisfaction, which fuel dyadic breakdown. We discuss two of these that seem particularly inflected by gender and sex and that are critical in fueling the dissatisfaction characteristic of dyadic breakdown.

Declines in Communication and Joint Activities

Riessman (1990) reported that women linked waning intimacy in marriages to declines in the quality and frequency of communication between partners. Women who have been socialized into feminine perspectives and values tend to become dissatisfied with relationships when they no longer feel that they and their partners are staying connected through communication, including talk about the relationship itself: "We don't communicate with each other any more." In contrast, men who have been socialized into masculine perspectives and values are more likely to become dissatisfied with relationships when there are declines in joint activities: "We don't enjoy doing things together any more."

The different sources of relational dissatisfaction that Riessman reports reflect a basic aspect of gender socialization. Masculine socialization tends to emphasize instrumental activities— doing things with and for others as routes to closeness. Feminine socialization places greater priority on expressive interaction and the *process* of relating—communicating with others as an ongoing means of achieving and sustaining closeness (Inman, 1995; Reissman, 1990; Wood & Inman, 1993). Thus, individuals who are socialized to hold masculine views and values may experience and appreciate what Swain (1989) calls "closeness in the doing," whereas individuals who are socialized to identify with feminine views and values are more inclined to experience and appreciate "closeness in dialogue" (Johnson, 1995).

Inequity in Homemaking and Child Care

Another major source of frustration and dissatisfaction in marriages and committed romantic relationships is inequitable divisions of labor in the home. Although the vast majority of heterosexual families today have two wage earners, the housework and care of children, parents, and other relatives continue to be done primarily by women who adopt feminine perspectives in partnerships with men who adopt masculine perspectives (Delamont, 2001; Gerson, 2004; Jena, 1999; Maushart, 2001; Risman & Godwin, 2001). Dubbing this the "second shift," sociologist Arlie Hochschild (2003) reported that the majority of wives employed outside of their homes have a second-shift job in the home. In dual-worker heterosexual families, women spend a mean of 27 hr each week on homemaking and child care whereas men spend a mean of 16 hr: Women are doing 70% more of the work involved in family life (Johnson, 2002). In stark contrast to women's juggling of their paid work and the second shift, the amount of housework and child care that husbands do weekly has risen by only 4 hr (from 12 to 16) since 1965 (Johnson).

Not only do most women work more than most men at home, but the work they do is generally more taxing and less gratifying. Many of the contributions men typically make are sporadic, variable, and flexible in timing (e.g., mowing the lawn), whereas the tasks women typically do are more repetitive, routine, and constrained by deadlines. Women are also more likely to do multiple tasks simultaneously—for example, helping a child with homework while preparing dinner. Whereas mothers tend to be constantly on duty, fathers more typically volunteer for irregular and relatively enjoyable child-care activities such as a trip to the zoo. The implications of this division can be very significant in the consideration of relationship breakdown.

One of the more subtle inequities in the second shift is the *buffer zone*, which is a period of time after returning home from a day's stress in the paid labor market in which a person does not engage in homemaking, child care, or relational interaction (Coulter & Helms-Erickson, 1997). When anyone first arrives home after a day's work, she or he may want some time to relax without any pressures or responsibilities to others. However, the likelihood that a person will feel entitled to time for relaxation, on the one hand, and that others will feel it is appropriate, on the other hand, is linked to sex. More often than women, men feel they deserve some unencumbered time after returning home. Furthermore, both women and men seem to feel it is appropriate for women to accommodate men's desires for buffer time and for women to assume the immediate responsibilities associated with home and family (Hochschild, 1997; Shellenbarger, 1997).

Several recent studies shed light on whether the typically inequitable division of labor is derived from sex or gender differences. Garrido and Acitelli (1999) reported that romantic partners—both men and women—who define themselves in relational terms, an identity fostered by feminine socialization, are more likely to engage in household and familial tasks traditionally associated with women. Further support for the importance of distinguishing between gender and sex when considering relationship dynamics comes from a study by Steiner-Pappalardo and Gurung (2002). They found that both women and men who were feminine have better quality relationships. Summing up what their findings suggest about published research on gender differences, Steiner-Pappalardo and Gurung stated that "many sex differences found in the literature may not have been due to the participants being female, but rather to those particular women in the study being high in femininity and the men low in femininity" (p. 321). Continuing, they cautioned that "sex and gender convey significantly different levels of information and cannot be used interchangeably" (p. 322).

Another way in which contributions to home life are inequitable is *psychological responsibility*, which is the responsibility to remember, plan, and make sure that things get done (Hochschild, 2003). For instance, partners agree to share responsibility for taking children to doctors and dentists, but it is typically partners who are feminine who assume the psychological responsibility for remembering when various inoculations are due, scheduling appointments, noticing when a child needs attention, and keeping track of whose turn it is to take a child. All of this planning and organization is a psychological responsibility that is often not counted in couples' agreements for sharing the work of maintaining a home and family. Further, the tasks composing psychological responsibility are ones generally considered "women's work" and they are generally performed by individuals—male or female—who have high relational identities, which are cultivated by feminine socialization (Garrido & Acitelli, 1999).

The phrase set off by dashes in the last sentence is important. Gender, not sex, is strongly allied with relational identities and the associated roles and responsibilities that partners assume. Vonk and van Nobelen (1993) reported that not all men behave in masculine ways within personal relationships, and Coleman and Ganong (1985) found that gender was a major influence on loving behaviors, whereas sex had little effect. Also demonstrating a strong link between gender and behaviors that nurture and maintain relationships are the results of a study by Stafford, Dutton, and Hass (2000). They found that biological sex was not a primary predictor of behaviors that support relationships, but that gender was. Specifically, for maintenance behaviors such as openness and sharing of tasks, "being female was not as strong a predictor as was femininity" (p. 317). Underlining the importance of distinguishing between sex and gender when considering relationship evolution, Acitelli and Young (1996) reported that women's greater tendencies to think about, care about, and spend energy on relationships probably result from feminine socialization—that is, gender. Because gender is learned (unlike sex), it is not surprising that men whose fathers were actively involved in tasks associated with home and family tend to see those tasks as compatible with masculinity (Schneider & Stevenson, 1999). Relatedly, both women and men whose mothers were actively involved in the paid labor force see women's career success as compatible with femininity (Cose, 2003; Schneider & Stevenson).

When one person is the primary or exclusive worker in the second shift, the consequences are substantial. Individuals who do the majority of homemaking and child-care tasks are often extremely stressed, fatigued, and susceptible to illness (Hochschild, 2003; Jena, 1999). Frustration, resentment, and conflict are also likely outcomes when only one person in a partnership is meeting the double responsibilities of jobs inside and outside of the home (Kluwer, Heesink, & Vliert, 1996; Knudson-Martin & Mahoney, 1996). In addition, the inequity of the arrangement is a primary source of relationship dissatisfaction and instability. Marital stability is more closely tied to equitable divisions of housework and child care than to income. The roughly 20% of heterosexual couples that share equitably in running a home and raising children are the most satisfied (Deutsch, 2001).

Duck (1982) and Rollie & Duck (chap. 12, this volume) argue that the first processes of breakdown involve ruminative, reflective activity. Here the person assesses rewards and costs and considers relational dynamics. Although Duck's (1982) original model evolved before substantial work on sex and gender had been published, it is now apparent that feminine individuals tend to reflect on relationships much more often than masculine individuals and that feminine individuals are therefore more likely to notice tensions and early symptoms of deterioration in the quality of relationships (Tavris, 1992). Because feminine individuals prefer to talk about relationships, they tend to perceive the absence of talk as problematic. Using sex as a proxy variable for gender, Acitelli (1988) found that husbands, who are typically socialized to be masculine, tend to see discussion of the relationship as indicative of problems, whereas wives, who are typically socialized to be feminine, perceive discussion of relationship issues to be an ongoing topic, whether or not there are perceived to be problems with the relationship.

Intrapsychic Processes

If not noticed and addressed, however, relational breakdown may lead to the *intrapsychic processes*, which involve reflecting, and sometimes brooding, about problems or dissatisfactions in a relationship. This set of processes tends to produce unbalanced appraisals of a relationship. Because the impetus for these processes is to be found in imagined or real problems and sources of dissatisfaction, relationship partners are likely to focus on undesirable facets of the relationship and to ignore positive aspects of it. For example, it is here that discussion of the inequity of distribution of housework or child care may become a significant talking point and where the good points of the relationship may recede into the shadows. One danger of this imbalance is the possibility of a self-fulfilling prophecy (Bradbury & Fincham, 1990; Fletcher & Fincham, 1991).

Given our discussion of relational breakdown processes, it is not surprising that the focus and frequency of brooding—what individuals dwell on—tends to differ along sex and gender lines. Individuals with feminine orientations tend to be preoccupied with declines in the quality and quantity of communication, whereas individuals with masculine perspectives are more likely to brood about lapses in shared activities, including sex (Riessman, 1990; Wood, 1986, 1993, 1994a, 1994b). Research shows that women who have been socialized into feminine perspectives are also more likely than men to see problems in a relationship as interrelated, whereas men who have been socialized into masculine perspectives are more likely to perceive problems as discrete, unconnected issues (Schaef, 1981; Wood 1986, 1993, 1994a, 1994b). A masculine perspective is also associated with regarding problems with relationships as unconnected to issues of self and self-image, whereas a feminine perspective encourages perceiving self and self-image as closely entwined with relational activity (Surrey, 1991). Research also shows that women are more likely than men to "get stuck" in negative feelings and brooding about an ailing relationship (Nolen-Hoeksema, 2003).

In addition to such psychological consequences of brooding, the Rollie and Duck model focuses also on the communication effects. A person who is preoccupied with brooding and ruminating about the partner and the relationship in a negative kind of way has, by definition, less time available for discussion with other people. For this reason, these intrapsychic processes are often accompanied and characterized by a social withdrawal that removes the person from his or her usual patterns of interaction (in ways that may be noticed by astute outsiders). At the same time as the person interacts less with others, the person is deprived of perspectives that others might offer in defense of the partner or the relationship's viability. The lack of outside perspective on and challenges to one's own views may lead a person to exaggerate the negative qualities of the partner and relationship. By the time the person emerges from intrapsychic processes and confronts the partner, the frame of mind may be substantially more negative than it would have been if discussion with other people had continued. Hence, when discussion between partners eventually takes place, dissatisfaction and conflict may be greater than they would have been if the partners had talked earlier or if the person feeling dissatisfaction had more fully availed herself or himself of outside perspectives.

Dyadic Processes

Not all deteriorating relationships actively go through the *dyadic processes*, but when these occur they can be dramatic and powerful, and sometimes enlightening. This activity is characterized by partners' efforts to manage their conflicts face to face and address their problems and to talk explicitly about whether to break up. If partners choose not to discuss or otherwise deal with the issues causing dissatisfaction, then these processes do not occur actively. Neglecting or refusing to discuss problems could be considered a passive method of enacting the dyadic phase, but there are known differences in male and female preferences for dealing with problematic issues in a relationship and these characteristic preferences are likely to be important. In general, men prefer not to discuss relationship issues and see any attempt to discuss the relationship as uncomfortable, whereas women, in general, see attempts to avoid such discussion as inherently problematic (Acitelli, 1988).

Active confrontation of the issues, however, creates a new dynamic in which complaints are presented and explained, and partners may offer alternative interpretations that may lead to a reappraisal of the complaint or its relevance to the relationship. In contrast, a presented complaint may be met with a countercomplaint that escalates tension and further jeopardizes the relationship's continuation. Whereas the discussion may start with expressions of personal concerns, it is all too easy for these discussions to get out of hand and for the "kitchen-sinking" noted by many therapists to occur. Issues not strictly relevant to the original concerns may be dragged into the conversation, which, in turn, may fuel anger and resentment, as well as perceptions that it is futile to try to restore the relationship because so much is wrong with it. For masculine persons, the very fact of discussing the relationship may be problematic, whereas for feminine persons the discussion may serve to alleviate concern and be taken as evidence that the partner cares enough to engage in conversation about it all. Thus, whatever the substance of the discourse, the fact of its occurrence may be differentially significant as a function of gender or sex.

Neither the Duck (1982) model nor the revised version in Rollie and Duck (chap. 12, this volume; also see Duck, 2005) proposes that there is only one outcome of the dyadic processes, namely the inevitable ending of the relationship. Clearly, many couples resolve differences by discussion even when these differences are strong, shocking, and unpleasant. Although there is not very strong guidance in the research literature about the resolution of such difficulties (because resolution and avoidance of potential breakups has seldom been studied), the tendency in studies of breakups is to assume an inevitability of breakup once the process begins. Of course, this assumption is partly an artifact of the methods of study, which start with participants who have broken up and then trace the pathways of those breakups. In such cases, it is entirely predictable that researchers will find an inevitable pathway because that is what they are asking about and is what the selected participants in fact experienced! All the same, real life provides numerous examples of partners who avoid a potential breakup, which underlines the point that the outcomes of dyadic processes are neither uniform nor certain.

Existing research indicates that women are more likely than men to want greater degrees of connection and emotional closeness (Feeney, 1999), which reflects the priority that feminine socialization accords to close relationships. Women are also more likely than men to identify relational problems and to want to resolve them through conversation, including demands for change (Acitelli, Rodgers, & Knee, 1999; Suh, Moskowitz, Fournier, & Zuroff, 2004). Men, in contrast, are more likely to minimize problems (or female partners' perceptions of problems), avoid conflict, and behave agreeably to foster reconciliation (Suh et al., 2004).

The communicative changes during the dyadic processes are relevant to gender and sex issues in several other ways also. First, dyadic processes may be marked by changes in topic and in distribution of communication time. If a couple is discussing its own relationship, then the two parties are either not spending as much time with other people as they perhaps once did or else during dyadic processes the amount of time they spend together is centered primarily on problems and dissatisfactions. If time spent together focuses on relational talks, as noted earlier, generally this will be regarded as better news by people with feminine rather than masculine orientations because the latter generally prefer to keep a lid on things. In addition, the topics of conversation are likely to be uncomfortable for masculine individuals because the topics involve discussion of feelings and relational attitudes in ways that are not part of the masculine norm. Furthermore, as Baxter (1985) and Wilmot, Carbaugh, and Baxter (1985) demonstrated, talks about The State of Our Relationship are typically hard for couples in distress and may lead to a definition of the future of the relationship that neither foresaw nor particularly desired. At this stage, then, things can run out of the control of the partners involved.

In those cases in which dyadic discussions lead partners either to decide to end their relationship or to believe that they simply cannot save it, there are options about how to terminate the relationship. Baxter (1985) and Wilmot et al. (1985) identified four strategies that people use to break up a long-distance romantic relationship:

- Withdrawal—reducing the amount of time spent together or frequency of interaction;
- Pseudodeescalation—stating a desire to see less of the partner while actually wanting to end the relationship entirely;
- Cost escalation—increasing what staying in the relationship costs the partner in the hope that the partner will initiate a breakup; and
- Fading away—mutually and implicitly letting the relationship end by gradually or abruptly ceasing to contact each other or to interact.

Are there sex or gender patterns in use of these strategies? Research suggests that there are several generalizable differences in how women and men, regardless of sexual orientation, act on a desire to end a relationship. First, as we have noted, feminine socialization, which most women experience, renders women more likely than men to recognize problems in a relationship (Acitelli, 1988; Cancian, 1987). Because feminine socialization teaches people to tune into relationship processes and rhythms, individuals who have been socialized to be feminine are likely to notice problems when they are minor—just slight variations from a relationship's previous patterns.

The recurrent finding that women tend to have greater awareness of relationship problems than men seems to reflect differences in gender socialization, whereby a majority of girls are socialized to be primarily feminine and a majority of boys are socialized to be primarily masculine. A classic study by Maltz and Borker (1982), which has been supported by more recent research (Austin, Salehi, & Leffler, 1987; Campbell, 1993; Clark, 1998; Coates, 1997; Harris, 1998; Johnson, 2000; Kovacs, Parker, & Hoffman, 1996; Leaper, 1991, 1994, 1996; Maccoby, 1998; Moller & Serbin, 1996), reported generalizable differences between feminine and masculine socialization. Interaction with peers, as well as immersion in the culture as a whole, encourages girls at early ages to build supportive relationships, engage in personal talk, pay attention to relationship processes, and be sensitive to others' needs and desires. In contrast, boys' interaction with peers, as well as their immersion in the overall culture, encourages them to assert themselves and their ideas, resist letting others gain attention or win arguments, and use talk to accomplish objectives rather than to form and nourish connections with others.

Second, women more than men are likely to want to confront and deal with relationship problems, and women are more interested in spending extensive time talking about problems in the relationships and options for its future. Thus, in general, women tend to use more direct strategies and men tend to rely on more indirect strategies (Eldridge & Gilbert, 1990; Huston & Schwartz, 1996; Kurdek & Schmitt, 1986; Rusbult, 1987; Rusbult, Zembrodt, & Iwaniszek, 1986; Wilmot, et al., 1985; Wood, 1986, 1994a, 1994b). For instance, women are more likely to tell a partner openly that a relationship is over or to explain why the relationship is not satisfying. Men, in general, are more likely to end a relationship by avoiding interaction or changing the subject when a partner mentions problems or asks where the relationship is going.

Gottman (1994a, 1994b) reported that men are more inclined than women to withdraw during times of marital distress. Men are more likely than women to refuse to discuss problems in relationships—a pattern Gottman calls "stonewalling." On the basis of both his research and his counseling of married couples, Gottman asserts that stonewalling is a particularly pernicious pattern because it slams the door on communication that might resolve or lessen tensions and sources of dissatisfaction in relationships. Although Gottman did not specifically identify or assess gender's influence on response to marital distress, the withdrawal and stonewalling patterns that he reports are more typical of men than women and have been linked to masculine socialization and perspectives on relationships (Stafford et al., 2000).

Social Support Processes

Failing to find satisfaction in discussions with each other, partners generally begin to seek comfort elsewhere and thus move into a crucial stage of relational breakdown in which relationship problems are aired to people outside of the relationship (Duck, 1982). This is a crucial step psychologically, because its enactment makes it much more difficult later for people to deny or play down the problems. Once the issues are aired to third parties, the problems are real and it is impossible to deny that they happened or that they matter. Before this step is taken, people can claim that the difficulties were merely "troubles" or "rough patches." After a public declaration, the relationship really is in trouble.

Social support processes involve a number of combined and subtle dynamics, the first of which we just noted. Telling others that there are problems in the relationship is, of course, also a means of seeking advice and comfort. Moreover, it is a means of presenting the problems in a way that protects the person presenting it, because she or he has a large amount of control over the ways in which the messages and descriptions about the relationship are conveyed to the audience. In social support processes, partners seek psychological support from friends and family members and decide how to present the breakup to the outside world if they cannot (or do not want to) enlist the supportive energy of their networks to protect the relationship from disintegration. Rubin (1985) reported that women are more likely than men to talk with friends about problems in a romantic relationship and to depend on them for support.

It is only at first that social support processes focus on getting sympathy and emotional sup-port regarding problems in the relationship (La Gaipa, 1982). Later, social support processes may involve seeking assistance, material and emotional, during the actual breakup. Although there is much difference between a sympathetic ear and a helping hand, both are forms of support sought—and often provided—as part of communal coping during relational deterio-ration. Studies by Burleson and his colleagues (Burleson, 2003; Burleson, Kunkel, Samter, & Werking, 1996; Kunkel & Burleson, 1998, 1999) found that women and men equally appreci-ate instrumental forms of support; both sexes perceive expressive, person-centered support as most valuable; and women place greater importance on affective support than men.

If a partner in a relationship moves from seeking sympathy to seeking assistance in imple-menting a breakup, the partner tends to be more interested in having his or her social supporters accept his or her account of how things went wrong and to take his or her side rather than just offer comfort. The subtle shift in the processes is one that finally clinches the breakup and is demonstrable in the changes of topics and communicative patterns that are associated with the social processes. Rollie and Duck (chap. 12, this volume) and Duck (2005) give more attention to the communicative topical shifts and communicative pattern changes than we can do here, but it is important to recognize that a public declaration that the relationship is in trouble carries consequences. When outsiders whose support is sought know both part-ners, the outsiders vividly report that they experience serious tensions over having to choose between the stories of two people known and perhaps liked equally well (La Gaipa, 1982). Much, then, depends on the type and structure of interpersonal network. Reis, Senchak, and Solomon (1985) showed that men had better health as a function of the number of women in their immediate network, and hence we can surmise that a person's success at acquiring support in these processes is also going to depend on the number of women in the person's network.

In some cases, partners collaborate to create a public presentation of the breakup that indicates their shared regret and mutual responsibility for the breakup that became inevitable as a consequence of inherent incompatibility. Alternatively, and more commonly, partners act individually, with each partner deciding for herself or himself how to announce and explain the breakup, including issues such as whether to present it as mutual or unilateral, in ways that save both partners' faces or attribute blame, and as permanent or trial.

Feminine socialization, which is more typical of women than men, explains why women are more likely than men to talk more with others about problems in their relationships and to seek support, sympathy, and perspective from friends throughout later parts of relational breakdown. However, it is less certain whether the sexes and genders have different styles of *reporting* breakup, and researchers would do well to investigate this issue more carefully in the future.

Grave-Dressing Processes

The *grave-dressing phase* was the final phase in Duck's (1982) original model. In his revised model, however, grave-dressing is conceived as a set of processes that precede the final work of ending a relationship. During the grave-dressing processes, each partner deals with any mourning that is necessary and begins to adopt a story whose repeated telling memorializes the relationship and defines its beginning and ending, rather like the headstone on a grave. As a rule, the memorial story presents the highlights and trajectory of the relationship in a way that offers a consistency that other people can accept. Typically, whatever was ultimately wrong with the relationship is presented in retrospect as evident from the start, inevitable because of circumstances or fate, or a completely unexpected betrayal. The person telling the story of the breakup usually portrays herself or himself as a responsible partner who endured suffering before finally getting out, or else who was so thoroughly betrayed that there was no choice in the matter (Weber, 1983).

Engagement in grave-dressing helps people to enter the next set of processes in which they prepare for future relationships or a voluntarily unpartnered life. Even when the result is ending a marriage, this point is not only an ending, but also a beginning. The word *divorce* comes from the Latin word *divortere*, which is a variant of *divertere* and means to divert or turn in a different direction, as people tend to do when they end a serious romantic relationship. Whatever new directions expartners follow, a key element of grave-dressing processes is to portray the individual who is doing the grave-dressing as worthwhile and whole without the former partner (La Gaipa, 1982). Kellas and Manusov (2003) demonstrated that people adjust better to breakups if they are able to craft narratives of relational dissolution that are coherent and complete. Given that there is a feminine proclivity for relational focus, it is likely that feminine individuals will cope better with these processes.

Grave-dressing processes thus involve a form of communication that offers self-justification and explanation to a greater extent than previous processes have done, but also the speaker is concerned to dress things up in a way that creates a socially respectable image. Unrestrained complaints about the partner of the form that are allowable during the dyadic and social processes are less suitable here, because they make the person look spiteful or obsessive about the failed relationship. To be attractive as a relational partner, these characteristics must be concealed beneath a self-presentation of positivity about other people in general and condemnation of the behavior of the partner as a specific deviation from accepted social norms. Thus, the expartner's behavior may be portrayed as reprehensible, which classifies the expartner, rather than the person presenting the account, as unworthy of future relational engagement by other people. Such narrations obviously connect to norms about the conduct of gossip as the application of moral standards in a community (Bergmann, 1993).

Resurrection Processes

The final set of processes in the new model is concerned with the activities that individuals pursue in order to move forward to a future without the former partner. Previous research has all too often made the assumption that the ending of a relationship is the ending of all processes to do with that relationship, but this is not necessarily the case. Individuals need to pick up the pieces and prepare themselves (and other people) for new relational enterprises, if they desire and expect to have them. In order to do this, they must resurrect themselves in a form that prepares them for unpartnered living or for new relationships. Often this preparation is lengthy and involves full distancing from the persona associated with the ended relationship. In any case, it is a complex set of processes that involve reconceptualizing the self, and preparing oneself either to avoid intimacy, either for the short or long term, or to seek new relationships (see Rollie & Duck, chap. 12, this volume).

Individuals who have been socialized into feminine perspectives—primarily but not exclusively women—may be globally unhappy and upset about relationship distress because feminine socialization emphasizes the central importance of relationships to self (Sedikides, Oliver, & Campbell, 1994; Surrey, 1991). However, research indicates that women and men do not differ in the distress they experience once a relationship ends. The likely reason is that women who are feminine are more attuned to relationships and relationship problems, so they begin accepting and preparing for a relationship's end before it actually occurs (Cross & Madsen, 1997). Women also report more personal growth than men following the ending of a serious relationship (Tashiro & Frazier, 2003; also see Tashiro, Frazier, & Berman, chap. 18, this volume). Individuals who have been socialized into masculine perspectives—primarily but not exclusively men—may experience more unhappiness that is specific to the ending of the relationship and not generalized to self or life overall because masculine socialization encourages compartmentalization. In either case, some form of psychological and behavioral adjustment may be necessary for new relationships to be perceived as safe and attractive. People often need time to heal, and the gender- and sex-related expectations and processes associated with the healing may be different. For example, feminine individuals are predicted to form support networks to reinforce the self as a worthy relational partner; masculine individuals are predicted to do something to take their minds off the previous partner. Such processes once more connect the individual to the groups of others with whom they habitually interact and who can perform various ego-related supportive tasks for the person.

CONTEXTUALIZING GENDERED PATTERNS

Our discussion of sex, gender, and relational dissolution has so far focused on individuals and their personal relationships, yet gendered patterns in relational dissolution cannot be fully understood as only individual or dyadic phenomena. They are also decisively social and cultural phenomena. They are social because relationships—including their endings—exist in and are affected by social networks and opportunities and constraints within the social context that creates gender in the first place. They are cultural because relationships exist in and are keenly shaped by broader cultural structures and practices that define gender and socialize individuals into gendered identities, and because larger cultural forces shape individuals and the relationships they create and inhabit.

In this final section of this chapter, we want to consider some of the ways in which the contexts within which relationships are embedded influence deterioration and dissolution. Historically, relationships have been conceived and studied as interpersonal entities that are largely isolated from contexts. In other words, relationship processes and dynamics have been viewed as being shaped almost exclusively by the individual partners and their relationship. However, research in recent years has offered correctives to the initial neglect of contexts and their influence on relationships. In 1993, Duck edited a collection of essays that made clear the relevance of social contexts to what happens *within* relationships.

Duck's volume instigated serious scholarly attention to contexts and their impact on relationships (Adams & Allan, 1998; Cohan & Bradbury, 1997; Cutrona, Russell, Hessling, Brown, & Murry, 2000; Vinokur, Price, & Caplan, 1996). Researchers quickly discovered that relationships were anything but independent of their environments. For example, downturns in the economy result in unemployment, which affects family life, satisfaction, and stability (Conger, Rueter, & Elder, 1999; Vinokur et al.). Life events such as work stress (Matthews, Conger, & Wickrama, 1996), becoming a parent (Goldstein, Diener, & Mangelsdorf, 1996), serious medical problems (Coyne & Anderson, 1999), and the death of a parent (Umberson, 1995) also affect marital stability, often by fueling negative emotions that, in turn, may lead to outbursts of anger and feelings of dissatisfaction (Abbey, Andrews, & Halman, 1995). Stressful life events are more likely to harm primary relationships if partners do not have a strong, supportive social network to help them weather difficult times (Cunningham & Barbee, 2000). A decade after Duck's volume appeared, sufficient research had been conducted on contexts to persuade Perlman and Surra (2003) to edit a special issue of *Personal Relationships* titled "Contextual Influences on Relationships." The eight articles in that issue reported additional evidence of the impact of contextual forces such as financial strain, social networks, social support, and neighborhoods.

We close by returning explicitly to our opening theme: the distinction between sex and gender. So far it has not been addressed well in research. As we have pointed out in this chapter, many researchers conflate the two concepts and infer the latter from identification of the former. The result is that we have little understanding of which relationship phenomena are related to sex, which are related to gender, and which are related to both. We have also called attention to a few studies that did distinguish between sex and gender and that reported that gender is a better predictor than sex of many relationship cognitions, feelings, and behaviors.

Future research should strive to recognize and take into account the distinction between sex and gender and in particular to be rigorous in reporting what was studied and what was found. When sex alone is measured (as in participant self-identification as male or female), then effects of gender may not be accurately inferred. When gender is assessed by such instruments as the Bem Sex Role Inventory, then conclusions about effects of gender are warranted, but conclusions about the effects of sex cannot be drawn from identification of gender. These careful practical and professional matters are prerequisites for advancing knowledge on the roles of sex and gender in relationships and hence in relationship dissolution.

In addition to taking better care in reporting variables and findings, what sorts of issues remain to be understood? First, we have noted that gender is a social construct and as such is much more likely than sex alone to be related to all issues surrounding the other social construct, conduct of relationships, which is inherently guided and bounded by whatever social norms and conventions prevail at the time. Insofar as the processes of relationship breakdown that have been identified by Duck (1982) and Rollie and Duck (chap. 12, this volume) can be linked to gender, then there will be advances in the understanding of relationship breakdown. For example, where men have been shown to be less capable than women at remembering relationship details (Holmberg & Holmes, 1993), we would predict that this sex difference will interact with the gender difference, indicating that feminine orientation tends to increase sensitivity to relational nuances. Hence, sex and gender will interact when it comes to both the intrapsychic processes (in which the person attends broodingly to relationship nuance and recalls details thereof) and the dyadic processes (in which the two partners necessarily confront one another's nuanced memories). Research on the influence of sex or gender on social support processes is limited and somewhat mixed. On the one hand, there are few unequivocal sex differences and only some suggestive gender differences in the manners of soliciting and responding to social support (Stafford et al., 2000; Helgeson, Novak, Lepore, & Eton, 2004). On the other hand, some research indicates that there may be sex or gender differences in modes of communicating or expressing support (Wood & Inman, 1993).

The distinction between sex and gender is a tough one to explore, because the overlap between the two concepts seems quite large at present. However, this is exactly why careful and precise research is needed to understand the role of the two concepts in relationship dissolution.

REFERENCES

Abbey, A., Andrews, F., & Halman, L. (1995). Provision and receipt of social support and disregard: What is their impact on the marital life quality of infertile and fertile couples? *Journal of Personality and Social Psychology, 68,* 455–469.

Acitelli, L. (1988). When spouses talk to each other about their relationship. *Journal of Social and Personal Relationships, 5,* 185–199.

Acitelli, L., Rogers, S., & Knee, R. (1999). The role of identity in the link between relationship thinking and relationship satisfaction. *Journal of Social and Personal Relationships, 16,* 591–618.

Acitelli, L., & Young, A. (1996). Gender and thought in relationships. In G. Fletcher & J. Fitness (Eds.), *Knowledge structures and interactions in close relationships: A social psychological approach* (pp. 147–168). Mahwah, NJ: Lawrence Erlbaum Associates.

Adams, R., & Allan, G. (Eds.). (1998). *Placing friendship in context*. New York: Cambridge University Press.

Austin, A., Salehi, M., & Leffler, A. (1987). Gender and developmental differences in children's conversations. *Sex Roles, 16,* 497–510.

Baxter, L. A. (1985). Accomplishing relational disengagement. In S. W. Duck & D. Perlman (Eds.), *Understanding personal relationships: An interdisciplinary approach* (pp. 243–265). Beverly Hills, CA: Sage.

Bergmann, J. R. (1993). *Discreet indiscretions: The social organization of gossip*. New York, de Gruyter.

Bradbury, T., & Fincham, F. (1990). Attributions in marriage: Review and critique. *Psychological Bulletin, 107,* 3–33.

Brown, L. (1997). *Two-spirit people*. Binghamton, NY: Haworth.

Burleson, B. (2003). The experience and effects of emotional support: What the study of cultural and gender differences can tell us about close relationships, emotion, and interpersonal communication. *Personal Relationships, 10,* 1–23.

Burleson, B., Kunkel, A., Samter, W., & Werking, K. (1996). Men's and women's evaluations of communication skills in personal relationships: When sex differences make a difference—and when they don't. *Journal of Social and Personal Relationships, 13,* 201–224.

Butler, J. (1990). Performative acts and gender constitution: An essay in phenomenology and feminist theory. In S. Case (Ed.), *Performing feminisms: Feminist critical theory and theatre* (pp. 270–282). Baltimore: Johns Hopkins University Press.

Butler, J. (1993). *Bodies that matter: On the discursive limits of "sex."* New York: Routledge.

Campbell, A. (1993). *Men, women, and aggression*. New York: Basic Books.

Canary, D., & Emmers-Sommer, T. (1997). *Sex and gender differences in personal relationships*. New York: Guilford.

Cancian, F. (1987). *Love in America*. Cambridge, England: Cambridge University Press.

Cancian, F. (1989). Love and the rise of capitalism. In B. Risman & P. Schwartz (Eds.), *Gender in intimate relationships* (pp. 12–25). Belmont, CA: Wadsworth.

Clark, R. (1998). A comparison of topics and objectives in a cross section of young men's and women's everyday conversations. In D. J. Canary & K. Dindia (Eds.), *Sex differences and similarities in communication: Critical essays and empirical investigations of sex and gender in interaction* (pp. 303–319). Mahwah, NJ: Lawrence Erlbaum Associates.

Coates, J. (Ed.). (1997). *Language and gender: A reader*. London: Blackwell.

Cohan, C., & Bradbury, T. (1997). Negative life events and the longitudinal course of newlywed marriage. *Journal of Personality and Social Psychology, 73,* 114–128.

Coleman, M., & Ganong, L. (1985). Love and sex-role stereotypes: Do macho men and feminine women make better lovers? *Journal of Personality and Social Psychology, 49,* 170–176.

Conger, R., Rueter, M., & Elder, G. (1999). Couple resilience to economic pressure. *Journal of Personality and Social Psychology, 76,* 54–71.

Cose, E. (2003, March 3). The Black gender gap. *Newsweek,* pp. 46–51.

Coulter, A. C., & Helms-Erikson, H. (1997). Work and family from a dyadic perspective: Variations in inequality. In S. W. Duck (Ed.), *Handbook of personal relationships* (2nd. ed., pp. 487–503). East Sussex, England: Wiley.

Coyne, J., & Anderson, K. (1999). Marital status, marital satisfaction, and support processes among women at high risk for breast cancer. *Journal of Family Psychology, 13,* 629–641.

Cross, S., & Madsen, L. (1997). Models of the self: Self-construals and gender. *Psychological Bulletin, 122,* 5–37.

Cunningham, M., & Barbee, A. (2000). Social support. In C. Hendrick & S. Hendrick (Eds.), *Close relationships: A sourcebook* (pp. 272–285). Thousand Oaks, CA: Sage.

Cutrona, C., Russell, D., Hessling, R., Brown, P., & Murry, V. (2000). Direct and moderating effects of community context on the psychological well-being of African American women. *Journal of Personality and Social Psychology, 79,* 1099–1101.

Delamont, S. (2001). *Changing women, unchanged men?* Buckingham, England: Open University Press.

Deutsch, F. (2001). Equally shared parenting. *Current Directions in Psychological Science, 10,* 25–28.

Duck, S. W. (1982). A topography of relationship disengagement and dissolution. In S. W. Duck (Ed.), *Personal relationships: Vol. 4. Dissolving personal relationships* (pp. 1–30). New York: Academic Press.

Duck, S. W. (Ed.). (1993). *Understanding relationship processes: Vol. 3. Social context and relationships*. Thousand Oaks, CA: Sage.

Duck, S. W. (2005). How do you tell someone you're letting go? A new model of relationship break up. *The Psychologist, 18,* 4, pp. 210–213. Leicester, UK: British Psychological Society.

Eldridge, N., & Gilbert, L. (1990). Correlates of relationship satisfaction in lesbian couples. *Psychology of Women Quarterly, 14,* 43–62.

Feeney, J. (1999). Issues of closeness and distance in dating relationships: Effects of sex and attachment style. *Journal of Social and Personal Relationships, 16,* 571–590.

Fletcher, G., & Fincham, F. (1991). Attribution in close relationships. In G. J. Fletcher & F. D. Fincham (Eds.), *Cognition in close relationships* (pp. 7–35). Hillsdale, NJ: Lawrence Erlbaum Associates.

Gaines, S. (1995). Relationships between members of cultural minorities. In J. T. Wood & S. W. Duck (Eds.), *Understanding relationship processes: Vol. 6. Off the beaten track: Understudied relationships* (pp. 51–88). Thousand Oaks, CA: Sage.

Garrido, E. F., & Acitelli, L. K. (1999). Relational identity and the division of household labor. *Journal of Social and Personal Relationships, 16,* 619–637.

Gerson, K. (2004). Moral dilemmas, moral strategies, and the transformation of gender: Lessons from two generations of work and family change. In J. Spade & C. Valentine (Eds.), *The kaleidoscope of gender: Prisms, patterns and possibilities* (pp. 413–424). Belmont, CA: Wadsworth.

Goldstein, L., Diener, M., & Mangelsdorf, S. (1996). Maternal characteristics and social support across the transition to motherhood: Associations with maternal behavior *Journal of Family Psychology, 10,* 60–71.

Gottman, J. M. (1994a). *What predicts divorce: The relationship between marital processes and marital outcomes.* Hillsdale, NJ: Lawrence Erlbaum Associates.

Gottman, J. M. (1994b). *Why marriages succeed or fail.* New York: Simon and Schuster.

Harris, J. (1998). *The nurture assumption.* New York: Simon & Schuster The Free Press.

Helgeson, V. S., Novak, S. A., Lepore, S. J., & Eton, D. T. (2004). Spouse social control efforts: Relations to health behavior and well-being among men with prostate cancer. *Journal of Social and Personal Relationships, 21,* 53–68.

Hill, C., Rubin, Z., & Peplau, L. (1976). Breakups before marriage: The end of 103 affairs. *Journal of Social Issues, 32,* 147–168.

Hochschild, A. (with Machung, A.). (2003). *The second shift: Working parents and the revolution at home* (rev. ed.). New York: Viking/Penguin.

Hochschild, A. (1997). *The time bind: When work becomes home and homes becomes work.* New York: Metropolitan Books.

Holmberg, D., & Holmes, J. G. (1993). Reconstruction of relationship memories: A mental models approach. In N. Schwartz & S. Sudman (Eds.), *Autobiographical memory and the validity of retrospective reports.* (pp. 267–288). New York: Springer-Verlag.

Huston, M., & Schwartz, P. (1996). Gendered dynamics in the romantic relationships of lesbians and gay men. In J. T. Wood (Ed.), *Gendered relationships* (pp. 163–176). Mountain View, CA: Mayfield.

Inman, C. (1995). Friendships among men: Closeness in the doing. In J. T. Wood (Ed.), *Gendered relationships* (pp. 95–110). Mountain View, CA: Mayfield.

Jena, S. (1999). Job, life satisfaction, and occupational stress of women. *Social Science International, 15,* 75–80.

Johnson, D. (2002, 25 March). Until dust do us part. *Newsweek,* p. 41.

Johnson, F. (1995). Friendships among women: Closeness in dialogue. In J. T. Wood (Ed.), *Gendered relationships* (pp. 79–94). Mountain View, CA: Mayfield.

Johnson, F. (2000). *Speaking culturally: Language diversity in the United States.* Thousand Oaks, CA: Sage.

Kessler, S. (1998). *Lessons from the intersexed.* New Brunswick, NJ: Rutgers University Press.

Kessler, S., & McKenna, W. (1978). *Gender: An ethnomethodological approach.* New York: Wiley.

Kellas, J., & Manusov, V. (2003). What's in a story? The relationship between narrative completeness and adjustment to relationship dissolution. *Journal of Social and Personal Relationships, 20,* 285–307.

Kessler, S., & McKenna, W. (1978). *Gender: An ethnomethodological approach.* New York: Wiley.

Kluwer, E., Heesink, J., & Vliert, E. (1996). The marital dynamics of conflict over the division of labor. *Journal of Marriage and the Family, 59,* 635–653.

Knudson-Martin, C., & Mahoney, A. (1996). Gender dilemmas and myths in the construction of marital bargains: Issues for marital therapy. *Family Process, 35,* 137–153.

Kovacs, P., Parker, J., & Hoffman, L. (1996). Behavioral, affective and social correlates of involvement in cross-sex friendships in elementary school. *Child Development, 67,* 2269–2286.

Kunkel, A., & Burleson, A. (1998). Social support and the emotional lives of men and women: An assessment of the different cultures perspective. In D. J. Canary & K. Dindia (Eds.), *Sex differences and similarities in communication* (pp. 101–125). Mahwah, NJ: Lawrence Erlbaum Associates.

Kunkel, A., & Burleson, B. (1999). Assessing explanations for sex differences in emotional support: A test of the different cultures and skill specialization accounts. *Human Communication Research, 25,* 307–340.

Kurdek, L., & Schmitt, J. (1986). Relationship quality of partners in heterosexual married, heterosexual cohabiting, and gay and lesbian relationships. *Journal of Personality and Social Psychology, 51,* 711–720.

La Gaipa, J. J. (1982). Rules and rituals in disengaging from relationships. In S. W. Duck (Ed.), *Personal relationships: Vol. 4. Dissolving personal relationships* (pp. 189–209). New York: Academic Press.

Leaper, C. (1991). Influence and involvement in children's discourse: Age, gender, and partner effects. *Child Development, 62,* 797–811.

Leaper, C. (Ed.). (1994). *Childhood gender segregation: Causes and consequences.* San Francisco: Jossey-Bass.

Leaper, C. (1996). The relationship of play activity and gender to parent and child sex-typed communication. *International Journal of Behavioral Development, 19,* 689–703.

Maccoby, E. (1998). *The two sexes: Growing up apart, coming together.* Cambridge, MA: Harvard University Press.

Maltz, D., & Borker, R. (1982). A cultural approach to male–female miscommunication. In J. J. Gumperz (Ed.), *Language and social identity* (pp. 196–216). Cambridge, England: Cambridge University Press.

Matthews, L., Conger, R., & Wickrama, K. (1996). Work–family conflict and marital quality: Mediating processes. *Social Psychology Quarterly, 59,* 62–79.

Maushart, S. (2001). *Wifework: What marriage really means for women.* New York: Bloomsbury.

McCloskey, D. (1999). *Crossing: A memoir.* Chicago: University of Chicago Press.

Mead, M. (1968). *Sex and temperament in three primitive societies.* New York: Dell. (Original work published 1935).

Moller, L., & Serbin, L. (1996). Antecedents of toddler gender segregation: Cognitive consonance, gender-typed toy preferences and behavioral compatibility. *Sex Roles, 35,* 445–460.

Nanda, S. (2004). Multiple genders among North American Indians. In J. Spade & C. Valentine (Eds.), *The kaleidoscope of gender* (pp. 64–70). Belmont, CA: Wadsworth.

Nolen-Hoeksema, S. (2003). *Women who think too much.* New York: Holt.

Perlman, D., & Surra, C. (2003). Special issue: Contextual influences on relationships. *Personal Relationships, 10,* 283–452.

Reis, H. T., Senchak, M., & Solomon, B. (1985). Sex differences in the intimacy of social interaction. *Journal of Personality and Social Psychology, 48,* 1204–1217.

Riessman, C. (1990). *Divorce talk: Women and men make sense of personal relationships.* New Brunswick, NJ: Rutgers University Press.

Risman, B., & Godwin, S. (2001). Twentieth-century changes in economic work and family. In D. Vannoy (Ed.), *Gender mosaics* (pp. 134–144). Los Angeles: Roxbury.

Rothenberg, P., Schafhausen, N., & Schneider, C. (Eds.). (2000). *Race, class and gender in the United States: An integrated study.* New York: Worth.

Rubin, L. (1985). *Just friends: The role of friendship in our lives.* New York: Harper and Row.

Rusbult, C. (1987). Responses to dissatisfaction in close relationships: The exit-voice-loyalty-neglect model. In D. Perlman & S. W. Duck (Eds.), *Intimate relationships: Development, dynamics, and deterioration* (pp. 209–238). London: Sage.

Rusbult, C., Zembrodt, I., & Iwaniszek, J. (1986). The impact of gender and sex-role orientation on responses to dissatisfaction in close relationships. *Sex Roles, 15,* 1–20.

Ryan, M. (1979). *Womanhood in America:From Colonial times to the present.* New York: New Viewpoints.

Schaef, A. W. (1981). *Women's reality.* St. Paul, MN: West.

Schneider, B., & Stevenson, D. (1999). *The ambitious generation.* Cambridge, MA: Yale University Press.

Sedikides, C., Oliver, M., & Campbell, W. (1994). Perceived benefits and costs of romantic relationships for women and men: Implications for exchange theory. *Personal Relationships, 1,* 23–43.

Shellenbarger, S. (1997, April 16). For many, work seems like a retreat compared with home. *Wall Street Journal,* p. B1.

Smith, V. (1998). *Not just race, not just gender: Black feminist readings.* New York: Routledge.

Stafford, L., Dutton, M., & Hass, S. (2000). Measuring routine maintenance: Scale revision, sex versus gender roles, and the prediction of relational characteristics. *Communication Monographs, 67,* 306–323.

Steiner-Pappalardo, N., & Gurung, R. (2002). The femininity effect: Relationship quality, sex, gender, attachment, and significant-other concepts. *Personal Relationships, 9,* 313–325.

Suh, E., Moskowitz, D., Fournier, M., & Zuroff, D. (2004). Gender and relationships: Influences on agentic and communal behaviors. *Personal Relationships, 11,* 41–59.

Surrey, J. (1991). The self-in-relation: A theory of women's development. In J. Jordan, A. Kaplan, J. Miller, I. Stiver, & J. Surrey (Eds.), *Women's growth in connection* (pp. 51–68). New York: Guilford.

Swain, S. (1989). Covert intimacy: Closeness in men's friendships. In B. J. Risman & P. Schwartz (Eds.), *Gender in intimate relationships* (pp. 71–86). Belmont, CA: Wadsworth/Brooks/Cole.

Tashiro, T., & Frazier, P. (2003). "I'll never be in a relationship like that again:" Personal growth following romantic relationship breakups. *Personal Relationships, 10,* 113–128.

Tavris, C. (1992). *The mismeasure of woman.* New York: Simon and Schuster.

Umberson, D. (1995). Marriage as support or strain? Marital quality following the death of a parent. *Journal of Marriage and the Family, 57,* 709–723.

Vinokur, A., Price, R., & Caplan, R. (1996). Hard times and hurtful partners: How financial strain affects depression and relationship satisfaction of unemployed persons and their spouses. *Journal of Personality and Social Psychology, 71,* 166–179.

Vonk, R., & van Nobelen, D. (1993). Masculinity and femininity in the self with an intimate partner: Men are not always men in the company of women. *Journal of Social and Personal Relationships, 10,* 627–630.

Weber, A. (1983, June). *The breakdown of relationships.* Paper presented at the conference on Social Interaction and Relationships, Nags Head, NC.

Wilmot, W., Carbaugh, D., & Baxter, L. (1985). Communication strategies used to terminate romantic relationships. *Western Journal of Speech Communication, 49,* 204–216.

Wood, J. T. (1986). Different voices in relationship crises: An extension of Gilligan's theory. *American Behavioral Scientist, 29,* 273–301.

Wood, J. T. (1993). Engendered relations: Interaction, caring, power, and responsibility in intimacy. In S. W. Duck (Ed.), *Understanding relationship processes, 3: Social context and relationships* (pp. 26–54). Newbury Park, CA: Sage.

Wood, J. T. (1994a). Engendered identities: Shaping voice and mind through gender. In D. Vocate (Ed.), *Intrapersonal communication: Different voices, different minds* (pp. 145–167). Hillsdale, NJ: Lawrence Erlbaum Associates.

Wood, J. T. (1994b). Gender and relationship crises: Contrasting reasons, responses and relational orientations. In J. Ringer (Ed.), *Queer words, queer images: The construction of homosexuality* (pp. 238–264). New York: New York University Press.

Wood, J. T., & Inman, C. (1993). In a different mode: Masculine styles of communicating closeness. *Journal of Applied Communication Research, 21,* 279–295.

10

Social Construction of Accounts in the Process of Relationship Termination

John H. Harvey
University of Iowa

Mark A. Fine
University of Missouri—Columbia

STORYTELLING–ACCOUNT-MAKING THEORETICAL BACKGROUND

A growing body of research has demonstrated that individuals eventually construct stories or accounts of how their relationship deteriorated and eventually ended. Because accounts serve different purposes for different individuals, partners may have very different accounts of the relationship deterioration process. This chapter explores account-making theory and the role of accounts in the process of dissolution and its aftermath.

Harvey, Weber, and Orbuch (1990) equated account-making with the more commonly used terms storytelling and narration. They defined account-making as the act of explaining, describing, and emotionally reacting to the major events in our lives in story-like form (p. 4), and they suggested that this account-making often begins in our private reflections and then is communicated in the form of an account to other people in whom we confide. In this theory, it has been argued that account-making plays a major positive role in dealing with life's major stresses.

When major loss occurs, both persons in a confiding situation may be telling stories of loss and comforting one another. People usually take turns discussing perceptions of what is happening, sometimes asking for input, sometimes asking the other person if he or she sees matters the same way, and sometimes asking if he or she has had similar experiences. It is the reciprocal communicative act that makes this experience a powerfully social event.

How important is it that the accounts or stories that people develop about major events in our lives are sometimes very distorted and inaccurate? It may matter a lot. For example, the issue of false memory regarding the occurrence of sexual abuse and incest early in a person's life is a prominent issue in the literature. Using the thesis of false memory, or implanted false memory, there have been legal suits by parents against children who had accused them of incest. In fact, when events are highly emotionally laden, they may be quite subject to distortion in memory

(Nigro & Neisser, 1983). Further, as the false memory syndrome issue highlights, people can even create memories (or be persuaded to create such memories by others) of events that did not occur. Thus, if one wanted *the* accurate account of how a couple's relationship deteriorated and eventually dissolved, one would not want to blindly accept as true what each of the relationship partners conveyed in his or her story.

For our purposes, however, we contend that people's accounts and stories influence them and others—whether or not they are true. In some circumstances, it certainly may be very important for the researcher to try to establish the truth and accuracy of an account. However, perhaps what is most important for the purposes of this chapter is that, regardless of whether or not the story is accurate, the researcher also may study how the account is related to factors such as psychological and physical health and its impact on others. In an account of a recent divorce, a person may choose to deemphasize personal culpability in the divorce to help himself or herself feel better about his or her role in the relationship termination. Thus, the development of the account may serve several purposes, such as assisting the person to feel better about his or her role in causing the termination, helping the person make sense of the events, aiding the individual in recovering from the pain of the loss, or presenting a socially acceptable story to those in the social network.

Harvey et al.'s (1990) use of the concept of account followed Weiss' (1975) persuasive use of this term to help us understand how people in the process of marital separation organized and managed their chaotic thoughts and feelings about why their marriage was ending. Weiss argued that work on the account or story often gives the survivor a greater sense of control over what are otherwise confusing and dismaying events. He suggested that the account begins to settle the issue of who is responsible for what and that it imposes on the events leading to separation a plot structure with a beginning, middle, and end. Thus, it organizes the events into a conceptually manageable and integrated entity. Once understood in this way, Weiss suggested, the events can be dealt with, and detachment from these emotionally searing stimuli can be achieved.

The concept of account has another root in sociological theory. On the basis of Goffman's (1959) influential writing about the presentation of self in everyday life, sociologists Scott and Lyman (1968) developed the concept of account to refer to people's use of justifications and excuse-making in general as they describe actions that have been associated with negative outcomes. For example, the driver may blame his running the red light on a bee that was chasing his hands as they negotiated the steering wheel. Orbuch (1997) developed a thorough analysis of this approach to account-making that emphasizes the justification of conduct as its central theme.

More generally, if we link the account to a story about why and how events occurred (whether it represents a justification for action, or a more general statement without reference to justification), there has been a plethora of recent writing in the social and behavioral sciences that emphasize the value of storytelling. Coles (1989) has written about the value of storytelling as a humanizing and meaning-giving force for human betterment in a variety of life contexts, such as education and medicine. Bruner (1990) suggested that the lives and selves we construct are the outcomes of the process of meaning construction, and that social scientists should give greater attention to how people construct and use meaning in different cultures.

In presenting what they term a *dramaturgical approach* to understanding emotion and understanding (which views life as a theater), Cochran and Claspell (1987) have written about how life is punctuated by overlapping and interweaving beginnings, middles, and ends of stories. They contend that we vacation, daydream, plot, love, meet challenges, do chores, pursue careers, seek redress, raise children, and play *in story*. We also grieve in story, a message that is at the heart of this book. Cochran and Claspell persuasively argue that to even object to viewing the story as the very root of what it is to be alive as a human would require enacting a counterargument in the form of a story!

The well-known counseling psychologist George Howard (1991) had this to say about storytelling:

> A life becomes meaningful when one sees himself or herself as an actor within the context of a story—be it a cultural tale, a religious narrative, a family saga, the march of science, a political movement, and so forth. Early in life we are free to choose what life story we will inhabit—and later we find we are lived by that story. (p. 196)

Still other important work on the storytelling metaphor has been done by scholars who emphasized the value of human narrative activity, such as Gergen and Gergen (1987). As an insight about the role of stories in life, the cognitive psychologist Frank Smith (1990) wrote the following:

> Most of the beliefs we have about the world and our place in it come in the form of stories. Most of the beliefs we have about other people, and the way we regard and treat them, are in the form of stories. Stories are the mortar that holds thoughts together, the grist of all our explanations, rationales, and values. Thought is inseparable from a literally fabulous conglomeration of person-alized stories—religious, political, social, economic, philosophical, and psychological. . . . Armies, terrorists, and bigots are motivated by the stories they believe—and so are peacemakers, philan-thropists, and martyrs. (p. 144)

ISSUES IN STUDYING STORIES, NARRATIVES, AND ACCOUNTS

By what means can we systematically and reliably study accounts, stories, and narratives? As we discuss later in this chapter, Berscheid wrote an important review of interpersonal relations in the 1994 *Annual Review of Psychology* and addressed what she called account narrative approaches to studying close relationships. Berscheid suggested that there were two main approaches in social psychology: (a) the ethnographic tradition represented by Gergen and Gergen (1988); and (b) the informational processing approach represented by Harvey et al. (1990). Although she did not clearly differentiate between these two traditions, one possible distinction is that the ethnographic tradition emphasizes participant observation techniques commonly used in cultural anthropology, whereas the information-processing technique in-volves a more removed, noninvolved approach in which the investigator presumably only observes and listens to the respondent. This distinction, however, is somewhat arbitrary. In the research by Harvey et al. (1990) or Harvey and Fine (2004) on accounts in different loss situa-tions, the investigators were partially removed from their respondents. Nevertheless, they also were close to being ethnographers in their seeking out of the respondents and then listening to or receiving their stories. Unless investigators developmentally evolve into confidants of research participants, they are also likely to remain at a distance from their respondents.

Another possible distinction is that ethnographic approaches involve the assumption that causal relations are recursive. That is, everything may causally affect everything else, and causal loops of reciprocal influences dominate in the real world. For example, a person's account may be influenced by the type of grief the person is experiencing, and the account then may affect the nature and extent of grief experienced. However, such an assumption fits well within the theoretical purview of account-making outlined in this chapter.

A final distinction is based on whether the data are handled in a quantitative or qualitative manner. With all approaches to accounts, stories, and narratives, respondents' written or spoken material may be coded and treated in the form of quantifiable indices. Certainly, the coding itself is an interpretative act, and, as Berscheid (1994) suggests, that act can distort the data and has to be carefully implemented and assessed. Alternatively, the investigator may leave the material as it is and report it, or excerpts of it, as is illustrated in the work of Harvey and Fine (2004) on young people's accounts of divorce in their families. However, even the decision about what to excerpt is an interpretive act itself. If one does not give the material a number or quantitative index, one can call that type of technique qualitative or descriptive research. We suggest that both approaches to stories, accounts, and narratives—the ethnographic and information-processing approaches—are tenable, depending on the objective of the investigator. What is important is that the material be representative of the phenomenon and people being investigated. If it is rich and evocative, either approach may pull out or present valuable insights about how the people think, feel, and behave (see Harvey, Orbuch, & Weber, 1992, for a number of types of methodological approaches to studying close relationships, all of which embrace accounts and narratives as key concepts). What may be most valuable is to use these two methodological approaches to complement each other, although this has not been frequently done in the social sciences.

A MODEL OF REACTIONS TO MAJOR LOSS
AND STEPS TOWARD RECOVERY

Figure 10.1 presents the model of theorized reactions to major loss and steps toward recovery formulated by Harvey et al. (1990). This model, which initially was adapted from Horowitz's (1976) model of coping with loss, is an idealized depiction. All people do not follow such a course in dealing with stressful events, such as the death of a loved one. In addition, people may jump around in the sequence. For example, a person may show little outcrying early, but then later will—after the traumatic event—exhibit signs of crying out to others for help, perhaps in an indirect way without knowing that the loss is still raw.

This model suggests that, in general, people experience states such as numbing, panic, despair, and hopelessness early after learning of a personally traumatic event. Very early, it is common for a person to show denial, isolation, and avoidance as the person tries to regroup. Over time, however, the individual may begin to accept the reality of the event and may begin looking to others for emotional support. We suggest that the type of support that is most helpful at first is simply being there for a person in shock from loss; the second is being a confidant— someone who listens well and offers suggestions when asked. Near the same time at which this early confiding may occur, the individual is doing his or her own private account-making about the loss. "Why did it happen?" "Why did it have to happen to her?" "Why me?" "If only. . . ." These are the kinds of questions that may not have good answers but that lead to thinking and feeling that center in on the best answers the individual can develop. The act of sharing confidences with a close other during this period may help the individual hone in on an acceptable account, and start the process of resolving the inquiry and achieving a degree of tranquility.

This model emphasizes the dual importance of private account-making and social interaction in the form of confiding as essential components of healing from a major loss. Either one alone may be insufficient. Both together may only advance the healing process to a certain point. All evidence indicates, however, that both are about the best type of medicine the survivor

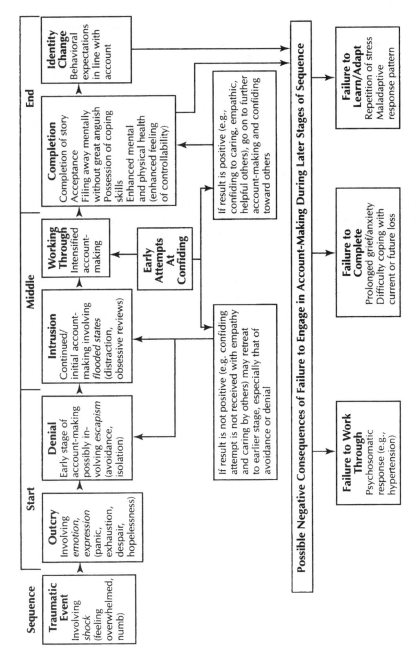

FIG. 10.1. Revision of Model in Harvey, Weber & Orbuch (1990)

can take. Each involves a process of thinking and feeling, and confiding involves a process of reaching out to others for assistance with the subsequent thinking and feeling that must occur.

The middle and final aspects of this model emphasize the importance of the psychoanalytically developed notion of *working through*, which centrally involves account-making and confiding and, one would hope, culminates in a sense of completion in one's story or understanding and greater acceptance of the facts surrounding the loss. Along with these feelings, we may believe that we have endured or become much more tenacious or hardened as a consequence of our grief and dealing with the issues of loss. Such beliefs probably represent positive outcomes, because now we think that we are stronger. We may even feel that we now can better help others because of our own experience and learning. Thus, the challenge to the survivor is to work on his or her story until the account *feels complete*, and along the way confide parts of the account to a close other. Completion, in fact, will have occurred to the extent that the survivor accepts what happened and its meaning for him or her. A sense of completion, though, does not mean that people do not continue to do some cognitive-emotional work on their accounts of major losses throughout their lives. It may, in fact, be the case that other losses at later points in time help the account-maker gain greater perspective about past losses.

Secondarily, the individual may see his or her losses in the broader spectrum of what humans lose in life and that a positive response to loss is to be there for others suffering similar losses (Harvey, 2002). Accounts help us understand the relative nature of losses. Major losses are relative in that they are relative to other losses we have experienced and to losses others have experienced as well. Understanding the relativity of loss helps us feel less naïve and shattered in our reactions to loss (Janoff-Bulman, 1992). Further, such understanding helps us recognize that we are not alone in our experience of loss.

The model further suggests that failure to work through the grieving process may eventuate in various negative consequences, including both physical (e.g., hypertension) and psychological (e.g., prolonged depression) difficulties. In a sense, the downside of completion, acceptance, and moving on is that of becoming "stuck." We may become stuck in an unending period of grieving, like the wife who 6 years after her husband's death still has left his room the way it was the day he died. That is, we persevere in grieving and fail to put our grief in a resting place after we have given it ample opportunity to exist and affect us. Or we may be stuck in the sense that we will not face up to the loss and what it means to us.

The last step is that of identity change. We argue and have provided some evidence (e.g., Harvey, Agostinelli, & Weber, 1989) that people change in significant ways when they incur major losses. This reality is especially true when we lose a loved one with whom we have a very close relationship, such as a spouse or primary partner. More generally, though, any truly major stressor changes who we are in some perceptible ways. Whether the stressor makes us less naive, less trusting, wiser, more confident, less apt to become seriously involved so quickly, "fed up with the system," or whatever, it exacts a change in some relatively permanent part of our identity.

This work on the importance of confiding is similar to the influential work of Pennebaker and his colleagues (e.g., Pennebaker, 1990; Pennebaker, Zech, & Rime', 2001). They provided impressive evidence that survivors of major loss experience improved psychological and physical health if they confide with others about their trauma. These researchers showed that confiding in the form of writing or talking about a trauma may positively affect physiological skin conductance (less reactivity reflecting nervousness), visits to a physician (less frequent visits), as well as self-reported improvement in feelings about the event. Pennebaker and associates do not emphasize the particular contents of stories or accounts, or reactions of confidants, to the extent that these factors are emphasized in the present model.

Harvey, Orbuch, Chwalisz, and Garwood (1991) found that middle-aged women who had experienced incest as young children and who had confided in family members or close others were better off only to the extent that the person in whom they confided showed empathy for them and believed in their story. If the confidant (usually a parent) was perceived as showing a lack of empathy or disbelief, it was an experience that led to the worst of outcomes: The women went into a shell with their hurt and did not come out until they reached midlife. Hence, a nonempathic confidant may be even worse than no confidant at all. As an example of the often elaborate account-making and confiding that we found among incest survivors who were in their 30s and 40s and who were working hard to deal with their wounds (Harvey et al.), consider this person's statement:

> I stayed a virgin for many years . . . [but I began to recover in my early 30s] after going to counseling, taking an emotional healing course . . . writing letters and making phone calls to my family, parents, sisters and brothers, to my brother the abuser. I'm right now making a tape and letter to my ex-husband who was emotionally and physically abusive. (p. 525)

This finding for female incest survivors was replicated by Orbuch, Harvey, Davis, and Merbach (1994), who found that male survivors also need to experience empathy among their confidants if the confiding behavior is to be effective.

THE ROLE OF ACCOUNTS IN THE DISSOLUTION PROCESS

An early finding in this literature is that males and female partners may diverge in their accounts of the problems in their relationship, and yet they do not recognize that divergence (Harvey, Wells, & Alvarez, 1978; Hopper, 1993; Orvis, Kelley, & Butler, 1976). These investigations provided suggestive evidence that spouses who could better recognize divergence in their accounts about the problems in their relationship were more effective in problem-solving activities, and hence less likely to separate.

A particularly intriguing qualitative study by Hopper (1993) suggests not only that narratives of the dissolution process may be quite different between spouses, but that certain types of narratives come to be associated with particular "motives of rhetoric." In particular, from a variety of data from 20 divorced individuals, he found that they tended to fall into one of two categories: those who felt that they were left by their partner and those who perceived that they left their partner. These two groups had very different narratives regarding the divorce process. The "left" group used more collectivist terms to describe their motives, as they characterized themselves as not wanting a divorce, as wanting to work through the marital problems, and as wanting to stay in the marriage for the collective good of the family. By contrast, the "leaver" group reported more individualistic motives, in that they stated that they had considered a divorce for some time, that they were unhappy with the marriage, and that they needed to leave the relationship for their own well-being. Perhaps most noteworthy was that, on the basis of the retrospective data available to him, Hopper could not identify any clear differences between the leaver group and the left group in terms of reported feelings, thoughts, and behaviors before the divorce. In other words, Hopper concluded that the experiences of the spouses in the two groups were quite similar (e.g., both considered divorce, and both were dissatisfied with the marriage), but that, after labeling themselves as either the leaver or the left, the spouses in the two groups constructed their narratives of their predivorce lives in the two very different ways. These findings illustrate that the narratives that are produced, both for oneself and for one's social network, may drift far from the actual circumstances that transpired, and that they serve the purposes of the individual in the role that he or she has come to occupy (e.g., left vs. leaver).

A case study may help elucidate how accounts play a role in the postdissolution phase of a relationship (this story was told to J. Harvey by a person attending a talk he gave on divorce to a local support group). This story concerns a relationship that ended in the late 1990s after 17 years of marriage. The marriage was officially dissolved after a year of separation in which the couple went to a few counseling sessions and tried to renew their connection. The primary ostensible issue at the time of separation was the discovery by the woman of the man's recent infidelity with a coworker. Later, in counseling attended by both parties, she also learned that he had had other short affairs earlier in the marriage, and that he felt he had "been in love" with one of the other women. The woman concluded over the year of separation that she could no longer trust the man, and she felt humiliated in her community given the public nature of his last affair and their standing in the community.

Accounts play several roles in the foregoing dissolution. As noted, the woman's development of an account about the man's lack of trustworthiness in the future was central to her decision to divorce him, even though he said he still loved her and wanted to be with her. She began to develop an account that characterized much of her husband's stated feelings for her and their future as lies. This type of account-making is similar to what Hopper (2001) described regarding a sample of people who had perceived themselves as having been left in their relationships. These individuals also interpreted their relationships as involving many lies on the part of their expartner.

Apparently, the woman in our story had a different account of the reasons for her divorce than the story entertained by her exhusband. Our information, based on the exwife's report of discussions with him, is that his account emphasized the fact that he had turned 50 and wanted new starts in all areas of his life—including the opportunity to be with younger women. He was done with raising children, and apparently he was done with the stability represented by his relatively long marriage. He also is alleged by his exwife not to have been happy with her as a sexual partner.

The exwife's ensuing account focused on male infidelity as a common theme in relationships. Thus, trust was a major issue for her in establishing new relationships. She also developed the theme that older men almost invariably prefer younger women. Further, she became very sexual herself in her early relationships out of divorce, and she discovered that sexuality was an element that she had missed in her marriage—attributing much of the problem to a combination of raising children and to her exhusband's inability to be expressive and free in his intimate activities. Hence, it can be seen that her behavioral pattern followed the type of account she developed, as well as her beliefs about her exhusband's account.

FUNCTIONS OF ACCOUNTS

There appear to be a number of functions of the account-making process. These include (a) experiencing catharsis, or the release of emotion about a topic that has caused a person pain; (b) trying to establish blame or exoneration about an event; (c) trying to clarify or resolve one's thinking about an event; (d) seeking to provide information about an event; and (e) receiving edification or instruction about future directions.

These functions are apparent in the subsequent account, which was presented to Harvey and Fine (2004) in their study of narratives of young adults whose parents had divorced. This account has as its theme "the lost father," as a young person recounts a major consequence of her parents' divorce. In this account, a 22-year-old woman describes her feelings that in time have become deep anguish, as she has tried and failed to make contact with her father, who seemingly could never love her after his divorce from her mother. She reflects both a degree of alienation often expressed by young women whose fathers have gone away after a divorce and an orientation to her own close relationships that involves being quite demanding in her expectations of men she dates. Perhaps what is most important is that her narrative illustrates the theme that it may be too late for previously absent fathers to enter their children's lives in a meaningful way. This story well reflects the theme of the father "being too late," or what might be viewed as a blaming function of the account. In terms of other functions of accounts, it is apparent that she is providing a release of emotion, information, and futuristic projections, as well as laying blame or making causal interpretations:

> When my parents told me they were getting a divorce I was only 4 years old, much too young and naive to know the implications it would have on the years ahead. I responded to their words by asking for permission to play at the neighbor's house, while my 7-year-old brother could not even utter through his tears. My mother eventually decided to arrange for my brother to attend therapy, although I suspect he has still not fully recovered and hides his pain with his hardened personality.
>
> My mother initiated the divorce proceedings when her tolerance of my father's alcoholism ceased. She wanted the best for her children and my father was never there to help her raise and nurture us. He had desired another son when I was born and could never find a way to bond with his new daughter. My mother noticed his actions and made an extra effort when she was with me. It must have hurt her to see me try so hard, even still in college, to create a relationship with my father where one could never exist.
>
> When we moved to Iowa two weeks before my freshman year in High School I said good-bye to my father, although I had no idea it would be one of my last face-to-face conversations with him. He arrived at the house, late as usual, that day to sign papers granting my mother full custody of my brother and me. He signed, without hesitation. We took a few pictures on the front lawn and then he was gone. Without a tear in his eye, it was almost as if he had already severed the relationship he had with us long before that day.
>
> My sophomore year in college I attempted to correspond with my father. I justified one last effort by telling myself that I wouldn't forgive myself if I hadn't tried and then found out one day that it was too late. I sat down at my computer in my dorm room and began to write him an e-mail. I asked him all the difficult questions to which I always wanted answers. Did he wish to even be a small part of my life? Why did he never initiate contact? The list went on.
>
> A few days after I wrote, I received a response. Indeed he wished to be a part of my life, he said he wanted to be a large part. He claimed he had no excuse for what had happened in the past, just that he was sorry. While years before this date I would have been thrilled with his statement, it was now much too late for him to want to get so involved. He had already missed so much of my life and the effort seemed too great to fill him in for what I would receive in return. He had missed my school plays, father–daughter functions, birthdays, graduation, holidays, the list goes on at length. Certainly he had excuses for not attending those events through the years. Usually it was that he had to take an exam to get his Master's Degree. I must have heard that excuse a dozen times, but to this day still haven't figured out how he could get his Masters without having an undergraduate degree. He had plenty of excuses then, but he was never as sorry as he seemed in that e-mail.
>
> We communicated via e-mail for a few months, exchanging a few messages. He told me all about his life, but never asked about mine. I was hurt, but later that summer I decided to give him a chance to redeem himself in a conversation over the phone. I kept his number for quite some time before calling. I was not sure what I would say. How would his voice sound? Would he recognize me? Would he be too busy to talk? Putting all these questions aside, I finally picked up the phone, I hesitatingly dialed and hung up. I was nervous. I tried again. I picked up the phone and slowly

dialed, but hoped he would not be home. The operator came on the line, "this number has been disconnected and is no longer in service" she said. He had escaped contact with me again.

I have not talked to my father since I tried calling him that day, nor has he continued e-mailing me. I do not know what his voice sounds like. I do not know if he is truly sorry. I do not know where he lives or even if a memory of me remains through the years of alcoholic lies and apologies.

While he may not be physically visible, he has certainly had a great influence on my life in regards to relationships. I no longer trust people as easily and innocently as I once did. I have learned to value proof when excuses are given. Most of all I have learned to value integrity in a man above all else. I do not date men simply because they are attractive as many college women do. I have high expectations for every man I date and if at any time in a relationship I cannot see myself ever marrying that person, I break that relationship because the effort seems wasted. I am not quick to commit and I know that the man I marry will be one whom I date many years before engagement.

I am sure I have hurt a few men along the way, but refuse to live the life of my parents. I could never live with myself if I knew that someday a child of mine was listening to the arguments from around the corner. Too many have already lived that horror. (pp. 94–96)

CONCLUSIONS, CAVEATS, AND FUTURE DIRECTIONS

At the heart of the account-making and confiding model is the act of working on one's story, possibly in the context of social interaction and confiding behavior. The theory suggests that account-making and confiding are positive for health and adaptation. These activities are precipitated by a loss event, which in the case of the material discussed here is a relationship ending. However, an emerging line of work in the loss and trauma literature suggests that some people do not grieve major losses (even the loss of a child) with deep and recurrent distress and depression, along with other standard indices of grief (Bonanno & Kaltman, 1999; Wortman & Silver, 1989). Further, some have contended that some people do not cope more effectively when they engage in emotional disclosures than when they do not engage in such disclosure (e.g., Pennebaker, Zech, & Rime', 2001). There appear to be many coping strategies and personality styles associated with dealing with major loss events, and there is no single blueprint best strategy for coping with major losses. It appears that a host of factors interact with both one's personality and repertoire of coping strategies to determine the effectiveness of adaptation to loss.

It follows, then, that the account-making and confiding model very likely has major limits in terms of whether it would work for all people in the throes of dissolution and at all times. No such claim is made here. We do believe that there is enough evidence at hand that people naturally feel compelled to engage in some type of accounting. They may do so privately, however. They also may do their account-making in bits and pieces over time, with no urgent motivation to achieve a sense of completion. The so-called silent generation of World War II survivors presumably shows well the stoic personality who does not readily communicate feelings about the losses experienced during that horrific period.

The importance of narratives and stories, at multiple stages of the dissolution process, illustrates the proactive and constructed way that people manage the termination of their romantic relationships. As opposed to a model that indicates that people passively and reactively respond in systematic, linear, and easily predictable ways to the experience of relationship dissolution, individuals are creative and active players who construct stories and accounts of their experiences. These accounts, therefore, both reflect experience and also shape subsequent experiences. The process of developing accounts of relationship termination is a uniquely human activity (communication scholars have referred to humans as *homo narans*) that not only records the veridical history of various experiences, but that alters and shapes past and present experiences. The constructed nature of accounts of relationship dissolution should make researchers and practitioners somewhat cautious in thinking that the stories reveal an accurate portrayal of events as they actually unfolded; indeed, all self-reports of dissolution-related events and experiences should be considered some combination of the individual's recollection of the actual events themselves and the person's active attempt to develop a story that helps him or her cope more effectively to such a major loss as one's primary romantic relationship.

REFERENCES

Berscheid, E. (1994). Interpersonal relationships. *Annual Review of Psychology, 45,* 79–129.

Bonanno, G. A., & Kaltman, D. (1999). Toward an integrative perspective on bereavement. *Psychological Bulletin, 125,* 760–776.

Bruner, J. (1990). *Acts of meaning.* Cambridge, MA: Harvard University Press.

Cochran, L., & Claspell, E. (1987). *The meaning of grief.* New York: Greenwood.

Coles, R. (1989). *The call of stories.* Boston: Houghton Mifflin.

Gergen, K., & Gergen, M. (1987). Narratives as relationship. In R. Burnett, P. McGhee, & D. C. Clarke (Eds.), *Accounting for relationships* (pp. 269–315). London: Methuen.

Gergen, K., & Gergen, M. (1988). Narrative and self as relationship. *Advances in Experimental Social Psychology, 21,* 17–56.

Goffman, E. (1959). *The presentation of self in everday life.* Garden City, NY: Doubleday-Anchor Books.

Harvey, J. H. (2002). *Perspectives on loss and trauma.* Thousand Oaks, CA: Sage.

Harvey, J. H., Agostinelli, G., & Weber, A. L. (1989). Account-making and the formation of expectations about close relationships. *Review of Personality and Social Psychology, 10,* 39–62.

Harvey, J. H., & Fine, M. A. (2004). *Children of divorce: Stories of loss and hope.* Mahwah, NJ: Lawrence Erlbaum Associates.

Harvey, J. H., Orbuch, T. L., Chwalisz, K., & Garwood, G. (1991). Coping with sexual assault: The roles of account-making and confiding. *Journal of Traumatic Stress, 4,* 515–531.

Harvey, J. H., Orbuch, T. L., & Weber, A. L. (1992). (Eds.). *Attributions, accounts, and close relationships.* New York: Springer-Verlag.

Harvey, J. H., Weber, A. L., & Orbuch, T. L. (1990). *Interpersonal accounts.* Oxford, England: Blackwell.

Harvey, J. H., Wells, G. H., & Alvarez, M. D. (1978). Attribution in the context of conflict and separation in close relationships. In J. H. Harvey, W. Ickes, & R. F. Kidd (Eds.), *New directions in attribution research* (Vol. 2, pp. 235–259). Hillsdale, NJ: Lawerence Erlbaum Associates.

Hopper, J. (1993). The rhetoric of motives in divorce. *Journal of Marriage and the Family, 55,* 801–813.

Hopper, J. (2001). The symbolic origins of conflict in divorce. *Journal of Marriage and the Family, 63,* 430–445.

Horowitz, M. J. (1976). *Stress response syndromes* (2nd ed.). Northvale, NJ: Aronson.

Howard, G. S. (1991). Cultural tales: A narrative approach to thinking, cross-cultural psychology, and psychotherapy. *American Psychologist, 46,* 187–197.

Janoff-Bulman, R. (1992). *Shattered assumptions.* New York: The Free Press.

Nigro, G., & Neisser, U. (1983). Point of views in personal memories. *Cognitive Psychology, 15,* 467–482.

Orbuch, T. L. (1997). People's accounts count: The sociology of accounts. *Annual Review of Sociology, 23,* 455–478.

Orbuch, T. L., Harvey, J. H., Davis, S. H., & Merbach, N. (1994). Account-making and confiding as acts of meaning in response to sexual assault. *Journal of Family Violence, 9,* 249–264.

Orvis, B. R., Kelley, H. H., & Butler, D. (1976). Attributional conflict in young couples. In J. H. Harvey, W. Ickes, & R. F. Kidd (Eds.), *New directions in attribution research* (Vol. 1, pp. 353–386). Hillsdale, NJ: Lawrence Erlbaum Associates.

Pennebaker, J. (1990). *Opening up.* New York: Morrow.

Pennebaker, J., Zech, E., & Rime', B. (2001). Disclosing and sharing emotion: Psychological, social, and health consequences. In M. Stroebe, R. O. Hansson, W. Stroebe, & H. Schut (Eds.), *Handbook of bereavement research: Consequences, coping, and care* (pp. 517–543). Washington, DC: American Psychological Association.

Scott, M. B., & Lyman, S. (1968). Accounts. *American Sociological Review, 33,* 46–62.

Smith, F. (1990). *To think.* New York: Columbia University Press.

Weiss, R. L. (1975). *Marital separation.* New York: The Free Press.

Wortman, C., & Silver, R. (1989). The myths of coping with loss. *Journal of Consulting and Clinical Psychology, 57,* 349–357.

11

Process of Disaffection in Relationship Breakdown[1]

Karen Kayser and Satya S. Rao
Boston College

> *Love is a shadow.*
> *How you lie and cry after it*
> *Listen: these are its hooves: it has gone off, like a horse.*[2]
>
> —Sylvia Plath (1960)

Many couples struggle to sustain love in their intimate relationships after the initial romance fades. In fact, it seems much easier to fall into love than to stay in love. Given the primacy of love in marriage in contemporary society, it is not surprising that the lack of love is the major reason reported for marital breakdown. In recent studies on divorce, separated and divorced individuals indicated that lack of love was one of the top two reasons for marital breakdown, second either to extramarital sex (de Munck & Korotayev, 1999) or communication difficulties (Gottman & Notarius, 2002). In fact, intimacy and love have been identified as the best indicators of whether couples plan to continue or terminate their relationships (Riehl-Emde, Volker, & Willi, 2003). These affective variables were more important than factors such as exchange of resources, conflict resolution, and self-disclosure.

For decades, social scientists have been examining the social and demographic predictors of divorce, such as age at marriage, parental status, social class, and race or ethnicity (Booth, Johnson, White, & Edwards, 1984; Kitson & Sussman, 1982; Kurdek, 1991, 1993; Martin & Bumpass, 1989; Spanier & Thompson, 1984; White, 1990). More recently, researchers have focused on social-psychological, interpersonal, and intrapersonal factors, and how conflict and destructive patterns of communication can lead to marital breakdown and divorce (Bodenmann, 1997; Bodenmann & Cina, 1999; Gottman, 1994; Gottman & Levenson, 1992, 2000; Leonard & Roberts, 1998; Lindahl, Clements, & Markman, 1998; Noller & Feeney, 1998).

---

[1]Portions of chapter 11 are reprinted from *When Loves Dies: The Process of Marital Disaffection* (Kayser, 1993, pp. 32–88) © Copyright. Reprinted by permission of Guilford Press.

[2]"Elm" from Ariel by Sylvia Plath © Copyright 1963 Ted Hughes. Reprinted by permission of HarperCollins Publishers.

201

The high divorce rate in Western societies attests to the fragility and vulnerability of love in marriage. Perhaps this is why some scholars of the family call marriage a "weakened" institution and ask what benefits marriage has to offer in the contemporary world (White, 1990). A question that has challenged social scientists, as well as couples therapists, is this: How does the love and emotional bond that couples claim existed at the beginning of their marriages gradually erode for many of these couples to reach the final point of apathy and emotional estrangement? What takes place within some marriages that extinguishes the joy and love that were felt so powerfully in the beginning? The breakdown of an emotional bond does not occur abruptly or immediately after the wedding; it can occur over months, or more likely years, of more or less continuing dissatisfaction with the relationship.

Although falling out of love does not occur in every marriage, the risk of it has been high enough to make some people think twice about "tying the knot." The purpose of this chapter is to examine the process of marital disaffection as it relates to the breakdown of marital relationships. We review several longitudinal studies on marital interaction and processes, present models of the process of disaffection, describe our findings identifying phases of the marital disaffection process, examine cultural and gender issues related to marital disaffection, and offer suggestions for practice. Although we focus on disaffection in marriage, there is research to support that a similar phenomenon and process can occur in other types of romantic relationships as well (Felmlee, 1995).

THE CONCEPT OF MARITAL DISAFFECTION

Marital disaffection consists of the gradual breaking down of an emotional attachment, a decline in caring about the partner, an emotional estrangement, and a sense of apathy and indifference toward one's spouse. During the process of disaffection, positive affect is replaced with neutral affect. This presumes that some positive feelings existed in the beginning of the relationship and that the feelings of love and affection die over time.

Disaffection provides a barometer of the emotional status of the couple. Assessing the level of disaffection is a central task in couples therapy. This information provides an indication about spouses' motivation to work on the marriage and the extent to which the couples therapist may be able to help rebuild emotional ties.

To understand the concept of marital disaffection, it is helpful to distinguish it from other similar concepts. These other states may occur along with marital disaffection, but they are not equivalent to marital disaffection. *Marital dissatisfaction* refers to a perceived low degree of adjustment or unhappiness with a relationship (Heaton & Albrect, 1991). Certainly, the spouse who is experiencing marital disaffection is also likely to be experiencing dissatisfaction. But dissatisfaction can be relatively transitory and can possibly occur simultaneously with some feelings of love and affection. Disaffection is the absence of loving feelings usually occurring after an accumulation of dissatisfactions with the marriage. Similarly, the term *marital breakdown* describes the decline in the attractiveness of the relationship, ambivalent feelings about the relationship, and marital conflict (Duck, 1981). But it does not necessarily indicate a lack of love and affection toward the partner. *Marital dissolution* involves the end of the relationship through separation or divorce (Sanchez & Gager, 2000). Marital disaffection does not mean that the spouses will dissolve their marriage. Many low quality marriages remain intact. However, marital disaffection often results in marital instability; that is, there is the propensity for the disaffected spouses to divorce their partners. Disaffection is an indicator of the spouse's *feelings* of love and affection for his or her partner; it does not indicate what a spouse will do or how he or she will behave in the marriage. Disaffection is often an internal or intrapsychic process that can be occurring within one spouse and not the other. Even when both spouses are feeling some disaffection, it is likely that they are not at the same level of disaffection or stage of emotional uncoupling.

REVIEW OF LONGITUDINAL STUDIES ON MARITAL SATISFACTION

Marital Interaction and Marital Distress

Over the past decade, there has been a tremendous interest in the processes in marriage, with a corresponding burgeoning of longitudinal studies on marriage (Bradbury, 1998). Karney and Bradbury, in their 1995 review of the longitudinal research on marriage, included 115 studies consisting of 68 independent samples and more than 45,000 marriages. These studies give us an in-depth understanding of when marital dissatisfaction sets in, how problems develop, and what leads to the consequence of marital dissolution.

Longitudinal studies on the early years of marriage report a common phenomenon: Marital satisfaction declines and conflict increases (Huston & Houts, 1998; Kurdek, 1998; Leonard & Roberts, 1998; Lindahl et al., 1998). Kurdek found that marital satisfaction for husbands and wives decreased over the first 6 years of marriage, with the steepest drop occurring in the first 2 years. Lindahl et al. (1998), in their 9-year study of the development of marriage, found a similar trend. Marital adjustment significantly declined during the first couple of years and then leveled out by approximately the third to fourth years. Several factors seem to account for this decline: commitment, conflict, and communication. In particular, husbands' and wives' low faith in the marriage at Year 1 predicted both spouses' long-term low marital satisfaction (Kurdek). Spouses with low faith at the start of the marriage may report low marital satisfaction 6 years later because they lack the motivation or the skill to engage in the kinds of relationship maintenance behaviors that foster high levels of satisfaction (e.g., being accommodating during conflict, managing jealousy, and being willing to sacrifice). Many researchers attribute the decline in marital satisfaction in the early years to the couple's transition to parenthood, and typically this factor has been a focus of their studies (Kurdek). However, this factor alone does not seem to account for the lower satisfaction, because many couples without children also experience a similar decline.

The occurrence of conflict appears as another critical variable in the course of marital satisfaction. Conflict is inevitable in any intimate relationship. How it affects satisfaction depends on the extent to which couples engage in conflict or withdraw from it. There are usually short-term negative effects to engaging in conflict, but there are long-term positive effects. If conflict is not openly addressed but is avoided, there are issues that can be left unresolved and further fuel feelings of resentment and anger. In their longitudinal study of 33 couples, Noller and Feeney (1998) found that, during the first 2 years of marriage, less happy couples made concerted attempts to improve their relationships during the first year of marriage, but gave up these efforts by the time of the third assessment in the study (approximately 1 year later). Noller and Feeney suggested that these new behaviors to improve the relationship were not being reinforced by the partner and hence did not become an integral part of the behavior repertoire. In particular, destructive conflict behaviors such as coercion, manipulation, and avoidance were likely to have negative effects on relationships.

Similarly, particular patterns of communication can have long-term effects on relationship satisfaction. In the Noller and Feeney (1998) study, communication behaviors predicted later satisfaction for wives only. Wives' reports of negativity, disengagement, and destructive processes at Time 1 predicted lower satisfaction at Time 2. These destructive patterns of communication that cause problems later in relationships had developed before the couple became married. Although most of the couples in this study were not living together prior to marriage, it appears that their patterns of communication and resolving conflict were established before they even had to handle particular issues involved in living together in a marriage.

Other researchers have also discovered that how couples behave prior to marriage indeed affects their satisfaction and stability during marriage. According to Lindahl et al. (1998), a variety of communication and conflict-related variables before marriage can predict who will stay married and who will divorce. In particular, they found that how couples communicate and regulate negative affect (anger, frustration, mistrust, and resentment) during conflict was significantly related to marital stability. The strategies that these couples used to handle conflict tended to improve over time. For example, the levels of withdrawal and verbal aggression decreased.

In their longitudinal studies of marital processes, Rusbult, Bissonnette, Arriage, and Cox (1998) found commitment to a relationship to be strongly predictive of feelings of satisfaction. Their study followed 123 married couples over the course of $3\frac{1}{2}$ years. They concluded that commitment is a central relationship-specific motive that promotes a wide range of prorelationship behaviors and that enhances dyadic adjustment. Strong commitment to a marriage promotes greater willingness to accommodate. Accommodation is defined as behavior in which individuals forgo self-interested behavior for the good of a relationship, place greater value on prorelationship behavior, and recognize the interdependence of the partners. It is one of several specific mechanisms through which committed individuals sustain their relationships.

Models of Relationship Deterioration

Two models of how intimate relationships develop and deteriorate were proposed by Houston and Houts (1998). In the first model, *disillusionment*, partners are compelled to put their best foot forward and overlook each other's—and the relationship's—shortcomings until after the wedding. During courtship, partners tend to view each other through rose-colored glasses and, when problems emerge, they are minimized so that they do not threaten the relationship (Huston & Houts). As incompatibilities and problems surface during the marriage, partners either accept each other's differences or the problems that are not resolved persist until the relationship dissolves.

The *perpetual problems* model views couples behaving similarly during courtship as they do after they are married, and consequently the problems that arise during courtship often persist into marriage. Thus, problems that persist from courtship through marriage erode partners' feelings toward one another. In contrast to the disillusionment model, the perpetual problems model proposes that courting couples are aware of each other's strengths and flaws as they enter marriage (Huston & Houts, 1998).

Alternative models of relationship deterioration emphasize that particular personalities of the partners are a root cause of marital happiness and distress. In these models, spouses view their partners', but not their own, personality as cause for marital disaffection. In particular, the partners with the personality trait of "negative affectivity" are more likely to be unhappy in their marriages. Negative affectivity reflects a tendency to be anxious and emotionally labile, to report distress or discomfort, to be introspective, and to dwell on one's own and other people's shortcomings (Watson & Clark, 1984). Husbands and wives high in negative affectivity tend to make more negative attributions for their partners' behavior (Karney, Bradbury, Fincham, & Sullivan, 1994). In the Karney et al. study, there was a relation between husbands' level of negative affectivity and their own and their wives' marital satisfaction. Wives' negative affectivity was related only to their own marital satisfaction. On the positive side, a personality quality that is related to marital satisfaction is expressiveness, which is a communal orientation that includes being kind, gentle, aware of others' feelings, warm, and emotional, and which might reduce conflict in relationships because one can respond constructively when one's partner behaves poorly (Rusbult, Verette, Whitney, Slovik, & Lipkus, 1991).

Utilizing the framework of these models and personality traits, Huston and Houts (1998) followed 168 couples from courtship into the early years of marriage. They examined personality and compatibility in courtship, marital behavior patterns, spouses' feelings about each other and their marriage, and spouses' characterizations of each other's personality qualities. Huston and Houts collected data 2 months after the couples wed and annually for the next 2 years. They took measures of personality, compatibility, and attitudes and dispositions toward the partner. They asked partners to construct a graph illustrating the development of their commitment to marriage and changes in the perceived likelihood of marriage over the course of the courtship.

The authors found support for the disillusionment model in that partners were more loving and less antagonistic during courtship and as newlyweds than after they were married for 1 or 2 years. They described the course of marriage as one in which men and women fell in love more deeply as they move from being a "couple" to being newlyweds, but then their love diminished somewhat during the first 2 years of marriage. Their perceived marital satisfaction, mutual attentiveness, and the expression of affection in marriage also declined over the first 2 years of marriage (Huston & Houts, 1998). Huston and Houts also observed that ambivalence declined from courtship into marriage and only increased over the first 2 years of marriage. Conflict, which was low during courtship and shortly after couples wed, increased during the first year of marriage and remained relatively high into the second year. Consistent with the disillusionment model, relationships did change over the first 2 years of marriage, both behaviorally and with regard to their affective tone. Love, satisfaction, affection, and maintenance, in particular, showed significant declines. Conflict increased over the first year of marriage and then leveled off. The strongest support for this model came from the increasingly strong inverse correlations between love and both negativity and conflict over the course of the marriage.

The perpetual problems model was supported by the data of Huston and Houts (1998), which showed that perpetual problems were the roots of marital distress. Couples who reportedly had trouble getting along while they were courting were more likely to experience relatively higher levels of conflict during each successive year of their marriage. Premarital conflict and ambivalence predicted how satisfied and how much in love spouses reported they were 2 years into marriage. Conflict, love, and ambivalence were intercorrelated during courtship, although not as strongly as they were later in marriage. The researchers concluded that, even as newlyweds, the bride and groom have images of each other's personality that reflect their courtship experiences and that remain relatively stable over the first 2 years of their marriage.

In the next section, we present findings from our study of the process of marital disaffection as reported by highly disaffected spouses through in-depth interviews. It is not a longitudinal study in that spouses were asked to recall the process, starting from when they first had doubts about their marriages to their current state of disaffection.

AN INVESTIGATION OF THE PROCESS OF MARITAL DISAFFECTION

A sample of highly disaffected spouses was recruited through newspaper advertisements asking for research participants who were experiencing marital difficulties or were recently separated. They were selected for interviews on the basis of their answers to several questions from the Marital Disaffection Scale (MDS; Kersten, 1990; also see Kayser, 1993, 1996), which determined their level of marital disaffection. Fifty spouses—36 women and 14 men—agreed to be interviewed. These spouses were not married to each other. When administered the entire MDS, it was determined that all except 1 spouse ranked very high on disaffection according to the scale's norms. The interview of the participant with the low score was deleted from the data analysis.

A semistructured interview schedule was used to chart changes in participants' satisfaction with their marriages over time, which ultimately led to their disaffection. We asked questions regarding major turning points in their marriage, during which the participants had doubts about their partner and their marriage. The events were not necessarily major crises, but they were perhaps crystallizing events after an accumulation of a number of seemingly minor events. In this respect, marital disaffection may be the result of the pileup effect of stress as described by stress and coping models (Boss, 2002; McCubbin & Patterson, 1983). For each turning point identified, participants were asked about their feelings, thoughts, and their own and their partner's behavior at the time. In addition, they were asked to what they attributed the problems in their relationship and how they coped with the situation.

Turning Point Events

The most frequently cited type of event involved situations in which the partner's behavior was very controlling. A common example of the partner's controlling behavior was unilateral decision-making, which disregarded the respondent's opinion. These decisions could be as minor as how the respondent should dress to major decisions about where he or she should live. The common element was the lack of consideration for the respondent's input, opinions, and feelings in making the decisions.

Two other frequently mentioned events included a partner's lack of responsibility and a partner's lack of emotional support. Partner's lack of responsibility was characterized by breaks of trust, unequal sharing of family responsibilities, and other irresponsible acts such as going to jail for drunk driving, leaving children unattended, losing jobs, and so on. Lack of emotional support involved a lack of care and concern for the respondent, usually during a stressful event such as during a pregnancy, the birth of a child, or the death of a family member.

As respondents reported specific turning points, their descriptions of these important events in their marriage often focused on something negative about their partner's behavior or personality. In other words, it was not a particular stressful event but how the partner behaved that made it notable in the history of the relationship. Although a stress may have been around a child's illness or the loss of a job, it was the partner's response to this that raised doubts in the respondent's mind about the marriage. This begs the question of whether it is the number of stressful events and level of stress that create havoc in a relationship, or the personality deficiencies of one or both partners. Recent research on dyadic stress and coping suggests that chronic stress significantly challenges the stability of marriages to the point that interpersonal skills alone may not be enough to maintain the relationship (Karney, Story, & Bradbury, 2005). Hence, it may not be the personalities of the spouses that are to blame, but the level of stress and its chronicity that produces a growing dissatisfaction with the relationship. However, the focus of this study was on the internal processes of the relationship, and one must keep in mind that it is from only the disaffected spouse's perspective.

Phase 1: Beginning Disappointments

The ink is barely dry on the marriage license when doubts and disillusionment about marriage and the partner can begin to set in. When asked about their first doubts about their marriage, approximately 40% of the individuals in the sample indicated that marital doubts occurred during the first 6 months of their marriage. Another 20% reported doubts between 6 months and 1 year. Thus, more than half (60%) of the participants were experiencing dissatisfactions and serious doubts about their marriages during the first year. For the remaining 40% of the respondents, disaffection started to set in later in their marriage.

This early onset of dissatisfaction corresponds with longitudinal studies (e.g., Kurdek, 1998; Lindahl et al., 1998) in which marital adjustment significantly declines during the first 2 years of marriage. Some of the research studies demonstrate that dissatisfaction can be traced back to the couple's interaction before marriage. Kelly, Huston, and Cate (1985) found that premarital conflict was the best predictor of conflict and dissatisfaction later in the marriage: The more premarital conflict, the less relationship satisfaction and the less the wives reported being in love at the follow-up assessment.

Regardless of when the disaffection started to set in, the accounts of the first phase in the study contained some common characteristics. During the first phase of disaffection, *disillusionment* was mentioned by respondents as a common feeling. They were disillusioned because their partners' behaviors were not what they had expected. Their marriages and partners were not living up to the dreams, fantasies, and expectations that they had prior to the wedding. Disillusionment is reflected in the following response:

> He was so different than when we first got married. And then I got pregnant so quickly—it was unplanned. We had been so close—emotionally and physically—and then he changed totally.

In general, the disaffected spouses were not individuals who hastily got married after a brief courtship or who married at a young age. The mean age at marriage was approximately 24 years, and the mean length of time the individuals had known their spouses before marriage was a little more than 2 years. Of the respondents, 16% had been previously married. However, they expressed a disappointment that sounded as though they were caught by surprise, tricked into the marriage, or cheated by love. What were these people expecting from their partners? Were their expectations too high, unrealistic, or unachievable? What explains this phenomenon of dramatic and inexplicable changes in the partner after the wedding?

Researchers of personal relationships suggest that what has changed, for the most part, is not the partner's behavior but the meaning that is given to a partner's behavior. The change in perception is as though a person is switching lenses through which he or she sees the partner (Beck, 1988). According to Felmlee (1995), an initial attracting quality is likely to be a characteristic that stands out and is readily noticed, but these extreme "positive" attributes may be likely to have negative dimensions that lead to "fatal attractions." Negative labels are now ascribed to the same characteristics that had been previously described with glowing terms. A wife's "bubbling, enthusiastic personality," as described by one respondent, was relabeled as "overemotional and destructive." This changing perspective is critical in relationships, because it results in a change in feelings, usually a negative change.

Felmlee (1995) offered three explanations for these changing perspectives. First, a person "does not know the partner well enough to accurately evaluate his or her qualities," (p. 308) and the true nature of the partner may become apparent only after some time in the relationship. Second, it is only after the relationship has become difficult or breaks down that the person "reinterprets" a positive attracting quality in a negative manner. Third, individuals may evaluate these attracting traits more positively when they are in a state of infatuation. Felmlee (1995) further argued that there may be social and situational factors that play a role in influencing a person's perception of these qualities. People in the person's social network may point out negative qualities. Stresses in the couple's lives may, over time, change the meaning of these positive traits as they adapt to changing circumstances. For example, qualities such as a partner's autonomy and independence may be assets in one situation, but they may be reassessed as deficits when a new situation requires more connection and dependence.

Not only do meanings of partners' behaviors change, but the behaviors themselves can actually change after the wedding. Huston and Houts (1998) found that behaviors such as a couple's attentiveness to each other and expression of affection declined during the first few years of marriage. Perhaps partners feel less of a need to prove their worthiness to be loved (as they felt during courtship) and they replace their good behavior with more realistic behavior. Being on "good behavior" is important to initiating relationships. Once marital vows are exchanged and the commitment to marriage is made, spouses are no longer in the initiation phase but move on to the maintenance phase. They no longer work to secure their partner's love on a daily basis. They have already achieved this goal, and they relax into a more casual mode of relating.

During this initial phase of disaffection, disillusionment and disappointment were often juxtaposed with hope and optimism about the future of the participants' relationships:

> I've committed myself for life with this person. Somewhere deep down I felt that everything will eventually be okay. We could always see a marriage counselor if it got to that point. He was going to change. He was going to see that I loved him so much. . . . I knew in my mind that if I worked hard enough, everything would be okay; this was going to be a good fruitful loving marriage.

> I tried to approach it with an open mind. The problems in the marriage itself do not seem to be insurmountable. If she and I could approach it from a reasonable basis, the problem can be solved.

When participants were asked how they had responded to the problems described during this early phase of their disaffection, a typical response was that they focused on trying to please their partners.

> I would always agree with his suggestions—whether I thought they were wrong or not, I would always agree.

> I tried to be more the perfect wife. To go home from work and bake a pie so that I could put a piece in his lunch. Basically providing him with the same home he had when he lived with his parents.

A sex difference seemed to emerge in terms of the disaffected spouses' response to problems during this initial phase. A sense of responsibility for the problems and self-blame were reflected in the voices of many of the women as they described the lengths to which they attempted to take care of the partner and relationship. The woman who baked pies for her husband stated, "I never blamed him. I felt the only problem was that I couldn't adjust. I was creating the problem."

Whereas women tended to assume responsibility for the problems and their solutions, the disaffected men tended to simply withdraw from their partners.

> I spent nights out to avoid her. I tried to stretch the work as long as possible before coming home.

> I might have said something in general to my drinking buddies. But as far as sitting down and being open to someone, I don't think I did that too often.

Unlike the previous female responses, the male responses do not convey a sense of responsibility for the relationship problems or their solutions. They give an impression of an avoidance of problems and a withdrawal from the partner.

Marital distress can take its toll on a spouse's well-being, as well as the well-being of the relationship. During the interview, respondents were asked how they coped with their marital distress. As they reflected on this initial phase of disaffection, denial and passive types of coping strategies were most frequently mentioned. More than half of the respondents reported that they kept silent, and about one third stated that they used denial as a means of coping.

> I just kept telling myself it would get better. Basically denial, I guess.

> I was pretty passive. I cried. But I didn't do anything active to cope with it. . . . I kept things inside.

It is apparent that many of these disaffected spouses suffered in silence. They were reluctant to admit marital problems to friends and family. Because the majority of respondents had experienced marital doubts during the first year of the marriage, it may have been too embarrassing to these spouses to admit dissatisfaction so early in their marriages. In addition, there is a taboo in Western culture that discourages spouses from talking about their marriages. This so-called intermarital taboo states that married sposes cannot talk openly to each other about their marriages (Mace & Mace, 1986). Unfortunately, because of this taboo, couples do not have the chance to share with one another the stresses of married life and the possible ways to cope effectively with them (Mace & Mace, 1986).

Summary

The emotions during the first phase focused on disillusionment with the marriage and disappointment in the partner. Disillusionment and disappointment do not necessarily mean that the spouses were disaffected and that love, affection, and caring had significantly diminished. However, the perceptions of the partner were changing. The rose-colored glasses that were worn during courtship were replaced with clear lenses through which to view their partner. Flaws that had been previously glossed over were now quite apparent. What were previously identified as positive traits were now relabeled as negative.

Although disappointed in the marriage, the disaffecting spouses were not contemplating leaving the marriage at this time, but were holding on to the hope that the marital relationship would improve. In general, the disaffecting spouses assumed responsibility for marital problems during this phase. They tried to change the marriage by pleasing and accommodating their partners—"trying to be a perfect spouse," in the words of one respondent.

In coping with their marital dissatisfactions during this early phase, respondents were primarily keeping silent and denying the gravity of the marital situation. Seeking support and help from their friends, family, or a professional helper rarely occurred.

Phase 2: Escalating Anger and Hurt

As the spouses in the study continued down the road of marital disaffection, the feeling of disillusionment dissipated and anger increased. The disaffected spouse was no longer shocked or surprised by the partner's behavior. In fact, having been let down so many times by their partners, by this time they were even expecting them to behave in certain negative ways and were pleasantly surprised when they did not. However, expecting the partner's misbehavior did not mean that the respondents were less upset or angry with their partner. Accounts of their anger not only increased in frequency but also in intensity, as exemplified by the following poignant statements:

> I had fantasies of killing him. . . . After I heard about the woman in Michigan putting her husband's bed on fire, I fantasized setting our bed on fire and burning my husband up.

> I could have killed him if I had the right vehicle. I didn't want to be around him—I wanted to just get out of his life.

These actions and feelings may appear quite extreme, but this was not the first time respondents had had to deal with some break of trust or other stressor. The process of disaffection may have been progressing for years, and this was just one more event that added to their growing anger.

Closely related to their anger was a sense of extreme hurt. The hurt appeared to stem from recurrences of the partner's negative and injurious behaviors. Often disaffected spouses interpreted these negative behaviors in a personal and intentional way, as if the partner was behaving in a way to purposefully hurt the spouse. Some respondents expressed hurt regarding feeling second to work or children in their partner's life. In general, there was a feeling of being unloved and uncared for.

> At first I thought, "I'm a fool to put that much trust in somebody. . . . I was let down." It wasn't what she had done that really got to me. What got to me was the fact that she lied to me for the whole time. That was what I was angry and hurt about.

Although in the first phase of disaffection there had been some doubts about their marriage, the respondents overall were quite hopeful and still cared about their partner. However, during the middle phase they started to question whether they still loved their partner, and the notion of "falling out of love" was entering their minds. Until this time respondents may not have used the phrase "falling out of love" or even recognized it as such. Interestingly, they were now viewing their relationship and feelings about it as a process—not as a static, isolated event but a sequence of events producing their current feelings about the marriage.

> It's such a gradual thing, I don't think I ever wanted to admit that I wasn't in love with him. . . . But romantically I didn't want him to touch me, and we fought continuously. And I preferred not to be around him unless we were with a group of people, and then we couldn't fight. I think all of a sudden one day I realized, "I'm just not in love with this man."

> At that time I was thinking that I didn't know if I loved her. I had lived with this so long. I didn't know what real love was. . . . If she left me, I wouldn't die.

Whereas in the previous phase it was easy to dismiss the problems and hurts as aberrations, now they were recurring, not easily forgiven or forgotten, and chipping away at the respondents' love. Accordingly, apathy also became increasingly evident during this phase.

The thoughts commonly accompanying these feelings of anger and hurt were primarily focusing on negative traits of the partners—their controlling behavior, drinking, lying, irresponsibility, and so on. This concentration on negative traits contrasts sharply with an earlier time, when the spouses were falling in love and rarely perceived anything wrong with their partner. Spouses previously shifted the negative traits to the background, but now they were shifting them to the foreground. Because they were experiencing a series of hurts, they may have become more vigilant and more sensitive to the potential hurtful actions in order to avoid further hurt. However, the resulting effect of this vigilance on the process of disaffection is that by accentuating the negative behaviors in the mind of the spouse, eventually the negative behaviors overshadow any positive actions of the partner.

Besides a preoccupation with the partner's negative attributes, the spouses during this stage spent a lot of time assessing the rewards and costs of the marriage. People are particularly mindful of the rewards and costs of a relationship during the courtship period, because they are making decisions about the continuation of the relationship. Similarly, during the breakdown of a relationship, individuals are carefully examining the reward–cost ratio as they are making decisions regarding the relationship's potential for change or the possibility of its dissolution.

The following response exemplifies this evaluation of rewards and costs during the middle phase:

> Do I really love her? I know I care about her; she was a very good friend of mine. I considered her on that basis, but I really questioned in my mind if I really loved her. She wasn't what I wanted, but does everybody get exactly what they want in a relationship? I've got a lot of good things here. Basically just trying to weigh things out.

Love, money, support, security, companionship, and validation are types of rewards desired in a close relationship. The costs of staying in a relationship may involve one's time, energy, and various other efforts. During the breakdown of a relationship, there is a drastic shift in perceived rewards or costs. This shift may be to the individual's view of fewer rewards, such as less time together and less money, as examples. Or what may have been perceived as a reward earlier in the marriage is no longer rewarding. For example, the continual care and attention given by a partner may have been viewed as rewarding in the beginning of the relationship, but later is viewed as smothering or manipulative.

What had previously been a fleeting thought—leaving—was being considered more seriously during this middle phase. Approximately 40% of the respondents in the study were contemplating leaving the marriage during the middle phase of disaffection. Often specific barriers to leaving, such as children, finances, or religion, were mentioned. The following thoughts of a respondent typify this dilemma of staying versus leaving:

> I really spent all those hours alone thinking about what I wanted to do. Did I want to leave him? Did I want to have a relationship with my brother-in-law, who I had always been close to? Did I want to meet someone totally different? What did I want to do with my life? And I really came to think that I wanted to put closeness back in my marriage. . . . I knew that he had to do something about the drinking.

Although she was spending much time thinking about leaving, this woman was not ready to give up on her husband or marriage yet. Despite the mounting doubts, she was still hopeful that he would change and that closeness would return to the marriage. The following quote illustrates a focus on the barriers to leaving rather than actually improving the marriage.

> I had made my mind up that I couldn't go anyplace. That I would just have to live with it until the kids were out of school or of an age where they could accept things. I was very close to the boys. We did a great many things with them. I just felt it would be devastating for them. And financially it would have put a bind on us. I was stuck.

From the beginning of their disaffection, the respondents were thinking about the barriers to ending the relationship. Barriers such as pressure from their social network to stay together, religious norms, and the consequences of divorce on children served to keep them in the marriage. However, in the beginning of the disaffection process, there were still attractions or rewards within the marriage that produced positive emotions and kept the couple together. As love and positive feelings began to die, barriers to leaving may have been the only factors holding the marriage together. One husband described it as a "partnership type of arrangement without any real emotional kind of thing about it." Goode (1966) coined the term *empty shell* for these marriages, as a shell or façade of a marriage is all that remains.

Most of the respondents in the study continued efforts to make changes in the marital relationships. Compared with the previous phase, their attempts at problem solving became more direct and assertive. The following response was typical of the confrontation of partners during this phase:

> I told him that I was ready to leave. I wanted a divorce then. So he enrolled himself into a hospital for drug and alcohol abuse. And he got out, and he was good for 6 months. He didn't touch a drop or do any kind of drugs. And then gradually at work he started drinking a little bit. And then he started smoking marijuana a little bit. And gradually he started going down hill again.

Furthermore, many respondents were no longer acquiescing to their partners' desires but were asserting their own needs and feelings. Especially for the women, a transformation from compliance and subservience to their husbands to expressing their own voice took place during this phase. This occurred as the women's self-esteem and confidence increased and as they became more aware of alternative ways of interacting in marriage. A woman who recently returned to work—an action of which her husband disapproved—stated that for the first time she felt "it was okay to have different ideas. I wasn't crazy." Another respondent found attending school to be both confidence building and liberating from her husband's domination.

Starting new jobs, going to school, making friends, and becoming involved in extracurricular activities boosted respondents' self-esteem so that they could stand up to their partners. However, these activities also provided alternatives to the marriage—a means of financial, social, or emotional support if the marriage ended.

Summary

By the middle phase, disillusionment had significantly dissipated and anger had intensified. The respondents were no longer shocked or surprised by their partner's behaviors, and to some extent they even expected it. Hurt also continued at the same high level as it had been experienced in the beginning phase, but in reaction to repeated hurts, the disaffecting spouses responded with more assertive behaviors or withdrew to protect themselves. Spouses were no longer trying to please the partner as much as they had in the beginning phase. They felt more free to assert their own opinions and feelings.

Their thoughts focused on the negative traits of the partner and the reward–cost ratio of the marriage. The oversensitivity to and vigilance of negative behaviors produced a tunnel vision effect; that is, the respondents could no longer see their partner's positive attributes because their shortcomings predominated. In addition, respondents began to see these shortcomings as inherent to the partner's personality and likely to be permanent. Although more time was spent in the calculation of the reward–cost ratio of the marital relationship to their personal happiness, most of the respondents were not ready to leave the marriage during the middle phase of marital disaffection. Barriers to leaving were keeping them in their relationships.

Phase 3: Reaching Apathy and Indifference

Increasing distance—both physical and emotional—characterized this final phase of the process of disaffection. Although the reports of anger declined from the middle phase, reports of apathy dramatically increased. Typical expressions of the apathy experienced include the following:

> It's too late to rekindle the feelings—I don't want to try. . . . I don't believe I love him anymore because I don't miss him since I've been gone.

> She's worn out my feelings. I don't care what she does—just leave me alone.

This is not worth it to me to go through this kind of aggravation and frustration. That's when I divorced him. I mean I have nothing on paper, but my feelings quit.

Other expressions of apathy included "gradually my love for him has been worn away," "My feelings are nothing," "I don't care if I ever see her again," and "Neutral—not hatred or anger." Apathy, not hate, is the opposite of love. As the psychoanalyst Theodore Reik (1976) stated, "The most serious enemy of love is not the hostility but the indifference that one feels toward the other" (p. 97). This experience of apathy is sometimes described as being decathected from a partner. Decathected spouses have no strong positive or negative affect regarding their partner.

Respondents also experienced feelings of sorrow about the relationship and pity for their partner during this phase. The expression of sorrow for the partner or the relationship sounded similar to the mourning of a loss or death.

It kinda feels like she's burned her bridges. The feelings may be there, but the bridge is burned. . . . There's a certain amount of sorrow.

It is very similar to the grieving process of death. I attended my first funeral during this time. . . . And all the words that were spoken by the minister I equated to my husband. . . . I let myself hurt and be sorrowful.

Sometimes the sorrow revolved around the loss of a fantasy:

We won't get to be Ozzie and Harriet the way my life has turned out.

I don't think I really grieved over the loss of him because I think our marriage was over a long time ago and we were just living together. I grieved over the loss of all these dreams, for example, taking trips.

Of the 50 respondents, 10 had no plans to leave their marriages and were resigned to live in marriages void of positive emotional connection. Perceived obstacles to leaving the relationship included the effects of divorce on children, increased financial stress, and violating a religious commitment. In these cases, disaffected spouses were facing another type of loss, namely, *ambiguous loss*. The partner was physically present, but the emotional bonding and intimacy once present in the relationship was absent. With ambiguous loss, there is a disconnect between psychological and physical—the image of what one wanted the marriage or family to be is replaced with a different image of what it is (Boss, 1999). "Ambiguous loss is always stressful and often tormenting. . . . Of all the losses experienced in personal relationships, ambiguous loss is the most devastating because it remains unclear, indeterminate. . . . People hunger for certainty" (pp. 5–6).

The remaining 40 respondents had actually made a decision to leave the marriage. Although some were struggling with exactly how it could be done, most respondents had thought out their plans, even if they were long range:

My youngest daughter is almost 10 years old, so I thought if I could just stick it out and make things work until she gets out of high school. Just hang around until then.

I'm biding my time. I want my wife to get her master's degree. Just waiting for the opportunity and best time to leave.

It's all in the thinking stages right now. We're moving now and will be locked into a year's lease. So I'm thinking when the year's lease will be over is when I'll want the divorce to be final. I went and spoke to a girlfriend of mine who's a lawyer and found out some information about what you have to do. . . . I'm not happy that I decided to stick it out for another year, but it's not practical for me to say to him, "I don't want this new apartment. I just want you to take off." There's no way I could support myself unless I had free rent somewhere.

Some were still vacillating between staying and leaving.

I'm not a quitter. . . . I find it very difficult to be in a situation where the end of the marriage exists. Because that spells failure to me—especially with the kids. . . . I can't make up my mind which way I want to go. It's not my style. I'm more of a decisive person.

I don't know what to do. I'm frightened. . . . Maybe there'll come a time when I'll leave him. I keep making excuses. First, I made the excuse that my daughter had to finish school. She finished school, and now I make the excuse about an operation. I don't have to stay for the operation, but I think that part of me wants to find some way to work this out.

These responses illustrate the ambivalence and despair that accompanies thoughts of ending a marriage. It is a difficult decision to make, and disaffected spouses were expending a great deal of cognitive activity and emotional energy on making it.

As expected, during the end phase, respondents spoke of fewer attempts to solve their marital problems. This was another indication that the respondents were moving away from repair toward dissolution. There may be no reason to discuss marital dissatisfactions if spouses are preparing to leave; there is no investment in resolving marital conflicts at this point.

Interestingly, disaffected spouses were more frequently turning to professional counselors for assistance during this phase. Until this stage, counseling was rarely pursued. However, in the final phase about one third of the respondents were seeking counseling. The last phase was the most common time for marital therapy to be sought, but the reason for seeking counseling was not necessarily to repair the marriage. Often other motives were underlying the counseling, more related to getting help to leave the marriage or relieving guilt around leaving:

I saw the psychiatrist—not to help him—but to make it look good in court records. I think more than anything, I didn't want his attorney to say, "Look, she's not even trying. The counseling would help him, and she's not doing that."

But I wanted to go to someone outside that didn't know us and see what they had to say. I don't think I went to counseling to work out the marriage because I really didn't think there was any hope for it. But I did want to see if they noticed the same thing in my husband that I did.

This outside opinion or social validation was important to the disaffected spouses. Receiving confirmation from a so-called expert would give them further reassurance that they were doing the right thing.

Summary

During this last phase, the strong emotions of anger and hurt had turned to apathy and indifference. Several respondents stated that they were "beyond hurt." Pity for the partner was more common, but not enough guilt was felt to keep many of the respondents from ending the relationship. The loneliness experienced in earlier phases was being alleviated through contacts with friends and family as the respondents were becoming more public with their discontent.

Ending the marriage became a more predominant thought during the final phase. This thought was being transformed into action as respondents took specific steps to end their marriage. There continued to be a focus on the negative traits of the partner as some respondents prepared their personal accounts for leaving.

During this last phase, efforts to solve problems with their partners were infrequent because many respondents had given up hope that their partners would change. Even in cases in which the partner made substantial changes, the respondents described a "point of no return," that is, a point beyond which feelings could not be restored. Unlike previous phases, many disaffected spouses were pursuing professional counseling. Counseling, however, was usually either a last desperate effort to salvage the marriage, an arena in which to receive assistance for leave-taking, or a means by which to leave the partner in good care.

MARITAL DISAFFECTION: ETHNICITY, RACE, AND GENDER

Effects of Ethnicity and Race on Disaffection

To understand the role of disaffection in the breakdown of marriages in other cultures, one has to exam the role of love in marriage. For example, marriage in non-Western cultures is based on many factors that are not always related to love as the primary category. Abraham (2002) stated that marriages in the United States are based on the notion of love and independence, where partners choose each other. This freedom of choice can, at times, make it easier to end a relationship when disaffection occurs than within a culture in which to end a relationship means dishonoring one's family. For immigrant families coming to the United States, especially many Asian families, marriage is an alliance between two families. The decision to marry is based on the following factors: economic worth, social status, education criteria, physical appearance, and family background. In these cultures, the compatibility of families comes first, and then love (Abraham).

Thus, in cultures in which the family is placed before the individual, women are expected to sacrifice their individual identity for the sake of preserving the family honor or family position in their native culture. The woman chooses to endure, when conflict arises, and in some instances when violence exists. She is more willing to sacrifice her own needs to pacify the partner in order to maintain the harmony in the home. Such gender relations are based on unequal power relations that, according to Sagrestano, Heavey, and Christensen (1999), can lead to increased incidents of violence. Thus, within a culture in which women are expected to be subordinate to the needs of men and their voices are less valued, there can be an increased probability of unequal power relations and in turn an increased vulnerability to marital disaffection.

In industrialized societies, romantic love causes the development of behaviors that hold couples together (Medora, Larson, Hortacsu, & Dave, 2002). Thus, in a culture that does not view romantic love as the primary basis of a marriage, spouses will develop alternative behaviors to keep their marriages together. The question in such arrangements is whether partners become dissatisfied with their marriage and whether such disaffection will lead to divorce or separation. According to Yelsma and Athappilly (1988), in a collectivistically driven society, such as India, "the quality of verbal, non-verbal communication, and sexual intimacy between partners was not influential in determining marital quality. In fact, they found that couples in traditional arranged marriages reported higher marriage satisfaction than couples in 'love marriages'" (Medora et al., p. 165). This could be due to the commitment of such couples to their native heritage rather than to the individual.

This influence of culture can also be seen with immigrant couples at various stages of acculturation to the mainstream culture. According to Snyder (1997), greater acculturation to the United States society was related to slightly higher marital dissatisfaction among Mexican American wives, but not for the husbands. Among West Indian couples in the United States, there was a negative correlation between ethnic identity and intimacy (Springer, 2000). For Mexican American spouses (regardless of their level of acculturation) passionate love predicted marital satisfaction more strongly than friendship- and altruistic-based loves they felt for their partners (Contreras, Hendrick, & Hendrick, 1996). Finally, Ying (1991) found that the greatest predictor of marital satisfaction occurred when spouses agreed on life aims and moral behaviors. Despite the limited research on ethnically diverse couples, there is a common theme that culture shapes marital satisfaction.

When understanding how marital disaffection manifests in minority couples, such as African Americans, we need to consider how the chronic stress of racism and oppression could affect a couple's ability to manage the internal stressors of marriage and family (McDowell & Jeris, 2004).[3] Although the Black poverty rate has fallen in the 1990s to under 24%, it is still at almost three times the level of White families, which is at 8.4% (Teachman, Tedrow, & Crowder, 2000). For Hispanic families, the rate of poverty has not changed significantly and still hovers around 25%. Furthermore, the distribution of family income has shown a general trend toward greater wage inequality in America, with the richest families getting richer and the poorest families getting poorer (Teachman et al.). To obtain economic security has become even more challenging for those couples that are in the lower socioeconomic classes. Job insecurity and dissatisfaction with their jobs have been reasons attributed to Black women's feeling less satisfied with their marriages than White women (Dillaway & Broman, 2001). This is despite the finding that Black men are more likely than their White counterparts to share in housework (Dillaway & Broman). Some researchers suggest that the decreased economic opportunities for a Black woman caused by institutional racism may increase her dissatisfaction with all aspects of her life, including her marriage (McDowell & Jeris). At least, we can speculate that the chronic strain from working at low-paying jobs with little autonomy and personal satisfaction may likely spill over to the marital relationship.

Unfortunately, there are too few studies on marital dissatisfaction among members of minority cultures to provide a thorough understanding of the dynamics involved in disaffection and marriage. However, the few studies that have been done have shown that minority group status can be a significant negative predictor of marital satisfaction (Robbins, Stoltenberg, Robbins, & Ross, 2002). Thus, future research in this area will have to look at external and internal stressors placed on minority couples, as well as the role of racism and oppression on marital dissatisfaction.

Disaffection and Gender

With an increasing number of women in the workforce, the division of labor in the households of dual-earner couples is becoming a greater challenge for women to negotiate and a source of greater marital dissatisfaction (Dillaway & Broman, 2001). The degree of marital dissatisfaction among women in a marriage is also mediated by the spouses' attitudes toward family life. If a couple upholds a more nontraditional or equalitarian view on family life and the wife perceives that there is an unequal division of labor, then she is more likely to experience

---

[3]Pinderhughes (2002) provides a thorough description of the social, economic, racial, and historical factors that stressed African American male–female relationships.

marital dissatisfaction than is her counterpart who has a more traditional view of family life (Kluwer, Heesink, & Van De Vliert, 1997; Lye & Biblarz, 1993). This is not surprising, given that women today are faced with more choices in regard to marriage, careers, and whether to have children. These choices come with shifting attitudes in women about their role in the life of the family and the role of their husbands in this equation.

However, with the increased choices women face around careers and family lives, the trend in marriages is still toward a gendered division of labor (Dillaway & Broman, 2001). As a result, the research has shown that men who are not confronted with housework decisions show greater marital satisfaction then men who participate in an equal division of household labor (Dillaway & Broman; Uebelacker, Courtnage, & Whisman, 2003). A plausible explanation for this finding can be attributed to a traditional view of marriage within the larger society in the United States. Despite greater opportunities for women in the workforce and education, society still views the household chores within the family as the role of women. As a result, women who adhere to a more equitable view of marriage and who are unable to achieve this expectation are more likely to experience symptoms associated with depression (Uebelacker et al.).

Literature has shown that women feel greater intimacy in their relationships when they feel connected with the human being they are sharing a life with. Uebelacker et al. (2003) suggest that "gender socialization is such that girls' [women's] sense of self is integrally tied to their relationships with other people, whereas boys may develop a sense of self that is relatively more independent" (p. 758). Thus, the differences in marital satisfaction between men and women are also linked to the degree of intimacy shared between the couple. Another factor that affects the degree of marital satisfaction experienced by women is self-esteem. Women who feel supported in the relationship experience higher self-esteem and lower levels of depression (Stevens, Kiger, & Riley, 2001; Uebelacker et al.). A woman can be supported by her partner in various ways, such as support for achievements, affirmation of personal qualities, or a willingness to participate in the completion of household chores that are considered by the larger society to be the responsibility of women.

Another source of marital dissatisfaction that is indirectly related to the division of labor is the demand–withdrawal communication pattern that emerges in some couples (Uebelacker et al., 2003). Women often are demanding in their method of communication in order to elicit change in the relationship. When the husband responds to this communication by withdrawing, the woman feels a sense of helplessness and hopelessness because she perceives the situation to be out of her control. The husband could also respond to this demanding role by changing his behaviors. This change in behaviors can help lower wives' levels of marital dissatisfaction and depression. Uebelacker et al. state that "it appears that husbands, regardless of gender ideology, education, or class status, remain satisfied with an unequal division of labor until their wives become dissatisfied, and only sometimes do they alter their own behavior and/or perceptions of family life in the face of their spouse's dissatisfaction" (p. 312).

In conclusion, gender role expectations and patterns of communication can play a significant role in the degree of marital disaffection that a spouse experiences. In contemporary society, the demands of women's increased participation in the labor force warrant a more equitable division of household labor. When a perceived equitable distribution of household labor is not achieved, the woman experiences greater marital dissatisfaction and depression. This can be addressed only when the couple can successfully negotiate a division of labor that meets the needs and expectations of both partners. Whether this can be achieved in a society that still views women as the primary caretakers for children and the household is questionable, unless greater awareness of the gendered roles that husbands and wives face is brought to the forefront in couples treatment.

IMPLICATIONS FOR PRACTICE

Restoring love in a disaffected marriage can be a daunting task. The phases of marital disaffection suggest that couples therapy must have different goals corresponding to each phase of the process of disaffection. Thus, interventions to assist couples have to be planned accordingly. An initial task of the clinician is to assess the loving feelings of each spouse toward the other and the level of commitment to the relationship to determine whether there is the motivation to build a stronger marriage. Once love and commitment are assessed, the clinician can select interventions appropriate for the particular phase.

During the beginning phase, when there is disillusionment but hope and optimism are high, interventions that teach relationship skills may be effective in preventing further deterioration in the relationship. Learning constructive communication skills and problem-solving behaviors assist couples in dealing with conflicts as they emerge in the relationship. Furthermore, examining marital expectations should help to challenge any preconceived expectations that are not realistic. These expectations or standards, as Baucom and Epstein (1990) refer to them, have to be analyzed by both partners in order for them to reach some agreement on what they expect of each other and the relationship.

The middle phase of disaffection is a critical phase for intervention. If hurt and anger escalate and positive changes are not realized, the disaffected spouse will start to lose hope and resentment will build. If there has been extensive hurt already, the disaffected spouse may already be reluctant to work on the marriage in order to avoid further disappointment and hurt should no changes be forthcoming. Therefore, interventions designed to increase the frequency of positive behaviors while reducing the frequency of negative, hurtful behaviors are crucial. Maintenance of positive change should be attended to because many of the disaffected spouses were further disappointed when changes made in the relationship were short lived. On a cognitive level, spouses need to modify their attributions for marital problems and attribute their marital problems to factors other than their partner.

In the final phase of disaffection, interventions have to address the long-standing anger and bitterness. Because attempts at changing the partner may have not worked in the past, a new focus may occur on taking care of oneself and learning to accept behaviors of the partner that seem immutable. If dissolution appears to be the only solution to the disaffected spouse, the goal of interventions in this case may be to facilitate the disengagement and not to repair the relationship. The interventions may have to focus on mediation of practical concerns (e.g., financial arrangements, visitation and child-custody arrangements, and the setting up of separate households) and postseparation adjustment.

CONCLUSIONS

Despite the struggles and challenges of maintaining a loving relationship, marriage and other committed relationships continue to be popular. However, greater anonymity, diminishing social capital, and economic pressures can place a couple under tremendous stress, resulting in greater demands on their relationship. Whereas stress may initially bring a couple closer together, chronic stress is likely to put undue strain on the relationship (Karney et al., 2005). Although there has been a plethora of research on marital distress and the internal processes occurring within the couple, at times this has been to the exclusion of considering external factors. To understand the process of disaffection fully, researchers need to continue to examine both these internal processes and the external context of the relationship. Improving communication and conflict resolution skills may have little effect on couples who are under the chronic stresses of poverty, unemployment, or violence. Intervention on a macrolevel involving family policies and programs may be effective ways to deal with these social problems.

Further longitudinal studies with couples that are not disaffected can shed light on the processes by which couples are able to deal with conflict and distress without having their love deteriorate. Love and marriage may not always be as inseparable as a "horse and carriage" (Cahn & VanHeusen, 1955), as the popular 1950s song declared. However, for many couples, with adequate nourishment, love has the strength and vitality of a horse to pull the institution of marriage—the carriage—down the road of life.

REFERENCES

Abraham, M. (2000). *Speaking the unspeakable: Marital violence among South Asian immigrants in the United States*. New Brunswick, NJ: Rutgers University Press.

Baucom, D. H., & Epstein, N. (1990). *Cognitive-behavioral marital therapy*. New York: Brunner/Mazel.

Berry, J. W. (2001). A psychology of immigration. *Journal of American Ethnic History, 14*(2), 38–59.

Bodenmann, G. (1997). Can divorce be prevented by enhancing coping skills in couples? *Journal of Divorce and Remarriage, 27*, 177–194.

Bodenmann, G., & Cina, A. (1999). *Divorce prediction based on stress and coping variables: A 5-year prospective longitudinal study* (Scientific Report No. 142). Fribourg, Switzerland: University of Fribourg.

Beck, A. T. (1988). *Love is never enough*. New York: Harper and Row.

Booth, A., Johnson, D. R., White, L., & Edwards, J. N. (1984). Women, outside employment, and martial instability. *American Journal of Sociology, 90*, 567–583.

Boss, P. G. (1999). *Ambiguous loss: Learning to live with unresolved grief*. Cambridge, MA: Harvard University Press.

Boss, P. G. (2002). *Family stress management: A contextual approach*. Thousand Oaks, CA: Sage.

Bradbury, T. N. (1998). (Ed.). *The develpomental course of marital dysfunction* NY: Cambridge University Press.

Cahn, S., & VanHeusen, J. (1955). *Love and marriage*. Los Angeles: Warner/Chappell Music.

Contreras, R., Hendrick, S. S., & Hendrick, C. (1996). Perspectives on marital love and satisfaction in Mexican American and Anglo-American couples. *Journal of Counseling and Development, 74*, 408–415.

Cramer, D. (2001). Destructive disagreement belief, disagreement, negative conflict, and relationship satisfaction in romantic relationships. *Genetic, Social, and General Psychology Monographs, 127*(3), 301–318.

Dillaway, H., & Broman, C. (2001). Race, class, and gender differences in marital satisfaction and divisions of household labor among dual-earner couples. *Journal of Family Issues, 22*, 309–327.

De Munck, V.C., & Korotayev, A. (1999). Sexual equality and romantic love: A reanalysis of Rosenblatt's study on the function of romantic love. *Cross-Cultural Research: The Journal of Comparative Social Science, 33*, 265–277.

Duck, S. (1981). Toward a research map for the study of relationship breakdown. In S. Duck & R. Gilmour (Eds.), *Personal relationships: Vol. 3. Personal relationships in disorder* (pp. 1–29). London: Academic Press.

Duck, S. (1982). A topography of relationship disengagement and dissolution. In S. Duck (Ed.), *Personal relationships: Vol. 4. Dissolving personal relationships* (pp. 1–30). London: Academic Press.

Felmlee, D. H. (1995). Fatal attractions: Affection and disaffection in intimate relationships. *Journal of Social and Personal Relationships, 12*, 295–311.

Gannon, M. J. (2001). *Understanding global cultures: Metaphorical journeys through 23 nations*. Thousands Oaks, CA: Sage.

Goode, W. J. (1966). Family disorganization. In R. K. Merton & R. A. Nisbet (Eds.), *Contemporary social problems* (pp. 479–552). New York: Harcourt Brace Jovanovich.

Gottman, J. M. (1994). *What predicts divorce? The relationship between marital processes and marital outcomes*. Hillsdale, NJ: Lawerence Erlbaum Associates.

Gottman, J. M., & Levenson, R. W. (1992). Marital processes predictive of later dissolution: Behavior, physiology, and health. *Journal of Personality and Social Psychology, 63*, 221–233.

Gottman, J. M., & Levenson, R. W. (2002). A two-factor model for predicting when a couple will divorce: Exploratory analyses using 14-year longitudinal data. *Family Process, 41*, 83–96.

Gottman, J. M., & Notarius, C. I. (2002). Marital research in the 20th century and a research agenda for the 21st century. *Family Process, 41*, 159–198.

Gurman, A. S., & Jacobson, N. S. (Eds.). (2002). *Clinical handbook of couples therapy* (3rd ed). New York: Guilford.

Heaton, T. B., & Albrecht, S. L. (1991). Stable unhappy marriages. *Journal of Marriage and the Family, 53*, 747–758.

Hughes, T. (Ed.). (1981). *The collected poems: Sylvia Plath*. New York: Harper and Row.

Huston, T. L., & Houts, R. M. (1998). The psychological infrastructure of courtship and marriage: The role of personality and compatibility in romantic relationships. In T. N. Bradbury (Ed.), *The developmental course of martial dysfunction* (pp. 114–151). Cambridge, England: Cambridge University Press.

Karney, B. R., & Bradbury, T. N. (1995). The longitudinal course of marital quality and stability: A review of theory, methods, and research. *Psychological Bulletin, 118*, 3–34.

Karney, B. R., Bradbury, T. N., Fincham, F. D., & Sullivan, K. T. (1994). The role of negative affectivity in the association between attributions and marital satisfaction. *Journal of Personality and Social Psychology, 66*, 413–424.

Karney, B. R., Story, L. B., & Bradbury, T. N. (2005). Marriages in context: Interactions between chronic and acute stress among newlyweds. In T. A. Revenson, K. Kayser, & G. Bodenmann (Eds.). *Couples' coping with stress: Emerging perspectives on dyadic coping*. Washington, DC: American Psychological Association.

Kayser, K. (1993). *When love dies: The process of marital disaffection*. New York: Guilford.

Kayser, K. (1996). The Marital Disaffection Scale: An inventory for assessing emotional estrangement in marriage. *The American Journal of Family Therapy, 24*, 81–86.

Kersten, K. K. (1990). The process of marital disaffection: Interventions at various stages. *Family Relations, 39*, 257–265.

Kelly, C., Huston, T., & Cate, R. (1985). Conceptual and methodological issues in studying close relationships. *Journal of Marriage and the Family, 44*, 901–925.

Kitson, G. C., & Sussman, M. B. (1982). Martial complaints, demographic characteristics and symptoms of mental distress in divorce. *Journal of Marriage and the Family, 44*, 87–101.

Kluwer, E. S., Heesink, J. A. M., & Van De Vliert, E. (1997). The marital dynamics of conflict over the division of labor. *Journal of Marriage and the Family, 59*, 635–653.

Kurdek, L. A. (1991). Predictors of increases in marital distress in newlywed couples: A 3-year prospective longitudinal study. *Developmental Psychology, 27*, 627–636.

Kurdek, L. A. (1993). Nature and prediction of changes in marital quality for first-time parent and nonparent husbands and wives. *Journal of Family Psychology, 6*, 22–35.

Kurdek, L. A. (1998). Developmental changes in martial satisfaction: A 6-year prospective longitudinal study of newlywed couples. In T. N. Bradbury (Ed.), *The developmental course of martial dysfunction* (pp. 180–204). Cambridge, England: Cambridge University Press.

Leonard, K. E., & Roberts, L. J. (1998). Martial aggression, quality, and stability in the first year of marriage: Findings from the Buffalo newlywed study. In T. N. Bradbury (Ed.), *The developmental course of martial dysfunction* (pp. 44–73). Cambridge, England: Cambridge University Press.

Lindahl, K., Clements, M., & Markman, H. (1998). The development of marriage: A 9-year perspective. In T. N. Bradbury (Ed.), *The developmental course of martial dysfunction* (pp. 205–236). Cambridge, England: Cambridge University Press.

Lye, D. N., & Biblarz, T. J. (1993). The effects of attitudes toward family life and gender roles on marital satisfaction. *Journal of Family Issues, 14*, 157–188.

Mace, D., & Mace, V. (1986). Marriage enrichment: Developing interpersonal potential. In P. W. Dail & R. H. Jewson (Eds.), *In praise of fifty years: The Groves Conference on the conversation of marriage and the family* (pp. 19–26). Lake Mills, IA: Graphic.

Martin, T. C., & Bumpass, L. L. (1989). Recent trends in martial disruption. *Demography, 26*, 37–52.

McCubbin, H. I., & Patterson, J. M. (1983), Family transitions: Adaptation to stress. In H. I. McCubbin & C. R. Figley (Eds.), *Stress and the family* (Vol. 1, pp. 5–25). New York: Brunner/Mazel.

McDowell, T., & Jeris, L. (2004). Talking about race using critical race theory: Recent trends in the *Journal of Marital and Family Therapy, Journal of Marital and Family Therapy, 30*, 81–94.

Medora, N. P., Larson, J. H, Hortacsu, N., & Dave, P. (2002). Perceived attitudes toward romanticism: A cross-cultural study of American, Asian-Indian and Turkish young adults. *Journal of Comparative Family Studies, 33*, 155–182.

Noller, P., & Feeney, J. A. (1998). Communication in early marriage: Responses to conflict, nonverbal accuracy, and conversational patterns. In T. N. Bradbury (Ed.), *The developmental course of martial dysfunction* (pp. 11–43). Cambridge, England: Cambridge University Press.

Pinderhughes, E. (2002). African American marriage in the 20th century. *Family Process, 41*, 269–282.

Reik, T. (1976). *Of love and lust*. New York: Pyramid Books.

Riehl-Emde, A., Volker, T., & Willi, J. (2003). Love, an important dimension in marital research and therapy. *Family Process, 42*, 253–267.

Robbins, R., Stoltenberg, C., Robbins, S., & Ross, M. J. (2002). Marital satisfaction and Cherokee language fluency. *Measurement and Evaluation in Counseling and Development, 35*, 27–34.

Rusbult, C. E. , Bissonnette, V. L., Arriaga, X. B., & Cox, C. L. (1998). Accommodation processes during the early years of marriage. In T. N. Bradbury (Ed.), *The developmental course of martial dysfunction* (pp. 74–113). Cambridge, England: Cambridge University Press.

Rusbult, C., Verette, J., Whitney, G. A., Slovik, L. F., & Lipkus, I. (1991). Accommodation processes in close relationships: Theory and preliminary empirical evidence. *Journal of Personality and Social Psychology, 60,* 53–78.

Sagrestano, L. M., Heavey, C. L., & Christensen, A. (1999). Perceived power and physical violence in marital conflict. *Journal of Social Issues, 55,* 65–72.

Sanchez, L., & Gager, C.T. (2000). Hard living, perceived entitlement to a great marriage and marital dissolution. *Journal of Marriage and the Family, 62,* 708–722.

Snyder, D. K. (1997). *Marital Satisfaction Inventory–Revised (MSI-R) manual.* Los Angeles: Western Psychological Services.

Spanier, G. B., & Thompson, L. (1984). *Parting: The aftermath of separation and divorce.* Beverly Hills, CA: Sage.

Springer, S. E. (2000). Ethnic identity, communication patterns and intimacy: An exploratory study of West Indian couples living in the United States. *Dissertations Abstracts International, 60*(12), 6426B.

Stevens, D., Kiger, G., & Riley, P. J. (2001). Working hard and hardly working: Domestic labor and marital satisfaction among dual-earner couples. *Journal of Marriage and Family, 63,* 514–526.

Teachman, J. D., Tedrow, L. M., & Crowder, K. D. (2000). The changing demography of America's families. *Journal of Marriage and the Family, 64,* 1234–1246.

Uebelacker, L. A., Courtnage, E. S., & Whisman, M. A. (2003). Correlates of depression and marital dissatisfaction: Perceptions of marital communication style. *Journal of Social and Personal Relationships, 20,* 757–769.

Vaughan, D. (1986). *Uncoupling.* New York: Oxford University Press.

Watson, D., & Clark, L. A. (1984). Negative affectivity: The disposition to experience aversive emotional states. *Psychological Bulletin, 96,* 465–490.

White, L. K. (1990). Determinants of divorce: A review of research in the eighties. *Journal of Marriage and the Family, 52,* 904–912.

Yelsma, P., & Athappilly, K. (1988). Marital satisfaction and communication practices: Comparisons among Indian and American couples. *Journal of Comparative Family Studies, 19,* 37–54.

Ying, Y. (1991). Marital satisfaction among San Francisco Chinese-Americans. *International Journal of Social Psychiatry, 37,* 201–213.

12

Divorce and Dissolution of Romantic Relationships: Stage Models and Their Limitations

Stephanie S. Rollie and Steve Duck
University of Iowa

Once formed, relationships do not simply exist or continue at a given level. Instead, they are always changing and evolving. In this chapter we consider relational change, focusing particularly on change associated with what has been labeled *relational dissolution, termination, breakup,* and *ending*. The fact that this change has been labeled suggests that there are specific, identifiable, and definable characteristics that allow individuals to point to this as a particular relational phenomenon. The recognition of potential commonalties associated with this relational change coupled with the social implications associated with divorce have made the understanding and modeling of relational dissolution important tasks for researchers.

In this chapter we examine various models of relational dissolution and consider their value in explaining relational change. We begin by discussing the appeal of stage models and some of the assumptions implicit in their creation. Before we begin, it is important to recognize the significance that the labeling has on perceptions of dissolution and research conducted on this change. Specifically, the social significance of the ending of relationships depends in part on the social expectations surrounding the social form itself. Not all ending is bad: dates can end in engagement, and engagements can end in marriage. However, in those cases we see the transformation and relabeling of the relationship as part of its growth and development, not as part of its ending. However, if one is to define stages of relationships, then one must impose those stages of dissolution on top of an understanding of the so-called normal stages of the development of intimacy in relationships. If the embedding culture describes marriage as a goal point rather than an undesired ending of an engagement, then one must account for it in terms different from the ones that apply to undesired and unexpected or unidealized relationship termination. In short, one must place the ending of a relationship in a framework for understanding the changes and continuities of life more generally. It is a mistake (as indicated by Duck, 1981) to separate breakup from all else that we know about human lives, as if breakup is a hermetic activity isolated from all other psychological, sociological, and everyday communicative processes. This thread runs throughout the chapter.

STAGE MODELS AS RESEARCH TOOLS

Researchers regularly construct models to understand relational phenomena. These models satisfy a need to reduce uncertainty about the world and to make relational phenomena predictable. In delineating common relational patterns, researchers are able to better understand, and to some extent forecast, how a relationship may unfold. Stage models take as their starting point that relationship breakdown is accomplished by (or is the result of) the effects of different activities over an extended process. That which starts the process may have no direct bearing on how the process finishes, or at least it may not be reflected in the processes occurring later. Nevertheless, the general goal of researchers in creating models is to discover and define basic laws of dissolution.

Another feature of stage models is parsimony. The goal is often to reduce relational processes to their basic, necessary, and universal components. In simplifying and identifying similarities across processes, researchers construct tools that can guide future research (and be used in introductory textbooks for years to come). Unfortunately, this goal is often at odds with goals of accuracy and usefulness. As models become more simplistic and parsimonious, they necessarily lose their ability to describe complex processes adequately. The problem, of course, is that many relational processes, including dissolution and divorce, are multifaceted, unpredictable, and messy processes, not easily relegated to a simple model. Accordingly, as knowledge of the complexity of dissolution increases, so necessarily does the complexity of the models and the urgency of the need to separate and delineate the "parts" relative to one another. Researchers' desire to account for as many different scenarios and trajectories as possible leads paradoxically to a decline in utility, as it becomes easy to get lost in a vast array of boxes, arrows, and preconditions. Thus, one issue we revisit throughout the chapter is the extent to which stage models are useful in understanding relational dissolution, even if they are simplified depictions. In keeping these issues in mind, we now provide an overview of various models of dissolution, followed by a general assessment of their value.

Divorce and Dissolution Models

Some basic principles of relational breakdown were first located by Simmel (1950, p. 123), who made the important observation that "a dyad depends on each of its two elements alone—in its death though not in its life: for its life it needs both, but for its death only one." Davis (1973), who noted that dissolution can be broadly broken into intentional and nonintentional breakup, followed up on this idea by indicating that there is an important difference between those researchers who regard dissolution as an *event* and those who regard it as a *process*. For those seeking to determine the cause (usually in the singular) of divorce and breakdown, the event of breakdown is all that matters to establish that it has occurred. For those involved in the activity, however, the process can be long and extended as well as painful and ambiguous. An implication of approaching breakdown in an extended way is that the extensive time taken to accomplish it in many cases points to the possibility that the process is itself made up of different components that kick in at different points or else can be simultaneously and perhaps divergently operative.

Although early work focused on causal attributions relating to breakdown (Harvey, Wells, & Alvarez, 1978; Orvis, Kelley, & Butler, 1976) or on the habitual styles of managing conflict (Gottman, Markman, & Notarius, 1977), this sort of focus for attention is different from the assessment of the stages and phases through which a disintegrating couple may pass. It may be perfectly true that poor styles of managing conflict lead to dissolution, but that, in itself, does not tell us how the resulting dissolution is accomplished, and is even less informative about the ways in which couples try to (or successfully do) achieve prevention of the dissolution in those cases in which it is predictable but does not actually eventuate.

Stage models arrived on the research scene partly in response to such concerns. Specifically, researchers creating various stage models expressed an interest in delineating the basic nature of relational dissolution, although inventive minds tended to settle on different elements without drawing maps of the process that laid these parts in relative context. In this sense, researchers focused on constructing broad frameworks that allowed for explanation and some degree of prediction in the dissolution process, but they did not characterize the whole process, often limiting discussion to whatever they were studying at the time. Thus, whether the dissolution process has been sufficiently well modeled has yet to be determined. The following sections describe some of these models and the ways in which they have shaped thinking about breakup and divorce.

Traditional Models

Traditional models can be described in several different ways. First, important distinctions have been made regarding differences in *marital* and *premarital* (dating) dissolution. Scholars such as Hill, Rubin, and Peplau (1976) emphasized that the processes and the factors influencing the two sorts of breakup are not necessarily the same. Premarital breakups often take place quite casually, with much less stress than marital dissolutions. Because there is typically no social stigma associated with premarital breakups, individuals usually recover from the loss and move on. Additionally, Hill et al. found that premarital breakups are more likely to be associated with *external* strains and life changes. Because of these important differences, some scholars (e.g., Lee, 1984; also see Bohannan, 1968) focused their research and modeling on the dissolutions of *either* marital *or* premarital romantic relationships. Others such as Duck (1982) focused on the process more generally, claiming that although levels of commitment, interdependence, and barriers may differ, the basic elements of the termination process are the same across various types of romantic relationships.

Models also differ in their temporal focus. In general, the models developed during this time focused primarily either on the period leading up to or the factors contributing to the decision to terminate the relationship (e.g., Levinger, 1976) or on the uncoupling process that focuses on movement (particularly on the legal movement) toward singlehood. Some models and typologies focus on one specific aspect of the process, such as the strength of resistance or on the strategies for handling breakup, whereas others attend to the pathways that are followed during its unfolding. Thus, the temporal focus of the breakup process differs from model to model. The following paragraphs describe in general progression the development of thinking about relational dissolution through the development of stage models.

One of the earliest frameworks of relational dissolution was Bohannan's (1968) six stations of divorce. Bohannan argued that divorce is a process rather than a simple result or outcome and that individuals move through or experience six different "stations" of divorce. The first station is the *emotional divorce*. This stage occurs before the legal process of relational dissolution begins and typically acts as an impetus for legal separation. Individuals become ambivalent toward each other and grow apart psychologically, socially, and emotionally. One or both individuals recognize that they do not have a so-called constructive future together. They may experience grief associated with the loss of relationship. The *legal divorce* is the response to the emotional divorce. Traditionally grounded in acts of spousal misbehavior, the legal or judicial divorce involves the socially and legally recognized process of uncoupling. Through interactions with lawyers and the court system, individuals become free of the joint obligations and interpersonal responsibilities of the marriage.

The *economic divorce* and aspects of the *coparental divorce* typically occur along with the legal divorce. The economic station involves the dividing of property and assets acquired during the marriage. It also includes the determining of provisions of alimony and child support. Similarly, the coparental divorce is the process of determining physical and legal custody of children. Typically one parent assumes primary responsibility for housing and making decisions on behalf of the children. The coparental divorce also includes the emotional strain of sharing children, running a single-parent household, or the process of living apart from one's children. Bohannan recognizes that this station is often enduringly painful for divorcees with children in that there is often no eventual resolution.

The fifth station is the *community divorce*. The divorce process often necessitates a change in network structure. Friendships and other family relationships are lost as individuals become uncoupled. Friends are often forced to choose between the two spouses. Bohannan argues that many divorcees feel obligated to develop "new communities." Finally, the sixth station, the *psychic divorce*, is "the separation of self from the personality and influence of the ex-spouse" (p. 60). Bohannan asserts that this is often the most challenging stage for divorcees. They must learn to become independent, autonomous individuals again. This often includes the process of objectively reflecting back on the marriage and the divorce in an effort to learn and grow from the experiences.

It is important to note that Bohannan's model focuses specifically on *marital* dissolution. He grounds his model on the material step-by-step process of divorcing. Although the model is useful as a guide for individuals moving through the divorce process, it says little about the uncoupling process or relational dissolution processes generally.

Altman and Taylor (1973) provided a more general model of relational dissolution. Within social penetration theory, Altman and Taylor proposed a model of relational *depenetration*. They argued that relational dissolution parallels the relational development process, but in reverse. They focused specifically on the role of "exchange" between members in the relationship. Altman and Taylor suggested that the relationship moves gradually and systematically to less intimate levels by decreasing the breadth, volume, and intimacy of verbal and nonverbal exchange. Relational members engage in more superficial exchanges until the relationship finally discontinues. Thus, the relationship essentially dissolves through the process of change in the type and frequency of communication that takes place in the relationship. In this sense, the ending of the relationship is similar to watching a film shown in reverse and is characterized by the progressive undoing of processes that had been the basis for the development of the relationship in the first place. Although this approach has an intuitive appeal and represents the breakdown in a graphic way, it is clear that the unpicking of relationships cannot be the reverse of their development, because things are learned in the process of growth that are not simply forgotten in breakdown. Instead, they are reformulated or recharacterized or given some other form of interpretation than the one that generated their existence in the first place.

The social exchange theory (interdependence theory) of Thibaut and Kelley (1959) has been widely used by scholars interested in studying how and why individuals continue or terminate relationships. Levinger (1979) built off of social exchange theory in developing his conceptual framework and model of marital dissolution. Levinger's model focuses primarily on factors that influence relational stability and dissolution. Specifically, the conceptual model depicts the important elements that influence whether or not an individual remains in a relationship. Levinger argued that cohesiveness in a relationship is a function of relational attractiveness, barriers to leaving, and alternative attractions. Relational attractiveness is based on rewards and costs. The extent to which the relationship provides or is expected to provide more rewards than costs is associated with the degree of attraction or desire to remain in the relationship. Attractiveness is positive when the rewards exceed costs, and it is negative when costs exceed the rewards.

Levinger identified a number of factors that make the relationship rewarding, such as income, social similarity, and companionship, which are types of material, symbolic, and affectional attractions, respectively. These factors act as cement that holds the marriage together.

Cohesiveness is also influenced by perceptions of barriers to leaving the relationship. Barriers are relevant only insofar as one of the members desires to discontinue the relationship. Again, these barriers can be material, symbolic, or affectional, and they include elements such as religious constraints, pressure from members of the social network or community to remain married, the presence of children, or a sense of obligation to the marital bond. These barriers actively restrain individuals from leaving the relationship. Finally, cohesiveness is influenced by individuals' perceptions of alternative attractions. Regardless of the degree of relational attractiveness and the presence of barriers, individuals are unlikely to leave a relationship unless alternatives to the relationship appear more attractive. These attractions may include independence, self-actualization, or perceptions of greater rewards from other persons.

Taken together, the relational attractiveness, barriers to leaving, and alternative attractiveness can be used to account for relational stability. When relational rewards are higher than costs, the barriers to leaving the relationship are high, and alternative attractions are low, individuals are highly unlikely to terminate their relationship. Conversely, when relational attractiveness and barriers are low or when alternative attractions are high, individuals are more likely to dissolve the relationship. Although Levinger focused this conceptual framework specifically on marital relationships, it is viewed as applying to relationship dissolution generally.

Important here is that, in describing barrier forces that a declining couple must overcome, Levinger's models recognized that the dissolving couple has to contend not only with a varied set of internal considerations (emotion, role, and routine) but also an external set of concerns about the reactions of those people who observe but do not directly participate in the relationship (e.g., parents, network, neighbors, and children). Although this is a simplification of the issue as people must deal with it in real life, Levinger at least suggested the idea that individuals might resist the possibility of dissolving a relationship and that concerned individuals might not be restricted to only the two in the relationship itself. Relationships are conducted in social environments where personal emotions may have only relative importance. For example, members of the community often have strong beliefs about marriage and its role in society or about the appropriate outcome of particular relational turmoil. Consequently, individuals in that community may be quite reluctant to violate network norms by seeking relational dissolution. Thus, an important part of the overall process of dissolution of a relationship might be consideration of whether and in what ways the dissolution could and should be presented to the surrounding network and what sorts of reactions and resistance might be expected.

However, the model is limited in that it explains *why* individuals may choose to terminate the relationship, but it says nothing about the dissolution process itself, merely the features that predispose people to enacting it. Levinger later offered a stage model describing the relational process as a whole (Levinger, 1980). His ABCDE model (attraction, building, continuation, deterioration, ending) implicitly assumes that each stage is a preparation for the next and that each follows its predecessor in ineluctable fashion. Particularly relevant here are his final two stages, deterioration and ending. Although Levinger does not elaborate on how the deterioration and ending processes occur, he does stress the importance of external environmental factors as important contributors to the process.

Although not a model per se, a further set of issues was raised by Hagestad and Smyer (1982), who pointed out that the tendency to focus on relationship breakdown as only an *emotional* matter missed some of the other important processes that get managed during relational dissolution. Specifically, they argue that divorcing couples not only handle the separation of their emotional attachments but also must manage the loss of status that comes with no longer being married. As noted earlier, our society prefers partnership and treats singles, divorcees, and widows as somewhat stigmatized. The pressure to enter and to stay in couplehood is quite strong, and Hagestad and Smyer rightly pointed to the importance of the loss of roles in the dissolution process. Enacting the role of boyfriend, wife, sister-in-law, son-in-law, and the like that is associated with one's role in a romantic relationship is often central to one's sense of self. Therefore, it can be quite difficult for individuals to lose valued roles associated with the relationship. Individuals may feel that they have lost a part of themselves.

Along with attachments and roles, Hagestad and Smyer pointed out that individuals lose the routines and rituals they established in the marriage. Many daily routines provide not only a structure for daily life but also a sense of identity and purpose. Often their value is not fully recognized until they can no longer be enacted. In short, loss of roles and routines is an important part of divorcing that theorists need to take into account, not only as part of a breakup process but as part of the broader enterprises of life as these are affected by breakup. This research further speaks to the complexity of relational dissolution and the need to recognize it as a process, rather than an event.

Duck's (1982) model attempted to address some of the weaknesses of earlier models and other relational dissolution work by emphasizing that the processual elements fall into phases through which relational partners pass in enacting a dissolution. He argued that relational dissolution is a process that occurs over time and that, although relationships differ, individuals tend to move through four phases or stages. Duck additionally suggested that the dissolution process generally moves from internal cognitions to the dyad to the social network.

First, the *intrapsychic phase* is an internal, individualistic process involving reflection on the state of the relationship generally and the partner more specifically, dealing with issues of equity, the partner's behavior, and the internal dynamics of the relationship. It is basically an internal decision-making process about the future of the relationship.

In the second, *dyadic phase*, the individual reveals to the partner his or her concerns regarding the relationship and forefronts a desire to redefine the relationship, something that may come as a surprise to the partner. At this point, the relationship can move in a number of directions in which dissolution is but one option because partners may choose to repair the relationship or to postpone immediate changes. If they do not make this choice, then the third phase begins.

The *social phase* recognizes that relationships are "embedded" and that dissolution must involve the network to some extent. In this phase, the news of dissolution is shared with members of the network, thus making the breakup official. Often, the termination of the relationship negatively affects relationships with other members, as friends and family members are forced to choose sides.

Finally, individuals enter into the *grave-dressing phase*. Here, individuals retrospectively make sense of the history of the life and death of the relationship by developing an account that is used to cast the individual in a favorable light, often focusing on the inevitability of the breakup. These stories act to cast the individual as a relationally responsible person who continues to be a so-called good catch for future relationships.

The models of both Baxter (1984) and Lee (1984) further developed aspects of Duck's (1982) model in attempting to account for individual differences in dissolution processes. Baxter developed a flowchart of relational disengagement that incorporates what she describes as the "six critical features" of the relational dissolution process: "(1) the gradual vs. sudden onset of relational problems; (2) the unilateral vs. bilateral desire to exit the relationship; (3) the use of direct vs. indirect actions to accomplish the dissolution; (4) the rapid vs. protracted nature of the disengagement negotiation; (5) the presence vs. absence of relationship repair attempts; and (6) the final outcome of relationship termination vs. relationship continuation" (p. 33). The flowchart accounts for different dissolution possibilities by allowing for various options at each of seven steps of the dissolution process.

Baxter's first step focuses on the onset of relational problems. It considers whether the decision to dissolve the relationship was based on a critical incident or the incremental combination of problems over time. Step 2 considers whether the decision to end the relationship is unilateral (one sided) or bilateral, in which both members want to dissolve the relationship. Step 3 focuses specifically on unilateral decisions and the method in which the decision is conveyed to the partner. An individual may use an indirect method such as *withdrawal, pseudodeescalation*, or *cost escalation*, in which the individual avoids having to directly discuss the decision with his or her partner. Alternatively, the individual may use a direct method such as *fait accompli* or *state-of-the-relationship talk*, in which the individual explicitly states dissatisfaction with the relationship or a desire to end the relationship. The fourth step considers the partner's initial reaction to the news and the degree to which the partner accepts or resists the termination. Resistance typically occurs in one of two forms: *reward-oriented resistance*, in which the partner offers to increase relational rewards, or *cost-oriented resistance*, in which the partner may threaten increased costs to the individual. Upon obtaining resistance, the initiator may choose to abandon the attempt to terminate the relationship, in which case the members may achieve a restoration or a transformation of the relationship. Thus, Step 5 may require several passes through the flowchart to gain the partner's acceptance.

Step 6 applies specifically to bilateral decisions. Here the dissolution may also be direct or indirect. Indirect bilateral dissolution in which relational members do not explicitly discuss ending the relationship typically occurs in one of two forms: *fading away* or pseudodeescalation. Alternatively, the bilateral dissolution may be directly conveyed through the use of *attributional conflict* or *negotiated farewell*. Finally, Step 7 considers final attempts to repair the relationship.

Baxter argued that the flowchart can be used to describe a wide range of relational trajectories based on whether the exit was unilateral or bilateral, direct or indirect, whether it involved one or multiple passes through the model, whether individuals attempted to repair the relationship, and whether the relationship was terminated or continued. This model, like others, has been criticized as being too forcefully sequential and as tending to describe a processual inevitability that faithfully captures retrospective appearances but not contemporary experiences of the dissolution. Events seen later as *turning points* do not necessarily seem to be so at the time, for instance.

Lee's (1984) model of dissolution focuses on five different "critical" events or stages in the relational termination process. In the *discovery of dissatisfaction* (or D) stage, one or both individuals become dissatisfied with the relationship to the extent that they consider ending the relationship. In the *exposure* (or E) stage, the individual discusses his or her dissatisfaction with the partner. This is followed by the *negotiation* (or N) stage, in which members discuss the issues of concern in the relationship. The process of making a decision about the future of the relationship occurs in the *resolution* (or R) stage. Finally, the *transformation* (or T) stage includes the actual occurrence of relational discontinuation or redefinition. Each stage includes individual, dyadic, and extradyadic (network) processes.

Lee also defined three parameters that shape the dissolution process. First, he noted that at each stage one or both individuals act as "agent(s) of action" that actively guide and shape that phase. Lee used the term *operator* to describe these individuals. The content of interaction is also specific to the stage. The *content* parameter considers the substance of interaction at each phase. Finally, *latency* refers to the length of time between stages and the overall dissolution process.

The combination of these four elements, stage (D-E-N-R-T), operator, content, and latency, can be used to characterize a wide range of termination processes or scenarios. For example, when individuals engage in each stage in order, the scenario can be characterized as a *simple format*. *Omission formats* occur when individuals do not engage in one or more of the inner (E-N-T) stages. Some stages may occur over an extended period of time; these are *extension formats*. When the scenario is overly complex, it may be described as a *mixed format* dissolution.

These models are mostly noncompetitive, in that some (e.g., Levinger's) describe conditions that surround dissolution, others (Lee's) describe critical events during dissolution, others (Baxter's or Duck's) focus on sequences of an extended process that goes beyond the decisions to leave, and still others (Bohannon's) essentially deal with types of consequences following relational endings. Although all legitimately count as stage models in some sense, they are really about different ways of approaching a complex topic. Indeed, there are other approaches not so far discussed that extend the variety even further and are strategic models such as Cody's (1982) five strategies to terminate the relationship—behavioral deescalation, deescalation, justification, positive tone, and negative identity management—that feature the means by which people achieve a dissolution once it is desired, or Kressel's (1985) "stages of psychic divorce," which offers a further perspective.

EVALUATING TRADITIONAL MODELS

So, what do these models tell us about relational dissolution? First, some of the similarities across models suggest that, at a most basic level, we are able to talk about *categories* of phenomena in most cases of relational dissolution. That is, if we step back far enough, the broad outlines of dissolution appear remarkably similar. As we get closer, it is apparent that the process becomes much more complex. As researchers try to incorporate this complexity, the models become equally complex. Thus, a basic issue here is that there is neither general agreement about the phenomena that should be modeled nor common acceptance of what it is that relationship dissolution encompasses most centrally. Also at issue is the level of specificity that models should incorporate.

Another common characteristic of these models is linearity. Traditional models of relational dissolution essentially provide a generic outline of the dissolution process as a linear sequential progression of steps and stages. After the first stage, individuals can be expected to be somewhere in the second stage and so forth. In this sense, although these models suggest that dissolution is a process rather than a singular event, that process becomes a sequence of single events that are strung together to form a path from couplehood to singlehood. They say little about *how* one actually moves from one stage to the next or whether researchers' convenient mappings and labels correspond with people's actual experiences. In addition, in focusing on pathways and the features of those pathways, many researchers overlook individuals' resistance to relational decline. From the point of view of the people in a ropey relationship, the expected pathway may not be as clear. People go to counselors, seek friendly advice, try reconciliations and trial partings, and do various things that suggest they do not see the inevitability about breakup that the models suggest. One thing to keep in mind, therefore, is that people very often resist the sense of decline in relationships, and that whatever topics researchers study, the resistance to decline should be one of them.

To accommodate different relational circumstances, researchers have adapted their models to be able to construct multiple trajectories. The events are the same but they may be strung together differently. Some couples may also repeat certain events or strings of events until they complete the path. Such attempts to capture the muddled experiences of separation do not successfully provide researchers with a map for depicting pathways—unless we simply conclude that there are many pathways and researchers should be satisfied with only the "weather forecasting" levels of certainty about them. Thus, although researchers naturally incline to metaphors of pathways, stages, sequences, and progression, one question that remains is whether this inclination is correct.

It is important to note that this notion of linearity results, in part, from the ways in which dissolution has been studied. Most models of relationship breakdown have been tested in ways that require respondents to report on the personal experience of a breakup. Such reports of course can be done only in retrospect, and hence the sense of ineluctable progression and inevitability may be a function of the reporting rather than of the experience at the time the breakup occurred. It is natural enough for human accounts of anything to be structured in a narrative form (Fisher, 1985), and the narrative form naturally contains a logic that forces certain relationships between events and characters in them. Hence it is much more likely that respondents will report a linear process after the breakup that does not reflect actual experience.

A further characteristic of traditional models is a focus on the *individual*. The story of relational dissolution tends to be told (and thus modeled) from one partner's perspective. As we have noted throughout, one feature of relational breakup is that individuals create accounts of the dissolution that tend to paint themselves in a favorable light (the protagonist) so that they are seen as desirable partners for future relationships. Because there is no such thing as *a* breakup in that each person experiences the breakup differently, accounts tend to represent aspects of this (individual) reality (Duck, 2005; Hill et al., 1976). To the extent that models are based on individual retrospective accounts of dissolution rather than actual relational experiences, they reflect an individualistic picture of the breakup, presented within an organizing narrative form.

In addition, models attempt to describe the process from beginning to end. As a result, most models provide a first-person point of view of dissolution based on the perspective of the person *doing* the breaking up. The model begins at the point at which one person decides to end the relationship, and it describes his or her path to singlehood. Although some stages may involve the partner, they tend to focus on what one individual is doing to or saying to the other. Traditional models also suggest that, to the extent that both individuals are involved in the dissolution process, they are at the same stage at the same time and move through the model at the same speed. This suggests a need for models to better depict *relational* processes.

Traditional models do not well incorporate notions of diversity. Although some models differentiate between the dissolution of dating relationships and that of married relationships, they do not address current variations in romantic relational forms. When research on the breakdown of relationships began to gather steam in the mid-1970s (e.g., Levinger & Moles, 1979), acceptance of alternative lifestyles was somewhat less developed than today. Cohabitational relationships and persons of opposite sex sharing living quarters were less frequent, or at least less frequently acknowledged (Cunningham & Antill, 1995). Acceptance of gay and lesbian romances was much less even than recently (Huston & Schwartz, 1995), and studies of relational breakdown tended to focus on the dominant forms of relationships then addressed by researchers, namely, heterosexual college romances and established White middle-class marriages (see Acitelli, Douvan, & Veroff, 1993, for a notable exception). Accordingly, the earliest forms of models of relational breakdown likewise tended to concentrate on the romances of heterosexual White middle-class adults. Given the basic restrictions on the relationships that were counted as important, relevant to theory or, more likely, readily accessible, studies that led to stage models of dissolution often failed to recognize the limitations on generality that were created by the respondents from whom the ideas were derived or from the social assumptions that beset researchers of the day. Along with variations in relational forms, traditional models of dissolution also fail to recognize potentially important distinctions associated with various ethnic and cultural groups for many of the same reasons. Scholars have generally failed to recognize stylistic differences when they have drawn up their models of dissolution.

Finally, traditional models do not focus on the role of communication in the breakup process. They tend to describe dissolution as a primarily psychological or cognitive process that may include bursts of communication, as in one person telling the other directly that he or she wants to terminate the relationship. As a result, individuals may communicate certain things at certain stages, but communication is often a secondary factor that results *because* of the stage the couple is in rather than creating the reality of the breakup process. Some newer models of relational dissolution attempt to address some of these issues.

"NEW" MODELS: A DYNAMIC APPROACH

More recent models have branched out in a number of ways, proposing both nonlinear (Conville, 1988, 1991; Weigel & Murray, 2000) and nonbehavioral, cognitive approaches (Honeycutt, 1993; Honeycutt & Cantrill, 2000), with a more recent model attending specifically to the communicative implications of interior considerations (Duck, 2005). We now consider these approaches in more detail.

Conville (1988, 1991) pointed to the importance of relational transitions within stage models generally. Rather than depicting the stages that individuals move through in developing or dissolving a relationship, Conville argued that transition points are particularly important. He found that, as relationships change, relational partners may move through an "interstage" between relational stages or phases. Conville also suggested that these relational transitions may have common underlying structures. One example of such structural sequence is anticipation, separation, discovery, and reconciliation. These relational transitions ultimately alter rules and expectations for relating as the individuals redefine their relationship. The key element here is in focusing on the *process* of change rather than the changes or stages themselves. An implicit message for research is that, beyond a basic framing by individuals of their experiences by means of sequences of expectation, the processes traditionally depicted by approaches to dissolution are actually quite shapeless.

Honeycutt (1993) proposed an approach based on the idea that memory organization packets (MOPS) are instrumental in shaping the experience of breakup and that schemas of various sorts lead people not only to report breakdown as systematic but also to experience parts of it that way. Honeycutt noted that the experiences of breakup are organized both post hoc and at the time by reference to cultural scripts about the nature of breakup, such that the parties tend to follow scripts for reporting their experiences. According to Honeycutt, these scripts are helpful in organizing a chaotic experience and providing a sense of structure and meaning to it all in ways that conform to societal beliefs and expectations. Accordingly, the reports given to researchers about breakup are likely to be organized in similar ways and do not necessarily tell us about the contemporaneous experiences of breakup so much as their processing after the fact according to accepted means of sense-making.

One message from Honeycutt's research, then, is the notion that a lot of breakup is in the mind. The organization of experience and chaotic events is one of the processes that spill over from the rest of everyday life to these particular events. Whether stages exist in any meaningful sense or are simply creative evocations by participants and researchers alike is thus a matter for future decision.

Duck (2005) has emphasized both communication and fluidity, stressing that partners do not at the time they are in the processes (identified post hoc as "breakup" by researchers) know that they are in fact breaking up. During the process for most relationships, there are moments of false dawn and reconciliation, as well as uncertainties about whether anything is really changed or a bad patch is simply showing up to be worked through. Breakdown of relationships occurs within the scope of everyday routines of pedestrian behaviors and communications and is not flagged by loud music and close focus on significant facial expressions as it is in the movies. Researchers are clearer now that there is *uncertainty in the pathways to dissolution* and the partners do not necessarily see themselves as "entering the *social phase*," so much as "having a chat with friends that might help them sorts things out." We must recognize that life presents our respondents with a great deal more uncertainty, lack of system, and informality than previous models of breakdown have suggested. Subjective awareness of the consequences of actions most often occurs after the event and not at the time, although people clearly recognize possible patterns and organized sequences (MOPs, as Honeycutt noted). The issue unresolved by such observations is the matter of what makes a person or couple decide that one available set of organizing scripts or MOPs defines their ambiguous experience rather than another equally applicable set.

As La Gaipa (1982) pointed out, a main concern for partners when they do recognize that the relationship is in trouble is an adjustment to the *problem of preparing for future relationships as one gets out of old ones*. At the point where Duck (1982) described them as entering the *grave-dressing phase*, people are not only getting out of one relationship but are preparing themselves socially for entry to others in the future, and it is not surprising that a significant part of breakup is the preparation of a good story that leaves the person dealing with issues of perception by others, as well as self-esteem, self-image, expectations, and self-goals, besides any effects on pure feelings and emotional attachments. Thus, the more recent version of the model suggests an additional stage labeled *resurrection*. In these processes, the person prepares for new relationships that replace or make up for loss of the old one.

Overlooked in previous accounts is the notion that *self-evaluation mediates the different stages*. A person with high self-esteem can be predicted to be affected differently from someone with a low self-esteem by the processes of breakup. One might also expect different steps along the way, and that the person will be influenced by advice from others to different extents and take more or less account of the image created in others' eyes by the breakup. We suggest that this can be mapped directly onto recent work in, for example, attachment theory such that people with secure attachment styles might draw less severe personal conclusions about what the ending meant and what the future holds for them.

Duck's new model also approaches questions of communication in the process of breakup, not only *changes in communication patterns* but also in conversational topics at the different stages. Unfortunately, research has given very little direct attention to the things that are discussed in everyday conversation (Dindia & Kennedy, 2004), and consequently we do not know about the ways in which people distribute their time talking to other people about specific topics that are the subject of everyday conversation under different conditions. We speculate in the context of examples provided by the *intrapsychic phase* that is supposed to involve inner thought, the *dyadic phase* devoted to discussing specific relational behaviors with the partner, and the *grave-dressing phase* featuring speaking out to outsiders. The new *resurrection phase* is proposed to project a generalized self who has learned from experience and is now ready for the fray once more. On top of these topical moves, there are proposed to be patterned differences in communication as a function of the process being accomplished at the time. Thus, for example, different audiences are assumed at the different stages, different topics of talk are likely to be presented to them, and different styles of talk will be used to accomplish those purposes. Examples are an increase in the expression of frustration and anger in the *dyadic phase*, and resignation and indignation in the *social phase*.

The new model also dispenses with the troublesome implications of the term *phase,* which implies a sequence and separateness to the processes that real life does not present. The term *processes* emphasizes a discernible pattern of behavior without suggesting that it is distinct from all other activity sequentially. In the *intrapsychic processes,* the individual is assumed to experience feelings of resentment and a feeling of being "*under*benefitted" (Hatfield, Traupmann, Sprecher, Utne, & Hay, 1984). Such feelings provide not only a psychological force but also affect *communicative* activity, in particular social withdrawal and rumination. *Social withdrawal* signifies isolation from the usual audiences with whom the person habitually communicates. Resentment of a partner is not the only reason for doing this, because it is well established that people tend to withdraw from society or social interaction when they are depressed (Segrin, 2000) or have other emotional, psychological, or personal issues (such as, grief, stress, or chronic illness; see Harvey, Barnes, Carlson, & Haig, 1995; Hobfoll & deVries, 1995; Lyons, Sullivan, & Ritvo, 1996). Thus, these processes of breakdown should be measurable in terms of changes to the patterns of interaction that the person inhabits.

In the *dyadic processes* that occur when the two partners are talking with one another about the problems that one person sees with the relationship, the future of their relationship together may be at stake. The presumed psychological state of the person is based partly on the reality that when this process starts, the two participants do not necessarily know how it will all end. They discuss mutual discontents in a context where one person might experience both shock and surprise, but they could both create a dramatic reconciliation based on acceptance of the validity of the partner's views. Indeed, the partner may experience the open expression of discontent as a betrayal that pains deeply. If nothing has been said before, then why not? Communication style and patterns in the *dyadic process* are of course dyadic and localized to "partner talks," or talks about "our relationship" (Acitelli, 1988; Baxter & Wilmot, 1985). Just as the increase of intimacy with a romantic partner is characterized by reduction of time available to friends and acquaintances (Milardo, 1982), so is the conduct of the relationship in the *dyadic process* likely to be characterized by withdrawal from discussion with other friends and acquaintances in order to spend time talking things out with the partner. The ability of couples to discuss things in a constructive, not a destructive, manner is critical here (Veroff, Young, & Coon, 2000).

The obvious ambiguity of topics here renders outcomes uncertain. In addition to style and pattern in communication, the communication topics in this process will be quite specific, dealing with attempts at understanding or justification, and becoming focused on history and patterns in the relationship; comparisons with what is known of other people's relationships and how they work to solve problems; what can be expected in relationships; and what sorts of satisfaction are to be anticipated. It seems most likely that this process offers the greatest chances for a general weighing up of costs and benefits, discussion of both partners' views of the equity levels in the relationship (as contrasted with the representation of only one person's view of equity in the *intrapsychic processes*), and feelings of guilt or anger. In other words, these processes are a communicative and psychological extension of some of the matters that arise in the *intrapsychic processes*, but the complaints are uttered in the presence of the partner and become the subject of discussion directly.

Much research concludes that, during discussions between troubled partners, there are attempts at redefining the relationship and behaviors in it, along with the predictable expressions of discomfort (Gottman, 1994). Typically, partners make resolutions to improve and promises to change, and they may form an agreement to try harder and make things work. The alternative that is always on the table here is the recognition that things cannot be changed and require reexamination of the validity of one person's or of both persons' distress with the relationship. Also at this point partners consider their relationship against the ideal, and this can entail reassessment of goals, both within relationships and relative to other things (family, career, alternative partners, and relational goals in general) in ways predicted by social exchange theory in terms of comparison level for alternatives. Part of the consideration here involves forces outside the feelings of the partners for one another, such as the relative costs of leaving and staying, setting up new relationships, implications of a breakup and fallout for others such as children and family (Johnson, 1982), and considerations of social consequences.

Several researchers have shown that, at some point, the couple (especially married couples) becomes aware of the social forces other than personal affection that bind them together, and partners may discuss staying together for the sake of the children, because of family or community pressure, or because of the fear of shame that attaches to relationship breakup (usually seen in Western cultures as a relational failure). Johnson (1999) has taught us that there are different sorts of reasons for feeling committed to a relationship: personal (such as affection), moral (such as duty or "doing the right thing") and social (such things as legal contracts or economic pressures such that one or both people in a couple may not be able to afford to start afresh in a life of singlehood). We propose that *dyadic processes* bring up all three types of reasons for staying in a relationship.

Somewhere about this point, there is a move to the *social processes* that make public the distress in the relationship by reporting it to outsiders. "Going public" of course makes it harder to deny that there really is a problem later, or to backtrack and reconcile. *Social processes* involve outsiders, who may be consulted for advice or support, although a key psychological process here involves denigration of the partner and the seeking of support for the account offered. When a third party learns about a split with a partner, the most normal response would be sympathy and a request for a full insight into the events. In a response to such a request, research suggests that a person would present the details in a way that allows full creative license, including a vivid account of the locations for the blame of the breaking up that focuses things away from self (Weber, 1983).

At this point the network is also likely to bring up some of the issues of social commitment already noted (Johnson, 1982), but a person may not experience any anxiety over the new relational state of separateness depending on his or her age, the type of relationship lost, and the reasonableness of expectations of replacing the relationship. Older teens and people in their early 20s might even expect relationships to end quite frequently as they test the market, as it were (Duck, 1999). For older people in long-term (presumably stable) relationships, however, there are likely to be much lower expectations of finding a replacement and perhaps also less desire to do so. For various reasons there may also be a considerable amount of repentance and oscillation as the full profundity of effects is considered.

One consequence of the social processes would be the prediction that communication patterns are changed by talking with third parties who know the relationship and both parties to it, possibly even having shared time with both people in the couple or perhaps even being couple friends. Attempts to scapegoat, or to attribute blame and seek plausible explanations for breakups, are human tendencies that also invite a response from others about the reasonableness of the person's accounting.

For these reasons, the style of communication in this process is likely to involve accounting, attributional narrative, relational narrative, self-narrative, attempts at coalition building, alliances, marketing of self, and negatively spinning the partner and the relationship. Establishment of a socially as well as a personally valid account of the ending is also important. Researchers have not examined the effects of the knowledge that people who are addressed will not always believe all of what they are told.

When the relationship has ended, there is still more work to be done in the *grave-dressing processes* in which persons address the task of facing up to the ending of the relationship in a socially acceptable way that leaves them still desirable as a future partner for other people. Topics in grave dressing are likely to be plausible stories about the betrayal of self by the partner, or else the difficulties of two honest folks working together on a relationship that requires more work than it is worth. In such cases it is likely that different audiences are addressed in different ways with relevant topics being hit for them (Masuda, 2000), rather than there being one consistent and repeated version offered to every listener.

The process here involves the tidying up of memories and reconceptualization of the pathway of the relationship from beginning to end, and to do so in a way that allows reconsolidation of social "face" that proposes the self as valuable as a future partner for someone else.

The new version of the model introduces a new set of processes (*resurrection processes*) focused on the needs of people with ended relationships to prepare themselves for the future. The end of a given relationship is not the end of social existence, except in extreme cases or in the very old (as when older people may reasonably see widowhood as the end of their romantic experience). In younger years, those who breakup one relationship probably expect to move on to another, although researchers have rarely taken account of the age of respondents in work on relationship dissolution. Neither have theorists so far taken account of the personality styles of those whose relationships have ended as this relates to the future. In the general case, if the broken relationship was a deep and serious one, we may expect that any preparation for the future constitutes a significant adjustment for everyone, and so we might be justified in predicting differential adjustment outcomes for people with different attachment styles.

We suggest that the *resurrection process* involves preparation for a different sort of future, based on beliefs about the significance to the self-image of the present breakup. Thus there is a concurrent second process here that makes the rewriting of unwanted history, that is to say, the reworking and reframing of those aspects of past relational life that represent stigmatic characteristics. A typical instance has been shown to be the representation of the expartner in a manner that presents the self as a person who has learned to deal more effectively with future relationships (Hopper, 1993). However, there is a largely rhetorical and symbolic function about such stories, all of which have something to do with identity and self-image (Hopper, 1999).

We suggest that communication patterns here will consist of advice seeking but also self-enhancing stories about present virtue and the foolish willingness to believe the best of others. In the *resurrection process*, we argue that the psychological state of the reporter will be reflected in the patterns of communication that ensue, where the goal is to enlist others as supporters for one's own view of the breakup. Such a view predicts that insecure persons would decrease social contact with all members of their network during the *resurrection process*, a prediction that could be tested against attachment theory.

The processes in the *resurrection process* are based on the idea that "everything will now be different." Research has already taught us that recent breakers tend to avoid conversation with anyone who reminds them of their former partner and that people claim less that they are looking for someone with particular characteristics so much as that they are avoiding anyone who reminds them of their former partner.

Some previous research has too readily assumed a discontinuity between the ending of relationships and the dissolution of all contact between the expartners. However, Masheter (1997) has shown that dissolved relational partners are very often necessarily in contact with one another after the breakup, even if they use legal intermediaries. Exspouses often need to maintain basic forms of communication to bring up their children and to sustain legal constraints about custody. Furthermore, divorcees often move to relationships that inevitably blend them with new familial groups (Fine & Demo, 2000). The study of blended families, although in its infancy, is relevant here (Coleman & Ganong, 1995). Indeed, Masuda (2000; also see chap. 6, this volume) has shown that even in the case of romantic relationships that are not marriage, individuals often sustain and develop friendships in place of their former romance, but they are acutely aware of the need to project such relationships in a form that defies easy social description. However, the message for research on breakup is clear: Not only is communication during the process significant, but it also has important roles afterward as people adjust themselves and their embedding social expectations and ease into the future form of their relational life.

THE VALUE OF STAGE MODELS

Throughout this chapter, we have raised a number of questions about the value of stage models in understanding dissolution and divorce. Is relational dissolution the same for various relational forms and situations? Do models adequately capture the actual experience of relational dissolution? Should models be able to account for the complexities of the dissolution process, or are they most useful as a basic guide to the critical components of the process? Is the concept of a stage any more than a research heuristic? Models of breakup are probably most useful as research tools, although a benefit of their assumptions is the representation of common experience in terms that are useful to everyday folks. Critical to both enterprises is the need to distinguish the various elements that are the focus of each model and not to see them as necessarily competitive models of the same process.

We have also pointed out a number of limitations of stage models. In focusing on common experiences, models necessarily neglect many of the details. In this way, models say very little about social context, network effects, daily routines, rituals and social performances, communication, and the fundamental ambiguity of the process at the time. Models presently are weakest at depicting the confusion and mess of the experience, and this result is partly because of the methodological emphasis on retrospective reports that necessarily smooth out the confusion as respondents look back, polish their hindsight, and report with certainty things that were much more unclear at the time that they happened. The dogged inexorability of movement from one stage to another has therefore probably been overestimated.

Although it is clear that they all seek to simplify the dissolution process by finding critical components that are universally applicable to a wide range of dissolution trajectories (that is, if they recognize that not every dissolution process is the same), what is unclear is the degree to which these models truly account for the complexities suggested herein.

In addition, as we noted earlier in the chapter, the great majority of stage models have been crafted from the experiences of White middle-class heterosexual college students and their relatives. An important question to consider, then, is this: To what extent can these experiences be expected to represent the experiences of other ethnic groups; the aged; members of low-income groups; gay, lesbian, or bisexuals; or persons of opposite sex sharing living quarters? Even in heterosexual relationships, there are different types of relationships, including married, dating, and cohabiting couples. Are the rules and processes of terminating these relationships the same?

When one is no longer tied to retrospective accounts and linear progressions associated with traditional research on relational breakup, it becomes possible to conceptualize dissolution in other ways. Although it is most often associated with finality (even the terms *dissolution*, *termination*, and *breakup* suggest permanence), many relationships never fully dissolve. Relationships are often redefined (e.g., as friendships) and continued under different relational rules and expectations. Many so-called dissolved relationships reemerge in similar or different (sometimes undesired) forms. Couples may break up only to get back together again, break up again, get married, get divorced, and then become friendly coparents. The point is that, rather than focusing on relational ending, scholars could focus on relational *change* more generally, because relationships do not necessarily end just because they are labeled as defunct. Future research should perhaps attend to the excellent article by Weigel and Murray (2000), who introduce chaos theory and its implications about types of change in relationships. Instead of seeking linearity of process, as stage models suggest, perhaps things really are a lot more disordered and much less discrete from other relationship processes than has been assumed.

A final thought concerns the matter of whether relational dissolution is a special sort of change in relationships or simply another example of processes of change that are broadly evident in growth as well. Although we are not making quite the same point as made by Altman and Taylor (1973), who suggested that breakdown is the reverse of development, we do see it as more likely than not that the processes of change are connected in some ways, whether the change takes the form of growth or termination of a relationship. It would be unlikely if human beings switched to an entirely new range of strategies in one form of relational change as distinct from another, especially when, at the time, they may not know which sort of change they are doing.

REFERENCES

Acitelli, L. K. (1988). When spouses talk to each other about their relationship. *Journal of Social and Personal Relationships, 5,* 185–199.

Acitelli, L. K., Douvan, E., & Veroff, J. (1993). Perceptions of conflict in the first year of marriage: How important are similarity and understanding? *Journal of Social and Personal Relationships, 10,* 5–19.

Altman, I., & Taylor, D. A. (1973). *Social penetration: The development of interpersonal relationships.* New York: Holt, Rinehart & Winston.

Baxter, L. A., & Wilmot, W. (1985). Taboo topics in close relationships. *Journal of Social and Personal Relationships, 2,* 253–269.

Baxter, L. A. (1984). Trajectories of relationship disengagement. *Journal of Social and Personal Relationships, 1,* 29–48.

Bohannan, P. (1968). The six stations of divorce. In P. Bohannan (Ed.), *Divorce and after* (pp. 33–62). Garden City, NY: Doubleday.

Cody, M. J. (1982). A typology of disengagement strategies and an examination of the role intimacy reactions to inequity and relational problems play in strategy selection. *Communication Monographs, 49,* 148–170.

Coleman, M., & Ganong, L. H. (1995). Family reconfiguring following divorce. In S. W. Duck & J. T. Wood (Eds.), *Understanding relationship processes: Vol. 5. Confronting relationship challenges* (pp. 73–108). Thousand Oaks, CA: Sage.

Conville, R. (1988). Relational transitions: An inquiry into their structure and functions. *Journal of Social and Personal Relationships, 5,* 423–437.

Conville, R. (1991). *Relational transitions: The evolution of personal relationships.* New York: Praeger.

Cunningham, J. D., & Antill, J. K. (1995). Current trends in non-marital cohabitation: In search of the POSSLQ. In J. T. Wood & S. W. Duck (Eds.), *Understanding relationship processes: Vol. 6. Under-studied relationships: Off the beaten track* (pp. 148–172). Thousand Oaks, CA: Sage.

Davis, M. S. (1973). *Intimate relations.* New York: The Free Press.

Dindia, K., & Kennedy, B. L. (2004). *Communication in everyday life: A descriptive study using mobile electronic data collection.* Unpublished manuscript.

Duck, S. W. (1981). Towards a research map for the study of relationship breakdown. In S. W. Duck & R. Gilmour (Eds.), *Personal relationships: Vol. 3. Personal relationships in disorder* (pp. 1–29). London: Academic Press.

Duck, S. W. (1982). A topography of relationship disengagement and dissolution. In S. W. Duck (Ed.), *Personal relationships: Vol. 4. Dissolving personal relationships* (pp. 1–30). London: Academic Press.

Duck, S. W. (1999). *Relating to others* (2nd ed.). Milton Keynes, England: Open University Press.

Duck, S. W. (2005). How do you tell someone you're letting go? A new model of relationship break up. *The Psychologist, 18*(4), 210–213.

Duck, S. W., & Lea, M. (1982). Breakdown of relationships as a threat to personal identity. In G. Breakwell (Ed.), *Threatened identities* (pp. 53–73). Chichester, England: Wiley.

Fine, M. A., & Demo, D. (2000). Consequences of divorce. In R. M. Milardo & S. W. Duck (Eds.), *Families as relationships* (pp. 135–156). Chichester, England: Wiley.

Fisher, W. R. (1985). The narrative paradigm: An elaboration. *Communication Monographs, 52,* 347–367.

Gottman, J. M. (1994). *What predicts divorce?* Hillsdale, NJ: Lawrence Erlbaum Associates.

Gottman, J. M., Markman, H., & Notarius, C. (1977). The topography of marital conflict: A sequential analysis of verbal and nonverbal behavior. *Journal of Marriage and the Family, 39,* 461–477.

Hagestad, G. O., & Smyer, M. A. (1982). Dissolving long-term relationships: Patterns of divorcing in middle age. *Personal relationships, 4: Dissolving personal relationships* (pp. 155–187). London: Academic Press.

Harvey, J. H., Wells, G. L., & Alvarez, M. D. (1978). Attributions in the context of conflict and separation in close relationships. In J. H. Harvey, W. Ickes, & R. F. Kidd (Eds.), *New directions in attribution research* (Vol. 2, pp. 235–260). Hillsdale, NJ: Lawrence Erlbaum Associates.

Harvey, J. H., Barnes, M. K., Carlson, H. R., & Haig, J. (1995). Held captive by their memories: Managing grief in relationships. In S. W. Duck & J. T. Wood (Eds.), *Understanding relationship processes: Vol. 5. Confronting relationship challenges* (pp. 181–210). Thousand Oaks, CA: Sage.

Hatfield, E., Traupmann, J., Sprecher, S., Utne, M., & Hay, J. (1984). Equity and intimate relations: Recent research. In W. Ickes (Ed.), *Compatible and incompatible relationships* (pp. 1–27). New York: Springer-Verlag.

Hill, C. T., Rubin, Z., & Peplau, L. A. (1976). Breakups before marriage: The end of 103 affairs. *Journal of Social Issues, 32,* 147–168.

Hobfoll, S. E., & deVries, M. W. (Eds.). (1995). *Extreme stress and communities: Impact and intervention.* Dordrecht: Kluwer.

Honeycutt, J., & Cantrill, J. (2000). *Cognition, communication, and romantic relationships.* Mahwah, NJ: Lawrence Erlbaum Associates.

Honeycutt, J. M. (1993). Memory structures for the rise and fall of personal relationships. In S. W. Duck (Ed.), *Understanding relationship processes: Vol. 1. Individuals in relationships* (pp. 60–86). Newbury Park, CA: Sage.

Hopper, J. (1993). The rhetoric of motives in divorce. *Journal of Marriage and the Family, 55,* 801–813.

Hopper, J. (1999). *The symbolic origins of conflict in divorce.* Chicago: University of Chicago, Population Research Center.

Huston, M., & Schwartz, P. (1995). Lesbian and gay male Relationships. In J. T. Wood & S. W. Duck (Eds.), *Understanding relationship processes: Vol. 6. Under-studied relationships: Off the beaten track* (pp. 89–121). Thousand Oaks, CA: Sage.

Huston, T. L., Surra, C. A., Fitzgerald, N. M., & Cate, R. M. (1981). From courtship to marriage: Mate selection as an interpersonal process. In S. W. Duck & R. Gilmour (Eds.), *Personal relationships: Vol. 2. Developing personal relationships* (pp. 53–88). New York: Academic Press.

Johnson, M. P. (1982). Social and cognitive features of dissolving commitment to relationships. In S. W. Duck (Ed.), *Personal relationships: Vol. 4. Dissolving personal relationships* (pp. 51–74). London: Academic Press.

Johnson, M. P. (1999). Personal, moral and structural commitment to relationships: Experiences of choice and constraint. In W. H. Jones & J. M. Adams (Eds.), *Handbook of interpersonal commitment and relationship stability* (pp. 73–87). New York: Plenum.

Kressel, K. (1985). *The process of divorce.* New York: Basic Books.

La Gaipa, J. J. (1982). Rules and rituals in disengaging from relationships. In S. W. Duck (Ed.), *Personal Relationships: Vol. 4. Dissolving personal relationships* (pp. 189–209). London: Academic Press.

Lee, L. (1984). Sequences in separation: A framework for investigating the endings of personal (romantic) relationships. *Journal of Social and Personal Relationships, 1,* 49–74.

Levinger, G. (1976). A social psychological perspective on marital dissolution. *Journal of Social Issues, 32,* 21–47.

Levinger, G. (1979). A social exchange view of the dissolution of pair relationship. In R. L. Burgess & T. L. Huston (Eds.), *Social exchange: Advances in theory and research* (pp. 169–193). New York: Academic Press.

Levinger, G. (1980). Toward the analysis of close relationships. *Journal of Experimental Social Psychology, 16,* 510–544.

Levinger, G., & Moles, O. C. (1979). (Eds.). *Divorce and separation: Context, causes and consequences.* New York: Basic Books.

Lyons, R. F., Sullivan, M. J. L., & Ritvo, P. G. (1996). *Relationships in chronic illness and disability.* Thousand Oaks, CA: Sage.

Masheter, C. (1997). Former spouses who are friends: Three case studies. *Journal of Social and Personal Relationships, 14,* 207–222.

Masuda, M. (2000). *Accounting for post-dissolution relationships.* Iowa City: University of Iowa.

Milardo, R. M. (1982). Friendship networks in developing relationships: Converging and diverging social environments. *Social Psychology Quarterly, 45,* 163–171.

Orvis, B. R., Kelley, H. H., & Butler, D. (1976). Attributional conflict in young couples. In J. H. Harvey, W. Ickes, & R. F. Kidd (Eds.), *New directions in attribution research* (Vol. 1, pp. 353–368). Hillsdale, NJ: Lawrence Erlbaum Associates.

Segrin, C. (2000). Interpersonal relationships and mental health problems. In K. Dindia & S. W. Duck (Eds.), *Communication and personal relationships* (pp. 95–111). Chichester, England: Wiley.

Simmel, G. (1950). *The sociology of Georg Simmel.* New York: The Free Press.

Thibaut, J. W., & Kelley, H. H. (1959). *The social psychology of groups.* New York: Wiley.

Veroff, J., Young, A. M., & Coon, H. M. (2000). The early years of marriage. In S. W. Duck (Ed.), *Handbook of personal relationships* (2nd ed., pp. 19–38). Chichester, England: Wiley.

Weber, A. (1983, May). *The breakdown of relationships.* Paper presented at the conference on Social Interaction and Relationships, Nags Head, NC.

Weigel, D., & Murray, C. (2000). The paradox of stability and change in relationships: What does chaos theory offer for the study of romantic relationships? *Journal of Social and Personal Relationships, 17,* 425–449.

13

Coparenting Following Divorce and Relationship Dissolution

Kari Adamsons
University of North Carolina at Greensboro

Kay Pasley
Florida State University

One of the biggest challenges faced by divorcing parents is how to continue parenting when the spousal relationship ends. These couples remain tied to one another through their parenting, even as they sever emotional, financial, and social ties associated with their marriage. How divorced parents interact over childrearing (referred to here as *coparenting*) has important implications for the well-being of both them and their children. Research consistently demonstrates the benefits for postdivorce adjustment of a cooperative coparental relationship versus one that is conflicted and hostile (Amato, 2000). In this chapter, we discuss several aspects of the coparental relationship following divorce. We begin with a discussion of how coparenting is defined and measured in the empirical literature. Next, we describe postdivorce coparenting patterns and some theoretical frameworks commonly used to explain and describe these relationships. We then discuss the factors influencing coparenting following divorce and the types of coparenting that work best (and for whom). Finally, we address limitations of the current research and suggest directions for future research.

WHAT IS COPARENTING?

Broadly speaking, coparenting refers to the interactions of parents regarding their children. It can include attitudes as well as behaviors; however, as noted by Feinberg (2003), it does not include "the romantic, sexual, companionate, emotional, financial, and legal aspects of the adults' relationship that do not relate to childrearing" (p. 96). Even beyond this basic distinction between the coparental and marital relationships, other distinctions are important regarding how coparenting is conceptualized and measured.

Conceptualizing Coparenting

We are not alone in suggesting that the coparental relationship be conceptualized as distinct from one's marital relationship (e.g., Ahrons & Wallisch, 1987; Feinberg, 2003); this

241

is especially important in divorced couples. More so than married couples, divorced couples have the opportunity to engage in coparenting as well as in "noncoparenting" (wherein one parent disengages entirely from childrearing). The phenomenon of noncoparenting is especially evident in the large body of research generated in the late 1970s and early 1980s (e.g., Blankenhorn, 1995; Furstenberg, Peterson, Nord, & Zill, 1983), which was largely deficit- oriented and focused on the negative impact of the absence of one parent (primarily fathers) from children's lives. More recent research has focused on the benefits to children of having two involved parents, and most parents do remain involved in parenting and coparenting. However, although estimates vary (e.g., Braver & O'Connell, 1995; Seltzer, 1991), there is a substantial minority of parents who disengage entirely from their children following divorce (e.g., the "dissolved duos" of Ahrons & Rodgers, 1987).

Coparental interactions should be conceptualized as distinct from marital or interparental interactions for other reasons as well. In general, research demonstrates that antagonistic marital interactions can spill over into coparenting and can affect coparental interactions in negative ways. Parents who have hostile interactions about financial, emotional, or other interpersonal matters (referred to by Ahrons and Wallisch, 1987, as "nonparental conflict") also tend to interact negatively about their children (Margolin, Gordis, & John, 2001). However, numerous studies (e.g., Cowan & McHale, 1996; Gable, Belsky, & Crnic, 1995; McHale, Kuersten-Hogan, Lauretti, & Rasmussen, 2000) have found that both married and divorced parents are capable of differentiating their broader interpersonal interactions from interactions specifically regarding their children. In fact, some research (e.g., Margolin et al.) suggests that the level of coparenting conflict, rather than the general level of interparental conflict, is most strongly associated with a variety of outcomes for both children and adults. However, to date this proposition has been tested only in married families. We argue that conceptualizing and studying coparenting as distinct from other interparental interactions is necessary because of the potential unique effect of coparental interactions on outcomes.

Typically, coparental interactions are characterized by (a) the openness or visibility of the interactions and (b) their affective quality. Coparental interactions can vary in the degree to which they are visible, as coparenting can occur in the presence of both parents and the child, both parents but not the child, or only one parent and the child. Coparental behaviors that are expressed in the presence of only one parent and the child and, thus, are invisible to one parent typically are labeled *covert* coparental behaviors. Coparental behaviors occurring in the presence of and visible to both parents and the child are *overt*. Interactions that take place between the two parents and outside the presence of the child are designated as *encapsulated* (Amato, 2000; Kelly, 2000). For example, a mother might react either positively or negatively to a father's disciplinary decision in the presence of both the father and the child (overt coparenting), in the father's absence but the child's presence (covert coparenting), or in the presence of the father but not the child (encapsulated coparenting).

The affective quality of an interaction is conceptualized as consisting of the level of supportiveness and or antagonism present in the interaction. For example, if a father revokes his child's television privileges, a mother might uphold a father's disciplinary decision by also refusing to let the child watch television (supportive), or she might criticize the father's decision in front of the child or undermine the father's action by letting the child watch television when the father is not present (antagonism). Research demonstrates that support and antagonism coexist in many relationships (Whiteside, 1998). Thus, we see antagonistic coparenting as more than the lack of supportive behaviors and supportive coparenting as more than a lack of antagonistic behaviors—supportive and antagonistic behaviors each exist in their own right, often independent of the presence or absence of the other. We argue that support and antagonism should be conceptualized as distinct constructs, rather than as opposing ends of a single continuum.

Measuring Coparenting

Although coparental relationships conceptually encompass both attitudes and behaviors, researchers have begun to distinguish between them when measuring coparenting. A significant body of research has examined the importance of coparental attitudes for parenting behaviors and, more specifically, how mothers' attitudes affect fathers' behaviors (often referred to as *maternal gatekeeping*). In fact, much of this literature has focused on the ways in which mothers' negative attitudes and behaviors toward fathers' involvement in childrearing adversely affect father involvement and father–child relationships (e.g., Fagan & Barnett, 2003; Pruett, Williams, Insabella, & Little, 2003). However, some researchers (e.g., Walker & McGraw, 2000) note that mothers also facilitate and benefit father–child relationships. Particularly following divorce, fathers tend to be more involved in both coparental interactions and with their children when mothers behave supportively and have attitudes that support father involvement (Ahrons & Miller, 1993; Arditti & Bickley, 1996; Madden-Derdich & Leonard, 2000).

Two studies have differentiated between coparental attitudes and behaviors in divorced families and found that they differentially affect parenting behaviors (interactions between parent and child that do not involve the other parent). Camara and Resnick (1989) found that coparenting behaviors are more strongly associated with parenting behaviors than are coparenting attitudes. Building on these findings, Fagan and Barnett (2003) found that coparenting behaviors actually mediate the relationship between mothers' coparental attitudes and fathers' parenting behaviors. These findings indicate that although attitudes and behaviors are both important components of the coparental relationship, their unique effects on fathering make it conceptually and methodologically advisable to differentiate between them.

Most research focuses on the spillover from mothers' coparenting to fathers' behaviors; little research exists regarding the influence of fathers' coparenting on mothers' behaviors. Some suggests that fathers' coparenting beliefs are not associated with mothers' parenting behaviors (e.g., Simons, Whitbeck, Conger, & Melby, 1990). Other research indicates that fathers' coparenting behaviors are associated with mothers' parenting behaviors, but that the spillover effect is stronger for fathers than for mothers (Katz & Gottman, 1996; Margolin et al., 2001). Although the degree of fathers' influence on mothers' parenting behaviors has yet to be determined, these findings suggest that mothers' coparenting appears more influential to fathers' parenting than vice versa.

Limitations of Current Conceptualizations and Measurement

One limitation of the way in which coparenting quality has been conceptualized and measured is the treatment of the affective quality of the coparental relationship as a dyadic-level variable—a holistic characteristic of the mother–father relationship rather than separate contributions made by each parent. Coparenting generally is operationalized as a single variable that describes the supportiveness or antagonism of the coparenting relationship or a particular coparenting interaction as a holistic event (e.g., Belsky, Crnic, & Gable, 1995). Each coparenting couple is assessed as having a supportive or antagonistic interaction or relationship; the score is assigned at the level of the dyad, and any differences in individual contributions to the interaction are averaged. However, coparenting could be disaggregated such that individual coparenting behaviors exhibited by each parent are assessed rather than global characteristics. We argue that this approach better reflects the true nature of coparenting. For example, a couple's interaction is assigned a dyadic coparenting score of *neutral* (neither supportive nor antagonistic) if both parents exhibit affectively neutral behaviors, the mother exhibits supportive behaviors and the father exhibits antagonistic behaviors, or the reverse. If only a composite score is derived (as is done with the dyadic or holistic approach), such individual variations are lost. Instead of taking this typical dyadic approach, we recommend obtaining individual-level coparenting scores and using these to create categories of interaction patterns (e.g., mother antagonistic–father antagonistic, mother neutral–father supportive), based on individual contributions to interactions rather than the overall or average quality of the exchange. Observational family interaction scales already exist (e.g., the Iowa Family Interaction Rating Scales; see Melby & Conger, 2001) that rate characteristics such as the warmth or support and hostility of dyadic or triadic family exchanges at the individual level. These scales even account for reciprocating or escalating behavior, so the dyadic nature of the exchanges is not lost through an exclusive focus on individual behaviors. Thus, the current failure of researchers to obtain or use individual scores in studies of coparental interactions primarily originates from the conceptualization of coparenting as a dyadic, relationship-level variable rather than from methodological limitations. By accounting for coparental behaviors at the individual level, measures of coparenting could account for both individual contributions to the interaction and which parent contributes which behaviors. Such additional information would allow us to (a) better identify couples wherein parents exhibit similar coparenting behaviors (vs. those who exhibit contradictory behaviors) and (b) learn more about the variations in coparenting that occur within and across dyads.

COPARENTING AND THEORY

Much of the research regarding coparenting following divorce has been atheoretical, as researchers have derived hypotheses from prior empirical literature rather than from theoretical frameworks (e.g., Belsky et al., 1995; Ehrenberg, 1996; Maccoby, Depner, & Mnookin, 1990). However, several theories have been used to explain coparenting processes, its predictors, and the ways in which they affect both adults and children. We present a brief overview of some of the more commonly used theoretical perspectives and demonstrate the ways in which they aid our understanding of postdivorce coparenting. We also identify the gaps resulting from their use, and then we suggest a more integrative approach to the use of theory.

Family Systems Theory

Perhaps the most common theoretical perspective in the coparenting literature is family systems theory (e.g., Kitzmann, 2000; Lindahl & Malik, 1999; McHale, 1995). Family systems theory (Minuchin, 1974) suggests that families consist of several different subsystems and are embedded in broader systems within society. For example, a family system consists of the subsystems of the spousal or parental subsystem (dyadic subsystem), the parent–child subsystem (dyadic subsystem), and the mother–father–child subsystem (triadic subsystem). Each of these subsystems influences and is influenced by the other subsystems within a family system. In turn, a family system is influenced by the broader suprasystems in which it is nested, such as the neighborhood in which the family lives or the school system with which they interact. Thus, systems, subsystems, and suprasystems are interdependent, such that interactions occurring within one affect interactions in others.

Family systems theory often is used to frame studies regarding coparenting between biological parents and coparenting arrangements involving grandparents. Regarding biological parents, research finds that hostile coparental interactions (negative interactions within the mother–father subsystem over child-related issues) often are associated with negative parenting interactions (negative interactions within the parent–child subsystem), and supportive coparenting is associated with positive parenting behaviors (e.g., Margolin et al., 2001). Such findings support the proposition that family systems are interdependent and mutually influential.

In addition to the situation in which biological parents act as coparents, there has been a recent increase in situations in which grandparents rear grandchildren, either as coparents with one or both of the biological parents or as replacement parental figures (Goodman & Silverstein, 2002; Saluter, 1996). This is particularly common following divorce and in other situations wherein biological parents are unmarried. Although studies regarding coparenting grandparents are limited, findings suggest that such grandparents generally act as supplements to the childrearing efforts of biological parents, creating a triangular and intergenerational system (Goodman, 2003; Goodman & Silverstein). Such coparenting systems involve similar issues of interdependence and power differentials as those existing among dyadic coparenting systems; however, the introduction of a third generation (grandparents) and its associated power issues, as well as the mere introduction of a third person into the coparenting system, make such coparenting interactions more complex.

Although power differentials are assumed between systems of differing levels (e.g., suprasystems vs. systems), there is no provision within family systems theory for power differentials within equivalent levels of systems. In the case of biological coparents, there likely exist power differentials between the parent–child subsystem (one member of the family system with high levels of power, i.e., parent, and one member with low levels of power, i.e., child) and the coparental subsystem (two members of the family system with high levels of power), although this is not specifically addressed within family systems theory. Regarding grandparents, family systems theory provides little guidance regarding how to balance the power differentials that exist between grandparents and their adult children (the grandchildren's parents) as a result of their parent–adult child relationship. Here, the grandparent is expected to have more influence over interactions than the adult child–biological parent. In addition, there is little guidance on balancing power differentials that result from the fact that the grandparents are not the grandchildren's biological parents, such that grandparents might take a backseat or supplemental coparenting role (Goodman, 2003; Goodman & Silverstein, 2002). Therefore, family systems theory provides little assistance in determining why certain subsystems might be more influential than others in determining the behaviors and interactions in other subsystems. Further, it is even less helpful in explaining how these differences might relate to personal characteristics of family members, such as gender (Goldner, 1988). Although family systems theory has guided numerous studies on coparenting, we believe that it has limited utility in the breadth and depth of its explanatory power.

Ecological Theory

In many ways, ecological theory (Bronfenbrenner, 1979) is similar to family systems theory in that it describes society as being made up of several overlapping and mutually influential systems. These systems include the individual, the family, and extrafamilial influences (both at a microlevel, e.g., teachers, and a macrolevel, e.g., the government). Like systems theory, each system is seen as interacting with the other systems. However, whereas family systems theory tends to focus on dyads or groups of individuals, ecological theory has the individual as its focus and examines the ways in which the various systems interact with the individual to create individual behaviors and outcomes. As conceptualized by Bronfenbrenner, an individual's behavior is a function of innate character traits in interaction with influences encountered in the environment.

Feinberg (2003) used ecological theory to propose a coparenting model, positing that coparenting is influenced by contextual influences (social support and stress), individual characteristics of the parent, the overall quality of the interparental relationship, and child characteristics.

In turn, coparenting is associated with parental adjustment, parenting behaviors, and child adjustment. Although Feinberg built his ecological model on the basis of prior empirical literature, the model has yet to be empirically tested.

We believe that, like family systems theory, ecological theory provides a strong foundation from which to conduct coparenting research. It allows for additional discussion about the influence of a variety of contexts on individuals' behavior, more so and more specifically than does family systems theory. However, the ecological framework does little to explain the processes through which interactions between the individual and his or her environment are translated into behavior. Therefore, it too is limited in its explanatory power regarding coparenting following divorce.

Symbolic Interactionism and Identity Theory

Although not as commonly used as family systems theory, symbolic interactionism (Mead, 1934) and its derivative, identity theory (Stryker, 1968), also provide useful frameworks for understanding coparenting. Research using these theories focuses on the subjective meanings that individuals assign to their coparenting experiences (e.g., appraisals rather than objective or third-party assessments of coparenting behaviors), as well as their attitudes and expectations regarding coparenting and the attitudes and expectations that they perceive others to hold (reflected appraisals). For example, Madden-Derdich and Leonard (2000) found that divorced fathers who were more satisfied with their parenting abilities (satisfaction here represents the subjective meaning assigned to their experiences as fathers) and who felt that they had more supportive coparental relationships were more involved in postdivorce coparenting interactions than were less satisfied fathers who had poorer coparental relationships. This finding built on the findings of McBride and Rane (1998), who reported that married fathers' reflected appraisals regarding their parenting abilities (i.e., what fathers thought their spouses thought about them as fathers) were significantly related to their involvement with their children. Thus, symbolic interactionism emphasizes understanding the meanings that individuals assign to coparenting interactions, as well as individuals' perceptions of others' intents and behaviors as a step toward understanding one's behavior.

Because of the focus on individuals and individual perceptions, symbolic interactionism is somewhat less successful in explaining the importance of context in determining behaviors. Particularly following divorce, contextual factors (e.g., geographic proximity, hours of employment, visitation schedules) can greatly influence the opportunities for and nature of coparenting (Pasley & Braver, 2003). We have argued elsewhere (Henley & Pasley, 2003) that such factors are not adequately addressed in symbolic interactionism or identity theory.

Further, although symbolic interactionism recognizes that interactions with others influence individuals' behaviors, the ways in which these influences are translated into behavior vary. For example, Burke (1991) described a self-verification model, wherein individuals enact behaviors and subsequently receive feedback from others that their behavior is either consistent or inconsistent with internalized identity standards (i.e., ideals about the ways in which they should behave in different roles). Because negative feedback (i.e., feedback indicating that behavior is inconsistent with identity standards) causes distress, his model suggests that individuals seek congruence. Applied to coparenting, in this model mothers and fathers would mutually negotiate the coparenting process, each giving and receiving appraisals of the others' behaviors and ultimately reaching a mutually agreeable and consistent pattern of coparental behavior. However, mothers and fathers do not always exhibit or report coparental behaviors that are similar in content, frequency, or intensity. For example, some research (Gable et al., 1995) suggests that fathers more frequently exhibit cooperative and supportive coparental behaviors than do mothers. There is little within symbolic interactionism or identity theory to explain such discrepancies. Thus, symbolic interactionism also leaves gaps in our understanding of and ability to explain coparental relationships.

Resource and Exchange Theories

Some coparenting research has used exchange theories as theoretical guides (e.g., Braver, Wolchik, Sandler, & Sheets, 1993; Rettig, Leichtentritt, & Stanton, 1999). The focus in these studies is on the costs and rewards associated with coparenting following divorce. Social exchange theory proposes that individuals weigh the benefits and drawbacks of various inter-action strategies, ultimately choosing those that result in the greatest personal benefits and the fewest personal costs. Within resource theory, also taken into consideration are the resources on which an individual may draw in a given interaction (e.g., income, social support). Braver et al. applied social exchange theory to explain postdivorce father involvement, noting the importance of the quality of the coparental relationship as a potential source of either costs (conflict and denigration) or rewards (cooperation and support for one's parenting). Also using an exchange model, Rettig et al. examined nonresident fathers' postdivorce satisfaction and found that both coparenting conflict (cost) and cooperation (reward) were highly associated with family and life satisfaction (i.e., low frequency of conflict and high cooperative coparent-ing communication were related to higher satisfaction). Although resource theory specifically has not been empirically tested, preliminary evidence from these studies suggests that exchange theory might be a helpful framework for understanding postdivorce coparenting.

However, like family systems theory and symbolic interactionism, resource and exchange theories do not provide adequate explanatory power for certain aspects of coparenting following divorce. For example, it is difficult to explain the existence of coparental relationships with high levels of both cooperation and conflict, as exchange theory generally assumes that individuals would seek to minimize conflict and maximize cooperation (although some people might not find conflict highly aversive and, therefore, would tolerate higher levels than others). Too, some research (e.g., Arendell, 1995) suggests that fathers who are highly involved with their children during the marriage are likely to either drastically reduce or disengage entirely from their children, despite the fact that these fathers find involvement with their children highly rewarding. Behaviors such as these appear to contradict the assumption of maximized rewards and minimized costs, and it is difficult to fully explain such findings through the lens of exchange theory. Furthermore, although resource theory implies the existence of an equation determining the amount of power possessed by an individual that is due to his or her control over various resources, it provides little guidance regarding the appropriate weighting of different types of resources, such as income (tangible) versus primary physical custody (intangible). In this way, it is difficult to predict individuals' relative levels of influence in interactions other than in a post hoc manner.

An Integrative Approach

Given the limitations of these commonly used theoretical frameworks in coparenting re-search, we suggest that an integrative approach might better explain postdivorce coparenting. Combining theoretical perspectives and integrating compatible constructs from different frame-works allows researchers to address some of the gaps left by using a single perspective. We provide one example of how limitations of one theoretical perspective (family systems theory) could be addressed by integrating a construct (power) from another theoretical perspective (resource theory).

Family systems theory introduces the concept of interdependence among family members, and this concept helps to explain why interactions between one dyad (e.g., parents) often spill over and affect interactions between other dyads within the family (e.g., parent–child, siblings). In addition, contextual influences from other systems and suprasystems can be considered, such as friends, employers, and legal or situational contexts (e.g., custodial status, geographic proximity). However, we noted earlier that systems theory does not address power differentials among systems, subsystems, or individuals. Resource theory might be useful here—like exchange theory, it assumes an imbalance such that individuals continually must negotiate the costs and rewards associated with possible outcomes of any given interaction, as well as the resources that they have to draw on to help them reach the desired outcome. According to this theoretical perspective, individuals who control more tangible or intangible resources (e.g., money, love) have more power within a relationship and, therefore, have more options in the behaviors they can enact (Sabatelli & Shehan, 1993). This proposition used in conjunction with family systems theory suggests that individuals or subsystems that control more resources would have more power and influence within the family system, particularly in interactions that directly relate to those resources. For example, because parents control financial resources in the family, the parental subsystem has more influence over financial decisions than does the sibling subsystem. Similarly, because mothers generally are granted primary physical custody of children following divorce (Hetherington & Stanley-Hagan, 1995), they have greater control over the intangible resource of access to the children; thus, from a resource perspective, mothers would be expected to have more power over child-related decisions than would noncustodial, nonresident fathers.

Much of the research regarding coparenting following divorce lacks a theoretical foundation. However, without theoretical underpinnings, it is difficult to move beyond basic descriptions of phenomenon to more complex explanations of processes and motivations (Klein & White, 1996). Thus, we argue that researchers in this area first must recognize the importance and utility of using a theoretical lens when conducting investigations of coparenting, particularly because several theoretical frameworks exist that can assist in explaining this phenomenon. Although there are useful theoretical perspectives for studying postdivorce coparenting, we further recommend using an integrative approach that combines constructs from several theories to create a framework that has greater explanatory ability than does any single theory. Specifically, our example of integrating the assumption of power imbalances from resource theory with family systems theory does not address all of the weakness of current coparenting studies, especially regarding coparenting processes. However, such integration of concepts and assumptions will help to address some of these gaps; we have provided only one example of an integrative approach. Because any number of theories and or permutations could be used, we believe that an integrated theoretical approach will give researchers better tools to explain the phenomenon of coparenting following divorce.

NATURE OF COPARENTING

Research has examined coparenting both within the context of committed relationships and following divorce. We begin with a discussion of the patterns that have emerged regarding coparenting within marriage and then discuss how these patterns are similar or different among families following divorce.

Types of Coparenting Within Marriage

Numerous studies have examined coparenting within the context of marriage (e.g., Abidin & Brunner, 1995; Bearss & Eyberg, 1998; Jouriles et al., 1991; McHale, 1995, 1997), identifying coparenting typologies that reflect patterns of supportive and antagonistic coparenting behaviors. Early research used primarily survey and interview techniques to investigate coparenting, but more recent research has used a variety of methodologies to study coparental communication and relationship styles in married families, such as observational techniques. As these observational studies both confirm and extend earlier findings regarding patterns of coparenting within married families, here we focus on two examples of such research. In one study, McHale et al. (2000) found evidence of three types of coparental relationships: oppositional, cohesive, and nonrestrictive. They characterized oppositional coparenting by low warmth and cooperation and high coparental antagonism; just under one fourth of their families fell into this category. In contrast, they characterized cohesive coparents by the highest levels of warmth and cooperation and low levels of antagonism, reflecting a little over half of their families. They categorized one fourth of their families as demonstrating nonrestrictive coparenting, having little coparental connection. These families showed low levels of warmth and cooperation and similar levels of antagonism to those in the oppositional group; however, their scores on all of these measures were not as extreme (scores generally were low on all three aspects of the coparental relationship).

Interestingly, McHale et al. (2000) also found that the coparenting behaviors of mothers and fathers differed greatly, depending on whether they were interacting with their child alone (i.e., in a dyadic parent–child interaction) or whether they both were involved with their child in a triadic family interaction. In addition, self-reports of coparental behaviors largely were uncorrelated with observed coparental behaviors. These findings have important implications for research regarding family processes such as coparenting, as they suggest that findings might differ across studies depending on the methodology (i.e., self-report vs. observational, dyadic-level vs. triadic-level task).

Some research also has investigated levels of supportiveness and antagonism in the coparental relationship and whether the resulting coparenting types remain stable over time. In their research regarding married parents of toddlers, Gable et al. (1995) found that supportive coparental interactions occurred more frequently than did antagonistic coparental interactions, occurring twice as often within a 2-hr period of observation. In addition, levels of supportive coparenting remained stable over a 6-month period, but antagonistic coparenting levels dropped by one third over the same period. Further, they found that fathers were supportive toward mothers almost twice as often as mothers were supportive toward fathers in their coparental interactions; however, both mothers and fathers were equally likely to engage in antagonistic coparenting. Thus, coparental behaviors might vary both across time and by sex of parent, with interactions becoming (relatively) more positive over time and fathers being more supportive of mothers than vice versa.

Notably missing from this research is an explanation of the processes through which these coparenting styles are created and negotiated, whether and how coparenting types change over extended periods, and what factors contribute to such change and or stability in coparental relationships. Therefore, despite improvements in both methodologies and statistics that have allowed researchers to investigate coparenting patterns and styles in more complex and interesting ways, many areas of inquiry remain unexplored.

Types of Coparenting Following Divorce

Like research regarding coparenting within the context of marriage, most research regarding postdivorce coparenting has categorized coparental relationships according to patterns of supportiveness and antagonism. Although this research has labeled the coparenting types in different ways, the general patterns of postdivorce coparenting behaviors are similar to those found for coparenting within marriage. In fact, the earliest research on coparenting was conducted with divorced families, having arisen out of findings within the divorce literature that it was not divorce per se but numerous other factors that were most strongly associated with child and adult outcomes following divorce.

Ahrons was among the first to investigate postdivorce coparenting, conducting the Binuclear Family Research Project. Findings from this study (Ahrons & Wallisch, 1987) demonstrated that coparental interactions occurred relatively frequently for the first year following divorce (20% of the families reported high levels of interaction, just under 60% reported moderate levels of coparental interaction, and only 20% reported low levels of interaction). Interactions declined over time, such that by 3 years following divorce, only 9% continued to report high levels of coparenting, and 24% reported low levels of coparenting.

Like studies of married families, studies of divorced families identified coparenting types. However, this research suggests the existence of additional categories for divorced parents beyond those described in the marital research. For example, Ahrons and Wallisch (1987) found that, although a majority of the divorced parents in their sample reported the presence of tension and anger during coparental interactions, close to half simultaneously reported feeling that their former spouses were understanding and supportive coparents, a pattern not noted in studies of marital coparenting. Ahrons and Rodgers (1987) argued that coparents could be placed into one of five types of coparental relationships (although they did not estimate the frequency with which each occurs): perfect pals (parents who get along well as friends and are cooperative in all aspects of their lives), cooperative colleagues (parents who are cooperative coparents but have little contact or high conflict in their other interpersonal dealings with one another), angry associates (parents whose relationship is characterized by a high level of anger and hostility, but who still attempt to coparent cooperatively and who often end up limiting their interactions to avoid conflict), fiery foes (parents who are extremely hostile and antagonistic and who experience high levels of conflict in the coparental relationship as well as their personal relationship), and dissolved duos (parents who sever contact with one another entirely, with one often moving to a distant geographic location). Although these types are similar to those found in the marital coparenting research, divorced parents have the potential to experience additional types of relationships as a result of their divorced status (e.g., dissolved duos).

In their widely cited study of postdivorce families, Maccoby and Mnookin (1992) interviewed 1,128 families and found four types of postdivorce coparental relationships: conflicted, cooperative, mixed, and parallel. Like the oppositional families of McHale et al. (2000) and the fiery foes of Ahrons and Rodgers (1987), Maccoby and Mnookin's conflicted families (approximately one third of their sample) had high levels of antagonistic coparenting and low levels of supportive coparenting. An additional one fourth of Maccoby and Mnookin's sample was classified as cooperative, having high levels of supportive coparenting and low levels of antagonistic coparenting. Although not as prominent as McHale's cohesive families, this difference in frequency is not surprising, as married parents tend to be more supportive and less antagonistic in their parenting and coparenting interactions than are divorced parents, so cooperative interactions would appear more often (and more often would characterize) married families than divorced families (Bronstein, Clauson, Stoll, & Abrams, 1993).

Approximately one third of the divorced couples were classified as being parallel coparents; like McHale's nonrestrictive group, these families had low levels of both supportiveness and antagonism, and they tended to interact with their children separately and minimize coparenting interactions. Unlike McHale's families, Maccoby and Mnookin included a fourth coparenting style of mixed. For these families (approximately 1/12 of the sample), coparents engaged in high levels of both supportive coparenting and antagonistic coparenting. The suggested category of Ahrons and Rodgers of angry associates overlaps elements of both the mixed and parallel coparents found by Maccoby and Mnookin, as angry associates were characterized as having high levels of conflict while still attempting to cooperate. Ahrons and Rodgers suggested that, when these parents could not balance coparental conflict and cooperation, they would minimize coparental contact as a strategy to avoid conflict. Thus, there is some evidence to suggest that divorced families experience greater variation in the levels and patterns of cooperation and conflict found within the coparental relationship.

Although families vary in their postdivorce coparental relationships, overall the research suggests that parallel coparenting is the most common type of postdivorce coparenting, and both conflicted and cooperative parents often move into parallel coparenting patterns over time (e.g., Hetherington & Stanley-Hagan, 1995; Maccoby & Mnookin, 1992). Although cooperative coparenting is associated with the best postdivorce outcomes for children, studies show that parallel coparenting is not associated with negative child outcomes (Hetherington & Stanley-Hagan). With limited coparental interactions, divorced parents can reduce the potential for conflict that might be created by their continuing regular interactions. Especially given the consistent finding that exposure to high levels of interparental conflict is harmful to children (Amato, 2000), children fare better when parents engage in parallel coparenting rather than continuing high levels of conflict.

FACTORS INFLUENCING COPARENTING

Parents vary widely in how they interact regarding childrearing issues following divorce, and different parents exhibit varying levels of antagonism and support. To explain such differences in postdivorce coparental relationships, we next review some of the factors associated with coparental interaction patterns and processes following divorce.

Quality of the Predivorce Relationship

The quality and nature of the postdivorce coparental relationship is closely tied to that of the predivorce coparental relationship. Parents who are supportive in their coparental interactions prior to divorce are more likely to be supportive following divorce, and those with highly conflicted predivorce relationships tend to continue such relationships following divorce (Maccoby et al., 1990). However, divorce is associated with reduced conflict for some couples, particularly those who experienced high levels of marital conflict (Booth & Amato, 2001).

Nature of the Divorce Process

The decision to divorce and the ensuing changes often spark changes in the coparental relationship, although whether these changes are positive, negative, or neutral varies among families. Some coparental patterns originate prior to divorce and simply continue through the divorce process (i.e., high-conflict couples remain high conflict through the divorce process and cooperative couples remain cooperative), whereas other couples experience changes in the coparental relationship following the decision to divorce (Booth & Amato, 2001; Kelly & Emery, 2003). Regardless of predivorce coparenting, research demonstrates that parents with highly hostile divorces are more likely to be hostile in their coparenting following the divorce, whereas couples who easily agree on custody and financial issues are more likely to have cooperative postdivorce coparenting (Arditti & Kelly, 1994; Braver et al., 1993; Emery, Lauman-Billings, Waldron, Sbarra, & Dillon, 2001). Similarly, parents who mediate their divorce settlement generally have more cooperative coparental relationships than those who litigate. The litigation process tends to exacerbate areas of disagreement and minimize cooperative communication between divorcing parents, whereas mediation emphasizes resolution of differences and cooperative, direct communication between parents (Emery et al.). Further, some research indicates that the degree of control one feels over the divorce process is associated with the level of conflict and cooperation in the coparental relationship following divorce (Braver et al.). Like the findings regarding ease of agreement, individuals who feel that they had more control over the divorce process also have higher levels of satisfaction with that process and, subsequently, are more likely to report cooperative rather than antagonistic coparental relationships.

Because some studies comparing mediated and litigated divorces used experimental designs (i.e., random assignment of divorcing couples to either litigation or mediation) and are longitudinal (e.g., Emery et al., 2001), we can conclude with relative confidence that mediation facilitates more cooperative postdivorce coparental relationships. However, we cannot determine the direction of the association between agreement and satisfaction with the divorce process and coparental quality following divorce. It might be that parents who coparented cooperatively before the divorce are more likely to agree on custody and financial issues and then simply continue being cooperative, and conflicted couples are more likely to have conflicts during the divorce. It also might be that, regardless of predivorce coparenting style, there is something about being able to agree easily on custody or financial issues that facilitates cooperative postdivorce coparenting. Unfortunately, without longitudinal research that includes controls for confounding factors, it is impossible to know the direction of these processes beyond simple associations.

Custody Arrangements

The amount of contact that divorced parents have with one another as a result of custody and visitation is associated with the opportunities for parents to engage in coparental interactions; thus it also is associated with the quality of these interactions. However, the direction and exact nature of these influences is unclear. Some research, such as that by Maccoby et al., (1990), suggests that when parents share joint physical custody of their children, they are not more likely to engage in antagonistic coparenting than when one parent has primary custody, and joint custody parents had slightly higher levels of supportive communication than primary custody parents. Further, Maccoby et al. reported that when one parent had primary physical custody, this was associated with higher levels of coparenting conflict, as such an arrangement often does not reflect the preferences of the noncustodial parent and dissatisfaction with custody arrangements generally is associated with higher levels of coparental conflict. However, other research, such as that by Arditti and Bickley (1996), finds that parents with joint physical custody arrangements tend to have higher levels of coparenting conflict and antagonism, which they interpreted as arising from the increased amount of contact between former spouses necessitated by joint physical custody.

The effects of joint custody on the coparental relationship likely are associated with whether the custodial arrangement is chosen freely by the divorcing couple or whether it is mandated by the court. Divorcing couples who agree on joint legal or physical custody likely already have a cooperative relationship, whereas those parents who have a joint custody agreement forced on them by the court (particularly joint physical custody) might experience ambivalence about the arrangement, creating potential conflicts. Too, official custody arrangements are not necessarily reflected in actual behavior. A parent legally might have primary physical custody but allow additional visitation beyond that which has been mandated, such that there is a de facto joint custody arrangement. As with research regarding the effects of the divorce process on coparenting, without experimental or longitudinal research that includes controls for other confounding factors, it is difficult to determine the exact nature of the relationship between custody and coparenting.

Postdivorce Relationship With the Former Spouse

As with married couples, the general quality of the relationship between former spouses is strongly associated with the quality of the coparental relationship. As such, divorced parents who generally are hostile and antagonistic in their interactions with one another also tend to be antagonistic over child-related issues specifically, whereas parents who generally are cooperative and supportive tend to be supportive coparents (Ahrons & Rodgers, 1987; Ahrons & Wallisch, 1987). As noted, parents are able to differentiate and distinguish between their overall interpersonal relationship and their coparental relationship (Margolin et al., 2001). Thus, although one's relationship with a former spouse is strongly associated with the coparenting, it alone does not determine the nature of one's postdivorce coparenting patterns.

A particular aspect of the postdivorce relationship that tends to be associated with the quality of the postdivorce coparental relationship is the attachment to the former spouse. An important task facing parents following divorce is disengaging from the former spouse as a romantic partner, while retaining the ability to partner in parenting children. Most parents appear to accomplish this goal, as research by Kitson (1992) suggested that 2 years following divorce only about 7% of divorced individuals reported still "loving" the former spouse. However, findings are somewhat mixed regarding the impact of such attachment to the former spouse. Some research suggests that divorced parents who cannot emotionally separate from their spouses (i.e., remain highly attached; they continue to think about them constantly or still feel romantically attracted to them) are more likely to have conflicted coparental relationships (Madden-Derdich, Leonard, & Scott, 1999; Masheter, 1997). Other research finds that, at least for women, lingering feelings of attachment to the former spouse (i.e., still feeling "in love") are associated with higher levels of supportive coparenting and more shared parenting interactions (Dozier, Sollie, Stack, & Smith, 1993; Kitson, 1992; Madden-Derdich & Arditti, 1999).

The research is more consistent regarding the influence of friendly relationships between former spouses. That is, parents who can remain friendly with one another without being emotionally attached generally have higher levels of supportive coparental behaviors, lower levels of antagonistic coparental behaviors, and engage in more frequent coparental interactions (Ahrons & Rodgers, 1987; Kitson, 1992; Dozier et al., 1993; Masheter, 1997). Although it is unclear whether remaining emotionally attached to a former spouse negatively affects the coparental relationship, emotional detachment from the former spousal relationship and coparenting as friends is beneficial.

Time Since Divorce

Generally, coparental antagonism and conflict decrease and cooperation or disengagement increase over time in most postdivorce families (Ahrons & Wallisch, 1987; Maccoby & Mnookin, 1992). Although some high-conflict couples remain so even several years following divorce, this is unusual (Ahrons & Rodgers, 1987; Maccoby & Mnookin). New, relatively stable coparenting patterns typically are reestablished within the first 2 years following divorce (Ahrons, 1980, 1981), and couples establish routines that are either cooperative or parallel in nature as the litigation ends and disputes are resolved regarding division of finances, households, custody, and visitation (Hetherington & Stanley-Hagan, 1995). Thus, for most couples the divorce process (separation, establishment of new residences, and creation of custody and visitation patterns) represents a temporary disruption of coparental relationships until new, stable routines are established over time.

Remarriage and New Family Formation

Following divorce, the remarriage of one or both partners affects coparenting, as this introduces an additional member into the coparental system (stepparent) and often additional family members as well (stepchildren). Unfortunately, research on how remarriage affects coparenting between biological parents is scant (see also chap. 20 by Ganong, Coleman, & Hans, this volume). There is some indication that remarriage fans old flames of contention, such that coparental relationships become more antagonistic, more conflictual, and less cooperative at least temporarily following remarriage, particularly if the father remarries and the mother does not (Buehler & Ryan, 1994; Hetherington, 2003). New family members compete for the time and resources of the remarried parent, sometimes generating a sense of competition between the old and new families and simultaneously generating conflict. Further, remarriage is associated with more infrequent coparental interactions and less supportive coparenting between former spouses (Christensen & Rettig, 1995). Thus, preliminary evidence suggests that remarriage, at least initially, might have a negative impact on postdivorce coparental relationships. However, the lack of research in general and longitudinal research in particular limits our knowledge of whether these patterns hold over time (i.e., coparental interactions remain at higher levels of antagonism), or whether this disruption, like that of divorce itself, is temporary. In the event that the latter scenario is accurate, it remains to be discovered whether coparental relationships after remarriage settle into more cooperative patterns, or whether, as generally is the case following divorce, they become more disengaged. Further, we do not yet know what factors determine these patterns.

Research regarding coparenting within stepfamilies is extremely limited as well, with only one such study having been conducted to date. Braithwaite, McBride, and Schrodt (2003) examined a variety of aspects of coparental relationships by using time diaries from a small sample of 22 parents and stepparents, including frequency and length of coparental interactions, topics discussed, and quality of the interactions. They found that stepfamilies had a moderate level of interaction, averaging six coparental interactions over the course of the 2-week study. They further found that these interactions were characterized by relatively low levels of conflict and tension. Because on average these stepfamilies had formed over 6 years earlier, this finding supports the idea that increases in coparental antagonism and conflict following a remarriage might be temporary. However, much work remains to be done regarding coparental relationships following stepfamily formation.

COPARENTING AND CHILD OUTCOMES

Most research regarding divorce generally and postdivorce coparental relationships specifically has focused on the effects on children. As noted, most research finds that exposure to high levels of interparental conflict is harmful to children, resulting in higher levels of behavior problems, poorer academic outcomes, and higher levels of emotional distress, particularly if conflict takes place in front of the children or is child related (see review by Amato, 2000; Amato & Rezac, 1994; Pruett et al., 2003). Even covert conflict, such as the denigration of the former spouse in front of the child or placing the children in the middle of parental conflict (triangulation), is detrimental to children. Denigration or triangulation creates loyalty conflicts and generally is associated with higher levels of internalized distress (Amato). In addition, whether the conflict is ultimately resolved is important for children, as unresolved conflict (particularly if such conflict occurs on a regular basis) is associated with higher levels of distress in children (Amato).

Conversely, supportive coparental relationships are associated with more positive child outcomes. When parents are more supportive of one another as parents, and if they resolve any conflicts or disagreements through compromise and negotiation rather than expressing hostility, children typically have fewer behavior problems (Belsky, Putnam, & Crnic, 1996; Floyd & Zmich, 1991; Hetherington & Clingempeel, 1992) and fewer internalizing problems (Camara & Resnick, 1989; Hetherington & Clingempeel).

Not surprisingly, research regarding coparenting and child outcomes generally suggests that coparental relationships that are high in cooperation and support and low in hostility and antagonism are associated with the best outcomes for children. However, we note that it is not the presence or absence of conflict or disagreement per se within the coparental relationship that is most strongly associated with children's well-being following divorce, but the content and nature of that conflict.

COPARENTING AND ADULT OUTCOMES

Fewer studies have focused on the effects of postdivorce coparental relationships on adults than have focused on child outcomes. However, some research has investigated the associations between postdivorce coparenting and fathering behaviors, including gatekeeping.

Coparenting and Paternal Involvement

Similar to the research regarding coparenting and child outcomes, fathers who report more cooperative and less antagonistic coparental relationships are more involved with their children, whereas fathers who have less cooperative and more antagonistic coparental relationships tend to be less involved with their children (Ahrons & Miller, 1993; Bouchard & Lee, 2000; Margolin et al., 2001). Importantly, some research suggests that low levels of involvement might not always be associated with a conflicted coparental relationship, as some fathers disengage entirely from both their children and their former spouses to reduce or avoid conflict (Ahrons & Rodgers, 1987; Ahrons & Tanner, 2003; Kruk, 1994). Further, some research found that high levels of coparental conflict are associated with high levels of father involvement, because high levels of involvement have correspondingly high levels of contact between former spouses and thus increase the potential for conflicted coparental interactions (McKenry, Price, Fine, & Serovich, 1992).

Coparenting and Maternal Involvement

Unlike the findings for fathers, research findings generally fail to support a relationship between coparental quality and maternal involvement. Following divorce, mothers tend to be equally involved with their children regardless of the quality of the coparental relationship (Maccoby, Buchanan, Mnookin, & Dornbusch, 1993), and fathers tend to view the parental and spousal roles as more closely tied than do mothers (Blair, Wenk, & Hardesty, 1994; Doherty, Kouneski, & Erickson, 1998). As noted, some research suggests that fathers' coparental beliefs are not associated with mothers' parenting behaviors (e.g., Simons et al., 1990), whereas other research indicates that fathers' coparental behaviors are associated with mothers' parenting behaviors

(Katz & Gottman, 1996; Margolin et al., 2001). However, even when such a relationship is found, findings indicate that fathers' coparenting tends to be less influential to mothers' parenting than vice versa.

Coparenting and Maternal Gatekeeping

One recent area of inquiry sheds light on why father involvement is so closely tied to the quality of the coparental relationship (and to marriage) compared with mother involvement. This area focuses on the phenomenon of maternal gatekeeping. Gatekeeping is conceptualized as the ways in which mothers restrict or encourage fathers' involvement with their children (Allen & Hawkins, 1999). Typically, mothers have more control over childrearing matters, especially following divorce, because they have physical custody of the children. Thus, mothers serve as gatekeepers of the father–child relationship, such that they control the amount and kinds of involvement that fathers can have. Although most of the research in this area has studied first-marriage families (Allen & Hawkins; DeLuccie, 1995, 1996), some research on divorced families also tends to support this argument (Fagan & Barnett, 2003). When mothers believe that father involvement in childrearing is important and act in ways that are supportive and encouraging of father involvement, fathers are, in fact, more involved with their children. When mothers do not emphasize the importance of father involvement or actively discourage fathers' involvement with their children, fathers are less involved. Importantly, this research is criticized (e.g., Walker & McGraw, 2000) for emphasizing the responsibility of mothers for fathers' involvement and failing to sufficiently address fathers' active participation in the construction of their roles and behaviors as fathers.

Coparenting and Parental Postdivorce Adjustment

Coparenting has implications for parents' behaviors with their children following divorce, but coparenting also has implications for parental well-being. Just as supportive coparenting is good for children, supportive coparenting generally is associated with positive adjustment and greater well-being postdivorce for both mothers and fathers (Amato, 2000; Blair et al., 1994). As noted, some research shows that supportive coparental interactions are associated with continued attachment between former spouses, and continued attachment is negatively associated with mothers' adjustment following divorce (Dozier et al., 1993; Madden-Derdich & Arditti, 1999). Similar to findings regarding children, antagonistic coparenting following divorce also is associated with poorer adjustment and well-being for both mothers and fathers (Amato, 2000). However, research also suggests that the simple presence or absence of disagreement or conflict is not what is most important for postdivorce adjustment. Rather, it is the level of antagonism and hostility in the coparental interaction that is most strongly associated with postdivorce adjustment among adults (Whiteside, 1998). Highly hostile conflict is more strongly associated with negative outcomes for both adults and children than is conflict that is neutral or that involves compromising behaviors by the parents.

Taken together, certain types of coparental relationships appear to be best for parents and children following divorce. Most research supports the proposition that cooperative coparenting is the most beneficial type of coparenting for both parents and children. Conversely, some degree of conflict is not harmful and often is expected following divorce, but antagonistic postdivorce coparenting appears particularly detrimental to both parents and children. Thus, although cooperative coparenting is the ideal, research suggests that avoiding antagonistic coparental interactions should be the primary goal of such interactions.

FUTURE DIRECTIONS
FOR COPARENTING RESEARCH

Despite the relative consistency of research findings regarding coparenting following divorce, several limitations and gaps remain in the literature that warrant our attention. First and foremost, research is scant regarding coparenting in family structures other than divorced families. Therefore, research is needed that explores coparenting between biological parents following remarriage, between new spouses within remarriage, between never-married parents (both those that are and are not involved in romantic relationships following the birth of their child, as well as during and following dissolution of such romantic relationships), between cohabiting parents, and between cohabiting parents following the end of their relationship. With research having focused on coparenting following only divorce and only divorce between biological parents, we lack certainty whether the patterns found also represent coparental relationships in other family structures. Further, much of the research regarding different family structures is descriptive in nature and/or makes simple comparisons among family structures on some outcome of interest. Thus, knowledge about processes in these families is omitted. Specifically relevant here is the lack of research regarding coparenting processes following dissolution of various relationships (e.g., romantic but never married, cohabiting, remarried).

Expanding the conceptualization of coparenting to include more than just the relationship between biological parents also is needed. For example, coparenting can and does occur in conjunction with grandparents, members of extended families, and nonrelatives, particularly for children in single-parent families. Therefore, research is needed that investigates these alternative coparents and the processes, patterns, and interactions that are characteristic of these diverse types of coparental relationships.

Further, given that preliminary research suggests that coparenting processes and outcomes might vary among coparenting biological parents and grandparents of different ethnic backgrounds (African American, Latino, White; see e.g., Goodman & Silverstein, 2002), greater attention has to be paid to issues of diversity in coparenting. Little has been done to further examine the differences or similarities among coparenting families of different ethnicities, socioeconomic statuses, or sexual orientations, nor have studies examined variability and homogeneity within diverse populations of coparents.

Finally, additional clarity in the conceptualization of the different aspects of coparental relationships under study (e.g., quality and frequency of interactions, attitudes vs. behaviors, whether coparenting is a dyadic-, triadic-, or individual-level construct) is essential, as is greater clarity in their measurement. As noted, research indicates differential effects of coparenting, depending on the ways in which it is conceptualized and measured (e.g., Fagan & Barnett, 2003; McHale et al., 2000). The recent growth in the use of observational research methods is encouraging, given the depth and amount of detailed information about coparental interactions that can be obtained. However, such methods have been used almost exclusively in studies of married couples. At least as currently implemented, observations of dyadic and triadic family interactions are not practical for use with nonmarried coparents, particularly those who experience high levels of antagonism and hostility in their relationships. Therefore, future research on coparenting following relationship dissolution would benefit from creative applications of existing methodologies, such as observational research, time diaries, or turning-points analyses. These methods would allow investigation of coparenting processes in more detail than currently is possible with the use of simple self-report and survey data.

Because marriages last for only one half of first-married couples and approximately one third of remarried couples, and a majority of dissolving marriages involve children, coparenting outside the context of marriage is now a normative experience in the United States. In this chapter, we summarized some of what is known regarding the phenomenon of postdivorce coparenting, and our beginning understanding of its importance in terms of both adult and child well-being. We also discussed some of the factors that help to shape the coparental relationship. Indeed, within this volume (see chap. 16 by Braver, Shapiro, & Goodman), our knowledge on this subject is expanded with the proposal of a midrange model of postdivorce coparental relationships. Much remains to be learned about coparenting following relationship dissolution, particularly regarding the processes that underlie coparental interactions and the ways in which coparental relationships are negotiated and maintained (or dissolved) over time. We remain optimistic—huge strides have been made in our knowledge of postdivorce relationships since the days when divorce research was dominated by deficit perspectives. The future of postdivorce coparenting research specifically, and of research regarding nonmarital coparenting more broadly, is promising.

REFERENCES

Abidin, R. R., & Brunner, J. F. (1995). Development of a Parenting Alliance Inventory. *Journal of Clinical Child Psychology, 24,* 31–40.

Ahrons, C. (1980). Joint custody arrangements in the postdivorce family. *Journal of Divorce, 3,* 189–205.

Ahrons, C. (1981). The continuing coparental relationship between divorced spouses. *American Journal of Orthopsychiatry, 5,* 415–428.

Ahrons, C. R., & Miller, R. B. (1993). The effect of the postdivorce relationship on paternal involvement. *American Journal of Orthopsychiatry, 63,* 441–450.

Ahrons, C. R., & Rodgers, R. H. (1987). *Divorced families: A multidisciplinary developmental view.* Markham, Ontario: Penguin.

Ahrons, C. R., & Tanner, J. L. (2003). Adult children and their fathers: Relationship changes 20 years after parental divorce. *Family Relations, 52,* 340–351.

Ahrons, C. R., & Wallisch, L. S. (1987). The relationship between former spouses. In D. Perlman & S. Duck (Eds.), *Intimate relationships: Development, dynamics, and deterioration* (pp. 269–296). Newbury Park, CA: Sage.

Allen, S. M., & Hawkins, A. J. (1999). Maternal gatekeeping: Mothers' beliefs and behaviors that inhibit greater father involvement in family work. *Journal of Marriage and the Family, 61,* 199–212.

Amato, P. R. (2000). The consequences of divorce for adults and children. *Journal of Marriage and the Family, 62,* 1269–1288.

Amato, P. R., & Rezac, S. J. (1994). Contact with nonresidential parents, interparental conflict, and children's behavior. *Journal of Family Issues, 15,* 191–207.

Arditti, J. A., & Bickley, P. (1996). Father's involvement and mothers' parenting stress postdivorce. *Journal of Divorce and Remarriage, 26*(1/2), 1–23.

Arditti, J. A., & Kelly, M. (1994). Fathers' perspectives of their co-parental relationships postdivorce. *Family Relations, 43,* 61–68.

Arendell, T. (1995). *Fathers and divorce.* Thousand Oaks, CA: Sage.

Bearss, K. E., & Eyberg, S. (1998). A test of the parenting alliance theory. *Early Education and Development, 9,* 179–185.

Belsky, J., Crnic, K., & Gable, S. (1995). The determinants of coparenting in families with toddler boys: Spousal differences and daily hassles. *Child Development, 66,* 629–642.

Belsky, J., Putnam, S., & Crnic, K. (1996). Coparenting, parenting, and early emotional development. In J. P. McHale & P. A. Cowan (Eds.), *Understanding how family-level dynamics affect children's development: Studies of two-parent families* (pp. 45–55). San Francisco: Jossey-Bass.

Blair, S. L., Wenk, D., & Hardesty, C. (1994). Marital quality and paternal involvement: Interconnections of men's spousal and parental roles. *The Journal of Men's Studies, 2,* 221–237.

Blankenhorn, D. (1995). *Fatherless America: Confronting our most urgent social problem.* New York: Basic Books.

Booth, A., & Amato, P. R. (2001). Parental predivorce relations and offspring postdivorce well-being. *Journal of Marriage and Family, 63,* 197–212.

Bouchard, G., & Lee, C. M. (2000). The marital context for father involvement with their preschool children: The role of partner support. In J. F. Gillespie & J. Primavera (Eds.), *Diverse families, competent families: Innovations in research and preventive intervention practice.* (pp. 37–53). New York: Haworth.

Braithwaite, D. O., McBride, M. C., & Schrodt, P. (2003). "Parent teams" and the everyday interactions of coparenting in stepfamilies. *Communication Reports, 16,* 93–111.

Braver, S. L., & O'Connell, D. (1998). *Divorced dads: Shattering the myths.* New York: Tarcher/Putnam.

Braver, S. L., Wolchik, S. A., Sandler, I. N., & Sheets, V. L. (1993). A social exchange model of nonresidential parent involvement. In C. E. Depner & J. H. Bray (Eds.), *Nonresidential parenting: New vistas in family living* (pp. 87–108). Thousand Oaks, CA: Sage.

Bronfenbrenner, U. (1979). *The ecology of human development: Experiments by nature and design.* Cambridge, MA: University Press.

Bronstein, P., Clauson, J., Stoll, M. F., & Abrams, C. L. (1993). Parenting behavior and children's social, psychological, and academic adjustment in diverse family structures. *Family Relations, 42,* 268–276.

Buehler, C., & Ryan, C. (1994). Former-spouse relations and noncustodial father involvement during marital and family transitions: A closer look at remarriage following divorce. In K. Pasley & M. Ihinger-Tallman (Eds.), *Stepparenting: Issues in theory, research, and practice* (pp. 127–150). Westport, CT: Greenwood.

Burke, P. J. (1991). Identity processes and social stress. *American Sociological Review, 56,* 836–849.

Camara, K. A., & Resnick, G. (1989). Styles of conflict resolution and cooperation between divorced parents: Effects on child behavior and adjustment. *American Journal of Orthopsychiatry, 59,* 560–575.

Christensen, D. H., & Rettig, K. D. (1995). The relationship of remarriage to post-divorce coparenting. *Journal of Divorce and Remarriage, 24*(1/2), 73–88.

Cowan, P., & McHale, J. (1996). Coparenting in a family context: Emerging achievements, current dilemmas and future directions. In J. P. McHale & P. A. Cowan (Eds.), *Understanding how family-level dynamics affect children's development: Studies of two-parent families.* (New directions for child development, No. 74, pp. 93–106). San Francisco: Jossey-Bass.

DeLuccie, M. F. (1995). Mothers as gatekeepers: A model of maternal mediators of father involvement. *Journal of Genetic Psychology, 156,* 115–132.

DeLuccie, M. F. (1996). Mothers: Influential agents in father–child relations. *Genetic, Social, & General Psychology Monographs, 122,* 287–308.

Doherty, W., Kouneski, E. F., & Erickson, M. F. (1998). Responsible fathering: An overview and conceptual framework. *Journal of Marriage and the Family, 60,* 277–293.

Dozier, B. S., Sollie, D. L., Stack, S. J., & Smith, T. A. (1993). The effects of postdivorce attachment on coparenting relationships. *Journal of Divorce and Remarriage, 19*(3/4), 109–123.

Ehrenberg, M. F. (1996). Cooperative parenting arrangements after marital separation: Former couples who make it work. *Journal of Divorce and Remarriage, 26*(1/2), 93–113.

Emery, R., Lauman-Billings, L., Waldron, M. C., Sbarra, D. A., & Dillon, P. (2001). Child custody mediation and litigation: Custody, contact, and coparenting 12 years after initial dispute resolution. *Journal of Consulting and Clinical Psychology, 69,* 323–332.

Fagan, J., & Barnett, M. (2003). The relationship between maternal gatekeeping, paternal competence, mothers' attitudes about the father role, and father involvement. *Journal of Family Issues, 24,* 1020–1043.

Feinberg, M. E. (2003). The internal structure and ecological context of coparenting: A framework for research and intervention. *Parenting: Science and Practice, 3,* 95–131.

Floyd, F. J., & Zmich, D. E. (1991). Marriage and the parenting partnership: Perceptions and interactions of parents with mentally retarded and typically developing children. *Child Development, 62,* 1434–1448.

Furstenberg, F., Peterson, J. L., Nord, C. W., & Zill, N. (1983). The life course of children of divorce: Marital disruption and parental contact. *American Sociological Review, 48,* 656–658.

Gable, S., Belsky, J., & Crnic, K. (1995). Coparenting during the child's 2nd year: A descriptive account. *Journal of Marriage and the Family, 57,* 609–616.

Goldner, V. (1988). Generation and gender: Normative and covert hierarchies. *Family Process, 27,* 17–31.

Goodman, C. C. (2003). Intergenerational triads in grandparent-headed families. *Journal of Gerontology: Social Sciences, 58B,* S281–S289.

Goodman, C. C., & Silverstein, M. (2002). Grandmothers raising grandchildren: Family structure and well-being in culturally diverse families. *The Gerontologist, 42,* 676–689.

Henley, K., & Pasley, K. (2003, November). *The role of context in identity theory: Making it more than background noise.* Paper presented at the Theory Construction and Research Methodology Workshop for the annual meeting of the National Council on Family Relations, Vancouver, BC.

Hetherington, E. M. (2003). Intimate pathways: Changing patterns in close personal relationships across time. *Family Relations, 52,* 318–331.

Hetherington, E. M., & Clingempeel, W. G. (1992). Coping with marital transitions: A family systems perspective. *Monographs of the Society for Research on Child Development, 57*(2/3), 1–242.

Hetherington, E. M., & Stanley-Hagan, M. M. (1995). Parenting in divorced and remarried families. In M. H. Bornstein (Ed.), *Handbook of parenting* (Vol. 3, pp. 233–254). Hillsdale, NJ: Lawrence Erlbaum Associates.

Jouriles, E. N., Murphy, C. M., Farris, A. M., Smith, D. A., Richters, J. E., & Waters, E. (1991). Marital adjustment, parental disagreements about child rearing, and behavior problems in boys: Increasing the specificity of the marital assessment. *Child Development, 62,* 1424–1433.

Katz, L. F., & Gottman, J. M. (1996). Spillover effects of marital conflict: In search of parenting and coparenting mechanisms. *New Directions for Child Development, 74,* 57–76.

Kelly, J. B. (2000). Children's adjustment in conflicted marriage and divorce: A decade review of research. *Journal of the American Academy of Child and Adolescent Psychiatry, 39,* 963–973.

Kelly, J. B., & Emery, R. (2003). Children's adjustment following divorce: Risk and resiliency perspectives. *Family Relations, 52,* 352–362.

Kitson, G. (1992). *Portrait of divorce: Adjustment to marital breakdown.* New York: Guilford.

Kitzmann, K. M. (2000). Effects of marital conflict on subsequent triadic family interactions and parenting. *Developmental Psychology, 36,* 3–13.

Klein, D. M., & White, J. M. (1996). *Family theories: An introduction.* Thousand Oaks, CA: Sage.

Kruk, E. (1994). The disengaged noncustodial father: Implications for social work practice with the divorced family. *Social Work, 39*(1), 15–26.

Lindahl, K. M., & Malik, N. M. (1999). Observations of marital conflict and power: Relations with parenting in the triad. *Journal of Marriage and the Family, 61,* 320–330.

Maccoby, E. E., Buchanan, C. M., Mnookin, R. H., & Dornbusch, S. M. (1993). Postdivorce roles of mothers and fathers in the lives of their children. *Journal of Family Psychology, 7,* 24–38.

Maccoby, E. E., Depner, C. E., & Mnookin, R. H. (1990). Coparenting in the second year after divorce. *Journal of Marriage and the Family, 52,* 141–155.

Maccoby, E. E., & Mnookin, R. H. (1992). *Dividing the child: Social and legal dilemmas of custody.* Cambridge, MA: Harvard University Press.

Madden-Derdich, D. A., & Arditti, J. A. (1999). The ties that bind: Attachment between former spouses. *Family Relations, 48,* 243–249.

Madden-Derdich, D. A., & Leonard, S. A. (2000). Parental role identity and fathers' involvement in coparental interaction after divorce: Fathers' perspectives. *Family Relations, 49,* 311–318.

Madden-Derdich, D. A., Leonard, S. A., & Scott, C. F. (1999). Boundary ambiguity and coparental conflict after divorce: An empirical test of a family systems model of the divorce process. *Journal of Marriage and the Family, 61,* 588–598.

Margolin, G., Gordis, E. B., & John, R. S. (2001). Coparenting: A link between marital conflict & parenting in two-parent families. *Journal of Family Psychology, 15,* 3–21.

Masheter, C. (1997). Healthy and unhealthy friendship and hostility between ex-spouses. *Journal of Marriage and the Family, 59,* 463–475.

McBride, B. A., & Rane, T. R. (1998). Parenting alliance as a predictor of father involvement: An exploratory study. *Family Relations, 47,* 229–236.

McHale, J. P. (1995). Coparenting and triadic interactions during infancy: The roles of marital distress and child gender. *Developmental Psychology, 31,* 985–996.

McHale, J. P. (1997). Overt and covert coparenting processes in the family. *Family Process, 36,* 183–201.

McHale, J. P., Kuersten-Hogan, R., Lauretti, A., & Rasmussen, J. L. (2000). Parental reports of coparenting and observed coparenting behavior during the toddler period. *Journal of Family Psychology, 14,* 220–236.

McKenry, P. C., Price, S. J., Fine, M. A., & Serovich, J. (1992). Predictors of single, noncustodial fathers' physical involvement with their children. *Journal of Genetic Psychology, 153,* 305–319.

Mead, G. H. (1934). *Mind, self, and society.* Chicago: University of Chicago Press.

Melby, J., & Conger, R. D. (2001). The Iowa Family Interaction Rating Scales: Instrument summary. In P. K. Kerig & K. M. Lindahl (Eds.), *Family observational coding systems: Resources for systemic research* (pp. 33–58). Mahwah, NJ: Lawrence Erlbaum Associates.

Minuchin, S. (1974). *Families and family therapy.* Cambridge, MA: Harvard University Press.

Pasley, K., & Braver, S. L. (2004). Measuring father involvement in divorced, nonresident fathers. In R. Day & M. Lamb (Eds.), *Conceptualizing and measuring father involvement* (pp. 217–240). Mahwah, NJ: Lawrence Erlbaum Associates.

Pruett, M. K., Williams, T. Y., Insabella, G., & Little, T. D. (2003). Family and legal indicators of child adjustment to divorce among families with young children. *Journal of Family Psychology, 17,* 169–180.

Rettig, K. D., Leichtentritt, R. D., & Stanton, L. M. (1999). Understanding noncustodial fathers' family and life satisfaction from resource theory perspective. *Journal of Family Issues, 20,* 507–538.

Sabatelli, R. M., & Shehan, C. L. (1993). Exchange and resource theories. In P. Boss, W. Doherty, R. LaRossa, W. Schumm, & S. Steinmetz (Eds.), *Sourcebook of family theories and methods: A contextual approach* (pp. 385–411). New York: Plenum.

Saluter, A. F. (1996). *Marital status and living arrangements: March 1994.* (Current Population Reports, Series P20-484, pp. A–7). Washington, DC: U.S. Government Printing Office.

Seltzer, J. A. (1991). Relationships between fathers and children who live apart: The father's role after separation. *Journal of Marriage and the Family, 53,* 79–102.

Simons, R., Whitbeck, L., Conger, R., & Melby, J. (1990). Husband and wife differences in determinants of parenting: A social learning and exchange model of parental behavior. *Journal of Marriage and the Family, 52,* 375–392.

Stryker, S. (1968). Identity salience and role performance: The relevance of symbolic interaction theory for family research. *Journal of Marriage and the Family, 30,* 558–564.

Walker, A. J., & McGraw, L. A. (2000). Who's responsible for responsible fathering? *Journal of Marriage and the Family, 62,* 563–569.

Whiteside, M. F. (1998). The parental alliance following divorce: An overview. *Journal of Marital and Family Therapy, 24,* 3–24.

14

Mechanisms of Distress and Dissolution in Physically Aggressive Romantic Relationships

Erika Lawrence, Eunyoe Ro,
Robin Barry, and Mali Bunde
University of Iowa

Physical aggression[1] (e.g., pushing, grabbing, slapping, or hitting a partner with an object) occurs in one fourth to one half of the couples in dating, cohabiting, engaged, and newlywed relationships (Eliot, Huizinga, & Morse, 1986; Lawrence & Bradbury, 2001, 2005; Leonard & Roberts, 1998; O'Leary et al., 1989), and it has harmful effects on the physical and psychological well-being of its victims and their children (e.g., Follingstad, Rutledge, Berg, Hause, & Polek, 1991; Kolbo, Blakely, & Engleman, 1996). The literature on physical aggression in intimate relationships provides many important clues about its prevalence, nature, and consequences, but this research also contains important limitations. For example, whereas replicable descriptive associations between physical aggression and relationship dissolution are beginning to emerge, conceptual frameworks for evaluating and integrating these findings remain to be developed. Whereas there exists an extensive literature informing the processes through which dissolution occurs in romantic relationships, there is little consideration of the potential contributory role of physical aggression in these models, let alone of the mechanisms through which relationship dissolution occurs when physical aggression is present. Finally, whereas extensive progress has been made in assessing the prevalence of aggression in intimate relationships, a number of methodological factors—such as a consideration of the heterogeneity of aggression and an examination of the relational and societal contexts in which aggression occurs—await further refinement. Thus, the body of research on physical aggression in intimate relationships is limited in its ability to explain dissolution in physically aggressive relationships.

---

[1]We use the term *aggression* throughout our chapter because, as Olson, Fine, and Lloyd (2005) explained, "it maintains a narrower focus on the acts themselves and, in so doing, also encapsulates a broader range of behaviors." Additional terms such as *battering*, *abuse*, and *violence* add important relational and social dynamics to the construct but do so in ways that exceed our chapter's thesis. Further, in our chapter we have chosen to focus exclusively on the unique aspects of physical aggression between adult romantic partners, although we acknowledge the importance of understanding other types of aggression (e.g., psychological aggression, sexual aggression) and other combinations of dyads within the family unit (e.g., child abuse and neglect, child-to-parent abuse).

Our purpose in this chapter is to review the existing literature relevant to our understanding of the mechanisms through which physical aggression leads to relationship distress and dissolution and to offer some suggestions for enhancing our understanding of these processes in the future. We organize our discussion first around conceptual issues and then methodological concerns, referring to recent efforts to explore the link between aggression and relationship dissolution.

THE ROLE OF PHYSICAL AGGRESSION IN RELATIONSHIP DISTRESS AND DISSOLUTION

Before reviewing the existing literature on physical aggression and relationship dissolution, we find it worthwhile to consider how aggression is viewed as a risk factor for relationship dissolution in the broader literature on intimate relationships. The divorce rate for first marriages is 40% to 45% in the United States, the United Kingdom, and Australia, and it is about 35% in Germany (Australian Bureau of Statistics, 2001; United States Census Bureau, 2002). Rates of dissolution are even higher among cohabiting couples (McDonald, 1995). Distressed couple relationships are a risk factor for a variety of mental and physical health problems for partners and their children (Ahlburg & DeVita, 1992; Amato & Keith, 1991a, 1991b; Burman & Margolin, 1992; Coie et al., 1993; Glenn et al., 2002; Halford & Markman, 1997; Larson, Sawyers, & Larson, 1995). Given the high prevalence rates and consequences of relationship dissolution, and given the high prevalence rates of physical aggression in young relationships, we find it reasonable to expect that efforts to address the question of how relationships succeed and fail would incorporate the role of physical aggression into their formulations. In addition to direct links between aggression and dissolution, physical aggression might be related to a number of factors that contribute to relationship deterioration, including difficulties with psychological aggression, emotional engagement, and attributional styles.

Despite these possible associations, most theoretical models of how relationships succeed and fail do not explicitly address the role of physical aggression in this process (see Bradbury, 1998; Karney & Bradbury, 1995; Weiss & Heyman, 1997). Attention has been given to individual and interactional variables that cross-sectionally discriminate aggressive and nonaggressive couples (e.g., Christopher & Lloyd, 2000; Holtzworth-Munroe & Hutchinson, 1993; Jacobson et al., 1994; Margolin, John, & Gleberman, 1988), and attention has been given to documenting the link between aggression and dissolution. Far less attention has been given to *how* aggression contributes to relationship dissolution. Thus, the establishment of a conceptual framework for examining the mechanisms through which physical aggression leads to relationship distress and dissolution holds the potential for refining our understanding of the role of aggression in broader models of relationship dysfunction that include a consideration of multiple disciplines, including psychology, sociology, family studies, and communication studies research.[2]

---

[2]Multiple theoretical perspectives have been used across disciplines to explain intimate aggression (e.g., biological, evolutionary, family systems, social learning, patriarchal, and relational control theories). For the purposes of this chapter, we have chosen to narrow our focus to a discussion of intrapersonal (i.e., cognitive), interpersonal–relational, and contextual (i.e., societal and cultural) factors, as we believe these factors to be most applicable to understanding the mechanisms through which relationships dissolve once physical aggression is present.

EXISTING RESEARCH ON PHYSICAL
AGGRESSION AND RELATIONSHIP DISSOLUTION

We now turn to a brief review of the cross-sectional and longitudinal research examining the role of physical aggression in understanding relationship distress and dissolution. First, we provide an overview of the research documenting the prevalence of physical aggression in intimate relationships and the few existing studies exploring the nature and temporal course of aggression among dyads. Then we turn to a review of the research examining the link between physical aggression and relationship dissolution.

Prevalence, Nature, and Longitudinal Course of Physical Aggression in Intimate Relationships

Prevalence rates of aggression against a partner have been studied across a variety of samples and have demonstrated that dating aggression starts as early as adolescence. Among high school students, rates of dating aggression range from 13% to 25% (Bergman, 1992; O'Keefe, Brockopp, & Chew, 1986; Smith & Williams, 1992), and among college students they range from 20% to 44% (Arias, Samios, & O'Leary, 1987; Lo & Sporakowski, 1989; Riggs, O'Leary, & Breslin, 1990). Rates of aggression among young adults (18–25 years of age) in cohabiting, engaged, and newlywed relationships are also quite high. For example, DeMaris (2001) found that 20% of cohabiting couples reported physical aggression. Elliot et al. (1986), in a large survey of cohabiting and newlywed couples, found that 37% of men and 43% of women reported aggressing against a partner in the year prior to assessment. In an examination of 272 community couples, O'Leary et al. (1989) found that 31% of men and 44% of women aggressed against their partners in the year before marriage. In a sample of 543 couples, Leonard and Roberts (1998) found that at least one instance of premarital male-to-female aggression was reported by 27% of the men and 28% of the women.

Although aggression is relatively common among dating, cohabiting, engaged, and newlywed couples, rates of aggression appear to decrease over time, and this decline is associated at least partially with age. Yllo and Straus (1981), in a national survey of 2,143 couples, found that cohabiting couples reported more aggression than married couples, but this difference was partially a function of age and length of relationship. Pan, Neidig, and O'Leary (1994) sampled 11,870 Anglo American men in the military and found that husband-to-wife aggression decreased by 19% for every 10-year increase in age. In sum, although cross-sectional data do not describe change for specific couples or for specific age cohorts, these prevalence rates suggest important trends such as the tendency for prevalence rates of aggression to decrease as individuals age.

However, when specific couples are tracked across time, a significant proportion of them do remain aggressive. Of individuals who report aggression in their dating relationships, 25% to 30% report an escalation in the severity of the aggression over time (Roscoe & Benaske, 1985; Woffordt, Mihalic, & Menard, 1994). In addition, the severity of the aggression early in the relationship is associated with the likelihood that it will continue, although the nature of this link is still unclear. Across several studies, women who reported severe aggression at the first assessment were significantly more likely to experience aggression at later time points (Feld & Straus, 1990; Quigley & Leonard, 1996; Woffordt et al.). Lawrence and Bradbury (2004), in a sample of 172 newlywed couples, examined the trajectories of physical aggression for couples initially classified as nonaggressive, moderately aggressive, and severely aggressive and found that spouses initially classified as severely aggressive (e.g., punching, kicking, or hitting a partner with an object) declined markedly in their aggression over the first 2 years of marriage (although most continued to be aggressive), whereas spouses initially classified as moderately aggressive (e.g., pushing, slapping, or shoving) continued to engage in moderate levels of aggression over time.[3] Thus, although the specific nature of the link between aggression early in a relationship and its maintenance over time is unclear, there is evidence that aggression does continue for most couples and that the severity of early aggression can help predict whether future aggression will occur. With that in mind, we now turn to a review of the literature examining the link between physical aggression and relationship dissolution.

Link Between Physical Aggression and Relationship Dissolution

The few studies that have explored the link between aggression and dissolution demonstrate strong and significant associations. Katz, Arias, Beach, Brody, and Roman (1995) found that physical aggression was significantly related to thoughts of divorce, especially for women. Kurz (1996) found that physical aggression was the primary reason cited for marital dissolution, particularly among wives. O'Leary et al. (1989) examined the association between the stability of aggression and marital satisfaction in newlyweds. They classified 8% of the men and 17% of the women as stably aggressive (i.e., they reported being aggressive at 1 month prior to marriage and at 18 and 30 months postmarriage). They found that 30% of the partners of stably aggressive men and 24% of the partners of stably aggressive women were maritally distressed at 30 months. In contrast, only 11% of the partners of stably nonaggressive men and 9% of the partners of stably nonaggressive women were in the maritally distressed range at 30 months. In a follow-up examination of this sample, Heyman, O'Leary, and Jouriles (1995) found that wives who were victims of serious premarital aggression (defined in this study as repeated acts of moderate aggression or any acts of severe aggression) reported significant declines in marital satisfaction and increases in divorce-related thoughts and actions from 6 to 18 to 30 months, even after premarital levels of relationship satisfaction were controlled for. In contrast, wives who had not experienced serious premarital aggression reported higher levels of marital satisfaction and fewer divorce-related thoughts and actions across this interval than wives who had experienced serious aggression. Because these samples were limited to newlywed couples, our ability to generalize these findings to other types of intimate relationships is limited. Nevertheless, they do suggest a strong link between aggression early in a relationship and severe distress and dissolution within approximately 3 years. Thus, the next step is to examine *how* aggression is associated with discord and dissolution. There have been some efforts to explore this link, and three explanations in particular are worth highlighting.

The first possible explanation for the consistent link between aggression and dissolution is that there are certain aspects of the aggression itself (e.g., based on frequency, severity, or context surrounding the aggressive episode) that are strongly predictive of relationship dissolution. Lo and Sporakowski (1989) examined 422 undergraduate dating couples and found that 56% reported verbal aggression and 44% reported both verbal and physical aggression. Of those in either verbally or physically aggressive relationships, 77% planned to stay in those relationships. Three of the most frequent reasons cited for continuing the relationships

---

[3]Trajectories of aggression were analyzed by use of hierarchical linear modeling techniques (see Bryk & Raudenbush, 1992). For spouses who were severely aggressive at the beginning of their marriages, the marked longitudinal declines in aggression were not deemed to simply be an artifact of regression to the mean. (See Lawrence & Bradbury, 2005, for more information on the statistical techniques used and the results of these analyses.)

were the type of aggressive behavior, the victim's reaction to the aggression, and whether others witnessed the episode. It is difficult to generalize the findings of Lo and Sporakowski to physically aggressive couples, because the reported results were not separated into (a) verbally aggressive only versus (b) verbally *and* physically aggressive couples. However, the results do suggest that specific aspects of the physical aggression itself and its immediate context may help predict whether victims stay in these relationships.

Lawrence and Bradbury (2001) examined physical aggression at the onset of marriage and subsequent marital outcomes. They found that spouses in marriages marked by physical aggression were at significantly greater risk for both severe, unremitting marital discord (Marital Adjustment Test scores below 80; Locke & Wallace, 1959) and dissolution over the first few years of marriage compared with spouses in nonaggressive marriages, and that this association was moderated by the severity of the aggression. Spouses engaging in severely aggressive behavior at the beginning of marriage and their victimized partners were significantly more likely to report severe distress and to report dissolution within the first 4 years of marriage compared with spouses in marriages classified as moderately aggressive or nonaggressive at the time of marriage. Specifically, 93% of couples reporting severe physical aggression experienced severe distress and dissolution compared with 46% of couples in moderately aggressive marriages and 39% of couples in nonaggressive marriages. Further, these marital outcomes occurred as early as within the first 2 years of marriage. In sum, there is preliminary evidence that understanding the specifics of the aggressive episodes themselves, in particular the severity of the aggression, can help predict whether subsequent distress and dissolution will occur.

A second possible explanation for the link between aggression and dissolution is that this association is moderated by the lingering threat of future aggression in the relationship, regardless of the actual continuing course of the aggression. Jacobson, Gottman, Gortner, Berns, and Shortt (1996) posited that, once male batterers have introduced physically aggressive tactics into the relationship, the threat of such aggression may remain over the course of the relationship, regardless of whether the batterer ever engages in physical aggression toward that partner again. We further propose that this threat of future aggression may be direct or indirect in nature. For example, once an individual has engaged in severely aggressive tactics, he may— either verbally or through nonverbal gestures—threaten the use of such tactics again during an argument. Alternatively, he might not make direct threats but the victim will continue to fear future victimization simply (and understandably) because it occurred previously in that relationship. The aggressor might never directly threaten to use physically aggressive tactics again and it might indeed never occur again, but the fear would forever exist for the victim, rendering it what we have termed an *indirect threat* and possibly leading to dissolution of the relationship.

A third explanation for the consistent link between aggression and dissolution is that relationship distress is mediating this association. Choice and Lamke (1999) studied individuals in physically aggressive dating relationships and found that relationship dissatisfaction was the strongest factor associated with an individual's decision to leave the relationship. DeMaris (2000) assessed 3,508 cohabiting and married couples twice over a 5- to 7-year period and found that male aggression (but not female aggression) predicted dissolution. However, the link between male aggression and dissolution could be accounted for by relationship distress.

In sum, the published research to date examining the link between physical aggression and relationship dissolution primarily has been descriptive in nature. There is some evidence to suggest that factors such as the severity of the aggression influence whether victims leave the relationship. There is also preliminary evidence to suggest that, once aggression has been exhibited in a relationship, its threat—whether it is direct or indirect—continues to affect the victim regardless of whether any further aggression exists. Finally, the link between aggression and dissolution may be mediated by relationship distress. These three possibilities may occur in proximity to one another, may influence each other, and may interact to lead to relationship distress and subsequent dissolution. Moreover, they are likely related to the proposed cognitive and behavioral mechanisms we delineate in the next section. We now incorporate these preliminary ideas into a conceptual framework that could provide a blueprint for future research targeting an understanding of the role of physical aggression in relationship dissolution.

UNDERSTANDING THE MECHANISMS THROUGH WHICH AGGRESSION PREDICTS RELATIONSHIP DISSOLUTION

In this section, we propose a cognitive-behavioral framework (presented in Fig. 14.1) for studying the role of physical aggression in relationship dissolution. This framework invokes two constructs—which we refer to as *behavioral engagement* and *attributions*—to account for variations in rates of dissolution when physical aggression is present. We next present a brief rationale for each of these constructs, followed by a discussion of how they interrelate.

We propose that the role of physical aggression in influencing dyadic distress and subsequent dissolution may be understood as a function of two types of processes. The first process is an interactional, behavioral one that can be conceptualized within a social learning framework. The second process is an intrapersonal, attributional one that can be conceptualized within a cognitive framework. These mediating processes are expected to lead to relationship distress, which in turn will lead to relationship dissolution. In this section, we describe the conceptual frameworks guiding each of these two constructs—the social learning model guiding the behavioral engagement construct and the cognitive model guiding the attributional construct—and the literature supporting the inclusion of each of the proposed mediators.

Social Learning Model of Physical Aggression in Intimate Relationships

Researchers have adapted Bandura's (1977) social learning model to help explain the onset of physical aggression in intimate relationships (e.g., O'Leary, 1988; Stith et al., 2000). The social learning model of physical aggression is based on the premise that aggression is learned

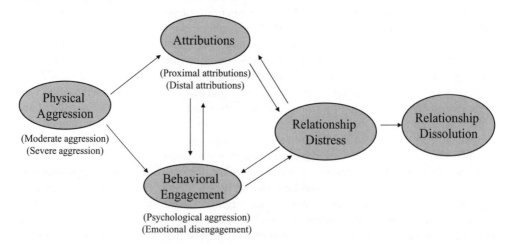

FIG. 14.1.   A Cognitive-Behavioral Framework for Understanding Mechanisms of Dissolution in Physically Aggressive Relationships.

and exhibited initially as an expression of anger. According to principles of social modeling, individuals who become aggressive learn to use such behavior in their families of origin, from their peers, and from the media. Moreover, individuals with aggressive, impulsive, or defensive personality styles are particularly vulnerable to being influenced by these models (e.g., O'Leary & Cascardi, 1998). Individuals who become aggressive toward romantic partners are believed to lack appropriate models for handling conflict effectively and for dealing with their feelings of frustration and anger. Consequently, as their attempts to generate constructive ways of resolving dyadic conflict are unsuccessful, negative behavior (e.g., negative reciprocity, negative escalation) becomes more frequent and severe, and partners eventually begin to use physically aggressive tactics as a means of anger expression. That is, mismanagement of negative affect during conflict contributes to the onset of physical aggression.

The social learning model provides a strong conceptual framework within which to understand the onset of physical aggression in intimate relationships, and there is quite a bit of evidence to support the model. For example, the link between aggression in one's family of origin and the likelihood that one will engage in aggressive behavior for men and women has been a consistent finding in the literature (e.g., Hotaling & Sugarman, 1986; Widom, 1989). This theory does not speak to the maintenance of aggression over time; however, the research of Lawrence and Bradbury (2005; Bradbury & Lawrence, 1999) demonstrates that the severity of the initial aggression may be used to predict its developmental course. If we interpret Lawrence and Bradbury's findings within the social learning framework, we might infer that individuals who engage in severe aggression early in their relationships lack appropriate conflict-resolution skills. Thus, even if the physical aggression declines over time among these individuals it does not mean that approaches to conflict resolution necessarily become constructive. Nevertheless, conflicts will inevitably arise and the use of physically aggressive tactics will therefore have to be replaced with some other behavioral strategy.

We posit that individuals who engage in severe aggression early on may engage in one of two behavioral replacement strategies. Specifically, declines in the severity and frequency of physical aggression will be concurrent with either (a) increases in psychologically aggressive tactics or (b) declines in emotional engagement more broadly such that couples not only stop engaging in problem-solving discussions—eliminating their ability to resolve disagreements— but also no longer engage in supportive, intimate, or sensual exchanges, leading to relationship distress and dissolution. We now examine each of these possibilities in turn.

Psychological Aggression as a Behavioral Mediator

Psychological aggression, defined by The Centers for Disease Control and Prevention (Saltzman, Fanslow, McMahon, & Shelley, 1999, pp. 12–13) as "a trauma to the victim caused by acts, threats of acts, or coercive tactics (including pure verbal and emotional acts such as humiliating, controlling the victim, getting annoyed if the victim disagrees, and also physically threatening acts such as smashing objects)," is highly prevalent in intimate relationships. Stets (1990) found that 65% of Anglo American men and 56% of African American men were psychologically aggressive toward their partner without concomitant physical aggression. In a national survey, 74% of men and 75% of women reported using at least one form of psychological aggression against their partner in the previous year (Gelles, 1997). In addition, psychological aggression is strongly related to relationship discord (e.g., Arias, Lyons, & Street, 1997), low self-esteem (e.g., Arias & Pape, 1999; Marshall, 1994), and depression (e.g., O'Leary & Jouriles, 1994).

Strong, positive associations between psychological aggression and physical aggression have been well documented across community samples of dating couples and newlyweds, and in samples of battered women (e.g., Capaldi & Crosby, 1997; Dutton, Goodman, & Bennett, 2001; Follingstad et al., 1990; Molidor, 1995; Straus & Sweet, 1992; Walker, 2000). Murphy and O'Leary (1989) assessed a non-treatment-seeking sample of 213 husbands and 184 wives at 1 month prior to marriage and at 6, 18, and 30 months after marriage. They found that spouses' initial levels of psychological aggression predicted first instances of physical aggression even after any previous partner physical aggression was controlled for.

Given (a) the high prevalence of psychological aggression in intimate relationships, (b) the link between psychological and physical aggression, and (c) the fact that physically aggressive individuals are believed to have poor conflict-resolution skills, it seems reasonable to posit that declines in physical aggression could be associated with an emergence of another poor interactional style, specifically increases in psychological aggression, which ultimately would lead to relationship distress and dissolution. There is evidence to suggest that psychological aggression is severely detrimental to its victims, lending support to the notion that it may function as a proximal contributor to relationship dissolution. For example, researchers have demonstrated that the impact of psychological aggression is often more detrimental to the victim than physical aggression. Walker (2000) found that most women described incidents involving psychological humiliation and verbal harassment as their worst "battering experiences." Indeed, women in battering relationships report that the psychological victimization they experience has a greater negative impact on their well-being (e.g., depression, self-esteem) than does the concurrent physical aggression they endure (e.g., Follingstad et al., 1990; Street & Arias, 2001).

There are also data to support longitudinal associations among physical aggression, psychological aggression, and relationship dissolution. Jacobson et al. (1996) examined levels of physical and psychological aggression as predictors of relationship dissolution over 2 years in a sample of 45 male batterers and their female spouses. All husbands exhibited severe physical aggression at the initial wave of data collection. At the 2-year follow-up, 62% of the couples were still married and living together and 38% had separated or divorced. Of the couples still living together at follow-up, 46% of the batterers had not reduced their levels of severe aggression and 54% significantly decreased the frequency and severity of their aggression. However, husband psychological aggression did not decrease over the 2-year period, even when levels of physical aggression did.

In sum, we suggest that psychological aggression may mediate the link between physical aggression and relationship distress and dissolution. Even if severely aggressive individuals markedly decline or desist in their physically aggressive behavior over the course of a relationship (e.g., Lawrence & Bradbury, 2005), in the absence of alternative models for managing their anger, they may wind up replacing the physical aggression with psychological aggression. Further, given that psychological aggression has been found to be extremely damaging to individual and dyadic adjustment (e.g., Follingstad et al., 1990; Straight, Harper, & Arias, 2003), increased psychological aggression is expected to contribute to declines in relationship satisfaction and stability. In contrast, individuals engaging in moderately aggressive behavior may maintain low levels of physical aggression, but they will also likely maintain low levels of psychological aggression. Thus, they are not affected by either severe aggression or by high levels of psychological aggression, so they do not experience erosion in relationship satisfaction or stability.

Emotional Disengagement as a Behavioral Mediator

Emotional disengagement is the process of increasing apathy, increasing withdrawal, declining feelings of love, and loss of emotional attachment toward one's partner over time, and these changes can be seen at the behavioral, cognitive, and affective levels of functioning. In a chapter in this volume (chap. 11), Kayser and Rao-Kelter posit that the process of disaffection begins with feelings of disillusionment with one's partner or with the relationship. Over time, disillusionment gives way to anger and hurt, and later to hopelessness and indifference, which often leads to dissolution of the relationship. Indeed, there is evidence to support links between certain features of emotional disengagement and relationship dissolution. For example, lack of love is one of the most frequently cited reasons for divorce (Albrecht, Bahr, & Goodman, 1983; Bloom & Hodges, 1981; Kingsbury & Minda, 1988). Smith, Vivian, and O'Leary (1990) found that disengagement behaviors exhibited at 1 month prior to marriage were associated with marital distress at 18 and 30 months after marriage. Similarly, Roberts (2000) found that wives' (but not husbands') withdrawal behaviors, particularly intimacy avoidance and angry withdrawal, predicted husbands' marital distress.

We posit that the link between declines in physical aggression and relationship dissolution may also be mediated by emotional disengagement. As we discussed earlier, individuals who are severely aggressive early in their relationships often decline or desist in their aggressive behavior over time. Once individuals no longer use physically aggressive behavior during dis-agreements, they will need to generate alternate ways of responding during dyadic conflict. However, according to social learning theory, aggressive individuals may not have learned more constructive ways of managing conflict and will be unable to substitute a more constructive behavioral response when disagreements arise. Consequently, for these couples, the immediate goal during a disagreement may be to avoid letting the conflict escalate to the point at which the individual would normally use physically aggressive tactics rather than generating a goal of using more constructive tactics when such disagreements arise. These couples might begin to avoid any discussion that has the perceived potential to become a disagreement, as disagreements have led to the use of physical aggression in the past. Initially, this strategy might be limited to problem-solving discussions. However, couples in highly conflictual re-lationships may believe that any interaction has the potential to become conflictual and to be marked by negative behavior. Couples may begin to generalize their avoidant behavior from simply known areas of disagreement to any emotionally engaging interaction. They would be-gin to avoid not only potential conflict discussions but also potentially supportive, sensual, or emotionally intimate interactions as well. Consequently, the relationship becomes one marked by emotional disengagement across a variety of domains, which leads to relationship distress and dissolution. In contrast, individuals engaging in moderate levels of aggression early on may maintain those low levels of aggression but are also able to maintain supportive and in-timate behaviors, allowing them to continue feeling emotionally engaged and satisfied with their relationships despite the continued presence of physical aggression.

Summary of Behavioral Mediators

We suggest that the link between physical aggression and relationship dissolution can be con-ceptualized as part of a larger interactional cycle such that physical aggression is followed by psychological aggression or behavioral disengagement rather than effective conflict reso-lution, leading to relationship distress and subsequent dissolution. It seems highly probable that individuals might even alternate between these two destructive interpersonal dynamics, yielding an emotionally labile and thus unstable relationship. We now turn to an examination of the proposed cognitive influences on this framework.

Attribution Model of Relationship Distress and Dissolution

Attribution theory has been used to help explain the link between behavior and relationship satisfaction in intimate relationships. The theory is based on the premise that partners in satisfied and distressed relationships can be distinguished by the attributions they make for each other's behaviors (e.g., Fincham, 1985; Jacobson, McDonald, Follette, & Berley, 1985). Dissatisfied individuals tend to view their partner as the cause of negative behaviors and find temporary, external causes for positive behaviors. In contrast, satisfied partners tend to view their partner's positive behaviors as the result of stable, internal causes and dismiss negative behaviors as the result of temporary, external causes. This association holds true even when researchers control for depressive symptoms (Fincham, Beach, & Bradbury, 1989) and neuroticism (Karney, Bradbury, Fincham, & Sullivan, 1994). On the basis of this research, attributions have been assigned a prominent role in theories of relationship development (e.g., Bradbury & Fincham, 1991) and have been described as a target of change in interventions designed to alleviate or prevent relationship distress and dissolution (e.g., Baucom, Sayers, & Sher, 1990; Markman, Stanley, & Blumberg, 1994).

Attribution theory has consistently been applied to global negative behavior in intimate relationships, but it has rarely been applied to physically aggressive behavior specifically. However, the studies that do exist suggest that such an adaptation might be useful. Ehrensaft and Vivian (1996) examined cognitive mechanisms (though not attributions specifically) relevant to physical aggression among treatment-seeking couples. They found that 60% of spouses seeking couple therapy reported experiencing physical aggression in their relationships. However, less than 10% of these spouses spontaneously identified the aggression as a problem. The primary explanations provided by individuals for this lack of reporting were: (1) physical aggression was not perceived to be a problem; (2) the aggression was unstable or infrequent; and (3) the aggression was either caused by other problems or was perceived as being secondary to other problems. Thus, individuals do not seem to be identifying a link between physical aggression and dyadic distress in their own relationships. One possible explanation for this disconnect might be the way partners think about aggression after it occurs. Specifically, victims of physical aggression may dismiss or minimize the role of the aggression to justify staying in their relationships. It seems reasonable to expect that attributions about a partner's aggression might be a key factor in understanding why one might remain in a relationship despite the presence of physical aggression. In sum, the types of attributions that victims make for partner aggression would likely have an impact on their relationship satisfaction and stability.

Byrne and Arias (1997) examined the role of attributions in understanding the relation between physical aggression and relationship satisfaction among married couples. They found that attributions of responsibility moderated the association between aggression and satisfaction for wives such that wives made negative responsibility attributions for their husbands' negative behavior. However, the attributions that they assessed were based on the Relationship Attribution Measure of Fincham and Bradbury (1992), limiting our ability to generalize these findings in two ways. First, the attributions assessed by means of this measure are relevant to global negative behaviors (e.g., criticism) and not to physically aggressive behavior specifically. Second, the attributions were made for hypothetical incidents rather than specific episodes experienced by the couples. Therefore, it is difficult to determine from this study whether the link between aggression and satisfaction is mediated by attributions specific to that aggression.

Holtzworth-Munroe, Jacobson, Fehrenbach, and Fruzzetti (1992) examined the types of attributions husbands and wives made for aggressive and nonaggressive behavior. They found that individuals were less likely to believe that physically aggressive behavior (relative to nonaggressive negative behavior) was likely to happen again in the future. Interestingly, husbands were more likely to excuse their own aggressive behavior compared with their own nonaggressive negative behavior. Finally, wives attributed responsibility for husbands' aggression to the husband, whereas both men and women blamed wives' aggression on the husband. In another study, Ehrensaft and Vivian (1999) compared appraisals made by individuals in physically aggressive and nonaggressive dating relationships. They found that individuals in aggressive relationships were more likely to perceive men's behavior as restrictive, domineering, or coercive, and less likely to appraise women's behavior as such. Moreover, compared with women, men tended to view these behaviors as less controlling overall.

We know of only one published study examining the role of attributions in explaining the link between physical aggression and relationship dissolution. Truman-Schram, Cann, Calhoun, and Vanwallendael (2000), in a retrospective assessment, compared women between the ages of 18 and 25 years who had left aggressive dating relationships and those who were still in such relationships. They found that women who had left their aggressive partners were more likely to blame their partners for the aggressive behavior than to blame themselves or relationship factors.

These studies support our contention that aggression-specific attributions may play a critical role in understanding how physical aggression affects relationship stability. We posit that victims of physical aggression may engage in one of two cognitive processes. First, following an aggressive interaction, victims will make attributions about their partner's aggression that allow them to justify remaining in the relationship despite the recent aggression. This tendency is expected to be particularly prevalent in the early stages of a relationship when satisfaction is still high. Second, declines in the severity or frequency of physical aggression over time will be followed by shifts in these attributions. Specifically, once the immediate threat of physical aggression has been removed, victims may feel freer to challenge their initial attributions such that they begin to blame their partner for his or her aggressive behavior. These revised attributions will lead to declines in satisfaction and ultimately to dissolution. We now examine each of these possibilities in turn.

Proximal Attributions as a Cognitive Mediator

We purport that a variety of different types of attributions will influence the link between physical aggression and concurrent relationship distress and dissolution. First, the types of attributions that victims make immediately following aggressive episodes—which we have termed *proximal attributions*—are likely to lead victims to stay in these relationships. For example, if a woman attributes her male partner's aggression to external factors (e.g., to a bad day at work), she might be less likely to think negatively of him for being aggressive. Moreover, she might blame herself for his aggression (e.g., for not being supportive when he has a bad day), making her more likely to stay in the relationship.

Second, attributions about the *reasons* for the presence of aggression in the relationship in general might be an important factor. A victim might feel that the aggression does not occur often enough to qualify as a problem, or that some aggression is acceptable (i.e., justified) based on his or her experiences in the family of origin or in prior relationships. Indeed, there is consistent evidence that men and women who have witnessed aggression in their families of origin and who have engaged in physical aggression in prior relationships are more likely to engage in aggression in their current relationships (Hotaling & Sugarman, 1986; Widom, 1989).

Third, individuals may make attributions about whether aggression is likely to occur in the future. For example, victims may make attributions that allow them to believe they have control over their partner's aggressive behavior, or that the reason the aggression occurred is due to something that will never happen again (i.e., an unstable influence). Either interpretation would likely lead victims to stay in these relationships. In sum, an understanding of such proximal attributions would likely allow us to better understand why individuals choose to stay in aggressive relationships, and why they often report concurrent physical aggression and relationship satisfaction early in these relationships.

Distal Attributions as a Cognitive Mediator

Lawrence and Bradbury (2001, 2005; Bradbury & Lawrence, 1999) found that severely aggressive individuals declined markedly in their aggression over the first 2 years of marriage, yet their relationships still became severely distressed and unstable; in contrast, moderately aggressive individuals continued to engage in such aggression over time, but neither partner experienced severe distress and the relationships did not dissolve. These findings suggest that the mere continuance of physical aggression over time does not explain the link between early physical aggression and subsequent distress and dissolution.

We posited that victims make proximal attributions for their partner's aggression that are external, unstable, and specific, which may explain why many victims of physical aggression remain in these relationships. However, we know that aggression declines over time in many relationships. If the severity or frequency of the aggression does indeed decline over time, the attenuation of the continued threat of physical aggression might create an environment in which the victim can consider the impact of the aggression on his or her psychological well-being in a more objective way. Consequently, the victim's *distal attributions* about the prior aggression may shift from external, unstable, and specific to internal, stable, and global in causality, and responsibility and blame may shift from the victim or from external factors to the aggressive partner. These latter attributions for partner aggression are expected to lead to relationship distress and ultimately to dissolution. In sum, changes in physical aggression over time trigger increased reflection on the history of the aggression in the relationship, which leads to changes in attributions about the aggression and subsequent relationship distress and dissolution.

Summary of Cognitive Mediators

We suggest that the link between physical aggression and relationship dissolution can be conceptualized as part of a larger attributional process. Specifically, physical aggression will be followed by attributions that lead to continued perceived relationship satisfaction (and consequently, relationship stability) for the victim. However, when declines in physical aggression occur over time, these declines will lead to changes in these initial attributions, triggering relationship distress and instability. It is expected that both types of attributions—proximal and distal—will influence relationship stability, such that initial levels and rates of change in each of the three key factors—aggression, attributions, and satisfaction—will interact to lead to relationship dissolution.

A Cognitive-Behavioral Framework to Explain How Physical Aggression Leads to Relationship Distress and Dissolution

A wealth of descriptive studies exists documenting the association between physical aggression and relationship dissolution, allowing us to now move to a more conceptual understanding of the mechanisms through which physical aggression contributes to the instability of romantic relationships. Herein we have proposed a cognitive-behavioral framework to help explain this link (see Fig. 14.1). Building on a social learning model previously used to explain the onset of physical aggression, we have proposed two potential behavioral interactional factors that may mediate the link between physical aggression trajectories and relationship dissolution. First, declines in physical aggression may be replaced with increases in psychological aggression, which then lead to dissatisfaction and instability. Second, declines in physical aggression may be followed by emotional and behavioral disengagement, leading to dyadic distress and dissolution. It is most likely that both mechanisms are at work such that partners alternate between these two behavioral approaches in an attempt to replace the physical aggression with another interactional strategy, or that a consecutive approach is used such that partners initially engage in psychological aggression in an attempt to remain emotionally engaged without using physically aggressive tactics, but, given the lack of effectiveness of such behavior, over time they transition to more emotional disengagement tactics that ultimately lead to relationship dissolution.

Building on an attribution model previously used to explain the link between global negative behavior and relationship distress, we have proposed two potential cognitive factors that may mediate the link between physical aggression trajectories and relationship distress and dissolution. First, victims may make proximal attributions for specific episodes of partner aggression that help explain why they stay in aggressive relationships and report concurrent relationship satisfaction. Specifically, partners in young relationships may feel the need to make external, unstable, and specific attributions to justify having entered into a relationship with an aggressive partner. This approach seems particularly likely for partners in the early stages of relationships when satisfaction typically is still high. Second, changes in aggression over time are expected to predict changes in attributions over time, which will ultimately lead to relationship dissolution. There is some evidence that individuals who engage in severe aggression early in relationships decline in their use of aggression over the next few years, but their relationships still dissolve (e.g., Bradbury & Lawrence, 1999; Lawrence & Bradbury, 2001, 2005). The removal of the immediate threat of physical aggression may allow victims to think about the aggression more objectively and begin making distal attributions. The victim is expected to begin making stable, global, and internal attributions for his or her partner's previous aggression, leading to declines in relationship satisfaction and ultimately to dissolution.

In conclusion, we have presented a cognitive-behavioral framework that may be useful in conceptualizing the mechanisms through which physical aggression leads to relationship dissolution. The proposed cognitive and behavioral mediating factors may occur in proximity to one another, may influence each other, and may interact to lead to relationship distress and subsequent dissolution.

INTERVENTION CONSIDERATIONS

We now consider some of the practical implications of better understanding the link between physical aggression and relationship dissolution. Specifically, we make three points related to intervention considerations. First, given that physical aggression occurs with such frequency among dating, cohabiting, engaged, and newlywed couples, and given the high rates of dissolution in these early stages of relationships, we assert that clinicians should target physical aggression in interventions designed to enhance relationship satisfaction. The findings reviewed in this chapter suggest that such a focused intervention component would be appropriate and beneficial for couples reporting aggression early in their relationships. Second, we believe that the high prevalence rates of aggression early in relationships support the need to pay greater attention to *prevention* efforts targeting physical aggression and subsequent dissolution in young relationships. Furthermore, aggression should be monitored over the first few years of the relationship, as levels change at different rates for different individuals. However, couples who do not report aggression at the beginning of their relationships typically do not report aggression at later data points (e.g., Bradbury & Lawrence, 1999; Lawrence & Bradbury, 2005). Thus, for couples who are initially nonaggressive, an intervention component targeting the aggression and its causes seems unnecessary. We therefore recommend that clinicians institute secondary prevention efforts rather than implement a widespread primary violence prevention program for couples.

Third, once these at risk couples have been identified, the question of exactly how to best intervene becomes paramount. According to the research presented in this chapter, existing behavioral interventions targeting global negative affect (e.g., anger) may be insufficient when the developmental course of aggression and the mechanisms through which aggression influences dissolution are considered. We suggest a two-part intervention strategy focused on (a) the causes of aggression and (b) its subsequent influences on relationship satisfaction and stability. Interventions targeting the causes of aggression might include psychoeducation about social modeling of aggression and the risk of continuing the patterns learned in one's childhood and adolescence, as well as inclusion of existing intervention components related to communication and problem-solving skills training. Assuming the immediate threat of physical aggression can be removed through these efforts, clinicians might then transition to interventions targeting psychological aggression, emotional disengagement, and attributional patterns. In sum, it is recommended that, when physical aggression is present, clinicians should incorporate a social learning model and a broader range of cognitive and behavioral approaches into existing interventions that are predominantly behaviorally focused (e.g., the Prevention and Relationship Enhancement Program, or PREP).

METHODOLOGICAL CONSIDERATIONS

Although the existence of a vast number of studies on physical aggression in intimate relationships suggests great potential for understanding the role of physical aggression in relationship dissolution, a wide array of methodological issues must be addressed if this potential is to be fully realized. We now transition from a discussion of conceptual issues to a discussion of methodological issues. Specifically, we discuss three methodological topics that are important to consider in conducting and evaluating research exploring physical aggression in intimate relationships, regardless of the conceptual orientation that is adopted. First, we discuss the emerging belief that physical aggression in intimate relationships may indeed consist of two types of phenomena, such that the inconsistencies reported in the literature may at least partially be a function of different sampling techniques. Second, we call for a more contextual approach to assessing physical aggression in intimate relationships, such as by using diary data or interviewing techniques, in order to better understand the relational circumstances surrounding the aggressive episodes themselves. Third, we review the literature relevant to the influence of factors such as gender roles, race and ethnicity, socioeconomic status (SES), and sexual orientation on the link between aggression and dissolution.

The Heterogeneous Nature of Physical Aggression in Intimate Relationships

Researchers have begun to view physical aggression as encompassing two types of phenomena (e.g., Chase, O'Leary, & Heyman, 2001; Johnson, 1995; Johnson & Ferraro, 2000; Straus, 1999). In the first type, referred to as *reactive aggression* or *situational violence*, prevalence rates are similar for men and women, and rates of reported injury and fear are low. Psychologically coercive tactics such as dominance and isolation are also presumed to be low. High numbers of aggressors and victims in this group report concurrent relationship satisfaction, and even couples in this group who are seeking marital therapy rarely report aggression as a problem (e.g., O'Leary, Vivian, & Malone, 1992). Most of the data presented in this chapter and the conceptual framework propos focus on situational aggression. In the second type, referred to as *proactive aggression, battering,* or *intimate terrorism*, men are primarily, if not exclusively, the aggressors. Rates of fear, physical injury, and psychological trauma are high for female victims, and psychologically coercive tactics such as dominance and isolation are common (e.g., Jacobson & Gottman, 1998; Koss et al., 1994; Walker, 2000).

A review of the literature on aggression suggests that situational aggression and battering are either not distinguished or that more theoretical writings and interventions focus on battering relationships. For example, almost all of the research regarding the physical and psychological impact of physical aggression on its victims has been conducted with samples of women in battering relationships (e.g., Koss et al., 1994; Walker, 2000). In addition, there have been recent efforts to distinguish among male batterers empirically (e.g., Jacobson & Gottman, 1998). Consequently, one of our key goals in this chapter was to increase understanding of situational aggression, a phenomenon that affects one fourth to one half of couples but that has been relatively ignored.

From a practical standpoint, situationally aggressive and battering relationships probably differ in the extent to which intervention might successfully decrease the aggression. Existing treatment programs targeting batterers have high rates of attrition and relatively low rates of effectiveness (e.g., Hamberger & Hastings, 1993; Rosenfeld, 1992). Researchers and clinicians are beginning to suggest that male batterers cannot be effectively rehabilitated (e.g., Jacobson, 1997). Regardless of one's stance on the treatment of male batterers, it is evident that treating these men is at best extremely difficult. Further, given that male batterers have been diagnosed as having antisocial personality traits (e.g., Gondolf, Fisher, & McFerron, 1988; Holtzworth-Munroe & Stuart, 1994), it seems likely that the prevention of battering also would be difficult. More promising are programs undertaken early in relationships to decrease situational aggression. For example, Avery-Leaf, Cascardi, O'Leary, and Cano (1997) piloted a prevention program in high schools targeting attitudes toward dating aggression. Markman, Renick, Floyd, Stanley, and Clements (1993) implemented a prevention program in which they teach constructive ways to handle marital conflict, although physical aggression was not directly targeted. Overall, however, few aggression prevention programs have been implemented let alone tested empirically. In sum, an understanding of the phenomenon of aggression cannot be successful without a consideration of the heterogeneity of the aggression.

Relational Context: Factors Relevant to Specific Aggressive Episodes

Our ability to answer most of the questions we have tackled to date as researchers (e.g., prevalence rates of aggression in relationships, the severity and frequency of aggression enacted by men and women, whether aggression continues over the course of a relationship) must be credited in large part to the Conflict Tactics Scales (CTS, Straus, 1979; CTS2, Straus, Hamby, Boney-McCoy, & Sugarman, 1995), the most widely used self-report questionnaire in studies of physical aggression in intimate relationships. However, many remaining questions may require novel methodological approaches in order for them to be adequately addressed. Questions about the relational context of aggression in particular may require a move beyond questionnaire data. Behavioral observation has allowed us to get closer to the phenomenon of aggression because we can examine constructs such as skills and affect displayed during conflictual discussions. However, physical aggression typically is not seen in these interactions, so our observation is still one step removed from the phenomenon under investigation. (A notable exception can be found in Capaldi's work, e.g., Capaldi & Crosby, 1997, in which she has evidence of couples actually engaging in moderate levels of physical aggression during their videotaped problem-solving interactions, allowing for a more direct investigation of the phenomenon.) In the absence of this type of evidence, shifts in methodological approaches, such as the use of diary data or individual interviews, might allow us to begin to answer questions about the context of aggressive episodes themselves. For example, we could begin to understand the antecedents or provoking factors that trigger aggression for men and women. We could explore the spontaneous strategies couples use to resolve aggressive conflicts. We could also more closely examine the attributions and emotional reactions that aggressors and victims experience before, during, and after aggressive episodes.

In addition to addressing novel contextual questions, we might begin to challenge existing theoretical approaches and implicit assumptions about aggression. For example, we have discussed the emergence of two qualitatively different types of physical aggression in intimate relationships. In an effort to further distinguish among types of aggressors or aggressive relationships, hypotheses attributed to one type of aggressive relationship could be tested empirically in another type. For example, are factors such as psychological domination, fear, and injury truly unique to battering relationships? Is aggression defensive for women in situationally aggressive relationships as well as in battering relationships? A contextual approach such as the use of individual interviews would allow such questions to be addressed.

Consideration of Cultural and Societal Influences

The second context that must be applied to any consideration of physical aggression in intimate relationships is the broader influence of societal and cultural factors such as gender roles, race and ethnicity, SES, and sexual orientation. Such factors are routinely considered in sociological studies of physical aggression but often ignored in psychological approaches to aggression, which tend to favor intrapersonal and interpersonal frameworks. Herein we summarize the few existing studies examining the roles of such contextual factors on physical aggression and relationship dissolution.

Sex and Gender

We have discussed the consistent evidence that men and women in young relationships use physically aggressive tactics at similar rates, and that the sampling techniques used and the relational context of the aggression moderate these sex differences. Specifically, in situationally aggressive or reactively aggressive relationships, women report rates of aggression that are similar to those reported by men, and reports of fear and injury are low, whereas in battering or intimate terrorist relationships, men are the primary aggressors and fear, injury, and psychological terrorism are common. Another explanation for the surprisingly high rates of female aggression is the difference in societal and cultural rules governing physical aggression by men and women in intimate relationships. Specifically, questions often arise about the factors that might explain the rates of aggression among women.

Straus (1999) identified seven societal and cultural influences that he believes might "facilitate" women's aggressive behavior in intimate relationships. First, cultural norms may support a woman's right to aggress against a man and even frame this behavior as a sign of femininity, such as the belief that it is acceptable for a woman to slap a man's face to defend herself against sexual advances. Such behavior is frequently modeled on television and in movies. Survey data from 1968, 1985, 1992, and 1995 (National Commission on the Causes and Prevention of Violence, 1969; Straus, Kaufman Kantor, & Moore, 1997) demonstrate that 22%

of respondents believe that there are times when it is acceptable for a woman to slap a man's face; rates of acceptability for a man to slap a woman's face were 20% in 1968 but dropped to 10% by 1995. Second, a woman's lesser size and strength may render her less likely to inhibit the use of aggression, as she may not feel the need to worry about hurting her male partner. In contrast, women's aggression may not have as strong an impact on the victim or the relationship precisely because of the lower risk of victim fear and injury. Fiebert and Gonzalez (1997) found that 29% of their sample of 978 female college students reported having hit a male partner. Of the women who had hit, two thirds (62%) checked as one of the reasons "I do not believe my actions would hurt my partner" or "I believe that men can readily protect themselves so I don't worry when I become physically aggressive." Third, women may often use aggression in self-defense or in retaliation after their male partner initiates aggressive behavior. Aggression in self-defense has been reported among women in battering relationships (e.g., Walker, 2000), but among women in situationally aggressive relationships, the explanations for aggression have rarely been examined empirically. The use of interview methods discussed earlier would be one way to examine this question. Fourth, Straus suggests that gender norms for conflict in general may differ for men and women. Men are more likely to use avoidance strategies and women are more likely to pursue conflictual discussions; this pattern has been called the "demand–withdraw cycle" and is common among distressed couples (Christensen & Heavey, 1990). Within this relational dynamic, women might be more likely to use a variety of strategies, including the use of physical aggression, in pursuit of their goal to have a discussion about the topic of disagreement. Fifth, Straus posited that the role of family in determining one's source of identity may differ for men and women. Women's identity, compared to men's identity, is as strongly or more strongly rooted in the relationship. Therefore, women may feel a strong need to defend their own interests in the relationship. Sixth, the criminal justice system punishes male aggression more than female aggression at present, which implies greater acceptability of female aggression than of male aggression. Male victims are less likely than female victims to call the police, and police are less likely to arrest women for aggressive behavior toward their partners.

We recommend consideration of a seventh factor—traditional gender roles. In short, we believe that the growing egalitarian nature of couple relationships may be related to the similarities in rates of male and female aggression. There is some support for this idea. In a sample of 85 college dating couples, stereotypically negative masculine characteristics were the best predictor of aggression for both men and women. Moreover, men who held more traditional beliefs about gender roles were more likely to be aggressive and women who held *less* traditional beliefs about gender roles were more likely to be aggressive (Jenkins & Aube, 2002). In sum, a variety of cultural and societal factors relevant to sex and gender differences may be influencing the seemingly surprisingly high rates of female aggression in situationally aggressive relationships.

Race, Ethnicity, and SES

To date, most research examining the role of physical aggression in relationship dissolution has been conducted on Anglo American, middle-class, heterosexual married couples. However, the few studies that have been conducted on samples of other types of individuals have been extremely useful in helping us understand the processes through which aggression may lead to dissolution. First, associations among race, SES, and rates of physical aggression have been inconsistent. Some studies have found that prevalence rates of physical aggression are highest among African American couples (23% and 30% for male and female aggressors, respectively), followed by Hispanic couples (17% and 21%, respectively) and then Caucasian couples (12% and 16%, respectively; see Caetano, Cunradi, Schafer, & Clark, 2000; Caetano, Nelson, & Cunradi, 2001; Rosen, Parmley, Knudson, & Fancher, 2002), and this difference exists even after SES has been accounted for (Cunradi, Caetano, & Schafer, 2002). Others have found that racial differences in prevalence rates disappear once SES and sex are accounted for (Rennison & Planty, 2003). For example, across racial and ethnic groups, factors related to SES—such as education, employment, and income—are predictive of aggression (Byrne, Resnick, Kilpatrick, Best, & Saunders, 1999; Hoffman & Demo, 1994; Schumacher, Feldbau-Kohn, Slep, & Heyman, 2001; Weinbaum et al., 2001). There is also some evidence demonstrating racial differences among the strength of the links between predictive factors and physical aggression. For example, the associations between aggression and cohabitation, and aggression and employment, were stronger among Hispanic couples than among Caucasian and African American couples (Jasinski, 2001).

There is some preliminary evidence that the cognitive strategies used by victims do not differ across different racial groups. Marshall, Weston, and Honeycutt (2000) assessed 717 African American, Anglo American, and Mexican American women who had experienced aggression from their male partners. They found that victimized women across groups weighted their perceptions of their partner's positive behavior (e.g., caring behavior) more heavily than the aggression, regardless of race, relationship status (dating, cohabiting, or married), or severity of the aggression.

Finally, there is some evidence that race, ethnicity, and SES have an impact on the consequences of aggression. Avakame and Fyfe (2001) found that the police were more likely to arrest the aggressor if the victim was female, affluent, Anglo American, older, or suburban. Further, there is evidence that early arrest functions as a deterrent to future aggression for Caucasian, upper-middle-class men. On the basis of these findings, we find it reasonable to posit that victims of physical aggression who are of color or of low SES are less likely to receive police assistance, which makes the likelihood of continued aggression greater. Moreover, the lack of interventions might make it more difficult for such victims to dissolve these relationships, as there are fewer resources in the community to assist them. In sum, there appear to be more intrapersonal and societal barriers to dissolution for low SES and non-Anglo-American victims of physical aggression.

Same-Sex Couples

Physical aggression among same-sex couples has also been relatively ignored. The research that does exist suggests that prevalence rates of aggression are similar across heterosexual and homosexual intimate relationships. Burke and Follingstad (1999) reviewed 19 studies and concluded that prevalence rates of aggression in same-sex romantic relationships are high and hold similar correlates to those identified in heterosexual intimate relationships. Freedner, Freed, Yang, and Austin (2002) found that 42% of men and 37% of women reported experiencing some sort of aggression (either psychological or physical), and that many of the barriers to dissolution are similar to those reported by victims of aggression in heterosexual relationships (e.g., financial dependence; see Cruz, 2003). However, preliminary evidence suggests that there may be additional barriers to dissolution for victims in same-sex relationships. Freedner et al. found that lesbian victims of aggression were more likely to report fearing for their safety from a date or romantic partner (31% of whom were male) compared with heterosexual female victims, and bisexual male and female victims were more likely to be threatened with outing compared with gay male and lesbian victims of aggression. In sum, although prevalence rates of physical aggression are similar across same-sex and opposite-sex dyads, there appear to be greater intrapersonal and societal barriers to dissolution for victims of aggression in same-sex relationships and possibly even greater barriers for bisexual victims.

Summary

Several significant methodological challenges must be recognized and resolved before the inferential benefits of clarifying the underlying processes governing the link between physical aggression and relationship dissolution can be realized. In this section, we discussed the need to consider physical aggression as a heterogeneous phenomenon and to consider the relational and societal contexts within which such aggression occurs. Such methodological shifts affect our ability to conduct descriptive research, to develop conceptual models such as the one proposed in this chapter, and to develop effective intervention programs targeting physical aggression and subsequent relationship distress and dissolution.

CONCLUSION

We hope that the prerequisites for advancing our understanding of relationship dissolution in physically aggressive couples are evident from this chapter. First, conceptual frameworks are likely to prove most useful to the extent that physical aggression and dyadic processes are assigned central roles in determining relationship outcomes. Prior research has provided consistent evidence documenting the prevalence of physical aggression in intimate relationships, the wide variety of longitudinal courses aggression may take over the course of a relationship, and the link between aggression early in a relationship and subsequent relationship distress and dissolution. Social learning models of physical aggression have provided a strong framework within which to understand the onset of physical aggression in intimate relationships, but they were never meant to address the developmental course of aggression once it began or the mechanisms through which aggression influences relationship dissolution. Attributional models of relationship distress have provided a strong framework within which to understand the link between behaviors and relationship distress, but they have never been applied directly to the physical aggression that partners experience in their own relationships. We have presented a cognitive-behavioral framework to help contextualize how interactional behavioral processes—by means of psychological aggression and emotional disengagement—and individual attributional processes—by means of proximal and distal aggression-specific attributions—might develop over time and contribute to relationship dissolution in couples experiencing physical aggression.

The significance of future studies will depend to a large degree on our ability to use sampling techniques that take into account the heterogeneous nature of physical aggression in intimate relationships, to include couples from a variety of races, ethnicities, socioeconomic environments, and sexual orientations, and to include consideration of both intrapersonal–cognitive and interactional–behavioral processes. The quality of efforts to prevent relationship distress and dissolution depends on our understanding of the processes through which couples arrive at relationship distress and dissolution. Although applied issues were not the focus of our chapter, we adopt the view that an emphasis on the dual components of intraindividual and interactional processes in intimate relationships will direct attention toward the content of prevention programs, whereas the consideration of the one fourth to one half of couples who engage in physically aggressive behavior at the beginning of their relationships can direct attention toward the couples who are most in need of early intervention. The social costs of physical aggression and relationship dissolution add to the urgency of conducting conceptually clear, methodologically rigorous research that will help solve this problem.

ACKNOWLEDGMENTS

Preparation of this chapter was supported by the following awards for Erika Lawrence: the University of Iowa Obermann Center of Advanced Studies Spelman Rockefeller Grant for the Study of Children and Families, a second Old Gold Summer Fellowship Award, and a Social Sciences Fellowship Program Award.

Correspondence concerning this article should be addressed to Erika Lawrence, Department of Psychology, University of Iowa, 11 Seashore Hall East, Iowa City, Iowa 52242-1407. E-mail: erika-lawrence@uiowa.edu

REFERENCES

Ahlburg, D. A., & DeVita, C. J. (1992). New realities of the American family. *Population Bulletin, 47,* 3–44.

Albrecht, S. L., Bahr, H. M., & Goodman, K. L. (1983). *Divorce and remarriage: Problems adaptations and adjustments.* Westport, CT: Greenwood.

Amato, P. R., & Keith, B. (1991a). Parental divorce and the well-being of children: A meta-analysis. *Psychological Bulletin, 110,* 26–46.

Amato, P. R., & Keith, B. (1991b). Parental divorce and adult well-being: A meta-analysis. *Journal of Marriage and the Family, 53,* 43–58.

Arias, I., Lyons, C. M., & Street, A. E. (1997). Individual and marital consequences of victimization: Moderating effects of relationship efficacy and spouse support. *Journal of Family Violence, 12,* 193–210.

Arias, I., & Pape, K. T. (1999). Psychological abuse: Implications for adjustment and commitment to leave violent partners. *Violence and Victims, 14,* 55–67.

Arias, I., Samios, M., & O'Leary, K. D. (1987). Prevalence and correlates of physical aggression during courtship. *Journal of Interpersonal Violence, 2,* 82–90.

Australian Bureau of Statistics. (2001). *Marriage and divorces, Australia.* Canberra, Australia: Author.

Avakame, E. F., & Fyfe, J. J. (2001). Differential police treatment of male-on-female spousal violence. *Violence against Women, 7,* 22–45.

Avery-Leaf, S., Cascardi, M., O'Leary, K. D., & Cano, A. (1997). Efficacy of a dating violence prevention program on attitudes justifying aggression. *Journal of Adolescent Health, 21,* 11–17.

Bandura, A. (1977). *Social learning theory.* Englewood Cliffs, NJ: Prentice-Hall.

Baucom, D. H., Sayers, S. L., & Sher, T. G. (1990). Supplementing behavioral marital therapy with cognitive restructuring and emotional expressiveness training: An outcome investigation. *Journal of Consulting and Clinical Psychology, 58,* 636–645.

Bergman, L. (1992). Dating violence among high school students. *Social Work, 37,* 21–27.

Bloom, B., & Hodges, W. W. (1981). The predicament of the newly separated. *Community Mental Health Journal, 17,* 277–293.

Bradbury, T. N. (1998). *The developmental course of marital dysfunction.* New York: Cambridge University Press.

Bradbury, T. N., & Fincham, F. D. (1991). A contextual model for advancing the study of marital interaction. In G. J. O. Fletcher & F. D. Fincham (Eds.), *Cognition in close relationships* (pp. 127–147). Hillsdale, NJ: Lawrence Erlbaum Associates.

Bradbury, T. N., & Lawrence, E. (1999). Physical aggression and the longitudinal course of newlywed marriage. In X. B. Arriaga & S. Oskamp (Eds.), *Violence in intimate relationships* (pp. 181–202). Thousand Oaks, CA: Sage.

Bryk, A. S., & Raudenbush, S. W. (1992). *Hierarchical linear models: Applications and data analysis methods.* Thousand Oaks, CA: Sage.

Burke, L. K., & Follingstad, D. R. (1999). Violence in lesbian and gay relationships: Theory, prevalence, and correlational factors. *Clinical Psychology Review, 19,* 487–512.

Burman, B., & Margolin, G. (1992). Analysis of the association between marital relationships and health problems: An interactional perspective. *Psychological Bulletin, 112,* 39–63.

Byrne, C. A., & Arias, I. (1997). Marital satisfaction and marital violence: Moderating effects of attributional processes. *Journal of Family Psychology, 11,* 188–195.

Byrne, C. A., Resnick, H. S., Kilpatrick, D. G., Best, C. L., & Saunders, B. E. (1999). The socioeconomic impact of interpersonal violence on women. *Journal of Consulting and Clinical Psychology, 67,* 362–366.

Caetano, R., Cunradi, C. B., Schafer, J., & Clark, C. L. (2000). Intimate partner violence and drinking patterns among White, Black, and Hispanic couples in the U.S. *Journal of Substance Abuse, 11,* 123–138.

Caetano, R., Nelson, S., & Cunradi, C. (2001). Intimate partner violence, dependence symptoms and social consequences from drinking among White, Black and Hispanic couples in the United States. *American Journal on Addictions, 10,* 60–69.

Capaldi, D. M., & Crosby, L. (1997). Observed and reported psychological and physical aggression in young, at-risk couples. S*ocial Development, 6,* 184–206.

Chase, K. A., O'Leary, K. D., & Heyman, R. E. (2001). Categorizing partner-violent men within the reactive-proactive typology model. *Journal of Consulting and Clinical Psychology, 69,* 567–572.

Christensen, A., & Heavey, C. L. (1990). Gender and social structure in the demand/withdraw pattern of marital conflict. *Journal of Personality and Social Psychology, 59,* 73–81.

Christopher, F. S., & Lloyd, S. A. (2000). Phsyical and sexual aggression in relationships. In C. Hendrick & S. S. Hendrick (Eds.), *Close relationships: A sourcebook* (pp. 331–343). Thousand Oaks, CA: Sage Publications, Inc.

Choice, P., & Lamke, L. K. (1999). Stay/leave decision-making processes in abusive dating relationships. *Personal Relationships, 6,* 351–367.

Coie, J. D., Watt, N. F., West, S. G., Hawkins, J. D., Asarnow, J. R., Markman, H. J., Ramey, S. L., Shure, M. B., & Long, B. (1993). The science of prevention: A conceptual framework and some directions for a national research program. *American Psychologist, 48,* 1013–1022.

Cruz, J. M. (2003). "Why doesn't he just leave?" Gay male domestic violence and the reasons victims stay. *Journal of Men's Studies, 3,* 309–323.

Cunradi, C. B., Caetano, R., & Schafer, J. (2002). Socioeconomic predictors of intimate partner violence among White, Black, and Hispanic couples in the United States. *Journal of Family Violence, 17,* 377–389.

DeMaris, A. (2000). Till discord do us part: The role of physical and verbal conflict in union disruption. *Journal of Marriage and the Family, 62,* 683–692.

DeMaris, A. (2001). The influence of intimate violence on transitions out of cohabitation. *Journal of Marriage and the Family, 63,* 235–246.

Dutton, M. A., Goodman, L. A, & Bennett, L. (2001). Court-involved battered women's responses to violence: The role of psychological, physical, and sexual abuse. In K. D. O'Leary & R. D. Maiuro (Eds.), *Psychological abuse in violent domestic relations* (pp. 177–195). New York: Springer.

Ehrensaft, M. K., & Vivian, D. (1996). Spouses' reasons for not reporting existing marital aggression as a marital problem. *Journal of Family Psychology, 10,* 443–453.

Ehrensaft, M. K., & Vivian, D. (1999). Is partner aggression related to appraisals of coercive control by a partner? *Journal of Family Violence, 14,* 251–266.

Elliot, D. S., Huizinga, D., & Morse, B. (1986). Self-reported violent offending: A descriptive analysis of juvenile violent offenders and their offending careers. *Journal of Interpersonal Violence, 1,* 472–514.

Feld, S. L., & Straus, M. A. (1990). Escalation and desistance from wife assault in marriage. In M. A. Straus & R. J. Gelles (Eds.), *Physical violence in American families: Risk factors and adaptation to violence in 8,145 families* (pp. 489–505). New Brunswick, NJ: Transaction.

Fiebert, M. S., & Gonzalez, D. M. (1997). College women who initiate assaults on their male partners and the reasons offered for such behavior. *Psychological Reports, 80,* 583–590.

Fincham, F. D. (1985). Attribution processes in distressed and nondistressed couples: 2. Responsibility for marital problems. *Journal of Abnormal Psychology, 94,* 183–190.

Fincham, F. D., Beach, S. R. H., & Bradbury, T. N. (1989). Marital distress, depression, and attributions: Is the marital distress-attribution association an artifact of depression? *Journal of Consulting and Clinical Psychology, 57,* 768–771.

Fincham, F. D., & Bradbury, T. N. (1992). Assessing attributions in marriage: The Relationship Attribution Measure. *Journal of Personality and Social Psychology, 62,* 457–468.

Follingstad, D. R., Brennan, A. F., Hause, E. S., Polek, D. S., & Rutledge, L. L. (1991). Factors moderating physical and psychological symptoms of battered women. *Journal of Family Violence, 6,* 81–95.

Follingstad, D. R., Rutledge, L. L., Berg, B. J., Hause, E. S., & Polek, D. S. (1990). The role of emotional abuse in physically abusive relationships. *Journal of Family Violence, 5,* 107–120.

Freedner, N., Freed, L. H., Yang, Y. W., & Austin, S. B. (2002). Dating violence among gay, lesbian, and bisexual adolescents: Results from a community survey. *Journal of Adolescent Health, 31,* 469–474.

Gelles, R. J. (1997). *Intimate violence in families* (3rd ed.). Thousand Oaks, CA: Sage.

Glenn, N. D., Nock, S., Waite, L., Doherty, W., Gottman, J. M., Markey, B., Galston, N. A., Markman, H. J., Popenoe, D., Rodriguez, G. G., Sawhill, I. V., Stanley, S. M., & Wallerstein, J. (2002). Why marriage matters: Twenty-one conclusions from the social sciences. *American Experiment Quarterly, 5,* 34–44.

Gondolf, E. W., Fisher, E., & McFerron, J. R. (1988). Racial differences among shelter residents: A comparison of Anglo, Black, and Hispanic battered women. *Journal of Family Violence, 3,* 39–51.

Halford, W. K., & Markman, H. J. (Eds.). (1997). *Clinical handbook of marriage and couples interventions.* Chichester, England: Wiley.

Hamberger, L. K., & Hastings, J. E. (1993). Personality correlates of men who batter and nonviolent men: Some continuities and discontinuities. *Journal of Family Violence, 6,* 131–147.

Heyman, R. E., O'Leary, K. D., & Jouriles, E. N. (1995). Alcohol and aggressive personality styles: Potentiators of serious physical aggression against wives? *Journal of Family Psychology, 9,* 44–57.

Hoffman, K. L., & Demo, D. H. (1994). Physical wife abuse in a non-Western society: An integrated theoretical approach. *Journal of Marriage and the Family, 56,* 131–146.

Holtzworth-Munroe, A., & Hutchinson, G. (1993). Attributing negative intent to wife behavior: The attributions of martially violent versus violent men. *Journal of Abnormal Psychology, 102,* 206–211.

Holtzworth-Munroe, A., Jacobson, N. S., Fehrenbach, P. A., & Fruzzetti, A. (1992). Violent married couples' attributions for violent and nonviolent self and partner behaviors. *Behavioral Assessment, 14,* 53–64.

Holtzworth-Munroe, A., & Stuart, G. (1994). Typologies of male batterers: Three subtypes and the differences among them. *Psychological Bulletin, 116,* 476–497.

Hotaling, G. T., & Sugarman, D. B. (1986). An analysis of risk markers in husband to wife violence: The current state of knowledge. *Violence and Victims, 1,* 101–124.

Jacobson, N. S. (1997, November). *Controversies in the treatment of domestic violence: Deriving clinical implications from basic research.* Paper presented at the 31st Annual Association for the Advancement of Behavior Therapy Conference, Miami Beach, FL.

Jacobson, N. S., & Gottman, J. M. (1998). *When men batter women.* New York: Simon and Schuster.

Jacobson, N. S., Gottman, J. M., Gortner, E., Berns, S., & Shortt, J. W. (1996). Psychological factors in the longitudinal course of battering: When do couples split up? When does abuse decrease? *Violence and Victims, 11,* 371–392.

Jacobson, N. S., Gottman, J. M., Waltz, J., Rushe, R., Babcock, J., & Hotzworth-Monroe, A. (1994). Affect, verbal content, and psychophysiology in the arguments of couples with a violent husband. *Journal of Consulting and Clinical Psychology, 62,* 982–988.

Jacobson, N. S., McDonald, D. W., Follette, W. C., & Berley, R. A. (1985). Attribution processes in distressed and nondistressed married couples. *Couples Therapy and Research, 9,* 33–50.

Jasinski, J. L. (2001). Physical violence among Anglo, African American, and Hispanic couples: Ethnic differences in persistence and cessation. *Violence and Victims, 16,* 479–490.

Jenkins, S. S., & Aube, J. (2002). Gender differences and gender-related constructs in dating aggression. *Personality and Social Psychology Bulletin, 28,* 1106–1118.

Johnson, M. P. (1995). Patriarchal terrorism and common couple violence: Two forms of violence against women. *Journal of Marriage and the Family, 57,* 283–294.

Johnson, M. P., & Ferraro, K. J. (2000). Research on domestic violence in the 1990s: Making distinctions. *Journal of Marriage and the Family, 62,* 948–963.

Karney, B. R., & Bradbury, T. N. (1995). The longitudinal course of marital quality and stability: A review of theory, methods, and research. *Psychological Bulletin, 118,* 3–34.

Karney, B. R., Bradbury, T. N., Fincham, F. D., & Sullivan, K. T. (1994). The role of negative affectivity in the association between attributions and marital satisfaction. *Journal of Personality and Social Psychology, 66,* 413–424.

Katz, J., Arias, I., Beach, S. R. H., Brody, G., & Roman, P. (1995). Excuses, excuses: Accounting for the effects of partner violence on marital satisfaction and stability. *Violence and Victims, 10,* 315–326.

Kingsbury, N. M., & Minda, R. B. (1988). An analysis of three expected intimate relationship states: Commitment, maintenance and termination. *Journal of Social and Personal Relationships, 5,* 405–422.

Kolbo, J. R., Blakely, E. H., & Engleman, D. (1996). Children who witness domestic violence: A review of empirical literature. *Journal of Interpersonal Violence, 11,* 281–293.

Koss, M. P., Goodman, L. A., Browne, A., Fitzgerald, L. F., Keita, G. P., & Russo, N. F. (1994). *No safe haven: Male violence against women at home, at work, and in the community.* Washington, DC: American Psychological Association.

Kurz, D. (1996). Separation, divorce, and woman abuse. *Violence Against Women, 2,* 63–81.

Larson, D., Sawyers, J. P., & Larson, S. S. (1995). *The costly consequences of divorce.* Rockville, MD: National Institute for Healthcare Research.

Lawrence, E., & Bradbury, T. N. (2001). Physical aggression and marital dysfunction: A longitudinal analysis. *Journal of Family Psychology, 15,* 135–154.

Lawrence, E., & Bradbury, T. N. (2005). *Trajectories of change in physical aggression and marital dysfunction.* Manuscript submitted for publication.

Leonard, K. E., & Roberts, L. J. (1998). Marital aggression, adjustment, and stability in the first year of marriage: Findings from the Buffalo Newlywed Study. In T.N. Bradbury (Ed.), *The developmental course of marital dysfunction* (pp. 44–73). New York: Cambridge University Press.

Lo, W., & Sporakowski, M. (1989). The continuation of violent dating relationships among college students. *Journal of College Student Development, 30,* 432–439.

Locke, H. J., & Wallace, K. M. (1959). Short marital adjustment and prediction tests: Their reliability and validity. *Journal of Marriage and Family Living, 21,* 251–255.

Margolin, G., John, R. S., & Gleberman, L. (1988). Affective responses to conflictual discussion in violent and nonviolent couples. *Journal of Consulting and Clinical Psychology, 56,* 24–33.

Markman, H. J., Renick, M. J., Floyd, F. J., Stanley, S. M., & Clements, M. (1993). Preventing marital distress through communication and conflict management training: A 4- and 5- year follow-up. *Journal of Consulting and Clinical Psychology, 61,* 70–77.

Markman, H. J., Stanley, S. M., & Blumberg, S. L. (1994). *Fighting for your marriage: Positive steps for preventing divorce and preserving a lasting love.* San Francisco: Jossey-Bass.

Marshall, L. L. (1994). Physical and psychological abuse. In W. R. Cupach & B. H. Spitzberg (Eds.), *The dark side of interpersonal communication* (pp. 281–311). Hillsdale, NJ: Lawrence Erlbaum Associates.

Marshall, L.L., Weston, R., & Honeycutt, T.C. (2000). Does men's positivity moderate or mediate the effects of their abuse on women's relationship quality? *Journal of Social and Personal Relationships, 17,* 660–675.

McDonald, P. (1995). *Families in Australia: A socio-demographic perspective.* Melbourne, Australia: Australian Institute of Family Studies.

Molidor, C. E. (1995). Gender differences of psychological abuse in high school dating relationships. *Child and Adolescent Social Work Journal, 12,* 119–134.

Murphy, C. M., & O'Leary, K. D. (1989). Psychological aggression predicts physical aggression in early marriage. *Journal of Consulting and Clinical Psychology, 57,* 579–582.

National Commission on the Causes and Prevention of Violence. (1969). *Report of the Media Task Force.* Washington, DC: Government Printing Office.

O'Keefe, N. K., Brockopp, K., & Chew, E. (1986). Teen dating violence. *Social Work, 31,* 465–468.

O'Leary, K. D. (1988). Physical aggression between spouses: A social learning theory perspective. In V. B. van Hasselt, R. L. Morrison, A. S. Bellack, & M. Hersen (Eds.), *Handbook of family violence* (pp. 31–55). New York: Plenum.

O'Leary, K. D., Barling, J., Arias, I., Rosenbaum, A., Malone, J., & Tyree, A. (1989). Prevalence and stability of marital aggression between spouses: A longitudinal analysis. *Journal of Consulting and Clinical Psychology, 57,* 263–268.

O'Leary, K. D., & Cascardi, M. (1998). Physical aggression in marriage: A developmental analysis. In T. N. Bradbury (Ed.), *The developmental course of marital dysfunction* (pp. 343–374). New York: Cambridge University Press.

O'Leary, K. D., & Jouriles, E. N. (1994). Psychological abuse between adult partners: Prevalence and impact on partners and children. In L. L'Abate (Ed.), *Handbook of developmental family psychology and psychopathology* (pp. 330–349). New York: Wiley.

O'Leary, K. D., Vivian, D., & Malone, J. (1992). Assessment of physical aggression against women in marriage: The need for multimodal assessment. *Behavioral Assessment, 14,* 5–14.

Olson, L. N., Fine, M. A., & Lloyd, S. A. (2005). A dialectical approach to theorizing about aggression between intimates. In V. Bengtson, A. Acock, K. Allen, P. Dilworth-Anderson, & D. Klein (Eds.), *Sourcebook of family theory and research: An integrative approach* (pp. 315–331). Newbury Park, CA: Sage.

Pan, H. S., Neidig, P. H., & O'Leary, K. D. (1994). Predicting mild and severe husband-to-wife physical aggression. *Journal of Consulting and Clinical Psychology, 62,* 975–981.

Quigley, B. M., & Leonard, K. E. (1996). Desistance of husband aggression in the early years of marriage. *Violence and Victims, 11,* 355–370.

Rennison, C., & Planty, M. (2003). Nonlethal intimate partner violence: Examining race, gender, and income patterns. *Violence and Victims, 18,* 433–443.

Riggs, D. S., O'Leary, K. D., & Breslin, F. C. (1990). Multiple correlates of physical aggression in dating couples. *Journal of Interpersonal Violence, 5,* 61–73.

Roberts, L. J. (2000). Fire and ice in marital communication: Hostile and distancing behaviors as predictors of marital distress. *Journal of Marriage and the Family, 62,* 693–707.

Roscoe, B., & Benaske, N. (1985). Courtship violence experienced by abused wives: Similarities in patterns of abuse. *Family Relations, 34,* 419–424.

Rosen, L. N., Parmley, A. M., Knudson, K. H., & Fancher, P. (2002). Gender differences in the experience of intimate partner violence among active duty U.S. Army soldiers. *Military Medicine, 167,* 959–963.

Rosenfeld, B. D. (1992). Court-ordered treatments of spouse abuse. *Clinical Psychology Review, 12,* 205–226.

Saltzman, L. E., Fanslow, J. L., McMahon, P. M., & Shelley, G. A. (1999). *Intimate partner violence surveillance uniform definitions and recommended data elements.* Atlanta, GA: Centers for Disease Control and Prevention, National Center for Injury Prevention and Control.

Schumacher, J. A., Feldbau-Kohn, S., Slep, A. M., & Heyman, R. E. (2001). Risk factors for male-to-female partner physical abuse. *Aggression and Violent Behavior, 6,* 281–352.

Smith, D. A., Vivian, D., & O'Leary, K. D. (1990). Longitudinal prediction of marital discord from premarital expressions of affect. *Journal of Consulting and Clinical Psychology, 58,* 790–798.

Smith, J. P., & Williams, J. (1992). From abusive household to dating violence. *Journal of Family Violence, 7,* 153–165.

Stets, J. E. (1990). Verbal and physical aggression in marriage. *Journal of Marriage and the Family, 52,* 501–514.

Stith, S. M., Rosen, K. H., Middleton, K. A., Busch, A. L., Lundeberg, K., & Carlton, R. P. (2000). The intergenerational transmission of spouse abuse: A meta-analysis. *Journal of Marriage and the Family, 62,* 640–654.

Straight, E. S., Harper, F. W. K., & Arias, I. (2003). The impact of partner psychological abuse on health behaviors and health status in college women. *Journal of Interpersonal Violence, 18,* 1035–1054.

Straus, M. A. (1979). Measuring intrafamily conflict and violence: The Conflict Tactics (CT) Scales. *Journal of Marriage and the Family, 41,* 75–88.

Straus, M. A. (1999). The controversy over domestic violence by women: A methodological, theoretical, and sociology of science analysis. In X. B. Arriaga & S. Oskamp (Eds.), *Violence in intimate relationships* (pp. 17–44). Thousand Oaks, CA: Sage.

Straus, M. A., Hamby, S. L., Boney-McCoy, S., & Sugarman, D. B. (1996). The revised Conflict Tactics Scales (CTS2): Development and preliminary psychometric data. *Journal of Family Issues, 17,* 283–316.

Straus, M. A., Kaufman Kantor, G., & Moore, D. W. (1997). Change in cultural norms approving marital violence: From 1968 to 1994. In G. Kaufman Kantor & J. L. Jasinski (Eds.), *Out of the darkness: Contemporary perspectives on family violence* (pp. 3–16). Thousand Oaks, CA: Sage.

Straus, M. A., & Sweet, S. (1992). Verbal/symbolic aggression in couples: Incidence rates and relationships to personal characteristics. *Journal of Marriage and the Family, 54,* 346–357.

Street, A. E., & Arias, I. (2001). Psychological abuse and posttraumatic stress disorder in battered women: Examining the roles of shame and guilt. *Violence and Victims, 16,* 65–78.

Truman-Schram, D. M., Cann, A., Calhoun, L., & Vanwallendael, L. (2000). Leaving an abusive dating relationship: An investment model comparison of women who stay versus women who leave. *Journal of Social and Clinical Psychology, 19,* 161–183.

United States Census Bureau. (2002). *Number, timing, and duration of marriages and divorces: 1996.* Washington, DC: Author.

Walker, L. E. (2000). *The battered woman syndrome.* New York: Springer.

Weinbaum, Z., Stratton, T. L., Chavez, G., Motylewski-Link, C., Barrera, N., Courtney, J. G., & California Department of Health Services Women's Health Survey Group. (2001). Female victims of intimate partner physical domestic violence (IPP-DV), California, 1998. *American Journal of Preventive Medicine, 21,* 313–319.

Weiss, R. L., & Heyman, R. E. (1997). A clinical-research overview of couples interactions. In W. K. Halford & H. J. Markman (Eds.), *Clinical handbook of marriage and couples interventions* (pp. 13–41). New York: Wiley.

Widom, C. S. (1989). Does violence beget violence? A critical examination of the literature. *Psychological Bulletin, 106,* 3–28.

Woffordt, S., Mihalic, D. E., & Menard, S. (1994). Continuities in marital violence. *Journal of Family Violence, 9,* 195–225.

Yllo, K., & Straus, M. A. (1981). Interpersonal violence among married and cohabiting couples. *Family Relations, 30,* 339–347.

IV

Consequences of Divorce and Relationship Dissolution

15

The Kids Are Alright (at Least, Most of Them): Links Between Divorce and Dissolution and Child Well-Being

Bonnie L. Barber
Murdoch University

David H. Demo
University of North Carolina at Greensboro

One week after my 16th birthday, over family supper, my parents told my brother, my sister and me that they were getting a divorce. This night would prove to have an amazing impact on the rest of my life. The last 4 years of my life have been a confusing, painful, and intense experience. (22-year-old woman's account of her parents' divorce; reported in Harvey & Fine, 2004, p. 44)

I have such a large family since the divorce. I can't imagine my life without all of them. I'm really glad I got to know and be around people who love me! (Adult's account of her parent's divorce; reported in Ahrons, 2004, p. 44)

Prompted in part by significant increases in the divorce rate in the 1960s and 1970s (and high but generally stable divorce rates since then), researchers across several disciplines have been energetic in examining the antecedents, correlates, and consequences of divorce. Amato's (2000) review documented that more than 9,200 studies examining divorce were published in the 1990s alone. The importance of conducting research that identifies consequences of divorce for children and adolescents is amplified by societal concerns for the well-being of children and by social policies and public expenditures intended to benefit children's health and well-being. To the degree that researchers are able to document the nature, magnitude, and sources of effects on children attributable to parental divorce, prevention and intervention programs can be designed to ameliorate child well-being.

Research on the effects of parental divorce for children has evolved from an initial emphasis on simple cross-sectional comparisons of children's well-being across two or more family types to more recent, more complex, and more sophisticated examinations of children's well-being prior to, during, and in the years following parental divorce. In this chapter, we describe four tiers characterizing research on the consequences of divorce for children and adolescents. We believe that research in this area has evolved and improved significantly over the past few decades, and we believe there are four clearly identifiable foci that have guided work on children's adjustment to divorce. However, we recognize the inherent limitations in any temporal classification scheme and thus refer to four *tiers* of research. It is perhaps ironic that, like a wedding cake, the tiers vary in size, with Tier 1 forming a huge foundation, Tiers 2 and 3 declining in size, and Tier 4 being by far the smallest. Tier 1 research concentrates on mean differences in children's well-being across family types, most commonly involving comparisons of children in first-marriage families with their peers in divorced families. Although some studies employ samples of children who live in single-parent families for reasons other than parental divorce (e.g., nonmarital childbearing, separation, death), far less is known about the consequences for children of the latter events because they have received relatively little attention. Further, studies using broader definitions of single-parent families typically rely on small, nonrepresentative samples, or they focus on comparisons between these families and two-parent families instead of distinguishing among types of single-parent families (e.g., McLanahan & Sandefur, 1994). Tier 2 research extends analysis to family processes and other predictor variables associated with children's adjustment to parental divorce. A more recent and still emerging body of work, which we call Tier 3, relies largely on within-group research designs and focuses on illustrating and explaining the substantial variability characterizing children's well-being both prior to and following parental divorce. Finally, Tier 4 work identifies and evaluates intervention strategies for children who have experienced their parents' divorce. We believe that one advantage of conceptualizing divorce research in terms of tiers, rather than using a temporal or multistage model, is that the former framework recognizes that some early studies focused on within-group variability or intervention, whereas many recent studies continue to focus on measures of central tendency across groups (Demo & Cox, 2000).

This chapter has several objectives. First, we summarize and describe the existing evidence for differences in adjustment between children in first-marriage families and their counterparts in divorced or separated families. In doing so, we attempt to cite and discuss representative and methodologically sound studies, but we do not attempt to be exhaustive or to repeat earlier, excellent reviews of this literature (e.g., see Amato, 2000; Emery, 1999). Second, we present research evidence for family processes that explain adjustment differences between divorced and first-marriage families, and factors that moderate divorce effects. Third, we discuss the processes and attributes that predict differences in child adjustment within the population of divorced families. Finally, we consider the use of preventive interventions guided by this research base on facilitative or undermining mechanisms, especially as such programs provide an experimental test of the correlational hypotheses derived from survey data.

DEMOGRAPHIC CONTEXT

Over the past 40 years, families in Western nations have changed considerably, as divorce and remarriage have become common experiences. Although the majority of children in the United States, Canada, Australia, United Kingdom, and New Zealand live with two parents, a growing proportion live with single parents. Between 1970 and 1999, the proportion of U.S. children living in two-parent households decreased from 85% to 68%, and by 1999, 23% of children lived with their mother only and 4% lived with their father only (U.S. Department of Health and Human Services, 2000). Single parents were more likely to be continuously single (40% of single mothers and 33% of single fathers) or divorced (34% and 44%) than widowed (4% and 4%) or separated (21% and 18%; U.S. Census Bureau, 2001). Single parenting has also increased in Canada, with almost one in five Canadian children living with a single parent in

1996. Divorce and separation account for an increasing proportion of single-parent households in Canada (roughly one third of single parents were divorced in 1996, and roughly one fifth were separated; Statistics Canada, 1997). Australian trends moved in the same direction, with the proportion of children in single-parent families increasing steadily from 12% in 1989 to 18% in 1997 (Kilmartin, 1997). Similarly, in the United Kingdom and New Zealand, the prevalence of single-parent families among parenting households increased from 7% in 1971 to 18% in 1991 in the United Kingdom and from 9% in 1976 to 19% in 1991 in New Zealand (Ringen, 1997; Shirley, Koopman-Boyden, Pool, & St. John, 1997).

Although divorce and single-parent families have been widely studied, and although many divorced adults and their children live in single-parent families for some period of time, it is important to recognize that divorce is a dynamic *process* that unfolds across the life course and, as such, is distinguishable from single-parent (or other) *family structures*. For example, continuously single adults and their children live in single-parent families without ever experiencing marriage or divorce. Similarly, children and adults live in a multitude of diverse and fluid postdivorce living arrangements that do not constitute single-parent families, such as cohabiting couples, childless adults, stepfamilies, and households headed by nonmarried adults, grandparents, or other relatives. Thus, an important caveat in reviewing research that relies on cross-sectional comparisons of children and adults living in different family structures (e.g., single-parent and two-parent families) is that such comparisons typically provide limited information on (a) family processes and individual adjustment prior to family disruption, (b) family processes and individual adjustment trajectories during and following disruption, and (c) how individuals and families respond over longer periods of time to changes in family composition, family relationships, and family resources (Demo, Aquilino, & Fine, 2005).

FIRST TIER: CHILDREN'S POSTDIVORCE ADJUSTMENT COMPARED WITH FIRST-MARRIAGE FAMILIES

In examining children's adjustment, researchers have devoted far more attention to children's initial adaptations to change than to their long-term adjustment. The latter is more difficult, time consuming, and expensive to study, because it is a product of the predivorce family, the transition process, and the subsequent family interactions. In addition, the literature on the effects of divorce and dissolution has primarily relied on the deficit family model, a perspective that assumes that deviations from married status will produce difficulties in adjustment (Barber & Eccles, 1992; Ganong & Coleman, 1994). However, literature reviews and meta-analyses of research conducted in the United States have consistently reported that, on average, parental divorce and remarriage have only a small negative impact on the well-being of children (Amato, 1994, 2000; Amato & Keith, 1991; Demo & Cox, 2000; Emery, 1999). Rodgers and Pryor's (1998) review of research conducted in the United Kingdom, Australia, and New Zealand corroborates this conclusion. An important limitation of these bodies of work is that, with few exceptions, the accumulated evidence is based on predominantly white, middle-class samples (Amato, 2000; Demo & Cox).

Divorce has been implicated in several areas of child and adolescent maladjustment, including social, emotional, behavioral, and academic problems. Negative effects attributed to divorce are most common around the period of the divorce, and many children and families recover from the initial distress and resume normal functioning within a few years (Emery, 1999; Hetherington & Kelly, 2002). However, many adolescents in divorced families remain at a disadvantage years after the divorce when compared with their peers in two-parent families, particularly in the areas of academic success, externalizing, internalizing, self-processes, and sexuality (Simons & Associates, 1996; Hetherington & Kelly). We briefly examine each of these domains.

Academic Achievement and Educational Attainment

Divorce has been linked to lower adolescent cognitive and scholastic performance, less attachment to school, decreased high school and college completion, and higher dropout rates (Biblarz & Gottainer, 2000; Demo & Acock, 1996; Hetherington et al., 1992; Simons & Associates, 1996; Teachman, Paasch, & Carver, 1996; Zimiles & Lee, 1991). Although scholastic performance differences between divorced and two-parent family groups are usually small and may decrease over time, they consistently favor children and adolescents in first-marriage families (for reviews, see Amato & Keith, 1991; Emery, 1999). The long-term implications of even small declines in school achievement and standardized test scores cannot be ignored, as decrements in achievement can contribute to the reduced educational attainment experienced by children in divorced families.

Conduct Problems (Externalizing)

Children and adolescents from divorced families are more likely to engage in externalizing, aggressive, noncompliant, and deviant behavior than children in first-marriage families (for reviews, see Amato & Keith, 1991; Emery, 1999). Hetherington's early work indicated that these behavioral differences were evident in childhood (Hetherington, Cox, & Cox, 1979), and those findings have been replicated in numerous subsequent studies (Healy, Stewart, & Copeland, 1993; Stolberg & Anker, 1983; Wyman, Cowen, Hightower, & Pedro-Carroll, 1985). More problem behavior and higher levels of delinquency and substance use have also been observed among adolescents from divorced families compared with those in first-marriage families (Doherty & Needle, 1991; Dornbusch et al., 1985; Kalter, Riemer, Brickman, & Chen, 1985; Kinard & Reinherz, 1984; Peterson & Zill, 1986; Simons & Associates, 1996).

Psychological Adjustment

Compared with adolescents in first-marriage families, increased depression and worse socioemotional adjustment are found among adolescents in divorced families (Demo & Acock, 1996; Kurdek, Fine, & Sinclair, 1994; Simons & Associates, 1996). However, this disadvantage does not generalize to adolescents living in continuously single-parent families (Demo & Acock). Long-term negative consequences of divorce for psychological adjustment have also been identified in adulthood (Amato, 2000; Chase-Lansdale, Cherlin, & Kiernan, 1995; Furstenberg & Teitler, 1994). Unlike aggressive behavior, which seems to be more common in boys after divorce, depression is more common among girls (Emery, 1999). Thus, those areas in which boys and girls differ (independent of parental divorce) are also the areas in which they experience more pronounced effects of the divorce (Allison & Furstenberg, 1989).

Self-Processes

A great deal of research has focused on competency beliefs and self-esteem. In some studies, parental divorce and father absence have been associated with lower self-esteem and feelings of competence in children and adolescents, especially in the short term (Long, Forehand,

Fauber, & Brody, 1987; Parish & Dostal, 1980; Smith, 1990). Other studies, however, fail to find such differences for children (Berg & Kelly, 1979; Kinard & Reinherz, 1984), adolescents (Clark & Barber, 1994), college students (Long, 1986), or adults (Amato, 1988). In their meta-analysis comparing divorced and continuously married families, Amato and Keith (1991) found a significant (but weak) negative effect of divorce on self-concept across 34 samples of children and adolescents. Thus, the differences in self-esteem between children in divorced and first-marriage families are not consistent, and, when there are differences, they decrease over time.

Intimate Relationships and Sexual Behavior

One area of concern to those who study the effects of divorce on children is the area of intergenerational transmission of divorce and relationship difficulties. Children from divorced families are more likely themselves to experience marital dissolution (Amato, 1999; Amato & Booth, 1997; Bumpass, Martin, & Sweet, 1991; Glenn & Kramer, 1987). Although this connection and possible mechanisms have been reviewed elsewhere (e.g., Emery, 1999), less has been written about the connections between divorce and adolescent sexual behavior.

Previous research has provided strong evidence of a link between family structure and adolescent sexual behavior. A number of scholars have demonstrated that the absence of a biological father in the home is an important risk factor for early sexual activity (Barber & Meschke, 2001; Billy, Brewster, & Grady, 1994; Ellis et al., 2003; Flewelling & Bauman, 1990; Hogan & Kitagawa, 1985; Ku, Sonenstein, & Pleck, 1993; Meschke, Zweig, Barber, & Eccles, 2000; Moore, Morrison, & Glei, 1995; Simons & Associates, 1996). This finding is especially true for girls. For example, Ellis et al. found a very strong relationship between early father absence and early sexual onset among girls (first intercourse before the age of 16 years). This relationship held across numerous controls for characteristics of the girls and their parents. The early onset of first intercourse has been related primarily to living with a single parent, but also moderately related to living with stepparents (Day, 1992; Thorton & Camburn, 1987; Upchurch, Aneschensel, Sucoff, & Levy-Storms, 1999). Unfortunately, research suggests that father absence is associated not only with earlier sexual debut but also with riskier sexual practices and teen pregnancy (Biglan, Metzler, Wirt, & Ary, 1990; Ellis et al., Russell, 2002). Just how big is the difference in age at first intercourse by family structure? Girls in father-present households have intercourse for the first time more than 1 year later than those in early father-absent households (Barber & Meschke). Girls in late father-absent households fall in between for timing of first intercourse. However, differences in the timing of first intercourse and teen pregnancy are substantially reduced or disappear when income, parental occupation, affiliation with deviant peers, mothers' permissive sexual attitudes, inept parenting, and measures of other theoretically relevant family processes are controlled (McLanahan & Sandefur, 1994; Simons & Associates; Smith, 1990; Zimiles & Lee, 1991).

SECOND TIER: PROCESSES THAT MAY EXPLAIN WHY SOME CHILDREN DO WELL WHEN OTHERS SUFFER

One reason for consistent but the generally weak associations between family context and developmental outcomes may be the research focus on family type rather than processes within families. Focus on family context or family process alone is incomplete. Family structure and processes are interconnected, as family structures create opportunities for certain kinds of interactions and decrease the likelihood of others (Amato, 1994). Because family types differ in their characteristic processes, they may offer different strengths and weaknesses for certain developmental outcomes (Barber & Eccles, 1992). As a result of structural and systemic differences, individuals in specific family structures may be more or less likely to experience certain processes, and these processes, in turn, may be linked to psychosocial adjustment. Tier 2 research has identified numerous family processes that serve as mediators of family structure effects on child and adolescent adjustment and behavior (e.g., Amato, 1993; Demo & Acock, 1996; Emery, 1999; Hetherington et al., 1992; Simons & Associates, 1996). Here, we review the potential mediating processes that have received the most empirical attention, and we offer a few promising directions for future research. First, we discuss mediating mechanisms that have received abundant attention and that are strongly supported by the accumulated evidence: financial resources, interparental conflict, residential and nonresidential parenting, and parental psychological adjustment. We then discuss a number of mediators for which there is substantial but not incontrovertible support—mechanisms that therefore require further attention. These potential mediators include parental role modeling, parental interpretations of reality, parental involvement in and structuring of adolescent activities, adolescent intrapersonal resources, and pubertal timing.

STRONGLY SUPPORTED MEDIATORS

Financial Resources

Divorce often leads to a dramatic decline in the economic situation of mothers and children, whereas divorced fathers often enjoy an improved financial situation (see Braver, Shapiro, & Goodman, chapter 16, this volume; Holden & Smock, 1991; Peterson, 1996). This reduction in family financial resources represents an important influence on the adjustment of children in divorced single-mother families, accounting for some of the decline in children's well-being (Barber & Eccles, 1992). Indeed, many studies of the effects of divorce on children have found that, if socioeconomic resources are controlled, the gap between children from divorced and first-marriage families is reduced sharply, often becoming nonsignificant (Carlson & Corcoran, 2001; Emery, 1999; McLanahan & Sandefur, 1994).

Interparental Conflict

High levels of conflict and hostility between parents frequently precede and accompany divorce, and these processes have consistently been related to internalizing problems such as anxiety disorders, withdrawal, low self-esteem, and depression in children and adolescents (Buchanan, Maccoby, & Dornbusch, 1996; Buehler et al., 1997; Davies & Cummings, 1994; Demo & Acock, 1988, 1996; Emery, 1999; Grych & Fincham, 1990; Simons & Associates, 1996). Interparental conflict has also been associated with externalizing problems such as aggression and conduct problems (Cummings, Goeke-Morey, & Papp, 2004; Davies & Cummings; Gerard & Buehler, 1999), as well as children's poorer school performance, lower social competence with peers, concerns about emotional security, and self-perceptions of lower levels of intelligence and popularity (Davies & Cummings, Long et al., 1987; McCombs & Forehand, 1989).

Many children experience harmful interparental conflict throughout sustained periods of their childhood and adolescence. Ahrons (2004) reports that one third of her sample of children of divorce lived in predivorce families characterized by frequent fighting between their parents. Sometimes, divorce can provide relief from that conflict. In fact, children raised in conflictual families with intact marriages can experience poorer adjustment than those in divorced families, particularly when divorce provides a reduction in the interparental conflict (Amato, 1993; Dunlop & Burns, 1988). However, divorce does not always reduce conflict, as research indicates there can be continuing tensions and heightened conflict during the first couple of years postseparation and postdivorce. Ahrons found that 60% of couples were angry and highly conflictual during the first few years following divorce, and Hetherington and Kelly (2002) found that 20% to 25% of couples were still highly conflicted 6 years after divorce. When divorce does not provide relief from the conflict, evidence suggests that continued conflict between parents postdivorce has deleterious consequences for children and adolescents; children can be drawn into the conflict, feel caught between parents, and experience loyalty conflicts (Buchanan et al., 1996; Hetherington & Kelly). As explored in greater detail in our subsequent discussion of Tier 3 research, many children's postdivorce behavior and achievement problems reflect developmental continuity of problems that predated the divorce. Interparental conflict prior to and after divorce is one of many possible contributing factors to children's predisruption and postdisruption maladjustment.

Residential Parenting: Decision Making, Support, Discipline, and Control

Across family types, child and adolescent development is enhanced by a warm, supportive relationship with a parent, accompanied by standards for mature behavior and consistent discipline (Grotevant, 1998). In single-parent families, the relationship with the residential parent is crucial, because there is only one parent in the household and that parent's connection to the adolescent may have more impact than when there is also daily input from a second parent. Processes such as parental control, discipline, and decision making are related to family structure, and these processes can influence outcomes posited to be more negative in divorced families, such as school performance, problem behavior, and maladjustment (Forgatch, Patterson, & Skinner, 1988; Patterson, 1986), or those considered to be more positive, such as independence and self-esteem (Weiss, 1979).

In two-parent families, there are many more opportunities for parents to collaborate on and reinforce each other's decisions about rules and discipline. Divorced-mother families experience a shift in the authority structure. Responsibilities are redistributed, and this change may lead to greater opportunities for the adolescent to participate in family decision making. In support of this idea, adolescents in divorced-mother families report experiencing less parental control and greater opportunity for involvement in several areas of decision making (Baumrind, 1989; Dornbusch et al., 1985; Flanagan, 1986; Hetherington, 1989; Steinberg, 1987).

This greater responsibility and input into decision making may have negative consequences, depending on its timing, its magnitude, and its embeddedness in a detached or authoritative family climate. If it is too early for the adolescent's level of maturity, and if it occurs in a nonauthoritative family environment, increased independence in divorced-mother families may lead to negative outcomes because it puts too much pressure on the child, or because it can be associated with inadequate monitoring, increased susceptibility to peer pressure, and tendencies toward delinquent behavior (Dornbusch et al., 1985; Newcomer & Udry, 1987; Whitbeck Simons, & Goldberg; 1996). If the increase in adult-like responsibility and decrease in parental control are timed appropriately and embedded in a warm, authoritative family environment, they can have positive consequences associated with increased self-esteem, confidence, and a sense of contribution to the family (Barber, 1995).

Decision making and parental control may be especially important during adolescence, when such processes normally are being renegotiated by parents and children. Parents who are warm, democratic, and demanding—a constellation described as *authoritative parenting*—may be more adept at negotiating with their adolescents a more independent role, thereby helping them to become self-reliant, behaviorally and academically competent, and mentally healthy young adults (Baumrind, 1991; Steinberg, 1990; Steinberg, Mounts, Lamborn, & Dornbusch, 1991). However, this does not imply that there is no need for limits and control. Depending on the outcome studied and the family context, authoritative parenting may be differentially beneficial. For example, there is evidence that authoritative parenting may be significantly more beneficial for adolescents in White, two-parent families than for those in African American and Hispanic middle class, single-parent families, or in Asian American, middle-class, two-parent families (Avenevoli, Sessa, & Steinberg, 1999). In fact, authoritativeness was related to *more* psychological distress and higher substance use in African American middle class, two-parent families (Avenevoli et al., 1999). With respect to authoritarian control, authoritarian parenting was positively related to grade point average in African American, single-parent, middle-class families, and predicted lower delinquency in African American, two-parent working class families (Avenevoli et al.).

Control may be especially important in explaining family structure differences in sexual debut. Parental control and regulation have been consistently related to adolescent sexual behavior (see the review by Miller, 1998). Some research suggests that growing up in a single-parent household may affect the sexual behavior of girls more than that of boys because girls' sexual behavior may be more subject to parents' control, and parental controls are lower in single-mother families (Dornbusch et al., 1985; Newcomer and Udry, 1987; Thornton, 1991). Certainly, research generally shows that higher levels of parental monitoring predict later onset of first sexual intercourse for both boys and girls (Capaldi, Crosby, & Stoolmiller, 1996; Danziger, 1995; Ku et al., 1993; Meschke, Bartholomae, & Zentall, 2000), fewer partners, and use of contraception (Luster & Small, 1994; Miller, Forehand, & Kotchick, 1999; Rodgers, 1999). This relation has been demonstrated not only for White adolescents, but also for African American and Hispanic youth (Hogan & Kitagawa, 1985; Hovell et al., 1994; Meschke et al., 2000; Miller et al.). The implications for divorced families are clear. Researchers have argued that the heightened risk of precocious sexual activity in single-mother families is a function of a decrease in the number of parents available to monitor the children (Wu & Martinson, 1993), and less opportunity for monitoring because residential parents (mostly mothers) typically work outside the home (Thornton). However, Hogan and Kitagawa found that, although parental supervision was an important predictor of sexual behavior, living in a mother-headed household was an important influence even when supervision was taken into account.

Nonresidential Father Involvement

We focus here on the father as the nonresidential parent because fathers represent the vast majority of nonresidential parents (Bray & Depner, 1993). Contact between fathers and children is a frequently studied indicator of the nature of the relationship, with a substantial proportion of children having little or no contact after the divorce (King, 1994; Seltzer, 1991). Examining a nationally representative sample of families with adolescents, King, Harris, and Heard (2004) found that overall levels of nonresident father involvement were similar across Hispanic, non-Hispanic White, non-Hispanic Black, and non-Hispanic Asian families. However, specific dimensions of involvement (talking, working on a project, engaging in religious activities) varied considerably across groups, and more negative consequences of family disruption were observed for Whites than for Black or Hispanic youth.

Despite the clear and substantial reduction in the quantity of contact with fathers after divorce, it does not appear that amount of contact is a primary mediator of divorce effects. The data are mixed concerning whether contact has positive or negative effects on children (Amato, 1993), with some studies finding positive effects, some negative, and some no association with children's well-being. In contrast to the uncertainty about contact effects, there is a clear positive impact of father's economic contribution by means of child support on the academic success and externalizing problems of children (Amato & Gilbreth, 1999). Furthermore, examining more substantive aspects of nonresidential fathers' parenting and their relationships with their children, Amato and Gilbreth's meta-analysis showed that aspects of authoritative parenting (closeness, advice, monitoring, noncoercive discipline) predicted higher academic achievement and fewer externalizing and internalizing problems among children.

Affective Climate and Parental Psychological Resources

The stressors associated with divorce may decrease parental adjustment, thus impairing ability to parent effectively. Divorced mothers report higher levels of depression, which in turn can be damaging to children's adjustment (Carlson & Corcoran, 2001; Demo & Acock, 1996; Simons & Associates, 1996). Amato's review (1993) indicated that children's adjustment after divorce was positively related to their custodial parent's adjustment, but that given methodological issues and direction of effect questions, support for the parent adjustment perspective is somewhat ambiguous. After divorce, children are especially likely to need emotional support, and in the face of socioemotional and economic stress, parents are especially unlikely to be able to provide it (Lamb, 1999). In support of such a cascade model, Degarmo and Forgatch (1999) found that chronically distressed divorced mothers had higher levels of confidant (friend, family member, or partner) negativity, and received less confidant support, which subsequently predicted poorer parenting practices. Effective parenting requires both parenting skills and self-beliefs of efficacy (Bandura, 1994). Because parental mental health problems and low sense of parenting efficacy have been found to undermine effective parenting behaviors (Furstenberg, Cook, Eccles, Elder, & Sameroff, 1999), single parents' lower sense of parenting efficacy and higher levels of depressed mood are likely mechanisms linking divorce and less positive parenting strategies.

POSSIBLE MEDIATORS

Parental Role Modeling

Parents may influence their children's attitudes toward various activities through role modeling (e.g., by the activities they engage in and by the messages they communicate regarding their own values and preferences). Some researchers have speculated that mothers who are dating provide role modeling of romantic and sexual interests and activities (Miller & Moore, 1990; Mott, Fondell, Hu, Kowaleski-Jones, & Menaghan, 1996; Whitbeck et al., 1996). If they date and participate in sexual relationships, single mothers convey a message about the value they place on sexual behavior and provide an example of how to interact with a partner. Through processes associated with social learning theory, such modeling could increase adolescents' motivation to be sexually active themselves (Bandura, 1986). These influences likely change as adolescents get older and begin to make important lifestyle decisions. These effects also likely depend on the quality of the parent–child relationship.

Data on stepfamilies support the idea that maternal repartnering may transmit messages regarding mothers' valuation of sexual behavior. Adolescents in remarried families report earlier sexual activities than those in first-marriage families (Flewelling & Bauman, 1990; Hogan, Sun, & Cornwell, 2000; Upchurch et al., 1999). In support of a social learning explanation, Thornton and Camburn (1987) found that adolescents in remarried families have more accepting attitudes toward sex, perceive their mothers as having more accepting attitudes regarding sex, and are more sexually active than children of nonremarried divorced parents.

Parental Interpretations of Reality

Parents can influence the ontogeny of adolescents' values and choices through the messages they provide regarding their view of their adolescents' world and experience (see Alexander & Entwisle, 1988; Eccles, Lord, Roeser, Barber, & Jozefowicz, 1997; Goodnow & Collins, 1990; Phillips, 1987). Parents help their adolescents to form an impression of their own potential achievement and values through communication (whether direct or indirect) of their beliefs about their adolescents' abilities and expectations for their conduct. One mechanism that may place children at risk is lowered maternal expectations for behavior and achievement. Parental expectations have been shown to be important predictors of children's academic performance (Parsons, Adler, & Kaczala, 1982). The beliefs that a mother holds about a child's ability and the accompanying expectations for that child's future success or failure in different domains could be important mediators of family structure effects. For example, divorced mothers have been found to have lower expectations for their children's school performance as well as satisfaction with lower school grades. Reduced expectancies such as these can play a mediating role between divorce and adolescents' lower achievement outcomes, but more research is needed to elucidate this connection (Barber, 1995).

Parental Structuring of Adolescent Experiences

Parents structure adolescents' experiences in a variety of ways that should impact preferences and choices (e.g., Eccles et al., 1997). Parents are key facilitators of activities (Schader, 2002) through their provision of specific experiences in and out of the home. This can include involvement in sports or other activities with their children; buying equipment, instruments, or materials; and arranging for their children's participation in clubs or activities. Family characteristics, including parental behaviors and attitudes (e.g., opportunity provision, involvement, and encouragement), as well as social class, have been shown to predict initiation and continuity of participation in youth development activities (Fletcher, Elder, & Mekos, 2000).

Divorced mothers, generally having fewer financial resources and more demands on their time, are less able to provide their children with the resources needed for participation in constructive activities. Single mothers may also be more likely to need the after-school help of their children to care for younger siblings or prepare meals. There has been little research on this topic, but there is evidence that youth from married families are more likely to participate in sports (Videon, 2002). Because youth development activities target not only adolescents' skills but also their self-beliefs and future aspirations (Moore & Brooks-Gunn, 2003), parental encouragement of such involvement may enhance children's development. Given the substantial evidence that participation in community and extracurricular activities is linked to better school achievement, higher educational attainment, lower levels of risk behavior, and better psychological adjustment (e.g., Barber, Eccles, & Stone, 2001; Mahoney & Cairns, 1997; Marsh & Kleitman, 2003), we find that parental provision of such opportunities is a mediator that deserves further study.

Adolescent Intrapersonal Resources

Differences in self-efficacy between divorced and first-marriage families are not limited to mothers, as children in divorced families also have been shown to have lower efficacy than those with married parents (Barber, 2003). Sandler and his colleagues have identified a number of intrapersonal factors that predict adolescent adjustment in divorced families, including active and avoidant coping, self-regulation, coping efficacy, cognitive appraisal biases, and fear of abandonment (e.g., Lengua & Sandler, 1996; Mazur, Wolchik, Virdin, Sandler, & West, 1999; Sandler, Tein, Mehta, Wolchik, & Ayers, 2000; Sandler, Tein & West, 1994; Wolchik, Tein, Sandler, & Doyle, 2002). Kurdek (1988) also found that generalized feelings of mastery and control were related to positive divorce adjustment. Other intrapersonal characteristics have been found to relate to adolescent adjustment in divorced families, including specific competencies such as divorce-related problem-solving skills and dimensions of emotional well-being including feeling stigmatized and isolated (Pedro-Carroll & Cowen, 1985).

Pubertal Timing

Some scholars have applied a biopsychosocial approach to explaining the externalizing behaviors and early onset of sexual intercourse of children in divorced families. Early pubertal timing has received attention as a mediator, given the consistent finding across a number of studies that girls experience accelerated pubertal development in single-mother families, particularly those in which the father is absent from an early age (Ellis, 2004; Ellis, McFadyen-Ketchum, Dodge, Pettit, & Bates, 1999; Jones, Leeton, McLeod, & Wood, 1972; Surbey, 1990). Expanding on the previous work of Draper and Harpending (1982), Belsky, Steinberg, and Draper (1991) articulated a theory for a potential hastening effect of stress on pubertal timing. They suggested that high levels of socioemotional stressors, triggered by such conditions as economic deprivation, marital discord, and psychological distress, especially in young children, would accelerate pubertal development. Certainly, many divorcing families are replete with such stressors. Earlier pubertal timing would facilitate leaving the stressful and uncertain environment sooner. In other words, early pubertal development ultimately allows adolescents to transition to adulthood earlier, including leaving the parental home and establishing their own families (Chisholm, 1993). Thus, early puberty, in addition to predisposing one to conduct problems and earlier sexual activity, has also been demonstrated to be environmentally triggered (for an excellent recent review, see Ellis).

THIRD TIER: VARIABILITY WITHIN DIVORCED FAMILIES AND OVER TIME

Many children in divorced-parent families experience a period of less than optimal growth characterized by increases in conduct problems and depression, and a decline in academic performance. However, many others demonstrate enhanced responsibility, mature self-reliance, and identification with positive goals and values. Why do some children develop successfully in divorced-parent families, whereas others experience serious difficulties? A third and still emerging research focus entails describing the substantial variation in children's short-term and long-term adjustment to parental divorce. Moving beyond the conventional reliance on measures of central tendency and the examination of mean differences across groups of children living in different family structures, many of these efforts have involved within-group rather than across-group research designs, as well as increased use of longitudinal analyses.

Tier 3 studies have been helpful in (a) documenting the wide range in children's adjustment; (b) elucidating the developmental trajectories in children's well-being from preseparation to decades following separation; (c) identifying preseparation family and child factors that are predictive of children's postdivorce adjustment; and (d) describing the risks for children of multiple transitions in parenting arrangements over time. In this section, we highlight insights gleaned from some illustrative studies.

Stewart, Copeland, Chester, Malley, and Barenbaum (1997) interviewed mothers and children and found that children (6–12 years of age) had widely differing reactions as early as the time when parents announced their plans to separate. According to mothers, 50% (one half) of children were distressed to hear the news, but 15% of children were relieved. Approximately 50% of the children described themselves as feeling sad a lot of the time, whereas 20% felt confused or scared, 13% felt angry, and 10% were glad. By 1 year postseparation, children were feeling significantly better and behavior problems had declined according to the reports of both mothers and teachers. Clearly, parental behavior during the transition process can facilitate or aggravate child adjustment. For example, Koerner's research examined boundary violations in the form of maternal disclosure to adolescents about financial concerns, personal concerns, and anger or complaints about the exhusband (Koerner, Jacobs, & Raymond, 2000). Using court records to recruit her sample of 255 mother–adolescent dyads, Koerner found that the frequency and depth of maternal disclosures regarding these sensitive topics were associated with adolescent psychological distress, as well as with disobedience to parents and substance use (Koerner, Wallace, Lehman, Lee, & Escalante, 2004). There were no interactions with sex or age of adolescent or time since the divorce.

In an early and excellent example of Tier 3 research, Buchanan et al. (1996) conducted telephone interviews with over 500 adolescents approximately 4.5 years after their parents separated, including substantial numbers of adolescents in father and dual residence. The Stanford Custody Project of Buchanan et al. focused on how adolescents integrated their lives in two households and highlighted the great diversity of circumstances after divorce. The heterogeneity of the Stanford Custody Project sample, with respect to both adjustment and postdivorce family arrangements, allowed Buchanan et al. to examine which family circumstances were most closely related to adolescent well-being. They examined three residential arrangements: primary mother, primary father, and dual residence, and they found that almost all residential differences in well-being were accounted for by differences in the family environments. In particular, they identified less conflictual interparental relationships, closeness with residential parent, and parental monitoring as being predictive of better adjustment. They also highlighted the positive role the nonresidential parent could play in adolescent well-being, both in terms of having a close relationship and in simply remembering special days (holidays or birthdays).

Following parents and children over nearly three decades, Hetherington and Kelly (2002) observed a wide variation in children's adjustment at 2 years, 6 years, and 20 years following parental divorce. Whereas about 10% of children in first-marriage families functioned below the normal range of adjustment, Hetherington and Kelly reported that 20% of children of divorce were maladjusted (i.e., troubled, impulsive, irresponsible, antisocial, or depressed). Similarly, Ahrons (2004) interviewed adult children of divorce and found that 20% of adult children were "devastated" by their parents' divorce. However, Ahrons found that more than three fourths of her sample of adult children of divorce felt that their parents' decision to divorce was a good one, that they did not wish their parents were still together, that their parents are better off today, and that they, as adult children, were either better off or not affected by their parents' divorce. Regarding relationships with their fathers, more than 33% of the individuals in Ahrons' sample reported that their relationships with their fathers worsened after the divorce, fully 50% felt that relationships with their fathers improved postdivorce, and 12% thought their relationships were unaffected by the divorce.

A number of pioneering studies suggest that children's postdivorce adjustment difficulties can be traced to predivorce family processes and child maladjustment. Block, Block, and Gjerde (1986) observed disturbed parent–child relationships and increased aggression in children 11 years prior to parents' separation. Similarly, Amato and Booth (1996) documented heightened problems in parent–child relationships 8 to 12 years prior to divorce. Importantly, growing evidence indicates that diminished parenting, elevated parent–child conflict, and lower levels of parent and child adjustment prior to divorce are significantly associated with child behavior problems postdivorce (Capaldi & Patterson, 1991; Cherlin et al., 1991; Hetherington & Kelly, 2002; Simons & Associates, 1996). Analyzing panel data from the National Education Longitudinal Study, Sun (2001) found that lower levels of adolescent well-being following divorce can be traced to poor family functioning and child maladjustment prior to marital disruption. Even with controls for demographic factors, adolescent boys and girls in predisrupted families scored lower on math and reading tests, and had lower educational expectations for themselves, lower self-concept and locus of control, and more behavior problems than their counterparts in families in which parents remained married. Sun found predisruption families to be characterized by worse interparental and parent–child relationships; parents were less involved in their children's education; and both mothers and fathers had lower educational expectations for their children. A key finding was that predisruption differences in adolescents' test scores and behavior problems were largely accounted for by lower levels of parental involvement and less favorable parent–child and interparental relationships in families in which parents subsequently separated, corroborating earlier studies suggesting that marital disruption per se has little or relatively little impact on adolescent well-being (Cherlin et al.; Morrison & Cherlin, 1995).

In support of both life course and risk and resilience explanations, the group of children and adolescents who appear to be at greatest risk for adjustment problems are those who experience multiple parenting transitions. Ahrons (2004) reported that a second parental divorce exacerbated losses that children felt during the first divorce. Hetherington and Kelly (2002) found that whereas 20% of children who experienced a single parental divorce suffered serious emotional or behavioral problems, the comparable figure for children experiencing multiple divorces was 38%. A small number of studies provide evidence that children who face no parenting transitions (i.e., no changes in their parents' marital status) enjoy the best adjustment and those who undergo multiple transitions have the poorest adjustment (Capaldi & Patterson, 1991; Kurdek et al., 1994; Kurdek, Fine, & Sinclair, 1995). Given the tremendous diversity and fluidity of children's living arrangements, we believe that significantly greater attention has to be directed to exploring the mechanisms underlying children's adjustment to multiple family transitions, including performing analyses of ways that family process variables interact with family structure, as well as developing more sensitive measures of the nature, frequency, and timing of parenting transitions (Demo, Aquilino, & Fine, 2005). Qualitative approaches are also underutilized but provide promising methods for illustrating the rich diversity of children's responses to family transitions (e.g., Harvey & Fine, 2004).

FOURTH TIER: INTERVENTION

The bodies of evidence summarized to this point highlight a number of mechanisms that statistically account for differences between and within family types. However, the causal inferences we can draw from these data are quite limited. One way to probe the causal links between the mediators and child outcomes is to conduct longitudinal studies that examine whether change in family processes is linked to change in child outcomes. An even more compelling method is to try to experimentally change intrapersonal resources or family processes and test whether those changes result in improved child adjustment (Bronfenbrenner, 1979; Pillow, Sandler, Braver, Wolchik, & Gersten, 1991). Such experiments can take the shape of intervention programs for children or parents after divorce, or more broad "experiments of nature" that result from policy changes such as mandatory parenting education sessions for divorcing parents (Bronfenbrenner). Publications outlining such research are much more rare than publications comprising the first three tiers that we have described, but here we summarize some of the most promising work in this fourth tier. First, we describe programs targeting intrapersonal resources of children. Second, we review programs that are focused on family process mediators of divorce effects. We also describe mandated parent education programs that have not been rigorously evaluated but that offer an opportunity to study a social reform as an experiment (Campbell, 1969).

Child-Focused Divorce Programs

Programs for children of divorce typically have educational as well as therapeutic goals for the children (e.g., Pedro-Carroll, 1997; Pedro-Carroll & Cowen, 1985; Stolberg & Cullen, 1983). However, the extent to which programs have been evaluated is quite limited (Barber, 2003; Grych & Fincham, 1992). Two well-evaluated programs have been reported: the Divorce Adjustment Project (DAP) for children and single parents by Stolberg and colleagues (Stolberg & Garrison, 1985; Stolberg & Walsh, 1988), and the Children of Divorce Intervention Project (CODIP) by Pedro-Carroll and Cowen (1985). The two programs target intrapersonal processes and resources. Both programs are based on the assumptions that divorce is a stressful event in children's lives, and that postdivorce adjustment can be facilitated by teaching cognitive-behavioral skills and providing emotional support. In particular, they emphasize acquiring specific competencies for dealing with divorce-related challenges.

Stolberg and Garrison (1985) evaluated the DAP by using a four-group design: child as participant, parent as participant, child and parent together, and a no-treatment control group. The immediate postgroup evaluation indicated higher self-esteem in the child-only group, and at the 5-month follow-up, this same group showed more positive social skills. Nonrandom assignment and preexisting group differences (combined group children were better adjusted prior to the program) may have accounted for less improvement in the combined group.

The CODIP places more emphasis on emotional support, problem-solving skills, and divorce-related feelings, places less emphasis on anger control, and relies more on experiential exercises such as discussions and role plays. The evaluation of this program has been extensive, beginning with an initial field trial with fourth- to sixth-grade children that found benefits in conduct, adjustment, and anxiety (Pedro-Carroll & Cowen, 1985). Replications (Alpert-Gillis, Pedro-Carroll, & Cowen, 1989; Pedro-Carroll, Alpert-Gillis, & Cowen, 1992; Pedro-Carroll, Cowen, Hightower, & Guare, 1986) have supported CODIP's role in enhancing children's postdivorce adjustment. The CODIP has most recently been modified for use with early adolescents (Pedro-Carroll, 1997). The 12-session school-based program aims to reduce the stress of parental divorce for adolescents and to foster coping through skill building (Pedro-Carroll & Black, 1993). The early adolescent version is composed of objectives common to all CODIP programs, such as supportive group climate, expression of feelings, and problem solving. In addition, the objectives for early adolescents incorporated age-appropriate targets of promoting realistic hopes for future relationships and the capacity to trust, as well as teaching strategies for disengaging from parent conflict and being "caught in the middle."

Pre-post evaluation of a pilot program suggested improved home environment and increases in adolescents' emotional adjustment, interpersonal skills, anger management, and hopefulness about future relationships and responsibilities (Pedro-Carroll & Black).

Programs for Postdivorce Parenting

There has been very little research evaluating the efficacy of parenting programs for children in divorced families (Barber, 2003; Emery, 1999). One program, designed by Wolchik and others (Wolchik, Sandler et al., 1993, 2000, 2002), has demonstrated program efficacy by using a strong research design. Wolchik et al. (1993, 2000) proposed a "small theory" for how a parenting program can prevent postdivorce child adjustment problems. They developed the theory from a strong base in the empirical divorce literature, and the theory guided program development and evaluation. The Children of Divorce Parenting Intervention targets five components of parenting that are hypothesized to be mediating factors in the relationship between divorce and child adjustment: parent–child relationships, interparental conflict, discipline, contact with and support from nonparental adults, and contact with the noncustodial parent (Wolchik, Sandler et al., 1993). The first evaluation by Wolchik et al. included a randomized field trial with children aged 8 to 15 years, and they found positive changes in participants' parenting practices, which in turn mediated program effects on children's adjustment and behavior. In a second trial, Wolchik, Sandler et al. (2000, 2002) evaluated a dual-component model for divorced mothers and their children aged 9 to 12. The mother-only program and the dual-component program for mothers and children were both effective in improving mother–child relationships, particularly for those who entered the program with worse relationships. The parenting program for mothers was also linked to more effective discipline strategies and to reductions in maternal reports of internalizing and externalizing problems in their children. A 6-year follow-up indicated that program participation led to reductions in externalizing problems (particularly for those with greater problems before they entered the program), diagnoses of mental disorder, drug and alcohol use, and number of sexual partners (Wolchik, Sandler, et al., 2002). The dual-component program led to few additive effects over and above the mother-only program. The evaluation approach of Wolchik et al. (2000, 2002) provides important information for future efforts with single parents and adolescents in that it identifies family characteristics empirically connected to child and adolescent maladjustment, targets those for change, and includes a theory-driven evaluation. Their data provide the strongest possible test of the causal links between the mediators and child outcomes.

There have been some efforts to support the single parents themselves (usually for mothers). This type of program targets the women's own adjustment to the divorce or single parenting (individual-level focus). Those programs aimed at the adjustment of the single mother, and not directly at modifying parenting behaviors, are based on the assumption that better maternal adjustment will lead to better parenting. One such program is the Single Parent Support Group (Stolberg & Garrison, 1985; Stolberg & Walsh, 1988), which is a 12-week support program for divorced custodial mothers. Evaluation results have shown that participants displayed better divorce adjustment than did those who did not receive the program. However, no changes in child adjustment were found.

Divorcing Parent Education

A number of U.S. states have begun to mandate parent education classes for divorcing parents (Blaisure & Geasler, chap. 28, this volume; Fine et al., 1999). However, despite widespread implementation, few evaluation studies have been conducted, and it is not known if children or adolescents benefit from their parents' attendance in these classes (Emery, 1999), other than evidence of strong consumer satisfaction with the programs (Fine et al., 1999; McKenry, Clark, & Stone, 1999). Pedro-Carroll, Nakhnikian, & Montes (2001) reported on a follow-up study of A.C.T.—For the Children (Assisting Children Through Transition). This skills-based parent education program was not targeted specifically to parents of any one age group, but the results suggest reductions in interparental conflict, increases in cooperative parenting behaviors, and improved child outcomes.

Opportunities Presented in Tier 4 Research

An evaluation of programs such as those described here could examine the effectiveness of different components of programs (Cook, Anson, & Walchli, 1993; Wolchik et al., 1993). The following four research questions should guide the evaluation of programs developed to test causal mediators. First, does the intervention program have an impact on the causal mechanisms it targets as proximal outcomes? This is a test of the action theory of the program, and negative results could be the result of flaws in the treatment as implemented, rather than in the basic conceptualization of causal mediators (Chen, 1990). Second do children improve with respect to the targeted adjustment outcomes over the course of follow-up evaluations? Third, do changes in specific features of the family environment (e.g., monitoring or communication) predict changes in distinct components of adjustment (e.g., risky behavior or emotional well-being)? Fourth, do the benefits for family processes and children's outcomes generalize across diverse racial, ethnic, and socioeconomic populations? These are tests of the conceptual theory (Chen). Research addressing these questions will complement evaluation efforts that describe program effectiveness without testing substantive theories for explaining program effects.

CONCLUSIONS

We have described four tiers of research examining the consequences for children of parental divorce and relationship dissolution. Tier 1 research documents consistent but weak effects of parental divorce, with children of divorced parents scoring lower on a broad range of measures of social, emotional, academic, and behavioral adjustment, thereby corroborating earlier reviews (Amato, 2000; Emery, 1999). A number of mediating processes were identified in Tier 2 research, notably including family financial resources, interparental conflict, the quality of residential and nonresidential parenting, parents' and children's psychological resources, and pubertal timing. Substantial variation in children's predivorce and postdivorce well-being was illustrated in Tier 3 research, with children's adjustment buffered by healthier parenting behaviors and closer, less conflictual family environments prior to, during, and following divorce. At greatest risk for maladjustment are children who experience multiple parenting transitions. Child- and parent-focused intervention programs were described and evaluated in Tier 4 research, but the overall effectiveness of these programs for ameliorating child well-being is largely unknown.

With changing family demographics and with the enormous attention that is being devoted to studying the consequences for children of parental divorce and relationship dissolution, we believe it is critical that researchers move beyond across-group designs and reliance on measures of central tendency. Ample and consistent evidence reviewed here and elsewhere has shown that, on average, children who experience their parents' divorce are slightly disadvantaged in a variety of domains. We also know there is tremendous variation within and across families in how individual children, adolescents, and adults respond. However, we know very little about developmental trajectories in domains of children's well-being over the course of their lives from preseparation through family disruption and for several years following the disruption. We suggest that important directions for future research focus on within-group, longitudinal examinations of children whose parents divorce and the impact on children of the changes in their family relationships, resources, and living arrangements over time. Evaluation research is also sorely needed to examine the effectiveness of programs designed to improve family environments and child well-being. Finally, we know far too little about the experience and consequences of parental divorce and relationship dissolution for non-White children and for children who live in economic circumstances outside the middle class. Although relatively privileged samples of White, middle-class children may be resilient, at least in the aggregate, to the stresses surrounding parental divorce, we urge researchers to be more aggressive in examining the possibility that the divorce process may be experienced differently by children in marginalized groups. Identifying similarities and differences across racial, ethnic, and socioeconomic groups provides enormous potential to broaden our understanding of how parental divorce and relationship dissolution affect children's lives.

ACKNOWLEDGMENTS

The writing of this chapter was partially funded by a grant to Bonnie Barber from the Department of Health and Human Services, Office of Adolescent Pregnancy Programs. We are grateful to Marion O'Brien for her constructive suggestions on this chapter.

REFERENCES

Ahrons, C. (2004). *We're still family*. New York: HarperCollins.

Alexander, K. L., & Entwisle, D. (1988). Achievement in the first two years of school: Patterns and processes. *Monographs of the Society for Research in Child Development, 53* (2, Serial No. 218).

Allison, P. D., & Furstenberg, F. F. (1989). How marital dissolution affects children: Variations by age and sex. *Developmental Psychology, 25*, 540–549.

Alpert-Gillis, L. J., Pedro-Carroll, J. L., & Cowen, E. L. (1989). The children of divorce intervention program: Development, implementation, and evaluation of a program for young urban children. *Journal of Consulting and Clinical Psychology, 57*, 583–589.

Amato, P. R. (1988). Long-term implications of parental divorce for adult self-concept. *Journal of Family Issues, 9*, 201–213.

Amato, P. R. (1993). Children's adjustment to divorce: Theories, hypotheses, and empirical support. *Journal of Marriage and the Family, 55*, 23–38.

Amato, P. R. (1994). The implications of research findings on children in stepfamilies. In A. Booth & J. Dunn (Eds.), *Stepfamilies: Who benefits? Who does not?* (pp. 81–87). Hillsdale, NJ: Lawrence Erlbaum Associates.

Amato, P. R. (1999). Children of divorced parents as young adults. In E. M. Hetherington (Ed.), *Coping with divorce, single parenting, and remarriage: A risk and resiliency perspective* (pp. 147–164). Mahwah, NJ: Lawrence Erlbaum Associates.

Amato, P. R. (2000). The consequences of divorce for adults and children. *Journal of Marriage and the Family, 62*, 1269–1287.

Amato, P. R., & Booth, A. (1996). A prospective study of parental divorce and parent–child relationships. *Journal of Marriage and the Family, 58*, 356–365.

Amato, P. R., & Booth, A. (1997). *A generation at risk: Growing up in an era of family upheaval*. Cambridge, MA: Harvard University Press.

Amato, P. R., & Gilbreth, J. G. (1999). Nonresident fathers and children's well-being: A meta-analysis. *Journal of Marriage and the Family, 61*, 557–573.

Amato, P. R., & Keith, B. (1991). Consequences of parental divorce for the well-being of children: A meta-analysis. *Psychological Bulletin, 110*, 26–46.

Avenevoli, S., Sessa, F. M., & Steinberg, L. (1999). Family structure, parenting practices, and adolescent adjustment: An ecological examination. In E. M. Hetherington (Ed.), *Coping with divorce, single parenting, and remarriage: A risk and resiliency perspective* (pp. 65–90). Mahwah, NJ: Lawrence Erlbaum Associates.

Bandura, A. (1986). *Social foundations of thought and action: A social cognitive theory.* Englewood Cliffs, NJ: Prentice-Hall.

Bandura, A. (1994). *Self-efficacy: The exercise of control.* New York: Freeman.

Barber, B. L. (1995). Preventive intervention with adolescents and divorced mothers: A conceptual framework for program design and evaluation. *Journal of Applied Developmental Psychology, 16,* 481–503.

Barber, B. L. (2003). Promoting healthy development of adolescents living in single parent families. In T. Gullotta and M. Bloom (Eds.) *Encyclopedia of primary prevention and health promotion* (pp. 788–795). New York: Kluwer/ Plenum.

Barber, B. L., & Eccles, J. S. (1992). Long-term influence of divorce and single parenting on adolescent family- and work-related values, behaviors, and aspirations. *Psychological Bulletin, 111,* 108–126.

Barber, B. L., Eccles, J. S., & Stone, M. R. (2001). Whatever happened to the Jock, the Brain, and the Princess? Young adult pathways linked to adolescent activity involvement and social identity. *Journal of Adolescent Research, 16,* 429–455.

Barber, B. L., & Meschke, L. L. (2001, September). *Parental divorce, family relations, and daughters' sexual activity: A biopsychosocial approach.* Invited talk presented at the Institute for Advanced Studies workshop on Advances in Human Evolution Ecology: Evolution and Development, Perth, Western Australia.

Baumrind, D. (1989, April). *Sex-differentiated socialization effects in childhood and adolescence in divorced and intact families.* Paper presented at the meeting of the Society for Research in Child Development, Kansas City, MO.

Baumrind, D. (1991). Effective parenting during the early adolescent transition. In P. A. Cowan & E. M. Hetherington (Eds.), *Family transitions* (pp. 111–163). Hillsdale, NJ: Lawrence Erlbaum Associates.

Belsky, J., Steinberg, L., & Draper, P. (1991). Childhood experience, interpersonal development, and reproductive strategy: An evolutionary theory of socialization. *Child Development, 62,* 647–670.

Berg, B., & Kelly, R. (1979). The measured self-esteem of children from broken, rejected, and accepted families. *Journal of Divorce, 2,* 363–369.

Biblarz, T. J., & Gottainer, G. (2000). Family structure and children's success: A comparison of widowed and divorced single mother families. *Journal of Marriage and the Family, 62,* 533–548.

Biglan, A., Metzler, C. W., Wirt, R., & Ary, D. V. (1990). Social and behavioral factors associated with high-risk sexual behavior among adolescents. *Journal of Behavioral Medicine, 13,* 245–261.

Billy, J. O. G., Brewster, K. L., & Grady, W. R. (1994). Contextual effects of the sexual behavior of adolescent women. *Journal of Marriage and the Family, 56,* 387–404.

Block, J. H., Block, J., & Gjerde. P. F. (1986). The personality of children prior to divorce: A prospective study. *Child Development, 57,* 827–840.

Bray, J. H., & Depner, C. E. (1993). Perspectives on nonresidential parenting. In C. E. Depner and J. H. Bray (Eds.), *Nonresidential parenting: New vistas in family living.* Newbury Park, CA: Sage.

Bronfenbrenner, U. (1979). *The ecology of human development: Experiments by nature and by design.* Cambridge, MA: Harvard University Press.

Buchanan, C. M., Maccoby, E. E., & Dornbusch, S. M. (1996). *Adolescents after divorce.* Cambridge, MA: Harvard University Press.

Buehler, C., Anthony, C., Krishnakumar, A., Stone, G., Gerard, J., & Pemberton, S. (1997). Interparental conflict and youth problem behaviors: A meta-analysis. *Journal of Child and Family Studies, 6,* 233–247.

Bumpass, L. L., Martin, T. C., & Sweet, J. A. (1991). The impact of family background and early marital factors on marital disruption. *Journal of Family Issues, 12,* 22–42.

Campbell, D. T. (1969). Reforms as experiments. *American Psychologist, 24,* 409–429.

Capaldi, D. M., Crosby, L., & Stoolmiller, M. (1996). Predicting the timing of first sexual intercourse for at-risk adolescent males. *Child Development, 67,* 344–359.

Capaldi, D. M., & Patterson, G. R. (1991). Relations of parental transitions to boys' adjustment problems: I. A linear hypothesis. II. Mothers at risk for transitions and unskilled parenting. *Developmental Psychology, 27,* 489–504.

Carlson, M. J., & Corcoran, M. E. (2001). Family structure and children's behavioral and cognitive outcomes. *Journal of Marriage and Family, 63,* 779–792.

Chase-Lansdale, P. L., Cherlin, A. J., & Kiernan, K. E. (1995). The long-term effects of parental divorce on the mental health of young adults: A developmental perspective. *Child Development, 66,* 1614–1634.

Chen, H. T. (1990). *Theory driven evaluations.* Newbury Park, CA: Sage.

Cherlin, A., Furstenberg, F., Chase-Lansdale, P., Kiernan, K., Robins, P., Morrison, D., & Teitler, J. (1991). Longitudinal studies of effects of divorce on children in Great Britain and the United States. *Science, 252,* 1386–1389.

Chisolm, J. S. (1993). Death, hope, and sex: Life history theory and the development of reproductive strategies. *Current Anthropology, 34,* 1–12.

Clark, J., & Barber, B. L. (1994). Adolescents in post-divorce and always-married families: Self-esteem and perceptions of their fathers' interest. *Journal of Marriage and the Family, 56,* 608–614.

Cook, T. D., Anson, A. R., & Walchli, S. B. (1993). From causal description to causal explanation: Improving three already good evaluations of adolescent health programs. In S. G. Millstein, A. C. Petersen, & E. O. Nightingale (Eds.), *Promoting the health of adolescents: New directions for the twenty-first century* (pp. 339–374). New York: Oxford University Press.

Cummings, E. M., Goeke-Morey, M. C., & Papp, L. M. (2004). Everyday marital conflict and child aggression. *Journal of Abnormal Child Psychology, 32,* 191–202.

Danziger, S. K. (1995). Family life and teenage pregnancy in the inner city: Experiences of African-American youth. *Children and Youth Services Review, 17,* 183–202.

Davies, P. T., & Cummings, E. M. (1994). Marital conflict and child adjustment: An emotional security hypothesis. *Psychological Bulletin, 116,* 387–411.

Day, R. D. (1992). The transition to first intercourse among racially and culturally diverse youth. *Journal of Marriage and the Family, 54,* 749–762.

Degarmo, D. S., & Forgatch, M. S. (1999). Contexts as predictors of changing maternal parenting practices in diverse family structures. In E. M. Hetherington (Ed.), *Coping with divorce, single parenting, and remarriage: A risk and resiliency perspective* (pp. 227–252). Mahwah, NJ: Lawrence Erlbaum Associates.

Demo, D. H., & Acock, A. C. (1988). The impact of divorce on children. *Journal of Marriage and the Family, 50,* 619–648.

Demo, D. H., & Acock, A. C. (1996). Family structure, family process, and adolescent well-being. *Journal of Research on Adolescence, 6,* 457–488.

Demo, D. H., Aquilino, W. S., & Fine, M. A. (2005). Family composition and family transitions. In V. Bengtson, A. Acock, K. Allen, P. Dilworth-Anderson, & D. Klein (Eds.), *Sourcebook of family theory and research* (pp. 119–142). Thousand Oaks, CA: Sage.

Demo, D. H., & Cox, M. J. (2000). Families with young children: A review of research in the 1990s. *Journal of Marriage and the Family, 62,* 876–895.

Doherty, W. J., & Needle, R. H. (1991). Psychological adjustment and substance use among adolescents before and after a parental divorce. *Child Development, 62,* 328–337.

Dornbusch, S. M., Carlsmith, J. M., Bushwall, S. J., Ritter, P. L., Leiderman, H., Hastorf, A. H., & Gross, R. T. (1985). Single parents, extended households, and the control of adolescents. *Child Development, 56,* 326–341.

Draper, P., & Harpending, H. (1982). Father absence and reproductive strategy: An evolutionary perspective. *Journal of Anthropological Research, 38,* 255–273.

Dunlop, R., & Burns, A. (1988). *Don't feel the world is caving in: Adolescents in divorcing families* (Monograph No. 6.) Melbourne: Australian Institute of Family Studies.

Eccles, J. S., Lord, S. E., Roeser, R. W., Barber, B. L., & Jozefowicz, D. M. (1997). The association of school transitions in early adolescence with developmental trajectories through high school. In J. Schulenberg, J. Maggs, & K. Hurrelmann (Eds.), *Health risks and developmental transitions during adolescence* (pp. 283–320). New York: Cambridge University Press.

Ellis, B. J. (2004). Timing of pubertal maturation in girls: An integrated life history approach. *Psychological Bulletin, 130,* 920–958.

Ellis, B. J., Bates, J. E., Dodge, K. A., Fergusson, D. M., Horwood, L. J., Pettit, G. S., & Woodward, L. (2003). Does father absence place daughters at special risk for early sexual activity and teenage pregnancy? *Child Development, 74,* 801–821.

Ellis, B. J., & Garber, J. (2000). Psychological antecedents of variation in girls' pubertal timing: Maternal depression, stepfather presence, and marital and family stress. *Child Development, 71,* 485–501.

Ellis, B. J., McFadyen-Ketchum, S., Dodge, K. A., Pettit, G. S., & Bates, J. E. (1999). Quality of early family relationships and individual differences in the timing of pubertal maturation in girls: A longitudinal test of an evolutionary model. *Journal of Personality and Social Psychology, 77,* 387–401.

Emery, R. E. (1999). *Marriage, divorce, and children's adjustment.* Thousand Oaks, CA: Sage.

Fine, M. A., Coleman, M., Gable, S., Ganong, L. H., Ispa, J., Morrison, J., & Thornburg, K. R. (1999). Research-based parenting education for divorcing parents: A university-community collaboration. In T. R. Chibucos & R. M. Lerner (Eds.), *Serving children and families through community–university partnerships: Success stories* (pp. 251–258). Norwell, MA: Kluwer.

Fine, M. A., & Demo, D. H. (2000). Divorce: Societal ill or normative transition? In R. M. Milardo & S. Duck (Eds.), *Families as relationships* (pp. 135–156). New York: Wiley.

Flanagan, C. (1986, November). *Early adolescent needs and family decision making opportunities: A study of person-environment fit.* Paper presented at the annual meeting of the American Educational Research Association, San Francisco, CA.

Fletcher, A. C., Elder, G. H., & Mekos, D. (2000). Parental influences on adolescent involvement in community activities. *Journal of Research on Adolescence, 10,* 29–48.

Flewelling, R. L., & Bauman, K. E. (1990). Family structure as a predictor of initial substance use and sexual intercourse in early adolescence. *Journal of Marriage and the Family, 52,* 171–181.

Forehand, R., Thomas, A. M., Wierson, M., Brody, G., & Fauber, R. (1990). Role of maternal functioning and parenting skills in adolescent functioning following parental divorce. *Journal of Abnormal Psychology, 99,* 278–283.

Forgatch, M. S., Patterson, G. R., & Skinner, M. L. (1988). A mediational model for the effect of divorce on anti-social behavior in boys. In E. M. Hetherington & J. D. Arasteh (Eds.), *Impact of divorce, single parenting, and stepparenting on children* (pp. 135–154). Hillsdale, NJ: Lawrence Erlbaum Associates.

Furstenberg, F. F., Cook, T. D., Eccles, J., Elder, G. H., & Sameroff, A. (1999). *Managing to make it: Urban families and adolescent success.* Chicago: University of Chicago Press.

Furstenberg, F. F., Jr., & Teitler, J. O. (1994). Reconsidering the effects of marital disruption: What happens to children of divorce in early adulthood? *Journal of Family Issues, 15,* 173–190.

Ganong, L. H., & Coleman, M. (1994). *Remarried family relationships.* Thousand Oaks, CA: Sage.

Gerard, J. M., & Buehler, C. (1999). Multiple risk factors in the family environment and youth problem behaviors. *Journal of Marriage and the Family, 61,* 343–361.

Glenn, N. D., & Kramer, K. B. (1987). The marriages and divorces of the children of divorce. *Journal of Marriage and the Family, 49,* 811–825.

Goodnow, J. J., & Collins, W. A. (1990). *Development according to parents: The nature, sources, and consequences of parents' ideas.* Hillsdale, NJ: Lawrence Erlbaum Associates.

Grotevant, H. D. (1998). Adolescent development in family contexts. In W. Damon (Ed.-in-chief) & N. Eisenberg (Vol. Ed.), *Handbook of child psychology: Vol. 3. Social, emotional and personality development* (5th ed., pp. 1097–1149). New York: Wiley.

Grych, J. H., & Fincham, F. D. (1990). Marital conflict and children's adjustment: A cognitive-contextual framework. *Psychological Bulletin, 108,* 267–290.

Grych, J. H., & Fincham, F. D. (1992). Interventions for children of divorce: Toward greater integration of research and action. *Psychological Bulletin, 111,* 434–454.

Harvey, J. H., & Fine, M. A. (2004). *Children of divorce: Stories of loss and growth.* Mahwah, NJ: Lawrence Erlbaum Associates.

Healy, J. M., Stewart, A. J., & Copeland, A. P. (1993). The role of self-blame in children's adjustment to parental separation. *Personality and Social Psychology Bulletin, 19,* 279–289.

Hetherington, E. M. (1989). Coping with family transitions: Winners, losers, and survivors. *Child Development, 60,* 1–14.

Hetherington, E. M., Clingempeel, W. G., Anderson, E. R., Deal, J. E., Hagan, M. S., Hollier, E. A., & Lindner, M. S. (1992). Coping with marital transitions: A family systems perspective. *Monographs of the Society for Research in Child Development, 57,* Nos 2–3, Serial 227.

Hetherington, E. M., Cox, M., & Cox, R. (1979). Play and social interaction in children following divorce. *Journal of Social Issues, 35,* 26–49.

Hetherington, E. M., & Kelly, J. (2002). *For better or for worse: Divorce reconsidered.* New York: Norton.

Hogan, D. P., & Kitagawa, E. M. (1985). The impact of social status, family structure, and neighborhood on fertility of Black adolescents. *American Journal of Sociology, 90,* 825–855.

Hogan, D. P., Sun, R., & Cornwell, G. T. (2000). Sexual and fertility behaviors of American Females aged 15–19 years: 1985, 1990, and 1995. *American Journal of Public Health, 90*(9), 1421–1425.

Holden, K. C., & Smock, P. J. (1991). The economic costs of marital dissolution: Why do women bear disproportionate costs? *Annual Review of Sociology, 17,* 51–78.

Hovell, M., Sipan, C., Blumberg, E., Atkins, C., Hofstetter, C. R., & Kreitner, S. (1994). Family influences on Latino and Anglo adolescents' sexual behavior. *Journal of Marriage and the Family, 56,* 973–986.

Jones, B., Leeton, J., McLeod, I., & Wood, C. (1972). Factors influencing the age of menarche in a lower socioeconomic group in Melbourne. *Medical Journal of Australia, 21,* 533–535.

Kalter, N., Riemer, B., Brickman, A., & Chen, J. W. (1985). Implications of parental divorce for female development. *Journal of the American Academy of Child Psychiatry, 24,* 538–544.

Kilmartin, C. (1997). Children, divorce, and one-parent families. *Family Matters, 48,* 34–35.

Kinard, E. M., & Reinherz, H. (1984). Marital disruption: Effects on behavioral and emotional functioning in children. *Journal of Family Issues, 5,* 90–115.

King, V. (1994). Nonresident father involvement and child well-being: Can dads make a difference? *Journal of Family Issues, 15,* 78–96.

King, V., Harris, K. M., & Heard, H. E. (2004). Racial and ethnic diversity in nonresident father involvement. *Journal of Marriage and Family, 66,* 1–21.

Koerner, S. S., Jacobs, S. L., & Raymond, M. (2000). When mothers turn to their adolescent daughters: Predicting daughters' vulnerability to negative adjustment outcomes. *Family Relations, 49,* 301–309.

Koerner, S. S., Wallace, S. R., Lehman, S. J., Lee, S., & Escalante, K. A. (2004). Sensitive mother-to-adolescent disclosures after divorce: Is the experience of sons different from that of daughters? *Journal of Family Psychology, 18,* 46–57.

Ku, L., Sonenstein, F. L., Pleck, J. H. (1993). Factors influencing first intercourse for teenage men. *Public Health Reports, 108,* 680–694.

Kurdek, L. A. (1988). Cognitive mediators of children's adjustment to divorce. In S. A. Wolchik & P. Karoly (Eds.), *Children of divorce: Empirical perspectives on adjustment.* New York: Gardner.

Kurdek, L. A., Fine, M. A., & Sinclair, R. J. (1994). The relation between parenting transitions and adjustment in young adolescents. *Journal of Early Adolescence, 14,* 412–432.

Kurdek, L. A., Fine, M. A., & Sinclair, R. J. (1995). School adjustment in sixth graders: Parenting transitions, family climate, and peer norm effects. *Child Development, 66,* 430–445.

Lamb, M. E. (1999). Parental behavior, family processes, and child development in nontraditional and traditionally understudied families. In M. Lamb (Ed.), *Parenting and child development in "nontraditional" families* (pp. 1–15). Hillsdale, NJ: Lawrence Erlbaum Associates.

Lengua, L., & Sandler, I. N. (1996). Self-regulation as a moderator of the relation between coping and symptomatology in children of divorce. *Journal of Abnormal Child Psychology, 24,* 681–701.

Long, B. H. (1986). Parental discord vs. family structure: Effects of divorce on the self-esteem of daughters. *Journal of Youth and Adolescence, 15,* 19–27.

Long, N., Forehand, R., Fauber, R., & Brody, G. H. (1987). Self-perceived and independently observed competence of young adolescents as a function of parental marital conflict and recent divorce. *Journal of Abnormal Child Psychology, 15,* 15–27.

Luster, T., & Small, S. A. (1994). Factors associated with sexual risk-taking behaviors among adolescents. *Journal of Marriage and the Family, 56,* 622–632.

Mahoney, J. L., & Cairns, R. B. (1997). Do extracurricular activities protect against early school dropout? *Developmental Psychology, 33,* 241–253.

Marsh, H. W., & Kleitman, S. (2003). School athletic participation: Mostly gain with little pain. *Journal of Sport and Exercise Psychology, 25,* 205–228.

Mazur, E., Wolchik, S. A., Virdin, L., Sandler, I. N., & West, S. G. (1999). Cognitive moderators of children's adjustment to stressful divorce events: The role of negative cognitive errors and positive illusions. *Child Development, 70,* 231–245.

McCombs, A., & Forehand, R. (1989). Adolescent school performance following parental divorce: Are there family factors that can enhance success? *Adolescence, 24,* 871–879.

McLanahan, S., & Sandefur, G. (1994). *Growing up with a single parent: What hurts, what helps.* Cambridge, MA: Harvard University Press.

McKenry, P. C., Clark, K. A., & Stone, G. (1999). Evaluation of a parent education program for divorcing parents. *Family Relations, 48,* 129–137.

Meschke L. L., Bartholomae, S., & Zentall, S. R. (2000). Adolescent sexuality and parent-adolescent processes: Promoting healthy teen choices. *Family Relations, 49,* 143–154.

Meschke, L. L., Zweig, J. M., Barber, B. L., & Eccles, J. S. (2000). Demographic, biological, social, and psychological correlates of the timing of first intercourse. *Journal of Research on Adolescence, 10,* 315–338.

Miller, B., & Moore, K. (1990). Adolescent sexual behaviors, pregnancy, and parenting: Research through the 1980s. *Journal of Marriage and the Family, 52,* 54–83.

Miller, B. C. (1998). *Families matter: A research synthesis of family influences on adolescent pregnancy.* Washington, DC: National Campaign to Prevent Teen Pregnancy.

Miller, K. S., Forehand, R., & Kotchick, B. A. (1999). Adolescent sexual behavior in two ethnic minority samples: The role of family variables. *Journal of Marriage and the Family, 61,* 85–98.

Moore, M. R., & Brooks-Gunn, J. (2003). Healthy sexual development: Notes on programs that reduce the risk of early sexual initiation and adolescent pregnancy. In D. Romer (Ed.), *Reducing adolescent risk* (pp. 284–292) Thousand Oaks, CA: Sage.

Moore, K. A., Morrison, D. R., & Glei, D. A. (1995). Welfare and adolescent sex: The effects of family history, benefit levels, and community context. *Journal of Family and Economic Issues, 16,* 207–237.

Morrison, D. R., & Cherlin, A. J. (1995). The divorce process and young children's well-being: A prospective analysis. *Journal of Marriage and the Family, 57,* 800–812.

Mott, F., Fondell, M., Hu, P., Kowaleski-Jones, P., & Menaghan, E. (1996). The determinants of first sex by age 14 in a high-risk adolescent population. *Family Planning Perspectives, 28,* 13–18.

Newcomer, S. F., & Udry, J. R. (1987). Parental marital status effects on adolescent sexual behavior. *Journal of Marriage and the Family, 49,* 235–240.

Parish, T., & Dostal, J. (1980). Evaluation of self and parent figures by children from intact, divorced, and reconstituted families. *Journal of Youth and Adolescence, 9,* 347–351.

Parsons, J. E., Adler, T. F., & Kaczala, C. M., (1982). Socialization of achievement attitudes and beliefs: Parental influences. *Child Development, 53*(2), 310–321.

Patterson, G. R. (1986). Performance models for antisocial boys. *American Psychologist, 41,* 432–444.

Pedro-Carroll, J. (1997). The Children of Divorce Intervention Program: Fostering resilient outcomes for school-aged children. In G. W. Albee & T. P. Gullotta (Eds.), *Primary prevention works* (pp. 213–238). Thousand Oaks, CA: Sage.

Pedro-Carroll, J., & Black, A. E. (1993). *The Children of Divorce Intervention Program: Preventative outreach to early adolescents* (Final report to the Gottschalk Mental Health Research Grant). Rochester, NY: University of Rochester, Center for Community Study.

Pedro-Carroll, J. L., Alpert-Gillis, L. J., & Cowen, E. L. (1992). An evaluation of the efficacy of a preventative intervention for 4th–6th grade urban children of divorce. *Journal of Primary Prevention, 13,* 115–130.

Pedro-Carroll, J. L., & Cowen, E. L. (1985). The Children of Divorce Intervention Program: An investigation of the efficacy of a school based prevention program. *Journal of Consulting and Clinical Psychology, 53,* 603–611.

Pedro-Carroll, J. L., Cowen, E. L., Hightower, A., & Guare, J. C. (1986). Preventive intervention with latency-aged children of divorce: A replication study. *American Journal of Community Psychology, 41,* 277–290.

Pedro-Carroll, J., Nakhnikian, E., & Montes, G. (2001). Court affiliated parent education: Assisting Children Through Transition: Helping parents protect their children from the toxic effects of ongoing conflict in the aftermath of divorce. *Family Court Review, 39*(4), 377–391.

Peterson, J. L., & Zill, N. (1986). Marital disruption, parent-child relationships, and behavior problems in children. *Journal of Marriage and the Family, 48,* 295–307.

Peterson, R. R. (1996). A re-evaluation of the economic consequences of divorce. *American Sociological Review, 61,* 528–536.

Phillips, D. A. (1987). Socialization of perceived academic competence among highly competent children. *Child Development, 58,* 1308–1320.

Pillow, D. R., Sandler, I. N., Braver, S. L., Wolchik, S. A., & Gersten, J. C. (1991). Theory-based screening for prevention: Focusing on mediating processes in children of divorce. *American Journal of Community Psychology, 19,* 809–836.

Ringen, S. (1997). Great Britain. In S. B. Kamerman & A. J. Kahn (Eds.), *Family change and family policies in Great Britain, Canada, New Zealand, and the United States* (pp. 29–102). Oxford, England: Clarendon.

Rodgers, B., & Pryor, J. (1998). *Divorce and separation: The outcomes for children.* York: Rowntree Foundation.

Rodgers, K. B. (1999). Parenting processes related to sexual risk-taking behaviors of adolescent males and females. *Journal of Marriage and the Family, 61,* 99–109.

Russell, S. T. (2002). Childhood developmental risk for teen childbearing in Britain. *Journal of Research on Adolescence, 12,* 305–324.

Sandler, I. N., Tein, J.-Y., Mehta, P., Wolchik, S., & Ayers, T. (2000). Coping efficacy and psychological problems of children of divorce. *Child Development, 71,* 1099–1118.

Sandler, I. N., Tein, J.-Y, & West, S. G. (1994). Coping, stress, and the psychological symptoms of children of divorce. *Child Development, 65,* 1744–1763.

Schader, R. (2002). Perceptions of elite female athletes regarding success attributions and the role of parental influence on talent development. *Dissertation Abstracts International, 62,* 4060A.

Seltzer, J. A. (1991). Relationships between fathers and children who live apart: The father's role after separation. *Journal of Marriage and the Family, 53,* 79–101.

Shirley, I., Koopman-Boyden, P., Pool, I., & St. John, S. (1997). New Zealand. In S. B. Kamerman & A. J. Kahn (Eds.), *Family change and family policies in Great Britain, Canada, New Zealand, and the United States* (pp. 207–304). Oxford, England: Clarendon.

Simons, R. L., & Associates. (1996). *Understanding differences between divorced and intact families: Stress, interaction, and child outcomes.* Thousand Oaks, CA: Sage.

Smith, T. E. (1990). Parental separation and the academic self-concepts of adolescents: An effort to solve the puzzle of separation effects. *Journal of Marriage and the Family, 52,* 107–118.

Statistics Canada. (1997, October 14). *The Daily—1996 Census: Marital status, common-law unions and families* [Online database]. Available at http://www.statcan.ca/Daily/English/971014/d971014.htm

Steinberg, L. (1987). Single parents, stepparents, and the susceptibility of adolescents to antisocial peer pressure. *Child Development, 58,* 269–275.

Steinberg, L. (1990). Autonomy, conflict, and harmony in the family relationship. In S. S. Feldman and G. R. Elliott (Eds.), *At the threshold: The developing adolescent.* Cambridge, MA: Harvard University Press.

Steinberg, L., Mounts, N. S., Lamborn, S. D., & Dornbusch, S. M. (1991). Authoritative parenting and adolescent adjustment across varied ecological niches. *Journal of Research on Adolescence, 1,* 19–36.

Stewart, A. J., Copeland, A. P., Chester, N. L., Malley, J. E., & Barenbaum, N. B. (1997). *Separating together: How divorce transforms families.* New York: Guilford.

Stolberg, A. L., & Anker, J. M. (1983). Cognitive and behavioral changes in children resulting from parental divorce and consequent environmental changes. *Journal of Divorce, 7,* 23–41.

Stolberg, A. L., & Cullen, P. M. (1983). Preventive interventions for families of divorce: The Divorce Adjustment Project. In L. A. Kurdek (Ed.), *Children and divorce: New directions for child development* (No. 19, pp. 71–81). San Francisco: Jossey-Bass.

Stolberg, A. L., & Garrison, K. M. (1985). Evaluating a primary prevention program for children of divorce. *American Journal of Community Psychology, 13,* 111–124.

Stolberg, A. L., & Walsh, P. (1988). A review of treatment methods for children of divorce. In S. A. Wolchik & P. Karoly (Eds.), *Children of divorce: Empirical perspectives on adjustment* (pp. 299–321). New York: Gardner.

Sun, Y. (2001). Family environment and adolescents' well-being before and after parents' marital disruption: A longitudinal analysis. *Journal of Marriage and Family, 63,* 697–713.

Surbey, M. K. (1990). Family composition, stress, and the timing of human menarche. In T. E. Ziegler & F. B. Bercovitch (Eds.), *Socioendocrinology of primate reproduction. Monographs in Primatology.* (Vol. XIII, pp. 11–32). New York: John Wiley-Liss.

Teachman, J. D., Paasch, K., & Carver, K. (1996). Social capital and dropping out of school early. *Journal of Marriage and the Family, 58,* 773–783.

Thomas, A. M., & Forehand, R. (1993). The role of paternal variables in divorced and married families: Predictability of adolescent adjustment. *American Journal of Orthopsychiatry, 63,* 126–135.

Thornton, A. (1991). Influence of the marital history of parents on the marital and cohabitational experiences of children. *American Journal of Sociology, 96,* 868–894.

Thornton, A., & Camburn, D. (1987). The influence of the family on premarital sexual attitudes and behavior. *Demography, 24,* 323–340.

Upchurch, D. M., Aneschensel, C. S., Sucoff, C. A., & Levy-Storms, L. (1999). Neighborhood and family contexts of adolescent sexual activity. *Journal of Marriage and the Family, 61,* 920–933.

U.S. Census Bureau. (2001). *Population profile of the United States: 1999* (Current Population Reports, Series P23–205). Washington, DC: U.S. Government Printing Office.

U.S. Department of Health and Human Services. (2000). *Trends in the well-being of America's children and youth.* Washington, DC: U.S. Government Printing Office.

Videon, T. M. (2002). Who plays and who benefits: Gender, interscholastic athletics, and academic outcomes. *Sociological Perspectives, 54,* 415–444.

Weiss, R. S. (1979). Growing up a little faster: The experience of growing up in a single-parent household. *Journal of Social Issues, 35,* 97–111.

Whitbeck, L. B., Simons, R. L., & Goldberg, E. (1996). Adolescent sexual intercourse. In R. L. Simons (Ed.), *Understanding differences between divorced and intact families: Stress, interaction, and child outcomes* (pp. 144–156). Thousand Oaks, CA: Sage.

Wolchik, S. A., Sandler, I. N., Millsap, R. E., Plummer, B. A., Greene, S. M., Anderson, E. R., Dawson-McClure, S. R., Hipke, K., & Haine, R. A. (2002). Six-year follow-up of preventive interventions for children of divorce: A randomized controlled trial. *Journal of the American Medical Association, 288,* 1874–1881.

Wolchik, S. A., Tein, J.-Y., Sandler, I. N., & Doyle, K. W. (2002). Fear of abandonment as a mediator of the relations between divorce stressors and mother–child relationship quality and children's adjustment problems. *Journal of Abnormal Child Psychology, 30,* 401–418.

Wolchik, S. A., West, S. G., Sandler, I. N., Tein, J., Coatsworth, D., Lengua, L., Weiss, L., Anderson, E. R., Greene, S. M., & Griffin, W. A. (2000). An experimental evaluation of theory-based mother and mother–child programs for children of divorce. *Journal of Consulting and Clinical Psychology, 68,* 843–856.

Wolchik, S. A., West, S. G., Westover, S., Sandler, I. N., Martin, A., Lustig, J., Tein, J., & Fisher, J. (1993). The children of divorce parenting intervention: Outcome evaluation of an empirically based program. *American Journal of Community Psychology, 21,* 293–331.

Wu, L. L., & Martinson, B. C. (1993). Family structure and the risk of a premarital birth. *American Sociological Review, 58,* 210–232.

Wyman, P. A., Cowen, E. L., Hightower, A. D., & Pedro-Carroll, J. L. (1985). Perceived competence, self-esteem, and anxiety in latency-aged children of divorce. *Journal of Clinical Child Psychology, 14,* 20–26.

Zimiles, H., & Lee, L. E. (1991). Adolescent family structure and educational progress. *Developmental Psychology, 27,* 314–320.

16

Consequences of Divorce
for Parents

Sanford L. Braver, Jenessa R. Shapiro,
and Matthew R. Goodman
Arizona State University

Although divorce rates have decreased a bit since about 1980, they increased so dramatically in the decade and a half before that as to make divorce unerringly register as a serious social problem. The divorce rate was about 15 per 1,000 married women aged 15 to 44 years in 1960; by 1980, it had risen to about 40 per 1,000, almost a threefold increase (Shiono & Quinn, 1994). Today, rates are about 35 per 1,000. As described in other chapters in this handbook (chap. 3 by Amato and chap. 4 by Teachman, Tedrow, & Hall), about 50% of marriages today are expected to end in divorce.

Starting in about the mid-1970s, social scientists and other scholars developed great interest in divorce and dissolution processes and outcomes, stirred no doubt by the flood of divorces near that time. In the decade of the 1990s alone, nearly 10,000 articles were published on the topic (Amato, 2000).

In this chapter, we trace the consequences of the process of becoming divorced on the parents. Thus, we trace the consequences for adults who divorce *who have children*. There is a separate and largely nonoverlapping literature on childless dissolutions. Generally, these impacts are milder and of shorter duration, in the sense that recovery is almost always rather swift (Masheter, 1991; Metts & Cupach, 1995). The consequences for the children of divorce are reviewed elsewhere in this handbook (chap. 15 by Barber and Demo).

The consequences of divorce for parents, mapped in the subsequent paragraphs, include the following:

- the legal process and consequences,
- the financial consequences,
- the psychological and emotional consequences,
- the consequences for the parental relationship, and
- the consequences for the interparental relationship.

As will be obvious, whereas some consequences are general and befall divorcing parents generally, most consequences are variable, depending on various factors. The most explored and obvious factors by which consequences differ are (a) the parent with custody versus the one without custody of the child(ren); (b) the sex of the parent (i.e., the mother vs. the father); and (c) the person who initiated the divorce versus the one who did not (and often did not want it; i.e., the "dumper" vs. the "dumpee").

It turns out that there is a great deal of overlap between these three dimensions: mothers generally are the parents who get custody; *and* mothers generally are the dumper. Whereas we present evidence for the first assertion in the subsequent section on legal consequences, we present evidence for the second assertion here. Virtually every study has shown that women initiate about two thirds of all divorces, and men one fourth of them; the remainder are mutual decisions (e.g., Ahrons, 1994; Braver, Whitley, & Ng, 1993; Kitson, 1992; Zeiss, Zeiss, & Johnson, 1980).

Accordingly, most of the following sections first give a description of the consequences for parents generally or *universally*, and then give a report that differentiates by sex, custodial status, or dumper–dumpee status.

LEGAL CONSEQUENCES OF DIVORCE FOR PARENTS: UNIVERSAL

When married couples dissolve their marriage, they must face and resolve a number of legal consequences. Because divorce is a formal, legal matter in which the government (at both the state and county level) has a central role, many of these consequences are resolved with the active participation, sanction, or even requirements of government agencies, such as judges, courts, and child support agencies. Existing statutes and case law, or court, governmental, and legal policies concern almost every aspect of divorce, including custody, visitation or access, child support, and the like.

What follows is a list of the seven legal issues that must, as a general rule, be resolved at the termination of a marriage with children. One way or another, most decrees of divorce will typically have provisions regarding each of the following items.

1. Physical or residential custody: This describes where the child (or children) will primarily live. It is typically either *sole* or *joint*, also termed *shared*. This last term often is reserved for those cases in which the child will live about an equal amount of time with both parents, typically in some alternation schedule, such as weekly, monthly, or semimonthly.

2. Legal custody: This refers to who has the legal authority to make decisions about the child regarding such matters as medical care, schooling, and religious issues.

3. Visitation or access: This refers to how often and under what circumstances the child will have contact with the nonresident parent. Only rarely will less than alternate weekends be specified.

4. Child support: Although administered by individual counties, as a result of federal mandates passed in 1988, financial guidelines are now set at a state level. These guidelines are "presumptive," meaning the formula the state sets must apply in every case unless a judge makes a written ruling that it would be unfair, given the particular circumstances of the family. The federal law also mandates that payments are normally ensured by automatic wage garnishment, much as income tax withholding.

5. Other financial issues concerning the child: These issues include, most importantly, who pays for the child's medical or dental insurance, how the child's medical expenses not covered by insurance are to be divided, and how child-care expenses are allocated. Since the 1988 federal mandates, by recommendation of the U.S. Commission on Interstate Child Support,

these three expenses are generally taken into account in the formal child support order, as an allocated addition, because "the *basic* child support guideline chart amount does *not* include the costs of child care or health insurance" (Elrod, 1994; emphasis added). Other items commonly covered in this portion are who pays for travel expenses associated with visitation when or if the parents move apart, and how college expenses, if any, will be divided (Fabricius, Braver & Deneau, 2003).

6. Spousal support–maintenance or alimony: As with child support, dollar amounts, method of payment, and the like are typically specified.

7. Property and debt division: The decree may contain a list of assets and debts and specify who gets what. The normal and virtually universal rule is equal or equitable division (Ellman, 1999).

The final two aforementioned issues, of course, are features of divorces both with and without children. It should also be noted that there is a movement to abolish custody and visitation provisions, replacing them with the more neutral terms *parenting plans* or *parenting time* (Emery, 2004).

How Issues Are Resolved

A common misconception is that these various legal consequences are typically decided for the family by a judge after each side presents its case in court. In fact, very few divorces are decided this way. Braver and O'Connell (1998) found that only 5% of couples had any of the aforementioned matters decided by a judge, whereas Maccoby and Mnookin (1992) found only 2.5%. Instead, there is a large and ever-growing menu of alternative methods of resolving these matters. According to the researchers mentioned here, in at least three fourths of cases, couples decide themselves, with or without (one or two) lawyers, how to resolve all of these matters, albeit sometimes only after protracted negotiations. The next most common alternative is mediation, in which a trained professional neutral third party attempts to help the couple arrive at a mutually acceptable compromise (see chap. 27 by Sbarra & Emery, this volume). For custody and visitation issues, a *custody evaluation* might be undertaken (Ackerman, 1995; Stahl, 1994), in which an expert makes nonbinding recommendations to the parties and the court concerning custody and access after a full psychological evaluation of the family. Although in the recent past each side could hire its own expert to "duel it out," current guidelines of the American Psychological Association discourage that practice, preferring instead only one evaluator, appointed by the court, whose code of ethics requires giving fair consideration to each side.

There is considerable variation from state to state, both in how frequently couples utilize each of the various dispute-resolution process options, and in what solutions they tend to come to regarding each of the discussed matters. Thus, how often lawyers are involved, mediators are used, and joint custody is awarded, for example, varies considerably among the states, from almost never to almost always. Partly this is a result of different statutes, case law precedents, or procedural options authorized or financially subsidized. Very frequently, however, this state-to-state variation occurs instead because of different informal "divorce cultures" within the state's professional groups. As an example, during the course of 2 years of data collection for one of Braver's studies (Braver & Griffin, 2000), joint legal custody increased from one third of all divorces to two thirds of divorces, though no laws or other formal specifications changed during the interim. Only the prevailing consensual views among judges, lawyers, mediators, and custody evaluators changed, likely as a result of the release of new research findings and professional workshops that built consensus.

Because about three fourths of divorces are settled by the parties as a result of bargaining, it might appear puzzling that a consensus shift among professionals can affect these decisions.

The answer appears to be both what these professionals counsel or urge the parties to agree to, as well as what the parties are told will befall them if they can't agree and instead go before a judge for the decision. The latter has been aptly called "bargaining in the shadow of the law" (Mnookin & Kornhauser, 1979).

LEGAL CONSEQUENCES OF DIVORCE: SEX DIFFERENCES

As a result of the processes leading them to resolution of the issues they must finalize, mothers and fathers typically experience far different legal consequences of divorce. According to a recent national study (Nord & Zill, 1996), in 75% of divorce cases, mothers become the sole custody parent, and fathers the nonresidential parent; in about 4% of cases, this is reversed (although this percentage appears to be slowly increasing; see Meyer & Garasky, 1993). About 17% of divorce cases have joint legal custody but mother residential custody. The most typical visitation provision allows for alternating weekend visitation by the noncustodial father (Lamb, 1999), but this is subject to considerable variability from couple to couple and from state to state.

In our economic section, we report the gender-related legal consequences for child support and child-related expenses. With respect to the remaining financial matters, the current trend is for spousal support to be ordered only rarely, when the two spouses have substantially unequal incomes, and one's is quite high, and especially when this is so because one parent tended not to work so as instead to care for the children (Ellman, 1989, 1991). When spousal support is ordered, it is normally time limited, until the spouse receiving it "rehabilitates" her (or his) work skills to the point where it's no longer necessary. For example, Braver and O'Connell (1998) found that only 7% of the Arizona decrees that they examined contained an alimony award. Of these, two thirds were scheduled to terminate within a specified period of time. Maccoby and Mnookin (1992) put the national rate of alimony awards at 8%, whereas the U.S. Census puts it at 15% (U.S. Bureau of the Census, 1986). Concerning property and debt division, little reliable data concerning gender related outcomes exist, except for the division of the house asset. One study (Braver & O'Connell) found that 39% of decrees contained the mention of a house as property to be allocated. Of these cases, 16% required the house to be put up for sale immediately for the equity to be divided. Of the remainder, in 58% of the families it was retained as a residence by the mother, and in 41% of families, it was retained by the father. Maccoby and Mnookin, studying a sample in northern California, where property values are extremely high, found that fully 37% required a sale and division of the financial equity. Of the remainder, the home was retained by the mother in 59% and by the father in 41%, which is almost identical to the previous investigation.

How are we to interpret these statistics, especially those pertaining to custody and access, relative to the question of whether either sex is disadvantaged? In fact, this is a highly debated issue in the field (e.g., Fineman, 1991; Mahoney, 1996; Mason, 1988; Weitzman, 1985). Gender-bias task forces have been established in 45 states, according to the National Center for State Courts (http://www.ncsconline.org/WC/Publications/KIS_RacEthStLnks.pdf). Most researchers like those mentioned here, have argued that "the system" is biased against women, because of their inability to afford competent representation and because of their alleged inadequate financial status after divorce. However, others scholars claim that fathers are the victims of gender bias, largely on the basis of alleged unfairness in custody and visitation decisions (Pruett & Jackson, 1999). Indeed, research has demonstrated that the great majority of fathers *feel* that the custody system is slanted toward mothers (Arendell, 1995; Neilson, 2004).

The two sides interpret the custody statistics in vastly different ways. The biased-against-fathers advocates presume that the 4% father custody figure itself indicates bias, because, if the system were gender blind, custody would be 50–50. The other side instead prefers the figures that show that in very few cases does a judge decide custody. They claim this implies that "most of the mothers who have custody attained it with the father's consent, presumably because the father understood and agreed that the best interest of the children was served by such an arrangement" (Tippins, 2001). In fact, among the few adjudicated cases, women and men win about equally (Maccoby & Mnookin, 1992; Pearson & Ring, 1982–1983), seemingly disproving the idea that courts are too mother friendly. However, the role that selection bias plays in this statistic has been raised by Warshak (1996): "If the perception exists of an uneven playing field favoring mothers, fathers with weaker cases are apt to drop their bid for custody early in the legal process" (p. 401). He argues that if, among the extremely highly selected and supposedly ironclad cases that make it to trial, fathers still lose half the time, that loss may be regarded as evidence of prejudice against fathers. Indeed, evidence from studies conducted very early in the divorce process and asking about the parties' preferences at that early time show that fathers get the arrangements they prefer far less often than mothers do (Braver & O'Connell, 1998; Maccoby & Mnookin). Further, there was no evidence that mothers had to trade off and make financial concessions in order to obtain the custody arrangement that they sought.

Evidence that it may well be lawyer advice concerning the likelihood of favorable custody decisions that indeed leads fathers to abandon the quest for custody arrangements they more prefer comes from a study by Braver, Cookston, and Cohen (2002). These authors distributed two versions of a questionnaire to family law attorneys at a state bar convention at random, describing a custody scenario in which the respondent was to imagine they represented either the mother or the father. They found that mothers would be advised that they had a greater chance for the higher custody and parenting-time scenarios than fathers, despite facts of the case that should advantage neither. Thus, attorneys appear to be advising clients what Maccoby and Mnookin (1992) declared: "when two competent parents—a fit mother and a fit father—each want to be primarily responsible for the child following divorce, mothers usually end up with the children" (p. 283).

Braver et al. (2002) also found that, when experienced attorneys were asked to "describe the 'slant' of the . . . legal system, as a whole, toward divorcing parents," only 5% thought it favors the father, 36% believed it is not slanted, and 59% perceived it favors the mother. This result corresponds well with what the fathers themselves answered in a separate investigation (Braver & O'Connell, 1998), in which three fourths thought that it favored mothers and not a single father thought that the system favored fathers. Mothers tended to agree that the system was slanted in their favor: although two thirds thought it was balanced, three times as many mothers thought it favored mothers as thought it favored fathers.

Perhaps related to this, Sheets and Braver (1996) found that mothers reported significantly greater satisfaction with the ultimate provisions of their divorce arrangements than fathers did on almost every one of the seven dimensions, and that this difference largely remained when the couples were retested 3 years later. Moreover, mediation analyses disclosed that mothers experienced this higher level of satisfaction both because they got the outcomes they preferred and because they felt more in control of the legal process.

ECONOMIC CONSEQUENCES
OF DIVORCE: UNIVERSAL

There are few parents who, at divorce, do not experience threats to their financial circumstances. First, there are the costs of the divorce itself. These costs can vary widely, depending on the state, the complexity of the case, the degree of contentiousness and disagreements, and the use of attorneys versus alternate modes of dispute resolution. On one hand, when there are few disagreements and the parties don't hire lawyers, the costs can be as little as a few hundred dollars. On the other hand, we have heard many reports of divorces costing well over $100,000 in legal and other costs. One popular estimate is that divorce is a $28 billion-a-year national industry with an average cost per couple of about $20,000 (http://www.bankrate.com/brm/news/advice/19990903a.asp). Absorbing such a cost is difficult financially for almost all couples. Second, and more enduringly, as the one household is split into two households, there will be added ongoing costs associated with running the second household. As Emery (1994) noted, because of economies of scale, two households are more expensive to maintain than one. These considerations might lead one to believe that the postdivorce finances of both parents are diminished after divorce.

ECONOMIC CONSEQUENCES OF DIVORCE: SEX DIFFERENCES

Nonetheless, the literature on the financial consequences of divorce is largely uniform in depicting substantial sex differences. Almost all studies show that custodial parents, that is, mothers, fare substantially worse economically after divorce than fathers do. Much of this literature is reviewed by Sayer (chap. 19) in this volume. The most well-known finding is that by Weitzman (1985), whose analysis showed that women (and children) suffered a 73% decline in standard of living after divorce, whereas fathers enjoyed a 42% increase. Her figures were extremely well publicized (Peterson, 1996) and characterized as "ranking among the most cited demographic statistics of the 1980s" (Hoffman & Duncan, 1988, p. 641), but they were later recanted as being in error (Weitzman, 1996; Peterson). One of the most recent findings of this sort is by Bianchi, Subaiya, and Kahn (1999), who found that divorced mothers' economic well-being is only 56% of that of the matched fathers. More findings that replicate the sex disparity of postdivorce financial circumstances are found in the research of Duncan and Hoffman (1985); Weiss (1984); Hoffman and Duncan (1985); Bianchi (1992); Sorensen (1992); Burkhauser, Duncan, Hauser, and Bernsten (1990, 1991); Holden and Smock (1991); David and Flory (1989); Corcoran (1979); Espenshade (1979); Smock, Manning, and Gupta (1999); Bartfeld (2000); and Teachman and Paasch (1994).

In this chapter, however, we present evidence and argument to the contrary. It is our contention that the postdivorce circumstances of fathers and mothers in the short term are largely equal, and neither is particularly worse off than before the divorce. In the longer term, moreover, it may well be that the majority of divorced mothers fare better than their exhusbands. Considering the voluminous literature documenting that a substantial mother disadvantage exists, this provocative and controversial proposition requires substantial context to be convincing.

Definition of Economic Well-Being

In order to empirically evaluate the relative economic well-being of the two parents, one needs an operational definition of the construct. Some possibilities that appear reasonable include gauging financial assets, debt, ownership, and so on. A difficulty with all these measures, however, is that they are too dependent on the lifestyle (spending vs. saving) *choices* that the respondent makes. Two individuals of the same means may spend, acquire, and save differently. Another possibility involves not inquiring about monetary amounts, but rather about the *perception* of economic hardship versus ease. As an example of the latter, Pearlin and Johnson (1977) asked respondents how often they did not have enough money to afford the kind of food, medical care, and the like that the household "should have." However, this judgment is not satisfying to the economists and demographers who have conducted most of the analyses in the literature, because it appears too subjective and dependent on what level of medical care (and so on) that the respondent believes the household *ought to* have.

Perhaps because of these considerations, most of the economic literature has taken a more objective numerical approach in which annual *income* is taken as the foundational component of economic well-being (or standard of living). In the case of divorced parents, because child support is very frequently paid by one and received by the other parent (and, less frequently, alimony is also paid), both are virtually always subtracted from the payer's income and added to the recipient's before any additional calculations are made. Henceforth, we term this corrected amount *transfer-corrected income*.

Let us concretize the discussion so far with an example. Assume that a noncustodial father earns $36,000/year, and a custodial mother earns $24,000/year. These two income values are realistic; they are the nearest rounded values found as average incomes in a random file review for 427 newly divorcing couples in 2001–2002 (Venohr & Griffith, 2003). As we can see in Table 16.1, the ratio of the father's income to the mother's is 1.5. Assume the couple has two children and resides in Wisconsin. In Wisconsin, the father would be ordered to pay $750/month in child support, or $9,000/year, which would be deducted from his payroll check and paid to the mother. (Wisconsin was chosen to illustrate the child support calculation both

TABLE 16.1

Calculation of Short-Term Relative Standard of Living for Average-Income Noncustodial and Custodial Households, by Various Criteria

		Average				
		NCP		CP		NCP:CP Ratio
Row	Criterion					
1	Income	36,000		24,000		1.50
2	Transfers (child support order)	(9,000)		9,000		
3	Transfer-corrected income	27,000		33,000		0.82
		Divide by	Result	Divide by	Result	
4	Per capita	1	27,000	3	11,000	2.45
5	BLS–LSB	0.36	75,000	.76	43,421	1.73
6	BLS–LSB under 35	0.35	77,143	.67	49,254	1.57
7	Expert panel	0.54	50,000	.80	41,250	1.21
8	Poverty threshold	0.513	52,632	.794	41,562	1.27
9	Formula .65	1	27,000	1.767	18,680	1.45
10	Formula .75	1	27,000	1.928	17,114	1.58
11	Federal and state taxes	(8,556)		262		
12	After-tax transfer-adjusted income	18,444		33,262		0.55
13	Poverty threshold	0.513	35,953	.794	41,892	0.86
14	Formula .7	1	18,444	1.846	18,022	1.02
15	Visitation-adjusted poverty threshold	0.581	31,768	.772	43,087	0.74
16	Visitation-adjusted formula .7	1.225	15,059	1.785	18,635	0.81

Note: NCP = noncustodial parent; CP = custodial parent.

because its formula is comparatively simple and because its child support guideline is at the exact average of all states' for the income case studied by Morgan & Lino, 1999, nearest to the present example). As seen in row 3 of the table, the transfer corrected incomes are $27,000 and $33,000, with a ratio of 0.82.

However, it is clearly inappropriate and unfair to mothers to compare these transfer-corrected incomes directly as an indication of their economic well-being, because in the custodial mother's household, the income must go to support more family members, the children as well as herself, whereas in the father's, it supports only one person, himself. An apparent potential corrective is to compute *per capita* transfer-corrected income, that is, the transfer-corrected income divided by the number of family members in the household, and compare these. As seen in row 4 of Table 16.1, because the family size of the noncustodial parent's home is 1, whereas that of the custodial parent's is 3, the ratio of per capita income is 2.45.

It is evident that this is an overcorrection, however, because the marginal financial burdens attributed to each *additional* family member are clearly diminishing (there exist so-called economies of scale). That is, it doesn't cost as much to feed and house the fourth person in the household as the first. The in-between method used in virtually all the empirical literature cited herein is the needs-adjusted income technique, in which the transfer-corrected income is divided by some other value than the number of people in the household, one which, although based on the family's size and composition, takes into account diminishing marginal living costs. Such a standard indicates what level of resources it takes to maintain identical standards of living for families of different composition. Comparing this needs-adjusted income index, also called the *income-to-needs ratio*, has thus been the method of choice to compare mothers' versus fathers' standards of living.

Three different such needs standards have been used by different analysts comparing economic well-being for divorced families. The early research (e.g., Duncan & Hoffman, 1985; Weitzman, 1985), as well as some more recent work (e.g., Blumberg, 1999; Peterson, 1996), used the Bureau of Labor Statistics "1977 lower standard budget" (BLS–LSB). The BLS–LSB depicted how much it cost to live (in 1977) at a "lower" economic level for families of different compositions. In arriving at these budgets, BLS analysts "used a mix of scientific standards, where available, and standards derived from actual spending patterns to specify lists of goods and services as well as the quantities of those items" (Johnson, Rogers, & Tan, 2001). After one divides the transfer-corrected income by this budget standard, the resulting index represents the ratio of what income the family *has* to what a family of that size *needs to have* to survive economically at a so-called lower level.

The equivalent calculations are shown in row 5 of Table 16.1. Rather than work in terms of absolute incomes, the calculation is in terms of the percentage of income the given family needs compared with that needed by an arbitrary base family—one that has two adults and two children. According to the BLS–LSB, the one-adult no-children household (i.e., the noncustodial's) needs 36% of what the base family needs to survive at the same level, whereas the custodial household, with one adult and two children, needs 76% of the base family's income. Using this figure as the divisor, one sees that the ratio is indeed intermediate between the 0.82 and the 2.45, 1.73, indicating that the father enjoys 1.73 times the standard of living as the mother.

The BLS–LSB's figures were for a householder over 35 years old; the BLS–LSB provides other percentages (35% and 67%, respectively) for those under 35. Row 6 shows the results of these under-35 figures being the denominator, a drop to a ratio of 1.57. No researcher we are aware of used the under-35 values. However, in the random case file review already referred to, age 35 was very close to the median age of the divorcing parents, so these values are arguably applicable to about half of all divorced families.

However, the BLS discontinued updating these BLS–LSB scales in 1978 and phased them out altogether in 1980, after a critical report by an expert panel (see Watts, 1980). The expert panel then proposed alternate values. For the two types of families in our example, these percentages were 54% and 80%, respectively (Johnson, Rogers & Tan, 2001, p. 34); the results of dividing by these percentages, a drop to a ratio of 1.21, are shown in row 7. Again, no published research we are aware of uses these expert panel values.

What most modern research (e.g., Amato, 1999; Bartfeld, 2000; Bianchi et al., 1999; Braver, 1999; Garfinkel et al., 1998; Rogers & Bieniewicz, 2004) does use instead is the federal poverty thresholds. For example, in 2003, the poverty levels were $18,660 for the base family of two adults and two children, $9,573 for the single-adult no-children family, (51.3% of the base family's poverty level threshold), and $14,824 for the one-parent, two-children family (79.4% of the base family's threshold; see http://www.census.gov/hhes/poverty/threshld/thresh03.html). The results of dividing by these two percentages of the base family are shown in row 8, with results quite close to the expert panel's, that is, a ratio of 1.27.

A few studies use a more modern index, one developed by the Panel on Poverty and Federal Assistance in response to a directive from the Joint Economic Committee of Congress in 1992. This index, endorsed by the National Research Council, was presented in Citro and Michael (1995) as the formula $(A + .7C)^F$, where A is the number of adults (set at 1 for both mother's and father's households), C is the number of children (set, for our example, at 0 for father's and 2 for mother's), and F is an economy of scale factor that "should be set at either 0.65 or 0.75" (Johnson et al., p. 39.) The .7 in the formula reflects that, according to the panel, children require only an average of .7 the expenditures that an adult does. Using the lower bound .65 value for F in the formula, we see that the divisor is 1 for father and 1.767 for mother. Using the .75 upper bound value for F, we find that the divisor remains 1 for father and becomes 1.928 for mother. Rows 9 and 10 of Table 16.1 show that the results of using these divisors in the calculations, respectively, are 1.45 and 1.58, intermediate between the BLS and the poverty threshold approach.

Comparative Standards of Living

What is apparent so far is that the comparative standards of living (i.e., the ratios in the final column) vary considerably for our average family depending on the methodology used, from a low of 1.21 (expert panel) to a high of 1.73 (BLS–LSB). Because all these methods (except those in rows 1, 3, and 4) are reasonable and recommended or used by some experts or researchers, it is difficult to say definitively exactly what the ratio of standards of living is for these two parents. By all methods, however, the ratio is greater than 1.0, suggesting that, consistent with the literature, the postdivorce standard of living of the father is higher than that of the mother.

The Two Omitted Factors

So how can we make the claim that the standards of living for the two parents are very similar? Because omitted from almost all calculations in the literature, including in every study cited in the Sayers chapter, are at least two crucial, yet obvious, factors. The first is taxes. All of the aforementioned calculations are based on gross income, yet only *after tax* income can be used to support the family. Because it is only what remains after the IRS, Social Security, and the states have reduced the parties' paychecks that can be spent to support the family, Espenshade (1979) argued that it is the *after-tax* income, not the *gross or pretax* income, that affects standard of living and hence should be used in any such calculation. However, only a few studies (Braver, 1999; Braver & Stockburger, 2004; Rogers & Bieniewicz, 2004) have heeded that advice. Taxes would not alter the results much, however, as long as divorced mothers and fathers were taxed about equally after divorce. They are not. Custodial parents are taxed differently, and far more advantageously, than noncustodial parents, in many respects.

We can estimate the taxes for these two families by making some simplifying assumptions (such as that both parents take the standard deduction, and that all income is earned income). The federal tax for the noncustodial parent would be $3,987 annually, whereas FICA takes $2,754. In Wisconsin, his state tax would be $1,814. The total of these three taxes is $8,556, as shown in row 11, leaving the parent $18,444 after-tax transfer-corrected (ATTC, or "spendable") income. The custodial parent, however, whose receipt of child support, though income, is *not taxed*, and whose employment (and investment) income is taxed at the lower, head-of-household rate, and who gets to take the children as exemptions, and who has a greater standard deduction, pays federal taxes of only $810. However, this is before the child tax credit, which, as of 2003, is $1,000 per child. Thus, not only does this cancel this parent's income tax debt of $810 completely, but she also *receives* a net $1,190 as a tax credit from the IRS. She also qualifies for the Earned Income Credit, which would pay her another $1,705 annually. Against this federal tax income of $2,895, she would pay FICA of $1,836 as well as $797 in state tax, leaving her a net tax income of $262. Now her ATTC income is $33,262, as seen in row 12. Rather than use all the preceding possible divisors to divide this spendable ATTC income, we show only two preferred ones. Using the poverty thresholds, as in row 13, we see that the standard of living ratio is now .86, implying hers is slightly higher than his. Even using the poverty panel's formula (set at .7, the value intermediate between the two reasonable ones), we see that the ratios are nearly identically equal. So one part of the answer to the above puzzle is clear: because the federal government (wisely?) treats custodial mothers so much better than noncustodial fathers for income tax purposes, mothers do far better when taking taxes into account than when not. In essence, the IRS is subsidizing to a degree the standard of living of the custodial household. In fact, a great many custodial parents have net tax *income*, not subtractions. No noncustodial fathers do. Until studies such as those reported in the Sayers chapter take taxes into account, they will show what we regard as seriously misleading findings.

The second factor the previous literature omitted is equally consequential. Almost all researchers assumed that, other than child support, 100% of the child's expenses are borne by the custodial parent, and 0% by the noncustodial one. That is, they assume the noncustodial parent pays for no child meals, has no child transportation costs, pays $0 to entertain the child, does not provide a room for the child in his home, and does not provide any medical insurance, share medical expenses, and so on. Thus, virtually none of the past analyses take into account any kind of visitation expense, nor payment of any kind directly by the noncustodial parent for the child.

This failure to account for these visitation and other child expenses further distorts the analyses in the literature. For example, in the random case file review (Venohr & Griffith, 2003), 62% of the files specified a visitation schedule for the child that exceeded 24% of the child's time. Thus, many if not most noncustodial parents must be bearing nontrivial expenses when the child is visiting, some of which (e.g., food and recreation) defray similar expenses by the custodial parent. Moreover, most states mandate that medical expenses, health insurance, and child-care costs be paid, at least in part, by the father, over and above the child support he pays the mother. In fact, Fabricius and Braver (2003) found that substantial expenses were being paid directly by noncustodial parents for their children. For example, according to their now-college-age children, 59% had a bedroom of their own (or shared with siblings) in their fathers' home, and 37% had had their own bicycle at their dad's house.

Braver and Stockburger (2004) specified a set of reasonable and robust assumptions—too detailed and technical to repeat here—that can be used to correct estimates for these expenses borne by the noncustodial parent. In the example at hand, 25% visitation by the noncustodial parent would raise his poverty threshold from 51.3% to 58% of the base family, whereas it would lower the custodial mother's from 79.4% to 77.2% of the base family, lowering the ratio to 74%, as shown in row 15. In the poverty formula, the figure is 81%, shown in row 16. (Rogers & Bieniewicz, 2004, use other assumptions that result in even greater lowering of the ratio.)

We have seen that the results change dramatically when taxes and visitation expenses are both taken into account, so that, for this hypothetical but average case, the custodial parent's standard of living goes from being seen as substantially inferior to that of the noncustodial parent to now being seen as substantially higher.

How well does this hypothetical case correspond to what is happening empirically? Recall that the income values (and the child support ordered amount and taxes that result) were chosen to reflect empirical reality. However, owed child support is not always fully paid, and scheduled visitation does not always occur. In order to reflect these actual events, Braver and O'Connell (1998) and Braver (1999) tracked an actual sample and substituted child support actually paid and visitation that actually occurred. (Of course, there are different ways of indexing both of these, and, most importantly, mothers' and fathers' reports of these quantities disagreed somewhat.) As expected, child support actually paid (in row 2) was not as much as was ordered, and visitation was a bit less than the 25% assumed in Table 16.1. These factors increased the average ratios shown in rows 15 and 16. In fact, they increased it by just enough to raise the ratios to close to 1.0 (a bit more or a bit less, depending on which of the multitude of specified operational definitions was used). However, this study, like virtually every other one in the literature, is outdated, because the divorces analyzed all occurred *before presumptive child support guidelines and mandatory wage garnishment* were enacted in 1988. Guidelines increased child support substantially (Bay, Braver, Fogas, Fitzpatrick, & Wolchik, 1988; Thoennes, Tjaden, & Pearson, 1991), and garnishment increased the chances that ordered child support was actually paid. These two factors will both favor mothers' standard of living. So, as a general statement, it appears warranted to claim that, when the omissions and oversights of the past empirical literature are properly accounted for, and the current child support policies are taken into account, the standards of living of the mother will be slightly above that of the father shortly after the divorce.

We also made the counterintuitive assertion near the beginning of this section that not only are the two parents about equally economically well off shortly after divorce, but that each has, on average, close to the same standard of living as when they were married. When Braver and O'Connell (1999) applied the same type of analyses as given here to what parents told us their family income was before the separation, the income-to-needs ratios for each parent were very similar before and after divorce.

How can this be so, despite the fact that they are now supporting two rather than one household? For the custodial parent, in addition to the very favorable tax treatment given to her, and the child support transfer she receives, another important factor is that she appears to earn more after divorce than she did while married (Braver, 1999). Thus, as a reasonable response to the standard of living threat posed by divorce, mothers work more hours or take jobs earning greater income. Fathers do not appear to do so, perhaps because they already earned near their maximum potential. This greater income, in combination with the tax subsidy, the child support, and the smaller household size that results when the father departs, appears to offset almost exactly the loss of the father's remaining income. For the father, the child support he pays, together with the greater tax burden a single noncustodial father bears, together with the expenses he pays directly for the child, appear to compensate nearly exactly for his smaller household size.

Long-Term Comparisons

Few of the studies in the literature have studied anything beyond about 18 months after the divorce. However, what we have been describing here, the nearly equal and remarkably steady standard of living of the two parents shortly after the divorce, appears not to remain constant throughout the "life" of the divorce (i.e., throughout the time the child remains a minor and therefore subject to child support and visitation). In particular, two very common events work to change matters as time progresses. The first is salary increases for the custodial mother. Duncan and Hoffman (1985) found that, by 5 years after divorce, women who remained single increased their standard of living 34%. Thus, as time progresses, fewer and fewer women remain out of the workforce, those who are in it work more hours, and they earn greater salaries in those jobs, partly because of advancement and experience, and partly because they have upgraded their education to command better salaries. This factor, as noted, does not work the same way for men, as they already earned far nearer their maximum capacity. Recall that we showed that that the average mother at the time of divorce earns 66% of her matched exhusband, which, when appropriately corrected for, led to approximately equal standards of living. However, the Census Bureau provides estimates of this relative *income* disparity that is not confined to the *immediate* postdivorce period for single parents. According to 1999 U.S. Census data, the median income of the closest category to divorced female custodial parents, "Family households with a female householder, no husband present," is 85% of that for the category closest to male noncustodial parents, "nonfamily households with a male householder" (Current Population Studies, 1999). Thus, with time alone, the income of the mothers gained appreciably on that of the fathers.

Will the greater earning by mothers be compensated for by their receiving less child support income? Legally, little or not at all. In states with a child support scheme like Wisconsin's, mothers' income plays no role whatever in the child support they are owed. In the majority of states, those that use the "income shares" approach, such as Kentucky and Oklahoma, the child support would drop about only about $22 per month in our scenario. Of course, fathers might decide to pay less child support than they owe if mothers earn more salary income, but they are subject to stringent child support collection machinery if they attempt to do so.

The second event, again one increasingly more likely as time progresses, is remarriage. According to Bumpass, Sweet, and Castro-Martin (1990), about two thirds of divorced mothers and about three fourths of divorced fathers will remarry. When they do, the economics will change again. Fabricius, Braver, and Deneau (2003) present evidence that the standard of living of remarried mothers is noticeably higher than that of remarried fathers, presumably because mothers, when they remarry, gain more income than they do expenses, whereas fathers, when they remarry, do the reverse. Child support obligations, however, do not change as a function of the remarriage of either parent, almost without exception. Thus, the factor of remarriage, too, will make mothers' standard of living higher than fathers', the more so as time passes after the divorce. Together, these two factors of greater income by custodial mothers and remarriage by either or both parents appear very likely to particularly favor the economic well-being of the mother, so that the long-term financial effects of divorce, on average, should result in a situation in which mothers' economic well-being is higher than fathers'. As yet, no definitive national study using long-term data, and corrections for taxes and for child expenses borne directly by fathers, has been conducted, so it is premature to say exactly how the two parents compare in economic well-being. These studies should soon be forthcoming.

The fact that child support does not change with remarriage represents an interesting but little noticed disconnect in public policy. As noted, the income of a stepfather does not affect the child support a father would be ordered to pay his exwife. However, once the child reaches the age of majority and seeks financial aid for college, the reverse holds true. The FASFA (Free Application for Student Financial Aid) form, used virtually universally for public colleges and universities to calculate students' so-called financial need for scholarships and loans, instructs that "if your parents are divorced or separated, answer the questions about the parent you lived with more during the past 12 months.... If this parent is remarried as of today, answer the questions on the rest of this form about that parent **and** the person whom your parent married (your stepparent)" (p. 6). Thus, in seeking college financial aid for children, stepfathers, but not fathers, are assumed in a position to provide financial support. In the years that the child remains a minor, however, exactly the reverse is true.

PSYCHOLOGICAL AND EMOTIONAL CONSEQUENCES OF DIVORCE ON PARENTS: UNIVERSAL

Divorce has been rated the number one life stressor (Dohrenwend & Dohrenwend, 1974; Holmes & Rahe, 1967). As a result, divorced parents in general are somewhat more likely than married ones to be afflicted with poor psychological well-being. Although the great majority of parents survive divorce with no permanent impairments, nonetheless divorced individuals have a higher risk of physical and mental illnesses, suicide, motor vehicle accidents, alcoholism, homicide, and overall mortality (e.g., Bloom, Asher, & White, 1978; Gove, Style, & Hughes, 1990; Hemstrom, 1996; Joung et al., 1997; Kposowa, Breault, & Singh, 1995). In addition, research shows that divorced parents report higher levels of depression, anxiety, and unhappiness (e.g., Aseltine & Kessler, 1993; Davies, Avison, & McAlpine, 1997; Gove & Shin, 1989; Kitson, 1992; Lorenz et al., 1997; Simon & Marcussen, 1999).

Greater rates of postdivorce adjustment are common to those individuals who are able to function well in new family and work roles, and those who have developed a new identity aside from their former marriage (Madden-Derdich & Arditti, 1999). Furthermore, certain psychological resources, such as self-efficacy, coping skills, and agency, have been shown to lessen the negative impact of divorce (Amato, 2000). Consistent with the concept of creating an identity that is independent from the former marriage, employment has been found to buffer against negative appraisal of postdivorce life and protect against effects of income decline (Wang & Amato, 2000). Holding religious or personal beliefs and values that do not oppose divorce make for an easier adjustment (Booth & Amato, 1991; Simon & Marcussen, 1999). Similarly, new relationships (e.g., Wang & Amato) and remarriage (e.g., Demo & Acock, 1996) are also shown to lead to increases in well-being. Some literature indicates that African Americans adjust better to divorce, mainly as a result of different norms regarding cohabitation, frequency of divorce, and the birth of children out of wedlock (Cherlin, 1992). However, other research suggests the timeline for the onset and the experience of psychological distress and coping for African Americans may be different from that of European Americans (Barrett, 2003).

Theories

Several writers have attempted to theorize about divorce's effect on psychological well-being. In a recent integration and review of the consequences of divorce on psychological well-being, Amato (2000) presented a divorce–stress–adjustment model. In this model, the path between divorce and adjustment is mediated by stressors such as sole parenting responsibility, loss of emotional support, continuing conflict with the exspouse, economic decline, and other stressful divorce-related events. The path to adjustment is also moderated by protective factors such as individual, interpersonal, and structural resources; definition and meaning of divorce to the individual; and demographic characteristics. In this model, Amato allowed for adjustment to divorce to be both short term (as generally argued in a divorce-as-crisis model, e.g., Booth & Amato, 1991; Tschann, Johnston, & Wallerstein, 1989) and long term (as generally argued in a divorce-as-chronic-strain model, e.g., McCubbin & Patterson, 1982). Amato argued that these opposing models of adjustment can coexist such that different types of people will utilize each strategy.

In contrast to Amato's (2000) model is a reverse causality argument—divorce may be driven by preexisting, stable personality characteristics. Individuals with poor adjustment, often those who divorce and never remarry, may select into divorce and out of remarriage. They may be more restless or mentally unstable prior to their first marriage (Davies et al., 1997; Kelly & Conley, 1987; Kitson, 1992; Kurdek, 1990; Mastekaasa, 1994).

Positive life changes and successful adjustment to divorce are also likely (e.g., Amato, 2000; Kitson, 1992; Kitson & Morgan, 1990). A second-chance perspective contends that divorce can be an opportunity for many individuals, and it can ultimately lead to increases in well-being. For example, divorce can provide the opportunity to get out of a troubled or abusive relationship, which in turn reduces stress levels (Aseltine & Kessler, 1993; Booth & Amato, 1991; Johnson & Wu, 2002; Wheaton, 1990). Moreover, divorce offers positive changes such as peace of mind, personal growth, and autonomy (Kitson, 1992; Marks, 1996). There are reported sex differences in the research on divorce as a second chance that are discussed in more detail in the following section.

EMOTIONAL CONSEQUENCES OF DIVORCE: SEX DIFFERENCES

Which sex does better emotionally after divorce? Despite media portrayals that present divorced fathers as comparatively content, coming through the whole divorce process with relatively few emotional scratches because they are free to pursue the happy-go-lucky single lifestyle they crave, while divorced mothers' burdens pushing them to the brink of emotional calamity (e.g., *The First Wives Club*; Braver & O'Connell, 1998), the empirical literature disagrees. The general finding in the literature is that, following divorce, women tend to show greater emotional adjustment and recovery than do men (Ahrons & Rodgers, 1987; Braver & O'Connell, 1998; Chiriboga & Cutler, 1977; Wallerstein & Kelly, 1980). There appear to be several reasons for this.

First, women tend to be more successful than men at seeking, building, and using social support networks that buffer the stresses that accompany divorce (Chiriboga, Coho, Stein, & Roberts, 1979; Hughes, 1988; Keith, 1986; Kitson, 1992; McKenry & Price, 1991; Pledge, 1992; Umberson, Chen, House, Hopkins, & Slaten, 1996). Women tend to turn to family, friends, close male friends, or an intimate other (McLanahan, Adelberg, & Wedemeyer, 1981). Men, however, are more likely to derive support from work, an intimate other, a former spouse, and in-laws of the former spouse (Stone, 2002). One important and often overlooked source of support for the custodial parent is the child (Blankenhorn, 1995; McKenry & Price). The noncustodial parent loses the child as a form of support, and also loses status as a parent, a process Blankenhorn (1995) refers to as becoming "unfathered." Mothers also must "hold it together" for the sake of the children they care for, whereas noncustodial fathers don't have this sobering responsibility.

Second, fathers tend to experience their highest levels of stress *following* the filing for divorce (Albrecht, 1980; Bloom & Caldwell, 1981), whereas mothers often experience more stress prior to the decision to divorce. Baum (2003) argues that this difference may be indicative of different mourning patterns in men and women.

Third, and related to the aforementioned items, it is usually the woman who initiates the divorce (Ahrons & Rodgers, 1987; Braver, Whitley, et al., 1993; Pettit & Bloom, 1984). The spouse who initiates the divorce tends to experience the greatest amount of stress *before* the actual decision to divorce and then experiences a relief period following this decision. In contrast, the spouse who does not initiate the divorce experiences the most amount of stress following the decision to divorce. Furthermore, greater levels of psychological adjustment are found in individuals who feel they had control over the breakup (Gray & Silver, 1990).

Fourth, men are more likely than women to use ineffective or harmful methods of coping with the stress of divorce. Thus, reports in the literature find divorced fathers more often turning to substance abuse and alcoholism as a form of coping (Baum, 2003; Umberson & Williams, 1993).

Fifth, role change may be one of the most important factors contributing to the distress and unsuccessful adjustment of fathers (Umberson & Williams, 1993) and the successful adjustment of mothers (Wallerstein & Kelly, 1980). Women are more likely to consider divorce as a second chance—mothers report improved work opportunities, social lives, happiness, and self-confidence (Demo & Acock, 1996). Along with divorce, women often gain higher status, within-family roles (e.g., head of the household, breadearner), whereas men often gain roles lower in status (e.g., they gain domestic roles in new house) in addition to confusion and frustration by the new role as a noncustodial parent (Braver & O'Connell, 1998; Umberson & Williams, 1993).

Finally, divorce settlement satisfaction is also found to differentially impact the emotional well-being of custodial and noncustodial parents (Sheets & Braver, 1996). As discussed earlier, fathers, often for the first time in their lives, frequently feel as though they have experienced gender discrimination at the hands of the legal system (Braver & O'Connell, 1998). In contrast, women tend to report higher levels of satisfaction with most divorce settlements, including custody, finances, visitation, and property (Sheets & Braver).

CONSEQUENCES OF DIVORCE FOR PARENTING: UNIVERSAL

The transitional period following a divorce has been characterized as a chaotic and stressful period for families as they experience many different changes within their family (Hetherington, 1993). This chaos in general disturbs the parent–child relationship (as well as the child) and lead to disruptions in parenting behaviors.

Research suggests that divorce generally leads to a deterioration of positive parenting strategies (responsiveness) and an increase in negative parenting strategies (e.g., harshness; Harold & Conger, 1997). This occurs for both custodial mothers as well as noncustodial fathers (Kline-Pruett, Williams, Insabella, & Little, 2003; Sturge-Apple, Gondoli, Bonds, & Salem, 2003). Nonetheless, there appear to be far different patterns to the eventual parenting practices of the two parents.

CONSEQUENCES OF DIVORCE FOR PARENTING: SEX DIFFERENCES

Custodial Parents

Research suggests that, immediately following divorce, custodial mothers are more likely to be inconsistent and punitive in their discipline strategies (Hetherington, 1993; Hetherington & Clingempeel, 1992). It is also common for divorced mothers to engage in coercive exchanges with their sons that are characterized by punitive discipline, irritability, an escalation of conflict, and aggressiveness (Hetherington).

Researchers also speculate that monitoring the activities of their youngsters and supervision is one of the biggest long-term challenges of custodial mothers (Hetherington & Stanley-Hagen, 2002). Part of this challenge is that children of divorce often have more autonomy than children in nondivorced families (Hetherington & Clingempeel, 1992). Furthermore, noncustodial mothers may allow children more power in decision making than mothers in nondivorced families. There is some evidence that this laxness in monitoring may change in adolescence, especially with girls, as children become involved in more sexualized or antisocial behavior (Hetherington, 1993).

Positive parenting strategies that are characterized by the emotional bond between parent and children, praise and warmth, may also be disrupted by divorce, although some research indicates that the warmth between custodial mothers and their children is just as strong as that between other mothers (Hetherington, 1993). Past research indicates that preadolescent girls and their mothers often have harmonious and close relationships (Hetherington & Clingempeel, 1992). Additionally, in some cases, custodial mothers may spend *more* time with their children than other mothers (Hetherington). Nonetheless, a substantial number of children also emotionally disengage from their families (Hetherington).

Although the majority of research on custodial parenting focuses on mothers, some research has also focused on custodial fathers. This research suggests that custodial fathers may have different challenges than custodial mothers. For example, research indicates that custodial fathers may have more difficulty than custodial mothers in supervising and monitoring their adolescents' behavior (Maccoby, Buchanan, Mnookin, & Dornbush, 1993). Furthermore, although adolescents reported having a close bond with both custodial mothers and custodial fathers, the strength of the bond may be greater for custodial mothers than for custodial fathers (Maccoby et al.).

Noncustodial Parents

Noncustodial parents face a radically different set of parenting challenges (Hetherington & Stanley-Hagen, 1997; Maccoby & Mnookin, 1992). For most, as described earlier, the amount of contact and involvement with their children will be dramatically reduced, despite the wishes of many of them to the contrary. The typical visitation clause of a divorce decree allows nonresidential fathers contact only on alternating weekends (Lamb, 1999), effectively setting a maximum legal limit on contact.

The amount of contact that noncustodial fathers ultimately have with their children is currently being debated in the research. Older research (e.g., Amato, 1986; Fulton, 1979; Furstenburg & Nord, 1985; Hetherington, Cox, & Cox, 1982; Hetherington & Hagan, 1986) had shown discouragingly low levels of contact, well below that allowed by the decree, and far too many fathers disengaging completely. However, much of this research failed to distinguish between never married fathers (40% of whom have no contact with their children) and divorced fathers (18% of whom have no contact with their children; see Seltzer, 1991). Some of the studies may have underreported paternal contact because they only used mother reports to estimate father contact. Past research indicates that mother estimates of paternal contact are as much as 40% lower than father estimates (Braver, Wolchik, Sandler, Fogas, & Zvetina, 1991; Seltzer & Brandreth, 1994). More current research correcting these methodological problems (Braver et al., 1991; Braver, Wolchik et al., 1993; Bray & Berger, 1990; Maccoby, Depner, & Mnookin, 1988; Seltzer) has shown higher levels of contact, and Cooksey and Craig (1998) have shown this discrepancy in part to be a cohort difference (i.e., current generations of divorced fathers visit more). Recent research (Fabricius & Hall, 2000) has also shown that both young adult children and their fathers reported that they wished for more contact. More contact was precluded because the divorce decree conformed closely to their mother's desires for more mother–child contact and, subsequently, less father–child contact. Although there remains some debate about the amount of paternal contact following divorce or separation, both sides would agree that fathers in general cope better with less contact with their children after a divorce or separation than do mothers.

Adjusting to this lack of contact may be particularly difficult because noncustodial fathers are put into a role that does not have an equivalent in the intact family (i.e., before divorce or separation, parents and children live together; see Wallerstein & Corbin, 1986). As a result, there may be no script or precedent for defining the relationship between children and their parents to guide a father's parental role (Wallerstein & Kelly, 1980). Furthermore, coping with less contact may be particularly difficult for fathers, when they feel that that they have a diminished level of control with their children and that their role is not valued (Braver, Griffin, Cookston, Sandler, & Williams, in press). Braver and O'Connell (1998) argued that a number of fathers feel "parentally disenfranchised:" They feel they that have only a limited amount of control over childrearing issues with their children, and that the role they do have is not valued by their children's mothers or by the legal system.

In addition to changes in the amount of contact with their children, noncustodial parents also must cope with changes in the quality of their relationship with their children (Amato & Gilbreth, 1999). Many become very permissive in their discipline style and assume more of a companion role than the role of a disciplinarian or teacher (Hetherington, 1993). Research indicates that, although children generally feel closer to their custodial than their noncustodial parent, they are nonetheless able to maintain close relationships with nonresident fathers even with only a small amount of contact (Maccoby et al., 1993).

Although the majority of research on noncustodial parents has focused on fathers, some research on noncustodial mothers indicates that they may not struggle as much with some parenting strategies. For example, although noncustodial mothers do not monitor their children as well as nondivorced mothers, they may not be as permissive as noncustodial fathers (Hetherington & Jodl, 1994). In addition, there is some evidence that children report feeling closer to noncustodial mothers than to noncustodial fathers (Gunnoe, 1993).

INTERPARENTAL CONSEQUENCES FOR PARENTS

A final common consequence of divorce is that most divorcing couples with children tend to experience high levels of conflict (commonly known as *interparental conflict*) immediately after the divorce (Fulton, 1979; Hetherington et al., 1982), and that hostility commonly persists for 3 years or more after the divorce is final (Ahrons & Wallisch, 1987; Masheter, 1991). The majority of couples appear to disengage from protracted conflict about then, and about half engage in parallel parenting (Ahrons, 1994; Maccoby & Mnookin, 1992). Another one fourth become coparental, which is more beneficial (Ahrons, 1981; Whiteside, 1998; also see chap. 13 by Adamsons & Pasley, this volume). Perhaps 25%, however, persist in high conflict more or less indefinitely (Ahrons).

Interparental conflict can be conceptualized as including three dimensions: legal conflict, behavioral conflict, and attitudinal conflict (Goodman, Bonds, Sandler, & Braver, 2004; Johnston, 1994). Legal conflict involves actions in the court system such as continued litigation, requests for change in decrees, and enforcement actions for noncompliance with the decree. Behavioral conflict refers to how the conflict is expressed in interpersonal relationships. Behavioral conflict may manifest through direct interactions between the parents, such as verbal and physical disputes, or through indirect interactions, such as bad-mouthing the other parent to the child. Finally, attitudinal conflict involves a parent's anger and hostility toward the exspouse, including negative attitudes toward the exspouse in the parenting role.

As parents adjust to new roles, divorce is likely to bring about changes in how interparental conflict is expressed. Legal family conflict will likely be much more prevalent in divorced families than in nondivorced families. The frequency of behavioral conflict may decrease because parents have less exposure to the other parent. Forehand and Thomas (1992) found that children from married families are exposed to more direct behavioral conflict than children whose parents divorced 2 or more years ago. However, the intensity of the conflict may be stronger for divorced families than for married families (Forehand & McCombs, 1989). In addition, although the amount of behavioral conflict may be reduced, the amount of attitudinal conflict may increase. For example, it is more common for a divorced parent to have more hostile and negative attitudes toward the child's other parent than in married families (Forehand & McCombs).

The result of these changes in interparental conflict not only changes the relationship that parents have with each other, but also the relationship that parents have with their children. For example, a characteristic of interparental conflict in divorced families is putting children in the middle of the conflict by bad-mouthing the other parent to the child or by sending messages to the other parent through the child (Arbuthnot & Gordon, 1996; Buchanan & Heiges, 2001). Such an experience may lead children to feel like they need to choose or take sides in the conflict.

CONCLUSION

The literature suggests that, as a result of divorce, there are many unique stresses on parents that require their adaptation. It is clear that most divorced parents ultimately master these adversities well (see chap. 18 by Tashiro, Frazier, & Berman, this volume), though in the short run, their lives are chaotic. Nonetheless, some parents will be more or less permanently damaged by these stresses (Umberson & Williams, 1993).

As we have shown, there are clearly somewhat different patterns of challenges faced by fathers and mothers. Because mothers most often are the initiators of divorce, they have different emotional reactions than fathers do. Because they almost invariably become the custodial parent, they face different problems in their parental relationship. Finally, although previous research stated that mothers also faced a far bleaker economic outlook, newer policies and research put that conclusion deeply into question.

Although the great volume of research on divorce since the mid-1970s has illuminated many matters, some still remain murky. In view of its importance to policy, we believe that high on the research agenda must be a more appropriate and definitive assessment of comparative standards of living. As we have argued, although existing research on this topic is voluminous, it shares four problems that make the consensus findings doubtful. For these problems to be corrected, a national study with a large and representative sample has to be undertaken in which (a) taxes are calculated and subtracted from both parents' incomes; (b) expenses borne by the father on behalf of the children during his visitation time with them (and sometimes defrayed from the mother) are factored into the calculations; (c) relatively *recent* divorces are assessed, that is, those finalized *after* child support reforms were enacted in about 1990 that both substantially raised levels of child support and increased its enforcement; and (d) long-term outcomes (5–10 years postdivorce) are assessed to take into account such long-term factors as remarriage and salary changes with time. Finally, because both child support payment levels and visitation are reported differently by mothers and fathers (Braver, Fitzpatrick, & Bay, 1991; Braver, Fitzpatrick, et al., 1991; Braver et al., 1993; Sonenstein & Calhoun, 1990), either some *objective* report of these has to be used, or, at minimum, both party's reports assessed, with an admission that each is biased, in opposite directions.

Although this issue requires further work to clarify a conclusion that remains highly debatable despite a substantial volume of research, other important issues are virtually unresearched. Amato (2000) commented on the lack of research on the impact of divorce among racial and ethnic minorities, and we certainly agree (see chap. 23 by Orbuch & Brown and chap. 25 by Umaña-Tayler). Relatedly, although we intended in this chapter to review consequences of dissolution for *unmarried* parents, we found very little literature to review. With about one third of all childbirths occurring to unmarried women (*National Vital Statistics Reports*, 2003), it is important that we quickly add to our understanding of unmarried parents.

Also awaiting much more rigorous research is the effect of various kinds of interventions, (both at the policy and legal level) and psychosocial programs, on divorced parents. As indicated herein, there is a great deal of difference from jurisdiction to jurisdiction on the prevailing laws and legal practices (see chap. 26 by Mahoney, this volume), yet we know little about how these differences play out in terms of differences among the families. Similarly, a number of programs have recently been designed by professionals to assist parents and families, such as divorce parent education programs, but the research lags in evaluating the effects of such programs (see chap. 28 by Blaisure & Geasler, this volume).

Finally, we call attention to one of the most important, thorny, and least understood questions: Why do some couples have relatively harmonious and amicable divorces, and others experience enormous and enduring conflict? The level of interparental conflict is one of the most consequential variables of all in predicting both child and adult outcomes after divorce. It is the aspect of divorce that is most important to the broad variety of professionals involved in divorce: judges, lawyers, divorce educators, and forensic mental health professionals. Not only is it crucially important, it is also immensely variable from family to family. What is not well understood is how couples arrive at the conflict levels they experience. What are the processes, and what are the predictors? Thus, one of the most important tasks for future research, in our view, is to formulate a coherent explanation of this "anatomy" of postdivorce interparental conflict. This endeavor would be most useful if it led to an efficacious intervention that would help to ameliorate conflict and defuse divorce. Such an intervention has so far been frustratingly elusive in work with divorcing parents.

REFERENCES

Ackerman, M. J. (1995). *Clinician's guide to child custody evaluations*. New York: Wiley.
Ahrons, C. R. (1981). The continuing coparental relationship between divorced spouses. *American Journal of Orthopsychiatry, 51,* 415–428.

Ahrons, C. R. (1994). *The good divorce: Keeping your family together when your marriage comes apart.* New York: HarperCollins.

Ahrons, C. R., & Rodgers, R. H. (1987). *Divorced families: A multidisciplinary developmental view.* New York: Norton.

Ahrons, C. R., & Wallisch, L. (1987). The relationship between former spouses. In S. Duck & D. Pearlman (Eds.), *Intimate relationships: Development, dynamics and deterioration* (pp. 269–296). Thousand Oaks, CA: Sage.

Albrecht, S. L. (1980). Reactions and adjustments to divorce: Differences in the experiences of males and females. *Family Relations, 29,* 59–68.

Amato, P. R. (1986). Marital conflict, the parent–child relationship and child self-esteem. *Family Relations, 35,* 403–410.

Amato, P. R. (1999). The postdivorce society: How divorce is shaping the family and other forms of social organization. In R. A. Thompson & P. R. Amato (Eds.), *The postdivorce family: Children, parenting, and society* (pp. 161–190). Thousand Oaks, CA: Sage.

Amato, P. R. (2000). The consequences of divorce for adults and children. *Journal of Marriage and the Family, 62,* 1269–1287.

Amato, P. R., & Gilbreth, J. G. (1999). Nonresident fathers and children's well-being: A meta-analysis. *Journal of Marriage and the Family, 61,* 557–573.

Arbuthnot, J., & Gordon, D. A. (1996). Does mandatory divorce education for parents work? A six-month outcome evaluation. *Family and Conciliation Courts Review, 34,* 60–81.

Arendell, T. (1995). *Fathers and divorce.* Thousand Oaks, CA: Sage.

Aseltine, R. H., & Kessler, R. C. (1993). Marital disruption and depression in a community sample. *Journal of Health and Social Behavior, 34,* 237–251.

Barrett, A. E. (2003). Race differences in the mental health effects of divorce. *Journal of Family Issues, 24,* 995–1019.

Bartfeld, J. (2000). Child support and the postdivorce economic well-being of mothers, fathers, and children. *Demography, 37,* 203–213.

Baum, N. (2003). The male way of mourning divorce: When, what, and how. *Clinical Social Work Journal, 31,* 37–49.

Bay, C., Braver, S. L., Fogas, B. S., Fitzpatrick, P., & Wolchik, S. A. (1988, April). *New child support guidelines: Changes and perceived fairness.* Paper presented at the Western Psychological Association, Burlingame, CA.

Bianchi, S. M. (1992). Marital separation and the economic well-being of children and their absent fathers. *Proceedings of the Social Statistics Section.* Alexandria, VA: The American Statistical Association.

Bianchi, S. M., Subaiya, L., & Kahn, J. R. (1999). The gender gap in the economic well-being of nonresident fathers and custodial mothers. *Demography, 36,* 195–203.

Blankenhorn, D. (1995). *Fatherless America: Confronting our most urgent social problem.* New York: Basic Books.

Bloom, B. L., Asher, S. J., & White, S. W. (1978). Marital disruption as a stressor: A review and analysis. *Psychological Bulletin, 85,* 867–894.

Bloom, B. L., & Caldwell, R. A. (1981). Sex differences in adjustment during the process of marital separation. *Journal of Marriage and the Family, 43,* 693–701.

Blumberg, G. G. (1999). Balancing the interests: The American Law Institute's treatment of child support. *Family Law Quarterly, 33,* 39–110.

Booth, A., & Amato, P. (1991). Divorce and psychological stress. *Journal of Health and Social Behavior, 32,* 396–407.

Braver, S. L. (1999). The gender gap in standard of living after divorce: Vanishingly small? *Family Law Quarterly, 33,* 111–134.

Braver, S. L., Cookston, J. T., & Cohen, B. R. (2002). Experiences of family law attorneys with current issues in divorce practice. *Family Relations, 51,* 325–334.

Braver, S. L., Fitzpatrick, P. J., & Bay, R. C. (1991). Non-custodial parent's report of child support payments. *Family Relations, 40,* 180–185.

Braver, S. L., & Griffin, W. A. (2000). Engaging fathers in the post-divorce family. *Marriage and Family Review, 29,* 247–267.

Braver, S. L., Griffin, W. A., Cookston, J. T., Sandler, I. N., & Williams, J. (in press). Promoting better fathering among divorced nonresident fathers. In W. F. Pinsof & J. Lebow, (Eds.), *Family psychology: The art of the science* (pp. 295–325). New York: Oxford University Press.

Braver, S. L., & O'Connell, D. (1998). *Divorced dads: Shattering the myth.* New York: Tarcher Penguin/Putnam.

Braver, S. L., & Stockburger, D. (2004). Child support guidelines and the equalization of living standards. In W. S. Comanor (Ed.), *The law and economics of child support payments* (pp. 91–127). Cheltenham, England: Edward Elgar.

Braver, S. L., Whitley, M., & Ng, C. (1993). Who divorces whom? Methodological and theoretical issues. *Journal of Divorce and Remarriage, 20,* 1–19.

Braver, S. L., Wolchik, S. A., Sandler, I. N., Fogas, B. S., & Zvetina, D. (1991). Frequency of visitation by divorce fathers: Differences in reports by fathers and mothers. *American Journal of Orthopsychiatry, 61,* 448–454.

Braver, S. L., Wolchik, S. A., Sandler, I. N., Sheets, V. L., Fogas, B. S., & Bay, R. C. (1993). A longitudinal study of noncustodial parents: Parents without children. *Journal of Family Psychology, 7,* 9–23.

Bray, J. H., & Berger, S. H. (1990). Noncustodial father and paternal grandparent relationships in stepfamilies. *Family-Relations, 39,* 414–419.

Buchanan, C., & Heiges, K. L. (2001). When conflict continues after the marriage ends: Effects of postdivorce conflict on children. In F. D. Fincham & J. H. Grych (Eds.), *Interparental conflict and child development: Theory, research, and applications.* (pp. 337–362). New York: Cambridge University Press.

Buchanan, C. M., Maccoby, E. E., & Dornbush, S. M. (1991). Caught between parents: Adolescents' experience in divorced homes. *Child Development, 62,* 1008–1029.

Bumpass, L., Sweet, J., & Castro-Martin, T. (1990). Changing patterns of remarriage in the U.S. *Journal of Marriage and the Family, 52,* 747–756.

Burkhauser, R. V., Duncan, G. J., Hauser, R., & Bernsten, R. (1990). Economic burdens of marital disruptions: A comparison of the United States and the Federal Republic of Germany. *The Review of Income and Wealth, 36,* 119–134.

Burkhauser, R. V., Duncan, G. J., Hauser, R., & Bernsten, R. (1991). Wife or frau, women do worse: A comparison of men and women in the United States and Germany after marital dissolution. *Demography, 28,* 353–360.

Cherlin, A. J. (1992). *Marriage, divorce, remarriage.* Cambridge, MA: Harvard University Press.

Chiriboga, D. A., Coho, A., Stein, J. A., & Roberts, J. (1979). Divorce, stress and social supports: A study in helpseeking behavior. *Journal of Divorce, 3,* 121–135.

Chiriboga, D. A., & Cutler, A. (1977). Stress responses among divorcing men and women. *Journal of Divorce, 1,* 95–106.

Citro, C. F., & Michael, R. T. (1995). *Measuring poverty: A new approach.* Washington, DC: National Academy Press.

Cooksey, E. C., & Craig, P. H. (1998). Parenting from a distance: The effects of paternal characteristics on contact between nonresidential fathers and their children. *Demography, 35,* 187–200.

Corcoran, M. (1979). The economic consequences of marital dissolution for women in the middle years. *Sex Roles, 5,* 345–353.

Current Population Studies. (1999). *Money income in the United States. Consumer income* (Document No. P60-209). Washington, DC: U.S. Bureau of the Census.

David, M., & Flory, T. (1989) Changes in marital status and short term income dynamics. In U.S. Bureau of the Census (Ed.), *Individuals and families in transition: Understanding change through longitudinal data* (pp. 15–22). Washington, DC: U.S. Bureau of the Census.

Davies, L., Avison, W. R., & McAlpine, D. D. (1997). Significant life experiences and depression among single and married mothers. *Journal of Marriage and the Family, 59,* 294–308.

Demo, D. H., & Acock, A. C. (1994). Singlehood, marriage, and remarriage: The effects of family structure and family relationships on mothers' well-being. *Journal of Family Issues, 17,* 388–407.

Dohrenwend, B. S., & Dohrenwend, B. (1974). *Stressful life events: Their nature and effects.* New York: Wiley.

Duncan, G. J., & Hoffman, S. D. (1985). Economic consequences of marital instability. In M. David & T. Smeeding (Eds.), *Horizontal equity, uncertainty, and economic well-being* (pp. 427–471). Chicago: University of Chicago Press.

Ellman, I. M. (1989). The theory of alimony. *California Law Review, 77,* 1–88.

Ellman, I. M. (1991). Should non-financial losses and motivations be included in the theory of alimony? *B.Y.U. Law Review, 259* (Symposium Issue).

Ellman, I. M. (1999). The maturing law of divorce finances: Toward rules and guidelines. *Family Law Quarterly, 33*(3), 801–814.

Elrod, L. H. (1994). Adding to the basic child support award. In *Child support guidelines: The next generation* (pp. 62–71). Washington, DC: U.S. Department of Health and Human Services, Office of Child Support Enforcement.

Emery, R. E. (1994). *Renegotiating family relationships: Divorce, child custody, and mediation.* New York: Guilford.

Emery, R. E. (2004). *The truth about children and divorce.* New York: Viking.

Espenshade, T. J. (1979). The economic consequences of divorce. *Journal of Marriage and the Family, 41,* 615–625.

Fabricius, W. V., & Braver, S. L. (2003). Non-child support expenditures on children by nonresidential divorced fathers: Results of a study. *Family Court Review, 41,* 321–336.

Fabricius, W. V., Braver, S. L., & Deneau, K. (2003). Divorced parents' financial support of their children's college expenses. *Family Court Review, 41,* 224–241.

Fabricius, W. V., & Hall, J. (2000). Young adults' perspectives on divorce: Living arrangements. *Family and Conciliation Courts Review, 38,* 446–461.

Fineman, M. A. (1991). *The illusion of equality: The rhetoric and reality of divorce reform.* Chicago: University of Chicago Press.

Forehand, R., & McCombs, A. (1989). The nature of interparental conflict of married and divorced parents: Implications for young adolescents. *Journal of Abnormal Child Psychology, 17,* 235–249.

Forehand, R., & Thomas, A. M. (1992). Conflict in the home environment of adolescents from divorced families: A longitudinal analysis. *Journal of Family Violence, 7,* 73–84.

Fulton, J. A. (1979). Parental reports of children's post-divorce adjustment. *Journal of Social Issues, 35,* 126–139.

Furstenberg, F. F. (1982). Conjugal succession: Reentering marriage after divorce. In P. B. Bates and O. G. Brim (Eds.), *Life-span development and behavior* (107–146). New York: Academic Press.

Furstenberg, F. F., & Cherlin, A. J. (1991). *Divided families: What happens to children when parents part.* Cambridge, MA: Harvard University Press.

Furstenberg, F. F., & Nord, C. (1985). Parenting apart: Patterns of childrearing after marital disruption. *Journal of Marriage and the Family, 47,* 893–904.

Garfinkel, I., McLanahan, S., & Hanson, T. (1998). A patchwork portrait of nonresident fathers. In I. Garfinkel, S. McLanahan, D. Meyer, & J. Seltzer (Eds.), *Fathers under fire: The revolution in child support enforcement* (p. 50). New York: Russell Sage Foundation.

Goodman, M., Bonds, D., Sandler, I. N., & Braver, S. L. (2004). Parent psychoeducational programs and reducing the negative effects of interparental conflict following divorce. *Family Court Review, 42,* 263–279.

Gove, W. R., & Shin, H. (1989). The psychological well-being of divorce and widowed men and women: An empirical analysis. *Journal of Family Issues, 10,* 122–144.

Gove, W. R., Style, C. B., & Hughes, M. (1990). The effect of marriage on the well-being of adults: A theoretical analysis. *Journal of Family Issues, 11,* 4–35.

Gray, J. D., & Silver, R. C. (1990). Opposite sides of the same coin: Former spouses' divergent perspectives in coping with their divorce. *Journal of Personality and Social Psychology, 59,* 1180–1191.

Gunnoe, M. L. (1993). *Noncustodial parents' contributions to the adjustment of adolescent stepchildren.* Unpublished doctoral dissertation, University of Virginia, Charlottesville.

Harold, G. T., & Conger, R. D. (1997). Marital conflict and adolescent distress: The role of adolescent awareness. *Child Development, 68,* 333–350.

Hemstrom, O. (1996). Is marriage dissolution linked to differences in mortality risks for men and women? *Journal of Marriage and the Family, 58,* 366–378.

Hetherington, E. M. (1993). An overview of the Virginia Longitudinal Study of divorce and remarriage with a focus on early adolescence. *Journal of Family Psychology, 7,* 39–56.

Hetherington, E. M., & Clingempeel, W. G. (1992). Coping with marital transitions: A family systems perspectives. *Monographs of the Society for Research in Child Development, 57* (2–3, Serial No. 227).

Hetherington, E. M., Cox, M., & Cox, R. (1982). Effects of divorce on parents and children. In M. E. Lamb (Ed.), *Nontraditional families.* Hillsdale, NJ: Lawrence Erlbaum Associates.

Hetherington, E. M., & Hagan, M. S. (1986). Divorced fathers: Stress, coping and adjustment. In M. E. Lamb (Ed.), *The father's role: Applied perspectives* (pp. 103–134). New York: Wiley.

Hetherington, E. M., & Jodl, K. (1994). Stepfamilies as settings for development. In A. Booth and J. Dunn (Eds.), *Stepfamilies: Who benefits? Who does not?* (pp. 55–80). Cambridge, MA: Harvard University Press.

Hetherington, E. M., & Stanley-Hagen, M. (1997). The effects of divorce on fathers and their children. In M. Lamb (Ed.), *The role of the father in child development* (pp. 191–211). New York: Wiley.

Hetherington, E. M., & Stanley-Hagen, M. (2002). Parenting in divorced and remarried families. In M. H. Bornstein (Ed.), *Handbook of parenting. Vol. 3: Being and becoming a parent* (2nd ed., pp. 287–315). Mahwah, NJ: Lawrence Erlbaum Associates.

Hoffman, S. D., & Duncan, G. J. (1985). A reconsideration of the economic consequences of marital dissolution. *Demography, 22,* 485–497.

Hoffman, S. D., & Duncan, G. J. (1988). What *are* the economic consequences of divorce. *Demography, 25,* 641–645.

Holden, K. C., & Smock, P. J. (1991). The economic cost of marital disruption: Why do women bear a disproportionate cost? *Annual Review of Sociology, 17,* 51–79.

Holmes, T. H. & Rahe, R. H. (1967). The Social Readjustment Rating Scale. *Journal of Psychosomatic Research, 11,* 213–218.

Hughes, R. (1988). Divorce and social support: A review. *Journal of Divorce, 11,* 123–145.

Johnson, D. R., & Wu, J. (2002). An empirical test of crisis, social selection, and role explanations of the relationship between marital disruption and psychological distress: A pooled time-series analysis of four wave panel data. *Journal of Marriage and the Family, 64,* 211–224.

Johnson, D. S., Rogers, J. M., & Tan, L. (2001). A century of family budgets in the United States. *Monthly Labor Review, 124*(5), 28–45.

Johnston, J. R. (1994). High-conflict divorce. *Future of Children, 4,* 165–182.

Joung, I. M., Stronks, K., van de Mheen, H., van Poppel, F. W. A., van der Meer, J. B. W., & Mackenbach, J. P. (1997). The contribution of intermediary factors to marital status differences in self-reported health. *Journal of Marriage and the Family, 59,* 476–490.

Keith, P. M. (1986). Isolation of the unmarried in later life. *Family Relations, 35,* 389–395.

Kelly, E. L., & Conley, J. J. (1987). Personality and compatibility: A prospective analysis of marital stability and marital satisfaction. *Journal of Personality and Social Psychology, 52,* 27–40.

Kitson, G. C. (1992). *Portrait of divorce: Adjustment to marital breakdown.* New York: Guilford.

Kitson, G. C., & Morgan, L. A. (1990). The multiple consequences of divorce: A decade in review. *Journal of Marriage and the Family, 52,* 913–924.

Kline-Pruett, M., Williams, T. Y., Insabella, G., & Little, T. D. (2003). Family and legal indicators of child adjustment to divorce among families with young children. *Journal of Family Psychology, 17,* 169–180.

Kposowa, A. J., Breault, K. D., & Singh, G. K. (1995). White male suicides in the United States: A multivariate individual level analysis. *Social Forces, 74*(1), 315–323.

Kurdek, L. A. (1990). Divorce history and self-reported psychological distress in husbands and wives. *Journal of Marriage and the Family, 52,* 701–708.

Lamb, M. E. (1999). Noncustodial fathers and their impact on the children of divorce. In R. A. Thompson & P. R. Amato (Eds.), *The postdivorce family: Children, parenting, and society* (pp. 105–126). Thousand Oaks, CA: Sage.

Lorenz, F. O., Simons, R. L., Conger, R. D., Elder, G. H., Johnson, C., & Chao, W. (1997). Married and recently divorced mothers' stressful events and distress: Tracing change over time. *Journal of Marriage and the Family, 59,* 219–232.

Maccoby, E. M., Buchanan, C. M., Mnookin, R. H., & Dornbush, S. M. (1993). Postdivorce roles of mothers and fathers in the lives of their children. *Journal of Family Psychology, 7,* 24–38.

Maccoby, E. E., Depner, C. E., & Mnookin, R. H. (1988). Custody of children following divorce. In E. M. Hetherington & J. D. Arasteh (Eds.), *Impact of divorce, single parenting, and stepparenting on children* (pp. 91–114). Hillsdale, NJ: Lawrence Erlbaum Associates.

Maccoby, E. E., & Mnookin, R. H. (1992). *Dividing the child: Social and legal dilemmas of custody.* Cambridge, MA: Harvard University Press.

Madden-Derdich, D. A., & Arditti, J. A. (1999). The ties that bind: Attachment between former spouses. *Family Relations, 48,* 243–249.

Mahoney, K. (1996). Gender issues in family law: Leveling the playing field for women. *Family and Conciliation Courts Review, 34,* 198–218.

Marks, N. F. (1996). Flying solo at midlife: Gender, marital status, and psychological well-being. *Journal of Marriage and the Family, 58,* 917–932.

Marks, N. F., & McLanahan, S. S. (1993). Gender, family structure, and social support among parents. *Journal of Marriage and the Family, 55,* 481–493.

Masheter, C. (1991). Postdivorce relations between ex-spouses: The roles of attachment and interpersonal conflict. *Journal of Marriage and the Family, 53,* 103–110.

Mason, M. A. (1988). *The equality trap.* New York: Simon and Schuster.

Mastekaasa, A. (1994). Psychological well-being and marital dissolution: "Selection effects?" *Journal of Family Issues, 15,* 208–228.

McCubbin, H., & Patterson, J. (1982). Family adaptation to crisis. In H. McCubbin, E. Cauble, & J. Patterson (Eds.), *Family stress, coping, and social support* (pp. 26–47). Springfield, IL: Thomas.

McKenry, P. C., & Price, S. J. (1991). Alternatives for support: Life after divorce—a literature review. *Journal of Divorce and Remarriage, 15*(3–4), 1–19.

McLanahan, S., Adelberg, T., & Wedemeyer, N. (1981). Network structure, social support and psychological well-being in the single parent family. *Journal of Marriage and the Family, 43,* 601–612.

Metts, S., & Cupach, W. R. (1995). Postdivorce relations. In M. A. Fitzpatrick & A. L. Vangelisti (Eds.), *Explaining family interactions* (pp. 232–251). London: Sage.

Meyer, D. R., & Garasky, S. (1993). Custodial fathers: Myths, realities, and child support policy. *Journal of Marriage and the Family, 55,* 73–89.

Mnookin, R. H., & Kornhauser, L. (1979). Bargaining in the shadow of the law: The case of divorce. *Yale Law Journal, 88,* 950–997.

Morgan L. W., & Lino, M. C. (1999). A comparison of child support awards calculated under states' child support guidelines with expenditures on children calculated by the U.S. Department of Agriculture. *Family Law Quarterly, 33,* 191–218.

National Vital Statistics Reports. (2003, December 17). Vol. 52, No. 10.

Neilson, L. C. (2004). Assessing mutual partner—abuse claims in child custody and access cases. *Family Court Review, 42*(3), 411–438.

Nord, C. W., & Zill, N. (1996). *Non-custodial parents' participation in their children's lives: Evidence from the Survey of Income and Program Participation. Volume I. Summary of SIPP Analysis.* Washington, DC: U.S. Department of Health and Human Services.

Pearlin, L. I., & Johnson, J. S. (1977) Marital status, life-strains and depression. *American Sociological Review, 42*(5), 704–715.

Pearson, J., & Ring, M. (1982–1983). Judicial decision-making in contested custody cases. *Journal of Family Law, 21,* 703.

Peterson, R. R. (1996). A re-evaluation of the economic consequences of divorce. *American Sociological Review, 61,* 528–536.

Pettit, E. J., & Bloom, B. L. (1984). Whose decision was it? The effects of initiator status on adjustment to marital disruption. *Journal of Marriage and the Family, 48,* 587–595.

Pledge, D. S. (1992). Marital separation/divorce: A review of individual responses to a major life stressor. *Journal of Divorce and Remarriage, 17,* 151–181.

Pruett, M. K., & Jackson, T. D. (1999). The lawyer's role during the divorce process: Perceptions of parents, their young children, and their attorneys. *Family Law Quarterly, 33,* 283–310.

Rogers, R. M., & Bieniewicz, D. J. (2004). Child support guidelines: Underlying methodologies, assumptions and the impact on standard of living. In W. S. Comanor (Ed.), *The law and economics of child support payments* (pp. 60–90). Cheltenham, England: Edward Elgar.

Seltzer, J. A. (1991). Relationships between fathers and children who live apart. *Journal of Marriage and the Family, 53,* 79–101.

Seltzer, J., & Brandreth, Y. (1994). What fathers say about involvement with children after separation. *Journal of Family Issues, 15,* 49–77.

Sheets, V. L., & Braver, S. L. (1996). Gender differences in satisfaction with divorce settlements. *Family Relations, 45,* 336–342.

Shiono, P. H., & Quinn, L. S. (1994) Epidemiology of divorce. *Future of Children, 4*(1), 15–28.

Simon, R. W., & Marcussen, K. (1999). Marital transitions, marital beliefs, and mental health. *Journal of Health and Social Behavior, 40,* 111–125.

Smock, P. J., Manning, W., & Gupta, S. (1999). The effect of marriage and divorce on women's economic well-being. *American Sociological Review, 64,* 794–812.

Sonenstein, F. L., & Calhoun, C. A. (1990). Determinants of child support: A pilot survey of absent parents. *Contemporary Policy Issues, 8,* 75–94.

Sorensen, A. (1992). Estimating the economic consequences of separation and divorce: A cautionary tale from the United States. In L. Weitzman & M. Maclean (Eds.), *The economic consequences of divorce: The international perspective* (pp. 264–282). New York: Oxford University Press.

Stahl, P. M. (1994). *Conducting child custody evaluations.* Thousand Oaks, CA: Sage.

Stone, G. (2002). Nonresidential father postdivorce well-being: The role of social supports. *Journal of Divorce and Remarriage, 36,* 139–150.

Sturge-Apple, M. L., Gondoli, D. M., Bonds, D. D., & Salem, L. N. (2003). Mothers' responsive parenting practices and psychological experience of parenting as mediators of the relation between marital conflict and mother–preadolescent relational negativity. *Parenting: Science and Practice, 3,* 327–355.

Teachman, J. D., & Paasch, K. M. (1994). Financial impact of divorce on children and their families. *The Future of Children, 4,* 63–83.

Thoennes, N., Tjaden, P., & Pearson, J. (1991). The impact of child support guidelines on award adequacy, award variability, and case processing efficiency, *Family Law Quarterly, 25,* 339–340.

Tippins, T. M. (2001, June 18). Are family courts prejudiced against fathers? No: Claims of gender bias tend to come from men who have gone to court and lost. Insightmag.com. Retrieved, April 25, 2005 from http://www.insightmag. com/news/2001/06/18/Symposium/Q.Are.Family.Courts.Prejudiced.Against.Fathersno.Claims.Of.Gender.Bias. Tend.To.C-161100.shtml

Tschann, J. M., Johnston, J. R., Wallerstein, J. S. (1989). Resources, stressors, and attachment as predictors of adult adjustment after divorce: A longitudinal study. *Journal of Marriage and the Family, 51,* 1033–1046.

Umberson, D., Chen, M. D., House, J. S., Hopkins, K., & Slaten, E. (1996). The effect of social relationships on psychological well-being: Are men and women really so different? *American Sociological Review, 61,* 837–857.

Umberson, D., & Williams, C. L. (1993). Divorced fathers: Parental role strain and psychological distress. *Journal of Family Issues, 14,* 378–400.

U.S. Bureau of the Census. (1986). *Child support and alimony: 1985 Current Population Reports, Series P23, No. 152).* Washington, DC: U.S. Government Printing Office.

Venohr, J. C., & Griffith, T. E. (2003). *Arizona child support guidelines: Findings from a case file review.* Denver: Policy Studies.

Wallerstein, J. S., & Corbin, S. B. (1986). Father–child relationships after divorce: Child support and educational opportunity. *Family Law Quarterly, 20,* 109–128.

Wallerstein, J. S., & Kelly, J. B. (1980). *Surviving the breakup.* New York: Basic Books.

Wang, H., & Amato, P. R. (2000). Predictors of divorce adjustment: Stressors, resources, and definitions. *Journal of Marriage and the Family, 62,* 655–668.

Warshak, R. A. (1996). Gender bias in child custody decisions. *Family and Conciliation Courts Review, 34,* 396–409.

Watts, H. W. (1980). Special panel suggests changes in BLS Family Budget Program. *Monthly Labor Review, 106*(12), 1–10.

Weiss, R. S. (1984). The impact of marital dissolution on income and consumption in single-parent households. *Journal of Marriage and the Family, 46,* 115–127.

Weitzman, L. (1996). The economic consequences of divorce are still unequal. *American Sociological Review, 61,* 537–538.

Weitzman, L. J. (1985). *The divorce revolution: The unexpected social and economic consequences for women and children in America.* New York: The Free Press.

Wheaton, B. (1990). Life transitions, role histories, and mental health. *American Sociological Review, 55,* 209–223.

Whiteside, M. F. (1998). The parental alliance following divorce: An overview. *Journal of Marital and Family Therapy, 24,* 3–24.

Zeiss, A. M., Zeiss, R. A., & Johnson, S. M. (1980). Sex differences in initiation of and adjustment to divorce. *Journal of Divorce, 4,* 21–33.

17

Influence of Parental Divorce on Romantic Relationships in Young Adulthood: A Cognitive-Developmental Perspective

Denise S. Bartell
University of Wisconsin—Green Bay

WHY EXAMINE THE EFFECTS OF PARENTAL DIVORCE ON ROMANTIC RELATIONSHIPS?

Parental divorce is a risk factor for romantic relationships in adulthood. By one estimate, the risk of divorce increases by almost 70% if the wife has experienced parental divorce and by almost 190% if both spouses have experienced parental divorce (Amato, 1996). Research also indicates that parental divorce is associated with more hesitancy toward commitment (Booth, Brinkerhoff, & White, 1984), lower trust in partners (Franklin, Janoff-Bulman, & Roberts, 1990), lower satisfaction in relationships (Ross & Mirowsky, 1999), poorer interpersonal skills (Amato, 1996), earlier involvement in relationships (Gabardi & Rosen, 1992), and greater acceptance of divorce (Kinnaird & Gerrard, 1986). A variety of potential divorce-related factors have been proposed to explain these findings, ranging from the socioeconomic decline that often accompanies parental divorce, to negative changes in parent–child relationships, to the observation of one's parents having a poor marital relationship, to the genetic transmission of problematic personality traits (Amato, 2000; Amato & Booth, 2001). However, we currently lack a broad conceptual model to identify which of these factors may be relevant or how they might exert an influence on romantic relationships. This chapter represents a preliminary attempt at the development of such a model. The cognitive-developmental model proposed here seeks to identify specific characteristics of parental divorce that are likely to exert an influence on romantic relationships and to propose a potential mechanism through which these characteristics exert an influence on romantic relationships. Before moving to the explication of the model, though, I first review in more detail the research introduced here.

339

REVIEW OF FINDINGS ON THE EFFECTS OF PARENTAL DIVORCE ON ROMANTIC RELATIONSHIPS

Research conducted over the past two decades indicates that experiences of parental divorce influence romantic relationships in a variety of ways. In this section, I briefly review these findings. However, it is important to keep in mind that, although I discuss them as part of distinct categories, some interdependence of effects among the findings certainly exists. For example, young adults from divorced families may have higher divorce rates than those from intact families because of both poorer conflict-resolution skills and a greater acceptance of divorce as a solution to an unsatisfying marriage. In addition, I discuss failures to find hypothesized effects alongside significant findings, because identifying the ways in which young adults from divorced families are similar to those from intact families is just as important to an understanding of the effects of parental divorce on romantic relationships as identifying the ways in which the two groups differ. Finally, the overwhelming majority of studies conducted on this topic have used samples of individuals in adolescence and early adulthood (with an approximate age range of 14–35 years); therefore, I use the term *young adults* to refer here to both groups.

Attitudes About Involvement

Compared with those from intact families, young adults from divorced families appear to be more hesitant about commitment in premarital and marital relationships. In terms of their generalized attitudes about involvement in romantic relationships, children of divorce report less of a desire for long-term relationships (Booth et al., 1984; Gabardi & Rosen, 1992; Kinnaird & Gerrard, 1986), as well as more difficulty committing themselves in romantic relationships (Wallerstein & Blakeslee, 1989). In a qualitative analysis of young adults' relationship attitudes and accounts of parental divorce experiences, a key theme in the narratives involved fears about the ability to have successful long-term relationships (Duran-Aydintug, 1997). Other studies have found that young adults from divorced families fear disappointment and betrayal in their romantic relationships (Mahl, 2001; Wallerstein, 1985). However, not all findings support this hypothesis. For example, one study found no differences between young adults from divorced and intact families on perceived difficulty of achieving an intimate relationship (Feldman, Gowen, & Fisher, 1998), another found no difference on fear of intimacy (Kirk, 2002), and a third found no difference on the perceived risk involved in romantic relationships (Johnston & Thomas, 1996). Although there are fewer relevant studies of relationship-specific attitudes, the available evidence also tends to indicate more hesitancy in young adults from divorced families, at least for young women. In a study of the development of commitment in dating relationships, women from divorced families reported more ambivalence about involvement in their dating relationship than did women from intact families (Jacquet & Surra, 2001).

Research on attachment has hypothesized that young adults from divorced families are less likely to have a secure romantic attachment style than are young adults from intact families, but results of empirical work have been less than conclusive. For example, although one study indicated that children of divorce are more likely to exhibit insecure romantic attachment styles than are children from intact families (Walker & Ehrenberg, 1998), others have failed to do so (Brennan & Shaver, 1993; Feldman et al., 1998; Hayashi & Strickland, 1998; Taylor, Parker, & Roy, 1995) or have found an effect only for women (Sprecher, Cate, & Levin, 1998).

Although disruptions in relationships in the family of origin during childhood certainly have the potential to influence the ways in which young adults approach romantic relationships, the lack of conclusive findings may indicate that there exists enough variability in the nature of parental divorce experiences that we cannot identify one global effect on attachment style.

Hesitancy toward commitment may apply more in the context of marital relationships than premarital romantic relationships. Young adults from divorced families appear more fearful of marriage (Wallerstein, 1985), have less favorable expectations about their future marital quality (Boyer-Pennington, Pennington, & Spink, 2001), and are more likely than their peers from intact families to report not wanting to marry (Gabardi & Rosen, 1992; Kinaird & Gerrard, 1986). Some research indicates that young adults from divorced families are more pessimistic about their chances of achieving a long-term, successful marriage than their chances of having successful dating relationships (e.g., Amato & Booth, 1991a; Franklin et al., 1990). This may be the case because they are applying the knowledge they gained from their parents' marital relationship quite narrowly to marital relationships, and less so to other forms of romantic relationships (Franklin et al.).

It is important here to address the fact that hesitancy about involvement is not inherently problematic. Part of this hesitancy in young adults from divorced families appears to manifest itself in less idealistic and more realistic views of marriage, as compared with the views of peers from intact families (Amato, 1988; Boyer-Pennington et al., 2001; Burgoyne & Hames, 2002; Franklin et al., 1990; Mahl, 2001). These more realistic views might help young adults from divorced families be more prepared to deal with the realities of courtship and marriage. For example, Booth et al. (1984) stated that individuals from divorced families may take the courtship process more seriously than their peers from intact families because they understand the importance of choosing well. Burgoyne & Hames hypothesized that the higher levels of caution in young adults from divorced families reflect the higher value that they place on marriage and their dedication to avoid making the same mistakes their parents made. In fact, a qualitative study of beliefs about romantic relationships in young adults from divorced families found that almost all respondents discussed their determination to do better than their parents had done, by not rushing into relationships and being careful to end relationships that become problematic, by developing effective communication skills, and by developing a strong sense of personal identity and financial stability before settling down (Darlington, 2001). Having experienced a parental divorce may also help young adults to feel more confident that they can deal with the dissolution of their romantic relationships, which might explain why, in one study (Riggio, 2004), young adults from divorced families exhibited less anxiety in dating relationships than did young adults from intact families.

Less idealistic views of marriage do not necessarily translate into more negative views of marriage. There appear to be few differences between young adults from divorced and intact families on the perceived advantages and disadvantages of marriage (Amato, 1988), on the perceived importance of marriage or the perception of marriage as a lifelong commitment (Burgoyne & Hames, 2002), or in the desire or the expectation to marry (Booth et al., 1984; Boyer-Pennington et al., 2001; Burgoyne & Hames). However, parental divorce may influence the types of factors that contribute to beliefs about marriage. For example, a belief in the benevolence of others was the strongest predictor of optimism about marriage for young adults from divorced families, whereas a strong perception of self-worth was the best predictor for young adults from intact families (Franklin et al., 1990). These findings may also indicate that young adults from divorced families perceive the characteristics of the partner as more important to a successful marriage than do young adults from intact families, a belief that may serve them well in the mate-selection process.

Attitudes About and Likelihood of Divorce

In addition to a general hesitance and sense of caution about involvement in romantic relationships, research indicates that young adults from divorced families are more fearful of divorce (Kirk, 2002), and are more likely to believe that their marriages may end in divorce (Duran-Aydintug, 1997; Kirk). Young adults from divorced families, however, are not more positive about divorce and do not perceive it to be an easier solution than their peers from intact families (Burgoyne & Hames, 2002). At the same time, they are more accepting of divorce as an option in unhappy marriages (Amato & Booth, 1991a; Franklin et al., 1990; Kinnaird & Gerrard, 1986). In their marital relationships, young adults from divorced families are more likely than their peers from intact families to report considering divorce when they are not happy (Amato & DeBoer, 2001). It is not surprising, then, that a variety of studies have found evidence for what has been called "the intergenerational transmission of divorce," in which adults from divorced families are more likely to experience divorce themselves than are adults from intact families (Amato, 1996; Amato & DeBoer; Ross & Mirowsky, 1999; Wolfinger, 2000).

Level of Involvement in Romantic Relationships

Although young adults from divorced families may be more hesitant or pessimistic about their romantic relationships, this hesitancy does not appear to discourage them from involvement in romantic relationships. Instead, compared with children from intact families, children from divorced families get involved more quickly in romantic relationships. They become sexually involved (Booth et al., 1984; Furstenberg & Teitler, 1994; Gabardi & Rosen, 1992; Sprague & Kinney, 1997) and emotionally involved (Gabardi & Rosen) in dating relationships more quickly than their peers from intact families, and they are more likely to marry young (Ross & Mirowsky, 1999). They also appear to be more involved in romantic relationships, as indicated by the greater number of dating relationships (Booth et al.; Duran-Aydintug, 1997) and sexual partners (Gabardi & Rosen; Sprague & Kinney) in young adults from divorced families as compared with those from intact families. However, one study found that young adults from divorced families were no more likely to currently be involved in a romantic relationship than were young adults from intact families (Brennan & Shaver, 1993). Young adults from divorced families also appear more likely to engage in premarital cohabitation (Booth et al.; Chase-Lansdale, Cherlin, & Kiernan, 1995). Although higher cohabitation rates may indicate a higher level of involvement in their relationships, it could also be that adults from divorced families see cohabitation as a lesser form of committed relationship, if they are fearful of marriage.

Interpersonal Characteristics of Romantic Relationships

Although young adults from divorced families are at least as likely to become involved in romantic relationships, some research indicates that parental divorce may cause them to trust their dating partners less than do their peers from intact families (Jacquet & Surra, 2001; Johnston & Thomas, 1996; Ross & Mirowsky, 1999; Sprague & Kinney, 1997). However, other research has either failed to find any association (King, 2002) or found that trust was lower for future spouses, but not for dating partners (Franklin et al., 1990). In addition, there appears to be no difference by parents' marital status on assumptions about the self or trust in the world (Franklin et al.). Once again, it appears that the effects of parental divorce may be stronger on beliefs (in this case, trust) in the context of marital relationships.

Parental divorce may influence the way in which young adults experience love for their romantic partners. One study found that young adults from divorced families reported less altruistic love for their dating partner than did their peers from intact families (Sprague & Kinney, 1997; Sprecher et al., 1998), and another found that women from divorced families had lower practical, dependent, and altruistic love for their dating partners than did women from happy intact families whereas men from divorced families had higher erotic love than did men from intact families (Sprecher et al.).

The relative pessimism of young adults from divorced families toward their romantic relationships may well be justified, if their relationship skills are any indication. Compared with young adults from intact families, those from divorced families display more negative interpersonal behaviors such as anger and problematic communication behaviors in their romantic relationships (Amato, 1996), and these problematic behaviors appear to extend into their marital relationships (Amato & DeBoer, 2001; Glenn & Kramer, 1987). However, there is some evidence that the effects on communication in romantic relationships may be stronger when the female partner experiences parental divorce than when the male partner does. Women, but not men, from divorced families reported poorer communication in their romantic relationships than did those from intact families (Herzog & Cooney, 2002). Another study found that couples in which only the female partner experienced parental divorce showed more negative communication patterns (e.g., higher rate of conflict, more withdrawal) than couples in which neither partner experienced parental divorce, or couples in which only the male partner experienced parental divorce (Sanders, Halford, & Behrens, 1999).

Given that they are more likely to engage in negative behavior patterns in romantic relationships, young adults from divorced families might be expected to report lower satisfaction with their relationships. However, the research support for this hypothesis is far from conclusive. Although some studies indicate that young adults from divorced families experience lower satisfaction in premarital romantic relationships (Ross & Mirowsky, 1999) and lower happiness in marital relationships (Glenn & Kramer, 1987), other studies have failed to do so (Kirk, 2002; Sanders et al., 1999). It is possible that this inconsistency reflects considerable variability in the effects of parental divorce on relational satisfaction. For example, young adults from divorced families who maintained high-quality relationships with both parents following the divorce may be more likely to develop high-quality romantic relationships, and to therefore be more satisfied with their relationships.

Conclusions From Research on Parental Divorce and Romantic Relationships

In conclusion, although young adults from divorced families appear more hesitant and even pessimistic about the success of their romantic relationships than do those from intact families, they are not dissuaded from involvement by these attitudes. In fact, existing research suggests higher levels of involvement in romantic relationships for young adults from divorced families. Although young adults from divorced families may be at least as likely to become involved in romantic relationships, research suggests that the characteristics of their relationships may differ in some ways, most notably in lower trust in marital partners, poorer communication skills, and perhaps even in lower satisfaction with romantic relationships.

It is interesting to note the contradictions within the findings on many relational characteristics (e.g., hesitance about commitment, trust, and satisfaction). Although it is likely that much of this variability is due to method variance, a portion may be due to untapped variability in parental divorce experiences that results from the operationalization of parental divorce as a dichotomous variable (i.e., divorced families or intact families). Parental divorce is not a uniform experience, and there exists much diversity in the types of experiences associated with parental divorce, diversity that likely leads to variability in outcomes. It is possible, then, that examining specific aspects of parental divorce experiences (e.g., changes in parent–child relationships) may help us to better understand how parental divorce influences romantic relationships by identifying, for example, how different aspects of the experience may be associated with different effects on romantic relationships.

Parental divorce experiences may exert a stronger influence on attitudes about and behaviors in marital relationships than on those in premarital romantic relationships, as young adults from divorced families appear particularly cautious, fearful, and distrustful about marital relationships. Franklin et al. (1990) suggested that young adults may cope with the experience of parental divorce by restricting its influence to only the most relevant relationships, namely marriage. Restricting the influence of parental divorce may be possible because the experience of parental divorce is more closely linked to marriage than to romantic relationships in general. Marriage is seen as the core social unit in our society and the primary source of personal fulfillment. Therefore, most individuals desire to marry. However, those who have experienced parental divorce may also be quite fearful about the very real possibility that their marriages will not succeed. At the same time, the purpose of dating relationships is becoming increasingly distanced from mate selection, as young adults now date more for temporary romantic companionship. In this social context, it may be easier for individuals who have experienced parental divorce to distance their negative beliefs about marital relationships and marital partners from their beliefs about dating relationships and dating partners, in effect making dating relationships feel somewhat "safer" to them. If this is indeed the case, then the effects of parental divorce on romantic relationships should be mediated by some sort of cognitive processing, whereby individuals appraise and evaluate their family of origin experiences and are able to make distinctions between, and develop different expectations for, different types of relationships.

THE NATURE OF THE INFLUENCE OF PARENTAL DIVORCE ON ROMANTIC RELATIONSHIPS

One of the primary goals of this chapter is to facilitate an understanding of what it is about the experience of parental divorce that influences children's romantic relationships. In order to do this, we need to understand at least two facets of the phenomenon: (a) the relevant characteristics of the parental divorce experience, and (b) the mechanisms through which these characteristics exert an influence on romantic relationships. I address the second facet first in order to provide a framework from which to discuss, in detail, how characteristics of the parental divorce experience exert an influence on romantic relationships.

Identifying a Causal Mechanism for the Association Between Parental Divorce and Romantic Relationships

The chronic strain model of the effects of divorce suggests that divorce creates a series of chronic strains for individuals, that these strains tend to persist indefinitely unless the situation changes, and that many individuals do not fully recover from the experience (Amato, 2000).

This model is quite useful in the examination of the effects of parental divorce, because it views divorce as a process instead of an event and assumes broad variability in divorce-related experiences. However, it may be more effective to discuss parental divorce as a *significant life process* for children, a term that is analogous to the term *significant life event* but better indicates the length of the experience, and to discuss chronic strains as the effects of the process on children's lives. Discussing parental divorce as a life course process allows us to move away from assuming negative effects for divorce-related experiences and view the experiences more evenhandedly, which may improve our ability to assess variability in outcomes. Research on the influence of parental divorce experiences on romantic relationships inherently tests the validity of a life course process perspective by examining characteristics that occur years after the parental divorce (e.g., commitment in romantic relationships). However, in order to understand the phenomenon fully, we must also understand which specific characteristics of parental divorce experiences influence romantic relationships in adulthood (e.g., changes in relationships with parents), as well as *how* these characteristics exert an influence on romantic relationships (e.g., how changes in the father–child relationship influence romantic relationship behaviors in adulthood).

In much of the research reviewed in the first section of this chapter, the observed effects of parental divorce on romantic relationships appear to be at least partially accounted for by characteristics of family relationships (e.g., Amato & DeBoer, 2001; Hayashi & Strickland, 1998; King, 2002; Mahl, 2001; Sprecher et al., 1998). Parental divorce-related characteristics of family relationships may be particularly influential to romantic relationships for at least two reasons. First, parental divorce should significantly influence the nature of parental marital relationships, and parental marital relationships are a primary source of information about the nature of romantic relationships, providing information about the characteristics of romantic relationships as well as models for behavior in romantic relationships (Conger, Cui, Bryant, & Elder, 2000; Furman & Simon, 1999). Second, parental divorce has the potential to significantly influence the nature of parent–child relationships, and parent–child relationships form the basis for conceptions about the nature of all close relationships (Collins & Read, 1994). In both of these cases, the characteristics of family relationships that result from parental divorce influence romantic relationships through their influence on conceptions of close relationships. In other words, cognitive representations of close relationships may be a causal mechanism through which these characteristics of parental divorce experiences influence romantic relationships.

Cognitive representations are organized knowledge structures about relationships that result from prior relational experiences and consist of autobiographical memories of past relational experiences (e.g., parental divorce experiences) as well as beliefs, attitudes, and expectations about the self and others in relationships (definition adapted from Collins & Read, 1994; Furman & Simon, 1999; Furman & Wehner, 1997; Surra & Bohman, 1991). These representations are activated during relevant social situations and affect cognitive processing of relational information (e.g., attention or interpretation), focusing attention on certain types of information and influencing whether it is stored in memory and how easily it can be retrieved (Collins & Read; Surra & Bohman). Representations also affect appraisals of and responses to social situations (Collins & Read; Surra & Bohman). More specifically, individuals are likely to appraise and explain relationship experiences in ways that are consistent with their existing representations (Collins & Read; Surra & Bohman). Once formed, therefore, cognitive representations are somewhat resistant to change. Cognitive representations also influence the selection of behavioral responses in relational situations (Collins & Read; Surra & Bohman). They include information about a variety of behavioral strategies that can be enacted in relevant situations, and they predispose individuals toward the use of certain strategies (Collins & Read; Surra & Bohman). The more experience an individual has with a given type of relationship, either direct or observational, the larger the repertoire of potential responses to situations in that type of relationship (Collins & Read). The more experience an individual has with particular types of strategies, the stronger he or she should become in representations and the more likely the individual should be to use those strategies in relevant social situations.

Three hierarchically organized types of cognitive representations influence romantic relationships: representations of the nature of close relationships in general, representations of specific types of close relationships (e.g., parent–child or romantic), and representations of specific relationships (e.g., one's relationship with one's father; Collins & Read, 1994; Furman & Wehner, 1997; see Fig. 17.1). The development of representations is continuous, occurring through a process of gradual differentiation. Representations of relationships with parents generally develop first, and higher order representations about the nature of this type of relationship as well as of relationships in general develop over time out of these early experiences, with general representations then forming the basis for representations of all other close relationships (Collins & Read). However, the different types of representations are truly interdependent, such that representations developed at every level may exert an influence on representations at every other level (Collins & Read; Furman & Simon, 1999).

Although they are resistant to change, representations are not immutable, and significant new experiences that are inconsistent with existing expectations may precipitate representational change (Furman & Simon, 1999; Surra & Bohman, 1991). In fact, new experiences act to continually refine representations, either strengthening existing beliefs and predispositions or triggering change (Collins & Read, 1994; Furman & Simon; Surra & Bohman). Information from new experiences that is more relevant to a specific type of relationship should be more influential in the development of representations for that relationship type (Collins & Read). For example, information from the observation of parents' marital relationship may be more influential than information from relationships with siblings to representations of romantic relationships. In addition, direct experience should be more influential than indirect experience to the development of relationship-type representations (Furman & Simon, 1999). For example, when individuals have little direct romantic experience from which to draw, information from the observation of others' romantic relationships (e.g., parents' marital relationship) should be relatively influential in the development of representations of romantic relationships. As the amount and depth of involvement in romantic relationships increases, the information that is derived from these direct experiences should become significantly more influential to representations of romantic relationships, whereas indirect experiences become less important (Furman & Simon). However, because earlier experiences in parent–child relationships form the basis for all cognitive representations of relationships, they should continue to exert an influence on romantic relationships even after extensive direct experience in romantic relationships.

Although much of the past work on cognitive representations considers appraisal, evaluation, explanation, and resolution processes as components of representations (e.g., Collins & Read, 1994; Surra & Bohman, 1991), in the cognitive-developmental model they are conceptualized as a distinct construct that moderates the influence of experiences on the development of cognitive representations (see Fig. 17.1). This has been done to underscore the importance of these processes in understanding the effects of parental divorce on romantic relationships. The way in which individuals account for, or make sense of, a significant life process should play an important role in the nature of its influence on their lives. In a qualitative study of young adults' retrospective accounts of their parents' divorce and their attitudes about romantic relationships, Duran-Aydintug (1997) found that, although most young adults reported blaming at least one parent for the divorce initially, many also reported that over time and with age they developed a more well-balanced understanding of the divorce and resolved their emotions about it, and were able to have successful relationships with both their parents. These results indicate that

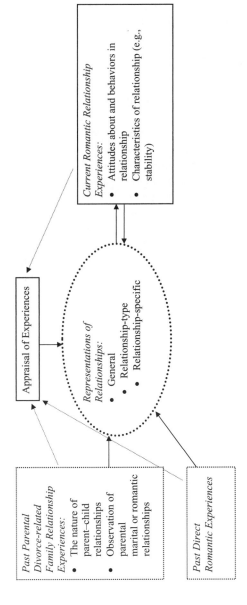

FIG. 17.1. Cognitive-Developmental Model of the Influence of Parental Divorce on Romantic Relationships.

appraisal and successful resolution of the parental divorce experience is, at the very least, important to the quality of parent–child relationships following divorce.

In a recent study on college students' narratives, Harvey and Fine (2004) suggested that perceiving parental divorce experiences as learning experiences that have contributed to personal growth may be important in facilitating good outcomes for young adults from divorced families. Recent research on romantic relationships supports this premise. For example, Walker and Ehrenberg (1998) found that young adults from divorced families who appraised the reasons for their parents' divorce as involving parental infidelity, parental anger, dissatisfaction with the marriage, and incompatibility between the parents were more likely to exhibit insecure romantic attachment styles, a component of representations about romantic relationships. In addition, in a study on young adults' descriptions of their parents' divorce, their own romantic experiences, and the connections between the two, Mahl (2001) found that individuals who see the divorce as a learning experience, something they could use as a source of information to help them identify both the warning signs of problems in relationships and the characteristics of healthy relationships, were more likely to report having healthy romantic relationships.

The research just described indicates that certain types of appraisal may be associated with better outcomes for young adults from divorced families, in terms of their romantic relationships. Positive relational outcomes appear to be associated with being able to move beyond a purely emotional response to the parental divorce and appraising it, and even the negative events associated with it, as a learning experience (Harvey & Fine, 2004; Mahl, 2001). Shulman, Scharf, Lumer, and Maurer (2001) proposed that three types of appraisal and resolution processes should be associated with better relational outcomes: (a) being able to coherently discuss any negative experiences; (b) recognizing the changes that have occurred since the parental divorce experience; and (c) understanding the complexity of the experience, which includes being able to see the experience from multiple perspectives (i.e., mother, father, self, sibling). Individuals who are successfully able to do these things are said to have developed an integrative perspective of their experiences. Shulman et al. suggested that these individuals should be less likely to exhibit negative effects in terms of current beliefs about the self, partners, and relationships and should therefore be less likely to have these past experiences interfere with current relationship functioning. In support of their hypothesis, they found that young adults from divorced families who had developed an integrative perspective reported fewer problems as well as more friendship and enjoyment in their romantic relationships. Successful appraisal of parental divorce experiences appears to be a relatively complex phenomenon, as neither age at divorce, gender, parental marital conflict, nor postdivorce parental romantic involvements were significantly associated with having an integrative perspective on the experience (Shulman et al.). Successful appraisal of parental divorce experiences may, then, require time, cognitive and emotional maturation, and continuing positive interaction with parents, as well as other significant relational experiences.

Relevant Characteristics of the Parental Divorce Experience

If a primary mechanism through which parental divorce exerts an influence on romantic relationships is through its influence on family relationships, then it appears particularly important to examine these relationships in greater detail. Doing so by using the cognitive-developmental model may allow us to better understand how these experiences influence romantic relationships in young adulthood and whether the different divorce-related characteristics of family relationships exert somewhat different influences on romantic relationships (e.g., whether observation of parental marital interactions exerts more of an influence than changes in the parent–child relationship on attitudes about marriage).

Characteristics of the Parent–Child Relationship

Parental divorce has the potential to significantly alter and even disrupt parent–child relationships. Parents are dealing with a host of issues (e.g., sense of loss, loneliness, economic strain, and loss of contact with the child) that may interfere with interactions with their children (Amato, 2000; Amato & Booth, 1991b; Clark & Kanoy, 1998; Feldman et al., 1998). Young adults from divorced families appear to recognize some of these effects, as they have described their relationships with parents as less positive than have adults from intact families, involving less frequent contact and less assistance exchange (Amato & Booth). These young adults also tend to attribute some of the characteristics of their current relationships with parents to the problems caused by their parents' divorce (Amato & Booth), including the situation in which parents became less available to them during and after the divorce as they dealt with their own emotional issues or their new postdivorce lives (Lee, 1995). The relationships that form between parents and child provide the child with information about the nature of the self, relational partners, and the social world in general (Collins & Read, 1994; Riggio, 2004). In addition, parenting practices contribute to a variety of traits and skills that are influential in close relationships, including achievement motivation, social competence, and self-esteem (Feldman et al.). Thus, parent–child relationships are powerful contributors to the general representations about close relationships that form the basis for representations about romantic relationships. Divorce-related changes in parent–child relationships may exert an influence on romantic relationships through their influence on these general representations.

Changes in the Quality of Parent–Child Relationships. One potential explanation for how parental divorce influences romantic relationships focuses on its effects on the quality of parent-child relationships, asserting that parental divorce negatively influences the degree of closeness and warmth in the parent–child relationship (e.g., Feldman et al., 1998; Mahl, 2001), or disrupts the attachment bond between parent and child (e.g., Taylor et al., 1995; Walker & Ehrenberg, 1998). From this perspective, declines in the quality of parent–child relationships contribute to the development of beliefs in children that make it more difficult for them to have healthy romantic relationships in young adulthood (Amato & Booth, 2001; Wallerstein & Blakeslee, 1989).

Disruptions in the quality of the parent–child relationship, as the primary close relationship in childhood, should influence general representations of close relationships. Specifically, significant family of origin experiences should influence generalized beliefs about self-worth in relationships, expectations for how others should behave in close relationships, as well as beliefs about the safety of the social world. As individuals get older and begin to get involved in romantic relationships, these generalized beliefs should play a significant role in romantic relationships through their influence on the development of relationship-type and relationship-specific representations. King (2002) suggested, for example, that children who have experienced disruptions in their attachment to parents as a result of parental divorce become less trusting of their parents, which then makes them less likely to trust other relational partners.

A brief hypothetical example may help to clarify the way in which these experiences may influence romantic relationships. Let's say that 17-year-old Amy experienced a parental divorce that led to significant declines in closeness with her father and her mother. These experiences have caused her to become less trusting of others, and also less certain that others will see her as worthy of love. In her first dating relationship, Amy may be more likely to attend to and remember her partner's forgetting to pick her up from school than his helping her little sister with her homework. In addition, she may be more likely to interpret his forgetfulness as a sign that he doesn't care for her, and to interpret his kindness to her sister as a ploy to get her to forgive him instead of as a gesture of his love for her. The tendency to attend to and interpret information in ways that are consistent with existing expectations may cause Amy to develop representations of romantic relationships and also of her current relationship that involve beliefs that romantic partners generally, and her partner specifically, cannot be trusted, and that she is not worthy of romantic partners who are trustworthy. In addition, Amy may respond to her partner's lateness with anger and hurt, accusing him of not caring about her. This response may influence her partner's feelings about Amy, perhaps making him feel wrongly accused and underappreciated. If the relationship ends as the result of these types of interactions, Amy's lack of trust in others and her negative beliefs about her own attractiveness, both aspects of her representations of romantic relationships, may be reinforced.

Existing research evidence supports the premise that declines in the quality of parent–child relationships following parental divorce are associated with more problematic romantic relationships. Poorer quality relationships with parents after a parental divorce are related to less satisfaction in romantic relationships (Booth et al., 1984; Riggio, 2004), more fear and anxiety about romantic relationships (Duran-Aydintug, 1997; Riggio), less trust in dating partners (Franklin et al., 1990; King, 2002), less happiness in love (Feldman et al., 1998), and lower perceived quality of romantic relationships in young adulthood (Booth et al.). A qualitative study found that young adults who reported having more distant relationships with parents after a parental divorce seemed to have more difficulty trusting and becoming attached to romantic partners, whereas those who reported a close relationship with parents desired romantic relationships with the same positive characteristics found in their parent–child relationships (i.e., intimacy, nurturance, and effective communication; see Mahl, 2001). These findings are quite consistent with the premises of the cognitive-development model. Declines in the quality of the parent–child relationship should influence beliefs about the safety of social relationships, the nature of relational partners, and the worth of the self in social relationships. We might, then, expect the influence of divorce-related changes in the quality of parent–child relationships to manifest itself more strongly in beliefs about the nature of romantic partners and romantic relationships than in, say, behavioral predispositions with regard to conflict resolution.

Loss of Contact With a Parent.   The loss of contact with a parent (usually the noncustodial parent) following parental divorce may be one relatively common cause of declines in the quality of parent–child relationships. Less contact with a parent following divorce has been found to be associated with lower well-being in childhood (Amato, 1993; Amato & Keith, 1991), more fearful attitudes about marriage (Duran-Aydintug, 1997), and an increased likelihood of cohabitation in young adulthood (Booth et al., 1984). However, the effects of contact with noncustodial parents appear to be somewhat complicated, as some studies have failed to find any association (Amato & Keith; Kline, Johnston, & Tschann, 1991), and at least one indicated that, in some cases, more frequent contact with the noncustodial parent was related to more negative outcomes for children (Amato). In and of itself, the amount of contact with parents following divorce may not account for much variance in outcomes for at least two reasons. First, the effects on children of contact with parents should be partially dependent on the nature of the relationship between the parents after the divorce. If the parents are in constant, open conflict with each other, more frequent visitation with the noncustodial parent means more exposure to conflict for the children (Amato). Second, the quality of the parent–child relationship may be more important than the frequency of contact for the romantic relationships of children of divorce. In support of this hypothesis, one study found that more frequent contact with noncustodial fathers who engaged in high-quality parenting was associated with better well-being in adulthood (Amato & Gilbreth, 1999). In contrast, if children have very problematic relationships with the parent, more frequent contact may do them more harm than good. Although the loss of contact with a parent following divorce may act to erode the quality of the parent–child relationship, it seems likely that the quality of the parent–child relationship is the more influential factor in terms of the effects on romantic relationships.

Declines in Effective Parenting. Another explanation for the negative effects of parental divorce on romantic relationships focuses on declines in effective parenting that result from the stressors associated with divorce for parents (e.g., loneliness or economic strain). This so-called socialization explanation proposes that poor parenting practices such as ineffective discipline or lack of empathy and nurturance cause less effective socialization of children, which leads them to be less socially competent (i.e., have less effective communication and conflict-resolution skills) and therefore to have more problematic romantic relationships (Conger et al., 2000). In support of this explanation, a longitudinal study conducted by Conger et al. found that authoritative parenting, in which parents were nurturant, consistent, and involved, predicted positive behaviors in romantic relationships 5 years later for young adults.

The parental socialization explanation for the effects of parental divorce on romantic relationships is also consistent with the premises of the cognitive-developmental model. Parental socialization may influence romantic relationships through its influence on beliefs about appropriate behaviors in close relationships and on the development of a repertoire of behavioral strategies. Using another hypothetical example for illustration, let's say that Jared's mother becomes relatively uninvolved in parenting after her divorce, and her limited interactions with Jared involve very little nurturance and empathy, providing Jared with little opportunity to learn such behaviors. When Jared becomes involved in his first romantic relationship at the age of 18, he does not interact well with his partner, as he understands neither how to exhibit empathy for his partner nor the importance of doing so for successful relationships. If his partner ends the relationship because she is unhappy with his lack of empathy, Jared may come to believe that partners in romantic relationships will require things of him that he is not capable of. Therefore, his socialization experiences with his mother have influenced not only his general representations about close relationships (i.e., through lack of development of interpersonal skills), but eventually his representations of romantic relationships and of relationships with specific partners.

In summary, it appears that the quality of parent–child relationships, amount of contact with parents, and parenting style all play some role in the effects of parental divorce on romantic relationships. However, the critical factors, in terms of positive influence on romantic relationships, appear to be the maintenance of close relationships with parents who enact authoritative parenting styles both during and after the parental divorce. In fact, in many of the studies just reported, the positive aspects of these types of parent–child relationships appear to have similar effects on romantic relationships regardless of parental marital status (see, e.g., Conger et al., 2000; Feldman et al., 1998; Hayashi & Strickland, 1998; King, 2002; Riggio, 2004; Taylor et al., 1995). From a cognitive-developmental perspective, high-quality parent–child relationships contribute to positive general representations of close relationships, which then positively influence the development of representations about romantic relationships as well as representations about specific romantic relationships. These more positive representations then contribute to more positive and healthy experiences in romantic relationships. These findings suggest, then, that a significant portion of the negative effects of parental divorce on romantic relationships can be ameliorated if the quality of parent–child relationships and parenting itself are protected during the divorce experience.

Exposure to Parental Romantic Relationships

A second characteristic of parental divorce experiences that has the potential to influence romantic relationships involves children's exposure to parental marital or nonmarital romantic relationships (e.g., Amato, 1996; Amato & Booth, 2001; Conger et al., 2000; Sanders et al., 1999). One of the primary ways that children learn about romantic relationships is through the observation of their parents' romantic relationships (Conger et al.; Furman & Simon, 1999). From a cognitive-developmental perspective, indirect experiences with romantic relationships, such as observation of parental relationships, influence romantic relationships primarily through their contribution to the development of representations of romantic relationships. These observations contribute to the repertoire of behavioral strategies that can be enacted in romantic situations, as well as to beliefs about the nature of romantic relationships and romantic partners, which then influence attitudes about and behaviors in specific romantic relationships.

Research indicates that children learn patterns of behavior in romantic relationships from observing their parents' romantic relationships. For example, children's exposure to parents' jealous, domineering, critical, angry, moody, and uncommunicative marital behaviors has been found to be a significant predictor of negative behaviors in their own marriages as young adults (Amato & Booth, 2001). Observation of parental romantic relationships also appears to influence beliefs about the nature of relationships, as recent studies have found evidence that individuals develop beliefs about the permanence of marriage through their observations of parents' divorcing (Amato & DeBoer 2001; Bartell & Surra, 1998; Wolfinger, 2000). In addition, the observation of negative parental marital interactions, such as discord, may exert more of an influence on romantic relationships than the observation of positive interactions, because negative behaviors are more likely to elicit strong emotional responses from children, and therefore are more likely to be cognitively attended to and processed (Amato & Booth).

The research just cited indicates that the observation of both parental marital discord and parental divorce influences romantic relationships for young adults from divorced families. In many respects, the observation of parental marital discord seems to exacerbate the effects of the observation of parents' ending their marriage. Compared with young adults from divorced families with lower levels of parental discord, those from divorced families with high discord reported lower quality dating relationships (Booth et al., 1984) and less altruistic love for their dating partners (Sprague & Kinney, 1997), were more fearful and negative about marriage (Duran-Aydintug, 1997; Gabardi & Rosen, 1992, respectively), and were more likely to believe that they would experience divorce in their own marriages (Kirk, 2002). Compared with young adults from intact families with little parental marital discord, those from divorced families with high discord perceived other people as less benevolent and dating partners as less dependable, and they were less optimistic and positive about their dating relationships (Amato, Spencer-Loomis, & Booth, 1995; Franklin et al., 1990). From a cognitive-developmental perspective, exposure to more parental marital discord with divorce may have an additive effect on romantic relationships, creating more negative and fearful beliefs about the nature of romantic partners and more fear about the ability to maintain successful romantic relationships, components of representations of romantic relationships.

Higher levels of parental marital discord, however, may not exacerbate the effects of observation of parental divorce in at least one area of romantic relationships, namely marital stability. In a study of the effects of parental marital discord on the intergenerational transmission of divorce, Amato and DeBoer (2001) found that the likelihood of divorce was greater in young adults from divorced families with low parental discord than in young adults from divorced families with high discord. In fact, young adults from divorced families with low discord were more likely to divorce than were any other group in the study (i.e., individuals from intact families with low or high discord and from divorced families with high discord). Amato and DeBoer suggested that individuals who observe parental divorce with little parental marital discord may learn that marriage is not a permanent institution and that it is acceptable to break a commitment if one is not satisfied in the relationship or feel that one could find a better partner elsewhere (Amato & DeBoer), beliefs that then negatively influence young adults' commitment in their own marital relationships. In contrast, individuals whose parents divorced after an extended period of discord may develop the belief that divorce is acceptable, but only under extreme conditions, making them less likely to divorce when they are not completely satisfied with their relationship (Amato & DeBoer). In this type of divorce-related experience, parental divorce and level of conflict appear to be exerting an interactive effect on young adults' romantic relationships. In addition, in this experience the observation of parents' marital relationship appears to be contributing specifically to representations about the nature of commitment in marital relationships, a component of representations of romantic relationships. Given the findings that some of the effects of parental divorce appear stronger in the context of marital relationships than in that of premarital romantic relationships (e.g., Boyer-Pennington et al., 2001; Franklin et al., 1990; Wallerstein, 1985), it is possible that parental divorce experiences that involve information about marital relationships exert a particularly strong influence on representations of marital relationships.

With some notable exceptions (e.g., Kinnaird & Gerrard, 1986; Shulman et al., 2001; Taylor et al., 1995), much of the existing research on exposure to parental marital discord indicates that it has a negative effect on romantic relationships independent of parental marital status. For example, higher levels of parental marital discord in both divorced and intact families were associated with more insecure romantic attachment styles (Hayashi & Strickland, 1998), more anxiety about personal relationships (Riggio, 2004), perceiving others and the world as less benevolent (Franklin et al., 1990), and perceiving romantic relationships as more risky (Johnston & Thomas, 1996). Higher discord was also associated with more fear of intimacy (Kirk, 2002), as well as less emotional intimacy (Westervelt & Vanderberg, 1997) and relational satisfaction in romantic relationships (Kirk). Young adults from families with greater parental marital discord were also more negative about marriage and more cautious about their own future in marriage (Burgoyne & Hames, 2002), exhibited more discord in their marriages (Amato & Booth, 2001; Amato & DeBoer, 2001), were less happy in their marriages (Amato & Booth), and contemplated divorce more often (Amato & DeBoer). Observing parental marital discord may influence representations about the nature of romantic relationships regardless of parental marital status. Specifically, observing high levels of discord between parents may contribute to the development of more negative beliefs about the risks involved in romantic relationships and the benevolence of partners and to the development of a repertoire of more problematic behavioral predispositions for romantic relationships. Because these observations are of marital relationships, they may exert a particularly strong influence on expectations about and behavioral predispositions in marital relationships.

The observation of parental marital interactions appears to have a significant and somewhat complex effect on romantic relationships in young adulthood. The observation of discord appears to have a negative effect on beliefs about and behaviors in romantic relationships independent of parental divorce, and it also appears to exacerbate many of the effects of observing parental divorce. However, the observations of parental discord and parental divorce appear to interact in their effects on marital stability, such that exposure to divorce with little marital discord is associated with the highest risk of divorce for young adults. Furthermore, observation of parental marital relationships may exert a particularly strong influence on representations of marital relationships, a component of representations of romantic relationships. These findings indicate that understanding the specific nature of the family relationship characteristics associated with parental divorce (e.g., amount of discord in marital relationships) is critical to understanding the effects of parental divorce on romantic relationships.

RECOMMENDATIONS FOR FUTURE RESEARCH

As the research reviewed here clearly indicates, parental divorce is best conceptualized as a process associated with a variety of experiences that have the potential to influence romantic relationships in adulthood. Although parental divorce, operationalized as a single dichotomous variable, is related to a variety of attitudes about and behaviors in romantic relationships, an examination of divorce-related family relationship characteristics such as the nature of parent–child relationships and exposure to parental marital or romantic relationships indicates that these experiences play a central role in the effects of parental divorce on romantic relationships. The cognitive-developmental model proposed here may be quite useful in identifying divorce-related characteristics that are likely to influence romantic relationships and in providing an explanatory mechanism for why these experiences should be influential to romantic relationships.

The model may also help us to explore further the variability associated with parental divorce and its effects on romantic relationships. Using this model, we can examine whether different types of parental divorce-related experiences (i.e., in parent–child relationships, through observation of parental relationships) operate through different pathways to exert an influence on romantic relationships. For example, the premises of the cognitive-developmental model suggest that experiences more relevant to representations of romantic relationships may exert more of an influence on these relationship-type representations, as opposed to general representations of close relationships. In support of this hypothesis, the research reviewed here indicates that observations of problematic parental marital interactions are more strongly related to beliefs about marriage and divorce than are experiences in parent–child relationships. In addition, the identification of different pathways of influence for different divorce-related experiences may be helpful in developing effective interventions for the negative effects of parental divorce on romantic relationships. If, for example, we know that a child has observed much parental marital discord surrounding a divorce, we can focus intervention efforts on identifying and improving the child's attitudes about and behavioral predispositions toward romantic relationships, as opposed to toward close relationships in general. The premises of the model also suggest that experiences in parent–child relationships may influence romantic relationships primarily through their influence on general representations of close relationships. To test this hypothesis further, future research could examine, longitudinally, whether changes in parent–child relationships with parental divorce exert a significant influence on attitudes about self-worth, the trustworthiness of others, and the safety of the social world during childhood, and then whether these general representations influence romantic relationships and the development of representations of romantic relationships in adulthood. Future research might also examine simultaneously the characteristics of parent–child relationships and the observation of parental marital behaviors in a divorce process, in order to clarify the extent and nature of each factor's influence on romantic relationships, as well as the ways in which they may interact with each other.

Although both the quality of parent–child relationships and the observation of parental marital interactions appear to have an influence on romantic relationships independent of parental marital status, the research reviewed here indicates that the observation of parental divorce exerts an independent influence on romantic relationships in young adulthood. Individuals who experience parental divorce appear to be more accepting of divorce regardless of parent–child relationship quality or observation of parental marital discord. In addition, observation of parental divorce appears to interact with the observation of discord to influence beliefs about the nature of marriage. Therefore, it appears that parental divorce is not merely a proxy variable for the host of other experiences (e.g., changes in the parent–child relationship and exposure to parental marital conflict) that are commonly associated with parental divorce, but that the observation of the divorce itself exerts an influence on young adults' romantic relationships.

The Need to Take a More Developmental Perspective in Future Research

Although the research reviewed in this chapter clearly indicates that parental divorce experiences in childhood exert an influence on romantic relationships in adulthood, we have really just begun to treat it as the developmental phenomenon it clearly is. Future research would benefit from a more developmental approach, exploring, for example, the way in which different aspects of life-span development (e.g., cognitive or emotional development) may moderate the effects of parental divorce experiences on romantic relationships or examining other factors that may contribute to the development of cognitive representations of close relationships, thereby moderating the effects of parental divorce on romantic relationships.

The effects of significant life processes such as parental divorce may differ at different phases of the life span. A more comprehensive understanding of the effects of parental divorce on young adult romantic relationships may, then, require consideration of the psychosocial developmental tasks of adolescence and young adulthood (i.e., the achievement of a firmly established and healthy identity; the development of healthy intimate relationships). For example, experiences with parental marital relationships may become especially significant during late adolescence and young adulthood because this is the age in which romantic experiences become especially salient, as individuals are striving to accomplish the developmental task of achieving a sense of intimacy (Burgoyne & Hames, 2002; Franklin et al., 1990). Future research might examine whether the nature of the influence of parental divorce differs at later phases of the life span, when the developmental tasks shift from a primary focus on romantic relationships. On the basis of the premises of the cognitive-developmental model as well as the proposition that romantic experiences in adolescence are crucial developmental precursors to romantic relationships in adulthood (e.g., Furman & Wehner, 1997), we might expect that parental divorce experiences continue to exert an influence on romantic relationships later in the life span. However, there is little empirical evidence with which to support such a claim at this time. The overwhelming majority of research conducted on this topic thus far has focused on late adolescents and young adults, and so future research must begin to examine older adults.

To better understand the influence of parental divorce on romantic relationships, we must also address the contribution of other relevant experiences to cognitive representations of relationships. One such factor is direct romantic experience. As a central contributor to cognitive representations about romantic relationships, direct romantic experiences may moderate the effects of parental divorce on romantic relationships by moderating its influence on representations of romantic relationships. In support of this possibility, some recent qualitative work has found that direct romantic experiences appear to be very important in the development of attitudes about romantic relationships (Burgoyne & Hames, 2002; Lee, 1995). In fact, young adults in one study reported that direct experiences moderated the influence of parental divorce on their attitudes about romantic relationships (Lee), and, in another, those who had experience in long-term romantic relationships attributed their views about marriage and divorce as much to their past and present romantic experiences as to their experiences in their family of origin (Burgoyne & Hames). Future research should examine the processes by which direct experiences in romantic relationships may moderate the influence of parental divorce on romantic relationships. For example, future studies should explore the conditions under which romantic relationship experiences are more or less likely to influence existing representations about the nature of romantic relationships (e.g., the length of the relationship, the stage of involvement, and the extent of the difference between the characteristics of the current relationship and existing representations about the nature of romantic relationships).

Although direct experiences in romantic relationships (as well as direct experiences in parent–child relationships and the observation of parental marital relationships) are likely to exert a strong influence on cognitive representations of close relationships, other relevant relationship experiences (e.g., observations of sibling's romantic relationships, or relationships with other close family members) should also contribute to the development of cognitive representations. Future research, therefore, should examine the extent to which these other experiences may moderate the nature of the influence of parental divorce on romantic relationships. For example, if a child observes a particularly negative and problematic parental marital relationship for the first 10 years of her life, but then observes a very positive and healthy marital relationship between her older brother and his wife for the next 10 years, it is possible that the negative effects on representations of romantic relationships of observing the parental marital relationship are moderated by the positive effects of observing the sibling marital relationship. As another example, if a child experiences a significant decline in the quality of her relationship with her mother after a parental divorce, but maintains a warm and nurturing relationship with a grandmother with whom she is in frequent contact, it is possible that the negative effects on general representations of relationships of the decline in the parent–child relationship are moderated by the positive effects of the relationship with the grandmother.

The Need to Conceptualize Romantic Relationships as Dyadic Phenomena in Future Research

Romantic relationships are the product of both partners' experiences and behaviors. Interaction with partners should influence the development of cognitive representations of close relationships, an influence that should increase in magnitude as the relationship continues over time and becomes more involved. Therefore, a better understanding of the influence of parental divorce on romantic relationships also requires consideration of the dyadic nature of romantic relationships. Some recent research has begun to make this consideration, and results indicate that partner characteristics play a role in the effects of parental divorce on romantic relationships. For example, Jacquet and Surra (2001) found that the parental marital status of female partners in premarital dating relationships was significantly more important than that of male partners in predicting both partners' perceptions of relational characteristics. Amato (1996) found that, although couples in which one partner's parents had divorced were somewhat more likely to divorce than couples from intact families, couples in which both partners' parents had divorced were significantly more likely to divorce. A fruitful path for future research may, therefore, involve further examination of whether and how specific partner characteristics such as personality or past family of origin experiences moderate the effects of parental divorce experiences on cognitive representations of relationships.

Relationships are also developmental phenomena. A given relationship continually develops over time, and this development is shaped by current experiences in the relationship as well as past experiences as manifested in relevant cognitive representations. Scientists who study romantic relationships, especially marriage, have called for the study of these relationships from a long-term developmental perspective, examining, for example, the characteristics of the premarital relationship in order to understand marital dynamics (e.g., Conger et al., 2000; Huston, 1994). If we seek to understand how parental divorce influences romantic relationships, future research must also take into consideration the dynamic nature of relationships and examine how the specific nature of development in a given romantic relationship may influence the effects of parental divorce on that relationship.

The Need for Continued Investigation of the Role of Appraisal

The appraisal of parental divorce experiences appears to exert a significant moderating influence on the effects of these experiences on romantic relationships. One factor that may be particularly important to successful resolution of parental divorce experiences is knowledge about why the divorce occurred. Existing research indicates that young adults who perceived having less information about the reasons for a parental divorce also reported more problems and stress in dealing with the parental divorce (Duran-Aydintug, 1997). Others have suggested that lack of knowledge about the reasons for parental divorce may make it more difficult for young adults to assess the quality and strength of their own romantic relationships, perhaps making it more difficult to form and maintain healthy romantic relationships (Bartell & Surra, 1998). Future research should investigate whether the perceived amount of knowledge about the parental divorce influences the probability of successful resolution of the experience, and also whether perceived knowledge is directly associated with the characteristics of romantic relationships in adulthood.

Future research should also empirically examine the factors that may determine different types of appraisal and be central to the successful resolution of parental divorce experiences. Shulman et al. (2001) suggested that individuals become more capable of interpreting and making meaning of their experiences over time, and we should examine whether length of time since the divorce and age play some role in resolution. In addition, we should examine whether coping resources such as social support from friends or psychological resiliency contribute to successful resolution, and whether different resources may be helpful for successful resolution in different types of parental divorce experiences (e.g., high vs. low parental marital conflict; negative changes vs. no change in the quality of the parent–child relationship). In addition, future research should continue to examine the significance of the three types of appraisal that Shulman et al. suggested are related to better relational outcomes.

The Need for a More Diverse Examination of the Phenomenon

A more comprehensive understanding of the nature of the influence of parental divorce on romantic relationships requires that we expand our samples to include individuals of different ages, from diverse racial, ethnic, and socioeconomic backgrounds, and even of different sexual orientations. The research conducted thus far on this topic predominantly involves young adult samples of individuals who are White and heterosexual. Obviously, these factors restrict our ability to generalize about the effects of parental divorce on the romantic relationships of Mexican Americans, for example, or on individuals in same-sex romantic relationships. Conducting studies on more diverse samples, including explicitly comparative work, could help us to understand the degree to which cultural socialization moderates the effects of parental divorce on cognitive representations about romantic relationships, for example. A consideration of more diverse samples is truly essential in order to gain a more comprehensive understanding of the factors that influence the nature of the effects of parental divorce on romantic relationships.

Finally, a comprehensive understanding of the influence of parental relational dissolution, as a phenomenon, would benefit from future exploration of the effects of other types of parental romantic relationship dissolution on romantic relationships. There exists some research that indicates that the observation of multiple parental relational dissolutions (i.e., the observation of divorce in parental remarriages or multiple partner changes) has a negative influence on attitudes about marriage and increases the probability of divorce (Duran-Aydintug, 1997 and Wolfinger, 2000, respectively). However, as far as I can tell, we have no empirical evidence about the effects of specific types of nonmarital parental romantic relationship dissolution, such as cohabiting heterosexual relationships or same-sex relationships, on romantic relationships in adulthood. Although we might hypothesize that the nature of the effects are similar to that observed in marital dissolutions, or that the extent of the influence may depend on the child's exposure to the parental romantic relationship as well as on the centrality of the relationship with the parent's romantic partner to the child's life, we cannot make these statements with any degree of certainty until we empirically test these assertions.

REFERENCES

Amato, P. R. (1988). Long-term implications of parental divorce for adult self-concept. *Journal of Family Issues, 9,* 201–213.

Amato, P. R. (1993). Children's adjustment to divorce: Theories, hypotheses, and empirical support. *Journal of Marriage and the Family, 55,* 23–38.

Amato, P. R. (1996). Explaining the intergenerational transmission of divorce. *Journal of Marriage and the Family, 58,* 628–640.

Amato, P. R. (2000). The consequences of divorce for adults and children. *Journal of Marriage and the Family, 62,* 1269–1287.

Amato, P. R., & Booth, A. (1991a). The consequences of divorce for attitudes toward divorce and gender roles. *Journal of Family Issues, 12,* 306–322.

Amato, P. R., & Booth, A. (1991b). Consequences of parental divorce and marital unhappiness for adult well-being. *Social Forces, 69,* 895–914.

Amato, P. R., & Booth, A. (2001). The legacy of parents' marital discord: Consequences for children's marital quality. *Journal of Personality and Social Psychology, 81,* 627–638.

Amato, P. R. & DeBoer, D. D. (2001). The transmission of marital instability across generations: Relationship skills or commitment to marriage? *Journal of Marriage and the Family, 63,* 1038–1051.

Amato, P. R., & Gilbreth, J. G. (1999). Nonresident fathers and children's well-being: A meta-analysis. *Journal of Marriage and the Family, 61,* 557–573.

Amato, P. R., & Keith, B. (1991). Consequences of parental divorce for children's well-being: A meta-analysis. *Psychological Bulletin, 110,* 26–46.

Amato, P. R., Spencer-Loomis, L., & Booth, A. (1995). Parental divorce, marital conflict, and offspring well-being during early adulthood. *Social Forces, 73,* 895–915.

Bartell, D. S., & Surra, C. A. (1998, November). Family background characteristics and stability of commitment to premarital romantic relationships. Paper presented at the meeting of the National Council on Family Relations, Milwaukee, WI.

Booth, A., Brinkerhoff, D. B., & White, L. K. (1984). The impact of parental divorce on courtship. *Journal of Marriage and the Family, 46,* 85–94.

Boyer-Pennington, M. E., Pennington, J., & Spink, C. (2001). Students' expectations and optimism towards marriage as a function of parental divorce. *Journal of Divorce and Remarriage, 34*(3/4), 71–87.

Brennan, K. A., & Shaver, P. R. (1993). Attachment styles and parental divorce. *Journal of Divorce and Remarriage, 21*(1/2), 161–175.

Burgoyne, C. B., & Hames, R. (2002). Views of marriage and divorce: An in-depth study of young adults from intact and divorced families. *Journal of Divorce and Remarriage, 37*(1/2), 75–100.

Chase-Lansdale, P. L., Cherlin, A. J., & Kiernan, K. E. (1995). The long-term effects of parental divorce on the mental health of young adults: A developmental perspective. *Child Development, 66,* 1614–1634.

Clark, K. J., & Kanoy, K. (1998). Parents' marital status, father-daughter intimacy and young adult females' dating relationships. *Journal of Divorce and Remarriage, 29*(1/2), 167–179.

Collins, N. C., & Read, S. J. (1994). Cognitive representations of attachment: The structure and function of working models. In K. Bartholomew & D. Perlman (Eds.), *Attachment processes in adulthood: Vol. 5. Advances in personal relationships* (pp. 53–90). London: Jessica Kingsley.

Conger, R. D., Cui, M., Bryant, C. M., & Elder, G. H. (2000). Competence in early adult romantic relationships: A developmental perspective on family influences. *Journal of Personality and Social Psychology, 79,* 224–237.

Darlington, Y. (2001). "When all is said and done": The impact of parental divorce and contested custody in childhood on young adults' relationships with their parents and their attitudes to relationships and marriage. *Journal of Divorce and Remarriage, 35*(3/4), 23–42.

Duran-Aydintug, C. (1997). Adult children of divorce revisited: When they speak up. *Journal of Divorce and Remarriage, 27*(1/2), 71–83.

Feldman, S. S., Gowen, L. K., & Fisher, L. (1998). Family relationships and gender as predictors of romantic intimacy in young adults: A longitudinal study. *Journal of Research on Adolescence, 8,* 263–286.

Franklin, K. M., Janoff-Bulman, R., & Roberts, J. E. (1990). Long-term impact of parental divorce on optimism and trust: Changes in general assumptions or narrow beliefs? *Journal of Personality and Social Psychology, 59,* 743–755.

Furman, W., & Simon, V. A. (1999). Cognitive representations of adolescent romantic relationships. In W. Furman, B. B. Brown, & C. Feiring (Eds.), *The development of romantic relationships in adolescence* (pp. 75–98). New York: Cambridge University Press.

Furman, W., & Wehner, E. A. (1997). Adolescent romantic relationships: A developmental perspective. In W. Damon (Series Ed.), S. Shulman, & W. A. Collins (Vol. Eds.), *New directions for child development: No. 78. Romantic relationships in adolescence: A developmental perspective:* (pp. 21–36). San Francisco: Jossey-Bass.

Furstenberg, F. F., Jr., & Teitler, J. O. (1994). Reconsidering the effects of marital disruption: What happens to children of divorce in early adulthood? *Journal of Family Issues, 15,* 173–190.

Gabardi, L., & Rosen, L. A. (1992). Intimate relationships: College students from divorced and intact families. *Journal of Divorce and Remarriage, 18*(3–4), 25–56.

Glenn, N. D., & Kramer, K. B. (1987). The marriages and divorces of the children of divorce. *Journal of Marriage and the Family, 49,* 811–825.

Harvey, J. H., & Fine, M. A. (2004). *Children of divorce: Stories of loss and growth.* Mahwah, NJ: Lawrence Erlbaum Associates.

Hayashi, G. M., & Strickland, B. R. (1998). Long-term effects of parental divorce on love relationships: Divorce as an attachment disruption. *Journal of Social and Personal Relationships, 15,* 23–38.

Herzog, M. J., & Cooney, T. M. (2002). Parental divorce and perceptions of past interparental conflict: Influences on the communication of young adults. *Journal of Divorce and Remarriage, 36*(3/4), 89–109.

Huston, T. L. (1994). Courtship antecedents of marital satisfaction and love. In R. Erber & R. Gilmore (Eds.), *Theoretical frameworks for personal relationships* (pp. 43–65). Hillsdale, NJ: Lawrence Erlbaum Associates.

Jacquet, S. E., & Surra, C. A. (2001). Parental divorce and premarital couples: Commitment and other relationship characteristics. *Journal of Marriage and Family, 63,* 627–638.

Johnston, S. G., & Thomas, A. M. (1996). Divorce versus intact parental marriage and perceived risk and dyadic trust in present heterosexual relationships. *Psychological Reports, 78,* 387–390.

King, V. (2002). Parental divorce and interpersonal trust in adult offspring. *Journal of Marriage and Family, 64,* 642–656.

Kinnaird, K. L., & Gerrard, M. (1986). Premarital sexual behavior and attitudes toward marriage and divorce among young women as a function of their mothers' marital status. *Journal of Marriage and the Family, 48,* 757–765.

Kirk, A. (2002). The effects of divorce on young adults' relationship competence: The influence of intimate friendships. *Journal of Divorce and Remarriage, 38*(1/2), 61–89.

Kline, M., Johnston, J. R., & Tschann, J. M. (1991). The long shadow of marital conflict: A model of children's postdivorce adjustment. *Journal of Marriage and the Family, 53,* 297–309.

Lee, M. (1995). Trajectory of influence of parental divorce on children's heterosexual relationships. *Journal of Divorce and Remarriage, 22*(3/4), 55–76.

Mahl, D. (2001). The influence of parental divorce on the romantic relationship beliefs of young adults. *Journal of Divorce and Remarriage, 34*(3/4), 89–118.

Riggio, H. R. (2004). Parental marital conflict and divorce, parent–child relationships, social support, and relationship anxiety in young adulthood. *Personal Relationships, 11,* 99–114.

Ross, C. E., & Mirowsky, J. (1999). Parental divorce, life-course disruption, and adult depression. *Journal of Marriage and the Family, 61,* 1034–1045.

Sanders, M. R., Halford, W. K., & Behrens, B. C. (1999). Parental divorce and premarital couple communication. *Journal of Family Psychology, 13,* 60–74.

Shulman, S., Scharf, M., Lumer, D., & Maurer, O. (2001). Parental divorce and young adult children's romantic relationships: Resolution of the divorce experience. *American Journal of Orthopsychiatry, 71,* 473–478.

Sprague, H. E., & Kinney, J. M. (1997). The effects of interparental divorce and conflict on college students' romantic relationships. *Journal of Divorce and Remarriage, 27*(1/2), 85–104.

Sprecher, S., Cate, R., & Levin, L. (1998). Parental divorce and young adults' beliefs about love. *Journal of Divorce and Remarriage, 28*(3/4), 107–120.

Surra, C. A., & Bohman, T. (1991). The development of close relationships: A cognitive perspective. In G. J. O. Fletcher & F. D. Fincham (Eds.), *Cognition and close relationships* (pp. 281–305). Hillsdale, NJ: Lawrence Erlbaum Associates.

Taylor, L, Parker, G., & Roy, K. (1995). Parental divorce and its effects on the quality of intimate relationships in adulthood. *Journal of Divorce and Remarriage, 24*(3/4), 181–202.

Walker, T. R., & Ehrenberg, M. F. (1998). An exploratory study of young persons' attachment styles and perceived reasons for parental divorce. *Journal of Adolescent Research, 13,* 320–342.

Wallerstein, J. S. (1985). Children of divorce: A preliminary report of a ten-year follow-up of older children and adolescents. *Journal of the American Academy of Child Psychiatry, 24,* 545–553.

Wallerstein, J. S., & Blakeslee, S. (1989). *Second chances: Men, women, and children a decade after divorce.* New York: Ticknor & Fields.

Westervelt, K., & Vanderberg, B. (1997). Parental divorce and intimate relationships of young adults. *Psychological Reports, 80,* 923–926.

Wolfinger, N. H. (2000). Beyond the intergenerational transmission of divorce: Do people replicate the patterns of marital instability they grew up with? *Journal of Family Issues, 21,* 1061–1086.

18

Stress-Related Growth Following Divorce and Relationship Dissolution

Ty Tashiro, Patricia Frazier, and Margit Berman
University of Minnesota

Recalling the pain of adolescent romantic relationship breakups often conjures up memories of weeks spent ruminating and depressed, wondering whether a relationship like that would *ever* be found again. Although relationship breakups are stressful, most people do eventually stop thinking about their expartner, their mood eventually improves, and they realize that there are "other fish in the sea." In fact, most people date more than one person—and in fact may marry more than one person—in their lifetimes. In retrospect, early relationships may never have had much of a chance. Poor partner selection, a poor fit between partners, or just a general lack of knowledge about how to make a relationship work can make it difficult for adolescent romances to endure. Ideally, years of trial and error in romantic relationships enable individuals to grow in their capacity to select and sustain satisfying, stable romantic relationships.

An emerging body of research suggests that one point at which such growth may occur is when individuals must come to terms with the loss of a relationship. Although relationship breakups can be distressing, they also can foster personal growth and positive changes in one's life (Hetherington & Kelly, 2002). The purpose of this chapter is to review research on personal growth following relationship dissolution. In the first section, we briefly review theory and research on growth following stressful life events. In the second section, we review research on personal growth specifically within the context of romantic relationship dissolution. Stress-related growth among divorcing partners is covered first, followed by research on growth in children of divorce. Next, we describe research on growth following nonmarital breakups, including our own program of research. We conclude by offering a methodological critique of existing research and future directions for research.

PERSONAL GROWTH FOLLOWING STRESSFUL LIFE EVENTS

Relationship dissolution is one of the most stressful life events one can encounter. Divorce and marital separation were ranked second and third, respectively, in an influential study of stressful life events, ranking higher than death of a close family member or being in jail (Holmes & Rahe, 1967). Experiencing divorce is associated with increased risk for pathology, including depression, anxiety, and substance abuse (Amato, 2000). Although nonmarital breakups may seem less important for individuals' psychological well-being, the impact of the loss of a nonmarital romantic relationship should not be underestimated. For example, a recent romantic relationship breakup greatly increases the risk for the initial onset of a major depressive disorder in adolescents (Monroe, Rohde, Seeley, & Lewinsohn, 1999).

Given the severity of symptoms that can accompany stressful events, including relationship dissolution, the primary goal of research and treatment has been to reduce their negative psychological impact. Although decreasing stress-related pathology is and should be a primary goal, *only* focusing on the pathology may limit our full understanding of the changes that take place following stressful events. Consistent with contemporary psychology's broadened focus on positive human adaptation (Seligman & Csikzentmihalyi, 2000), researchers have begun to explore how stressful or traumatic life events can lead to personal growth.

Many terms are used to describe the process of growth following stressful events, including *posttraumatic growth*, *thriving*, *positive life changes*, and *stress-related growth*. All of these terms refer to *improvements* in psychological functioning after a stressful event compared to preevent functioning. The term *resilience* is sometimes used interchangeably with these terms, but it is distinct in that resilience refers to maintaining or returning to a baseline level of functioning despite experiencing a stressful event (Masten, 2001). We focus on stress-related growth (i.e., improvements in functioning compared with before the divorce or dissolution), rather than resilience. In the brief overview of the broader stress-related growth literature that follows, we review prevalence, types, and correlates of growth.

Research on stress-related growth indicates that most individuals who have experienced traumatic events report positive life changes (Tedeschi & Calhoun, 1995). Importantly, studies that have compared the prevalence of growth across events have *not* found that those who experienced relationship dissolution reported less growth than those who experienced stressors generally considered more severe (see e.g., Park, Cohen, & Murch, 1996). Descriptive data derived from participants experiencing a range of stressors, including relationship dissolution, suggest that growth often occurs in three domains: the self (e.g., increased self-efficacy), interpersonal relationships (e.g., closer to friends and family), and philosophy of life (e.g., spiritual growth; Tedeschi & Calhoun).

Although self-reported growth is common, it is by no means universal. Thus, several studies in the broader stress-related growth literature have tried to identify factors that explain why some people and not others report finding benefits in traumatic events. The correlates reviewed here—sex or gender, social support, personality, and attributions—are factors that have been examined in the broader stress-related growth literature as well as in research on stress-related growth following relationship dissolution. The most consistent finding with respect to demographic variables has been that women report more growth than do men, although there is little evidence to suggest which factors mediate this association (Tashiro & Frazier, 2003). Social support also is consistently associated with more growth across a number of studies (e.g., Frazier, Tashiro, Berman, Steger, & Long, 2004; Park et al., 1996). Personality variables, including extraversion and agreeableness, have also demonstrated significant, positive associations with growth (Tedeschi & Calhoun, 1996). Finally, cognitive appraisals, such as causal attributions for the stressful event, have also been investigated, although the findings in the broader stress-related growth literature have been inconsistent (see e.g., Affleck, Allen, Tennen, McGrade, & Ratzan, 1985; Frazier, Tashiro, et al., 2004; Thompson, 1985).

The investigation of stress-related growth following relationship dissolution moves us beyond theory and research focused solely on distress reduction to a broader conceptualization of the impact of dissolution that includes the promotion of healthier relationships. Given the high probability that individuals will form new relationships following dissolution, as well as the elevated risk of divorce in second marriages (Cherlin, 1992), research that elucidates mechanisms that improve the probability of success in subsequent relationships is critical. In the following sections we review research on the prevalence and correlates of stress-related growth following dissolution, including growth for divorcing partners and children of divorce, and growth following nonmarital breakups.

STRESS-RELATED GROWTH IN DIVORCING PARTNERS

Amato (2000) described divorce scholarship as "polemical," because divorce scholars (and public commentators) can be divided along ideological lines into those who believe that the stable two-parent family is foundational to social order and personal well-being and those who believe that adults and children can be nurtured in a variety of familial constellations. This polemical quality has profoundly shaped research on the effects of divorce, such that the greatest body of research focuses on the negative effects of divorce on children and (secondarily) on parents, with little emphasis on either positive effects for children or adults or the experiences of adult divorcees apart from their role as parents.

Any research (as well as any review) of the positive effects of divorce on adult expartners is thus going to be strongly flavored by arguments and controversies on both sides: According to the first, more conservative perspective, the negative effects of divorce are expected to be dire and long-lasting, with any (rare) positive effects found only among those few divorcees who learn from and atone for their mistakes; according to the second, more permissive perspective, we might expect a variety of mostly positive effects of divorce as adults reorder their relationships to better meet their individual needs. Following Amato (2000), we have tried to synthesize research from a variety of ideological and theoretical perspectives as objectively as possible in exploring the potential positive outcomes of divorce, with the caveat that, as is true of most stressful life events, we expect to find positive effects coexisting with negative ones.

It is important to distinguish between two potential pathways by which adults' postdivorce outcomes might be improved relative to their predivorce functioning. We call the first the *crisis–growth* pathway. In this model, the divorce is a painful or even traumatic and worldview-shattering experience with long-term effects. Nevertheless, some people are able to capitalize on the growth opportunity presented by this stressful event to become stronger, better people in various ways. We call the second the *stress-relief pathway*. In contrast to the previous model, in this pathway the divorce is *not* conceptualized primarily as a stressful event. Instead, the divorce represents the end of a miserable or abusive partnership and the beginning of a clearly better life alone or with another partner. Divorce, for at least half of all adults who experience it, is very unlike most other stressful experiences (and also unlike the experiences of the divorcing partners' children) in that it is a *deliberately chosen* event. If partners who choose to divorce did not anticipate deriving some important benefit from divorcing, it is difficult to understand why they would undertake the costly and difficult process of uncoupling from a spouse. Partners' anticipation of benefits from the divorce process may be more or less carefully considered and more or less accurate, but partners who believe that divorce offers no benefits likely do not choose to end their marriages.

Most research on positive outcomes of divorce in adults has been piecemeal and lacking a theoretical framework. Much of the existing research explores positive outcomes only incidentally, either to account for scores in the normal range on adjustment measures, or as part of qualitative research, where participants' self-reported growth or feelings of relief are difficult to ignore. Several researchers have mentioned that failure to find positive outcomes as a routine part of adults' divorce experience is partly due to researchers' failure to assess such outcomes (Ahrons, 1994; Amato, 2000). In the following sections, we review existing research on growth and stress-relief outcomes for adults following divorce, including their prevalence and correlates.

Prevalence of Stress-Related Growth Following Divorce

How common are positive outcomes of divorce? One might guess, from the intensity of focus on negative outcomes in the divorce literature, that they must be rare. Although, as mentioned, positive outcomes are somewhat rarely *assessed*, they are frequently reported when divorces are asked specifically about them. For example, Hetherington and Kelly (2002), in their longitudinal study of divorced families, classified roughly 30% of their divorced adults as either Enhancers—people who, by 10 years postdivorce, had become more successful and resilient in many areas of their lives, and were currently involved in a satisfying remarriage—or Competent Loners, individuals who were "enhanced" in most areas of their lives postdivorce, but did not remarry (and often did not wish to). Rates in other studies are even higher, with 70% to 93% of samples of individuals reporting some pleasant change or benefit (Colburn, Lin, & Moore, 1992; Kitson, 1992; Reissman, 1990; Stewart, Copeland, Chester, Malley, & Barenbaum, 1997). One thing that is clear from the existing research on positive outcomes following divorce, whether conceptualized as growth or as stress-relief, is that it is at least as common to experience positive outcomes following divorce as negative ones, and that positive outcomes can coexist with even substantial psychological pain and stress. If we accept that positive outcomes do sometimes (or even usually) occur following divorce, it is important to understand the pathways that divorcees may take in acquiring benefits from what has always been conceptualized as among the most difficult of stressful life events (Holmes & Rahe, 1967).

Stress-Relief Pathway

Does growth occur because of the lessons learned through the difficult divorce process, or because the divorce is not a stressor at all, but a blessed relief, at least for some individuals? Certainly many divorcees describe themselves as relieved, and report that this sense of relief is among their most predominant reactions to the divorce. For example, among a sample of 205 recently divorced individuals, relief was as commonly reported as distress (Spanier & Thompson, 1983). In a similar survey conducted with a sample of divorced Israeli kibbutz members, the two most commonly endorsed reactions were "full acceptance of divorce" (74%) and "feeling of relief" (60%), whereas the next most commonly endorsed reaction was "high spirits—euphoria" (endorsed by 34%). None of the negative reactions on the list—including sadness, jealousy, anger, revenge, guilt, and fear—were reported by more than 13% of the participants (Kaffman, Elizur, Shoham, Gilead-Roelofs, & Shefatya, 1992). Similarly, 2 years after the divorce, 75% of the women in the Virginia Longitudinal Study of Divorce and Remarriage reported being happier in their present situations than in the final year of the marriage (Hetherington, 1993).

Wheaton (1990) laid out the most persuasive argument for divorce as a stress reliever, rather than a stressor itself, as part of a larger discussion of the importance of contextual factors in considering whether an event is stressful. In his stressful event as stress relief model, he pointed out that the mental health impact of any so-called stressful role transition depends on the stressfulness of the preceding role—being fired from a job or divorcing a partner you hated are likely to be beneficial to you, whereas losing a job or a partner you loved is likely to cause harm. Wheaton found support for this model as it pertains to divorce in a prospective, longitudinal panel survey with a large representative sample of Canadian adults. Specifically, among men and women who divorced in the first wave of his study (earlier divorces), psychological symptoms increased from the first interview to the last interview 4 years later only among those who reported at the first interview that they had good marriages; for those who reported at the initial interview that the marriage had problems, psychological symptoms were actually reduced 4 years later. In general, his work suggested that, in the short term, most men and some women (especially those with demanding lives) did experience the divorce as a stressor. However, over the long term, among men and women whose marriages were unhappy, divorce could relieve stress and "have a beneficial effect on mental health, possibly acting as a catharsis that resolves the earlier problems" (p. 217).

Crisis–Growth Pathway

Still, it is difficult to see how people who truly cherished what they believed to be good partnerships could possibly reap benefits from the pain of an unwanted divorce. In the short term, even for those who will ultimately see it as a positive step forward in their lives, divorce can be enormously stressful. Despite the short-term stress and long-term pain of the experience (or perhaps because of it), however, many people do report growing from and becoming better people as a result of the divorce. In many cases, the positive changes they report parallel those reported by participants who have experienced other, less controllable traumatic events, such as rape (e.g., Frazier, Conlon, & Glaser, 2001; Frazier, Tashiro, et al., 2004) or serious illness (Mohr et al., 1999), with self-reported growth in relationships, the self, and personal philosophies commonly reported. In other instances, the types of growth reported are unique to the divorce experience (such as increased freedom and independence).

Positive Changes in Relationships

Kaslow and Hyatt (1982) provided an early description of divorce as a potential growth experience, although their article had a clinical focus and did not include any data. They suggested that divorce may provide benefits not only to the divorcees and their children but also to the extended family, because divorcees may activate their social support networks, allowing parents and other extended family of the divorcing adults an opportunity to become closer by means of their helping activities. In addition, they suggested that divorcees who cope well with the experience might provide a model for their children and for others in their social networks to emulate, allowing those in unsatisfying relationships, for example, to reevaluate and change them. Likewise, children of divorce who cope well may provide impetus to their parents to treat each other better and become more mature individuals.

Such a model seems unusual in comparison with models that emphasize ongoing negative interactions that reverberate through the family prior to and following divorce, but adults do report improved relationships with others as one of the benefits of divorce. For example, a substantial minority (30%) of the mothers in a small sample of divorcing African American women mentioned better ability to parent their children as an outcome of the divorce (Molina, 1999); all of the mothers in another qualitative study of the effects of divorce on battered Israeli women also reported this (Eldar-Avidan & Haj-Yahia, 2000). The battered Israeli women also frequently described improved intimacy with parents, extended family, and friends as an outcome of the divorce process, echoing the formulation by Kaslow and Hyatt (1982). Others also have found that, for women in particular, divorce is associated with strengthening of kin ties and increased instrumental social support by kin—support that is associated for women with increased well-being (Gerstel, 1988; Reissman, 1990).[1]

Even relationships with exspouses may improve following divorce in ways that add to divorcees' well-being. Goldsmith (1980) reported that, by 1 year postdivorce, the vast majority (95%) of divorcees reported positive feelings toward their exspouse. Such feelings evidently go beyond fond wishes for the spouse's independent future: 33% of the individuals in one community sample chose to maintain regular contact with their exspouses for the purpose of keeping up a friendship. In addition, reporting that friendship was a reason for contact was associated with *less* preoccupation with the exspouse, which in turn was associated with increased well-being (Masheter, 1997). Ahrons (1994) described divorced parents who collaborate civilly with one another in the raising of children as "the binuclear family" and suggested that successful cocreation of this new family structure helps to promote happiness for all family members.

Remarriage is one particularly important way individuals may seek to demonstrate growth following a divorce, and one that has important implications for their well-being. Several researchers have found that remarried individuals resemble first-married individuals in psychological, financial, and physical health (Acock & Demo, 1994; Booth & Amato, 1991; Hetherington & Kelly, 2002), or even that stepfamilies are stronger in some ways than first-marriage families. Acock and Demo, for example, reported that stepmothers in their sample reported having less conflict and more interaction with their husbands, as well as more frequent sexual intercourse, than first-married wives. However, most research on remarriage has focused on risk factors that explain the higher rate of failure in remarriages compared with initial marriages. No work that we know of has systematically assessed improvements in relationship skills learned in the first marriage or in the divorce process that divorcees might apply to new relationships, although Reissman (1990) reported some suggestive qualitative data. Men in particular in her sample reported learning the importance of good communication skills, and they reported that the divorce served as an impetus to actively improve these skills by seeking out communication "mentorship," either from a nonsexual female friend or confidante or from involvement in psychotherapy. Some men in her sample described therapy as "the only good thing" to come out of divorce. Because the risk for divorce is higher in remarriages than first marriages, assessing the validity of these self-reported experiences of relationship growth is of the utmost importance, as is identifying factors that differentiate individuals who remarry and redivorce from those who demonstrate real relationship growth by maintaining a stable and satisfying second marriage.

---

[1] Divorced men in Gerstel's (1988) sample also reported increased reliance on kin for support; however, the support men sought tended to be social and emotional rather than instrumental, and support from kin was associated with increased depression rather than improved well-being.

Positive Changes in the Self

Another important area of postdivorce growth is improvement within the self. Whereas it may be difficult to believe that a person's relationships will improve following the loss of a significant marital relationship, we might expect some personal growth among divorcees. Indeed, Marks and Lambert (1998), in a large, nationally representative sample of individuals assessed across 5 years, found that participants who were continuously divorced or separated during the study reported slightly greater autonomy and personal growth than continuously married individuals, although, interestingly, the effects were stronger for men than for women. A small study likewise found divorcees reporting more recent positive changes in enjoyment of life, in self-esteem and personal competence, and in their careers (as well as more positive changes in general) than married or widowed mothers (Nelson, 1982). In another particularly intriguing study of changes in the self, Bursik (1991) reported that women who initially adjusted poorly to a recent divorce, but whose adjustment had improved 1 year later, experienced an accompanying increase in ego development (e.g., personal maturity and self-awareness). Women who found ways to better adjust to divorce, despite an initially poor adjustment, progressed to an average of a half-stage higher level of ego development over the course of the year.

Experiences of self-improvement and personal growth following divorce, like other types of positive change, may be fairly common: Approximately 20% to 30% of the participants in two studies reported personal growth or positive self-changes in their postdivorce lives (Colburn et al., 1992; Kitson, 1992). Reissman (1990) described two prominent areas of positive intrapersonal change among divorced participants in her qualitative study: developing competence in managing daily life alone and creating a positive self-identity apart from the old spousal role. Women in her sample described "learning to fix things," and discovering other abilities as they entered the workforce (some for the first time) or returned to school. They also described increases in self-esteem as they coped with life successfully and developed richer self-identities beyond the home. The men in her sample commonly reported increased occupational success (as they spent more time at work, freed from family demands), new leisure interests, and changes in self-image as they "spruced themselves up" both externally, through new clothes, diets, and other improvements, and internally, through efforts to change the personal flaws that many identified as ending their marriages. Both sexes in her sample described relishing their solitude, and their newfound opportunity to make their own decisions and choices.

Changes Unique to Divorce

Freedom and independence are other commonly reported benefits of divorce. In two studies, 19% to 38% of women described increased freedom and independence as positive changes resulting from the divorce, as did 16% to 25% of the men (Colburn et al., 1992; Stewart et al., 1997). In Reissman's (1990) study, freedom was among the most common themes mentioned by participants in her interviews; for women, the freedom generally was from subordination and their husbands' control, whereas men more commonly described it as freedom from obligation to their wives and families. Increased freedom postdivorce may be an especially important benefit for members of groups whose freedom often is curtailed by oppression or discrimination: Kitson (1992) found that 42% of non-White participants (compared with 33% of White participants) mentioned "more freedom" as a benefit of divorce. Increased freedom and independence may be one area where divorcees may actually be better off than their married or remarried counterparts: Recall that Marks and Lambert (1998) found that continuously single divorcees (over a 5-year period) reported greater autonomy than continuously married individuals.

Because benefits of divorce are common and may have important implications for divorcees' future well-being, it particularly important to determine to whom and under what circumstances they are most likely to accrue. To address this question, we turn to several potential correlates of positive outcomes following divorce. We focus specifically on correlates of positive outcomes, rather than correlates of good divorce adjustment more generally.

Correlates of Positive Outcomes

One factor that has been frequently suggested as predictive of the likelihood of positive outcomes following divorce is the divorcee's status as initiator of the divorce. Initiating the divorce process ought to be associated with better adjustment and increased benefits from a divorce for a variety of reasons, including initiators' presumably greater sense of dissatisfaction with the marriage and greater sense of personal control over the divorce process (Pettit & Bloom, 1984; Vaughan, 1986). However, the research findings regarding the impact of initiator status on positive outcomes following divorce have been mixed. Two studies have reported few differences between initiators and noninitiators in postdivorce adjustment (Buehler, Hogan, Robinson, & Levy, 1986; Spanier & Thompson, 1984), whereas another found that differences in overall adjustment immediately following divorce had largely disappeared 18 months later (Pettit & Bloom). However, initiators, particularly if they were women, did report increasing benefits from divorce over time (Pettit & Bloom). Similarly, in the large longitudinal study by Wang and Amato (2000), initiators were more likely than noninitiators to view the divorce process itself more positively (e.g., to think it was a good idea).

Several authors have suggested that initiators and noninitiators may not differ so much in their reactions to the divorce process as in the time course of adjustment. Buehler (1987), for example, found that, whereas noninitiators and initiators shared similar emotional reactions to the divorce, initiators experienced more change, stress, and personal growth 6 months to 1 year following divorce, whereas noninitiators experienced these changes 18 months to 2 years following the divorce. Initiators may mourn the loss of the marriage and experience much of the stress of divorce while still married, leaving them free to take advantage of benefits and opportunities for growth when the divorce becomes final, whereas noninitiators may begin the stress–growth process only when the marriage actually ends (Amato, 2000; Emery, 1994). Initiators and noninitiators may also travel different pathways to positive outcomes, with divorce serving as a stress reliever for initiators, but as a crisis with attendant opportunities for growth for noninitiators. Hopper (1993, 2001) suggested that initiator status, rather than being a characteristic of the partners' prior to divorce, may sometimes be socially constructed by the partners following the divorce to explain reactions to the divorce process. Nonetheless, it is likely that differences in growth trajectories following divorce will be found for self-identified initiators and noninitiators, because initiator status, whether constructed before or after divorce, likely has implications for how much growth divorcees experience, and by what pathways.

Other variables that may promote positive postdivorce outcomes are the material, social, and coping resources the divorcing spouse possesses at the time of the divorce. Veevers (1991) suggested that divorce may sometimes be a "stren" (i.e., a strengthening, personality-enhancing experience) rather than a trauma, provided adequate resources are available to the divorcing partners. From a review of the then-current divorce literature, she identified 17 resources that promote the experience of divorce as a stren rather than a stressor, including high income and broad educational options, presence of nontraditional gender roles, supportive peer networks, and intimacy with a new romantic partner. Intimacy and remarriage with a new romantic partner may be the most powerful of these resources in promoting emotional and economic well-being among divorcees (Hetherington & Kelly, 2002; Wang & Amato, 2000). As mentioned, Acock and Demo (1994) found few differences between remarried and first-married mothers, with both groups being much better off in most respects than single mothers, whereas Stewart et al. (1997) reported similar results for divorced fathers. Large social support networks of peers and family are also an important resource for divorcees (Cotton, 1999; DeGarmo & Forgatch, 1999), with the caveat that receiving social support can be unhelpful if it comes with strings attached or from disapproving network members. For men in particular, the embarrassment and stigma of needing emotional support following divorce may account for the largely negative relationship between social support and growth or well-being that has been reported for men (Stewart et al.).

Cognitive appraisals, such as attributions for the divorce, may also affect the experience of positive outcomes following divorce. Amato and Previti (2003) found that attributing the cause of the divorce to oneself or to factors external to the relationship (such as a demanding job) was associated with poorer postdivorce adjustment and greater attachment to the exspouse, whereas attributing the causes of the divorce to the relationship itself (rather than to either partner) was associated with feeling that the divorce had caused improvements in one's life and was generally a good idea. Amato and Previti suggested that it may be easier to develop a separate identity and begin to grow apart from the relationship if the problems that precipitated the divorce were seen as being due to irreconcilable differences within the relationship for which neither partner was to blame, rather than to personal or external factors that presumably could have been changed by one of the partners.

Rather than one's status as a divorce initiator, one's personal resources, or one's appraisals about the divorce, however, partner sex has received the most attention as a correlate of positive (and negative) outcomes following divorce. Men consistently report deriving fewer (or no) benefits from the divorce compared with women (Colburn et al., 1992; Kitson, 1992; Reissman, 1990; Marks & Lambert, 1998), although findings are mixed with regard to the overall adjustment of men and women divorce.[2] Why might men report fewer positives from the divorce experience?

Amato and Previti (2003) found consistent sex differences in the attributions individuals made about the divorce, such that women were about twice as likely as men to attribute the cause of the divorce to their partners. Only 1.5% of women (versus 10% of men) attributed the cause of the divorce to their own behavior. Although it is possible that women, more than men, are displaying a self-enhancing attributional bias in their divorce accounts, it is perhaps more likely that this sex difference reflects the greater likelihood of men to behave badly in marriage—in terms of specific causes of divorce, women were also more likely than men to mention infidelity, mental or physical abuse, and alcohol or drug use (generally by their husbands, not themselves) as causing the divorce, a finding that echoes similar results in other studies (Bloom, Niles, & Tatcher, 1985; Cleek & Pearson, 1985; Kitson, 1992). These transgressions on the part of men may partially explain why women are more likely to initiate divorce (Kitson), and they may also serve to explain why men derive fewer benefits from the divorce process. If, as Amato and Previti suggested, feeling that one could have done something to avoid the divorce leads to greater preoccupation with the expartner and a feeling that the

---

[2]See Amato (2000) for a detailed review of sex differences in divorce adjustment. The largest and highest quality studies generally found few or no sex differences in overall adjustment to divorce (e.g., Booth & Amato 1991).

divorce was a mistake, then men are at greater risk for such feelings to the degree that they are aware that their own behavior caused the divorce.

Summary

Whether conceptualized as stress relief or growth, it is clear from the existing research on positive outcomes following divorce that it is at least as common to experience positive outcomes following divorce as negative ones, and that positive outcomes can coexist with even substantial psychological pain and stress. Types of positive outcomes reported are generally similar to those reported following other stressful events, including positive changes in the self and in one's relationships, with some changes distinct to divorce, such as increased freedom and independence, or relief that a bad marriage is over. With regard to correlates of positive outcomes, the most consistent finding to date is that women are more likely to report benefits of divorce than are men, although having greater access to social and personal resources also seems to be important.

STRESS-RELATED GROWTH IN CHILDREN OF DIVORCE

As is the case with research on the effects of divorce on the divorcing partners, research on children of divorce is ideologically driven and biased toward finding negative effects (Gately & Schwebel, 1991, 1992; chap. 15 by Barber & Demo, this volume). Specifically, studies may more often find negative than positive effects because they are designed to do so—they use measures of distress, clinical samples, and informants (such as teachers) who expect more negative outcomes among children from divorced families (Gately & Schwebel). Media images also focus on loss and trauma following divorce, which can prevent researchers and the public from seeing that divorce can initiate growth (Stewart et al., 1997). This narrow focus on the negative consequences of divorce creates stereotypes and self-fulfilling prophecies that adversely affect divorced families and children (Barber & Eccles, 1992; Dreman, 2000).

Although several authors have noted the need to assess the positive as well as negative effects of divorce on children (e.g., Dreman, 2000; Gately & Schwebel, 1991, 1992; Stewart et al., 1997), like the research on adults, existing data are piecemeal and unsystematic. Nonetheless, they do show that, for some children, divorce can lead to positive outcomes. We review this evidence by using the two pathways described before—namely, stress relief and crisis–growth. The studies reviewed in this section are of two types: (a) studies in which children from divorced families describe the positives that came out of the experience for them, and (b) studies that compare children from divorced and intact families by using standardized measures of adjustment and that find better functioning in children of divorce. Because we only review studies that find better adjustment among children of divorce, we also compare the findings of these selected studies to those of recent meta-analyses. We begin with a discussion of the overall prevalence of growth outcomes among children of divorce.

Prevalence of Stress-Related Growth for Children of Divorce

Because few studies have specifically asked about positive outcomes and there are no standard measures of growth outcomes for children of divorce, it is difficult to estimate the frequency with which children are enhanced in at least some area of their life as a result of a divorce. Some researchers have assessed growth by asking *parents* about their children's adjustment.

In one study, Kurdek and Siesky (1979) asked a direct question about growth, and 84% of parents reported that their children had acquired strengths that could be due to the divorce. In another study, Stewart et al. (1997) asked parents a more neutral question about major changes in their children, and 39% of the mothers reported that their child's behavior or personality had improved. In that same study, two thirds of the children could think of something that was better after the separation. Interestingly, when Rosen (1977) asked children the extent to which they had been *adversely* affected by the divorce, 43% reported that they did not feel they had been negatively affected in any way and 24% felt they had benefited. Other studies have asked children structured questions, some of which could be construed as positive consequences. For example, the majority (55–60%) of the children in another study by Kurdek and Siesky (1980a) agreed with items that could be seen as evidencing growth (e.g., "Mother and I have a better understanding"). Finally, as noted in the paragraphs that follow, about half of the college students in one sample felt that the divorce had relieved tensions in their life (Laumann-Billings & Emery, 2000). In sum, although the exact frequency of growth following divorce cannot be estimated, the potential clearly exists. We now turn to a description of studies that assess growth outcomes in specific areas, and in terms of the stress-relief and crisis–growth pathways.

Stress-Relief Pathway

When considering adults who have divorced, the stress-relief pathway conceptualizes the divorce as a stress reliever as opposed to a stressor per se. As noted, people who initiate divorce may do so because they anticipate that they will derive benefits. Unlike the adults who are divorcing, children do not generally have a choice in the matter. Nonetheless, the data suggest that, like their parents, children at times view divorce as involving the relief of stress. For example, when asked about their initial reactions to the news of the divorce, 10% of the children in one study said they were relieved and 31% said they were glad their parents had divorced (Stewart et al., 1997). When children were interviewed 2 years later, when asked about what was better, more than 25% said the absence of conflict (implying a relief from stress). Similarly, when children were asked about some of the good things about the divorce, the most common answer (43%) in another study was that "Mom and Dad don't fight" (Kurdek & Siesky, 1980a). In Wallerstein's (1985) study, 30% of the sample of children reported relief at being separated from a tyrannical parent. This theme was also evident in the narratives of college students whose parents had divorced (Harvey & Fine, 2004). Students described their parents' separation as the happiest time of their lives, said their home was more peaceful as a result, and that they were glad they didn't have to continue to live with constant fighting. In another study of college students, Laumann-Billings and Emery (2000) developed a measure of feelings about the divorce that included questions related to stress relief. In two samples, 62% to 81% of the participants agreed that divorce was the right thing for their parents, 62% to 74% agreed that their parents seemed happier, and 46% to 48% agreed that the divorce relieved a lot of tensions in their own lives. The notion of divorce as stress relief for children also is consistent with the finding that parental conflict has a more negative effect on children than does divorce (e.g., Doucet & Aseltine, 2003; Hetherington & Elmore, 2003; Stewart et al., 1997) and that, when parental conflict is high, divorce is associated with positive outcomes for children (Amato & Booth, 1997).

Crisis–Growth Pathway

Unlike the stress–relief pathway, the crisis-growth pathway views the divorce as a traumatic event but one nonetheless from which individuals can grow. As with the literature on the effects of divorce on the divorcing partners, research on the effects of divorce on children reveals growth in many of the same areas reported by individuals who have experienced other traumatic life events, particularly positive changes in one's relationships and in one's self, as well as some unique changes.

Positive Changes in Relationships

The most commonly reported positive change in relationships involves improved relationships with parents. In comparison with their relationships before the divorce, children whose parents have divorced report being closer to and having better relationships with both their custodial (usually the mother) and noncustodial parents (Harvey & Fine, 2004; Kurdek & Siesky, 1980a; Stewart et al., 1997). Consistent with the stress-relief theme, they also feel that their parents are "nicer" following the divorce (Kurdek & Siesky, 1980a). The majority (55% to 60%) report being more understanding and accepting of their parents (Kurdek & Siesky; Reinhard, 1977). Children of divorce also see themselves as having increased concern and empathy for their custodial parent (again, usually their mother; Harvey & Fine; Kurdek & Siesky, 1979; Reinhard). In one study, children also reported seeing their fathers more after the divorce (Stewart et al.). These positive changes reported by children whose parents have divorced have been reflected in studies that have compared children from divorced and intact families. For example, in one study, children from divorced families reported better parent–child relationships than did children in unhappy intact homes (Nye, 1957). In another, boys (but not girls) from divorced homes rated their families more positively on some dimensions (e.g., conflict) than did boys from intact families (Slater, Stewart, & Linn, 1983). Finally, Amato and Booth (1997) found that girls from divorced families had better relationships with their mothers than did girls from intact families.

Because we are focusing only on studies that find positive effects for children of divorce, it is important to compare these outcomes to meta-analytic findings when available. Two meta-analyses, one by Kunz (2001) and one by Reifman, Villa, Amans, Rethinam, and Telesca (2001), have analyzed studies comparing children from divorced and intact families in terms of parent–child relationships. Both found very small between-group differences (ds $= -.04$ to $-.13$) with regard to mother–child relationships (with children from intact families reporting slightly better relationships with their mothers). Because effect sizes varied across studies, Kunz also examined factors that might explain this heterogeneity. These analyses revealed positive effect sizes (differences favoring divorced children) in some comparisons. For example, in studies of 18- to 25-year-old children, children from divorced homes had better mother–child relationships than did those from intact homes ($d = .12$). Effect sizes in studies that used random ($d = .39$) or large ($d = .12$) samples also were positive. With regard to father–child relationships, however, differences between groups were negative and in the small to medium range (ds $= -.35$ to $-.49$), indicating that children from divorced families had poorer relationships with their fathers than did children from intact families. Nonetheless, there were positive effect sizes in studies that used clinical ($d = .32$), random ($d = .71$), or small ($d = .53$) samples. Similarly, in the first-meta-analysis, by Amato and Keith (1991), mother–child relationships were better in divorced than in intact families ($d = .18$) when studies controlled for other variables (e.g., socioeconomic status).

A similar positive change in relationships is developing closer relationships with one's siblings. For example, in the study by Stewart et al. (1997), 25% of the children reported that their relationships with their siblings had improved following the divorce. This theme was also present in the narratives of college students whose parents had divorced (Harvey & Fine, 2004). This group also mentioned having stepsiblings as a positive aspect of the divorce (and subsequent remarriage). Although Wallerstein (1985) generally has focused on the negative effects of divorce in her writings, she noted being "impressed with the... love, intimacy, and loyalty among brother and sisters" (p. 552). We also located one study that found better sibling relationships in divorced families than in intact families (Brady, Bray, & Zeeb, 1986). In Kunz's (2001) meta-analysis, the overall effect size was small but positive for sibling relationships ($d = .07$), indicating slightly better sibling relationships in divorced versus intact families. Moderators of this difference were not separately examined because of the small number of studies.

Children of divorce also have reported growth in general relationship skills. These include being more compassionate, empathic, adaptable, outgoing, understanding, aware, and tolerant (Kurdek & Siesky, 1979; Reinhard, 1977; Rosen, 1977; Wallerstein & Kelly, 1976). One study that compared children who lived with their fathers with children in intact families found that boys who lived with their fathers were more socially competent (e.g., warmer, more sociable) in a laboratory interaction than were boys in intact families (Santrock & Warshak, 1979). However, girls living with their fathers were less socially competent than girls in intact families. In contrast, in the Virginia Longitudinal Study (Hetherington & Elmore, 2003; Hetherington & Kelly, 2002), girls living with their divorced mothers were especially likely to be exceptionally welladjusted and socially responsible. Thus, whether a child shows increased social competence following a divorce may depend on the sex of the child and the custodial parent. Across three meta-analyses, the effect sizes for peer relationships–social relations were generally small and negative ($ds = -.05$ to $-.16$; Amato, 2001; Kunz, 2001; Reifman et al., 2001), indicating slightly worse peer relations among children of divorce.

A final aspect of relationships in which children of divorce have reported positive outcomes is in terms of seeking to ensure that their own future relationships are healthy and satisfying. For example, interviews with children of divorce revealed that the divorce seemed to have made them more aware of the importance of selecting a compatible partner (Kurdek & Siesky, 1980a). Narratives of college students whose parents had divorced also suggested that they were resolved to avoid the problems they had experienced in their own families (Harvey & Fine, 2004). One comparative study found that children from multiple-divorce homes reported more control over the success of their own future marriage than did children from intact or single-divorce homes (Boyer-Pennington, Pennington, & Spink, 2001). The authors interpreted this to mean that children whose parents had divorced multiple times were determined to avoid their parents' mistakes.

Of course, the findings from these studies only show that children from divorced homes want to avoid their parents' mistakes, not that they are necessarily able to do so. Kunz's (2001) meta-analysis revealed essentially no difference between children from divorced and intact families in terms of dating relationships ($d = -.04$), suggesting that divorce does not harm children's relationship skills. Another recent study also sheds some light on the extent to which children of divorce may be successful in their relationship goals. Specifically, Doucet and Aseltine (2003) examined the relations among parental marital status (intact, divorced, or remarried), parental conflict, and young adults' own marital relationships. There were no differences between the divorced and intact groups with regard to marital support or dissatisfaction, although young adults whose parents had divorced reported more disagreements with their own spouse. In general, parental conflict was more strongly related to poorer offspring marital relationships than was parental divorce per se.

Positive Changes in the Self

Another area of change commonly reported in the literature on posttraumatic growth is personal growth, or positive changes in one's self. The particular positive changes reported depend to some extent on the nature of the event.[3] Among children whose parents have divorced, the most common positive self-changes revolve around themes of increased responsibility, maturity, strength, and independence. For example, in Kurdek and Siesky's (1980a) study of children and their divorced parents, the majority of children said that they had taken on new responsibilities (83%) and that they had become more self-reliant (79%). The majority (72%) of parents also reported that their children had responsibilities that other children did not have (Kurdek & Siesky, 1979). When parents were asked what strengths their children had acquired as a result of adjusting to the divorce, their most common response (73%) was that their children had become more independent and mature (Kurdek & Siesky, 1979). These themes also were mentioned by children of divorce in several more qualitative studies (e.g., Harvey & Fine, 2004; Reinhard, 1977; Rosen, 1977; Wallerstein, 1985). For example, Wallerstein mentioned that "many" of the children in her study described themselves as being stronger and more independent as a result of taking on new responsibilities. These new responsibilities are seen as contributing to a sense of self-esteem and social competence (Hetherington & Elmore, 2003; Weiss, 1979).

Some studies that have compared children from divorced and intact families have corroborated these self-reports from children and parents. Children from divorced families have been found to have higher self-esteem (Santrock & Warshak, 1979; Slater et al., 1983), greater ego identity (Grossman, Shea, & Adams, 1980), higher levels of moral development (Kogos & Snarey, 1995), more maturity and independence in a laboratory interaction with their custodial parent (Santrock & Warshak), and greater functional, emotional, and attitudinal independence from their parents (Lopez, Campbell, & Watkins, 1988). Interestingly, three of these studies found better functioning in children of divorce only among boys (Grossman et al; Santrock & Warshak; Slater et al.). In the meta-analyses by Amato (2001) and by Reifman et al. (2001), the effect sizes for self-concept (self-esteem and self-efficacy) revealed very small differences favoring children from intact families ($ds = -.12$).

Although increased responsibility and maturity have been described as positive changes stemming from the divorce by both parents and children, others have commented that these increased responsibilities can come at a cost. For example, on the basis of interviews with single parents and their adolescent children, Weiss (1979) concluded that, although these children may be proud of themselves for having mastered new responsibilities, they regret having had to do so. Wallerstein (1985) also noted that the children she interviewed were proud of their maturity, but they also had a sense of missing out on childhood and growing up too fast. Nonetheless, a minority (24–34%) of college students whose parents had divorced thought that their childhood had been cut short (Laumann-Billings & Emery, 2000), which is less than the percentage who said the divorce relieved tensions in their life (46–48%). The effects of increased responsibilities may depend on the age of the child and the amount of responsibility (Hetherington & Elmore, 2003; Weiss). In general, moderate levels of age-appropriate responsibilities are seen as promoting social competence. Parents also may view these increased responsibilities more positively than do the children themselves, however (Kurdek & Siesky, 1979, 1980a; Stewart et al., 1997; Weiss).

A final consequence of divorce that might be considered a positive change concerns gender roles among children of divorce. Specifically, three studies have found that children in divorced families have less traditional gender roles than do children in intact families, including less traditional attitudes toward women (Kiecolt & Acock, 1988; MacKinnon, Stoneman, & Brody, 1984) and more androgynous self-concepts (Kurdek & Siesky, 1980b). Interestingly, becoming

---

[3]For example, following sexual assault, one of the most commonly reported positive life changes is being more cautious (Frazier et al., 2001; Frazier & Burnett, 1994).

less traditional was not reported as a positive change by the children of divorce themselves in the studies we reviewed. Although becoming less traditional may not seem to be a positive (or negative) change, Barber and Eccles (1992) made a compelling case for studying the effects of living with a single parent (particularly a single mother) on children's career aspirations, gender roles, plans to integrate work and family roles, and achievement behaviors. They viewed these as areas in which children living with a single mother may have an advantage over their peers.

Correlates of Stress-Related Growth in Children of Divorce

Although a great deal of research has examined factors associated with adjustment in children of divorce, data on correlates of growth outcomes among children of divorce are very limited. It is important to specifically assess correlates of growth, because they may differ from the correlates of adjustment or distress (Frazier, Steward, & Mortensen, 2004). The most extensive information on correlates of growth outcomes comes from Hetherington's large-scale studies of divorce and remarriage (see, e.g., Hetherington, 1993; Hetherington & Elmore, 2003; Hetherington & Kelly, 2002). She identified several patterns of adjustment and found that children of divorce were overrepresented in both the multiproblem and high-competency clusters. The best functioning cluster, which she called the "caring-competent" cluster, was described as socially skilled, self-sufficient, and very sensitive and responsive to others' feelings. This group consisted mainly of girls. Other factors associated with being in the caring-competent cluster were having an easy temperament, having a supportive parent, and experiencing low levels of family conflict. It was also helpful to have some stress (in order to learn coping skills), but not so much that it was overwhelming. Girls in the caring-competent cluster were often responsible for caring for others, such as younger siblings, early in life. Again, however, it was best if the tasks were age appropriate and not overwhelming. If taking on responsibilities is associated with growth, this might partly explain why parents in the study by Kurdek and Siesky (1979) study were more likely to describe older than younger children as acquiring strengths (see also Weiss, 1979). Thus, the factors that appear to be related to growth for children of divorce replicate findings in the broader posttraumatic growth literature, such as being female (e.g., Tedeschi & Calhoun, 1996), having more social support (e.g., Frazier et al.), and having personality factors such as agreeableness (e.g., Tedeschi & Calhoun).

Summary

This review illustrates that positive change in the form of stress relief or crisis–growth can, and does, occur in children following a parental divorce. This is particularly evident in the words of the children themselves, some of whom, when asked about adverse effects of the divorce, report that they have in fact benefited. They report that the divorce relieved tensions in their life and that they have better relationships with their parents and their siblings, and that they are more compassionate, empathic, mature, and independent. Nonetheless, self-reports of positive changes cannot necessarily be taken at face value, as they may represent a positive reframing of the event rather than actual growth. Several studies do show better functioning in children of divorce compared with children from intact families, although selectively focusing on these studies may be misleading. Meta-analytic reviews of the literature generally show small differences between groups, suggesting that children from divorced and intact families are more alike than different. Most effect sizes indicate slightly poorer functioning among children of divorce, although some indicate slightly better functioning. These meta-analyses may underestimate functioning in children of divorce because they have not reviewed research in areas in which divorced children may thrive, such as maturity and independence. In addition, grouping studies into broad categories such as "self-concept" may mask positive effects of divorce in specific areas. Nonetheless, the overall picture that emerges from this research is that, on average, differences between children from divorced and intact families are small, that there is a great deal of diversity in how children are affected by a divorce, and that divorce can be a growth-promoting experience. Unfortunately, we know little about the factors that promote growth outcomes for children of divorce.

STRESS-RELATED GROWTH FOLLOWING NONMARITAL ROMANTIC RELATIONSHIPS

Compared with the research on divorce, there has been even less investigation of stress-related growth following nonmarital romantic relationship dissolution. However, given the level of distress associated with breakups, it seems logical to suspect that stress-related growth may occur following nonmarital breakups as well. We focus here on our own ongoing program of research on adolescent and young adult nonmarital dissolution, citing other research on the prevalence and correlates of growth when available. The primary goal of this research program is to identify factors that facilitate growth following breakups during adolescence and young adulthood so that adaptive relationship attitudes and behaviors are acquired prior to lifelong partnership decisions and family formation. The research reviewed is conceptualized in terms of the crisis–growth pathway, because to our knowledge there have been no studies examining the stress-relief pathway.

Because most research on nonmarital breakups has focused on distress and its correlates, in our first study of stress-related growth following breakups we sought to investigate how frequently positive changes occur (if at all), what types of changes are most prevalent, and the correlates of positive change (Tashiro & Frazier, 2003). Participants experiencing a recent breakup were asked to describe in an open-ended format what positive changes had occurred following their recent breakup that might improve the quality of future relationships, and what negative changes occurred that might negatively affect the quality of future relationships. Although we hypothesized that positive changes would occur, we were surprised by the proportion of positive to negative changes reported. Specifically, participants reported five positive changes to every one negative change. The most common domains of positive change included improved ability to regulate emotions, more self-confidence, improved partner selection, increased wisdom about relationships, and improved friendships. The most common domains of negative change included finding it harder to trust, having decreased self-esteem, experiencing a negative impact on friendships, and ruminating about the expartner. The only other studies we are aware of that have found evidence for both positive and negative changes have examined emotional reactions. Common positive emotions following breakups have included joy, love, and relief, whereas some of the common negative emotions were guilt, hurt, frustration, and depression (Choo, Levine, & Hatfield, 1996; Sprecher, 1994).

Although every participant in our first study (Tashiro & Frazier, 2003) reported growth following his or her breakup, there was substantial variability in the amount of growth reported. Several factors have been examined as potential correlates of growth in our own and others' research, including who initiated the breakup, sex, social support, personality, and causal attributions. These factors are discussed in turn.

In the broader literature on stress-related growth, the event characteristic most often studied is the severity of the event. In research on relationship dissolution, the focus has been on who initiated the breakup. On one hand, given that more severe events have been found to trigger more growth (e.g., Armeli, Gunthert, & Cohen, 2001), and that breakups are likely to be perceived as more distressing by noninitiators (Sprecher, 1994), we might expect more growth among noninitiators. On the other hand, initiators may begin making positive changes in anticipation of the dissolution (Amato, 2000), resulting in more positive changes once the breakup occurs. Initiators may also report more growth in terms of stress relief. However, we found no difference between initiators and noninitiators in reported growth (Tashiro & Frazier, 2003). In contrast, Helgeson (1994) found that initiators reported more growth than did noninitiators and that female noninitiators reported more growth than did male noninitiators.

Like Helgeson (1994), we found that women reported more growth than did men following nonmarital breakups (Tashiro & Frazier, 2003). Originally, we had hypothesized that this might be because they perceive that they have more social support. However, social support was not associated with growth, and women did not report more social support than men following a breakup (Tashiro & Frazier, 2001).

We also examined personality as a correlate of growth because substantial evidence suggests that personality can predict how well individuals cope with stressful events (Watson & Hubbard, 1996), and because several personality factors (e.g., Extraversion, Openness, Agreeableness) are positively associated with self-reports of growth (Tedeschi & Calhoun, 1996). However, in our study, of the Big Five personality traits, only Agreeableness was related to reporting more growth (Tashiro & Frazier, 2003).

Finally, we have investigated attributions for why the relationship ended, because an individual's ability to remedy problems from previous relationships may depend in part on his or her ability to correctly identify causal factors. Participants completed a measure on which they attributed the breakup to the self (e.g., "my mood"), their former partner (e.g., "my expartner's mood"), relational factors (e.g., "poor communication"), or environmental factors (e.g., "work stress"). Only environmental attributions were associated with the tendency to report growth. The mechanisms underlying this relation will be explored in future studies.

Summary

In sum, little research has investigated stress-related growth following nonmarital relationship dissolution. Our initial research in this area suggests that perceptions of positive change following dissolution are common and are reported more frequently than negative changes. Women, people higher in agreeableness, and individuals who make more environmental attributions report more growth. Although this initial work is encouraging, a number of methodological limitations have to be addressed. In our current program of research, we are addressing these limitations by developing and validating a new measure of stress-related growth that is specific to nonmarital breakups, correlating participant reports of growth on this measure with reports from multiple informants to assess the validity of self-reports of growth, and using experimental designs to develop and test theories regarding the stress-related growth process.

LIMITATIONS AND FUTURE DIRECTIONS

The preceding review illustrates that the potential for growth following divorce and relationship dissolution certainly exists. It also illustrates that systematic data on the frequency with which individuals change in positive ways following relationship dissolution, the types of changes they experience, and factors that facilitate growth are all seriously lacking. In this section we first describe various ways in which the assessment of growth following relationship dissolution can be improved, as well as a few of the key research questions that have to be addressed. We conclude with a summary of research to date and implications for future research.

Assessment of Growth

Self-Report Measures

A major limitation of current research is that most studies do not use standardized measures of stress-related growth. Good general measures are available (see Frazier, Oishi, & Steger, 2003, for a review), but to our knowledge no studies of relationship dissolution have used these measures. Although use of these measures would allow for comparisons with other traumatic events, some types of growth are unique to divorce and dissolution and would not be tapped by these broader measures. Thus, measures specifically designed to assess growth following relationship dissolution are needed. As mentioned, we have developed a measure to assess positive (and negative) changes following nonmarital breakups, but similar measures have to be developed for divorced partners and children of divorce. These measures should tap the domains revealed in the previous review, although it would be useful to first more systematically assess self-reported growth by using open-ended responses in samples of divorced partners and children of divorced parents.

When one is assessing self-reports of growth, a central question is whether these self-reports represent real changes in cognition or behavior or merely rationalization or denial. We suggest four criteria for assessing the validity of these self-reports. First, given the assumption that it is the divorce or breakup that spurs growth, individuals experiencing a recent dissolution should report more positive life changes than those not experiencing a recent dissolution. Second, if stress-related growth represents real changes in cognition and behavior, reports of growth should remain relatively stable or even increase over time. Third, positive changes in cognition should manifest in positive changes in behavior that are observable to other people. Ideally, this information would come from multiple informants. Gathering data from parents and children in divorced families might also reveal discrepancies in what parents and children see as positive change (e.g., increased responsibility). Finally, self-reports of growth should predict more adaptive, domain-specific behaviors in the future. For example, if individuals report that they choose better partners following a breakup, there should be greater satisfaction with the new partner than with the previous partner. Although these criteria are not exhaustive, meeting all of them would certainly provide more confidence that self-reported growth is "real." However, most studies of stress-related growth do not provide information about any of these criteria.

Cross-Sectional Between-Group Comparisons

Another way to assess growth, particularly following divorce, is to compare divorced partners and children with other groups on standardized measures of relevant constructs. If, for example, children really become more mature as a result of a divorce, then they should score higher than other children on measures of maturity. However, it is important to think clearly about the proper comparison group to use in studies of this type. For example, divorced individuals have been compared with never-married singles, to married individuals with and without significant problems (or married couples heterogeneous with respect to marital quality), to the divorcees' own predivorce adjustment, to unmarried single parents who may or may not have a cohabiting romantic partner, and to remarried individuals. These diverse comparison groups have profound implications for what kinds of adjustment we are likely to expect, and to find. One large longitudinal study makes this point in a fascinating way (Marks & Lambert, 1998). Whereas continuously divorced individuals reported somewhat poorer adjustment on most measures than did continuously married individuals, continuously married individuals scored less favorably than expected, especially when compared with newly first-married individuals. In addition, differences in well-being between continuously divorced, never married, and widowed individuals were small. The researchers commented that mean differences in adjustment between married and divorced individuals may well be inflated by the inclusion of newlyweds in married comparison groups. What comparison group is most appropriate will likely depend on particular researchers' aims, but a rationale for the choice should in all instances be provided.

In making comparisons between groups, one has to take other factors into account as well. For example, divorced families in which the mother is the custodial parent may well differ from intact families with regard to income, which may explain some of the differences between groups in well-being. Thus, differences in income have to be controlled. As we mentioned, Amato and Keith (1991) found positive effect sizes (favoring children of divorce) in studies that used such controls. In general, the complexities of postdivorce family life have to be taken into account, including custody arrangements, the sex of the custodial parents and children, and the age of the children (both current and at the time of the divorce), given that these factors consistently affect outcomes.

Longitudinal Studies

Although between-group comparisons are useful, just because divorced children score higher on measures of some outcome does not necessarily mean that they have grown as a result of the divorce. To truly assess "growth," it is necessary to conduct prospective studies that assess functioning prior to and following the dissolution. Prospective studies can be used to study divorce as a *process* rather than as a discrete event (Amato, 2000). For example, they can elucidate whether most growth occurs during the relationship or if it is the actual dissolution that spurs growth. Prospective studies also can be used to assess the validity of self-reports of growth by comparing these reports with change scores derived from assessments taken before and after the dissolution occurred. If individuals report that they are more self-confident as a result of a divorce or breakup, then their scores on standard measures of self-confidence also should increase from before the breakup to after it. This is very important to establish given that reports of stress-related growth may actually reflect derogations of the past rather than posttraumatic growth (McFarland & Alvaro, 2000). Prospective studies with multiple assessment points also allow researchers to assess the course of growth and distress over time, which may differ across subgroups of divorced individuals (e.g., initiators and noninitiators; see Buehler, 1987). Unlike other traumatic events, divorce and particularly nonmarital romantic relationship breakups are amenable to prospective designs because of the high probability of relationship dissolution.

Additional Research Questions

Although there are many additional research questions that have to be addressed with regard to growth outcomes following relationship dissolution, here we highlight four that we feel are particularly important. The first concerns who is most likely to grow and change in positive ways following a marital or nonmarital breakup. Although a few variables have been studied (e.g., initiator status, personality, social support), data so far are sparse and inconsistent. In addition, several variables that are related to growth following other stressful life events have yet to be studied in this domain, including coping strategies and perceived control (e.g., Frazier, Tashiro, et al., 2004). A second, and related, question concerns how growth outcomes may vary across diverse groups. As we have seen, women tend to report more growth than do men. However, other diversity issues have received little attention in research on growth following relationship dissolution. In the broader stress-related growth literature, individuals with higher socioeconomic status tend to report more growth (Updegraff, Taylor, Kemeny, & Wyatt, 2002). Findings regarding ethnic groups differences are mixed (Frazier, Tashiro et al.; Updegraff et al.). Age tends not to be related to growth outcomes (e.g., Tedeschi & Calhoun, 1996) following other traumas, but the relation between this and other variables has to be studied specifically with regard to relationship dissolution. The third question concerns the relation between the adjustment of parents and their children, particularly with regard to growth outcomes. For example, Amato (2001) cited data showing that children have poorer outcomes if there was not overt conflict between their parents. If parents who divorce in the absence of overt conflict do so for reasons of "personal growth," then growth on the part of parents may be associated with poorer outcomes for their children. Indeed, at least one study found that positive adjustment in recently divorced custodial parents was associated with maladjustment among their children (Stolberg, Camplair, Currier, & Wells, 1987). The final question concerns how to foster genuine growth in relationship skills, both to help prevent divorce from occurring in the first place and to lessen the risk of divorce following remarriage.

Summary and Implications

Our review suggests that, although divorce clearly is stressful, divorcing partners—and even children of divorce—generally recover after a year or two and many emerge better off as a result. There are two general pathways by which this appears to occur: (a) the stress-relief pathway, in which the divorce relieves the stress of an unhappy marriage for partners and for children, and (b) the crisis–growth pathway, in which the divorce, although traumatic, nonetheless serves as an impetus for growth. We have highlighted the need for more systematic investigation of these growth outcomes, as well as of factors that might facilitate or hinder the growth process. In addition, we agree with the conclusions of several authors that interventions with divorcing partners and their families have to focus on enhancing growth as well as on ameliorating distress (e.g., Coleman, Ganong, & Fine, 2000).

Research on growth following nonmarital breakups is in its infancy but suggests that young adults in dating relationships also report a number of positive life changes following these breakups. Importantly, this growth carries the promise of improving adolescents' relationship skills, which may increase their chances of maintaining satisfying relationships in the future. As Doucet and Aseltine (2003) noted, troubled family relationships beget troubled adolescent dating relationships, which beget conflictual marital relationships. Teaching relationship skills to adolescents, before problematic behaviors really take root, can help us to intervene in this cycle.

Finally, it is important to note the ways in which studying growth following relationship dissolution can increase our understanding of stress-related growth more generally. Because relationship breakups are more frequent than other traumas, and in fact are normative experiences most individuals will undergo, it is easier to conduct prospective studies that are important to establishing that growth has actually occurred. Further, because most people begin new relationships after a divorce or breakup, it is possible to track individuals over time to see if self-reported growth really results in better future relationships. In addition, there are often multiple observers of any one relationship who are privy to the intimate details of the relationship. In sum, unlike other stressors, it is possible to conduct prospective studies, make clear predictions about future behaviors, and get multiple informants following relationship dissolution. Doing so will greatly advance our knowledge of stress-related growth, its validity, and correlates, knowledge that ideally will lead to more effective interventions.

REFERENCES

Acock, A. C., & Demo, D. H. (1994). *Family diversity and well-being*. Thousand Oaks, CA: Sage.

Affleck, G., Allen, D. A., Tennen, H., McGrade, B. J., & Ratzan, S. (1985). Causal and control cognitions in parents' coping with chronically ill children. *Journal of Social and Clinical Psychology, 3,* 367–377.

Ahrons, C. R. (1994). *The good divorce: Keeping your family together when your marriage comes apart.* New York: Harper.

Amato, P. (2001). Children of divorce in the 1990s: An update of the Amato and Keith (1991) meta-analysis. *Journal of Family Psychology, 15,* 355–370.

Amato, P., & Booth, A. (1997). *A generation at risk: Growing up in an era of family upheaval.* Cambridge, MA: Harvard University Press.

Amato, P., & Keith, B. (1991). Parental divorce and the well-being of children: A meta-analysis. *Psychological Bulletin, 110,* 26–46.

Amato, P. R. (2000). The consequence of divorce for adults and children. *Journal of Marriage and the Family, 62,* 1269–1287.

Amato, P. R., & Previti, D. (2003). People's reasons for divorcing: Gender, social class, the life course, and adjustment. *Journal of Family Issues, 24,* 602–626.

Armeli, S., Gunthert, K., & Cohen, L. (2001). Stressor appraisals, coping, and post-event outcomes: The dimensionality and antecedents of stress-related growth. *Journal of Social and Clinical Psychology, 20,* 366–395.

Barber, B., & Eccles, J. (1992). Long-term influence of divorce and single parenting on adolescent family- and work-related values, behaviors, and aspirations. *Psychological Bulletin, 111,* 108–126.

Bloom, B. L., Niles, R. L., & Tatcher, A. M. (1985). Sources of marital dissatisfaction among newly separated persons.*Journal of Family Issues, 6,* 359–373.

Booth, A., & Amato, P. R. (1991). Divorce and psychological stress. *Journal of Health and Social Behavior, 32,* 396–407.

Boyer-Pennington, M., Pennington, J., & Splink, C. (2001). Students' expectations and optimism toward marriage as a function of parental divorce. *Journal of Divorce and Remarriage, 34,* 71–87.

Brady, C. P., Bray, J., & Zeeb, L. (1986). Behavior problems of clinic children: Relation to parental marital status, age and sex of child. *American Journal of Orthopsychiatry, 56,* 399–412.

Buehler, C. (1987). Initiator status and the divorce transition. *Family Relations, 36,* 82–86.

Buehler, C., Hogan, M. J., Robinson, B., & Levy, R. (1986). The parental divorce transition: Divorce-related stressors and well-being. *Journal of Divorce, 9,* 61–81.

Bursik, K. (1991). Adaptation to divorce and ego development in adult women. *Journal of Personality and Social Psychology, 60,* 300–306.

Cherlin, A. J. (1992). *Marriage, divorce, remarriage.* Cambridge, MA: Harvard University Press.

Choo, P., Levine, T., & Hatfield, E. (1996). Gender, love schemas, and reactions to romantic break-ups. *Journal of Social Behavior and Personality, 11,* 143–160.

Cleek, M. G., & Pearson, T. A. (1985). Perceived causes of divorce: An analysis of interrelationships. *Journal of Marriage and the Family, 47,* 179–183.

Colburn, K., Lin, P. L., & Moore, M. C. (1992). Gender and divorce experience. *Journal of Divorce and Remarriage, 17,* 87–108.

Coleman, M., Ganong, L., & Fine, M. (2000). Reinvestigating remarriage: Another decade of progress. *Journal of Marriage and the Family, 62,* 1288–1307.

Cotton, S. R. (1999). Marital status and mental health revisited: Examining the importance of risk factors and resources. *Family Relations, 48,* 225–233.

DeGarmo, D. S., & Forgatch, M.S. (1999). Contexts as predictors of changing maternal parenting practices in diverse family structures: A social interactional perspective of risk and resilience. In E.M. Hetherington (Ed.), *Coping with divorce, single parenting, and remarriage: A risk and resiliency perspective* (pp. 227–252). Mahwah, NJ: Lawrence Erlbaum Associates.

Doucet, J., & Aseltine, R. (2003). Childhood family adversity and the quality of marital relationships in young adulthood. *Journal of Social and Personal Relationships, 20,* 818–842.

Dreman, S. (2000). The influence of divorce on children. *Journal of Divorce and Remarriage, 32,* 41–71.

Eldar-Avidan, D., & Haj-Yahia, M. M. (2000). The experience of formerly battered women with divorce: A qualitative descriptive study. *Journal of Divorce and Remarriage, 32,* 19–40.

Emery, R. E. (1994). *Renegotiating family relationships: Divorce, child custody, and mediation.* New York: Guilford.

Frazier, P., & Burnett, J. (1994). Immediate coping strategies among rape victims. *Journal of Counseling and Development, 72,* 633–639.

Frazier, P., Conlon, A., & Glaser, T. (2001). Positive and negative life changes following sexual assault. *Journal of Consulting and Clinical Psychology, 69,* 1048–1055.

Frazier, P., Oishi, S., & Steger, M. (2003). Assessing optimal human functioning. In B. Walsh (Ed.), *Counseling psychology and optimal human functioning* (pp. 251–278). Mahwah, NJ: Lawrence Erlbaum Associates.

Frazier, P., Steward, J., & Mortensen, H. (2004). Perceived control and adjustment to trauma: A comparison across events. *Journal of Social and Clinical Psychology, 23,* 303–324.

Frazier, P., Tashiro, T., Berman, M., Steger, M., & Long, J. (2004). Correlates of levels and patterns of posttraumatic growth among sexual assault survivors. *Journal of Consulting and Clinical Psychology, 72,* 19–30.

Gately, D., & Schwebel, A. (1991). The challenge model of children's adjustment to parental divorce: Explaining favorable postdivorce outcomes in children. *Journal of Family Psychology, 4,* 60–81.

Gately, D., & Schwebel, A. (1992). Favorable outcomes in children after parental divorce. *Journal of Divorce and Remarriage, 18,* 57–78.

Gerstel, N. (1988). Divorce and kin ties: The importance of gender. *Journal of Marriage and the Family, 50,* 209–221.

Goldsmith, J. (1980). Relationships between former spouses: Descriptive findings. *Journal of Divorce, 4,* 1–20.

Grossman, S., Shea, J., & Adams, G. (1980). Effects of parental divorce during early childhood on ego development and identity of college students. *Journal of Divorce, 3,* 263–272.

Harvey, J., & Fine, M. (2004). *Children of divorce: Stories of loss and growth.* Mahwah, NJ: Lawerence Erlbaum Associates.

Helgeson, V. S. (1994). Long-distance romantic relationships: Sex differences in adjustment and breakup. *Personality and Social Psychology Bulletin, 20,* 254–265.

Hetherington, E. M. (1993). An overview of the Virginia Longitudinal Study of Divorce and Remarriage with a focus on early adolescence. *Journal of Family Psychology, 7,* 39–56.

Hetherington, E. M., & Elmore, A. M. (2003). Risk and resilience in children coping with their parents' divorce and remarriage. In S. Luthar (Ed)., *Resilience and vulnerability: Adaptation in the context of childhood adversities* (pp. 182–212). New York: Cambridge University Press.

Hetherington, E. M., & Kelly, J. (2002). *For better or for worse: Divorce reconsidered.* New York: Norton.

Holmes, T. H., & Rahe, R. H. (1967). The Social Readjustment Rating Scale. *Journal of Psychosomatic Research, 2,* 213–218.

Hopper, J. (1993). The rhetoric of motives in divorce. *Journal of Marriage and the Family, 55,* 801–813.

Hopper, J. (2001). The symbolic origins of conflict in divorce. *Journal of Marriage and the Family, 63,* 430–445.

Kaffman, M., Elizur, E., Shoham, S., Gilead-Roelofs, N., & Shefatya, L. (1992). Divorce in the kibbutz: Affective responses to separation. *Contemporary Family Therapy, 14,* 51–74.

Kaslow, F., & Hyatt, R. (1982). Divorce: A potential growth experience for the extended family. *Journal of Divorce, 6,* 115–125.

Kiecolt, K. J., & Acock, A. C. (1988). The long-term effects of family structure on gender-role attitudes. *Journal of Marriage and the Family, 50,* 709–717.

Kitson, G. C. (1992). *Portrait of divorce: Adjustment to marital breakdown.* New York: Guilford.

Kogos, J., & Snarey, J. (1995). Parental divorce and the moral development of adolescents. *Journal of Divorce and Remarriage, 23,* 177–186.

Kunz, J. (2001). Parental divorce and children's interpersonal relationships: A meta-analysis. *Journal of Divorce and Remarriage, 34,* 19–47.

Kurdek, L., & Siesky, A., Jr. (1979). An interview study of parent's perceptions of their children's reactions and adjustments to divorce. *Journal of Divorce, 3,* 5–17.

Kurdek, L., & Siesky, A., Jr. (1980a). Children's perceptions of their parent's divorce. *Journal of Divorce, 3,* 339–378.

Kurdek, L., & Siesky, A., Jr. (1980b). Sex role self-concepts of single divorced parents and their children. *Journal of Divorce, 3,* 249–261.

Laumann-Billings, L., & Emery, R. (2000). Distress among young adults from divorced families. *Journal of Family Psychology, 14,* 671–687.

Lopez, F., Campbell, V., & Watkins, C. E., Jr. (1988). The relation of parental divorce to college student development. *Journal of Divorce, 12,* 83–98.

MacKinnon, C., Stoneman, Z., & Brody, G. (1984). The impact of maternal employment and family form on children's sex-role stereotypes and mother's traditional attitudes. *Journal of Divorce, 8,* 51–60.

Marks, N. F., & Lambert, J.D. (1998). Marital status continuity and change among young and midlife adults: Longitudinal effects on psychological well-being. *Journal of Family Issues, 19,* 652–686.

Masheter, C. (1997). Healthy and unhealthy friendship and hostility between ex-spouses. *Journal of Marriage and the Family, 59,* 463–475.

Masten, A. S. (2001). Ordinary magic: Resilience processes in development. *American Psychologist, 56,* 227–238.

McFarland, C., & Alvaro, C. (2000). The impact of motivation on temporal comparisons: Coping with traumatic events by perceiving personal growth. *Journal of Personality and Social Psychology, 79,* 327–343.

Mohr, D. C., Dick, L. P., Russo, D., Pinn, J., Boudewyn, A. C., Goodkin, D., & Likosky, W. (1999). The psychosocial impact of multiple sclerosis: Exploring the patient's perspective. *Health Psychology, 18,* 376–382.

Molina, O. (1999). The effect of divorce on African American working women. *Journal of Divorce and Remarriage, 32,* 1–15.

Monroe, S. M., & Rohde, P., Seeley, J. R., & Lewinsohn, P. M. (1999). Life events and depression in adolescence: Relationship loss as a prospective risk factor for first onset of Major Depressive Disorder. *Journal of Abnormal Psychology, 108,* 606–614.

Nelson, G. (1982). Coping with the loss of father: Family reaction to death or divorce. *Journal of Family Issues, 3,* 41–60.

Nye, F. I. (1957). Child adjustment in broken and in unhappy unbroken homes. *Marriage and Family Living, 19,* 356–361.

Park, C. L., Cohen, L. H., & Murch, R. (1996). Assessment and prediction of stress related growth. *Journal of Personality, 64,* 71–105.

Pettit, E.J., & Bloom, B. L. (1984). Whose decision was it? The effects of initiator status on adjustment to marital disruption. *Journal of Marriage and the Family, 46,* 587–595.

Reifman, A., Villa, L., Amans, J., Rethinam, V., & Telesca, T. (2001). Children of divorce in the 1990s: A meta-analysis. *Journal of Divorce and Remarriage, 36,* 27–36.

Reinhard, D. (1977). The reaction of adolescent boys and girls to the divorce of their parents. *Journal of Clinical Child Psychology, 6,* 21–23.

Reissman, C. K. (1990). *Divorce talk: Men and women make sense of personal relationships.* New Brunswick, NJ: Rutgers University Press.

Rosen, R., (1977). Children of divorce: What they feel about access and other aspects of the divorce experience. *Journal of Clinical Child Psychology, 6,* 24–27.

Santrock, J., & Warshak, R. (1979). Father custody and social development in boys and girls. *Journal of Social Issues, 35,* 112–125.

Seligman, M. E. P., & Csikszentmihalyi, M. (2000). Positive psychology: An introduction. *American Psychologist, 55,* 5–14.

Slater, E., Stewart, K., & Linn, M. (1983). The effects of family disruption on adolescent males and females. *Adolescence, 18,* 931–942.

Spanier, G., & Thompson, L. (1984). *Parting: The aftermath of separation and divorce.* Beverly Hills, CA: Sage.

Spanier, G. B., & Thompson, L. (1983). Relief and distress after marital separation. *Journal of Divorce, 7,* 31–49.

Sprecher, S. (1994). Two sides to the breakup of dating relationships. *Personal Relationships, 1,* 199–222.

Stewart, A. J., Copeland, A. P., Chester, N. L., Malley, J. E., & Barenbaum, N. B. (1997). *Separating together: How divorce transforms families.* New York: Guilford.

Stolberg, A., Camplair, C., Currier, K., & Wells, M. (1987). Individual, familial, and environmental determinants of children's post-divorce adjustment and maladjustment. *Journal of Divorce, 11,* 51–70.

Tashiro, T., & Frazier, P. (2001, August). Personal growth following relationship dissolution. Paper presented at the Positive Psychology Summer Institute, Sea Ranch, CA.

Tashiro, T., & Frazier, P. (2003). "I'll never be in a relationship like that again": Personal growth following relationship breakups. *Personal Relationships, 10,* 113–128.

Tedeschi, R. G., & Calhoun, L. G. (1995). *Trauma and transformation: Growing in the aftermath of suffering.* Thousand Oaks, CA: Sage.

Tedeschi, R. G., & Calhoun, L. G. (1996). The posttraumatic growth inventory: Measuring the positive legacy of trauma. *Journal of Traumatic Stress, 9,* 455–471.

Tedeschi, R. G., Park, C. L., & Calhoun, L. G. (1998). *Posttraumatic growth.* Mahwah, NJ: Lawrence Erlbaum Associates.

Thompson, S. (1985). Finding meaning in a stressful event and coping. *Basic and Applied Social Psychology, 6,* 279–295.

Updegraff, J. A., Taylor, S. E., Kemeny, M. E., & Wyatt, G. E. (2002). Positive and negative effects of HIV infection in women with low socioeconomic resources. *Personality and Social Psychology Bulletin, 28,* 382–394.

Vaughan, D. (1986). *Uncoupling: Turning points in intimate relationships.* New York: Oxford University Press.

Veevers, J. E. (1991). Traumas versus strens: A paradigm of positive versus negative divorce outcomes. *Journal of Divorce, 15,* 99–126.

Wallerstein, J. (1985). Children of divorce: Report of a ten-year follow-up of older children and adolescents. *Journal of the American Academy of Child Psychiatry, 24,* 545–553.

Wallerstein, J., & Kelly, J. (1976). The effects of parental divorce: Experiences of the child in later latency. *American Journal of Orthopsychiatry, 46,* 256–269.

Wang, H., & Amato, P.R. (2000). Predictors of divorce adjustment: Stressors, resources, and definitions. *Journal of Marriage and the Family, 62,* 655–668.

Watson, D., & Hubbard, B. (1996). Adaptational style and dispositional structure: Coping in the context of the Five-Factor model. *Journal of Personality, 64,* 737–774.

Weiss, R. (1979). Growing up a little faster: The experience of growing up in a single-parent household. *Journal of Social Issues, 35,* 97–111.

Wheaton, B. (1990). Life transitions, role histories, and mental health. *American Sociological Review, 55,* 209–223.

19

Economic Aspects of Divorce and Relationship Dissolution

Liana C. Sayer
Ohio State University

Although the century-long increase in divorce rates stabilized in the mid-1980s, high levels of divorce appear to be an established aspect of family structure in the United States. Of all first marriages, 20% end after 5 years and 33% end after 10 years (Bramlett & Mosher, 2001). Levels of relationship instability are also high in cohabiting unions: About 50% of cohabiting unions end within 5 years, including cohabiting unions that became marriages (Bumpass & Lu, 2000). Concern about high levels of union instability and increasing numbers of children growing up outside of marriage has spurred polemical debates about the causes and consequences of marital dissolution. Much attention has focused on the changing nature of men's and women's economic roles within marriage and their relationship with union dissolution and well-being outside of marriage. A large body of research documents the economic, psychological, and social gains associated with marriage (see Waite, 1995, 2000 for reviews), although the causal relationship of marriage with these positive outcomes is the subject of some dispute. Nonetheless, empirical evidence indicates that economic well-being and marital status are intertwined: Women and children are economically vulnerable outside of marriage. Moreover, contrary to conventional wisdom, recent research also indicates that many men experience economic losses after divorce.

Marriage and divorce remain economic arrangements with economic consequences. These economic aspects are obscured in the popular discourse that frames unions as being based on romantic love and commitment, not on base financial motives. Nonetheless, economic calculations figure prominently in women and men's decisions about whom to marry, when to marry, and whether to remain married. Economic considerations also affect decisions about entering a cohabiting union, formalizing the union through marriage, or dissolving the union.

In this chapter I review recent scholarly work on the economic aspects of divorce in the United States. I also review the small number of studies that have examined the economic consequences of cohabiting union dissolution. Instead of presenting an exhaustive review of all published literature, I focus on major findings. I begin the review with an overview of theory and findings about the relationship between women and men's economic resources, union formation, and union dissolution. Next, I discuss empirical findings about the economic consequences of union dissolution for women, men, and children. I conclude the chapter with suggestions for future research.

ECONOMIC RESOURCES, MARRIAGE, AND UNION DISSOLUTION

Economic resources are central to theories of union formation and dissolution. One theoretical perspective is Becker's (1991) economics of the family. Becker argues that the gains to marriage are greatest when spouses are selected within the framework of positive and negative assortative mating, or "complementarity" and "substitutability." In other words, optimal mating occurs when spouses share certain noneconomic traits, such as intelligence, education, family background, and race, and differ on other traits, such as wage earning and caregiving abilities. The perspective thus posits differentiated marital roles, with men specializing in market work and women specializing in nonmarket work, as the foundation for marital satisfaction and stability. The reason specialization is more efficient, and the reason men specialize in market work whereas women specialize in nonmarket work, is because of human capital and biological differences that result in a comparative advantage for men in paid work and women in household work. Hence, any decrease in specialization is presumed to reduce efficiency and thus reduce the gains to marriage (Becker, 1991, Becker, Landes, & Michael, 1977).

A second theoretical approach comes from exchange or bargaining models (England & Kilbourne, 1990; Lundberg & Pollak, 1996). These ideas are similar to those derived from sociologists' exchange theory (Cherlin, 2000; Molm & Cook, 1995). In this perspective, marital bargains are negotiated in the shadow of the possibility of divorce, and the external so-called threat point is established on the basis of what an individual has to fall back on if the marriage dissolves. The fallback position is influenced by personal earnings, access to other sources of income (e.g., state-provided support or child support), marriage market position, and other skills and preferences related to the utility of being single. Hence, individuals decide whether to remain in or leave a relationship by comparing the utility they experience in marriage to the anticipated utility they would experience if they exited the relationship. The same resources that provide more leverage to drive better bargains also provide the means by which individuals can leave a relationship with less loss.

Becker's gains-to-marriage thesis predicts that higher economic resources among women indicate less specialization and thus should be associated with lower marital gains and higher risks of divorce. This assumption has been criticized by feminist scholars, however, because it overlooks sharp gender differences in power within marriage and economic well-being outside of marriage. The gains to marriage for women may be lower than they are to men, because women make marriage-specific investments that are not portable (e.g., childrearing skills that cannot easily be transferred to other relationships), whereas men make individual-specific investments in human capital that they retain if the relationship ends (England, 2000). Bargaining perspectives assume a gender-neutral process, in which either partner, male or female, can use resources to negotiate favorable bargains or to exit a relationship. Men's greater resource portability also means that women are less able than men to drive satisfactory bargains. Historically, the lower levels of women's labor force participation and earnings have translated into less advantageous threat points for married women and consequently a weaker bargaining position vis-à-vis their husbands. Weak enforcement of child support laws and limited public transfers available to divorced women and children also reduce women's bargaining power (Lundberg & Pollak, 1996). Additionally, men's reluctance to assume responsibility for some household labor may stymie the ability of women with relatively high earnings and education to drive equitable bargains (England & Kilbourne, 1990). Hence, a bargaining perspective that accounts for sex inequality predicts that the higher economic resources of men and of women will be used either to negotiate favorable marital bargains that result in high levels of marital satisfaction, or to leave the relationship when bargaining breaks down.

In contrast to economic perspectives, gender scholars posit that similar economic and household roles of spouses increase empathy and companionship (England & Farkas, 1986; Goldscheider & Waite, 1991), in particular among husbands and wives with more egalitarian gender ideologies (Risman & Johnson-Sumerford, 1998). Indeed, Oppenheimer (1994, 2000) contends that the specialization of wives in household labor and husbands in market work is increasingly risky in modern societies because of the growing economic interdependence between spouses. The stagnation of male wages and the difficulty in maintaining consumption patterns of a middle-class standard of living on a single income have reduced and in many cases removed the ability of husbands to be sole breadwinners. Similar economic roles of wives and husbands buffer nuclear households against job loss and financial strain and thus reduce marital discord that typically accompanies shifts in economic circumstances. Hence, comparable, rather than complementary, spousal roles augment women's and men's emotional gains from marriage, reduce economic risks, and, by extension, increase marital stability. Men's gains to marriage may actually increase as a result of the presence of another wage earner coupled with men's lesser involvement in household chores and childrearing.

In sum, each of these perspectives predicts that the altered economic circumstances of men and women since the 1950s are driving changes in marriage and divorce patterns (Bianchi & Casper, 2000; Farley, 1996; White & Rogers, 2000). The direction of the hypothesized relationship between women's and men's resources differs, however. Becker's gains-to-marriage perspective posits that higher economic resources among women indicate less specialization and thus signal lower marital gains and higher risks of divorce. Bargaining models predict that macrolevel gender inequality may hinder women's ability to use economic resources as leverage in the bargaining process, and thus higher economic resources among women may also be associated with higher risks of divorce. In contrast, gender theorists predict that dissimilar levels of spousal economic resources hinder intimacy and marital satisfaction and thus are associated with higher risks of divorce.

Prior empirical research has found that men's higher education, earnings, and stable employment increased entry into marriage from singlehood or cohabiting unions (Goldscheider & Waite, 1991; Oppenheimer, 2003; Oppenheimer, Kalmijn, & Lim, 1997; Sassler & Schoen, 1999). Empirical work on the association between women's economic characteristics and marriage entry has found less consistent results. Studies that used aggregate data on marriage and labor market trends have generally found a negative association between women's employment and marriage (McLanahan & Casper, 1995), whereas those that used individual panel data found that women with better employment prospects were more likely to marry, not less, as compared with women with more constrained employment options (Goldscheider & Waite, 1991; Ono, 2003; Oppenheimer, 1995; Sweeney, 2002). Historically, women with more education have had lower probabilities of marriage compared with less educated women; however, they now appear to be more likely to marry compared with less educated women, regardless of race (Goldstein & Kenney, 2001; Kreider & Fields, 2001).

Numerous studies have also documented how men's and women's economic resources affect divorce. Divorce has consistently been found to be more likely when men's earnings are lower (Hoffman & Duncan, 1995; South & Lloyd, 1995) or declining (Weiss & Willis, 1997). One recent study reported that uncertainty about men's employment and earnings trajectories was associated with entry into cohabiting unions instead of marriage, and employment instability was associated with greater risks of cohabiting unions ending instead of transitioning to marriage (Oppenheimer, 2003). Interactions with race have also been noted in the literature. Yeung and Hofferth (1998) found that husbands' unemployment or reduced work hours had a stronger effect on divorce in Black than in White families. It is unclear how much racial differences are a result of differences in economic status. For example, although many studies have found that differences between Blacks and Whites persisted after controls for both spouses' earnings (Bumpass, Martin, & Sweet, 1991), South (2001) found that differences between Blacks and Whites disappeared once home ownership was considered.

The relationship between wives' economic resources and increased likelihood of divorce is less conclusive (White & Rogers, 2000). Some studies have reported a positive association between a wife's relative contribution to family income or wages and increased risks of marital disruption (Cherlin, 1979; D'Amico, 1983; Heckert, Nowak, & Snyder, 1998; Hiedemann, Suhomlinova, & O'Rand, 1998; Moore & Waite, 1981; Ono, 1998; Ross & Sawhill, 1975; Spitze & South, 1985). Others have found no effect of women's earnings (Greenstein, 1995; Mott & Moore, 1979; Sayer & Bianchi, 2000; South & Lloyd, 1995; Tzeng & Mare, 1995), and a few have suggested that women's earnings, like men's, stabilize marriage (Greenstein, 1990; Hoffman & Duncan, 1995; Weiss & Willis, 1997). Thus, no clear conclusion can be drawn regarding the effects of women's earnings on divorce.

The inconclusive results do not appear to stem from differences in data quality or the indicator used to measure women's economic independence: Studies have used comparable measures and analyzed nationally representative, longitudinal data. Instead, differences may stem from incomplete models that overlook important noneconomic variables associated with divorce. Studies that have found a positive association between women's economic resources and likelihood of divorce have not typically included measures of gender ideology or marital quality in their multivariate models. Both variables have been found to moderate the effect of women's economic resources on divorce (Rogers, 2004; Sayer & Bianchi, 2000; Schoen, Astone, Rothert, Standish, & Kim, 2002).

The decision to separate or divorce, although made on the basis of a cost-benefit analysis, also takes noneconomic factors into consideration. Measures of the quality of the marital relationship have been found to be strongly related to risk of divorce (Amato & Rogers, 1997; Blair, 1993; 1986; Booth, Johnson, White, & Edwards, 1985; Greenstein, 1995; Huber & Spitze, 1980; Spitze & South, 1985; Vannoy & Philliber, 1992). For example, Booth et al. reported that individuals who rated their marriage as unhappy had odds of divorce 9 times higher than individuals in happy marriages. Additionally, wives' economic resources have been found to increase risks of divorce only among couples in which marital satisfaction was low (Rogers, 2004; Sayer & Bianchi, 2000; Schoen et al., 2002).

Some scholars have posited that women's employment or earnings lead to marriages of poor quality, which are then more prone to disruption. This conjecture is not supported by the literature. Studies done before 1970 found some association, but recent analyses based on large national samples have reported no effect of wife's employment on the marital satisfaction of either the wife or the husband. In an analysis of panel data, Rogers (1999) reported that marital problems led women to take moves to increase their earnings, but increases in women's earnings had no adverse effects on reports of marital problems by either spouse. Similarly, Greene and Quester (1982) and Johnson and Skinner (1986) reported no effect of women's employment on marital dissolution. Individuals who perceived few benefits from and little cost to leaving their marriage, however, have been found to be more likely to separate or divorce (Heaton & Albrecht, 1991; Nock, 1995).

In sum, women and men with higher economic resources are more likely to marry than they are to remain single. Uncertainty over men's economic prospects is also associated with entry into cohabiting unions instead of marriage. Men with higher economic resources are more likely to transition from cohabitation into marriage and also less likely to divorce, but the effects of women's resources on divorce are mixed. Clearly, economic factors are related to decisions about marriage and union dissolution—decisions that have economic consequences for women, men, and children.

ECONOMIC CONSEQUENCES OF UNION DISSOLUTION

Marriage enhances a couple's economic resources through three mechanisms: specialization, economies of scale, and greater access to social institutions and networks (Hao, 1996; Waite, 1995). Specialization enhances economic well-being by increasing the joint output of couples more so than the sum of outputs produced individually. The economies of scale that result from sharing household and living expenses yield a higher standard of living on the same income level than each partner would realize if each maintained separate households. Married individuals are also more likely than single persons to have access to health insurance and pensions by means of their spouse (Wilmoth & Koso, 2002). Each of these factors is associated with higher rates of savings among married individuals compared with single persons, even net of other demographic and socioeconomic characteristics that are associated with earnings (Hao).

Consequently, after marital dissolution, some decline in economic well-being should result. Former partners now have two households with two sets of associated expenses to maintain instead of one. Sorensen (1992) noted that, even assuming that former partners continue to share economic resources equally following dissolution—an unlikely assumption—income would have to increase by 31% for individuals to maintain the same standard of living after marital dissolution compared with that enjoyed within marriage. Marital dissolution also removes gains associated with specialization.

Because both former spouses are no longer benefiting from specialization and economies of scale, women and men alike should experience a loss in economic status after divorce. However, research through the 1980s conclusively documented that women and children experienced declines in economic well-being following marital dissolution, whereas men's economic well-being increased (see Holden & Smock, 1991, for a review).

Recent research has focused on three themes: first, documenting the extent of economic change following divorce for women and for men; second, assessing reasons for the unequal gendered economic consequences of divorce; and third, examining the relationship between child support and children's economic well-being after divorce.

Economic Well-Being of Women After Divorce

The fact that poverty rates are higher and family incomes are lower for unmarried women compared with married women is well established in the social science literature (Casper & Bianchi, 2002). Measures of economic well-being at only one point in time, however, cannot be used to assess the extent of change in economic status associated with the event of divorce. Longitudinal studies instead typically document change in three measures of economic well-being after marital dissolution: family income, per capita income, and income-to-needs ratios. Estimates of well-being following marital dissolution differ across the three measures, because of different assumptions about economies of scale (Sorensen, 1992). Family income assumes the largest economies of scale, whereas per capita income assumes no economies of scale. Income-to-needs ratios adjust family income to take economies of scale into account, as well as the varying consumption patterns of household members by age. Most studies typically report multiple measures and consider both separation and legal divorce as instances of marital disruption. A minority of separations never transition to divorce: 6 years after separation, 98%

TABLE 19.1

Summary of Findings About Change in Women's and Men's Family Income, Per Capita Income,
and Income-to-Needs Ratios After Marital Dissolution

Study	Data	% Change Between $T - 1$ and $T + 1$	
		Women	*Men*
Family income			
McManus & DiPrete (2001)	PSID 1980–1993		−40 (Whites)
	(avg. % change)		−41 (Blacks)
Hanson, McLanahan, & Thomson (1998)	NSFH 1987–1988, 1992–1994 (avg. % change)	−27	
Smock (1993)	NLSY 1979–1988	−46 to −43 (Whites)	−8 to +7 (Whites)
	NLSYW 1968–1978	−51 to −45 (Blacks)	−13 to −29 (Blacks)
	NLSYM 1966–1978		
	(median % change)		
Morgan (1991)	NLSMW 1967–1982 (median % change)	−29	
Per capita income			
McManus & DiPrete (2001)			+34 (Whites)
			+68 (Blacks)
Smock (1994)	NLSY 1979–1988	−35 to −20	+18 to +61
Smock (1993)		−22 to −21 (Whites)	+93 to +62 (Whites)
		−44 to −35 (Blacks)	+80 to +47 (Blacks)
Income-to-needs ratio			
McManus & DiPrete (2001)			−14 (Whites)
			−3 (Blacks)
Bianchi, Subaiya, & Kahn (1999)	SIPP 1984–1990 (excl. 1989)	−36	+28
Hanson, McLanahan, & Thomson (1998)		−20	
Peterson (1996)	Reanalysis of Weitzman (1985)	−27	+10
Burkhauser, Duncan, Hauser, & Berntsen (1991)	PSID 1981–1985	−24	−6

Note: PSID = Panel Study of Income Dynamics; NSFH = National Survey of Families and Households; NLSY = National Longitudinal Survey of Youth; NLSYW = National Longitudinal Surveys of Young Women; NLSYM = National Longitudinal Surveys Young Men; NSLMW = National Longitudinal Surveys Mature Women; SIPP = Survey of Income and Program Participation.

of separations have ended in divorce for White women, compared with 80% among Hispanic women and 72% among Black women (Bramlett & Mosher, 2001).

Table 19.1 summarizes the results of recent studies that compare the economic status of women and men after marital dissolution relative to their predissolution status. The table shows estimates of the percentage change in family income, per capita income, and income-to-needs ratios. All of the studies found that women and children experience substantial declines in economic well-being on each of the three measures, across studies using different sample criteria (parental status and age restrictions), different sources of data, and different methods.

Estimates of declines in family income range from 27% to 51%, declines in per capita income range from 20% to 44%, and declines in income-to-needs ratios range from 20% to 36%. These results are consistent with those found prior to the 1990s. Holden and Smock (1991) reported that, prior to 1990, declines in family income ranged between 30% and 50%, declines in per capita income ranged between 20% and 35%, and declines in income-to-needs ranged between 7% and 30%.

This suggests that the economic costs of divorce for women have not changed over recent decades. Smock (1993) compared the economic consequences of divorce between women who divorced in the late 1960s and 1970s (early cohort) to those who divorced in the 1980s (late cohort). Her comparison of predissolution status and postdissolution status indicated that declines in family income and per capita income were similar across the early and the late cohorts. Among White women who divorced in the 1970s, per capita income declined 22%, whereas among White women who divorced in the 1980s, per capita income declined 21%.

Women have increased their educational attainment and employment; fertility has declined within marriage, which has reduced conflict between childrearing and employment; and normative acceptance of outside employment among mothers has increased. Despite these changes, though, the costs of divorce for women remain severe. One reason may be the stagnation of labor force participation rates and hourly wages during the 1990s among divorced women (Zimmer, 2004). Another reason for the continued high economic costs of divorce is the strong association in recent decades between characteristics associated with economic disadvantage, such as low levels of education and shaky employment histories, and union dissolution. As a result, union instability has increased most among the women who are least able to maintain their economic position subsequent to divorce: About 60% of marriages of women who did not complete high school end in divorce, compared with 36% among women with college degrees (Raley & Bumpass, 2003).

Recent research has attempted to disentangle the relationship among the event of divorce, women's predissolution characteristics, and their postdissolution economic well-being. Evidence is accumulating that higher human capital characteristics offer some protection against economic deprivation after divorce. Multivariate analyses from past studies have indicated that education, years of work experience, and number of weeks worked in the year prior to dissolution increased postdisruption family income, per capita income, and income-to-needs ratios (Bianchi, Subaiya, & Kahn, 1999; Mauldin, 1990; Smock, 1993; 1994; Smock, Manning, & Gupta, 1999). In particular, continuous labor force experience increased postdissolution income (Bianchi et al.; Peterson, 1989). Women who were worse off economically prior to marriage and during marriage fared worse after divorce compared with economically more advantaged women (Smock, 1994).

The question remains, however, whether there is a causal relationship between union dissolution and subsequent economic hardship. Recall that women who are economically disadvantaged are more likely to divorce than those who are economically better off. Women who divorce have lower family incomes, personal incomes, and income-to-needs ratios than women who remain married. Furthermore, women who divorce have lower predissolution levels of human capital characteristics correlated with economic well-being (age, education, and earnings trajectories) compared with women who remain married (Duncan & Hoffman, 1985; Hanson, McLanahan, & Thomson, 1998; Peterson, 1996).

One innovative study by Smock et al. (1999) addresses this issue by assessing two questions: First, would divorced women fare as well economically compared with continuously married women if, in fact, they had not divorced but instead had remained married? Second, would continuously married women be in the same state economically as divorced women if, in fact, they had divorced instead of remaining married? The results indicated that, even if women who divorced had remained married, they would not be as well off economically as women who remained married. Assuming divorced women had not divorced, their family incomes would have been about $5,000 lower than those of women who remained married ($46,861 vs. $51,976) and their income-to-needs ratio would have been only 90% that of continuously married women (3.5 vs. 3.9). The conclusion by Smock et al. was that prior investigations of the economic status of women before and after dissolution somewhat overstated the extent of economic gain that was directly associated with marriage. Nonetheless, the study found that divorce carried economic costs: Assuming that divorced women had not divorced, their family income would have been $29,000 higher ($46,861 vs. $17,480, assuming no remarriage) and their income-to-needs ratio would have been about 46% higher (3.5 vs. 1.6). Moreover, if married women had divorced instead of remaining married, they would have suffered similar declines in family income and income-to-needs ratios as did women who actually divorced. The findings of this study suggest that the economic costs of divorce are pervasive and not due solely to the lower human capital characteristics of women that divorce.

Economic Well-Being and Entry Into New Unions

Women can improve their economic circumstances after marital dissolution by increasing their personal earnings (the largest proportion of women's income after dissolution), by increasing child support payments from former husbands, and by entering a new heterosexual union and thus gaining access to another man's earnings. Studies have conclusively documented that the short-term economic consequences of divorce persist unless women remarry (Duncan & Hoffman, 1985; Hanson et al., 1998; Hoffman & Duncan, 1988; Smock et al., 1999; Weiss, 1984). For example, Hanson et al. (1998) found that the family income of divorced mothers who did not enter new unions was about $30,000 less than that of married couple families (in 1992 dollars), whereas no significant differences in family income between married couple families and remarried couple families were found. Remarriage also appears to compensate for the negative effect of marital disruption on wealth (Wilmoth & Koso, 2002). Three fourths of divorced women have remarried within 10 years after divorce, and younger women and Whites are more likely to remarry (Bramlett & Mosher, 2001).

Whether the economic advantages that accompany remarriage persist if the remarriage also ends in divorce is an open empirical question. Studies have not yet examined whether the economic consequences of union dissolution of higher order marriages are similar to those of first-union dissolution. One study reported that mothers who have divorced more than once and who have dependent residential children had lower median family incomes compared with mothers in stable remarriages, and entry into cohabiting unions after a divorce did not result in long-term economic benefits (Morrison & Ritualo, 2000). Comparisons of wealth accumulation among the continuously married, never married, and individuals who have experienced multiple union transitions have also found additional economic penalties that follow the disruption of remarriages (Wilmoth & Koso, 2002). These findings indicate that the economic advantages of remarriage stem almost entirely from renewed access to male wages. The selection into cohabiting unions instead of remarriages of individuals with less education and lower earnings capabilities also suggests that the economic returns to cohabitation are less than those to remarriage.

Investigating the economic outcomes that are associated with entry into and exit from cohabiting unions is important, given the growing prominence of cohabitation both prior to and subsequent to marriage. For example, the majority of marriages are preceded by cohabitation, and cohabitation is now more common than remarriage after divorce. About 50% of people in cohabiting unions have been previously married (Raley & Wildsmith, 2004). Nevertheless, most analyses of the economic consequences of union dissolution for women have not considered differences between cohabiting and marital unions. Marital and cohabiting relationships are similar in that partners share a residence and some living expenses; hence, as in marriage, cohabiting unions may have financial benefits from economies of scale (Lerman, 2002).

Cohabiting unions typically feature lower levels of specialization, however, and this may reduce economic returns. Women in cohabiting unions have higher labor force participation rates and contribute a larger proportion of household income compared with women in marital unions, and household labor is divided more equally between women and men in cohabiting unions compared with those in marital unions (Bianchi & Casper, 2000). Individuals in cohabiting unions are also less likely to pool income than are married persons (Heimdal & Houseknecht, 2003), and the assumption of permanence that is implicit in marital relationships is absent from many cohabiting unions, most of which are of short duration. Hence, the dissolution of cohabiting unions may not lead to sharp economic declines in well-being among women or men, because the economies of scale and mutual financial interdependence are not as high in cohabiting unions vis-à-vis marital unions.

Economic Well-Being of Men After Divorce

Table 19.1 also summarizes changes in men's family income, per capita income, and income-to-needs ratios and indicates that estimates are more varied for men than for women. Similar to women, men experience a decline in family income after divorce that ranges from 8% to 41%. Hence, both women and men suffer from the loss of their former spouse's financial contributions. In contrast to women, however, men's per capita income increases after divorce, with estimates ranging from 18% to 93%. One study has examined economic outcomes following cohabiting union dissolution and reports similar patterns: among Whites, men's family income declined 42% following exit from cohabitation (vs. 40% following divorce) and per capita income increased 29% after ending a cohabiting relationship, versus a 34% increase after a divorce (McManus & DiPrete, 2001).

Men's per capita income increases after divorce in part because their household size postdissolution is smaller, because fathers rarely have physical custody of children after divorce. Fertility has decreased, resulting in smaller differences in predivorce and postdivorce household size, however, meaning that men who divorced in the 1980s experienced smaller increases in per capita income compared with those who divorced in the 1970s (Smock, 1993). Another reason per capita income generally increases among men after a divorce stems from men's greater earnings capacity relative to women. Even in 2000, men continued to earn higher wages than women: Among workers aged 25 to 54 who were employed full time, year round, men's annual salary was $38,700 compared with only $28,000 for women (Cotter, Hermsen, & Vanneman, 2004).

Socioeconomic Status Differences in Men's Outcomes

The average consequences of divorce on men's economic well-being mask significant variation in outcomes by men's socioeconomic status. In terms of income-to-needs ratios, Table 19.1 shows that, in some samples, men experienced mean increases that ranged from 10% to 28% (Bianchi et al., 1999; Peterson, 1996), whereas, in other samples, they experienced mean declines that ranged from 6% to 14% (Burkhauser, Duncan, Hauser, & Berntsen, 1991; McManus & DiPrete, 2001). The wide range of estimates is associated with the increased heterogeneity in men's financial contributions to marriage prior to divorce. Among men who divorced between 1981 and 1992, only those contributing more than 80% of predissolution household income experienced increases in their standard of living after divorce (McManus & DiPrete). Compared with increases of 12% among those contributing between 80% and 100% of household income, living standards declined among men contributing lower proportions of predissolution household income: 27% among those contributing less than 40%; 17% among those contributing between 40% and 59%; and 5% among those contributing between 60% and 79% (McManus & DiPrete). Smock (1994) also found that men who contributed the largest amount of household income prior to divorce experienced the smallest decline in gross household income. Hence, economically advantaged men—those with high levels of education and high earnings—fare relatively well after a divorce, whereas economically disadvantaged men experience declines in economic well-being.

It is possible that these results signal the increasing economic interdependence of women and men within marriage, in particular among those without a college education. Less educated men's labor market prospects and earnings have declined since the mid-1970s (White & Rogers, 2000). Even among better educated men, it is increasingly difficult to maintain an adequate standard of living on only one income. For example, prior to 1980, the higher family income of married couple families compared with other family types was the result of the presence of a male earner; and the man would retain most of these earnings in case the marriage dissolved. After 1980, though, higher married couple family income resulted from the presence of two earners (Cancian & Reed, 1999)—each of whom would presumably retain his or her own income following a divorce.

Differences by Race

The economic well-being of women and men after marital dissolution also varies by race, which is not surprising given the economic disparities in income and earnings linked to race and ethnicity. Because of data limitations, studies typically have assessed the economic consequences of divorce only for Blacks and Whites (but see Smock, 1994, for an exception). Following marital disruption, Black women experienced larger declines in family income and per capita income than White women (Smock, 1993). Black men also experienced larger decreases in family income and smaller increases in per capita income after divorce compared with White men (McManus & DiPrete, 2001). Although the determinants of postdissolution personal and per capita income have not been found to differ by race, Blacks have lower per capita income after divorce net of human capital characteristics. In addition, non-White men experienced greater economic downturns after disruption relative to White women, which suggests that economic disadvantages associated with race may be as pronounced as gender disparities (Smock, 1994). Blacks are also less likely to remarry than are Whites (in part because they are more likely to remain separated rather than obtaining a legal divorce), and they are also more likely than Whites to divorce following remarriage (Bramlett & Mosher, 2001). Hence, the long-term economic disadvantage from divorce may be more pronounced for Black women than for White women.

Economic Consequences of Divorce on Wealth Accumulation

A few studies have examined the effect of divorce on wealth disparities. This is important, because family wealth has a more direct association with consumption patterns than does current income (Hao, 1996). Wealth reflects access to or control of economic resources and is also more stable over time, whereas income fluctuates from year to year. Furthermore, measures of economic well-being such as family income, per capita income, and income-to-needs ratios reflect economic status at only one point in time. Studies typically have measured wealth as the current value of all marketable assets minus debt. Divorce has been found to reduce wealth because of the costs associated with separation, such as dividing household assets,

TABLE 19.2

Summary of Findings About Sex Differences in Family Income, Per Capita Income,
and Income-to-Needs Ratios Following Marital Dissolution

		Post Dissolution Income Measures		
Study	*Data*	*Women*	*Men*	*Ratio (women : men)*
Family income ($ monthly)				
Bianchi, Subaiya, & Kahn (1999)	SIPP 1984–1990	1,598	2,197	.73
Per capita income ($ monthly)				
Bianchi, Subaiya, & Kahn (1999)		459	1,211	.38
Income-to-needs ratio				
Bartfeld (2000)	SIPP 1986–1991	1.57	3.55	.44
Bianchi, Subaiya, & Kahn (1999)		1.51	2.98	.51
Peterson (1996)	Weitzman sample (1985)	3.34	4.88	.68

Note: SIPP = Survey of Income and Program Participation

including the family home in some cases, which may leave spouses with no home equity or savings (Hao; Wilmoth & Koso, 2002). One study found that a separation or divorce reduced wealth between 70% and 80%, and individuals who did not remarry had wealth accumulations 75% lower than continuously married individuals. The negative effects of divorce on wealth accumulation persisted even when individuals subsequently remarried or cohabited: Remarried individuals had 29% less wealth and cohabiting individuals had 59% less wealth compared with continuously married persons (Wilmoth & Koso). Additionally, one third of mothers with residential children who owned homes prior to marital disruption did not own them afterward, because of the negative effect of divorce on economic assets (Hanson et al., 1998). There is some evidence that individuals are increasingly selected into marriage on the basis of characteristics also associated with wealth accumulation, such as high educational attainment and stable employment histories (Goldstein & Kenney, 2001; Oppenheimer, 2003; Sweeney, 2002). Still, wealth differences between married and divorced or separated individuals persist, even accounting for higher education and earnings potential among married persons (Hao; Wilmoth & Koso).

Gendered Costs of Marital Dissolution

Most longitudinal studies do not collect information on all family members either predissolution or postdissolution. As a result, the majority of the research documenting women's (and children's) economic disadvantage and men's economic advantage after marital dissolution has compared the average experience of women to the average experience of men, instead of making direct comparisons between the economic well-being of former husbands and wives. Given that some men are worse off economically after dissolution, vis-à-vis their status within marriage, it is possible that the economic declines experienced by women after divorce may not translate into economic gains for men (McManus & DiPrete, 2001).

Table 19.2 summarizes the results of three studies that directly compared the economic well-being of former spouses. The estimates indicate that former wives' family income, per capita income, and income-to-needs ratio are lower than those of their former husbands, suggesting that the economic costs of divorce are not shared equally by women and men. For example, past research reports that following marital dissolution divorced women's family income was only 73% as high as that of their former husband, per capita income was only 38% of that of their former husband, and estimates of the sex gap in income-to-needs ratio ranged from 44% to 68% (Bartfeld, 2000; Bianchi et al., 1999; Peterson, 1996).

A small minority of women, however, fare better economically after divorce compared with their former husbands. One analysis of parents who divorced in the 1980s found that, in 10% of divorces postdissolution, per capita income was higher among former wives than among former husbands, and in 19% of cases, former wives' income-to-needs ratio was greater than that of their former husbands (Bianchi et al., 1999). Nonetheless, the same study reports the flip side of these estimates: The postdivorce median family income of former husbands was greater than that of former wives in 65% of divorces; former husbands' median per capita income was greater than that of former wives in 90% of divorces; and former husbands' median income-to-needs ratio was greater than that of their former wives in 81% of divorces. Furthermore, whereas one fifth of former wives experienced an increase in their standard of living after marital disruption, two thirds of former husbands' standards of living increased postdissolution. Divorced mothers were also more likely to become poor as a result of divorce compared with their former spouses (19% of mothers vs. 3% of fathers), and three fourths of mothers with incomes below the poverty line predissolution remained poor after divorce compared with one fourth of fathers (Bianchi et al.). Peterson's (1996) reanalysis of data from the Weitzman study of couples living in Los Angeles that divorced in 1977 also found that, on average, postdissolution family income declined 27% among former wives whereas that of former husbands increased 10%.

Although estimates vary somewhat, results from studies that have compared the economic well-being of separate samples of women and men who have divorced are consistent with results from studies that directly compared the economic well-being of former spouses. For example, one analysis of women and men that divorced between 1981 and 1985 reports that 42% of men but only 26% of women experienced increased living standards, and only 10% of men experienced a 50% or greater drop in living standards compared with 22% of women (Burkhauser et al., 1991). Additionally, divorce reduced assets and wealth much less for men than for women (Hao, 1996; Wilmoth & Koso, 2002).

Some scholars have suggested that sex differences in economic outcomes following divorce are overstated, because analyses have used pretax income comparisons that have not accounted for the tax advantages realized by custodial parents or voluntary financial transfers from nonresidential fathers to their children (see Braver, Sharpiro, & Goodman, chap. 16, this volume). Measures used in recent studies, however, have considered public and private transfers (Burkhauser et al., 1991; McManus & DiPrete, 2001) and have *still* found that, on average, former husbands were economically advantaged following divorce compared with their former wives. In addition, dollar amounts of voluntary support provided by nonresidential fathers, such as expenses for food, clothing, and presents, appear to be relatively small. The majority of fathers provided no voluntary support for children's clothes, vacations, or uninsured medical expenses, and only one third included children on health insurance coverage (Paasch & Teachman, 1991).

Compulsory child support payments have a larger effect on nonresidential fathers' economic fortunes compared with voluntary support, but even so, the size of the effects are small: Child support and alimony reduced high-earning fathers' income by 5 percentage points, and voluntary support amplified the decline by only an additional 2 percentage points (McManus & DiPrete, 2001). Burkhauser et al. (1991) also found that only one third of divorced women received private transfers of income, and the dollar amount of transfers amounted to only 7% of wives' postdivorce income. Even after accounting for the more advantageous tax situation of custodial parents and private financial transfers from nonresidential fathers to custodial mothers, Braver et al. (chap. 16, this volume) reported that fathers experienced a 2% increase in postdivorce standards of living, whereas mothers experienced an 8% decline. To be sure, though, child support payments reduce sex disparities in economic well-being of former wives and husbands after a divorce.

One might expect that sex differences in economic well-being would be smaller among recent cohorts experiencing divorce because of women's increased human capital and lower fertility, both of which should have narrowed sex gaps in earnings capabilities after dissolution. Nonetheless, Smock (1993) found that sex differences in per capita income were similar for cohorts that divorced in the 1980s compared with those that divorced in the 1970s. Substantial sex differences in postdissolution economic well-being persisted even among young women and men with similar human capital investments (Smock, 1994).

Three factors explain why women suffer disproportionate economic costs of marital disruption: sex inequality in wages and employment opportunities; the gendered division of labor within marriage that increases men's portable marriage-specific capital while reducing women's; and the high proportion of mothers with physical custody of children after divorce, along with low levels of postdissolution child support (Bianchi et al., 1999; Smock, 1993). Macrolevel sex inequality in employment reduces all women's economic resources relative to all men's. Married women continue to be dependent on husbands for economic support, even though dependency has declined over time (Nock, 2001), because it remains difficult for most women to combine having a career with being a wife and mother (Goldin, 1997; Moen & Sweet, 2003). Women with children continue to have lower employment rates compared with childless women: only 38% of married mothers with children are employed full time, year round, compared with 55% of single women without children (Sayer, Cohen, & Casper, 2004). Marriage and parenthood increase men's wages, whereas they reduce women's (Budig & England, 2001; Light, 2004; Nock, 1998). Although men earn more than women among both married and unmarried individuals, the difference is greater within marriage than among single women and men (England, 2000), and sex differences in income increase with marital duration (Joshi, 1998). Husbands earn more than wives in 72% of all dual-earner couples, and in 68% of all dual-earner couples in which both husbands and wives work full time (Ameristat, 2003).

Children have direct and indirect effects on women's economic well-being after divorce. They affect women's well-being indirectly by dampening their labor force participation during marriage (Sayer et al., 2004). They affect women's postdissolution economic well-being directly, because most children live with their mothers after divorce, and thus decrease per capita income. Child support provides some assistance, but most fathers do not provide the same level of economic support postdissolution as they did predissolution (assuming that all family members share equally in family income prior to dissolution, an assumption past research suggests is *not* true in all marital families; see Treas, 1993). Because men contribute a larger proportion of family income within marriage, their family income does not decline as much after a divorce as does women's, and because most children live with their mothers after divorce, the number of individuals in men's households is typically smaller after a divorce compared with women's. Fathers have relatively more income on which to support relatively fewer people, compared with their former wives. As a result, mothers shoulder more of the cost of supporting children on lower earnings. Furthermore, the inverse relationship between presence of children and lower postdissolution per capita income has not been found for custodial fathers, because of men's higher earnings (Smock, 1994; Sorensen, 1992).

Consequences of Divorce on Children's Economic Well-Being

The gendered costs of divorce are of concern, not only because of the negative effect on women's well-being but also because divorce leads to inadequate economic resources for children. Because children are more likely to live with their mothers than with their fathers following a divorce, the economic well-being of children after marital dissolution largely mirrors that of women. In 2002, 21.5 million children under the age of 21, or 28%, were living with only one of their parents; 84% of custodial parents were mothers and 16% were fathers, proportions that have not changed since 1994 (Grall, 2003). Over the course of their childhood, more than 50% of all children will live with only one of their parents, typically their mother (Garfinkel, McLanahan, Meyer, & Seltzer, 1998). In addition, the proportion of children residing in a cohabiting family household has increased 50% since 1990 (Brown, 2002).

Children's economic well-being varies by the marital status of their parents. In 2002, 69% of custodial mothers were divorced whereas 31% were never married; among custodial fathers, 80% were divorced and 20% were never married (Grall, 2003). Children living with divorced mothers fare better economically compared with those living with never-married mothers, both those living without a partner and those living in cohabiting unions. Divorced mothers have more education, higher rates of employment, higher rates of home ownership, and lower rates of poverty than never-married mothers (Casper & Bianchi, 2002). The economic status of children in cohabiting family households is precarious in part because of less income pooling in cohabiting households than in marital households (Brown, 2004).

In an ideal world, both mothers and fathers would provide for their children after marital disruption. Child support payments are the primary way in which divorced fathers share economic resources with their children. The majority of guidelines for child support are based on the principle that parents should provide the same level of economic resources to children that they would if they were still living together (Bartfeld, 2000). Nonetheless, many fathers provide little to no economic support for their children. Children's economic vulnerability has been linked with poor nutrition, health problems, poor academic performance, including dropping out of high school, and psychological and behavioral problems (Marsiglio, Amato, Ray, & Lamb, 2000; McLanahan & Sandefur, 1994). Consequently, much public debate and legislation has focused on increasing compliance with child support orders and increasing levels of child support payments.

Divorced mothers are more likely to be awarded child support than are never-married mothers: 74% of ever-married mothers compared with only 26% of never-married mothers were awarded child support payments in 2001 (Grall, 2003). Divorced mothers are also more likely to actually receive child support payments compared with never-married mothers. Table 19.3 compares child support receipt among mothers by marital status. It indicates that, in 2001, among mothers who were supposed to receive child support payments, 79% of divorced mothers, 74% of separated mothers, and 64% of never-married mothers actually received payments. About one half of divorced mothers and around one third of separated and never-married mothers receive no child support payments from their children's father (see percentage of total receiving support). In absolute and relative terms, child support payments are minimal. For example, child support payments provide only 15% of total income among divorced mothers.

One reason amounts are so low is because many fathers do not provide the full amount of monetary support. In 2001, of divorced and separated mothers who were supposed to receive child support, 51% received full payment, 27% received partial payment, and 22% received no child support payments (Grall, 2003). Fathers of children born in cohabiting unions have

TABLE 19.3
Child Support Received by Mothers by Marital Status, 2001

	Marital Status		
Characteristic	Divorced	Separated	Never Married
Percent of all mothers with an award who were supposed to receive support in 2001	64	44	45
Percent with award who received support	79	74	64
Percent of total receiving support	51	33	29
Mean annual dollar amount per recipient	5,148	4,417	2,864
Percent of total money income	15	16	14

Note: From Grall (2003), Internet Tables 4 and 5.

less contact after the cohabiting union ends, as compared with divorced fathers, and low levels of visitation are associated with lower probabilities of providing child support (Seltzer, 2000). New biological children born within remarriages also reduce the amount of nonresidential fathers' support for children from a previous marriage (Manning & Smock, 2000). Clearly, the "costs" of children are falling disproportionately on mothers after marital disruption.

Since the 1970s, federal legislation has established guidelines for child support levels and enforcement across states that are designed both to make it more difficult for fathers to evade paying child support and to shift some financial support of children from the state to biological fathers (Garfinkel et al., 1998). Child support enforcement featured prominently in the Personal Responsibility and Work Opportunity and Reconciliation Act (PRWORA) of 1996, and, in 1998, the federal government passed the Deadbeat Parents Act, which made it a felony for anyone who crosses a state line to evade child support obligation (Garfinkel et al.).

Some evidence suggests that child support payments increased between 1996 and 2001, primarily for children in families with incomes 200% or less of the poverty threshold (Sorensen, 2003). Still, as shown in Table 19.3, many fathers are not in compliance with legal child support orders. Some fathers do not pay child support because of conflict with their former wives over child visitation rights and issues pertaining to lack of control over how child support payments are spent (Arendell, 1992). Other fathers, however, are providing less (or no) child support than legally mandated because of informal modifications agreed to by both parents. Child support compliance fluctuates substantially from year to year because many divorced parents have agreed to informally alter payments to take into account changed economic circumstances of the father or changes in custodial arrangements (Peters, Argys, Maccoby, & Mnookin, 1993). Hence, fathers' actual transfers of resources to children may be higher than indicated by official statistics.

In addition, some fathers are assuming more day-to-day responsibility for their children after disruption. Shared physical custody of children has become more common as state courts have determined custody based on the "best interests" of children in contrast to prior explicit preferences for maternal custody. One analysis of custody decisions in divorces that occurred in Wisconsin between 1986 and 1992 indicates that the proportion of mothers awarded sole custody declined from 80% to 74%, whereas shared custody increased from 7% to 14% over the same period. The proportion of fathers who were granted sole custody remained at about 10% over the period (Cancian & Meyer, 1998). Shared physical custody has implications for improving children's well-being and lessening economic disparities between former spouses: Father-headed families have higher incomes compared with mother-headed families, and fathers with shared custody may provide more resources to children compared with fathers without shared custody (Cancian & Meyer).

Does Child Support Improve Children's Economic Status?

The evidence is mixed on whether increases in child support improve children's economic well-being. On the one hand, divorced mothers who did not receive child support income had incomes only 77% as high as mothers who did receive child support payments ($26,815 compared with $34,974; Grall, 2003). Child support also has positive long-term effects on characteristics intertwined with economic well-being in adulthood, such as children's educational and developmental outcomes (Amato & Gilbreth, 1999).

On the other hand, ensuring that all nonresidential parents pay child support will not, by itself, increase all children's economic well-being. Payment of child support and levels of support are strongly correlated with nonresidential fathers' educational attainment, employment status, and earnings (Case, Lin, & McLanahan, 2003; Nelson, 2004; Smock & Manning, 1997). Enforcement of child support payments appears to have reduced welfare costs rather than raising children's living standards, in part because enforcement efforts have concentrated more on increasing compliance among never married, low-income fathers rather than among relatively better off divorced fathers (Garfinkel et al., 1998). According to the Office of Child Support Enforcement, 70% of the $70 billion child support debt is owed by noncustodial parents with no or very low earnings. Some additional evidence suggests that many nonresidential fathers are not able to support themselves, much less their children, adequately (Meyer, 1998; Nelson). Higher earning fathers have been found to be more likely to make child support payments than lower earning fathers (Smock & Manning; Teachman, 1991).

Economically disadvantaged fathers are usually never married, however, and Sorensen (1997) suggested that many divorced fathers can afford to pay higher levels of child support. Obviously, child support payments reduce fathers' economic resources, but, even assuming higher payment levels, divorced fathers had more income and higher living standards compared with former wives and children (Bartfeld, 2000; Meyer, 1998). Furthermore, levels of child support were only weakly associated with poverty levels among nonresidential fathers (Meyer). Hence, at least one subgroup of fathers could afford to transfer more resources to children. Nonetheless, assuming that all fathers could afford to fully comply with the most generous child support guidelines, mothers and children would still have lower living standards and higher poverty rates than fathers (Bartfeld).

The route to economic recovery among children of divorced mothers appears to be their mother's remarriage. Compared with children whose mothers remained single or entered cohabiting unions, children whose mothers remarried had higher living standards and lower poverty rates (Morrison & Ritualo, 2000). The economic well-being of children has also been found to be closely related to the stability of postdivorce unions. Five years after divorce, 19% of children had transitioned into and out of two or more cohabiting or marital unions, and these children had lower median family incomes and higher rates of poverty compared with those living with their mothers in postdivorce stable unions (Morrison & Ritualo).

Research on the economic consequences of divorce for children has not specifically focused on differences by race or ethnicity, socioeconomic status, or parents' sexual orientation. Because the economic well-being of children largely mirrors that of their mothers, however, some inferences about children's well-being can be drawn from studies that have examined racial or ethnic and socioeconomic status variation in mothers' and fathers' economic well-being following divorce. The short- and long-term economic consequences of divorce have been found to be more severe for Black women than for White women. In addition, Black men experience greater declines in economic well-being following a divorce compared with White men. Hence, Black children likely suffer more economic disadvantage after divorce compared with White children. In terms of socioeconomic differences, women who were worse off economically prior to marriage and during marriage fare worse than more advantaged women postdivorce, and economically disadvantaged women are less likely to remarry than better off women. Men who contributed less than 80% of predivorce family income experienced drops in living standards after a divorce. These findings suggest that children in families of low socioeconomic status are likely to face greater long-term economic deprivation following a divorce compared with children in higher status families. Studies have yet to examine variation in the economic consequences of divorce for children of gay or lesbian parents.

CONCLUSION

Findings from recent analyses of the economic consequences of divorce indicate that two of the central findings from the review by Holden and Smock (1991) still hold: Most women and children are economically disadvantaged following divorce, and the route to economic recovery is remarriage. Divorce itself appears to lead to economic disadvantage because the average married woman—were she to divorce—would experience a reduced standard of living. Nonetheless, women's characteristics do cushion economic deprivation after divorce. Women with more education, years of work experience, and higher weeks worked have higher postdisruption family income, per capita income, and income-to-needs ratios compared with women with weaker human capital characteristics.

Recent research also suggests heterogeneity in outcomes for men, with divorce disadvantaging some men, but not others. Husbands' greater reliance on wives' economic contributions within marriage and more heterogeneity in family structure (fewer men living with biological children and more living with stepchildren, older children, and nonrelatives) are associated with negative economic consequences of divorce among men. The economic well-being of husbands and wives in marriage increasingly depends on financial contributions of both partners. The economic interdependencies of low-earning wives and husbands may be particularly strong. Among wives, declines in public assistance, increases in the stigma of receiving welfare, and more limited employment opportunities among the less educated reduce their ability to support themselves and dependent children outside of marriage. At the same time, the economic dependence of low-earning husbands has increased because they have been the hardest hit by economic upheavals since the 1970s. Today, then, many men, similar to most women, may fare better economically within marriage than outside marriage.

Still, direct comparisons between spouses indicate large sex disparities in economic well-being following divorce, even when child support payments and other private and public transfers are taken into account. Compared with their former spouses and children, most men fare better after divorce. The specialized sex division of labor within marriage continues to be a key factor in women's greater economic disadvantage after divorce. During the 1990s, little changed in terms of sex differences in labor force participation, occupational segregation, and the wage gap (Cotter et al., 2004; Sayer et al., 2004). Marriage and parenthood continue to differentiate women's and men's labor force participation, wages, and career opportunities, albeit to a lesser extent than in prior decades. Without further improvement in women's wages and labor market opportunities, or additional public support provision to mothers and children, gender disparities in the economic consequences of divorce are likely to persist, even among recent cohorts.

SUGGESTIONS FOR FUTURE RESEARCH

The negative economic consequences of divorce on women and children have been well-documented. A growing body of work also suggests that although on average men's economic well-being increases following divorce, some men's economic well-being declines. This review highlights several gaps in the literature that warrant additional research.

First, variability in the economic consequences of divorce for women and for men should be investigated further. The greater diversity in work and family arrangements within unions appears to be associated with how women and men fare after union dissolution. Greater attention should be focused on the determinants of positive and negative economic outcomes after dissolution among women and men. In particular, new research that examines variability in outcomes with matched couple data is needed. We know that some men's economic circumstances decline after divorce in comparison with their predissolution economic situation, and some women fare better economically after divorce relative to their predissolution situation. Whether one spouse's economic disadvantage translates directly into the other spouse's economic advantage remains an intriguing open empirical question. In addition, little work has focused on heterogeneity in economic consequences associated with race, social class, or partners' sexual orientation. Given that economic arrangements within unions vary along these dimensions, investigations focusing on the intersecting effects of gender, race or ethnicity, social class, and sexual orientation on postdissolution economic well-being would be particularly useful. Finally, this area would also benefit from additional cross-national research that could illuminate the linkages between private and public transfers and postdissolution economic well-being.

Second, we know far less about the economic consequences of exiting cohabiting unions and remarriages than we do about the consequences of divorce. This is a critical area for further research, given the prominence of cohabitation in the family formation process. The majority of first marriages are now preceded by cohabitation, remarriages have declined as more women and men enter cohabiting unions after divorce, and about two fifths of children will live with a parent and their cohabiting partner at some point during their childhood. New research should also explore the implications of multiple union transitions for the economic well-being of women, children, and men.

Third, new research should consider whether postdissolution economic circumstances vary depending on which partner initiates the divorce. Women's and men's economic resources may not only affect marital processes and outcomes differently, but may also differentially moderate the relationship between men's and women's marital quality, marital dissolution, and postdissolution outcomes. That women initiate the majority of divorces is an interesting issue in its own right, but even more so in light of women's persistent economic disadvantage after dissolution.

Although divorce rates have stabilized, approximately 50% of first marriages end in divorce. Union instability is also high among cohabiting relationships and remarriages. The need for additional research on the economic consequences of union dissolution is likely to be more enduring than many unions themselves.

REFERENCES

Amato, P. R., & Gilbreth, J. G. (1999). Nonresident fathers and children's well-being: A meta-analysis. *Journal of Marriage and Family, 61,* 557–573.

Amato, P. R., & Rogers, S. J. (1997). A longitudinal study of marital problems and subsequent divorce. *Journal of Marriage and the Family, 59,* 612–624.

Ameristat. (2003). *Dual-earner households in which the wife earned more than the husband, by work status, 2001.* Washington, DC: Population Reference Bureau.

Arendell, T. (1992). After divorce: Investigations into father absence. *Gender and Society, 6,* 562–586.

Bartfeld, J. (2000). Child support and the postdivorce economic well-being of mothers, fathers, and children. *Demography, 37,* 203–213.

Becker, G. S. (1991). *A treatise on the family.* Cambridge, MA: Harvard University Press.

Becker, G. S., Landes, E. M., & Michael, R. T. (1977). An economic analysis of marital instability. *Journal of Political Economy, 85,* 1141–1187.

Bianchi, S. M., & Casper, L. M. (2000). American families. In *Population Bulletin* (Vol. 55 pp. 1–42). Washington, DC: Population Reference Bureau.

Bianchi, S. M., Subaiya, L., & Kahn, J. R. (1999). The gender gap in the economic well-being of nonresident fathers and custodial mothers. *Demography, 36,* 195–203.

Blair, S. L. (1993). Employment, family, and perceptions of marital quality among husbands and wives. *Journal of Family Issues, 14,* 189–212.

Booth, A., Johnson, D. R., White, L. K., & Edwards, J. N. (1985). Predicting divorce and permanent separation. *Journal of Family Issues, 6,* 331–346.

Booth, A., Johnson, D. R., White, L. K., & Edwards, J. N. (1986). Divorce and marital instability over the life course. *Journal of Family Issues, 7,* 421–442.

Bramlett, M. D., & Mosher, W. D. (2001). *First marriage dissolution, divorce, and remarriage: United States* (Advanced Data From Vital and Health Statistics, No. 323). Washington, DC: U.S. Government Printing Office.

Brown, S. L. (2002). Child well-being in cohabiting families. In A. Booth & A. C. Crouter (Eds.), *Just living together: Implications of cohabitation for children, families, and social policy* (pp. 173–187). Mahwah, NJ: Lawrence Erlbaum Associates.

Brown, S. L. (2004). Family structure and child well-being: The significance of parental cohabitation. *Journal of Marriage and Family, 66,* 351–367.

Budig, M. J., & England, P. (2001). The wage penalty for motherhood. *American Sociological Review, 66,* 204–225.

Bumpass, L., & Lu, H.-H. (2000). Trends in cohabitation and implications for children's family contexts in the United States. *Population Studies—A Journal of Demography, 54,* 29–41.

Bumpass, L. L., Martin, T. C., & Sweet, J. A. (1991). The impact of family background and early marital factors on marital disruption. *Journal of Family Issues, 12,* 22–42.

Burkhauser, R. V., Duncan, G. J., Hauser, R., & Berntsen, R. (1991). Wife or frau, women do worse: A comparison of women and men in the United States and Germany after marital dissolution. *Demography, 28,* 353–360.

Cancian, M., & Meyer, D. R. (1998). Who gets custody? *Demography, 35,* 147–157.

Cancian, M., & Reed, D. (1999). The impact of wives' earnings on income inequality: Issues and estimates. *Demography, 36,* 173–184.

Case, A. C., Lin, I.-F., & McLanahan, S. S. (2003). Explaining trends in child support: Economic, demographic, and policy effects. *Demography, 40,* 171–189.

Casper, L. M., & Bianchi, S. M. (2002). *Continuity and change in the American family.* Thousand Oaks: Sage.

Cherlin, A. J. (1979). Work life and marital dissolution. In G. Levinger & O. C. Moles (Eds.), *Divorce and separation: Context, causes, and consequences* (pp. 151–166). New York: Basic Books.

Cherlin, A. J. (2000). Toward a new home economics of union formation. In L. J. Waite, C. Bachrach, M. Hindin, E. Thomson, & A. Thornton (Eds.), *The ties that bind: Perspectives on marriage and cohabitation* (pp. 126–146). New York: de Gruyter.

Cotter, D. A., Hermsen, J. M., & Vanneman, R. (2004). *Gender inequality at work.* Washington, DC: Population Reference Bureau/Russell Sage Foundation.

D'Amico, R. (1983). Status maintenance or status competition? Wife's relative wages as a determinant of labor supply and marital instability. *Social Forces, 61,* 1186–1205.

Duncan, G. J., & Hoffman, S. D. (1985). A reconsideration of the economic consequences of marital dissolution. *Demography, 22,* 485–497.

England, P. (2000). Marriage, the costs of children, and gender inequality. In L. J. Waite (Eds.), *The ties that bind: Perspectives on marriage and cohabitation* (pp. 320–342). New York: de Gruyter.

England, P., & Farkas, G. (1986). *Households, employment and gender: A social, economic and demographic view.* Hawthorne, NY: Aldine.

England, P., & Kilbourne, B. S. (1990). Markets, marriages, and other mates: The problem of power. In R. Friedland & A. F. Robertson (Eds.), *Beyond the marketplace: Rethinking economy and society* (pp. 163–188). New York: de Gruyter.

Farley, R. (1996). *The new American reality: Who we are, how we got here, where we are going.* New York: Russell Sage Foundation.

Garfinkel, I., McLanahan, S., Meyer, D. R., & Seltzer, J. A. (1998). Introduction. In I. Garfinkel, S. McLanahan, D. R. Meyer, & J. A. Seltzer (Eds.), *Fathers under fire: The revolution in child support enforcement* (pp. 1–10). New York: Russell Sage Foundation.

Goldin, C. (1997). Career and family: College women look to the past. In F. D. Blau & R. G. Ehrenberg (Eds.), *Gender and family issues in the workplace* (pp. 20–58). New York: Russell Sage Foundation.

Goldscheider, F., & Waite, L. J. (1991). *New families, no families: The transformation of the American home.* Berkeley: University of California Press.

Goldstein, J. R., & Kenney, C. T. (2001). Marriage delayed or marriage forgone? New cohort forecasts of first marriage for US women. *American Sociological Review, 66,* 506–519.

Grall, T. S. (2003). *Custodial mothers and fathers and their child support: 2001* (Current Population Reports, Series P60–225). Washington, DC: U.S. Government Printing Office.

Greene, W. H., & Quester, A. O. (1982). Divorce risk and wives' labor supply behavior. *Social Science Quarterly, 63,* 16–27.

Greenstein, T. N. (1990). Marital disruption and the employment of married women. *Journal of Marriage and the Family, 52,* 657–676.

Greenstein, T. N. (1995). Gender ideology, marital disruption, and the employment of married women. *Journal of Marriage and the Family, 57,* 31–42.

Hanson, T. L., McLanahan, S., & Thomson, E. (1998). Windows on divorce: Before and after. *Social Science Research, 27,* 329–349.

Hao, L. (1996). Family structure, private transfers, and the economic well-being of families with children. *Social Forces, 75,* 269–292.

Heaton, T. B., & Albrecht, S. L. (1991). Stable unhappy marriages. *Journal of Marriage and the Family, 53,* 747–758.

Heckert, D. A., Nowak, T. C., & Snyder, K. A. (1998). The impact of husbands' and wives' relative earnings on marital disruption. *Journal of Marriage and the Family, 60,* 690–703.

Heimdal, K. R., & Houseknecht, S. K. (2003). Cohabiting and married couples' income organization: Approaches in Sweden and the United States. *Journal of Marriage and Family, 65,* 525–538.

Hiedemann, B., Suhomlinova, O., & O'Rand, A. M. (1998). Economic independence, economic status, and empty nest in midlife marital disruption. *Journal of Marriage and the Family, 60,* 219–231.

Hoffman, S. D., & Duncan, G. J. (1988). What are the economic consequences of divorce? *Demography, 25,* 641–645.

Hoffman, S. D., & Duncan, G. J. (1995). The effect of incomes, wages, and AFDC benefits on marital disruption. *The Journal of Human Resources, 30,* 19–41.

Holden, K. C., & Smock, P. J. (1991). The economic costs of marital dissolution: Why do women bear a disproportionate cost? *Annual Review of Sociology, 17,* 51–78.

Huber, J., & Spitze, G. (1980). Considering divorce: An expansion of Becker's theory of marital instability. *American Journal of Sociology, 86,* 75–89.

Johnson, W. R., & Skinner, J. (1986). Labor supply and marital separation. *The American Economic Review, 76,* 455–469.

Joshi, H. (1998). The opportunity costs of childbearing: More than mothers' business. *Journal of Population Economics, 11,* 161–183.

Kreider, R. M., & Fields, J. M. (2001). *Number, timing and duration of marriages and divorces: Fall 1996* (Current Population Reports, Series P70–80). Washington, DC: U.S. Government Printing Office.

Lerman, R. I. (2002). *Marriage and the economic well-being of families with children: A review of the literature.* Washington, DC: The Urban Institute.

Light, A. (2004). Gender differences in the marriage and cohabitation income premium. *Demography, 41,* 263–284.

Lundberg, S., & Pollak, R. A. (1996). Bargaining and distribution in marriage. *Journal of Economic Perspectives, 10,* 139–158.

Manning, W. D., & Smock, P. J. (2000). "Swapping" families: Serial parenting and economic support for children. *Journal of Marriage and the Family, 62,* 111–122.

Marsiglio, W., Amato, P. R., Day, R. D., & Lamb, M. E. (2000). Scholarship on fatherhood in the 1990s and beyond. *Journal of Marriage and Family, 62,* 1173–1191.

Mauldin, T. A. (1990). Women who remain above the poverty level in divorce: Implications for family policy. *Family Relations, 39,* 141–146.

McLanahan, S., & Casper, L. (1995). Growing diversity and inequality in the American family. In R. Farley (Eds.), *State of the Union: America in the 1990s* (pp. 1–45). New York: Russell Sage Foundation.

McLanahan, S., & Sandefur, G. (1994). *Growing up with a single parent: What hurts, what helps.* Cambridge, MA: Harvard University Press.

McManus, P. A., & DiPrete, T. A. (2001). Losers and winners: The financial consequences of separation and divorce for men. *American Sociological Review, 66,* 246–268.

Meyer, D. R. (1998). The effect of child support on the economic status of nonresident fathers. In I. Garfinkel, S. McLanahan, D. R. Meyer, & J. A. Seltzer (Eds.), *Fathers under fire: The revolution in child support enforcement* (pp. 67–93). New York: Russell Sage Foundation.

Moen, P., & Sweet, S. (2003). Time clocks: Couples' work hour strategies. In Phyllis Moen name of editor (Ed.), *Its about time: Couples and careers* (pp. 17–34). Ithaca: ILR Press.

Molm, L., & Cook, K. (1995). Social exchange and exchange networks. In K. Cook, G. Fine, & J. S. House (Eds.), *Sociological perspectives on social psychology* (pp. 209–235). Needham Heights, MA: Allyn & Bacon.

Moore, K. A., & Waite, L. J. (1981). Marital dissolution, early motherhood and early marriage. *Social Forces, 60,* 20–40.

Morgan, L. A. (1991). *After marriage ends: Economic consequences for midlife women.* Newbury Park, CA: Sage.

Morrison, D. R., & Ritualo, A. (2000). Routes to children's economic recovery after divorce: Are cohabitation and remarriage equivalent? *Demography, 65,* 560–580.

Mott, F. L., & Moore, S. F. (1979). The causes of marital disruption among young American women: An interdisciplinary perspective. *Journal of Marriage and the Family, 41,* 355–365.

Nelson, T. J. (2004). Low-income fathers. *Annual Review of Sociology, 30,* 427–451.

Nock, S. L. (1995). Commitment and dependence in marriage. *Journal of Marriage and the Family, 57,* 503–514.

Nock, S. L. (1998). *Marriage in men's lives.* New York: Oxford University Press.

Nock, S. L. (2001). The marriages of equally dependent spouses. *Journal of Family Issues, 22,* 756–777.

Ono, H. (1998). Husbands' and wives' resources and marital dissolution. *Journal of Marriage and the Family, 60,* 674–689.

Ono, H. (2003). Women's economic standing, marriage timing, and cross-national contexts of gender. *Journal of Marriage and Family, 65,* 275–286.

Oppenheimer, V. K. (1994). Women's rising employment and the future of the family in industrial-societies. *Population and Development Review, 20,* 293–342.

Oppenheimer, V. K. (1995). The role of women's economic independence in marriage formation: A skeptic's response to Annemette Sorensen's remarks. In H.-P. Blossfeld (Eds.), *The new role of women: Family formation in modern societies* (pp. 236–243). Boulder, CO: Westview Press.

Oppenheimer, V. K. (2000). The continuing importance of men's economic position in marriage formation. In L. J. Waite, C. Bachrach, M. Hindin, E. Thomson, & A. Thornton (Eds.), *The ties that bind: Perspectives on marriage and cohabitation* (pp. 283–301). New York: de Gruyter.

Oppenheimer, V. K. (2003). Cohabiting and marriage during young men's career-development process. *Demography, 40,* 127–149.

Oppenheimer, V. K., Kalmijn, M., & Lim, N. (1997). Men's career development and marriage timing during a period of rising inequality. *Demography, 34,* 311–330.

Paasch, K. M., & Teachman, J. D. (1991). Gender of children and receipt of assistance from absent fathers. *Journal of Family Issues, 12,* 450–466.

Peters, H. E., Argys, L. M., Maccoby, E. E., & Mnookin, R. H. (1993). Enforcing divorce settlements: Evidence from child support compliance and award modifications. *Demography, 30,* 719–735.

Peterson, R. R. (1989). *Women, work, and divorce.* Albany, NY: State University of New York Press.

Peterson, R. R. (1996). A re-evaluation of the economic consequences of divorce. *American Sociological Review, 61,* 528–536.

Raley, R. K., & Bumpass, L. L. (2003). The topography of the plateau in divorce: Levels and trends in union stability after 1980. *Demographic Research, 8,* 245–259.

Raley, R. K., & Wildsmith, E. (2004). Cohabitation and children's family instability. *Journal of Marriage and Family, 66,* 210–219.

Risman, B. J., & Johnson-Sumerford, D. (1998). Doing it fairly: A study of postgender marriages. *Journal of Marriage and the Family, 60,* 23–40.

Rogers, S. J. (1999). Wives' income and marital quality: Are there reciprocal effects? *Journal of Marriage and the Family, 61,* 123–132.

Rogers, S. J. (2004). Dollars, dependency and divorce: Four perspectives on the role of wives' income. *Journal of Marriage and Family, 66,* 59–74.

Ross, H. L., & Sawhill, I. V. (1975). *Time of transition: The growth of families headed by women.* Washington, DC: The Urban Institute.

Sassler, S., & Schoen, R. (1999). The effect of attitudes and economic activity on marriage. *Journal of Marriage and the Family, 61,* 147–159.

Sayer, L. C., & Bianchi, S. M. (2000). Women's economic independence and the probability of divorce—A review and reexamination. *Journal of Family Issues, 21,* 906–943.

Sayer, L. C., Cohen, P. N., & Casper, L. M. (2004). *Women, men, and work*. Washington, DC: Population Reference Bureau/Russell Sage Foundation.

Schoen, R., Astone, N. M., Rothert, K., Standish, N. J., & Kim, Y. J. (2002). Women's employment, marital happiness, and divorce. *Social Forces, 81,* 643–662.

Seltzer, J. A. (2000). Families formed outside of marriage. *Journal of Marriage and the Family, 62,* 1247–1268.

Smock, P. J. (1993). The economic costs of marital disruption for young women over the past two decades. *Demography, 30,* 353–371.

Smock, P. J. (1994). Gender and the short-run economic consequences of marital disruption. *Social Forces, 73,* 243–262.

Smock, P. J., & Manning, W. D. (1997). Nonresident parents' characteristics and child support. *Journal of Marriage and the Family, 59,* 798–808.

Smock, P. J., Manning, W. D., & Gupta, S. (1999). The effect of marriage and divorce on women's economic well-being. *American Sociological Review, 64,* 794–812.

Sorensen, A. (1992). Estimating the economic consequences of separation and divorce: A cautionary tale from the United States. In L. J. Weitzman & M. Maclean (Eds.), *Economic consequences of divorce: The international perspective* (pp. 262–282). Oxford, England: Clarendon.

Sorensen, E. (1997). A national profile of nonresident fathers and their ability to pay child support. *Journal of Marriage and the Family, 59,* 785–797.

Sorensen, E. (2003). *Child support gains some ground*. Washington, DC: The Urban Institute.

South, S. J. (2001). The geographic context of divorce: Do neighborhoods matter? *Journal of Marriage and the Family, 63,* 755–766.

South, S. J., & Lloyd, K. M. (1995). Spousal alternatives and marital dissolution. *American Sociological Review, 60,* 21–35.

Spitze, G., & South, S. J. (1985). Women's employment, time expenditure, and divorce. *Journal of Family Issues, 6,* 307–329.

Sweeney, M. M. (2002). Two decades of family change: The shifting economic foundations of marriage. *American Sociological Review, 67,* 132–147.

Teachman, J. D. (1991). Who pays? Receipt of child support in the United States. *Journal of Marriage and the Family, 53,* 759–772.

Treas, J. (1993). Money in the bank: Transaction costs and the economic organization of marriage. *American Sociological Review, 58,* 723–734.

Tzeng, J. M., & Mare, R. D. (1995). Labor market and socioeconomic effects on marital stability. *Social Science Research, 24,* 329–351.

Vannoy, D., & Philliber, W. W. (1992). Wife's employment and quality of marriage. *Journal of Marriage and the Family, 54,* 387–398.

Waite, L. J. (1995). Does marriage matter? *Demography, 32,* 483–507.

Waite, L. J. (2000). The family as a social organization: Key ideas for the twenty-first century. *Contemporary Sociology, 29,* 463–469.

Weiss, R. S. (1984). The impact of marital dissolution on income and consumption in single-parent households. *Journal of Marriage and the Family, 46,* 115–127.

Weiss, Y., & Willis, R. J. (1997). Match quality, new information and marital dissolution. *Journal of Labor Economics, 15,* S293–S329.

Weitzman, L. (1985). *The Divorce Revolution*. New York: Free Press.

White, L. K., & Rogers, S. J. (2000). Economic circumstances and family outcomes: A review of the 1990s. *Journal of Marriage and the Family, 62,* 1035–1051.

Wilmoth, J., & Koso, G. (2002). Does marital history matter? Marital status and wealth outcomes among preretirement adults. *Journal of Marriage and Family, 64,* 254–268.

Yeung, W. J., & Hofferth, S. L. (1998). Family adaptation to income and job loss in the U.S. *Journal of Family and Economic Issues, 19,* 255–283.

Zimmer, M. (2004). How did divorced women fare in the 1990s? Analysis of work and hourly earnings. *The Social Science Journal, 41,* 267–277.

V

Coping With Divorce and Relationship Dissolution

20

Divorce as Prelude to Stepfamily Living and the Consequences of Redivorce

Lawrence Ganong and Marilyn Coleman
University of Missouri—Columbia

Jason Hans
University of Kentucky

Many researchers who have studied divorce, especially those who launched longitudinal projects, have gradually become stepfamily researchers. By the same token, many of us who started out primarily studying stepfamilies have "reached back" to explore divorce because of its importance as a precursor of remarriage and stepfamily living. Furthermore, redivorce, because of its frequency, is increasingly becoming a subject of interest for stepfamily researchers. Although often thought of by researchers and clinicians as separate processes, divorce and stepfamily dynamics are inexorably intertwined in the lives of many adults and children.

In the first section of this chapter, we examine the influences of prior divorce on repartnering, remarriage, stepfamily development, and stepfamily relationship maintenance. In the second section, we examine what is known about causes and consequences of redivorce in stepfamilies. Even though divorce occurs more frequently in remarried stepfamilies than in first-married families, the process of remarital dissolution has received minimal attention by researchers. We focus on intrapersonal, cultural, and interpersonal factors as causes of redivorce. Next, we will discuss implications of redivorce for practitioners and for policy-makers. Finally, we will suggest methods, theories, and research questions that need to be addressed in future scholarship on stepfamily dissolution.

DIVORCE AS A PRECURSOR OF REMARRIAGE: DEMOGRAPHICS

Approximately 40% to 50% of first marriages in the United States will end in divorce. This is the highest rate of divorce in the Western world, but it is an underestimate, because permanent separations are not included (Bramlett & Mosher, 2001). The majority of those who divorce eventually cohabit or remarry (Allan, Hawker, & Crow, 2004; Wu & Penning, 1997), although the rates for repartnering vary by ethnic and racial background, the sex and age of the persons divorcing, and other factors such as the presence of children, religious values, education, labor force participation, attractiveness, and opportunity (deGraff & Kalmijn, 2003).

Remarriage

Most divorced adults eventually remarry. For instance, in the Netherlands, 60% of men and a little over 40% of women remarry after divorce (deGraff & Kalmijn, 2003); in the United States, approximately 85% of people who divorce eventually remarry (Kreider & Fields, 2002). Of those who do remarry in the United States, 50% to 60% divorce again at least once. Nevertheless, many divorcees apparently remain optimistic about the institution of marriage—the rate of third and higher order marriages has increased dramatically over the past two decades, and these now make up 10% of all U.S. marriages (National Center for Health Statistics, 1993). Many people appear to keep trying until they "get it right."

Using three large random samples from the Netherlands (one sample of first-married persons, one of divorced persons who were not remarried, and one of divorced persons who were remarried), deGraff and Kalmijn (2003) examined the social, economic, and cultural determinants of repartnering by using discrete-time event-history analysis. For men, there was a significant downward trend in remarriage and an increase in cohabitation; for women, the remarriage rate remained the same but the rates of cohabitation went up. Both men and women who had been married longer were more likely to repartner after divorce. For men, more education was related to repartnering, but education was not related to women's chances of repartnering. Women who engaged in more activities outside the home or who attended church more often were significantly more likely to repartner. Divorced men who attended church more often were also more likely to repartner, but those who frequented bars were significantly less likely to remarry than those who did not. Having children at home negatively affected repartnering for both men and women.

Women's economic conditions after divorce affected their repartnering probabilities, but not in expected ways. Women with restricted finances were no more likely to repartner than other women. It was suggested that low-income women may be less attractive partners in the remarriage market, which tends to be less traditional in terms of gender-role expectations than the marriage market for first-time marriages. Working women actually had the highest repartnering rate, women on welfare, the lowest, and those who worked part time were in the middle in terms of repartnering. The reason seemed to be that work provides a social setting that favors repartnering, rather than anything related to socioeconomic status (SES) or financial security. The prestige of men's jobs also had no significant effect on repartnering, and men who owed child support or had financial obligations to their former wives were no less likely to repartner than those who did not. Therefore, economic theories of remarriage received little support. Cultural theories of remarriage were more important in that women with an individualistic orientation were less likely to remarry but just as likely to cohabit. Religious persons were not more or less likely to remarry, but they were less likely to cohabit after divorce.

Marital Transition Cycles

In addition to divorcing and remarrying often, people in the United States engage and disengage quite quickly. The median time from first marriage to divorce is 8 years, and from remarriage to divorce is 7 years (Kreider & Fields, 2002). The median length of time between the first divorce and remarriage is 3 years (Kreider & Fields), and this does not account for the fact that nearly 75% of people who remarry cohabit first, at least for a short time (Wilson & Clarke,

1992). The probability of cohabiting within 10 years of divorce in the United States is 70% (Bramlett & Mosher, 2001), and in Europe postdivorce cohabitation may be even higher (Allan et al., 2004). It also appears to be the case that a growing number of those who cohabit are doing so as an alternative to legal remarriage, and not as part of the courtship process (Ganong & Coleman, 2004). These defacto stepfamilies are widespread in Europe, North America, New Zealand, and Australia, although statistics regarding the prevalence of cohabiting stepfamilies are hard to come by.

Data are not available on the prevalence of multiple cohabiting relationships between marriages, so we have little idea of how many new partners divorced persons may typically have before they remarry. "Informal divorces" (i.e., the ending of a cohabiting relationship) are probably as important to the welfare of children, and perhaps the adults, as are legal divorces. Using data from the 1995 National Survey of Family Growth, Raley and Wildsmith (2004) found that adding transitions into and out of cohabitation to those into and out of marriage increased their measure of family instability by 30% for White children and over 100% for Black children. By age 12, White children have experienced 0.69 marital transitions and 0.90 marital and cohabitation transitions. Black children have experienced 0.55 marital transitions and 1.18 marital and cohabitation transitions.

Raley and Wildsmith (2004) noted that their measure of family instability was likely an underestimate because it ignored mothers' relationships with noncohabiting boyfriends. These men may spend considerable time in the household, including overnight stays, creating frequent transitions of people in and out of the household. It is critically important that researchers consider contextual factors such as race, ethnicity, SES, and family transitions other than marriage, divorce, and remarriage when they are investigating how children are affected by family changes. Much of the research about divorce and remarriage focuses on samples of White middle-class families or mixes different groups without analyzing subsets of data.

There is controversy over whether rapid remarriage following divorce is positive, neutral, or negative. Some have argued that, when children are involved, remarrying rapidly is positive because it does not allow time for the custodial parent and children to develop a family culture that may be difficult to change following remarriage (Rodgers & Conrad, 1986). If the single-parent-headed household has already established rules, rituals, and routines, it may not only be difficult for a new person to adjust to or assimilate into this culture, but any attempts to change the culture may be met with defiance and resentment. Others argue that adults need a period of personal assessment and contemplation regarding the previous marriage before leaping into the fray again, and that children need time to adjust to one major family transition (divorce) before being forced into another major family transition (remarriage). Both of these arguments are theoretical rather than data based, however, and they need to be explored further. In any event, regardless of whether or not it is a good idea, the fact remains that people tend to repartner or remarry rather quickly after divorce.

There are a number of potential reasons why remarriage occurs so rapidly after divorce in Western societies. First, in spite of the prominence of divorce and remarriage in Western culture, the stigma surrounding both remains strong (Ganong & Coleman, 2004). It is little wonder that people are anxious to quickly move from a status that they may view as branding them as "losers" or "damaged goods" to remarriage, which they may believe reestablishes them within the mainstream, especially if they mask their status by presenting themselves as a first-married family. This is not the only reason that people remarry quickly, however. There is evidence that men quickly begin seeking new partners because they tend to be emotionally dependent on their wives and seldom have other confidants (Hulbert & Acock, 1990). As a result of losing their confidant and emotional connection, men may become lonely and thus seek a replacement—someone who will listen to them and share emotions and a social life with them. Women also may be lonely, but they are more likely to have a well-developed friendship network that provides emotional connections and allows them to maintain an active social life (Baber & Allen, 1992), so their need for a partner is less salient strictly in social terms. Women with minor-age children, however, are often tied to the home. These women may seek partners not only because of loneliness, but because they need help meeting the financial responsibilities of caring for their children (Sweeney, 1997). Although there is controversy about the equity of postdivorce finances, it is often difficult for mothers to support their children at the level that was possible prior to the divorce (McManus & Diprete, 2001). The U.S. Census Bureau recently reported that only 45% of custodial parents who were owed child support payments received the full amount in 2001, and the average received was $5,800, so child support does not amount to a large sum; furthermore, often it is not paid in full or at all (Grall, 2003). Therefore, it is perhaps not surprising that remarried mothers frequently mention the importance of finances in in-depth interviews, although they seldom blatantly state that they remarried for financial reasons (e.g., to provide financial security for their children; see Schmeige, Richards, & Zvonkovic, 2001; Weaver & Coleman, 2004). A careful examination of the transcripts in the study by Weaver and Coleman highlighted the importance that finances played in the thinking of these remarried women, and it was clear that, for the majority of them, family breadwinning was primarily the responsibility of men.

The rapidity of postdivorce remarriage also appears to be related to who initiated the divorce in the prior marriage, particularly among women over the age of 35 years (Sweeney, 2002). Older women in unsatisfying marriages may be more likely than younger women to postpone initiating separations until they have determined that their prospects for another relationship are good. Age may be less of a factor for men in repartnering because social norms about gender and marriage (i.e., men marry younger partners, women marry older) tend to increase the potential pool of eligible partners for men as they age, whereas they diminish the pool for women. Divorce initiators may have been less happy in their prior marriages and thus more motivated to develop relationships with a new partner, and they may be more adjusted to divorce than noninitiators and thus ready for another relationship earlier than their former spouses. Other hypotheses are that divorce initiators may have more resources (e.g., confidence, high self-esteem) and are more capable of attracting new partners than noninitiators, and they may be drawn psychologically to change and stimulation. Finally, some of the initiators of divorce may have found a new partner before they started the divorce process (Ganong & Coleman, 2004).

A final reason for short durations between divorce and remarriage that we have observed but have only anecdotal evidence to report is that extremely religious couples who do not believe in cohabiting or having sexual relations outside of marriage remarry more quickly than others once they find a potential partner. This is a matter of short courtships once a suitable partner is found, however, rather than one of quick remarriages after divorce.

In general, divorced individuals make relatively quick decisions about future partners. It is unknown whether this is because they have a clear idea of what they want in a relationship and, when they find a person with the qualities they seek, they move with haste, or whether, because opportunities are few, they settle quickly when *any* potential partner appears. Ambert (1989), in a longitudinal study, found that multiply divorced persons remarried much more quickly, and after a shorter acquaintance, than once-divorced individuals. She concluded that getting married was important to the multiply divorced, whereas marrying the *right* partner was the goal of the once divorced. Although hasty remarriages have generally been viewed as problematic, data from the British General Household Survey showed that longer rather than shorter durations between divorce and remarriage were linked to redivorce (Lampard & Peggs, 1999).

POSTDIVORCE REMARRIAGE

We have speculated that how individuals evaluate and cope with divorce is related to how they adjust to postdivorce family life, which, in turn, is related to the functioning of postdivorce stepfamilies (Ganong & Coleman, 2004). There are a number of ways in which the evaluation of divorce might affect stepfamily living—for instance, adults and children who perceived that a divorce was basically a good transition for themselves and their family may view a subsequent remarriage and accompanying stepfamily relationships as a chance for a new start. If there has been spousal violence and a great deal of conflict and stress in the household, divorce may bring welcome relief for both children and adults, and remarriage may be seen as the inclusion of new people and additional resources (e.g., finances, affection). In contrast, some individuals who perceive divorce as good for themselves may be reluctant to reenter another marriage, especially if they have children. In addition, individuals who perceive the divorce as a crisis may not be motivated by the prospect of beginning again with a new partner, or they may welcome remarriage as an opportunity to return to the family life they miss.

Several studies conducted by Mavis Hetherington and her colleagues illustrate the relation between adjustment to divorce and remarriage and stepfamily living. Hetherington proposed six patterns of responses to divorce—Enhancers, Competent Loners, Good Enoughs, Seekers, Libertines, and The Defeated (Hetherington & Kelly, 2002). About 20% of the divorced adults in her studies reported that their lives were enhanced by divorce (Enhancers); their lives were improved in many ways, and their subsequent romantic relationships, including remarriage, were better than their first marriages had been. The Competent Loners, a smaller group of divorced adults, found greater success professionally and personally after their marriages ended, but they differed from the Enhancers in their desire to remarry. The marital experiences of the Competent Loners may have discouraged them from considering remarriage. Another group that avoided remarriage was the Defeated—these individuals were devastated by their divorce, depressed, and barely able to function. They probably lacked both energy and motivation to pursue new relationships, and in their depressed and embittered states would not be especially attractive to potential new partners. They also were more likely to be poor, which probably did not enhance their value as potential partners. In sharp contrast, Seekers remarried quickly after divorce. Nearly 40% of divorced adults in Hetherington's studies eagerly sought a new spouse, and many remarried within 1 year. The perceived security and regularity of married life appealed to these individuals. The Libertines also pursued relationships after divorce, but these were often limited to sexual encounters and seldom led to remarriage. The pursuit of sensual experiences was relatively short lived, however; more than 6 years after divorce, many of the Libertines were in faithful remarriages. Finally, a large group, the Good Enoughs, consisted of people who coped fairly well, adjusted to the challenges of divorce, and did their best to move on with their lives. They functioned adequately at childrearing, jobs, and interpersonal relationships, and they were able to resolve most of their problems. Their remarriages often were no better than their prior marriages, and they had similar problems as in their first marriages. Hetherington's typologies shed some light on postdivorce remarriages, but much more has to be known about the connections among first-marriage dynamics, divorce, and remarital dynamics.

Courtship for Remarriage

We do know several things about postdivorce remarriage courtship: Previously married individuals court for brief periods of time, they do little to prepare for remarriage, they tend to live together before remarriage, and their reasons for remarriage are apt to be pragmatic

(Ganong & Coleman, 2004). We also know that there are gender differences in remarriage courtship behaviors, and we know that remarriers are more likely than individuals in first marriages to wed someone who is different from themselves (e.g., age discrepancies, racial differences). Researchers generally report that remarriages are no more satisfying than first marriages (Rogers, 1996), and they are less stable (Amato & Rogers, 1997). Why does remarriage not lead to stronger, more stable marriages? Remarried individuals are typically older than those in first marriages and presumably wiser and more mature; they have had experience with the intense interpersonal relationships of marriage; and they may have learned from those experiences and gained insight into their expectations for marriage. Unfortunately, there is little evidence that such insights occur. Instead, there are numerous indicators that remarriage is viewed as a chance to reestablish the nuclear family with a new partner and to get it "right" this time—attributions are often that it was the previous partner who was flawed and not the person who divorced (Hopper, 2001). We found that couples who plan to remarry discuss practical things such as finding a large enough house to accommodate everyone, but they do not discuss much else. Ignored or avoided are subjects such as how to handle parenting (especially discipline) and finances (Ganong & Coleman, 1989), which are two areas that create the most conflict for remarried couples (Coleman, Fine, Ganong, Downs, & Pauk, 2001).

Why do people do so little preparation for remarriage? We speculate that several factors may come into play: (a) naivete, (b) avoidance, (c) lack of available resources in the community, and (d) adherence to societal myths about marriage, divorce, and remarriage (Ganong & Coleman, 2004). First, divorced adults are often naïve when contemplating the challenges of remarriages with children. If they have decided that their former partner was the "cause" of the divorce or that they were too young the first time, then the added complexity of melding households with children from prior unions is often not seen as much of a challenge; after all, this time the partner is the right one and they are older and wiser. Second, there is a tendency for divorced individuals to avoid discussing stressful, potentially toxic topics (Ganong & Coleman, 1989). For many people, as long as there are no overt conflicts, they can assume or pretend that any problems will be relatively simple to solve. Third, there may not be adequate resources for people to consult prior to remarriage. We have required graduate students taking a course on remarriage and stepfamilies to search our community for available stepfamily resources; they report being challenged to find informative materials and knowledgeable professionals (e.g., counselors, clergy) in a well-educated community that has three institutions of higher learning, a large regional public library, and two dozen bookstores. Although the Internet is readily available to many people, it does not appear to be heavily accessed and the quality of Web resources varies greatly. Finally, we argue that prevailing societal myths about marriage and divorce also affect how individuals think about remarriage. For example, the remarriage myths that "What is best for us is best for the children" and "Having a real family again is best for everyone" deny that children will have to make adjustments and may experience stress when a parent remarries. These myths allow adults to confuse their own joy and pleasant anticipation regarding the new partner with the children's reactions to the acquisition of a new stepparent. Unrealistic expectations often lead to a lack of remarriage preparation.

There are differences in how postdivorce remarriages in stepfamilies function compared with first marriages. Although there probably are many distinctions between the two, research on remarriage dynamics generally reveals two fundamental differences: (a) women tend to seek and gain more power in remarriages than they did in their prior marriages, and (b) remarriages develop and are maintained under the intimate watch of third parties who hold intense interests in the quality and stability of the remarriage, namely children from prior relationships and former spouses (or partners).

Marital Power in Stepfamilies

Decision Making

Divorced men and women think differently about marital roles as a result of earlier marital or relational experiences, which leads them to interact with new partners in more egalitarian ways (Burgoyne & Morison, 1997; Ishii-Kuntz & Coltrane, 1992). Many remarried women seek a greater decision-making role and more power than they had in their prior (first) marriages (e.g., Coleman & Ganong, 1989; Pyke, 1994), and remarried men share decision making with their wives more than first-marriage husbands do. The connections between prior divorce and single-parenting experiences and subsequent remarital behaviors are clearer for women than for men. Remarried women have been reported by researchers to exercise more control and power in regard to finances and childrearing than in other areas of stepfamily living.

Remarried women are more likely to be employed outside of the home than women in first marriages, and their financial contributions to the household tend to provide these women with more bargaining power (Pasley, Sandras, & Edmondson, 1994). They may have encountered financial difficulties in prior marriages when they did not have as much control over money (Burgoyne & Morison, 1997; Coleman & Ganong, 1989; Pyke, 1994), and, having managed finances for themselves and their children as single mothers, they are reluctant to lose financial power in a remarriage. Men also seek more egalitarian remarriages if they think marital power imbalances contributed to problems in their first marriages (Pyke & Coltrane, 1996). Remarried or repartnered individuals appear to use their previous marriage(s) or relationship(s) as a baseline by which to compare their current relationship.

Giles-Sims (1987) argued that ideology may help determine remarital power relations. Remarried couples may hold less traditional views about how marital roles should be performed. A more equitable contribution of resources coupled with a desire to share power or, at least, to share more power than they did in first marriages lead to marital processes that include implicit and explicit negotiations around issues of power and control.

Children

Unlike the more egalitarian decision-making processes in many aspects of remarriage, parenting is an area in which power is less often shared than in first marriages—women want to retain control of their children (Weaver & Coleman, 2004). Mothers may be unwilling to relinquish decision making over their children because they enjoy childrearing and consider themselves to be good parents that do not need help from their partners (Bray & Kelly, 1998). It may also be the way these women establish power within their household (Kranichfeld, 1987). Moreover, early in the remarriage, children generally do not welcome parenting behaviors exhibited to them by stepparents. Fathers are more willing to share responsibilities for childrearing, however, as can be seen in the studies of division of labor in stepfamilies.

Division of Labor in Stepfamily Couples

A trend toward more marital sharing of decisions about finances and women's exerting more power in remarriages does not necessarily mean that the division of household labor is equitable in remarriages. Although some researchers have found more sharing of household responsibilities in remarriages compared with first marriages, which were generally attributed to the greater resources brought to remarriages by wives (Ishii-Kuntz & Coltrane, 1992; Sullivan, 1997), other researchers have found that women do more household tasks in remarriages, including most of the care of their stepchildren (Demo & Acock 1993; Guisinger, Cowan, & Schuldberg, 1989). Other researchers have reported that labor is more evenly distributed in stepfather households than in first-marriage families (Deal, Stanley Hagen, & Anderson, 1992), although women do more than men do in both types of households.

Pyke and Coltrane (1996) argued that remarried individuals make judgments about gender-based entitlements and obligations to a spouse within the context of prior marital experiences. Remarried women may seek a more equitable power-sharing marriage when they move into greater involvement in the labor force, if this type of arrangement is what they and their spouses want. Other women may seek more shared power in remarriage than they had in their first marriage, but move out of the labor force, particularly if they had been employed in low-skill jobs in their first marriages and had felt forced to work outside of the home by dominant husbands. Pyke (1994) found that these divorced women purposefully sought men who would appreciate their unpaid family work and who made enough money to support that choice. Women who were reluctant to remarry gained bargaining power in these remarriages, which helped them assert more decision-making power. The men in these marriages wanted a stay-at-home wife and were willing to share power in exchange. Regardless of what couples chose to do, both men and women implicitly and explicitly compared their current spouses' participation in household labor and decision making to that of their former spouses (Pyke & Coltrane).

Clinicians have long asserted that stepfamilies fare better when the adults do not adhere to gendered stereotypes to guide their beliefs and behaviors (Carter, 1988). Exploring the links among decision making, equity, and the distribution of power in remarriage holds considerable potential for future research. Moreover, knowing the meanings that people have regarding work roles and family roles should yield a clearer understanding of the dynamics of remarried couples.

Remarriage Relationships Have an Intimate Audience

In newly formed remarriages, the relationship develops under the watch of intimate third parties who have vested interests in the quality and perhaps the stability of the remarriage. As the partners in a remarriage are developing new relationships with stepchildren and extended kin as well as with each other, they do so in the context of ongoing ties with their former spouses (as their children's other parent) and with their children. The presence of children from prior unions means that remarried couples have an audience of interested and potentially powerful third parties all or most of the time.

Children may have little motivation to help make the remarriage relationship strong, because they view the stepparent as an intruder into their relationship with the parent (Visher & Visher, 1996). In addition, because the parent–child bond is generally stronger and more durable than the couple relationship, at least early in remarriage, parents' loyalties may lie with their children more than with the partner. Children may want the couple to fail because the stepparent may represent lost status, power, and time with the parent. Even if they do not succeed in ending the couple relationship, children can disrupt adults' efforts to maintain a strong relationship, and they can divert attention away from efforts to build a satisfying couple relationship.

For example, clinicians (Visher & Visher, 1996) and researchers (Weaver & Coleman, 2004) have observed that, in single-parent households, sometimes a child becomes the parent's confidant. Children often enjoy their elevated status—sometimes older children in a single-parent household are allowed or even encouraged to discipline and supervise younger children. In essence, single parents sometimes promote a child or children to fulfill some of the functions of the nonresidential or absent parent. When this is the case, children may see a new stepparent as a competitor who has caused them to be demoted. Children may resent this demotion, even when they feel relief from the burdens of overseeing younger children and being responsible for mom or dad's emotional stability, and it may be difficult for the adult couple to establish the legitimacy of the new partner in the minds of the children (Visher & Visher). When children are jealous of the new stepparent, they may attempt to sabotage the new marriage in their efforts to regain their previous status.

Former partners can also be intrusive and disruptive to couples' relationship maintenance efforts. Relationships with former partners can make it difficult to establish boundaries around the remarried dyad, particularly when former partners are actively coparenting (Coleman, Ganong, & Weaver, 2001). Remarried persons who share parenting tasks with former partners have to figure out how to maintain a working relationship as parents, yet not let the former spouse intrude on the remarriage (Ganong, Coleman, & Weaver, 2002). This may be difficult for some individuals because, in first-marriage families, the married couple usually fulfills both parental tasks and marital tasks. In remarriages, the couple fulfills marital tasks but parental tasks may continue to be split between the children's parents (i.e., the residential parent and the children's nonresidential parent), or shared between the children's parents and the stepparent(s), or in the control of the residential parent only. Over time, especially when children are young, stepparents eventually do a large share of the childrearing in many stepfamilies, so there is not a clear-cut boundary between the marital and parental subsystems in all stepfamilies, but initially there often is.

Clearly, more studies are needed of the process of building satisfying remarriages after divorce. In particular, the effectiveness of couples' strategies to build close bonds has to be assessed. Given the theoretical and pragmatic importance of the adult couple relationship in stepfamilies, the lack of attention by researchers on bonding processes represents a major gap in understanding stepfamily development.

STEPRELATIONSHIPS IN POSTDIVORCE STEPFAMILIES

The stepparent–stepchild relationship in postdivorce stepfamilies is an important one for the stability and quality of the stepfamily. Stepparent–stepchild relationships that are characterized by hostility or passive aggressive resistance (by either party) create enough tension that virtually all other stepfamily relationships are adversely affected, as is the entire stepfamily.

The steprelationship obviously is affected by the behaviors, attitudes, and cognitions of both the stepparent and the stepchild, but other family members also are influential in the development of these relationships, most particularly the child's genetic parents and any children the stepparent might have from prior unions. Other factors also affect the development and quality of steprelationships, such as the length of time between parental marriages, the age and sex of stepchildren, the sex of stepparents, and how frequently the stepparents and stepchildren share a residence (Ganong & Coleman, 2004). Given the limited space we have in this chapter, we focus on three aspects related to steprelationships—stepparents' behaviors and stepchildren's reactions, the influences of the nonresidential parent, and the residential parents' roles in facilitating or preventing the development of the steprelationship.

Stepparents' Affinity Seeking

One challenge facing postdivorce stepfamilies is to determine which roles the stepparents will fulfill in children's lives. In many postdivorce stepfamilies, a stepparent is a third (or even a fourth, if both parents remarry) parent figure in a child's life. Is the stepparent going to be another parent, a friend, an acquaintance, or will there be any functional role for him or her to play? Stepfamily members may have thought about this very little, assuming that stepparents will replace nonresidential parents or that stepparents will have little to do in raising children from prior unions. In many cases, stepfamily members hold quite distinct expectations from each other regarding how the stepparent will interact with the stepchild, a situation that leads to much strife and stress (Coleman, Ganong, & Fine, 2000).

In an in-depth study that we conducted of a small number of stepfamilies, we found that the most successful stepparent–stepchild relationships were those in which the stepparent made a deliberate effort to get the stepchild to like him or her. The stepparents did this by engaging in activities that the stepchild enjoyed, by helping the stepchild do tasks such as homework, and by spending fun time together as a dyad (Ganong, Coleman, Fine, & Martin, 1999). Stepparents were most successful when they started these affinity-seeking and affinity–maintaining behaviors from the very start of the relationship and did not stop once they had remarried; stepparents who had engaged in affinity-seeking behaviors but terminated them when they remarried found that engaging in discipline and reducing the extent of friendship-maintaining activities resulted in more conflicted and distant relationships with stepchildren. Stepparents who had never engaged in efforts to develop friendships with their stepchildren had the most distant relationships.

Relational development is a bidirectional process. Stepparents' actions are only part of the process—good steprelationships are created when stepchildren respond to affinity-building efforts (Ganong et al., 1999). Much more research needs to be done on why stepchildren do or do not respond to stepparents' overtures to them. How stepchildren define their relationships with nonresidential parents and stepparents may be a key. White and Gilbreath (2001) examined three perspectives on the importance of residential stepfathers and nonresidential fathers on stepchildren, and they found support for what they called an accumulation model in which stepchildren incorporated both men into their lives. They recommended that researchers pay attention to how stepchildren feel about *all* of their parents and stepparents. White and Gilbreath also argued that how children *feel about* their parents and stepparents predicts children's outcomes better than does contact or involvement with stepfathers and fathers.

In contrast, how the adults *feel about* their roles has remained relatively unexplored as well. Marsiglio (2004) interviewed 36 stepfathers and, using grounded theory methodology, examined what he labeled paternal claiming, which he defined as "the stepfather's investment as a social father and represents a meaningful way for him to orient himself toward stepfamily life" (p. 23). According to Marsiglio, paternal claiming is broader than affinity seeking and affinity maintaining (Ganong et al., 1999) and is equated somewhat to a sense of "we-ness." The work of Weaver and Coleman (2004) reported earlier in this chapter indicates that mothers have influence over the development of a sense of we-ness and the ability of the stepfather to "claim" the stepchildren. Data from biological mothers indicate that fathers would have a difficult time with paternal claiming, especially those men in Marsiglio's study who indicated it was "all or nothing. . . . all father or nothing at all" (p. 29). Such men were not willing to marry a woman with children unless they could assume the father role. Marsiglio, in general, seemed to conclude that paternal claiming (and the subsequent embracing of the nuclear family model) was positive—that stepfathers who claimed their stepchildren as their own loved, nurtured, provided for, and served as advocates for their stepchildren in healthy ways. As a caveat, he said, "Of course, stepfathers may make significant contributions to stepchildren without claiming them." This view and the father's quotes contrasted sharply with those of nonresidential stepmothers, who felt great ambivalence about their role and were extremely careful *not* to claim their stepchildren as their own (Weaver & Coleman, in press). Although

Marsiglio indicated that some of the stepfathers in his study experienced feelings of ambiguity, it seemed to permeate his data much less than it permeated the data of Weaver and Coleman. He did state that, in most of the cases in which the stepfather claimed the stepchild as his own, the biological father was not involved with the child or only marginally so. That was not the case with the biological mothers in the Weaver and Coleman study. Data from these two qualitative studies would indicate that stepfathers are more invested than stepmothers in recreating nuclear family roles, but this may be confounded by where the stepchild lives most of the time. More in-depth qualitative investigations of various stepfamily structures are needed to gain insight into process in these variously configured families.

The Nonresidential Parent and Steprelationships

The ease with which a stepparent is welcomed into a stepchild's life or, conversely, the difficulty encountered by a stepparent trying to develop a positive steprelationship is partly affected by the presence or absence of the child's genetic nonresidential parent in the child's life, and partly by the quality of the nonresidential parent–child tie. If stepchildren feel opening themselves to developing a warm relationship with the stepparent is a betrayal of their nonresidential parent, then they are more likely to reject stepparents' overtures (Hetherington & Clingempeel, 1992) and to feel guilty when they do not reject them. Conversely, when stepchildren feel abandoned by their nonresidential parent or if they have a distant or hostile connection with them, then stepparents are often, but not always, more readily accepted by stepchildren. In such cases stepparents can fulfill many parental functions and children do not feel torn loyalty between their father and stepfather, or mother and stepmother.

There is some research evidence that nonresidential parents, particularly fathers, may reduce their involvement in children's lives after their own remarriage or their exwife's remarriage (Cooksey & Craig, 1998). Some nonresidential fathers withdraw from their children and transfer or substitute their paternal feelings and behaviors to stepchildren or to children born in new unions (Smock & Manning, 2000). It is not at all clear, however, that children are able to transfer filial feelings from a nonresidential parent to a stepparent, or even if they want to do so, unless they feel rejected by the parent.

The Residential Parent and Steprelationships

Residential parents can serve as gatekeepers to their children or they can facilitate the development of close stepparent–stepchild relationships (Bray & Kelly, 1998). Most residential parents in stepfamilies are mothers, because women are more likely to get physical custody of children following divorce. In an in-depth study of remarried mothers, Weaver and Coleman (2004) reported that, when remarriages began, being a mother was much more salient to the women's identity than her spousal role was. In general, remarried mothers saw their responsibilities as that of a *protector* for their children. They did this through four role functions: *gatekeeper*, *defender*, *mediator*, and *interpreter*. Gatekeeping regulated stepfathers' involvement in childrearing. Whether this is harmful to stepfamily functioning or not may depend on the stepfathers' role expectations. When stepfathers expect to be involved with children and make an effort to do so, then continued gatekeeping may be detrimental to stepfamily integration and individuals' well-being. The effect of the defender role on stepfamily integration is less ambiguous. Mothers who clearly valued the role of mother over the spousal role became defenders. Although defending lessened as children got older and the mothers determined the children could look after their own interests, the constant triangulation of mother and child against the stepfather places a strain on marriages (Browning, 1994). Defending suggests a lack of trust in the stepfather's abilities to raise children or an unwillingness to allow stepfathers and stepchildren to work out disagreements without the mother as a referee or child advocate. Defending creates coalitions that inhibit the growth of a family identity (Browning), mothers express discomfort at feeling the need to defend (Weaver & Coleman), and other studies have reported that stepfathers who are uncertain about how to relate to their stepchildren are less satisfied with their stepfamilies (Erera-Weatherly, 1996). Stepfathers' uncertainty may be a consequence of the lack of clear communication between mothers and stepfathers about desired childrearing roles—stepfathers may be asked to do some parenting duties (e.g., pay for school lunches, enforce curfews), but defended against when they overstep the mothers' preferences (Visher & Visher, 1996). Although the women Weaver and Coleman interviewed were remarried, we speculate that the marriages of mothers who continue to defend their children from the stepfather will be unstable. Although the mediator role of mothers was appreciated by stepchildren, the women found it to be stressful. Conversely, they perceived that the interpreter function worked well over time. We hypothesize that mothers do not engage in mediating or interpreting unless they are invested and committed to a long-term remarriage. We also hypothesize that cohabiting mothers would be less likely to engage in mediating and interpreting than remarried mothers, because cohabiting mothers are likely to be less committed to their partners than remarried mothers are to their spouses (Bumpass & Lu, 2000) and thus are less likely to make the added efforts demanded by mediating and interpreting.

Coparental Relationships and Stepparent–Stepchild Relationships

Most divorced parents are able to work together to some extent, although 20% to 30% of divorced couples' interactions can be classified as high conflict (Whiteside, 1998). Longitudinal studies suggest that disagreements between parents are highest in the first 2 years following separation, but that these gradually decrease in frequency (e.g., Hetherington, Cox, & Cox, 1982) because parents figure out how to cooperate better and because, in some families, they interact less often.

However, it is not unusual for divorced parents to continue to fight with each other because of resentment about the past marriage as well as the divorce process. For some couples, their mutual anger is an integral part of their postdivorce relationship. Mothers may use their control of children by means of physical custody by limiting fathers' access to children, and fathers may use child support to continue fighting (Visher & Visher, 1996). In these situations, children often get caught in the middle, and remarriage by either exspouse is likely to exacerbate the hostility.

One of the most robust findings we have about coparenting is that conflict between coparents is related to negative child outcomes (e.g., Amato & Booth, 1996; Clingempeel & Brand-Clingempeel, 2004). Stepfamilies formed by adults who are engaged in angry interactions with their expartners over coparenting are more likely to have children who are having problems. Children who are having interpersonal or intrapersonal problems are likely to present more challenges for parents and stepparents and to create more stressful stepfamily household dynamics (Tzeng & Mare, 1995).

Sometimes stepparents can help by serving as a neutral go-between for the children, but they also may team up with their spouse in the continuing battle with the expartner. Jealousies among the (step)parents make it difficult for children to establish positive relationships with any of the adults (Crosbie-Burnett, 1984). It is difficult for a stepparent to enter such a volatile situation. A parent may say damaging things to the children about the other household's stepparent as a means of upsetting the exspouse. These efforts, in turn, may make it difficult for the stepparent–stepchild relationship to positively evolve.

In contrast, when coparents get along too well, a stepparent might find it difficult to define roles within the stepfamily for himself or herself because there may be little room for another parent figure. Conflicts and jealousy may be more common between the parent and the stepparent (i.e., between father and stepfather or between mother and stepmother), and, ironically, loyalty conflicts for the children may be more common as well. However, cooperative coparent relationships may provide the most functional postdivorce stepfamily relationships for the original family members. Cooperative coparents are the most likely to make compromises for the sake of the children and to not let conflicts escalate into power struggles (Ahrons, 1994).

STEPFAMILY DEVELOPMENT AND RELATIONSHIP MAINTENANCE IN POSTDIVORCE STEPFAMILIES

Although all families face barriers to growing positively as a unit, it should be somewhat clear by now that the development and maintenance of stepfamilies is a complex business that often goes awry. Compared with first-marriage family relationships, which benefit from clear cultural norms, well-defined relational and household boundaries, and an abundance of social support, stepfamily relationships are ambiguous and inherently more complex. There are few established norms for stepfamilies to follow, and as a result the first-marriage family model is the default template on which stepfamily members measure success. This often leads to frustration for stepfamily members, because only a small percentage of stepfamilies (those in which a nonresidential parent has removed himself or herself from the child's life) are able to fit into the mold of a nuclear family. Trying to enact family roles that develop slowly over time in nuclear families has destined many stepfamilies for disappointment and failure. For example, the men in Marsiglio's study who only felt the we-ness of family when the stepchildren called them "Dad" are likely to be disappointed if the stepchildren do not do that. The very definition of we-ness, feeling "like a family" (Braithwaite, Olson, Golish, Soukup, & Turman, 2001), and other definitions that stepfamily members use to describe their experiences are often based on the nuclear family model rather than the evolving more ambiguous nature of stepfamily relationship development.

The fact that research indicates that stepparents have to work at building a relationship with a child in their care is anathema to many people's senses of family. Those who expect family feelings to evolve without proactively pursuing relationship development are bound to be disappointed. It is unrealistic to expect a stepfamily, especially one formed when the children are school age or older, to have the same relationship dynamics as a first-married family. We forget that nuclear family relationships build over time, and that our bonding with biological children is no more instant than our bonding with stepchildren—it may seem that way because bonds begin to develop even before a child is born. The development and maintenance of stepfamily relationships then hinge greatly on realistic expectations, education, and hard work.

Clinical Implications of Stepfamily Research

Clinicians have long made pleas to stepfamily members to avoid trying to re-create the first-married nuclear family, but perhaps more attention has to be devoted to how those who are successful at doing this have accomplished their goal. It is also critical that more assistance be provided to those who are trying new and creative ways to manage stepfamily living. Clearly defined concrete suggestions for attempting innovative family strategies will greatly assist stepfamily members in achieving their family goals. Suggestions that the stepparent not take a disciplinary role, at least early in family formation, is about as specific as the advice gets. And in many ways, stepfamilies, by virtue of being a family, have to function similarly to all families—children have to be fed, houses have to be cleaned, yards have to be mowed, children have to be sent off to school and be helped with homework. There is nothing particularly unique about much of the process that must occur in stepfamilies. Perhaps greater attention to those ways that stepfamilies are like other or "normal" families (as the individuals in stepfamilies often refer to traditional nuclear families) will help partially normalize the experience and allow them to be more open to suggestions regarding the stepfamily process that probably needs to diverge from traditional nuclear family models.

Hetherington's (2002) found that the Good Enough pattern, in which remarriages were very similar to first marriages, was the most frequent pattern in her sample. These findings suggest that the re-creation of past family patterns is a powerful dynamic influencing the quality of remarriages and stepfamily life. These repeated family patterns may go back much further than just the previous marriage. Family systems and attachment theories suggest that family patterns are likely to be repeated across generations (Boszormenyi-Nagy & Spark, 1973), and there is a growing body of research that has provided empirical support for the intergenerational transmission of family patterns (Kretchmar & Jacobvitz, 2002; van IJzendoorn, 1995). Some of the patterns of interaction that stepfamilies are repeating from first marriages may actually have their roots in previous generations. Thus, clinicians may be able to help stepfamilies prevent the re-creation of problematic patterns by helping them to identify relationship patterns that are rooted in previous generations, determine which patterns are beneficial and which are likely to lead to similar problems that were experienced in previous relationships, and acquire skills for changing problematic relationship patterns. Working to change intergenerational patterns is clearly a process that requires a large investment of time and effort. It is not a quick-fix solution, but the payoff may be substantial.

Characteristics of Successful Stepfamilies

On the basis of a connection between the previous family and the new stepfamily, Visher and Visher (1990) delineated six characteristics of successful stepfamilies that can serve as a guide to stepfamily members. The six characteristics are as follow: (a) family members have grieved the loss of the previous family; (b) the remarried couple presents a unified front; (c) family members have realistic expectations; (d) family members have good relationships with each other; (e) relationships between households are cooperative; and (f) productive rituals are enacted. Thus far, however, there has been little guidance on how family members can actually implement these suggestions. We briefly explore areas for application within each of the six characteristics.

Loss and Grieving

Grieving for a previous family is a task that is often lost on the remarrying adults. Rather than processing the relationship failure, some adults remarry quickly to avoid the discomfort associated with being perceived (by others or by themselves) as inadequate partners. They are typically happy to have another chance at loving and being loved by a partner. Children, in contrast, may be upset about losing their family of origin forever, especially if adults are not aware of and respectful of their distress. Children's grief is probably exacerbated by the fact that they had no control over their parents' decisions to either divorce or remarry.

Presenting a United Front

It is often difficult for a remarried couple to present a united front to the children. The biological parent knows much more about her or his children than a stepparent is likely to know for many years. Because of this, biological children and parents often form a coalition against the stepparent when there are disagreements regarding the children. Most children are sharp enough to know that, when the remarried couple (in a united front) presents new rules, the stepparent was the instigator. Why, for example, would Mom all of a sudden decide that the kids cannot watch TV at the dinner table when they had been doing that for 3 years? Did Mom suddenly decide that it was not cool to do that? A united front is certainly a good idea, but couples need to think carefully about what changes need to be made and why. It is likely that if the stepparent requests too many household rule changes that the parent will start breaking rank and begin siding with the children anyway.

Realistic Expectations

Having realistic expectations is certainly an excellent piece of advice. The problem, however, is that stepfamily members are often unaware of which expectations are realistic and which are not. Solving the expectation problem is a challenge for even the most skilled therapist and can be likened to a detective looking for clues to an ancient murder. The stepparent who has always been well liked by children and has perhaps had a career as a popular teacher, may expect his or her stepchildren to like them as well. This would not seem like an unreasonable or unrealistic expectation, but stepchildren may associate the stepparent with the pain, anger, frustration, and loss of their family of origin—or they may see the person as the reason they can no longer watch TV during dinner. They may decide in advance that they are not going to like a stepparent for fear it will upset their nonresidential parent—it is hard in our society to be accepting of more than two parents at a time. Unfortunately, remarrying individuals seldom share their expectations for their newly forming stepfamily, and they tend to neither solicit nor share expectations even when the adults share. It is difficult to meet expectations if you feel insecure about what you are doing, but it is impossible to meet unexpressed expectations. Perhaps, for this reason, stepfamilies that are re-creating nuclear families have the easiest time—they repeat old patterns and this brings comfort to some stepfamily members.

Good Relationships Within and Across Households

It is certainly helpful when stepfamily members have good relationships with each other and with those in the other household. However, once again, individuals are not always sure what good relationships should look like. Do good relationships with each other replicate biological relationships? Do you go to the movies together, share holidays, keep contact to a minimum but be pleasant when contact is unavoidable? Therapists have made suggestions, but research on how to maintain good relationships between households is quite limited. There is evidence that frequent contact is not a good thing when the contact is conflictual, but how much contact is appropriate when it is not conflictual?

The quality of relationships within the household is probably quite interrelated with expectations. Some women remarry because they want a partner for themselves; they do not want their husband to take an active role with the children. Some women remarry because they want a partner to help with the burden of childrearing, especially when those children are adolescent males, it seems. Others may remarry to secure financial stability for their children. A good relationship with the spouse might look quite different in these three scenarios, and we have only included one side of the equation. Clinicians have suggested that a stepparent reprise the role of friend with her or his stepchildren, but some adults have no clue what it means to be a friend with a child. It also is a bit unrealistic if the adult takes the notion of friend seriously. For example, few adults remind their friends to brush their teeth before they go to bed, to do their homework, or to remember their mother's birthday. Yet, stepparents often find themselves in a role in which these tasks are required of them.

Rituals

Enacting rituals is something that we have discovered few stepfamilies think much about. Some try to incorporate all the rituals from the old families, some drop rituals completely, and others have instigated new rituals without even realizing it. Having rituals is an important part of family life, and it is especially hard for children to lose rituals that were important to them. If they always went to the country with their dad to cut down a Christmas tree, they may resent it if their stepfather tries to take them to a Christmas tree farm. Sometimes children find security or comfort in mundane or uncommon activities that adults fail to recognize as rituals. Children may have a difficult time understanding or expressing their sense of loss when adults unknowingly abandon those covert rituals, leaving parents perplexed by children's behavior. For example, the nonresidential dad may have gotten the children up by singing a funny song in the morning while mom was cooking breakfast. Mom may not even have been aware that he did this, nor would she have necessarily thought of it as an important ritual. Children may feel otherwise and be grouchy in the morning when either the mom or stepdad tries to get them up. The mom may be mystified by the grouchy behavior and the stepdad may think the kids are just unpleasant in the morning.

Unearthing the clues to building and maintaining relationships in remarriage is not easy, and researchers have probably not been concrete enough in some of their investigations and reporting of the data to provide much assistance to stepfamilies. There is little evidence that divorce, remarriage, and other forms of family diversity will lessen over time. It is important that more specific attention be given to relationship development in stepfamilies by researchers and practitioners alike. It is also important that the suggestions be at a level that is concrete enough that stepfamily members can understand and practice them.

REDIVORCE IN STEPFAMILIES: CAUSES OF REDIVORCE

Although there have been few studies of the processes surrounding redivorce per se, it is possible to examine a few likely causes for redivorce. Among the causes of redivorce that researchers have proposed and examined are (a) intrapersonal factors that predispose individuals to leave relationships quickly; (b) cultural factors, such as inadequate societal support for stepfamilies; and (c) interpersonal factors, such as family and relational conflicts and the stress that ensues from such strife (Ganong & Coleman, 2004).

Intrapersonal Factors

Some researchers have proposed that remarriages are more likely to end than first marriages because there are a greater proportion of remarried individuals who possess personality characteristics that predispose them to marital dissolution (Johnson & Booth, 1998). Characteristics such as need for stimulation, low frustration tolerance, and intolerance of ambiguity have been mentioned as possible intrapersonal factors that do not predict stable relationships. Other personal problems, such as substance abuse or depression, have been found to occur more often among remarried adults, and these may be either contributors or consequences of redivorce. There is some support for these hypotheses, but the evidence is not overwhelming that intrapersonal factors are major causes of redivorce.

Cultural Factors

Cherlin (1978) wrote long ago that stepfamilies were incomplete institutions that lacked norms to guide the behaviors of stepfamily members and social support from legal and social institutions. Cherlin's contention was that the absence of societal aids (i.e., norms and institutionalized social support) made it harder for stepfamilies to solve problems and avoid redivorce. Although this argument has not always been sustained by subsequent research, most researchers who have examined the incomplete institutionalization hypothesis have found evidence that supports it (e.g., Fine, Coleman, & Ganong, 1998; Hequembourg, 2004).

Other researchers have argued that social stigma and stereotypes related to stepfamily membership add stress, which thus makes it harder for stepfamilies to function well and discourages them from seeking outside support when they encounter problems (Scanzoni, 2004). Although few have investigated the effects of social stigma on stepchildren, there is some evidence to support this proposition (Lansford, Ceballo, Abbey, & Stewart, 2001).

It should be noted that most research on stepfamilies has been based on middle class, European American samples, although there has been a marked increase in recent years of studies conducted in countries other than the United States. Cultural factors may affect re-marriages and stepfamilies differently in diverse contexts. For example, some scholars have speculated that African Americans, because of their collectivistic cultural values and shared historical experiences with discrimination and marginalization, are generally more accepting of stepfamilies than other ethnic groups in the United States and are more flexible in creating functional stepfamily processes (Crosbie-Burnett & Lewis, 1993). These ideas are intriguing, but they have yet to be examined empirically. Given the diversity of values and experiences between different racial and ethnic groups in any given society, it seems probable that cultural influences on postdivorce stepfamilies may vary between different racial and ethnic groups.

Research evidence from studies outside the United State suggests that postdivorce step-families share more similarities than differences across societies (e.g., Church, 1999; Dunn, Davies, O'Connor, & Sturgess, 2001; Flinn, 1999; Russell & Searcy, 1997; Wu, 1994). More-over, cultural stereotypes and attitudes about stepfamilies are generally similar across societies (e.g., Claxton-Oldfield, Goodyear, Parsons, & Claxton-Oldfield, 2002; Ganong, Coleman, & Mapes, 1990). Clinical evidence from abroad also supports this conclusion that postdivorce families are more the same than different (e.g., Batchelder, Dimmock, & Smith, 1994; De'Ath, 1997; Webber, 1991). However, it would be premature to conclude that postdivorce stepfamily dynamics are the same all over the world—differences in social policies and laws regarding postdivorce obligations of parents diverge markedly between countries, as do social policies and laws about stepparents' rights and responsibilities, so it appears unlikely that cultural and societal influences are unimportant in understanding stepfamily dynamics. It may be that cultural effects on postdivorce stepfamilies are so subtle that researchers have yet to uncover them, or perhaps we know so little about cultural influences on stepfamilies because study designs and measurements have yet to be developed to achieve this goal.

Gay and Lesbian Stepfamilies

Postdivorce stepfamilies headed by gay and lesbian couples illustrate the importance of societal factors on relational dynamics. Although accurate statistics are difficult to obtain, estimates are that between 7% (Blumstein & Schwartz, 1983) and 21% (Bryant & Demian, 1994) of lesbian couples have children in their care—estimates of gay couples with children are generally lower (9%), mostly because women tend to get physical custody of children after divorce (Bryant & Demian).

Gays and lesbians can potentially create stepfamilies in one of three ways: (a) one or both adults have reproduced in heterosexual relationships or adopted children that they bring to the union; (b) donor insemination (mostly for lesbians) or surrogate mothers (for gays) allow for reproduction after the couple has gotten together; and (c) adoption, either second-parent (one adult partner adopts the other's child) or stranger adoption. Adoption by gay and lesbian individuals is still relatively rare in the United States (Hequembourg, 2004), because living parents must give up parental rights in second-parent adoptions and laws in some states make stranger adoptions difficult for homosexual individuals (and impossible for homosexual couples). Social stigma is a barrier for all types of adoptions by gay and lesbian individuals. Consequently, having children from prior relationships and eliciting aid from outsiders to reproduce after the formation of the homosexual union are the most frequent avenues to forming gay and lesbian stepfamilies.

One societal effect on gay and lesbian stepfamilies is that few members of such families think of themselves as being in stepfamilies, partly because the concept of stepfamilies to most gay and lesbian individuals implies remarriage (L.A. Kurdek, personal communication, June 18, 2003), a legal status that has not been available to homosexuals (in the United States, at least). Instead, first-marriage (nuclear) families appear to be the implicit model used by many gay and lesbian couples in stepfamilies. Some scholars have argued that using the nuclear family model is an attempt by gays and lesbians to avoid further stigma (Berger, 1998; Lynch, 2000; Lynch & Murray, 2000).

Tasks that gay and lesbian stepfamilies face in common with heterosexual postdivorce stepfamilies include the following: Negotiating childrearing with nonresidential parents, developing positive stepparent–stepchild relationships, coping with children's loyalties to both genetic parents, helping stepparents and nonresidential stepchildren feel that they belong, and developing a comfortable identity as a stepparent or stepchild (Berger, 1998; Erera & Fredriksen, 1999; Hall & Kitson, 2000; Hequembourg, 2004). These challenges are primarily faced by gays and lesbians with children from prior relationships, because when children are born after the formation of the homosexual union, nonresidential parents are rarely involved in children's lives (e.g., they may be anonymous sperm donors), the nonparent in the household rarely identifies himself or herself as a stepparent, and children consider both adults to be their parents (Hare & Richards, 1993; Lynch & Murray, 2000; Nelson, 1996). However, all gay and lesbian stepfamilies must deal with the absence of legal obligations and rights (Mason, Fine, & Carnochan, 2004). Marriage, and the legal rights and responsibilities attendant to marriage, is not available to gay and lesbian couples, and this lack of legal ties creates problems, especially when children are involved. When an adult and a child or children are not legally related, as is the case with stepparent–stepchild relationships, than the dissolution of the adult couple from death or separation can and often does sever the stepparent–stepchild relationship. Although heterosexual stepparents are slowly gaining legal rights to be involved with stepchildren after the dissolution of their marriage by filing for third-party visitation or by filing civil suits to gain access to stepchildren (Mason et al.), these are not likely to be successful strategies for homosexual stepparents. Finally, given the social stigma faced by gay and lesbian couples, and the challenges they face in establishing individual and family identities that are acceptable to themselves and to the society as a whole, it is not surprising that several scholars have applied Cherlin's (1978) notion of incomplete institutionalization to gay and lesbian stepfamilies (Hall & Kitson, 2000; Hequembourg, 2004).

Interpersonal Factors

There are potentially many interpersonal causes for redivorce, ranging from conflicts between spouses, stepparent–stepchild problems, interference of the former spouses into remarriage and stepfamily dynamics, parent–child difficulties, and the widespread complexity of stepfamilies (Ganong & Coleman, 2004). Most of the interpersonal explanations focus on conflicts and the ensuing stress as pressures that wear down remarriages; in the case of stepfamily complexity, stress is a by-product of people's feeling confused and overwhelmed by the number of roles and relationships for which they are unprepared, leading to redivorce.

The two primary sources of conflict in remarriages are finances and children (Coleman, Fine, et al., 2001). These two sources of conflict may underlie many, if not most, remarital dissolutions.

Remarital Conflicts Over Finances

Although many couples in stepfamilies face economic hardships because they lack sufficient resources to meet family members' needs, lack of funds may not be the primary source of financial problems for stepfamily couples. Instead, deciding how resources will be distributed has been reported to be a major source of conflicts (Coleman, Fine, et al., 2001). Although women generally have more say in financial matters in their remarriages than they had in their prior marriages (e.g., Burgoyne & Morison, 1997), the ways in which finances are managed by stepcouples are incredibly diverse (Burgoyne & Morison). Partly because of financial commitments to support children from present and from prior unions (who may or may not reside in the stepfamily household), and partly because of remarried individuals' desires to retain some degree of financial independence, remarried couples are more likely than those in first marriages to maintain at least part of their economic resources under the individual control of each partner.

In addition to the complexity of multiple "pots" of money to manage, there is the issue that, in many stepfamilies, remarried couples' decisions about finances are connected to, and sometimes dependent on, economic decisions and behaviors of former partners (e.g., paying or not paying child support; asking for more financial aid for children's expenses). This means that remarried couples may have to delay or forgo purchases because of decisions made by a former spouse (e.g., about children's health care or education). It is frustrating to remarried individuals when former spouses or children from earlier unions make decisions about how their household income or how a partner's income will be spent. Even when the individuals in a stepcouple have negotiated decisions about distributing their household finances that are agreeable to each other, stress and conflict can ensue if expected child support payments are not received or are late.

Remarital Conflicts Over Children

Arguments related to raising stepchildren are a major source of stress in stepfamilies. The classic issues are when parents perceive that stepparents are too strict in setting rules and too punitive in enforcing rules, or when parents and stepparents hold widely disparate expectations for the proper behavior of children.

As we noted earlier in this chapter, stepparents are often unsure how to interact with stepchildren, and they often define their roles in ways that are not compatible with others' definitions for stepparent roles (Ganong & Coleman, 2004). Conflicts that lead to marital dissolution may occur when stepparents, usually stepfathers, attempt to take a more active role than biological parents think is appropriate. If stepparents persist, then children and parents may form alliances against the stepparent, leading to tension and the breakdown of the step-family household along prior family lines. Stepparents are treated as outsiders, which leads to increasingly uncomfortable marital relationships, and, possibly, dissolution. These dynamics are more common in stepfather–mother households (they are more common than stepmother–father households); they also occur in complex stepfamily households in which both adults bring children from prior unions into the stepfamily. In complex households, having different rules for children from different original families leads to marital conflicts that can threaten marital stability.

It should be noted that most of what we know about remarital conflict over stepchildren is from clinicians rather than researchers. There is a great need for research that examines the processes by which disputes over childrearing in stepfamilies lead to remarital problems.

Stepparent-Stepchild Conflicts

Conflicts in stepfamilies often are related to adolescents' externalizing and internalizing behaviors (Doyle, Wolchik, & Dawson-McClure, 2002). Researchers speculate that stepchil-dren may move out or withdraw from others as a way to keep peace in the family and to try to maintain their own well-being (Hanson, McLanahan, & Thomson, 1996). However, not all researchers have found that stepfamilies have more conflicts than do first-marriage families (Salem, Zimmerman, & Notaro, 1998). The amount of conflict in stepfamilies may be greater when stepchildren are adolescents than when they are younger. This may be because adoles-cents resist directions and discipline from a stepparent more than do younger stepchildren. Regardless of the reason, adolescent stepchildren often report more conflict with stepparents than do adolescents in first-marriage families (e.g., Kurdek & Fine, 1993).

CONSEQUENCES OF REDIVORCE

We know of no research on the outcomes of redivorce, other than the studies that have found that the more their residential parent experiences relational transitions, the more poorly the children fare (Martinez & Forgatch, 2002; Wu & Thomson, 2001). Anecdotally, we know that former stepparents and stepchildren tend to sever relationships with each other after redivorce, but there have been no studies of what happens to stepfamily relationships following redivorce.

IMPLICATIONS OF REDIVORCE FOR PRACTICE AND POLICY

Redivorce has become increasingly common, and it probably results at least partially from un-realistic expectations on the part of the remarried couple. These expectations, many emanating from attempts to replicate a nuclear family model, can be remedied with skillful intervention by practitioners who are well versed in stepfamily dynamics. It is critical that therapists, family life educators, and other professionals who work with families have knowledge of stepfamily dynamics so they do not collude with stepfamily members in their attempts to replicate the nuclear family model. Therapists and faculty in counseling programs continue to be somewhat unaware that helping professionals need special training to fully understand stepfamily dynam-ics. It is not known if stepfamily members now feel better served than was true over a decade ago (Ganong & Coleman, 1989), but there is little evidence that programs have done much to incorporate this information into their curriculum. Therapists such as Papernow (2001) and

Browning (1994) have developed excellent materials related to stepfamily intervention, and the Stepfamily Association of America publishes relevant information (www.saafamilies. org).

One of the long-standing challenges that clinicians have grappled with is how to intervene with stepfamilies *before* they run into serious problems. Noted stepfamily clinicians Visher and Visher (1996) contended that most stepfamily problems were preventable, and yet, as we noted earlier in this chapter, most adults do little to prepare themselves prior to remarriage (Ganong & Coleman, 1989). Consequently, many efforts to educate stepfamily couples and prevent problems before they reach crisis proportions have been tried, and, for the most part, they have not been widely successful. In our view, their lack of success is not because of deficits in the quality of interventions but because they have not been utilized. Perhaps the Web will yield new opportunities for stepfamily interventions.

Clinicians and educators, as well as stepfamilies themselves, would be well advised to attend to resilience strategies used by other types of marginalized families, such as Blacks and gay and lesbian stepfamilies. It may be that new paradigms of teaching about and doing therapy with stepfamilies are needed—perhaps by focusing on interpersonal strategies such as intentionality and affirming redefinitions (Oswald, 2002). Intentionality strategies are used by gay and lesbian stepfamilies, and they include creating a kin network of friends and members of the family of origin, managing disclosure of family identity and relationships, building community with supportive resources within and outside of kin networks, and engaging in rituals that affirm identities and create supportive environments. Redefining includes conceptualizing and envisioning family in more inclusive ways than just biological or legal relationships.

It is more difficult to speculate about policy than it is to speculate about intervention. Policies related to the definition of family are necessary. For example, we know of many cases in which stepfamily relationships are not honored as immediate family by hospitals in intensive care units. This is clearly not appropriate policy on the part of institutions. It is our impression that public schools have improved greatly in recognizing that the families of school-aged children are complex and varied. It is much less common now for children to have to make the painful decision of which parents to list when only one line is available on information forms. Family law is slowly addressing issues such as child visitation between stepparent and stepchild after redivorce (Hans, 2002), but there are no universal policies about this as yet. As a result, all ties between stepchildren and stepparents are often severed after redivorce, which may seem more normal to the stepparent than to the stepchild. To a 10-year-old child who was raised by a stepparent for 7 or 8 years of her or his life, the child is potentially losing a major figure of importance; 7 or 8 years is a much smaller proportion of the adult's life. Because we have no policies about maintaining ties after divorce, it may even seem an inappropriate thing to do to some stepfamily members. Clearly, given the prevalence of remarriage and redivorce, policies are needed that help children maintain ties with stepfamily members who have been important to them. Policies that legitimate stepfamily members as "family" are also important in relation to institutions such as schools, health care, and religious organizations.

FUTURE DIRECTIONS FOR RESEARCH ON STEPFAMILY DISSOLUTION

The processes of divorce, remarriage, and redivorce are relatively common experiences, and yet to our knowledge there have been few studies of the processes that connect these transitions (Coleman et al., 2000). Researchers have focused on transition outcomes for both adults and children; discussions about transitional processes have generally been left to clinicians. However, in recent years, there has been an increase in qualitative research designs that emphasize processes in stepfamilies (e.g., Coleman, Fine, et al., 2001; Marsiglio, 2004). We are optimistic that this trend will continue, and that future studies using grounded theory methods and other approaches will continue to shed light on stepfamily changes such as divorce, remarriage, and redivorce. Future studies of postdivorce stepfamily relationships and stepfamily processes over time should include *interhousehold* negotiations and communications, and these studies should include the perspectives and experiences of multiple family members, including nonresidential parents and other family members who do not live in the stephousehold. Stepfamily living varies remarkably across family members—there are multiple, often competing agendas held by stepfamily members, so gathering data from parents, stepparents, and stepchildren yields a more comprehensive picture than when only one family position is studied.

In addition, there is a need for demographic studies that provide a better understanding of where and with whom people live after divorce, whether it be in remarried or in cohabiting stepfamilies. For instance, demographic studies are needed that distinguish between first and higher order remarriages, that capture the complexity of postdivorce stepfamily households, and that include cohabiting heterosexual couples with children from prior marriages, gay and lesbian couples with children, and large subsamples of African American, Asian American, and Latino stepfamilies.

There is a need for scholars to expand and build on previous research. For instance, we know that few people prepare for remarriage (Ganong & Coleman, 1989), but we do not know why this is the case. We also do not know what, if anything, cohabiting couples do to prepare for living together. In addition, what kinds of information do divorced individuals want who are planning to marry again? Are there particular delivery systems that would work better than others for these busy adults? What are the barriers to remarriage preparation? What motivates some individuals to seek help or advice?

Earlier in the chapter we mentioned several other areas that should be expanded on. For example, Rodgers and Conrad's (1986) hypothesis about the length of time between divorce and remarriage and stepfamily adjustment has yet to be investigated; more studies are needed that explore the effects of personality characteristics on remarital stability and satisfaction (e.g., Johnson & Booth, 1998); and the influence of religious beliefs on remarriage and stepfamily dynamics has been underinvestigated. In addition, stepchildren's affinity-seeking efforts and their responses to the affinity-seeking behaviors of stepparents need to be explicated.

Issues around gender and postdivorce stepfamily living also should be investigated. What are the similarities and differences between men and women in their motivations and expectations to remarry or repartner? Once in a new union, how do men and women negotiate power in the relationship? How are childrearing decisions made, and by whom? These and many other questions may be raised that examine the experiences of men and women in postdivorce stepfamilies.

There are also issues that have yet to be investigated. For instance, what are the relational outcomes of redivorce? We know that multiple transitions place children at risk for certain problems, but what happens to relationships? How do stepfamily members redefine their relationships following redivorce?

In recent years, several scholars have developed empirically derived typologies of stepfamilies (e.g., Berger, 1995; Bray & Kelly, 1998; Erera-Weatherly, 1996; Hetherington, 2002). These typologies are usually based on variations in stepfamily processes that distinguish stepfamilies on specific characteristics. Future researchers, using longitudinal designs, could explore the outcomes of different stepfamily "types" to see which, if any, sets of family processes lead to identifiable outcomes for children and adults.

Researchers also could compare successful and unsuccessful stepfamilies, using clearly identified criteria to define the groups, to examine similarities and differences in family processes. Researchers could test clinicians' assertions regarding the characteristics of successful stepfamilies (e.g., realistic expectations, productive rituals), or they could examine other family dynamics that were identified from theory or prior research.

Researchers should make special efforts to include racially and ethnically diverse samples in their investigations of stepfamilies. Structural diversity is also important, as is the inclusion of gay and lesbian stepfamilies. However, given the frequent difficulty that researchers face in finding stepfamilies, future researchers would be well advised to focus their studies on specific groups of stepfamilies (e.g., lesbian stepfamilies, stepmother households), particularly when they are using qualitative methods or mixed method designs.

The study of postdivorce stepfamily processes is an area of investigation rich with possibilities. The findings of such investigations should be helpful to practitioners, researchers, policy-makers, and even to stepfamily members. There are many areas that researchers could investigate in the future (see Coleman et al., 2000 and Ganong & Coleman, 2004 for additional suggestions); we have mentioned but a few.

REFERENCES

Ahrons, C. (1994). *The good divorce*. New York: HarperCollins.

Allan, G., Hawker, G., & Crow, S. (2004). Britain's changing families. In M. Coleman & L. Ganong (Eds.), *Handbook of contemporary families* (pp. 302–316). Thousand Oaks, CA: Sage.

Amato, P., & Booth, A. (1996). A prospective study of parental divorce and parent–child relationships. *Journal of Marriage and the Family, 58,* 356–365.

Amato, P. R., & Rogers, S. J. (1997). A longitudinal study of marital problems and subsequent divorce. *Journal of Marriage and the Family, 59,* 612–624.

Ambert, A. M. (1989). *Ex-spouses and new spouses.* Greenwich, CT: JAI.

Baber, K. M., & Allen, K. R. (1992). *Women and families.* New York: Guilford.

Batchelder, J., Dimmock, B., & Smith, D. (1994). *Understanding stepfamilies: What can be learned from callers to the stepfamily telephone counseling service.* London: Stepfamily Publications.

Berger, R. (1995). Three types of stepfamilies. *Journal of Divorce and Remarriage, 24,* 35–49.

Berger, R. (1998). The experience and issues of gay stepfamilies. *Journal of Divorce and Remarriage, 29*(3/4), 93–102.

Blumstein, P., & Schwartz, P. (1983). *American couples: Money, work, sex.* New York: Morrow.

Boszormenyi-Nagy, I., & Spark, G. M. (1973). *Invisible loyalties.* New York: Harper and Row.

Braithwaite, D., Olson, L. N., Golish, T. D., Soukup, C., & Turman, P. (2001). "Becoming a family": Developmental processes represented in blended family discourse. *Journal of Applied Communication Research, 29,* 221–247.

Bramlett, M. D., & Mosher, W. D. (2001). *Cohabitation, marriage, divorce, and remarriage in the United States* (U.S. Center for Disease Control, Series 23, No. 22). Hyattsville, MD: U.S. Department of Health and Human Services.

Bray, J., & Kelly, J. (1998). *Stepfamilies.* New York: Broadway Books.

Browning, S. W. (1994). Treating stepfamilies: Alternatives to traditional family therapy. In K. Pasley & M. Ihinger-Tallman (Eds.), *Stepparenting: Issues in theory, research, and practice* (pp. 175–198). Westport, CT: Greenwood.

Bryant, A. S., & Demian, (1994). Relationship characteristics of American gay and lesbian couples: Findings from a national survey. *Journal of Gay and Lesbian Social Services, 1,* 101–117.

Bumpass, L. L., & Lu, H. (2000). Trends in cohabitation and implications for children's family contexts in the United States. *Population Studies, 54,* 19–41.

Burgoyne, C. B., & Morison, V. (1997). Money in remarriage: Keeping things simple and separate. *Sociological Review, 45,* 363–395.

Carter, E. A. (1988). Counseling stepfamilies effectively. *Behavior Today, 19,* 1–2.

Cherlin, A. (1978). Remarriage as an incomplete institution. *American Journal of Sociology, 84,* 634–650.

Church, E. (1999). Who are the people in your family? Stepmothers' diverse notions of kinship. *Journal of Divorce and Remarriage, 31,* 83–105.

Claxton-Oldfield, S., Goodyear, C., Parsons, T., & Claxton-Oldfield, J. (2002). Some possible implications of negative stepfather stereotypes. *Journal of Divorce and Remarriage, 36*(3/4), 77–88.

Clingempeel, W. G., & Brand-Clingempeel, U. (2004). Pathogenic conflict families and children: What we know, what we need to know. In M. Coleman & L. Ganong (Eds.), *Handbook of contemporary families: Considering the past, contemplating the future* (pp. 244–261). Thousand Oaks, CA: Sage.

Coleman, M., Fine, M., Ganong, L., Downs, K., & Pauk, N. (2001). When you're not the Brady Bunch: Identifying perceived conflicts and resolution strategies in stepfamilies. *Personal Relationships, 8,* 55–73.

Coleman, M., Ganong, L., & Fine, M. (2000). Reinvestigating remarriage: Another decade of progress. *Journal of Marriage and the Family, 62,* 1288–1307.

Coleman, M., Ganong, L., & Fine, M. (2004). Communication in stepfamilies. In A. Vangilisti (Ed.), *Handbook of family communication* (pp. 215–232). Mahwah, NJ: Lawrence Erlbaum Associates.

Coleman, M., Ganong, L., & Weaver, S. (2001). Maintenance and enhancement in remarried families. In J. Harvey & A. Wenzel (Eds.), *Close romantic relationships: Maintenance and enhancement* (pp. 255–276). Mahwah, NJ: Lawrence Erlbaum Associates.

Cooksey, E. C., & Craig, P. H. (1998). Parenting from a distance: The effects of paternal characteristics on contact between nonresidential fathers and their children. *Demography, 35,* 187–200.

Crosbie-Burnett, M. (1984). The centrality of the step relationship: A challenge to family theory and practice. *Family Relations, 33,* 459–464.

Crosbie-Burnett, M., & Lewis, E. (1993). Use of African-American family structures and functioning to address the challenges of European-American postdivorce families. *Family Relations, 42,* 243–248.

deGraaf, P. M., & Kalmijn, M. (2003). Alternative routes in the remarriage market: Competing-risk analyses of union formation after divorce. *Social Forces, 81,* 1459–1498.

De'Ath, E. (1997). Stepfamily policy from the perspective of a stepfamily organization. In I. Levin & M. Sussman (Eds.), *Stepfamilies: History, research, and policy* (pp. 265–280). Binghamton, NY: Haworth.

Deal, J. E., Stanley Hagan, M., & Anderson, J. C. (1992). The marital relationships in remarried families. *Monographs of the Society for Research in Child Development, 57*(2–3, Serial No. 227), 73–93.

Demo, D. H., & Acock, A. C. (1993). Family diversity and the division of domestic labor: How much have things really changed? *Family Relations, 42,* 323–331.

Doyle, K. W., Wolchik, S. A., & Dawson-McClure, S. (2002). Development of the stepfamily events profile. *Journal of Family Psychology, 16,* 128–143.

Dunn, J., Davies, L. C., O'Connor, T. G., & Sturgess, W. (2001). Family lives and friendships: The perspectives of children in step-, single-parent, and nonstep families. *Journal of Family Psychology, 15,* 272–287.

Erera, P. I., & Fredriksen, K. (1999). Lesbian stepfamilies: A unique family structure. *Families in Society, 80,* 263–270.

Erera-Weatherly, P. I. (1996). On becoming a stepparent: Factors associated with the adoption of alternative stepparenting styles. *Journal of Divorce and Remarriage, 25,* 155–174.

Fine, M. A., Coleman, M., & Ganong, L. (1998). Consistency in perceptions of the stepparent role among stepparents, parents, and stepchildren. *Journal of Social and Personal Relationships, 15,* 810–828.

Flinn, M. V. (1999). Family environment, stress, and health during childhood. In C. Panter-Brick & C. Worthman (Eds.), *Hormones, health, and behavior* (pp. 105–138). Cambridge, England: Cambridge University Press.

Ganong, L., & Coleman, M. (1989). Preparing for remarriage: Anticipating the issues, seeking solutions. *Family Relations, 38,* 28–33.

Ganong, L., & Coleman, M. (2004). *Stepfamily relationships.* New York: Kluwer/Plenum.

Ganong, L., Coleman, M., & Mapes, D. (1990). *A meta-analytic review of family structure stereotypes. Journal of Marriage and the Family, 52,* 287–298.

Ganong, L., Coleman, M., Fine, M., & Martin, P. (1999). Stepparents' affinity-seeking and affinity-maintaining strategies with stepchildren. *Journal of Family Issues, 20,* 299–327.

Ganong, L., Coleman, M., Fine, M. A., & McDaniel, A. K. (1998). Issues considered in stepparent adoption. *Family Relations, 47,* 63–72.

Ganong, L., Coleman, M., & Weaver, S. (2002). Maintenance and enhancement in remarried families: Clinical applications. In J. Harvey & A. Wenzel (Eds.), *A clinicians' guide to maintaining and enhancing close relationships* (pp. 105–129). Mahwah, NJ: Lawrence Erlbaum Associates.

Giles-Sims, J. (1987). Social exchange in remarried families. In K. Pasley & M. Ihinger-Tallman (Eds.), *Remarriage and stepparenting today* (pp. 141–163). New York: Guilford.

Grall, T. (2003). *Custodial mothers and fathers and their child support: 2001* (Current Population Report P60-225). Washington, DC: U.S. Government Printing Office.

Guisinger, S., Cowan, P., & Schuldberg, D. (1989). Changing parent and spouse relations in the first years of remarriage of divorced fathers. *Journal of Marriage and the Family, 51,* 445–456.

Hall, K. J., & Kitson, G. C. (2000). Lesbian stepfamilies: An even more "incomplete institution." *Journal of Lesbian Studies, 4*(3), 31–47.

Hans, J. D. (2002). Stepparenting after divorce: Stepparents' legal position regarding custody, access, and support. *Family Relations, 51,* 301–307.

Hanson, T. L., McLanahan, S. S., & Thomson, E. (1996). Double jeopardy: Parental conflict and stepfamily outcomes for children. *Journal of Marriage and the Family, 58,* 141–154.

Hare, J., & Richards, L. (1993). Children raised by lesbian couples: Does context of birth affect father and partner involvement? *Family Relations, 42,* 249–255.

Hequembourg, A. (2004). Unscripted motherhood: Lesbian mothers negotiating incompletely institutionalized family relationships. *Journal of Social and Personal Relationships, 21,* 739–762.

Hetherington, E. M. (2002). *For better or for worse: Divorce reconsidered.* New York: Norton.

Hetherington, E. M. (2003). Intimate pathways: Changing patterns in close personal relationships across time. *Family Relations, 52,* 318–331.

Hetherington, E. M., & Clingempeel, W. G. (1992). Coping with marital transitions: A family systems perspective. *Monographs of the Society for Research in Child Development, 57*(2–3, Serial No. 227).

Hetherington, E. M., Cox, M., & Cox, R. (1982). Effects of divorce on parents and children. In M. Lamb (Ed.), *Nontraditional families* (pp. 233–285). Mahwah, NJ: Lawrence Erlbaum Associates.

Hetherington, E. M., & Kelly, J. (2002). *For better or for worse.* New York: Norton.

Hopper, J. (2001). The symbolic origins of conflict in divorce. *Journal of Marriage and Family, 63,* 430–445.

Hulbert, J. S., & Acock, A. C. (1990). The effects of marital status on the form and composition of social networks. *Social Science Quarterly, 71,* 163–174.

Ishii-Kuntz, M., & Coltrane, S. (1992). Remarriage, stepparenting, and household labor. *Journal of Family Issues, 13,* 215–233.

Johnson, D. R., & Booth, A. (1998). Marital quality: A product of the dyadic environment or individual factors? *Social Forces, 76,* 883–904.

Kranichfeld, M. L. (1987). Rethinking family power. *Journal of Family Issues, 8,* 42–56.

Kreider, R. M., & Fields, J. M. (2002). *Number, timing, and duration of marriage and divorce: 1996* (Current Population Reports, Series P70-80). Washington, DC: U.S. Government Printing Office.

Kretchmar, M. D., & Jacobvitz, D. B. (2002). Observing mother–child relationships across generations: Boundary patterns, attachment, and the transmission of caregiving. *Family Process, 41,* 351–374.

Kurdek, L. A., & Fine, M. A. (1993). Parent and nonparent residential family members as providers of warmth and supervision to young adolescents. *Journal of Family Psychology, 7,* 245–249.

Lampard, R., & Peggs, K. (1999). Repartnering: The relevance of parenthood and gender to cohabitation and remarriage among the formerly married. *British Journal of Sociology, 50,* 443–465.

Lansford, J. E., Ceballo, R., Abbey, A., & Stewart, A. J. (2001). Does family structure matter? A comparison of adoptive, two-parent biological, single-mother, stepfather, and stepmother households. *Journal of Marriage and Family, 63,* 840–851.

Lynch, J. M. (2000). Considerations of family structure and gender composition: The lesbian and gay stepfamily. *Journal of Homosexuality, 39,* 81–96.

Lynch, J. M., & Murray, K. (2000). For the love of the children: The coming out process for lesbian and gay parents and stepparents. *Journal of Homosexuality, 39,* 1–24.

Marsiglio, W. (2004). When stepfathers claim stepchildren: A conceptual analysis. *Journal of Marriage and Family, 66,* 22–39.

Martinez, C. R., & Forgatch, M. S. (2002). Adjusting to change: Linking family structure transitions with parenting and boys adjustment. *Journal of Family Psychology, 16,* 107–117.

Mason, M. A., Fine, M. A., & Carnochan, S. (2004). Family law for changing families. In M. Coleman & L. Ganong (Eds.), *Handbook of contemporary families: Considering the past, contemplating the future* (pp. 432–450). Thousand Oaks, CA: Sage.

McManus, P., & Diprete, T. (2001). Losers and winners: The financial consequences of separation and divorce for men. *American Sociological Review, 55,* 246–268.

National Center for Health Statistics. (1993). 1988 marriages: Number of the marriage by bride by groom [Computer program]. Washington, DC: National Center for Health Statistics Computer Center.

Nelson, F. (1996). *Lesbian motherhood.* Toronto: University of Toronto Press.

Oswald, R. F. (2002). Resilience within the family networks of lesbians and gay men: Intentionality and redefinition. *Journal of Marriage and the Family, 64,* 374–394.

Papernow, P. (2001, February). *Working with stepfamilies.* Paper presented at the National Conference on Stepfamilies, New Orleans, LA.

Pasley, K., Sandras, E., & Edmondson, M. E. (1994). The effects of financial management strategies on the quality of family life in remarraige. *Journal of Family and Economic Issues, 15,* 53–70.

Pyke, K., & Coltrane, S. (1996). Entitlement, obligation, and gratitude in family work. *Journal of Family Issues, 17,* 60–82.

Pyke, K. D. (1994). Women's employment as a gift or burden? Marital power across marriage, divorce, and remarriage. *Gender and Society, 8,* 73–91.

Raley, R. K., & Wildsmith, E. (2004). Cohabitation and children's family instability. *Journal of Marriage and Family, 66,* 210–219.

Rodgers, R. H., & Conrad, L. (1986). Courtship for remarriage: Influences on family reorganization after divorce. *Journal of Marriage and the Family, 48,* 767–775.

Rogers, S. J. (1996). Marital quality, mothers' parenting and children's outcomes: A comparison of mother/father and mother/stepfather families. *Sociological Focus, 29,* 325–340.

Russell, A., & Searcy, E. (1997). The contribution of affective reactions and relationship qualities to adolescents' reported responses to parents. *Journal of Social and Personal Relationships, 14,* 539–548.

Salem, D., Zimmerman, M., & Notaro, P. (1998). Effects of family structure, family process, and father involvement on psychosocial outcomes among African American adolescents. *Family Relations, 47,* 331–341.

Scanzoni, J. (2004). Household diversity: The starting point for healthy families in the new century. In M. Coleman & L. Ganong (Eds.), *Handbook of contemporary families: Considering the past, contemplating the future* (pp. 3–22). Thousand Oaks, CA: Sage.

Schmiege, C., Richards, L., & Zvonkovic, A. (2001). Remarriage: For love or money? *Journal of Divorce and Remarriage, 36,* 123–140.

Smock, P., & Manning, W. D. (2000). Swapping families? Serial parenting and economic support for children. *Journal of Marriage and the Family, 62,* 111–22.

Sullivan, O. (1997). The division of housework among "remarried" couples. *Journal of Family Issues, 18,* 205–226.

Sweeney, M. (2002). Remarriage and the nature of divorce. *Journal of Family Issues, 23,* 410–440.

Sweeney, M. M. (1997). Remarriage of women and men after divorce: The role of socioeconomic prospects. *Journal of Family Issues, 18,* 479–502.

Tzeng, J. M., & Mare, R. D. (1995). Labor market and socioeconomic effects on marital stability. *Social Science Research, 24,* 329–351.

van IJzendoorn, M. H. (1995). Adult attachment representations, parental responsiveness, and infant attachment: A meta-analysis on the predictive validity of the adult attachment interview. *Psychological Bulletin, 117,* 387–403.

Visher, E. B., & Visher, J. S. (1990). Dynamics of successful stepfamilies. *Journal of Divorce and Remarriage, 14,* 3–12.

Visher, E. B., & Visher, J. S. (1996). *Therapy with stepfamilies.* New York: Brunner/Mazel.

Weaver, S., & Coleman, M. (2004). *Caught in the middle: Mothers and stepfamilies.* Unpublished manuscript.

Weaver, S., & Coleman, M. (in press). A mothering but not a mother role: A grounded theory study of the nonresidential stepmother role. *Journal of Social and Personal Relationships.*

Webber, R. (1991). Life in stepfamilies: Conceptions and misconceptions. In K. Funder (Ed.), *Images of Australian families* (pp. 88–101). Melbourne: Longman Cheshire.

White, L. K., & Gilbreth, J. G. (2001). When children have two fathers: Effects of relationships with stepfathers and noncustodial fathers on adolescent outcomes. *Journal of Marriage and Family, 63,* 155–167.

Whiteside, M. (1998). The parental alliance following divorce: An overview. *Journal of Marital and Family Therapy, 24,* 3–24.

Wilson, B. F., & Clarke, S. C. (1992). Remarriages: A demographic profile. *Journal of Family Issues, 13,* 123–141.

Wu, Z. (1994). Remarriage in Canada: A social exchange perspective. *Journal of Divorce and Remarriage, 21,* 191–224.

Wu, Z., & Penning, M. J. (1997). Marital instability after midlife. *Journal of Family Issues, 18,* 459–478.

Wu, Z., & Thomson, E. (2001). Race differences in family experience and early sexual initiation: Dynamic models of family structure and family change. *Journal of Marriage and Family, 63,* 682–696.

21

Communication Processes That Promote Risk and Resiliency in Postdivorce Families

Tamara D. Afifi and Kellie Hamrick
Pennsylvania State University

Divorce often produces a chain of stressors (e.g., decline in income, loneliness, role burden, parenting across households, loss of social networks, parental conflict, and moving to a new neighborhood) that challenge family members' ability to cope with everyday life. Although the precise impact of these stressors on family functioning continues to be a point of contention (see Amato, 2000), most scholars, practitioners, and family members agree that divorce is a stressful experience. Divorce provides opportunities to escape an unhealthy environment and build new relationships for some people, perhaps enhancing their well-being. For others, it creates an acute and often chronic source of stress that can persist years before and after the physical separation (see Amato; Hetherington, 1999; Lamb, Sternberg, & Thompson, 1999). Regardless of the extent of the stress, divorce is never a victimless process (Lamb, 1999). Most people suffer a deep sense of personal, familial, or relational loss as the result of a divorce (Lamb et al.).

As family networks are being nurtured, strained, and adjusted during divorce, the communicative dynamics within them are also undergoing change. The interactions that transpire among family members during these delicate times can place them at risk for, or protect them against, a variety of adverse effects. Children, in particular, are sensitive to their family communication environment because they are often affected by, and can adopt, their parents' negative interaction patterns. Explicating the specific communication patterns that help and hinder family members' ability to adapt to divorce is important in an attempt to better understand the wide range of individuals' responses to divorce. Because divorce has become so prevalent in today's American families and because it can often have a debilitating effect on family members' emotional and physical well-being (Booth & Amato, 2001; Chase-Lansdale, Cherlin, & Kiernan, 1995; Deater-Deckard & Dunn, 1999), we are compelled to further delineate, and consequently improve, the interpersonal behavior patterns that complicate this process. Therefore, using a risk and resiliency perspective, in this chapter we provide an overview of some of the communication characteristics that foster resilience and those that contribute to poor functioning in postdivorce families.

RISK AND RESILIENCY

Numerous researchers have attempted to address the variability in family members' responses to divorce by adopting a risk and resiliency approach (e.g., Afifi & Keith, 2004; Deater-Deckard & Dunn, 1999; Forehand, Biggar & Kotchick, 1998). What has become clear in the research on divorce is the diversity of people's responses to similar postdivorce circumstances (Hetherington, 1999). For instance, Amato and Keith (1991) found in their meta-analysis of the impact of divorce on children that, although there were short-term and long-term differences between offspring of divorced and nondivorced families, the effect sizes were quite small. Children varied considerably in how they responded to divorce, with some children faring better than others. What this and other research (e.g., Deater-Deckard & Dunn; Hetherington) suggests is that, rather than determining the generative impact of divorce and the seemingly inherent debilitating effects of it on children as a whole, perhaps a more useful approach is to decipher the specific processes and conditions, and their interactive effects, that contribute to differential degrees of functioning.

Risk and resiliency perspectives attempt to address the diversity in family members' responses to divorce by exploring the interactions among individual, familial, and extrafamilial risk and protective factors (Hetherington, 1999). As Amato (1999) noted, numerous factors influence people's responses to stress, resulting in a variety of outcomes among children and adults. At a very general level, exposure to stress increases the likelihood of adverse psychological and physical outcomes, but a more complex picture of the stress and coping process can be garnered when a host of factors are considered (Amato). As Amato mentioned, individuals' responses to stress depend on the resources that are available to them and their willingness to implement these resources. These resources include psychological attributes of the individual (e.g., self-efficacy, negativity), interpersonal and familial relationships (e.g., social support), and the larger societal and demographic context in which the stress is subsumed (e.g., school systems, economy, government policies, and financial resources within the family). In essence, risk and resiliency approaches can help explain variance in people's reactions to divorce by examining the individual, interdependent, and cumulative contributions of the different levels of the family system on these reactions.

In addition to explaining the variance in individual family members' responses to divorce, risk and resiliency models also help decipher variables that predict positive family functioning as well as those that deter it. As scholars interested in family strengths have argued (e.g., Coleman, Ganong, & Fine, 2000; DeFrain & Stinnett, 1992; Golish, 2003), researchers often focus on the problematic behavior patterns of divorced families at the expense of those behaviors that make them function well. Moreover, although differences between first-marriage families and divorced families are important and necessary to fully understand family functioning, within-group differences and similarities among divorced families can also shed light on this process. Thus, some risk and resiliency models may tap into what Visher and Visher (1979) labeled a *normative-adaptive approach* to studying divorced and remarried families. A normative-adaptive approach does not preclude comparisons of divorced families to first-marriage families, but it does place emphasis on what makes some divorced families function better than others (Ganong & Coleman, 1994). Thus, a risk and resiliency framework can be used to examine differences and similarities between first-marriage families and divorced families or within divorced families themselves.

Although a comprehensive risk and resiliency approach would probably examine the psychological, environmental, and relational factors that promote risk and resiliency in postdivorce families, in this chapter we more closely explore one of these dimensions: relational or familial factors. More specifically, we examine the impact of family communication on individual and family functioning. Examining families from a communication approach means that families are defined through their communication, verbally and nonverbally, rather than solely through their biological or kinship ties (Whitchurch & Dickson, 1999). By interacting together as a family, family members coconstruct a sense of family. Consequently, communication scholars do not view communication as only one variable among many to be analyzed in a family, but as "the central process through which people construct and maintain themselves as a family" (Whitchurch & Dickson, p. 688). Because of the specificity of the processes being investigated, those who study communication tend to examine it from a "micro" approach— paying attention to the detail of the verbal and nonverbal behaviors that occur within families. However, it is also important to note that communication is inherently linked to cognition and larger sociological forces and also often emerges in other seemingly noncommunicative actions. For example, even though family rituals and routines may not seem highly communicative, what family members talk about during these activities and what the nonverbal behaviors enacted in them symbolize to family members are based in communication. Thus, for the purpose of this chapter, we are interested in a wide variety of communicative behaviors, attitudes, norms, rituals, and actions that promote risk and resiliency in postdivorce families.

Research on the specific role of communication in postdivorce families is rather limited, with most of it also being interdisciplinary. The scholarship that is available has tended to focus on communication in a general sense or has made it a tertiary variable in analyses. However, communication plays a critical role in family members' ability to cope with various divorce-related stressors. Communication is an antecedent and a consequence of coping, but it is also a primary way in which family members cope with one another and generate meaning from their experiences (Afifi, Hutchinson, & Krouse, 2005; Afifi & Nussbaum, in press). Whether it is through avoidance, problem solving, disclosure, social support, or affirmation, family members often enact their stress and attempt to cope with it through their communication with each other (see Afifi et al.). The communicative nature of stress and coping is also revealed within the dynamic interplay of multiple family members. How effectively or ineffectively family members cope with divorce is often dependent on how they react to one another's stress and implementation of certain coping strategies. These communicative processes are discussed in the sections that follow.

COMMUNICATION PROCESSES THAT PROMOTE RISK AND RESILIENCY IN POSTDIVORCE FAMILIES

Although we are only detailing some of the communication processes that foster risk and resiliency in postdivorce families, they must be understood within the psychological capacity of the individual and the larger societal forces in which they are embedded. Communication processes in postdivorce families can be categorized in many ways, but a review of the literature in this area appears to produce three very broad themes: interpersonal skill deficiencies, balancing appropriate boundaries, and family rituals, maintenance, and coping. These general domains encompass specific communication characteristics (e.g., disclosure, conflict, and social support) that have been shown to promote varying levels of risk and resiliency in postdivorce families. Although these areas may appear somewhat heterogeneous, when they are taken together they provide a rather comprehensive overview of the communication patterns that contribute to stress in postdivorce families, as well as those that help build resolve.

Interpersonal Skill Deficiencies

Personality Characteristics That Can Influence Interpersonal Skills in Divorced Families

At a very basic level, family members may simply lack certain communication skills, ones that are both learned from their environment and ingrained as a part of their personality or genetics, that not only make divorce more stressful but more probable. Numerous studies on divorce have shown that inadequate interpersonal communication skills, such as aggressiveness, criticism, negativity, demand–withdraw patterns, and a lack of impulse control, are risk factors for divorce (Amato, 1996; Amato & DeBoer, 2001; Amato & Rogers, 1997; Caughlin, Huston, & Houts, 2000). For example, self-differentiation and narcissism have been found to affect a person's responses to disagreement and have been linked to marital discord and divorce (Baum & Shnit, 2003). Negativity has also been shown to have a debilitating effect on marital quality (Caughlin et al.; Huston & Vangelisti, 1991). A pessimistic personality often reveals itself as greater negativity in one's communication. In fact, Gottman (1994) argued that couples that have less than a 5:1 ratio of positive to negative comments are more likely to divorce than couples that have more favorable ratios. Over time, negativity can wear away at the fabric of a marriage and family. Family members who are able to maintain affirming communication with one another are also better able to cope with divorce-related challenges (Braithwaite, Olson, Golish, Soukup, & Turman, 2001; Golish, 2003).

Although many personality traits may promote greater risk for divorce and difficulty coping with the stressors associated with it, other personality traits may promote resilience in post-divorce families. For instance, one factor that may influence how family members are able to adjust to the ambiguity that often accompanies divorce transitions is uncertainty orientation. Certainty-oriented persons are more comfortable when there is a great deal of clarity and little uncertainty; uncertainty-oriented individuals are more comfortable with uncertainty and are motivated to learn from new situations and acquire information to manage it (Neuberg, Judice, & West, 1997). Research has shown that certainty-oriented individuals are more likely than uncertainty-oriented individuals to have greater difficulty coping with uncertainty and avoid situations that are unpredictable (Sorrentino, Hewitt, & Raso-Knott, 1992). What this research suggests is that uncertainty-oriented individuals may have a greater ability to cope with the uncertainty that often ensues after divorce and may be more apt to seek information in order to manage it. As Lengua and Sandler (1996) discovered, preadolescents who were positively oriented toward change, or who evidenced approach flexibility, were more likely than other preadolescents to adapt to divorce and think about divorce-related stressors in alternative ways that enhanced their self-efficacy and control.

In addition to the degree of approach flexibility or uncertainty orientation, research suggests that individuals who engage in more active coping compared with avoidant coping tend to have greater self-efficacy and less physical and mental distress after divorce (Sandler, Tein, & West, 1994). Even though avoidance has been found to be productive under certain circumstances, such as when the stress is deemed to be out of one's control (e.g., controlling a former spouse's anger; see Holloway & Machida, 1991), active coping in general tends to be a more functional approach to managing stress (Folkman & Lazarus, 1988; Herman-Stahl & Petersen, 1996). Certain personality types may also be better apt to use active coping rather than avoidant coping. For instance, Miller (1992) noted that there are individual differences in preferences for control that determine if and when a person seeks information to reduce stress. For instance, high "monitors" tend to cope with stress by focusing on and disclosing their emotions, are less avoidant when faced with uncertainty, and are more likely to seek out social support for instrumental reasons. To the contrary, "blunters" often prefer to avoid and distract from highly threatening or stressful situations and threat-relevant information. Miller went on to note, however, that even though monitors may often feel less anxious after receiving information, blunters can also be satisfied with the information they receive, primarily because they believe they have received enough knowledge. In some situations, people may not desire to actively reduce their uncertainty (e.g., "ignorance is bliss").

Interpersonal Communication Skills in Divorced Families

Personality characteristics such as those described herein can translate into other interpersonal communication skills that promote risk and resiliency. In particular, conflict-management strategies are integral to the success of a marriage and postdivorce family life. Some scholars (e.g., Gottman, 1994; Stanley, Markman, & Whitton, 2002) contend that how couples argue is a stronger predictor of the health of their relationship than what they actually argue about. Conflict-management strategies that appear to pose the greatest risk for couples and families include the frequency and intensity of the conflict, negativity, avoidance, aggression, criticism, contempt, invalidation, stonewalling, and demand–withdrawal patterns. For instance, escalation, which concerns the intensity of an argument, and invalidation, which leads to criticizing and belittling a partner, often deter positive relationship factors such as satisfaction, commitment, and confidence in relationships (Stanley et al.). John Gottman's work (e.g., Gottman, 1994; Gottman & Levenson, 2000) also points to the importance of couple's not criticizing each other's shortcomings, becoming defensive, cross-complaining, removing one's self emotionally or physically from conflict situations with a lack of verbal and nonverbal responses (stonewalling), and communicating contempt.

Parents' hostility and aggression toward one another can also create a host of risk factors for children. Children who are exposed to negative amounts and types of conflict, whether it is through direct or indirect exposure, are at a heightened risk for emotional and behavioral difficulties (Amato, Loomis, & Booth, 1995; Laumann-Billings & Emery, 2000; Richardson & McCabe, 2001). Research indicates that the amount of interparental conflict is one of the strongest predictors of children's well-being after divorce, perhaps more so than the divorce itself (Ahrons & Rodgers, 1987; Amato et al.). In fact, growing evidence suggests that some children may be better off psychologically if their parents divorce than if they remain in a high-discord marriage (Amato & DeBoer, 2001; Booth & Amato, 2001; Jekielek, 1998). For instance, Jekielek discovered that, when children were removed from a high-conflict marriage, they were less anxious and depressed 4 years later than if their parents remained married. In a series of studies from their longitudinal work on divorce, Booth and Amato (Amato & DeBoer; Amato et al.; Booth & Amato) also found that children fared better after divorce if their parents had a high-discord marriage, primarily because they were removed from an unhealthy family environment. They were worse off, however, if their parents divorced from a low-discord marriage. Interparental conflict, regardless of whether the parents are divorced or not, is an important mediating factor in children's development. In general, this research seems to suggest that the extremities of conflict—either a high amount of conflict or a complete lack of any indication that anything is wrong—tend to contribute to adult children's psychological well-being later in life (see Amato & DeBoer).

One aspect of conflict, in particular, that has received considerable attention from relational and family scholars is the demand–withdraw pattern, in which one spouse criticizes or demands to talk about certain issues while the other spouse withdraws or avoids them (Heavey, Layne,

& Christensen, 1993). Oftentimes, it is women who have been found to assume more of a demanding role, whereas men withdraw from the interactions (Christensen & Heavey, 1990). Although there are numerous reasons why couples engage in demand–withdraw patterns, one explanation is individuals who are in a demanding role desire change in the relationship, which is a reflection of various inequities and social-structural barriers (Caughlin & Vangelisti, 1999; Christensen & Heavey; Heavey et al.). There is some research that suggests that demand–withdraw patterns can be effective if the demands produce positive behavioral change (Caughlin & Vangelisti). For instance, Golish (2003) found that, in new stepfamilies, stepparents who continually demanded that their spouse become more authoritative were able to help the family as a whole address its problems more directly and take greater responsibility for household rules. Other research (e.g., Caughlin, 2002) indicates that demand–withdraw patterns can be associated with satisfaction for wives over time. Nevertheless, most of the research on demand–withdraw patterns suggests that such patterns are indicative of distressed couples (Schaap, Buunk, & Kerkstra, 1988) and are predictive of relational dissatisfaction (Caughlin & Huston, 2002; Heavey, Christensen, & Malamuth, 1995) and divorce (Gottman & Levenson, 2000).

Although most of the research on demand–withdraw patterns has focused on the interactions of couples who are still married and their ability to predict marital distress and divorce, this body of literature has strong implications for post–divorce families. Former spouses, who are often involuntarily linked to one another through their children, may perceive that their role in the family has become especially inequitable since the divorce (Afifi & Schrodt, 2003a). Even though these inequities may truly exist, they are also often intensified because of former spouses' heightened emotional connections to one another. Their desires for change may reveal themselves in a situation in which one parent demands changes in custody arrangements, household rules, parenting styles, or child support payments and the other parent either demands back or avoids the issue altogether in order to detach himself or herself emotionally from the relationship (Emery, 1994). The fact that both spouses often do not want the divorce and that many of them also do not perceive their child support payments or custody arrangements as equitable (Greif, 1995; Hoffman, 1995) may also foster a habitual cycle of demand–withdraw patterns in some postdivorce families (Afifi & Schrodt). The demand–withdraw patterns of married couples may also be transferred onto their interactions with their children. For instance, children can be drawn into such interactions when one parent demands to communicate with the former spouse about a particular issue and the parent, refusing to talk about the matter further, indirectly places the children in the role as mediators. In general, postdivorce families provide a rich context in which to study the "tugs and pulls" of such interactions and the conditions in which they are beneficial or harmful.

Another important interpersonal skill that can foster varying levels of risk and resiliency in postdivorce families is communication competence. Communication is often considered competent to the degree that it consists of an adequate combination of assertiveness, appropriateness, social skill, other-orientation, patience, flexibility, and adaptation (Gross & Guerrero, 2000; Guerrero, 1994; Rubin, 1985; Spitzberg & Cupach, 1984). The shifting parental and spousal roles that often accompany divorce can be stressful and can challenge parents' ability to communicate competently (Madden-Derdich & Arditti, 1999). Parents who are skillful communicators in most situations may become incompetent communicators within the context of a specific relationship (i.e., with their former spouse). This competence, or lack thereof, becomes particularly salient when researchers examine its impact on children. For instance, research indicates that adolescents and young adults who perceive their parents as incompetent communicators are more likely than children who perceive their parents as competent to feel caught between their parents' conflict (Afifi & Schrodt, 2003a; Buchanan, Maccoby,

& Dornbusch, 1991). Children whose parents are able to cooperate with one another, are consistent in their parenting, respect one another's household rules, and who communicate frequently about their children are better able to maintain a healthy postdivorce family environment (Ahrons & Rodgers, 1987; Maccoby & Mnookin, 1992).

Long-Term Implications for Divorced Families

As much of the aforementioned research suggests, interpersonal communication skills become especially important because they have implications beyond the couple to children and the postdivorce family as a whole. Social learning theory (Bandura, 1977) suggests that children learn to model many of their communication patterns by observing the adults around them. Children learn about the construct of marriage and the specific behaviors that build, maintain, and deteriorate it by observing their parents' relationship (Amato & DeBoer, 2001). As Amato and DeBoer noted, it is largely because of these socialization processes that children whose parents divorce may have fewer opportunities than children whose parents remain happily married to learn positive interaction skills (e.g., social support, constructive conflict management, and affection).

Research suggests that communication deficiencies can be transmitted intergenerationally from parents to their children (Amato, 1996; Caspi & Elder, 1988; Wolfinger, 2000). More specifically, offspring of divorced parents can develop personality traits and interpersonal skills from their parents that make it difficult to maintain relationships and cope with relational stressors in adulthood. For instance, Amato found that adult offspring of divorced parents who evidenced interpersonal skill deficiencies (e.g., criticism, revealing anger easily, jealousy, dogmatism, and lack of compromise) were more likely to develop these deficiencies themselves in their own marriages, which in turn increased the likelihood that their marriages would also end in divorce. Caspi and Elder also discovered that offspring of discordant parents were likely to develop interpersonal skill deficiencies (becoming aggressive easily, lacking impulse control, or being critical) from their parents, enhancing the likelihood that they would eventually divorce. Developing interpersonal skills (such as effective communication and the ability to compromise) and personality traits (such as trust and the ability to commit) are important in childhood and promote emotional security. What these studies suggest is that divorce and the interpersonal behaviors that often accompany it can teach children destructive communication patterns that undermine their own intimate relationships.

Balancing Appropriate Boundaries

Often a lack of interpersonal skills can translate into inappropriate boundary regulation among family members involved in the divorce process. Boundaries have been conceptualized, and subsequently operationalized, in several ways in the family literature. From a systems perspective (Minuchin, 1974; Satir, 1972; von Bertalanffy, 1968), boundaries are often described as physical boundaries from one system or subsystem to another (e.g., having a permeable boundary or physical access between noncustodial parents and their children) and as intimacy boundaries (e.g., emotional boundaries with one's former spouse or child) or role–relational boundaries (e.g., rules and norms for appropriate parenting). A fourth type of boundary is what Petronio (1991, 2000, 2002) referred to as a privacy boundary in her communication privacy management theory. According to this theory, people often experience a dialectical tension of the desire to reveal information but simultaneously conceal it. In this sense, the boundaries become the means of disclosing or regulating information by monitoring the kind of private information they reveal and the people to whom they reveal it. Although many of the boundaries that are discussed here involve the regulation of privacy issues, they are often intertwined with physical and relational boundaries.

Boundaries Between Former Spouses

As much of the research that has applied attachment theory to divorce indicates (e.g., Masheter, 1997), parents' difficulty coping with the divorce often revolves around the inability to successfully renegotiate intimacy and relational boundaries with their former spouse. The ongoing emotional connection to one's former spouse on separation has been identified in the clinical and empirical literature as a significant source of distress and depression (Cole & Cole, 1999; Graham, 1997; Maccoby & Mnookin, 1992). Even though most people recognize that their partner was not the appropriate person for them, it does not diminish the feelings of confusion, sadness, loss, intimacy, and anger that encompass divorce (Madden-Derdich & Arditti, 1999).

The emotional connection with one's previous partner often manifests itself in two types of behavior patterns: preoccupation with one's former spouse and hostility toward him or her (Madden-Derdich & Arditti, 1999). Some clinical observations, such as those by Emery (1994), suggest that conflicts between former spouses that appear to be about parenting children or finances do not have to do with children or money, but are actually indications of ill-defined feelings of intimacy for one another. As Emery noted, spouses' intense anger can sometimes represent greater intimacy, not less intimacy, particularly during the separation process. Because of the confusion that such feelings create, parents may be unable to contain or regulate their emotional reactions and use the most salient part of their partner's identity as a form of retribution. Consequently, fathers may threaten to change custody arrangements and mothers may propose greater financial support as a way to "get even" with one another (Emery).

The inability to redefine intimacy boundaries with one's partner creates ambiguity in other types of boundaries. As Madden-Derdich, Leonard, and Christopher (1999) found, individuals who had a high degree of emotional intensity toward their former partner after their divorce had difficulty adjusting from their role as spouses to coparents. Research indicates that healthy postdivorce parents are able to reframe their relationship as a married couple to that of parents who construct and communicate clear role expectations and boundaries for one another and their children (Madden-Derdich & Arditti, 1999). Clinical treatment of former spouses who were having difficulty with emotional attachments has been used to promote a complete dissolution of the relationship (Ahrons, 1983; Cole & Cole, 1999). However, parents were also told to continue to provide access to the other household for their children. As a result, redefining one's relationship and communication with the other spouse can be confusing for parents who are supposed to foster open communication boundaries between households and yet communicate less with each other to reduce their level of intimacy (Emery, 1994). Current research and clinical assessments suggest (Madden-Derdich & Arditti), however, that some degree of attachment is necessary for the partners to act as effective parents.

A continued and redefined attachment with one's former spouse subsequently translates into a renegotiation of privacy boundaries. To redefine their relationship effectively for themselves and their children, former spouses must renegotiate their privacy regulation rules (Petronio, 2000, 2002) with one another. That is, parents must construct rules for what constitutes appropriate and inappropriate communication with each other. In particular, they must determine what information should be kept private or disclosed with one another and their children (Afifi, 2003). But, what happens when one spouse decides not to adhere to the privacy rules that were originally coconstructed? Even though some degree of contact is beneficial and necessary for parents, when one's partner does not abide by specific rules for privacy boundaries, the emotions that this can produce can sometimes be too overwhelming to manage. In cases in which spouses have a volatile relationship, minimization strategies may be effective (Afifi, 2003; Amato & Rezac, 1994). For instance, Afifi (e.g., Afifi, 2003; Afifi et al., 2004; Golish, 2003) found that spouses may be able to remove some of the emotion from personal exchanges with their former spouse by using e-mail and minimizing the amount of face-to-face contact.

Enmeshed Privacy Boundaries Between Parents and Children

When parents are unable to regulate appropriate privacy rules with one another, this inability can reveal itself in inappropriate disclosures to their children about each other or the divorce process. It is important for parents to share information about the divorce with their children in order to reduce their uncertainty (Thomas, Booth-Butterfield, & Booth-Butterfield, 1995). For instance, Thomas et al. found that, if young adults perceived a lack of parental openness regarding their parents' impending divorce, it negatively affected their self-esteem and satisfaction with their parents' communication with them. As these authors noted, if children feel as if they have been deceived about the divorce process, it can affect parent–child relations.

The question that is often raised, however, is this: How much information is too much information? What constitutes appropriate disclosures to one's children about the divorce process? In addition, what topics do parents talk to their children about with regard to the divorce? Although it remains to be tested empirically, the association between disclosure and various outcomes for children's well-being and parent–child relations may be curvilinear. That is, too much disclosure about the divorce process and one's feelings toward it may be detrimental to children and parent–child relationships, but some information is necessary in order to facilitate understanding. Moreover, the literature on disclosure, secrets, and topic avoidance indicates that how people respond to the revelation of certain topics depends on how much people identify with the topic and the salience and valence of it, as well as the responsiveness of the target to the disclosure (Afifi & Guerrero, 2000; Vangelisti, Caughlin, & Timmerman, 2000).

Parents are also often unsure how permeable their privacy boundaries should be, or what and how they should communicate about divorce-related issues with their children (Afifi et al., 2004). On one hand, they want to provide information about the divorce and the reasons for the divorce to them. On the other hand, they often do not want to reveal too much information about why it happened or how they feel about the divorce. Furthermore, compared with their adolescent children, parents have also been found to overestimate the appropriateness of their disclosures (Sandler, Wolchik, & Braver, 1988). Many parents are not consciously aware that their children are uncomfortable with how they talk about divorce-related issues with them (Golish, 2003). As Sandler et al. argued, parents not only tend to underestimate the impact that their disclosures about divorce have on their children, but they also provide inadequate and potentially inappropriate information to them.

The privacy boundaries between parents and children can become particularly problematic when the intergenerational intimacy boundaries between them become enmeshed (Emery & Dillon, 1994). A violation of intergenerational boundaries often occurs when parents turn to their children as confidants, by sharing too much private information about their sadness, financial or personal worries, relationship problems, or criticisms about their former spouse (Koerner, Jacobs, & Raymond, 2000). One potential outcome of such disclosures that is typically described in the literature is role reversals or parentification whereby children assume a "peerlike" relationship with their parent and are given too much of a parental role in the family hierarchy (Aquilino, 1994; Biblarz & Gottainer, 2000; Mann, Borduin, Henggeler, & Blaske, 1990). The parent's boundary assumes a level of permeability that is equivalent to that of a friendship or close adult relationship (Koerner et al.). This enmeshment of boundaries is especially prominent for mothers and daughters (Arditti, 1999), who may form an increasingly cohesive bond following divorce because of the greater amounts of disclosure typically exhibited in their relationship. Exposure to parents' continual disclosures about relational or financial difficulties can sometimes consume children with worry about their parents' well-being, contributing to greater symptoms of psychological distress (e.g., anxiety, depression; see Koerner et al.).

Parents' reliance on their children as confidants has been examined primarily by practitioners within clinical populations. In general, clinicians and systems theorists have noted that parents often turn to their children for emotional support following a divorce and warn that this can compromise children's psychological and physical well-being (Minuchin, 1974; Satir, 1967). Much less research has been conducted with empirical research from the general population, especially within diverse populations (Arditti, 1999; Koerner et al., 2000). As Arditti contended, the majority of this research has emphasized the problems that can be associated with the intergenerational boundaries between parents and children. Unlike previous researchers, Arditti discovered in her qualitative interviews with 58 young adult children who experienced divorce that their mothers' reliance on them for emotional support enhanced their closeness and was predominantly valued by the participants. Other research also suggests that parents and children, especially mothers and daughters, maintain close relationships and potentially even increase their closeness after divorce (Amato, 2000).

The majority of the research that is available on this topic, however, tends to support the finding that role enmeshment can pose psychological risks for children (e.g., Alexander, 2003). For instance, in their research with a sample of 62 adolescent girls and their mothers 2 years after divorce, Koerner and Lehman (e.g., Koerner et al., 2000; Koerner, Wallace, Lehman, & Raymond, 2002; Lehman & Koerner, 2002) found that most of the mothers had disclosed to their daughters about five primary topic areas: financial concerns, negativity toward their former spouse, difficulties with their job, personal concerns, and parenting challenges. They discovered that financial concerns, negativity toward their former spouse, difficulties with their job, and personal concerns were associated with their daughter's psychological distress, but not greater closeness as other research suggests. They also found that the daughters' worrying about their mothers' welfare as a result of the disclosures mediated the association between maternal disclosure and the daughter's psychological distress.

The transitions and social context of divorce provide insight into why the enmeshment of parent–child boundaries is more likely in divorced, single-parent families than in two-parent families. Custodial mothers' roles are expanded from working and taking care of the children to being the major breadwinners for the family, managing the daily routines of the children and their activities, maintaining family rituals and routines, and managing the emotional impact of the divorce (Ladd & Zvonkovic, 1995). Parents are also attempting to grieve for their former relationship and cope with the adjustments of divorce with fewer social networks for support. Consequently, parents may disclose to their children and rely on them for additional responsibilities around the home in order to cope with the cumulative stressors they are experiencing. Because parents and children may undergo much of the effects of these stressors and the divorce process together, they can experience a type of traumatic bonding, which can further solidify their relationship—in both positive and negative ways (Afifi, 2003; Biblarz & Gottainer, 2000). Single parents also lack an additional parental authority to help them buffer some of the stress (Larson & Gilman, 1999). When parents are unable to contain their stress, it can "spill over" onto their children, producing a kind of stress contagion effect (Larson & Almeida, 1999; Larson & Gilman).

Of future interest to researchers studying communication is the degree to which parents' disclosure of divorce-related issues, and subsequent anxiety and stress, becomes transferred to their children and the conditions under which this occurs. Such discussions become especially complex when the circumstances of divorce are sensitive, negatively valenced, or identity threatening. For instance, gay and lesbian parents who have not told their children about their sexual orientation may choose to do so when they get a divorce from their heterosexual partner: How and when should such information be revealed to a child? Research suggests that parents' disclosures about their sexual orientation, if they do not occur at the time of the divorce, may be less stressful at earlier or later points in a child's development (Patterson, 1995). Future research is required, however, that assesses the generative impact of layers of disclosures on children.

There is also considerable research that has to be conducted to assess whether families of various ethnicities experience the stress of these divorce-related transitions differently and how their access to social networks may shape what and how much information they disclose to their children about the divorce. For instance, African Americans are more likely to divorce and form single-parent families than are Whites (Augustine, 1998; Orbuch & Brown, chap. 23, this volume). However, they also tend to have a larger kinship network than Whites, which may help to moderate some of the extent of their stress and sensitive disclosures to their children. These questions require additional attention from family scholars.

To cope effectively with the divorce process, parents and young adult children must successfully learn to renegotiate their privacy boundaries with one another. The parentification that may result for mothers and children after divorce can make it especially difficult for a new stepparent to penetrate their relational and communicative boundaries (Braithwaite et al., 2001). Stepparents often feel as if they are outsiders because of the previously established, cohesive bond and disclosures between the parent and the children (Anderson & White, 1986; Banker & Gaertner, 1998). Research has demonstrated that it is important for parents and stepparents to create a unified front or impermeable boundary (regarding their marriage) to the children (Cissna, Cox, & Bochner, 1990). This helps to prevent loyalty conflicts from resulting and to enhance new stepfamily ties. Research incorporating communication privacy management (e.g., Afifi, 2003; Afifi et al., 2004) also illustrates that parents and children, and potentially a new stepparent, from strong families tend to engage in problem solving together about how to reconstruct appropriate privacy boundaries.

Interparental Conflict, Coparenting and Children's Feelings of Being Caught

Current research suggests that interparental conflict may be particularly harmful when children become caught in the middle of their parents' disputes and negative disclosures. When the boundaries for appropriate revelation of information become ambiguous and parents begin to form alliances with their children, whether consciously or subconsciously, children may "feel caught" between their parents (Afifi & Schrodt, 2003b; Amato & Afifi, 2004; Buchanan et al., 1991; Johnston & Campbell, 1987). When parents are unable to encapsulate their conflict, their negative interaction patterns can spill over onto their children (Hetherington, 1999; Hetherington, Cox, & Cox, 1982). This interaction often includes negative disclosures about the other parent, accounts that substantiate one's point of view at the expense of the other parent, tests of allegiance, using children as messengers of information or mediators, and probing for information about the other parent (Afifi, 2003; Buchanan et al.). When such communication patterns emerge, children often describe themselves as "torn," "caught," or "put in the middle" of their parents' conflict. Children often experience a dialectical tension of loyalty–disloyalty, because in their attempt to be loyal to both of their parents, they are simultaneously disloyal to each of them (Afifi).

Because of the stressful nature of such interactions, it is often difficult for children to maintain equitable relationships with both of their parents. In high-discord marriages, children have been found to form an alliance with one parent over another over time (Booth & Amato, 1994; Johnston & Campbell, 1987; Mann et al., 1990), perhaps because of the difficulty of continuing to balance the competing needs of one parent with the other. Nevertheless, this is an undesired and anxiety-producing alliance for children (Amato & Afifi, 2004; Hetherington, 1999). In fact, feelings of being caught have been associated with externalizing behavior, depression, and feelings of self-blame in adolescents and young adults (Buchanan & Waizenhofer, 2001). For example, Buchanan et al. (1991) found that children from divorced families whose parents had a highly conflicted relationship with little cooperation were more likely to feel caught than children from divorced families whose parents had a cooperative relationship. Parental conflict, however, was only associated with children's depression, and deviance through children's feelings of being enmeshed in it.

There is also some evidence to suggest that children's feelings of being caught affect parent–child relations for children in first-marriage and divorced families and that these effects may carry over into adulthood (Afifi & Schrodt, 2003a; Amato & Afifi, 2004; Mann et al., 1990; Lopez, Campbell, & Watkins, 1989). In general, research suggests that adolescents and young adults who feel caught between their parents report more problematic parent–child relations compared with other adolescents and young adults (Afifi & Schrodt; Amato & Afifi; Buchanan et al., 1991). Afifi and Schrodt discovered that adolescents' and young adults' feelings of being caught mediated the association between divorce and children's avoidance and satisfaction with their parents. The children's feelings of being caught were a by-product of their parents' demand–withdraw patterns and lack of communication competence. Their general model of communication patterns held true for adolescents and young adults of divorced and nondivorced households. Similarly, Amato and Afifi found that adult offspring (aged 19–37 years) with highly conflicted, but not divorced, parents were more likely than other adult offspring of low-conflict parents and divorced parents to feel caught in the middle. These feelings were indicative of psychological distress and weakened parent–child relationships. Additional analyses revealed that children's feelings of being caught appeared to fade approximately 10 years after divorce. These results suggest that, unlike children of divorce who may be apt to remove themselves from a turbulent parental environment, children whose parents have a high-conflict marriage and who remain together may be unable to escape their parents' marital difficulties.

Children respond to the internalization of their parents' conflict in numerous ways. In particular, children seem to respond to such loyalty conflicts, and interparental conflict more generally, with avoidance and escape behaviors. When confronted with parental conflict, adolescents' initial reaction is often one of wanting to remove themselves from the aversive environment (Afifi et al., 2004). For example, they may physically walk away from their parent(s) and go into their room, play video games, turn up the volume on their television, or read a book to escape. They may also avoid confrontation with their parents by refusing to discuss the matter, changing the topic, providing evasive responses, or simply not bringing up the topic for discussion. As research indicates (Afifi, 2003; Golish & Caughlin, 2002), children often avoid talking about one parent to another in order to prevent conflict or being pulled further into their parents' disputes. Avoidance may often be an automatic response when children simply do not know how they should respond to a difficult circumstance.

Nevertheless, children also respond to interparental conflict and their feelings of being caught in other, more confrontational ways. Children may respond aggressively to their parents' interparental conflict, modeling their parents' behavior (Cummings, Goeke-Morey, & Papp, 2001). They may simply attempt to confront their parents' negative interaction patterns. They may ask their parents to leave them out of their problems and to take responsibility for them. However, many young adolescents may lack the communication competence or cognitive complexity necessary to confront their parents in such a way (Buchanan et al., 1991). They have also been socialized not to challenge their parents' authority, making confrontation especially difficult.

The research on interparental conflict and children's feelings of being caught points to the importance of constructive coparenting for positive family functioning. The initial level of conflict between spouses before and during separation is predictive of the quality of coparenting in the years following divorce (Maccoby, Depner, & Mnookin, 1990; Maccoby & Mnookin, 1992). Maccoby et al. found that parents' ability to cooperate with each other 18 months after their divorce was linked to their degree of hostility toward one another at the time of their physical separation. Even though approximately 24% percent of divorced spouses report having inadequate support and some conflict in their relationship and 20% have intense, ongoing conflict, 57% rate themselves as having at least a cooperative alliance (Whiteside, 1998). Although reducing the amount and intensity of conflict between parents are important first steps toward effective parenting, a positive coparental alliance is more than simply low levels of conflict (Whiteside).

Even though most of the research on coparenting following divorce tends to describe characteristics of its ineffectiveness, there is some research that has examined what constitutes effective coparenting (see chap. 13 by Adamsons & Pasley, this volume). According to Ahrons (Ahrons, 1980, Ahrons & Rodgers, 1987; Camara & Resnick, 1989) and others (e.g., Maccoby & Mnookin, 1992), central components of positive coparental alliances include communicating respect for the other parent, being able to control anger, maintaining constructive information exchange and problem solving about the children when confronted with stressors, and creating ways to share responsibility for everyday childrearing tasks, parenting, and movement between households. Parents who are successful at coparenting recognize that a harmonious relationship is best for their children and communicate in a way that facilitates secure attachments with them (Whiteside, 1998). Effective coparents are also likely to believe that their former spouse is a good parent and that his or her role as a parent is completely separate from the spousal relationship (Masheter, 1997; Whiteside). This sense of respect is communicated through parents' verbal and nonverbal communication to their former spouses and to their children.

Issues surrounding coparenting become even more complex when one assesses the multiple forms that coparental relationships can assume. Cohabitation and childrearing outside of marriage have become increasingly common in the United States (Seltzer, 2000a). Children can often solidify the union between cohabiting partners, especially couples that may not be able to legally recognize their relationship through marriage or couples that do not feel a need to conform to societal proscriptions for marriage. However, because cohabiting relationships tend to be more short lived than marriages, it can increase the number of family disruptions that children experience in their lifetime (Seltzer). There are also fewer barriers to maintaining the relationship and family life in cohabiting relationships, which may affect the effectiveness of coparenting practices when a couple is together and if they separate. For instance, fathers of children born in cohabiting relationships pay less child support and communicate with their children less often than do divorced fathers (Seltzer, 2000b). Nevertheless, research suggests that divorced gay fathers tend to parent with greater warmth, reasoning, and limit setting (or authoritative parenting) than divorced heterosexual fathers (Bigner & Jacobsen, 1989). Moreover, unlike what popular culture suggests, few differences in parenting behaviors have been found between divorced lesbian mothers and divorced heterosexual mothers and their former partners (see Patterson, 2000). Therefore, when assessing the effectiveness of coparenting behaviors following separation, one must consider the type of family.

Family Rituals, Maintenance, and Coping

Families as Collective, Interactive Systems

Much of the work on resilience in postdivorce families can be found in the research on family rituals, maintenance behaviors, and collective coping. Although research on communication in postdivorce families as social units remains limited (see Socha, 1999), researchers have long realized the importance of assessing the communication patterns of families rather than assessing only isolated individuals. Determining the interdependence of various family members' behaviors as set within larger, systemic influences can shed light on how family members cope with divorce-related stressors and how they can foster greater resilience as a collective unit.

Many of the stressors that families experience throughout the divorce process affect both the individual and the family. For instance, even though parents may attempt to shield their children from some of the financial difficulties they encounter after divorce, children are still often able to detect their parents' stress. Postdivorce families must also learn to adapt to their changes in family structure, routines, and relationships in order to regain a sense of family. As Hutchinson, Afifi, and Krouse (2005) contend, when we conceive of families as primarily physical structures, we obstruct our understanding of how families sustain and even grow in the face of adversity. These authors argue that in order to truly comprehend how these families cope, researchers must examine the communicative and behavioral practices that encourage *family making*. According to Bella (in press), family making refers to the process that families engage in that helps them create, maintain, and strengthen the bonds that constitute their family. In essence, research is necessary that focuses on what families actually do that helps them cope with stress and build resilience as a family (Hutchinson et al.).

As Bella (in press) goes on to suggest, family making is composed of acts of caring, enduring and intimate relationships, and shared physical space. Caring involves family members caring for each other through affection and affirming communication, care-taking activities, domestic labor, and reciprocal care in which family members actively care for one another. Bella also argues that family making means that the ties between family members are able to endure and that members "stick together" through crises. Finally, shared domestic space refers to the space that is composed of the everyday rituals and practices that family members engage in that help build a sense of routine and cohesion. Hutchinson et al. (2004) found that parents and adolescents engaged in numerous types of communicative and leisure-based practices that helped them reconstruct a sense of family after divorce. In particular, they found that family rituals and routines were essential to creating continuity during times of stress. Their findings validated the existing scholarship on relationship maintenance (Duck, 1990) that illustrates that, in addition to the activities themselves, it was the talk during the activities that helped individuals maintain their relationships.

Other research also points to the importance of family rituals in the family-making process (Braithwaite, Baxter, & Harper, 1998; Bruess & Pearson, 1997; Imber-Black, 2002). Rituals can be especially important for families that are undergoing crises (Johnson, 1988), because they promote stability while simultaneously encouraging adaptation and growth (Braithwaite et al.).

For instance, Braithwaite et al. found that one of the ways that stepfamilies were able to adapt to their transition was by creating new family rituals and blending them with the predictability of their old ones. Similarly, research indicates that families spending time together, sharing activities, talking about their daily routines, and having regular family meetings to discuss their stress promotes resilience against stress (Golish, 2003; Kelley, 1992).

Communication Processes That Foster Resilience and Strength in Divorced Families

The research on family rituals and practices echoes scholarship that assumes a strengths perspective (Coleman, Fine, Ganong, Downs, & Pauk, 2001; Golish, 2003; Stinnett & DeFrain, 1985). Although their research was not specifically focused on postdivorce families, Stinnett and DeFrain (e.g., DeFrain & Stinnett, 1992; Stinnett & DeFrain; Stinnett, 1979) identified characteristics of strong families that have been found to be predictive of positive family functioning across family types. Their Family Strengths Inventory consists of six underlying characteristics of strong families: appreciation for one another, spending time together, open communication patterns, commitment, high degree of religious orientation, and the ability to handle stress in a constructive manner. Building on their work, Kelley and Sequeira (1997) compared functional and dysfunctional families and discovered that their findings verified those of Stinnett and DeFrain. Families that were functional were open in their communication, managed conflict assertively, spent time together, created a supportive environment, were religious, and felt a sense of unity. Other research has focused on strengths or varying degrees of functionality in postdivorce families (e.g., Baxter, Braithwaite, & Nicholson, 1999; Duncan & Brown, 1992; Golish, 2003) and has found that families with higher levels of functioning engage in greater degrees of openness, direct confrontation of stressors, compromise, problem solving, family rituals, and affirming communication; they have realistic expectations, allow the family to develop at its own pace, and use open displays of affection.

A common theme across these studies is the collective and interactive efforts that family members use to overcome adversity. Most of the processes that help postdivorce families function well appear to occur at the individual and the family level and often do so through family members' communication and activities with one another. Nevertheless, most of the research on stress and coping has focused primarily on the cognitive capacities of the individual to cope rather than the coping abilities of the family (Skinner & Edge, 1998). As other scholars (e.g., Lyons, Mickelson, Sullivan, & Coyne, 1998; Wells, Hobfoll, & Lavin, 1997) have argued, the continued overemphasis on individualistic coping diverts attention away from other important collective coping practices. For instance, problem solving typically emphasizes the active cognitive efforts that individuals use to directly address their stress, instead of also attending to the predominantly interactive process with family, friends, and outside support networks that encompasses it. Although it is often the individual who decides to take action to control the stress, how this problem solving is accomplished is largely the result of collective, interactive efforts with others.

Research on social support sheds some light on the jointly constructed nature of coping in postdivorce families. Research on social support more generally (e.g., Brashers, Haas, Klingle, & Neidig, 2000; Ford, Babrow, & Stohl, 1996; Gore & Aseltine, 1995) suggests that access to social networks can buffer some of the extent of individuals' stress. Similarly, research on coping on postdivorce families suggests that family members can moderate some of the physical and psychological stress that family members experience after a divorce (e.g., Brown, Eichenberger, Portes, & Christensen, 1991; Richmond & Christensen, 2000). For instance,

Brown et al. found that adolescents adapted to divorce better when their family was nurturing and supportive in its communication and provided a sense of security and routine. Families that provide a warm environment where open, confirming, and comforting communication is encouraged can help its members cope more effectively with the divorce process.

As Lyons et al. (1998) noted, however, communal coping involves more than one family member's simply providing help to another. Research on communal coping, or the active, jointly shared coping mechanisms that groups of people use together to confront adversity (Lyons et al.), could provide further insight into the interactive nature of coping in families and corresponding health benefits. This construct has been studied in contexts such as wars (e.g., Khalaf, 2002), natural disasters (e.g., Kaniasty & Norris, 1993), pregnancy (e.g., Wells et al., 1997), HIV support groups (e.g., Brashers et al., 2000), and family members with chronic illnesses (e.g., Lyons & Meade, 1995), but it can also be used to determine the extent to which families take collective responsibility for their stressors and confront them together in order to foster resilience as a social group. For instance, Afifi et al. (2004) discovered that families that engaged in communal coping strategies used problem solving, communicated resolve, and directly confronted and assumed responsibility for stressors following divorce. As this research suggests, communal coping may further enhance postdivorce families' ability to actively address their stress.

AVENUES FOR FUTURE RESEARCH

Communication is incredibly important for determining how family members respond to, and cope with, divorce-related stressors. Family members rely on one another to validate, console, reduce their uncertainty, and problem solve about their stress. Future research efforts should be directed at explicating the specific ways that family members cope communicatively with one another in order to cope with the divorce process. The way that family members cope communicatively with one another could also have unique implications for family functioning. When communication is ineffective, it can hinder adaptation to divorce and even place individuals at risk for getting divorced. When it is effective, however, it can promote resilience against some of the adverse effects of stress.

As the previous sections in this chapter illustrate, most of the divorce literature tends to focus on the communicative factors that promote risk rather than those that foster resilience in postdivorce families. To better understand how postdivorce families can create strong relational bonds and cope effectively with the stressors they encounter, researchers must begin to detail the communicative processes that strengthen them. An extensive amount of research has focused on the stress and problematic behavior patterns of divorced families that make them distinct from first-marriage families (Coleman et al., 2000). As Coleman et al. contend, however, these differences are often highlighted at the expense of the similarities to first-marriage families or the properties that make some postdivorce families more functional than others. Although these studies are extremely important and necessary for understanding the impact of divorce on families, especially for prevention purposes, we are often resigned to knowledge of strategies that can minimize and prevent dysfunction rather than strategies that can also promote resilience.

Research is also required that produces greater specificity in the communication variables that promote risk and resiliency in postdivorce families. To decipher which communication processes foster varying levels of risk and resilience, researchers must make a microscopic examination of the communication phenomenon under consideration. For example, much of the work on interparental conflict has focused on the amount of conflict instead of also delineating the different types of conflict that make it more or less problematic (Cummings et al., 2001). Because conflict differs in its form, functionality, and intensity and is dependent on the particular outcome being investigated, not all conflict is likely to be equally harmful (Afifi & Schrodt, 2003a). Similarly, further research is necessary that details what constitutes appropriate disclosure about the divorce process and the amount and types of disclosures that are destructive or beneficial for children. What and how much information should parents provide to their children about the divorce process? What impact do the type and valence of the topic have on children's responses to such disclosures?

Valuable knowledge could also be garnered from a better understanding of what constitutes effective coparenting practices and how they can be best be achieved by parents. Parents may be aware that they *should* communicate competently, but have difficulty knowing *how* to do that when they feel as if their former spouse's communication is out of their control. For instance, they may desire open and cooperative communication with their former spouse, but after several failed attempts caused by emotional outbursts or aggressiveness, they resort to minimization tactics as a way to better manage the stress. However, when is avoidance beneficial and when is it harmful to coparental and parent–child relationships? How can parents maintain cooperative relationships when the rules for appropriate privacy are violated? These, and other issues, could provide further insight into the functionality of communication in the coparental alliance.

Finally, there are also aspects of communication that are rooted in genetics and physiological differences. Future research efforts could be directed at determining the role of physiology in family members' ability to cope effectively with the divorce process. For example, what happens to children's anxiety levels when their parents disclose negative information to them about their other parent? Do people who have elevated anxiety levels have greater difficulty coping communicatively with others about the divorce process? Furthermore, do families that actively engage in communal coping strategies respond physiologically with greater resilience to stress than other families? These, and many other questions, may provide additional insight into the communicative nature of the stress and coping process in postdivorce families. However, because communication is largely socially constructed, it illustrates the importance of differentiating the communication processes that promote risk and resiliency in postdivorce families. If children learn communication skill deficiencies from their parents that make them susceptible to divorce themselves, then they can also be taught functional patterns of communication that facilitate healthy relationships.

REFERENCES

Afifi, T., & Keith, S. (2004). A risk and resiliency model of ambiguous loss in post-divorce stepfamilies. *Journal of Family Communication, 4,* 65–98.

Afifi, T. D. (2003). "Feeling caught" in stepfamilies: Managing boundary turbulence through appropriate privacy coordination rules. *Journal of Social and Personal Relationships, 20,* 729–756.

Afifi, T. D., Hutchinson, S., & Krouse, S. (2005). *A contextual model of communal coping in post-divorce families.* Manuscript submitted for publication.

Afifi, T. D., & Nussbaum, J. F. (in press). Family career theories: Family stress and adaptation across the lifespan. In D. Braithwaite & L. Baxter (Eds.), *Family communication theories.* Thousand Oaks, CA: Sage.

Afifi, T. D., & Schrodt, P. (2003a). "Feeling caught" as a mediator of adolescents' and young adults' avoidance and satisfaction with their parents in divorced and non-divorced households. *Communication Monographs, 70,* 142–173.

Afifi, T. D., & Schrodt, P. (2003b). Uncertainty and the avoidance of the state of one's family/relationships in stepfamilies, post-divorce single parent families, and first marriage families. *Human Communication Research, 29,* 516–533.

Afifi, W. A., & Guerrero, L. K. (2000). Motivations underlying topic avoidance in close relationships. In S. Petronio (Ed)., *Balancing the secrets of private disclosures* (pp. 165–180). Mahwah, NJ: Lawrence Erlbaum Associates.

Ahrons, C. R. (1980). Joint custody arrangements in the postdivorce family. *Journal of Divorce, 3*, 189–205.

Ahrons, C. R. (1983). Divorce: Before, during and after. In H. I. McCubbin & C. R. Figley (Eds.), *Stress and the family. Vol. 1: Coping with normative transitions* (pp. 102–115). New York: Brunner/Mazel.

Ahrons, C. R., & Rodgers, R. H. (1987). *Divorced families*. New York: Norton.

Alexander, P. C. (2003). Parent–child role reversal: Development of a measure and test of an attachment theory model. *Journal of Systemic Therapies, 22*, 31–43.

Amato, P., & Afifi, T. D. (2004). *Adult children's feelings of being caught between their parents in divorced and nondivorced families: Consequences for parent–child relations and children's well-being*. Manuscript submitted for publication.

Amato, P. R. (1996). Explaining the intergenerational transmission of divorce. *Journal of Marriage and the Family, 58*, 628–640.

Amato, P. R. (1999). Children of divorced parents as young adults. In E. M. Hetherington (Ed.), *Coping with divorce, single parenting, and remarriage: A risk and resiliency perspective* (pp. 147–164). Mahwah, NJ: Lawrence Erlbaum Associates.

Amato, P. R. (2000). The consequences of divorce for adults and children. *Journal of Marriage and the Family, 62*, 1269–1287.

Amato, P. R., & Booth, A. (1996). A prospective study of parental divorce and parent–child relationships. *Journal of Marriage and the Family, 58*, 356–365.

Amato, P. R., & DeBoer, D. D. (2001). The transmission of marital instability across generations: Relationship skills or commitment to marriage? *Journal of Marriage and Family, 63*, 1038–1051.

Amato, P. R., & Keith, B. (1991). Parental divorce and the well-being of children: A meta-analysis. *Psychological Bulletin, 110*, 26–46.

Amato, P. R., Loomis, L., & Booth, A. (1995). Parental divorce, marital conflict, and offspring well-being during early adulthood. *Social Forces, 73*, 895–915.

Amato, P. R., & Rezac, S. J. (1994). Contact with nonresident parents, interparental conflict, and children's behavior. *Journal of Family Issues, 15*, 191–207.

Amato, P. R., & Rogers, S. J. (1997). A longitudinal study of marital problems and subsequent divorce. *Journal of Marriage and the Family, 59*, 612–624.

Anderson, J. Z., & White, G. D. (1986). An empirical investigation of interaction and relationship patterns of functional and dysfunctional nuclear families and stepfamilies. *Family Process, 25*, 407–422.

Aquilino, W. S. (1994). Impact of childhood family disruption on young adults' relationships with parents. *Journal of Marriage and the Family, 56*, 295–313.

Arditti, J. A. (1999). Rethinking relationships between divorced mothers and their children: Capitalizing on family strengths. *Family Relations, 48*, 109–119.

Augustine, J. K. (1998). The impact of race on divorce in the United States. *Journal of Comparative Family Studies, 29*, 529–549.

Bandura, A. (1977). *Social learning theory*. Englewood Cliffs, NJ: Prentice-Hall.

Banker, B. S., & Gaertner, S. L. (1998). Achieving stepfamily harmony: An intergroup-relations approach. *Journal of Family Psychology, 12*, 310–325.

Baum, N., & Shnit, D. (2003). Divorced parents' conflict management styles: Self-differentiation and narcissism. *Journal of Divorce and Remarriage, 39*, 37–58.

Baxter, L. A., Braithwaite, D. O., & Nicholson, J. H. (1999). Turning points in the development of blended families. *Journal of Social and Personal Relationships, 16*, 291–313.

Bella, L. (Ed.). (in press). *Family making*. Halifax, NS: Fernwood Press.

Biblarz, T. J., & Gottainer, G. (2000). Family structure and children's success: A comparison of widowed and divorced single-mother families. *Journal of Marriage and the Family, 62*, 533–548.

Bigner, J. J., & Jacobsen, R. B. (1989). Parenting behaviors of homosexual and heterosexual fathers. In E. W. Bozett (Eds.), *Homosexuality and the family* (pp. 173–186). New York: Harrington Park Press.

Booth, A., & Amato, P. R. (1994). Parental marital quality, parental divorce, and relations with parents. *Journal of Marriage and the Family, 56*, 21–34.

Booth, A., & Amato, P. R. (2001). Parental predivorce relations and offspring postdivorce well-being. *Journal of Marriage and Family, 63*, 197–212.

Braithwaite, D. O., Baxter, L. A., & Harper, A. M. (1998). The role of rituals in the management of the dialectical tension of "old" and "new" in blended families. *Communication Studies, 49*(2), 101–120.

Braithwaite, D. O., Olson, L., Golish, T., Soukup, C., & Turman, P. (2001). Developmental communication patterns of blended families: Exploring the different trajectories of blended families. *Journal of Applied Communication Research, 29*, 221–247.

Brashers, D. E., Haas, S. M., Klingle, R. S., & Neidig, J. L. (2000). Collective AIDS activism and individu-als' perceived self-advocacy in physician–patient communication. *Human Communication Research, 26,* 372–402.

Brown, J. H., Eichenberger, S. A., Portes, P. R., & Christensen, D. N. (1991). Family functioning factors associated with the adjustment of children of divorce. *Journal of Divorce and Remarriage, 17,* 81–96.

Bruess, C. J. S., & Pearson, J. C. (1997). Interpersonal rituals in marriage and adult friendship. *Communication Monographs, 64,* 25–46.

Buchanan, C. M., Maccoby, E. E., & Dornbusch, S. M. (1991). Caught between parents: Adolescents' experience in divorced homes. *Child Development, 62,* 1008–1029.

Buchanan, C. M., & Waizenhofer, R. (2001). The impact of interparental conflict on adolescent children: Considerations of family systems and family structure. In A. Booth, A. C. Crouter, & M. Clements (Eds.), *Couples in conflict* (pp. 149–161). Mahwah, NJ: Lawrence Erlbaum Associates.

Camara, K. A., & Resnick, G. (1989). Styles of conflict resolution and cooperation between divorced parents: Effects on child behavior and adjustment. *American Journal of Orthopsychiatry, 59,* 560–575.

Caspi, A., & Elder, G. H., Jr. (1988). Emergent family patterns: The intergenerational construction of problem behavior and relationships. In R. A. Hinde & J. Stevenson-Hinde (Eds.), *Relationships within families* (pp. 218–240). New York: Oxford University Press.

Caughlin, J. P. (2002). The demand/withdraw pattern of communication as a predictor of marital satisfaction over time: Unresolved issues and future directions. *Human Communication Research, 28,* 49–85.

Caughlin, J. P., & Huston, T. L. (2002). A contextual analysis of the association between demand/withdraw and marital satisfaction. *Personal Relationships, 9,* 95–119.

Caughlin, J. P., Huston, T. L., & Houts, R. M. (2000). How does personality matter in marriage? An examination of trait anxiety, interpersonal negativity, and marital satisfaction. *Journal of Personality and Social Psychology, 78,* 326–336.

Caughlin, J. P., & Vangelisti, A. L. (1999). Desire for change in one's partner as a predictor of the demand/withdraw pattern of marital communication. *Communication Monographs, 66,* 66–89.

Chase-Lansdale, P. L., Cherlin, A. J., & Kiernan, K. E. (1995). The long-term effects of parental divorce on the mental health of young adults: A developmental perspective. *Child Development, 66,* 1614–1634.

Christensen, A., & Heavey, C. L. (1990). Gender and social structure in the demand/withdraw pattern of marital conflict. *Journal of Personality and Social Psychology, 59,* 73–81.

Cissna, K. N., Cox, D. E., & Bochner, A. P. (1990). The dialectic of marital and parental relationships within the stepfamily. *Communication Monographs, 37,* 44–61.

Cole, C. L., & Cole, A. L. (1999). Boundary ambiguities that bind former spouses together after children leave home in post-divorce families. *Family Relations, 48,* 271–272.

Coleman, M., Fine, M. A., Ganong, L. H., Downs, K., & Pauk, N. (2001). When you're not the Brady Bunch: Identifying perceived conflicts and resolution strategies in stepfamilies. *Personal Relationships, 8,* 55–73.

Coleman, M., Ganong, L., & Fine, M. (2000). Reinvestigating remarriage: Another decade of progress. *Journal of Marriage and the Family, 62,* 1288–1307.

Cummings, E. M., Goeke-Morey, M. C., & Papp, L. M. (2001). Couple conflict, children, and families: It's not just you and me, babe. In A. Booth, A. C. Crouter, and M. Clements (Eds.), *Couples in conflict* (pp. 117–147). Mahwah, NJ: Erlbaum.

Deater-Deckard, K., & Dunn, J. (1999). Multiple risks and adjustment in young children growing up in different family settings: A British community study of stepparent, single mother, and nondivorced families. In E. M. Hetherington (Ed.), *Coping with divorce, single parenting, and remarriage: A risk and resiliency perspective* (pp. 47–65). Mahwah, NJ: Lawrence Erlbaum Associates.

DeFrain, J., & Stinnett, N. (1992). Building on the inherent strengths of families: A positive approach for family psychologists and counselors. *Topics in Family Psychology and Counseling, 1,* 15–26.

Duck, S. (1990). Relationships as unfinished business: Out of the frying pan and into the 1990s. *Journal of Social and Personal Relationships, 7,* 3–28.

Duncan, S. F., & Brown, G. (1992). RENEW: A program for building remarried family strengths. *Families in Society: The Journal of Contemporary Human Services, 73,* 149–158.

Emery, R. E. (1994). *Renegotiating family relationships: Divorce, child custody, and mediation.* New York: Guilford.

Emery, R. E., & Dillon, P. (1994). Conceptualizing the divorce process: Renegotiating boundaries of intimacy and power in the divorce family system. *Family Relations, 43,* 374–379.

Folkman, S., & Lazarus, R. S. (1988). Coping as a mediator of emotion. *Journal of Personality and Social Psychology, 54,* 466–475.

Ford, L. A., Babrow, A. S., & Stohl, C. (1996). Social support messages and the management of uncertainty in the experience of breast cancer: An application of problematic integration theory. *Communication Monographs, 63,* 189–202.

Forehand, R., Biggar, H., & Kotchick, B. A. (1998). Cumulative risk across family stressors: Short and long-term effects for adolescents. *Journal of Abnormal Child Psychology, 26,* 119–128.

Ganong, L. H., & Coleman, M. (1994). *Remarried family relationships.* Thousand Oaks, CA: Sage.

Golish, T. D. (2003). Stepfamily communication strengths: Examining the ties that bind. *Human Communication Research, 29,* 41–80.

Golish, T. D., & Caughlin, J. (2002). I'd rather not talk about it: Adolescents' and young adults' use of topic avoidance in stepfamilies. *Journal of Applied Communication Research, 30,* 78–106.

Gore, S., & Aseltine, R. H. (1995). Protective processes in adolescence: Matching stressors with social resources. *American Journal of Community Psychology, 23,* 301–315.

Gottman, J. M. (1994). *What predicts divorce? The relationship between marital processes and marital outcomes.* Hillsdale, NJ: Lawrence Erlbaum Associates.

Gottman, J. M., & Levenson, R. W. (2000). The timing of divorce: Predicting when a couple will divorce over a 14-year period. *Journal of Marriage and the Family, 62,* 737–745.

Graham, E. E. (1997). Turning points and commitment in post-divorce relationships. *Communication Monographs, 64,* 351–367.

Greif, G. L. (1995). When divorced fathers want no contact with their children: A preliminary analysis. *Journal of Divorce and Remarriage, 23,* 75–85.

Gross, M. A., & Guerrero, L. K. (2000). Managing conflict appropriately and effectively: An application of the competence model to Rahim's organizational conflict styles. *International Journal of Conflict Management, 11,* 200–226.

Guerrero, L. K. (1994). "I'm so mad I could scream": The effects of anger expression on relational satisfaction and communication competence. *The Southern Communication Journal, 59,* 125–141.

Heavey, C. L., Christensen, A., & Malamuth, N. M. (1995). The longitudinal impact of demand and withdrawal during marital conflict. *Journal of Consulting and Clinical Psychology, 63,* 797–801.

Heavey, C. L., Layne, C., & Christensen, A. (1993). Gender and conflict structure in marital interaction: A replication and extension. *Journal of Consulting and Clinical Psychology, 61,* 16–27.

Herman-Stahl, M. A., & Petersen, A. C. (1996). The protective role of coping and social resources for depressive symptoms among young adolescents. *Journal of Youth and Adolescence, 25,* 733–753.

Hetherington, E. M. (1999). Family functioning and the adjustment of adolescent siblings in diverse types of families. In E. M. Hetherington, S. H. Henderson, and D. Reiss (Eds.), Adolescent siblings in stepfamilies: Family functioning and adolescent adjustment. *Monographs of the Society for Research in Child Development, 64,* 1–25.

Hetherington, E. M., Cox, M., & Cox, R. (1982). *Effects of divorce on parents and children. Nontraditional families: Parenting and child development* (pp. 233–259). Hillsdale, NJ: Lawrence Erlbaum Associates.

Hoffman, C. D. (1995). Pre- and post-divorce father–child relationships and child adjustment: Noncustodial fathers' perspectives. *Journal of Divorce and Remarriage, 23,* 3–19.

Holloway, S. D., & Machida, S. (1991). The relationship between divorced mothers' perceived control over child rearing and children's post-divorce development. *Family Relations, 40,* 272–295.

Huston, T. L., & Vangelisti, A. L. (1991). Socioemotional behavior and satisfaction in marital relationships: A longitudinal study. *Journal of Personality and Social Psychology, 61,* 721–733.

Hutchinson, S., Afifi, T. D., & Krouse, S. (2005). *"Family making" following divorce: Parent and adolescent perspectives.* Manuscript submitted for publication.

Imber-Black, E. (2002). Family rituals—From research to the consulting room and back again: Comment on the special section. *Journal of Family Psychology, 16,* 445–446.

Jekielek, S. (1998). Parental conflict, marital disruption and children's emotional well-being. *Social Forces, 76,* 905–936.

Johnson, C. L. (1988). Socially controlled civility: The functioning of rituals in the divorce process. *American Behavioral Scientist, 31,* 685–701.

Johnston, J. R., & Campbell, L. E. G. (1987). Instability in family networks of divorced and disputing parents. In E. J. Lawler & B. Markovsky (Eds.), *Advances in group processes* (Vol. 4, pp. 243–269). Greenwich, CT: JAI.

Kaniasty, K., & Norris, F. H. (1993). A test of the social support deterioration model in the context of natural disasters. *Journal of Personality and Social Psychology, 64,* 395–408.

Kelley, D. L., & Sequeira, D. L. (1997). Understanding family functioning in a changing America. *Communication Studies, 48,* 93–107.

Kelley, P. (1992). Healthy stepfamily functioning. *Families in Society: The Journal of Contemporary Human Services, 11,* 579–587.

Khalaf, S. (2002). *Civil and uncivil violence: A history of the internationalization of communal conflict in Lebanon.* Cambridge, MA: Columbia University Press.

Koerner, S. S., Jacobs, S. L., & Raymond, M. (2000). When mothers turn to their adolescent daughters: Predicting daughters' vulnerability to negative adjustment outcomes. *Family Relations, 49,* 301–309.

Koerner, S. S., Wallace, S., Lehman, S. J., & Raymond, M. (2002). Mother-to-daughter disclosure after divorce: Are there costs and benefits? *Journal of Child and Family Studies, 11,* 469–483.

Ladd, L. D., & Zvonkovic, A. (1995). Single mothers with custody following divorce. *Marriage and Family Review, 20,* 189–207.

Lamb, M. E., Sternberg, K. J., & Thompson, R. A. (1999). The effects of divorce and custody arrangements on children's behavior, development, and adjustment. In M. E. Lamb (Ed.), *Parenting and child development in "nontraditional" families* (pp. 125–136). Mahwah, NJ: Lawrence Erlbaum Associates.

Larson, R. W., & Almeida, D. M. (1999). Emotional transmission in the daily lives of families: A new paradigm of studying family process. *Journal of Marriage and the Family, 61,* 5–20.

Larson, R. W., & Gilman, S. (1999). Transmission of emotions in the daily interactions of single-mother families. *Journal of Marriage and the Family, 61,* 21–37.

Laumann-Billings, L., & Emery, R. E. (2000). Distress among young adults from divorced families. *Journal of Family Psychology, 14,* 671–687.

Lehman, S. J., & Koerner, S. S. (2002). Family financial hardship and adolescent girls' adjustment: The role of maternal disclosure of financial concerns. *Merrill-Palmer Quarterly, 48,* 1–15.

Lengua, L. J., & Sandler, I. N. (1996). Self-regulation as a moderator of the relation between coping and symptomatology in children of divorce. *Journal of Abnormal Child Psychology, 24,* 681–701.

Lopez, F. G., Campbell, V. L., & Watkins, C. E. (1989). Effects of marital conflict and family coalition patterns on college student adjustment. *Journal of College Student Development, 30,* 46–52.

Lyons, R. F., & Meade, D. (1995). Painting a new face on relationships: Relationship modeling in response to chronic illness. In S. W. Duck & J. T. Wood (Eds.), *Confronting relationship challenges* (pp. 181–210). Thousand Oaks, CA: Sage.

Lyons, R. F., Mickelson, K., Sullivan, J. L., & Coyne, J. C. (1998). Coping as a communal process. *Journal of Social and Personal Relationships, 15,* 579–607.

Maccoby, E. E., Depner, C. E., & Mnookin, R. H. (1990). Coparenting in the second year after divorce. *Journal of Marriage and the Family, 52,* 141–155.

Maccoby, E. E., & Mnookin, R. H. (1992). *Dividing the child: Social and legal dilemmas of custody.* Cambridge, MA: Harvard University Press.

Madden-Derdich, D. A., & Arditti, J. A. (1999). The ties that bind: Attachment between former spouses. *Family Relations, 48,* 243–249.

Madden-Derdich, D. A., Leonard, S. A., & Christopher, F. S. (1999). Boundary ambiguity and coparental conflict after divorce: An empirical test of a family systems model of the divorce process. *Journal of Marriage and the Family, 61,* 588–598.

Mann, B. J., Borduin, C. M., Henggeler, S. W., & Blaske, D. M. (1990). An investigation of systemic conceptualizations of parent-child coalitions and symptom change. *Journal of Consulting and Clinical Psychology, 58,* 336–344.

Masheter, C. (1997). Healthy and unhealthy friendship and hostility between ex- spouses. *Journal of Marriage and the Family, 59,* 463–475.

Miller, S. M. (1992). Individual differences in the coping process: What to know and when to know it. In B. N. Carpenter (Ed.), *Personal coping: Theory, research, and application* (pp. 77–91). Westport, CT: Praeger.

Minuchin, S. (1974). *Family and family therapy.* Cambridge, MA: Harvard University Press.

Neuberg, S. L., Judice, T. N., & West, S. G. (1997). What the need for closure scale measures and what it does not: Toward differentiating among related epistemic motives. *Journal of Personality and Social Psychology, 72,* 1396–1412.

Patterson, C. J. (1995). Lesbian mothers, gay fathers, and their children. In A. R. D'Augelli & C. J. Patterson (Eds.), *Lesbian, gay and bisexual identities over the lifespan* (pp. 262–290). New York: Oxford University Press.

Patterson, C. J. (2000). Family relationships of lesbians and gay men. *Journal of Marriage and the Family, 62,* 1052–1070.

Petronio, S. (1991). Communication boundary management: A theoretical model of managing disclosure of private information between marital couples. *Communication Theory, 1,* 311–335.

Petronio, S. (2000). The boundaries of privacy: Praxis of everyday life. In S. Petronio (Ed.), *Balancing the secrets of private disclosures* (pp. 37–49). Mahwah, NJ: Lawrence Erlbaum Associates.

Petronio, S. (2002). Boundaries of privacy: Dialectics of disclosure. Albany, NY: SUNY Press.

Richmond, L. S., & Christensen, D. H. (2000). Coping strategies and postdivorce health outcomes. *Journal of Divorce and Remarriage, 34,* 41–59.

Richardson, S., & McCabe, M. P. (2001). Parental divorce during adolescence and adjustment in early adulthood. *Adolescence, 36,* 467–489.

Rubin, R. R. (1985). The validity of the communication competency assessment instrument. *Communication Monographs, 52,* 173–185.

Rubinstein, D., & Timmins, J. (1979). Narcissistic dyadic relationship. *The American Journal of Psychoanalysis, 39*(2), 125–136.

Sabourin, T. C., Infante, D. C., & Rudd, J. E. (1993). Verbal aggression in marriages: A comparison of violent, distressed but not violent, and nondistressed couples. *Human Communication Research, 20,* 245–267.

Sandler, I. N., Tein, J., & West, S. G. (1994). Coping, stress and the psychological symptoms of children of divorce: A cross-sectional and longitudinal study. *Child Development, 65,* 1744–1763.

Sandler, I. N., Wolchik, S. A., & Brave, S. L. (1988). The stressors of children's postdivorce environments. In S. A. Wolchik & P. Karoly (Eds.), Children of Divorce:Empirical perspectives on adjustment (pp. 111–143). New York: Gardner Press, Inc.

Satir, V. (1972). *Peoplemaking.* Palo Alto, CA: Science and Behavior Books.

Schaap, C., Buunk, B., & Kerkstra, A. (1988). Marital conflict resolution. In P. Nollar & M. A. Fitzpatrick (Eds.), *Perspectives on marital interaction* (pp. 203–244). Clevedon, England: Multilingual Matters.

Seltzer, J. A. (2000a). Families formed outside of marriage. *Journal of Marriage and the Family, 62,* 1247–1269.

Seltzer, J. A. (2000b). Child support and child access: Experiences of divorced and nonmarital families. In J. T. Oldham & M. S. Melli (Eds.), *Child support: The next frontier* (pp. 69–87). Ann Arbor, MI: University of Michigan Press.

Skinner, E., & Edge, K. (1998). Reflections on coping and development across the lifespan. *International Journal of Behavioral Development, 22,* 357–366.

Socha, T. J. (1999). Communication in family units. In L. R. Frey, D. S. Gouran, & S. M. Poole (Eds.), *The handbook of group communication theory and research* (pp. 475–492). Thousand Oaks, CA: Sage.

Sorrentino, R. M., Hewitt, E. C., & Raso-Knott, P. A. (1992). Risk-taking in games of chance and skill: Informational and affective influences on choice behavior. *Journal of Personality and Social Psychology, 62,* 522–533.

Spitzberg, B. H., & Cupach, W. R. (1984). *Interpersonal communication competence.* Beverly Hills, CA: Sage.

Stanley, S. M., Markman, H. J., & Whitton, S. W. (2002). Communication, conflict, and commitment: Insights on the foundations of relationship success from a national survey. *Family Process, 41,* 659–675.

Stinnett, N. (1979). In search of strong families. In N. Stinnett, B. Chesser, & J. DeFrain (Eds.), *Building family strengths* (pp. 23–30). Lincoln: University of Nebraska Press.

Stinnett, N., & DeFrain, J. (1985). *Secrets of strong families.* Boston: Little, Brown.

Thomas, C. E., Booth-Butterfield, M., & Booth-Butterfield, S. (1995). Perceptions of deception, divorce disclosures, and communication satisfaction with parents. *Western Journal of Communication, 59,* 228–242.

Vangelisti, A. L., & Caughlin, J. P. (1997). Revealing family secrets: The influence of topic, function, and relationships. *Journal of Social and Personal Relationships, 14,* 679–707.

Vangelisti, A. L., Caughlin, J. P., & Timmerman, L. (2001). Criteria for revealing family secrets. *Communication Monographs, 68,* 1–17.

Visher, E. B., & Visher, J. S. (1979). *Stepfamilies: A guide to working with stepparents and stepchildren.* New York: Brunner/Mazel.

von Bertalanffy, L. (1968). *General systems theory.* New York: Braziller.

Weiss, R. (1975). *Marital separation.* New York: Basic Books.

Wells, J. D., Hobfoll, S. E., & Lavin, J. (1997). Resource loss, resource gain, and communal coping during pregnancy among women with multiple roles. *Psychology of Women Quarterly, 21,* 645–662.

Whitchurch, G. G., & Dickson, F. C. (1999). Family communication. In M. Sussman, S. K. Stinmetz, & G. W. Peterson (Eds.), *Handbook of marriage and the family* (pp. 687–704). New York: Plenum.

Whiteside, M. F. (1998). The parental alliance following divorce: An overview. *Journal of Marital and Family Therapy, 24,* 3–24.

Wolfinger, N. H. (2000). Beyond the intergenerational transmission of divorce: Do people replicate the patterns of marital instability they grew up with? *Journal of Family Issues, 21,* 1061–1086.

22

No Breakup Occurs on an Island: Social Networks and Relationship Dissolution

Susan Sprecher
Illinois State University

Diane Felmlee
University of California—Davis

Maria Schmeeckle
Illinois State University

Xiaoling Shu
University of California—Davis

Relationships begin, develop, and are maintained in a social context. People often meet romantic partners and friends through other friends, acquaintances, and family members. They also are more likely to develop those relationships that are approved of by family and friends, and that are linked with existing social connections, than those that exist in isolation from social networks (Schmeeckle & Sprecher, 2004; Sprecher, Felmlee, Orbuch, & Willetts, 2002). Although the social network literature has focused on how social networks propel relationships forward toward greater intimacy (e.g., Sprecher & Felmlee, 1992), the more neglected side of this literature is that social networks also play a role in the termination of relationships. Two people may explore the possibility of a relationship with each other but never officially start dating (i.e., they end their "relationship") because their network members express disapproval of their relationship. Furthermore, couples that progress to an intimate partnership or marriage may later dissolve their relationship, in part because they are encouraged by friends and family to break up or because the network provides an alternative relationship.

In this chapter, we discuss theory and empirical literature that address how social networks, including family and friends, either prevent or possibly *contribute* to the breakup of relationships, ranging from early developing relationships to long-term marriages. We also discuss the role of social networks in the *process* and *aftermath* of relationship dissolution. As individuals go through a breakup, they involve others in the breakup process. In addition, other relationships and patterns of affiliations in the larger social network are affected when a relationship is terminated. Although most of the literature reviewed in this chapter focuses on heterosexual dating or marital couples, in a later section of the chapter we also discuss the unique social network aspects of the dissolution of same-sex couples. We also examine diversity in network influences by considering the role of social networks in the dissolution of two other specific types of couples: interracial relationships and couples formed through arranged marriages. We end our chapter with suggestions for future research.

CONCEPTUAL BACKGROUND TO SOCIAL NETWORK ATTRIBUTES AND PROCESSES

In this first section, we provide a conceptual background to the social network attributes and processes likely to be associated with relationship dissolution. *Social networks* have been defined and measured in a variety of ways (e.g., Felmlee, 2004), but they generally consist of family members (e.g., parents, siblings) as well as nonfamily members (e.g., friends, co-workers, neighbors). Each member of a couple has his or her own social network, but there is often considerable overlap between partners' social networks. *Network overlap* refers to the degree to which the two partners (or friends) have social network members in common (Milardo & Helms-Erickson, 2000). Network overlap generally increases as the relationship develops (Kalmijn & Bernasco, 2001).

Surra and Milardo (1991) distinguished between the *psychological network*, which consists of people defined to be important or significant, and the *interactive network*, which consists of people with whom one interacts on a frequent basis. Both types of social networks are likely to influence whether and how a relationship dissolves and the experiences in the aftermath of the breakup. Other network attributes include size (number of distinct individuals included in the network), composition (breakdown of the social network on dimensions such as proportion of kin to nonkin), density or interconnectedness (the degree to which the network members have connections with each other separate from their ties with the particular individual), and cross-network contact (the degree to which the partner knows and communicates with members of the other's network; e.g., Milardo & Helms-Erikson, 2000; Parks, 2000; Schmeeckle & Sprecher, 2004). As we discuss in a later section of this chapter, these network attributes are likely to change in the process and aftermath of the relationship dissolution.

Social networks exert influence on couples through various processes, including opportunity, information, and reactions (Sprecher et al., 2002). Social networks provide opportunities (for new relationships and interactions), information (e.g., about the partner), and reactions directed toward the couple that are likely to have an impact on the relationship's outcome. There are also more indirect ways by which social networks may influence the intimate dyad and the likelihood that it remains intact or ends. For example, networks provide norms about appropriate relationship behavior, including under which conditions a relationship termination might be acceptable and whether it is normative for members in the network to be coupled.

Most of the prior social network literature has focused on the relationship-building dimensions of these network processes (Felmlee & Sprecher, 2000)—that is, how opportunities lead to the initiation and development of relationships, and how positive information and explicit social approval obtained from the network strengthen the relationship. However, there are also relationship-undermining aspects to these processes. Network members may try to block opportunities for two people to spend time together and may even present opportunities for one or both partners to meet alternative partners. Network members could offer negative information about the partner. Network members also may express negative reactions (interference) for the relationship rather than positive support. Furthermore, network peer groups may strongly encourage singlehood over couplehood. When network members engage in the undermining side of these network processes, the effects are likely to be detrimental to the romantic relationship.

Nevertheless, what is a negative effect for the relationship may have a positive outcome for one or both individuals in the relationship, for example if the relationship is dysfunctional or abusive.

We also distinguish between network influence that occurs because the locus of influence is the social network itself, and network influence that occurs as a result of an action taken by one or both members of the dyad in order to obtain a particular type of social network reaction or opportunity. The former has been referred to as *exogenous network effects* because they originate outside the couple, within the network. The latter is referred to as *endogenous network effects* because they originate within the dyad, in one or both partners (Berscheid & Lopes, 1997). Furthermore, exogenous and endogenous network influences may vary in the degree to which they are intentional and planned (e.g., network members intentionally try to change the course of the relationship) versus happenstance (e.g., a chance meeting with a new attractive partner, facilitated by the social network, leads to the demise of a relationship). We know very little about how individuals manipulate their social (and physical) environments in order to either facilitate or hinder the development and continuation of their relationship, but it may be a common occurrence (e.g., Berscheid & Lopes, 1997).

THE INFLUENCE OF SOCIAL NETWORKS
ON RELATIONSHIP TERMINATION
(VERSUS STABILITY)

In this section, we begin with a discussion of the general neglect of the social environment in the study of predictors of relationship dissolution and a review of the importance of alternatives, a variable that is to some degree embedded in the social network. We then consider how social network reactions may lead to the breakup of a relationship at different stages: (a) the developing stage of the relationship; (b) after a relationship has developed and the partners have become an established couple; and (c) after marriage (i.e, a divorce). Although network processes probably operate similarly across the different stages, there are some issues unique to specific relationship stages that will be highlighted in the paragraphs that follow. The last topic addressed in this section is the degree to which people who have experienced a breakup perceive, in hindsight, that social networks played a role in their breakup process.

The Neglect of the Social Environment in Research on Predictors of Relationship Dissolution

Close relationship scholars have long been interested in identifying the factors that contribute to the breakup (vs. the stability) of intimate relationships (Berscheid & Reis, 1998). In the typical design, one or both members of a sample of couples are surveyed at one time about several aspects of their relationship, and then they are contacted again at least one additional time in order to see which variables measured at Time 1 best predict the likelihood of a breakup at a later time. Most of this research has focused on factors internal to the relationship, such as satisfaction, commitment, love, sexual intimacy, equity, and self-disclosure (for a review, see Cate, Levin, & Richmond, 2002). Generally neglected in this research are social network variables. This blindness to the role of social network variables is also characteristic of research focusing on other relationship outcomes, including relationship development and commitment. Several relationship scholars, in reviews of the close relationships literature, have criticized relationship researchers for ignoring the role of social networks and other social context factors in the development, maintenance, and dissolution of personal relationships (Berscheid, 1999; Huston & Levinger, 1978; Ridley & Avery, 1979). For example, Berscheid (1999) criticized social psychologists who study relationship stability as having "been prey to the fundamental attribution error" by an "overemphasis on the causal role of individual dispositions" and the "neglect of relationships' environment" (pp. 263–264). In our view, these critiques are warranted; we believe that network aspects are deserving of additional attention.

Alternatives: A Social Network Variable?

One variable that is external to the relationship that has received considerable attention in prior research on relationship stability is access to desirable alternatives. Comparison level for alternatives, or quality alternatives, is a variable central to interdependence theory (Rusbult, 1983; Thibaut & Kelley, 1959) and related theoretical models (e.g., Levinger, 1976) that focus on predictors of relationship satisfaction and stability. Research has indicated that quality alternatives are one of the strongest predictors of relationship stability versus termination. Those who believe they have desirable alternatives are more likely to break up over time than those who do not (e.g., Felmlee, Sprecher, & Bassin, 1990; Rusbult, 1983).

Although alternatives are not always considered to be a social network variable, most alternatives are probably embedded in or related to existing social networks. Research indicates that many people say that they are introduced to their current romantic partner by someone in their social network or at least knew about their partner prior to meeting him or her based on information from members of their network (e.g., Laumann, Gagnon, Michael, & Michaels, 1994; Parks & Eggert, 1991). Thus, people currently in a relationship who perceive that they have desirable alternatives are likely to base these perceptions in part on those who are available or known to them in their social network. They may even perceive some network members to be alternatives, as when good friends of the opposite sex (or the same sex for those who are homosexual) are available for a romantic relationship. In addition, peripheral members of the social network—such as friends of friends—contribute to the assessment of the availability of alternatives.

Although alternatives are an important factor affecting the dissolution of relationships, in the remainder of this section we focus on variables most often associated with social networks. In particular, we focus on the degree to which network members offer support for the relationship, or, conversely, the degree to which they try to interfere with or hinder the relationship. In addition, we discuss the extent to which partners have overlapping network members and spend time with these friends and family members and the degree to which this overlap affects the likelihood that the relationship remains intact versus ends.

The Specific Behaviors of Social Network Members

What types of behaviors do social network members engage in that are likely to influence a couple's relationship? Most of the research examining the degree to which network members support or hinder relationships has focused on overall support. For example, a typical question that has been asked in survey research is, "To what degree do you think your family disapproves or approves of this relationship?" (e.g., Sprecher & Felmlee, 1992). Perceptions of overall approval or disapproval for the relationship, however, usually arise from specific behaviors engaged in by network members. Leslie, Johnson, and Huston (1986) asked young adults about the type of actions their parents engaged in to influence their relationship. Approving behaviors included such actions as asking how the partner is doing and asking about the future of the relationship. Disapproving behaviors included talking about other people they could date, cautioning them about getting involved with this partner, and not talking to the partner. Many years ago, Lewis (1973) created a social reactions scale that included questions that asked about specific network reactions, such as "How often are you invited alone to a party or another social event without the other person being invited?" and "How often do members of your family make comments about how nice a pair you make together?"

Although network members may engage in a variety of behaviors to try to influence a couple's relationship, the partners may also attempt to solicit reactions from their network members in order to facilitate particular types of interactions in their relationship (e.g., Berscheid & Lopes, 1997). For example, if a person is considering breaking up with his or her partner, he or she may make negative statements about the partner to others, show up at social events alone, and in other ways encourage behaviors from network members that will support the breakup of the relationship. These types of behaviors are recognized as part of the dissolution process in Duck's (1982) process model of relationship dissolution. During the "social phase" of the breakup process, one or both partners discuss their dissatisfaction with the relationship with their network members, often for the purpose of obtaining support for the breakup. As described in Rollie and Duck (chap. 12, this volume), communication with social network members at this stage often involves attributing blame, providing explanations for the pending breakup, and providing positive information about the self and negative information about the partner and the relationship.

Social Networks and the Termination of Developing Relationships

Relationship scholars do not agree on what constitutes the "beginning" of a relationship between two people. However, Berscheid, Levinger, and other scholars have referred to mutual awareness and superficial contact as minimum criteria for there to be a relationship (e.g., Berscheid & Graziano, 1979; Levinger & Snoek, 1972). If we consider awareness and superficial contact to be the start of a relationship, many developing relationships that might have developed into significant relationships, because the two partners were attracted to each other after minimal interaction, may not in fact develop. In other words, many relationships are terminated at an early stage. Although a newly developing relationship may end for a variety of reasons, the absence of social network support or actual interference from the network may play a role. If the developing relationship is not anchored sufficiently in the social environment, two people may perceive they do not have enough in common to continue interaction, despite attraction to each other. Furthermore, without the benefit of mutual friends serving as intermediaries and providing support for the relationship, two people may suffer from what has been called "pluralistic ignorance" (Vorauer & Raner, 1996) and assume that the other is not interested in pursuing the relationship. In addition, in cases in which family members and friends are aware of the relationship but actually express disapproval and interference, the relationship is probably even more likely to end at a very early stage of relationship development.

Unfortunately, the role of the social network in the dissolution of naturally occurring relationships in the very early stages of relationship development is almost impossible to assess directly because of the difficulty in obtaining a sample of pairs shortly after their initial interactions. However, research conducted on existing relationships indicates that a large proportion of dating, cohabiting, and marital relationships begin through an introduction from a network member (Laumann et al., 1994), which suggests that many fleeting but positive encounters between strangers who do not have social network connections end at an early stage of relationship development. Otherwise, a national sample, such as that in the study by Laumann et al., would be apt to yield a greater proportion of long-term relationships existing between individuals who had met without prior social connections. In addition, research on premarital relationships, ranging from casual dating to engagement, indicates a linear association between stage of relationship and level of social approval, with casual dating relationships perceived to receive the least amount of social support (Leslie et al., 1986). These results suggest that if a sample of "predating relationships" could be obtained, these pairings would be characterized by the least amount of social support or the lowest level of involvement with a larger social network.

Social Networks and the Termination of Developed and Established Relationships

Social networks have a powerful influence on the trajectory of intimate relationships that have reached a developed stage (e.g., dating or cohabiting). In particular, the affective approval of family members and friends decreases the likelihood that a couple breaks up, whereas their disapproval enhances this likelihood.

Social support and approval from network members are likely to be important once the couple is in a serious relationship for several reasons. Network support for a couple is apt to aid in the process of developing a "couple identity," in which people move from viewing themselves as separate and autonomous individuals to envisioning themselves as a bonafide pair (Felmlee & Sprecher, 2000). Having an established and firm identity as a couple is likely to assist a pair in withstanding relationship threats. In addition, approving networks can provide a wide range of support that is beneficial for committed couples, such as emotional support, instrumental aid, and advice. Supportive network members can also help individuals reframe the potentially problematic characteristics of their romantic partner in a more flattering light. More generally, social ties act as a source of information about a partner, which can reduce uncertainty about a relationship (Berger, 1988). Frequent communication with a partner's network has been linked to greater certainty and the reduction of breakups (Parks & Adelman, 1983).

Disapproving friends and family members, in contrast, may play an opposite role in a couple's development and maintenance. Unsupportive network participants can provide a negative rather than a positive interpretation of a partner's personality and actions. They also may fail to come to a couple's aid in times of need. In addition, disgruntled network members might engage in more overtly negative actions that work to undermine a pair, such as lying about one partner to the other, providing information that is wrong or misleading, or engaging in acts of betrayal.

Positive social reactions are strongly predictive of the stability of premarital relationships, whereas negative reactions are predictive of instability, according to research. For example, in a short-term longitudinal study of dating individuals (Felmlee et al., 1990), perceptions of approval from a partner's social network decreased the rate of breakup over a period of several months, when other factors were controlled for. Network support was one of the strongest predictors of couple stability in two other longitudinal studies (Parks & Adelman, 1983; Parks, Stan, & Eggert, 1983). Furthermore, perceived approval from an individual's friends, perceived approval from a partner's family and friends, and actual approval from a best friend were all significantly and positively associated with the stability of intimate relationships over a 5-month time period in a longitudinal study (Felmlee, 2001).

Approval and support from the female partner's network, in particular, may be important for the development of heterosexual relationships. Agnew, Loving, and Drigotas (2001) found that perceptions of support on the part of the friends of the female member of couples were especially successful in predicting relationship longevity, particularly for highly self-disclosing individuals. According to Sprecher and Felmlee (1992), level of approval from the female partner's social network significantly forecasts breakups even over a period as long as 5 years for a sample of romantic couples.

Why may women's networks be especially relevant to relationship development and stability in some cases? Perhaps network members of women are more involved and invested in a couple's relationship; networks may give men more leeway in their romantic encounters but monitor more closely those of women. It is also quite possible that women talk more about their relationships to their friends and family members than do men, including when they are having problems (i.e., "troubles talk"; see Tannen, 1990). Therefore, network members have additional information on which to base assessments of women's relationships. Research also indicates that women are more aware of the state of their relationship, and this probably includes how others view their relationship (Acitelli, 1992).

Contrary to the bulk of theoretical and empirical research, some research suggests that negative social network reactions are not always detrimental to couples' long-term stability and instead can strengthen a pair's bonds. The "Romeo and Juliet effect" (Driscoll, Davis, & Lipetz, 1972), for instance, may occur when network opposition to a pair drives partners closer together, rather than tearing them asunder. In such cases, lack of support on the part of family or friends sets off a process of psychological reactance, in which individuals respond negatively to what is perceived of as unfair attempts to control their lives. These individuals then intensify, rather than withdraw, their involvement in the disapproved of relationship.

An early study on the Romeo and Juliet effect found that parental interference was associated with feelings of romantic love, and that increases in interference on the part of parents were significantly related to increases in perceptions of love over time (Driscoll et al., 1972). In another investigation, participants who reported slight opposition from their mothers or fathers were more involved in their relationships than those reporting neutral responses, although the predominant link between romantic involvement and responses from parents, as well as from other network sectors, tended to be positive (Parks, Stan, & Eggert, 1983). In a study by Felmlee (2001), parental disapproval increased the stability of an individual's intimate relationship over a period of several months, but only in situations in which this opposition occurred at the same time that friends were close and approving of the couple. In other words, psychological reactance to parental disapproval appeared to be activated only when parents had negative opinions that conflicted with the positive reactions of close friends. Thus, there is some support for the Romeo and Juliet effect in empirical work, but only in certain limited situations.

An additional general process by which social networks may enhance couple instability, as opposed to their stability, is that of social competition. Individuals have general needs for emotional intimacy, and those needs may be satisfied, at least in part, by someone other than a romantic partner. Close friends, therefore, may compete with intimate partners for the role of confidante to an individual. Networks also vary as to their degree of substitutability, that is, the degree to which network members engage in the same patterns of social exchange (Marsiglio & Scanzoni, 1995). If friends or family members can readily substitute for a partner in meeting an individual's emotional needs, then a breakup may be more likely, particularly if the romantic relationship is dissatisfying. In support of this argument, there is some evidence in the literature that there is competition, or substitutability, between best friends and intimate partners that influences intimate couples. In one study (Felmlee, 2001), the rate of relationship dissolution increased substantially over time for a sample of dating individuals as closeness to a best friend intensified. However, having other sources of companionship and social support may, under some conditions, promote the stability of the relationship. For example, Rubin (1985) found through in-depth interviews conducted with middle-aged married individuals that many women reported that friends filled in the gaps of their marriage, which allowed them to appreciate their marriage for what it did offer.

Overlap that occurs between two partners' social networks is another aspect of couples' social environment that influences the relationship's development and stability over time. As romantic couples become more involved, their social networks tend to become more overlapping and interdependent (Milardo, 1982). Network interdependence is likely to decrease the chances of a breakup because two individuals become embedded in a joint network that is relatively highly invested in their future as a couple. In addition, individuals in overlapping networks have fewer opportunities to meet potential new partners, particularly if the network consists of many other couples rather than single individuals. However, the other side of this is that, if couples fail to develop intertwined networks, they may be more likely to break up. In one longitudinal study, relationships deteriorated over time when network overlap with partners decreased, whereas relationships developed when network overlap increased (Milardo, 1982). The importance of overlapping networks for relationship stability may be one reason that long-distance relationships have a higher failure rate than geographically close relationships (Rohlfing, 1995); long-distance relationships have less opportunity to develop overlapping social networks.

Social Networks and the Termination of Marriages

Compared with the research on the breakdown of dating relationships, less research has been conducted on how social networks affect the likelihood of marital dissolution. As noted by Sprecher et al. (2002), research on the role of social networks in the breakdown of marriage may be scant, both because of the assumption that the influence of social networks may be less significant once relationships enter a more committed stage and because of the difficulty in conducting prospective studies of marital relationships through to divorce (researchers would need to follow a sample of couples for a very long time in order to obtain enough divorces for analyses). However, theories of divorce or commitment argue that social networks can serve as barrier forces keeping couples in their marriage (e.g., Johnson, 1991; Levinger, 1976), and cross-sectional studies indicate that engaged and married individuals report more social pressure to remain in their relationships than do dating individuals (e.g., Cate & Sprecher, 2005).

Although social networks are generally approving of couples once they reach marriage (e.g., Sprecher & Felmlee, 2000), there is still likely to be variation in the degree of positive social reactions (Bryant & Conger, 1999). Furthermore, disapproval for the relationship can develop over time as a result of problems that emerge, including unemployment, infidelity, infertility, geographical moves, and perceived unhappiness in the couple. Cross-sectional research indicates that couples who remain married report more network support (and less opposition) before and during marriage than those who divorce (e.g., Thornes & Collard, 1979). In addition, in a study of long-term relationships, Bryant and Conger (1999) found that the more support husbands and wives reported for their relationships, the greater their satisfaction and commitment, and the greater the stability of the marriages. Couples who reported lower levels of support for their relationship had lower levels of stability.

In marriage and other long-term relationships, individuals are likely to vary in the degree to which they integrate themselves with their partner's friends and family members, feel close to them, and develop new friends together. Couples that are able to do this are probably more likely to stay committed to the relationship. For example, a study based on the Early Years of Marriage Project, conducted with a sample of 199 Black couples and 174 White couples, showed that closeness with family was associated with marital stability for Black couples although not for White couples (Veroff, Douvan, & Hatchett, 1995). Another study based on the same sample showed that, among wives from a divorced family, closeness to husband's family was positively associated with the couple's marital happiness. Furthermore, a couple's closeness to the husband's family appears to reduce the risk of divorce, particularly when the wife is from a divorced family. These results suggest that when the husband and wife forge and maintain close ties with the husband's family, they also enhance the well-being in their own marital relationship, thus reducing marital instability (Timmer & Veroff, 2000), at least among some sectors of the population.

Insiders' Perspectives of the Role of the Social Network in Breakups

In the previous sections, we discussed how measures of social support (e.g., social reactions, closeness to family) are related to relationship stability versus breakups. However, do divorced and former dating partners *perceive* that their social networks played a role in the termination of their relationships? In retrospective studies, in which divorced individuals are asked why their relationships ended, many respondents report that interference from their network (in-laws, in particular) played at least some role in the breakup (e.g., Burns, 1984; Cleek & Pearson, 1985; Kitson & Sussman, 1982). Furthermore, some people say that they would not want to divorce unless they had the support of their network for the breakup. For example, in a national sample of married individuals, 11% of the respondents reported that they considered whether family or friends would approve or disapprove of a divorce as "very important," and 22% thought it is "somewhat important" as barriers to divorce (Knoester & Booth, 2000).

Interference from the network is also reported as a factor that is a possible influence on the ending of dating relationships. For example, Sprecher (1994) asked a sample of former romantic dating partners to indicate the importance of each of several possible reasons for their breakup, and "others' disapproval of the relationship" was rated as slightly important; its mean importance was 13th in a list of 19 factors. The primary reasons given for the breakup of a romantic relationship, however, are such factors as incompatibility, lack of communication, and the development of conflicting interests (Hortacsu & Karanci, 1987; Sprecher, 1994; Stephen, 1987).

THE EFFECT OF RELATIONSHIP DISSOLUTION ON SOCIAL NETWORKS

Thus far in this chapter, we have focused on how social networks contribute to the breakup of intimate relationships. In this section, we focus on the reverse direction: how relationship dissolution affects social networks.

Studies find that, in several ways, divorce significantly reshapes the social environment of men and women who were once married. First, divorce often leads to some degree of atrophy in social networks. According to research based on a national representative sample from the United States, divorced or separated individuals have social networks that are of lower density and are of shorter duration when compared with those of the married or widowed (Hurlbert & Acock, 1990). Second, the composition of an individual's social arrangements alters in various ways following the dissolution of a marriage. One noteworthy change is that the social ties of divorced mothers include fewer relatives and relatively more companions who are not related by kinship or marriage. In general, when compared with those who are married or widowed, U.S. citizens who divorce or separate have a lower proportion of kin in their interactive social networks (Hurlbert & Acock, 1990; Milardo, 1987; Rands, 1988).

In-depth studies with smaller samples also find evidence of shifts in network composition in the advent of a marital breakup. The networks of divorced mothers, for instance, change from being composed of a number of married friends and couples when the women were married to include more unmarried friends who are either divorced or single (Albeck & Kaydar, 2002). Another apparent shift is that the workplace emerges as a particularly important source of network connections and support for both divorced mothers (Albeck & Kaydar, 2002) and divorced fathers (Stone, 2002).

Not only do structural aspects of social networks change after a couple's dissolution, but the well-being of other couples, friends, and family members in the larger social network also can be affected. For example, divorce dramatically influences the social ties of children of the once-married couple. Social networks differ substantially for children and adolescents who live with both of their biological parents when compared with those whose residence is with a divorced or remarried mother. An in-depth study of 30 young people found that the role of the father and the paternal network was reduced in such situations, no matter how close the father remained to the adolescent (Stinson, 1991). Adolescents whose parents were divorced also were more likely to include at least one unrelated adult in their network than were those whose parents remained married. Furthermore, the ending of a couple's relationship affects other relationships. Expartners withdraw from their former partner's networks; alliances change; and two additional people enter the social network as potential partners (Berscheid & Campbell, 1981; Sprecher & Felmlee, 2000). In addition, social network members are sometimes used to help end the relationship, and they may serve as confidants of the problems that are occurring (Duck, 1982; chap. 12 by Rollie & Duck, this volume).

ROLE OF SOCIAL NETWORKS IN THE BREAKUP OF SPECIfiC TYPES OF COUPLES

Some couples are less likely than others to receive support from their networks and from society in general. They may be violating endogamy rules, or they may be stigmatized for having certain personal characteristics (e.g., race, sexual orientation). In this section, we discuss the role of social networks in same-sex couples and interracial and interethnic couples. We also discuss the influence of social networks in cultures (e.g., China) in which there has traditionally been a high degree of family involvement in marital choices, through arranged marriages.

Same-Sex Couples

The key features that seem to set gay and lesbian partnerships apart from heterosexual ones is the lack of institutional recognition (such as the right to marry) and the social stigma still attached to these relationships (Peplau & Beals, 2004). Although tolerance for and visibility of these relationships has increased in a number of countries, gay and lesbian couples still have a long way to go to achieve equal access to rights that heterosexuals take for granted. In the United States, Massachusetts recently became the first state to legalize same-sex marriage. Although activists in many other states are pushing for legalization as well, as of this writing they have yet to be successful.

Historically, it has been difficult to find representative samples of these partnerships, and breakups have not been as easily tracked as they are for heterosexual marriages (Huston & Schwartz, 1995; Peplau & Spalding, 2000). Despite this, research on gay and lesbian relationships is growing (Peplau & Beals, 2004), but the focus thus far has been more on intact relationships than on relationship dissolution. For example, research has compared levels of satisfaction and correlates of satisfaction in different couple types (lesbian, gay, and hetero-sexual) and generally found no differences (Peplau & Spalding, 2000).

The larger social networks of heterosexuals versus those of homosexuals have also been compared. Research suggests that, compared with heterosexuals, gay and lesbian individuals place higher importance on friendship (Nardi, 1999) and have a tendency to include "chosen family" members (fictive kin) as family (Muraco, 2004; Weston, 1991). Therefore, gays and lesbians may be more likely to turn to their friends than to their family members for social support for their romantic alliances.

Breakup rates among gay and lesbian couples have been found to be higher than those among heterosexual couples in some studies (Kurdek, 1998). How might social networks be involved in homosexual couples' higher breakup rates? There are several ways that networks may be related to relationship dissolution in unique ways for gay and lesbian couples. First, because of intoler-ant attitudes or perceived intolerant attitudes, networks (or subsets of networks) may be ignorant about the very existence of some homosexual partnerships, and thus may not be in a position to provide support when these partnerships are developing or ailing (Peplau & Beals, 2004). The corresponding lower level of social support may contribute to the likelihood of breakups, includ-ing at early stages of development when mutual friends could help legitimize the relationship.

Second, scholars have pointed out that there are fewer barriers to ending gay and lesbian relationships compared with heterosexual ones (Huston & Schwartz, 1995; Kurdek, 1998; Peplau & Spalding, 2000). This would include less pressure from family and friends to keep relationships intact, but also fewer institutional level barriers (such as laws). The lower level of barriers may change as countries incrementally move toward greater legal recognition and benefits and the public becomes more tolerant of these relationships (Graff, 1999).

Third, the closeness of ties in some gay communities may have mixed effects on relation-ship stability. Communities provide social support for same-sex partnerships, but they may also facilitate the meeting of alternative partners (Huston & Schwartz, 1995). One study found that, for 301 lesbian couples, availability of alternatives was negatively associated with psy-chological commitment, which in turn was associated with relationship stability (Beals & Peplau, 2002, cited in Peplau & Beals, 2004). Assessments of the availability of alternatives across relationship types reveal mixed results; one study found that gay men and heterosex-ual cohabitors have more alternatives than lesbians and married couples (Kurdek & Schmitt, 1986), whereas another found moderately poor alternatives across sexual orientation groupings (Duffy & Rusbult, 1986).

Fourth, it has been suggested that gay couples may have somewhat different expectations about fidelity than other types of couples (Huston & Schwartz, 1995). For some gay couples, it is not the presence of alternative sexual partners that is threatening to the relationship, but the presence of alternatives who might threaten the emotional commitment within the existing relationship (Weeks, Heaphy, & Donovan, 2001). Thus, for gay men, in particular, same-sex others met through their social network may be viewed as alternative sexual partners as well as alternative emotional partners.

The dissolution of gay and lesbian partnerships may affect their social networks in unique ways. Compared with the dissolution of a heterosexual relationship, networks or partial net-works may be less affected by the dissolution of a gay or lesbian relationship, if the relationship that is coming to an end is a hidden one (Peplau & Beals, 2004). Even if the relationship is known about, sympathy and support after a breakup may not be as forthcoming for homosexual partnerships as they are for heterosexual couples (Huston & Schwartz, 1995).

Another frequently discussed issue in the literature on gay and lesbian partnerships is that same-sex former partners may be more likely than heterosexual former partners to transition to becoming part of the broader friendship network (Huston & Schwartz, 1995; Peplau &

Spalding, 2000). There seems to be a heightened emphasis on maintaining friendship or fictive kin ties with expartners among gay networks (Weeks et al., 2001; Weston, 1991). In Nardi's (1999) study of 161 gay men, 19% said their best friend was an exlover.

In sum, social networks are probably just as important to the relationships of gays and lesbians are they are to heterosexual couples, although in slightly different ways. A focus on how networks influence gay and lesbian relationships seems particularly important and appropriate given the larger sociopolitical context surrounding them. It will be quite interesting to see how relationship stability might change as industrialized countries continue to award more rights and benefits to same-sex partners over time. (For more discussion of same-sex relationships and dissolution issues, see chap. 24 by Oswald and Clausell, this volume.)

Interracial or Interethnic Couples

Another couple type that may have unique challenges in obtaining social network support is interracial or interethnic couples. Historically there has been a great deal of societal hostility directed towards couples that cross traditional, socially constructed, racial boundaries. For years, laws against such interracial marriages were prevalent in a majority of states throughout the United States, and it was not until 1967 that the Supreme Court finally banned these types of "antimiscegenation" laws. One state, Alabama, managed to retain its law against interracial marriage (even though it was unenforceable) until it was finally abolished in 2000. Opposition to interracial courtship also has been common, and an official policy against interracial dating at a southern college, Bob Jones University, was not repealed until public pressure led to its demise in 2000. Today, interracial marriages and romances are still relatively rare, and they often continue to be considered socially inappropriate. For example, a large majority of White Americans in 1991 (66%) reported that they would oppose a marriage between one of their close relatives and a Black American (Pinkney, 1993).

Although interracial unions remain relatively rare, they are growing in numbers. In spite of a heritage of widespread social opposition, there has been an increase in the rate of interracial marriages over the past few decades in the United States, from approximately 1% in 1960 to 5% more recently (Gaines & Leaver, 2002). Interracial dating may be increasing to an even greater degree than interracial marriages, although it is difficult to enumerate the exact percentage of dating couples that are interracial.

Social networks probably influence the likelihood that an individual enters into a relationship with someone from a different ethnic or racial background. A study of the romantic relationships of a sample of California university students (Clark-Ibanez & Felmlee, 2004) found that those individuals whose friendship networks were ethnically diverse were more prone to engage in interethnic dating than were those whose friends were of the same ethnicity or race. In addition, individuals whose parents had ethnically diverse friends were more likely to frequently date interethnically than were those whose parents' networks were relatively uniform. Having an ethnically varied social network presumably enhances the chances of meeting and accepting an interethnic partner.

Not only do social networks affect the likelihood that people will enter relationships with someone of a different race, but reactions from the social network can influence the likelihood that a developing relationship between two individuals of different ethnic or racial backgrounds will either end or remain stable. In the Clark-Ibanez and Felmlee (2004) study, the respondents provided open-ended responses that indicated that a majority believed that social network pressure made it difficult to date outside of their ethnicity. One White man, for instance, explained why interethnic dating was difficult for him: "My family is conservative and elite in the community and it would not look good socially." A Latina female noted that "[my family and my Hispanic friends]... all told me not to mix blood. Stay with your own." Thus, even if two people of different races are attracted to each other, they may end their relationship early because their family and friends do not approve.

Interethnic or interracial couples that do stay together and eventually marry despite opposition from some sectors of their networks or from society in general may continue to be affected by negative reactions from family and friends. A study of 21 interracial married couples from Minnesota found evidence of opposition from social networks (Rosenblatt, Karis, & Powell, 1995). Similar to findings from an earlier study (Porterfield, 1978), the large majority of White spouses experienced hostile or fearful initial reactions to their relationship on the part of their family members. Some reasons for the lack of support included social disapproval, safety, and problems with children. Family members of the Black partners, in contrast, expressed less disapproval, although they also may have been more "veiled" in their opposition than Whites. One reason for less open hostility on the part of the Black spouse's network may have been that the Black partner was usually the husband, a male. Family members of both races tended to be less protective of men than women, and they afforded men more latitude in their intimate relationships. White racism is another likely explanation for greater levels of opposition on the part of White network members.

The social opposition to interethnic relationships is likely to influence the demise of interracial pairings, although there has been very little direct research on this topic. One study of a sample of 600 midwesterners found that interracial romantic relationships had higher breakup rates than did relationships that occurred between those of the same race, even after other factors were controlled for (Felmlee et al., 1990). The reason for this relatively high rate of breakup is unclear, but it may be due to unmeasured social disapproval of interracial romance.

Nevertheless, not all studies suggest that interracial relationships have particularly high dissolution rates. A study of 446 students at a western university found no significant differences in the breakup rate over a period of 5 months for those in interracial, as compared with intraracial, relationships (Felmlee, 2001). There are several possible reasons for the departure in findings between this study and those of the earlier, midwestern study that identified interracial effects (Felmlee et al., 1990). Explanations include regional differences (more challenges for the midwest, as opposed to Californian, interracial couples), time trends (a growing acceptance of interracial romance with time), or differences in the types of interracial couples in the two studies (more Black–White than Asian–White couples in the midwestern sample).

Although interracial couples may receive more negative than positive social reactions, the social acceptance they receive from at least some network members may be particularly important and play a salient, supportive role in the degree to which they are successful in crossing racial divides in our society. In the aforementioned study of Minnesota couples, a number of married individuals in multiracial marriages, including several Whites, reported a good deal of acceptance and support from their family members; the opposition that did occur for many couples almost always lessened with time (Rosenblatt et al., 1995). Furthermore, in approximately one fourth of the cases, individuals at a California university reported that their social networks were supportive of their interracial romance (Clark-Ibanez & Felmlee, 2004). In other words, social networks do not always attempt to interfere with interracial intimate contact, and, in some cases, friends and family members may even help to keep such couples together.

Further research is needed to determine the extent to which, and under what conditions, social networks may help to cement interracial relationships or, in other cases, may act to tear them apart. Another intriguing question worthy of study is the manner in which certain interracial couples manage to thrive in spite of network opposition. The Romeo and Juliet effect, discussed earlier, may operate in some interethnic couples (i.e., greater opposition may actually lead them to love each other even more).

Arranged Marriages: An International Perspective

Traditional Asian societies have high tolerance toward networks' influence on marriage, so much so that marriages are sometimes arranged with little or no input from the marriage partners themselves. Because of these distinctive characteristics of the role of social networks in marriage in these societies, in this section, we focus our review on findings from Asian countries to shed light on the degree to which the role of social networks in such marital relationships differs from Western societies.

Because these societies emphasize strong interpersonal relationships, particularly family relationships, marriage is considered to be an important part of a family's strategy for network building and expansion. Through marriage, new alliances between families are formed and old alliances are strengthened (Ebrey, 1991). This networking function of marriage is believed to have contributed to the high levels of marriage found throughout Asian societies (Smith, 1980) and the prevalence of arranged marriage on the part of parents or other relatives (Blood, 1967; Xu & Whyte, 1990).

Although most young adults today play a dominant role in selecting whom they marry, kin relationships continue to be valued in the process of the formation of conjugal unions, and marriage continues to serve an important function by which new family ties are formed and new bases of social relations are created in China (Riley, 1994) and in other Asian countries (Blood, 1967; Cheal, 2002). Parents still play a substantial role in mate selection, and they influence when and whom their children marry. In countries in which kin are expected to take an important part in the selection and approval of a mate, romantic relationships that fail to receive approval from this network are less likely to lead to marriage unions.

After union formation, marriage in traditional societies continues to involve a great deal of cooperation on the parts of married children and their parents. In such societies, married individuals and their parents are constantly exchanging financial and nonfinancial assistance. For example, parents influence the fertility decisions of young couples in Taiwan (Thornton, Freeman, Sun, & Chang, 1986) and live with their married children in China (Logan, Bian, & Bian, 1998). In-laws' approval has been found to be positively associated with marriage quality in China (Pimentel, 2000), and marital satisfaction is not only influenced by conjugal interaction, but also by family and community support systems that lead to resolution of conjugal conflicts in Taiwan (Wu & Yi, 2003).

In an extended family system, the social ties of married couples act as a barrier force keeping couples in their marriage. Strong kinship-based social ties can sometimes help to override incompatibility or conflict within the conjugal relationship. This is evident in the low percentages of divorce among arranged marriages, even when such marriages are not based primarily on love or personality compatibility between the partners. For example, a probability sample of 586 ever-married Chinese women from one city interviewed in 1987 showed only a modest negative correlation of $-.11$ between scores on a freedom of mate choice scale (measured by six items such as whether the marriage is a traditional arranged marriage, and who, such as parents, mixed, or respondent, played a dominant role in mate choice) and having been divorced from the first husband (Xu & Whyte, 1990). A 1991 Chinese national sample showed that only 2.6% of the respondents whose first marriage was arranged reported being divorced or remarried, and only 6.5% of those whose first marriage was arranged against their own wills were either divorced or remarried. These rates were only modestly higher than the remarriage and divorce rate of 1.3% among those whose first marriages were love marriages (Sha, 1994). In other words, divorce rates are low in China, even in arranged marriages, and one possible explanation for this low rate is that extended family networks aid in bonding spouses together.

The erosion of such a family-based social network support system has been seen as being associated with the rising world divorce rates (Goode, 1963). According to this argument, the nuclear family is increasingly isolated from its wider kinship network in the emergence of an industrial economic system. This isolation makes the nuclear family unit fragile, because social networks have a cushioning effect on the known marriage stressors: housework and childcare, financial concerns, and emotional conflicts. The worldwide trend toward a convergence on the nuclear family thus correlates with sharp increases in divorce rates throughout West Europe, in Russia, and in Latin America prior to 1980 (Goode, 1993).

DISCUSSION AND FUTURE RESEARCH DIRECTIONS

In this final section, we discuss two issues: (a) the degree to which historical and other broad contextual factors affect the role of social networks in relationship dissolution, which has been a neglected issue in the literature; and (b) specific suggestions for future research.

A Larger Contextual Perspective on the Influence of Social Networks

In this chapter, we discussed theory and empirical research connecting social networks with the dissolution of courtship and marital relationships. We see that an individual's network of friends and family members often plays a substantial and significant role in the likelihood that an intimate relationship either dissolves or remains intact. Social networks are highly instrumental in developing romantic interests in the first place, and, for the most part, they act in ways that tend to enhance the stability of dating relationships and marriages. In addition, we explored the ways in which relationship dissolution affects social networks. Research shows that divorce is associated with reductions in the proportion of relatives and married friends and increases in the importance of workplace associates and unmarried friends in people's networks.

Much of our focus in this chapter was on the microlevel of social networks—friends and family and how they influence and are influenced by relationship dissolution. However, these microlevel influences are occurring in a much larger societal context. Our focus on same-sex and interracial relationships makes the larger context visible, by highlighting the idea that network support for couples in our society does not occur evenly. Some relationship types (opposite sex and same race) are celebrated more than other types. Our international focus, revealing the low levels of dissolution for arranged marriages in China, further shows the importance of the larger societal context in which network influences on relationships occur. It also makes visible the degree to which assumptions about the role of social networks in relationships differ in western contexts from those in other societies, such as assumptions involving the degree to which network influence on marital relationships would be welcome.

The larger societal context that shapes network responses to relationships is also itself changing in significant ways across historical time. For instance, as relationship types previously hidden or shunned become more acceptable, network effects on the stability of these relationships are likely to change as well. This would apply to same-sex relationships and interracial relationships, which are far more acceptable and supported today than they were a few decades ago, and which may become more acceptable in the future. There are other macrohistorical developments, including trends in the areas of divorce, singlehood, and additional options for partnership, that are likely to affect social network processes. The context around divorce has changed over the past few decades, and therefore the behavior of networks surrounding divorcing individuals also is likely to have changed correspondingly. For example, married couples have been found to receive more support from their networks than those who divorce. However, is this changing as divorce becomes more acceptable? Might networks today be more accepting of divorce, and, consequently, more supportive after a divorce has taken place? Research showing significant family aid to single mothers (Cheal, 2002) would suggest that divorced mothers receive a significant amount of support from their networks.

Attitudes about the necessity of being in relationships have also changed across time. In the 1950s, those who remained single in the United States were often thought to be emotionally immature, irresponsible, narcissistic, deviant, or homosexual (Mintz & Kellogg, 1988). Today, staying single is not only acceptable but is preferable in some network situations. Popular culture sources are beginning to celebrate this, as in discussions about"urban tribes" (Watters, 2001) and "quirkyalones" (Cagen, 2004). More research has to be done on how social networks provide norms for being coupled versus being single.

More options have emerged for partnership as well, across historical time. Cohabitation, considered scandalous during the 1960s, has become commonplace. Other more recent partnership types include civil solidarity pacts in parts of Europe, which provide an easy-to-get-out-of middle ground between cohabitation and marriage (Lyall, 2004), and civil unions in states such Vermont, which give legal recognition and benefits to gay and lesbian couples (Sneyd, 2004). These recent options make it all the more challenging to capture the breadth of relationship formation, to track breakups, and to examine network connections to these as well.

A focus on serial monogamy across the life course also reveals many network complexities related to partnership. Much of our chapter has focused on issues pertinent to young and previously unmarried couples. As a result of longer life expectancy and relaxed attitudes about divorce, many people are experiencing multiple partners and marriages across their lifetimes. Different network issues come into play with partnerships formed after the demise of previous ones. Expartners, children, and even grandchildren may become part of the social network providing opportunities for, information about, and reactions to relationships. Strong connections with a child's former spouse (especially former daughters-in-law) may play a role in the acceptance of that child's more recent spouse or partner (Johnson & Barer, 1987). The webs of network interaction can become very complex, with children, expartners, former in-laws, former stepkin, and others collected along the way weighing in on new relationships. Although complex, this area is one in which future study could be revealing.

Other Suggestions for Future Research

Network concepts deserving of further research include distinguishing between the effects of psychological versus interactive networks on relationship stability. For instance, are there ways in which geographically distant yet emotionally close (psychological) network members' reactions about a relationship might have more or less of an impact than geographically close (interactive) network members? Another valuable avenue of research would explore the distinction between active and passive ties. For instance, under what circumstances do passive ties become active again because they become relevant support for a new relationship? How do network members fade in and fade out on the basis of transitions in relationships? Furthermore, there are a number of additional specific types of relationships for which networks may play a significant role but that we did not have the space to explore in this chapter. These include network connections with relationship dissolution of those who are incarcerated; those battered and fleeing their partners; those working or living in separate locations from their partners; and those involved in affairs.

A relatively new interaction tool, the computer, has brought with it speculation and research about the effects of the Internet and e-mail for relationship stability. Virtual social networks formed on the Internet have unique properties, including communication across great distances, a lack of nonverbal cues, the development of online groups, and the possibility of exchanges in which individuals' social demographic characteristics are unknown or hidden (Wellman et al., 1996). Internet networks differ significantly from face-to-face networks, in other words, and thus may have unique effects on intimate relationships over time. Some questions for future research include these: Do the social ties and virtual intimacies that develop over e-mail serve as a replacement for a connection to a live-in partner? Or is involvement in the Internet more likely to act as a mechanism that increases a couple's solidarity, perhaps by expanding couples' supportive, social ties? Do chat groups or other Internet groups lead to infidelity more often than other forms of human interaction? Is it possible that relationship maintenance is improved by Internet communication with couples' friends and relatives? These questions represent just the beginning of issues worthy of investigation regarding computer networks and intimate dyads.

An additional opportunity for future research involves gathering more data from couples' social network members, regardless of whether these ties are formed in person or online. Many network studies obtain information from individuals, or couples, regarding perceptions of their network, and rarely do researchers get data from friends and family members themselves. It is possible that relying solely on individuals' perceptions of network variables introduces error into analyses. For example, individuals may believe that network members are supportive of a relationship when they are not, or fear that they are opposed when they are approving. Data from network constituents also would allow an investigation of the question as to which is more influential in shaping the course of a couple's relationship—the actual attitudes of network members or the individuals' perceptions of these attitudes. One study found that individuals' perceptions of their networks are more powerful in shaping their relational behavior than are the actual attitudes of their network members (e.g., Felmlee, 2001). However, this evidence is limited, and more research is needed along these lines. Other salient questions that could be addressed with more data from a couple's joint network include the following: What are the reasons that network members support, or fail to support, a friend or family member's relationship? Which methods do network members use to attempt to influence the outcome of a particular couple's tie? Which sectors of individuals' networks are more likely to affect a couple's success over time—family or friends? In what ways have couples attempted to change the attitudes of their family and friends about a spouse or partner?

One of the points made in this chapter is that social networks do not always have a uniformly beneficial effect on intimate couples, and this topic represents an additional line of inquiry for future scholarly work. As discussed previously, for example, network members can compete with a partner for emotional intimacy with an individual. Network members also sometimes disapprove strongly of relationships solely because the members are not from the same racial or ethnic backgrounds or because the members are of the same sex. Nevertheless, this possible shadow side of social networks has received relatively little attention in the literature; most network research on relationships emphasizes the positive, social support dimension of networks, similar to the positive bias that exists in close relationship research more generally. There is a range of topics in this genre that would benefit from more attention, such as the use of lies and betrayal on the part of network members, situations in which a friend or family member engages in "mate poaching," that is, taking someone else's romantic partner, and other techniques used by network participants to instigate or hasten a breakup or divorce.

At a theoretical level, there is also room for development. A social network perspective on relationship dissolution represents a quintessential, social structural approach to social relationships. In a network framework, couples are viewed as pairs that are embedded in an intricate web of social ties that molds and shapes their functioning over time. A long-standing debate within social science, however, involves the role of social structure versus that of agency in influencing individual behavior. The agency side of this debate tends to be underrepresented in a social network approach. A more complete theory of the link between social networks and romantic dyads would do well to conceptualize about both the structured ways that networks influence couples as well as the active manner in which couples shape their social environment. As noted earlier, little theoretical or empirical research has been done regarding these latter, endogenous network effects (Berscheid & Lopes, 1997).

There are a number of possible ways in which couples could manipulate their social networks in order to affect the trajectory of their relationship over time. For instance, individuals are likely to encourage support on the part of their social networks for a relationship that they value. They may do so by providing appealing information about a partner, inviting network members and their partner to social events, and by withholding negative information about the relationship. Some also may cut off ties entirely with disapproving network members. Couples are apt to create new friendships with those who approve of their relationship and, in particular, form close ties with other, sympathetic twosomes. When individuals are dissatisfied with a relationship, in contrast, they too may work to shape their networks, but in this case the goal is to garner support for a breakup. They may exchange disparaging remarks about their mate, drop friends the two have in common, and so on. Little is known about these various ways by which individuals and pairs may manipulate the social environment that surrounds their relationship. However, it seems likely that social networks are both a force that shapes couples' long-term development as well as a product that evolves out of couples' actions.

More theoretical research is also needed to integrate a social network perspective with those of other significant theories of relationship demise. Contextual approaches are under-represented in much of social relationship research, and a network perspective is useful in partially remedying that problem—yet social context is not the whole story. Clearly, couples themselves, and the individuals within them, also affect the trajectory of their courtship, cohab-iting, or marital relationship. They do so no doubt by means of a range of social psychological mechanisms that are detailed in alternative theoretical approaches, such as social exchange, cognitive approaches, and evolutionary theory. Furthermore, certain individuals and couples appear to be immune to network opposition, such as some in same-sex relationships, interracial pairings, and other types of liaisons that challenge societal norms. Under what circumstances do networks fail to affect couples? Additional theoretical research is needed to detail the limits of a social network perspective of relationship dissolution and also the ways in which this approach dovetails with more traditional theories of intimate development.

In conclusion, it is evident from the network research that has been done that "no breakup occurs on an island." Partnerships are affected in numerous ways by the social networks in which they are embedded, and couple breakups cause ripple effects among these social networks. Network influences reflect the current norms and attitudes of the broader societal context, and as a result we can expect them to change over time as new developments in laws and customs are realized.

AUTHOR NOTE

For correspondence on this chapter, write to S. Sprecher at the Department of Sociology and Anthropology, Illinois State University, Normal, IL 61790-4660. E-mail: Sprecher@ilstu.edu We thank Jesse Rude for his assistance in library research for this chapter.

REFERENCES

Acitelli, L. K. (1992). Gender differences in relationship awareness and marital satisfaction among young married couples. *Personality and Social Psychology Bulletin, 18,* 102–110.

Agnew, C. R., Loving, T. J., & Drigotas, S. M. (2001). Substituting the forest for the trees: Social networks and the prediction of romantic relationship state and fate. *Journal of Personality and Social Psychology, 81,* 1042–1057.

Albeck, S., & Kaydar, D. (2002). Divorced mothers: Their network of friends pre- and post-divorce. *Journal of Divorce and Remarriage, 36,* 111–138.

Beals, K. P., & Peplau, L. A. (2002, July). *Conceptualizing and measuring the disclosure of sexual orientation.* Poster presented at the International Conference on Personal Relationships, Halifax, Nova Scotia.

Berger, C. R. (1988). Uncertainty and information exchange in developing relationships. In S. Duck (Ed.), *Handbook of personal relationships: Theory, research, and interventions* (pp. 239–256). Chichester, England: Wiley.

Berscheid, E. (1999). The greening of relationship science. *American Psychologist, 54,* 260–266.

Berscheid, E., & Campbell, B. (1981). The changing longevity of heterosexual close relationships: A commentary and forecast. In M. J. Lerner & S. C. Lerner (Eds.), *The justice motive in social behavior* (pp. 209–234). New York: Plenum.

Berscheid, E., & Graziano, W. (1979). The initiation of social relationships and interpersonal attraction. In T. Huston (Ed.), *Social exchange in developing relationships* (pp. 31–60). New York: Academic Press.

Berscheid, E., & Lopes, J. (1997). A temporal model of relationship satisfaction and stability. In R. J. Sternberg & J. Hojjat (Eds.), *Satisfaction in close relationships* (pp. 129–159). New York: Guilford.

Berscheid, E., & Reis, H. T. (1998). Attraction and close relationships. In D. T. Gilbert, S. T. Fiske, & G. Lindzey (Eds.), *The handbook of social psychology* (4th ed., Vol. 2, pp. 193–281). New York: McGraw-Hill.

Blood, R. O., Jr. (1967). *Love match and arranged marriage: A Tokyo-Detroit comparison.* New York: The Free Press.

Bryant, C. M., & Conger, R. D. (1999). Marital success and domains of social support in long-term relationships: Does the influence of network members ever end? *Journal of Marriage and the Family, 61,* 437–450.

Burns, A. (1984). Perceived causes of marriage breakdown and conditions of life. *Journal of Marriage and the Family, 46,* 551–562.

Cagen, S. (2004). *Quirkyalone: A manifesto for uncompromising romantics.* San Francisco: Harper.

Cate, R. M., Levin, L. A., & Richmond, L. S. (2002). Premarital relationship stability: A review of recent research. *Journal of Social and Personal Relationships, 19,* 261–284.

Cate, R. M., & Sprecher, S. (2005). *Commitment in dating and engaged/married couples: A contextual analysis.* Manuscript submitted for publication.

Cheal, D. (2002). *Sociology of family life.* New York: Palgrave.

Clark-Ibanez, M., & Felmlee, D. (2004). Interethnic relationships: The role of social network diversity. *Journal of Marriage and Family, 66,* 293–305.

Cleek, M., & Pearson, T. A. (1985). Perceived causes of divorce: An analysis of interrelationships. *Journal of Marriage and the Family, 47,* 179–191.

Driscoll, R., Davis, K. E., & Lipetz, M. E. (1972). Parental interference and romantic love: The Romeo and Juliet effect. *Journal of Personality and Social Psychology, 24,* 1–10.

Duck, S. (1982). A topography of relationship disengagement and dissolution. In S. Duck (Ed.), *Personal relationships: Vol. 4. Dissolving personal relationships* (pp. 1–30). London: Academic Press.

Duffy, S. M., & Rusbult, C. E. (1986). Satisfaction and commitment in homosexual and heterosexual relationships. *Journal of Homosexuality, 12,* 1–24.

Ebrey, P. (1991). Introduction. In R. Watson & R. Ebrey (Eds.) *Marriage and inequality in Chinese society* (pp. 1–23). Berkeley: University of California Press.

Felmlee, D., & Sprecher, S. (2000). Close relationships and social psychology: Intersections and future paths. *Social Psychology Quarterly, 63,* 365–376.

Felmlee, D., Sprecher, S., & Bassin, E. (1990). The dissolution of intimate relationships: A hazard model. *Social Psychology Quarterly, 53,* 13–30.

Felmlee, D. H. (2001). No couple is an island: A social network perspective on dyadic stability. *Social Forces, 4,* 1259–1287.

Felmlee, D. H. (2004). Interaction in social networks. In J. DeLamater (Ed.), *Handbook of Social Psychology* (pp. 389–409). Kluwer-Plenum.

Gaines, S. O., & Leaver, J. (2002). Interracial relationships. In R. Goodwin & D. Cramer (Eds.), *Inappropriate relationships: The unconventional, the disapproved, & the forbidden* (pp. 65–78). Mahwah, NJ: Lawrence Erlbaum Associates.

Goode, W. J. (1963). *World revolution and family patterns.* Englewood Cliffs, NJ: Prentice-Hall.

Goode, W. J. (1993). *World changes in divorce patterns.* New Haven, CT: Yale University Press.

Graff, E. J. (1999, July 12). Same-sex spouses in Canada. *The Nation,* pp. 23–24.

Hortacsu, N., & Karanci, A. N. (1987). Premarital breakups in a Turkish sample: Perceived reasons, attributional dimensions and affective reactions. *International Journal of Psychology, 22,* 57–64.

Hurlbert, J. S., & Acock, A. C. (1990). The effects of marital status on the form and composition of social networks. *Social Science Quarterly, 71,* 163–174.

Huston, M., & Schwartz, P. (1995). The relationships of lesbians and gay men. In J. T. Wood & S. Duck (Eds.), *Understudied relationships: Off the beaten track* (pp. 89–121). Thousand Oaks, CA: Sage.

Huston, T. L., & Levinger, G. (1978). Interpersonal attraction and relationships. *Annual Review of Psychology, 29,* 115–156.

Johnson, C. L., & Barer, B. M. (1987). Marital instability and the changing kinship networks of grandparents. *The Gerontologist, 27,* 330–335.

Johnson, M. P. (1991). Commitment to personal relationships. In W. H. Jones & D. W. Perlman (Eds.), *Advances in personal relationships* (Vol. 3, pp. 117–143). London: Jessica Kingsley.

Julien, D., Chartrand, E., & Begin, J. (1999). Social networks, structural interdependence, and conjugal adjustment in heterosexual, gay, and lesbian couples. *Journal of Marriage and the Family, 61,* 516–530.

Kalmijn, M. (2003). Shared friendship networks and the life course: An analysis of survey data on married and cohabiting couples *Social Networks, 25,* 231–249.

Kalmijn, M., & Bernasco, W. (2001). Joint and separated lifestyles in couple relationships. *Journal of Marriage and Family, 63,* 639–654.

Kitson, G., & Sussman, M. (1982). Marital complaints, demographic characteristics and symptoms of mental distress in divorce. *Journal of Marriage and the Family, 44,* 87–101.

Knoester, C., & Booth, A. (2000). Barriers to divorce: When are they effective? When are they not? *Journal of Family Issues, 21,* 78–99.

Kurdek, L. A. (1998). Relationship outcomes and their predictors: Longitudinal evidence from heterosexual married, gay cohabiting, and lesbian cohabiting couples. *Journal of Marriage and the Family, 60,* 711–720.

Kurdek, L. A., & Schmitt, J. P. (1986). Relationship quality of partners in heterosexual married, heterosexual cohabiting, and gay and lesbian relationships. *Journal of Personality and Social Psychology, 51,* 711–720.

Laumann, E. O., Gagnon, J. H., Michael, R. T., & Michaels, S. (1994). *The social organization of sexuality: Sexual practices in the United States.* Chicago: University of Chicago Press.

Leslie, L. A., Johnson, M. P., & Huston, T. L. (1986). Parental reactions to dating relationships: Do they make a difference? *Journal of Marriage and the Family, 48,* 57–66.

Levinger, G. A. (1976). A social psychological perspective on marital dissolution. *Journal of Social Issues, 3,* 21–47.

Levinger, G., & Snoek, J. D. (1972). *Attraction in relationships.* Morristown, NJ: General Learning Press.

Lewis, R. A. (1973). Social reactions and the formation of dyads: An interactionist approach to mate selection. *Sociometry, 36,* 409–418.

Logan, J. R., Bian, F., & Bian, Y. (1998). Traditional and change in the urban chinese family: The case of living arrangements. *Social Forces, 76,* 851–882.

Lyall, S. (2004, February 16). In Europe, lovers say: Marry me, a little. *The International Herald Tribune,* p. 3.

Marsiglio, W., & Scanzoni, J. (1995). *Families and friendships: Applying the sociological imagination.* New York: HarperCollins.

Milardo, R. M. (1982). Friendship networks in developing relationships: Converging and diverging social environments. *Social Psychology Quarterly, 45,* 162–172.

Milardo, R. M. (1987). Changes in social networks of men and women following divorce. *Journal of Family Issues, 8,* 78–96.

Milardo, R. M., & Helms-Erikson, H. (2000). Network overlap and third-party influence in close relationships. In C. Hendrick & S. S. Hendrick (Eds.), *Close relationships: A sourcebook* (pp. 33–45). Thousand Oaks, CA: Sage.

Mintz, S., & Kellogg, S. (1988). *Domestic revolutions: A social history of American family life.* New York: The Free Press.

Muraco, A. (2004). *Friendship matters: A study of close intersectional friendships.* Unpublished doctoral dissertation, University of California, Davis.

Nardi, P. M. (1999). *Gay men's friendships: Invincible communities.* Chicago: University of Chicago Press.

Parks, M. R. (2000). Communication networks and relationship life cycles. In K. Dindia & S. Duck (Eds.), *Communication and personal relationships* (pp. 56–75). New York: Wiley.

Parks, M. R., & Adelman, M. B. (1983). Communication networks and the development of romantic relationships: An expansion of uncertainty reduction theory. *Human Communication Research, 10,* 55–79.

Parks, M. R., & Eggert, L. (1991). The role of social context in the dynamics of personal relationships. In W. H. Jones & D. Perlman (Eds.), *Advances in personal relationships* (Vol. 2, pp. 1–34). London: Jessica Kingsley.

Parks, M. R., Stan, C., & Eggert, L. (1983). Romantic involvement and social network involvement. *Social Psychology Quarterly, 46,* 116–130.

Peplau, L. A., & Beals, K. P. (2004). The family lives of lesbians and gay men. In A. L. Vangelisti (Ed.), *Handbook of family communication* (pp. 233–248). Mahwah, NJ: Lawrence Erlbaum Associates.

Peplau, L. A., & Spalding, L. R. (2000). The close relationships of lesbians, gay men, and bisexuals. In C. Hendrick & S. Hendrick (Eds.), *Close relationships: A sourcebook* (pp. 111–123). Thousand Oaks, CA: Sage.

Pimentel, E. E. (2000). "Just how do I love thee?: Marital relations in urban China. *Journal of Marriage and the Family, 62,* 32–47.

Pinkney, A. 1993. *Black Americans* (4th ed.). Englewood Cliffs, NJ: Prentice-Hall.

Porterfield, E. 1978. *Black and white mixed marriages.* Chicago: Nelson-Hall.

Rands, M. (1988). Changes in social networks following marital separation and divorce. In R. M. Milardo (Ed.), *Families and social networks* (pp. 127–146). Newbury Park, CA: Sage.

Ridley, C. A., & Avery, A. W. (1979). Social network influence on the dyadic relationship. In R. Burgess & T. Huston (Eds.), *Social exchange in developing relationships* (pp. 223–246). New York: Academic Press.

Riley, N. (1994). Interwoven lives: Parents, marriage, and guanxi in China. *Journal of Marriage and the Family, 56,* 791–803.

Rohlfing, M. E. (1995). "Doesn't anyone stay in one place anymore?": An exploration of the under-studied phenomenon of long-distance relationships. In J. T. Wood & S. Duck (Eds.), *Understanding relationship processes: Vol. 6. Under-studied relationships: Off the beaten track* (pp. 173–196). Thousand Oaks, CA: Sage.

Rosenblatt, P. C., Karis, T. A., & Powell, R. D. (1995). *Multiracial couples: Black and white voices.* Thousand Oaks, CA: Sage.

Rubin, L. B. (1985). *Just friends.* New York: Harper and Row.

Rusbult, C. E. (1983). A longitudinal test of the investment model: The development (and deterioration) of satisfaction and commitment in heterosexual involvements. *Journal of Personality and Social Psychology, 45,* 101–117.

Schmeeckle, M., & Sprecher, S. (2004). Extended family and social networks. In A. Vangelisti (Ed.), *Handbook of family communication* (pp. 349–375). Mahwah, NJ: Lawrence Erlbaum Associates.

Sha, J. (1994). *Sampling survey data of women's status in contemporary China.* Beijing: International Academic Publishers.

Smith, P. C. (1980). Asian marriage patterns in transition. *Journal of Family History, 5,* 58–96.

Sneyd, R. (2004, March 5). Civil unions go from radical to conservative in four years. *The Associated Press State and Local Wire.*

Sprecher, S. (1994). Two sides to the breakup of dating relationships. *Personal Relationships, 1,* 199–222.

Sprecher, S., & Felmlee, D. (1992). The influence of parents and friends on the quality and stability of romantic relationships: A three-wave longitudinal investigation. *Journal of Marriage and the Family, 54,* 888–900.

Sprecher, S., & Felmlee, D. (2000). Romantic partners' perceptions of social network attributes with the passage of time and relationship transitions. *Personal Relationships, 7,* 325–340.

Sprecher, S., Felmlee, D., Orbuch, T. L., & Willetts, M. C. (2002). Social networks and change in personal relationships. In A. Vangelisti, H. Reis, & M. A. Fitzpatrick (Eds.), *Stability and change in relationships* (pp. 257–284). New York: Cambridge University Press.

Stephen, T. (1987). Attribution and adjustment to relationship termination. *Journal of Social and Personal Relationships, 4,* 47–61.

Stinson, K. M. (1991). *Adolescents, family, and friends: Social support after parents' divorce or remarriage.* New York: Praeger.

Stone, G. (2002). Nonresidential father postdivorce well-being: The role of social supports. *Journal of Divorce and Remarriage, 36,* 139–150.

Surra, C., & Milardo, R. (1991). The social psychological context of developing relationships: Psychological and interactive networks. In D. Perlman & W. Jones (Eds.), *Advances in personal relationships* (Vol., 3, pp. 1–36). London: Jessica Kingsley.

Tannen, D. (1990). *You just don't understand: Women and men in conversation.* New York: Morrow.

Thibaut, J. W., & Kelley, H. H. (1959). *The social psychology of groups.* New York: Wiley.

Thornes, B., & Collard, J. (1979). *Who divorces?* London: Routledge and Kegan Paul.

Thornton, A., Freeman, R., Sun, T. H., & Chang, M. H. (1986). Intergenerational relations and reproductive behavior in Taiwan. *Demography, 23,* 185–197.

Timmer, S. G., & Veroff, J. (2000). Family ties and the discontinuity of divorce in black and white newlywed couples. *Journal of Marriage and the Family, 62,* 349–361.

Veroff, J., Douvan, E., & Hatchett, S. (1995). *Marital instability: A social and behavioral study of early years.* Westerport, CT: Praeger.

Vorauer, J. D., & Raner, R. K. (1996). Who's going to make the first move? Pluralistic ignorance as an impediment to relationship formation. *Journal of Social and Personal Relationships, 13,* 483–506.

Watters, E. (2001, October 14). In my tribe. *The New York Times*, p. 25.

Weeks, J., Heaphy, B., & Donovan, C. (2001). *Same sex intimacies: Families of choice and other life experiments.* New York: Routledge.

Wellman, B. Salaff, J., Dimitrova, D., Garton, L., Gulia, M., & Haythornthwaite, C. (1996). Computer networks as social networks: Collaborative work, telework, and virtual community. *Annual Review of Sociology, 22,* 213–238.

Weston, K. (1991). *Families we choose: Lesbians, gays, kinship.* New York: Columbia University Press.

Wu, M., & Yi, C. (2003). A marriage is more than a marriage: The impacts of familial factors on marital satisfaction. *Journal of Population Studies, 26,* 71–95.

Xu, X., & Whyte, M. K. (1990). Love matches and arranged marriages: A Chinese replication. *Journal of Marriage and the Family, 2,* 709–722.

VI

Variations in Divorce and Relationship Dissolution Patterns and Processes

23

Divorce in the Context of Being African American

Terri L. Orbuch
Oakland University and University of Michigan

Edna Brown
University of Michigan

There is a growing body of research that examines marital stability and quality in the United States. Over the past several decades, this research has been concerned primarily with (a) who is most likely to divorce or the demographic or life course variables that affect the risk of divorce (e.g., age at marriage, social class), (b) factors that affect marital stability and quality over time (Amato & Rodgers, 1997; Gottman, 1994; Karney & Bradbury, 1995; Orbuch, Veroff, Hassan, & Horrocks, 2002), and (c) stories from individuals that account or tell the story of divorce (Kitson, 1992; Weiss, 1975).

The literature on marital stability and quality has been quite comprehensive in nature and scope, but it has primarily emphasized White marriages. Little research attention has been given to African American marriages and even less to divorce within the African American community. According to Billingsley (1992), relatively little attention has been given to African American marriages because of researchers' inability to go beyond the pathological approach to African American families, which emphasizes single-parent families and teen pregnancies within this cultural group. Billingsley argued that the thesis of the vanishing African American family is neither supported nor empirically grounded. Research needs to move beyond the pathological model and investigate factors specific to African Americans and other minority groups.

The few studies to date that have examined divorce among African Americans rarely go beyond a mere description of differences between African Americans and White Americans. In addition, these studies focus primarily on the structural conditions (e.g., occupational and educational opportunities, financial resources, or network support) under which divorce takes place to explain the differential rates of divorce among African Americans and White Americans. We have argued repeatedly (see Orbuch et al., 2002) that, although the structural context and environment within which relationships reside is critical to the behaviors and interactions within those relationships, the norms and meanings surrounding relationships and relational processes also are important to the study of marriage and divorce among African Americans. Thus, any study investigating marital stability and quality among African Americans must consider the distinct rather than the universal processes that underlie divorce (Orbuch, Veroff, & Hunter, 1999).

In addition, divorce can be challenging to individuals, to families, and to society because growing up in a single-parent family puts children and adults at risk for developing social, emotional, and behavioral problems (Kitson & Morgan, 1990; Wang & Amato, 2000). Research findings indicate that children raised in mother-headed households are three times more likely to live in poverty than those raised by two parents. Given the high separation or divorce rates among African Americans (Sweet & Bumpass, 1987), these rates have major implications for the emotional and social development of African American children. Although we do not believe that the nuclear family or an intact marital dyad is the best or only family structure that leads to healthy and happy individuals or children, it is still important for investigators to determine the major factors that lead to divorce, particularly among African Americans.

Numerous conceptual and methodological challenges arise when social scientists begin to examine divorce and other relational phenomena for African Americans or other minority cultures. First and foremost, it has been quite problematic for social scientists to make distinctions among the concepts of race, ethnicity, and culture. Orbuch and Fine (2003) stated that "even though the concept of race may have little biological support (i.e., there are few, if any, clear-cut biological distinctions or markers of traditional racial categories), the concept of race/ethnicity has important psychological and social meaning. Thus, rather than abandoning and ignoring the concept, we argue that we need to conceptualize race and ethnicity in ways that are responsive to the meanings attached to these concepts" (pg. 150). James and Tucker (2003) further argued that the concepts of race and ethnicity are difficult and ambiguous to define, but nonetheless important to the operational measurement and sample design of any research study. We agree that the concepts have to be defined and conceptualized, but it is not our aim in this chapter to accomplish such a task. Further, we recognize that there are subtle and sometimes important differences among the constructs of *race*, *ethnicity*, and *culture*, but we use the terms interchangeably in this chapter.

Another challenge for social scientists stems from the difficulty in obtaining large representative samples for study. Teachman, Tedrow, and Crowder (2000) argued that it is very difficult to obtain data on any family transformation by race or ethnicity, because the information is too often based on anecdotal and small, nonrepresentative samples. More specifically, Veroff and Orbuch (in press) maintained that representative samples of African American couples can be very difficult to obtain and track over time. They also stated that it is one thing to start with an interesting population from which to draw a sample that could be representative of that population, but it is another thing to get the individuals in that sample to participate in the study so that it remains representative.

There also is the challenge of whether scholars should study a particular relational phenomenon, such as divorce, among members of only one single racial or ethnic group, such as African Americans, or compare the risk of divorce between minority (African American) and majority (White American) groups. We contend that studies that gather information from both between-group and within-group designs are important to understanding divorce in the context of being Black in American society. Despite these challenges and others (see Orbuch & Fine, 2003), studies have moved slowly forward to highlight variations in marital quality and stability by race or ethnicity, particularly among African Americans.

Our goal in this chapter is to highlight research that examines divorce in the context of being African American. Although few research programs have this focus, those that do indicate that race or ethnicity is critical to understanding the meaning of relationships and marriage in the lives of individuals and couples. These relationship meanings lay the groundwork for how individuals evaluate relationships, the importance of relationships to overall well-being, and

NEW DIRECTIONS IN RESEARCH

There have been several recent theoretical and conceptual advances in the literature on divorce among African Americans. We recognize that it is not possible to review all of the relevant research in this chapter, so, instead, we focus on several new directions that we argue are most relevant to an audience of researchers studying divorce. We start our discussion with the larger theoretical advances or directions, concentrating on (a) cultural explanations beyond structure to explain the differential rates of divorce among African American and White American marriages, and (b) a risk and resilience framework for the study of divorce among African Americans. More specifically, within the risk and resilience perspective, we examine three factors that have been found to promote resilience among African American families. We then move on to a specific topic that has recently received a great deal of research attention—the effects of divorce on African American children.

Recognition of Explanations Beyond Structure

One predominant new direction in this area of research is to examine the influence of both structural and cultural factors on the risk of divorce over time. It is surprising that past research has given so little attention to potential cultural factors beyond structure for their role in explaining differential rates of quality and stability among African American and White American marriages. Relationships are embedded within a racial or ethnic culture, consisting of norms or expectations that help determine the meaning and interpretation of interpersonal processes and experiences in and out of relationships (e.g., parenthood, social network ties, and conflict). These interpersonal processes and experiences have different meanings for the stability of marriage over time, depending on whether the process is being interpreted by an African American or White American spouse.

In fact, Bruner (1990) long ago stated that people search for meaning—of themselves, of others, and of the world in which they live. He further argued that any science of human behavior would be more effective to the extent that it recognizes the human as meaning making, meaning using, and embedded within cultures of meanings. Even though there is considerable diversity in these cultural norms, within and between groups, the normative expectations and meanings of relationships in an African American minority community may differ in critical ways from the expectations of a dominant White American society. These expectations and meanings would inevitably place a different light on the interpretations that members of each community make of marriage and divorce (Broman, 2002; Orbuch et al., 1999; Veroff, Douvan, & Hatchett, 1995).

Orbuch et al. (2002) argued that both structural and interactional factors can independently affect divorce (Veroff et al., 1995). Although structural conditions can set the stage for divorce and can be mediated by interactional processes, structural factors can also act as contexts in which to understand the quality and effect of the interactional process being studied. Their findings show that styles of interaction can affect marital outcomes including divorce differentially, depending on whether one is a man or woman, African American or White, and at different points in the life course of a marriage. Thus, it can be argued that structural components set the context for an individual's sense of commitment, satisfaction, and dependency on relationships.

Similarly, Broman (2002) reported that divorce has different meanings for African Americans and White Americans. He found that spouses in African American couples are more likely to think about getting a divorce (and are less satisfied with their marriages), but less likely to actually get one, than are those in White American couples. He contended that this may be due to the level of independence among African American spouses, or it may be the result of different expectations and meanings regarding the institution of marriage itself. These differential meanings are learned in the African American community, and the result is that being unhappy with a spouse becomes less of a problem in one's daily life. African American spouses may be able to tolerate more dissatisfaction in this way. In contrast, when White American spouses think about getting a divorce, it indicates a level of dissatisfaction with their marriage that increases the likelihood that they will actually be divorced in the future.

Tucker and Mitchell-Kernan (1995) also proposed that, although the structural explanation of unbalanced sex ratios may influence African American divorce rates and the overall marriage market, there is a cultural component to this approach. There are a range of interpersonal and interactional outcomes given the sex ratio that affect an individual's potential for relationship formation and dissolution. Tucker and Taylor (1989) further stated that, "In the case of African Americans, male availability, as well as suitability, for marriage have been especially compromised in recent decades as increasing differential mortality has been compounded by decreasing economic viability" (p. 83).

In addition, Teachman et al. (2000) expanded the economically based conception of mate availability. They stated that the lack of available occupational opportunities and the increasing economic marginality of African American men constrain their ability to perform the provider role in marriage. This situation increases the probability of unmarried African American women and the available pool of mates for African American men. Orbuch et al. (1999) further stated that, because the unbalanced sex ratio among African Americans decreases the available pool of marriageable men, this sex ratio may influence the selection of a mate or one's decision to stay within a marriage. One might value one's present marriage more or less if the potential for meeting another available mate is compromised or benefited given the sex ratio (Kiecolt & Fossett, 1997).

Thus, there is the recent recognition in the literature that any study examining divorce, particularly in the context of being African American, must address two sets of factors affecting the stability of marriages over time: (a) structural conditions connected to the couple's lives (e.g., occupational opportunities, racial discrimination, and social network ties), and (b) interpersonal or interactional processes within marriages (e.g., conflict, division of household labor, and commitment). Bradbury et al. (2000) proposed that, in order to fully understand relational phenomena and their meaning and consequences to relationship partners, researchers must attend to the "sociocultural ecology" that relationships reside in. These sociocultural ecologies are the norms, cultural meanings settings, social or economic circumstances, and people outside the relationship that are likely to affect the functioning and success of the relationship (Berscheid & Reis, 1998; Bradbury et al.).

The Early Years of Marriage Project (see Veroff et al., 1995; Orbuch et al., 2002), of which we are a part, was designed to assess the sociocultural ecology of both African American and White American marriages. The project focuses on cultural factors beyond structure in explaining differential rates of quality and stability among African American and White American marriages. We now turn to a discussion of this project and some of its recent findings.

The Early Years of Marriage Project

The original project began in 1986, with a sample of newly married African American couples and White American couples that filed for marriage licenses in Wayne County Michigan, during the period from April to June in 1986. The project started with 199 African American couples and 174 White American couples. To be eligible for the study, the partners had to be of the same race; both had to be entering their first marriage; and the wife had to be younger than 35 years of age. Because we wanted to track the development of couples' marriages over time, the couples were interviewed on multiple occasions. The first interview took place just a few months after their marriage, at a time when most couples are firmly in the glow of the honeymoon period. We then returned to interview the still married couples in Years 2, 3, 4, 7, and 16 of their marriage. We also did a brief survey with everyone, married or divorced, in Year 14 of the marriage. In Years 2 and 4, brief telephone interviews were conducted. In Years 1, 3, 7, and 16, married couples were interviewed at their homes by a race-matched interviewer, in which each individual was first interviewed separately and then with his or her spouse. A novel feature of the Year 16 interviews was the fact that, for the first time, we were able to conduct extensive interviews with many of the participants who had divorced over the years.

There are several unique features of the project that enhance the significance and contributions it can make to research on divorce, especially in the context of being African American. The Early Years of Marriage Project concentrates on both structural and interactional factors as important determinants of marital quality and stability. The project also has a reasonably large and representative sample. When we compare this sample to national Census data, we find that it corresponds to married individuals in the United States, by race, on income, education, parental status, and other demographic qualities. Further, the project is the first of its kind because of its focus on how an individual's being an African American in American society affects the way his or her marriage develops and dissolves, especially in contrast to the individual's being a member of the dominant society. Next, this project analyzes both members of the couple, rather than just one spouse reporting on both persons' perspectives. Reports were obtained for the first time right after the marriage began. Futhermore, whereas most studies on marriage gather information at one (or perhaps two) time point, so far this project has collected seven waves of data at various points in time. Finally, the project gathers qualitative and quantitative information from married and divorced individuals. Besides a structured interview, married individuals also are asked to tell the joint story of their relationship, from the beginning when it first began, up to the present, and to plans for the future. Divorced individuals also are asked to tell the story of their divorce, from events leading up to the divorce, to the present and future. These narrative techniques are unique to this project; we wanted to gather the meanings of marriage and divorce from the voices of the couples or individuals themselves.

The Early Years of Marriage Project has focused on differential structural and interactional processes that affect marital quality and stability over time. Further, we have investigated multiple structural and interactional factors within a cultural and gendered context. We make the following propositions. First, we argue that to truly understand the meaning of marriage and divorce to individuals, we first need to recognize the cultural context within which the individual and couple are embedded. For example, we discuss in our recent book, *Thrice Told Tales: Married Couples Tell Their Stories* (Holmberg, Orbuch, & Veroff, 2004), that African American and White American couples present different themes and concerns surrounding marriage and divorce in their relationship stories. In the book, we argue that because the divorce or separation rate among African Americans is higher than it is among White Americans, this fact may cause many courting and newlywed African American partners to doubt and question their relationship. These doubts and questions seem to surface when African American married couples are asked to tell the story of their courtship. In fact, after analyzing the Year 1 relationship narratives, we found that African American couples, at least in the initial stories of courtship, focused on making sense of their relationship. White American couples took their relationship more for granted, and their courtship stories contained themes about the couple's work and accomplishments. Consider what Denise and Try, an African American couple, said about their courtship in Year 1 (Holmberg et al., 2004, p. 139):

Denise: We just kept seeing each other after that. And then, I guess our relationship got stronger and everything, you know.

    Try: We just enjoyed going out together.

Denise: And then, we stayed together so long, everybody kept staying, we are not going to get married. We are not going to get married. Eventually, we started talking about marriage.

    Try: Yes, we began talking about getting married. We were finally there.

In contrast, Joy and Steve, a White American couple (p. 0), discussed the need for individuality and independence before they got married:

    Joy: I just wasn't ready to get married. There were things I wanted to do and I wanted all that stuff. At the beginning, we didn't really see each other a whole lot, you know, maybe once a week. Sometimes not for a couple of weeks. With working and school, we had busy schedules.

Steve: I've always been a hard worker, save my money. I was, you know, content with staying busy. I had my own car, paid for my first car, by myself and all that. I also had enough brothers and sisters that were married and things. I didn't really need that, you know.

    Joy: Yeah, I don't know. I didn't like the guys my age. They were immature. I like guys who were more settled, less wild. When I met Steve, although I wasn't ready to get married right away, he was stable and a hard worker. He kept saying, well, not until I get out of school and things like that. Luckily, some things came up and then he gave me a ring. I was surprised at that time, because I didn't think he wanted to right then, that early, and then I had said to him, I want to finish school. I was afraid if I got married, I wouldn't finish school.

Second, we further propose that the experiences of being male or female in a marriage have unique meanings depending on the cultural or ethnic context. For example, Orbuch et al. (1999) found that, after analyzing the narrative styles of storytelling for both White and Black stable marriages, wives are supportive of their husbands, but the meaning of these supportive behaviors varied depending on the race or ethnicity of the couple. For White stable marriages, wives' supportive behaviors were conceptualized as whether she was perceived as *cooperative* (i.e., making any direct statement indicating agreement, such as "I like what you said") by both husband and wife. In contrast, for Black stable marriages, when wives were *collaborative* (i.e., picking up words or ideas of the spouse and adding to them, or answering questions in ways that furthered the story or that confirmed what the spouse thought was happening) in their style of interaction, these behaviors were seen as supportive by both husbands and wives.

We maintain that African American women and men organize their lives differently from White American women and men, specifically around issues of power and gender that affect patterns of marriage and divorce. Our findings indicate that the cultural context may filter ways that men and women experience the power they have within their marriages (Hunter & Davis, 1992; Orbuch & Sprecher, 2003). For example, we have found that Black couples are more egalitarian than White couples in their attitudes toward women and gendered roles (Orbuch & Eyster, 1997). African American men seem to place great value on the input of women and men inside and outside the home, perhaps in response to their lack of structural opportunities. They also are more likely than White men to criticize gender inequality and more traditional views of masculinity and femininity (Collins, 1990; Hunter & Sellers, 1998; Kane, 1992; Orbuch & Eyster). In addition, other findings (Orbuch & Eyster) indicate that African American husbands are more likely to participate in household tasks, including child care, than White husbands. Relatedly, we also found (Orbuch et al., 2002) that African American husbands' participation in home labor and child care reduces the risk of divorce for Black couples.

Our project findings also indicate that the meaning of particular structural factors, such as parental status, income, educational attainment, and social network ties, are different in the two ethnic groups (and for husbands and wives), which leads to differential connections to marital risk in the two communities. Even more importantly, this project has found that the norms surrounding marriage, divorce, and parenthood are different depending on the racial or ethnic culture. Although most of the literature on marriage and divorce has been geared toward developing universal assumptions about what keeps marriages together and happy and what breaks them apart, our project has taken a divergent path and emphasized the need to examine marital interactional processes through both a cultural and gendered lens. For example, Veroff et al. (1995) found that, although there were some instances in which identical variables were associated with instability over the first 4 years of marriage in both African American and White American couples (e.g., the wife having an affair, interferences experienced from wives' friends, and the experience of marital unhappiness among wives), these similarities were few and far between. Instead, there appear to be numerous subtle ways in which the determinants of marital instability are different for the two groups. Most of these themes implicate important interactive phenomena that are critical for stable marriages, gender-power phenomena that can destabilize marriages, or both. Findings from the Early Years of Marriage Project (e.g., Orbuch et al., 2002) conclude that the meaning of specific interactional factors contributing to the risk of divorce (e.g., frequency of conflict, division of household labor, and affective affirmation) must always be examined within a cultural and gendered context.

In addition, a more recent focus of our project has been how the cultural context within which divorce occurs (e.g., meaning, social support from others, and stigmatization) also may differ between the two ethnic groups (African American and White American). Studies suggest that, within the African American community, the norms surrounding divorce are more tolerant and accepting of individuals who divorce. Further, the availability of single-parent models (Ruggles, 1994) and the important emphasis on kin networks and support (Stack, 1974) allow for greater inclusion and less blaming of individuals in the African American community. We argue that these factors may lead to less stigmatization, more supportive resources, and more effective coping strategies for managing the dissolution of a marriage for African Americans. Studies have provided strong evidence that support from social networks is significantly linked to parent–child relationship quality and better adjustment after divorce in White American families (McLanahan & Sandefur, 1994; Orbuch, Thornton, & Cancio, 2000). Thus, further research is needed to address how factors such as social support or stigmatization embedded in the cultural context of a divorce may influence coping and adjustment to divorce for adults and children in African American and other minority families.

Risk and Resilience Perspective

Another new development in the literature, from a theoretical perspective, has been to apply a risk and resilience framework to the study of divorce among African Americans. McCubbin and McCubbin (1993, 1996) define resiliency as the ability and competency of individuals or families to exhibit positive consequences given the stress and hardship associated with adverse and distressing situations, such as divorce. More specifically, a research program that applies a risk and resilience perspective to the study of divorce would examine the processes and factors that lead to individuals' and families' ability to cope and adjust to marital transitions and life in a single-parent family. Hetherington (1999) maintained that "although divorce, growing up in a single-parent family, and remarriage put children at risk for developing social, emotional, behavioral, and academic problems, most children eventually emerge from these experiences as competent, reasonably well-adjusted individuals" (p. viii). This ability to emerge as a well-adjusted and functional individual or family, given the multiple risk factors associated with divorce, is the direct result of certain strength-based factors that promote positive outcomes in the individual or family. Thus, although African Americans may divorce at twice the rate of White Americans, African American families also have resources and strengths that protect them from the possible risks associated with divorce.

Taylor, Jackson, and Chatters (1997) stated that the literature has often ignored the resiliency of African American families and has failed to examine specific family or couple strengths that can positively affect African American family life and functioning. We turn now to the literature that has examined specific family or couple strengths among African American families. Although there are several family strength-based factors that have been examined in the literature, we focus on three that have been found to lead to positive outcomes during or after divorce and that have been widely supported in the literature: (a) multigenerational households, (b) ties to grandparents, and (c) church and friend support. These strength-based factors have made important contributions to research in this area of study.

Multigenerational Households

One particular strengths-based factor that is evident in African American and other minority families and that has received a great deal of attention lately is multigenerational households (Wilson, 1996). Studies (Brown & Jackson, in press; Taylor et al., 1990) indicate that African Americans are more likely than White Americans to reside in extended family or multigenerational households, which provide a number of benefits to adults and children, especially during times of extreme stress such as divorce.

Taylor, Tucker, Chatters, and Jayakody (1997) stated that multigenerational living arrangements are beneficial in that they provide extra resources, including economic, emotional, and social support for all family members. The additional resources are important for maintaining a healthy standard of living or for meeting the basic needs of family members, and for providing a healthy exchange of assistance across generations (Taylor et al., 1990). Further, the presence of more than one adult provides help with child care, elder care, and household responsibilities.

In addition, compared with White American divorced single mothers, child support and alimony are practically nonexistent for African American divorced single mothers (Taylor et al., 1990). The lack of economic support from children's fathers or exhusbands, coupled with other economic disparities (e.g., expensive child-care costs, low-paying jobs), contributes to high poverty rates among African American female-headed households. Given that African American single mothers are likely to live in larger multigenerational households than White single mothers, this living arrangement often provides necessary child care so that single African American mothers can pursue and maintain employment or attain higher educational status. Research suggests that when single mothers live in multigenerational households, they are more likely to be employed outside the home than single mothers in nonmultigenerational households (Taylor, Tucker, et al., 1997).

Some studies find (Adkins, 1999; Hatchett, Veroff, & Douvan, 1995) that generations in ethnic minority families may live together because of economic necessity caused by low SES, poverty, and generally having few resources and opportunities. In contrast, other researchers assert that intergenerational households may be more the product of cultural norms, such as familialism, filial piety, or familial obligation. Brown and Jackson (in press) state that, in any case, the large family provides a functional, mutually beneficial network from which to give and receive care. Further, evidence indicates that extended family is the primary source of support and protection in the face of economic stress and problems and that a greater number of African Americans turn to family for help during stressful life events than to professionals (Taylor, Tucker, et al., 1997).

As we already discussed, multigenerational extended family households have several benefits. However, the arrangement also may have its disadvantages. Child-care advice can often turn into child-care criticism, causing conflict and arguments between generations as well as between genders (Jayakody & Chatters, 1997). In addition to childrearing conflicts, extended periods of coresidency can result in other challenging outcomes, including a lack of privacy, overreliance on others, overcrowding, and fragile economic viability. Nonetheless, despite the negative consequences of multigenerational households, in general the research suggests that a diverse, functional multigenerational network is essential for coping with adverse conditions, such as divorce, for most African American families (Caldwell & Koski, 1997; Jayakody & Chatters).

Ties to Grandparents

The role of grandparent ties and their beneficial links to African American individuals undergoing adverse or stressful circumstances, such as divorce (Taylor, Keith, & Tucker, 1993), is another strengths-based resiliency factor that has been explored widely in this area. Studies find that the majority of African American children have greater opportunities to interact and be involved with their grandparents than White American children (Taylor et al., 1990). Results support the notion that African American grandmothers are critically important for their grandchildren's mental and physical health, as well as academic achievement (Adkins, 1999; Taylor et al., 1990). Grandparents teach younger children to read and write, help adult children, and strengthen family intergenerational bonds. Grandparents also can provide direct emotional and financial support to younger needy family members, serve as confidants and sources of advice and socialization agents, and be responsible for caring for the sick. Research findings indicate that African American adult children depend on older family members for economic and housing assistance (Hudson, 1986; Pillemer & Finkelhor, 1989). Further, other recent studies have found that, when adult children are in the divorce process or experiencing temporary unemployment, older generations are usually their first source of help (Baron & Welty, 1996; Pillemer & Finkelhor). According to Taylor, Tucker, et al. (1997), grandmothers have been (and will continue to be) the primary support for unmarried single mothers and their children in the African American community.

Church and Friend Support

A third strengths-based factor promoting resilience after divorce for African Americans that has received a great deal of recent attention is the influence of church and friend support. Research provides a wealth of information concerning the importance of church support for the resiliency of African American family life and functioning in general (Taylor, Chatters, & Levin, 2004). Thus, one of the aims of the literature on divorce among African Americans has been to examine the supportive role that religion may play in the family functioning and lives of African Americans, specifically during the divorce process. The majority of this research suggests that the church can provide a religious role in individuals' lives, but what is even more important for positive adaptation in times of stress is the special support system that the church itself and its members provide. Black churches have proven to be responsive to the needs of communities that have limited access to general societal support systems (Taylor, Tucker, et al., 1997). Church members exchange instrumental, financial, emotional, and spiritual assistance with each other. This support includes food, clothing, and care for the sick, as well as advice, encouragement, and information and referrals (Taylor et al., 2004).

Keith (1997) further found that, among separated and divorced African American individuals, reports of close friendships and of family closeness are associated with optimal feelings of individual well-being. The results indicate that although family was the primary source of financial support, friends were an important resource for affective support during stressful events, such as divorce. Keith concluded that, during a marital dissolution, friends become a critical source of emotional support for African Americans to cope with the potential divorce-related risks. Because family relationships often become distant during a marital dissolution or separation, friends and their support may become even more critical to positive adjustment (Keith). Taylor, Tucker, et al. (1997) also found that friends become a closer and more reliable source of emotional support if individuals are not connected to the family network.

African American Children and Divorce

Lastly, research in this area also has focused on the effects of divorce for African American children. The rise in divorce rates has increased the number of children living in single-parent families and has implications for children's social, emotional, and academic development (see chap. 16 by Barber & Demo, this volume). Divorce has important implications for all children; however, because of the low incidence of remarriage in the African American community, African American children of divorce are especially disadvantaged. Using 1995 U.S. Census data, Taylor, Tucker, et al. (1997) reported that three fourths of White children and two thirds of Hispanic children lived with two parents, whereas only one third of African American children lived with both parents.

The outcomes of divorce on children's development are complex and depend on various factors such as the sex and age of the child at the time of divorce, residential neighborhood, income, whether parent(s) remarries or not, and the social or economic resources of the custodial parent (Orbuch et al., 2001; South, Crowder, & Trent, 1998). Further, there is recent evidence to suggest that the outcomes of divorce on children's development also may vary by ethnicity or race. For example, African American wives are more likely to have sole custody of their children than are White wives, who are likely to share custody of children with fathers (Taylor, Tucker, et al., 1997). This custodial issue may place African American divorced mothers and their children in financial jeopardy, particularly given that they are less likely to receive alimony and child support than White American divorced mothers.

In addition, numerous studies indicate that an immediate consequence of divorce for children is a change in their SES. Children in divorced families tend to move to lower SES residential neighborhoods (South et al., 1998), and accompanying this change in residential status is usually a decline in the quality of schools—lower teacher expectations, poorer school performance, decrease in educational attainment, and higher incidences of delinquent behaviors (Brooks-Gunn, Duncan, Klebanov, & Sealand, 1993). More recent studies suggest that African American children experience even greater neighborhood economic decline than White American children after divorce and are more likely to remain in economically and socially disadvantaged neighborhoods with low social resources (South et al.).

Although most studies have focused extensively on the negative effects of divorce and single parenting on children, particularly for African American children, other studies have discussed some of the positive outcomes for African American children in single-parent households

(Fine & Schwebel, 1987; 1991). For example, several researchers propose that the extended family networks of Black families serve to provide additional economic, social, and material resources for single parents and their children (Caldwell & Koski, 1997; Fine & Schwebel, 1991; Jayakody & Chatters, 1997). The impressive review by Fine and Schwebel (1991) of resiliency in Black children presents evidence that various protective factors from single mothers have beneficial effects on African American children's personality characteristics. Their review indicates that some African American children from single-parent families often have the same as or higher perceptions of self-image, self-esteem, and levels of assertiveness than children in two-family or White American single-family households. In African American communities, children of divorce and never-married parents are not considered "illegitimate" or stigmatized and ostracized as in other communities (Fine & Schwebel, 1987; 1991; Fine, Schwebel, & James-Myers, 1987; McAdoo, 1997). Additionally, as discussed previously, African American children of single mothers are more likely than White American children to live in households with grandparents who may help to alleviate some of the negative economic and social consequences of single parenthood for African American children (Fine & Schwebel, 1987; Taylor, Tucker, et al., 1997; South et al., 1998).

Furthermore, research has just begun to acknowledge the contribution of nonresidential African American fathers to children (Majors & Gordon, 1994; McAdoo, 1997). Grandfathers, uncles, and male friends of the family also often provide guidance and counseling for young boys in mother-headed households (Taylor, Jackson, & Chatters, 1997). Moreover, studies indicate that African American children benefit socially, cognitively, and academically when their single mothers are employed (Parcel & Cornfield, 2000). Other factors that have been found to contribute to African American children's ability to cope with divorce is high parental involvement and supervision and the social support network that exists within their families and throughout their neighborhoods (Fine & Schwebel, 1991).

Although current research on divorce among African Americans has begun to expand beyond mere descriptions of differences in divorce rates between African Americans and White Americans, even this research is limited. We presented several interesting new research directions, but additional research is needed in this area of study. Some of the recent advances in this field originate from our own project, The Early Years of Marriage Project. We continue to argue that by expanding these new directions of study, investigators will gain a more comprehensive understanding of divorce in the context of being African American.

CONCLUSIONS AND FUTURE RESEARCH DIRECTIONS

Recently, there has been a growth of research investigating divorce in the context of being African American. As stated previously, most of this work has concentrated on divorce rates among White Americans and African Americans and has emphasized the structural factors that account for these differences. Consequently, it is not surprising then that we encourage more research on the topic of divorce among minority groups other than African Americans. It is important to note that the literature continues to be restricted by what Collins (1990) called a "biracial or dichotomous thinking, in which the normative work is conducted using European American relationships and the 'minority' perspective is represented via an examination of African American relationships" (as cited by McLoyd, Cauce, Takeuchi & Wilson, 2000, p. 1071).

Second, we encourage more researchers to move from examining only structural predictors to exploring both structural and interactional factors, which may interact to predict divorce and relationship dissolution outcomes. For example, in the Early Years of Marriage Project,

we plan to analyze marriages that progress to the early middle years (using the recently collected Year 16 data) and ask how structural factors (e.g., education, income, network ties, and
religious involvement) along with the nature of interpersonal relationships (e.g., communication, conflict, and affirmation) account for marital outcomes (perceived marital quality and
stability) and patterns of family life (parental involvement and family cohesion) over time.
We are especially interested in finding out whether the determinants of these marital and
family outcomes are different or similar for White American and African American married
couples.

Third, the existing work on divorce has tried to account for the influences of diverse socioeconomic backgrounds (e.g., class, employment status), but several controversies and unanswered questions still exist. There is always the challenge of isolating race and ethnicity effects
from other sociodemographic effects (Orbuch & Fine, 2003), but additional research has to
be conducted to examine how variations in psychological strain or pressures within various
socioeconomic contexts have different consequences and meanings within various racial or
ethnic groups. As we have stated elsewhere (Orbuch & Fine; Orbuch & Sprecher, 2003), we
also encourage researchers to examine these diverse cultural memberships for within- and
between-group differences. Too often we think of differences, but commonalities between and
among groups are important to examine as well.

Fourth, the research has to be expanded on how the predictors of divorce within various
ethnic or racial groups may vary across the life course of a relationship. Orbuch, House, Mero,
and Webster (1996) argued that there is an abundance of literature on why there is a gradual
decline in marital quality and stability in the early years of marriage, but little is known on
how and why marriages are maintained or dissolved in the middle and later years. In addition,
the factors that contribute to divorce early on in a marriage may be different or a variation of
those factors that determine divorce in the early middle years of marriage or beyond. Although
some research has begun to examine these processes (Gottman & Levenson, 2000; Orbuch
et al., 2002), additional research is needed, especially among African Americans.

Fifth, as research becomes more concerned with nonmarital unions and their dissolutions,
we need to examine the meaning of cohabitation, especially for African Americans. Taylor,
Tucker, & Mitchell-Kernan (1999) argued that given more tolerant attitudes in the African
American community toward nonmarital unions, cohabitation has become a substitute for
marriage. In fact, many have argued that the decline in the rates of marriage and remarriage
among African Americans is partially explained by the rise in the number of cohabiting couples
(Bumpass, Sweet, & Cherlin, 1991; Taylor, Jackson, et al., 1997). Taylor, Jackson, et al. (1997)
reported that similar numbers of White American and African American women, about one
third, have cohabited from adolescence to midlife. However, whereas about 50% of White
women's first cohabitation experience ends in marriage, only approximately 40% of African
American women's first cohabitation has the same marital outcome. In addition, research
suggests that among cohabiting couples, African American couples are more likely to have
children than White American couples (Hunter, 1997; McLanahan & Casper, 1995).

Lastly, as we have stated previously (Orbuch & Sprecher, 2003), additional efforts have to
be made to utilize larger and more representative groups of African Americans (and other racial
or ethnic groups). Further, social scientists who study divorce and the dissolution of romantic
relationships need to consistently take race or ethnicity into account when they consider their
samples, measures, and interpretations of findings (Orbuch & Fine, 2003). Most of the empirical
work on this topic continues to examine individuals, rather than reports from both members of
the couple. The samples we use in our research have to be seriously considered in any study
that examines divorce in the context of race or ethnicity.

ACKNOWLEDGMENTS

We wish to thank the following individuals for their comments and assistance on this chapter: Jonathan Blair, Rachel Barr, Lisa Byrd and the two handbook editors, Mark Fine and John Harvey.

REFERENCES

Adelmann, P. K., Chadwick, C., & Baerger, D. R. (1996). Marital quality of Black and White adults over the life course. *Journal of Social and Personal Relationships, 13*, 361–384.

Adkins, V. K. (1999). Grandparents as a national asset: A brief note. *Activities, Adaptation and Aging, 24*, 13–18.

Amato, P. R., Johnson, D. R., Booth, A., & Rogers, S. J. (2003). Continuity and change in marital quality between 1980 and 2000. *Journal of Marriage and the Family, 65*, 1–22.

Amato, P. R., & Rogers, S. T. (1997). A longitudinal study of marital problems and subsequent divorce. *Journal of Marriage and the Family, 59*, 612–624.

Baron, S., & Welty, A. (1996). Elder abuse. *Journal of Gerontological Social Work, 25*, 33–57.

Berscheid, E., & Reis, H. (1998). Attraction and close relationships. In D. T. Gilbert, S. T. Fiske, & G. Lindzey (Eds.), *The handbook of social psychology* (4th ed., pp. 193–281). New York: McGraw-Hill

Billingsley, A. (1988). *Black families in White America*. New York: Simon & Schuster.

Billingsley, A. (1992). *Climbing Jacob's ladder: The enduring legacy of African-American families*. New York: Simon & Schuster.

Bradbury, T. N., Fincham, F. D., & Beach, S. R. H. (2000). Research on the nature and determinants of marital satisfaction: A decade in review. *Journal of Marriage and the Family, 62*, 964–980.

Broman, C. L. (1993). Race differences in marital well-being. *Journal of Marriage and the Family, 55*, 724–732.

Broman, C. L. (2002). Thinking of divorce, but staying married: The interplay of race and marital satisfaction. *Journal of Divorce and Remarriage, 37*(1/2), 151–161.

Brooks-Gunn, J. Duncan, G., Klebanov, P., & Sealand, N. (1993). Do neighborhoods influence child and adolescent development? *American Journal of Sociology, 99*, 353–395. '

Brown, E., & Jackson, J. S. (in press). Age-related issues among minority populations. In C. Spielberger & R. K. Lee (Eds.), *Encyclopedia of applied psychology* (pp. 79–90). New York: Elsevier.

Bruner, J. (1990). *Acts of meaning*. Cambridge, MA: Harvard University Press.

Bumpass, L., & Sweet, J. (1989). National estimates of cohabitation. *Demography, 26*, 615–625.

Bumpass, L., Sweet, J., & Cherlin, A. (1991). The role of cohabitation in declining rates of marriage. *Journal of Marriage and the Family, 53*, 913–927.

Caldwell, C. H., & Koski, L. R. (1997). Child rearing, social support, and perceptions of parental competency among African American mothers. In R. J. Taylor, J. S. Jackson & L. M. Chatters (Eds.), *Family life in Black America* (pp. 185–200). Thousand Oaks, CA: Sage.

Cherlin, A. J. (1998). Marriage and marital dissolution among black Americans. *Journal of Comparative Family Studies, 29*, 147–158.

Collins, P. H. (1990). *Black feminist thought*. Boston: Unwin Hyman.

Duncan, G. (1994). Families and neighbors as sources of disadvantage in the schooling decisions of white and black adolescents. *American Journal of Education, 103*, 20–53.

Elder, G., & Caspi, A. (1988). Economic stress in lives: Developmental perspectives. *Journal of Social Issues, 44*, 25–45.

Farley, R., & Allen, W. (1987). *The color line and the quality of life in America*. New York: Russell Sage Foundation.

Fine, M. A., & Schwebel, A. I. (1987). An emergent explanation of differing racial reactions to single parenthood. *Journal of Divorce, 11*, 1–15.

Fine, M. A., & Schwebel, A. I. (1991). Resiliency in black children from single-parent families. In W. A. Rhodes & W. K. Brown (Eds.), *Why some children succeed despite the odds* (pp. 23–40). New York: Praeger.

Fine, M. A., & Schwebel, A. I., & James-Myers, L. (1987). Family stability in Black families: Values underlying three different perspectives. *Journal of Comparative Family Studies, 18*, 1–23.

Gottman, J. M. (1994). *What predicts divorce? The relationships between marital process and marital outcomes*. Hillsdale, NJ: Lawrence Erlbaum Associates.

Gottman, J. M., & Levenson, R.W. (2000). The timing of divorce: Predicting when a couple will divorce over a 14-year period. *Journal of Marriage and the Family, 62*, 737–745.

Hatchett, S., Veroff, J., & Douvan, E. (1995). *Marital stability among Black and White couples in early marriage.* In M. B. Tucker & C. Mitchell-Kernan (Eds.), The decline in marriage among African-Americans (pp. 177–218). New York: Russell Sage Foundation.

Hetherington, E. M. (1999). *Coping with divorce, single parenting, and remarriage: A risk and resiliency perspective.* Mahwah, NJ: Lawrence Erlbaum Associates.

Holmberg, D., Orbuch, T. L., & Veroff, J. (2004). *Thrice told tales: Married couples tell their stories.* Mahwah, NJ: Lawrence Erlbaum Associates.

Hudson, M. F. (1986). Elder mistreatment: Current research. In K. A. Pillemer & R. S. Wolf (Eds.), *Elder abuse: Conflict in the family* (pp. 125–166). Dover, MA: Auburn House.

Hunter, A. (1997). Living arrangements of African American adults. In R. J. Taylor, J. S. Jackson, & L. M. Chatters (Eds.), *Family Life in Black America* (pp. 94–116). Thousand Oaks, CA: Sage.

Hunter, A. G., & Davis, J. (1992). Constructing gender: An exploration of Afro-American men's conceptualization of manhood. *Gender and Society, 6,* 464–479.

Hunter, A. G., & Sellers, S. L. (1998). Feminist attitudes among African-American men's conceptualization of manhood. *Gender and Society, 12,* 81–99.

James, A. D., & Tucker, M. B. (2003). Racial ambiguity and relationships formation in the United States: Theoretical and practical considerations. *Journal of Social and Personal Relationships, 20,* 153–169.

Jayakody, R., & Chatters, L. M. (1997). Differences among African American single mothers: Marital status, living arrangements, and family support. In R. J. Taylor, J. S. Jackson, & L. M. Chatters (Eds.), *Family life in Black America* (pp. 167–184). Thousand Oaks, CA: Sage.

Kane, E. W. (1992). Race, gender, and attitudes toward gender stratification. *Social Psychology Quarterly, 55,* 311–320

Karney, B. R., & Bradbury, T. N. (1995). The longitudinal course of marital quality and stability: A review of theory, methods, and research. *Psychological Bulletin, 118,* 3–34.

Keith, V. M. (1997). Life stress and psychological well-being among married and unmarried blacks. In R. J. Taylor, J. S. Jackson, & L. M. Chatters (Eds.), *Family life in Black America* (pp. 94–116). Thousand Oaks, CA: Sage.

Kiecolt, K. J., & Fossett, M. A. (1997). The effects of mate availability on marriage among Black Americans. In R. J. Taylor, J. S. Jackson, & L. M. Chatters (Eds.), *Family life in Black America* (pp. 94–116). Thousand Oaks, CA: Sage.

Kitson, G. C. (1992). *Portrait of divorce.* New York: Guilford.

Kitson, H. D., & Morgan, H. K. (1990). Social structural and psychological correlates of interethnic dating. *Journal of Applied Psychology, 8,* 446–450.

Kposwa, A. J. (1998). The impact of race on divorce in the United States. *Journal of Comparative Family Studies, 29,* 529–548.

Kreider, R. M., & Fields, J. M. (2001). *Number, timing, and duration of marriages and divorces: Fall 1996* (Current Population Reports, Series P70–80). Washington, DC: U.S. Government Printing Office.

Lawson, E. J., & Thompson, A. (1999). *Black men and divorce.* Thousand Oaks, CA: Sage.

Lichter, D. T., McLaughlin, D. K., Kephart, G., & Landry, D. J. (1992). Race and the retreat from marriage: A shortage of marriageable men? *American Sociological Review, 57,* 781–799.

Majors, R., & Gordon, J. (1994). *The American black male: His present status and his future.* Chicago: Nelson-Hall.

McAdoo, H. P. (1997). *Black families.* Thousand Oaks, CA: Sage.

McCubbin, M., & McCubbin, H. (1993). Family coping with health crises: The resiliency model of family stress, adjustment and adaptation. In C. Danielson, B. Hamel-Bissel, & P. Winstead-Fry (Eds.), *Families, health and illness* (pp. 3–63). St. Louis, MO: Mosby.

McCubbin, M., & McCubbin, H. (1996). Resiliency in families: A conceptual model of family adjustment and adaptation in response to stress and crisis. In H. McCubbin, A. Thompson, & M. McCubbin (Eds.), *Family assessment: Resiliency, coping and adaptation—Inventories for research and practice* (pp. 1–64). Madison: University of Wisconsin.

McLanahan, S., & Casper, L. (1995). Growing diversity and inequality in the American family. In R. Farley (Ed.), *State of the union: America in the 1990s. Vol. 2: Social trends* (pp. 1–45). New York: Russell Sage Foundation.

McLanahan, S., & Sandefur, G. (1994). *Growing up with a single parent: What hurts, what helps.* Cambridge, MA: Harvard University.

McLoyd, V. C., Cauce, A. M., Takeuchi, D., & Wilson, L. (2000). Marital processes and parental socialization in families of color: A decade review of research. *Journal of Marriage and the Family, 64,* 1070–1093.

Orbuch, T. L. (1992). *Relationship loss: Theoretical perspectives.* New York: Springer-Verlag.

Orbuch, T. L., & Eyster, S. (1997). Division of household labor among Black couples and White couples. *Social Forces, 76*(1), 301–322.

Orbuch, T. L., & Fine, M. A. (2003). The context of race/ethnicity in interpersonal relationships: Crossing the chasm. *Journal of Social and Personal Relationships, 20,* 147–152.

Orbuch, T. L., House, J. S., Mero, R. P., & Webster, P. S. (1996). Marital quality over the lifecourse. *Social Psychology Quarterly, 59,* 162–171.

Orbuch, T. L., & Sprecher, S. (2003). *Attraction and interpersonal relationships. Handbook of social psychology.* New York: Kluwer Academic/Plenum.

Orbuch, T. L., Thornton, A., & Cancio, J. (2001). The impact of marital quality, divorce, and remarriage on the relationships between parents and their children. *Marriage and Family Review, 29,* 247–263.

Orbuch, T. L., Veroff, J., Hassan, H., & Horrocks, J. (2002). Who will divorce? A 14-year longitudinal study of Black couples and White couples. *Journal of Social and Personal Relationships, 19,* 179–202.

Orbuch, T. L, Veroff, J., & Hunter, A. G. (1999). Black couples, White couples: The early years of marriage. In E. M. Hethington (Ed.), *Coping with divorce, single parenting, and remarriage: A risk and resiliency perspective.* (pp. 23–43). Mahwah, NJ: Lawrence Erlbaum Associates.

Parcel, T., & Cornfield, D. (2000). *Work and family: Research informing policy.* Thousand Oaks, CA: Sage.

Pillemer, K., & Finkelhor, D. (1989). Causes of elder abuse: Caregiver stress versus problem relatives. *American Journal of Orthopsychiatry, 59,* 179–187.

Ruggles, S. (1994). The origins of African-American family structure. *American Sociological Review, 59,* 136–151.

South, S., Crowder, K., & Trent, K. (1998). Children's residential mobility and neighborhood environment following parental divorce and remarriage. *Social Forces, 77,* 667–693.

Sprecher, S., & Toro-Morn, M. (2002). A study of men and women from different sides of earth to determine if men are from mars and women are from Venus in their beliefs about love and romantic relationships. *Sex Roles, 46,* 131–147.

Stack, C. B. (1974). *All our kin: Strategies for surviving in a black community.* New York: Harper & Row.

Staples, R., & Johnson, L. B. (1993). *Black families at the crossroads.* New York: Harper & Row.

Sweet, J., & Bumpass, L. (1987). *American families and households.* New York: Russell Sage Foundation.

Taylor, R. J., Chatters, L. M., & Levin, J. (2004). *Religion in the lives of African-Americans: Social, psychological, and health perspectives.* Thousand Oaks, CA: Sage.

Taylor, J. T., Chatters, L. M., Tucker, L. M., & Lewis, E. (1990). Developments in research on Black families: A decade in review. *Journal of Marriage and the Family, 52,* 993–1014.

Taylor, R. J., Jackson, J. S., & Chatters, L. M. (1997). *Family life in Black America.* Thousand Oaks, CA: Sage.

Taylor, R. J., Keith, V. M., & Tucker, M. B. (1993). Gender, marital, familial, and friendship roles. In. J. S. Jackson, L. M. Chatters, R. J. Taylor (Eds.), *Aging in Black America* (pp. 49–68). Newbury Park, CA: Sage.

Taylor, R. J., Tucker, M. B., Chatters, L. M., & Jayakody, R. (1997). Recent demographic trends in African American family structure. In R. J. Taylor, J. S. Jackson, & L. M. Chatters (Eds.), *Family life in Black America* (pp. 94–116). Thousand Oaks, CA: Sage.

Taylor, P. L., Tucker, M. B., & Mitchell-Kernan, C. (1999). Ethnic variations in perceptions of men's provider role. *Psychology of Women Quarterly, 23,* 741–761.

Teachman, J. D., Tedrow, L. M., & Crowder, K. D. (2000). The changing demography of America's families. *Journal of Marriage and the Family, 62,* 1234–1246.

Tein, J., Sandler, I. N., & Zautra, A. J. (2000). Stressful life events, psychological distress, coping, and parenting of divorced mothers: A longitudinal study. *Journal of Family Psychology, 14,* 27–41.

Tucker, M. B., & Mitchell-Kernan, C. (1995). Social structural and psychological correlates of interethnic dating. *Journal of Social and Personal Relationships, 12,* 341–361.

Tucker, M. B., & Taylor, R. J. (1989). Demographic correlates of relationship status among Black Americans. *Journal of Marriage and the Family, 51,* 655–665.

Tucker, B. M., & Taylor, R. J. (1997). Gender, age, and marital status as related to romantic involvement among African American singles. In R. J. Taylor, J. S. Jackson, & L. M. Chatters (Eds.), *Family life in Black America* (pp. 94–116). Thousand Oaks, CA: Sage.

Tucker, M. B., Taylor, R. J., & Mitchell-Kernan, C. (1993). Marriage and romantic involvement among aged African Americans. *Journal of Gerontology: Social Science, 48,* S123–S132.

Veroff, J., Douvan, E., & Hatchett, S. (1995). *Marital instability: A social and behavioral study of the early years.* Westport, CT: Praeger.

Veroff, J., & Orbuch, T. L. (in press). Studying marital relationships. In J. Jackson & C. Howard (Eds.), *Research methodologies in African American communities.* Newbury Park, CA: Sage.

Wade, L. D., & DeLamater, J. D. (2002). Relationship dissolution as a life stage transition: Effects on sexual attitudes and behaviors. *Journal of Marriage and Family, 64,* 898–914.

Walker, H. A. (1988). Black–White differences in marriage and family patterns. In S. M. Dornbusch & M. H. Strober (Eds.), *Feminism, children and the new family* (pp. 87–112). New York: Guilford.

Wang, H., & Amato, P. R. (2000). Predictors of divorce adjustment: Stressors, resources and definitions. *Journal of Marriage and the Family, 62,* 655–668.

Weiss, R. S., (1975). *Marital separation.* New York: Basic Books.

White, L. K. (1990). Determinants of divorce: A review of research in the eighties. *Journal of Marriage and the Family, 53,* 904–912.

Wilson, W. J. (1996). *When work disappears: The world of the new urban poor.* New York: Random House.

Yang, B., & Lester, D. (1991). Correlates of statewide divorce rates. *Journal of Divorce and Remarriage, 15,* 219–223.

24

Same-Sex Relationships and Their Dissolution

Ramona Faith Oswald and Eric Clausell
University of Illinois

What is the strongest predictor of divorce? Marriage! This joke was a graduate school favorite, and it has remained amusing because of the same-sex relationship conundrum that it reveals—How can one divorce if one cannot marry in the first place? The legally insecure status of gay and lesbian couples has been one motivation for scholars to document that same-sex couples exist, and to investigate the dynamics of these relationships. Considerably less scholarly attention has been paid to the dissolution of same-sex couples. The two seminal studies of "gay divorce" that continue to be cited (Blumstein & Schwartz, 1983; Kurdek, 1992) were conducted more than 10 years ago, well before the current "gayby boom" or battle for marriage rights. Given the increasing visibility and legalization of same-sex couples (and their children), a closer examination of lesbian and gay divorce certainly seems overdue. Our goal in this chapter is to present what is currently known about the dissolution of same-sex relationships and, perhaps more importantly, to articulate what we do not know so that relationship dissolution scholars can consider ways of expanding their research to include same-sex relationships. Before we do this, however, we believe it is important to put relationship dissolution in context by summarizing what we know about the prevalence, formation, and relational dynamics of gay and lesbian couples.

WHAT ARE THE DEMOGRAPHICS OF SAME-SEX COUPLES?

The 2000 Census counted 601,209 same-sex partner households across 99.3% of all U.S. counties (Smith & Gates, 2001). These households constitute approximately 5% of the nation's population; however, this estimate is probably an undercount because many same-sex cohabiting couples did not reveal themselves on the Census, because not all committed couples live together, and because of measurement error (Gates & Ost, 2004).

Complete analyses of the race, income, and educational demographics of same-sex partner households have yet to be completed (Smith & Gates, 2001). However, same-sex couples are two times more likely than heterosexual married couples to be of mixed race or ethnicity (Simmons & O'Connell, cited in Gates & Ost, 2004), and same-sex couples, especially gay men, are more likely than heterosexual married couples to live in ethnically diverse communities (Gates & Ost). The number of interracial relationships in the lesbian and gay community may partly reflect the fact that, among ethnic minority gays and lesbians, fewer opportunities to find homogamous partners exist in communities of origin. It may be the case that, by simply migrating to more cosmopolitan urban settings, gays and lesbians intermingle with diverse cultural groups, increasing possibilities for dating outside of their race or ethnicity (Peplau, Cochran, & Mays, 1997).

According to the 2000 Census, minor children reside in one third of the female–female, and one fifth of the male–male, households (Gates & Ost, 2004). Again, this is likely an undercount for the reasons already described, as well as because gay and lesbian parents and their children do not necessarily fit neatly into the "two parents with kids" household mold. For example, Weston's (1991) ethnography of gay and lesbian kinship in San Francisco describes a myriad of relationship structures, including lesbian couples who coparent with gay couples. African Americans and Latinos may be more likely to parent than gays and lesbians of other races (Battle et al., 2000; Gates & Ost).

The residential context of same-sex couples may vary by parental status. Though same-sex couples are more likely than heterosexual couples to live in urban areas, same-sex couples with minor children tend to live in communities characterized by greater numbers of children, and fewer same-sex couple households (Gates & Ost, 2004). For example, California has the most same-sex partner households, but Mississippi is the state with the highest proportion of same-sex partner households that include minor children relative to all same-sex partner households (Gates & Ost).

Despite the demographic diversity counted by the 2000 Census, most research on same-sex couples is severely limited by the oversampling of White, highly educated, and financially secure, "homosexually identified" urban people who are connected to gay and lesbian organizations (Allen & Demo, 1995; Meyer & Colten, 1999; Peplau, 1983). Readers should understand that our knowledge of same-sex relationships is constrained by these limitations.

HOW DO GAY MEN AND LESBIANS FORM RELATIONSHIPS?

Heterosexual marriage conflates cohabitation, legalization, and ritualization. Though the advent of nationally recognized legal same-sex marriage would change this for many individuals, same-sex committed couples do not automatically incorporate these three dimensions of institutionalization into their relationships at this point in history. Even those same-sex couples that have legally married in the past few months face an enduring legal limbo as all levels of our government battle over how to recognize or nullify these rites. Whereas marriage is the conventional so-called start date for heterosexual relationships, gay and lesbian relationships may be experienced on a completely different clock. The question "How long have you been together?" may bring a complicated answer as same-sex partners try to decide whether to count time from the point at which they first met for coffee, had their first sexual encounter, moved in together, had a commitment ceremony, or other noninstitutionalized marker. It is also a mistake to presume that all committed same-sex couples are cohabiters. Further, commitment ceremonies, though presented in such forums as the *New York Times* society page as "wedding equivalents," are typically understood by those involved as markers of long-standing commitment rather than beginnings of them (Lewin, 1998; Stiers, 1999). Given this complexity and the lack of research on this topic, it is difficult to make generalizations about how and when same-sex commitment begins or progresses. We can, however, cite a few surveys that included questions about relationship formation and progress.

Berger's (1990) survey of 92 male couples (race was not reported) found that 41% met in a gay bar (the only location mentioned by more than 10% of their sample). Across all settings, men were most likely to meet by self-introduction (53%) or introduction by a mutual friend (34%). All couples cohabited, and the time between first meeting and moving in together ranged from less than 1 week to 6 years, with a median time of approximately 4 months. Of the couples, 50% had written wills, and 13% had a commitment ceremony.

Bryant and Demian (1994; $N = 1,749$, 95% White) found that lesbian partners most often met through work or mutual friends, whereas gay men were more likely to have met in a bar or other "sexually charged" arena. Of the couples, 90% reported some degree of cohabitation in the past year, but the length of time between first meeting and cohabitation was not assessed. Forty-three percent of the couples had executed at least one legal document to protect their relationship, and 16% had a commitment ceremony.

According to the survey by Oswald, Gebbie, and Culton (2001) of 527 nonmetropolitan gay, lesbian, bisexual, and transgender individuals (93% White), 62% had a same-sex partner. Seventy-three percent of those coupled also cohabitated, 55% had taken steps to legalize their relationship, and 19% had a commitment ceremony. Ceremonies were held when respondents were a mean age of 40 years old and had been partnered for a mean of 4 years (Oswald, Grossman, & Chung, 2003).

In contrast to these findings based on overwhelmingly White samples, the National Black Pride survey ($N = 2,645$) found that 27% of respondents were in committed relationships, and 16% were cohabiting with someone of the same sex (Battle et al., 2000). Legalization and ritualization were not assessed. The Black Women's Relationship Project ($N = 530$; Mays & Cochran, 1988/1991) found that 66% of Black lesbians were in committed relationships, with 35% cohabiting. Clearly, we have much to learn about the prevalence, onset, progress, and formalization of same-sex commitment, and how these are related to subsequent relationship dissolution.

WHAT ARE THE DYNAMICS OF SAME-SEX COUPLES?

According to Patterson's (2001) decade review, research on committed relationships has found that same-sex and opposite-sex couples report similar levels of happiness and relationship satisfaction (see also Peplau, Veniegas, & Campbell, 1996). Correlates of same-sex relationship satisfaction include intimacy, equity, and commitment (Patterson), as well as the ability to show affection to one's partner in front of parents and siblings (Caron & Ulin, 1997). Same-sex and opposite-sex couples have similar conflict-resolution styles, although lesbians report being more optimistic and constructive during relationship conflict than do heterosexual women (Gottman et al., 2003; Metz, Rosser, & Strapko, 1994).

Gay men and lesbians typically expect to share power and domestic chores with their partners (Patterson, 2001). Despite this ideal, power imbalances have been found when one partner has greater resources or less dependency (Patterson). Further, although researchers using self-report measures have found egalitarian patterns of domestic labor, especially for lesbians (e.g., Kurdek, 1993), more intensive ethnographic methods have identified a mismatch between self-report and actual behavior. For example, after living with 52 different gay and lesbian San Francisco Bay Area couples for 1 week per household and interviewing partners separately and in depth, Carrington (1999) exquisitely documented that partners with more flexible or less prestigious employment performed more domestic labor, even if they believed that chores were shared equally.

Same-sex couples may relate to their families of origin differently than do heterosexual couples. For example, the social networks of same-sex couples include more friends than those of heterosexual couples (Julien, Chartrand, & Begin, 1999). Further, same-sex couples receive social support from their friends more than from their families of origin (Crosbie-Burnett & Helmbrecht, 1993), whereas heterosexual couples report the inverse pattern (Kurdek, 2001; Kurdek & Schmidtt, 1987). In fact, friends may be considered "true family" as a way to offset the varying degrees of rejection that gay and lesbian people may experience from their families of origin (Weston, 1991). Actual or feared rejection may lead couples to hide or minimize their relationship (Caron & Ulin, 1997). In addition, partners may be pressured to deny their relationships in specific family of origin contexts, for example by receiving wedding invitations that instruct one to leave his or her same-sex partner at home (Oswald, 2000, 2002). Berger (1990) reported that families of origin were the second most common source of conflict for same-sex couples.

Research on ethnic minority gays and lesbians implies that tensions between same-sex couples and families of origin may be negotiated differently when implicit acceptance, rather than overt affirmation, is a cultural norm (Cantú, 2001; Greene, 1998; Peplau, et al., 1997; Waller & McAllen-Walker, 2001; Weston). Overt affirmation implies a celebration of uniqueness and self-definition that is highly compatible with the mainstream American values of personal choice and independence, but potentially incompatible with cultural contexts that prioritize the group over the individual. For example, the study by Chung, Oswald, and Wiley (2005) of Korean heritage lesbians in the United States found that being more Americanized was related to pursuing more overt parental acceptance, whereas being more embedded within an ethnic enclave was related to consciously hiding one's sexuality or relationships in an effort to protect parents from community censure. Although research utilizing a dominant-group sample found that overt acceptance had a positive effect on lesbian couples (Caron & Ulin, 1997), to our knowledge no study has examined the impact of family support on ethnic minority same-sex couples.

As implied by our discussion of demographics, same-sex couples may have birthed, surrogated, adopted, or fostered children into their current relationship. Partners may also have children from previous relationships (e.g., Crosbie-Burnett & Helmbrecht, 1993; Tasker & Golombok, 1997). In addition to negotiating the childrearing terrain shared by all parents, gay and lesbian coparenting couples have some unique strengths and concerns. Strengths include becoming parents intentionally rather than accidentally (Gartrell et al., 1996), flexibly sharing the tasks of parenting rather than assigning each partner a static role (Patterson, 1995; Patterson, Sutfin, & Fulcher, 2004; Reimann, 1997), and having close and warm communication with children (Golombok, Tasker, & Murray, 1997; Mitchell, 1998).

Concerns include managing coparent invisibility as well as antigay hostility. Though it is possible in some jurisdictions for children to have two legal mothers or two legal fathers, many, if not most, children of same-sex couples have only one legal parent. Further, though couples may conscientiously establish within-family parenting roles and routines for both partners (Reimann, 1997), others may not treat them as equal parents (Sullivan, 2001). This may be social, such as a neighbor who insists on knowing which partner is the "real" mother or father. It may also be legal or institutional, such as the school that will not allow a nonlegal coparent to enroll his or her child. To protect their families from hassles and harm, both parents and children may selectively reveal the truth of parental sexual orientation (Hare, 1994; Lott-Whitehead & Tully, 1999; Wright, 2001). In addition, parents may actively socialize their children to manage prejudice and to respect diversity in others (Hare; O'Connell, 1993; Tasker & Golombok, 1995, 1997; Wright).

Though the literature that is identified as being about gay and lesbian relationships never mentions violence, there is a separate body of research suggesting that rates of intimate partner violence are similar for both same-sex and opposite-sex couples (West, 2002). Though same-sex couples may be gaining societal visibility despite prejudice, abused gay men and lesbians continue to be a hidden group. They may be reluctant to reveal their situation to others for many reasons, including a fear of being politically incorrect by exposing intimate partner violence (Renzetti, 1992). Though the overall dynamics of same-sex and opposite-sex abuse may be similar (Cruz, 2003), gay or lesbian perpetrators may additionally use so-called homophobic control to prevent their partners from leaving or seeking help, for example by threatening to "out" a partner, which could result in negative consequences such as loss of employment or child custody (Renzetti noted that one third of her sample were mothers). When seeking help, the most common responses that the individuals in Renzetti's sample received were denial (e.g., not defining the experience as battering) and rejection. Such reactions reinforced the notion that the violence was their fault and made it difficult for them to leave the relationship. It would be helpful for gay and lesbian couple and intimate partner violence researchers to collaborate so that we can gain a much better understanding of how the dynamics of abuse may relate to relationship dissolution.

The 2000 Census notwithstanding, most research on gay and lesbian relationships ignores context. There is, however, a growing body of research that situates relationship dynamics within specific and diverse residential and cultural milieus. For example, Lott-Whitehead and Tully (1999) found that lesbian mothers increased social support by moving their families to "diverse" and "friendly" Atlanta neighborhoods. In contrast, participants in Oswald's ethnography in rural Illinois largely defined themselves as intentionally not urban, even though this meant living with fewer resources and supports (Oswald, 2000, 2002; also see Cody & Welch, 1995). In a similar vein, Yip (1996) found that gay Christian couples were more likely to participate in a gay Christian group than a mainstream gay organization or commercial gay "scene." These couples did not want to choose between their gay identities and their relatively conservative Christian values. Though much more research linking relational dynamics to context is needed, it seems plausible that positive same-sex couple relationships are facilitated by partners having access to contexts that fit their values and identities, and not merely access to gay- or lesbian-identified resources (see Oswald & Culton, 2003).

A final issue that has to be addressed is HIV–AIDS. More than 1 million people have been infected with HIV in the United States alone, including more than 500,000 who have died and another estimated 850,000 to 950,000 people who are living with HIV–AIDS (Kaiser Family Foundation, 2004). Though lesbians have been affected by HIV–AIDS, the epidemic has utterly devastated portions of the gay male community, especially African American and Latino men who have sex with men, and gay men of all races who have been involved in the gay networks of New York, San Francisco, and other large cities (Kaiser Family Foundation). In terms of couple relationships, those affected by HIV–AIDS may be grappling with posttraumatic stress disorder brought on by previous losses (Martin, Dean, Garcia, & Hall, 1989), as well as challenges to the current relationship, such as reconciling discordant diagnoses, caregiving and its attendant losses of privacy and control, and preparing for possible death (Powell-Cope, 1995). Active involvement in private (Richards, Wrubel, & Folkman, 1999–2000) and public (Lewis & Fraser, 1996) commemoration rituals may be integrated into the lives of male couples. In contrast, Peplau et al. (1997) found no relationship between HIV status and overall relationship satisfaction. The extent to which HIV–AIDS affects relationship stability is unclear. Peplau and her colleagues provided one example of collaboration between couple and health researchers, and more such endeavors would be very worthwhile.

HOW MANY SAME-SEX RELATIONSHIPS BREAK UP, AND AT WHAT POINT IN THE RELATIONSHIP?

The end of same-sex relationships can be as difficult to note as the beginning, because it is culturally familiar for expartners to remain friends and even be considered family (Nardi, 1999; Weston, 1991). For example, expartners may act as "surrogate grandparents" to one's children (Patterson, Hurt, & Mason, 1998). That said, a few authors have provided some estimates of relationship dissolution rates. When contacting all couples who had obtained civil unions in Vermont the first year that these became available, Solomon, Rothblum, and Balsam (2004) found that 1% had separated after 1 year. Kurdek (1992) found a 19% dissolution rate during a 4-year study of same-sex cohabiters. Though he did not calculate the length of time the couples were together before dissolution, his baseline data on length of time cohabitating at Year 1 of data collection suggest that dissolution for these couples typically occurred after 6–11 years of cohabitation. The longitudinal study by Gartrell (2000) of the transition to lesbian parenthood found that 31% of the coparenting couples had separated by the time their children were 5 years old. They had been together for a mean of 8 years, and those who separated had been together significantly less time than those who remained a couple. The findings of Blumstein and Schwartz (1983) suggest that the 10-year mark is significant for relationship longevity: Same-sex couples that had been together for more than 10 years were less likely to break up than those who had been together for 0–10 years (6% vs. 21% for lesbians; 4% vs. 16% for gay men). Although not systematically controlled for in past relationship research, the limited data available imply that length of relationship is a salient variable for researchers to explore when researching the end of same-sex relationships.

We do not know the extent to which having a civil union or other legal or ritual marker has an impact on relationship stability—nor do we know anything in depth about the impact of children on same-sex dissolution. Our limited knowledge about why same-sex couples break up is addressed in the next section.

WHY AND HOW DO SAME-SEX COUPLES BREAK UP?

Virtually everything we know in answer to the question of why and how same-sex couples break up has come from the research program of Kurdek. His overall approach is to study cohabitating committed and child-free same-sex couples (often comparing them to heterosexual cohabiting or married couples) by using the investment model derived from exchange theory. In other words, he investigates whether relationships continue because partners are more satisfied, perceive fewer alternatives to the relationship, and perceive more barriers to leaving. In the paragraphs that follow, we summarize Kurdek's studies that specifically examined same-sex relationship dissolution, and we also reference other supporting research.

Using data from six gay and seven lesbian couples (92% White) who had separated during the course of a longitudinal study, Kurdek (1991) analyzed reasons for the relationship's ending, emotions experienced since the separation, and problems encountered since the separation. In addition, Kurdek sought to identify predictors of postseparation adjustment. The top two participant-supplied reasons for ending the relationship were nonresponsiveness (73%; i.e., "there was no communication between us and little support," p. 269), and partner problems (50%; i.e., "he/she had a drug and alcohol problem," p. 269). When presented with a list of reasons for separating and asked to rate how much each one contributed to their breakup, participants agreed on average that the following reasons had contributed to their situation: Frequent absence, sexual incompatibility, and mental cruelty. The top three emotional reactions to separation were personal growth, loneliness, and relief from conflict. Managing relationships with expartners and experiencing financial stress were the top two problems encountered since the breakup. Partners who expected the breakup reported more positive emotional adjustment and fewer postseparation problems. Further, managing well after the breakup was associated with higher education, less time knowing and cohabitating with the expartner, maintaining independent finances, reporting low levels of love for, and attachment to, the partner, and reporting less psychological distress. There were no significant differences between lesbian and gay male couples.

In another study focused on adjustment to relationship dissolution, Kurdek (1997) further confirmed the "reasons for leaving" findings by using a comparative sample of 26 gay, 24 lesbian, and 46 heterosexual couples. In this study, no significant differences among gay, lesbian, and heterosexual couples regarding their reasons for ending relationships were found. In a similar vein, Blumstein and Schwartz (1983) found that couples who argued about money matters, had discrepant income levels, and did not pool finances were more likely to break up than other couples. In terms of work-related factors, couples who articulated that work "intruded" on the relationship were more likely to break up, and the more ambitious partner, careerwise, was more likely to leave the relationship. Finally, sexually dissatisfied couples were more likely to break up.

In 1992, Kurdek used longitudinal data (94% White) to compare 22 couples (12 lesbian, 10 gay male) that had separated with 92 (61 gay male, 31 lesbian) couples whose relationship remained intact over the 4 years of data collection. At Year 1, gay male couples had cohabitated for a mean of 7 years, whereas lesbian couples had cohabited for a mean of 5 years. Partners in separated couples differed in six ways from partners in intact couples: They reported more negative emotions, less relationship satisfaction, fewer pooled finances, and less emotional commitment, and they invested less time in the relationship and placed a higher value on personal autonomy. Kurdek argued that these findings show remarkable similarity to research on heterosexual relationship dissolution.

In a project that was the first of its kind, Kurdek (1996) prospectively addressed the deterioration of relationship quality of cohabiting gay and lesbian couples. For this study, Kurdek traced the predictors associated with relationship dissolution over a period of 5 years. Relationship quality was composed of three factors—positivity, relationship conflict, and personal autonomy. Compared with couples that remained together, same-sex couples that eventually separated reported a decrease in positivity with an increase in relationship conflict, and an increase in personal autonomy. These data address questions neither of causality nor directionality, such as whether a decrease in positivity triggers increases in autonomy, or vice versa.

In one of his most recent studies comparing heterosexual married partners with same-sex cohabiting couples, Kurdek (1998) again used data collected during a 5-year longitudinal study to assess whether members of married couples differed from those of either gay or lesbian cohabiting couples on five dimensions of relationship quality (intimacy, autonomy, equality, constructive problem solving, and barriers to leaving), and two relationship outcomes (the trajectory of change in relationship satisfaction and relationship dissolution over 5 years). Further, he examined whether each dimension of relationship quality was linked with each relationship outcome. Partners in lesbian couples did report significantly higher levels of intimacy than partners in heterosexual couples, and partners from both gay and lesbian couples reported higher autonomy and more equality than did partners from heterosexual couples. There were no couple-type differences in constructive problem solving. Heterosexual couples reported significantly more barriers to leaving than did partners in same-sex couples.

In sum, Kurdek's research suggests that same-sex and opposite-sex couples are similar in that partners seem to stay together when they find the relationship rewarding and perceive fewer alternatives to being together. In contrast to heterosexual couples, partners in same-sex couples perceive fewer barriers to leaving, and this is perhaps largely due to their lack of institutionalization.

Kurdek's research has provided ground-breaking knowledge regarding same-sex relationships, and he has clearly paved the way for more investigators in this area. Like all research programs, however, his has a specific focus and thus provides only a piece of the whole relationship puzzle. For one, he has overwhelmingly relied on White, educated, gainfully employed, "homosexually identified," cohabiting, and child-free same-sex couple samples, and thus his findings should be generalized at most to a specific niche within the overall gay and lesbian population. As Bell and Weinberger (1978) declared a quarter of a century ago, and as the 2000 Census confirmed (Gates & Ost, 2004), "homosexual adults are a remarkably diverse group" (p. 217). A related limitation is that Kurdek's samples are overlapping; for example, his 1997 data set was extracted from three of his other longitudinal studies. Although this is not inherently a problem, it does highlight the remarkably small pool of people from which information about same-sex relationship dissolution has been gathered.

A further limitation is Kurdek's sole use of quantified self-report measures, rather than physiological or behavioral measures, or in-depth interviews with same-sex couples. Our knowledge of same-sex relationships and their dissolution would be greatly enhanced by studies of dyadic, network, and community interactions, as well as meaning-making processes, within everyday contexts.

Finally, Kurdek's consistent finding of similarity between same-sex and opposite-sex couples may be due to his choice of variables normed on heterosexual couples. For example, Kurdek's (1996) measure of reasons for separation was derived from heterosexual respondents' subjective descriptions of why their relationships ended. This seems particularly problematic if we take the position that, although there may be similarities among lesbian, gay, and heterosexual couples, there are still salient differences that researchers will necessarily obscure by incorporating measures normed on heterosexual samples when they research lesbian and gay couples. Kurdek does acknowledge that differences among the separation-related experiences of gay and lesbian versus heterosexual partners seem *possible* given that same-sex and heterosexual relationships develop in different social contexts. However, no attempt has been made to assess reasons that previously committed partners from same-sex couples give for why their relationships end. Might we find differences between same-sex and opposite-sex couples if we attended to the quality of relationships with families of origin? Looking only at same-sex couples, might we find differences if we compared those with children with those without? Do legalization and ritualization increase the barriers to leaving for same-sex partners?

Reviewing Kurdek's research in light of our prior discussion of same-sex relationship demographics and processes reminds us of both the importance of his research and the limitations of our knowledge. We did locate one unpublished dissertation that helps fill this gap, and we present it in the next section.

WHAT HAPPENS WHEN CHILDREN ARE INVOLVED?

Turteltaub (2002) interviewed 10 mothers (5 former couples separated for at least 1 year) and their 7 children (4 sons and 3 daughters). All mothers were White and had college degrees; their mean age was 45 years, and they had been separated from their expartner for a mean of

Not only do researchers need to work harder to locate and build the trust of racially diverse participants, they need to conceptualize same-sex relationships and their dissolution within the complexities of race, class, and geography. For example, are Korean American same-sex couples organized by age hierarchies that parallel other forms of relating within Korean immigrant culture? If the answer is yes, in what ways does this hierarchy contribute to stability or dissolution? Are relationship trajectories different for African American couples depending on whether they are more integrated into their ethnic communities versus gay or lesbian communities? Does support from female kin have a stabilizing effect on Black couples? Are White or middleclass couples more likely to pursue legalization because they stand to reap more benefit from legal recognition and legal dissolution than those in less privileged positions? Are interracial or interethnic couples more likely to break up?

There are innumerable questions about same-sex relationships and their dissolution that could be asked and answered, and we hope that this chapter has provided both inspiration and direction. Any motivated researcher is capable of building the knowledge and social competence needed for the task. Larry Kurdek has spent the past decade opening the door to research on same-sex couples. It is time for other relationship scholars to join him.

REFERENCES

Allen, K., & Demo, D. (1995). The families of lesbians and gay men: A new frontier in family research. *Journal of Marriage and the Family, 57,* 111–127.

Battle, J., Cohen, C., Warren, D., Fergerson, G., & Audam, S. (2000). *Say it loud I'm Black and I'm proud: Black Pride Survey 2000.* New York: Policy Institute of the National Gay and Lesbian Task Force.

Bell, A. P., & Weinberger, M. S. (1978). *Homosexualities: A study of diversity among men and women.* New York: Simon & Schuster.

Berger, R. (1990). Men together: Understanding the gay couple. *Journal of Homosexuality, 19*(3), 31–49.

Blumstein, P., & Schwartz, P. (1983). *American couples.* New York: Morrow.

Bryant, A., & Demian. (1994). Relationship characteristics of American gay and lesbian couples: Findings from a national survey. *Journal of Gay and Lesbian Social Services, 1*(2), 101–117.

Cantú, L. (2001). A place called home: A queer political economy of Mexican immigrant men's family experiences. In M. Bernstein & R. Reimann (Eds.), *Queer families, queer politics: Challenging culture and the state* (pp. 112–136). New York: Columbia University Press.

Carrington, C. (1999). *No place like home: Relationships and family life among lesbians and gay men.* Chicago: University of Chicago Press.

Caron, S. L., & Ulin, M. (1997). Closeting and the quality of lesbian relationships. *Families in Society. 78,* 413–419.

Cherlin, A. (1978). Remarriage as an incomplete institution. *American Journal of Sociology, 84,* 634–650.

Chung, G., Oswald, R., & Wiley, A. (in press). Being a good daughter? Korean American lesbians and their parents. *Journal of GLBT Family Studies.*

Cody, P., & Welch, P. (1995). Rural gay men in northern New England: Life experiences and coping styles. *Journal of Homosexuality, 33,* 51–67.

Crosbie-Burnett, M., & Helmbrecht, L. (1993). A descriptive empirical study of gay male stepfamilies. *Family Relations, 42,* 256–262.

Cruz, M. (2003). Why doesn't he just leave? Gay male domestic violence and the reasons victims stay. *Journal of Men's Studies, 11,* 309–323.

Dolan, E., & Stum, M. (2001). Economic security and financial management issues facing same-sex couples. In J. Lehmann (Ed.), *The gay and lesbian marriage and family reader: Analyses of problems and prospects for the 21st century* (pp. 7–24). New York: Gordian Knot Books.

Gartrell, N., Banks, A., Reed, N., Hamilton, J., Rodas, C., & Deck, A. (2000). The national lesbian family study III: Interviews with mothers of 5-year-olds. *American Journal of Orthopsychiatry, 70,* 542–548.

Gartrell, N., Hamilton, J., Banks, A., Mosbacher, D., Reed, N., Sparks, C., & Bishop, H. (1996). The national lesbian family study I: Interviews with prospective mothers. *American Journal of Orthopsychiatry, 66,* 272–281.

Gates, G., & Ost, J. (2004). *The gay and lesbian atlas.* Washington, DC: The Urban Institute Press.

Golombok, S., Tasker, F., & Murray, C. (1997). Children raised in fatherless families from infancy: Family relationships and the socioemotional development of children of lesbian and single heterosexual mothers. *Journal of Child Psychology, 38,* 783–791.

Gottman, J. M., Levenson, R. W., Gross, J., Frederickson, B. L., McCoy, K., Rosenthal, L., Ruef, A., & Yoshimoto, D. (2003). Correlates of gay and lesbian couples' relationship satisfaction and relationship dissolution. *Journal of Homosexuality, 45*(1), 23–43.

Greene, B. (1998). Family, ethnic identity and sexual orientation: African American lesbians and gay men. In C. Patterson & A. D'Augelli (Eds.), *Lesbian, gay, and bisexual identies in families: Psychological perspectives* (pp. 40–52). New York: Oxford University Press.

Hall, M. (1998). The *lesbian love companion: How to survive everything from heartthrob to heartbreak.* San Francisco, CA: HarperCollins.

Hare, J. (1994). Concerns and issues faced by families headed by a lesbian couple. *Families in Society: Journal of Contemporary Human Services, 75,* 27–35.

Julien, D., Chartrand, E., & Begin, J. (1999). Social networks, structural interdependence, and conjugal adjustment in heterosexual, gay, and lesbian couples. *Journal of Marriage and the Family, 61,* 516–530.

Kaiser Family Foundation. (2004). *HIV/AIDS policy fact sheet.* Menlo Park, CA: Henry J. Kaiser Family Foundation. Available online at www.kff.org.

Kitzinger, C., & Coyle, A. (1995). Lesbian and gay couples: Speaking of difference. *Psychologist, 8,* 64–69.

Kurdek, L. (2001). Differences between heterosexual-nonparent couples and gay, lesbian, and heterosexual-parent couples. *Journal of Family Issues, 22,* 727–754.

Kurdek, L., & Schmitt, J. (1987). Perceived emotional support from family and friends in members of homosexual married and heterosexual cohabiting couples. *Journal of Homosexuality, 14,* 57–68.

Kurdek, L. A. (1991). The dissolution of gay and lesbian couples. *Personal Relationships, 8,* 265–278.

Kurdek, L. A. (1992). Relationship stability and relationship satisfaction in cohabiting gay and lesbian couples: A prospective longitudinal test of the contextual and interdependence models. *Journal of Social and Personal Relationships, 9,* 125–142.

Kurdek, L. A. (1993). The allocation of household labor in gay, lesbian, and heterosexual married couples. *Journal of Social Issues, 49*(3), 127–139.

Kurdek, L. A. (1995). Lesbian and gay couples. In A. R. D'Augelli & C. J. Patterson (Eds.), *Lesbian, gay, and bisexual identities over the lifespan: Psychological perspectives* (pp. 243–261). New York: Oxford University Press.

Kurdek, L. A. (1996). The deterioration of relationship quality for gay and lesbian cohabiting couples: A five-year prospective longitudinal study. *Personal Relationships, 3,* 417–442.

Kurdek, L.A. (1997). Adjustment to relationship dissolution in gay, lesbian, and heterosexual partners. *Personal Relationships, 4,* 145–161.

Kurdek, L. A. (1998). Relationship outcomes and their predictors: Longitudinal evidence from heterosexual married, gay cohabiting, and lesbian cohabiting couples. *Journal of Marriage and the Family, 60,* 553–568.

Lewin, E. (1998). *Recognizing ourselves: Ceremonies of lesbian and gay commitment.* New York: Columbia University Press.

Lewis, J., & Fraser, M. (1996). Patches of grief and rage: Visitor responses to the NAMES Project AIDS Memorial Quilt. *Qualitative Sociology, 19,* 433–451.

Lott-Whitehead, L., & Tully, C. (1999). The family lives of lesbian mothers. In J. Laird (Ed.), *Lesbians and lesbian families* (pp. 243–259). New York: Columbia University Press.

Martin, J. L., Dean, L., Garcia, M., & Hall, W. (1989). The impact of AIDS on a gay community: changes in sexual behavior, substance use, and mental health. *American Journal of Community Psychology, 17,* 269–293.

Mays, V., & Cochran, S. (1991). The Black women's relationship project: A national survey of Black lesbians. In R. Staples (Ed.), *The Black family: Essays and studies* (pp. 92–100). Belmont, CA: Wadsworth. (Reprinted from *A sourcebook of gay/lesbian health care,* pp. 54–62, by M. Shernoff & W. Scott, Eds., 1988, Washington, DC: National Gay and Lesbian Health Foundation.)

Metz, M., Rosser, B. R., & Strapko, N. (1994). Differences in conflict resolution styles among heterosexual, gay, and lesbian couples. *The Journal of Sex Research, 31,* 293–308.

Meyer, I., & Colten, M. (1999). Sampling gay men: Random digit dialing versus sources in the gay community. *Journal of Homosexuality, 37,* 99–110.

Mitchell, V. (1998). The birds, the bees . . . and the sperm banks: How lesbian mothers talk with their children about sex and reproduction. *American Journal of Orthopsychiatry, 68,* 400–409.

Morton, S. B. (1998). Lesbian divorce. *American Journal of Orthopsychiatry, 68,* 410–419.

Nardi, P. (1999). *Gay men's friendships: Invincible communities.* Chicago: University of Chicago Press.

O'Connell, A. (1993). Voices from the heart: The developmental impact of a mother's lesbianism on her adolescent children. *Smith College Studies in Social Work, 63,* 281–299.

Oswald, R. (2000). A member of the wedding? Heterosexism and family ritual. *Journal of Social and Personal Relationships, 17,* 349–368.

Oswald, R. (2002). Inclusion and belonging in the family rituals of gay and lesbian people. *Journal of Family Psychology, 16,* 428–436.

Oswald, R., & Culton, L. (2003). Under the rainbow: Rural gay life and its relevance for family providers. *Family Relations, 52,* 72–81.

Oswald, R., Gebbie, E., & Culton, L. (2001). *Report to the community: Rainbow Illinois survey of gay, lesbian, bisexual, and transgender people in central Illinois.* Urbana: University of Illinois.

Oswald, R., Grossman, R., & Chung, G. (2003). Same sex commitment ceremonies. Paper presented at the National Council on Family Relations annual conference, Vancouver, BC

Patterson, C. (1995). Families of the lesbian baby boom: Parents' division of labor and children's adjustment. *Developmental Psychology, 31,* 115–123.

Patterson, C., Hurt, S., & Mason, C. (1998). Families of the lesbian baby boom: Children's contact with grandparents and other adults. *American Journal of Orthopsychiatry, 68,* 390–399.

Patterson, C., Sutfin, E., & Fulcher, M. (2004). Division of labor among lesbian and heterosexual parenting couples: Correlates of specialized versus shared patterns. *Journal of Adult Development,* 179–189.

Patterson, C. J. (2001). Family relationships of lesbians and gay men. In R. M. Milardo (Ed.), *Understanding families into the new millennium: A decade in review* (pp. 271–288). Lawrence, KS: National Council on Family Relations.

Peplau, L. A. (1983). Research on homosexual couples: An overview. *Journal of Homosexuality, 8*(2), 3–8.

Peplau, L. A., Cochran, S. D., & Mays, V. M. (1997). A national survey of the intimate relationships of African American lesbians and gay men: A look at commitment, satisfaction, sexual behavior, and HIV disease. In B. Greene (Ed.), *Ethnic and cultural diversity among lesbians and gay men: Psychological perspectives on lesbian and gay issues* (Vol. 3., pp. 11–38). Thousand Oaks, CA: Sage.

Peplau, L. A., Veniegas, R. C., & Campbell, S. M. (1996). Gay and lesbian relationships. In R. C. Savin-Williams & K. M. Cohen (Eds.), *The lives of lesbians, gays, and bisexuals: Children to adults* (pp. 250–273). New York: Harcourt Brace.

Powell-Cope, G. (1995). The experiences of gay couples affected by HIV infection. *Qualitative Health Research, 5,* 36–62.

Reimann, R. (1997). Does biology matter? Lesbian couples' transition to parenthood and their division of labor. *Qualitative Sociology, 20,* 153–185.

Renzetti, C. (1992). *Violent betrayal: Partner abuse in lesbian relationships.* Newbury Park, CA: Sage.

Richards, T., Wrubel, J., & Folkman, S. (1999–2000). Death rites in the San Francisco gay community: Cultural developments of the AIDS Epidemic. *Omega, 40*(2), 335–350.

Shernoff, M. (1997). Unexamined loss: An expanded view of gay break-ups. *In The Family, 3*(2), 10–13.

Smith, D. M., & Gates, G. (2001). *Gay and lesbian families in the United States: Same-sex unmarried partner households.* Washington, DC: Human Rights Campaign Fund.

Solomon, S., Rothblum, E., & Balsam, K. (2004). Pioneers in partnership: Lesbian and gay male couples in civil unions compared with those not in civil unions, and married heterosexual siblings. *Journal of Family Psychology, 18,* 275–286.

Stiers, G. (1999). *From this day forward: Commitment, marriage, and family in lesbian and gay relationships.* New York: St. Martin's Press.

Sullivan, M. (2001). Alma mater: Family "outings" and the making of the modern other-mother. In M. B. R. Reimann (Ed.), *Queer families, queer politics: Challenging culture and the state* (pp. 231–253). New York: Columbia University Press.

Tasker, F., & Golombok, S. (1995). Adults raised as children in lesbian families. *American Journal of Orthopsychiatry, 65,* 203–215.

Tasker, F., & Golombok, S. (1997). Young people's attitudes toward living in a lesbian family: A longitudinal study of children raised by post-divorce lesbian mothers. *Journal of Divorce and Remarriage, 28,* 183–202.

Turteltaub, G. (2002). *The effects of long-term primary relationship dissolution on the children of lesbian parents.* Unpublished clinical dissertation, Alliance University, San Francisco.

Waller, M., & McAllen-Walker, R. (2001). One man's story of being gay and Dine' (Navajo): A study in resiliency. In M. Bernstein & R. Reimann (Eds.), *Queer families, queer politics: Challenging culture and the state* (pp. 87–103). New York: Columbia University Press.

West, C. M. (2002). Lesbian intimate partner violence: Prevalence and dynamics. *Journal of Lesbian Studies, 6,* 121–127.

Weston, K. (1991). *Families we chose: Lesbian, gays, kinship.* New York: Columbia University Press.

Wright, J. (2001). "Aside from one tiny little detail, we are so incredibly normal": Perspectives of children in lesbian step-families. In M. Bernstein & R. Reimann (Eds.), *Queer families, queer politics: Challenging culture and the state* (pp. 272–290). New York: Columbia University Press.

Yip, A. (1996). Gay Christians and their participation in the gay subculture. *Deviant Behavior: An Interdisciplinary Journal, 17,* 297–318.

25

Divorce and Relationship Dissolution Among Latino Populations in the United States

Adriana J. Umaña-Taylor and Edna C. Alfaro
Arizona State University

Existing research has documented the benefits of marriage and the costs of divorce for men, women, and children (for a review, see Bramlett & Mosher, 2001). The psychological costs of divorce for men and women include poorer psychological adjustment, increased health problems, and lower levels of happiness (Amato, 2000). Furthermore, existing research has also documented poorer outcomes among children of divorce, when compared with children living in two-parent families, with regard to social competence, academic achievement, and psychological adjustment (Amato; Coleman, Ganong, & Fine, 2000). Although it is unclear whether the negative outcomes associated with divorce are causal or due to selection effects (Amato; Bramlett & Mosher), an undisputed reality is that current rates of marital disruption are considerably higher than they were 50 years ago (Amato & Irving, chap. 3, this volume; Kreider & Fields, 2001; Teachman, Tedrow, & Crowder, 2000). This is a reality for all major ethnic or racial populations in the United States, including Latinos. Current estimates for first marriages suggest that 48% of Whites' marriages, 52% of Latinos' marriages, and 63% of Blacks' marriages end in divorce within the first 20 years of marriage (Bramlett & Mosher).

Although rates of divorce are similar for Whites and Latinos, the existing research available about Latinos' experiences is limited. Given the possible negative consequences of marital disruption, it is critical that we gain a fuller understanding of Latinos' divorce experiences and outcomes associated with this transition. The current chapter reviews current trends regarding divorce and relationship dissolution among Latino populations, summarizes the existing empirical research in which Latinos' experiences have been examined, and provides directions to consider for future research. Although we conducted an exhaustive review of the literature on relationship dissolution among Latinos, we were only able to locate a few studies that focused on nonmarital relationships. Thus, our review tends to focus more heavily on dissolution among marital relationships (e.g., divorce); nevertheless, wherever possible, we have included information pertaining to nonmarital relationships as well (e.g., cohabiting unions).

DEMOGRAPHICS

The shifting ethnic composition of U.S. demographics is attributed largely to high rates of immigration and fertility among Latino populations. Projections indicate that, by the year 2060, Latino individuals will comprise 27% of the U.S. population (U.S. Census, 2000). In addition to the rapid growth of this panethnic group, the composition of Latino national origin groups in the United States is also shifting, as individuals with Central American, South American, and Dominican backgrounds increase in number (Guzman, 2001). Although empirical research on divorce among Latinos has not kept pace with the rapid growth of the populations, demographers have continually monitored rates of divorce and separation among Latino groups in the United States.

Early reports of divorce statistics grouped all Latinos into one category and often compared Latinos with Whites and African Americans. When Latinos were categorized in this way, researchers found that they had the lowest rates of divorce and that the rate of divorce slowly increased from the 1970s to the present (Eberstein & Frisbie, 1976; Teachman et al., 2000). Although this information was valuable, the vast diversity within Latino populations was not being considered or acknowledged with these statistics. For example, our own examination of 1979 Census data revealed that, although only 4.5% of Mexican Latinos were divorced, 7.8% of Cubans were divorced (U.S. Bureau of the Census, 1980). Thus, this diversity was masked with early research on Latinos.

Another oversimplification that occurred in early work pertained to the term *separated*; however, in the late 1990s the U.S. Census began to qualify the separated category by including the category "married–spouse absent" and considering it distinct from the separated category. An examination of these data revealed interesting divergent trends between Latinos and the general U.S. population. For instance, data from 2002 indicated that 3.2% of the Latino population reported that their spouse was absent, 3.4% reported that they were separated, and 6.6% reported that they were divorced (U.S. Bureau of the Census, n.d.). Although the rates of divorce for the Latino population as a whole remain lower when compared with those of the general population (i.e., 6.6% vs. 9.5%), the rates for the separated (3.4% vs. 2.0%) and spouse absent (3.2% vs. 1.4%) categories are higher among Latinos. Furthermore, when this is examined by national origin, we see vast diversity within the Latino community. For example, 5.9%, 2.9%, and 3.2% of Mexican-origin Latinos reported being divorced, separated, and married–spouse absent, respectively, in 2002. This differs greatly from the figures of 10.5%, 6.2%, and 2.1% for Puerto Ricans.

Thus, these figures suggest that, although Latinos appear less likely to divorce, they may be more likely to use separation as a proxy for union dissolution. We also find that, within Latino subgroups, there is great diversity in the rates of divorce, separation, and married–spouse absent categories. Researchers should pay particular attention to these differences, as research questions may have to differ based on the national origin group under investigation (e.g., Mexican vs. Cuban).

HISTORICAL OVERVIEW: HOW HAVE WE VIEWED DIVORCE AMONG LATINOS IN EXISTING RESEARCH?

Here, we present a historical overview organized in chronological order; although the initial studies reviewed may appear dated, they are followed by more recent studies in subsequent sections. In line with the demographic information already provided, early research on Latinos' relationship dissolution focused almost exclusively on an examination of national trends and comparisons of rates of relationship dissolution by ethnicity and race (e.g., Bean & Tienda, 1987; Eberstein & Frisbie, 1976; Frisbie, Bean, & Eberstein, 1980; Norton & Moorman, 1987; Uhlenberg, 1972). Nevertheless, a few early studies explored the psychological effects of divorce on families. First, we present the research that examined exclusively demographic aspects of divorce. Next, we present studies that explored the psychological effects of divorce.

Rates of Dissolution: Demographics

Conclusions from one study in which 1960 Census data were examined (Uhlenberg, 1972) indicated that Mexican Americans had levels of marital instability [1] (i.e., divorced, separated, or spouse absent) comparable with those of Whites; when only Mexican Americans in California were examined, levels of marital instability were comparable with those of Blacks. Uhlenberg concluded that geographical location appeared to be important, as rural Mexican Americans displayed the lowest levels of instability. Furthermore, he suggested that perhaps the higher rates of marital instability in urban areas in California were a result of women being less dependent on men for economic support because of their comparatively higher rates of employment.

A few years later, using 1970 Census data, Eberstein and Frisbie (1976) noted that rates of marital instability (i.e., divorced, separated) were lower for Mexican American women than for Black and White women. This finding remained after they controlled for age, age at first marriage, residence, and education. Eberstein and Frisbie concluded that Mexican Americans' strong familial bonds promote cohesion despite economic instability. They noted that it was important to consider that divorce rates tended to be higher in western states and that estimates should not include the separated category because this produced an inflated estimate for Mexican Americans, whose spouses were disproportionately represented in this category because they tended to be employed away from home.

Upon closer examination of two decades of Census data (i.e., 1960 and 1970), Frisbie et al. (1980) reported that Mexican Americans had the lowest levels of divorce for both first-time marriages and remarriages; however, they also found a higher prevalence of separation among Mexican women than Anglo women. Thus, it appeared that Mexicans were turning more toward separation as a mechanism for relationship dissolution than were Anglos. One possibility that scholars did not consider is that perhaps separation allowed Mexican women to achieve consistency between their traditional values regarding divorce and their behaviors; if they divorced, they would be going against the sacred institution of marriage.

Almost a decade later, Bean and Tienda (1987) also reviewed the 1960 and 1970 Census data and concluded that Spanish-origin groups had higher percentages in the married–spouse absent category. They looked more closely at specific Latino groups and concluded that rates of marital instability (i.e., remarried and previously divorced, divorced, or separated) were much higher for Puerto Ricans (36.2%) and much lower for Central and South Americans (15.5%), whereas rates were similar for Whites (23.3%), Mexicans (21.2%), and Cubans (23.2%).

Analyses of 1980 Census data provided similar conclusions, as Frisbie (1986) found that Mexican American women had the lowest rates of marital instability (i.e., remarried divorced, divorced, or separated), followed closely by Anglos and Cubans. Furthermore, Frisbie found that whereas educational attainment was positively related to marital stability for Puerto Rican women, these variables were negatively related for Mexican and Cuban women. Findings from both studies (i.e., Bean & Tienda, 1987; Frisbie) underscore the need to consider variability in relationship dissolution by national origin.

---

[1] Because of the varied definitions of the term *marital instability*, we have specified how the term is used in each study that we review. Where we have not provided this detail, we use the term to mean divorced or legally separated.

In an examination of three decades of Census data (i.e., 1960, 1970, and 1980), Frisbie, Opitz, and Kelly (1985) concluded that marital instability (i.e., remarried divorced, divorced, or separated) was much less frequent among Mexican American women than among Blacks and Whites. Furthermore, Frisbie et al. found that Mexican American women had the lowest levels of marital instability across all three decades. Finally, when important demographic variables such as current age, age at first marriage, and education were controlled for, the odds of stability of marriage for Mexican American women were 2 times greater than the odds for White women, and 4 times greater than the odds for Black women. Frisbie et al. suggested that a couple of factors may explain these findings. First, differences could be due to a familistic orientation that emphasized the maintenance of strong kinship ties, which was more typical of Mexican Americans. Second, religion could partly explain this finding, as a large proportion of Mexican Americans adhere to Catholicism and therefore may be more opposed to divorce.

Finally, Norton and Moorman (1987) explored the 1985 Current Population Survey and reported an upward trend in the divorce rate after first marriage for Spanish-origin women, although rates of divorce were still lower than those for White or Black women. Norton and Moorman also explored a different aspect of separation (i.e., length of separations) and found that Spanish-origin women were separated a mean of 3.4 years, compared with 1.8 years for White women and 5.7 years for Black women. This finding corroborated previous findings, which suggested that Latinos may be more likely than whites to use separation as a way to functionally end marriage (Norton & Moorman).

Psychological Effects of Divorce on Families

In a different line of work, scholars examined the effects of divorce on Latino children and adults. Findings suggested that adolescents whose fathers were absent as a result of divorce scored similarly on measures of self-concept when compared with adolescents whose fathers were absent as a result of imprisonment (Moerk, 1973). Furthermore, when comparing Blacks, Whites, and Mexican Americans who had experienced divorce, Mirowski and Ross (1980) found that Mexicans reported the lowest levels of distress. Finally, a third study found that although divorce was the best predictor of depression scores among Anglos, separation (not divorce) predicted depression among Mexicans (Vega, Warheit, & Meinhardt, 1984). This finding was not surprising, given that Mexicans tended to rely more on separation than divorce, a pattern that has emerged in previous research and was evident in the study by Vega et al.

Limitations

Although this early research made significant contributions by providing an arena in which Latino populations' relationship experiences could be examined, a number of limitations were evident. First, the studies conducted prior to the 1980s tended to use the term *Mexican American* to describe their samples; however, a more thorough examination of their method suggested that Mexican American ethnicity was determined by using the Census category of "Whites of Spanish surname." This is a limitation primarily because respondents with Spanish surnames were not necessarily Mexican (e.g., Cubans). Furthermore, because data were gathered from women in the majority of these studies, this method does not account for the possibility that a non-Latina woman could have assumed her Latino spouse's surname.

Another limitation, which was evident in several of the studies, is that lower rates of marital instability among Latinos were consistently interpreted as representing more traditional family values among Latinos, compared with other groups. An important possibility that may have been overlooked was that Latinos were merely avoiding formal divorce as a result of financial considerations. Another possibility could be that a cohesive family unit was a mechanism for survival that assisted with difficulties the couples encountered based on their immigrant status. Thus, it may not be that Latinos were culturally more resilient with regard to marriage, but rather that they needed to stay married in order to cope with other concerns.

A third limitation is the focus on Mexican-origin Latinos and the lack of attention to non-Mexican Latino groups. Although two studies (i.e., Bean & Tienda, 1987; Frisbie, 1986) included an analysis and discussion of various Latino groups in their study, the remainder focused on a homogenous Latino or Mexican population. This was perhaps due to the fact that Mexicans were a majority of the Latino population in the United States during the 1970s and 1980s when this research was conducted. Nevertheless, as will be noted in the subsequent review of more recent research, we have made little progress in this area. Although Mexican Latinos are currently the majority Latino population in the United States, recent estimates suggest that this is changing as Central and South American Latinos have emerged as the fastest growing Latino groups. Thus, there is a need to become more inclusive in terms of Latino populations examined.

Finally, early research, which was based almost exclusively on demographic data, tended to conclude that differences found between Latino and White populations were a result of psychological processes (i.e., familism). For example, Bean and Tienda (1987) concluded that larger household sizes, higher rates of people between the ages of 18 and 24 years who lived with their parents, and greater number of adults in households were all consistent with the idea that Latinos are more familistic. Similarly, Frisbie (1986) implied that the negative relationship that was found between educational attainment and marital stability was consistent with a cultural interpretation such that, with higher levels of education, Latinos become more acculturated and, therefore, less likely to follow their culture's more traditional and familistic orientation. Although it is valuable and expected that scholars use theory to build possible explanations for demographic differences found between populations, what makes this a limitation is that researchers did not take the next step. For over a decade, scholars focused on demographic differences among ethnic groups, without a more detailed examination of the social and psychological processes that may be associated with these differences. Recent research, however, has begun to move in this direction.

OVERVIEW OF MAJOR FINDINGS FROM RECENT LITERATURE

Although early research focused almost exclusively on examining Census data, more recent studies (1990s to the present) have begun to explore other data sources, in addition to conducting studies in which individuals' social and psychological characteristics are explored. The studies conducted since the late 1980s can be categorized by the type of Latino populations examined. For example, whereas some researchers have focused on a homogenous Latino population, in which they make no distinction between the national origins of the Latinos included in their samples, others have focused on specific Latino national origin groups (e.g., Puerto Rican). Accordingly, we have organized our review in this manner.

Homogenous Latino Population

In line with previous findings, which suggested that Latinos relied more heavily on separation rather than divorce as a method of ending their relationships, the examination by del Carmen and Virgo (1993) of 1990 Census data indicated that the primary cause of single-parent households among Latinos was separation without divorce, whereas the primary cause for Whites was divorce.

Similarly, an examination of divorce petitions and decrees (Neff, Gilbert, & Hoppe, 1991) in a southwestern city indicated that divorce petitions from those with Spanish surnames involved longer delay times between filing and receipt of decree. Furthermore, petitions from those with Spanish surnames involved significantly more children and greater likelihood of filing a pauper's oath (indicating limited financial resources). Thus, it is possible that children and finances partially explain the longer delay times between filing and receipt of decree, as these may serve as barriers to divorcing (Neff et al.).

Scholars have also attempted to understand how individual and family functioning vary on the basis of family structure. Amato (1991) examined depression in adulthood and found a significant relationship between parental absence during childhood and adult depression among Blacks and Whites, whereas there was no such relationship between these variables for Hispanics. Amato suggested that perhaps this finding emerged as a result of Hispanic culture emphasizing a closely knit extended family, which could serve a protective function by providing high levels of support that would minimize the consequences of living in a single-parent family.

Researchers focusing on earlier developmental periods (i.e., adolescence) found that family structure was associated with family conflict and cohesion such that Latino adolescents in single-parent households reported higher levels of conflict and lower levels of family cohesion than their counterparts living in two-parent family households (Baer, 1999). In a second study, researchers found that Latino adolescents living in two-parent households were less likely to initiate drug use than their counterparts living in single-parent homes (Amey & Albrecht, 1998; Gil, Vega, & Binafora, 1998). We turn to research with mainstream populations to understand the possible connection between these studies. Specifically, previous research suggests that higher levels of family conflict are associated with increased deviance and delinquency (Henggeler, 1989). Furthermore, higher levels of family cohesion have been associated with lower levels of deviance (Tolan, 1988). Taken together, it is possible to conclude that the higher levels of conflict and lower levels of cohesion associated with single-parent households among Latinos may be leading to more delinquency and deviance for adolescents in these households, which helps to explain the greater likelihood of drug use. Thus, family structure may be indirectly associated with adolescent drug use by means of its negative influence on family functioning (e.g., conflict, cohesion). Given the lack of research available, this conclusion is speculative and future research should explore the connections among these variables.

Finally, using a national probability sample, Stroup and Pollock (1999) examined the economic consequences of martial dissolution for Latinos. Their results mirrored existing research on Whites (Weitzman, 1985), which suggested that women experienced negative economic consequences following divorce. Specifically, average income was significantly higher for Latina women who were married than it was for their divorced counterparts. Finally, although men did not experience negative economic consequences following divorce, they also did not gain an economic advantage over their married counterparts. That is, average income levels of Latino divorced men were comparable with the income levels of Latino married men.

Specific Latino Groups

Puerto Rican Latinos

Of particular concern within the broad Latino population are Puerto Rican families. In particular, scholars suggest that rising divorce rates and out-of-wedlock births have led to increases in female family headships, which have been associated with increased risks for poverty (Landale & Ogena, 1995; Lichter & Landale, 1995). For instance, one study found that over two thirds of Puerto Rican children who live in single-parent households live in poverty (Landale & Ogena). A second study found that 55% of the poverty gap between Latino children and White children was due to differences in family structure (Lichter & Landale). Given the possible negative consequences of family structure on children's lives, a number of studies have been conducted in which Puerto Rican women's experiences with relationship formation and dissolution have been examined.

In a study of Puerto Rican women, Landale and Forste (1991) found that a large proportion (i.e., 46%) of women between the ages of 15 and 29 years began their first union through co-habitation. Furthermore, only 12% of these unions resulted in legal marriage; of the remaining 88%, 65% eventually dissolved. For Puerto Rican women whose first union occurred between the ages of 30 and 39, and was a cohabiting union, 28% of their relationships resulted in legal marriage, whereas 88% of the relationships that did not result in marriage eventually dissolved. Finally, for Puerto Rican women whose first union experience occurred between the ages of 40 and 49, 16% of the unions were informal, 22% of these resulted in eventual marriage, and 85% of those that did not result in marriage eventually dissolved. Thus, the rates of instability of cohabitation were relatively high and consistent across all age groups. Furthermore, previous research examining a national sample of White participants indicated that 75% of first unions that began informally eventually resulted in legal marriage (Willis & Michael, 1988, as cited in Landale & Forste), and, with an ethnically and racially diverse national sample, Bumpass and Sweet (1989) concluded that 60% of cohabiting couples eventually married; these figures are considerably higher than the percentages of 12, 28, and 22 evidenced in the study by Landale and Forste of Puerto Rican women (already described). Although the purpose of the study by Landale and Forste was to examine union formation, their data also lent themselves to an exploration of union dissolution for the different union types.

There is an increasing trend toward cohabitation as a method of union formation among Puerto Rican women, and although this trend is evident in the general U.S. population, the implications of cohabitation as a method of first union formation are different for Puerto Ricans (Landale & Forste, 1991). Specifically, Puerto Ricans are less likely to transform informal first unions into marriage, and a vast majority of informal first unions result in eventual dissolution, as described earlier. Landale and Forste suggested that informal union formation may serve an adaptive function for family formation among Puerto Ricans, because it has fewer expectations of the man, who may be facing economic uncertainty. Landale and Forste also suggested that, for Puerto Ricans, cohabitation may not hold the same meaning as another form of singlehood or a precursor to marriage; rather, it functions as a context for family building. In line with this idea, a follow-up study (Landale & Fennelly, 1992) found that approximately 75% of cohabiting Puerto Rican women viewed their unions as a form of marriage. Nevertheless, it is important to consider that the trend toward cohabitation may contribute to negative outcomes among Puerto Rican women and children, as the rate of dissolution is higher for cohabitation than for legal marriage (Landale & Forste).

An examination of Puerto Rican children's experience with their mothers' relationship dissolution indicated that a majority of Puerto Rican children born into an intact union (i.e., legal marriage or cohabitation) were likely to experience family disruption (Landale & Hauan, 1992). For example, for 15-year-old children born either into a legal marriage or an informal union in the 1970s, 62% and 85% experienced family disruption, respectively. Furthermore, Puerto Rican children born into intact unions were more likely to experience family disruption if their mothers (a) were born on the mainland, (b) were younger at the time of birth, (c) conceived them prior to coresidence, (d) had not planned for them, and/or (e) were in an informal union at the time of birth (Landale & Hauan).

Finally, Landale and Ogena (1995) examined the factors associated with Puerto Rican women's relationship dissolution. They found that women who entered legal marriages had disruption rates that were 50% lower than those who entered cohabiting relationships. Furthermore, women who experienced a pre-union pregnancy or who were not employed prior to the union were more likely to experience union disruption. Finally, having children under the age of 6 in the household was associated with a reduced likelihood of union disruption.

Taken together, findings from these studies suggest that the correlates and incidence of cohabitation and marital disruption must be examined with attention to variations by national origin. As evidenced by the data presented in these studies, Puerto Ricans are more likely to begin their relationships with cohabitation; these unions are less likely to result in eventual marriage, yet they are more likely to end in eventual dissolution.

Although these studies add to the very limited scholarship on Latino families, a couple of limitations should be acknowledged. First, all studies were conducted by the same research team (i.e., Landale and colleagues); thus, the findings reflect the focus of one team and it is possible that additional perspectives or issues were not investigated or discussed because they were not within the scope of their research program. In addition, all studies were conducted with Puerto Rican women living in the Northeast, which is where the majority of the Puerto Rican population is concentrated on the U.S. mainland. This limits our ability to generalize these findings to other Puerto Rican populations (e.g., those living in Puerto Rico or in the Southeast), given that the studies comprise a restricted range of the population in the United States. Regardless of these limitations, however, it is encouraging to find scholarship on a specific Latino population; it will be important for other researchers to follow this lead. In addition to research with Puerto Rican families, a few studies have focused exclusively on Mexican families.

Mexican Latinos

Parra, Arkowitz, Hannah, and Vazquez (1995) examined experiences with separation and divorce among Mexican-origin and Anglo women. Their findings indicated that Mexican women living primarily in the United States were more likely to rely on family members for support during the divorce than White women or Mexican women living primarily in Mexico. Furthermore, Mexican women reported relationships with relatives as a cause for divorce significantly more frequently than their White counterparts. Finally, whereas the main causes of divorce for Mexican women were infidelity and relatives, the main cause of divorce for White women was alcoholism. It appears that relational factors predict divorce for Mexican women and individual factors may be better predictors for White women. This coincides with the notion that Latino families follow a more collectivistic orientation, whereas White families follow more individualistic ideals. Interestingly, Mexican women reported relying on family significantly more than White women, but they also tended to report family as a main cause of divorce. This is similar to previous findings on premarital commitment to marriage in which Latina women's commitment to marrying their dating partner was negatively related to familial support toward the relationship (Umaña-Taylor & Fine, 2003). Specifically, the more familial support Latinas reported for their dating relationship, the lower was their commitment to marrying their partner. Thus, although families may serve as a resource, they may also serve as a source of relationship conflict. Because there is limited research in this area, it is unclear why Latinos may rely more heavily on family support, or how this support may eventually lead to the dissolution of their relationships.

Another interesting feature of the study by Parra et al. (1995) was the finding that Mexican women who were living primarily in the United States tended to rely on family support more than women living primarily in Mexico. This raises important issues regarding within-group variability. It will be important to examine residential patterns and generational status in future research with Latinos, as the increased reliance on family could be a result of the immigrant context as opposed to an adherence to cultural values.

Second, in a detailed analysis of a national longitudinal survey, Bean, Berg, and Van Hook (1996) found that, although there was a negative relationship between education and marital disruption for first-generation Mexican immigrants, for second- and third-generation Mexicans this relationship was positive. Furthermore, Bean et al. found that, for Mexicans living in Mexico, the relationship between these variables was positive. Thus, perhaps it is a condition of migration that inverses the relationship between education and disruption, but the nature or direction of the relationship is restored to mirror patterns in the native country in later generations. Similar to the research by Parra et al. (1995), this research highlights the within-group variability that exists with regard to national origin, and it underscores the importance of examining processes in multiple generational cohorts of Latinos.

Finally, Bean et al. (1996) indicated that conclusions that suggest that Mexicans have the lowest levels of marital disruption are driven by data from immigrants, who tend to have the lowest levels of martial disruption. Therefore, it is possible that using immigrants' data leads to more positive portrayals of the general Latino population. It is possible that low levels of divorce among immigrants are a result of a family adaptation strategy, which emphasizes stability in the conjugal unit. Thus, marital stability is not a cultural pattern, but rather a survival mechanism or family adaptation strategy adopted to cope with difficult economic and social circumstances.

Limitations

Overall, this research is promising, in that we are moving toward examining within-group differences as opposed to examining a homogenous Latino population. Nevertheless, the existing work is not without limitations. For instance, these within-group analyses are exclusive to Mexican and Puerto Rican populations. As the presence of Central and South American populations increases, we will need to expand our studies to include these populations. In addition, the existing studies tend to focus on one Latino population in a geographical location where that group is heavily represented (e.g., Puerto Ricans in New York, Mexicans in the Southwest). In order to gain a more complete understanding of relationship dissolution among Latino populations, we will need to implement multisite studies in which the diversity within specific national origin groups is considered.

Furthermore, the majority of research on Latinos' relationship dissolution focuses on the dissolution of marital relationships. As evidenced by this review, nonmarital unions have higher rates of dissolution (at least among Puerto Ricans) than marital unions. However, we have yet to conduct a systematic examination of this difference. Thus, there is a vast need to focus attention on nonmarital relationships and the dissolution process of these unions.

Moving beyond these methodological limitations, however, is the major limitation that the works are not grounded in family theories and paradigms. Demographers have contributed substantially to our knowledge about the prevalence of relationship dissolution among Latino populations; however, we must move beyond demographics and into family processes underlying dissolution. It is critical that we begin to understand how Latinos' experiences regarding relationship dissolution can or cannot be examined with existing theoretical studies on relationship dissolution.

For example, do existing theories of relationship stability and dissolution (e.g., Johnson, 1991; Levinger, 1976; Rusbult, 1980; Stanley & Markman, 1992) apply to the relationships of Latinos? It seems logical that Latino couples will experience many of the same barriers to dissolution as White couples (e.g., children, legal marriage); however, it is also possible that certain barriers (e.g., marriage recognized by the Church) may influence Latino couples more heavily than they do White couples. However, scholars have yet to test the validity of these theories with Latino populations.

Although we must begin to think about how Latinos' relationships fit with current theoretical notions, an important consideration involves the use of an inductive approach. Existing theories, although valuable, may have to be altered considerably in order to be relevant to the experiences of U.S. Latinos. For example, we need to tease apart how migration and immigration play roles in this process (i.e., migration within the United States and immigration to the United States from other countries). Furthermore, we need to understand the role of social networks and familial support on individuals' experiences with divorce and relationship dissolution. A review of existing literature (del Carmen & Virgo, 1993) suggested that familial relationships can serve both supportive and unsupportive functions for Hispanic women going through divorce or dealing with single parenthood. Because of limited research, conclusions are tentative, but nonetheless they demonstrate the need for more research in this area. Finally, we must understand how immigration fits into existing models; specifically, we need to develop an understanding of how immigration processes and experiences are related to relationship functioning patterns. In the following paragraphs we introduce specific suggestions for future research, and we recommend that scholars consider these issues as they begin to formulate new theories (or extend existing theories) to understand Latinos' relationship dissolution experiences.

SUGGESTIONS FOR FUTURE RESEARCH: WHERE DO WE GO FROM HERE?

Although suggestions have been interwoven throughout this chapter, here we provide specific recommendations for future research. Specifically, we recommend that future studies on Latinos' relationship dissolution should (a) explore national origin groups independently, (b) examine variability within national origin groups, and (c) study Latinos in their respective countries of origin.

Exploring National Origin Groups Independently

A great deal of diversity exists within Latinos in the United States, partly in terms of national origin (Umaña-Taylor & Fine, 2001). Specific Latino populations are concentrated in distinct regions across the United States. For example, larger proportions of Cubans are found in the Southeast, large populations of Puerto Ricans are found in the Northeast, and close to two thirds of Mexicans are found in the Southwest (Sullivan, 2000). Furthermore, although diversity exists within national origin groups with regard to reasons for immigration and reception in the United States, larger proportions of certain national origin groups immigrate for similar reasons (e.g., political refuge, or economic or educational reasons). For example, whereas a majority of Cuban Latinos come to the United States seeking political refuge, a majority of Mexican Latinos come to the United States to seek economic prosperity. Finally, important differences in union formation may exist based on national origin. For example, previous research suggests that the majority of cohabiting Puerto Rican women view their informal unions as a form of marriage (Landale & Fennelly, 1992). In addition, scholars have suggested that the unique economic circumstances of Puerto Ricans (e.g., highest rates of poverty), compared with other

Latino groups, may discourage entry into legal marriage and thus explain the high rates of cohabitation (Landale & Fennelly). Given the differential rates of dissolution by type of union (e.g., cohabitation vs. legal marriage) and the variation in types of union by national origin (e.g., Puerto Rican's high level of cohabitation), it will be important for researchers to consider these national origin differences when they examine trends in and processes of divorce and relationship dissolution among Latinos.

Exploring Diversity Within National Origin Groups

In addition to attending to the diversity that exists among Latinos as a result of national origin, we must acknowledge the diversity that exists within national origin groups. For example, although Mexican-origin Latinos may have a common ancestry, experiences in the United States will vary as a result of generational status, conditions of immigration, educational status in the United States and socioeconomic status in Mexico prior to immigration, and ethnic identity.

Generational Status

Latinos of the same national origin may have different U.S. experiences because of the amount of time that they or their families have been in the country. Whereas some families may have been in the United States before the Mexican–American war, when a large part of the Southwest was Mexican territory, others may have immigrated to the United States in the past year. Generational status may be associated with adherence to values, beliefs, and traditions. For example, a Mexican family that recently immigrated to the United States may adhere to more collectivist notions than a Mexican family that has been in the United States for five generations and perhaps adheres more to individualistic values. Thus, predictors of relationship dissolution may be ultimately driven by these worldviews such that the relationship processes of those who adhere to more collectivistic ideals will be driven more by relational factors (e.g., family support toward the relationship), whereas the relationships of those who adhere to more individualistic ideals will be driven more by individual factors (e.g., personal gain in the relationship).

Similarly, families that recently immigrated to the United States may have a smaller family support network than families that have been in the United States for many generations. With this in mind, we find it important to consider that the barriers that protect against relationship dissolution may vary on the basis of generational status. For instance, it is possible that partners who have been in the United States for many generations and who have a more established familial support network may rely more heavily on family influence when making decisions regarding their relationships than those who are more recent immigrants and who do not have the established network. In the latter case, partners may be more heavily influenced by their values and ideologies regarding marriage than by their familial network. Finally, recent immigrants may have various constraints associated with their immigrant status that could affect their relationships. Immigration status may strain marital relations, or it may serve as a buffer against relationship dissolution because of the need to maintain a cohesive family unit. Given the lack of research in this area, these ideas are speculative; future studies should explore how these factors affect individuals' decisions to divorce or end their romantic relationships.

Immigration Experiences

Regardless of national origin group, individuals may experience different conditions when immigrating to the United States. Furthermore, individuals' experiences with the reception of immigrants in the United States during the particular historical period of their immigration will also vary. For example, Hondagneu-Sotelo (1992) compared the effects of migration experiences on Mexican couples that had migrated to the United States prior to 1965 with those migrating after 1965. She found that families that had migrated prior to 1965 exhibited more egalitarian relationships, which were particularly due to the conditions of immigration during that time period. Specifically, for Mexican men who migrated prior to 1965, U.S. social networks were composed almost exclusively of men; as a result, men had to incorporate into their lives activities that were traditionally women's, such as cooking, doing laundry, and grocery shopping. In contrast, men who migrated after 1965 entered U.S. networks that were primarily composed of families, in which women conducted the gendered labor. Although this study did not focus on relationship dissolution, the findings highlight the importance of considering the timing and conditions of immigration, and how these affect relationship functioning and roles.

With regard to relationship dissolution, it is possible that the timing and conditions of immigration (such as those just described) may be differentially related to the likelihood of divorce or relationship termination as a result of their impact on family functioning. For instance, immigration experiences that may affect family relationships include length of separation if family members immigrated at different times, availability of the social network in the receiving country, current climate toward immigrants in the receiving country, and social and economic resources available to the family during immigration. These experiences could lead to the strengthening of a relationship or to its deterioration. Specifically, partners in a couple experiencing a hostile reception by the host country as a result of their immigration status may experience high levels of stress, which could eventually result in increased marital conflict and eventual separation or divorce. In contrast, partners in an immigrant couple that entered into an established ethnic community and that have numerous opportunities to prosper in the new country may experience positive mental health, which could positively influence relationship satisfaction.

Finally, it will be important to acknowledge the confound that is introduced in research in which the married–spouse absent category is treated as a separation or divorce, especially in the case of immigrant families that are still in the process of immigrating (i.e., one spouse is still in the sending country) or for families in which the economic conditions require a spouse to work in a different part of the country or in another country. These conditions may bring additional stress into the relationship, which could eventually lead to relationship termination.

Educational Attainment–Socioeconomic Status

Previous research has demonstrated that educational attainment is negatively associated with relationship dissolution for certain Latino groups, although it is positively associated with relationship dissolution for other Latino groups. We need to consider how educational attainment influences relationship experiences not only among specific Latino national origin groups but also within national origin groups. For example, it is possible that variation exists because of the socioeconomic status of families in their sending countries. Although members of a Guatemalan family may not have a high level of education in the United States because they migrated prior to completing their education, their social status in Guatemala may be high. The socioeconomic status in the country of origin will help us understand the values that individuals bring with them to the United States. Although U.S. educational status may not be high, the couple may have numerous social resources that will affect their relationship. For instance, the ability to send their children to study in Guatemala while they establish themselves in the United States could potentially reduce the financial strain on a family and, in turn, the strain on the relationship.

Ethnic Identity

In addition to considering generational status, experiences with immigration, and socioeconomic resources, we must acknowledge that a great deal of diversity exists within national origin groups in terms of ethnic identity. Individuals' identification with their ethnic group may be associated with the degree to which they espouse and adhere to cultural values regarding relationship issues such as divorce and marriage. Existing studies have not examined variation in ethnic identification and, rather, have used group labels to identify individuals as *Latino*, *Mexican*, *Puerto Rican*, and so forth. As we begin to develop a clearer understanding of divorce and relationship dissolution experiences among Latino populations, it will be important for us to consider the degree of ethnic identification and how it relates to adherence to values regarding marriage and relationship outcomes.

Geographical Locale

Finally, researchers suggest that western states have a higher incidence of divorce. However, because certain Latino groups are disproportionately located in certain geographical areas (e.g., the majority of the Mexican-origin U.S. population lives in the Southwest), we must conduct multisite studies with the same national origin groups (e.g., Mexicans in New York, California, Chicago, and Florida) in order to understand whether the higher incidence of divorce is associated with a particular geographical area or with a particular national origin group.

Considering an International Perspective

Our final recommendation involves the need to study Latinos in their respective countries of origin, especially if we will continue to explain our findings in terms of cultural patterns, values, or beliefs. It may be that what we are evidencing is not a cultural pattern but an adaptation strategy. We will begin to understand the answer to this question only by studying patterns in countries of origin and gaining a more international understanding of processes across cultures. In fact, Landale (1994) studied Puerto Ricans in Puerto Rico and on the mainland. Her findings suggested that, if one were to examine patterns of union formation only among Puerto Ricans living on the mainland, one would conclude that first-generation migrants adhere to a traditional pattern of early and informal coupling, whereas second-generation Puerto Ricans adhere less to this, which means they are being influenced by U.S. norms and exposure. However, when pooled data from Puerto Rico and the mainland were examined, results indicated that the behavior of Puerto Rican women was more similar to that of second-generation Puerto Ricans on the mainland than to first-generation Puerto Rican immigrants. Thus, without data from Puerto Rico, one would have incorrectly concluded that patterns exhibited by first-generation immigrants were a result of more traditional behaviors that immigrants brought with them from Puerto Rico. Although Landale did not examine the effects of migration on union formation, she alluded to the possibility that the different behaviors between first- and second-generation Puerto Ricans in the mainland were a result of the migration process, as opposed to a stronger adherence to cultural values.

Similarly, Parra et al. (1995) found that Mexican immigrants living in the United States were more likely to rely on family support during divorce than Mexicans living in Mexico and Whites living in the United States. Had they only examined Mexicans living in the United States and compared them with Whites, they may have concluded that Mexicans were adhering to traditional familistic values. Finally, findings from Bean et al. (1996) also underscore the importance of considering processes in the country of origin. Their research suggested that the relationship between education and marital disruption was negative for first-generation Mexican immigrants, but positive for second- and third-generation immigrants. An examination of this relationship among Mexicans living in Mexico, however, suggested that this relationship was positive. As illustrated by findings from these multiple studies, we must move toward examining family relationships internationally in order to make any conclusions about immigrants' behaviors representing values resulting from their cultures of origin.

CONCLUSION

Early research on relationship dissolution among Latinos focused almost exclusively on demographic comparisons. This research tended to conclude that Latinos were at a lower risk for marital disruption. However, studies conducted within the past two decades have begun to uncover the vast diversity that exists within Latino populations. Although a number of studies have informed us of demographic trends regarding Latinos' relationship dissolution, a vast gap in our knowledge remains. Given that the Latino population is now the second largest ethnic group in the United States and continues to grow at unprecedented rates, there is a strong need to advance our knowledge in this area.

REFERENCES

Amato, P. R. (1991). Parental absence during childhood and depression in later life. *Sociological Quarterly, 32,* 543–556.

Amato, P. R. (2000). The consequences of divorce for adults and children. *Journal of Marriage and Family, 62,* 1269–1287.

Amato, P. R., & DeBoer, D. D. (2001) The transmission of marital instability across generations: Relationship skills or commitment to marriage? *Journal of Marriage and Family, 63,* 1038–1051.

Amey, C. H., & Albrecht, S. L. (1998). Race and ethnic differences in adolescent drug use: The impact of family structure and the quantity and quality of parental interaction. *Journal of Drug Issues, 28,* 283–298.

Baer, J. (1999). The effects of family structure and SES on family processes in early adolescence. *Journal of Adolescence, 22,* 341–354.

Bean, F. D., Berg, R. R., & Van Hook, J. V. W. (1996). Socioeconomic and cultural incorporation and marital disruption among Mexican Americans. *Social Forces, 75,* 593–617.

Bean, F. D., & Tienda, M. (1987). Marriage, family, and household. In *The Hispanic population in the United States* (pp. 178–204). New York: Russell Sage Foundation.

Bramlett, M. D., & Mosher, W. D. (2001). *First marriage dissolution, divorce, and remarriage: United States.* Advanced data from Vital and Health Statistics, No. 323. Washington, DC: U.S. Government Printing Office.

Bumpass, L. L., & Sweet, J. A. (1989). National estimates of cohabitation. *Demography, 26,* 615–625.

Coleman, M., Ganong, L., & Fine, M. (2000). Reinvestigating remarriage: Another decade of progress. *Journal of Marriage and Family, 62,* 1288–1307.

del Carmen, R., & Virgo, G.N. (1993). Marital disruption and nonresidential parenting: A multicultural perspective. In C.E. Depner & J.H. Bray (Eds.), *Nonresidential parenting: New vistas in family living* (pp. 13–36). Newbury Park, CA: Sage.

Eberstein, I. E., & Frisbie, W. P. (1976). Differences in marital instability among Mexican Americans, Blacks, and Anglos: 1960 and 1970. *Social Problems, 23,* 609–321.

Frisbie, W. P. (1986). Variation in patterns of marital instability among Hispanics. *Journal of Marriage and the Family, 48,* 99–106.

Frisbie, W. P., Bean, F. D., & Eberstein, I. W. (1980). Recent changes in marital instability among Mexican Americans: Convergence with Black and Anglo trends? *Social Forces, 58,* 1205–1220.

Frisbie, W. P., Opitz, W., & Kelly, W. R. (1985). Marital instability trends among Mexican Americans as compared to Blacks, and Anglos: New evidence. *Social Science Quarterly, 66,* 587–601.

Gil, A. G., Vega, W. A., & Binafora, F. (1998). Temporal influences of family structure and family risk factors on drug use initiation in a multiethnic sample of adolescent boys. *Journal of Youth and Adolescence, 27,* 373–393.

Guzman, B. (2001). *The Hispanic population: Census 2000 brief* (Publication No. C2KBR/01-3). Washington, DC: U.S. Census Bureau.

Henggeler, S. W. (1989). *Delinquency in adolescence.* Newbury Park, CA: Sage.

Hondagneu-Sotelo, P. (1992). Overcoming patriarchal constraints: The reconstruction of gender relations among Mexican Immigrant women and men. *Gender and Society, 6,* 393–415.

Johnson, M. P. (1991). Commitment to personal relationships. *Advances in Personal Relationships, 3,* 117–143.

Kreider, R. M., & Fields, J. M. (2001). *Number, timing, and duration of marriages and divorces: Fall 1996.* (Current Population Reports, Series P70–80). Washington, DC: U.S. Government Printing Office.

Landale, N. S. (1994). Migration and the Latino family: The union formation behavior of Puerto Rican women. *Demography, 31,* 133–157.

Landale, N. S., & Fennelly, K. (1992). Informal unions among mainland Puerto Ricans: cohabitation or an alternative to legal marriage? *Journal of Marriage and the Family, 54,* 269–280.

Landale, N. S., & Forste, R. (1991). Patterns of entry into cohabitation and marriage among mainland Puerto Rican women. *Demography, 28,* 587–607.

Landale, N. S., & Hauan, S. M. (1992). The family life course of Puerto Rican children. *Journal of Marriage and the Family, 54,* 912–924.

Landale, N. S., & Ogena, N. B. (1995). Migration and union dissolution among Puerto Rican women. *International Migration Review, 29,* 671–692.

Levinger, G. (1976). A social psychological perspective on marital dissolution. *Journal of Social Issues, 32,* 21–47.

Litcher, D. T., & Landale N. S. (1995). Parental work, family structure, and poverty among Latino children. *Journal of Marriage and the Family, 57,* 346–354.

Mirowski, J., II, & Ross, C. E. (1980). Minority status, ethnic culture, and distress: A comparison of Blacks, Whites, Mexicans, and Mexican Americans. *American Journal of Sociology, 86,* 479–495.

Moerk, E. L. (1973). Like father like son: Imprisonment of fathers and the psychological adjustment of sons. *Journal of Youth and Adolescence, 2,* 303–312.

Neff, J. A., Gilbert, K. R., & Hoppe, S. K. (1991). Divorce likelihood among Anglos and Mexican Americans. *Journal of Divorce and Remarriage, 15*(1–2), 75–98.

Norton, A. J., & Moorman, J. E. (1987). Current trends in marriage and divorce among American women. *Journal of Marriage and the Family, 49,* 3–14.

Parra, E. B., Arkowitz, H., Hannah, M. T., and Vazquez, A. M. (1995). Coping strategies and emotional reactions to separation and divorce in Anglo, Chicana, and Mexicana women. *Journal of Divorce and Remarriage, 23*(1/2), 117–129.

Rusbult, C. E. (1980). Commitment and satisfaction in romantic associations: A test of the investment model. *Journal of Experimental Social Psychology, 16,* 172–186.

Stanley, S. M., & Markman, H. J. (1992). Assessing commitment in personal relationships. *Journal of Marriage and the Family, 54,* 595–608.

Stroup, A. L., & Pollock, G. E. (1999). Economic consequences of marital dissolution for Hispanics. *Journal of Divorce and Remarriage, 30*(1/2), 149–166.

Sullivan, T. A. (2000). A demographic portrait. In P. Cafferty & D. Engstrom (Eds.), *Hispanics in the United States* (pp. 1–29). New Brunswick, NJ: Transaction Publishers.

Teachman, J. D., Tedrow, L. M., & Crowder, K. D. (2000). The changing demography of America's families. *Journal of Marriage and Family, 62,* 1234–1246.

Tolan, P. H. (1988). Socioeconomic, family and social stress correlates of adolescent antisocial and delinquent behavior. *Journal of Abnormal Child Psychology, 16,* 317–331.

Uhlenberg, P. (1972). Marital instability among Mexican Americans: Following the patterns of Blacks? *Social Problems, 20,* 49–56.

Umaña-Taylor, A. J., & Fine, M. A. (2001). Methodological implications of grouping Latino adolescents into one collective ethnic group. *Hispanic Journal of Behavioral Sciences, 23,* 347–362.

Umaña-Taylor, A. J., & Fine, M. A. (2003). Predicting commitment to wed among Hispanic and Anglo partners. *Journal of Marriage and Family, 65,* 117–139.

U.S. Bureau of the Census. (n.d.). Index of /population/socdemo/Hispanic. Retrieved January 22, 2004, from http://www.census.gov/population/socdemo/hispanic

U.S. Bureau of the Census. (1980). *Marital status of the Spanish-origin population: 1970 to 1979.* (No. 53; Statistical abstract of the United States: 1980). Washington, DC: Author.

U.S. Bureau of the Census. (2000). Projections of the Resident Population by Race, Hispanic Origin, and Nativity: Middle Series 2050 to 2070. Retrieved January 22, 2004, from: http//www.census.gov/population/projections/nation/summary/np-t5-g.pdf

Vega, W. A., Warheit, G. J., & Meinhardt, K. (1984). Marital disruption and the prevalence of depressive symptomatology among Anglos and Mexican Americans. *Journal of Marriage and the Family, 46,* 817–823.

Weitzman, L. (1985). *The divorce revolution: The unexpected social and economic consequences for women and children in America.* New York: The Free Press.

VII

Policy Issues Pertaining to Divorce and Relationship Dissolution

26

The Law of Divorce and Relationship Dissolution

Margaret M. Mahoney
University of Pittsburgh

In the eyes of the law, marriage is a complex status that entails a wide array of rights and responsibilities. The termination of this legal status occurs either on the death of a spouse, or on the entry of a court order of divorce or marriage dissolution. Beyond the power to terminate the couple's marriage relationship, divorce courts also have the authority to address other legal issues that typically arise at this time of family transition. The additional issues include spousal maintenance or alimony, division of marital assets, child support, and child custody.

All of these legal issues arising in the context of a divorce or dissolution proceeding are governed by state law. As described in the following sections, laws governing the issues of grounds for divorce, spousal maintenance, property distribution, child support, and child custody have undergone radical change in every state during the past few decades. Collectively, many of the changes are referred to as the *no-fault divorce revolution*. Notably, although the reforms in each state addressed the same important topics, there is little uniformity among the resulting state laws governing the divorce-related issues discussed in this chapter.

Recently, in 2002, the American Law Institute (ALI) published the *Principles of the Law of Family Dissolution*, which surveyed current state laws and made thoughtful proposals for additional reform. Widespread adoption of the ALI proposals by the state legislatures, which would result in a uniform body of law for the first time in this field, is unlikely. Nevertheless, the *Principles* is discussed throughout this chapter, because it contains thoughtful approaches to many divorce-related issues.

State court judges, whose orders terminate a couple's marriage and describe their post-divorce rights and duties, must apply the laws of the state establishing grounds for divorce and governing economic and child-related issues. These rules of law play a crucial role in another context as well. Namely, in the large majority of divorce cases, the spouses negotiate a settlement agreement (also called a *separation agreement* in some jurisdictions), usually with the assistance of lawyers, which addresses many of the issues between them (Weisberg & Appleton, 2002, p. 786). The divorce court then reviews the couple's agreement to be sure that its provisions are reasonable and fair to all family members, especially the children (Uniform

533

Marriage and Divorce Act, 1973, sec. 306). If the judge determines that the settlement agreement satisfies this standard, then the divorce decree will embody the couple's agreements as to grounds for divorce, the financial affairs of the family, and future parenting plans for minor children. In this context, the rules of law governing each of these issues play an important role in shaping the negotiation between the spouses leading to their settlement agreement. As described throughout this chapter, in settled cases, the spouses and their attorneys bargain "in the shadow of the law" (Mnookin & Kornhauser, 1979).

The final section of this chapter describes the legal treatment of unmarried cohabitants at the time of relationship dissolution. Outside of formal registration systems for domestic partners, unmarried cohabitation is generally not recognized as a legal status in the United States (ALI, 2002, sec. 6.01 cmt. a). Not surprisingly, then, the state courts do not regulate the termination of nonformalized cohabiting relationships; there is no counterpart to divorce for unmarried couples. Furthermore, as a general rule, no financial rights between the cohabitants, based on status, are recognized either during their relationship or on its dissolution. Indeed, one explanation for the increase in unmarried cohabitation, as an alternative to marriage for opposite-sex couples in the United States, highlights the desire of many individuals and couples to avoid the legal requirements of divorce in the event of relationship dissolution (Wardle, 2001, p. 1210).

The field of family law, including the laws governing relationship dissolution, remains in constant flux, as rule-makers attempt to balance and rebalance the interests of individual family members, family units, and the larger society. As to certain topics discussed in this chapter involving the termination of marriage relationships, which underwent major reform during the no-fault divorce revolution, a counterrevolution is brewing. As to other divorce-related topics, the process of continuing reform has unfolded in a more incremental fashion in recent decades. Finally, the issue of legal recognition for unmarried cohabitants, including their rights and duties at the time of relationship dissolution, is receiving renewed attention. The pressure for same-sex couples to receive legal recognition has resulted in their access to marriage (and divorce) for the first time in certain U.S. jurisdictions. Elsewhere, the debate has focused on the creation of a new, nonmarital legal status for cohabitants, involving certain rights and duties during the intact relationship and at the time of dissolution. This type of ongoing change in the field of family law, along with the continuing lack of uniformity among the states as to many important issues, reinforces the view that there are no final or definitive answers to the difficult questions discussed herein.

GROUNDS FOR DIVORCE

The divorce law of each state lists the grounds for divorce for married couples residing within the state. A marriage can be legally terminated only if one of these statutory grounds for divorce is established in a legal proceeding. This requirement reflects the strong interest of the state and the public in the relationship of each married couple. That is, the state will grant a divorce only under the limited circumstances delineated in the divorce statute (Clark, 1988, pp. 496–497).

Prior to the no-fault divorce revolution in the 1970s, the grounds for divorce available under the laws of most states involved marital fault on the part of one spouse. Typical fault grounds included adultery, cruelty, desertion, and imprisonment for a crime (Gregory, Swisher, & Wolf, 2001, sec. 8.03B). Within this fault system, the spouse filing for divorce had to allege and prove to the satisfaction of the divorce court that the other spouse had engaged in one of these behaviors. If the nonfiling spouse contested the claim and prevailed by proving his or her so-called innocence, then the judge would deny the divorce. If the judge believed the filing spouse's allegations, in spite of the other partner's denials, the divorce would be granted.

Many divorces granted under the fault-based system were not contested by the nonfiling spouse. In many of these cases, both spouses wished to end their marriage. If neither partner had engaged in behavior that would constitute a statutory ground for divorce, the couple could obtain a divorce only by making misrepresentations to the divorce court. The filing spouse would allege that the other had been adulterous or cruel or whatever. The nonfiling spouse would not deny and might actively support this (false) statement. Unless the court questioned the spouses' veracity for some reason, a divorce would be granted to the filing spouse (Krause & Meyer, 2003, pp. 249–250).

As the number of divorces increased during the 1960s, critics of the fault-based system became increasingly vocal (Krause & Meyer, 2003, pp. 253–254). The first major criticism focused on uncontested divorce cases in which the spouses, often with the knowledge of their attorneys, willfully lied to the court as the only means of obtaining a divorce decree. Critics believed that a legal regime that fostered such a pattern of conduct was intolerable. The second major criticism focused on the state's interest in marriage and divorce. According to the critics, the use of marital fault to identify those marriages to which the state would grant legal termination was misguided. The more appropriate criteria, they believed, related to the vitality of the marriage in each case. Thus, the state should grant divorces, in both contested and uncontested cases, following a judicial determination that the marriage had no possibility of continuation (Krause & Meyer, p. 254). Absent such a finding, the state would have a continuing interest in preserving the marriage, and divorce should not be granted.

During the period of the no-fault divorce revolution, in the 1970s and early 1980s, the state legislatures responded to these criticisms by reforming the laws setting forth grounds for divorce. The new divorce laws (in many states redesignated *marriage dissolution* laws) introduced no-fault grounds, such as "irretrievable breakdown" of the marriage and "irreconcilable differences" between the spouses. There are significant variations from state to state in the current no-fault divorce statutes (Gregory et al., 2001, sec. 8.03E). First, some states simply added the new no-fault provisions to existing fault grounds (23 Pa. Cons. Stat. Ann. § 3301, 2003), whereas other states moved to a strictly no-fault system (Uniform Marriage and Divorce Act, 1973, sec. 302). Second, many state no-fault laws required the filing spouse's allegation of marital breakdown to be supported by specified evidence, such as a designated period of living separate and apart (Uniform Marriage and Divorce Act, 1973, sec. 302a 2). Other state statutes have no such evidentiary requirement, allowing any type of evidence to establish the grounds for divorce (Cal. Fam. Code § 2310, 2004).

Not surprisingly, a no-fault divorce case becomes more complicated if one spouse contests the grounds for divorce asserted by his or her partner. On the one hand, if both parties allege that their marriage is beyond repair, and support the allegation with evidence of the legally required period of separation or other evidence of sustained incompatibility, a divorce will inevitably be granted (Krause & Meyer, 2003, pp. 256–257). If one party simply fails to participate, the result will likely be the same. On the other hand, if the nonfiling party contests the allegation of marital breakdown, he or she can attempt to prove that the marriage still has vitality in spite of a period of separation or other evidence to the contrary introduced by the filing party. Furthermore, the laws in many states enable the contesting spouse to request court-ordered marital counseling or additional time to heal the marriage (Mont. Code Ann. § 40-4-107 2b, 2003). Most observers have concluded, however, that the contesting spouse can delay the divorce, but not prevent it, unless the other partner has a change of heart. Ultimately, the filing spouse's sustained insistence on ending the marriage constitutes the requisite proof of marriage breakdown (Krause & Meyer, 2003, p. 257).

The rules of law governing the grounds for divorce inform divorce court judges as to when marriages in the state are legally terminable. These laws also influence the negotiation of separation agreements in some cases. In a purely fault-based system, a so-called innocent spouse has the right to keep his or her marriage intact. The only way the other partner can obtain a divorce is with the consent and participation of the innocent spouse. This fact confers bargaining leverage on the innocent partner, who may agree to the divorce in exchange for economic or other benefits (Krause & Meyer, 2003, pp. 228–229). In a similar fashion, in the no-fault context, if one spouse is more interested than the other in ending the marriage quickly, the latter spouse's ability to cause delay empowers him or her. This bargaining chip may be exchanged for some other concession from the eager-to-divorce spouse. The rules governing grounds for divorce are least likely to influence the negotiation process in the no-fault context when both spouses desire a divorce.

In recent years, the system of no-fault grounds for divorce has come under attack in many states. The critics maintain that no-fault divorce laws have established a regime of divorce on demand, which abdicates the traditional role of the state in regulating who is entitled to divorce. Furthermore, critics contend that many persistent social problems, especially those relating to poverty in single-parent families, are related to the divorce-on-demand phenomenon. The proposed solution, embodied in legislative reform proposals in many states, involves a return to fault-based divorce grounds (Weisberg & Appleton, 2002, pp. 590–591). In Louisiana, for example, the state legislature has established *covenant marriage* as an option for couples who marry. Among the differences between covenant marriages and other marriages in Louisiana is a more fault-based set of grounds for terminating the covenant marriage (La. Rev. Stat. Ann. § 9:972, 2000). In a second example, in the state of Michigan, a bill has been introduced for several years in the state legislature that would change the grounds for divorce in contested cases from the current no-fault grounds to an exclusive list of fault-based grounds (H.B. 5217, 1997).

The proposed return to fault-based divorce grounds is controversial. Proponents of the current no-fault system point to the discussions of a few decades ago, which highlighted the many weaknesses of the fault-based system in place at that time. Those discussions, of course, led to the nationwide introduction of the current no-fault grounds for divorce. Today's opponents of reform believe that a return to the problematical fault-based system of 30 years ago would be misguided. Furthermore, these proponents of the status quo do not believe that the existing divorce laws are the cause of the persistent social problems that reformers hope to address through a return to fault-based grounds for divorce (Wardle, 2000, pp. 784–793).

The current debate about divorce reform clearly illustrates the importance assigned by the public and by policy-makers to this field of law, in stating and shaping societal values.

ALIMONY OR SPOUSAL MAINTENANCE

The laws of every state provide that the divorce court may, under certain circumstances, require one former spouse to pay alimony (often called *spousal maintenance* in the no-fault divorce system) to the other following their divorce. The rationale for this type of award is not well defined (Ellman, 1989). Furthermore, there is wide variation from state to state as to the circumstances in which one spouse is entitled to an alimony award, and the form that it should take (Gregory et al., 2001, sec. 9.03–9.04).

In the fault-based era of divorce, alimony was a gender-based (payable by men) continuation of the spousal support obligation of marriage. In this context, there was little clarity in the laws describing the circumstances in which an award would be appropriate, and the amount and duration of such an award. Clearly, fault mattered. If the wife obtained a divorce based on the marital fault of her husband, the divorce court would be more likely to order substantial alimony. Conversely, if the husband obtained a divorce based on his wife's behavior during marriage, alimony for the wife was less likely. Besides fault, courts in the pre-no-fault era frequently relied as well on a second consideration, namely, the respective economic positions of the partners. A husband with sufficient economic ability to pay alimony would likely be required to provide ongoing support to his wife if she lacked significant income and resources, especially if he was the faulty defendant in the divorce case (Ellman, Kurtz, & Scott, 1998, pp. 368–369).

As to the amount and duration of alimony awards, divorce courts in the fault-based era generally exercised wide discretion in individual cases, unrestrained by any statutory guidelines. An award labeled *permanent* was generally intended to endure until the death of either party or the recipient's remarriage. Permanent awards also remained modifiable (upward or downward) in the future, based on the changed economic circumstances of either former spouse (Gregory et al., 2001, sec. 9.05). The rules providing for the modification of alimony awards in this manner illustrate an important feature of divorce court jurisdiction. Not just as to alimony, but also as to child-related issues, the rules of law anticipate that the parties may need to return to court in the future as the circumstances of family members change over time.

At the time of the no-fault revolution, when the grounds for divorce shifted away from a focus on fault, the lawmakers in most states also reformulated their alimony laws. First, although many states had already introduced the principle of gender neutrality into their family law systems, the remaining states implemented the principle at the time of divorce reform. Indeed, a 1979 U.S. Supreme Court decision, which struck down a gender-based alimony statute in Alabama, required this result (*Orr v. Orr*, 1979). Second, many state legislatures reformed the rules governing the availability, duration, and amount of alimony awards.

One set of changes in the rules governing alimony and spousal maintenance awards focused on the goal of ending, in a just manner, the economic dependencies formed during marriage. Thus, the theory of rehabilitative alimony found widespread acceptance early in the no-fault era (Krause & Meyer, 2003, pp. 262–263). According to this theory, in appropriate cases, the divorce court would best serve the interests of both former spouses by awarding time-limited alimony with the goal of enabling the recipient to enhance his or her own future earning capacity. Of course, in some families, this type of award is simply inadequate to achieve a just realignment of the former spouses' economic circumstances.

Another change in the alimony laws in many states, geared toward the goal of fairly disentangling the financial interests of former spouses, highlighted the priority of property distribution orders vis-á-vis alimony awards. As described in the next section, the "equitable distribution of property" laws, introduced in most states at the time of the no-fault revolution, empowered divorce courts to reassign ownership of the spouses' assets. In reformulating the alimony laws, many lawmakers clearly anticipated that the availability of such a property distribution would obviate the need for long-term alimony awards in many cases. Of course, reliance on the equitable distribution of property in order to address the economic needs and equities between former spouses has no application in families in which few assets, or few unmortgaged assets, are available for distribution by the court.

The following Colorado maintenance law (Colo. Rev. Stat. § 14-10-114 3, 2003), which describes the circumstances under which spousal maintenance may be awarded by the courts, reflects both of these changes in the alimony laws of the no-fault era. The first section (a) embodies the priority assigned to property distribution as the mechanism for adjusting the economic claims of former spouses. The second section (b) reflects the concept of mutual self-sufficiency, which also provides the basis for the theory of rehabilitative alimony.

> In a proceeding for dissolution of marriage . . . , the court may grant . . . a maintenance order . . . only if it finds that the spouse seeking maintenance:
>
> (a) Lacks sufficient property, including property apportioned to him or her, to provide for his or her reasonable needs; and
> (b) Is unable to support himself or herself through appropriate employment or is the custodian of a child whose condition or circumstances make it appropriate that the custodian not be required to seek employment outside the home.

If the spouse claiming maintenance in Colorado can pass this threshold test for lack of self-sufficiency, then the divorce court may enter a maintenance order. Whether to do so and the amount and duration of the award are based on the judge's consideration of "all relevant factors," including several factors set out in the Colorado maintenance statute (Colo. Rev. Stat. § 14-10-114 4, 2003), as follows:

> [A] maintenance order . . . shall be in such amounts and for such periods of time as the court deems just, without regard to marital misconduct, and after considering all relevant factors including:
>
> (a) The financial resources of the party seeking maintenance, including marital property apportioned to such party, and the party's ability to meet his or her needs independently, including the extent to which a provision for support of a child living with the party includes a sum for the party;
> (b) The time necessary to acquire sufficient education or training to enable the party seeking maintenance to find appropriate employment and that party's future earning capacity;
> (c) The standard of living established during the marriage;
> (d) The duration of the marriage;
> (e) The age and physical and emotional condition of the spouse seeking maintenance;
> (f) The ability of the spouse from whom the maintenance is sought to meet his or her need while meeting those of the spouse seeking maintenance.

The alimony statutes in some states omit the threshold test for self-sufficiency, which appears in the first portion of the Colorado statute set out here, and require the divorce judge to determine the availability of alimony as well as the amount of each award solely by reference to this type of list of factors (Uniform Marriage and Divorce Act, 1973, sec. 308).

Clearly, the divorce court must exercise a great deal of discretion in individual spousal maintenance cases under a standard that involves numerous, and frequently qualitative, factors. As in the pre-no-fault era, the results in many alimony and maintenance cases remain unpredictable in the modern context. This type of uncertainty has an impact on the negotiation process, in cases in which the divorce-related issues between the spouses are settled by their agreement. Economic issues like alimony, where the respective rights of the parties under the law are an uncertain matter, may operate as wild cards in the negotiation process. Predictably, the party who is more risk averse, and fearful of an undesirable result if the case goes to trial, will be more likely to settle the issue, even for a result that he or she considers unfair (Mnookin & Kornhauser, 1979, pp. 969–971, 979 —custody context).

Notably, the language of the Colorado maintenance statute, set out earlier, excludes the consideration of marital misconduct from judicial determinations about spousal maintenance. This approach is consistent with the general movement in the law toward a regime of no-fault divorce. Many other states similarly eliminated the fault factor, which had played such an important role in the law of alimony prior to the no-fault revolution, from their modern alimony statutes. However, not all state laws took this approach. According to a recent survey of state laws, 27 states retain marital misconduct as a factor for the court to consider in setting alimony awards, and 18 states include fault as a factor in the formulation of equitable distribution of property orders, the subject of the next section (Ellman, 1996, pp. 776–784). The proper place of fault considerations in the laws governing divorce and its consequences remains a controversial issue. The ambivalence of lawmakers is reflected in state laws that restrict the grounds for divorce to no-fault standards, but allow the spouses to tell the judge about hurtful behavior in the economic phase of the divorce proceeding.

As discussed throughout this section, lawmakers and policy-makers have never articulated a satisfactory justification for the existence of alimony and spousal maintenance laws. Alimony is frequently characterized as a continuation of the support duties that exist between spouses during marriage. This characterization leads to the following question: Why should the marital support duty survive divorce when all of the other legal incidents of marriage (e.g., inheritance rights and the authority to give consent for a partner's medical treatment) terminate with the relationship? Explanations for the ongoing financial responsibility between former spouses have frequently focused on notions of fairness between the parties and the state's interest in allocating the responsibility for financially needy persons to family (or former family) members. These rationales are reflected in the list of factors in the Colorado maintenance statute, set out herein.

In the process of rethinking the functions and proper terms of the alimony and spousal maintenance laws, the recent ALI project rejected these current rationales for the alimony doctrine. Indeed, in the *Principles of the Law of Family Dissolution*, the ALI rejected the concept of alimony itself. The *Principles* proposes a substitute for alimony, called *compensatory payments*, which has the sole purpose of compensating spouses for certain specified types of financial losses resulting from marriage dissolution (ALI, 2002, chap. 5). The eligibility of one spouse for compensatory payments from the other is determined by reference to a list of objective criteria, such as a wide disparity between the spouses' income levels following marriage of a designated duration. Furthermore, the amount and duration of compensatory payments in each case is determined by reference to quantitative guidelines, similar to the state law child support guidelines. The judge in each case may adjust the compensatory payment amount established under the *Principles*, if fairness to both parties requires such an adjustment.

To date, no state legislature has reformed the state alimony or spousal maintenance statute by adopting the ALI's compensatory payment doctrine. Nevertheless, the ALI proposal highlights the features of the existing state laws that are problematical: the lack of a clear theory for the alimony doctrine, and lack of certainty and predictability about alimony or spousal maintenance awards in individual cases. The ALI compensatory payment doctrine, which proposes a radical change to existing state laws, has reopened the debate about the nature and function of economic awards between former spouses.

PROPERTY AWARDS

The laws of every state authorize the divorce courts to make certain orders affecting the assets and debts of the divorcing couple. Prior to the introduction of the no-fault divorce laws in the 1970s, this judicial function was limited, for the most part, to determining and declaring the title to each asset, by reference to the general principles of property law (Gregory et al., 2001, sec. 10.01). This property-related function of the divorce court was called the title theory of property distribution. The relevant property law principles, which informed the court about the title to marital assets, were different in the eight community property states, on the one hand, and the remaining states that have a common law property system, on the other. The eight traditional community property states are Arizona, California, Idaho, Louisiana, New Mexico, Nevada, Texas, and Washington. Wisconsin joined this group in 1983, when the state legislature enacted a statute that created a new system of marital property law that follows the community property model (Gregory et al., 2001, sec. 3.06). The common law marital property regime defines the ownership rights of married couples in the remaining 41 states and the District of Columbia.

In the common law property states, in both the pre-no-fault era and in the modern setting, an individual's property rights during marriage are generally unaffected by the existence of the marriage (Singer, 2001, pp. 379–380). If, for example, the wife in a common law property state earns a salary, her husband has no legal interest in this income. If she places the entire amount of her salary each month into a bank account in her name, her husband has no ownership interest in the bank account while they are married. Under the title theory of property distribution in the pre-no-fault era, the function of the divorce court as to this asset would be simply to declare the title to it, namely, that the asset belonged exclusively to the wife. At the time of divorce, as during marriage, the husband had no claim to this asset of the wife.

With the no-fault divorce revolution, in the 41 common law property states, a new doctrine entitled *equitable distribution* replaced the old title theory of property distribution. Under the theory of equitable distribution, the divorce court has the power to order one spouse to transfer his or her assets to the other, in order to achieve financial equity between them (Singer, 2001, pp. 380–381). Thus, for example, as to the wife's bank account just described, the divorce court may order the wife (who clearly had exclusive ownership during marriage) to transfer some or all or none of the account balance to her husband at the time of divorce. The equitable distribution laws governing this process must provide the answers to two obvious questions. First, over what assets does the divorce court have this authority? Second, on what basis or by what standard must the divorce court exercise this authority to reassign the ownership of property?

As to the first question, a major split exists among the 41 common law property states. One set of state laws provides that the divorce court has authority to distribute any or all of the assets owned by one or both spouses at the time of divorce, however and whenever the assets were acquired (Uniform Marriage and Divorce Act, 1973, sec. 307, alt. A). By way of contrast, many state equitable distribution laws provide that only property acquired *during the marriage* is distributable, so that assets owned by either spouse prior to marriage are excluded. Furthermore, these state laws typically impose a further limitation by excluding any assets acquired by one spouse during marriage as a gift from a third party (23 Pa. Cons. Stat. Ann. § 3501, 2003). In this second category of states statutes, the restricted pool of assets subject to equitable distribution is often labeled *marital property*, and the assets of the parties *not* subject to the court's authority are called *separate property* of the titled spouse.

However the pool of distributable assets is defined, the equitable distribution law must provide guidance to the divorce court in determining the share of the pool that each spouse will receive. As a general rule, the state equitable distribution statutes set out a list of factors to be considered by the court in determining the two shares. For example, the Pennsylvania statute sets out the following factors (23 Pa. Cons. Stat. Ann. § 3502a, 2003):

In an action for divorce . . . the court shall . . . equitably divide, distribute or assign . . . the marital property between the parties without regard to marital misconduct in such proportions and in such manner as the court deems just after considering all relevant factors, including:

1) The length of the marriage.
2) Any prior marriage of either party.

3) The age, health, station, amount and sources of income, vocational skills, employability, estate, liabilities and needs of each of the parties.
4) The contribution by one party to the education, training or increased earning power of the other party.
5) The opportunity of each party for future acquisitions of capital assets and income.
6) The sources of income of both parties, including, but not limited to, medical, retirement, insurance or other benefits.
7) The contribution or dissipation of each party in the acquisition, preservation, depreciation or appreciation of the marital property, including the contribution of a party as homemaker.
8) The value of the property set apart to each party.
9) The standard of living of the parties established during the marriage.
10) The economic circumstances of each party, including Federal, State and local tax ramifications, at the time the division of property is to become effective.
11) Whether the party will be serving as the custodian of any dependent minor children.

As with the lists of factors in the state alimony and maintenance statutes described in the previous section, the application of numerous factors in the property distribution setting requires the exercise of discretion by the divorce court in individual cases. It is up to the judge to determine the relative weight assigned to each factor, and how the weighted factors translate into an order dividing the pool of distributable assets into two shares, one for each spouse. In order to inject greater certainty and predictability into the equitable distribution laws, the courts and legislatures in some states have adopted a presumption that the pool of assets should be divided into two equal shares (a 50:50 distribution), unless this result would clearly be unfair in a particular case (Ind. Code Ann. § 31-15-7-5, 2003). This more certain rule inevitably influences negotiated settlements, as well as the results in cases decided by the court.

The concept of equal ownership of assets is the hallmark of the second marital property regime in the United States, the community property system. In the nine community property states, during marriage, the spouses share equal ownership of the assets they acquire (Mennell & Boykoff, 1988, pp. 6–11). Excluded from this community of assets are the items owned by one spouse prior to marriage and any gift received by one spouse from a third party during the marriage. The excluded assets are regarded as the acquiring spouse's "separate property" (Mennell & Boykoff, pp. 30–39). In the pre-no-fault era, the function of the divorce court was to determine who owned what, under these principles of law governing the ownership of property in marriage. In the community property states, unlike the common law states, each spouse entered the divorce proceeding (and left the proceeding) owning one half of the assets acquired during marriage. In the modern no-fault era, some community property states retain this title theory of property distribution at the time of divorce. Other community property states have conferred equitable distribution powers on the divorce court, in cases in which the reallocation of property ownership is necessary to achieve an equitable result (Mennell & Boykoff, pp. 307–310).

Following the widespread enactment of equitable distribution of property statutes during the 1970s and early 1980s, important questions arose about the meaning of the term *property* for this purpose. First, most of the equitable distribution laws made no reference to liabilities owed by the spouses individually or jointly at the time of divorce. In many families, financial equity between divorcing spouses would be difficult to achieve, absent judicial authority to allocate responsibility for the repayment of debts. Over time, most states have included liabilities within the scope of "property subject to equitable distribution" by the divorce court, either by legislation or by judicial fiat (Turner, 1991, pp. 29–32). Notably, an equitable distribution order assigning responsibility to one spouse for repayment of a joint liability does *not* affect the creditor's right to collect the debt from either spouse. As a general rule, in the event that the divorce court a assigns a debt to one spouse, and the creditor collects the debt from other, the paying spouse can seek reimbursement pursuant to the terms of the equitable distribution order (Turner, p. 31).

Another key question that arose about the meaning of "property" under the state equitable distribution laws related to the deferred financial rights of a working spouse under his or her pension program. Could these economic rights, which would not be realized and enjoyed by the working spouse until retirement, perhaps many years following the divorce, be regarded as an asset subject to distribution by the court? On the one hand, the pension rights of one or both spouses, along with equity in the family home, constitute the most valuable assets of many families. Furthermore, the pension benefits, although deferred, represent compensation for the working spouse(s)' efforts during marriage. On the other hand, practical problems arise in many cases in the valuation and actual distribution of deferred pension benefits. Over time, the courts in most states concluded that these practical problems must not prevent the divorce courts from exercising authority over, and making an appropriate distribution of, the pension rights earned by each partner during marriage (McKnight, 2002, sec. 18.03 2b).

A final test of the scope of the term "property" asked whether the equitable distribution statutes could be used to reach the future income of the higher earning spouse. In many families, even families with a high standard of living, there are few real assets to distribute at the time of divorce. The expensive home and cars may be subject to mortgages and security interests, which do not leave any significant equity value available for distribution between the divorcing spouses. Similarly, credit card debts may approximate the value of the other major assets of the marriage. At the same time, the higher earning spouse may have a sizeable income, at the time of divorce and for the foreseeable future. In these circumstances, the future earning capacity of one or both spouses far exceeds the value of all assets available for current distribution.

The narrow formulation and application of alimony laws in the no-fault era, described in the previous section, limited the rights of the lower earning spouse in many cases to the future earnings of the other spouse under the theory of alimony. Thus, a question inevitably arose as to whether future earning capacity could be divided between the spouses under the theory of equitable distribution of property (McKnight, 2002, sec. 18.03 2e). The lawyers posing this question in the courts argued that a spouse whose earning capacity was significantly enhanced during the period of his or her marriage had thereby acquired a valuable marital asset. This position took a somewhat more concrete form in cases in which the enhanced earning capacity resulted from the completion of an academic or professional degree program during the period of the marriage. In these cases, the nondegreed spouse would argue that the other spouse's professional degree or license was an asset acquired during marriage that was subject to valuation and distribution by the court, along with other assets of the marriage.

With one major exception, the state courts and legislatures have been unreceptive to claims that enhanced earning capacity, academic degrees, and professional licenses are property under the equitable distribution statutes (McKnight, 2002, sec. 18.03 2e). The exception appears in New York State, where the state high court has accepted this theory (*O'Brien v. O'Brien*, 1985). Elsewhere, the equitable adjustment of financial interests between the spouses must be made by a reallocation of existing assets (including deferred assets acquired during marriage, such as pension rights) and by the establishment of alimony or maintenance awards in appropriate cases.

The ALI's *Principles* follows the majority rule in excluding future earning capacity from the definition of property subject to equitable distribution (ALI, 2002, sec. 4.07). The *Principles* also follows the majority of current state laws in drawing a distinction between separate property (acquired by one spouse prior to marriage or as a third-party gift during the marriage) and marital property subject to equitable distribution. Unlike existing law in the states that draw this distinction, however, the *Principles* provides for the automatic recharacterization of separate property as marital property in marriages of substantial duration. In this regard, the *Principles* proposes that state lawmakers adopt a formula to specify the percentage of separate assets to be recharacterized in each case, which would vary with the length of the marriage (ALI, 2002, sec. 4.12). Finally, the *Principles* adopts a rule of *equal* distribution of marital property, except in certain designated circumstances, such as the case in which one spouse wasted or destroyed marital assets (ALI, 2002, sec. 4.10). The equitable adjustment of the spouses' financial interests at the time of divorce under this equitable distribution of property model is supplemented under the *Principles* by the compensatory payment system, described in the previous section, which establishes automatic access to future earnings of the higher earning spouse in designated categories of cases.

CHILD SUPPORT

Under the laws of every state, parents have a legal obligation to provide financial support to their minor children. The duty is imposed on both biological parents, whether they are married to each other, never married, or divorced. As a general rule, the parent is permanently relieved of the support obligation to a minor child only on legal termination of the parent–child relationship (Gregory et al., 2001, sec. 9.06). In some cases, termination of the biological parent(s)' rights and obligations is followed by adoption of the child by new parent(s). Adoptive parents have all of the same rights and duties as biological parents, including the child support obligation (Hollinger, 1997, sec. 1.01). In some states, the nonadoptive stepparent has a duty to support minor stepchildren in certain circumstances while residing with the stepchildren's parent, but the obligation ceases on the stepparent's divorce from the child's parent (Mahoney, 1994, pp. 16–41).

The divorce courts in every state have the authority to enter child support orders, which reduce the parental support obligation to a concrete debt, owed to the child. The key issues arising in this context include the relationship between parental support and custody, the amount of child support awards in individual cases, and the procedures established by the state for collecting and enforcing postdivorce child support.

The state laws governing these issues underwent radical change during the 1980s, when Congress became involved in the field of child support. Prior to that time, the state child support laws left wide discretion to the family court judge in each case to determine the proper amount of support to be paid by divorced parents. Congress became involved in the field of child support as a result of nationwide dissatisfaction with the existing state of the law. Members of Congress criticized the lack of uniformity in child support awards. They also criticized the low level at which many child support awards were set by state court judges in the exercise of their discretion (Morgan, 1996 & Supp. 2001, sec. 1.01).

Congress has no authority to enact child support laws or to require the states to enact particular child support laws. During the 1980s, Congress nevertheless caused the states to completely reform their child support systems. Specifically, Congress enacted several laws providing that each state would lose billions of dollars in public assistance funding, unless that state made specified changes to its child support laws. Not surprisingly, all states complied (Morgan, 1996 & Supp. 2001, sec. 1.02a–b).

The first change indirectly mandated in this fashion by Congress involved the adoption by each state of numerical guidelines to establish the amount of child support awards. Importantly, the guideline system removed much of the discretion of the divorce courts and turned the calculation of support awards into a largely mechanical function (Morgan, 1996 & Supp. 2001, sec. 1.02e). For example, a simple guideline model might require that the support calculation be made in the following fashion: (a) Determine the parents' combined gross income, and subtract only their social security and income tax deductions to reach a "net income" figure. (b) Multiply the fraction provided in the established guideline for the number of children to be supported (perhaps 25% for one child) times the net income figure from Step a. The resulting dollar amount is the amount of child support to which the child is entitled. Other models for calculating child support are more complex, but they generally take a similarly quantitative approach. That is, the guidelines in each state provide the exclusive list of numerical factors that enter into the calculation of child support awards.

The resulting guideline amount in each case is a presumptive calculation. Either parent is entitled to request an adjustment (upward or downward) because of some special and involuntary circumstance of the family (Morgan, 1996 & Supp. 2001, sec. 1.02c 2–3). For example, the fact that one parent has an expensive house and a large mortgage payment is not the likely basis for a downward adjustment in child support, because the circumstance of owning an expensive house is not a special or involuntary circumstance of the parent. By way of contrast, a family member's ongoing and uninsured medical expenses are more likely to result in an adjustment to the presumptive amount of child support calculated under the guideline.

In the next step, a determination must be made as to how the support obligation will be allocated between the parents. As a general rule, under the simple combined-income guideline model just described, each parent's financial obligation to the child is proportional to his or her share of the combined income figure. Furthermore, the portion of the obligation that is transferable between parents depends on the amount and nature of the time spent by the child in the home of each parent. In a simple example, if mother and father have equal incomes totaling $80,000, and the presumptive award is $20,000, then each parent owes $10,000 in child support. If the child spends all of his or her time with the mother, except for a few days per year, the father will likely be required to transfer $10,000 per year for the benefit of the child. The mother may be regarded as providing her share of the child's support "in kind." If the equal-income parents also have equal custodial responsibilities following divorce, the court might determine that no transfer payments are required because the parents provide equal in-kind child support (Morgan, 1996 & Supp. 2001, sec. 3.03).

Additional state law changes indirectly mandated by Congress during the 1980s and 1990s involved the enforcement of child support orders. Prior to this Congressional intervention, the custodial parent who was entitled to collect support payments from the other parent had essentially the same legal rights as a credit card company seeking to collect payments from its cardholder. One additional remedy in the family support setting was a contempt order from the court, which could result in temporary imprisonment or fines to coerce compliance with the court's earlier child support order. In many cases, however, if the obligated parent did not voluntarily comply with court-ordered child support obligations, the child's representative (usually the custodial parent) did not pursue the available debt-enforcement remedies. The debt-collection system was not a user-friendly place for the parent in these circumstances. In mandating change in the state laws governing collection and enforcement, Congress noted that a high percentage of court-ordered child support obligations went unpaid and unenforced (Krause & Meyer, 2003, pp. 153–154).

The changes in state law regarding child support enforcement, indirectly mandated by Congress during the 1980s and into the 1990s (by means of the threat to cut off state funding), were designed to enable the custodial parent to more easily collect support payments on behalf of the child. The laws in every state now provide numerous support enforcement mechanisms, including streamlined mechanisms for garnishing the obligated parent's wages or other sources of income, and judicial authority to require the obligated parent to post a bond or other security to guarantee regular support payments (Gregory et al., 2001, sec. 9.06F 1–2 & 5).

Other devices have been created at the state level to assist the custodial parent in child support collection cases, in response to the federal intervention in this field. First, the obligated parent may be required to send child support payments to a designated court administrator, who then disburses the payment to the child's custodian. If payments are not made in a timely fashion, the court administrator is immediately aware of the problem and can initiate enforcement procedures. Other administrators associated with the family court are available to assist in locating missing obligated parents. In interstate cases, the states have established cooperative procedures for locating parents and collecting support debts across state lines (Gregory et al., 2001, sec. 9.06F 3–4).

A final question about the child support obligations of divorced parents involves their responsibility for the costs of higher education. In the intact family in which married parents reside with their common children, state laws are clear about the duration of the parental support duty: The obligation terminates on the child's age of majority (typically, age 18) or on the child's earlier emancipation. The only circumstance in which the legal obligation of married parents might extend beyond the child's age of majority arises in the case of a child with disabilities (Clark, 1988, pp. 716–719). Thus, married parents do not have a legal obligation to support their child during the years of higher education following the child's 18th birthday.

By way of contrast, the laws in a number of states authorize the divorce courts to order divorced parents to support a child beyond the age of majority while the child pursues a higher education (Morgan, 1996 & Supp. 2001, sec. 4.05d). The premise here is that many divorced parents, especially divorced noncustodial parents, will be less likely to pay for a child's higher education than their married counterparts. Therefore, a legal parental duty is necessary to ensure that the children of divorced parents will receive this additional support from parents who can afford it.

Notably, Congress left this matter to the discretion of the states, and there is considerable variation among state laws describing the obligation of divorced parents to pay for their children's higher education. First, many states do not impose this obligation. Second, the obligation usually endures for just 3 or 4 years beyond the child's age of majority (i.e., until age 21 or 22). Next, the child may be required to be a full-time student and may be required to contribute to his or her own support during this period. Finally, unlike the support awards calculated pursuant to guidelines during the child's minority, the existence, amount, and duration of this additional obligation is established on a case-by-case basis through the exercise of judicial discretion (Morgan, 1996 & Supp. 2001, sec. 4.05d).

Divorcing parents may include the issue of financial responsibility for a child's higher education in their separation agreement. They may also reach an agreement regarding postdivorce support prior the child's 18th birthday. As a general rule, the divorce courts are deferential to the decisions of the couple about the various issues between them that must be resolved at the time of divorce. As to child support issues, however, courts tend to carefully scrutinize the terms of a separation agreement, to be sure that the parents are not waiving the child's financial rights under state law (Uniform Marriage and Divorce Act, 1973, sec. 306).

CHILD CUSTODY

The laws of every state authorize the divorce courts to make orders regarding the custody of minor children following their parents' divorce. Determinations must be made about two primary topics involving the postdivorce parenting of children. First, where will the children spend their time? Second, which parent(s) will make the important decisions affecting the children's future?

In the intact family, all members typically reside in a single household. Furthermore, they develop some method for making decisions about medical care, education, and other important matters affecting the children. For the most part, the government and the courts are not involved in and are unavailable to resolve family disputes about these matters, as long as the family remains intact (Krause & Meyer, 2003, pp. 27–30).

Once married parents divorce, however, the state believes that judges must have the authority to address custodial issues, in order to ensure the well-being of children. In recent years, the question has arisen whether the category of children for whom the state feels this concern includes unadopted stepchildren who reside in the home of the divorcing couple. The legal issue that arises most often is whether the stepparent is entitled to visitation rights with the child following the divorce. Although there is no final consensus among the states, the trend is clearly toward allowing the divorce court to enter stepparent visitation orders based on a determination of the child's best interests (Mahoney, 1994, pp. 129–137).

The laws of each state provide substantive standards to guide judges in making decisions about the future parenting of minor children following divorce. These standards play an important role as well in the large majority of cases in which the issues are resolved not by a judge, but through negotiation or mediation between the parents. The rules of law in this field—both the statutes enacted by the state legislatures and the opinions of the state appellate courts—have undergone numerous changes during the past several decades.

Prior to the early 1970s, gender played an important role in the formulation of custody standards by state lawmakers (Little, 1998 & Supp. 2004, sec. 1.05 2a). The so-called tender years presumption provided the basis for preferring the mother as the primary custodian of minor children, especially younger children, in many cases. The model of postdivorce parenting contemplated by the custody laws in this era assumed that one parent (usually the mother) would become the primary or sole custodian.

Sole custody entailed physical custody as well as most of the decision-making authority (sometimes called legal custody) for the child. The other parent (usually the father) was referred to as the secondary parent. Parenting rights and responsibilities associated with this role typically involved limited time with the child (visitation rights) and limited decision-making responsibility spelled out in the custody order of the divorce court or the agreement of the parents. The noncustodial parent was frequently required to make child support payments. This dominant legal model was presumed to best serve the interests of children in most cases decided by the courts, unless some special facts pointed to a different result (Gregory et al., 2001, sec. 11.04a). Of course, parents who made their own custody arrangements could also deviate from the traditional custody model described here, subject to judicial approval.

During the 1970s, gender was widely rejected as an appropriate basis for assigning rights and duties under the law, and this reform had major effects on the family law field. As discussed earlier, family support responsibilities during and after marriage were extended to wives and husbands in an evenhanded fashion, based on their respective financial circumstances. Furthermore, custody preferences based solely on gender were abolished (Little, 1998 & Supp. 2004, sec. 1.05 3). The dominant gender-neutral custody standard in the United States is "the best interests of the child." Divorce courts using this standard generally look to all relevant circumstances of each parent and the children in formulating orders about both physical and legal (decision-making) custody rights on a case-by-case basis (Little, 1998 & Supp. 2004, sec. 1.05 1).

The obvious difficulty associated with the best interests of the child standard is the lack of certainty and predictability of results in cases involving two fit and loving parents. Theoretically, the list of relevant considerations in a custody case is unlimited. Many family court judges feel burdened by the extent of their discretion in these circumstances. Families themselves may feel that court-ordered parenting arrangements are arbitrary, because the rules of law provided no clear-cut guide. Several developments in the law have taken place that seek to inject more certainty into the law while staying focused on the child's interests.

First, a primary-caretaker presumption has entered the law in many states, either by legislative enactment or by order of the state high court (Ellman et al., 1998, pp. 660–665). According to this doctrine, in families where one parent was primarily responsible for parenting children during the parents' marriage, the law assigns a custodial preference to that parent at the time of divorce. The divorce court assumes the child's best interests will be served following divorce by continuing the primary parenting role of the parent who was more active during the marriage, absent specific reasons why the assumption is incorrect in a particular case. The custody orders regarding both physical and legal custody in each case will then be formulated around this starting premise, to accommodate the specific needs and circumstances of the family.

Generally speaking, the significance of the primary-caretaker presumption in the law of child custody has waned since its introduction into the law of many states a couple of decades ago (Ellman et al., 1998, pp. 663–665). First, although the child's past history with each parent remains an important consideration in custody cases, the scope of inquiry about past relationships under the best interests standard frequently transcends the question of caretaking. Furthermore, best interests inquiries in many cases focus as well on the future, that is, on the placement and parenting for the child that each parent can make available following divorce.

Notably, the recently drafted *Principles of the Law of Family Dissolution* proposes a custody standard that would assign postdivorce parenting responsibilities on the basis of each parent's predivorce involvement with the children (ALI, 2002, sec. 2.08). This "approximation standard," like the primary-caretaker doctrine, assigns weight to the family's past practices in assessing the family model that will best serve the children's interests in the future.

A second development in the law of child custody, following the abandonment of gender as a relevant consideration, was the introduction of joint custody doctrines in many states. The basic concept here is that the interests of many children are best served if both of their parents remain actively involved in their children's upbringing following divorce. State law joint custody provisions require judges to consider alternatives to the traditional primary custodian–secondary parent model for postdivorce parenting. Judges must consider a more flexible division of parental decision-making authority, and perhaps physical custody as well, depending on the circumstances of the family. The mechanisms in the law for establishing these requirements vary from state to state, ranging from a strong presumption in favor of joint custody awards to laws that simply authorize judges to enter such orders (Ellman et al., 1998, pp. 672–677).

Joint custody doctrines and the notion of flexible parenting plans have affected the vocabulary for discussing children's issues in divorce proceedings. Thus, the language of *custody* and *visitation* have been replaced in many contexts by language referring to *parenting*, *decision making*, and *residence* in the postdivorce family (Ellman et al., 1998, p. 680).

The primary-caretaker and joint custody doctrines, like all of the other substantive doctrines that establish rights and duties at the time of divorce, have an impact on the negotiation of separation agreements between the spouses. For example, if one parent is committed to obtaining sole custody in a jurisdiction with a strong joint custody presumption, the parent may trade economic rights to the other spouse in exchange for a release of joint custody rights. Many state courts and legislatures have grown increasingly sensitive to this dimension of the rules they formulate, especially in the field of child custody.

A final set of developments in substantive custody law in the modern context involves the imposition of certain limits on the court's inquiry about each parent, under the best interests of the child standard. As a general rule, as noted earlier, the best interests of the child standard invites the judge in a custody case to consider all relevant factors relating to the circumstances of the children, their relationships with each parent, and the placement option for the children presented by each parent. Within this wide framework of inquiry, parents have argued that certain matters, such as the parent's sexual orientation, religion, or race, should be removed from consideration in all custody cases between parents at the time of divorce. The rationale for limiting the judicial inquiry may be based in the state or federal constitution, state public policy, or a view that the particular factor simply has no relevance to the welfare of children. With the exception of the factor of race (*Palmore v. Sidoti*, 1984), very few blackletter rules of exclusion have emerged from these efforts (Krause & Meyer, 2003, pp. 184–188). The legislatures and courts are typically reluctant to limit the scope of inquiry under the best interests of the child standard in individual cases. Thus, for example, a parent's sexual orientation may be considered by the court in most states, if there is evidence that the child's well-being has been affected by it, in the same manner that other aspects of the parent's circumstances are deemed relevant.

Given the importance of the interests involved in custody cases, and the difficulty for judges in applying an open-ended best interests of the child standard, many states have established procedures to encourage the settlement of custody issues by the parents. First, the courts generally encourage divorcing couples to negotiate a settlement agreement addressing all of the issues between them, especially when there are children from the marriage. Furthermore, a number of family court systems provide, and strongly encourage parents to utilize, mediation or other dispute-resolution services in custody cases. Of course, any resulting settlement agreement between the spouses must be reviewed by the court.

Like the issues of family support in the postdivorce family, discussed earlier, the arrangements made for the custody of children may be modified by the court sometime later. The laws of each state provide a substantive standard, such as changed circumstances that seriously affect the well-being of the child, to govern judicial decisions in modification cases (Clark, 1988, pp. 836–847). Clearly, the interests of the child and the family in regard to stability following the parents' divorce counsels in favor of the conservative application of modification doctrines.

As to each of the divorce-related issues over which the courts retain postdivorce authority, jurisdictional complications may arise if some of the family members move to another state. During recent years, state lawmakers have come to understand the need for interstate cooperation in these circumstances, and they have enacted uniform laws to govern interstate custody and support cases (Uniform Child Custody Jurisdiction Act, 1968; Uniform Child Custody Jurisdiction Enforcement Act, 1997; Uniform Interstate Family Support Act, 1996).

PREMARITAL CONTRACTS

As noted in the preceding sections of this chapter, the large majority of divorcing couples negotiate settlement agreements, which address the important economic and child-related issues that must be resolved at the time of divorce. Most divorce courts encourage this type of informal dispute-resolution process, although the court in each case must review and approve the terms of the couple's agreement. Absent such a settlement between the spouses, the divorce judge is required to hear evidence and make its own ruling as to each of the couple's divorce-related issues.

In a growing number of marriages, couples execute contracts *prior to* marriage that address their respective economic rights in the event of a subsequent divorce. The question of whether such a contract should be enforceable by the divorce court, in place of the typical settlement agreement negotiated at the time of marriage breakdown, is a difficult one. There is no uniform answer to the question of enforceability of prenuptial contracts in the United States today (Rutkin, 2003, sec. 59.04–59.06).

Most antenuptial contracts address the economic issues that arise between the spouses at the time of divorce, namely, property distribution and alimony or spousal maintenance. Generally speaking, the divorce courts are less likely to accept and enforce these provisions in a couple's antenuptial contract than the corresponding terms of a settlement agreement. The reluctance to enforce premarital contracts relates to both the likely manner of contract execution and the likely passage of time between execution and enforcement. Neither of these concerns arises as to the typical settlement contract executed while a divorce is pending.

First, the separation agreement or settlement contract is generally negotiated following the couple's decision to terminate their marriage. At that time, each spouse is likely to see his or her own interests as distinct from those of the partner. By way of contrast, the antenuptial or prenuptial contract is usually negotiated at a time, shortly before marriage, when the partners are more likely to lose sight of their individual interests. The possibility exists that "arm's-length bargaining," an essential ingredient for meaningful contract negotiation, will be lost in these circumstances. For example, one partner may be reluctant to insist on full access to the financial records of the other, for fear of being perceived as distrustful of the person he or she is about to marry. As a result, when the question of enforcement arises at the time of a later divorce, the court may be skeptical that the agreement was the result of a genuine bargaining process. For this reason, the courts in some states require proof that each party was represented by a lawyer, or that full disclosure and other procedural requirements were met, before enforcing an antenuptial contract (Developments in the Law, 2003, pp. 2082–2087).

The second concern about the enforcement of antenuptial contracts relates to the inability of the couple, even if they engaged in a good faith, arm's-length bargaining process at the time of contract formation, to know what their future would hold. The agreement executed prior to marriage may have been based on expectations about the future that, in fact, were not realized over time. The classic example is the marriage of partners who anticipate that they will concentrate on their careers and not have children. As time passes, however, they raise a family, and one partner devotes full time to domestic duties. If their prenuptial contract provided for no spousal support or property distribution in the event of divorce, this result may appear to be unfair in light of the couple's changed goals at the time of divorce. As a result of this concern, the law in some states requires a determination by the divorce court that the terms of the premarital contract are not unjust at the time of divorce. In the absence of such a judicial determination, the contract will be set aside (Developments in the Law, 2003, pp. 2082–2087).

A couple interested in ensuring the enforceability of their antenuptial contract may be advised to comply with procedural requirements regarding full disclosure of financial matters and obtaining separate legal advice. Furthermore, many legal advisors may suggest that the couple revisit and revise the contract periodically during their marriage, especially if family circumstances undergo changes such as the birth of a child or loss of employment. Absent such measures, the enforceability of an antenuptial contract at the time of divorce is an uncertain matter in many U.S. jurisdictions.

DISSOLUTION OF THE RELATIONSHIP
BETWEEN UNMARRIED COHABITANTS

Generally speaking, nonformalized cohabiting relationships in the United States do not constitute a legal status giving rise to legal consequences between the partners or vis-á-vis third parties and the government. Because the relationship of unmarried cohabitants is not recognized by the legal system, no court order or other legal intervention is required or available to terminate the relationship.

The exception to these rules about legal noninvolvement in unmarried relationships can be found in various municipal domestic partnership ordinances and in the state statutes enacted in California (Cal. Fam. Code § 2310, 2004), Hawaii (Reciprocal Beneficiaries Act, Haw. Rev. Stat. Ann. §§ 572–1–7, 1997), New Jersey (N.J. Stat. Ann. § 26:8A–4, 2004), and Vermont (Vt. Stat. Ann. tit. 15, § 2000, 2001), which entitle eligible couples to register as domestic partners. Each domestic partnership law establishes a particular set of benefits for registered couples. The laws creating domestic partnership registration systems also provide a mechanism for legally terminating these relationships (Duncan, 2001, p. 975). Most of the municipal domestic partnership registration systems provide for formal termination of the relationship on the filing of a termination document by the partners. By way of contrast, the Vermont civil union statute, which confers all of the rights and duties of marriage under Vermont law upon same-sex domestic partners who enter a civil union, requires that their legal status be terminated in the same manner as a marriage (i.e., by order of the family court). Furthermore, in Vermont, all of the laws governing the financial relationship of spouses at the time of divorce, such as the alimony and equitable distribution of property laws, also apply to partners dissolving a civil union.

Outside the context of formal registration systems, the law recognizes no legal status between unmarried cohabitants, which could become the subject matter of a divorce or other termination proceeding. In the informal context, no alimony or equitable distribution claims are available between cohabitants at the time of relationship dissolution. (The exception to this general statement appears in the state of Washington, where the courts have established the right of "meretricious partners" to obtain a court order equally dividing the assets acquired during their cohabiting relationship (*Connell v. Francisco*, 1995).

Beginning with the California Supreme Court case of *Marvin v. Marvin* in 1976, most states have opened their courtrooms to cohabitants dissolving their relationships, for the limited purpose of enforcing contracts between them. In the most clear-cut case, if the couple signed a contract promising to divide their property in a certain fashion, or providing for postseparation support payments, and the obligated partner refuses to comply, the court has the authority to enforce their agreement. The basis for finding an enforceable contract is less clear in cases in which there is no written contract. Here, one cohabitant must rely on the couple's conversations and behavior to establish an agreement about property rights on dissolution of their relationship. The willingness of the courts to entertain claims to property in these circumstances on the basis of oral or implied contract varies a great deal from state to state (Rutkin, 2003, sec. 65.04–65.05). Notably, even the broad enforcement of cohabitants' contracts based on words and conduct does not establish cohabitation as a legally significant status. That is, claims between partners are established under these theories by virtue of the existence of their contract, *not* by virtue of their relationship.

When a cohabiting relationship dissolves, questions arise about future parenting of the couple's common children, just as child-related issues arise when married parents divorce. Although no legal proceeding is available to terminate the nonformalized relationship of unmarried cohabitants, cohabiting couples may initiate a judicial proceeding specifically to address issues of child support and the future parenting of their common children. The laws in every state generally provide that these issues should be resolved according to the same rules, already described, which are applied for the benefit of minor children in cases of divorce (Little, 1998 & Supp. 2004, sec. 1.05 2b).

Notably, in 2002 the ALI addressed the subject of cohabitants' rights in the *Principles of the Law of Family Dissolution*. Contrary to current state law, the *Principles* takes the position that qualifying unmarried cohabitants should enjoy the same financial rights as spouses on relationship dissolution (chap. 6). Those rights are the equitable distribution of assets acquired during the relationship and entitlement to the compensatory payments that replace alimony and spousal maintenance under the *Principles*. The ALI proposal first establishes standards for identifying those unmarried couples who are eligible for this type of legal recognition. These standards involve the consideration of numerous factors including the length of relationship, whether the couple had common children, and other matters relating to the nature of the cohabiting relationship in each case.

Unlike the existing state domestic partnership laws in California, Vermont, Hawaii, and New Jersey, the ALI proposal extends evenhandedly to opposite-sex couples along with same-sex couples. The inclusion of opposite-sex couples, who unlike their same-sex counterparts are generally free to marry, raises difficult questions about the impact of recognizing a new status for marriage-eligible couples on the institution of marriage. In part for this reason, to date, the ALI's proposal to establish financial claims between unmarried cohabitants at the time of relationship dissolution has not been enacted by any state legislature. Indeed, most of the pressure for legal recognition of cohabiting couples in the recent past has come from same-sex couples who were ineligible to marry. At the present time, many of the key legal distinctions of the past are beginning to blur. Same-sex couples are on the verge of obtaining the right to marry in several states. It remains to be seen how this major development affects the creation and recognition of an alternative, unmarried, cohabiting status for marriage-eligible couples under state law.

CONCLUSION

The decision of spouses to terminate their marriage relationship marks a time of dramatic transition for the members of their family. The legal system, which generally respects the privacy of intact families, becomes involved with various aspects of the family in the context of a marriage dissolution. Thus, as discussed in this chapter, the rules of law in each state govern the grounds for divorce, the economic rights of the spouses, and important child-related issues in the divorce context. In formulating these rules, state lawmakers must balance the sometimes conflicting interests of individual family members, the family as a unit, and the larger society. Given the importance of the interests at stake, the many and ongoing changes in modern family life, and public awareness of the laws in this field, the relevant rules of law are much discussed and often revised.

The related topic of dissolution of unmarried, cohabiting relationships presents a different picture. Outside the limited number of local and state domestic partnership laws, unmarried cohabitation is not a status recognized by the legal system. The courts generally become involved in the unwinding of a nonformalized cohabiting relationship only if the partners raise economic claims based on the existence of a contract or issues involving the welfare of their children. For some, but certainly not all, unmarried partners, the noninvolvement of the state at the time of relationship dissolution is a welcome feature of their nonformalized relationships.

In this field, lawmakers must formulate rules that involve an appropriate degree of state involvement in the affairs of the family and the most appropriate forms of regulation. As revealed by the discussion in this chapter of the laws governing relationship dissolution, the achievement of these goals has presented many challenges for the state courts and legislatures.

REFERENCES

American Law Institute. (2002). *Principles of the law of family dissolution.* Philadelphia, PA: LexisNexis.

Cal. Fam. Code §§ 297-299 (Supp. 2004).

Cal. Fam. Code § 2310 (2004).

Clark, H. H., Jr. (1988). *The law of domestic relations in the United States* (2nd. ed.). Minneapolis, MN: West.

Colo. Rev. Stat. §§ 14-10-114(3)-(4) (2003).

Connell v. Francisco, 898 P. 2d 831 (Wash. 1995).

Developments in the Law. (2003). Marriage as contract and marriage as partnership. *Harvard Law Review, 116,* 2075–2098.

Duncan, W. C. (2001). Domestic partnership laws in the United States: A review and critique. *Brigham Young University Law Review, 2001,* 961–992.

Ellman, I. M. (1989). The theory of alimony. *California Law Review, 11,* 1–81.

Ellman, I. M. (1996). The place of fault in a modern divorce law. *Arizona State Law Journal, 28,* 773–837.

Ellman, I. M., Kurtz, P. M., & Scott, E. S. (1998). *Family law* (3rd ed.). Charlottesville, VA: Lexis Law.

Gregory, J. D., Swisher, P. N., & Wolf, S. L. (2001). *Understanding family law* (2nd ed.). New York: Bender.

Hollinger, J. H. (1997). *Adoption law and practice* (Vol. 1). New York: Bender.

H. B. 5217, 1997–1998 Sess. (Mich. 1997).

Ind. Code Ann. § 31-15-7-5 (2003).

Krause, H. D., & Meyer, D. D. (2003). *Family law: In a nutshell* (4th ed.). Minneapolis, MN: West.

Little, S. M. (1998). *Child custody and visitation* (Vol. 1). New York: Bender. (Supp. 2004)

La. Rev. Stat. Ann. § 9:772 (West 2000).

Mahoney, M. M. (1994). *Stepfamilies and the law.* Ann Arbor: University of Michigan Press.

Marvin v. Marvin, 557 P. 2d 106 (Cal. 1976).

McKnight, J. W. (2002). *Valuation and distribution of marital property* (Vol. 1). New York: Bender.

Mennell, R., & Boykoff, T. M. (1988). *Community property: In a nutshell.* Minneapolis, MN: West.

Mnookin, R. H., & Kornhauser, L. (1979). Bargaining in the shadow of the law: The case of divorce. *Yale Law Journal, 88,* 950–997.

Mont. Code Ann. § 40-4-107(2)(b) (2003).

Morgan, L. W. (1996). *Child support guidelines: Interpretation and application.* New York: Aspen Law and Business (Supp. 2001).

N.J. Stat. Ann. § 26:8A-4 (2004).

O'Brien v. O'Brien, 489 N.E. 2d 712 (N.Y. Ct. App. 1985).

Orr v. Orr, 440 U.S. 268 (1979).

Palmore v. Sidoti, 466 U.S. 429 (1984).

Reciprocal Beneficiaries Act, Haw. Rev. Stat. Ann. §§ 572-1–7 (1997).

Rutkin, A. H. (2003). *Family law and practice* (Vol. 5–6). New York: Bender.

Singer, J. W. (2001). *Introduction to property.* New York: Aspen Law and Business.

Turner, B. R. (1991). The hidden part of the marital estate: Classifying, valuing, and dividing marital debts. *Divorce Litigation, 3,* 21–32.

23 Pa. Cons. Stat. Ann. (2003).

Uniform Child Custody Jurisdiction Act (1968). 9 *Uniform Laws Annotated* 261 (1998).

Uniform Child Custody Jurisdiction Enforcement Act (1997). 9 *Uniform Laws Annotated* 649 (1998).

Uniform Interstate Family Support Act (1996). 9 *Uniform Laws Annotated* 235 (1998).

Uniform Marriage and Divorce Act (1973). 9A *Uniform Laws Annotated* 159 (1998).

Vt. Stat. Ann. tit. 15, § 2000 (2001).

Wardle, L. D. (2000). Divorce reform at the turn of the millennium: Certainties and possibilities. *Family Law Quarterly, 33,* 783–800.

Wardle, L. D. (2001). Deconstructing family: A critique of the American Law Institute's "Domestic Partners" proposal. *Brigham Young University Law Review, 2001,* 1189–1234.

Weisberg, D. K., & Appleton, S. F. (2002). *Modern family law* (2nd ed.). New York: Aspen Law and Business.

27

In the Presence of Grief:
The Role of Cognitive-Emotional
Adaptation in Contemporary
Divorce Mediation

David A. Sbarra
University of Arizona

Robert E. Emery
University of Virginia

Any professional—an attorney, psychologist, social worker, family physician, accountant—working to assist couples make the transition out of marriage quickly realizes that, if not already present in full force, the psychological pain of relationship dissolution rests quite close to the surface. After a period of initial upheaval, most adults and children fare well following divorce and other separation experiences (Amato, 2000; Emery, 1999, 2004; Hetherington & Kelly, 2002). However, for parents, this transition period characterized by financial, contextual, and psychological crisis and change is precisely when important family decisions have to be made: How should custody arrangements be divided? What is a good visitation plan? How much child support or alimony should paid? For this reason, therapeutic interventions designed to treat, ameliorate, or otherwise counteract the potentially deleterious effects of divorce must be deeply rooted in empirical research on the cognitive-emotional sequelae of relationship dissolution. Said differently, practitioners need to know where people can get *emotionally* stuck following the end of their marriage and what to do about it.

Any "treatment" for divorce, be it family mediation, parenting education, or individual psychotherapy, is implicitly charged with balancing an understanding of dissolution-specific psychological outcomes with appropriate intervention strategies. The primary thesis of this chapter is that contemporary divorce mediation, the most systematic and well-established form of alternative dispute resolution for divorcing couples, can and should be more deeply grounded in a scientific understanding of postrelationship psychological functioning and associated processes of cognitive-emotional recovery. This perspective calls for a blending of applied interventions with the basic science of relationship dissolution; appropriate treatments should build off existing research while simultaneously pushing relationship researchers to ask and answer treatment-relevant questions (Emery, 1990). Heretofore, a complete and integrated psychology of divorce that includes both basic science and applied intervention research has been difficult to achieve because court-mandated or court-involved interventions emerged largely without the necessary input from empirical science (Beck & Sales, 2001).

Conceptually, this chapter is organized around two broad questions. First, what is the state of the science regarding divorce mediation? Second, how can the basic science of relationship dissolution more completely inform contemporary mediation interventions? We view understanding the role of divorce-related grief and emotion regulation following relationship dissolution as a critical process for building effective interventions (Emery, 1994; Sbarra & Emery, 2004, in press). Hence, we begin with an eye toward these topics when we consider the empirical research on family mediation. As a form of alternative dispute resolution, mediation services for divorcing parents formally emerged in the early 1980s in response to growing discontent with adversarial litigation practices (Beck & Sales, 2001; Emery, 1994; Myers, Gallas, Hanson, & Keilitz, 1988). In addition to mediation, a variety of other programs now exist to assist adults make the transition out of marriage and to help parents develop effective coparenting skills following divorce (e.g., Wolchik et al., 2000). Because research on parenting and related programs is limited, only newly emerging (Emery, Kitzmann, & Waldron, 1999; Wolchik et al., 2002), and covered in its own chapter in this handbook (chap. 28, Blaisure & Geasler), we focus our discussion on divorce mediation services, which are widely adopted in many states although hardly uniform in practice (Tondo, Coronel, & Drucker, 2001).

Following a review of mediation history, research on outcomes, and mention of methodological limitations, we turn to the question of how basic science can broaden and expand therapeutic models of mediation and, in particular, address the need for cognitive adaptation and the ever-present topic of emotional grief when marriage comes to an end. We consider these issues from both theoretical and empirical perspectives by reviewing relevant literature within the divorce and larger coping literatures, as well as by discussing a model of postdivorce emotional grief we have developed and begun testing over the past decade (Emery, 1994; Sbarra & Emery, 2004). Finally, we return to the topic of mediation interventions and, in the spirit of provoking and encouraging more complete treatment research (cf. Beck & Sales, 2001), offer four individual- and couple-level treatment recommendations that we believe are important but understudied. Overall, our goal in this chapter is to provide a concise, up-to-date review of divorce mediation research while also illustrating how basic science on relationship dissolution can inform interventions and assist families in transition.

DIVORCE MEDIATION: STATE OF THE SCIENCE

In the first portion of this chapter, we define and outline the scope of divorce mediation as it is currently practiced; review evidence on the process and content outcomes of mediation; underscore three key methodological issues complicating mediation research; and introduce a model of therapeutic mediation focused on parents' main postdivorce challenge of renegotiating family relationships. Central to all mediation services is the idea that contesting parties can come together with a neutral person or persons in order to reach a consensus decision on isolated issues of dispute (Beck & Sales, 2001). As practiced, mediation is typically task oriented and time limited (usually ranging from 1 to 10 sessions but varying considerably, depending on whether the mediation is voluntary or court ordered). It seeks to provide parties with an alternative form of dispute resolution that does not exacerbate the very problems leading them to seek a formal dispute resolution in the first place. In contrast, traditional adversarial litigation might be considered formalized competition in which one party needs to lose in order for the other to win. Although several studies have found that mediation can be more cost effective than litigation, Beck and Sales have noted that no definitive conclusions can be made about differences in costs to litigants.

Family mediation services are provided by a wide range of professionals (including attorneys, psychologists, social workers, and other trained professionals working for the court or independently) and can cover a wide range of topics. Beck and Sales (2001) stated that "At the heart of mediation ... is the opportunity for each parent (a) to completely air her or his concerns while the other parent listens, (b) to do so in front of a neutral third party, and (c) to do so in a less adversarial forum than a courtroom" (p. 27). Custody mediation is limited to negotiating children's issues, specifically residence and decision making (physical and legal custody). Comprehensive mediation includes disputes about the children, as well as financial issues of spousal support, property division, and child support. Comprehensive mediation may be used with childless couples or couples that have grown children. When mediation is successful, both parents ratify and sign the agreement, and each party is encouraged to contact his or her attorney for a final review. Mediation can fail for a variety of reasons. Parents can disagree over the central problem to be mediated, fight over the details of the agreement, decide to reconcile, refuse court-mandated services, or undermine the process in many other ways.

Mediation Outcome Research: Process and Content

Rather than reviewing research already well synthesized (Beck & Sales, 2001; Emery, Sbarra, & Grover, 2004), our aim in this section is to underscore a few key themes that we believe are particularly relevant to understanding and broadening therapeutic mediation models. Like other investigators in this area (Bickerdike, 1998; Bickerdike & Littlefield, 2001), we view the distinction between process and content outcomes as an important one; process-focused research examines the mechanisms of mediation, whereas content research concentrates on broad-based outcome domains. Understanding why and how mediation works, or does not work for that matter, has key implications for adopting appropriate intervention strategies.

Mediation Process Outcomes

Within the process arena, Bickerdike and Littlefield (2001) recently completed the most ambitious study to date on the psychological and relationship-level factors impacting mediation outcomes. Partners from 110 divorcing couples who were voluntarily attending comprehensive mediation services in Victoria, Australia rated their ongoing attachment (to their former partner), anger, and sadness prior to beginning the dispute-resolution program. Chief among the findings were that individuals reporting higher mean anger and couples evidencing greater attachment disparity (operationalized at the difference between former partners' individual attachment scores) were significantly less likely to reach a satisfactory mediation agreement, and that couples that engaged in high levels of contentious behavior and low levels of problem solving and that exhibited a high disparity in problem solving were less likely to reach a successful mediation outcome. In addition, attachment disparity prior to entering mediation predicted problem-solving disparity within the mediation sessions (Bickerdike & Littlefield). High attachment disparity prior to mediation also was associated with poor outcomes, which the authors speculated could be due to highly attached spouses' obstructing the settlements (and thereby forestalling the dissolution of marriage) by engaging in prolonged discussions about what to talk about and how the process of mediation works rather than actually negotiating substantive issues (Bickerdike & Littlefield).

Process-focused and mechanistic research of the kind conducted by Bickerdike and Littlefield (2001; also see Bickerdike, 1998) is important for several reasons. First, Bickerdike and Littlefield tested competing theoretical models about mediation processes. If psychological factors do not impact the process of mediation (as argued by some, e.g., Mathis & Yingling, 1991), there would be little need for therapeutic models that seek to help adults manage and potentially resolve their psychological distress while working toward mediation outcomes. Thus, theory-driven work is essential for understanding the mechanisms of divorce mediation (Beck & Sales, 2001). Second, process-focused research has clear implications for modifying applied interventions. Following Bickerdike and Littlefield, hypotheses can be made and tested regarding particular intervention strategies for dealing with anger and attachment disparity. Finally, Bickerdike and Littlefield have moved beyond static individual-level variables to consider the emergent properties of the dyad by investigating attachment and problem-solving disparity. The degree of one's attachment to a former spouse alone is not corrosive to the mediation process perse. Rather, it is the *disconnect* in ongoing attachment between former spouses that hampers the process (Bickerdike & Littlefield). If one person holds on to the relationship and resists the end of the marriage while the other strongly wants out and feels much less attached, the success of a satisfactory settlement is at increased risk.

Mediation Content Outcomes

In the context of broader mediation research, attachment and longing for one's former partner are typically considered among the psychological outcome variables mediation is hypothesized to impact, rather than a predictor of mediation outcomes. (Obviously, in this arena, psychological outcome variables can be thought of as important independent *and* dependent variables.) Overall, the corpus of available research does not indicate that mediation (relative to more traditional litigation) serves to either decrease general psychological distress (e.g., anger, sadness or depression, or attachment to one's former spouse) or improve coparenting relationships (see Beck & Sales, 2001; Emery, Laumann-Billings, Waldron, Sbarra, & Dillon, 2001). A number of hypotheses have been offered to explain the lack of differences between mediation and litigation samples on general adjustment variables, including the methodological argument that subtle differences in adjustment between groups may not be adequately assessed by means of typically used outcomes measures that assess the presence of broad-based psychopathology (Emery, 1994).

Beyond measurement issues, a more parsimonious explanation for the lack of mediation and litigation differences is that expectations for overall decreases in psychological distress may be too great (Emery, 1994). As it is generally practiced, especially in court-mandated jurisdictions, custody mediation is a short-term, focused intervention designed to reach a negotiated agreement and not to improve mental health generally. Even when intentionally therapeutic, the overarching goal of mediation is to give voice to parents' concerns and, if necessary, allow them to process their psychological distress in the service of reaching a negotiated agreement. Thus, therapeutic mediation could be said to address mental health outcomes in the short term (in order to move toward an agreed-on dispute resolution), but it does not aim to ameliorate the distress of divorce more generally. In sum, compared with traditional adversarial litigation, the evidence that divorce mediation *causes* better psychological outcomes for adults is equivocal, with many possible explanations for a lack of differences between traditional court services and contemporary alternative dispute practices.

Mediation has proven beneficial in other outcome domains. In our own research from the Charlottesville Mediation Study, we studied whether parents would prefer the mediation process over an adversarial settlement or whether they would favor one dispute resolution alternative in some respects but not in others. In this study (discussed more in the next subsection),

71 couples that petitioned a Juvenile and Domestic Relations Court in Virginia for a contested custody hearing were randomly assigned to either mediate or litigate their dispute. Among the most consistent findings from the study were that, on average, parents preferred mediation to an adversarial settlement, and this relation held on items assessing both the assumed strengths of mediation (e.g., "Your feelings were understood") and the assumed strengths of an adversarial settlement (e.g., "Your rights were protected"). On *both* types of items, mediation consistently came out ahead. Furthermore, parents were more satisfied with mediation than with an adversarial settlement 6 weeks after dispute resolution (Emery, Matthews, & Wyer, 1991; Emery & Wyer, 1987), 1.5 years later (Emery, Matthews, & Kitzmann, 1994), and 12 years following the initial settlement (Emery et al., 2001). Other researchers have also reported finding greater satisfaction with mediation in comparison with an adversarial settlement, and, in general, parties report a high degree of satisfaction with mediation (Beck & Sales, 2001; Jones & Bodtker, 1999; Kelly, 1996). Thus, it can be confidently said that, on the basis of our own findings and those of others, mediation produces higher levels of satisfaction than adversarial methods.

In a long-term follow-up of the Charlottesville sample, parents were recontacted 12 years after their initial custody dispute and interviewed again regarding postdivorce family life (Emery et al., 2001). At follow-up, striking differences were observed between the mediation and litigation groups for continued noncustodial parent involvement in the children's lives. Twelve years after the initial dispute, 30% of nonresidential parents who mediated saw their children once a week or more often, in comparison with only 9% of parents in the adversarial group. At the opposite extreme, 39% of nonresidential parents in the adversarial group had seen their children only once or not at all in the past year compared with 15% in the mediation group. These differences are both substantively important and statistically significant (Emery et al., 2001).

We found an even larger difference for telephone contact, perhaps a better measure of nonresidential involvement given the geographic mobility of both parents over a 12-year period and their children who, at the time of the 12-year follow-up, ranged in age from adolescence to young adulthood. In the mediation group, 54% of nonresidential parents spoke to their children on the telephone once a week or more often, in contrast to 13% in the adversarial group. Once again, at the opposite extreme, 54% of nonresidential parents in the adversarial settlement group had *not* spoken with their children on the telephone in the past year, or had done so only once, in comparison with 12% in the mediation group. These differences are statistically significant (Emery et al., 2001) and, in many ways, startling. Because of the random assignment design of the study, we can conclude with confidence that the overall differences between the mediation and litigation settlement procedures (Emery et al., 1991) *caused* the differences in contact 12 years later. At this time, it is unclear whether these long-term effects are direct or mediated by other factors. Moreover, it remains to be seen whether the causal ingredients for these positive outcomes rest in what is "good" about mediation as opposed to what is "bad" about litigation (a point to which we return later in the chapter).

Although the long-term effects for noncustodial parent involvement and contact are positive, a second report from the follow-up study indicated that mediation may have the unintended effect of keeping participants attached to each other (and nonaccepting of their divorce) over time (Sbarra & Emery, in press). The second follow-up study focused on adults' psychological adjustment more explicitly and used a relatively novel method for addressing incomplete data called multiple imputation (MI), to address sample attrition over time. MI strategies (see Schafer & Olsen, 1998) allow researchers to make the most of limited or incomplete data by statistically imputing complete data sets based on the multivariate relations among the available data. Complete data sets are then simulated, analyses conducted on a subset of complete data sets, and the resulting outcomes then summarized to account for studywise missingness. In this study, our analyses revealed that, compared with parents who litigated their custody dispute, those who mediated reported significantly greater attachment to their former partner at the 12-year follow-up assessment; depression at the follow-up was a significant predictor of concurrent attachment for mothers, and, for fathers, conflict at the follow-up was significantly negatively associated with concurrent attachment, indicating that fathers who reported a cooperative, stable coparenting relationship with their former partner also reported considerably more attachment and regret over the end of the marriage (Sbarra & Emery). These findings underscore a point we have made repeatedly in our work on mediation and grief. Mediators and other who advocate cooperation ask parents to do something emotionally *unnatural* in divorce. Anger, it seems, helps people to disengage emotionally from each other; it may also, at least temporarily, protect individuals from the pain of depression. Put another way, parents who succeed in cooperating in divorce do this for the sake of their children, not themselves. Along with the many benefits for their children, one long-term consequence for themselves is increased longing and regret about what might have been in their marriage. Indeed, considerable research has demonstrated that, following marital dissolution, continued attachment to a former partner is a risk factor for poor mental health outcomes (Amato, 2000; Kiecolt-Glaser et al., 1987; Wang & Amato, 2000).

Although it is not clear from these results whether mediation *caused* increased attachment (by enhancing positive coparenting relationships) or litigation *caused* decreased attachment (by exacerbating acrimony and promoting win–lose solutions, thus further polarizing former partners), one obvious concern for mediation practitioners is whether attending to relationship-level dynamics can compromise individual-level psychological outcomes. It is easy to imagine how former partners who describe their relationship as good and their coparenting as open, warm, and successful may begin to wonder why they decided to end the relationship in the first place, which may result in pining for a former partner or a failure to accept the end of the relationship. By enhancing the relationship, then, mediation may also maintain individual-level attachment and preoccupation with a former partner. Although a degree of connection is likely necessary for maintaining a successful coparenting relationship, the strong association between continued attachment and poor mental health outcomes suggests that mediators should seek to encourage and enhance positive coparenting relationships while also attending to individual-level difficulties in accepting the marital dissolution.

Mediation Research: Methodological Conundrums

From a methodological perspective, three practical obstacles make conducting and evaluating mediation research difficult, and these challenges have to be considered when the extant research literature is interpreted. First, family mediation is practiced in a striking array of different settings by using a number of different intervention models. According to Beck and Sales (2001), in 1997 there were roughly 2,000 alternative dispute programs offered nationwide and roughly 4,500 separate court jurisdictions mandating mediation in contested custody and visitation disputes. Currently, 38 states have legislation regulating family mediation, yet no two states practice mediation in precisely the same way (Tondo et al., 2001). The situation is further complicated by differences in overarching treatment models. All mediation is not created equally, and several different models exist for guiding intervention practices, each making a series of underlying assumptions about how couples negotiate as well as the necessary and sufficient ingredients for reaching a consensus agreement (e.g., Kressel, Frontera, Florenza, Butler, & Fish, 1994). For instance, the legal model of mediation outlined by Coogler (1978) holds that parties are rational and will engage in cooperative mediation practices if mandated to do so. In this form of mediation, few direct efforts are made to deal with the psychological fallout of divorce; mediation is limited to topical content, and very little attention is paid to psychological process variables.

In contrast to legalistic mediation, therapeutic models of mediation hold that the capability for rational decision making can be impinged by underlying relational dynamics. From this perspective, divorcing couples come to the negotiation table with a variety of emotional or cognitive barriers, making adaptive decision making difficult, if not impossible. In such situations, person- or couples-level factors (e.g., depression or continued attachment in one adult, or intense, ongoing acrimony between former partners) impede effective attempts at problem solving (Bickerdike, 1998; Bickerdike & Littlefield, 2001; Emery, 1994; Irving & Benjamin, 1992, 1995). Thus, when the psychological outcomes of mediation for adults are considered the type or kind of mediation and associated assumptions for change and the negotiation process are important factors.

Beyond issues of standardization and differences in intervention models, two other methodological concerns are relevant to answering questions of absolute efficacy, or whether divorce mediation works. Few studies of divorce mediation have relied on random assignment to different treatment conditions, which ultimately limits any conclusions about the effectiveness of mediation services (relative to more traditional litigation) for solving custody or other divorce-related disputes. Consequently, divorce mediation's efficacy remains understudied. The Charlottesville Mediation Study, conducted by Emery and colleagues and described elsewhere (Emery et al., 1991, 1994, 2001; Emery & Wyer, 1987), is the only series of published reports that relied on complete random assignment. In this study, parents petitioning a Juvenile and Domestic Relations Court in Virginia for a child custody hearing were approached at random and asked either to try a program of mediation as an 11th-hour settlement attempt (and also to let us study them) or to participate in a study of the court (i.e., to continue with an adversarial process, but to let us study them). A key to the success of random assignment was obtaining a high degree of agreement to participate. In the end, 71% of the families agreed to try mediation, and 84% of the families agreed to participate in the court study. These rates were imperfect, but no differences were found between those who accepted and those who rejected participation (Emery et al., 1991).

A natural follow-up to the efficacy question is to consider the outcome domains of interest. Typically, mediation is hypothesized to increase party satisfaction, decrease burden on the administration of justice by decreasing rates of relitigation and increasing compliance with court orders, and reduce acrimonious parental relationships by increasing the emotional stability of parents, which is hypothesized to have a positive, downstream effect on the development of children whose parents attend mediation. Thus, determining whether mediation *works* is highly dependent on the outcome in question. Additionally, like other psychological interventions, the question of moderation is also important but understudied. Do some parents but not others report increased satisfaction or emotional stability following mediation? If so, why? One example of moderating effects is sex differences in party satisfaction with mediation and litigation settlements. Among the most robust findings from the Charlottesville study was that mothers were consistently more satisfied with litigation and mediation than fathers (Emery & Wyer, 1987; Emery et al., 1991, 1994). In contrast, Kelly's study of comprehensive mediation in California (Kelly, 1989; Kelly & Gigy, 1989) found few sex differences between mediation or litigation parents. Importantly, a number of differences between the samples may serve to explain the observed sex discrepancies in party satisfaction. The Charlottesville project included a sample of individuals of low socioeconomic status who agreed to mediate only after partitioning the court for a custody hearing; in contrast, the individuals in Kelly's sample had a considerably larger family income and voluntarily sought comprehensive mediation (see Emery, 1994, for a more complete discussion). The background legal environment, although more difficult to characterize, may also explain differences between these studies. Mothers were likely to be the preferred custodians in Virginia, where law changes more slowly, whereas California more rapidly advanced more equal access for both mothers and fathers. This background surely influences mothers' and fathers' experiences of adversary settlement, so the legal backdrop naturally affects parents' experience of mediation relative to litigation (Emery). Hence, a key and nuanced methodological challenge is understanding for whom and under what circumstances mediation works best. In this arena, research is only newly emerging (Beck & Sales, 2001).

Therapeutic Intervention Models: The Practice of Renegotiating Relationships

Research is clear in demonstrating that anger, sadness, and ongoing attachment to one's former partner negatively impact negotiation efforts and agreements within mediation (Bickerdike, 1998; Bikerdike & Littlefield, 2001). As mentioned earlier, therapeutic mediation models seek to address these process variables in the service of enhancing outcomes (Emery, 1994; Irving & Benjamin, 1989, 1995; Schwebel, Gately, Milburn, & Renner, 1994). In this section, we outline the underlying assumptions of this model in greater detail by touching on the importance of separating marital and parenting roles following separation or divorce. To begin, we contend that parents often have difficulty resolving custody disputes effectively because they cannot solve the individual or interpersonal conflicts brought about by their marital distress, separation, and divorce. Thus, negotiating a child custody agreement is as much a psychological task as it is a legal one. Although emotional distress greatly complicates the negotiation of a custody agreement, it is conversely true that the resolution of custody and other legal issues is an important step toward abandoning past conflicts and redefining future family relationships. In this regard, negotiation of a custody settlement is inseparable from the renegotiation of family relationships following divorce.

The main idea underpinning the importance of renegotiating relationships is that partners who are also parents can never fully divorce. The divorced family is still a family (see Emery, 1994), and the feelings, thoughts, and actions of individual family members cannot be understood apart from the broader family system. Although the notion that divorced parents can never be fully divorced may seem ironic, many of the interpersonal and emotional processes involved in divorce can be conceptualized in terms of the family's need to renegotiate and maintain their relationships (Emery). Foremost, this renegotiation process involves the reworking of relationships with children, including the practicalities of how and when each parent will now spend time with the children as well as any new rules for affection, discipline, and household responsibilities. Furthermore, parents need to redefine their relationship with each other, and mediation interventions have the potential to assist individuals negotiate this transition, one that begins well before the "official" end of the marital relationship (cf. Vaughan, 1986). For instance, parents need to make new, practical determinations about how child exchanges will be handled or how to share basic information about the children. At a deeper level, adults need to redefine their boundaries for closeness or distance, frequency and intensity of contact, and ongoing involvement in each other's lives. Some divorced parents remain close, talking frequently on the phone and amiably sharing special family occasions (see Ahrons & Rodgers, 1987). Other parents make a shift toward a more businesslike arrangement for sharing children and discussing the practicalities of parenting. Good coparenting relationships come in a variety of forms, but the key ingredient of a successful relationship is mutual agreement between spouses on what works best for managing their relationship. If one person is consistently fighting his or her partner's efforts to increase distance (by calling frequently, showing up at unexpected times, failing to meet parenting responsibilities, petitioning the court for continued custody disputes, etc.), the renegotiation process cannot be said to be successful.

Therapeutic mediation models of mediation (Emery, 1994; Irving & Benjamin, 1995) can thus be described as assisting parents begin the process of renegotiating their relationship through a formal custody settlement, which plays a central role in redefining boundaries of intimacy between former partners. Emery noted the following:

> A good custody agreement not only spells out boundaries in parent–child relationships by providing very specific information about times and exchanges, but in so doing, it also helps to redefine the boundaries of the former spouses' relationships. By indicating when the children will be with each parent, a carefully written custody agreement helps to establish each parent's autonomy from the other. (p. 40)

Mediation strategies that address the psychological barriers to reaching such an agreement are at the heart of more therapeutic interventions. For example, within the therapeutic family mediation model of Irving and Benjamin, premediation assessments and, if need be, therapy (sometime lasting upward of 10 sessions) are conducted to assess couples' and individuals' levels of psychological readiness to enter into the mediation process. If individuals enter the mediation process resistant to change or ending the marriage, individual premediation therapy is conducted to discuss readiness, explore options, air concerns, and treat underlying depressive symptoms (see Irving & Benjamin, 1989, 1995).

Within Emery's (1994) mediation treatment model, the first few sessions are dedicated to joining with parents to focus on the best interests of their children, allowing the expression of emotion (especially anger) during a problem definition, and holding individual caucuses to provide a further opportunity for emotional ventilation, which is often necessary after affectively charged cojoint sessions defining the topics for dispute resolution. During the first mediation session, typically lasting 2 hr, mediators are also encouraged to highlight parents' shared interests (usually in terms of finding the best possible custody solution for their children). Custody problems are redefined as parenting problems, thus highlighting parents' need and ability to more effectively solve their parenting disputes about custody issues. As mediation continues, Emery's treatment model holds that sessions focus explicitly on the identification and pursuit of specific problems (to be solved) rather than intense emotions. Although emotion is always recognized in later sessions, redirection toward the main goal of mediation (i.e., creating and ratifying an agreeable parenting plan) happens quickly in the later sessions. When strong emotions occur, the goal is not to be therapeutic per se but to prevent strong feelings from clouding substantive discussions by allowing the parents' feelings to be ventilated in a controlled manner. Thus, therapeutic mediation can be said to be solution focused but process minded.

Although the *relative efficacy* of mediation strategies that do versus do not focus on potential psychological barriers to custody settlements remains in question, therapeutic mediation has proven advantageous to traditional adversary settlement procedures in assisting both parents feel like they won what they wanted from the dispute resolution. Emery et al. (1991) tested competing hypotheses about the win–win orientation of mediation versus the win–lose orientation of litigation by calculating the correlations within each group between mothers' and fathers' ratings on the item "[you] won what you wanted." In the mediation sample, the correlation between mothers' and fathers' reports was .33 ($p < .05$), whereas a significant negative relation of $-.43$ ($p < .01$) was observed in the litigation sample. Within the mediation intervention that focused on addressing parents' emotional responses to the marital dissolution experience, the more one parent felt he or she won, the more the other parent felt similarly (Emery et al.).

RELATIONSHIP DISSOLUTION AND GRIEF: THE BASIC SCIENCE OF COGNITIVE-EMOTIONAL ADAPTATION

Thus far, we have surveyed the literature on divorce mediation by highlighting several important methodological challenges, reviewing process and content outcome research, and outlining the basic strategies of therapeutic mediation. Although we have discussed intervention approaches for dealing with postdissolution grief, we have yet to offer a detailed model for understanding how such cognitive-emotional processes operate in the wake of separation or divorce experiences. In this section, we address these topics and argue that basic theoretical and empirical research on the divorce recovery process has much to offer intervention science. We assume that understanding the mechanisms of positive adaptation and elucidating how adults cope (or fail to cope) with dissolution experiences can assist in the pinpointing of the most effective targets for mediation and other applied treatments.

To this end, our discussion and commentary are focused largely around two topics. First, we consider research on cognitive adaptation in the wake of dissolution experience. Applied most completely to the study of chronic illness, cognitive adaptation theory (Helgeson, 1999) holds that successful adjustment to traumatic experiences hinges on individuals' abilities to maintain or develop a positive outlook, gain a sense of personal control or mastery, and restore self-regard. With respect to relationship dissolution, the extent to which adults construct a coherent and organized narrative of their separation experience is expected to be an important predictor of both psychological and physical health outcomes. Mediation interventions, we contend, can play a major role in assisting adults narrate their divorce experience and develop an improved sense of control and heightened self-efficacy. Second, we expand on a model of emotional adaptation that hypothesizes that affective responses to separation experiences are largely cyclical (rather than stagelike), and we review research indicating that within-person variation in emotional recovery is at least as large as between-person differences. In the final section of the chapter, we use these ideas to inform and expand therapeutic models of family mediation.

The Organizing Role of Cognitive Adaptation

Among the vast array of available coping strategies for dealing with stressful life events, the study of cognitive adaptation (Helgeson, 1999), or how individuals come to understand and appraise their experiences, has received considerable research attention, especially with respect to how people cope with loss and other traumas. Stressful life events have a high potential to disturb psychological balance, and, in particular, cognitive worldviews of life as meaningful and comprehensible (Baumeister, 1991). Traumatic events, including divorce, threaten one's sense of self and beliefs that the world is just and life events are controllable and nonrandom (Taylor, 1983). Several studies have found that the positive beliefs typically associated with control are linked to positive physiological states (Futterman, Kemeny, Shapiro, & Fahey, 1994; Segerstrom, Taylor, Kemeny, & Fahey, 1998; Taylor et al., 1992). Reed and colleagues (Reed, Kemeny, Taylor, & Visscher, 1999), for instance, found that positive expectations regarding one's health, feelings of confidence and optimism, and a greater sense of control over one's disease were associated with a slower progression of HIV-related illness among HIV-positive bereaved men. Alternatively, numerous laboratory studies have found that both experimentally induced unpredictability and stable individual differences of personal mastery promote greater physiological arousal to acutely stressful events (see Pham, Taylor, & Seeman, 2001).

The notion of cognitive processing suggests that something happens over time—a process unfolds that moves individuals from a state of uncertainty to one of confidence, optimism, and self-efficacy (see Harvey & Fine, chap. 10, this volume). Research on narratives following loss and other stressful life events suggests that individuals who are able to construct an organized and coherent account of a painful event benefit, because thoughts and feelings can be more completely integrated (Capps & Bonanno, 2000; Pennebaker & Francis, 1996; Pennebaker, Mayne, & Francis, 1997; Pennebaker & Seagal, 1999). In one of the only studies connecting cognitions to health outcomes following social loss, Bower, Kemeny, Taylor, and Fahey (1998) reported that finding meaning by making a major shift in values, priorities, or perspective in response to loss by means of cognitive processing (e.g., defined as verbal statements reflecting deliberative, effortful, or lasting thinking about the death) was associated with less rapid CD4+ decline and rates of AIDS-related mortality among 40 HIV-seropositive men who lost a close friend or partner to AIDS within the past year. For these men, finding meaning following AIDS-related bereavement proved biologically protective, even after a number of known predictors of HIV progression were controlled for (Bower et al.). Bower et al. concluded that finding meaning may buffer stress-related changes in the Autonomic Nervous System, Hypothalmic-pituitary Axis, or may have direct beneficial effects on these systems (also see Taylor, Kemeny, Reed, Bower, & Gruenewald, 2000).

Although no studies to date have detailed how these processes might operate following marital dissolution, mediation interventions aimed at assisting adults gain a sense of cognitive adaptation, control, and personal mastery may attenuate *both* physical and psychological stress responses by providing a sense of limited or partial closure to the divorce experience. In other words, mediation can help adults close the first stressful chapter of their divorce experience. Furthermore, successful mediation agreements may help parents redefine new roles within the postdivorce family, a process that enhances control and self-efficacy (Emery, 1994). Of course, such interventions are not panaceas, and it is expected that the stress of dissolution and the associated emotions of love, anger, sadness, guilt, and frustration will emerge again over time. In fact, as we suggest in the next section, the potentially *revocable* nature of the divorce experience virtually ensures that the emotional pain of marital separation will emerge as parents continue to negotiate the transition out of marriage and into postdivorce family life.

The Emotional Sequelae of Marital Dissolution

The concept of grief has a long and rich tradition in clinical psychology and clinical lore (Averill, 1968; Freud, 1957), and, as an organizing construct, it is commonly invoked to understand the affective, cognitive, behavioral, and physiological or somatic responses that characterize how individuals cope with loss (Nolen-Hoeksema & Larson, 1999). Grief responses are typically regarded as the cognitions and behaviors that people use to assess, reduce stress, and moderate the affective tensions that accompany stressful loss events (Bonanno, 2001). In an effort to provide a winning theoretical account of affective responses to marital dissolution, Emery (1994) proposed a normative theoretical model for understanding how individuals emotionally cope with divorce. The model has a number of direct implications for the practice of family mediation: It specifies typical and atypical patterns of emotion regulation over time, points to important emotional differences between partners who leave the marriage and who feel left, and operationalizes the construct of resolution of loss.

An underlying and important component of Emery's (1994) conceptualization is that the loss of a close romantic relationship is potentially revocable. This perspective differs from common conceptualizations of grief that concentrate on coping following permanent and ir-revocable losses, such as the death of one's partner (Wortman & Silver, 2001). Investigators

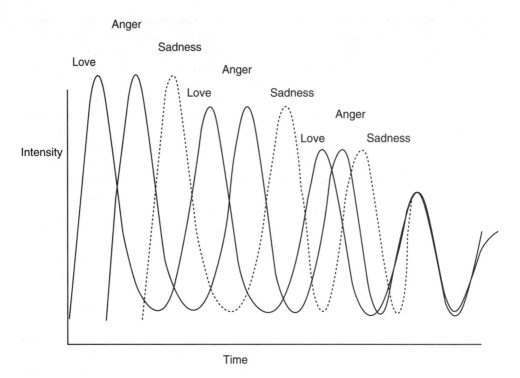

FIG. 27.1. Process Model Depicting Cyclical Changes in Love, Anger, and Sadness Following Relationship Dissolution.

have increasingly acknowledged that how individuals cope with or grieve potentially revocable losses, such as the dissolution of romantic bonds, represents an important area of study (Crosby, Lybarger, & Mason, 1986; Hazan & Shaver, 1992; Weiss, 1975, 1976, 2001) and one that can inform research on both attachment and emotion regulation (Fraley & Shaver, 1999; Vormbrock, 1993). However unrealistic, the possibility of reunion is always present among divorced couples and, in many cases, the emotional sequelae of dissolution can be easily activated and reactivated well after final dispute resolution. A phone call (wanted or unwanted), a child exchange, or a shared holiday all provide repeated opportunities for reexperiencing the pain of separation. Admittedly, individuals grieving permanent losses are also charged with negotiating potent reminders of their relationship—important dates or anniversaries, for example—but it is our contention that the always present possibility of reconciliation (following divorce) fundamentally changes the nature of the emotional grief process by inhibiting a stagelike resolution of loss.

The distinction between revocable and irrevocable loss has important implications for the coping process. Emery's (1994) model, shown in Fig. 27.1, is organized around three main assumptions that capitalize on the potentially revocable nature of the end of romantic relationships. First, central to this model is the simultaneous existence of three competing emotions: love, anger, and sadness. From this perspective, *love* includes the intense longing that follows separation from a loved one, as well as vague hopes for reconciliation, guilt-ridden concern, and related emotions that cause one person to want to move closer to another. *Anger* refers to a variety of affective states ranging from feelings of frustration and resentment to the far more intense fury or rage that is commonly experienced in divorce. *Sadness* refers to a constellation of associated feelings including loneliness, depression, and despair. Unlike anger, these feelings are directed inward toward the self, rather than outward toward the other. Rather than a linear progression from distress to resolution, the grief process, as shown in Fig. 27.1, is characterized by constant cycling back and forth between the conflicted feelings of longing for a partner, being saddened by the end of the relationship, and feeling frustrated with and resentful toward this person. The model also allows for specific hypotheses regarding atypical patterns of emotional grief reactions. An individual who maintains, for example, elevated levels of anger and frustration with a former partner without experiencing associated feelings of longing or sadness would be described as being "stuck" in anger. Hence, the predominance or maintained elevation of any one emotional state is hypothesized to portend an atypical grief reaction.

The second underlying assumption of the model is that, as the process unfolds over time, it is expected that competing emotions come into phase and diminish in intensity. The resolution of grief thus represents an ability to simultaneously recognize and experience the triad of emotional states without getting stuck on any one set of feelings. Grieving can be assumed to be complete (or as complete as it ever will be) when individuals can acknowledge that they are saddened by the loss of their marriage, and that they are angered by all that has happened, and yet they can also experience some warm memories about the past and regrets about what might have been in the future. Emery (1994) described this state of emotional integration in which a person has access to the array of feelings associated with divorce but is not overwhelmed by or trying to suppress any one of them.

Finally, consistent with evidence in the divorce literature indicating that adults who perceive themselves as left by their partner frequently report increased distress and nonacceptance of relationship termination (Kiecolt-Glaser et al., 1987; Thompson & Spanier, 1983; Wang & Amato, 2000), key differences exist in the experience of grief for the leaver and the left. The leaver's emotions are expected to be less intense because they typically evolve over the course of preparing to end the relationship (Vaughn, 1986). The partner who is left has had little time to prepare for the loss and experiences an elevated rate of emotional intensity based on this suddenness.

The Emery (1994) conceptualization of grief also can be understood as a control systems theory of affect regulation (see Simpson & Rholes, 1998). From this perspective, the oscillatory nature of the model represents a person's emotional dysregulation following a separation experience. One of the primary purposes of normative attachment across the life span is the maintenance of felt security, and the importance of adult love relationships for affect regulation has been repeatedly demonstrated (Diamond, 2001; Feeney, 1995). From this perspective, the emotional disorganization that individuals frequently experience when dissolving a love relationship can be conceptualized in terms of the removal of the functional components of the attachment system. Following relationship dissolution, adults are charged with attempting to maintain and regain emotional homeostasis (i.e., felt security) while battling multiple pangs of separation distress. A critical point underlying control systems models is that differences in the observable emotion may serve the same underlying function, and this issue is frequently discussed in terms of the functional purpose of individual differences in child and adult attachment styles (see Weinfield, Sroufe, Egeland, & Carlson, 1999). Hence, following divorce, understanding person-level emotional dynamics is as critical as making broad nomothetic generalizations (Sbarra & Emery, 2004). From this perspective, patterns of intraindividual, within-person variations in love, anger, and sadness can become important between-person grouping variables.

Grieving Relationship Loss: An Empirical Example

In an effort in investigate these ideas empirically, Sbarra and Emery (2004) conducted a daily diary investigation of emotional coping among 58 young adult college students who recently dissolved a committed dating relationship lasting a mean of 20 months. Although the emotional response to nonmarital breakups and divorce likely differ in amount and kind, investigating the affective experiences of college students provides a controlled setting for studying short-term responses to breakup experiences. Following recruitment into the study, the 58 participants (48 women, 10 men) completed an initial intake interview that assessed their history in the most recent relationship, their attachment styles, the emotional impact of the dissolution event, and their continued longing for their former partner. Then, each person was equipped with a beeper signaling device and paper-and-pencil daily diary assessing four key emotions: love, anger, sadness, and relief. In addition to the emotion scales, a single diary item assessed whether participants had any contact with their former partner. Participants were signaled once a day at random times (between 10 a.m. and 10 p.m.), at which time they were asked to make a brief rating of their current emotions regarding the breakup experiences.

For the purposes of the current discussion of emotional grief and consideration of potential applications to divorce mediation, we discuss two findings from this study (for more details, see Sbarra & Emery, 2004). First, the results demonstrated that underlying emotional change processes can be identified and modeled, and that contact with one's former partner (be it "good" or "bad") stalls the trajectory of recovery for love and sadness over time. Multilevel growth modeling was used to identify the underlying model of change for each of the four core emotions, and the results indicated that reports of love, anger, and sadness could all be charac-terized as variants of linear growth over time, whereas relief followed a quadratic decreasing and then increasing trend. Time-varying and time-invariant covariates were then added to the models to determine whether within-occasion contact with a former partner stalls the decline of these emotions and whether between-person variables (such as attachment style, emotional intrusion, and ongoing longing) measured at intake predict individuals' initial starting point for each emotion and the rate of decline over time. For love and sadness, contact was significantly positively associated with within-occasion reports of these emotions, indicating that partic-ipants reporting personal contact (vs. no contact) with their former partner at any occasion also had significantly higher love and sadness scores. Of particular interest is that the type of contact was irrelevant to the association; whether individuals reported positive or negative experiences with their former partner, they reported increased love and sadness, which slowed the underlying trajectory of recovery.

Second, consistent with the Emery (1994) model, within-person variation in daily emotion played an important role in predicting between-person mental health outcomes, and this relation was especially true for sadness variability. In hierarchical regressions predicting general emo-tional disturbance (measured by the Mood and Anxiety Symptom Checklist, Watson & Clark, 1991, which assesses features common to both mood and anxiety disorders) at the end of the 28-day diary person, mean sadness variability (computed as the average daily variability around one's mean sadness score over time) explained 7% of adjusted variance after other significant covariates and mean sadness were controlled. Thus, the extent to which participants varied in their daily reports of sadness predicted depression and anxiety at the end of the dissolution study. Although this variability–outcome relation was observed only for sadness and not for love or anger, considering intraindividual variability as a predictor of psychological adjustment offers a potentially useful way of thinking about how adults regulate their emotions following breakup. Divorcing adults, for example, commonly report feeling lost, confused, and emotionally scat-tered (Weiss, 1975). Hetherington and Kelly (2002) suggested that this type of emotional lability is much more of the norm than the exception in the first year after divorce. Although these ideas are appealing from a clinical perspective, few investigations have tackled them em-pirically, and even fewer efforts have been made to conceptualize this process as one of basic emotion regulation. The evidence from the present study suggests that, at least for generalized mood disturbance, patterns of intraindividual variability can emerge as important predictors of between-person outcomes.

REVISITING DIVORCE MEDIATION: TREATMENT IMPLICATIONS FROM BASIC SCIENCE

In this final section of the chapter, we turn our attention back to mediation interventions and pull from the larger literature on adaptation to divorce in order to make recommendations for continued mediation practice and research. Although research on cognitive adaptation and cyclical emotional responding following divorce clearly awaits more detailed study, several treatment implications for mediation can be culled from these areas of basic science. Recently, Beck and Sales (2001) argued for improving mediation research by borrowing from available research strategies in the larger psychotherapy treatment literature. One important element of treatment outcome research is component or dismantling studies, which compare treatment as usual (TAU) conditions to an enhanced or alternative version of the TAU that includes the addition of a few specific ingredients. If the new treatment improves on the TAU in a randomized controlled research study, strong causal conclusions can be drawn about the power of the specific ingredients for promoting change.

In mediation research, TAUs come in a variety of forms; nonetheless, component studies that add additional interventions provide an excellent means of determining which types of mediation work and for whom (see Beck & Sales, 2001). (It should be noted that making specific ingredient conclusions when comparing mediation with traditional litigation is extremely difficult because, even in a random assignment situation, it is unclear whether differences in outcomes can be attributed to the benefits of alternative dispute resolution or the potentially harmful consequences of adversarial litigation.) Given the importance of component designs, the four clinical and research recommendations we outline here can be used as add-ons to clinical research studies to determine if enhancing therapeutic mediation leads to increased consumer satisfaction, improved mediation process, and better coparenting. Although we describe each of these recommendations as a distinct phenomenon, there are many areas of overlap.

1. Mediation Should be Psychoeducational

Most therapeutic mediation programs begin with a degree of education, outlining the divorce process, highlighting the importance of stable coparenting for child development, and generally discussing appropriate expectations for postdivorce family life (see Beck & Sales, 2001; Emery, 1994; Emery et al., 2004; Irving & Benjamin, 1995). We believe the process of educating parents can go further still and be therapeutic in and of itself. One successful example of therapeutic psychoeducation comes from research on interpersonal psychotherapy, or IPT (Klerman, Chevron, & Weissman, 1994), which has proven to be an effective intervention for the treatment of clinical depression. Chief among IPT interventions is the identification and explanation of the "sick" role in depression, which is specifically designed to educate patients by helping them view depression as a medical illness, relieving some of the pressure that depressed patients put on themselves for their own recovery, and describing depression as a problem outside of them rather than a core character deficit. Like the IPT benefits of clarifying the so-called sick role for depressed patients, we believe that helping adults understand two important components about their divorce process can enhance positive adaptation and the process of mediation. First, we hypothesize that normalizing the stress associated with marital dissolution can promote calm and resolution of loss by increasing self-efficacy and perceived control. To this end, we have found that the following explanation is useful for separating adults and can be easily explained during individual caucuses within mediation:

> This experience of being in a relationship like marriage helps us stay calm and maintain a degree of psychological security, even in the face of a great deal of acrimony. When relationships dissolve, the resulting stress can be wide ranging. Some people feel physically ill; some people feel a vague sense of physical discomfort; some people feel like their heart is truly broken. All of these outcomes are an expectable part of the divorce process. Despite the pain of dissolution, we are ultimately charged with finding new ways to regulate ourselves. Overall, you might think of the process as one of being off balance; your central job during this postdivorce period is to find a way to establish balance without getting stuck in anger or sadness over the end of the relationship.

Normalizing the dysregulation process can go a long way toward helping adults view the stressful disruptions of divorce as natural and expectable outcomes while also communicating to individuals that they are now responsible for calming themselves and finding balance. Our second psychoeducational suggestion is to discuss the social psychology of loss and individuals' fundamental need to see the world as meaningful and controllable. Divorce shatters many adults' expectations for themselves and their relationships, and helping divorcing parents understand the ways in which their separation experience has violated their assumptions of the social world can assist in the recovery process. Viewing divorce from this perspective necessarily involves a discussion of loss. Some parents are so entrenched in ongoing custody battles that they have trouble recognizing that divorce is, indeed, a loss event and, like all loss events, involves redefinition of the self (Emery, 1994). From this perspective, helping adults view their separation experience as one that requires a personal redefinition can also help them begin the process of renegotiating family relationships in a more complete way.

2.   Mediation Can Assist in the Narration of One's Divorce

Considerable research evidence indicates that adults who are able to make sense of stressful live events by creating coherent, organized, and meaningful personal narratives demonstrate improved psychological and physical health outcomes (see Harvey & Fine, chap. 10, this volume). Our second recommendation builds off the first by suggesting that satisfactory mediation agreements can enhance adults' narration of their divorce experience by providing parents with a rule-governed contract that is coherent, organized, and personally meaningful. Of course, even therapeutic mediation does not seek, nor should it, to assist adults understand why they got divorced, what role they played in the end of the marriage, and what they now want out of their life from here. When we suggest that mediation can assist in the narration of divorce, we are referring to the importance of a mutually satisfying problem definition in the practice of mediation (see Emery, 1994). Parents come to the mediation negotiation with a variety of wants and hopes, and, in many cases, feeling that deeply entrenched custody disagreements cannot be solved. In assisting parents identify and outline *solvable* parenting problems to be discussed, mediators instill a degree of hope and control while promoting cognitive adaptation. In turn, parents can replace "this is terrible, we always fight and never solve anything" ideas with more adaptive beliefs such as "this is hard, but I think we can get together on this . . . in fact, I know we can and we've already done it." Research aimed at these outcomes should seek to measure them explicitly. If therapeutic mediations interventions designed to assist the narration and cognitive adaptation process work well, then corresponding changes in perceived control and self-efficacy should be observable.

3. Mediation Should Attend to the Reactivation of Attachment

Earlier in this chapter, we reviewed evidence suggesting that a possible unintended effect of improving coparenting abilities by means of divorce mediation may be to keep parents attached to each other in a potentially unhealthy way by (Sbarra & Emery, in press). More proximally, our prospective study of nonmarital breakups indicated that contact with one's former partner slows the underlying trajectories of recovery for love and sadness over time (Sbarra & Emery, 2004). Both sets of results have direct implications for mediation practice. As an overarching framework, mediators need to attend to both couple- and individual-level psychological dynamics. Although enhancing coparenting is among the main goals of therapeutic mediation, addressing only relationship-level topics or problems fails the individuals within the relationship. Indeed, being aware of the emotional sequelae of contact with one's former partner is critical for both mediators and divorcing adults.

Practically, these issues can be explained to adults in terms of the need to separate marital and parental roles, and Emery (1994) has outlined a model for doing so. Adults who are stuck on longing for their former partner cannot be said to have let go their role as a married partner, at least in terms of their psychological adjustment. Furthermore, because divorced parents can never truly divorce, we believe a useful heuristic for renegotiating the marital and parental roles is the concept of autonomy-relatedness. Parents who seek a successful divorce (i.e., one that exists without intense, unsolvable acrimony or that does not exacerbate longing and regret) have two relational goals: become autonomous from their former partners and begin a new life while also maintaining a degree of relatedness that enables successful coparenting without compromising their own autonomy. Mediation can help parents understand that the risk of ongoing contact or cooperation also is ongoing attachment to one's former partner, which can ultimately compromise individual well-being. Armed with this knowledge and the twin mantras of renegotiating marital and parental roles and maintaining autonomy with relatedness, we believe that many parents will be able to attend to the coparenting relationships while also monitoring their own potential feelings of longing or regret. Elsewhere (Emery, 1999, 2004; Emery et al., in press), we have suggested that this process involves developing a businesslike relationship between former partners. Viewing the coparenting relationship from this perspective often helps parents contain fighting as well as their own hopes and expectations for better outcomes. A difficult and stressful interaction with one's former partner is attributed to the business of coparenting.

4. Mediation Can Promote Emotional Integration

Emery's (1994) model of cyclical emotional adaptation to divorce suggests that the experience of being stuck in a single emotional state (which, following divorce, typically involves one of three major affective states: love, anger, and sadness) signifies an atypical grief reaction. Emotional resolution of the divorce, in contrast, is seen when adults have easy access to their feelings and can simultaneously experience love, anger, and sadness. From this model, it can be hypothesized that therapeutic mediation interventions seeking to promote emotional integration would enhance the process of mediation and lead to increased agreements over TAUs that do not focus on emotion within mediation. The research of Bickerdike and Littlefield (2001) demonstrates that adults stuck on anger have difficulty engaging in the process of mediation, as do individuals who remain highly attached (i.e., stuck on love) when their partners are not.

Emery (1994) has argued that mediators can address atypical grief in individual caucus meetings providing empathy, support, and reflection as well as allowing for the venting of varied emotions and pulling for missing affective states. Regarding the latter point, a husband who presents to mediation furious at his wife for seeking sole custody of their children is likely harboring a great deal of sadness and regret. Although the anger is certainly real and justified, the process of legitimizing other affective states may loosen the husband's hold on anger and thereby enhance the process of mediation. A treatment strategy we use to address this topic is asking every mediation client, prior to an individual caucus, to think about the associated feelings of love, anger, and sadness, and, when parents seem willing and able, come to session prepared to discuss their emotions about their divorce as well as their practical hopes for mediation. For practitioners, it is important to realize one does not need to be a clinical psychologist to implement this kind of emotional support. We believe that providing a nonjudgmental and supportive forum for the airing of emotional grievances is both necessary and sufficient to exact emotional change. Creating this environment is never easy, but it is an endeavor that can enhance mediation agreements by helping adults move from positions of emotional distress to a greater degree of emotional resolution.

REFERENCES

Ahrons, C. R., & Rodgers, R. H. (1987). *Divorced families: A multidisciplinary developmental view.* New York: Norton.

Amato, P. R. (2000). The consequences of divorce for adults and children. *Journal of Marriage and the Family, 62,* 1269–1287.

Aseltin, R. H., & Kessler, R. C. (1993). Marital disruption and depression in a community sample. *Journal of Health and Social Behavior, 34,* 237–251.

Averill, J. R. (1968). Grief: Its nature and significance. *Psychological Bulletin, 70,* 721–748.

Baumeister, R. F. (1991). *Meanings of life.* New York: Guilford.

Beck, C. J. A., & Sales, B. D. (2001). *Family mediation: Facts, myths, and future prospects.* Washington, DC: American Psychological Association.

Bickerdike, A. J. (1998). *Conflict resolution in divorce mediation: The impact of the divorce adjustment process and negotiation behaviour on mediation outcomes.* Unpublished doctoral dissertation, LaTrobe University, Melbourne, Australia.

Bickerdike, A. J., & Littlefield, L. (2001). Divorce adjustment and mediation: Theoretically grounded process research. *Mediation Quarterly, 18,* 1–23.

Bonanno, G. A. (2001). Grief and emotion: A social-functional perspective. In M. Stroebe, R. O. Hannson, W. Stroebe, & H. Schut (Eds.), *Handbook of bereavement research: Consequences, coping, and care* (pp. 493–515). Washington, DC: American Psychological Association.

Bower, J. E., Kemeny, M. E., Taylor, S. E., & Fahey, J. L. (1998). Cognitive processing, discovery of meaning, CD4+ decline, and AIDS-related mortality among bereaved HIV-seropositive men. *Journal of Consulting and Clinical Psychology, 66,* 979–986.

Capps, L., & Bonanno, G. A. (2000). Narrative bereavement: Thematic and grammatical predictors of adjustment to loss. *Discourse Processes, 30,* 1–25.

Coogler, O. J. (1978). *Structured mediation in divorce settlement: A handbook for marital mediators.* Lexington, MA: Heath.

Crosby, J. F., Lybarger, S. K., & Mason, R. L. (1986). The grief resolution process in divorce: Phase II. *Journal of Divorce and Remarriage, 10,* 17–40.

Diamond, L. M. (2001). Contributions of psychophysiology to research on adult attachment: Review and recommendations. *Personality and Social Psychology Review, 5,* 276–295.

Emery, R. E. (1990). Divorce mediation: A practice in search of a theory. *Contemporary Psychology, 35,* 373–374.

Emery, R. E. (1994). *Renegotiating family relationships: Divorce, child custody, and mediation.* New York: Guilford.

Emery, R. E. (1999). *Marriage, divorce, and children's adjustment* (2nd ed.). Thousand Oaks, CA: Sage.

Emery, R. E. (2004). *The truth about children and divorce: Dealing with the emotions so you and your children can thrive.* New York: Viking/Penguin.

Emery, R. E., Kitzmann, K. M., & Waldron, M. (Eds.). (1999). *Psychological interventions for separated and divorced families.* Mahwah, NJ: Lawrence Erlbaum Associates.

Emery, R. E., Laumann-Billings, L., Waldron, M., Sbarra, D. A., & Dillon, P. (2001). Child custody mediation and litigation: Custody, contact, and co-parenting 12 years after initial dispute resolution. *Journal of Consulting and Clinical Psychology, 69,* 323–332.

Emery, R. E., Matthews, S. G., & Kitzmann, K. M. (1994). Child custody mediation and litigation: Parents' satisfaction and functioning one year after settlement. *Journal of Consulting and Clinical Psychology, 62,* 124–129.

Emery, R. E., Matthews, S. G., & Wyer, M. M. (1991). Child custody mediation and litigation: Further evidence on the differing views of mothers and fathers. *Journal of Consulting and Clinical Psychology, 59,* 410–418.

Emery, R. E., Sbarra, D. A., & Grover, T. (2005). Divorce mediation: Research and reflections. *Family and Conciliation Courts Review, 43,* 22–37.

Emery, R. E., & Wyer, M. M. (1987). Child custody mediation and litigation: An experimental evaluation of the experience of parents. *Journal of Consulting and Clinical Psychology, 55,* 179–186.

Feeney, J. A. (1995). Adult attachment and emotional control. *Personal Relationships, 2,* 143–159.

Fraley, R. C., & Shaver, P. R. (1999). Loss and bereavement: Attachment theory and recent controversies concerning "grief work" and the nature of detachment. In J. Cassidy & P. R. Shaver (Eds.), *Handbook of attachment: Theory, research, and clinical applications.* (pp. 735–759). New York: Guilford.

Freud, S. (1957). Mourning and melancholia. In J. Strachey (Ed.), *The standard edition of the complete psychological works of Sigmund Freud, vol. 14* (pp. 152–170). London: Hogarth. (Original work published in 1917)

Funder, K., Harrison, M., & Weston, R. (1993). *Settling down: Pathways of parents after divorce.* Melbourne, Australia: Australian Institute of Family Studies.

Futterman, A. D., Kemeny, M. E., Shapiro, D., & Fahey, J. L. (1994). Immunological and physiological changes associated with induced positive and negative mood. *Psychosomatic Medicine, 56,* 499–511.

Gotlib, I., & McCabe, S. B. (1990). Marriage and psychopathology. In F. D. Fincham & T. N. Bradbury (Eds.), *The psychology of marriage* (pp. 226–257). New York: Guilford.

Hazan, C., & Shaver, P. R. (1992). Broken attachments: Relationship loss from the perspective of attachment theory. In T. L. Orbuch (Ed.), *Close relationship loss* (pp. 90–110). New York: Springer-Verlag.

Heister, J. W. (1985). Sequential mediation—a necessary therapeutic intervention technique. *Mediation Quarterly, 9,* 57–61.

Helgeson, V. S. (1999). Applicability of cognitive adaptation theory to predicting adjustment to heart disease after coronary angioplasty. *Health Psychology, 18,* 561–569.

Hetherington, E. M., & Kelly, J. (2002). *For better or for worse: Divorce reconsidered.* New York: Norton.

Irving, H. H., & Benjamin, M. (1989). Therapeutic family mediation: Fitting the service to the interactional diversity of client couples. *Mediation Quarterly, 7,* 115–131.

Irving, H. H., & Benjamin, M. (1992). An evaluation of process and outcome in a private family mediation service. *Mediation Quarterly, 10,* 35–55.

Irving, H. H., & Benjamin, M. (1995). *Family mediation: Contemporary issues.* Thousand Oaks, CA: Sage.

Jones, T. S., & Bodtker, A. (1999). Agreement, maintenance, satisfaction and relitigation in mediated and non-mediated custody cases: A research note. *Journal of Divorce and Remarriage, 32,* 17–31.

Kelly, J. B. (1989). Mediated and adversarial divorce: Respondents' perceptions of their processes and outcomes. *Mediation Quarterly, 24,* 71–88.

Kelly, J. B. (1990). Is mediation less expensive? *Mediation Quarterly, 8,* 15–25.

Kelly, J. B. (1996). A decade of divorce mediation research: Some answers and questions. *Family and Conciliation Courts Review, 34,* 373–385.

Kelly, J. B., & Gigy, L. (1989). Divorce mediation: Characteristics of clients and outcomes. In K. Kressel & D. G. Pruitt (Eds.), *Mediation research* (pp. 263–283). San Francisco: Jossey-Bass.

Kiecolt-Glaser, J. K., Fisher, L. D., Ogrocki, P., Stout, J. C., Speicher, C. E., & Glaser, R. (1987). Marital quality, marital disruption, and immune function. *Psychosomatic Medicine, 49,* 13–34.

Kiecolt-Glaser, J. K., Kennedy, S., Malkoff, S., Fisher, L., Speicher, C. E., & Glaser, R. (1988). Marital discord and immunity in males. *Psychosomatic Medicine, 50,* 213–229.

Kitson, G. C. (1982). Attachment to the spouse in divorce: A scale and its application. *Journal of Marriage and the Family, 44,* 379–391.

Klerman, G. L., Chevron, E. S., & Weissman, M. W. (1994). *Interpersonal psychotherapy of depression.* New York: HarperCollins.

Kressel, K., Frontera, E. A., Florenza, S., Butler, F., & Fish, L. (1994). The settlement oriented vs. the problem-solving style in custody mediation. *Journal of Social Issues, 50,* 67–84.

Mathis, R. D., & Yingling, L. C. (1991). Spousal consensus on the divorce decision and mediation outcome. *Family and Conciliation Courts Review, 29,* 56–62.

Monroe, S. M., Rohde, P., Seeley, J. R., & Lewinsohn, P. M. (1999). Life events and depression in adolescence: Relationship loss as a prospective risk factor for first onset of major depressive disorder. *Journal of Abnormal Psychology, 108,* 606–614.

Myers, S., Gallas, G., Hanson, R., & Keilitz, S. (1988). Divorce mediation in the states: Institutionalization, use, and assessment. *State Court Journal, 4,* 17–25.

Nolen-Hoeksema, S., & Larson, J. (1999). *Coping with loss.* Mahwah, NJ: Lawrence Erlbaum Associates.

Pennebaker, J. W., & Francis, M. E. (1996). Cognitive, emotional, and language processes in disclosure. *Cognition and Emotion, 10,* 601–626.

Pennebaker, J. W., Mayne, T. J., & Francis, M. E. (1997). Linguistic predictors of adaptive bereavement. *Journal of Personality and Social Psychology, 72,* 863–871.

Pennebaker, J. W., & Seagal, J. D. (1999). Forming a story: The health benefits of narrative. *Journal of Clinical Psychology, 55,* 1243–1254.

Pham, L. B., Taylor, S. E., & Seeman, T. E. (2001). Effects of environmental predictability and personal mastery on self-regulatory and physiological processes. *Personality & Social Psychology Bulletin, 27,* 611–620.

Reed, G. M., Kemeny, M. E., Taylor, S. E., & Visscher, B. R. (1999). Negative HIV-specific expectancies and AIDS-related bereavement as predictors of symptom onset in asymptomatic HIV-positive gay men. *Health Psychology, 18,* 354–363.

Sbarra, D. A., & Emery, R. E. (in press). The emotional sequelae of non-marital relationship dissolution: Analysis of change and intraindividual variability over time. *Personal Relationships.*

Sbarra, D. A., & Emery, R. E. (in press). Co-parenting conflict, nonacceptance, and depression among divorced adults: Results from a 12-year follow-up study of child custody mediation using multiple imputation. *American Journal of Orthopsychiatry.*

Schafer, J. L., & Olsen, M. K. (1998). Multiple imputation for multivariate-missing data problems: A data analyst's perspective. *Multivariate Behavioral Research, 33,* 545–571.

Schwebel, A. L., Gately, D. W., Milburn, T. W., & Renner, M. A. (1993). PMI-DM: A divorce mediation approach that first addresses interpersonal issues. *Journal of Family Psychotherapy, 4,* 69–90.

Segerstrom, S. C., Taylor, S. E., Kemeny, M. E., & Fahey, J. L. (1998). Optimism is associated with mood, coping and immune change in response to stress. *Journal of Personality and Social Psychology, 74,* 1646–1655.

Simpson, J. A., & Rholes, W. S. (1998). Attachment in adulthood. In J. A. Simpson & W. S. Rholes (Eds.), *Attachment theory and close relationships* (pp. 3–24). New York: Guilford.

Taylor, S. E. (1983). Adjustment to threatening events: A theory of cognitive adaptation. *American Psychologist, 38,* 1161–1173.

Taylor, S. E., Kemeny, M. E., Aspinwall, L. G., Schneider, S. G., Rodriguez, R., & Herbert, M. (1992). Optimism, coping, psychological distress, and high-risk sexual behavior among men at risk for acquired immunodeficiency syndrome (AIDS). *Journal of Personality and Social Psychology, 63,* 460–473.

Taylor, S. E., Kemeny, M. E., Reed, G. M., Bower, J. E., & Gruenewald, T. L. (2000). Psychological resources, positive illusions, and health. *American Psychologist, 55,* 99–109.

Thompson, L., & Spanier, G. B. (1983). The end of marriage and the acceptance of marital termination. *Journal of Marriage and the Family, 45,* 101–113.

Tondo, C.-A., Coronel, R., & Drucker, B. (2001). Mediation trends: A survey of states. *Family Court Review, 39,* 431–753.

Vaughan, D. (1986). *Uncoupling: Turning points in intimate relationships.* New York: Vintage Books.

Vormbrock, J. K. (1993). Attachment theory as applied to wartime and job-related marital separation. *Psychological Bulletin, 114,* 122–144.

Wang, H., & Amato, P. R. (2000). Predictors of divorce adjustment: Stressors, resources, and definitions. *Journal of Marriage and the Family, 62,* 655–668.

Watson, D., & Clark, L. A. (1991). *The mood and anxiety symptom questionnaire.* Unpublished manuscript, University of Iowa, Department of Psychology.

Weinfield, N. S., Sroufe, L. A., Egeland, B., & Carlson, E. A. (1999). The nature of individual differences in infant–caregiver attachment. In J. Cassidy & P. R. Shaver (Eds.), *Handbook of attachment: Theory, research, and clinical applications* (pp. 68–88). New York: Guilford.

Weiss, R. S. (1975). *Marital separation.* New York: Basic Books.

Weiss, R. S. (1976). The emotional impact of marital separation. *Journal of Social Issues, 32,* 135–145.

Weiss, R. S. (2001). Grief, bonds, and relationships. In M. Stroebe, R. O. Hannson, W. Stroebe, & H. Schut (Eds.), *Handbook of bereavement research: Consequences, coping, and care* (pp. 47–62). Washington, DC: American Psychological Association.

Wolchik, S. A., Sandler, I. N., Millsap, R. E., Plummer, B. A., Greene, S. M., Anderson, E. R., Dawson-McCluve, S. R. Hioke, K., & Haine R. A. (2002). Six-year follow-up of preventive interventions for children of divorce. A randomized controlled trial. *Journal of the American Medical Association, 288,* 1874–1881.

Wolchik, S. A., West, S. G., Sandler, I. N., Tein, J.-Y., Coatsworth, D., Lengua, L., Weiss, L., Anderson, E. R., Greene, S. M., & Griffin, W. A. (2000). An experimental evaluation of theory-based mother and mother–child programs for children of divorce. *Journal of Consulting and Clinical Psychology, 68,* 843–856.

Wortman, C. B., & Silver, R. C. (2001). The myths of coping with loss revisited. In M. Stroebe, R. O. Hansson, W. Stroebe, & H. Schut (Eds.), *Handbook of bereavement research: Consequences, coping, and care* (pp. 405–430). Washington, DC: American Psychological Association.

28

Educational Interventions for Separating and Divorcing Parents and Their Children

Karen R. Blaisure and Margie J. Geasler
Western Michigan University

In the United States, approximately 2.3 million couples marry each year and 1.2 million divorce (Kreider & Fields, 2002; Sutton, 2003). Twenty percent of couples in first marriages divorce or separate after 5 years, and 33% do so within 10 years (Bramlett & Mosher, 2001). Over half of divorces occur to families with minor children, resulting in over 1 million children experiencing parental divorce annually (Amato, 2000). Cohabiting unions are even more likely to dissolve than marriages, and 46% of these unions include children under the age of 18 (Simmons & O'Connell, 2003). Parents who dissolve their intimate relationship with one another must attend to practical, emotional, and legal matters concerning their children. Parents who have never lived together and who choose to dissolve their relationship also face these matters, including establishment of paternity (Seltzer, 2000). Given the challenges that may result from adult relationship dissolution, legal and family professionals have developed interventions to ease the transition for families, reduce destructive conflict, and facilitate progress through the legal system. This chapter describes court-affiliated educational programs and locates them within a larger context of court and community services for families experiencing parental relationship dissolution.

NEED FOR EDUCATIONAL INTERVENTIONS

Since the 1960s, interventions for families experiencing divorce and relationship dissolution have increased in number and complexity, driven by concern for children's welfare and a need to divert a growing number of cases from costly litigation. Children, parents, and courts all have a stake in educational interventions that effectively help them adjust to adult relationship dissolution. Research on adjustment of children and adults to relationship dissolution, other than to divorce, is meager (Amato, 2000); therefore, our brief discussion on child and adult adjustment focuses on the family transition of divorce.

Children

Children are resilient, and a majority of children from divorced families develop into individuals who function within normal ranges of adjustment (Hetherington, Bridges, & Insabella, 1998). However, approximately 20% to 25% of children in divorced or remarried families, in comparison with 10% of children in nondivorced families, display social and psychological problems (Hetherington & Kelly, 2002). Divorce is most stressful for children when they perceive they are being blamed for the divorce and when there is parental conflict, including physical violence and arguing. Children report being stressed when parents complain about each other, parents become angry with the child, one parent moves away, and daily routines change (Grych & Fincham, 1997).

Whether children experience divorce as a crisis from which they bounce back or as a chronic strain depends on the presence and intensity of mediating or stressor variables and moderating or protective factors. Poor-quality custodial and noncustodial parenting, high parental conflict and low cooperation, economic difficulties, and other life events such as changing schools or moving away from support systems are mediating variables. Moderating variables include coping skills (i.e., solving problems actively, obtaining social support), lack of self-blame for the divorce, perceived control (i.e., can provide input into the decision-making process regarding details that affect their lives), and interventions such as school-based programs (Amato, 2000; Kelly & Emery, 2003). When parents engage in high levels of conflict, children can be protected from negative outcomes if they experience a close relationship with at least one parent, parental warmth, and encapsulated parental conflict (i.e., parents do not allow their conflict to spill over into their children's lives; see Kelly & Emery).

Children can benefit from reduction in postdivorce interparental conflict even when that conflict has been present for a number of years. For example, 20-year follow-up research with adult children indicates that, when interparental conflict decreases and coparenting support increases over the years, adult children's relationships with their fathers remain the same or improve. Conversely, interparental conflict that continues or intensifies over time interferes with children's future relationship with their fathers (Ahrons & Tanner, 2003).

Although some studies reveal poignant tales of pain and destroyed lives, fueling to some degree the development of interventions for separating parents and their children (Walker, 2003), overall, research tells a more complex and promising tale about adult and child adjustment to divorce and relationship dissolution (Ahrons & Tanner, 2003; Amato, 2003; Coltrane & Adams, 2003; Harvey & Fine, 2004; Kelly & Emery, 2003).

Adults

Divorce or relationship dissolution may bring substantial turmoil into adults' lives, but as with children, adult reactions and long-term well-being vary. Some adults experience divorce as a crisis, with a postdivorce adjustment lower, equal to, or even above their predivorce well-being, whereas others experience it as chronic strain that negatively affects the rest of their lives (Amato, 2000; Hetherington, 2003). A combination of mediators and moderators determine whether adults experience divorce as a crisis or a chronic strain. Interparental conflict, parenting difficulties (e.g., child care, misbehavior, number of children in the household, and loss of contact with children), loss of economic resources or emotional support, and pileup of life changes are the stressors most often associated with divorce and relationship dissolution for adults. Education, social support, employment, government policies, and personal beliefs about divorce moderate its effects (Amato).

As in children's adjustment, the postdivorce relationship is an important factor in adult's adjustment. In the Binuclear Family Study, Ahrons (1994) studied the variability of postdivorce parental relationships and highlighted the possibility of amicable and cooperative parenting postdivorce. Labels given to these five relationship types convey a sense of how the parents communicate and interact. *Perfect pals* remain friends and are able to interact well in private and public. *Cooperative colleagues* contain their anger in order to protect their children and carry out parental responsibilities; compromise over issues, such as parenting time and caring for children's needs; are able to attend the same events that involve their children (e.g., concerts, graduations, and weddings); and distinguish between former marital issues and current parenting tasks. *Angry associates*, however, are unable to limit anger related to their marriage and allow it to interfere with family relationships. *Fiery foes* continue their conflict for years, devastating their families' lives. *Dissolved duos* are those in which one parent does not maintain contact with the children.

Most parental conflict lessens 2 to 3 years after the divorce, and 25% to 30% of parents carry out a cooperative relationship, typified by joint coordination and adequate communication. However, over 50% of parents use parallel parenting, typified by emotional disengagement, minimal communication, and low conflict. Children benefit from cooperative parenting but also benefit from parallel parenting when it is combined with "nurturing care and appropriate discipline" (Kelly & Emery, 2003, p. 357). Although research analogous to that of Ahrons has not been completed with parents who have cohabited before dissolving their relationships or who have never lived together, it is reasonable to expect that a comparable typology exists, although the frequency of relationship types may differ.

Research suggests that educational interventions should aim to increase protective factors and decrease the effect of stressors for both adults and children. Strengthening parent–child relationships, enhancing coping skills, and decreasing destructive interparental conflict are appropriate intervention goals (Amato, 2000).

Courts

Because of the legal aspects associated with relationship dissolution, court systems have become the primary location for dispute resolution, creating a "legalization" of family problems and a congregating point for those experiencing family transitions related to adult relationship dissolution (Firestone & Weinstein, 2004). Courts have become overloaded, if not overwhelmed, with the caseloads presented by family transitions (Schepard, 1994). These caseloads pose particular problems for smaller court systems that do not have mediation, custody evaluation, and visitation supervision services (Braver, Salem, Pearson, & DeLuse, 1996). Another frequent problem for courts is that many are *pro per* filings; that is, they are filings by parents who are not represented by attorneys (Braver et al.). The highly charged emotional nature of relationship dissolution, accompanied by an increase in litigation, produced a situation in which courts in the early 1990s were desperate for other approaches as they recognized the limitations of a legal solution to a primarily psychological and social situation.

COURT- AND COMMUNITY-BASED INTERVENTIONS

Legal, family, and mental health professionals have initiated court-related interventions in an attempt to improve family relationships for the benefit of children and to use public resources wisely. This collaboration has resulted in an increase in and access to services, even when such services are based in the community rather than in the court. Although family transition services exist in communities, anecdotal reports indicate that it is largely the result of referrals through the court, encouraged or mandated, that families find their way to educational and therapeutic interventions. The following section reviews the interventions available through contact with the legal system, recognizing that these services are a result of multidisciplinary collaborations and that families can and do find their way to community-based services without going through attorneys, judges, and court workers.

Family Courts

The legal system's traditionally adversarial approach to conflict is undergoing a transformation, requiring and resulting in multidisciplinary partnerships to support families. For example, family courts are designed to funnel cases related to a particular family (e.g., family violence, child support, paternity, custody conflicts, juvenile crime, and child molestation) to one judge rather than to many judges in different courts. Moreover, family courts are assuming leadership in initiating a process whereby parents, attorneys, court workers, and community professionals work toward parental cooperation and positive parent–child and family relationships (Johnston, 2000).

Numerous case examples exist in which the court, the local bar association, and community professionals are collaborating to design and implement interventions in order to accommodate a growing and more troubling domestic relations caseload and to address the heightened risk for negative outcomes experienced by children in high-conflict families. Through this collaborative process, courts are shifting from being a place of adversarial dispute resolution to a place where community resources intersect to assist families (Johnston & Roseby, 1997; Schepard, 1998, 2004).

Parent Education Programs

Education programs for separating and divorcing parents have been accepted by courts at an "impressive rate" in the hopes of assisting parents to better meet the needs of their children, while at the same time providing some relief for overloaded courts (Braver et al., 1996). Since their inception, parent or divorce education programs have had an educational and preventive, rather than a counseling or mediation, purpose. Programs primarily focus on the developmental needs of children, coparenting, and child and parental adjustment to divorce (Blaisure & Geasler, 1996; Braver et al.).

Universal Programs

Court-affiliated programs for divorcing parents began appearing in the 1970s, first focusing on families with continuing conflict and then expanding to all divorcing families with minor children (Roeder-Esser, 1994). By the late 1990s, nearly 50% of U.S. county court systems sponsored either court- or community-based programs for parents (Geasler & Blaisure, 1999), an increase from less than 20% in 1994 (Blaisure & Geasler, 1996). Education programs for separating parents are often developed and implemented by a collaboration of many disciplines and professions. Community-wide involvement increases program exposure and educates the public about the needs of children experiencing parental separation (Heilmann, 2000).

The majority of programs for separating or divorcing parents in the early 1990s consisted of one session of 2.5 hr or less and cost parents less than $30 (Blaisure & Geasler, 1996). By the end of the 1990s, programs averaged 4 hr in length and were offered in one or two sessions. Likewise, a majority of programs that were initially conducted in house by the court were later subcontracted or referred to community providers. The extent to which programs are theoretically and empirically grounded varies (Geasler & Blaisure, 1998, 1999).

Mandated attendance at a parent education program prior to litigation or relitigation has increased since the early 1990s. Eleven states have legislated mandatory attendance at programs for divorcing parents with minor children. Fourteen states have granted discretionary powers to courts to require parental attendance on an individual case basis (2 of these 14 states do require attendance when custody or contact is contested). Three states allow judicial districts to decide whether to implement a program. Finally, courts in 18 states rely on local court rules to provide the necessary authority to require attendance (Clement, 1999). As might be expected, mandated programs are less likely to report problems with attendance or funding (Geasler & Blaisure, 1999).

The content of basic programs can be classified as child focused, parent focused, and court focused (Geasler & Blaisure, 1998). Adult emotional adjustment; family, economic, work, and social changes; coparenting models, such as cooperative and parallel parenting; communication and conflict-management skills; and resource referrals are topics in parent-focused content. Child-focused content consists of topics such as children's reactions to divorce, symptoms of problems at various developmental stages, and assistance in children's adjustment. Court-focused content includes information about court processes; alternative dispute-resolution options; and procedures related to separation, custody, contact, and support. However, program providers differ in their willingness to provide court-focused content. Some providers feel that it is helpful to parents to be familiar with court procedures and invite a local judge or attorney to discuss court procedures. Other program providers prefer to avoid introducing a subject that may have negative associations for parents or is outside their area of expertise (Geasler & Blaisure). A number of prepared materials and training models are available (see the Appendix for a list of resources).

Divorce education programs are presented by a variety of professionals, including social workers, counselors, marriage and family therapists, psychologists, mediators, court workers, attorneys, teachers, family life educators, and nurses. A majority of programs use two presenters, with many of the mandated programs requiring that one be male and the other female (Braver et al., 1996).

Programs for Families in High Conflict

Special interventions have been developed for an exigent minority of parents who are described as high conflict. It is estimated that 70% to 80% of divorcing parents reach custody agreements without litigation, whereas the remaining families require some amount of further court involvement. About 10% pursue extended litigation, court hearings, and trials as ways to resolve their hostility (Johnston, 2000). In California, over half of the families in court resolve custody decisions through state-mandated mediation, and one fourth settle after a custody evaluation. Custody decisions for the remaining families are made by a judge or as a result of a trial. Although a minority of separating or divorcing families fall into these highest conflict categories, as Johnston notes, they represent an accumulating subpopulation of children who live amid high conflict year after year. These families consume a disproportionate share of court resources, and reliance on these traditionally adversarial and expensive legal processes often fails to truly resolve conflict or heal hurts (Johnston; Johnston & Campbell, 1988). Up to one third of parents continue to experience hostility regarding the care of children years after separation. As noted earlier, high parental conflict is predictive of negative outcomes for children (Amato & Booth, 1997; Ayoub, Deutsch, & Maraganore, 1999; Cummings & Davies, 1994; Grych & Fincham, 1997; Hetherington et al., 1998; Kelly, 1998).

High-conflict families typically demonstrate high rates of litigation and relitigation; mutual anger, distrust, and fear; occasional verbal abuse; intermittent physical aggression; and inability to cooperate in caring for their children. Domestic violence, varying in severity, is present in approximately 75% of high-conflict families; child molestation is a concern in 10% and child abuse in 30%. Explanations for continuing conflict between some parents include unresolved grief, an adversarial court system, a litigious cultural context, changing amounts of parenting time in order to manipulate the amount of child support received or paid, lack of awareness of how children are affected by destructive conflict, personality disorders, and individual challenges (e.g., substance abuse; see Johnston, 2000; Neff & Cooper, 2004). Certainly the conflict in some of these families represents "realistic responses to the other parent's violent, neglectful, or substance abusing behavior" (Johnston, p. 455). However, more commonly, the high level of conflict represents parents' negative views of one another; feelings of rejection, loss, humiliation, and anxiety; and desire to blame the other and obtain vindication through the legal system (Johnston).

Given the demands placed on court resources by high-conflict families and poor outcomes when they are left to the adversarial legal system, an increasing number of court systems are implementing educational interventions specifically designed to assist these parents to coparent more appropriately. Programs range in length from one 4-hr session to six or more sessions of varying length (Neff & Cooper, 2004; B. L. Bacon & B. McKenzie, personal communication, March 1, 2004).

In contrast to other programs for high-conflict parents that are multisession, the Parental Conflict Resolution (PCR) Program in Maricopa County, Arizona is a one session, 4-hr program. PCR take-home materials include a copy of *Healing Hearts* (Hickey & Dalton, 1997), a list of parenting classes, a list of readings, and copies of program overheads (Neff & Cooper, 2004). The PCR program is based on the assumption that many high-conflict parents are personality disordered and so can benefit from the application of cognitive principles, such as explicating the negative consequences for children of continuing the present course of action (e.g., alienating children from the other parent, continued destructive conflict). Parents are ordered by a judge to attend the program and are placed in separate classes. A parent's new partner is encouraged to attend and sometimes is also ordered to attend.

Both cooperative and parallel coparenting skills have been taught to assist high-conflict parents to continue in their parental role even as they dissolve their intimate relationship. Judges in Los Angeles and Oregon have ordered high-conflict parents to attend 5- to 6-week cooperative parenting classes. The overarching goal of cooperative parenting is to enable parents to work together to resolve their disagreements. In contrast, parallel parenting is encouraged for high-conflict parents by educational programs in Massachusetts and Colorado. The goal of parallel parenting is to have parents reduce conflict by disengaging from each other, at least initially until conflict subsides, rather than seeking cooperation too quickly (Kibler, Sanchez, & Baker-Jackson, 1994; McIsaac & Finn, 1999; Neff & Cooper, 2004).

Culturally Responsive Programs

The availability and use of culturally appropriate curricula by court systems is unknown at this time. The last nationwide survey did not reveal curricula designed for specific cultural groups, although explicit questions asking about such curricula were not included in the questionnaire sent to counties (Geasler & Blaisure, 1999). A few studies, however, have examined whether parents' reactions to the divorce education program differed according to demographic variables. Parents' high level of satisfaction with the Focus on Kids Program did not differ according to race or ethnicity, household income, education, and sex (Feng & Fine, 2000). Parents reported a more positive feeling about attendance at the completion of the Families in Transition program than at the beginning of the program, regardless of race or sex.

However, level of education did have an effect on parents' reactions. Parents with college degrees or some graduate school were less likely to believe that the Families in Transition program could help them, other families, or their children than were parents with only as elementary education (Yankeelov, Bledsoe, Brown, & Cambron, 2003).

Parent education is offered in Spanish for separating parents in U.S. jurisdictions where there is a large Spanish-speaking population. Court officials in Howard County, Maryland have requested that the National Family Resiliency Center develop and present their basic program in Spanish to meet the needs of the many Spanish-speaking parents who are involved in court battles over child issues (R. Garon, personal communication, February 26, 2004). Canada, Quebec, and New Brunswick, among others, offer programs in French. Interpreters are integral to programs in many jurisdictions in Canada, in order to ensure that persons understand the laws, their rights and responsibilities, and future options. Obstacles to presentation of parent education programs in a language other than English include the following: finding trained presenters who speak the language; overcoming cultural bias against attending meetings related to personal issues; generating groups large enough to make the program feasible; and locating presentations in a familiar environment.

Culturally sensitive parent education programs should be offered in languages of the major ethnic groups represented in the community. They should also reflect definitions of family beyond a nuclear model; integrate members of the local community into the program as codevelopers of programs, advisory group members, presenters, and actors in videos; and be easily accessible, perhaps through neighborhood community centers. If the local population includes immigrants, then additional instruction about the legal system is warranted (Zegarra, 1998).

Programs for Gay, Lesbian, Bisexual, or Transgender Parents

No programs for gay, lesbian, bisexual, or transgender (GLBT) parents were identified in the national surveys of county court systems (Geasler & Blaisure, 1999). However, it is assumed that some communities are beginning to serve this population. For example, The KidsFirst Center, located in Maine, offers a 6-week group for GLBT parents who are experiencing separation. This program emphasizes the legitimacy and validity of their families, heterosexism and homphobia faced by parents, and positive ways to protect children from being in the middle of adult conflict. Begun about 3 years ago by Frank Brooks and Susan Wiggin, this program has been run on three separate occasions. It does take time to have enough parents to form a group. Beginning in the summer of 2004, staff will offer a once-a-month drop in time for GLBT parents as a way to serve parents in the interim (Frank Brooks, personal communication, May 27, 2004; see www.kidsfirstcenter.org).

Programs for Never-Married Parents

Attendance at education programs is not limited to separating parents of minor children. Married, divorced, or never-married parents who are disputing custody, child support, or contact may be included in an education program. Forty-five percent of the counties with a divorce education program send or invite never-married parents involved in paternity, custody, support, or visitation cases to the program. It is unclear whether GLBT parents are included. When serving never-married parents, court-connected programs are more likely to adapt program materials or design their own than use a commercially available program (Geasler & Blaisure, 1999). A few jurisdictions and community providers have offered separate programs for never-married parents in which more focus is given to developing trust between parents who may have never lived together and explaining parental legal rights and responsibilities (F. Nicholson, personal communication, February 14, 2004). Judges believe that content must be made relevant to never-married parents in order to improve programs (Fischer, 1997).

Programs for Parents in Domestic Violence Situations

A debate exists over whether parents with domestic violence issues should attend basic parent education programs. Domestic violence service providers have criticized court-connected parent education programs for encouraging parents to cooperate with and trust their coparent when to do so may jeopardize the safety of women who live in situations of control-instigated violence (Fuhrmann, McGill, & O'Connell, 1999). However, at least one study found that attendance at an educational program for parents who are divorcing does not lead to an increase in domestic violence (Kramer, Arbuthnot, Gordon, Rousis, & Hoza, 1998). Another study found that parents who have experienced domestic violence do not differ from other parents in their perceptions of a program's helpfulness (McKenzie & Bacon, 2002).

Most parent education programs have procedures to screen for domestic violence, provide waivers, or hold separate meetings; however, additional adjustments for increased security may be necessary. Suggestions include the following: prohibit partners from attending a program at the same time; avoid disclosure of when the other parent is attending a program; obtain the names of both parents on any registration forms to ensure that parents are not scheduled for the same program; train program leaders in domestic violence issues; conduct classes in public locations (e.g., hospitals, colleges, or courthouses) where security is present and visible; and phrase program content to make it clear that trust, cooperation, and nurturing of children by both parents is encouraged *when it is safe*. An example of wording that is sensitive to domestic violence would be this: "Parents who have a businesslike relationship that is focused on the business of raising children generally fare well. For families where there has been violence, however, the businesslike relationship may be best conducted through a third party such as a parent coordinator" (Fuhrmann et al., 1999, p. 31; Lutz & Gady, 2004).

Continuum of Services

Researchers, practitioners, courts, and community agencies are recognizing the benefit of conceptualizing interventions along a continuum, loosely grouping services according to intensity of parental difficulties. With a continuum of services, parents can either progress through each intervention until they are helped (e.g., agree on parenting issues, reduce conflict) or be directed to services that best address their family situation. Johnston (2000) raised the point that perhaps families are best served if they are screened and sent directly to the services that fit their needs so that they do not experience "failure" at primary interventions. Such an approach requires an initial assessment of families' needs. At least one court system (Homrich, Glover, & White, 2004) and one agency (Garon, Donner, & Peacock, 2000) have introduced an assessment phase into their range of services.

A few models for organizing a continuum of services have been advanced. Johnston and Roseby (1997) suggested that families proceed through a triage and referral process to five groups of services: parenting and divorce education programs; consultations and mediation programs; therapeutic mediation or custody evaluations; special master or parenting coordination; and finally, ancillary services such as domestic violence programs, supervised visitation and monitoring, community mental health, and substance abuse programs. A public health model suggests three levels of services: universal services for those at a lower risk of developing future problems but who likely will experience initial distress during separation and divorce, selected prevention services for those at risk of developing future problems, and treatment services for individuals or families already exhibiting problems (Haine, Sandler, Wolchik, Tein, & Dawson-McClure, 2003). Schepard (1998) applied a public health model to programs available through the legal system, beginning with couple education programs before marriage.

Using the multidoor courthouse concept as inspiration, Firestone and Weinstein (2004) proposed a freestanding private–public program that enables families to choose dispute-resolution services that are best suited to their needs. Families would enter the program through a visit to a so-called dispute-resolution coordinator located in the community rather than in a courthouse. The coordinator would rely on the court system for its rights-based dispute-resolution capabilities and the filing of legal paperwork, but he or she would otherwise proceed with assisting families in identifying and addressing their dilemmas. The authors argue that such a program would promote a culture of problem solving with its focus on the family's future, and it would empower parents, ultimately replacing the win-lose culture that is fostered by the current adversarial system.

Supporting this range or continuum of services are the recommendations issued by the participants of the Wingspread Conference (2001a, 2001b) held in 2000 and sponsored by the Family Law Section of the American Bar Association and The Johnson Foundation. The conference produced recommendations for mental health professionals, lawyers, and the court system. It was recommended that the court system provide the following services and programs to all families: mediation; custody evaluations; investigations; education programs; parenting coordination; group and individual mental health treatment; interventions and services tailored to individuals' or families' needs; and literature on laws, procedures, and community resources. These programs and services should exist within a system that identifies high-conflict cases, provides structure, facilitates connection to community resources, and prioritizes them within the court calendar.

Building on a model of family involvement that differentiates education from therapy (Doherty, 1995), the divorce education intervention model offers courts and community agencies a way to conceptualize variations in program goals and structure, curricula, and resource allocation (Blaisure & Geasler, 2000). These levels also require increasing levels of professional skills.

Minimal Level

A minimal level of intervention is not considered education, but rather an efficient means of processing parents through the legal system with a minimum of individual attention. A minimal level of service may include brochures and general information for parents, but it would discourage any individual or group interactions between parents and court workers. A limitation inherent in this level of programming is that parents who receive minimal help may rely on the legal system to resolve their family disputes and, in so doing, require multiple court appearances.

Basic Level

A basic level of intervention is typified by parents attending a one- or two-session education program that conveys information didactically and through printed materials. Advantages of this level are that, compared with longer or more intense programs, it demands fewer resources on the part of the community and the parents, and it can convey information to a large number of persons within a short period of time. A majority of court-connected programs for separating parents fit this intervention level.

Active Level

Programs at the active level require parent involvement in skill-building exercises and usually a longer overall time commitment by parents. Key features are opportunities for skill building and conflict reduction. An additional advantage is that parents who are found to require a higher level of involvement can be identified and referred to other services. This level of parent involvement necessarily requires more resources both on the part of the program provider (e.g., increased skills and knowledge of the presenter, and space and wage commitments) and on the part of the parent (e.g., increased time commitment and fees).

Intense Level

Programs with an intense level of parental involvement provide time and opportunities for high-risk and high-conflict parents to focus on coping with their specific situations. This level requires multisession, small group settings with presenters who have backgrounds in assessment and family systems and knowledge of referral options. More courts are implementing intense intervention for those families characterized by persistent high conflict. Intense-level programming requires higher levels of resources than other educational interventions.

Therapeutic Level

The therapeutic level of parent involvement by definition precludes classifying it as an educational intervention. It is included here in order to recognize that some parents may require more assistance in their adjustment and with coping skills than can be provided through educational programs. This level is characterized by ongoing therapy sessions with or without the coparent.

Models of Continuum of Services

The following case examples illustrate how a court and a nonprofit community agency have each implemented a continuum of services for separating parents. The first case uses the divorce education intervention model as a starting point, and the second case demonstrates the web of services available in a community context.

Court Care Center for Divorcing Families, Orange County Florida

The Ninth Judicial Circuit Court in Orange County, Florida recently implemented the Court Care Center for Divorcing Families (CCCDF) within the domestic court system (Homrich et al., 2004). This multifaceted program, based on the divorce education intervention model (Blaisure & Geasler, 2000), provides services beyond the state-mandated 4-hr parent education program required of all divorcing parents with minor children. The goals of the CCCDF are to reduce conflict and unnecessary litigation and to encourage responsible coparenting and emotional stability. Parents are referred into the CCCDF program by court judges or another court agent when parents use court actions inappropriately, do not resolve issues that most parents are able to resolve, place children in the middle of conflicts, or fail in attempts at alternative dispute resolution.

Parents meet with a CCCDF staff member for an assessment, resulting in necessary referral or crisis counseling, and then enrollment in one or more of the CCCDF groups. The staff member first assesses family members' functioning and redirects to agencies any individuals who need to address confounding issues (e.g., mental illness, substance abuse, domestic violence, or child protective services investigation). Parents then are enrolled in the Cooperating for Your Kids group (for parents demonstrating mild to moderate levels of conflict) or the Focus on the Children—Orlando group (for parents with high levels of conflict). Both of these groups meet for 2 hrs over 8 weeks and include a 6-month follow-up session. When necessary, parents are referred to family, individual, or group therapy. Another unique aspect of the CCCDF model is that the family therapy referral base was partially developed from those mental health practitioners who attended an 11-hr training on the emotional needs of divorcing or divorced adults.

The National Family Resiliency Center, Maryland

The National Family Resiliency Center (NFRC) examplifies a multidisciplinary model that provides a constellation of services to families transitioning through separation and divorce. Originally called Children of Separation and Divorce, the organization was renamed the NFRC in 2003 to reflect the focus on facilitating family transitions for all parents, not just for those associated with separation and divorce (R. Garon, personal communication, February 26, 2004). The NFRC follows a family-focused decision-making model called the National Family Resiliency Program (NFRP) developed by center staff (Garon et al., 2000). Moreover, the NFRC trains and works with attorneys, judges, and mediators who believe in a nonadversarial, child-focused approach and consults with attorneys and mediators who are working with families (with parents' informed consent).

The NFRP begins with an orientation and an intake assessment of the presenting issues of parents and children. This initial step is followed by a basic 6-hr parent education program that includes the use of child and adult peer counselors who have experienced the NFRP and are willing to talk about the process with others. When orientation and parent education have been completed, parents, together with a practitioner, develop a Family Action Plan, in which individual, group, or family therapy may be recommended. High-conflict counseling and anger management are additional options for parents.

Before a parenting agreement is written, two to six sessions are held with the parents in which planning for the future of the child or children is addressed. Extensive needs assessments for each child are developed in consultation with teachers, pediatricians, child-care providers, and other helping professionals. The child's self-concept, intellectual functioning, interpersonal functioning, and safety and security needs at various developmental stages are addressed as a parenting agreement takes shape. The parenting agreements completed through the NFRP are more detailed than typical parenting agreements and are likely to address children's needs through postsecondary education. Sessions to develop parenting agreements are limited to child issues, although some parents are concurrently linked with mediators (who are trined with a child focus) to provide short-term relief of financial matters and reduce their anxiety about finances.

On completion of a parenting agreement, mediation of money and property issues takes place. If mediation is successful, a final meeting is held to discuss explaining the parenting agreement to the children. If mediation is unsuccessful, impasse counseling may be called for. The members of the NFRC staff continue their involvement with families as long as the families desire, working through timely renegotiations, family sessions, and other counseling and education programs. Figure 28.1 illustrates the process.

As parents proceed through the program model the NFRC provides comprehensive services for children. These services include 12-week therapy groups for 6- to 7-, 8- to 10-, 11- to 13-, and

Family Resiliency Program Model

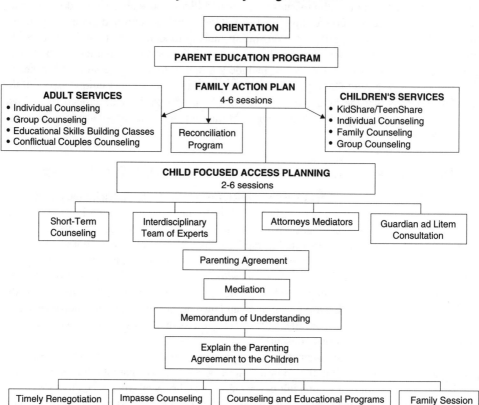

FIG. 28.1.   NFRP Model. (Copyright 2003 by Risa Garon, NFRC, Inc. Used With Permission.)

14- to 15-year olds; each parent is involved throughout the proess. Multiple family therapy is involved in each age group. Participation in KidShare/TeenShare is also an option for children.

Children's Programs

The late 1990s marked an increase in the number of court systems sponsoring programs for children; however, children's programs are more likely to be found in schools or through profit or not-for-profit organizations (Geelhoed, Blaisure, & Geasler, 2001; Grych & Fincham, 1992). A minority of courts have programs for children or are affiliated with programs for children, although many would like to add this service (Cookston, Braver, Sandler, & Genalo, 2002; Geasler & Blaisure, 1999).

A typical children's program is composed of 15 children who meet for four sessions for a total of 5.5 hr. Average yearly attendance is 353 children in one location. Programs most commonly serve early and late elementary ages; however, programs for preschool children and teenagers do exist. Some programs do not charge fees but rather rely on court funding, grants, or fees collected from the parents' program. For those programs that charge a fee, the average is under $50. Sliding scales or family caps also are used.

Facilitation of feelings, development of coping skills, adjustment to changes, provision of information, normalization of the experience, and provision of support are reported goals of court-connected children's programs. Examples of exercises used in a majority of children's programs include writing a newsletter for parents, practicing communication skills, role-playing a talk with parents, and writing a letter to parents (Geelhoed et al., 2001). See the Appendix for a list of materials.

International Programs

Canada

Canada's provinces and the Yukon and Northwest Territories offer education programs for separating parents, providing widespread but not complete coverage of all judicial areas. These programs are administered through provincial government departments, some of which offer the program directly and some of which subcontract the program to local agencies. Attendance is required in Alberta and in some jurisdictions in other provinces. Certain judges order attendance, and, in two provinces, Manitoba and Newfoundland, parents must attend programs if they wish to use government-provided mediation (Bacon & McKenzie, 2001, 2004). In Quebec and New Brunswick, programs are offered in French and English, and a number of programs incorporate interpreters, especially to ensure the understanding of laws, rights, and legal options (B. L. Bacon & B. McKenzie, personal communication, March 1, 2004).

Programs range in length from 3 to 12 hr, with a mode of 6 hr and an average length slightly less because some voluntary programs have two sessions and some parents do not attend the second session. Two provinces, Manitoba and New Brunswick, allow parents to select either a low-conflict or a high-conflict seminar for the second session. Alberta offers a program designed for those exposed to domestic violence. Separating but never-married individuals regularly attend programs. The Manitoba program is available on an interactive CD and is sent to persons in isolated areas. Saskatchewan is piloting a 6-hr program for high-conflict couples (B. L. Bacon & B. McKenzie, personal communication, March 1, 2004).

United Kingdom

In January of 2005, the Secretaries of State for Constitutional Affairs, Education and Skills, and Trade and Industry published their agenda to improve court, judicial, and social services for separating and divorcing parents in England and Wales (see www.dfes.gov.uk/childrensneeds; Falconer, Kelly, & Hewitt, 2005). This publication included responses to an earlier green paper that was issued for a 3-month consultation period (Falconer, Clarke, & Hewitt, 2004). Among other items in this agenda are plans to enhance the advice and information offered to separating parents through a variety of avenues, including marriage and relationship support organizations and schools; to continue offering and evaluating the Family Resolutions Pilot Project, and to enhance the Family Advice and Information Service (FAInS). Additional plans call for online diaries as a means for family communication, a legal advice helpline, a collaborative law approach for publicly funded cases, extended in-court conciliation services as a routine step before formal court hearings, and improved case management by the courts.

Information services, counseling, mediation, and classes are present in the UK but accessibility has been limited and coverage incomplete. Moreover, programs typically have not been affiliated with the court system, except for the voluntary, two-hour Parenting Information Programme (PIP), offered by Family Mediation Scotland, initiated through the legal system, and supported by the Sheriff Courts (Hawthorne, Jessop, Pryor, & Richards, 2003) and the current Family Resolutions Pilot Project. The government intends to empower courts in England and Wales with the authority to refer parents in conflict to available educational classes and programs (e.g., information meetings, counseling, and parenting programs designed to re-solve disputes about contact) and to require parents' attendance before issuing contact orders (Falconer, Kelly, & Hewitt, 2005).

The Family Resolutions Pilot Project includes a three-stage process for parents undergoing separation. First they receive an information packet that describes court operations and expec-tations for a meaningful and sustained relationship between children and each parent. Parents then separately attend two group sessions focused on assisting children's adjustment through decreased parental conflict. Finally, parents meet with a family court advisor to develop a parenting plan.

The group sessions are being piloted at three locations during 2004 and 2005. As a joint project, Relate (the UK's largest provider of relationship counseling and services, see www.relate.org.uk) and the Parenting Education and Support Forum (a professional associa-tion for those who work in parenting education and support, see www.parenting-forum.org.uk) developed materials and trained facilitators for the group sessions that are focusing on chil-dren's needs, co-parenting skills, and strategies for good contact. Parents are being directed to the sessions while waiting for court hearings; cases involving non-contact disputes, domestic violence allegations, and repeat applications are being screened out. An evaluation report on the Family Resolutions Pilot Project is due in April 2006 (Falconer, Kelly, & Hewitt, 2005).

The FAInS program in England and Wales is another pilot project recently initiated. It emerged from research indicating that 80% of persons experiencing family or relationship dif-ficulties visit family solicitors and that individuals experiencing relationship separation wanted information about the emotional, family, and legal processes tailored to their particular situa-tion (Smart, Wade, & Neale, 1999; Walker, 2001). In the FAInS model, family solicitors serve as case managers who explore not only the legal issues facing clients, but also emotional, finan-cial, relationship, and other needs that affect the well-being of clients' and their children. Family solicitors identify clients' needs and ensure that clients obtain access to the specialist services that can address these needs. The goals of FAInS are to facilitate the process of relationship dis-solution, promote cooperative parenting, tailor information to client needs, and facilitate access to community services. Central to meeting these goals is the development of interdisciplinary networks of services so clients have easy access to legal, financial, mediation, and children and adolescent services; welfare benefits and housing advice; relationship and parenting support; and other services (e.g., domestic violence, therapy, anger management). Evaluation of FAInS is underway and the intention is to expand access points to FAInS by training other professional groups (e.g., mediators) (Walker, 2003; see www.legalservices.gov.uk/civil/fains.asp).

Australia

The Australian Family Law Act of 1996 focuses on children's rights and parents' respon-sibilities, encouraging parents to use mediation and counseling rather than courts during the process of separation and divorce. Australian government policy encourages communities and agencies to "think first" of alternative dispute-resolution services rather than litigation. As a result, many family agencies have designed and are offering multisession education programs for separating and divorcing parents and their children, individual counseling sessions, and mediation (Dickinson & Murphy, 2000; Mackay, 2001).

Other Court-Based Interventions

In addition to education programs, U.S. courts have initiated a variety of interventions and services to assist families experiencing the transition of separation and divorce. Mediation and therapy, the most widely known noneducational interventions available, are described in the paragraphs that follow, along with variations of these interventions.

Parenting Coordinator

The past decade has seen the growth of parenting coordinators (also called arbitrators, coparenting counselors, custody commissioners, family court advisors, special masters, and wisepersons) who work closely with high-conflict and relitigating families (Association of Family and Conciliation Courts [AFCC] Task Force on Parenting Coordination, 2004; F. Nicholson, personal communication, March 13, 2004). In the early 1990s, a high-conflict study group of attorneys and mental health professionals in the Denver area developed a parenting coordination model for working with families involved in contentious relitigation. Meanwhile, in northern California, counties were also developing a similar model (AFCC Task Force on Parenting Coordination). Three states now have parenting coordination statutes, and other states have used existing statutory authority regarding mediators, special masters, guardians ad litem, and referees to appoint parenting coordinators (AFCC Task Force on Parenting Coordination).

Parenting coordinators have a law or mental health background, depending on the region of the country. Additional training in divorce mediation, parenting, child development, and high-conflict divorce is expected. Parenting coordinators may be based in either the court or the community (AFCC Task Force on Parenting Coordination). In Michigan, for example, there is a growing number of parenting coordinators in private practice. Judges order parents to parenting coordination when high-conflict or chronic litigation becomes apparent. In addition, when clients' hostility prevents a settlement, some attorneys have agreed to send clients to parenting coordination (M. Banning, personal communication, February 25, 2004).

Parenting coordinators may work intensively with high-conflict parents to reduce conflict, teach communication and conflict-resolution skills, educate parents on adult and child adjustment to separation and divorce, stabilize the family, provide mediation, respond to crises, monitor the family situation on behalf of the court, submit progress reports, and make recommendations to the court. In addressing these tasks, parent coordinators blend assessment, case management, mediation, and arbitration. They often follow a parallel parenting model that encourages low engagement and low conflict between parents, and they become the link between parents (Coates, Deutsch, Starnes, Sullivan, & Sydlik, 2004). Many parenting coordinators are empowered to make court orders that are binding; however, more major decisions (e.g., parenting time, parental moves) require approval by the judge (Coates et al.; Sullivan, 1997).

The length of time a parenting coordinator works with a family in transition differs across the country, although a 2-year appointment is typical (AFCC Task Force on Parenting Coordination, 2004). The Family Law Division of the Superior Court in Pima County, Arizona, is exploring the use of special masters who would offer quick assistance to parents stuck on a variety of relatively minor parenting time issues or group of issues (e.g., schooling, vacations, or religious instruction). Special masters will make recommendations to the court that generally will be binding unless an objection is upheld by the court. Other services in Arizona include a state-mandated parenting information program, mandatory divorce mediation for parents who cannot agree on a parenting plan, and conciliation counseling to assess the marriage and make appropriate referrals (F. Nicholson, personal communication, March 14, 2004).

The Cooperative Parenting Program in Atlanta, Georgia features longer contact between parents and professionals. First, it offers a 2.5-hr psychoeducational didactic group that meets weekly for 8 weeks. This group intervention is geared to couples experiencing mild to moderate levels of conflict, and it focuses on skill development, using discussion, parent interaction, and assignments. One or both parents can attend. In addition, the court orders high-conflict couples into a 14- to 16-session parenting coordination program that combines education, mediation, monitoring of the family's progress, and enforcement of court orders. The goal is for parents to learn how to cooperate and problem solve and to create a workable parenting plan. Parents can be involved with the parenting coordination for over a year and must agree to participate in 2 joint sessions with the parent coordinator before initiating litigation against the other parent (Boyan, 2000).

Mediation

Mediation is conducted by legal, mental health, or human service professionals who have obtained training and have met state requirements. Mediation is a structured, alternative dispute-resolution strategy built on a mutually beneficial process rather than an adversarial one. The goal is for former partners to reach agreement concerning children, property, and financial issues by using a third party. In addition, it is hoped that individuals will also learn skills in the areas of communication, problem identification, and negotiation. Mediation is mandatory in some jurisdictions when parents cannot agree on a parenting plan. In comparison with traditional litigation, mediation results in a greater likelihood of reaching settlements in areas of parental time, support, and division of property; decreases in the number of court hearings; faster resolution of issues; greater compliance with parenting and child support agreements; and more detailed parenting plans. Less money is spent using mediation than litigation, and client satisfaction is high (Benjamin & Irving, 1995; Emery, 1994, 1995; Hahn & Kleist, 2000; Pearson, 1993; Sbarra & Emery, chap. 27, this volume).

Therapeutic Mediation

Therapeutic mediation combines counseling and mediation and is conducted by mental health or human services professionals trained in mediation for high-conflict families. In addition to conducting mediation, the mediator also uses therapeutic interventions when the process comes to an impasse as a result of emotional reasons. Courts refer parents who are involved in ongoing litigation. Mediators use a combination of individual and joint sessions, augmented at times by group sessions with other parents (Johnston & Roseby, 1997).

Collaborative Law

More recent than mediation is the practice of collaborative law. With roots in Minnesota and California, collaborative law changes how attorneys practice. Two adults and their attorneys agree to meet until they reach a settlement and agree to forego litigation. Clients are able to fire the attorneys if no settlement is reached; however, clients must hire other attorneys if they decide to pursue litigation. Other professionals, such as mental health professionals, child advocates, and financial advisors, assist parents in negotiating their way through the divorce. The goal of collaborative law is to decrease the amount of hostility and polarization that can be fueled by an adversarial approach (Lande & Herman, 2004; Tessler, 1999; Thompson & Nurse, 1999). Fewer attorneys practice cooperative law, a variation of collaborative law. Cooperative law is similar to collaborative law except that attorneys will agree to represent clients who, after attempting to reach a settlement and appearing to fail, wish to at least threaten litigation (Lande & Herman).

Legal Therapist Counselor

A legal therapist counselor is a mental health professional, employed by a legal firm, who offers psychoeducational rather than therapeutic services to clients. The legal therapist counselor assesses a client's emotional well-being, provides information and readings on adjustment, assists the client in preparing to meet with the attorney, describes legal processes, reviews any custody evaluations with the client, attends hearings along with the client and attorney, and responds to crisis calls. The cost of this service is either billed separately or as part of the attorney's hourly fee (Burrows & Buzzinotti, 1997).

Community-Based Resources

Resources outside of the court system exist for families that are transitioning through separation or divorce. Secular and religious support groups, facilitated by human services or mental health professionals or supervised laypersons, provide information on adjustment and emotional support (e.g., www.rebuilding.org). For example, in one Midwest community, a 10-session divorce adjustment program follows a similar format each week: for the first hour, a guest speaker addresses the large group of 40 to 60 attendees, who then divide into small groups of 7 to 10 individuals for discussion during the second hour. Topics covered include personal adjustment issues, facing reality, letting go of the past, negotiating, forgiveness, children and parenting, self-responsibility, being single, and relationships (J. Poppe, personal communication, March 9, 2004).

Other resources available include online and published materials that address emotional, legal, financial, and parenting aspects of separation and divorce (for recommended books and internet sites, see Norcross et al., 2003). The Children, Youth and Families Education and Research Network provides links to numerous resources developed at universities and extension services (see www.cyfernet.org).

EFFECTIVENESS OF EDUCATIONAL INTERVENTIONS

The need for rigorous studies of court-connected parent education programs persists. Few studies use research designs that allow researchers to draw solid inferences concerning program effects (Amato, 2000). Outcome studies ideally would include random selection from the population of separated or divorcing parents and random assignment to program and control groups, or the use of program and demographically matched comparison groups from equivalent geographical areas; pretests and posttests; multiple and psychometrically sound measures; multiple means of data collection (e.g., observer report; court, school, and medical records; and observed interactions) beyond self-report; sample sizes large enough to detect treatment effects; and field rather than laboratory settings. Challenges in conducting such research include the reluctance of public officials to allow probability sampling; the relative ease and low cost of self-report when compared with the demands of using multiple measures and data-collection processes; the expense of longitudinal research caused by high mobility of this population; and the need for consistent cross-program measures (Goodman, Bonds, Sandler, & Braver, 2004; Kramer et al., 1998; Whitworth, Capshew, & Abell, 2002).

Universal Programs

Short-Term Programs

In their recent review of outcome research, Goodman et al. (2004) identified five studies of four short-term parent education programs (i.e., Children in the Middle, Children First, Kids, and Mandated Divorce) that had met their criteria for evidence of program effects (i.e., use of program and control or comparison groups, pretests and posttests, quantitative measures, and appropriate statistical tests). These studies also included sample sizes large enough to detect treatment effects. The researchers considered the evidence of program effects on quality of parenting, attitudinal conflict, children's adjustment, interparental conflict, and relitigation. Researchers concluded that there was no evidence suggesting that short-term programs effect the quality of parenting (primarily because programs are not designed with this goal in mind), parents' attitude toward the other parent, or children's adjustment. However, some evidence exists that demonstrate program effects on interparental conflict and relitigation.

Children in the Middle, a divorce education program that has earned the model program rating from the Substance Abuse and Mental Health Services Administrative (see http://modelprograms.samhsa.gov), demonstrates some evidence, and the other programs produced "sparse" evidence, of reducing interparental conflict (Goodman et al., 2004). For example, parents who attended a Children in the Middle program reported more improvement in parental communication and less exposure of children to destructive parental conflict than parents in the comparison group (Arbuthnot & Gordon, 1996; Kramer et al., 1998). Although no differences in the level of interparental conflict were found between parents attending the Children First program and those in a control group, additional analyses identified benefits for families initially reporting high conflict (Kramer & Washo, 1993).

Evidence is split on whether parent education programs decrease litigation rates. In a 6-year follow-up study of Children First, Kramer and Kowal (1998) noted no differences in litigation rates for those who attended the program and those in a comparison group. However, when examining the subsample of attending and nonattending parents who reported high levels of parental conflict, triangulation of children into parental conflict, and low levels of adaptive parenting, they found that relitigation rates were lower for attendees than nonattendees. Results of a Utah study indicated that there was a moderately decreased likelihood of relitigation for those who attended the program, but that relitigation was likely to increase as the number of children increased, perhaps because of an increased potential for conflict given more persons in the family or given child support concerns (Criddle, Allgood, & Piercy, 2003).

An analysis of 1,010 divorce cases for postjudgment petitions revealed that participation at a 2.5-hr parent education program did not speed up time to settlement and was associated with increased adversarial relitigation. It is speculated that the curriculum reinforced parents' motivation to take action to protect their children, but its passive teaching strategy did not ensure that parents acquired the skills that may reduce conflict (McClure, 2002). Studies on Children in the Middle offered some evidence that the likelihood of relitigation does depend on the parents' level of skill mastery. Those who did not demonstrate evidence of skills (e.g., keeping children from the middle of parental conflict) were more likely to relitigate, suggesting the importance of skill-building emphasis in programming (Arbuthnot & Gordon, 1996; Arbuthnot, Kramer, & Gordon, 1997).

Relitigation, an indirect and crude measure, is not a clear indicator of program (in)effectiveness. For example, it is possible that those involved in hostile conflict may not use the court to resolve their disputes, whereas others who relitigate may do so in cooperation as they adjust family arrangements to best meet the needs of their children. In addition, confounding variables may occur during the time litigation rates are tracked, such as changes in laws, legal practice, and community awareness of children's adjustment. However, relitigation rates are positively correlated with high parental conflict and are independent of parental self-reports. Relitigation requires substantial court resources, potentially exposes children to continued parental conflict, indicates that families are unable to resolve conflict without a third party's decision making, and may escalate further relitigation. It is likely that demonstrating a reduction in costly litigation may translate into further community support for such programs (Kramer & Kowal, 1998).

In the field, questionnaires issued at the end of programs or within a few months of attendance are commonly used as means of program evaluation (Braver, Smith, & DeLuse, 1997; Buehler, Betz, Ryan, Legg, & Trotter, 1992; Geasler & Blaisure, 1999; Thoennes & Pearson, 1999). Although limitations of field-based evaluations are easily highlighted, studies of programs in different regions of the United States and Canada suggest similar parental experiences. In general, parents who have attended programs report (a) positive feelings about the program even when initially resistant; (b) beliefs that programs should be required; (c) increased awareness of the harmful effect of poorly managed parental conflict; (d) intention to use knowledge or skills covered in the program; and (e) increased parental cooperation (Criddle et al., 2003; Feng & Fine, 2000; Frieman, Garon, & Garon, 2000; McKenzie & Bacon, 2002; Pedro-Carroll, Nakhnikian, & Montes, 2001; Petersen & Steinman, 1994; Schepard, 1998; Thoennes & Pearson, 1999; Yankeelov et al., 2003). Regardless, more extensive and systematic research beyond these parental self-reports is desperately needed.

Long-Term Programs

Although the typical education program for separating parents is 4 hr in length, longer programs have been developed and evaluated at Prevention Research Centers funded by the National Institute of Mental Health. These studies include more rigorous research designs than those typically applied to short-term programs, including a randomized experimental design, multiple measures, and multiple reporters. Weaknesses of these studies are that the programs are located in research settings rather than in the field, and none of the studies examined effects on legal conflict. Program content focused primarily on improving the quality of parenting and secondarily on the reduction of interparental conflict (Goodman et al., 2004; Haine et al., 2003).

At Arizona State University, two versions of the New Beginnings Program for custodial mothers, one with and one without their 9- to 12-year-old children present, were offered and compared with a control group that received divorce adjustment literature. The program included 11 group sessions and 2 individual sessions. Randomized controlled studies show positive program effects on children's externalizing behaviors at a 6-month and 6-year follow-up, especially for children at greatest risk for poor outcomes. Maintenance of these gains was dependent on the level of mothers' psychological distress and children's regulatory skills; researchers recommend modifying the curriculum to address these points (Cookston et al., 2002; Hipke, Wolchik, Sandler, & Braver, 2002; Wolchik et al., 2002). Meanwhile, an intervention for noncustodial fathers also appears to produce positive effects on children's behavior, especially for the most troubled families, and has provided evidence of the importance of addressing parental conflict and coparenting issues in programs (Braver & Gordon, 2002).

Randomized, experimental evaluations of a 14-session parent training program of custodial mothers, offered through the Oregon Social Learning Center, demonstrated reductions in coercive parenting and prevention of decay in positive parenting for intervention mothers, and a decrease in positive parenting for mothers in the control group 12 months postintervention. Children's behavior, as rated by teachers, showed a trend in positive changes in prosocial interactions, externalizing behaviors, and adaptive functioning. The program was effective in preventing an increase in boys' noncompliance 30 months postintervention, by promoting positive parenting and avoidance of coercive discipline (Cookston et al., 2002; Forgatch & DeGarmo, 1999; Martinez & Forgatch, 2001).

Research on these longer programs provides evidence that interventions can positively affect parenting and, in turn, have positive effects on children. Evidence is mixed concerning program effects on attitudinal and interparental conflict. The challenge is transferring these programs, with fidelity, into court systems. Some evidence exists that courts may be interested in implementing longer, evidenced-based education programs for separating parents and that these programs may best serve those parents having difficulty with parenting or coparenting (Cookston et al., 2002).

Targeted Programs

Little research is available on short- or long-term programs specifically designed for high-conflict families. To our knowledge, no studies using control groups have been published (Goodman et al., 2004). Meanwhile, results of a follow-up, self-report study indicated that the attitudes of parents who attended a program designed for high-conflict parents mirrored those of parents who attended universal programs. Follow-up telephone calls were completed with 135 parents who had attended the PCR program in Maricopa County, Arizona 6 to 15 months before the interview. Prior to attendance, 76% of the parents reported not working well together in meeting their children's needs. A majority of the 135 parents agreed or strongly agreed that they learned a lot from the class; have a better understanding of how children are affected by long-term conflict; have made changes in relating to their children and to the other parent; believe their children are doing better; and have less hostility toward the other parent (Neff & Cooper, 2004).

Children's Programs

Court-connected children's programs are relatively new, and systematic evaluations are clearly needed. Meanwhile, randomized experimental studies of school-based programs for children have demonstrated program effects on adjustment (Emery, Kitzmann, & Waldron, 1999; Stolberg & Mahler, 1994). Longitudinal studies have been conducted on the Children of Divorce Intervention Program (CODIP), a school-based, 12-session program designed for 9- to 12-year-olds, with versions for 5- and 6-year-olds and 6- and 8-year-olds. Studies of the CODIP include the use of matched comparison groups, data collection from multiple sources, and inclusion of instruments with established validity and reliability data. In one study of the CODIP with 5- and 6-year-olds, independent ratings from group participants, teachers, parents, and group leaders indicated improvements in adjustment in school (e.g., getting along with classmates, tolerating frustration, being less anxious and disruptive) and at home (e.g., behaving appropriately, being less moody, and being more open to sharing feelings). Participants reported feeling less worried and more positive about themselves. They enjoyed the group experience and were talking more with their parents. Group leaders indicated that children showed a better understanding of divorce (e.g., it's not the child's fault) and handled problems better. Studies with other ages also indicate improvements in children's adjustment (Pedro-Carroll & Alpert-Gillis, 1997; Pedro-Carroll & Cowen, 1987; Pedro-Carroll et al., 2001; Pedro-Carroll, Sutton, & Wyman, 1999).

FUTURE DIRECTIONS

The last third of the 20th century saw the introduction of educational interventions and related services for separating parents into court systems and the wider community. The beginning of the 21st century is seeing some improvements in evaluation and refinement of programs (Fuhrmann, McGill, & O'Connell, 1999). Theory-driven programs emerging from universities and research institutes are advancing knowledge about prevention interventions, demonstrating that programs can be effective in teaching conflict-reducing techniques, maintaining and enhancing parenting, and improving children's adjustment to family transitions. Meanwhile, evaluations of court-connected programs in the field consistently indicate that parents are receptive to mandatory programs, satisfied with them, and report finding programs useful in promoting positive interactions with their children and reducing conflict with the other parent (Arbuthnot & Gordon, 1996; Braver & Gordon, 2002; Goodman et al., 2004; Haine et al., 2003).

Professional Practice

The growth of alternative dispute-resolution services, collaborative law, and family courts point to the continuing shift in perspective, from the narrow definition of family transitions as a legal matter to the wider consideration of family transitions as a process with emotional and social dimensions (Johnston, 2000). As education programs for separating and postdivorce parents and parenting coordination are becoming more common, practice guidelines and regulations are under consideration (Coates et al., 2004; Schepard, 1998, 2004; Wingspread Conference, 2001a, 2001b). The more court and community professionals work to assist families in relationship transition, the more imperative it will be for those professionals to triage families' needs and coordinate with one another in order to avoid mirroring and escalating parental disputes. Professionals are expected to collaborate with one another, to agree regarding preferred outcomes for the family and the services required, and to contact one another when different professional opinions surface (Johnston, 2004). To accomplish these expectations, professionals must have specialized training, especially on working with high-conflict families, in order to encourage a shared perspective and the skills necessary for successful collaboration (Wingspread Conference).

Program Development

It is imperative that program developers design and modify parent education curricula according to theoretical advancements, empirical evidence, and cultural processes. Research on adult and child adjustment provides insight into those moderating and mediating factors that influence well-being (Amato, 2000, 2003; Hetherington et al., 1998). Developers should incorporate content and teaching strategies that address interparental conflict, quality of parenting, attitudinal support of the other parent, legal conflict, and children's adjustment (Goodman et al., 2004; Haine et al., 2003).

Program refinement and expansion are necessary to meet the increasing needs of various cultural groups. Many jurisdictions recognize that their populations are heterogeneous and reflect a range of family customs and expectations and therefore require culturally appropriate interventions. For example, program facilitators may need to overtly invite and welcome extended family members, such as aunts, uncles, grandparents, and others who may play significant roles in the well-being of children and in the process of a couple's separation. The integration of interpreters, the translation of written and audiovisual materials, and the presentation of programs in languages other than English are beginning points for making programs more responsive to an ethnically diverse population. Over time, it may become apparent that some services are more attractive than others to particular cultural groups (e.g., preferring a parenting coordinator over a multisession education group). Making a thorough assessment of family needs and matching them with the most appropriate services will be a growing challenge for courts and communities.

Online Directory of Programs

In 1997, the Association of Family and Conciliation Courts published the *Directory of Parent Education Programs*, which provides basic information about programs by county and state. The next step is to expand the information available and develop a national and international database accessible on the Internet by families and professionals. The database could provide an overview of educational intervention services; Web pages for counties or jurisdictions to describe their services; and links to curricula, materials, and other services (e.g., those who provide training in parenting coordination). Visitors to the site could search by location, program, or other variables. This database would also provide a means to collect descriptive data about programs (e.g., number of attendees, fees, or curricula). The feasibility of such a project would depend on funding for initial development and widespread cooperation from courts and program developers.

Research

Future research efforts should focus on strengthening evaluations of court-connected education programs and other interventions such as parenting coordination and collaborative law. To do so requires the funding, personnel, and opportunity to implement rigorous research designs in the study of interventions found in court systems and community services. The following model is suggested as a way of overcoming some of the evaluation challenges that divorce education interventions face. A coalition of courts could become evaluation demonstration sites to illustrate the systematic application of an evaluation standard (i.e., assessing evaluability of the program, articulating a theory of change, creating logic models, and developing empirically guided outcomes and indicators of those outcomes). These sites could progress from formative to summative evaluation that focuses on program effectiveness (Treichel, 2003). To facilitate comparisons of program outcomes across studies, researchers could recommend a package of psychometrically sound instruments that are easily administered through community institutions (Bacon & McKenzie, 2004; Hughes & Kirby, 2000).

Likewise, it is important to incorporate conceptual advances in defining concepts such as interparental conflict, attitudinal conflict, relitigation, and intensity of conflict in order to identify program effects more precisely; use results to refine theories of change; and allow comparisons among educational programs and interventions. In addition, as lengthier education programs transition from universities to communities, attention to program fidelity will be paramount, requiring formative evaluation to examine and illustrate the extent to which laboratory research designs can transfer into the field (see, Goodman et al., 2004; McClure, 2002; Yankeelov et al., 2003). The implementation of services for separating and divorcing couples in other countries provides the potential for cross-cultural research.

Parenting coordination and collaborative law are becoming more available, and evaluation is needed to determine their effectiveness. More research is needed to determine the most effective interventions for families with varying levels of conflict and at-risk factors. Finally, basic research on parents in high conflict continues to be needed (Wingspread Conference, 2001a, 2001b).

Public Policy

Although proponents of alternative dispute-resolution models note their benefit over traditional adversarial processes, mandatory participation in parent education programs or in other interventions poses a potential threat to civil liberties (Johnston, 2000). It also raises questions about the financial burden placed on families.

Clement (1999) noted that states have a right to prescribe the conditions under which marriages and divorces are granted, and as long as mandatory attendance is allowed for in the enacted legislation, such a condition is not an impediment to divorce. For example, a class-action suit in Illinois successfully challenged a local court rule mandating attendance before granting the divorce decree because the state statute only granted authority to the court to make a case-by-case decision and not to require attendance of all parents. With a change in legislation, mandatory attendance becomes possible. In Kentucky, plaintiffs argued that mandatory attendance at a program offered by Catholic Social Services violated the Establishment Clause of the First Amendment by endorsing the Catholic religion. The district court found no violation because the law had a secular purpose (i.e., supporting families and minimizing litigation) and the benefit provided was neutral and nonideological (i.e., the program content did not encourage a religious belief, and parents could substitute another program; see Clement).

It is acknowledged by professionals in law and family-related professions that legal representation and access to high-quality interventions should be available to all families regardless of income (Wingspread Conference, 2001a, 2001b). If attendance is mandatory and a fee is charged, then courts must provide indigent parents access to the program or be in violation of the Fourteenth Amendment (Clement, 1999). Fee waivers for indigent parents are a common means of making programs accessible to those who demonstrate indigence (Geasler & Blaisure, 1999).

However, financial support for families in transition remains a need when we consider the landscape of possible interventions. Currently, interventions are paid for by grants, court filing fees, and families. If a single-session education program poses a financial problem for families, then longer term interventions, such as parenting coordination and organized groups for high-conflict parents, will pose an even greater challenge. Proponents argue that these alternatives to the adversarial approach save families money, and they do so for many families (i.e., mediation), especially in terms of legal fees. However, the scenario created by the possible court adoption of more comprehensive intervention models, in which families are assessed and directed to appropriate interventions, exemplifies a good news–bad news situation. It means that an increasing number of families will be expected to pay for services that will support them and their children in reaching a successful and less contentious transition, but that will also saddle them with a financial burden that they might not necessarily choose. Certainly, it can be argued that, under a continuum of services system, these families will be better off; the reduction in psychological pain and increased children and parental adjustment will offset any fees. Potential benefits to the communities in which these families live, for example, in terms of fewer days of work and school missed, must not be overlooked. Clearly, this cost–benefit ratio is an important question for the future.

Separating parents and their children are more likely to find support services now than ever before. Educational interventions are expanding in an increasing number of locales. A menu of interventions is becoming available to meet the needs of families facing relationship dissolution. Challenges for the future include matching parents with the services they need, when and where they need them; documenting program outcomes; and funding the services in the most equitable way possible.

APPENDIX

Children of Divorce Intervention Program
www.childrensinstitute.net/programs/CODIP/

Children in the Middle
www.divorce-education.com

Families in Transition
www.kycourts.net/Courts/JeffFITabout_text.shtm

Family Mediation Canada—Web site for kids and teens
www.fmc.ca/?p=Families

New Beginnings and Dads For Life
www.asu.edu/clas/asuprc/projects.html

Rainbows
www.rainbows.org

National Family Resiliency Center
www.divorceABC.com

Parents Forever
www.parenting.umn.edu

Parent Education and Custody Effectiveness (PEACE) Program
www.hofstra.edu/academics/law/law_center_family.cfm

REFERENCES

Ahrons, C. (1994). *The good divorce*. New York: HarperCollins.
Ahrons, C. R., & Tanner, J. (2003). Adult children and their fathers: Relationship changes 20 years after parental divorce. *Family Relations, 52,* 340–351.
Amato, P. R. (2000). The consequences of divorce for adults and children. *Journal of Marriage and the Family, 62,* 1269–1287.
Amato, P. R. (2003). Reconciling divergent perspectives: Judith Wallerstein, quantitative family research, and children of divorce. *Family Relations, 52,* 332–229.
Amato, P. R., & Booth, (1997). *A generation at risk: Growing up in an era of family upheaval*. Cambridge, MA: Harvard University Press.
Arbuthnot, J., & Gordon, D. A. (1996). Does mandatory divorce education work: A six-month outcome evaluation. *Family and Conciliation Courts Review, 34,* 60–81.
Arbuthnot, J., Kramer, K. M., & Gordon, D. A. (1997). Patterns of relitigation following divorce education. *Family and Conciliation Courts Review, 35,* 269–279.
Association of Family and Conciliation Courts Tasks Force on Parenting Coordination. (2004). Parenting coordination: Implementation issues. *Family Court Review, 41,* 533–564.
Ayoub, C. C., Deutsch, R. M., & Maraganore, A. (1999). Emotional distress in children of high-conflict divorce: The impact of martial conflict and violence. *Family and Conciliation Courts Review, 37,* 297–314.
Bacon, B., & McKenzie, B. (2001, February). *Best practices in parent information and education programs after separation and divorce: Final report*. Kitchener, ON: Family Mediation Canada. Retrieved March 12, 2004, from http://www.fmc.ca/main.asp?p=Families/ParentEducation.htm
Bacon, B. L., & McKenzie, B. (2004). Parent education after separation/divorce: Impact of the level of parental conflict on outcomes. *Family Court Review, 42,* 85–98.
Bramlett, M. D., & Mosher, W. D. (2002). *Cohabitation, marriage, divorce, and remarriage in the United States* (Vital and Health Statistics, Series No. 22). 23, Washington, DC: U.S. Government Printing Office.
Benjamin, M., & Irving, H. H. (1995). Research in family mediation: Review and implications. *Mediation Quarterly, 13,* 53–82.
Blaisure, K. R., & Geasler, M. J. (1996). Results of a survey of court-connected parent education programs in U.S. counties. *Family and Conciliation Courts Review, 34,* 23–40.
Blaisure, K. R., & Geasler, M. J. (2000). The divorce education intervention model. *Family and Conciliation Courts Review, 38,* 501–513.
Boyan, S. (2000, June–July). What is a parent coordinator? *Family Therapy News,* pp. 14–15.
Bramlett, M. D., & Mosher, W. D. (2001). *First marriage dissolution, divorce, and remarriage: United States* (Advanced Data from Vital and Health Statistics, No. 323). Washington, DC: U.S. Government Printing Office.

Braver, S., Smith, M., & DeLuse, S. (1997). Methodological considerations in evaluating family court programs. *Family and Conciliation Courts Review, 35,* 9–36.

Braver, S. L., & Gordon, D. (2002, November). *What works and what doesn't? A critical review of the parent education literature.* Paper presented at the Fifth International Congress on Parent Education and Access Programs of the Association of Family and Conciliation Courts, Tucson, AZ.

Braver, S. L., Salem, P., Pearson, J., & DeLuse, S. R. (1996). The content of divorce education programs: Results of a survey. *Family and Conciliation Courts Review, 34,* 41–59.

Buehler, C., Betz, P., Ryan, C. M., Legg, B. H., & Trotter, B. B. (1992). Description and evaluation of the orientation for divorcing parents: Implications for postdivorce prevention programs. *Family Relations, 41,* 154–162.

Burrows, R. K., & Buzzinotti, E. (1997). Legal therapists and lawyers. *Family Advocate, 22,* 33–36.

Clement, D. A. (1999). 1998 nationwide survey of the legal status of parent education. *Family and Conciliation Courts Review, 37,* 220–239.

Coates, C. A., Deutsch, R., Starnes, H., Sullivan, M. J., & Sydlik, B. (2004). Parenting coordination for high-conflict families. *Family Court Review, 42,* 246–262.

Coltrane, S., & Adams, M. (2003). The social construction of the divorce "problem": Morality, child victims, and the politics of gender. *Family Relations, 52,* 363–372.

Cookston, J. T., Braver, S. L., Sandler, I., & Genalo, M. T. (2002). Prospects for expanded parent education services for divorcing families with children. *Family Court Review, 40,* 190–203.

Criddle, M. N., Jr., Allgood, S. M., & Piercy, K. W. (2003). The relationship between mandatory divorce education and level of post-divorce parental conflict. *Journal of Divorce and Remarriage, 39,* 99–110.

Cummings, E. M., & Davies, P. (1994). *Children and marital conflict: The impact of family dispute and resolution.* New York: Guilford.

Dickinson, J., & Murphy, P. (December, 2000). Mums and dads forever: A cooperative parenting initiative. *Family Service Newsletter,* pp. 33–36.

Doherty, W. (1995). Boundaries between parent and family education and family therapy: The levels of family involvement model. *Family Relations, 44,* 353–358.

Emery, R. E. (1994). *Renegotiating family relationships: Divorce, child custody, and mediation.* New York: Guilford.

Emery, R. E. (1995). Divorce mediation: Negotiating agreements and renegotiating relationships. *Family Relations, 44,* 377–383.

Emery, R. E., Kitzmann, K. M., & Waldron, M. (1999). Psychological interventions for separated and divorced families. In E. M. Hetherington (Ed.), *Coping with divorce, single parenting, and remarriage: A risk and resiliency perspective* (pp. 323–344). Mahwah, NJ: Lawrence Erlbaum Associates.

Falconer, C., Clarke, C., & Hewitt, P. (2004). *Parental separation: Children's needs and parents' responsibilities.* London: Crown.

Falconer, C., Kelly, R., & Hewitt, P. (2005). *Parental separation: Children's needs and parents' responsibilities—next steps: Report of the responses to consultation and agenda for action.* London: Crown.

Feng, P., & Fine, M. A. (2000). Evaluation of a research-based parenting education program for divorcing parents: The focus on kids program. *Journal of Divorce and Remarriage, 34,* 1–23.

Firestone, G., & Weinstein, J. (2004). In the best interests of children: A proposal to transform the adversarial system. *Family Court Review, 42,* 203–215.

Fischer, R. L. (1997). The impact of an educational seminar for divorcing parents: Results from a national survey of family court judges. *Journal of Divorce and Remarriage, 28,* 35–48.

Forgatch, M. S., & DeGarmo, D. S. (1999). Parenting through change: An effective prevention program for single mothers. *Journal of Consulting and Clinical Psychology, 67,* 711–724.

Frieman, B. B., Garon, H. M., & Garon, R. J. (2000). Parenting seminars for divorcing parents: One year later. *Journal of Divorce and Remarriage, 33,* 129–143.

Fuhrmann, G. S. W., McGill, J., & O'Connell, M. E. (1999). Parent education's second generation: Integrating violence sensitivity. *Family and Conciliation Courts Review, 37,* 24–35.

Garon, R. J., Donner, D. S., & Peacock, K. (2000). From infants to adolescents: A developmental approach to parenting plans. *Family and Conciliation Courts Review, 38,* 168–191.

Geasler, M. J., & Blaisure, K. R. (1998). A review of divorce education program materials. *Family Relations, 47,* 167–175.

Geasler, M. J., & Blaisure, K. R. (1999). 1998 Nationwide survey of court-connected divorce education programs. *Family and Conciliation Courts Review, 37,* 36–63.

Geelhoed, R. J., Blaisure, K. R., & Geasler, M. J. (2001). Status of court-connected programs for children whose parents are separating or divorcing. *Family Court Review, 39,* 393–404.

Goodman, M., Bonds, D., Sandler, I., & Braver, S. (2004). Parent psychoeducational programs and reducing the negative effects of interpersonal conflict following divorce. *Family Court Review, 42,* 263–279.

Grych, J. H., & Fincham, F. D. (1992). Interventions for children of divorce: Toward greater integration of research and action. *Psychological Bulletin, 111,* 434–454.

Grych, J. H., & Fincham, F. D. (1997). Children's adaptation to divorce: From description to explanation. In S. A. Wolchik & I. N. Sandler (Eds.), *Handbook of children's coping: Linking theory and intervention* (pp. 159–193). New York: Plenum.

Hahn, R. A., & Kleist, D. M. (2000). Divorce mediation: Research and implications for family and couples counseling. *The Family Journal, 8,* 165–171.

Haine, R. A., Sandler, I. N., Wolchik, S. A., Tein, J.-Y., & Dawson-McClure, S. R. (2003). Changing the legacy of divorce: Evidence from prevention programs and future directions. *Family Relations, 52,* 397–405.

Harvey, J. H., & Fine, M. A. (2004). *Children of divorce: Stories of loss and growth.* Mahwah, NJ: Lawrence Erlbaum Associates.

Hawthorne, J., Jessop, J., Pryor, J., & Richards, M. (2003). *Supporting children through family change: A review of interventions and services for children of divorcing and separating parents.* York, England: Joseph Rountree Foundation.

Heilmann, R. W. (2000). A community-based parent education program for separating parents. *Family and Conciliation Courts Review, 38,* 514–524.

Hetherington, E. M. (2003). Intimate pathways: Changing patterns in close personal relationships across time. *Family Relations, 52,* 318–331.

Hetherington, E. M., Bridges, M., & Insabella, G. M. (1998). What matters? What does not? Five perspectives on the association between marital transitions and children's adjustment. *American Psychologist, 53,* 167–184.

Hetherington, E. M., & Kelly, J. (2002). *For better or for worse.* New York: Norton.

Hickey, E., & Dalton, E. (1997). *Healing hearts: Helping children and adults recover from divorce.* Seattle, WA: Gold Leaf Press.

Hipke, K. N., Wolchik, S. A., Sandler, I. N., & Braver, S. L. (2002). Predictors of children's intervention-induced resilience in a parenting program for divorced mothers. *Family Relations, 51,* 121–129.

Homrich, A. M., Glover, M. M., & White, A. B. (2004). Program profile: The court care center for divorcing families. *Family Court Review, 41,* 141–161.

Hughes, R., Jr., & Kirby, J. (2000). Strengthening evaluation studies for divorcing family support services: Perspectives of parent educators, mediators, attorneys, and judges. *Family Relations, 49,* 53–61.

Johnston, J., & Campbell, L. (1988). *Impasses of divorce: The dynamics and resolution of family conflict.* New York: The Free Press.

Johnston, J., & Roseby, V. (1997). *In the name of the child: A developmental approach to understanding and helping children of conflicted and violent divorce.* New York: Collier Macmillan.

Johnston, J. R. (2000). Building multidisciplinary professional partnerships with the court on behalf of high-conflict divorcing families and their children: Who needs what kind of help? *University of Little Rock Law Review, 22,* 453–479.

Kelly, J. B. (1998). Marital conflict, divorce, and children's adjustment. *Child and Adolescent Psychiatric Clinics of North America, 7,* 259–271.

Kelly, J. B., & Emery, R E. (2003). Children's adjustment following divorce: Risk and resilience perspectives. *Family Relations, 52,* 352–362.

Kibler, S., Sanchez, E., & Baker-Jackson, M. (1994). Pre-contempt/contemnors group diversion counseling program: A program to address parental frustration of custody and visitation orders. *Family and Conciliation Courts Review, 32,* 62–71.

Kramer, K. M., Arbuthnot, J., Gordon, D. A., Rousis, N. J., & Hoza, J. (1998). Effects of skill-based versus information-based divorce education programs on domestic violence and parental communication. *Family and Conciliation Courts Review, 36,* 9–31.

Kramer, L., & Kowal, A. (1998). Long-term follow-up of a court-based intervention for divorcing parents. *Family and Conciliation Courts Review, 36,* 452–465.

Kramer, L., & Washo, C. A. (1993). Evaluation of a court-mandated prevention program for divorcing parents: The Children First Program. *Family Relations, 42,* 179–186.

Kreider, R. M., & Fields, J. M. (2002, February). *Number, timing, and duration of marriages and divorces: 1996* (Current Population Reports, Series P70-80). Washington, DC: U.S. Government Printing Office.

Lande, J., & Herman, G. (2004). Fitting the forum to the family fuss: Choosing mediation, collaborative law, or cooperative law for negotiating divorce cases. *Family Court Review, 42,* 280–291.

Lutz, V. L., & Gady, C. E. (2004). Domestic violence and parent education: Necessary measures and logistics to maximize the safety of victims and domestic violence attending parenting education programs. *Family Court Review, 42,* 363–374.

Mackay, M. (2001). *Through a child's eyes: Child inclusive practice in family relationship services.* Canberra: Commonwealth of Australia. Retrieved May 19, 2004, from http://www.facs.gov.au/internet/facsinternet.nsf/ family /frsp-through_childs_eyes.htm

Martinez, C. R., Jr., & Forgatch, M. S. (2001). Preventing problems with boys' noncompliance: Effects of a parent training intervention for divorcing mothers. *Journal of Consulting and Clinical Psychology, 69,* 416–428.

McClure, T. E. (2002). Postjudgment conflict and cooperation following court-connected parent education. *Journal of Divorce and Remarriage, 38,* 1–16.

McIssaac, H., & Finn, C. (1999). Parents beyond conflict: A cognitive restructuring program model for high conflict families in divorce. *Family and Conciliation Courts Review, 37,* 74–82.

McKenzie, B., & Bacon, B. (2002). Parent education after separation: Results from a multi-site study on best practices. *Canadian Journal of Community Mental Health* (Spec. Suppl. 4), 73–88.

Neff, R., & Cooper, K. (2004). Parental conflict resolution: Six-, twelve-, and fifteen-month follow-ups of a high-conflict program. *Family Court Review, 42,* 99–114.

Norcross, J. C., Santrock, J. W., Campbell, L. F., Smith, T. P., Sommer, R., & Zuckerman, E. L. (2003). *Authoritative guide to self-help resources in mental health* (rev. ed.). New York: Guilford.

Pearson, J. (1993). Ten myths about family law. *Family Law Quarterly, 27,* 279–299.

Pedro-Carroll, J., Nakhnikian, E., & Montes, G. (2001). Assisting children through transition: Helping parents protect their children from the toxic effects of ongoing conflict in the aftermath of divorce. *Family Court Review, 39,* 377–392.

Pedro-Carroll, J. L., & Alpert-Gillis, L. J. (1997). Preventive interventions for children of divorce: A developmental model for 5 and 6 year old children. *Journal of Primary Prevention, 18,* 5–23.

Pedro-Carroll, J. L., & Cowen, E. L. (1987). The children of divorce intervention program: Implementation and evaluation of a time-limited group approach. *Advances in Family Intervention, 4,* 281–307.

Pedro-Carroll, J. L., Sutton, S. E., & Wyman, P. A. (1999). A two-year follow-up evaluation of a preventive intervention for young children of divorce. *School Psychology Review, 28,* 467–476.

Petersen, V., & Steinman, S. B. (1994). Helping children succeed after divorce: A court-mandated educational program for divorcing parents. *Family and Conciliation Courts Review, 32,* 27–39.

Roeder-Esser, C. (1994). Families in transition: A divorce workshop. *Family and Conciliation Courts Review, 32,* 40–49.

Schepard, A. (1994, September). *The emergence of parent education programs.* Paper presented at the meeting of the First International Congress on Parent Education Programs, Chicago.

Schepard, A. (1998). Parental conflict prevention programs and the unified family court: A public health perspective. *Family Law Quarterly, 32,* 95–130.

Schepard, A. (2004). *Children, courts, and custody: Interdisciplinary models for divorcing families.* Boston: Cambridge University Press.

Seltzer, J. A. (2000). Families formed outside of marriage. *Journal of Marriage and the Family, 62,* 1247–1268.

Simmons, T., & O'Connell, M. (2003, February). *Married-couple and unmarried-partner households: 2000* (Census 2000 Special Reports). Washington, DC: U.S. Department of Commerce.

Smart, C., Wade, A., & Neale, B. (1999). Objects of concern?—children and divorce. *Child and Family Law Quarterly, 11,* 365–376.

Stolberg, A., & Mahler, J. (1994). Enhancing treatment gains in a school-based intervention for children of divorce. *American Journal of Community Psychology, 12,* 111–124.

Sullivan, M. J. (1997). Have a problem? Hire a special master as decision-maker. *Family Advocate, 21,* 41–44.

Sutton, P. D. (2003). *Births, marriages, divorces, and deaths: Provisional data for October–December 2002* (National Vital Statistics Reports, 51, No. 10). Hyattsville, MD: National Center for Health Statistics.

Tessler, P. H. (1999). Collaborative law: What it is and why family law attorneys need to know about it. *American Journal of Family Law, 13,* 215–225.

Thoennes, N., & Pearson, J. (1999). Parent education in the domestic relations court: A multisite assessment. *Family and Conciliation Courts Review, 37,* 195–218.

Thompson, P., & Nurse, A. R. (1999). Collaborative divorce: A new, interdiscliplinary approach. *American Journal of Family Law, 13,* 226–234.

Treichel, C. J. (2003). In the best interests of children and their families: Merging program development and program evaluation. In D. J. Bredehoft & M. J. Walcheski (Eds.), *Family life education: Integrating theory and practice* (pp. 32–43). Minneapolis, MN: National Council on Family Relations.

Walker, J. (Ed.). (2001). *Information meetings and associated provisions within the Family Law Act 1996: Final evaluation report.* London: Lord Chancellor's Department.

Walker, J. (2003). Radiating messages: An international perspective. *Family Relations, 52,* 406–417.

Whitworth, J. D., Capshew, T. F., & Abell, N. (2002). Children caught in the conflict: Are court-endorsed divorce-parenting education programs effective? *Journal of Divorce and Remarriage, 37* (3/4), 1–18.

Wingspread Conference. (2001a). High-conflict custody cases: Reforming the system for children—conference report and action plan. *Family Law Quarterly, 34,* 589–606.

Wingspread Conference. (2001b). High-conflict custody cases: Reforming the system for children—conference report and action plan. *Family Court Review, 39,* 146–157.

Wolchik, S. A., Sandler, I. N., Millsap, R. E., Plummer, B. A., Greene, S. M., Anderson, E. R., Dawson-McClure, S. R., Hipke, K., & Haine, R. A. (2002). Six-year follow-up of preventive interventions for children of divorce: A randomized controlled trial. *Journal of the American Medical Association, 288,* 1874–1881.

Yankeelov, P. A., Bledsoe, L. K., Brown, J., & Cambron, M. L. (2003). Transition or not? A theory-based quantitative evaluation of Families in Transition. *Family Court Review, 41,* 242–256.

Zegarra, G. (1998). Educando a la familia Latina: Ideas for making parent education programs accessible to the Latino community. *Family and Conciliation Courts Review, 36,* 281–293.

VIII

Commentaries

Trying to Understand Close Relationships

Robert S. Weiss
University of Massachusetts, Boston

In this commentary I want to describe my own experience in trying to achieve an understanding of close relationships, their provisions, and the consequences of their absence. As I reconstruct this experience, I am impressed by the extent to which my work was directed and informed by the work of others. I want then to consider ways in which published research reports can be incomplete in their effort to contribute to understanding and in need of augmentation, perhaps by the work of others.

Theodore Newcomb, one of the pioneers of empirical social psychology, taught that the central problem of social psychology was interaction: why it happened, how it happened, and what resulted from it. For him, it was interaction that made social psychology social. I took courses with him and he was my thesis chairman. It was his influence that led me to decide to study the nature of social relationships.

At the time I began work on the nature of social relationships, the dominant idea in the field was that people formed two kinds of relationships: on the one hand, primary relationships that were face to face, ends in themselves, persisting, emotionally expressive, and capable of maintaining morale and structuring perception; on the other hand, relationships that were more incidental and had little emotional importance. Consistent with this outlook, a paper had been published that argued that people required a certain amount of emotionally significant contact to sustain their morale and functioning—they required that a certain level in a fund of sociability be maintained—but that it did not matter how they obtained it. They would do equally well with interactions with a spouse, interactions with friends and members of their families, or a mix of these.

The fund of sociability idea could be phrased as a hypothesis that any mix of primary relationships can make for well-being as long as it provides, in aggregate, an adequate amount of sociability. This hypothesis seemed to be reasonable and testable and so a good place to begin research.

Different methodological approaches could have been used to decide whether the fund of sociability hypothesis held. A survey study might have looked at the correlation between how people organized their relational lives and what they said about their morale. An experimental study could be imagined in which the marriages of experimental participants were replaced by friendships, although ethically it could not have been done even if participants could be found who would go along with it. However, a field study that would resemble this experimental study was entirely possible.

The Parents Without Partners organization brought together parents whose marriages had ended. (Only a small proportion of those who became members were parents but had never been married). The organization then provided the new members with a supportive community within which they could form close friendships. Thus, many members of the organization had lives from which the primary relationship of marriage had been removed and new primary relationships of friendship added.

I was accepted as a research person by a chapter of Parents Without Partners. I attended meetings and discussion groups and interviewed members. At one point, the president of the chapter asked me to help draft the chapter's by-laws. This kind of partial induction into membership is not unusual when people study an organization by hanging around.

Only a bit of investigation was needed to discover that the fund of sociability hypothesis is thoroughly false. Members who were without belief that their lives included a pair-bond relationship—marriage or a dating relationship in which there was at least the beginnings of commitment—complained of loneliness. Most members, of course, were in this situation.

One woman said to me, "My friends and I get together and we talk about how lonely we are." Many members formed friendships with other members, but the friendships did not compensate for the absence of a pair bond. The friendships helped them sustain their morale, but the members remained lonely until they found someone with whom they could at least begin to establish a new pair bond.

However, the fund of sociability hypothesis was nevertheless of value to me in that it focused my attention on what happened after marital separation, and—once I learned that confusion, volatility, and loneliness were common consequences—on the processes by which people returned to their ordinary stable selves. A false hypothesis can be a better guide for research than no hypothesis at all.

I later interviewed married couples who had moved to the Boston area from more than two states away and so could not easily maintain contact with the friends and family they had left behind. They felt isolated and adrift within the world they had moved to. It turned out that, just as friends and family did not compensate for the absence of marriages, so marriages did not compensate for the absence of friends and family: Both a pair bond and membership in a community were needed if people were to escape feeling that their lives were deficient.

It was easy to get members of Parents Without Partners to describe the loneliness that was a consequence of the absence of a pair-bond relationship. They said that there was a sense of being painfully alone despite being in the midst of others. One woman described being at a Christmas celebration with her family and finding herself so lonely she had to leave. Part of the experience of loneliness was great restlessness. This could show itself as a kind of compulsion to move from one's setting, whatever that might be, or it might show itself as an inability to give full attention to anything other than one's loneliness. Nothing could fully engage the lonely person's attention except the possibility of a new pair bond developing. Some people complained of feeling empty inside. Some people spoke of a constriction in their throats.

I was unable to explain why this condition, with its particular expressions, developed among people without a pair bond. The literature on loneliness was sparse, and much of it was influenced by philosophical concerns about people's inescapable aloneness. One discussion of loneliness suggested learning to find strength in solitude; another saw loneliness as a universal condition that was fully perceived primarily by those unable to maintain engagement with active life. None of this helped.

A related question was what it was about a pair-bond relationship that fended off loneliness. It was not intimacy or closeness or the ability to talk about one's deepest feelings: People could tell things to friends that they could not tell someone they were newly dating, but it was the dating relationship, not the friendship, that fended off loneliness.

I was perplexed by these puzzles when I began a year as a Visiting Fellow at the Tavistock Institute in London. Then, at the Tavistock, I happened to hear John Bowlby, a senior figure there, lecture on the attachment system in children. Bowlby described how small children who felt secure when in their mothers' presence would display what he called separation anxiety—I came to call it separation distress—when separated from their mothers. This was especially likely, he said, if they encountered a threat such as a person they did not know or were in a setting that was strange. Bowlby described how separation anxiety displayed itself: There was a fixity of attention on the direction from which the attachment figure (Bowlby's characterization of the child's mother) had left and so might be thought to return. The child was tense and restless, seemingly driven to regain the mother's presence, and utterly unable to give attention to anything else. After a time, the child would lapse into despair. This was, of course, exactly the way loneliness displayed itself.

It was as if a bulb hanging over my head suddenly turned on. Loneliness was a form of separation distress: the same restlessness, the same fixity of attention on the possibility of being joined by someone who would thereupon be part of one's life. The loneliness of adults was different from the separation distress of children because it was not triggered by the absence of a particular figure, the mother; it was separation distress without an object. However, it was certainly separation distress. No wonder lonely people said they felt empty; they were without the warmth that the adult equivalent of maternal love might have provided. And that constriction in their throat? They wanted to cry, although there was no one to hear.

I could now see what was essential in marriage and other pair bonds. They contributed an attachment figure to life. The attachment figure became linked to a security-fostering system, the attachment system, that had once bound children to parents (mothers, especially), but now required someone different, an age peer.

How did it happen that the attachment system in adults had released its childhood linkage to a parental figure and made it available for a new kind of figure? Having found a solution to the earlier puzzle, I was confronted by a new puzzle. Indeed, although I did not realize it at the time, there were many new puzzles implied by my initial recognitions. There was the puzzle of the way the attachment system could be modified by early experience so that, as adults, people would display characteristic attachment styles. There was the puzzle of grief as a consequence of loss of attachment relationships: Why did grief happen and how long did it last, and was it invariably the case that it was loss of an attachment figure that produced grief? There was the puzzle of the emotional upset that quite regularly followed marital separation even when the separation seemingly had been desired. Many of these new puzzles have been explored by other investigators, including those whose work is presented in this volume. Some became a basis for my further work.

While at the Tavistock, in addition to attending seminars chaired by John Bowlby, I sat in on a seminar for therapists that was led by a widely recognized psychoanalyst. Several times, a member of the seminar described a patient who was in the throes of marital separation. The members of the seminar, as they discussed the patient's behavior, tried to make sense of the patient's ambivalence, indecision, and wide mood swings. After my work with Parents Without Partners, the stories of irrational behavior following marital separation were familiar to me; to the therapists, they were bizarre. Members of the seminar agreed, with mine the lone demurral, that the patients were severely disturbed. I became aware that what happened in marital separation was little understood.

With Bowlby's work in mind, it seemed to me that the confusions of marital separation could be explained as expressions of attempts to break a bond of attachment. Someone trying to break away from a marriage that he or she no longer wanted would be like a child trying to become emotionally independent of an abusive parent. The marital break would make the person vulnerable to fears and fantasies associated with abandonment, even though the break was desired. Ambivalence would be entirely normal. Mood swings were, I thought, the consequence of shifting from feeling complete without the attachment figure to feeling abandoned and back again.

When I returned to my Boston job with Harvard's Laboratory for Community Psychiatry, I set up a program for people going through marital separation. Its premise was that these people were no more abnormal than any other randomly selected group, but they were dealing with a situation that gave rise to severe emotional cross-currents. The program, which I called Seminars for the Separated, was found to be helpful by those who participated in it and was adopted by other service-providing groups.

Here was a first application of the understanding that Bowlby's work had provided. Until I heard Bowlby's lecture, I knew that people without a pair-bond partner were vulnerable to loneliness but I did not know why. Until I had some understanding of what was happening, I could not see how it played itself out in, notably, marital separation. Once Bowlby's lecture showed me what was happening, it seemed likely that the self-doubt people must feel when they see themselves behaving irrationally could be allayed by providing them, too, with understanding.

My sense of what it means to understand something is that you can see what is going on and you have a good idea of what produced it. For example, you have good descriptive information of how loneliness expresses itself and what it feels like and, in addition, a satisfactory explanation of its causation. When I now read research papers, I sometimes feel they provide useful information but fall short of providing understanding. They don't adequately describe the phenomenon or don't explain how it came about. Of course, a single study can't do everything, but it may nevertheless be useful to identify some ways in which studies can leave inportant further work to be done.

Investigators sometimes organize descriptive information through use of a conceptual framework. An example is the proposal that there are three necessary elements in the process of marital dissolution: first, a couple must confront challenges or stressors; second, the couple must be unsuccessful in its attempt to cope with the challenges or stressors; and, third, the constraints against dissolution must prove too weak to prevent the dissolution from happening.

This might appear to be a theory explaining marital dissolution: A challenge or other stressor occurs, the couple cannot cope with it, and there is no insurmountable barrier to dissolution. However, this line of thought cannot be invalidated. Any process of relational dissolution must have had a challenge or stressor that got it going. Whatever the reaction to the challenge or stressor, it can be characterized as an effort at coping. Because the process ended in dissolution, the coping must have been unsuccessful, and whatever the barriers against dissolution, they were not strong enough to prevent it. One of the spouses is a compulsive drinker, gambler, or adulterer and so the marriage moves, slowly or rapidly, to dissolution? That fits. The spouse tried and failed to be understanding or insisted on change and it did not happen, or the spouse sought counseling but it was unsuccessful? They all fit. Anything fits.

An account that cannot be invalidated is not a theory about reality: rather, it is an accounting scheme, a way of organizing observations and thought that provides a place in a conceptual framework for whatever is learned. Like the financial categories that acountants use, it is a method for giving order to observation.

An accounting scheme provides a template for a narrative. The scheme of my example gives us a way to tell the story of a marital dissolution; it gives us a way of sorting observations and establishes the order in which we should report them. Sometimes people propose improvements in accounting schemes that permit the schemes to take account of more variables or previously unacknowledged complexities. This may make the accounting schemes better—but not truer.

It might be thought that findings of a definite relationship between one variable and another would escape the vacuity of the accounting scheme and so contribute more effectively to our understanding. If, for example, we could establish that some things that preceded marital dissolution were strongly connected to it, would not this help us understand how marital separation comes about? Not necessarily.

Correlation does not mean causation. We might, for example, find that those among the married whose parents had divorced are more likely themselves to divorce. But suppose the correlation occured because divorce is more common in some regions than others, or is linked to familial characteristics like religiosity. If we had concluded from the correlation that unstable parental marriages fostered unstable marriages in the next gineration, we would have been mistaken. The issue is what produces the connection between the correlated variables. Unless the connection is clear, the contribution of the correlation to our understanding is limited.

The correlation between social class and relational dissolution does not especially help us understand what it is that makes for relational dissolution, because there is no clear connection through which the status of being working class rather than middle class triggers a causal chain that leads to relational dissolution.

One indication that, despite the correlation between class status and likelihood of marital separation, there is no clear connection between the two is that their correlation could have been brought about in many ways. There might be more stress in low-income marriages because of shift work or job loss or financial trouble (as Rodriguez, Hall, & Fincham, chap. 5, this volume, suggest). There also could be less concern in working-class settings with maintaining the family's position in the larger community or greater reliance on a network of kin that weakens commitment to the marriage. Indeed, the number of possible processes leading to a correlation between working-class status and marital dissolution is limited only by the ingenuity of the investigator.

Another indication that social class is not closely linked to marital dissolution is that the association between social class and divorce has changed over the years and may be changing again (according to Teachman, Tedrow, & Hall, chap. 4, this volume). However, if social class is not determinative of marital dissolution, what are we to make of the (perhaps ended) correlation between social class status and marital dissolution? I would propose that the correlation tells us that some difference within social classes made for differences in the likelihood of marital dissolution. This suggests that we examine the possible linkage with marital dissolution of things that social class implies, such as ability to obtain satisfactory employment, aims in life, consistent with commitment to marriage, and mutually acceptable definitions of male and female responsibilities in marriage. The social class variable has suggested where we should look for causal determinants. It is, one might say, a "locator variable."

In a similar way, the greater likelihood that two-career marriages will end in dissolution suggests that we examine two-career marriages to find what is in them that is hostile to marriage (or not in them that might be protective to marriage). Is the two-career marriage burdened by the stress of inadequate time, or by tensions between a husband and wife who have different expectations of the marriage, or are barriers to the marriage's dissolution reduced by the ability of the wife to support herself if need be, or are husbands and wives who form two-career marriages more individualistic to begin with? A locator variable does not tell us which processes might be responsible.

A surprising number of correlates of marital dissolution can be seen as locator variables. They include ethnicity (African–American couples are more likely to divorce), ethnic differences between the spouses, cohabitation before marriage, having had parents who divorced, and a low rate of church attendance. Locator variables aid us in our search for understanding, but they do not provide understanding themselves.

Some variables that survey research shows to be correlated with marital dissolution might better be called proxy variables than locator variables, because they seem to take the place of something that is truly determinative. Neuroticism, for example, might be seen as a stand-in for something else: perhaps depressive states that burden the relationship, perhaps diminished ability to maintain a marital partnership, perhaps diminished desire for one.

It would seem that careful qualitative study of the processes leading to marital dissolution would avoid these difficulties of survey research. Indeed, qualitative study of causal processes may make the processes seem entirely understandable, even obvious. I shared a qualitative chapter from this volume that describes the process of relational dissolution with a friend who was in process of ending a long-standing close relationship. He was grateful to the chapter's author for making the difficulties of breaking up so clear. He had not before understood how common and natural was his own experience. Here was a triumph for qualitative research.

However, the qualitative study was narrowly bounded. It said nothing about what sort of relationships are likely to get into trouble, nor about the many relationships that hit road bumps but nevertheless maintain their stability and continue as before. In addition, the number of cases was too small to permit confident extrapolation from subgroups such as those who had been in long-term counseling. Qualitative work tends to be like the zoom control on a camera—it gives a close-up look at a limited part of the scene. If quantitative work often fails to come to grips with causal processes, qualitative work—while dealing with such processes—often does so in a small and narrowly defined group.

One implication of this discussion might be to attempt to integrate qualitative and quantitative work. Quantitative work could give us the large picture, qualitative the small; quantitative work could display the paths leading to marital dissolution, for example, and qualitative work then provide the observations that would make evident the causal elements signaled by locater variables or proxy variables.

It is not necessary to do both quantitative work and qualitative work oneself. It seems almost certain that whatever one wants to do, there will be earlier work using every variety of method on which one can build. I began my own study of marital dissolution with qualitative work, but there had already been quantitative work that demonstrated how distressing marital dissolution was. What is important is to keep in mind the ultimate objective of understanding how the system works.

As I think about my own search for understanding of social relationships, I was fortunate to have let my graduate school experience direct my attention to a problem, the extent to which primary relationships were substitutable, one for another, whose resolution would be of value to the larger area of concern. Then, as my research developed, I was led to focus attention on loneliness as a response to the absence of certain kinds of close relationships. At that point I found myself perplexed.

It was not too difficult to develop a description of loneliness and to recognize that loneliness appeared when there was neither the reality nor the promise of a pair bond. But I found it very difficult to identify the reasons for loneliness appearing then. "Absence of a pair bond" was a kind of locator variable. There was something in it or associated with it that produced loneliness. But as to what that was, I hadn't a clue.

John Bowlby's work provided the answers I was looking for. I could not have found those answers myself because they came from a field—child development—about which I knew little. In addition, Bowlby was just making his ideas widely known. I was made aware of them at a conference in which he presented his most recent observations.

It may be worth emphasizing that in our efforts to achieve understanding of the dynamics of our lives, none of us are lone explorers. We are all participants in a community of investigators engaged in a shared enterprise. Conference addresses, like the one given by Bowlby, and the papers that appear in journals and in volumes like this one, are the reports of research in progress by which we learn from each other.

The Changing Reasons for Marriage and Divorce

Ellen Berscheid
University of Minnesota

To understand any close relationship, including whether and how it dissolves, it is necessary to understand the conditions under which it was initiated (Berscheid & Graziano, 1979). Of prime importance among those initiation conditions is the partners' expectations of the benefits they are likely to receive from the relationship, because the relationship becomes vulnerable to dissolution when those expectations are violated. Thus, to understand marital and other close romantic relationships, it is necessary to understand the social definition of these relationships, particularly their raison d'être as perceived both by the partners and by society.

The basis on which most marriages in the United States are contracted today, at the beginning of the 21st century, is quite different from the basis on which they were contracted at the beginning of the 20th century and, thus, the conditions leading to their dissolution are also different. The social definition of marriage and other romantic relationships, many of which lead to marriage, has undergone a rocky and contentious evolutionary process that continues today, as is illustrated by recent deliberations of the U.S. Senate. In the summer of 2004, the U.S. Senate voted to end debate on a constitutional amendment proposed by President Bush to bar same-sex marriages, thus "assuring the issue renewed prominence in the fall campaign for the White House and control of Congress" (O'Rourke, 2004, p. A1).

Almost everyone has an opinion about whether the U.S. constitution should be amended to make same-sex marriages illegal. Many, in fact, hold an opinion strong enough to get them off the couch and on the phone to their Congressional representatives. Within the 2 days preceding the Senate vote, for example, nearly 10,000 Minnesotans contacted their Republican senator (who supported the amendment) and an equal number contacted their Democratic senator (who opposed it); in Washington, DC, "The Senate switchboard was overwhelmed ..., taking calls from people across America staking out their ground on a constitutional amendment defining marriage as between a man and a woman" (George, 2004). This latest marital cause célèbre illustrates that state and federal governments in the United States have always, even since colonial times (see Gadlin, 1977), legislated in numerous ways to promote and protect the stake of society at large in marriage. It also illustrates that almost everyone is interested in marriage and that the evolutionary process by which the social definition of marriage changes is usually marked by controversy.

The battleground on which most of the current debate is taking place concerns the extent to which legalization of same-sex marriage presents a threat to so-called traditional marriage. Traditional marriage has long been characterized as American society's fundamental unit of organization—"the bedrock of our society," as majority leader Bill Fritz put it in the Senate's debate (Bieber & Delan, 2004). Many Americans agree. They fear that legalization of same-sex marriage would grind society's bedrock into gravel. For example:

> Wynne Schendel, a Shoreview homemaker, called both of Minnesota's senators to say her family feels threatened by the absence of an amendment banning same-sex marriage. "It's not just an issue of homosexual versus traditional marriage," Schendel said. Allowing a same-sex union, she added, "just has a lot of impact on marriage as an institution." (George, 2004, p. A19)

When people use the phrases *traditional marriage* and *marriage as an institution*, they rarely elaborate on what they mean. They usually are referring, however, not only to a legal contract representing certain rights and obligations between a man and a woman, as opposed to between two men or two women, but also the couple's personal daily living arrangement— one in which each individual's roles and responsibilities in the relationship are allocated on the basis of the individual's biological sex. In a traditional marriage, for example, the man is expected to take major responsibility for the economic welfare of himself, his partner, and any children they have and also for such domestic activities as car maintenance and garbage and pest removal, whereas the woman is expected to take primary responsibility for management of the house and rearing the children. The so-called traditional form of marriage is in contrast to egalitarian marriage, in which the partners share roles and responsibilities and divisions of labor in their personal relationship life are assigned on the basis of the partners' preferences and skills (e.g., see Peplau, 1983/2002). Moreover, whereas in traditional marriages both partners often draw heavily on relatives and same-sex friends for companionship and emotional support, in egalitarian marriages they rely primarily on each other.

Although impassioned warnings that the actions of some states (e.g., Massachusetts) and cities (e.g., San Franciso) to legalize same-sex marriage will result in the death of marriage (and, hence, a constitutional amendment banning same-sex marriages is necessary), the legalization of same-sex marriage is simply the threat du jour. Two more long-standing and potent threats to marriage—the dramatic rise in the practice of cohabitation and the increase in the divorce rate, both of which have been evident for some time not only in the United States but throughout the world—are discussed by sociologists Paul Amato and Shelley Irving in their extraordinarily valuable review, "Historical Trends in Divorce in the United States" (chap. 3, this volume).

Amato and Irving discuss the rise in cohabitation and divorce with reference to the growing "deinstitutionalization of marriage," a prophesy made long ago by Ernest Burgess, a pioneer in the study of marriage and the family (e.g., Burgess, Locke, & Thomes, 1963). Burgess believed that the institutional basis of marriage was weakening as a result of the industrialization and urbanization of the United States, and he predicted that a new model of marriage, "companionate marriage," would become increasingly popular. In contrast to traditional marriages, based on economic necessity and masculine and feminine sex roles, companionate marriages are contracted and endure on the basis of the partners' emotional ties, such as their love for each other and friendship. Companionate marriages also tend to be egalitarian in that decisions usually are made by both partners.

Few will read the historical review by Amato and Irving without recognizing that the seeds of the movement for same-sex marriage, which appeared to suddenly bubble to the surface of the American body politic, have been germinating for almost a century when the social definition of marriage began to change. The demand for same-sex marriage is an inevitable outgrowth of widespread acceptance of the companionate model of marriage and the belief that marriages should be contracted on the basis of the partners' love for each other and their commitment to each other's welfare and happiness.

Same-sex marriage is not the first challenge the growing dominance of the companionate model of marriage has presented to governments in the United States. As the conditions under which a relationship is contracted change, so, too, do the conditions under which the relationship is likely to be dissolved. Moreover, just as the evolution of public opinion concerning the appropriate basis on which a marriage should be contracted has been accompanied by controversy, so too has the evolution of public opinion concerning the appropriate grounds for dissolution of a marriage. Margaret Mahoney's review of the current hodge-podge of divorce laws instituted by the states ("The Law of Divorce and Relationship Dissolution," chap. 26, this volume) chronicles attempts by state governments to adapt to growth in the belief that marriages contracted on the basis of the spouses' emotional ties to each other should be dissolved when those emotional ties break. As a consequence, the grounds on which the states permit marriages to be dissolved have become increasingly amorphous and permissive. It should be noted, however, that all states retain the right to govern the dissolution of a marriage, which testifies to the fact that society at large wishes marriage to remain an institution over which it retains local control. In fact, some senators departed from their party's stance and voted against the proposed constitutional amendment banning same-sex marriage because, as the senator from Arizona, John McCain, put it, "It usurps from the states a fundamental authority they have always possessed" (O'Rourke, 2004, p. A19).

The changing social definition of marriage—namely, the shift from the traditional model of marriage to the companionate model and the concomitant rise in cohabitation and in divorce— also has created a number of changes in the approach researchers have taken to the study of marital phenomena. To the changes discussed by Gay Kitson in "Divorce and Relationship Dissolution Research: Then and Now" (chap. 2, this volume) should be added the fact that the advent of companionate marriage required expansion of the kinds of expertise needed to understand and predict phenomena associated with the formation and dissolution of marriages, as is illustrated by the variety of disciplinary affiliations represented by the contributors to this handbook. Particularly significant has been the growth in the number of psychologists now conducting marital and family research, formerly the almost exclusive province of sociological scholars of marriage and the family. Sociologists tend to view the marital and family unit from the macroperspective of large societal trends (e.g., economic conditions; see Levinger, 1994). As more and more marriages became based on the expectation of companionship and emotional fulfillment, the microperspective of psychologists—a focus on the properties of the partners and the properties of their interaction with each other—became important, as is illustrated by the fact that the lion's share of chapters in this handbook focus on relationship internals, or the causes and consequences of the nature of the partners' interactions with each other.

The shift in focus from the marital relationship to the so-called close relationship also is a result of the rise in cohabitation and divorce (see Berscheid, 1999). As divorce and serial marriage became frequent, as increasing numbers of children were separated from their biological parents, and as increasing numbers of persons cohabited without marrying, it became necessary for researchers to identify a close relationship by means other than the appearance of two persons' names on the same marriage certificate or three persons' names on the same birth certificate (Berscheid, Snyder, & Omoto, 1989). Hence, there has been remarkably rapid growth of the multidisciplinary field of relationship science—a field to which scholars of marriage and the family remain important contributors but to which the expertise of scholars in many of the other behavioral, social, and health sciences is required for an understanding of all close relationships, marital and otherwise, and their impact on the individual's behavior, happiness, and health (see Berscheid & Regan, 2005).

Forecasting the outcome of the same-sex marriage controversy or, indeed, the form and fate of marriage and other close romantic relationships is extraordinarily hazardous. For the present volume, Jay Teachman, Lucky Tedrow, and Matthew Hall drew the short straw ("The Demographic Future of Divorce and Dissolution"). Their analysis prudently begins and ends with warnings of the impossibility of accurately predicting divorce and dissolution given the difficulty of identifying the great number of events and forces that may affect relationship stability, as well as the lack of knowledge concerning how each of these events and forces may interact. After providing their caveats, however, Teachman and his colleagues bravely offer a useful framework for thinking about trends in divorce. Their predictive equation includes what they call a "period factor" that acts on all persons or couples during a specific time period (e.g., an economic depression or war) to increase or decrease the chances that a marriage will be happy or unhappy (in recognition of the fact that the happiness of the marital relationship has become an important variable to consider in predicting marital stability given that companionate marriage has become the most usual ground on which marriages are currently contracted and dissolved).

Predicting the occurrence of a period factor is difficult, and even more difficult is predicting its effects on close romantic relationships. Nevertheless, a period factor that some see looming on the horizon concerns global fertility rate, which is very likely to have an impact on the social definition of marriage and other close romantic relationships and thus deserves more attention than it has yet received. Longman (2004), in his article "The Global Baby Bust," published by the Council on Foreign Relations, notes that fertility rates in all countries (particularly the Middle East, China, and Mexico, but also the United States) are falling rapidly and dramatically. According to projections by the United Nations, by 2045 the world's fertility rate will have fallen below replacement levels. Longman makes this statement:

> Some biologists now speculate that modern humans have created an environment in which the "fittest," or most successful, individuals are those who have few, if any children. As more and more people find themselves living under urban conditions in which children no longer provide economic benefit to their parents, but rather are costly impediments to material success, people who are well adapted to this new environment will tend not to reproduce themselves. (p. 76)

The worldwide spread of urbanization and industrialization appears to have not only produced companionate marriage but also a precipitous decline in fertility.

When fertility falls beneath replacement levels, Longman observes, the number of productive workers also drops and the number of dependent elderly persons increases. This combination of events puts severe strains on government budgets. Among the consequences named by Longman are the inability of governments to sustain a large military as well as the inability to spend on education, research, and development. In other words, financial exigency makes it difficult for a government to provide for the common defense and to promote domestic tranquillity and well-being—the two essential purposes of governments in democratic societies. Thus, severe financial constraints are rarely suffered passively for long. Among the actions Longman suggests governments might take when their citizens' fertility falls below replacement level is to exempt parents from contributing to social security systems under the rationale that by raising and educating their children, parents have already contributed. Many other avenues to increasing fertility by governmental action are possible, including legislation that reduces the tensions that parents currently experience when they attempt to simultaneously participate in the workforce and raise children (e.g., provision of child care support and child health insurance).

Forecasting precisely how the impending fertility period factor will affect the social definition of marriage and other close romantic relationships is difficult, but it likely will have a number of effects. It may, for example, cast a different light over the current same-sex marriage controversy. Given modern reproductive technology and increasing evidence that a stable close relationship environment is necessary for optimal human infant development, particularly brain development (see Siegel, 1999), whether the child's parents are same or opposite sex may become less important than the fact that two people are committed to a stable relationship within which they are willing to raise children. More generally, governmental actions may make it once again an economic necessity for people to participate in some form of marriage or enduring close relationship that puts children at its center—in other words, certain aspects of traditional marriage may make a comeback.

Although it is difficult to forecast the shape of marriage in the future, one prediction can be made with some confidence: However much marriage may seem to be threatened, some form of marriage will survive and be nurtured by society. Evolutionary psychologists believe that the dyad—the two-person group—is the most basic and ancient configuration of humans because it was, and still is, necessary for the survival of the species (e.g., Brewer & Caporael, 1990). As a consequence, over evolutionary time the human was wired biologically for small-group living and acquired a fundamental motivation for interpersonal attachments, or a "need to belong" (Baumeister & Leary, 1995).

Yet another prediction can be made without resort to a crystal ball: Given that the social definition of marriage and other close romantic relationships continues to evolve, volumes addressed to divorce and romantic relationship dissolution will require frequent updates.

REFERENCES

Baumeister, R. F., & Leary, M. R. (1995). The need to belong: The desire for interpersonal attachments as a fundamental human motivation. *Psychological Bulletin, 117,* 497–529.

Berscheid, E. (1999). The greening of relationship science. *American Psychologist, 54,* 260–266.

Berscheid, E., & Graziano, W. (1979). The initiation of social relationships and interpersonal attraction. In R. L. Burgess & T. L. Huston (Eds.), *Social exchange in developing relationships* (pp. 31–60). New York: Academic Press.

Berscheid, E., & Regan, P. (2005). *The psychology of interpersonal relationships.* New York: Prentice-Hall.

Berscheid, E., Snyder, M., & Omoto, A. M. (1989). Issues in studying relationships: Conceptualizing and measuring closeness. In C. Hendrick (Ed.), *Close relationships:Vol 10. Review of Personality and Social Psychology* (pp. 63–91). Newbury Park, CA: Sage.

Bieber, J., & Delan, D. (Executive Producers). (2004, July 16). *Washington Week* [Television broadcast]. New York and Washington, DC: Public Broadcasting Service.

Brewer, M. B., & Caporeal, L. R. (1990). Selfish genes vs. selfish people: Sociobiology as origin myth. *Motivation and Emotion, 14,* 237–243.

Burgess, E. W., Locke, H. J., & Thomes, M. (1963). *The family: From institution to companionship.* New York: American Book Company.

Gadlin, H. (1977). Private lives and public order: A critical view of the history of intimate relations in the United States. In G. Levinger & H. L. Raush (Eds.), *Close relationships: Perspectives on the meaning of intimacy* (pp. 33–72). Amherst: University of Massachusetts Press.

George, L. (2004, July 15). Dayton, Coleman flooded with calls. *Star Tribune,* p. A19.

Levinger, G. (1994). Figure versus ground: Micro- and macroperspectives on the social psychology of personal relationships. In R. Erber & R. Gilmour (Eds.), *Theoretical frameworks for personal relationships* (pp. 1–28). Hillsdale, NJ: Lawrence Erlbaum Associates.

Longman, P. (2004). The global baby bust. *Foreign Affairs, 83,* 64–79.

O'Rourke, L. M. (2004, July 15). Move to ban gay marriage rejected. *Star Tribune,* pp. A1, A19.

Peplau, L. A. (2002). Roles and gender. In H. H. Kelley, E. Berscheid, A. Christensen, J. H. Harvey, T. L. Huston, G. Levinger, E. McClintock, L. A. Peplau, & D.R. Peterson(Eds.), *Close relationships* (pp. 220–264). Clinton Corners, NY: Percheron Press. (Original work published 1983)

Siegel, D. J. (1999). *The developing mind: Toward a neurobiology of interpersonal experience.* New York: Guilford.

Proposals for Research on the Consequences of Divorce for Children

Alan Booth
Pennsylvania State University

This book is a testament to the great strides that have been made in increasing our understanding of divorce and its aftermath. Read in another way, it is also a call for new research emphases. Although there is still much to be learned about the causes and processes of divorce, recent policy and program initiatives notwithstanding, I elect to focus on the consequences of parental marital dissolution for children. Children are most vulnerable to divorce, and responsive to intervention. The purpose of this commentary is to suggest topics that should be included in our research agenda as we examine the current gaps in this topic. I frame these areas through the following questions. First, what are the consequences of different parent marital trajectories for the well-being of the children of divorce? Second, to what extent are the children of divorce disadvantaged? Third, how does divorce affect third and higher order generations? Fourth, what role does biology play in helping us understand the consequences of divorce for children?

WHAT ARE THE CONSEQUENCES OF PARENT MARITAL TRAJECTORIES FOR THE CHILDREN OF DIVORCE?

The research on marital trajectories following divorce is extensive but seldom takes into account all of the components in a systematic fashion. Studies of marital trajectories should simultaneously take into account the types of families in which children reside following divorce (e.g., single parent, cohabiting parent, and stepfamily), the number of transitions, the age of the child at the time of transition, and the duration of each new role. Each of these marital trajectory components has the potential to affect child well-being. The literature is replete with studies that show that children of divorce have lower psychological adjustment, social competence, academic achievement, and self-concept (e.g., Amato & Keith, 1991). The problems often extend into adulthood and include low socioeconomic attainment, low self-esteem, and high risk of premarital birth, cohabitation, marital problems, and divorce (e.g., Teachman, 2004). With notable exceptions (e.g., Aquilino, 1996), family scholars have not studied more than one transition (change in family type) at a time. However, as Aquilino demonstrates, the type of family makes a big difference in the transition. For example, living with a single parent is preferable to living with other relatives or in a household in which the child must continually adjust to the mother's or father's serial live-in dating partner.

The divorce of biological parents is often associated with a number of family transitions (e.g., single parenthood, cohabitation, remarriage, and a second divorce followed by single parenthood). Several studies indicate that multiple transitions put the child at higher risk of problem behavior (e.g., Wu & Martinson, 1993). The aspects of multiple transitions that are so damaging to child well-being have yet to be identified. Evidence suggests that such damage may be due to parental neglect or poor parenting practices (Brown, 2002). They may also be due to long-term insecurity about family living arrangements or a lifetime of observing and modeling adults with limited interpersonal skills.

Linked to the number of transitions is duration, or the amount of time spent in any one role. One long role, such as a remarriage, adds stability to the child's life and is preferable to multiple transitions.

Timing of the initial transition may also be a factor affecting offspring well-being. Studies indicate that divorce in the preteen years tends to be more damaging than dissolution during the teen years (Amato & Booth, 1997).

Thus, parent marital trajectories reflect not only the kind and number of family types, but the amount of time spent in any one type of family as well as the age of the child at the time of each transition. What researchers in this area of study need now are studies that simultaneously examine the type of family, the number of transitions, the timing of the transition with respect to the child's age, and the duration of each family structure (see also Demo, Aquilino, & Fine, 2005). Such information will reveal to researchers exactly what it is about parents' postdissolution trajectories that lowers child well-being, and the reasons for this state.

Typically, marital trajectory studies create typologies that combine various aspects of the four dimensions of marital trajectories of concern. Often these typologies are time invariant and mask the effect of parents' marital status over the life span. The use of event-history analysis allows researchers to model all four dimensions of each parent's marital trajectory simultaneously and to fill in the deficiencies in our knowledge about the consequences of divorce for children.

The research recommended here will identify the family change or combination of changes following parental divorce that are most likely to influence child outcomes. Further, it will overcome the misspecification found in studies utilizing typologies of parents' marital histories. With such information in hand, we may design better intervention programs that both increase stability in the child's life and lower the chance of declines in well-being.

TO WHAT EXTENT ARE THE CHILDREN OF DIVORCE DISADVANTAGED?

Following divorce, children may find themselves in a single-parent family (with or without other relatives), a stepfamily, a family composed of the biological parent and a cohabiting partner, and other less common caretaking arrangements. Compared with the gold standard of living with two biological parents, offspring in all other family forms are at greater risk of enduring lower levels of well-being. However, there are children in every family type who

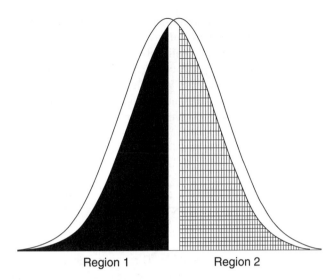

Region 1   Region 2

FIG. C.1. Distribution of scores on a typical measure of well-being for children in intact two-parent families (Region 1—children who score below the mean of children in stepfamilies) and stepfamilies (Region 2—children who score above the mean of children in two-parent families). (Taken from P. R. Amato, 1994. Copyright 1994 by Lawrence Erlbaum Associates. Reprinted with permission.)

have excellent caretakers and children who are more resilient to the changes following parental divorce. The question is this: what proportion of children of divorce suffer well-being deficits compared with children in two biological married-parent families, and what is the process by which they become disadvantaged?

In a meta-analysis, Amato and Keith (1991) estimated that children in stepfamilies scored below those in continuously intact two-parent families on six well-being and developmental outcomes, with a mean difference of 0.17 *SD* (the mean difference between the two groups divided by the standard deviation of the outcome). In another publication, Amato (1994) superimposed the distribution of well-being for stepchildren onto the distribution for children in two-parent intact families (Fig. C.1).

Note that a substantial proportion of children (43%) in intact two-parent families scored below the average of disadvantage experienced by children in stepfamilies. Note too that 43% of the children in stepfamilies were better off than children in intact two-parent families. As Fig. c1 indicates, many children grow up in dysfunctional intact families and many grow up in well-functioning stepfamilies. The study highlights the importance of knowing the mean difference between family structures as well as the overlap in the distributions.

These findings suggest three lines of research that would improve child well-being. The first line should focus on the well-being of children in a variety of family types (living with stepfamilies, single parents, cohabiting parents, two parents, or relatives). The purpose of this research would be to compare mean differences in effect sizes for various family types. Such analyses would estimate the relative disadvantage among children in different family structures and would identify the most disadvantaged populations of children.

A second line of research should investigate whether the factors that influence lower levels of child well-being are different for those in stepfamilies (and other family structures) than for those in intact two-parent families. Differences suggest that there should be separate policies for different populations. If there are similarities, it suggests the effectiveness of a single policy directed at all disadvantaged families with children.

A third research focus should be the identification of those factors that account for why some children, say in stepfamilies, experience a lower level of well-being whereas others in stepfamilies do not. Does this have to do with the competence of the child (e.g., intelligence, problem-solving ability, social skills, and locus of control), the quality of the parent–child relationship, low social economic resources, other factors, or some combination of these indicators?

HOW DOES DIVORCE AFFECT THE THIRD
AND SUBSEQUENT GENERATIONS?

The bulk of research on the impact of divorce on children has focused on two generations—parents and their offspring. This is as it should be. Direct experience has the greatest potential for affecting offspring life chances, whether positive (e.g., escaping conflict and abuse) or negative (e.g., having lower educational achievements, more behavior problems, or less self-esteem; see Amato & Booth, 1997). Very little is known about the effects of grandparents' (G1) divorce on grandchildren (G3) or subsequent generations and the extent to which they are mediated by the effect of the divorce on the parents (G2).

The only study to deal with this topic using a large data set was conducted by Amato and Cheadle (2005) using Marital Instability Over the Life Course data. They found that G1 divorce had a direct effect on G3 educational attainment. Links between G1's divorce and G3's marital discord and the quality of her or his relationship with her or his parents were entirely mediated by disrupted family processes in G2. Although the study was limited by incomplete information from each generation, it was especially severe from G1. Nevertheless, this pioneering study is an excellent model on which to base subsequent studies.

There are a number of things that might prevent or enhance divorce's influence on the well-being of subsequent generations. Genetics is one such factor. The mating of G2 and his or her spouse results in a unique combination of genetic material that may influence offspring behavior predispositions in G3. The unique combination of genetic material may lead to G3's being more resilient (e.g., having personal competencies such as intelligence, social skills, and locus of control) than G2 and therefore be less likely to suffer from the problems developed by G2 in response to parental divorce. In addition, G2 may have a spouse who invests heavily in maintaining a stable marriage and creating an environment favorable to the development of G3.

At the same time, society is much more accepting of divorce in contemporary G3's generation than in G2's, and G2's is more accepting than G1's. Professionals and lay persons alike are more sensitive to the needs of divorced individuals and their offspring. Counseling services, school policies, and the law, as well as common wisdom, are much more in tune with the needs of the children of divorce. This knowledge may result in a situation in which each succeeding generation is less disadvantaged by parental divorce than earlier generations.

In contrast, it is possible that each generation's problems as they stem from parents' divorce may be exacerbated by that event. Further, the disadvantages of divorce may multiply. Some researchers view divorce as part of a much larger pattern of family disorganization and believe that the growth in unstable cohabiting relationships and the increase in nonmarital births are linked to marital instability. In short, we do not have enough research extending to three or four generations to use in making informed judgments about the long-term impact of parental divorce.

Estimating the impact of divorce and its aftermath on G3 and higher orders is essential if we wish to assess the impact of divorce on children accurately. Such estimations are the only way to ascertain the extent to which the influence is cumulative or limited to one or two generations. Linked with knowledge about cultural change, we can better estimate the longevity of current trends or possible new directions. Ultimately, the information will be a key to designing interventions that lower the risk of divorce leading to declines in offspring well-being.

WHAT ROLE DOES BIOLOGY PLAY IN HELPING US UNDERSTAND THE CONSEQUENCES OF DIVORCE FOR ADULTS AND CHILDREN?

Social and behavioral scientists have long assumed that physiological processes are critical components of human behavior. However, the nature of many behaviorally relevant biological processes was unknown until recently. Technical and theoretical advances achieved during the 1990s have provided new opportunities to integrate biological science into social science research. A series of conceptual shifts have placed new emphasis on the contributions of both nature *and* nurture to individual development (see Magnusson & Cairns, 1996; Plomin & Rutter, 1998; Rutter et al., 1997). Leading the cutting edge of this paradigm shift are behaviorally and socially oriented scientists testing "biosocial" alternatives to traditional models of individual differences and intraindividual change in behavior. This new biosocial perspective is built on living systems theory (Ford, 1987). That is, individual differences are considered to be products of individual and interactive influences among genetic, environmental, social, and biological processes over time (Cicchetti & Dawson, 2002). More specifically, Gottlieb (1992) speculates that biological functions set the stage for behavioral adaptation to environmental challenge. Simultaneously, environmental challenges may induce behavioral change that in turn affects fast-acting (e.g., hormone secretion) and slower responding (e.g., gene expression) biological processes. It is important that these biological activities are not considered determinants of behavior; rather, their action influences the likelihood that preexisting behavioral tendencies are expressed. A central tenet of the overarching model is that the expression of biobehavioral relationships can be amplified or attenuated by social forces.

The ability to measure some biological variables noninvasively (e.g., in saliva) has created many opportunities for behavioral scientists to test biosocial models in the naturalistic settings of everyday social worlds. The additional advantage of this measure is that hormone (e.g., testosterone) levels in saliva reflect the unbound or biologically active fraction of the hormone in circulation (Granger, Schwarz, Booth, & Arentz, 1999). Thus, there is an immediate need for the development of midlevel models that will enable us to specify, test, and refine hypotheses regarding the integration of biological processes with behavioral and social-contextual levels of analysis. The need is particularly acute with respect to understanding family relationships.

No research involving biological variables has focused directly on the children of divorce, but several relevant studies suggest models that could guide such endeavors. In the field of genetics, studies suggest that divorce is heritable (Jockin, McGue, & Lykken, 1996; McGue & Lykken, 1992). The interesting aspect of this research is the way in which the environment moderates this link. On one hand, when divorce is unacceptable, as reflected in a low divorce rate, heritability of divorce is low. The prevailing values suppress genetic predispositions. On the other hand, when divorce is widespread, as reflected in a high divorce rate, the impact of heritability is high. This is an example of how the environment plays a significant role in the expression of genetic predispositions. It is unlikely that there is a gene for divorce. Instead, a complex set of genetic material may predispose offspring to unstable romantic relationships.

One of the consequences of divorce is socioeconomic deprivation, which is associated with offspring's antisocial behavior and intelligence. Note, though, that some children are more resilient to socioeconomic deprivation than others. Kim-Cohen, Moffitt, Caspi, and Taylor (2004) studied the genetic and environmental factors influencing children's resilience to socioeconomic deprivation. Factors found to be associated with children's resilience were maternal warmth, children's outgoing temperament, and a stimulating home environment. The National Longitudinal Study of Adolescent Health (Add Health) is a public-use data set that includes a large representative sample of monozygotic and dizygotic twin pairs that are needed to study genetic and environmental sources of influence on child well-being. Using data from this sample of 1,116 twins, the researchers were able to identify the proportion of variance in resilience (by means of the three protective factors) attributable to genetic and environmental roots. Seventy-one percent of the behavioral resilience was accounted for by genetic factors, whereas 46% of the cognitive resilience was accounted for by genetic factors, which suggests that the environment also plays an important role. The study demonstrates that resilience to socioeconomic deprivation is partly heritable and that the protective factors (maternal warmth, child's outgoing temperament, and stimulating activities) have both genetic and environmental roots. The study also suggests that family as well as individual processes are partly heritable and that children can act in evocative ways (which are partly heritable) that shape the family environment in ways that make offspring more resilient. This study indicates the value of studying genetics as well as environmental variables in understanding the resilience of the child of divorce. Behavioral endocrinology has also made significant inroads into understanding family processes that have the potential to chart the way in which the aftermath of divorce affects children. Testosterone is of interest to social and behavior scientists because it is one of a few hormones (out of several hundred) with many links to behavior. The others are cortisol (a reliable measure of hypothalamic–pituitary–adrenal axis activation in response to stress) and oxytocin (linked to high levels of affiliation). Testosterone has links to positive as well as negative behavior; the fact that the hormone's links to behavior are moderated by social context is even more reason to include it in studies of the consequences of divorce for youth.

Why is it important to include hormones in studies of social behavior? First, hormones increase the explained variance in many dependent variables. Second, their inclusion lowers the possibility of attributing the wrong cause to behavior. Third, interaction between social variables and hormones adds a new dimension to our understanding of biological behavior–social context links.

Here are some examples of recent advances in family research involving testosterone that have implications for the well-being of children of divorce. Studies of youth have not taken into account a potentially key moderating variable that is consistently related to problem behavior—parent–child relationship quality. Three studies indicate that our understanding of testosterone's link to problem behavior would be greatly enhanced if we included parent–child relationship quality in the analysis.

Drawing on the risk and resilience perspective (e.g., Masten, Best, & Garmezy, 1990), Booth, Johnson, Granger, Crouter, and McHale (2003), in an analysis of 608 children (ages 7–18) from working- and middle-class two-parent families, revealed that testosterone had little direct effect on their reports of risk behavior or symptoms of depression. In contrast, testosterone's positive relationship with risk behavior and negative relation with depression were conditional on the quality of parent–child relations. When the parent–child relationship quality was high, testosterone-related adjustment problems were less evident. When relationship quality was low, testosterone-linked risk taking and symptoms of depression were more in evidence. These findings suggest that the relationship between testosterone and problem behavior in children is likely to be moderated by family context. Divorce may lower parent–child relationship quality, at least from the nonresident parent, and in turn increase the level of risk behavior and depression.

Peers figure prominently in adolescents' daily lives. They provide companionship, opportunities to develop interpersonal skills, and a source of social support (Hartup, 1993). What scholars seldom consider is that moderate amounts of assertiveness are necessary to initiate and maintain positive social relationships. Active engagement in a new or existing intimate relationship is essential to understanding and responding to another's needs, and thereby maintaining or enhancing the quality of the peer relationships. A handful of small, nonrepresentative sample studies suggest that testosterone may have positive links with peer associations. In a study of college students, men and women with high testosterone had a more forward and confident interaction style than those with low testosterone (Dabbs, Bernieri, Strong, Campo, & Milun, 2001). Testosterone has been linked to helpful, engaging, and outgoing behavior (Dabbs & Ruback, 1988). In adult women, testosterone is related to being confident (Baucom, Besch & Callaan, 1985).

In a study of 331 adolescents residing in intact working- and middle-class families, the social environment proved to be an important moderator for understanding testosterone's association with adolescent peer relationships (Updegraff, Booth, & Bahr, in press). Above average levels of testosterone were associated with perceived peer competence, romantic relationships, popularity, and time spent alone with girls. However, this occurred only if boys had a positive relationship with their mother or an older sister. In the absence of a positive relationship with a female family member, testosterone had no relation to the extent or quality of affiliation with peers. These findings suggest that mothers whose involvement with children is diminished by divorce may be less able to provide the support that facilitates testosterone's link with the development of peer relationships.

Although research on family–peer linkages has a long history of highlighting the connections between parent–child and peer relationship quality (Parke & Buriel, 1998), studies from the biosocial perspective have focused almost exclusively on problematic peer interaction and behavior. Findings highlight the potential for exploring how biological and family factors interact to predict adolescent interpersonal competence.

In a sample of 308 established working- and middle-class families with school-age children, neither husbands' nor wives' testosterone showed a direct connection with marital quality (Booth, Johnson, & Granger, 2005). Rather, the association between husbands' testosterone and positive and negative marital quality was conditional on husbands' perceptions of role overload. When role overload was elevated, higher testosterone levels were associated with lower levels of marital quality. When role overload was low, higher testosterone was linked to higher levels of marital quality. By what mechanism could men's perceptions of the demands of the environment moderate the association between testosterone and marital quality? We suggest that testosterone enables the expression of high levels of social engagement, but that this engagement may be positive or negative depending on men's perceptions of the environment. As it applies to marriage, when stress is low, men with higher levels of testosterone may devote more attention to their spouses, take the initiative in expressing positive interaction, and make a greater overall investment in the relationship. High-testosterone men under considerable stress are more likely to disagree, be less responsive to affective cues, and take risks that may lead to divorce.

Other research links a father's testosterone with family involvement. For instance, a father's testosterone level declines following the birth of a child and remains low for an extended period (Story, Walsh, Quinton, & Wynne-Edwards, 2000). Another study reveals that fathers with low testosterone are more attuned to their infant's cries (Fleming, Corter, Stallings, & Steiner, 2002). Although the studies involve different samples of men, it is possible that the social context of fatherhood may bring about testosterone changes that are associated with being an attentive parent. Further study is needed to identify factors that may moderate links between testosterone and father–infant relationship quality and how it changes following divorce.

Some researchers are now examining the impact of within-family testosterone levels as they affect marital communication. In a study of 93 newly married couples that involved videotaping problem-solving and support tasks, it was found that similarities and differences in partners' testosterone (relative to their gender) predicted the extent to which partners exhibited less positive and more negative behavior in discussing marital problems (Cohan, Booth, & Granger, 2004). Husbands exhibited more adaptive behavior when husbands and wives were concordant for lower testosterone. In addition, wives exhibited more positive support when they had higher levels and husbands had lower levels of testosterone.

Many social scientists believe that hormone research would require laboratory work that is difficult to perform. In fact, it is relatively easy. Saliva-collection procedures are noninvasive and straightforward. There are excellent labs that perform saliva assays so that the social scientist do not have to do the assays themselves. The literature is now developing to the point that major advances in knowledge can be made in a relatively short period of time.

I have identified four areas requiring further research. Others merit attention but seem to take us in relatively unexplored directions. Some have policy implications that may, if borne out by further research, lead us toward new interventions.

REFERENCES

Amato, P. (1994). The implications of research findings on children in stepfamilies. In A. Booth and J. Dunn (Eds.), *Stepfamilies: Who benefits? Who does not?* (pp. 81–87). Hillsdale, NJ: Lawrence Erlbaum Associates.

Amato, P., & Booth, A. (1997). *Generation at risk: Growing up in era of family upheaval.* Cambridge, MA: Harvard University Press.

Amato, P., & Cheadle, J. (2005). The long reach of divorce: Tracking marital dissolution and child well-being across three generations. *Journal of Marriage and Family, 67,* 191–206.

Amato, P., & Keith, B. (1991). Consequences of parental divorce for children's wellbeing: A meta-analysis. *Psychological Bulletin, 110,* 26–46.

Aquilino, W. (1996). The life course of children born to unmarried mothers: Childhood living arrangements and young adult outcomes. *Journal of Marriage and the Family, 58,* 293–310.

Baucom, D., Besch, P., & Callaan, S. (1985). Relation between testosterone concentration, sex role identity and personality among females. *Journal of Personality and Social Psychology, 48,* 1218–1226.

Booth, A., Johnson, D., Granger, D., Crouter, A., & McHale, S. (2003). Testosterone and child and adolescent adjustment: The moderating role of parent–child relationships. *Developmental Psychology, 39,* 85–98.

Booth, A., Johnson, D., & Granger, D. (2005). Testosterone and marital quality. *Journal of Marriage and Family, 67,* 483–498.

Brown, S. (2002). Child well-being in cohabiting families. In A. Booth & A. Crouter (Eds.), *Just living together: Implications of cohabitation for children, families, and social policy* (pp. 173–188). Mahwah, NJ: Lawrence Erlbaum Associates.

Cicchetti, D., & Dawson, G. (2002). Multiple levels of analysis. *Developmental Psychopathology, 14,* 417–420.

Cohan, C., Booth, A., & Granger, D. (2004). Gender moderates the relationship between testosterone and marital interaction. *Journal of Family Psychology, 17,* 29–40.

Dabbs. J., & Ruback, B. (1988). Saliva testosterone and personality of male college students. *Bulletin of the Psychonomic Society, 26,* 244–247.

Dabbs, J. M., Bernieri, F. J., Strong, R. K., Campo, R., & Milun, R. (2001). Going on stage: Testosterone in greetings and meetings. *Journal of Research in Personality, 35,* 27–40.

Demo, D. H., Aquilino, W. S., & Fine, M. A. (2005). Family composition and family transitions. In V. Bengsten, A. Acock, K. Allen, P. Dilworth-Anderson, & D. Klein (Eds.), *Sourcebook of family theories and methods: An interactive approach* (pp. 119–142). Newbury Park, CA: Sage.

Fleming, A., Corter, C., Stallings, J., & Steiner, M. (2002). Testosterone and prolactin are associated with emotional responses to infant cries in new fathers. *Hormones and Behavior, 42,* 399–413.

Ford, D. H. (1987). *Humans as self-constructing living systems.* Hillsdale, NJ: Lawrence Erlbaum Associates.

Gottlieb, G. (1992). *Individual development and evolution: The genesis of novel behavior.* New York: Oxford University Press.

Granger, D., Schwarz, E. B., Booth, A., & Arentz, M. (1999). A reliable, simple, and highly sensitive radioimmunoassay for salivary T determination in studies of child development. *Hormones and Behavior, 35,* 8–27.

Hartup, W. W. (1993). Adolescents and their friends. In B. Laursen (Ed.), *Close relationships in adolescence* (pp. 3–22). San Francisco: Jossey-Bass.

Jockin, V., McGue, M., & Lykken, D. (1996). Personality and divorce: A genetic analysis. *Journal of Personality and Social Psychology, 71,* 288–299.

Kim-Cohen, J., Moffitt, T., Caspi, A., & Taylor, A. (2004). Genetic and environmental processes in young children's resilience and vulnerability to socioeconomic deprivation. *Child Development, 75,* 651–668.

Magnusson, D., & Cairns, R. B. (1996). Developmental science: Toward a unified framework. In R. B. Cairns, G. H. Elder, & E. J. Costello (Eds.), *Developmental science* (pp. 7–30). Cambridge, England: Cambridge University Press.

Masten, A., Best, K., & Garmezy, N. (1990). Resilience and development: Contributions from the study of children who overcome adversity. *Development and Psychopathology, 2,* 425–444.

McGue, M., & Lykken, D. (1992). Genetic influence on risk of divorce. *Psychological Science, 6,* 368–373.

Parke, R. D., & Buriel, R. B. (1998). Socialization in the family: Ethnic and ecological perspectives. In N. Eisenberg (Ed.), *Handbook of child psychology* (5th ed., pp. 463–552). New York: Wiley.

Plomin, R., & Rutter, M. (1998). Child development, molecular genetics, and what to do with genes once they are found. *Child Development, 69,* 1223–1242.

Rutter, M., Dunn, J., Plomin, R., Simonoff, E., Pickles, A., Maughan, B., Ormel, J., Meyer, J., & Eaves, L. (1997). Integrating nature and nurture: Implications of person–environment correlations and interactions for developmental psychopathology. *Developmental Psychopathology, 9,* 335–364.

Story, A., Walsh, C., Quinton, R., & Wynne-Edwards, K. (2000). Hormonal correlates of paternal responsiveness in new and expectant fathers. *Evolution and Human Behavior, 21,* 79–95.

Teachman, J. (2004). The childhood living arrangements of children and the characteristics of their marriages. *Journal of Family Issues, 25,* 86–111.

Updegraff, K., Booth, A., & Bahr, S. (in press). *Hormones and adolescents' peer experiences: The moderating roles of the parent–adolescent relationship.* Family Psychology.

Wu, L., & Martinson, B. (1993). Family structure and the risk of pre-marital birth. *American Sociological Review, 58,* 210–232.

Author Index

Subject Index